Guide to Gale Literary Criticism Series

For criticism on	Consult these Gale series
Authors now living or who died after December 31, 1999	*CONTEMPORARY LITERARY CRITICISM (CLC)*
Authors who died between 1900 and 1999	*TWENTIETH-CENTURY LITERARY CRITICISM (TCLC)*
Authors who died between 1800 and 1899	*NINETEENTH-CENTURY LITERATURE CRITICISM (NCLC)*
Authors who died between 1400 and 1799	*LITERATURE CRITICISM FROM 1400 TO 1800 (LC)* *SHAKESPEAREAN CRITICISM (SC)*
Authors who died before 1400	*CLASSICAL AND MEDIEVAL LITERATURE CRITICISM (CMLC)*
Authors of books for children and young adults	*CHILDREN'S LITERATURE REVIEW (CLR)*
Dramatists	*DRAMA CRITICISM (DC)*
Poets	*POETRY CRITICISM (PC)*
Short story writers	*SHORT STORY CRITICISM (SSC)*
Black writers of the past two hundred years	*BLACK LITERATURE CRITICISM (BLC)* *BLACK LITERATURE CRITICISM SUPPLEMENT (BLCS)*
Hispanic writers of the late nineteenth and twentieth centuries	*HISPANIC LITERATURE CRITICISM (HLC)* *HISPANIC LITERATURE CRITICISM SUPPLEMENT (HLCS)*
Native North American writers and orators of the eighteenth, nineteenth, and twentieth centuries	*NATIVE NORTH AMERICAN LITERATURE (NNAL)*
Major authors from the Renaissance to the present	*WORLD LITERATURE CRITICISM, 1500 TO THE PRESENT (WLC)* *WORLD LITERATURE CRITICISM SUPPLEMENT (WLCS)*

Poetry Criticism

Contents

Preface

Poetry Criticism (*PC*) presents significant criticism of the world's greatest poets and provides supplementary biographical and bibliographical material to guide the interested reader to a greater understanding of the genre and its creators. Although major poets and literary movements are covered in such Gale Literary Criticism series as *Contemporary Literary Criticism* (*CLC*), *Twentieth-Century Literary Criticism* (*TCLC*), *Nineteenth-Century Literature Criticism* (*NCLC*), *Literature Criticism from 1400 to 1800* (*LC*), and *Classical and Medieval Literature Criticism* (*CMLC*), *PC* offers more focused attention on poetry than is possible in the broader, survey-oriented entries on writers in these Gale series. Students, teachers, librarians, and researchers will find that the generous excerpts and supplementary material provided by *PC* supply them with the vital information needed to write a term paper on poetic technique, to examine a poet's most prominent themes, or to lead a poetry discussion group.

Scope of the Series

PC is designed to serve as an introduction to major poets of all eras and nationalities. Since these authors have inspired a great deal of relevant critical material, *PC* is necessarily selective, and the editors have chosen the most important published criticism to aid readers and students in their research. Each author entry presents a historical survey of the critical response to that author's work. The length of an entry is intended to reflect the amount of critical attention the author has received from critics writing in English and from foreign critics in translation. Every attempt has been made to identify and include the most significant essays on each author's work. In order to provide these important critical pieces, the editors sometimes reprint essays that have appeared elsewhere in Gale's Literary Criticism Series. Such duplication, however, never exceeds twenty percent of a *PC* volume.

Organization of the Book

Each *PC* entry consists of the following elements:

- The **Author Heading** cites the name under which the author most commonly wrote, followed by birth and death dates. Also located here are any name variations under which an author wrote, including transliterated forms for authors whose native languages use nonroman alphabets. If the author wrote consistently under a pseudonym, the pseudonym will be listed in the author heading and the author's actual name given in parenthesis on the first line of the biographical and critical introduction. Uncertain birth or death dates are indicated by question marks. Single-work entries are preceded by the title of the work and its date of publication.

- The **Introduction** contains background information that introduces the reader to the author and the critical debates surrounding his or her work.

- A **Portrait of the Author** is included when available.

- The list of **Principal Works** is ordered chronologically by date of first publication and lists the most important works by the author. The first section comprises poetry collections and book-length poems. The second section gives information on other major works by the author. For foreign authors, the editors have provided original foreign-language publication information and have selected what are considered the best and most complete English-language editions of their works.

- Reprinted **Criticism** is arranged chronologically in each entry to provide a useful perspective on changes in critical evaluation over time. All individual titles of poems and poetry collections by the author featured in the entry are printed in boldface type. The critic's name and the date of composition or publication of the critical work are given at the beginning of each piece of criticism. Unsigned criticism is preceded by the title of the source in which it appeared. Footnotes are reprinted at the end of each essay or excerpt. In the case of excerpted criticism, only those footnotes that pertain to the excerpted texts are included.

- Critical essays are prefaced by brief **Annotations** explicating each piece.
- A complete **Bibliographical Citation** of the original essay or book precedes each piece of criticism.
- An annotated bibliography of **Further Reading** appears at the end of each entry and suggests resources for additional study. In some cases, significant essays for which the editors could not obtain reprint rights are included here. Boxed material following the further reading list provides references to other biographical and critical sources on the author in series published by Gale.

Cumulative Indexes

A **Cumulative Author Index** lists all of the authors that appear in a wide variety of reference sources published by the Gale Group, including *PC*. A complete list of these sources is found facing the first page of the Author Index. The index also includes birth and death dates and cross references between pseudonyms and actual names.

A **Cumulative Nationality Index** lists all authors featured in *PC* by nationality, followed by the number of the *PC* volume in which their entry appears.

A **Cumulative Title Index** lists in alphabetical order all individual poems, book-length poems, and collection titles contained in the *PC* series. Titles of poetry collections and separately published poems are printed in italics, while titles of individual poems are printed in roman type with quotation marks. Each title is followed by the author's last name and corresponding volume and page numbers where commentary on the work is located. English-language translations of original foreign-language titles are cross-referenced to the foreign titles so that all references to discussion of a work are combined in one listing.

Citing *Poetry Criticism*

When writing papers, students who quote directly from any volume in the Literary Criticism Series may use the following general format to footnote reprinted criticism. The first example pertains to material drawn from periodicals, the second to material reprinted from books.

Sylvia Kasey Marks, "A Brief Glance at George Eliot's *The Spanish Gypsy,*" *Victorian Poetry* 20, no. 2 (Summer 1983), 184-90; reprinted in *Poetry Criticism,* vol. 20, ed. Ellen McGeagh (Detroit: The Gale Group), 128-31.

Linden Peach, "Man, Nature and Wordsworth: American Versions," *British Influence on the Birth of American Literature,* (Macmillan Press Ltd., 1982), 29-57; reprinted in *Poetry Criticism,* vol. 20, ed. Ellen McGeagh (Detroit: The Gale Group), 37-40.

Suggestions are Welcome

Readers who wish to suggest new features, topics, or authors to appear in future volumes, or who have other suggestions or comments are cordially invited to call, write, or fax the Managing Editor:

Managing Editor, Literary Criticism Series
The Gale Group
27500 Drake Road
Farmington Hills, MI 48331-3535
1-800-347-4253 (GALE)
Fax: 248-699-8054

Acknowledgments

The editors wish to thank the copyright holders of the excerpted criticism included in this volume and the permissions managers of many book and magazine publishing companies for assisting us in securing reproduction rights. We are also grateful to the staffs of the Detroit Public Library, the Library of Congress, the University of Detroit Mercy Library, Wayne State University Purdy/Kresge Library Complex, and the University of Michigan Libraries for making their resources available to us. Following is a list of the copyright holders who have granted us permission to reproduce material in this volume of *PC*. Every effort has been made to trace copyright, but if omissions have been made, please let us know.

COPYRIGHTED EXCERPTS IN *PC*, VOLUME 32, WERE REPRODUCED FROM THE FOLLOWING PERIODICALS:

The Americas, v. XIV, October, 1957; v. XVII, January, 1961. Copyright, 1957, 1961 by The Academy of American Franciscan History. Both reproduced by permission.—***Borges Studies on Line,*** January 13, 2000 for "Spinoza in Borges' Looking-Glass," by Marcelo Abadi. Translated by Leila Yael. © Borges Studies on Line 2000. © Marcelo Abadi 1989. Retrieved March 30, 2000 from http://www.hum.au.dk/romansk/borges/bsol/abadi.htm. Reproduced by permission of the author.—***Bulletin of Hispanic Studies,*** v. LXXIV, January, 1997. Reproduced by permission of Liverpool University Press.—***CLA Journal,*** v. 37, 1993. Copyright, 1993 by The College Language Association. Used by permission of The College Language Association.—***Commonweal,*** v. 35, December, 1941. Copyright 1941, renewed 1969 Commonweal Publishing Co., Inc. Reproduced by permission of Commonweal Foundation.—***Current Bibliography on African Affairs,*** v. 17, 1984-85 for "Transcendence: The Poetry of Maya Angelou" by Priscilla R. Ramsey. © 1985, Baywood Publishing Co., Inc. Reproduced by permission of the publisher and the author. Excerpts from "No, No, No," and "Country Lover," (And Still I Rise, 1978), "The Calling of Names," "When I Think About Myself," "To a Man," "Remembrance," and "Diverse Deviations," (*Just Give Me a Cool Drink of Water 'fore I Diiie,* 1971) and (*I Know Why the Caged Bird Sings,* 1970), all reproduced by permission of Random House, Inc.—***ELH,*** v. 36, March, 1969; v. 49, Winter, 1982; v. 58, Autumn, 1991; v. 63, 1996. Copyright © 1969, 1982, 1991, 1996 by The Johns Hopkins University Press. All reproduced by permission of The Johns Hopkins University Press.—***English Language Notes,*** v. XIV, June, 1977; v. XV, September, 1977. © copyrighted 1977, Regents of the University of Colorado. Both reproduced by permission.—***English Literary Renaissance,*** v. 2, Winter, 1972. Copyright © 1972 by English Literary Renaissance. Reproduced by permission.—***English Studies,*** Netherlands, v. 55, February, 1974. © 1974 by Swets & Zeitlinger B. V. Reproduced by permission.—***Essays in Criticism,*** v. XXIV, October, 1974. Copyright © 1974 by *Essays in Criticism.* Reproduced by permission.—***The Explicator,*** v. 34, May, 1976; v. 46, Winter, 1988; v. 51, Spring, 1993. Copyright © 1976, 1988,1993 Helen Dwight Reid Educational Foundation. All reproduced with permission of the Helen Dwight Reid Educational Foundation, published by Heldref Publications, 1319 18th Street, NW, Washington, DC 20036-1802.—***Hispanofila,*** v. 98, January, 1990; v. 109, September, 1993. Both reproduced by permission.—***The Nation,*** New York, v. 268, May 31, 1999. © 1999 *The Nation* magazine/ The Nation Company, Inc. Reproduced by permission.—***Nineteenth Century French Studies,*** v. 27, Fall 1998 & Winter 1999. © 1998 by Nineteenth-Century French Studies. Reproduced by permission.—***Notes on Contemporary Literature,*** v. XXVIII, January, 1999. Copyright 1998 by William S. Daxey. Reproduced by permission.—***Papers on Language and Literature,*** v. 7, Summer, 1971. Copyright © 1971 by The Board of Trustees, Southern Illinois University at Edwardsville. Reproduced by permission.—***Parnassus,*** v. 8, Fall-Winter, 1979. Copyright © 1979 Poetry in Review Foundation, NY. Reproduced by permission.—***PMLA,*** v. 87, October, 1972. Copyright © 1972 by the Modern Language Association of America. Reproduced by permission of the Modern Language Association of America.—***Publication of the Arkansas Philological Association,*** v. 22, Fall, 1996 for "What to Make of an Even More Diminished Thing: A Borgesian Sonnet Considered in a Frosty Light" by Johnny Wink. Reproduced by permission of the publisher and the author.—***Readerly/Writerly Texts,*** v. 1, Fall-Winter, 1993. Copyright © 1993 *Readerly/Writerly Texts.* Reproduced by permission.—***Revista Hispanica Moderna,*** v. 50, December, 1997. Reproduced by permission.—***Romance Notes,*** v. XX, Winter, 1979; v. XXXVI, Fall, 1995; v. XXIX, Spring, 1999. All reproduced by permission.—***Romance Quarterly,*** v. 29, 1982; v. 38, May, 1991. Copyright © 1982, 1991 Helen Dwight Reid Educational Foundation. Both reproduced with permission of the Helen Dwight Reid Educational Foundation, published by Heldref Publications, 1319 18th Street, NW, Washington, DC 20036-1802.—***Romanic Review,*** v. 77, March, 1986. © 1986 The Trustees of Columbia University. Reproduced by permission.—***Studies in Philology,*** v. 72, April, 1975. Copyright © 1975 by the University of North Carolina Press. Reproduced by permission of the publisher.—***Studies in the Literary Imagination,*** v. XI, Spring, 1978. Copyright 1978 Department of English, Georgia State University. Reproduced by permission.—***The Times Literary Supplement,*** n. 5019, June 11, 1999. © The Times Supplements Limited 1999. Reproduced from *The Times Literary Supplement*by permission.—***The Wilson Quarterly,*** v. XXII, Autumn, 1991 for "Jorge Luis Borges" by Edward Hirsch. Reproduced by permission of the author.—***World Literature Today,*** v. 58, Autumn, 1984; v. 69, Autumn, 1995. Copyright 1984, 1995 by the University of Oklahoma Press. Both reproduced by permission of the publisher.

COPYRIGHTED EXCERPTS IN *PC*, VOLUME 32, WERE REPRODUCED FROM THE FOLLOWING BOOKS:

Alazraki, Jaime. From ***Borges and the Kabbalah: And Other Essays on His Fiction and Poetry.*** Cambridge University Press, 1988. © Cambridge University Press 1988. Reproduced by permission of the Cambridge University Press and the author.—Arce de Vazquez, Margot. From ***Gabriela Mistral: The Poet and Her Work.*** Translated by Helene Masslo Anderson. New York University Press, 1964. © 1964 by New York University. Reproduced by permission.—Arce de Vazquez, Margot. From ***Gabriela Mistral: The Poet and Her Work.*** Translated by Helene Masslo Anderson. New York University Press, 1964. © 1964 by New York University. Reproduced by permission.—Bastos, Maria Luisa. From "Whitman as Inscribed in Borges," translated with Daniel Balderston, in ***Borges the Poet.*** Edited by Carlos Cortinez. The University of Arkansas Press, 1986. Copyright © 1986 by the Board of Trustees of the University of Arkansas. All rights reserved. Reproduced by permission of Carlos Cortinez.—Canas, Dionisio. From "The Eye of the Mind: Borges and Wallace Stevens," in ***Borges the Poet.*** Edited by Carlos Cortinez. The University of Arkansas Press, 1986. Copyright © 1986 by the Board of Trustees of the University of Arkansas. All rights reserved. Reproduced by permission of Carlos Cortinez.—Carter, A. E. From ***Paul Verlaine.*** Twayne Publishers, Inc., 1971. Copyright © 1971 by Twayne Publishers, Inc. The Gale Group.—Coleman, Alexander. From "The Ghost of Whitman in Neruda and Borges," in ***Walt Whitman of Mickle Street: A Centennial Collection.*** Edited by Geoffrey M. Sill. University of Tennessee Press, 1994. Copyright © 1994 by The University of Tennessee Press/Knoxville. All rights reserved. Reproduced by permission of Geoffrey M. Sill.—Erickson, Peter. From ***Rewriting Shakespeare, Rewriting Ourselves.*** University of California Press, 1991. © 1991 by The Regents of the University of California. Reproduced by permission of the publisher and the author.—Evans, Maurice. From "Divided Aims in the 'Revised Arcadia,'" in ***Sir Philip Sidney and the Interpretation of Renaissance Culture: A Poet in His Time and Ours.*** Edited by Gary F. Waller and Michael D. Moore. Croom Helm, 1984. Copyright © 1984 G. F. Waller and M. D. Moore. Reproduced by permission.—Freer, Coburn. From "The Style of Sidney's Psalms," in ***Essential Articles for the Study of Sir Philip Sidney.*** Edited by Arthur F. Kinney. Archon Books, 1986. Copyright © 1986 Arthur F. Kinney. Reproduced by permission.—Gullberg, H. J. From "Noble Prize Citation," in ***Selected Poems of Gabriela Mistral.*** Translated by Langston Hughes. Indiana University Press, 1957. Copyright © 1957 by Indiana University Press.—Hagen, Lyman B. From ***Heart of a Woman, Mind of a Writer, and Soul of a Poet: A Critical Analysis of the Writings of Maya Angelou.*** University Press of America, Inc., 1997. Copyright © 1997 by University Press of America, Inc. Reproduced by permission.—Holditch, W. Kenneth. From "Borges and Emerson: The Poet as Intellectual," in ***Borges the Poet.*** Edited by Carlos Cortinez. The University of Arkansas Press, 1986. Copyright © 1986 by the Board of Trustees of the University of Arkansas. All rights reserved. Reproduced by permission of Carlos Cortinez.—Hughes, Langston. From in an introduction to ***Selected Poems of Gabriela Mistral.*** Translated by Langston Hughes. Indiana University Press, 1957. Copyright © 1957 by Indiana University Press. Introduction copyright © 1957 by Langston Hughes. Reproduced by permission of Harold Ober Associates Incorporated.—Jones, Julie. From "Borges and Browning: A Dramatic Dialogue," in ***Borges the Poet.*** Edited by Carlos Cortinez. The University of Arkansas Press, 1986. Copyright © 1986 by the Board of Trustees of the University of Arkansas. All rights reserved. Reproduced by permission of Carlos Cortinez.—Kalstone, David. From ***Sidney's Poetry.*** Harvard University Press, 1965. Copyright © 1965 by the President and Fellows of Harvard College. All rights reserved. Reproduced by permission Harvard University Press.—Kodama, Maria. From "Oriental Influences in Borges' Poetry: The Nature of the Haiku and Western Literature," in ***Borges the Poet.*** Edited by Carlos Cortinez. The University of Arkansas Press, 1986. Copyright © 1986 by the Board of Trustees of the University of Arkansas. All rights reserved. Reproduced by permission of Carlos Cortinez.—Lisandrelli, Elaine Slivinski. From ***Maya Angelou: More Than a Poet.*** Enslow Publishers, Inc., 1996. Copyright © 1996 by Elaine Slivinski Lisandrelli. All rights reserved. Reproduced by permission.—Montgomery, Jr., Robert, L. From ***Symmetry and Sense: The Poetry of Sir Philip Sidney.*** University of Texas Press, 1961. Copyright © 1961 by Robert L. Montgomery, Jr. Reproduced by permission.—Peschel, Enid Rhodes. From ***Four French Symbolist Poets: Baudelaire, Rimbaud, Verlaine, Mallarme.*** Translated by Enid Rhodes Peschel. Ohio University Press, 1981. © Translations 1981 by Enid Rhodes Peshel. All rights reserved. Reproduced by permission of the Literary Estate of Enid Rhodes Peschel.—Porter, Laurence M. From ***The Crisis of French Symbolism.*** Cornell University Press, 1990. Copyright © 1990 by Cornell University. Reproduced by permission of the publisher, Cornell University Press.—Rosenbaum, Sidonia Carmen. From ***Modern Women Poets of Spanish America.*** Hispanic Institute in the United States, 1945. Copyright 1945 by Sidonia Carmen Rosenbaum. Reproduced by permission.—Stabbs, Martin S. From ***Borges Revisited.*** Twayne Publishers, 1991. Copyright 1991 by G. K. Hall & Co. The Gale Group.—Stephan, Philip. From ***Paul Verlaine and the Decadence, 1882-90.*** Manchester University Press, 1974. © 1974 Philip Stephan. Reproduced by permission of the author.—Strong,

Beret E. From ***The Poetic Avant-Garde: The Groups of Borges, Auden, and Breton.*** Northwestern University Press, 1997. Copyright © 1997 by Northwestern University Press. Reproduced by permission.—Tate, Claudia. From ***Black Women Writers at Work.*** Edited by Claudia Tate. Continuum, 1983. Copyright © 1983 by Continuum. Reproduced by permission.—Virgillo, Carmelo. From ***Woman as Myth and Metaphor in Latin American Literature.*** Edited by Carmelo Virgillo and Naomi Lindstrom. University of Missouri Press, 1985. Copyright © 1985 by The Curators of the University of Missouri. All rights reserved. Reproduced by permission.—Wall, Cheryl. From an interview in ***Women Writers Talking.*** Edited by Janet Todd. Holmes & Meier, Publishers, 1983. Copyright © 1983 by Holmes & Meier Publishers, Inc. Reproduced by permission of the publisher.

PHOTOGRAPHS AND ILLUSTRATIONS APPEARING IN *PC*, VOLUME 32, WERE RECEIVED FROM THE FOLLOWING SOURCES:

Angelou, Maya, 1970, photograph. UPI/Corbis-Bettmann. Reproduced by permission.—Angelou, Maya, photograph. AP/Wide World Photos. Reproduced by permission.—Mistral, Gabriela, photograph. AP/Wide World Photos. Reproduced by permission.—Verlaine, Paul, photograph by Popperfoto/Archive Photos, Inc. Reproduced by permission.

Maya Angelou
1928-

(Born Marguerite Johnson) American poet, autobiographer, screenwriter, playwright, actress, singer, and political activist.

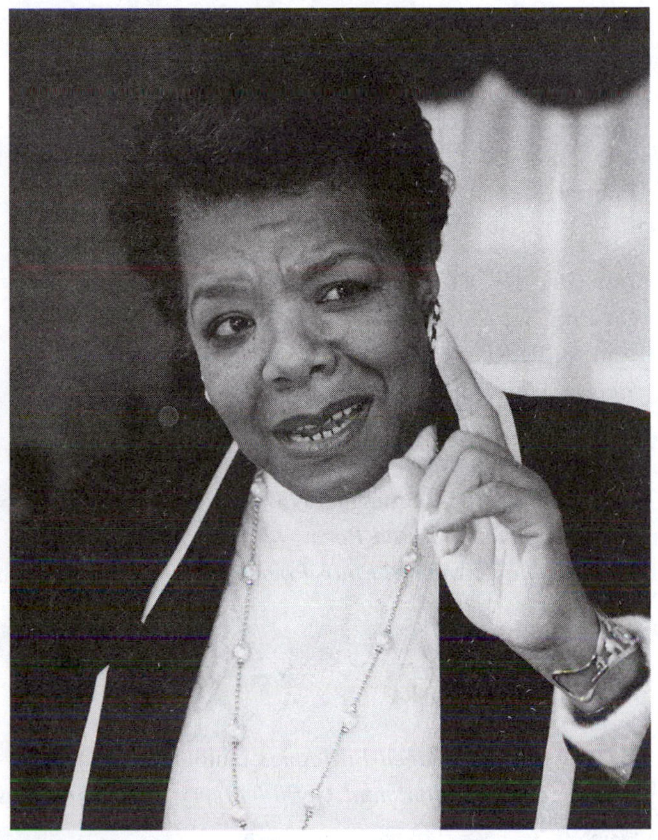

INTRODUCTION

In her poetry, as in the five volumes of autobiography upon which her fame rests, Angelou's primary concern is with the distillation of experience into immediately accessible language. Her writing attempts to capture and preserve the determining forces, vicissitudes, and ambiance of her own life story and of the ongoing African-American story, which helped to shape her and which she reflects and illuminates.

BIOGRAPHICAL INFORMATION

Born Marguerite Johnson in St. Louis, Missouri, in 1928, abandoned by both her parents when they divorced, Angelou early experienced the twin forces that would determine the shape of her life and the nature of her career: personal rejection and institutional racism. Until her teen years when she lived with her mother in San Francisco, she lived with her paternal grandmother, a strong independent woman who ran a grocery store, in Stamps, Arkansas. On a visit to her mother in St. Louis, when Angelou was eight, she was raped by her mother's boyfriend. After his murder by her uncles, she returned to her grandmother in Arkansas. Traumatized by the events, she stopped speaking, and only regained her voice in her early teens. At sixteen, soon after her high school graduation, Angelou became the single mother of a son. Her life continued to present her ample material for autobiography. She has been at various times in her life a streetcar conductor, Creole cook, madam, prostitute, junkie, singer, actress, and civil-rights activist. Angelou toured Europe for the U.S. State Department in *Porgy and Bess*, and appeared on Broadway and Off-Broadway in the Negro Ensemble Theater Company's famous production of Jean Genet's *The Blacks*. She wrote for the theater, the movies, television, and achieved celebrity with the first volume of her autobiography *I Know Why the Caged Bird Sings*. Married and divorced several times, Angelou has lived and worked in Ghana and in Egypt, where she was associate editor of the English language *Arab Observer*. Angelou has written plays, composed musical scores, written television programs, and lectured on literature. She achieved national prominence in 1993 when she read "On the Pulse of the Morning," a poem she had written, at his request, for Bill Clinton's presidential inauguration.

MAJOR WORKS

As in her volumes of autobiography, Angelou's poems suggest a context of experiences and character of incidents that give them meaning, rather than being autonomous creations independent of external, experiential reference. As with her volumes of autobiography, they, too, show twin concerns: the effects and consequences of individual desire, experience, oppression, and loss, and the social, psychological, and spiritual responses to racial and sexual brutality.

CRITICAL RECEPTION

Despite the popular success of her poetry, general critical consensus holds that Angelou would be hardly known as a poet were she not famous for the chronicles of her life. Her poems are considered by some critics to be thin in substance, lacking in poetic invention, and lackluster in language. Others, however, argue that the poems belong to a neglected oral tradition, incorporate elements of African-

American slave songs and work songs, and must be seen as lyrics which require performance to reveal their depth and riches. As critic Lyman B. Hagen has observed, "Angelou may rank as a poet of moderate ability, but her poetry is praised for its honesty and for a moving sense of dignity."

PRINCIPAL WORKS

Poetry

Just Give Me A Cool Drink of Water 'fore I Diiie 1971
Oh Pray My Wings Are Gonna Fit Me Well 1975
And Still I Rise 1978
Shaker, Why Don't You Sing? 1983
Now Sheba Sings the Song 1987
I Shall Not Be Moved 1990
"On the Pulse of Morning" 1993
The Complete Collected Poems of Maya Angelou 1994
Phenomenal Woman: Four Poems Celebrating Women 1995

Other Major Works

I Know Why the Caged Bird Sings (autobiography) 1970
Singin' and Swingin' and Gettin' Merry Like Christmas (novel) 1976
The Heart of a Woman (autobiography) 1981
Gather Together in My Name (autobiography) 1983
All God's Children Need Travelling Shoes (autobiography) 1986

Other Works

Cabaret for Freedom [with Godfrey Cambridge] (drama) 1960
The Least of These (drama) 1966
Black, Blues, Black (television series) 1968
Georgia, Georgia (screenplay) 1972
Ajax (drama adapted from Sophocles) 1974
All Day Long (screenplay) 1974
Assignment America (television series) 1975
And Still I Rise (drama) 1976
"The Inheritors" (television script) 1976
"Sister, Sister" (television script) 1982
"The Legacy" 1983
I Shall Not Be Moved 1990

CRITICISM

R. B. Stepto (essay date 1979)

SOURCE: A review of *And Still I Rise*, in *Parnassus*,Vol. 8, No. 1, Fall–Winter, 1979, pp. 313–15.

[*In the following review, Stepto finds the poems in Angelou's third volume "woefully thin," but significant because of their relation to her autobiographical writing.*]

. . . ***And Still I Rise*** is Angelou's third volume of verse, and most of its thirty-two poems are as slight as those which dominated the pages of the first two books. Stanzas such as this one,

> In every town and village,
> In every city square,
> In crowded places
> I search the faces
> Hoping to find
> Someone to care.

or the following,

> Then you rose into my life,
> Like a promised sunrise.
> Brightening my days with the light in your eyes.
> I've never been so strong,
> Now I'm where I belong.

cannot but make lesser-known talents grieve all the more about how this thin stuff finds its way to the rosters of a major New York house while their stronger, more inventive lines seem to be relegated to low-budget (or no-budget) journals and presses. On the other hand, a good Angelou poem has what we call "possibilities." One soon discovers that she is on her surest ground when she "borrows" various folk idioms and forms and thereby buttresses her poems by evoking aspects of a culture's written and unwritten heritage. **"One More Round,"** for example, gains most of its energy from "work songs" and "protest songs" that have come before. In this eight-stanza poem, the even-number stanzas constitute a refrain—obviously, a "work song" refrain:

> One more round
> And let's heave it down.
> One more round
> And let's heave it down.

At the heart of the odd-number stanzas are variations upon the familiar "protest" couplet "But before I'll be a slave / I'll be buried in my grave," such as the following: "I was born to work up to my grave / But I was not born / To be a slave." The idea of somehow binding "work" and "protest" forms to create new art is absolutely first rate, but the mere alternation of "work" and "protest" stanzas does not, in this instance, carry the idea very far.

Other poems, such as **"Willie,"** cover familiar ground previously charted by Sterling Brown, Langston Hughes, and

Gwendolyn Brooks. Indeed, Angelou's Willie, despite his rare powers and essences ("When the sun rises / I am the time. / When the children sing / I am the Rhyme"), approaches becoming memorable only when he is placed in that pantheon where Brooks's Satin-Legs Smith and Brown's Sportin' Beasly are already seated. Similarly, **"Through the Inner City to the Suburbs," "Lady Luncheon Club,"** and **"Momma Welfare Roll"** bear strong resemblances to several poems of Brooks's pre-Black Aesthetic period in *Annie Allen* and *The Bean-Eaters.*

Up to a point, **"Still I Rise,"** Angelou's title poem, reminds us of Brown's famous "Strong Men," and it is the discovery of that point which helps us define Angelou's particular presence and success in contemporary letters and, if we may say so, in publishing. The poetic and visual rhythms created by the repetition of "Still I rise" and its variants clearly revoice that of Brown's "strong men . . . strong men gittin' stronger." But the "I" of Angelou's refrain is obviously female and, in this instance, a woman forthright about the sexual nuances of personal and social struggle:

> Does my sexiness upset you?
> Does it come as a surprise
> That I dance like I've got diamonds
> At the meeting of my thighs?

Needless to say, the woman "rising" from these lines is largely unaccounted for in the earlier verse of men and women poets alike. Most certainly, this "phenomenal woman," as she terms herself in another poem, is not likely to appear, except perhaps in a negative way, in the feminist verse of our time. Where she *does* appear is in Angelou's own marvelous autobiographies, *I Know Why The Caged Bird Sings* and *Gather Together in My Name.* In short, Angelou's poems are often woefully thin as poems but they nevertheless work their way into contemporary literary history. In their celebration of a particularly defined "phenomenal woman," they serve as ancillary, supporting texts for Angelou's more adeptly rendered self-portraits, and even guide the reader to (or back to) the autobiographies. With this achieved, Angelou's "phenomenal woman," as persona *and* self-portrait, assumes a posture in our literature that would not be available if she were the product of Angelou's prose or verse alone.

Maya Angelou with Cheryl Wall (essay date 1981)

SOURCE: "Women Writers Talking," edited by Janet Todd, Holmes & Meier Publishers, 1983, pp. 59–67.

[In the following interview, originally conducted in 1981, Angelou talks about her writing habits and the values by which she is guided, and those which she wishes to pass on.]

In 1969 Maya Angelou published *I Know Why the Caged Bird Sings*, a memoir of her girlhood in Stamps, Arkansas, and San Francisco, California. The book quickly became a contemporary classic. More fully than any writer before her, Angelou laid bare the pain of the black girl's coming of age. She counted the costs of being doubly disenfranchised in a society that denied black women's beauty and worth. Yet interlaced with the sadness was joy, conveyed in the spiritual peace and power of her grandmother and in the élan with which her mother lived her life. Ultimately, *Caged Bird* is a song of triumph: the young Maya's triumph over self-hatred, the triumph of the black communities that sustained themselves despite the white world's racism, and the triumph of a writer whose love and command of language are profound.

Three subsequent volumes, *Gather Together in My Name, Singin', Swingin', and Gettin' Merry Like Christmas*, and *The Heart of a Woman*, document Angelou's womanhood. They record her successful careers as dancer, singer, actress, and civil rights administrator as well as her extensive travels in Africa and Europe. With the last book she has chronicled her life and times up until the early 1960s.

Over the last decade she has published three books of poetry, ***Just Give Me a Cool Drink of Water 'fore I Diiie, Oh Pray My Wings Are Gonna Fit Me Well***, and ***And Still I Rise***. In addition she has written several movie and television scripts, including the adaptation of *Caged Bird.*

Yet, it is on her four memoirs that her literary reputation mainly rests. In the following pages, Angelou discusses the art of autobiography—her sources and her method. Her claims for the originality of her form prove unexpectedly convincing. Hers is an audacious experiment. While the results have been uneven, the best of her books—like *The Heart of a Woman*—blend the individual and the collective, the witty and the wise, in an inimitable style. Angelou subscribes fully to her own dictum: "A good autobiographer seems to write about herself and is in fact writing about the temper of the times."

Assisted by Wendy Kuppermann, I interviewed Maya Angelou in New York in December, 1981. Angelou's calendar was characteristically full. She was to fly to Ghana the next day to arrange for a course, "African Culture and Its Impact on the West," she will offer next fall at Wake Forest University where she has accepted a professorship. Work in progress includes a book of narrative, free-verse poems that signal a new direction for her poetry. Although it will be a year or two before she starts writing the next one, she promises that more volumes of her memoir will be forthcoming.

Cheryl Wall: *You have just published* The Heart of a Woman, *the fourth volume of an autobiography that began with* I Know Why the Caged Bird Sings *in 1969. Yet from passages in all four books, a reader may infer that Maya Angelou is a private person. If this inference is correct, how difficult has it been to relinquish, that privacy in order to share your experiences with readers?*

Maya Angelou: The difficulty is met early on by making a choice. I made a choice to become an autobiographer. You know the saying, "You make your bed and do whatever you want in it." I find autobiography as a form little used. I know no serious writer in the United States who has chosen to use autobiography as the vehicle for his or her most serious work. So as a form, it has few precedents. But I decided to use it. Now, I made that choice, I ain't got no choice. Unless I found it totally untenable—if it was running me totally mad or if I lost the magic—then that would be a different matter. I would start to look at fiction or go back to plays. But having said I'm going to write autobiography as literature and to write history as literature, then I have made that agreement with myself and my work and I can't be less than honest about it. So I have to tell private things, first to remember them and then to so enchant myself that I'm back there in that time.

I love teaching Caged Bird *because the voice of the child from the very beginning is so authentic. I understand that as a part of the PBS television series,* Creativity, *you returned to Stamps and once there, you said, "became twelve years old again." Did you revisit the scenes of your childhood before writing that book? How did you reawaken that part of your past?*

It's a kind of enchantment. It's a scary one, whether it was in that book or in *Gather Together in My Name.* I go to work everyday about 6:30 in the morning. I keep a hotel room and I go to the same room each day, and it takes about a half hour to shuffle off the external coil and all that. Before I go—it's like a trip in a time machine—my concern, my hesitation in fact, is that I won't be able to come out. It is truly strange. But to write it so that the reader is there and *thinks* he's making it up, to make the reader believe that she is the one who is doing that, or is the one to whom it is being done, you have to be there in the place. Ohhh!

Can you elaborate on the process? When you have finished for the day, is it easy then, or is it possible to put the past aside, to leave it in the hotel room?

I always leave no earlier than 12:30, even when the work is going poorly; if the work is going well, I'll stay until 1:30. Then I leave the hotel and go shopping for my food. And *that's* real! And I'm six foot tall and my face is somewhat known. In a little town (and I always manage to live in small towns), people will have maybe the day before or week before seen me on the Merv Griffin show, but since I operate in the town I'm not a celebrity from whom people feel separate. So people see me and they say, "Hello, Miss Angelou. I saw you on the so and so." But they have also seen me in the gardening shop and in the old folks home and playing with children, so I'm kind of a celebrity with honor. But that means that when I come out of that hotel room and go to the market, suddenly my feet get the familiarity of the place. I'm encouraged back into the time in which I live. And it's real again.

Then I go home and have a drink or two or however many and prepare dinner. I love to cook. I am a cook. I write, cook, and drive. Those are my accomplishments.

All of which you started early.

That's true, too true. After I've put dinner on and showered, then I read the work. So by 4:30 or 5 o'clock in the afternoon, I read what I have written that day. I start then to cut extraneous "ands," "ifs," "toos," "fors," "buts," "howevers"—all those out! Any repetition of description, out. Just cut, cut, cut. And then I leave it and set the table and sit down to dinner. And about nine o'clock I pick up the work again, now with all those cuts, and look at it again and start making marginal notes. And I'm finished with the yellow pad. The next morning I take a fresh yellow pad and go out and start the thing all over again. And I do that five days a week.

In about a month, when I've got stacks of yellow pads, I will pull all the pages off and put them in order and I will take one day to read it all. Then I start to write again. As I write it the second time, I see how cavalier I have been with the language, with the craft, so I try to make that one really clean, hot, terse. And then when I've finished that, I go back to work. But at least in the period, I'm not doing that going down inside and it's a lot like a vacation in a way.

How long does the entire process take, for instance with this last book?

About a year and eight months.

Autobiographies by black women have been exceedingly rare, and to my knowledge, none of the few before yours has probed personal experience very deeply. Why and how did you select the form?

The form is intriguing. Maybe third, certainly half into *Caged Bird*, I realized that a good autobiographer (whatever that means and I don't know what that means *yet*—I'm learning the form. I am molding the form and the form is molding me. That's the truth of it.), a good autobiographer seems to write about herself and is in fact writing about the temper of the times. A good one is writing history from one person's viewpoint. So that a good one brings the reader into a historical event as if the reader was standing there, bridled the horse for Paul Revere, joined Dred Scott, actually was there. What I'm trying to do is very ambitious, because I am trying, I hope, to lay a foundation for a form. And I know it's ambitious, it's egomaniacal. I know all that, I don't mind. There it is. I mean, I do mind; I'd love to be nice and sweet and loved by everyone, but there it is.

There are writers now and coming who will develop that form. It is important to remember how new the novel as a form is. So somebody in the next twenty, thirty, five years, or next year will write autobiography going through the door I have opened, or cracked anyway, and really show us what that form can be. One has to see it as stemming from the slave narrative and developing into a new American literary form. It's ambitious, I told you, it's ambitious. . . .

By the time I left Momma, I knew what was right and what wasn't. I have a painting now by Phoebe Beasley called *Sister Fannie's Funeral.* It depicts women sitting on fold-up chairs, and it reminds me of all the women in my grandmother's prayer-meeting group. There's one empty chair that for me is Momma's. Whenever I have a debate within myself about right action, I just sit down and look at that and think now, what would Momma say? So, morals and generosity, good things, I believe I got at Momma's lap.

Your grandmother and her teachings seem always to have been an anchor. Many black children coming of age today don't have that link to their past; is there anything that can replace it?

Nothing. I see nothing. It's tragic. There is no substitute for parental and/or family love. And by love, I do not in any way mean indulgence. I mean love . . . that quality so strong it holds the earth on its axis. The child needs that carrying over of wisdom from the family to the child directly, and there is no substitute. Society cannot do it, despite the 1984 concepts of Big Brother and a larger society caring for a child and imbuing the child with values. One needs it from someone to whom one is physically attached.

That whole theme of the maternal figure is apparent in the work of many black women writers and white women as well. That leads me to wonder, is there a community of writers of which you feel a part—Afro-American writers, women writers, particular individual writers?

That's a question . . . I'm a member of the community of writers, serious writers; I suppose much like a drug addict is a member of a community. I know what it costs to write . . . as soon as that is so, one is part of that community.

I'm part of the Afro-American writing community, because that is so. I'm writing out of my own background, but it is also the background of Toni Morrison, Toni Cade Bambara, Nikki Giovanni, Carolyn Rodgers, Jayne Cortez. All the black women who are writing today and who have written in the past: we write out of the same pot.

I know that the title of Caged Bird *is taken from a poem by Paul Laurence Dunbar. Does the new book's title allude to the poem by Georgia Douglas Johnson, the poet of the Harlem Renaissance?*

It certainly does. "The heart of a woman goes forth with the dawn . . ." I love that woman. I have *Bronze* [Johnson's second book, published in 1922]. It's in my nightstand. I will not put it even in my own private bookcases, let alone in the library. It's in my nightstand and there it will stay.

How long have you known of her work?

Since I was a very young person. I love Anne Spencer too. So different . . . born a year apart . . . but so different.

Many Afro-American writers cite music as a primary influence on their work. References to music recur in your prose and poetry. In fact, you begin Singin', Swingin', and Gettin' Merry Like Christmas *with the statement: "Music was my refuge." Do you believe Afro-American music in particular has shaped your work as well as your life?*

So much. I listen for the rhythm in everything I write, in prose or poetry. And the rhythms I use are very much like the blues and the spirituals. So that more often than not they are in 3/4 or 4/4 time. For example: [she reads from *The Heart of a Woman*] "The drive to the airport was an adventure in motoring and a lesson in conversational dissembling" [p. 76]. "His clear tenor floated up over the heads of the already-irate passengers. The haunting beauty of the melody must have quelled some of the irritation, because no one asked Liam to shut up" [p. 77]. "It seemed to me that I washed, scrubbed, mopped, dusted and waxed thoroughly every other day. Vus was particular. He checked on my progress. Sometimes he would pull the sofa away from the wall to see if possibly . . ." [p. 141]. It is *always* there, wherever; it seems to me that there is the rhythm. And the melody of the piece, I work very hard for that melody.

A young woman told me that I had it easy because I have the art which Graham Greene has of making writing, a complex thing, seem so simple. So I said yes, it's hard work, and she replied, yes, but you have the art. But [to paraphrase Hemingway] "easy reading is damned hard writing."

Until I read The Heart of a Woman, *I had not realized how very much involved you had been with the civil rights movement. In this book you really capture the incredible sense of momentum, the vitality, and the hope. How important were those experiences as catalysts for your art?*

I suppose it's so important for me in my life that it must come through in the work. Despite living in the middle of murk, I am an optimist. It is *contrived* optimism; it is not pollyanna. I have to really work very hard to find that flare of a kitchen match in a hurricane and claim it, shelter it, praise it. Very important. The challenge to hope in a hopeless time is a part of our history. And I take it for myself personally, for me, Maya. I believe somewhere just beyond my knowing now, there is knowing and I shall know. *This* I shall overcome. There is a light, no larger than a pinhead, but I shall know. When I say I take it personally, I take that tradition of hoping against hope, which is the tradition of black Americans, for myself.

That may perhaps be defined as a spiritual quality. Do you see your writing as political as well as spiritual?

Well, yes. In the large sense, in that everything is political. If something I write encourages one person to save her life, then that is a political act. I wrote *Gather Together in My Name*—the most painful book until *The Heart of a Woman.* In the book I had to admit, confess; I had to talk about prostitution, and it was painful. I talked to my son, my mother, my brother, and my husband, and they said, "Tell it." I called the book *Gather Together in My Name,* because so many people lie to young people. They say, "I have no skeletons in my closet. Why, when I was young I always obeyed." And they lie like everything. So I thought all those people could gather together in my name. I would tell it.

I had a lot of really ugly things happen as a result right after the book's publication. Then I arrived in Cleveland, Ohio, and I was doing a signing in a large department store. Maybe one hundred fifty people were in line. Suddenly I looked and there were black fingers and long fingernails that had curved over in the mandarin style. And I looked to follow those up and the woman had a wig down to here, a miniskirt, a fake-fur minicoat, which had been dirtied—it might have been white once—false eyelashes out to there. She was about eighteen, maybe twenty. She leaned over and said, "Lady, I wanna tell you something, you even give me goddamn hope." If she was the only person . . . The encouragement is: you may encounter defeats, but you must not be defeated.

Apart from your grandmother, can you identify what gave you that belief?

My mom, my mom is outrageous. And I'm a Christian or trying to be. I'm very religious. I try to live what I understand a Christian life to be. It's my nature to try to be larger than what I appear to be, and that's a religious yearning.

Although all your books give insight into a quintessentially female experience, The Heart of a Woman *seems to explore the most explicitly feminist themes. For example, your treatment of single motherhood and the portrayal of your marriage to a South African freedom fighter. Has the feminist movement influenced your reflections on your past?*

No. I am a feminist, I am black, I am a human being. Now those three things are circumstances, as you look at the forces behind them, over which I have no control. I was born as a human being, born as a black, and born as a female. Other things I may deal with, my Americanness for example, or I may shift political loyalties. But, these three things I *am.* It is embarrassing, in fact insulting, for a woman to be asked if she's a feminist, or a human, if he's a humanist, or a black if he's black inside. It goes with the territory. It is embarrassing for a woman to hear another woman say, "I am not a feminist." What do you mean?! Who do you side with?

The book is about a woman's heart, about surviving and being done down, surviving and being done down. If I were a man, I hope I would have the presence of mind to write "The Heart of a Man" and the courage to do so. But I have to talk about what I see, what I see as a black woman. I have to speak with my own voice.

One of the most moving passages in The Heart of a Woman *involves a conversation among women married to African freedom fighters. You and the other women—most of whom are African, one of whom is West Indian—forge a powerful common bond. Is there a broader lesson in that scene; are there bonds linking black women on several continents?*

If you have the luck to encounter women who will tell. That experience had to do in particular with African women. In Egypt, through the poet Hanifa Fahty, I met a group of Egyptian women involved with the Arab Women's League. They were at once struggling against the larger oppressor, colonialism, and against a history of masculine oppression from their own men. I understood it. Unfortunately. I would like to say it's such a rare occurrence that it was exotic; unfortunately, I understood it clearly. It would be the same if I were in Vietnam and talked to the Vietnamese women. It is one of the internationally pervasive problems, and women today are choosing to take courage as their banner. Courage is the most important virtue because without it you can't practice any of the other virtues with consistency.

Do you see alliances being formed among women in various societies who are facing like problems?

I haven't seen them yet. It must happen. But you have to consider that certain movements are very new. One of the many American problems built into the fabric of the country, beyond the woven-in lie of "we hold these truths to be self-evident that all men are created equal," beyond the inherent lie that the people who were writing those statements owned other human beings, one of the serious problems has been looking at the idea of freedom as every human being's inherent right. Just by being born, you've got it. It is ridiculous as a concept. It is wishful, wistful, and foolish. Freedom and justice for a group of animals is a dream to work toward. It is not on every corner waiting to be picked up with the Sunday paper.

As a species we have not evolved much beyond the conceiving of the idea. Now that's fabulous, and for that we need to salute ourselves. But to say that we have conceived the idea and the next moment it is in our laps is ridiculous. We have to work diligently, courageously, without ceasing, to bring this thing into being. It is still in the mind. It will take us hundreds of years, if not thousands, to actually bring it so that we can see it. We need to tell our children that this quality which has been conceived of most recently by human beings is something wonderful to work for. And your children's children and your children's children's children and everybody will be working to pull this order out of disorder.

The joy then is in the struggle.

Yes, yes, then you begin to understand that you love the process. The process has as its final end the realization, but you fall in love with the process.

We are new as a species. We just got here yesterday. The reptiles were on this little ball of spit and sand 300 million years. We just grew an opposing thumb—I think it was last week—and grew it by trying to pick up something to beat somebody down.

The terrifying irony is that we live such a short time. And it takes so long for an idea to be realized. Can you imagine the first person who had these fingers and saw this little nub growing and said, "Got the nub, pretty soon we're going to be able to hold on to the whole hatchet?" Not to know that it was to be another three million years. You see?

Thomas Wolfe calls us "dupes of time and moths of gravity." We're like fireflies—lighted by an idea and hardly any time to work at it. Certainly no time if we don't realize it has to be worked for. At least in this brief span, we can try to come to grips with how large an idea it is and how much work it demands, and try to pass it on to one other person. That's more than some people can achieve in a lifetime.

J. T. Keefe (review date 1983)

SOURCE: A review of *Shaker, Why Don't You Sing?* in *World Literature Today*, Vol. 58, No. 4, Autumn, 1984, p. 607.

[*In the following thumbnail review, Keefe praises Angelou's poems in* Shaker, Why Don't You Sing?]

Deceptively light and graceful, Maya Angelou's poems are lyrical, emotional, melancholy. They move to inner tunes—"I wait in silence / For the bridal croon," we read in the title poem—and chart a stoic angst reminiscent of Piaf. As in Piaf, there is here deep gut feeling based on history and myth. **"Family Affairs"** is a poem that encapsulates the story of the poet's painful origins, beautifully realized in contrapuntal harmony against the legend of Rapunzel (she of the folktale who let down her golden hair for her lover to climb to her tower). With an enviable economy, Angelou contrasts black/white tensions, using this myth as a framework. It is a wise and deeply felt poem. Again, **"Caged Bird"** expresses this poet's central motif. A rhythmical and hypnotic chant that cries out to be sung, the actual form of the poem echoes its theme.

> The caged bird sings
> with a fearful trill
> of things unknown
> but longed for still
> and his tune is heard
> on the distant hill
> for the caged bird
> Sings of freedom.

These poems are full of shining hurt as, like curving scimitars, they skillfully pierce the hearts of their readers.

Maya Angelou with Claudia Tate (interview date 1983)

SOURCE: "Conversations with Maya Angelou," edited by Jeffrey M. Elliot, University Press of Mississippi, 1989, pp. 146–56.

[In the following interview, originally conducted in 1983, Angelou discusses the influence of other writers, social conditions, and her own experience upon her work.]

Maya Angelou: Image making is very important for every human being. It is especially important for black American women in that we are, by being black, a minority in the United States, and by being female, the less powerful of the genders. So, we have two areas we must address. If we look out of our eyes at the immediate world around us, we see whites and males in dominant roles. We need to see our mothers, aunts, our sisters, and grandmothers. We need to see Frances Harper, Sojourner Truth, Fannie Lou Hamer, women of our heritage. We need to have these women preserved. We need them all: . . . Constance Motley, Etta Motten. . . . All of these women are important as role models. Depending on our profession, some may be even more important. Zora Neale Hurston means a great deal to me as a writer. So does Josephine Baker, but not in the same way because her profession is not directly related to mine. Yet I would imagine for someone like Diahann Carroll or Diana Ross, Miss Baker must mean a great deal. I would imagine that Bessie Smith and Mammie Smith, though they are important to me, would be even more so to Aretha Franklin.

If I were a black male writer, I would think of Frederick Douglass, who was not just a politician, but as a writer was stunning. In the nineteenth century I would think of William Wells Brown, Martin Delaney, and certainly David Walker, who showed not only purpose but method. In the twentieth century I would think of Richard Wright, Jean Toomer, and so on. They mean a great deal to me. I'm black, and they experienced America as blacks. These particular writers may mean more to the black male writer, just as I imagine Jack Johnson would mean a great deal to Jesse Owens, and Jesse Owens a great deal to Arthur Ashe.

Claudia Tate: When you write, are you particularly conscious of preserving certain kinds of images of black people?

Well, I am some time, though I can't actually say when this happens in the creation of the work. I make writing as much a part of my life as I do eating or listening to music. Once I left church, and as I walked down the street, three young black women stopped me and asked if I would have a glass of wine with them. I said, "Yes." One is a painter; one is an actress, and one a singer. We talked, and when I started to leave, I tried to tell them what it means to me to see young black women. I tried to tell them, but I could hardly explain it. My eyes filled with tears. In one way, it means all the work, all the loneliness and discipline my work exacts, demands, is not in vain. It also means, in a more atavistic, absolutely internal way, that I can never die. It's like living through children. So when I approach a piece of work, *that* is in my approach, whether it's a poem that might appear frivolous or is a serious piece. In my approach I take as fact that my work will be carried on.

Did you envision young Maya as a symbolic character for every black girl growing up in America?

Yes, after a while I did. It's a strange condition, being an autobiographer and a poet. I have to be so internal, and yet while writing, I have to be apart from the story so that I don't fall into indulgence. Whenever I speak about the books, I always think in terms of the Maya character. When I wrote the teleplay of *I Know Why the Caged Bird Sings,* I would refer to the Maya character so as not to mean me. It's damned difficult for me to preserve this distancing. But it's very necessary.

What has been the effect of the women's movement on black women?

Black women and white women are in strange positions in our separate communities. In the social gatherings of black people, black women have always been predominant. That is to say, in the church it's always Sister Hudson, Sister Thomas and Sister Witheringay who keep the church alive. In lay gatherings it's always Lottie who cooks, and Mary who's going over to Bonita's where there is a good party going on. Also, black women are the nurturers of children in our community. White women are in a different position in their social institutions. White men, who are in effect their fathers, husbands, brothers, their sons, nephews and uncles, say to white women, or imply in any case: "I don't really need you to run my institutions. I need you in certain places and in those places you must be kept—in the bedroom, in the kitchen, in the nursery, and on the pedestal." Black women have never been told this. Black women have not historically stood in the pulpit, but that doesn't undermine the fact that they built the churches and maintain the pulpits. The people who have historically been heads of institutions in black communities have never said to black women—and they, too, are their fathers, husbands, brothers, their sons, nephews and uncles—"We don't need you in our institutions." So there is a fundamental difference.

One of the problems I see that faces black women in the eighties, just as it has in the past two decades, has been dealt with quite well in Michele Wallace's *Black Macho and the Myth of the Superwoman.* A number of black men in the sixties fell for a terrible, terrible ploy. They felt that in order to be total and free and independent and powerful, they had to be like white men to their women. So there was a terrible time when black men told their women that if you really love me, you must walk three steps behind me.

I try to live what I consider a "poetic existence." That means I take responsibility for the air I breathe and the space I take up. I try to be immediate, to be totally present for all my work. *I try.* This interview with you is a prime example of this. I am withdrawing from the grief that awaits me over the death of someone dear so that I can be present for you, for myself, for your work and for the people who will read it, so I can tell you exactly how I feel and what I think and try to answer your questions cheerfully—if I feel cheerful—as I can. That to me is poetic. I try for concentrated consciousness which I miss by more than half, but I'm trying.

How do you fit writing into your life?

Writing is a part of my life; cooking is a part of my life. Making love is a part of my life; walking down the street is a part of it. Writing demands more time, but it takes from all of these other activities. They all feed into the writing. I think it's dangerous to concern oneself too damned much with "being an artist." It's more important to get the work done. You don't have to concern yourself with it, just get it done. The pondering pose—the back of the hand glued against the forehead—is baloney. People spend more time posing than getting the work done. The work is all there is. And when it's done, then you can laugh, have a pot of beans, stroke some child's head, or skip down the street.

What is your responsibility as a writer?

My responsibility as a writer is to be as good as I can be at my craft. So I study my craft. I don't simply write what I feel, let it all hang out. That's baloney. That's no craft at all. Learning the craft, understanding what language can do, gaining control of the language, enables one to make people weep, make them laugh, even make them go to war. You can do this by learning how to harness the power of the word. So studying my craft is one of my responsibilities. The other is to be as good a human being as I possibly can be so that once I have achieved control of the language, I don't force my weaknesses on a public who might then pick them up and abuse themselves.

During the sixties some lecturers went to universities and took thoughtless liberties with young people. They told them "to turn on, tune in and drop out." People still do that. They go to universities and students will ask them, "Mr. So-and-So, Ms./Miss./Mrs./Brother/Sister So-and-So, these teachers here at this institution aren't happening, like what should we do?" Many lecturers have said, "Don't take it! Walk out! Let your protest be seen." That lecturer then gets on a plane, first-class, with a double scotch on-the-rocks, jets off to San Juan, Puerto Rico, for a few days' rest, then travels to some other place where he or she is being paid two to three thousand dollars to speak. Those young people risk and sometimes lose their scholastic lives on that zoom because somebody's been irresponsible. I loathe that. I will not do it. I *am* responsible. I *am* trying to be responsible.

So first, I'm always trying to be a better human being, and second, I continue to learn my craft. Then, when I have something positive to say, I can say it beautifully. That's my responsibility.

Do you see any distinctions in the ways black male and female writers dramatize their themes and select significant events? This is a general question, but perhaps there is some basis for analysis. Gayl Jones responded to this question by saying she thought women tended to deal with events concerning the family, the community, personal events, that were not generally thought to be important by male writers. She said that male writers tended to select "representative" events for the significant events in their works. Toni Bambara said she thought women writers were concerned with developing a circumscribed place from which the story would unfold. Have you observed such patterns in your reading?

I find those observations interesting. In fact, the question is very interesting. I think black male writers do deal with the particular, but we are so conditioned by a sexist society that we tend to think when they do so that they mean it representationally; and when black females deal with the particular they only mean it as such. Whether we look at works by Richard Wright, James Baldwin, or John Killens—I'm thinking of novelists—we immediately say this is a generalization; this is meant as an overview, a microcosmic view of the world at large. Yet, if we look at works by Toni Morrison or Toni Bambara, if we look at Alice Walker's work or Hurston's, Rosa Guy's, Louise Meriwether's, or Paule Marshall's, we must say that these works are meant as general statements, universal statements. If *Daddy Was a Numbers Runner* [by Louise Meriwether] is not a microcosm of a macrocosm, I don't know what it is. If Paule Marshall's *Chosen Place and Timeless People* is not a microcosm, I don't know what it is. I don't know what *Ruby* [by Rosa Guy] is if it is not a microcosm of a larger world. I see everybody's work as an example of the particular, which is indicative of the general. I don't see any difference really. Whether it's Claude Brown's or Gayl Jones's. I can look at *Manchild in the Promised Land* and at *Corregidora* and see that these writers are talking about particular situations and yet about the general human condition. They are instructive for the generalities of our lives. Therefore, I won't indulge inherent distinctions between men and women writers.

Do you consider your quartet to be autobiographical novels or autobiographies?

They are autobiographies. When I wrote *I Know Why the Caged Bird Sings,* I wasn't thinking so much about my own life or identity. I was thinking about a particular time in which I lived and the influences of that time on a number of people. I kept thinking, what about that time? What were the people around young Maya doing? I used the central figure—myself—as a focus to show how one person can make it through those times.

I really got roped into writing *The Caged Bird.* At that time I was really only concerned with poetry, though I'd written a television series. Anyway, James Baldwin took me to a party at Jules Feiffer's house. It was just the four of us: Jimmy Baldwin and me, Jules Feiffer and his wife, at that time Judy Feiffer. We sat up until three or four o'clock in the morning, drinking scotch and telling tales. The next morning Judy Feiffer called a friend of hers at Random House and said, "You know the poet, Maya Angelou? If you can get her to write a book . . ." Then Robert Loomis at Random House phoned, and I said, "No, I'm not interested." I went out to California and produced my series for WNET. Loomis called two or three times, and I said, "No, I'm not interested. Thank you so much." Then, I'm sure he talked to Baldwin because he used a ploy which I'm not proud to say I haven't gained control of yet. He called and said, "Miss Angelou, it's been nice talking to you. I'm rather glad you decided not to write an autobiography because to write an autobiography as literature is the most difficult thing anyone could do." I said, "I'll do it." Now that's an area I don't have control of yet at this age. The minute someone says I can't, all my energy goes up and I say, what? What? I'm still unable to say that you may be wrong and walk away. I'm not pleased with that. I want to get beyond that.

How did you select the events to present in the autobiographies?

Some events stood out in my mind more than others. Some, though, were never recorded because they either were so bad or so painful, that there was no way to write about them honestly and artistically without making them melodramatic. They would have taken the book off its course. All my work, my life, everything is about survival. All my work is meant to say, "You may encounter many defeats, but you must not be defeated." In fact, the encountering may be the very experience which creates the vitality and the power to endure.

You are a writer, poet, director, composer, lyricist, dancer, singer, journalist, teacher and lecturer. Can you say what the source of such creative diversity is?

I don't do the dancing anymore. The rest I try. I believe talent is like electricity. We don't understand electricity. We use it. Electricity makes no judgment. You can plug into it and light up a lamp, keep a heart pump going, light a cathedral, or you can electrocute a person with it. Electricity will do all that. It makes no judgment. I think talent is like that. I believe every person is born with talent. I believe anyone can learn the craft of painting and paint.

I believe all things are possible for a human being, and I don't think there's anything in the world I can't do. Of course, I can't be five feet four because I'm six feet tall. I can't be a man because I'm a woman. The physical gifts are given to me, just like having two arms is a gift. In my creative source, whatever that is, I don't see why I can't sculpt. Why shouldn't I? Human beings sculpt. I'm a human being. I refuse to indulge any man-made differences between myself and another human being. I will not do it. I'm not going to live very long. If I live another fifty years, it's not very long. So I should indulge somebody else's prejudice at their whim and not for my own convenience! Never happen! Not me!

How do you integrate protest in your work?

Protest is an inherent part of my work. You can't just not write about protest themes or not sing about them. It's a part of life. If I don't agree with a part of life, then my work has to address it.

I remember in the early fifties I read a book, *Dom Casmurro.* It was written by Machado De Assis, a nineteenth-century Brazilian. I thought it was very good. A month later I thought about the book and went back and reread it. Two months later I read the book again, and six months later I realized the sensation that I had had while reading the book was as if I had walked down to a beach to watch a sunset. I had watched the sunset and turned around, only to find that while I had been standing there the tide had come in over my head. I decided to write like that. I would never get on a soapbox; instead, I would pull in the reader. My work is intended to be slowly absorbed into the system on deeper and deeper levels.

Would you describe your writing process?

I usually get up at about 5:30, and I'm ready to have coffee by 6, usually with my husband. He goes off to his work around 6:30, and I go off to mine. I keep a hotel room in which I do my work—a tiny, mean room with just a bed, and sometimes, if I can find it, a face basin. I keep a dictionary, a Bible, a deck of cards and a bottle of sherry in the room. I try to get there around 7, and I work until 2 in the afternoon. If the work is going badly, I stay until 12:30. If it's going well, I'll stay as long as it's going well. It's lonely, and it's marvelous. I edit while I'm working. When I come home at 2, I read over what I've written that day, and then try to put it out of my mind. I shower, prepare dinner, so that when my husband comes home, I'm not totally absorbed in my work. We have a semblance of a normal life. We have a drink together and have dinner. Maybe after dinner I'll read to him what I've written that day. He doesn't comment. I don't invite comments from anyone but my editor, but hearing it aloud is good. Sometimes I hear the dissonance; then I'll try to straighten it out in the morning. When I've finished the creative work and the editing and have six hundred handwritten pages, I send it to my editor. Then we both begin to work. I've kept the same editor through six books. We have a relationship that's kind of famous among publishers, since oftentimes writers shift from one publisher to another for larger advances. I just stay with my own editor, and we'll be together as long as he and I are alive. He understands my work rhythm, and I understand his. We respect each other, but the nitpicking does come. He'll say, "This bothers me—on page twelve, line three, why do you have a comma there? Do you mean to break the flow?"

How do you feel about your past works?

Generally, I forget them. I'm totally free of them. They have their own life. I've done well by them, or I did the best I could, which is all I can say. I'm not cavalier about work anymore than I am about sitting here with you, or cooking a meal, or cleaning my house. I've tried to be totally present, so that when I'm finished with a piece of work, I'm finished. I remember one occasion when we were in New York City at the Waldorf Astoria some years ago. I think I was with my sister friends—Rosa [Guy], Paule [Marshall] and Louise [Meriwether]. We were sitting at a table near the bandstand during some tribute for someone, and I felt people staring at me. Someone was singing, say, stage left, and some people were performing a dance. It was very nice, but I felt people staring; so I turned around, and they were. My sister friends were all smiling. I wondered what was happening. I had been following the performance. Well, it turned out that the singer was doing a piece of mine, and they had choreographed a dance to it. I had forgotten the work altogether. The work, once completed, does not need me. The work I'm working on needs my total concentration. The one that's finished doesn't belong to me anymore. It belongs to itself.

Would you comment on your title selections?

As you probably know, the title *I Know Why the Caged Bird Sings* is from [Paul Lawrence] Dunbar's "Sympathy." *Gather Together in My Name,* though it does have a biblical origin, comes from the fact I saw so many adults lying to so many young people, lying in their teeth, saying, "You know, when I was young, I never would have done . . . Why I couldn't . . . I shouldn't . . . " Lying. Young people know when you're lying; so I thought for all those parents and non-parents alike who have lied about their past, I will tell it.

Singin' and Swingin' and Gettin' Merry Like Christmas comes from a time in the twenties and thirties when black people used to have rent parties. On Saturday night from around nine when they'd give these parties, through the next morning when they would go to church and have the Sunday meal, until early Sunday evening was the time when everyone was encouraged to sing and swing and get merry like Christmas so one would have some fuel with which to live the rest of the week.

Just Give Me a Cool Drink of Water 'Fore I Diiie refers to my belief that we as individuals in a species are still so innocent that we think we could ask our murderer just before he puts the final wrench upon the throat, "Would you please give me a cool drink of water?" and he would do so. That's innocence. It's lovely.

The tune of ***Oh, Pray My Wings Are Gonna Fit Me Well*** originally comes from a slave holler, and the words from a nineteenth-century spiritual:

Oh, pray my wings are gonna fit me well.
  I'm a lay down this heavy load.
I tried them on at the gates of hell.
  I'm a lay down this heavy load.

I planned to put all the things bothering me—my heavy load—in that book, and let them pass.

The title poem of ***And Still I Rise*** refers to the indomitable spirit of black people. Here's a bit of it:

You may write me down in history
With your bitter, twisted lies,
You may trod me in the very dirt
But still, like dust, I'll rise.

Can black women writers help clarify or help to resolve the black sexist debate that was rekindled by Ntozake Shange's For Colored Girls Who Have Considered Suicide When the Rainbow Is Enuf *and Michele Wallace's* Black Macho and the Myth of the Superwoman?

Neither Miss Shange nor Miss Wallace started the dialogue, so I wouldn't suggest any black woman is going to stop it. If anything could have clarified the dialogue, Toni Morrison's *The Song of Solomon* should have been the work to do that. I don't know if that is a chore or a goal black women writers should assume. If someone feels so inclined, then she should go on and do it.

Everything good tends to clarify. By good I mean well written and well researched. There is nothing so strong as an idea whose time has come. The writer—male or female—who is meant to clarify this issue will do so. I, myself, have no encouragement in that direction. There's a lot that hasn't been said. It may be necessary to hear the male view of *For Colored Girls* in a book or spoken upon the stage. It may be necessary, and I know it will be very painful.

What writers have influenced your work?

There were two men who probably formed my writing ambition more than any others. They were Paul Lawrence Dunbar and William Shakespeare. I love them. I love the rhythm and sweetness of Dunbar's dialect verse. I love "Candle Lighting Time" and "Little Brown Baby." I also love James Weldon Johnson's "Creation."

I am also impressed by living writers. I'm impressed with James Baldwin. I continue to see not only his craftsmanship but his courage. That means a lot to me. Courage may be the most important of all the virtues because without it one cannot practice any other virtue with consistency. I'm impressed by Toni Morrison a great deal. I long for her new works. I'm impressed by the growth of Rosa Guy. I'm impressed by Ann Petry. I'm impressed by the work of Joan Didion. Her first collection, *Slouching Toward Jerusalem,* contains short pieces, which are absolutely stunning. I would walk fifty blocks in high heels to buy the works of any of these writers. I'm a country girl, so that means a lot.

Have any of your works been misunderstood?

A number of people have asked me why I wrote about the rape in *I Know Why the Caged Bird Sings.* They wanted to know why I had to tell that rape happens in the black community. I wanted people to see that the man was not totally an ogre. The hard thing about writing or directing or producing is to make sure one doesn't make the negative person totally negative. I try to tell the truth and preserve it in all artistic forms.

Priscilla R. Ramsey (essay date 1984–5)

SOURCE: "Transcendence: The Poetry of Maya Angelou," in *Current Bibliography on African Affairs*, Vol. 17, No. 2, 1984–85, pp. 139–53.

[*In the following essay, Ramsey argues that Angelou creates transcendent meaning from oppressive experience in her poetry.*]

Maya Angelou's physical shifts from Stamps, Arkansas' Lafayette County Public School to the Village Gate's stage in Manhattan and from New York to a teaching podium at Cairo University in Egypt represent an intellectual and psychological voyage of considerable complexity—one of unpredictably erratic cyclic movement. She has chronicled some of this voyage in her three autobiographies: *I Know Why the Caged Bird Sings,*[1] a bestseller (in 1970), *Gather Together in My Name* (1974),[2] and *Singin' and Swingin' and Gettin' Merry Like Christmas* (1976).[3] Her final and most recent autobiography is *The Heart of a Woman* (1982).[4] Additionally she has written three collections of poetry: ***Oh Pray My Wings are Gonna Fit Me Well*** (1975),[5] ***And Still I Rise*** (1978),[6] and ***Just Give Me a Cool Drink of Water 'fore I Diiie*** (1971).[7]

In addition to her full length creative writing there have been so many additional accomplishments characterized by so much variety one can only speak of them superficially in this limited space. After acting in "Cabaret for Freedom," she wrote the original television screen play for "Georgia, Georgia." Angelou performed on the stage in Genet's "The Blacks" and Sophocles' "Ajax." Additionally, she explored the parallels between American life and African tradition in a ten-part series she wrote for national television in the 1960's. She worked as a journalist for national newspapers in both Ghana and Cairo.

The public achievements have been many and yet the private motivation out of which her writing generates extends beyond the mere search for words as metaphors for purely private experience. Her poetry becomes both political and confessional. Significantly, one sees in her autobiographies a role-modeling process—one paradigmatic for other women—while not allowing the didactic to become paramount in either the poetry or the autobiographies.

Her autobiographies and poetry reveal a vital need to transform the elements of a stultifying and destructive personal, social, political and historical milieu into a sensual and physical refuge. Loneliness and human distantiation pervade both her love and political poetry, but are counterposed by a glorification of life and sensuality which produces a transcendence over all which could otherwise destroy and create her despair. This world of sensuality becomes a fortress against potentially alienating forces, i.e., men, war, oppression of any kind, in the real world. This essay examines the outlines of this transcendence in selected examples from her love and political poetry with additional thought and experience where relevant, from her autobiographical narratives.

Drawing upon her scholarly and gifted understanding of poetic technique and rhetorical structure in modern Black poetry, Ruth Sheffey explains:

> Genuine rhetoric, indeed all verbal art, coexists with reason, truth, justice. All of the traditions of rational and moral speech are allied to the primitive idea of goodness, to the force of utterance. Because the past is functional in our lives when we neither forget it nor try to return to it, the new Black voices must reach the masses in increasingly communal ways, must penetrate those hidden crevices of our beings only recognizable and reachable by poetry.[8]

Professor Sheffey speaks here to the fundamental meaning and significance Black poetry holds for its private community. Sheffey's remarks could not more appropriately describe Maya Angelou's poetic voice in terms of motive, content and audience. By way of example consider:

"No No No No"

No
the two legg'd beasts
that walk like men
play stink finger in their crusty asses
while crackling babies
in napalm coats
stretch mouths to receive
burning tears
on splitting tongues
JUST GIVE ME A COOL DRINK OF WATER 'FORE
I DIE

No
the gap legg'd whore
of the eastern shore
enticing Europe to COME
in her
and turns her pigeon shit back to me
to me
Who stoked coal that drove the ships
which brought her over the sinnous cemetery
Of my many brothers

No
the cocktailed afternoons
of what can I do.
In my white layed pink world.
I've let your men cram my mouth
with their black throbbing hate
and I swallowed after
I've let your mammies
steal from my kitchens
(I was always half-amused)
I've chuckled the chins of
your topsy-haired pickaninnies.
What more can I do?
I'll never be black like you.
(Hallelujah)

No
the red-shoed priests riding
palanquined
in barefoot children country.
the plastered saints gazing down
beneficently
on kneeling mothers
picking undigested beans
from yesterday's shit.

I have waited
toes curled, hat rolled
heart and genitals
in hand
on the back porches
of forever
in the kitchens and fields
of rejections
on the cold marble steps
of America's White Out-House
in the drop seats of buses
and the open flies of war

No More
The hope that
the razored insults
which mercury slide over your tongue
will be forgotten
and you will learn the words of love
Mother Brother Father Sister Lover Friend

My hopes
dying slowly
rose petals falling
beneath an autumn red moon
will not adorn your unmarked graves

My dreams
lying quietly
a dark pool under the trees
will not carry your name
to a forgetful shore
And what a pity

What a pity
that pity has folded in upon itself
an old man's mouth
whose teeth are gone
and I have no pity

[7, pp. 38–41].

Once having recited the horrors of capitalistic wars, Angelou continues her narrative focusing then on Black people who were forced, for economic reasons, to "stoke" America's coals. (Her money hungry "gapped legg'd whore" has never beckoned to Blacks as she did to Europe's ethnics promising them her materialistic fruits.) From the beginning, slavery defined a Black involuntary coming, one far alienated from an American dream. Rather than enjoy the dream, Black people were relegated to the drudgery of its death and destruction. Despite the fact that Black men stoked the coals that drew the ships which helped make the "gapped legg'd whore" possible, Black historical victimization cannot be undone "assures" the quasi-liberalized persona's voice in the third stanza. This voice echoes values dramatically different from any we have heard up to this point. For this reason its callousness toward the conditions of Black people dramatizes, all the more, its particular irony: the white liberal voice—whose consolation extends compassion only to the point at which it is convenient—no further.

Her metonymic body imagery functions as poetic referent further chronicling and transporting her prophetic message: stop the assault on Black people and recognize their humanness. As prophecy, her succinct assertions for change beginning with napalmed babies, epitomized in hopeful dreams as the poem progresses—disintegrate ironically into the decayed emptiness of an old man's "gaping mouth."

Again Ruth Sheffey seems relevant to the reading of this poem when she explains:

> The audience must read with the poet's passion and reason, must relish his poignant metaphors, his sensitive ironies, his percussive and passionate repetitions, his urgent suppressions, deletions, the wry humor of his syllables and understatements, his paradoxes—"Have you ever said 'Thank you, sir' for an umbrella full of holes?"
>
> [8, p. 107]

The audience, a Black one, cannot help but understand the universal message this poem imports. It is a collectively oriented statement (the persona's "I" operating synecdochically for the group), and one of hope, although a hope which ironically collapses at poem's end.

A similar transcendence becomes the ironically complicated prophetic message in:

"The Calling of Names"

He went to being called a Colored man
after answering to "hey nigger,"
Now that's a big jump,
anyway you figger,
    Hey, Baby, Watch my smoke.
From colored man to Negro.

With the "N" in caps
was like saying Japanese
instead of saying Japs.

    I mean, during the war.

The next big step
was change for true
From Negro in caps
to being a Jew.

    Now, Sing Yiddish Mama.

Light, Yello, Brown
and Dark brown skin,
were o.k. colors to
describe him then,

    He was a bouquet of Roses.

He changed his seasons
like an almanac,
Now you'll get hurt
if you don't call him "Black"

    Nigguh, I ain't playin' this time

[7, p. 43].

As significant referents, words are used to recreate a personal reality, but as verbal discourse they remain very close to the writer's understanding of truth. Maya Angelou brings to the audience her own perceptions of historical change and their relationship to a new reality. With the exception of a long ago Phyllis Wheatley, whose poems speak almost exclusively of God, nature and man, few Black artists have focused their poetic gifts outside history, politics and their changing effects upon Black life. Here Maya Angelou engages in this lifelong tradition of speaking to the concerns of a historical and political Black presence in World War II, Voter and Civil Rights legislation of the fifties; finally the Black Power Movement of the sixties—these events name only a few of the historical and political meanings the synecdochic imagery of naming has signalled for Blacks in America.

From the ancient African rituals which gave a child a name harmonious with his or her chi to the derogatory epithets coming out of slavery's master-servant relationships—naming has always held a reality redefining importance for black people. It has reached the level contemporarily with the recreation of one's destiny, an incantation signalling control over one's life. Hence the proliferation of African names with significant meanings.

But as the incantation and the structure of the poem's ideas have evolved out of historical and political event, one hears the old degrading epithets merging into new and more positive meanings.

Her title with its article "the" and preposition "of" signal, perhaps, the only formalizing or distancing aesthetic techniques in the poem. Her emphasis is primarily upon the concrete, the substantive movement back to a derogatory black history and a clearly assertive statement about a more positive future. Like many of the poems in this collection this one also works toward the notion of a positive identity, a positive assertion of what and who Black people have decided they will be. Her formal rhyme scheme here is one in which the initial stanzas rhyme the second and fourth lines, a rhyming pattern more constricted than in much of her other political poetry. Less metaphorical transformation and less abstraction appear in this poem, however, and while that makes it aesthetically less pleasing, its meaning speaks more directly to the concrete issues of evolving importance to Afro-American history and politics. The abstractions of metaphor perhaps then do not apply here.

A self-defining function continues in **"When I Think about Myself."** We hear the definitions through a narrative she frequently uses in her poetry: Angelou's persona assumes an ironic distance toward the world. As a result, her relationship to the world loses its direct, i.e., literal quality. She steps back into this distance and can laugh at its characteristics no matter how politically and socially devastating:

"When I Think About Myself"

When I think about myself
I almost laugh myself to death.
My life has been one big joke.
A dance that's walked
A song that's spoke,
I laugh so hard I almost choke
When I think about myself.

Sixty years in these folks' world
The child I works for calls me girl.
I say "Yes Ma'am" for working's sake
Too proud to break,
I laugh until my stomach ache,
When I think about myself.

My folks can make me split my sides,
I laughed so hard I nearly died,
The tales they tell, sound just like lying,
They grow the fruit,
But eat the rind,
I laugh until I start to crying,
When I think about my folks

[7, p. 25].

Out of the emotional distance comes the paradox upon which the persona's insights rest. Dances are walked and songs are spoken reinforcing the dialectical nature of this paradox: an illusion which keeps sacrosanct a much more complicated racial reality.

Both Stephen Henderson's *Understanding the New Black Poetry* and Ruth Sheffey argue that the "I" of Black poetry is not a singular or individualistic referent but a symbol for the ideas of a Black collective. With that point in mind, it becomes clear she is ultimately talking about the ironies of economic oppression which trap Black people provided they allow them, i.e., the ironies to define them rather than their gaining the distance from the oppression to define themselves. An unending tension exists between haves and have-nots—one which the have-nots cannot allow to erupt into open violence and conflict (excluding certain mass exceptions like Watts, New York and Washington in the 1960's). Having once gained an understanding of the absurdity, the have-nots gain superiority in that ironic distance which creates freedom and a partial definition of one's superiority over the oppressor's blind myopia. Perhaps as a further illumination of the ideas generating this poem, Maya Angelou told an illustrative story to George Goodman, Jr. who was reviewing her autobiography, *Caged Bird* for the *New York Times* [9]. He remarked that Angelou consistently expressed the sickness of racism like a thread running throughout all her work. Her reply took an illustrative form as she told him about an elderly Black domestic worker in Montgomery, Alabama during Martin Luther King's 1955 Montgomery bus boycotts. The worker solemnly assured her white employer that in spite of the boycotts, she had instructed her husband and children to ride the daily busses. Afterwards, behind the closed, protective doors of the kitchen the employer's liberal, more realistic daughter asked the Black woman why she needed to hide the truth (the Black woman had, in reality, told her family to absolutely stay away from public transportation busses in Montgomery.) The elderly maid (a prototype not divorced from this poem's persona by any flight of the imagination) told her, "Honey when you have your head in a lion's mouth, you don't jerk it out. You scratch him behind the ears and draw it out gradually." Like the conclusion of the woman's story, this persona speaks a similarly paradigmatic truth in all its ironic and varied implications. Psychological distance becomes the persona's mightiest weapon, a distance born of years of slowly drawing one's head out of the proverbial lion's mouth.

While Maya Angelou's political poetry suggests the irony of emotional distantiation by using bodily imagery as her objective correlative, her love poetry almost equally as often employs this series of patterns to capture an image, an instant, an emotional attitude. Moreover, fantasy often rounds out the missing parts of the human whole when reality fails to explain fully what she sees. Here in the following poem, **"To a Man"** she explores this mystery, this distantiation from the understanding of a man:

"To a Man"

My man is
Black Golden Amber
Changing.
Warm mouths of Brandy Fine
Cautious sunlight on a patterned rug
Coughing laughter, rocked on a whirl of French tobacco
Graceful turns on wollen stilts

Secretive?
A cat's eye.
Southern, Plump and tender with navy bean sullenness
And did I say "Tender?"
The gentleness
A big cat stalks through stubborn bush
And did I mention "Amber"?
The heatless fire consuming itself.
Again. Anew. Into ever neverlessness.
My man is Amber
Changing
Always into itself
New. Now New.
Still itself.
Still

[7, p. 6]

If indeed this poem talks about a man and not some more hidden and abstract object we cannot define, then **"To a Man"** explores the mysteries of a baffling and emotionally distant human being through a persona's fantasy, her worshipping recreation of an artifice rather than of any more luminous understanding of his many selves. And while she does not name him in the poem and he could be reminiscent of any of the men she knew, her description of him evokes a picture of Make, a South African freedom fighter and the man who became her second husband. She recounts this marriage and its end in her final autobiography, *The Heart of a Woman.* Whether a husband or not, his mystery constitutes her poem's ostensible statement, through her persona's particular visual gestalt, i.e., approach. The persona's failure to (penetrate) her subject's overpreoccupation with his own personal style as a wall against intimacy becomes a source of the poem's interesting aesthetic and emotional tension. Her subject cannot be captured, i.e., "understood" and he is cut off from the persona's concentrated engagement by this barrier that she creates—his personal style. The word choices she selects to describe or rather, guess at what she comprehends about him are words suggesting the altering and varying nature of his physical and psychic characteristics. She looks at him seeing only the qualities of an ambiance he creates around himself through the deliberateness of his studied poses. He moves "Cat like." She images his moving dynamism concretely in "woolen stilts" which both regalize and thrust him backward spatially and temporally to a time when he could have been a royal African chieftain dancing on tall stilts.

She magnificently combines the auditory, tactile and visual into the imagery of his ". . . coughing laughter rocked on a whirl of French tobacco" graphically capturing what we take to be—given all she has said before—still, his moving and elegant dynamism. His sight, sound, smell—even his smoke concretized in French rather than in some ordinary domestic. This is no:

"Country Lover"

Funky blues
Keen toed shoes
High water pants
Saddy night dance
Red soda water
and anybody's daughter

[6, p. 4]

A man of expediency, the **"Country Lover,"** clearly he is not the sophisticated and subtle, previous "amber" man.

Like a musical recitative, she repeats in the earlier **"To a Man,"** descriptions framed in rhetorical questions drawing attention all the more to his stolid mystery. In using the repeated rhetorical questions, she counterposes her technique against the traditional way in which modern Black poets use repetition. Modern Black poets use repetitious phrasing for emphasis, clarity and to signal an end to complexity. In Angelou's work the rhetorical questions increase tension and complexity and build upon his opaque mystery. Why?

Some of the explanation might lie in the fact that writers often repeat the issues and conflicts of their own lives throughout much of their art until either concrete conditions or the art brings insight and resolution. Witness Richard Wright's unending preoccupation with the Communist Party's orthodoxy and demanding control over his work, or Gwendolyn Brooks' mid-career, philosophical redirection after attending the Fisk University Black Writer's Conference. The seeds for a similar obsession lie in her autobiographies and project into Angelou's poetry. She berates herself for her overly romantic ability to place men on pedestals, to create a rose-colored fantasy around them at a distance only to later discover her cognitive error. Her relationships with men in *Caged Bird* and *Gather Together* have this fantasy quality where she overelaborates their personalities in her own mind confusing their concrete behaviors with her day-dream. She does this, sometimes out of her own unconscious desire for their unconditional love—wanting almost a symbiotic object-subject attachment to them. In the final analysis, each of these men exploits her because all are morally and characterologically flawed in ways her own emotional neediness causes her to miss as her fantasy life recreates their personalities. One lover, temporarily stationed close to her home in San Diego, uses her companionship while his naval assignment lasts then leaves her. He returns to his wife. A fast living "sugar daddy" cons her into prostitution to "help" him with a non-existent gambling debt. Again concrete conditions force her into looking beneath the surface he presents. She finds that her "giving" provided pretty dresses for his wife. Nothing more! Finally, when at last she marries, and her fantasies tell her she has found nirvana in the white-picket-fenced cottage she has dreamed of she learns its hidden price: she will become prisoner rather than mistress of the house and husband.

In her autobiographies, Angelou presents her flaws head-on not once rationalizing away her own complicity or the details of her own mistakes. The irony and wisdom typical of autobiographies written retrospectively bare the exposed nerves, the humiliating flaws of her experience. But this brutal honesty seems part and parcel for Black female autobiography. A Black psychological self gets created who for all its painful error and insight reveals an enduring depth and strength—one at which readers marvel. Mary Burgher confirms the idea when she says:

> Doubtless Maya Angelou . . . and other Black women autobiographers write about experiences more varied, much harsher, and at times more beautiful than most others encounter. They create incisive and sensitive images of womanhood that remain meaningful to all Black women who struggle to come to terms with the hardships and violence just beneath the surface in the Black experience. *The Caged Bird*, like other autobiographies of Black women, is a valuable resource to the understanding of Black women because it reveals and symbolizes the Black woman's daring act of remaking her lost innocence into invisible dignity, her never-practiced delicacy into quiet grace, and her forced responsibility into unshouted courage.[10]

Throughout Stephen Butterfield's study of Black autobiography he repeatedly voices statements paralleling Mary Burgher's observation on the important role Black autobiographers play as explorers and purveyors of the Black feminine self and its community.[11] Even Maya Angelou herself reinforced this idea in a newspaper interview when she said:

> "Now I'm going to do what I can to help clear the air in Black America, because as I see it, that's what needs to be done. I'm going to write . . . *Caged Bird* . . .
>
> [Goodman, p. 28]

Maya Angelou did in her autobiography just what she promised, she did what "needed to be done," in all its complexity. Given the nature of autobiographical rationalization which critics like Roy Pascal and Stephen Butterfield have pointed out in their work, one which demands a certain tendency to under or overemphasize certain elements for the sake of a unified work of art—despite her compelling honesty—still her autobiographies cannot help but suggest parallels—speculative at best between her poetic themes and her autobiographical. These themes, nevertheless, parallel the pattern of fantasy motivated attachment to men as saviors then the inevitable consequent disillusioning disappointment which one finds both in the autobiographical stories of her life and in the themes of her confessional love poetry.

Erik Erikson provides another possible explanation, and while not an infallible one, it might contribute to further understanding the sources of her romanticism. His discussion of the intricate psychoanalytic dynamics of ego experience sheds some light on Angelou's yearning for undifferentiated attachment to men. First he must ascertain the social nature of our worlds—worlds which include the egos of those most significant to us when he explains:

> They (the egos of others) are significant because on many levels of crude or subtle communication my whole being perceives in them a hospitability to the way in which they order their world and include me—a mutual affirmation, which can be depended upon to activate my being as I can be to activate theirs.[12]

Unfortunately for Angelou, her fantasy of this ego interaction or mutuality is often inaccurate where her perception of men is concerned. She perceives them as the complement of her ego dynamic but far too overwhelmingly so. In other words, she becomes too attached to them too quickly before giving them space and time to prove that, indeed, they are her complements. She is repeatedly hurt by men who are far more experienced than she, who are far more able to see her neediness and exploit it before she is able to see it in herself.

The narcissistic male is always the one most attractive to her and the one most mysterious—ultimately he will always turn out to be the man most destructive to her and her capacity to invest too much of her dependency and need in him too quickly. The wonder which underlies her perceptions in **"To a Man"** are not surprising provided one has read her autobiographies and identified this common psychic pattern she recurringly illustrates. What she identifies as mystery—and wonder are part of the guardedness and distance he sustains—keeping her always at a safe length away from himself. One would expect anger from her rather than wonder.

Anger would have been more appropriate toward his self-protection and yet she does not express anger. Perhaps also the absence of anger affirms the passivity Lillian Arensberg has seen in Angelou's writing.[13] We must, however, not overlook another important factor which accounts for what may be occurring here from an aesthetic and artistic rather than a purely psychic point of view. Her persona's opportunity to draw attention to it—rather than to her male subject. Thus, in doing this, she can draw upon her female audience's alleged universal bafflement with the mysterious male psyche. The poem would be better called "To a Woman" in that case, if one accepts this less direct reading of the poem.

Again fantasy subsumes reality in the distance-keeping strategy which provides space for her imaginative elaborations:

"Remembrance"

Your hands easy
weight, teasing the bees
hived in my hair, your smile at the
slope of my cheek. On the
occasion, you press
above me, glowing, spouting
readiness, mystery rapes
my reason.

When you have withdrawn
yourself and the magic, when
only the spell of your
love lingers between

my breasts, then, only
then, can I greedily consume
your presence

[7]

She infuses bodily imagery with the poem's primary work as vehicle of expression concluding finally with the notion that her subject's residual, i.e., his memory (her fantasized version of him) is far preferable to his actual presence. Again full physical and psychological mutuality are missing, and she can only experience him within her own grasp of what she rounds but he is in her mind rather than in his physical reality after "the occasion" as she so euphemistically alludes to sex. The bees hived in her hair where mystery rapes her signals her chaos, her madness and anxiety toward his impending physical engulfment.

Her persona's fear of physical overwhelming and her wish for estrangement from him counterpoints her earlier **"To a Man."** What seemed the male's distance keeping desire in the former poem becomes what the female persona wants in the second. In either case, the issue in both is the mistrust of intimacy because men are perceived as engulfing rather than mutual. She desires to maintain psychic boundaries fearing her own vulnerability while paradoxically wanting trusting attachment to men.

Finally, she again raises the recurring psychic remoteness idea, the ambiguity which here defines her only possible conception of love's nature within a changing and undecipherable world:

"On Diverse Deviations"

When love is a shimmering curtain
Before a door of chance
That leads to a world in question
Wherein the macabrous dance
Of bones that rattle in silence
Of blinded eyes and rolls
Of thick lips thin, denying
A thousand powdered moles,
Where touch to touch is feel
And life a weary whore
  I would be carried off, not gently
  To a shore,
  Where love is the scream of anguish.
  And no curtain drapes the door

[7, p. 18].

The hyperbolic thousand moles further disguising the already cloaked ambiguous nature of things and the door with its drapes torn away all evoke a naked death. Angelou well could be allusively playing here with the Neo-Classical synonymous relationship between death and consummation.

Furthermore, love as intellectual labyrinth becomes the poem's underlying motif, pervading its progressive movement of ideas. Only at poem's end does the resolution come to this Medea-headed series of ambiguous images synecdochically representing love. In the last line, love as the scream of anguish—although terrible in itself—at least becomes something more distinct than all of the varying forms it has taken up to this point.

While Maya Angelou's poetry may not have taken us into every nook and cranny of her long and complex life starting with the Lafayette County Training School—its various movements and insights have nonetheless helped us understand the themes, the issues even some of the conflicts which have pervaded her inner life. Thus, while we could not share the objective events in all their entirety (the autobiographies have helped to partially illuminate these), her various poetic stances have given us some lead into parts of that subjective voyage.

Her autobiographies, the clues they give suggest a self image which as Sidonia Smith points out in her essay, "The Song of the Caged Bird: Maya Angelou's Quest after Self-Acceptance," provides Angelou a strategy for attempting to answer her fundamental and basic questions about the self.[14] Moreover, that self determines the pattern of her writing as Smith also summarily points out. Her autobiographies do indeed present a dislocated self image. But that self image becomes a new and assertive one as she transcends the singular self through a wide and compassionate direct assertion of her statements against political injustice. Her love poetry—on the other hand—suggests her relationship to a world which can be stultifying, mystifying and oppressive, but one she will not allow to become these things and overwhelm her. The voyage through her life has not been filled with soft and pliable steps each opening into another opportunity for self acceptance. Her voyage has instead been anything but that and yet she has filled those voids with fantasy, song, hope and the redefinition of her world's view through art.

Notes

1. Maya Angelou. *I Know Why the Caged Bird Sings,* Random House, New York, 1970.
2. ———. *Gather Together in My Name,* Bantam Books, New York, 1974.
3. ———. *Singin' and Swingin' and Gettin' Merry Like Christmas,* Harper and Row, New York, 1976.
4. ———. *The Heart of a Woman,* Random House, New York, 1982.
5. ———. *Oh Pray My Wings are Gonna Fit Me Well,* Bantam Books, New York, 1975.
6. ———. *And Still I Rise,* Random House, New York, 1978.
7. ———. *Just Give Me a Cool Drink of Water 'fore I Diiie,* Random House, New York, 1971.
8. R. Sheffey. "Rhetorical Structure in Contemporary Afro-American Literature," *College Language Association Journal, XXIV:*1, p. 97, 1980.
9. G. Goodman, Jr. "Maya Angelou's Lonely Black Out-Look," *The New York Times,* p. 28, March 24, 1972.

10. M. Burgher. "Images of Self and Race in Autobiographies of Black Women," in *Sturdy Black Bridges: Visions of Black Women in Literature,* R. P. Bell, B. J. Parker, and B. Guy-Shefftall (eds.), Anchor Books, New York, 1979.

11. S. Butterfield. *Black Autobiography in America,* The University of Massachusetts Press, Amherst, 1974.

12. E. Erikson. *Identity, Youth and Crisis,* W. W. Norton, New York, p. 219, 1968.

13. L. Arensberg. "Death as Metaphor of Self, in 'I Know Why the Caged Bird Sings,'" *Journal of the College Language Association, 20,* pp. 273–291, December 1976.

14. S. Smith. "The Song of the Caged Bird: Maya Angelou's Quest after Self-Acceptance," *Southern Humanities Review, 7,* pp. 365–375, Fall 1973.

Peter Erickson (essay date 1991)

SOURCE: "Shakespeare, Angelou, Cheney: The Administration of the Humanities in the Reagan-Bush Era," in *Rewriting Shakespeare, Rewriting Ourselves*, University of California Press, 1991, pp. 111–23.

[*In the following excerpt, Erikson explores Angelou's remarks on Shakespeare, and their implications, challenging how they were employed by Lynne Cheney, Ronald Reagan's director of the National Endowment for the Humanities, in a report about the conflict in academia over determining the scope, nature, and value of the Western Literary Canon.*]

The emotional high point of Lynne V. Cheney's *Humanities in America* is her quotation of an extended passage from an address by Maya Angelou in which Angelou quotes Shakespeare's Sonnet 29 and asserts: "'I *know* that William Shakespeare was a black woman.'"[1] In this heightened moment, Cheney links and fuses three voices—Shakespeare's, Angelou's, and her own—thus creating the conjunction to which my title refers. However, my purpose is to challenge the impression Cheney conveys of a unified canon of Western literature, and I shall do so by suggesting that there are significant differences between Angelou's use of Shakespeare and Cheney's representation of Angelou's Shakespeare. My procedure will be, first, to examine the overall structure of the report of which the Angelou quotation is a part and, second, to consider this quotation in the larger context of Angelou's work as a whole.

I

Humanities in America touches on a number of educational issues, including the priority given to research over teaching and the arcane nature of post-structuralist theory. But these have little bearing on Cheney's core concern—the emergence of political interpretation in the humanities. Political analysis is very clear, not arcane; and it is conducive rather than resistant to the increased emphasis on teaching that Cheney advocates. As she herself warns, "teaching becomes a form of political activism" (p. 12).

Cheney's specific focus is on political interpretation as it relates to the status of the traditional canon. The title of the section for which the Maya Angelou passage serves as climax makes this connection between "Politics and the Curriculum" (p. 11). In Cheney's view, the whole educational structure is threatened because political analysis erodes support for the established classics: "It makes more difficult a task that is already hard: determining a substantive and coherent plan of study for undergraduates" (p. 12); "the newly politicized nature of debate in the humanities has made it more difficult" (p. 14). Cheney's objective is to remove this difficulty.

Despite her opposition to the intrusion of politics into the humanities, Cheney's own argument is explicitly political in two ways. First, given her administrative power as a presidentially appointed head of a federal agency that disburses funds, Cheney has an agenda that can fairly be called political in the familiar sense of politics as governmental activity. Her report is an intervention and intended as such. As the final heading, "Recommendations" (p. 31), makes plain, she is not merely presenting a neutral description but rather actively signaling the views to which she wishes to lend her institutional support.

Second, the report directly acknowledges the political dimension of literature: "The humanities provide context for the decisions we must make as a people by raising questions of social purpose: What is a just society, and how is it achieved?" (pp. 2–3). In this opening moment, the terms of Cheney's approach overlap with those of the political critics she opposes. The concepts of "social purpose" and of "a just society" are relevant, Cheney agrees, to the study of literature. The contrast, then, is not between political and nonpolitical approaches but between different political views. It is therefore appropriate to pursue the question "What are Cheney's politics?" where politics are understood as the intellectual vision that gradually unfolds over the course of the report.

The body of Cheney's discussion is organized as an evaluation of three areas—higher education, television, and cultural institutions such as museums, libraries, historical societies, humanities councils, and theater festivals. The order of this three-part structure dramatizes a distinct progression from the negative review of higher education through the ambivalent survey of television to the decidedly upbeat assessment of the other cultural institutions. Shakespeare figures as an index to the tone of each of the three sections, which may be summarized, respectively, as Shakespeare endangered, Shakespeare abundant, and Shakespeare redeemed.

In the middle section, television occasions mixed feelings: reservations are strongly expressed; benefits, however tentative, are duly noted. In general, the effort here is to put the best face on things. Shakespeare, for example, is given the limited test of commercial availability:

> Classics are amazingly easy to obtain. In neighborhood bookstores, one can find volumes of Aeschylus and Sophocles, Dickens and Shakespeare selling for under five dollars. Observed Michael Novak, "The very best books ever produced in the history of the human race are available for many times less than a pair of basketball shoes. . . ."
>
> Facets, a nonprofit Chicago organization, . . . is able to rent videotapes by mail for $10. Four versions of "Macbeth" are available, three of "King Lear."
>
> (pp. 19–22)

This reassurance about the successful operation of our cultural economy may seem an inconsequential digression. However, the conspicuous avoidance of larger economic problems in the analysis of television is relevant to the political stance of the report as a whole, for it suggests how constrained Cheney's intellectual vision is by the need to affirm an economic philosophy congenial to the Reagan administration. The role of commercials in television and the contrast in this regard between commercial and public television require a deeper economic discussion than Cheney is prepared to give. Moreover, her economic thinking elsewhere in the report: for example, in the praise for the role of private philanthropy in the creation of the Alabama Shakespeare Festival theater complex (pp. 24–25); in the application of market principles to college education so that parents can be encouraged to use their purchase power to influence the curricular products that are offered to their children (pp. 14, 32).

At the beginning of the third part of the report, Cheney invokes the motif of an expanding economy to underwrite a more general image of social unity:

> Carl Raschke, a philosophy professor from the University of Denver, pointed to similarities between our own time and the late 1870s. . . . "We were then, as we are now, about fifteen years after a devastating war that had divided the country," Raschke noted. "The American people seemed to have been emerging out of a kind of cynicism and slumber and dispiritedness with a hunger for a new vitality and vision. There was a hunger to reappropriate and to understand anew values, traditions, and history that had been set aside during the period of conflict."
>
> (pp. 23–24)

Details of this analogy between the Civil and Vietnam wars and their aftermaths are never specified and clarified, but the gist of the attitude adopted toward the period of the 1960s through 1980s is evident. The divisiveness associated with the Vietnam War has been put behind us, superseded and canceled by a reawakening of social harmony. Reinstatement of the canon fits into and reinforces the purported historical shift by fulfilling the desire to recover traditions. This projected overview of the past three decades receives its gesture of confirmation in the quotation from Matthew Arnold that concludes the report's third section: "'Again and again I have insisted,' he wrote, 'how those are the happy moments of humanity, how those are the marking epochs of a people's life, how those are the flowering times for literature and art and all the creative power of genius, when there is a *national* glow of life and thought'" (p. 29).

Cheney's interpretation of the present as one of "the happy moments" hinges on the contrast—around which the entire report is constructed—between the negative view of higher education in part 1 and the positive view of "public programming in the humanities" (p. 27) in part 3. According to Cheney, we face a situation in which the new "'two cultures' are the academy and society" (p. 10). The public cultural institutions have filled the gap, becoming "a kind of parallel school, one that has grown up outside established institutions of education" (p. 27). Since public humanities organizations are more closely involved with and responsive to diverse general audiences, they represent a populist trend that can be trusted to counteract the political interpretation prevailing in the academy.

How the constituencies cultivated by public humanities institutions operate as a corrective, Cheney indicates by example:

> Overly narrow interpretations are also likely to be challenged by an audience that has the authority of maturity. "I once watched a young scholar try to draw an ideological conclusion from a passage in a Doris Lessing novel," says Victor Swenson, executive director of the humanities council in Vermont. "The discussion group wasn't confrontational about objecting, but they weren't having any of it either."
>
> (p. 29)

Cheney implies that this disagreement proves that the scholar's position was invalid and should be retracted, but this does not necessarily follow. Cheney goes on, however, openly to encourage the development of a pressure group capable of supplying political leverage: "Millions of adult Americans, through their participation in public programs, have come to affirm the importance of the humanities. They can be a force for change" (p. 33).

This movement also secures the recuperation of the 1960s because managers of public humanities organizations are drawn from graduate students for whom the academy could not provide employment: "Many of those who received humanities Ph.D.'s in the 1960s and 1970s when the academic job market was tight, now work in public humanities institutions" (p. 26). These "new scholars"—in Cheney's phrase (p. 26)—are supposed to have adjusted their views to the requirements of their new environments and, in particular, to have rejected subservience to academic scholars.

Two difficulties remain, however. Quoting Sidney Hook's assertion in her initial defense of the canon, Cheney appears to value the criticism it incorporates: "The Western tradition *is* a debate. . . . 'It would hardly be an exaggeration to say that of all cultures of which we have knowledge, Western culture has been the most critical of itself'" (pp. 12–13). Yet Cheney celebrates and denies this critical inquiry in the same breath. In a characteristic move, she first concedes, then negates, the importance of a critical perspective: "There will probably always be in our colleges and universities some sense of estrangement from society, a sense that flows from a critical attitude toward human affairs which is crucial to preserve. But the extreme alienation of some faculty members may well be tempered by closer involvement with our culture" (p. 29). Cheney's previous appreciation of criticism is converted by the vaguely negative terminology of "estrangement" and "alienation" into a dangerous tendency that should be curbed. In the end, Cheney's scheme can provide no adequate account of, or place for, the critical spirit she had earlier seen as an essential feature of Western tradition.

Moreover, the antidote suggested by Matthew Arnold's "happy moments of humanity" is itself immediately undercut by a less sanguine version of the role of the classics in a democratic society:

> With no small and permanent ruling class to uphold standards, democratic literature, he [Tocqueville] thought, would exhibit "a rude and untutored vigor of thought," a fascination with the facile and vivid, rather than the rigorous and subtle. Loving liberty as he did, Tocqueville sought ways to counter-balance such tendencies. He recommended looking back to classical literature, for example, for models of excellence from which we could learn.
>
> (p. 31)

Gone is Cheney's original view of the social purpose of the humanities as facilitating explorations of "a just society" (p. 3). Emphasis now falls on literature as a vehicle for maintaining social order. The phrases "uphold standards" and "such tendencies," eloquent in their vagueness, communicate a built-in bias against the lower-class instability potential in a democratic system. The tension in Matthew Arnold's polarized title *Culture and Anarchy* comes to the fore, with democracy as the anarchy and culture as the equivalent of ruling-class control.[2] The populace that Cheney has just celebrated for its capacity to oppose and curtail disaffected academics is itself in need of control. The apparent democratic appeal of Cheney's populism is thus vitiated; in its place is a politics of suspicion toward democracy.

II

I return to my starting point—the long passage from Maya Angelou that concludes the first part of Cheney's report. I find this moment more deeply compelling than the corresponding climax at the end of part three when Cheney cites Matthew Arnold. My questions are: what purpose does the Angelou quotation serve in Cheney's report? and is Cheney's use of Angelou justified by Angelou's work as a whole?

Cheney's lengthy quotation of Angelou has a twofold function: it is meant both to bolster Cheney's opposition to political readings and to validate Cheney's defense of a traditional canon. The first purpose is signaled by the preface with which Cheney frames the excerpt from Angelou: "What gives them [the humanities] their abiding worth are truths that pass beyond time and circumstance; truths that, transcending accidents of class, race, and gender, speak to us all" (p. 14). Cheney's earlier concession to political analysis—"The key questions are thought to be about gender, race, and class. . . . These are, of course, legitimate questions" (p. 12)—proves to be a throwaway gesture. The substance of the concession is subsequently withdrawn and canceled by the way the term "accidents" trivializes and dismisses the conceptual significance of gender, race, and class.

For Cheney, Angelou's ability to make Shakespeare's Sonnet 29 speak her own situation as a black woman shows that gender, race, and class do not really matter, are irrelevant. But neither the sonnet itself nor Angelou's use of it support Cheney's point of view. The different class positions of the poet and the highborn young man are central, not incidental, to the sonnets because they articulate a social dynamic that works against simple transcendence. The poet's expressions of love do not triumphantly dissolve the class barrier; rather, the class difference helps to underscore the love's wishfulness and pathos. The couplet of Sonnet 29—"For thy sweet love rememb'red such wealth brings / That then I scorn to change my state with kings"—may assertively announce the power of love; but the couplet of Sonnet 87 employs the imagery of class hierarchy to insist with equal authority on the opposite: "Thus have I had thee as a dream doth flatter, / In sleep a king, but waking no such matter." Moreover, contrary to Cheney's interpretation, Angelou herself does not set aside class. Her identification with Shakespeare here is a statement about the lower-class position of many black women.

The special value of Angelou for Cheney's reinvigoration of the traditional canon involves the proposition that, if the emergence of black women writers threatens the established canon, then the most powerful response will be to have a black woman in her own voice endorse that canon and, further, to ratify it as a nonracial, nongendered tradition. To have Shakespeare quoted by Angelou and the two together quoted by Cheney constructs an impressive linear effect. This lining up of authors symbolically enacts a unified tradition, but the question remains of how well Angelou fits.

Cheney's conception of the canon blurs and conflates a key distinction between access and content, as though access to a certain set of works guarantees their communication of a self-evident, fixed meaning. When Cheney insists that "students should be knowledgeable about texts" (p. 12), she assumes that the outcome of this process will be a certain form of knowledge. To be knowledgeable means to possess a specific content that falls within a specified range. But acquaintance and content are two separate steps:

one can accept the point about the need to engage traditional authors, yet disagree with the particular interpretations Cheney wishes to derive from them. Angelou's identification with Shakespeare primarily signifies a belief in access. "I suggest to you that an entire species depends upon keeping the arts alive and accessible. It is imperative that the arts are accessible and not other, not elite but available to everybody," she stresses in her 1985 address (p. 12). It does not follow that Angelou's vision of Shakespeare coincides with Cheney's. Angelou is unwilling to be limited to black culture and claims her right to the entire spectrum of cultural heritage. But this does not imply her denial of black culture as a distinct tradition, nor does it constitute an endorsement of the restricted concept of tradition advanced by Cheney.

When we put Angelou back in context—her own context—we see that the context of Cheney's report and the context of Angelou's work do not, in significant respects, match up. Taken in isolation, in the context with which Cheney surrounds it, Angelou's evocation of the moment when she overcomes her grandmother's stipulation that she choose black authors and satisfies her love for Shakespeare can be read as a triumph over the grandmother's provincial and separatist attitudes and as a one-way development of educational liberation. But this impression cannot be sustained when the passage is returned to its original context in Angelou's 1985 address. For in the address as a whole there can be no doubt that the representation of the grandmother has an overwhelmingly positive resonance. The grandmother is not a narrow, blocking figure but a source of support and survival.

In particular, Angelou's grandmother serves as a resource by embodying the specific Afro-American tradition of church music and ritual:

> So I started a song Momma [the grandmother] sang every Sunday. Now, it never occurred to me when she sang this song that it would be important to me, but of course I recorded it. . . . In Morocco all alone on the stage I sang her song. . . . It is important to remember that the first blacks were brought to this country in 1619. . . . How did we survive except by art.
>
> (pp. 8–10)

This passage counterbalances the Shakespearean one that Cheney chooses; the voice made possible by the grandmother's words is even stronger than the voice enabled by Shakespeare's language.

The cultural and political authority for Angelou of black religious expression is reinforced by the larger context of her five-volume autobiography.[3] Her allegiance to her religious heritage contributes to the dissolution of her interracial marriage when her husband opposes it, as she recounts in *Singin' and Swingin' and Gettin' Merry Like Christmas:*

> I tucked away the memory of my great-grandmother (who had been a slave), who told me of praying silently under old wash pots, and of secret meetings deep in the woods to praise God . . .
>
> I planned a secret crawl through neighborhood churches . . .
>
> The spirituals and gospel songs were sweeter than sugar. I wanted to keep my mouth full of them and the sounds of my people singing fell like sweet oil in my ears . . .
>
> After watching the multicolored people in church dressed in their gay Sunday finery and praising their Maker with loud voices and sensual movements, Tosh and my house looked very pale. Van Gogh and Klee posters which would please me a day later seemed irrelevant.
>
> (pp. 28–29)

The tension marked here between the Afro-American church and Western art implies an experience of multiple traditions instead of a single great tradition. Angelou's desire to embrace both traditions does not eliminate the multiplicity; no easy amalgamation or synthesis is possible.

The conflict between alternate traditions is dramatized in Angelou's account in *I Know Why the Caged Bird Sings* of her eighth-grade graduation from a segregated black school. The mood of the ceremony is destroyed by a representative from the white world: "Owens and the Brown Bomber were great heroes in our world, but what school official in the white goddom of Little Rock had the right to decide that those two men must be our only heroes?" (p. 151). What rescues the moment is not the planned allusion to Shakespearean heroism, but rather the spontaneous affirmation of a specifically Afro-American perspective:

> There was a shuffling and rustling about me, then Henry Reed was giving his valedictory address, "To Be or Not to Be". . . .
>
> . . . The English teacher had helped him to create a sermon winging through Hamlet's soliloquy. . . .
>
> I had been listening and silently rebutting each sentence with my eyes closed; then there was a hush, which in an audience warns that something unplanned is happening. I looked up and saw Henry Reed, the conservative, the proper, the A student, turn his back to the audience and turn to us (the proud graduating class of 1940) and sing, nearly speaking,
>
> "Lift ev'ry voice and sing
> Till earth and heaven ring
> Ring with the harmonies of Liberty . . . "
>
> It was the poem written by James Weldon Johnson. It was the music composed by J. Rosamond Johnson. It was the Negro national anthem.
>
> (pp. 154–55)

Angelou concludes without reference to Shakespeare: "Oh, Black known and unknown poets, how often have your auctioned pains sustained us? . . . We survive in exact relationship to the dedication of our poets (include preachers, musicians and blues singers)" (p. 156). Three poems—"Lift Ev'ry Voice and Sing," Johnson's "O Black and Unknown Bards," to which Angelou obliquely alludes, and Paul Laurence Dunbar's "Sympathy," from which Angelou takes the title of her book—combine to emphasize the equation of poetry with singing. Through this motif Angelou joins three elements that will define her own career: religious music, entertainment, and writing.

Twenty years later in New York City, in 1960, when Angelou organizes *Cabaret for Freedom,* a theatrical presentation to benefit Martin Luther King's Southern Christian Leadership Conference, James Weldon Johnson's lyric again plays a key role. As Angelou portrays it in *The Heart of a Woman,* the initial effort calls forth Shakespearean inspiration: "'Well, hell, you start with Act I, Scene I, same way Shakespeare started'" (p. 65). But the Shakespearean model is sharply qualified: "We needed a story which had the complexity of *Hamlet* and the pertinence of *A Raisin in the Sun*" (p. 63). In the end, pertinence lacking in Shakespeare is achieved through the invocation of black literary tradition: "The entire cast stood in a straight line and sang 'Lift every voice and sing . . . '" (p. 68). Angelou affirms this tradition not only in her account of the Harlem Writers Guild (pp. 37–43), but also in the title, drawn from Georgia Douglas Johnson's poem, that frames the entire volume.[4]

Seen from the perspective of Angelou's work as a whole, Cheney's rendering of Angelou's Shakespearean passage in the NEH report has the effect of blunting, even of eliminating, the force of multiple traditions. Where Angelou's work presents dual traditions in tension, Cheney promotes a canon that is unified and harmonious. Canon formation is a political issue because there is a direct correlation between one's image of the canon and one's image of society. Cheney's version of the canon carries with it a vision of social harmony. Her cultural assumptions imply political assumptions since her canon asks us to act as though the "just society" (p. 3) she evokes is already achieved. By contrast, Angelou does not adopt the premature, self-congratulatory view of an American society whose major conflicts have been substantially moderated and resolved. Appealing instead to James Baldwin's phrase "these yet to be united states" (1985 address, p. 11), she implies that the 1960s she so vividly recalls in *The Heart of a Woman* are not over, that the issues raised in the sixties are still outstanding.

III

In the choice between the two models of a unitary canon or conflicting multiple traditions, Angelou's work—contrary to Cheney—does not lend support to the first over the second. The complexity that Cheney's selective presentation leaves out includes Angelou's problematic reliance on Shakespeare as one of the two most important authors who "formed my writing ambition."[5] In her discussion of the Angelou-Shakespeare connection, Christine Froula notes how precarious the voice is—because of the identification with Lucrece—to which Angelou's love of Shakespeare gives access in the case of *The Rape of Lucrece*: "But if Shakespeare's poem redeems Maya from her hysterical silence, it is also a lover that she embraces at her peril."[6]

In another instance, in *Singin' and Swingin' and Gettin' Merry Like Christmas*, Angelou's enthusiasm for Shakespeare seems excessive because of the way it uncritically enacts the realization of a fantasy of upward mobility. Arriving in Verona with the touring company of *Porgy and Bess*, Angelou exults: "I was so excited at the incredible turn of events which had brought me from a past of rejection, of slammed doors and blind alleys, of dead-end streets and culs-de-sac, . . . into a town made famous by one of the world's greatest writers" (pp. 140–41). But after this excitement over *Romeo and Juliet*, the arrival in Venice brings no mention of *Othello.* When on a return visit to Venice, two volumes later in *All God's Children Need Traveling Shoes*, Angelou imagines herself as "a sister to Othello," she does so with a deliberate reduction of awareness: "For a short while I let my Black American history sink beneath the surface of the city's sluggish water" (p. 175). As Angelou's Jewish companion in Berlin had remarked, "'Neither you nor I can afford to be so innocent'" (p. 173).

Notes

1. Cheney's quotation of Angelou occurs on pp. 14–15 of *Humanities in America: A Report to the President, the Congress, and the American People* (Washington, D.C.: National Endowment for the Humanities, September 1988). The original passage appears on pp. 4–5 of Angelou's "Journey to the Heartland" (address delivered at the National Association of Local Arts Agencies Convention, Cedar Rapids, Iowa, June 12, 1985) and is an amplification of Angelou's declaration of love for Shakespeare at the outset of the first volume of her autobiography, *I Know Why the Caged Bird Sings* (p. 10).
2. Raymond Williams's "A Hundred Years of Culture and Anarchy" (1970), in his *Problems in Materialism and Culture* (London: Verso, 1980), pp. 3–8, stresses this tension.
3. The five volumes of Maya Angelou's autobiographical sequence to date are: *I Know Why the Caged Bird Sings* (New York: Random House, 1970); *Gather Together in My Name* (New York: Random House, 1974); *Singin' and Swingin' and Gettin' Merry Like Christmas* (New York: Random House, 1976); *The Heart of a Woman* (New York: Random House, 1981); and *All God's Children Need Traveling Shoes* (New York: Random House, 1986).
4. Angelou's comment on the allusion in the title *The Heart of a Woman* appears in *Conversations with Maya Angelou,* ed. Jeffrey M. Elliot (Jackson: University Press of Mississippi, 1989), p. 117.
5. See Claudia Tate's interview of Angelou in *Black Women Writers at Work* (New York: Continuum, 1983), p. 11.

6. Christine Froula, "The Daughter's Seduction: Sexual Violence and Literary History," *Signs* 11 (1986): 621–44, quotation from p. 636. Using Alice Walker's *Color Purple* to provide a comparative perspective on Angelou, Froula remarks that Walker's work is "more powerful" because it involves a more fundamental cultural revision (p. 637). See also Marjorie Garber's discussion of Angelou in "Shakespeare as Fetish," *Shakespeare Quarterly* 41 (1990): 242–50.

Sandra Cookson (essay date 1995)

SOURCE: A review of *The Complete Collected Poems of Maya Angelou* and *Phenomenal Woman: Four Poems Celebrating Women*, in *World Literature Today*, Vol. 69, No. 4, Autumn, 1995, p. 800.

[*In the following review, Cookson praises Angelou's use of black-speech rhythms, inflections and patterns in her poetry.*]

Maya Angelou's five volumes of poems are here collected, reset in a handsome typeface, and produced in a collector's first edition. As a sort of companion volume, her publisher, Random House, has brought out a separate, pocket-size volume of "four poems celebrating women," entitled ***Phenomenal Woman*** (after the title poem). It too is handsomely designed; the publisher no doubt hopes to capitalize on the wider recognition of the poet, following her reading of her poem **"On the Pulse of Morning"** at the inauguration of President Clinton in 1993.

Angelou's poems celebrate black people, men and women; at the same time, they bear witness to the trials of black people in this country. Implicitly or directly, whites are called to account, yet Angelou's poetry, steeped though it is in the languages and cultures of black America, does not exclude whites. Quite the reverse: the poems are generous in their directness, in the humor Angelou finds alongside her outrage and pain, in their robust embrace of life. They are truly "celebratory."

Though Angelou's repertory is wide, she is at her best when working in the rhythms and highly inflected speech patterns of black Southern dialect, or being street-wise hip. She prefers strong, straightforward rhyme to free verse. The musical currents of blues and jazz, the rhythm of rap songs, and the language of the Bible mingle in her poems. The rhetoric of the pulpit is here too, though Angelou sometimes turns it to secular purposes. **"Still I Rise,"** a poem about the survival of black women despite every kind of humiliation, deploys most of these forces, as it celebrates black women while simultaneously challenging the stereotypes to which America has subjected them since the days of slavery. "Does my sassiness upset you?" "Does my haughtiness offend you?" "Does my sexiness upset you?" the poet demands in an in-your-face tone through successive stanzas, leading to the poem's inspirational conclusion. The penultimate stanza is especially strong: "Out of the huts of history's shame / I rise / Up from a past that's rooted in pain / I rise / I'm a black ocean, leaping and wide, / Welling and swelling I bear in the tide."

Angelou is master of several poetic idioms, and her voices are many. From the admonitory "Letter to an Aspiring Junkie" ("Let me hip you to the streets, / Jim, / Ain't nothing happening") to the simple prayer of a black man giving thanks for another day on earth ("Thank You, Lord"), she provides her readers direct access to her poems.

> I was once a sinner man,
> Living unsaved and wild,
> Taking my chances in a dangerous world,
> Putting my soul on trial.
> Because of Your mercy,
> Falling down on me like rain,
> Because of Your mercy,
> When I die I'll live again,
> Let me humbly say,
> Thank You for this day.
> I want to thank You.

Maya Angelou does not stint and she does not spare the often painful details of her people. Still, she somehow gives hope.

Elaine Slivinski Lisandrelli (essay date 1996)

SOURCE: "The Pulse of Morning," in *Maya Angelou: More Than a Poet*, Enslow Publishers, Inc., 1996, pp. 5–13.

[*In the following vignette, Slivinski Lisandrelli depicts Angelou's composition and presentation of the Clinton inauguration poem* "In the Pulse of Morning."]

In a country store in the dusty town of Stamps, Arkansas, a young girl sits near the candy counter. Outside, a sharp wind rustles through the shingles, but inside a potbellied stove warms the small store. Between customers she often writes poetry or reads from her beloved books.[1] These pursuits take her mind off the pain of growing up in the segregated South of the 1930s, where opportunities are denied to her because she is African American. On this day she memorizes the Presidents of the United States in chronological order.[2]

A tap on the counter disturbs her concentration. She never intended to ignore the customer who came to patronize her grandmother's store.[3] With a sigh, she closes the book. She accurately scoops up a half-pound of flour, and gently places it into a thin paper sack.[4]

Years later, after she journeyed far away from this Arkansas town, and overcame many hardships, a special opportunity was presented to this child who grew up to be Maya Angelou—author, playwright, professional stage and screen producer, director, performer, and singer. On a November day in 1992, the future forty-second President of the United States, William Jefferson Clinton, invited Angelou to compose and deliver a poem for his Inauguration Day ceremony. Her talent earned her the distinction of being the first African American and the first woman in the history of our nation to do so.

Maya Angelou felt grateful.[5] No poet had participated in a presidential inauguration swearing-in ceremony since 1961, when Robert Frost read his work at President Kennedy's inauguration. But Angelou was terrified, too.[6] Creating a poem that must touch the hearts of millions is a difficult task. Throughout her sixty-four years, Angelou had encountered many difficult tasks, and each time she embraced the challenge as an opportunity.

In preparation, Angelou spent weeks reading the works of scholar W. E. B. DuBois, abolitionist Frederick Douglass, poet Frances Ellen Watkins Harper, and sermons of African-American preachers. Often she left her beautiful home in Winston-Salem, North Carolina, and checked into a quiet hotel room to write. With her Bible, dictionary, and thesaurus by her side, she wrote and rewrote the poem on yellow legal pads, soon filling two hundred pages. As she searched for more ideas and reflected upon what she had already written, she played a game of solitaire.

Between her writing sessions, people asked about her progress and suggested topics she should address. Angelou remembers, "Even on an airplane, people would pass by my seat and say: 'Mornin,' finish your poem yet?'"[7]

Angelou kept writing. The themes she longed to impress upon the nation—that we human beings "are more alike than unalike"[8] and that "we may encounter many defeats but we must not be defeated,"[9] flowed through the 668 well-chosen words of the poem she called **"On the Pulse of Morning."**

The delivery of the poem was crucial, too. Bertha Flowers, a special woman from Angelou's past, had once told Angelou, "Words mean more than what is set down on paper. It takes the human voice to infuse them with the shades of deeper meaning."[10] And on that cold Inauguration Day of January 20, 1993, Angelou took her carefully crafted poem and eloquently gave meaning to her written words.

After being introduced to the audience as a "noted educator, historian, and author," Maya Angelou began with images that would speak throughout the poem:

> A Rock, a River, a Tree
> Hosts to species long since departed[11]

The January sun reflected off her hoop earrings and the metal buttons of her navy blue coat. Her deep, rich voice, once described as "the sound of summer evening thunder rumbling somewhere off in the distance,"[12] gave power to the alliterations of "distant destiny," "Marked the mastodon," and "wall of the world."[13] Maya Angelou's vision of each of us as a "descendant of some passed-on traveler"[14] reminded many of the suffering of those who came to this country, "arriving on a nightmare, / Praying for a dream."[15]

She encouraged us to have hope for the future even though our past has been troubled.

> History, despite its wrenching pain,
> Cannot be unlived, but if faced
> With courage, need not be lived again.[16]

Millions across the nation listened to their radios or watched as TV cameras focused on the faces in the crowd whose differences in race, color, creed, profession, and persuasion make up our nation. Tears filled some eyes. To each listener, Angelou seemed to speak personally.

> Lift up your eyes
> Upon this day breaking for you.
> Give birth again
> To the dream.[17]

The television camera captured President Clinton smiling and nodding approvingly at these lines:

> Here, on the pulse of this fine day,
> You may have the courage
> To look up and out and upon me,
> The Rock, the River, the Tree, your country.
> No less to Midas than the mendicant.
> No less to you now than the mastodon then.[18]

Novelist Louise Erdrich praised Angelou's forceful delivery. "Her presence was so powerful and momentous, she made a statement that I was personally longing to see and hear."[19]

> Here, on the pulse of this new day,
> You may have the grace to look up and out
> and into your sister's eyes,
> And into your brother's face,
> Your country,
> And say simply
> Very simply
> With hope—
> Good morning.[20]

As Maya Angelou concluded her poem, loud cheers, enthusiastic applause, a standing ovation, and a hug by the new President greeted her. "I loved your poem," President Clinton remarked, and he promised to hang a copy in the White House.[21] Television news correspondent Peter Jennings referred to Maya Angelou's poem as her "vision of America."[22]

This poem that "electrified the nation"[23] symbolized the hope President Clinton wanted to instill in the country—the hope that one person can overcome hardships and injustices and still look at the world with love and forgiveness.

She once told television journalist Bill Moyers, "You can never leave home. You take it with you wherever you go."[24] Maya Angelou's vision of America, first formed in Stamps, Arkansas, had come with her to Washington, D.C., in the form of a poem.

Many who listened to her eloquence that historic day did not realize that she had endured a long and often painful journey to arrive at this shining moment.

Notes

1. Esther Hill, "Maya Angelou: Resolving the Past, Embracing the Future," *The Student* (student literary magazine, Wake Forest University, Winston-Salem, North Carolina), Spring 1981, p. 8.
2. Maya Angelou, *I Know Why the Caged Bird Sings* (New York: Random House, 1969), p. 168.
3. Jeffrey M. Elliot, *Conversations with Maya Angelou* (Jackson, Miss.: University Press of Mississippi, 1989), p. 112.
4. Angelou, *I Know Why the Caged Bird Sings,* p. 15.
5. Howard G. Chau-Eoan and Nina Burleigh, "Moment of Creation," *People Magazine,* January 18, 1993, p. 62.
6. Ibid.
7. Karima Haynes, "Maya Angelou: Prime Time Poet," *Ebony,* April 1993, p. 72.
8. Susan Cahill, ed., *Writing Women's Lives: An Anthology of Autobiographical Narratives by Twentieth-Century American Women Writers* (New York: Harper Perennial, 1994), p. 210.
9. Elliot, p. 192.
10. Angelou, *I Know Why the Caged Bird Sings,* p. 95.
11. Maya Angelou, *The Complete Collected Poems of Maya Angelou* (New York: Random House, 1994), p. 270.
12. Haynes, p. 68.
13. Angelou, *Collected Poems,* p. 270.
14. Ibid., p. 271.
15. Ibid., p. 272.
16. Ibid.
17. Ibid.
18. Ibid., p. 273.
19. Judith Graham, ed., *Current Biography* (New York: H. W. Wilson), February 1994, Vol. 55, no. 2, p. 10.
20. Angelou, *Collected Poems,* p. 273.
21. Haynes, p. 70.
22. ABC News live broadcast of President William Jefferson Clinton's inauguration, January 20, 1993.
23. "Oprah Throws a Party," *Ebony,* June 1993, p. 120.
24. *Creativity with Bill Moyers: Maya Angelou.* Corporation for Entertainment and Learning, WNET Theater, 1982. Videotape.

Lyman B. Hagen (essay date 1997)

SOURCE: "Poetry: Something About Everything," in *Heart of a Woman, Mind of a Writer, and Soul of a Poet: A Critical Analysis of the Writings of Maya Angelou*, University Press of America, Inc., 1997, pp. 118–36.

[*In the following excerpt, Hagen presents an anatomy of Angelou's poetry and its subject matter.*]

Of Maya Angelou's six published volumes of poetry, the first four have been collected into one Bantam paperback volume, titled ***Maya Angelou: Poems*** (1986). Her early practice was to alternate a prose publication with a poetry volume, and a fifth "collection" follows her fifth autobiography. Unlike the four previous volumes of poetry, this fifth work titled ***Now Sheba Sings the Song*** (1987), adds a new dimension. Here fifteen or so short poems are responses to sketches of African-American women done by artist Tom Feelings, whom Angelou has known for many years. The combined talents of these two are highly complementary and the results are particularly appealing. A sixth volume, ***I Shall Not Be Moved*** (1990), contains new love poems and praise poems. A four poem inspirational collection has been available under the title ***Phenomenal Woman.*** These four are previously published poems.

Angelou's poems are a continuum of mood and emotion. They go from the excitement of love to outrage over racial injustice, from the pride of blackness and African heritage to suffered slurs. Angelou follows Countee Cullen's literary perspective that black authors have the prerogative to "do, write, create what we will, our only concern being that we do it well and with all the power in us."[1] Angelou indeed speaks out in many ways and with the best of words she can summon.

Angelou's poetry is generally brief, in the tradition of Langston Hughes who believed that a poem should be short—the shorter the better. Forty percent of the 135 poems in the Bantam edition are 15 lines or less. Of this forty percent, fifteen poems contain three stanzas, twelve have two stanzas, and eleven poems are unstructured. These eleven seem rather forced and rhetorical. Another dozen poems contain between eleven and fifteen lines each. The remainder of her 135 collected poems range from 30 to 50 lines. Angelou never indulges in lengthy narrative poems. She chooses words frugally. The length of line in her poems is also short. Most lines of her three-stanza poems are trimeter; others, particularly those in the unstructured poems, are from two to four syllables long. Some critics do cite her poetry as "oversimplistic or slight because of the short lines, easy diction, and heavy dependence on rhythm and rhyme in her poetry."[2] But Angelou herself has frequently commented on the difficulty of reducing complex thoughts and ideas to a poetic format. She says she begins with many pages of words on her yellow legal pad and works long and hard at distilling them.

Total poetic meaning stresses both emotional content and rhythmical elements. If the emotional content can be considered the bricks of the poem, the rhythm would be the mortar that binds. Angelou is a natural builder of poetry for she not only has a keen sensitivity to feeling, but also a marvelous sense of rhythm. Her musical awareness is so strong that she claims she *hears* music in ordinary, everyday circumstances. A rhythmical awareness has been reinforced by four important influences on her: first, her many readings of the lyrical King James Bible; second, acknowledged reading of traditional white writers such as Edgar Allan Poe, William Thackeray, and particularly William Shakespeare; and of prominent black writers such as Paul Laurence Dunbar, Langston Hughes, James Weldon Johnson, Countee Cullen, and of W. E. B. DuBois' "Litany at Atlanta." A third strong influence grew out of her participation in the rhythmical shouting and singing in African-American church services with their emotional spirituals; and the strong, moving sermons preached in those churches, whose tones she absorbed into her being. The fourth shaping force derives from childhood chants, songs and rhyme games long familiar in folklore.

With her keen sense of feeling, it is natural for Angelou, when she decides to compose a poem, first to find the rhythm of a subject, however mundane that subject may be. This approach is outlined in an interview with Arthur Thomas as Angelou explains the lengthy procedure she follows to produce a poem:

> When I write a poem I try to find a rhythm. First, if I wanted to write a poem about today. . . . I would write everything I know about today.
>
> Then I find the rhythm. Everything in the universe, Art, has rhythm. The sun rises and sets. The moon rises and sets. The tides come, they go out. Everything moves in rhythm. Tangentially, I would like to say that when people say of black people, "You have rhythm," it is not an insult. . . .
>
> It means that you are close to the universe. . . . I will find that maybe the rhythm changes. . . . This rhythm is slow and simple, and then maybe it's faster, more complex; and then there's the audience, and then—it's marvelous! Exciting!
>
> *Then* I start to work on the poem, and I will *pull* and *push* it and *kick* it and *kiss* it, *hug* it, everything. Until finally it reflects what this day has been.
>
> It costs me. It might take me three months to write that poem. And it might end up being six lines.[3]

Angelou has often spoken about this painful process of distilling her thoughts and the flow of her words. She mentions that 15 pages of notes might end up producing four lines of poetry. She has explained that the effort involved encompasses a discipline that is very difficult. But she finds the results rewarding and is still attracted to this means of expression.

A few of her poems seem pretentious with somewhat forced language, but most of her poetry has the spritely diction of the vernacular and the dialectical. It is with this language mode that she is most successful. She has no objection to using dialect, as long as it does not denigrate. She admires the dialect poems of Paul Laurence Dunbar because of "the sweetness of them." The high regard for this kind of poetry might have astonished Dunbar. He was dismayed that his vernacular poems were more appreciated than his romantic and cultured ones.

Of the poetry Angelou has published, only a few poems first appeared in journals or literary reviews, the usual path to publication for poets. Her work finds its way immediately into books. R. B. Stepto waspishly observes that Angelou's slight poems "cannot but make lesser-known talents grieve all the more about how this thin stuff finds its way to the rosters of a major New York house while their stronger, more inventive lines seem to be relegated to the low-budget (or no-budget) journals and presses."[4] Angelou's 'thin stuff' is not so thin if read with an eye to inner meaning. Her deliberate distillations are effective. They are written for people, not other poets. Some of the poems in her first volume, ***Just Give Me a Cool Drink of Water 'fore I Diiie,*** were originally published as songs. The volume includes many of the lyrics from her 1969 recording of "The Poetry of Maya Angelou" for GWP Records. Most of her other poetry could easily be set to music. It is purposely lyrical. It is designed to elicit stirring emotional responses. Much of it is meant to show fun with the familiar.

There has been little critical attention given to Angelou's poetry beyond the usual book reviews. A scattering of negative responses have greeted each book of poetry. Ellen Lippman writes that ". . . Angelou is more adept at prose than verse."[5] Janet Blundell agrees: "This ***Shaker, Why Don't You Sing?*** poetry is no match for Angelou's prose writings."[6] A third reviewer, J. A. Avant, judges that ". . . this ***Just Give Me a Cool Drink of Water*** isn't accomplished, not by any means. . . ." But he concedes that ". . . some readers are going to love it."[7] And S. M. Gilbert suggests publishers have exploited Angelou. Gilbert comments that her second poetry book, ***Oh, Pray My Wings Are Gonna Fit Well*** ". . . is such a painfully untalented collection of poems that I can't think of any reason other than the Maya myth for it to be in print; it's impossible indeed."[8] It is not unusual to capitalize on a successful author's name. A new book by a currently popular writer generally guarantees at least minimum sales with minimum promotion. But Angelou had been writing poetry long before her prose ventures and has considered herself basically a poet. These negative reviewers have failed to look beyond the apparent simplistic lines to discover the power of their message. Angelou tries to reach readers not attuned to soaring poetics but comfortable with sparse exchanges.

Contrary to the negative criticism, positive comments have also appeared. The reviewer in *Choice* magazine finds that Angelou's work is ". . . craftsmanlike and powerful (though not great poetry)."[9] Chad Walsh says the work in ***Just Give Me*** is ". . . a moving blend of lyricism and harsh social observation."[10] The reviewer of ***Shaker, Why***

Don't You Sing? in *Publishers Weekly* says, her "poems speak with delicacy and depth of feeling."[11] Robert Loomis, Angelou's long-time editor at Random House, supports her with his well-taken remarks:

> I've always believed that those who have reservations about Angelou's poetry simply don't understand what she's doing. She is very strongly in a certain tradition of Black American poetry, and when I hear her read or declaim the works of other Black American poets, I can see very clearly what her heritage is and what her inspiration is. Furthermore, Maya is not writing the sort of poetry that most of us grew up in school admiring. What she is writing is poetry that is very definitely in what I would call the oral tradition. That is, what she writes can be read aloud and even acted. When her words are spoken, they are extremely effective and moving. They always sound just right.[12]

Although few critics have found great merit in her poetry, Angelou has acquired a dedicated audience. Her work seems to have a special appeal to college students. At her public readings, a generally balanced cross-section, male and female, black and white, is in attendance. She delights and enchants the entire group with her timing and her powerful delivery. Some admirers of her poetry have been so impressed with its rhymes, rhythms, and content that they themselves have been encouraged to write. Many poets manque have sent Angelou their unsolicited creations. Quite a few of these can be found stored with her collected papers at the Wake Forest University library. Angelou encourages young people to express themselves openly and seeks to inspire them.

The titles of Angelou's first four books of poems are attention getters. They are catchy black vernacular expressions. Her first volume, ***Just Give Me A Cool Drink of Water*** (1971), refers to Angelou's belief that "we as individuals . . . are still so innocent that we think if we asked our murderer just before he puts the final wrench upon the throat, 'Would you please give me a cool drink of water?' and he would do so. That's innocence. It's lovely."[13]

Angelou covers a wide range of subject matter. In Angelou's writings, poetry or prose, she holds to tradition and makes a special effort to dispel false impressions about African Americans, but does not use this as her sole motivation.

Angelou's poetry belongs in the category of "light" verse. Her poems are entertainments derived from personal experiences and fall into one of two broad subject areas. First, she writes about everyday considerations—the telephone, aging, insomnia—topics that are totally neutral. Second, she writes with deep feeling about a variety of racial themes and concerns.

"The Telephone," for example, exemplifies her universally identifiable reflections on an ordinary subject. She admits in verse that she is dependent on it. Its importance to her daily life is notable by a contrast to its periods of silence.

But she can't stand the quietude long, nor the isolation implied, and so she impatiently demands that the phone ring. This demand follows three structured stanzas: the first physically describes the telephone; the second, its active effect on people's lives; and the third, the effect of its silence. In the second stanza, she emphasizes the familiar and the feminine by employing a metaphor of sewing, tatting, crocheting, hemming, and darning. The intrinsic themes of black and blue and week-end loneliness are often found in popular blues songs.

Another light general rumination is **"On Reaching Forty."** In somewhat stuffy language Angelou regrets the passage of time and expresses tongue-in-cheek admiration for those departing this world early and by this bestows upon the poem an unexpected conclusion. She is saddened by the passing of youthful milestones. The years forward will weigh even more heavily.

Inasmuch as Angelou is an accomplished cook, it is not surprising to find that she addresses the appreciation of traditional foods. In **"The Health-Food Diner"** exotic, faddish health food items are rejected in favor of standard fare such as red meat. In alternating tetrameter and trimeter quatrains, Angelou concludes each stanza with a food preference. Her reader finds life must be sustained by solid values, not notional influences.

Angelou not only has a keen ear for dialogue and dialect, but she also evidences a keen psychological understanding of an adolescent girl's romantic concerns and possessiveness. The speaker in **"No Loser, No Weeper"** expresses in the vernacular a universal sentiment. Again Angelou carefully structures her poem. In each stanza, the speaker notes how her reaction to losing something, beginning with childish items and advancing to that of major worth: in the first stanza, a dime; then a doll; then a watch; but especially in the last stanza when she truly hates to lose her boy friend.

The same subject matter—the loss of a boy friend—is expressed in **"Poor Girl."** The speaker is a teenager who addresses a fickle fellow playing the field. She's afraid there will be another disappointed girl in a long line of disappointed girls, just like her. One girl, she says, will believe the lies but can't be forewarned because of a possible misunderstanding. Eventually the truth will be realized and awareness will set in.

Angelou is a realist. She knows that a married man who sees other women usually returns home to his wife in spite of the attraction and charm of the Other Woman. The speaker in **"They Went Home"** is aware that she plays a loser's role. While the sentiment is psychologically sound, the lines are prosaic, reflecting the pitiful state of the abandoned.

Sometimes Angelou uses contrasting pairs in her poetry. For example, in **"Phenomenal Woman,"** considered a personal theme-poem, she asserts the special qualities of a particular woman. The woman described is easily matched to the author herself. Angelou is an imposing woman—at least six feet tall. She has a strong personality and a compelling presence as defined in the poem. One can accept the autobiographical details in this poem or extend the reading to infer that all women have qualities that attract attention. Angelou's dramatic presentation of this poem always pleases her audience and is frequently the highlight of her programs.

Angelou pairs this poem with **"Men."** The speaker is a woman whose experience has taught her the games men play. In this she uses a raw egg metaphor to contrast fragile femininity with dominant masculinity, but the female speaker has perhaps learned to be cautious.

Other contrasting poetic pairs are **"America"** and **"Africa"; "Communication I"** and **"Communication II"**; and **"The Thirteens (Black and White)."**

In *Gather Together in My Name*, Angelou describes being shown a room full of dope addicts and the impact this picture had on her. In both **"A Letter to An Aspiring Junkie"** and in **"Junkie Monkey Reel"** she details the dangerous consequences of using drugs. In both poems the slave master of today is drugs, and the junkie is tied to the habit as if he were the monkey attached to the street vendor's strap. Both poems contain particularly disturbing images.

Angelou uses every opportunity to build African-American pride and in **"Ain't That Bad?"** she praises black culture, mores, customs, and leaders. Its short lines, its repetition of imperatives, and its repetition of the title help constitute a chant, which categorizes it as a "shouting poem."

In black West African English (Sierra Leone) *i gud baad* means "it's very good." Thus "bad" as used extensively in this poem carries a favorable connotation, meaning to be "very good, extremely good." This meaning has been incorporated into everyday black vernacular and therefore is commonly understood. The last word in the last line of the poem sustains the positive connotations and provides a closure.

As detailed in an earlier chapter, a number of children's activities and responses have been handed down through the years in all cultures and are considered folk materials and light entertainments. This wealth of rhyming folklore, so important in Angelou's childhood, provides an indigenous and unconscious source of much of the style and the flow of both her poetry and prose. It dictates the structure of much of her poetry.

Angelou's second group of meditations is concerned with racial subjects and themes. This group allies poetry with morality by continuing the themes of protest and survival found in her autobiographies. These poems are not excessively polemical; they voice only mild protest.

In this category is Angelou's favorite poem and theme, **"Still I Rise,"** the same title as that of a play she wrote in 1976. The title, Angelou says, refers "to the indominable spirit of the black people." She often quotes this poem in interviews and includes it in public readings. The poem follows Angelou's customary fashion of incremental repetition, and catalogues injustices.

In spite of adversity, dire conditions and circumstances; in spite of racial epithets, scorn, and hostility, Angelou expresses unshakable faith that one will overcome; one will triumph; one will Rise! The lines remind us of the black spiritual "Rise and Shine" as well as other religious hymns that express hope: "Oh, rise and shine, and give God the glory, glory! / Rise and shine, and give God the glory, glory!" In **"Our Grandmothers"** Angelou voices a similar sentiment contained in another dearly loved spiritual: "Like a tree, down by the riverside, I shall not be moved."

The "I" in **"Still I Rise**' is designated female by Angelou herself as she numbers this poem as one of the four about women in ***Phenomenal Woman.*** She speaks not only for herself but also for her gender and race. This extension of self occurs in Angelou's autobiographies and protest poetry. It is in keeping with a traditional practice of black writers to personalize their common racial experiences. Moreover, Angelou implies that the black race will not just endure, but that in the words of Sondra O'Neale, "will triumph with a will of collective consciousness that Western experience cannot extinguish."[14] Angelou's most militant poems are contained in the second section of her first volume of poetry, "Just Before the World Ends." They have "more bite—the anguished and often sardonic expression of a black in a white dominated world," Chad Walsh observes.[15] In her moving address **"To a Freedom Fighter,"** Angelou again as a spokesperson for all blacks acknowledges a debt owed to those who fought earlier civil rights battles. They did more than survive; they endured all indignities for the maintenance of their race.

In **"Elegy,"** the speakers are early black activists, Harriet Tubman and Frederick Douglass, who proudly observe successors to their cause, the torch bearers they spawned.

In their battles for status, African Americans have experienced disappointment with political and social liberals. In her early twenties, Angelou wrote **"On Working White Liberals,"** which expressed the prevailing cynical view of their broken promises. Liberal words have often been empty words, and so the black came to doubt their sincerity. The poem challenges white liberals to an extreme action to prove their racial tolerance. Words are not enough. Angelou has since disavowed the poem's sentiments; she says she was a young "hot-head" at the time she wrote it.

Angelou comes to the defense of Uncle Toms, people censured by black activists because they do not overtly resist unfair treatment. In **"When I Think About Myself,"** Angelou explains why a black woman responds with a simple "Yes, ma'am" for the sake of a job, even to a young white who insults her with the offensive word "girl." The servant does not pity herself and knows she is keeping her race alive. By being servile for an entire lifetime, she has provided sustenance for another generation who may find better conditions. Whenever appropriate, Angelou voices approval of those who endured indignities to feed, shelter, clothe, and educate the family.

Angelou also praises the black slaves who helped build America. In **"To a Husband,"** she reminds readers of this, and that the black man proudly reflects his African roots, while contributing to the physical growth of this country.

Angelou also idealizes black men and enhances their pride in her love poems. Two poems in particular in the first section of ***Just Give Me*** present admirable images of black men—their color: Black Golden Amber; and their behavior—gentle and grave. In **"A Zorro Man"** love is found to be exciting; the speaker is delighted that her man is courageous and thrilled with her. **"To a Man"** admires a man's special qualities: he is Southern, gentle, and always changing. That Angelou dedicated her first book of poems to Amber Sam and the Zorro Man is not at all surprising.

Her best poem in the section on love is **"The Mothering Blackness."** In incremental repetition and with biblical allusions, the speaker observes that black mothers forgive their prodigal children. A black mother loves her children simply because they are her children. These mothers refrain from condemning and warmly welcome their wanderers. Angelou's poem praises such unconditional love. Whenever Angelou found herself troubled, she went home to her mother or grandmother for nurturing; the bond between them was always strong and supportive. It is a natural consequence of motherhood in Angelou's mind.

Angelou speaks positively about women in various mundane settings. **"Woman Work"** reinforces the saying that "women's work is never done." It's a list of the endless daily chores faced by a housewife and mother. Its lines do not explain or complain. They merely list.

In **"Momma Welfare Roll,"** Angelou tells how brave a mother is when she accepts welfare. Circumstances force survival to depend upon government largesse, but pride dictates an attitude toward it. This poem acknowledges the demeaning turmoil endured when accepting welfare benefits. Malcolm X blamed his mother's death on the bureaucratic bungling of social workers.

Angelou's poems are dramatic and lyrical. Her style is open, direct, unambiguous, and conversational. The diction is plain but sometimes the metaphors are quite striking. The most successful of her poems are those that "have language close to speech or more nearly song,"[16] those written in the vernacular. When she steps outside this level of language, the resulting effort appears affected. An example is **"Unmeasured Tempo."** In this poem we find awkward, forced lines. Some of Angelou's best "poetry" might well be her song lyrics such as **"They Went Home."**

When Paul Laurence Dunbar complained that his vernacular poems were better received than his romantic, he was referring to vernacular as the everyday language of the street as opposed to dialect—that is, the black dialect of the "comic minstrel" tradition. The phonology of "yo" for "your" and the grammar of "be's" for "is" or of the zero copula are examples.

The use of the vernacular can convey a maturity, while the dialectical can imply a childishness, an inferiority. Angelou avoids anything that might make her race an object of ridicule, and the use of black dialect—or soul talk—might compromise dignity. Therefore, she chooses a language level perceived to be more dignified.

Angelou's poems read easily and smoothly by utilizing both rhyme and repetition, particularly incremental repetition. However, out of 39 poems in ***Just Give Me*** she uses rhyme in only seven and the rhymes she chooses are rather ordinary and unimaginative: approaches/coaches; weaving/leaving; or in another volume, cake with steak. She shows a keen ear for sound as when in **"Harlem Hopscotch"** she rhymes the words "left" and "hisself." There is also an occasional internal rhyme such as "Carrot straw" and "spinach raw" in **"The Health-Food Diner."**

Her theatrical sense exemplifies itself in her rhythms. In an interview with Bill Moyers on National Educational Television where they discussed black writers and white critics, Angelou said,

> Quite often there are allusions made in black American writing, there are rhythms set in the writing and counter-rhythms that mean a great deal to blacks. A white American can come in and he will hear, he will understand hopefully, the gist. And that's what one is talking about. The other is sort of "in" talk.[17]

As the fundamental appeals in poetry are the emotion, the feeling, and the rhythm, anyone can appreciate them in a successful poem, even poetry of different cultures. The "in" talk, on the other hand, refers to "signifying" wherein certain phrases evoke a response from an African-American reader but might be unknown to other readers. For example, the phrase "cigar-box guitar" means a string instrument associated with the devil but that most consider merely a primitive musical device. There are also words in black linguistic lore that have restricted meanings such as the word "dichty" in **"Weekend Glory,"** which means "snooty," "high-hat," or "snobbishness." Line six in **"Harlem Hopscotch"** recalls a popular jingle of black origin:

> If you're white, all right
> If you're brown, hang around
> If you're black stand back.

A knowledge of black linguistic regionalisms and folklore enhances the appreciation of Angelou's poems. Thus a Whorfian "linguistic relativity" in which language shapes the way we view the world may be at work here. But most of Angelou's poems can be understood and appreciated on their own merits, sans special insight. Her topics of simple universal concerns embrace the breadth of everyday worldly encounters, and, through poetic presentation, uplift these ordinary experiences to special status for the ordinary reader.

The tone in many of Angelou's poems is somewhat muted and reserved. There is frequently a melancholy, a blues feeling. There are no explosive outbursts like John Donne's "Batter My Heart, Three Personed God" or "For God's Sake, Hold your Tongue"; nor outrage as in John Milton's "On the Massacre at Piedmont." Perhaps her restraint derives from the African-American attitude of fatalism which has been noted by many scholars and particularly evidenced in black folklore. Perhaps it is merely for the emphasis related to a mutual response.

The sound should echo the sense, as Alexander Pope suggested, and Angelou does achieve a correspondence of sound and sense in many of her poems. The monotonous rhythms and diction of her poem **"Greyday"** seem to echo the feeling of loss and emptiness without the presence of a loved one. The lines clearly depict the perception of a time of loneliness.

R. B. Stepto points out parallels between Angelou's poetry and that of Sterling Brown, Langston Hughes, and Gwendolyn Brooks, particularly "Annie Allen" and "the Bean-Eaters" of Brooks' pre-Black aesthetic period. He also notes Angelou's marriage of "work song" refrains and "protest" couplets and wishes she had developed this further.[18] In Angelou's latest collection, ***I Shall Not Be Moved***, she does give testimony to hard work in the poem, **"Worker's Song."** This poem sings the praises of those whose work contributes to the orderly function of vital activities. African Americans do have a long history of hard work. In Angelou's writings, rarely is there anyone who does not work. Everyone of her characters—singers, dancers, railroad workers, etc.—works hard.

While Angelou's poetry is not generally acclaimed as great poetry, it is nevertheless highly enjoyable as J. A. Avant observes. Angelou may rank as a poet of moderate ability, but her poetry is praised for its honesty and for a moving sense of dignity. Angelou is consistently understandable, enlightening, and entertaining. Her personal readings of her poetry are moving events and greeted with great enthusiasm. Angelou plays an audience masterfully and her delivery enhances the most simple rhyme. It is little wonder she inspires novices; she makes the difficult seem simple and touching. This in itself is an accomplishment reflecting more than moderate ability.

Angelou discussed her crowning moment as a poet with Oprah Winfrey on a recent television interview. A telephone call came from Harry Thomason shortly after Bill Clinton's election as president. Clinton had asked to have Maya Angelou compose a special poem to be read, by her, at his inauguration. Angelou said she was overwhelmed, but went to work. She rented a hotel room, as is her practice when composing, took her pads and pencils and closeted herself from early morning to afternoon. She first settled on her theme, America, and then wrote down everything she could think of about the country. Those thoughts were then pushed and squeezed into a poetic form. The resultant poem, **"On the Pulse of the Morning,"** was read by Maya Angelou from the ceremonial balcony at President Clinton's swearing in. Angelou herself does not consider it a great poem. She says it is a good public poem and carries the message of unity she intended. She has a frequently recurring theme that, as people of diversity, we are more alike than unalike. This idea is contained in the inaugural poem. Angelou feels that one day she will rework this material into a more important private poem. This distinction she draws between public and private poetry is worthy of note.

The notoriety attendant upon being only the second poet, and the first African American and first female, asked to be a part of such an important public event, has spilled into Angelou's life of quietude at Wake Forest University and put her again high on the demand list for public speakers. It also has led to renewed interest in her books and poetry and should result in greater academic evaluation of her lifetime accomplishments.

Angelou again went public with a specially written poem, **"A Brave and Startling Truth,"** for the San Francisco celebration of the 50th birthday of the United Nations. She once more violated her stated belief that "'public' and 'poem' go together like buttermilk and champagne." She prefers her poetry to be a private experience, but answers when called upon if the cause is noble. The African-American Million Man March in Washington, D. C., in October 1995 was another request for a specially tailored tribute. She could not refuse her brothers and agreed to read on their program.

Maya Angelou has served her people well and has informed and entertained untold numbers of us. Hopefully, she will continue to do so and to point out our "alikes" and oneness.

Notes

1. Countee Cullen, *Color* (New York: Arno Press, 1969) vi.
2. "Maya Angelou." *Contemporary Literary Criticism* 35 (Detroit: Gale, 1985) 29.
3. Arthur E. Thomas, *Like It Is. Arthur E. Thomas Interviews Leaders on Black America* (New York: Dutton, 1981) 5.
4. R. B. Stepto, "The Phenomenal Woman and the Severed Daughter," *Parnassus: Poetry in Review* 8, 1 (Fall/Winter 1979) 313–15.
5. Ellen Lippman, *School Library Journal* 25 (1978): 83.
6. Janet Blundell, *Library Journal* 108 (1983): 746.
7. J. A. Avant, *Library Journal* 96 (1971): 3329.
8. S. M. Gilbert, *Poetry* (August 1976): 128–129.

9. *Choice* 9 (1972): 210.
10. Chad Walsh, *Book World* 9 (1972): 12.
11. *Publishers Weekly* 11 Feb. 1983: 59.
12. Robert Loomis, "Letter to L. B. Hagen," 3 June 1988.
13. Jeffrey M. Elliot, ed., *Conversations with Maya Angelou* (Jackson, MS: University Press of Mississippi, 1989) 155.
14. Sondra O'Neale, "Reconstruction of the Composite Self: New Images of Black Women in Maya Angelou's Continuing Autobiography," *Black Women Writers 1950–1980,* ed. Mari Evans (New York: Anchor Books/Doubleday, 1984) 28.
15. Walsh, 12.
16. Blundell, 1640.
17. "Maya Angelou," *Current Biography* (New York: H. W. Wilson, 1974) 14.
18. Stepto, 313–315.

A. R. Coulthard (essay date 1999)

SOURCE: "Poetry as Politics: Maya Angelou's Inaugural Poem, 'On the Pulse of Morning,'" in *Notes on Contemporary Literature,* Vol. XXVIII, No. 1, January, 1999, pp. 2–5.

[*In the following essay, Coulthard argues that* "On the Pulse of Morning" *is a bad poem, sloppy in construction, and hackneyed in content.*]

Since Maya Angelou delivered her Clinton inaugural poem, she has shot onto the bestseller list, performed in a film titled (ironically enough) "Poetic Justice," and, if a mind-boggling news snippet is correct, reported 1995 earnings of 4.2 million dollars. **"On the Pulse of Morning"** recently was set to music and performed by the Winston-Salem Symphony as testimony to its enduring fame. When I ask my literature majors to nominate the best living American poet, Ms. Angelou always gets several enthusiastic mentions. Never in the long course of literary history has so much been made of, and from, so little.

Polemical is almost always bad art because it assumes that worthy ideas are enough. Literary political crusaders who also honor the craft of their work, as Shelley did in some of his proletarian poems, are rare. More typically, the dogma-driven poet pays insufficient heed to artistic demands, such as the excellent one expressed by the poet-priest Gerard Manley Hopkins when he defined poetry as "speech framed . . . to be heard for its own sake over and above its interest in meaning" (see *Handbook to Literature,* ed. C. Hugh Holman [Indianapolis: Odyssey Press, 1972], 404). The hack polemicist expects his or her words to soar on noble ideas rather than on the wings of poesy. **"On the Pulse of Morning"** perfectly exemplifies this attitude. The poem is virtually devoid of "speech" shaped in such a way that it provides pleasure in and of itself. Quite the contrary. The interest of **"On the Pulse of Morning"** depends entirely upon the audience's agreement with its sociopolitical content. Only the most unstudied of liberals (or conservatives, for that matter) could glean a new insight from it, nor is there anything in the poem's style to inspirit the feelings of the initiated for the values dutifully incorporated. Roseanne Barr gushed over **"Pulse"** on "Letterman," but it's hard to imagine a thoughtful liberal being moved by it. The poem therefore fails not only as poetry but also as politics. It contains no ideas of any conceivable interest to anyone not already in agreement with them, and the poem is so poorly expressed that it more likely anesthetized rather than vitalized even that interest among those who heard or read it. Comparing such a poem to the one Robert Frost delivered at John Kennedy's inauguration says something about what has happened to American verse over the intervening decades. "The Gift Outright" transcends politics by catering to no party line, and it still stands up today as poetry. But I am not judging **"Pulse"** on its political content or the worthiness of its ideas, most of which I agree with. Just as good art can give evil values a dangerous appeal, so can bad art honorable ones. Angelou's poem makes even the cherished liberal totems of tolerance, long-suffering endurance, and brave new beginnings sound superficial and mundane. Take, for instance, this near-parody of the melting-pot ideal:

> There is a true yearning to respond to
> The singing River and the wise Rock.
> So say the Asian, the Hispanic, the Jew
> The African and Native American, the Sioux,
> The Catholic, the Muslim, the French, the Greek,
> The Irish, the Rabbi, the Priest, the Sheikh,
> The Gay, the Straight, the Preacher
> The privileged, the homeless, the Teacher.
> They hear. They all hear
> The speaking of the Tree.

Aside from the sophomoric predictability of this list, the craft of the passage is embarrassingly amateurish. A river can "sing," metaphorically, but the "Rock" is made "wise" just to endow it with arbitrary symbolism. (Steadfastness may link figuratively with a rock, but does wisdom?) A clean poetic line, with no word wasted, was once valued, but Angelou bathetically and redundantly tells us that her Rainbow Coalition's yearning to respond to Rock and River is a "true" one and that "They hear. They all hear" the loquacious Tree. The "Sioux" is illogically listed as separate from the "Native American" standing just beside him, and "the Sheik" may or may not hear the words of the wise Tree, but he does rhyme conveniently with "the Greek.' One of the many oddities of this basically free-verse poem is how often rhyme pops up at seemingly accidental moments. These accidents are far from happy ones. The doggerel chiming of "The Gay, the Straight, the Preacher, / The privileged, the homeless, the Teacher," for example, further cheapens the sentiment of what already looks like some pretty strange bedfellows, even for politics. Such stanzas are pedestrian in style and content, but

Angelou fares no better when she employs an elevated "literary" voice that does not seem her own, as in the opening stanza:

> A Rock, A River, A Tree
> Hosts to species long since departed,
> Marked the mastodon.
> The dinosaur, who left dry tokens
> Of their sojourn here
> On our planet floor,
> Any broad alarm of their hastening doom
> Is lost in the gloom of dust and ages.

In addition to the confusing grammar (the missing punctuation after line one, the statement beginning with "The dinosaur" which is never completed but instead comma-splices into the stanza's concluding generalization), this passage is deadened by inflated style. The image of "dry tokens" for either fossils or bones flirts with comedy, and the fancy noun "sojourn" is mismatched with the homely "planet floor." "Marked the mastodon" alliterates better than it communicates, for "Hosts" don't mark anything, not even in poetry. Yeats once said that a poet's words must seen inevitable (see *Writers on Writing,* ed. Walter Allen [Boston: The Writer, 1988], 102), but there is nothing natural, necessary, or even very clear about "Any broad alarm of their hastening doom." (The line does make some sense if the vague, superfluous adjectives are omitted.) Such writing passes for poetry only if style is ignored and content isn't scrutinized very closely. The April 1993 issue of *The Writer* quotes Ms. Angelou's pronouncement that "One of the problems in the West is that people are too busy putting things under microscopes," but only inferior literature suffers from such examination.

Some of my students mistakenly believe that symbolism equates with profundity, and such thinking may have produced Angelou's Rock, River, and Tree. But symbolism enriches a poem only if it springs naturally from the poem's rhetoric. These symbols don't. They are instead self-consciously and erratically invoked, at times almost as afterthoughts. Instead of adding variety, the symbols are redundant even within themselves. All three "speak" with essentially the same voice and message. Within the first four stanzas, the Rock twice "cries out" invitations to break free of our chains and realize our destiny; then the River "sings" a long sixth stanza to much the same effect. At times, Angelou even forgets that her symbols are meant to represent the oracular. When "the first and last of every Tree / Speaks to humankind," it becomes both the voice of inspiration and the high and low humans it is meant to inspire. Finally, the symbolic trio merges into a solo ("I am the Tree planted by the River, / Which will not be moved. / I, the Rock, I the River, I the Tree"), which apparently represents the hackneyed "inspirational" Voice of America: "the / Rock, the River, the Tree, your country."

Instead of providing unity and thematic heft, these clumsily-incorporated symbols merely add to the muddle. Since their function is basically the same and the poem is at least twice as long as it should be for what it says, the poet might better have picked any one of the three to do the talking and thereby tightened structure, point of view, and metaphorical consistency. But a nonchalant confidence in the message apparently took precedence over care with the medium.

"Pulse" is overdone in expression as well as conception. It is filled with modifiers, which would have been better deleted, for a cleaner, stronger line. Tacked-on adverbs, for example, weaken rather than strengthen "But today, the Rock cries out to us, clearly, forcefully." The adjective "distant" adds nothing but alliteration to "face your distant destiny," and it even reverses the appeal for action. Such cliched modifiers as "*piercing* need," "*wrenching* pain," and "*bright* morning" blunt other statements, and entire lines like "A River sings a beautiful song" and "The River sings on and on" are merely insipid.

Parts of the poem make little or no sense. What does it mean, for instance, to be "strangely made proud," and what is a "passed / On traveler"? One long passage has beleaguered humanity crouching in "bruising darkness" and lying "Face down in ignorance" at the same time. This cowed figure spills out-of-character "words / Armed for slaughter," then rises to his feet to become "a bordered country" that is "thrusting [?] perpetually under siege" in a bizarre melange of metaphors. It gets worse. These besieged victims suddenly transform into capitalistic victimizers fighting "armed struggles for profit," in a battle that abandons the military analogy and rounds the speaking River's shoreline into polluted "collars of waste." As this passage is completed, however, the river is flowing again, and feminized too, with currents of debris upon its "breast." This is, to put it bluntly, very sloppy writing.

Edward Rothstein, in a *New York Times* article, called the choice of inaugural music "bombastic and artificial" (reprinted in *The Charlotte Observer* 14 Feb. 1993: 5F). These words also describe Maya Angelou's poem. It may be exceptional in its undistinguished style, but it is of an ilk with the propagandist poetry favored by today's literary social engineers. The poem is so poorly crafted that it would be fatuous to take it apart were it not put together to the faulty specifications of the politically correct school of thought that is debilitating the study and production of literature in the United States.

This trend will continue unless the newly-empowered literary establishment comes to its critical senses and tolerates a compromise between the politically palatable and the aesthetically acceptable. Barring that unlikely event, a presidential inauguration will not be the only occasion for honoring bad writing in the name of a good cause. Check any current college anthology to see what I mean.

FURTHER READING

Criticism

Saher, Annette D., Sebastian M. Brenninkinmeyer and Daniel C. O'Connel. "Maya Angelou's Inaugural Poem." *Journal of Psycholinguistic Research*, Vol. 26, No. 4 (1997), 448–63.

The authors use Angelou's inaugural poem as a database for a linguistic analysis of the meaning generated in a text by its performance.

Additional coverage of Angelou's life and career is contained in the following sources published by the Gale Group: *Authors and Artists for Young Adults*, Vol. 20; *Black Literature Criticism*, Vol. 1; *Black Writers*, second edition; *Contemporary Authors*, Vols. 65–68; *Contemporary Authors New Revision Series*, Vol. 19; *Contemporary Black Biography*, Vol. 1; *Contemporary Literary Criticism*, Vols. 12, 35, 64, 77; *Dictionary of Literary Biography*, Vol. 38; *DISCovering Authors*; *DISCovering Authors: British*; *DISCovering Authors: Canadian*; *DISCovering Authors Modules: Most-Studied Authors, Multicultural, Poets,* and *Popular Fiction and Genres Authors*; *Major 20th-Century Writers*; *Something About the Author,* Vol. 49; and *World Literature Criticism Supplement*.

Jorge Luis Borges
1899-1986

(Also wrote under the pseudonym F. Bustos, and, with Adolfo Bioy Casares, under the joint pseudonyms H[onorio]. Bustos Domecq, B. Lynch Davis, and B. Suarez Lynch.) Argentine poet, short-story writer, essayist, critic, translator, biographer, and screenwriter.

For further discussion of Borges's works, see *PC*, Vol. 22.

INTRODUCTION

During his lifetime, Borges was highly regarded as a writer of baroque and labyrinthine short fictions often written in the form of metaphysical detective stories. Characteristically, they blur the distinction between reality and the perception of reality, between the possible and the fantastic, between matter and spirit, between past, present, and future, and between the self and the other. They are usually situated in the nebulous confines of allegorical locations, whether identified as bizarre dimensions of the universe, Arabian cities, English gardens, the Argentine pampa, amazing libraries, or the neighborhoods of Buenos Aires. Since his death, Borges has attained the status of one of the major literary figures of the twentieth century, a master poet and essayist, as well as an architect of the short story. His work has influenced not only how Latin American and non-Latin American writers write, but also the way readers read. Associated with the avant-garde Spanish *Ultraístas* in the 1920s, Borges rejected the Spanish poetry of the nineteenth century, and wrote a baroque verse free of rhyme, surrealistic, even brutal, in imagery and metaphor, dedicated to the incorporation of Argentinean locations, locutions and themes, and establishing the poet as the soul of his subject. By the end of the thirties, however, Borges repudiated his early verse, abandoning local color, nationalism, and the desire to shock. Thereafter, until his death, he worked with traditional devices: rhyme, meter, elucidation, and time-honored metaphors in traditional forms such as the sonnet and haiku. He strove for simplicity of expression through the use of common language and colloquial word order, and projected a tone of tranquil irony, and a wisdom concerned with, but tempered by, an indifference to, time, desire, and mortality.

BIOGRAPHICAL INFORMATION

Borges was born August 24, 1899, into an old, Argentinean family of soldiers, patriots, and scholars, in Buenos Aires, where he spent most of his childhood. His father was an intellectual, a university professor of psychology and modern languages, a lawyer, and a writer. He possessed an extensive library, which was the boy's delight. Borges, whose paternal grandmother was English, was raised bilingual and read English before Spanish. His first encounter with Cervantes, for example, was in English, and when he was seven, his Spanish translation of Oscar Wilde's "The Happy Prince" appeared in a Uruguayan newspaper. A visit to Switzerland in 1914 became an extended stay when the outbreak of the first World War made it impossible for the family to return to Argentina. Borges enrolled in the College de Geneve, where he studied Latin, French and German, as well as the European philosophers. he was especially taken with Schopenhauer and Bishop Berkley, whose dark pessimist and anti-materialist world view was reflected in Borges's literary work. After receiving his degree in 1918, Borges traveled to Spain where he joined with the avant-garde *Ultraístas*, who combined elements of Dadaism, Imagism, and German Expressionism in their reviews, essays, and highly metaphorical poetry. Borges returned to Buenos Aires in 1921, and, with the publication of his first books of poetry, *Fervor de Buenos*

Aires (1923), *Luna de Enfrente* (1925), and *Cuaderno San Martín* (1929), was recognized as a leading literary figure in Argentina. During these years, too, Borges helped establish several literary journals, and published essays on metaphysics and language. In 1938, the same year his father died, Borges himself nearly died from blood poisoning, after the wound he received from knocking his head against the casement of an open window while running up a flight of steps was poorly treated. Fearful that his ability to write might have been impaired by his illness, Borges took up short fiction rather than poetry, intending to attribute possible failure to inexperience in the genre rather than diminished literary skill. The result was "Pierre Menard, autor del Quijote," a story highly acclaimed both as a fiction and as a precursor to deconstructionist textual analysis. In the period following this publication, Borges wrote many of the works now considered to be among his masterpieces. Though he spoke of his disdain for politics, Borges was always politically outspoken. He opposed European fascism and anti-Semitism, and the dictatorship of Juan Perón in Argentina. In 1946, Perón removed Borges from his post as an assistant at the National Library of Argentina, due to his opposition to the regime; in 1955, however, following the overthrow of Perón, Borges, now almost totally blind from a condition he inherited from his father, was made director of the National Library. In 1957, he was appointed professor of English literature at the University of Buenos Aires. In 1961, he was a co-recipient, with Samuel Beckett, of the Prix Formentor, the prestigious International Publishers Prize. Borges did not oppose the Argentinean military coup or the terrorism of the Videla junta in the seventies until 1980, when, apologetically, he signed a plea for those whom the regime had caused to "disappear." Similarly, he supported the Pinochet dictatorship in Chile, calling the general a "gentleman," and commending his imposition of "order" in the face of communism. It was for these failings, rather than for any failure as an artist, many believe, that Borges was never awarded the Nobel Prize. The catalog of his awards and honors, nevertheless, is long and distinguished. He spent his last years as a literary celebrity, traveling and lecturing. Totally blind, he continued to write by dictation: to his mother, who died, in 1975, at the age of ninety-nine, and to his student and companion, María Kodama, whom he married shortly before his death. His enduring love of languages was marked by his late study of Icelandic. Borges died of cancer of the liver in 1986, and was buried in Geneva.

MAJOR WORKS

Borges's literary output spanned seven decades, from the 1920s–1980s, during which he published more than fifty volumes of short stories, poetry, and essays. In his first collection of poetry, *Fervor de Buenos Aires* (Passion for Buenos Aires), published in 1923, Borges, an early adherent to the *Ultraísta* literary movement, took his native city as his subject matter. Subsequent collections of poetry published in the 1920s include *Luna de enfrente* (1925; Moon Across the Way), and *Cuaderno San Martín* (1929; San Martín Copybook). Turning to the works of short fiction that eventually won him international praise, Borges virtually ceased to publish poetry throughout most of the 1930s and 40s. His best-known short-story collections include *El jardin de senderos que se bifurcan* (1941; The Garden of Forking Paths), *Ficciones* (1944), and *El Aleph* (1949), although the first English language translations of his work did not appear until 1962, with two collections, titled *Labyrinths* and *Ficciones*. Borges began publishing poetry again in the 1950s, when, as Edward Hirsch describes it: "The fabulist returned to poetry . . . with a more direct and straightforward style, a beguiling and deceptive simplicity." Jay Parini asserts that, "his finest poems appeared between 1955 and 1965," while Martin S. Stabbs observes, "By the mid-1960s Borges seems to have regained considerable momentum as a poet. Both thematically and technically his work displays a richness not seen since the 1920s." In these later poems, "a notion that recurs almost obsessively in his poetry as well as in his prose" is "the idea of the world as a complex enigma, expressed at times in the form of a labyrinth, or as the dream-made-real of a capricious creator." Borges's poetry volumes of the 1960s include *El hacedor* (1960; Dreamtigers), *Obra poética* (1964), and *El otro, el mismo* (1969; The Other, the Same), among others. This period of prolific poetic output continued into the 1970s, with the collections, *The Gold of Tigers* (1972), *In Praise of Darkness* (1974), and *Historia de la noche* (1977), among others. Borges's second-to-last volume of poetry, *La cifra*, was published in 1981. His last collection, *Los conjurados* (1985; The Conspirators), includes a combination of short prose pieces and poetry, often blurring the distinction between the two. Of this volume Stabbs states, "The very fact that Borges, then eighty-five, was still exploring that fascinating no-man's-land between prose and poetry, was still writing fine sonnets, and was continuing to rework the rich metal of earlier texts suggests that even though death was close, he remained a poet of substantial talent and considerable vigor." A volume of new translations, *Selected Poems: Jorge Luis Borges*, was released in 1999.

CRITICAL RECEPTION

Borges was not well known outside of literary circles in Buenos Aires until 1961, when he was awarded the prestigious Formentor Prize, earning him international recognition and leading to his current status as one of the foremost short fiction writers of the twentieth century. Borges met members of the *Ultraísta* literary movement while in Spain in 1919, and, as a young writer in the 1920s, is sometimes credited with having introduced ulráism to Argentina. Jay Parini, writing in 1999, notes that, "With Pablo Neruda and Alejo Carpentier, Jorge Luis Borges set in motion the wave of astonishing writing that has given Latin American literature its high place in our time," adding, "Yet Borges stands alone, a planet unto himself, resisting categorization." Marcelo Abadi refers to Borges as, "one of the most prominent writers in any tongue," observing, "in his poems, stories and essays our century can detect a voice that stirs the dormant wonder which, according to the Greeks, lies at the source of the love of knowledge and wisdom." Edward Hirsch opines that Borges, "was a rapturous writer, a literary alchemist who emerged as an explorer of labyrinths, an adventurer in the fantastic, a poet of mysterious intimacies who probed the infinite postponements and cycles of time, the shimmering mirrors of fiction and reality, the symbols of unreality, the illusions of identity, the disintegration of the self into the universe, into the realm of the Archetypes and the Splendors." However, critics frequently note that, to this day, Borges's accomplishments as a poet are largely overshadowed by his reputation as a master of short fiction. Beret E. Strong describes "the international literary community's portrait of 'Borges'" as "that of a great short story writer and mediocre poet of conservative political and traditional literary values," adding that critics have agreed with Borges's own assessment of his early poetry and essays "as less valuable than the later fiction," and have, therefore, opted "not to write about them much." Mark Couture, writing in 1999, states the case more strongly: "Borges, like Cervantes, has the reputation in some circles of being a 'bad' poet," but adds, "I don't think this label is quite fair." Couture points out that Borges's poems "have a quiet, metaphysical intensity and a thematic complexity that can be overlooked in superficial readings." Parini, observing that, while "One tends to think of Borges as the writer of a dozen or so classic stories . . . Yet Borges was a well-known poet long before he tried his hand at fiction." Stabbs, acknowledging that, "Today he is usually thought of first as the creator of fictional labyrinths, then as the writer of erudite essays . . . and only last as a poet," defends Borges's poetry in adding: ". . . he began as a poet and has worked more or less continuously in this genre. Most important, he reveals more of himself in his verse than in any other kind of writing."

PRINCIPAL WORKS

Poetry

Fervor de Buenos Aires [*Passion for Buenos Aires*] 1923
Luna de enfrente [*Moon across the Way*] 1925
Cuaderno San Martín [*San Martín Copybook*] 1929
Poemas, 1923–1943 1943
Poemas, 1923–1953 1954
El Hacedor [*Dreamtigers*] (poetry and prose) 1960
Obra poetica, 1923–1964 1964
Para las seis cuerdas [*For the Six Strings* (verses for Milangas)] 1965
Seis poemas escandinavos [*Six Scandinavian Poems*] 1966
Siete poemas [*Seven Poems*] 1967
Elogio de la sombra (poetry and prose) 1969
El otro, el mismo [*The Other, the Same*] 1969
El oro de los tigres [*The Gold of Tigers*] 1972
Selected Poems, 1923–1967 1972
In Praise of Darkness 1974
Siete poemas sajones [*Seven Saxon Poems*] 1974
La rosa profunda [*The Unending Rose*] 1975
La moneda de hierro [*The Iron Coin*] 1976
Historia de la noche [*History of Night*] 1977
The Gold of Tigers: Selected Later Poems 1977
Obras Completas (poetry and prose) 1977
La cifra 1981
Antologia poetica, 1923–1977 1981
Los conjurados [*The Conspirators*] 1985
Selected Poems: Jorge Luis Borges 1999

Short Stories

Historia universal de la infamia 1935
El jardin de senderos que se bifurcan 1941
Ficciones, 1935–1944 1944
El Aleph 1949
Ficciones (includes The Garden of Forking Paths) 1962
Labyrinths: Selected Stories and Other Writings (short stories and essays) 1962
The Aleph and Other Stories, 1933–1969 1970
El informe de Brodie 1970
El matrero 1970
Dr. Brodie's Report 1971
El congreso [*The Congress*] 1971
A Universal History of Infamy 1972
El libro de arena 1975
The Book of Sand 1977
Rosa y azul (contains "La rosa de Paracelso" and "Tigres azules") 1977
Veinticinco agosto 1983 y otros cuentos de Jorges Luis Borges 1983
Collected Fictions: Jorges Luis Borges 1999

Collaborations and Pseudonymous Stories

Seis problemas para Isidro parodi [with Adolfo Bioy Casares, under joint pseudonym H. Bustos Domecq] (short stories) 1942
Dos fantasias memorables [with Bioy Casares, under joint pseudonym H. Bustos Domecq] (short stories) 1946
Manual de zoologia fantastica [with Margarita Guerrero] (essays) 1955
Cronicas de Bustos Domecq [with Bioy Casares] (short stories) 1967
The Book of Imaginary Beings [with Margarita Guerrero] (essays) 1969
Chronicles of Bustos Domecq [with Bioy Casares] (short stories) 1976
Nuevos cuentos de Bustos Domecq [with Bioy Casares] (short stories) 1977
Six Problems for Don Isidro Parodi [with Adolfo Bioy Casares] (short stories) 1983
Atlas [with Maria Kodama] (prose and poetry) 1985

Essays

Inquisiciones [*Inquisitions*] 1925
El tamano de mi esperanza [*The Measure of My Hope*] 1926
El idioma de los argentinos [*The Language of the Argentines*] 1928
Evaristo Carriego (biography) 1930
Discusión 1932
Las Kennigar 1933
Historia de la eternidad [*History of Eternity*] 1936
Nueva refutacion del tiempo 1947
Aspectos de la literatura gauchesca 1950
Otras inquisiciones 1952
La poesia gauchesca [*Gaucho Poetry*] 1960
Other Inquisitions, 1937–1952 1964
Nuevos ensayos dantescos [*New Dante Essays*] 1982
Selected Non-Fiction: Jorge Luis Borges 1999

CRITICISM

María Luisa Bastos (essay date 1986)

SOURCE: "Whitman as Inscribed in Borges," translated with Daniel Balderston, in *Borges the Poet*, edited by Carlos Cortinez, The University of Arkansas Press, 1986, pp. 219–30.

[*In the following excerpt, Bastos argues that Walt Whitman is a major influence on Borges's poetry.*]

1. The Wish to Express the Totality of Life

In 1925, referring to the extreme subjectivity typical of nineteenth century esthetics, Borges pointed out: ". . . any frame of mind, however extraneous, can become the focus of our attention; in its brief totality, it may be our essence. If translated into the language of literature, this means that trying to express oneself and having the wish to express the totality of life are but one and the same thing." Whitman was the first Atlas attempting to bring such a challenge into action, and he lifted the world upon his shoulders.[2]

Years before, the young Borges, astounded by Whitman's ambitious task,[3] wrote verses that, according to the sarcastic reflection of the mature Borges, instead of echoing Whitman echoed the Peruvian Post-*Modernista* poet, Chocano.[4] Here is a sample of those verses, from **"Himno del mar,"** written in 1919:

> I have longed for a hymn of the sea with rhythms
> as ample as the screming waves;
> Of the sea when on its waters the sun flutters as
> a scarlet flag;
> Of the sea when it kisses the golden breasts of
> virgin, thirstily waiting, beaches;
> Of the sea when its forces howl, when winds shout
> their blasphemes;
> When the polished, bloody moon shines on the steel
> waters. . . .
>
> Oh, protean, I have sprung from you.
> Both of us shackled and nomadic;
> Both of us intensely thirsty of stars;
> Both of us hopeful and deceived;
> Both of us air, light, strength, darkness;
> Both of us with our great desire,
> and both of us with our great misery![5]

However, in spite of the deliberate grandiloquence with which Borges tried to render the Whitmanesque rhythm, the statements in **"Himno del mar,"** like blurred copies, lessen the optimism of the original. It is useful to compare Borges' verses to Whitman's:

> You sea! I resign myself to you also—
> I guess what you mean,
> I behold from the beach your crooked inviting fingers,
> I believe you refuse to go back without feeling
> of me,
> We must have a turn together, I undress, hurry me
> out of sight of the land,
> Cushion me soft, rock me in billowy drowse,
> Dash me with amorous wet, I can repay you.
>
> Sea of stretch'd ground-swells,
> Sea breathing broad and convulsive breaths,
> Sea of the brine of life and of unshovell'd yet
> always-ready graves,
> Howler and scooper of storms, capricious and dainty
> sea,
> I am integral with you, I too am of one phase and
> of all phases.[6]

"Himno del mar" is interesting as a part of the prehistory of Borges' poetry, but the fact remains that many of his lasting early poems are firmly guided by the enticing invitation at the beginning of "Song of Myself": "Stop this day and night with me and you shall possess the origin of all poems" (25).

Also, both ***Fervor de Buenos Aires*** and ***Luna de enfrente*** have many echoes of Whitman's decision: "Creeds and schools in abeyance / Retiring back a while sufficed at what they are, but never forgotten" (24). For the Borges who wrote ***Fervor de Buenos Aires*** to turn away from the schools meant, among other things, having too many different objectives, which he himself mockingly summarized in 1969: ". . . to copy some of Unamuno's awkardnesses (which I liked), to be a Seventeenth Century Spanish writer, to be Macedonio Fernández, to find out metaphors already found out by Lugones, to sing of a Buenos Aires with one story houses and, towards the West or the South, villas surrounded by iron fences."[7] Underlying those contradictory objectives it is possible, however, to detect one guiding principle, an adaptation of Whitman's ambitious plan: "With the twirl of my tongue I encompass worlds and volumes of worlds" (45).

From the very beginning, it is also clear that Borges' project has been designed on a scale totally different from Whitman's. In Borges' first two books of poems and even in ***Cuaderno San Martín***, the totality of life has been, paradoxically, envisioned in minute dimensions: the universe is viewed with a very limited focus. Moreover, it is looked for, pointed out and expressed within boundaries. Borges already knew that the poet is not identical to his universe—that he can, and must, keep his distance, accepting the limited dimensions of the poem in relation to the limitless world, to the limitless sectors of the world:

> Africa's destiny lies in eternity, where there are
> deeds, idols, kingdoms, arduous forests and swords.
> I have attained a sunset and a village.
>
> (66; transl. MLB)

Even before these lines in **"Dakar,"** from ***Luna de enfrente***, in **"Las calles,"** the opening poem of ***Fervor de Buenos Aires***, one can see some sort of a reduction of the Whitmanesque world. In fact, Whitman's "worlds and volumes of worlds" have been replaced by the humble streets which will be Borges' only topography:

> Towards the West, the North, and the South
> streets, which are also the native land, have unfurled:
> may those flags be in the verses I design.
>
> (16; transl. MLB)

As echoes of Whitman's project and of Whitman's voice, even the more grandiloquent poems—particularly those collected in ***Luna de enfrente:*** **"Una despedida," "Jactancia de quietud," "Dakar," "La promisión en alta mar"**—render the tone of the model at a lower pitch. One could point out the poem, **"Casi Juicio Final" ("Almost Last Judgment")** as the epitome of that change:

> In my heart of hearts, I justify and praise myself:
> I have witnessed the world; I have confessed the strangeness of the world.
> I have sung the eternal: the clear returning moon and the cheeks longed for by love.
>
> (69; transl. MLB)

In ***Elogio de la sombra,*** Borges acknowledges that he "once coveted the ample breath of the psalms or of Walt Whitman" (975; transl. MLB). The lines quoted above do, in my opinion, recall the almighty Adamic Whitmanesque breath. But it is as if Borges' reproduction had undergone a filtering process. Borges has pointed out very often that language is succession: it can only render a simplified, reduced universe, it cannot reproduce the universe's concurrences. A comparison between Whitman's and Borges' declarations will show the modesty of Borges' project. Whitman says in *Leaves of Grass:*

> My voice goes after what my eyes cannot reach,
> With the twirl of my tongue I encompass worlds and volumes of worlds.
> Speech is the twin of my vision, it is unequal to measure itself.
>
> (45)

In **"Casi Juicio Final,"** the poetic voice sums up its accomplishments, its originality:

> I have commemorated with verses the city that embraces
> me and the shredding outskirts.
> I have expressed wonder where others have merely expressed custom.
> I have held up in firm words my feeling which could have been easily scattered in tenderness.
>
> (69; transl. MLB)

It is also worth remembering that **"Casi Juicio Final"** is like a disturbing anticipation, a matrix of other Last Judgments in Borges' poetry in addition to that in **"Mateo, XXV, 30."** For instance, in **"Otro poema de los dones,"** from ***El otro, el mismo*** (***The Self and The Other***), Whitman is a double symbol; his name is equivalent to gratitude and it is also an equivalent of the power of Grace:

> I want to thank the divine
> Labyrinth of effects and causes . . .
> For Whitman and Francis of Assisi
> Who already wrote the poem.
>
> (936; transl. MLB)

All of the above can be summarized very briefly: if one had to choose only one poem from Borges' early poetry as an emblem of the powerful, yet silent presence of Whitman—presence explicitly reinforced in other texts—**"Casi Juicio Final"** could be that poem. In it, Whitman's ambition to witness the world is clearly inscribed. This vision, however, expressed through the modest confines of the topography of Buenos Aires has become typically Borgesian.

2. Self-Definition through Opposition

One of Borges' practices has been to define his own literary objectives when characterizing the literature of other writers. This, he has done while dealing with Whitman's poetry; in two notes included in ***Discusión***—"El otro Whitman"; and "Nota sobre Walt Whitman"—in his lectures on the poet;[8] in the preface to his selection and translations from *Leaves of Grass* (1969);[9] and in his essay," Valéry como símbolo."

In his essay, "El otro Whitman," written in 1929, Borges wrote that Whitman's themes render "the peculiar poetry of arbitrariness and loss," (208; transl. DB) a phrase which would describe his own poetry with accuracy and concision. He also pointed out the failure of Whitman's critics to see the basic merit of his enumerations, "a merit lying not in their length but in their delicate verbal balance" (206; transl. D.B.), a description which is perhaps ultimately more appropriate for Borges' enumerations than for Whitman's. The essay on Valéry—written on the poet's death in 1945, and collected in *Otras Inquisiciones* in 1952—is an excellent sample of Borges' technique. He defines by closeness or by opposition—*simpatías y diferencias*. He develops an opposition Whitman/Valéry which might serve as a base to define Borges' literature; "Valéry personifies in an illustrious way the labyrinths of the spirit; Whitman, the interjections of the body" (686; transl. DB). Borges says of Whitman: ". . . he wrote his rhapsodies by means of an imaginary self, formed partly from himself, partly from each of his readers." Borges continues that in the face of that quest, of that fiction of a "possible man . . . of unlimited and careless happiness Valéry glorifies the virtues of the mind." Finally, in Valéry's predilections (the antithesis of Whitman's), are without a doubt Borges' pleasures: "The lucid pleasures of thought and the secret adventures of order."

3. The Memory of an Unending Poem

In the early poetry of Borges one can notice the presence of Whitman's diction; but these versions even in the young Borges' display of *Ultraísta* baroque, already announce the future Borges. It is well-known that in the work of both Whitman and Borges free verse, marked by the use of long lines, has Biblical resonances. It is also known that such a resonance largely derives from the anaphoric repetitions and the enumerations. (I think it is appropriate to recall here that Michel Foucault, in *The Order of Things*,[10] has aptly described Borges' enumerations as heteroclite, a term more adequate, in my view, than the stylistic "chaotic enumeration" popularized by Leo Spitzer, who, by the way, never mentioned Borges in his essay written in 1944, when Borges had already published twelve books.[11]) Like Whitman's, Borges' diction interweaves somewhat unexpected colloquial language with rather audacious images, linked together by a syntax of a paradoxically grandiloquent ease. That syntax, nonetheless, shows a degree of control which is the privilege of brevity: "he was a poet of a tremulous and sufficient laconism" (207; transl. DB), Borges said of Whitman, a singularly apt characterization of his own poetry. With tremulous and sufficient pithiness, Whitman had announced: "Tenderly will I use you, curling grass" (28), which Borges translated: "Te usaré con ternura, hierba curva."[12] Raised from its elementary condition to a pantheist motif, and ultimately to the level of symbol, the "curling grass" sums up the whole of *Leaves of Grass*, and perhaps provides the main clue to it:

> These are really the thoughts of all men in all ages
> and lands, they are not original with me,
> If they are not the riddle and the untying of the
> riddle they are nothing,
>
> If they are not as close as they are distant they
> are nothing.
> This is the grass that grows wherever the land is
> and the water is,
> This the common air that bathes the globe.
>
> (38)

It is striking to note that Whitman's verses are particularly close to the reflections on "La nadería de la personalidad" ("The Nothingness of Personality") in *Inquisiciones*[13] and, above all, to Borges' concept of the author of the poem. That concept, repeated so many times, was set forth in the early inscription to the reader in ***Fervor de Buenos Aires***: "Our nothings differ little: it is a trivial and chance circumstance that you are the reader of these exercises, and I the writer of them" (16; transl. DB).

Nonetheless, it must be recognized that the point of contact is at once more subtle and more solid than the comparison of the texts might suggest at first sight. The two concepts of poetry depend essentially on a similar intention: on a way of looking at humble and insignificant elements and raising them to poetic stature, to make them poetically prestigious. It is possible to go still further, and one will note that the deeper connection between Whitman's voice and that of the early Borges will be revealed moreover in the echoes of the first Borges in his later work. Such a connection can be established, I think, once the links are found between the early poems by Borges and later reworkings of them. To be sure, here it is necessary to attempt a reading which would reach for one of those secret traces I referred to previously. Like Whitman's grass, some humble and insignificant elements belong for Borges in the category of symbols. The streets of the out-of-the-way neighborhood, the outskirts—the *arrabal*—are one of those symbols. And just as there is a recognizable echo of "tenderly will I use you, curling grass" in the first line of **"Para una calle del Oeste"** (**"For a street in the West"**): "You will give me an alien immortality, lonely street" (72; transl. DB). That echo, that exaltation of something insignificant, similar to Whitman's, is repeated when the neighborhood street—freed of its literal meaning—is endowed with symbolic value.[14]

The preceding remarks are based on the following hypothesis: in **"La noche cíclica"** (**"The Cyclical Night"**), one of Borges' most characteristic and striking poems dated in 1940, Whitman is subtly inscribed in the affinity of the poetic quest, and in the will to specify a totalizing vision. There is no doubt, to begin with, that formally the regular quatrains of **"La noche cíclica"** could not be farther from Whitman's free verse. Besides, it is obvious that there are poems in ***El otro, el mismo*—"Insomnio,"** for instance, with which the book begins—in which the influence of Whitman, a "presence" that Borges acknowledges in the preface, is undeniable. But I think that the affinity should also be traced on a more profound level. Perhaps the affinity lies above all in the way of looking at, or in the way of looking for, the substance of poetry. In that respect, Borges transfigures the insignificant neighborhood into a meaningful, relevant poetic symbol:

> They knew it, the fervent pupils of Pythagoras. . . .
>
> But I know that a vague Pythagorean rotation
> Night after night sets me down in the world
>
> On the outskirts of the city. A remote street
> Which might be either north or west or south,
> But always with a blue-washed wall, the shade
> Of a fig tree, and a sidewalk of broken concrete.

This, here, is Buenos Aires. Time, which brings
Either love or money to men, hands on to me
Only this withered rose, this empty tracery
Of streets with names recurring from the past

In my blood. . . .[15]

These stanzas show that, under the umbrella of other much more explicit shades—Pythagoras, Hume, Anaxagoras—Whitman springs forth to give deeper meaning to the non-prestigious sign (the grass / the neighborhood street). But, also, there is another trace of Whitman in the poem: Whitman is also present in the design of Borges' text. The design by which the last stanza (cyclically) returns to the first line of the poem is a version of Whitman's faith in poetic writing:

It returns, the hollow dark of Anaxagoras;
In my human flesh, eternity keeps recurring
And the memory, or plan, of an endless poem
beginning:
"They knew it, the fervent pupils of Pythagoras . . ."[16]

Borges had commented many times on Whitman's intention that his entire work be a single book or poem, and also on the unattainable nature of such an intention: **"La noche cíclica"** appears to me as a metaphor, a Borgesian transposition of that ambition.

An earlier reference was made to Borges' desire to transcend Whitman's ambition by a process of moderation or restraint, and to conceive of poetry not as the complex expression of a luxuriant world but limiting himself to recording and simplifying an already essential universe; in ordering an "enigmatic abundance."[17] In his works on Whitman, Borges insists on the failures of an ultimately unattainable conception of a poem which would embrace the whole universe. In the preface to the selection from *Leaves of Grass*, he states: "To speak of literary experiments is to speak of exercises which have failed in some more or less brilliant way . . . Whitman's experiment worked out so well that we tend to forget that it was an experiment."[18]

In the work of Borges, there is at least one significant example of failure to which we might say that Whitman is secretly, almost cunningly, inscribed. This is the wild project of the second rate, amateurish character in "El Aleph," Carlos Argentino Daneri, bitten with the idea of composing a poem about "La Tierra" ("The Earth"). It is not by chance that this grotesque imitation, this caricature of a Whitman who has failed completely—or, better perhaps, of a barely embryonic Whitman—provides Borges, the character-narrator, with the experience of the Aleph; that Borges should perceive the qualities of that Aleph from Carlos Argentino's place; and, that he should transmit them in a paradigmatic enumeration. That enumeration not only proves the impossibility of rendering the universe's concurrences, but is at once a culmination and a negation of Carlos Argentino's (and Whitman's) unattainable project.[19]

4. Exorcism and Generative Power

To a certain extent, to write, or to speak about the familiar presences in this work was a fertile exorcism, which led Borges to find his own literary voice. The exorcism of the name of Whitman, like that of the other names which are signs in Borges, began early, perhaps becoming intensified during the hiatus in his poetic production after ***Cuaderno San Martín* (*San Martín Copybook*)**—as is proven by the two notes included in *Discusión* mentioned above—and culminating when Whitman appears as an explicit sign in poems and prefaces. A final confrontation between a poem by Whitman and a poem by Borges will be useful to show to what extent the exorcism was successful: it will provide an example of how Whitman's name, an explicit sign starting from ***El otro, el mismo*** keeps on inspiring the poet, as a secret cipher, as in the texts of Borges' prehistory. In his "Nota sobre Walt Whitman," included in *Discusión*, Borges included a Spanish version of "Full of Life, Now":

Full of life now, compact, visible,
I, forty years old the eighty-third year of the States,
To one a century hence or any number of centuries hence,
To you yet unborn these, seeking you.

When you read these I that was visible am become invisible,
Now it is you, compact, visible, realizing my poems, seeking me,
Fancying how happy you were if I could be with you and become your comrade;
Be it as if I were you. (Be not too certain but I am now with you.)

(109)

So Borges addresses himself, in ***El otro, el mismo*, "To My Reader"**:

You are invulnerable. Have they not shown you,
The powers that preordain your destiny,
The certainty of dust? Is not your time
As irreversible as that same river
Where Heraclitus, mirrored, saw the symbol
Of fleeting life? A marble slab awaits you
Which you will not read—on it, already written,
The date, the city, and the epitaph.
Other men too are only dreams of time,
Not everlasting bronze nor shining gold;
The universe is, like you, a Proteus.
Dark, you will enter the darkness that expects you,
Doomed to the limits of your traveled time.
Know that in some sense you by now are dead.[20]

Certainly the dialogue of these two texts can be interpreted as a summary of the generative power of poetry, and as a synthesis of a continuity—ultimately beyond all analysis—of a poetic text combined with an idealist belief and with a clear baroque certainty: the continuity which prevents us from separating this poem from the whole of Borges' poetry, a poetry in which Whitman's name is a permanent force, and perhaps more so when it is not spelled out.

Notes

1. Guillermo Sucre, "Borges: el elogio de la sombra," *Revista Iberoamericana*, 72 (1970): 372.
2. Jorge Luis Borges, *Inquisiciones* (Buenos Aires: Proa, 1925):91. Translated by MLB.
3. James E. Irby, *Encuentro con Borges* (Buenos Aires: Galerna, 1968): 12–13.
4. César Fernández Moreno, "Harto de laberintos," *Mundo Nuevo*, 18 (1967):10.
5. In Carlos Meneses, *Poesía juvenil de Jorge Luis Borges* (Barcelona: Otañeta Editor, 1978): 57–8. Translated by MLB.
6. Walt Whitman, "Song of Myself," 3. In *Leaves of Grass* and *Selected Prose* (New York: the Modern Library, 1950):25. Further references to Whitman belong to this edition, and the page number is given in parenthesis in the text. As I have said, in this paper I refer only to poems by Whitman which Borges chose to translate into Spanish for his selection of *Leaves of Grass.*
7. Jorge Luis Borges, *Obras completas* (Buenos Aires: Emecé, 1969): 13. Translated by MLB. Further references to this edition are given in parenthesis in the text.
8. Apparently, the first public lecture that Borges gave on Whitman took place in Buenos Aires in 1958. Cf. *La Prensa*, Buenos Aires, August 2, 1958, p. 3. To my knowledge, there is a transcription of another lecture on Whitman he gave in Chicago in 1968. Cf. Jorge Luis Borges, "Walt Whitman: Man and Myth," *Critical Inquiry*, 1 (1975): 708–711. James East Irby has mentioned Borges' project to give a lecture on Whitman in Texas in 1961. Cf. Irby, *Encuentro con Borges*, 12. Irby has told me that Borges lectured on Whitman at Princeton University in 1968 or 1969.
9. Walt Whitman, *Hojas de hierba.* Selección, traducción y pró-logo de Jorge Luis Borges (Buenos Aires: Juárez Editor, 1969).
10. Michel Foucault, Preface. *The Order of Things* (New York: Vintage Books, 1973): XVII.
11. Leo Spitzer, *La enumeración caótica en la poesía moderna* (Buenos Aires: Facultad de Filosofía y Letras, 1945).
12. Whitman, *Hojas de hierba*, 45.
13. Borges, *Inquisiciones*, 84–95.
14. I have developed this idea in "La topografía de la ambigüedad: Buenos Aires en Borges, Bianco, Bioy Casares," *Hispamérica*, 27 (1980): 33–46. The opposition: Literal meaning/symbolic value is based in A. J. Greimas' theory, in *Du Sens* (Paris: Seuil, 1970): 7–17.
15. Jorge Luis Borges, *Selected Poems, 1923–1967* (New York: Dell, 1972): 79. Translation by Alastair Reid.
16. Borges, *Selected Poems*, 81.
17. Borges wrote in "Examen de metáforas," *Inquisiciones* 65: "Language is an efficient ordering of the world's enigmatic abundance." Translation by MLB.
18. Jorge Luis Borges, "Prólogo," Walt Whitman, *Hojas de hierba*, 29. Translation DB.
19. There is, I think, another echo of that unattainable project in the drama in verse, *The Enemies* by the second-rate writer Jaromir Hladíc, victim of the Nazis, protagonist of "El milagro secreto" ("The Secret Miracle") in *Ficciones.*
20. Borges, *Selected Poems*, 183. Translated by Alastair Reid.

Dionisio Cañas (essay date 1986)

SOURCE: "The Eye of the Mind: Borges and Wallace Stevens," in *Borges the Poet*, edited by Carlos Cortinez, The University of Arkansas Press, 1986, pp. 254–59.

[*In the following essay, Cañas explores affinities between Borges and Wallace Stevens.*]

I don't know what mysterious reason Borges had in his 1967 *Introduction to American Literature* by not mentioning the name of Wallace Stevens; to solve the enigma is irrelevant. Nevertheless, it is this omission that impelled me to do a simultaneous reading of the two poets.

In 1944, the literary magazine *Sur* published a translation of the famous Stevens poem "Sunday Morning"; the translators were Bioy Casares and Borges, and some lines from this poem are very close to Borges' own poetry:

> What is divinity if it can come
> Only in silent shadows and in dreams?

At the end of the poem, once more, the obscurity so dear to the author of ***In Praise of Darkness*** appears in all of its sublimity:

> And, in the isolation of the sky,
> At evening, casual flocks of pigeons make
> Ambiguous undulations as they sink,
> Downward to darkness, on extended wings.

In the twenties, two poetic works were created over the foundations of European verse that would play a preponderent role among American and European writers. Robert Alter, in his article "Borges and Stevens: a Note on Post-Symbolist Writing" (*Prose for Borges*), points out the affinity between Borges and Stevens as part of post-modern literature and its anti-symbolist movement. He writes: "Borges and Stevens are great imaginists whose exercise of imagination—in Borges' case, often fantastication—is directed by a fine skepticism not only about the world of brute matter but also about the imagination itself."

Borges writes about himself, about men and their activities as the splendor and mockery of a god, of gods; Stevens, with irony, writes about the splendor of the world and the presence of the "I" as a mind surrounded by beings created through poetry. Both are solitary poets, but generous in their gifts, and with their poetry they give us abundant fruits of the mind.

In **"Poem of the Gifts"** Borges writes:

> Let no one debase with pity or reprove
> This declaration of God's mastery
> Who with magnificent irony
> Gave me at once books and the night . . .
>
> Within my darkness I slowly explore
> The hollow half light with hesitant cane,
> I who always imagined Paradise
> To be a sort of library.

Stevens, in "Of Mere Being," writes that Paradise is

> The palm at the end of the mind,
> Beyond the last thought, rises
> In the bronze decor
>
> A gold-feathered bird
> Sings in the palm, without human meaning
> Without human feeling, a foreign song.

We are facing here a humanistic philosophy, but paradoxically, the human being is absent, and it is his achievements and his imagination that create an Eden for these poets.

As Borges states in his **"Ars Poetica,"** poetry is "humble and immortal," "Art is that Ithaca, / of green eternity." But what does Borges mean by eternity? To what place does the finger of his poetry point? Is a library his eternity, his Paradise? And after all, doesn't a library provide the only surviving visions of the minds of writers from the past? In *The Necessary Angel* Wallace Stevens writes: "The mind of the poet describes itself as constantly in his poems."

But in the poems of Stevens that Borges translated, a more drastic dichotomy appears; blood is a symbol of life which opens a possible space for Paradise:

> Shall our blood fail? Or shall it come to be
> The blood of paradise? And shall the earth
> Seem all of paradise that we shall know?

The answer to Stevens' question is given by Borges in his article "Valéry as Symbol." This article is most illuminating and if we replace the name of the French poet with that of Stevens: ". . . a man who, in an age that worships the chaotic idols of blood, earth and passion, preferred always the lucid pleasures of thought and the secret adventures of order."

Indeed, both poets are the last consequence of a certain faith in the human mind, not as a reasoning form, but rather as an imagining reason. They are the last members of the aristocracy of an imagining wisdom.

Borges and Stevens represent the other side and the ultimate expression of Romantic poetic thought. For both poets the domesticated imagination occupies a principal place in their poetry. In this way, they have overcome the long debate between imagination and reason, and have created the imagining reason.

The two poets have the tendency to claim for their poetry the same essential outlook: one that appears to the eyes as it is—the ordinary, everyday scene. At the same time, this commonplace is projected into an imaginative level, fabulous and mythical. Borges, for example, refers to "the celestial moon of every day," but nevertheless believes that "better than real nighttime moons, I can / recall the moons of poetry" (**"The Moon"**). Stevens, in "An Ordinary Evening in New Haven" writes: "The moon rose in the mind . . ."

What moon is this that looks like the ordinary moon but is not? What eye that looks like the ordinary eye but is not, describes these moons? It is the moon of the mind, the eye of the mind and it is the sun "half sun, half thinking of the sun; half sky, / Half desire for indifference about sky" ("Extracts From Addresses to the Academy of Fine Ideas"). As a result of this, Stevens writes: "the mind / is the eye, and . . . this landscape of the mind / is a landscape only of the eye" ("Crude Foyer").

For both poets, the poem is a kind of iceberg in which the world seen or thought has been frozen, making it always available to the reader's eyes. For Borges and Stevens poetry is also a sort of window in which the frame creates specific limits. Things are perceived by means of their changing aspects, with their lights and shadows, but circumscribed by a frame, by the boundaries of a precise form. This window can be a book, a word, a painting, a song, a legend or a myth: in any case, always with very clearly defined outlines.

Borges, as a poet, describes himself as someone sitting in a dark room from which he observes the outside world or the world of the mind. And from the darkness he can see without being seen. Stevens, in "Of Modern Poetry," refers to poetry as "metaphysician in the dark." The poet as well as the poem, for both writers, represents poetic form, art and the world, its limitations, its *trompe l'oeil.* In truth, the ultimate raison d'être for writers is a longing to find themselves or a description of the mind that does this.

Borges in his **"Ars Poetica"** writes:

> Sometimes at evening there's a face
> that sees us from the deeps of a mirror.
> Art must be that sort of mirror,
> disclosing to each of us his face.

Stevens in "An Ordinary Evening in New Haven" views "reality as a thing seen by the mind" and continues:

> Not that which is but that which is apprehended,
> A mirror, a lake of reflections in a room,
> A glassy ocean lying at the door, . . .

And it is because the eye of the mind is what we see reflected in the poem, that every object described in it is sustained by the self of the poet. Simultaneously the separation of the otherness and the self has vanished into the new space of poetic fiction.

> Suppose these houses are composed of ourselves,
> So that they become an impalpable town, full of
> Impalpable bells, transparencies of sound.

The attitude of the two poets originated in an *a priori:* that of a "confidence in language as self sufficient" (as Guillermo Sucre has pointed out in *Borges el poeta*). But it is not a faith in the tautological values of language. Harold Bloom writes in *Figures of Capable Imagination:* "what Wittgenstein means when he speaks of a *deep* tautology, which leads to a true realism, Stevens too knows, as Emerson knew, that what he *says* is wrong, but that his meaning is right."

When Borges wants to talk about the tiger **"El otro tigre"** (**"The Other Tiger"**) he establishes that his tiger is "a system and arrangement of human language." Conscious about the fallacy of poetic fiction he says:

> . . . I keep on looking
> throughout the afternoon for the other tiger,
> the other tiger which is not in this poem.

Stevens also describes a tiger as "lamed by nothingness and frost." Therefore a faith in language indicates at the same time a distrust of the world that conceived it. This tragic consciousness of an excision between language and world, and the consequent retreat of the poet into an imagining reason, is resolved by Borges and Stevens through irony and sarcasm.

The works of the two poets is modulated by the eye of the mind that sees the world in its totality. This may be sensorial and intellectual in the way of Wallace Stevens, or profoundly intellectual in the manner of Jorge Luis Borges. To quote Borges, though he was talking about Valéry, both poets are: ". . . the symbol of [men] infinitely sensitive to every phenomenon and for whom every phenomenon is a stimulus capable of provoking an infinite series of thoughts."

The concept of the eye of the mind is the ultimate result of the creative impulse formulated by the emotional eye of the Romantic movement. It is possible that the poetry of Borges and Stevens derives from the "Majestic Intellect" mentioned by William Wordsworth in the poem of the same title:

> When into air had partially dissolved
> That vision, given to spirits of the night
> And three chance human wanderers, in calm thought
>
> Reflected, it appeared to me the type
> Of a majestic intellect, its acts
> And its possessions, what it has and craves,
> What in itself it is, and would become . . .

If, as Borges said in his poem **"Cambridge,"**

> We are our memory,
> we are this chimerical museum of shifting forms,
> this heap of broken mirrors,

I am convinced that in some remote region of his memory Wallace Stevens is looking at Borges with consciousness from the eye of his mind.

Works Cited

Bloom, Harold. *Figures of Capable Imagination.* New York: Seabury Press, 1976.

Borges, Jorge Luis. "El otro tigre," in *Obra Poética.* Buenos Aires: Emecé, 1977.

———. *In Praise of Darkness.* New York: E. P. Cutton, 1974.

———. *Introduction to American Literature.* Translated by L. Clark Keating and Robert O. Owens. Lexington: University of Kentucky Press, 1973.

Kinzie, Mary. *Prose for Borges.* Evanston: Northwestern University Press, 1974.

Stevens, Wallace. *The Necessary Angel.* New York: Knopf, 1951.

Sucre, Guillermo. *Borges: el poeta.* México: Unam, 1967.

Kenneth Holditch (essay date 1986)

SOURCE: "Borges and Emerson: The Poet as Intellectual," in *Borges the Poet,* edited by Carlos Cortinez, The University of Arkansas Press, 1986, pp. 197–206.

[*In the following essay, Holditch examines Borges's appreciation of and affinity with Ralph Waldo Emerson as a poet.*]

Perhaps the most remarkable aspect of Borges' deep love for the literature of the United States is the high position in which he has repeatedly, in writing and in interviews, placed Ralph Waldo Emerson as poet. One is certainly not surprised at his appraisal of Walt Whitman as an epic poet, or Emily Dickinson as "perhaps the greatest poet that America . . . has as yet produced," or when he speaks with admiration of the ideas expressed in Emerson's essays; but the praise for Emerson as a poet is another thing altogether. Traditionally Emerson has been admired by American readers and critics, rightly or wrongly, as a philosopher, thinker, and creator of pithy and memorable aphorisms that generously pepper the prose of his famous essays. His poetry, however, interesting insofar as it conveys some of the same philosophical concepts belonging to American romanticism, has generally been relegated to a distant second place. Yes, we remember the farmers who gathered by "the rude bridge that arched the flood" and "fired the shot heard round the world" and may even recall isolated lines such as "Things are in the saddle / And ride mankind," but when we quote Emerson, it is usually from unforgetable lines in his prose; and such essays as "Nature," "Self-Reliance," and "The American Scholar," for example. Borges' praise for the poems, then, places them in a new and intriguing light in which we can identify those aspects of Emerson's poetry Borges finds of particular interest and merit; examine specific poems which he singles out for comment or commendation; and distinguish any Emersonian elements which are present as allusions or influences in Borges' own works.

The one aspect of Emerson's poetry most often commented upon by Borges is its intellectual quality. His most recent published remarks on the subject appear in *Borges at Eighty* in which he states that Emerson, like Walt Whitman, is "one of those men who cannot be thought away," that "literature would not be what it is today" without Poe, Melville, Whitman, Thoreau and Emerson, then singles out Emerson for particular commendation: "I love Emerson and I am very fond of his poetry. He is to me the one intellectual poet—in any case the one intellectual poet who has ideas. The others are merely intellectual with no ideas at all. In the case of Emerson, he had ideas and was thoroughly a poet."[1] The "intellectual poet who has ideas"—this is the characterization that surfaces again and again whenever Borges has written or spoken of the great Transcendentalist.

What exactly does Borges mean by the phrase "intellectual poet"? Is his definition of the word *intellectual* a restrictive one, or are we to accept it as meaning merely rational as opposed to emotional, merely possessed of ideas as opposed to being devoid of same? Part of the answer may be found in his assertion that the "breadth of his mind was astonishing,"[2] and his comparison of Emerson to three other writers may illuminate this evaluation. In 1949, in the prologue to *Representative Men*, which he had translated into Spanish, Borges identifies Emerson as a classical writer in opposition to Thomas Carlyle the romantic—whom Borges had earlier loved but later declared unreadable—and asserts that Emerson is far superior to those "compatriots who have obscured his glory: Whitman and Poe."[3] In *An Introduction to American Literature* he states that Friederich Nietzsche had remarked "that he felt himself so close to Emerson, that he did not dare to praise him because it would have been like praising himself."[4] Borges counters that identification between the two philosophers, however, by observing that Emerson is "a finer writer and a finer thinker than Nietzsche, though most people wouldn't say that today."[5] Granted that Borges reserves much of his praise and respect related to philosophers for that other German master, Schopenhauer, his comparison of Nietzsche to Emerson attests surely to his admiration for the philosophy of the American and suggests that it is in the philosophical realm, not only in his prose but also in his poetry, that Emerson excels intellectually. This is true especially in poetry, one might argue, since Borges has elsewhere asserted that Emerson's prose has a "disconnected character" and suffers from the fact that he does not construct valid, sequential arguments in the essays but merely strings together "memorable sayings, sometimes full of wisdom, which do not proceed from what [has] come before nor prepare for what [is] to come."[6]

When he mentions Emerson in connection with Poe, Borges observes rather ambiguously that "the most curious" volume of the twelve that contains Emerson's collected works is the one devoted to his poetry, then reiterates his belief that Emerson was "a great intellectual poet" and that Poe, "whom he called, not without disdain, the 'jingle man,' did not interest him."[7] In the short fiction entitled "The Other Death," the persona argues that Emerson is "a poet far more complex, far more skilled, and truly more extraordinary than the unfortunate Poe."[8]

In the preface to *Doctor Brodie's Report*, Borges states that "the art of writing is mysterious" and "the opinions we hold are ephemeral." He prefers, he continues, "the Platonic idea of the Muse of that of Poe, who reasoned, or feigned to reason, that the writing of a poem is an act of the intelligence. It never fails to amaze me that the classics advance a romantic theory of poetry, and romantic poets a classical theory."[9] Here he is referring, of course, to Poe's famous "explanation" in "The Philosophy of Composition" of the allegedly rational procedure through which he wrote that seemingly irrational poem "The Raven."

Later Borges was to reaffirm this belief when in a 1980 conversation he stated that "opinions come and go, politics come and go, my personal opinions are changing all the time. But when I write I try to be faithful to the dream, to be true to the dream."[10] This rejection of Poe's belief that writing a poem is "an act of the intelligence" and the assertion that our opinions are "ephemeral" might seem markedly contrary to his praise for Emerson as an intellectual poet: a paradox, and how should it be solved? Probably Borges would not want it solved, since much of his work attests to love of the paradoxical, but critics never tire of trying.

The answer to the seeming dilemma lies perhaps in "A Vindication of the Cabala" where writers are categorized as journalists, verse writers, and intellectuals. The journalist, Borges states, in his "ephemeral utterances . . . allows for a noticeable amount of chance," while the verse writer subjects "meaning to euphonic necessities (or superstitions)," but the intellectual is another matter. Although he has not eliminated chance, either in prose or verse, "he has denied it as much as possible, and limited its incalculable concurrence. He remotely resembles the Lord, for Whom the vague concept of chance holds no meaning, the God, the perfected God of the theologians, Who sees all at once (*uno intelligendu actu*), not only all the events of this replete world, but also those that would take place if even the most evanescent of them should change, the impossible ones also."[11] This presumably is the kind of poet that Borges believes Emerson to be, and the introduction of the notion that the intellectual poet sees all—not only that which exists, but that which might have been—relates to a favorite theme of Borges' own poetry. His admiration for the intellectual process as exemplified in Emerson's versifying surely relates to the idea of the nineteenth-century writer that all poetry derives from "meter-making arguments" rather than from meter.

Emerson is admired by Borges not only for his intellectuality, but, as Ronald Christ points out, for being a "man of letters" of the caliber of G. K. Chesterton, H. G. Wells, Thomas DeQuincey, George Bernard Shaw, and Robert Louis Stevenson—all, the critics note, "lovers of words, poets, or storytellers, weavers of theories, manifestations of the writer as *grammaticus.*" In addition, Borges has commented on the writer as *vate* or *místico* the writer, as Christ defines him, "who looks through the solidness of our reality and reveals another world and perhaps a secret scheme or logic which controls our world." Emerson's transcendentalism, the critic concludes, "is explicitly vatic in the Borgesian sense. . . ."[12] In his discussion of Transcendentalism in *An Introduction to American Literature* Borges points out that the New England version of Romanticism has its origin in, among other sources, Hindu pantheism and "the visionary theology of Swedenborg"—a favorite of Borges', of course—who proposed a belief that "the external light is a mirror of the spiritual."[13]

Emerson's theory of art obviously holds an appeal for Borges, since he refers often to its principles. In *Borges at Eighty,* he is quoted as observing, "I remember what Emerson said: language is fossil poetry. He said every word is a metaphor. You can verify that by looking a word up in the dictionary. All words are metaphors—a fossil poetry, a fine metaphor itself." In the same work, he remarks that "a book, when it lies in the bookshelf—I think Emerson has said so (I like to be indebted to Emerson, one of my heroes)—a book is a thing among things . . . A book is unaware of itself until the reader comes."[14] Often he has reiterated his agreement with Emerson that creative reading is as important as creative writing, the reader as essential in the scheme of things as he who writes the poetry. Another aspect of Emerson's esthetic, as Christ points out, is the belief that "a work of art is an abstract of the epitome of the world" and Borges has created in "The Aleph" "one of the points of the universe which contains all the points" so that it becomes "a symbol of all Borges' writing."[15]

The works of Emerson to which Borges most often refers in his own writing include three remarkable poems, "Days," "The Past," and "Brahma." The first two are concerned with the passage of time and its relationship to man, the third embodies the doctrine of the unity of all that exists.

In "Days," the persona describes the subjects as "Daughters of Time," hypocritical, dumb, like dervishes, who offer to each man "gifts after his will." Forgetting his own "morning wishes," the persona accepts from one of them "a few herbs and apples" and the day departs, a look of scorn upon her face. The poem is decidedly ambiguous, open to at least two interpretations. Certainly the persona may be complaining that he has not taken full advantage of the opportunities offered to him by the days (and months and years) of his life, but has settled rather for something less than the rewards accorded kings and martyrs. On the other hand, the two items he employs to symbolize his choice—herbs and apples—are objects of nature, not worldly baubles, and given Emerson's devotion to the natural world, to the simple; given his belief that man even in his most trivial activities may be involved in the serious labor of eternity, it is surely at least as likely that he is arguing that his decision is correct and the scorn of the "hypocritic" Daughter of Time is not to be accorded credence.

Borges has opted for the former interpretation. In a 1967 interview with Cesar Fernández Moreno, cited by Carlos Cortínez in his study of Borges' poem **"Emerson,"** Borges interprets "Days" as meaning that when Emerson, offered anything he wants on earth, takes only "a few herbs and apples," the days make fun of the poet's absurd moderation ("*la absurda moderación del poeta*"). This leads Borges to speculate that there was in Emerson a secret discontent ("*una secreta insatisfacción*"), and that he regretted having chosen the life of the mind over the life of action.[16]

The powerful sonnet to Emerson portrays the "tall New Englander" closing a volume of Montaigne and going out into the fields one evening. The walk, as much a pleasure for him as reading, takes him toward the sunset, as well as through the memory of Borges who writes of him. Emerson thinks of the important books he has read, the imperishable books he has been granted the privilege to write, and of his national fame and concludes, surprisingly, that "I have not lived. I want to be someone else." In his note to the poem, Emir Rodríguez Monegal observes that the sonnet was written in 1962 after Borges had visited New England and that in the work the North American poet becomes a "mask" for the Argentine poet. Cortínez has argued that Borges creates a contrast in the poem between Emerson, the contemplative man, and Don Quixote, the man of action. Although as I have suggested, the opposite interpretation may be given to "Days," Emerson's belief in the necessity for action certainly was often expressed; consider, for example, his criticism of Thoreau, even as he eulogized him, for being content to be "the captain of a huckleberry-party" when he could have been "engineering for all America."[17]

The opening line of "The Other Death," Borges' story of the soldier who behaved in a cowardly manner in battle and may—or may not—be allowed to relive the event and die bravely, refers to a proposed first translation of Emerson's "The Past" into Spanish. In that poem, Emerson's intellectual idea is that what is past is finished; there is no altering any event: "All is now secure and fast; / Not the gods can shake the Past. . . ." "The Other Death" would seem to posit as one of the interpretations of the strange events it contains, a contradiction of Emerson's argument; to offer the possibility, at least, that the past can be relived.

The nostalgic and rather tragic recognition of the immutability of things and events that have been, however, is on other occasions, in other works, embraced by Borges. In **"Things That Might Have Been,"** for example, the poet envisions literary masterpieces that were never written, empires that never existed and "History without the afternoon of the Cross and the afternoon of hemlock. / History without the face of Helen." Or, after "the three labored days of Gettysburg, the victory of the South." In the conclusion of the poem, the persona envisions the "son I did not have."[18] In **"Things That Might Have Been,"** Borges obviously concurs with Emerson's past that "is now secure and past," even though he may elsewhere assert, as in a 1980 conversation, that "as to the past, we are changing it all the time. Every time we remember something, we slightly alter our memory."[19] On the other hand, remember that one of the attributes of the "intellectual poet," as noted above, is the ability to see "all at once," not only what was, but what might have been; and it is to this category, of course, that he assigns Emerson.

The poem "Brahma" is based on the pantheistic unity which Emerson had derived from his reading of Hindu scriptures. Borges quotes the entire poem in *An Introduction to American Literature* and in *Other Inquisitions* identifies as "perhaps the most memorable line" that in which the persona, Brahma, states paradoxically "When me they fly, I am the wings."[20] The concept of the contradictory unity of all things as Emerson conveys it in the poem manifests itself often in Borges' works. Consider the passage in ***Dreamtigers*** called **"A Problem"** in which he speaks of the possibility of Don Quixote's having been reincarnated as a Hindustani king who stands over the body of the enemy he has slain and understands "that to kill and beget are divine or magical acts which manifestly transcend humanity. He knows that the dead man is an illusion, as is the bloody sword that weighs down his hand, as is he himself, and all his past life, and the vast gods, and the universe."[21] Not only is the idea of the passage parallel to the argument of "Brahma," but the phrase "the vast gods" is surely an echo of Emerson's line "The strong gods pine for my abode."

In addition to Emerson's concepts reflected in the poems considered above, other themes of his that have been influential in the works of Borges include the doctrines of the Over-Soul and the Universal Poet and man; of Compensation and Undulation; the concepts of Illusions and Miracles, and the ethical considerations of the Concord genius. Of these, Emerson's most important influence on the thought and work of Borges would seem to be the basic Transcendental concept of the Over-Soul, particularly as embodied in the Universal Man, or, more to the point here, the Universal Poet.

In "The Flower of Coleridge," Borges quotes Paul Valéry as saying that literary history should not be constituted by the lives of poets and their careers but rather "the history of the Spirit as the producer or consumer of literature." Borges adds that "It was not the first time that the Spirit had made such an observation," for in 1844, "one of its amanuenses in Concord" wrote,

> I am very much struck in literature by the appearance that one person wrote all the books; . . . there is such equality and identity both of judgement and point of view in the narrative that it is plainly the work of one, all-seeing, all-hearing gentleman.[22]

This passage from Emerson's essay "Nominalist and Realist" introduces a theme that obviously has a strong appeal for Borges, since he turns to it again and again. In a 1980 conversation, for example, he commented on how little we know of Shakespeare's life, a fact which does not trouble us, he insists, because Shakespeare has converted that life into plays and sonnets. The best thing for any author is to be a part of a tradition, a part of the language, which is in itself a kind of immortality, he argues, since language and tradition go on, while the books may be forgotten: "or perhaps every age rewrites the same books, over and over again. . . . Perhaps the eternal books are all the same books. We are always rewriting what the ancients wrote, and that should prove sufficient."[23] Emerson makes exactly the same point in his essay "The Poet" where he states that "poetry was all written before time was."

A more generalized implication of the Over-Soul concept—the belief that not only are all poets one poet, but all men are one man—has intrigued Borges and provided inspiration in several works. In *An Introduction to American Literature* he observes that for Emerson, every man is a microcosm and the "soul of the individual is identified with the soul of the world," so that all "each man needs is his own profound and secret identity."[24] The prologue to Borges' translation of *Representative Men* contains the observation that since the tragedy of human life results from individuals being "restricted by time and space," nothing is "more gratifying than a belief that there is no one who is not the universe."[25] This being the case, for Emerson, men are immortal through their universality; and for Borges, as he states elsewhere, "my days and nights are equal in poverty and richness to those of God and those of all men."[26]

Any attempt to make a case for Borges as a Transcendentalist in the Emersonian sense would be foolish and futile, but what is apparent from the evidence offered above, incomplete as it may be, is the fact that Borges feels for that "tall gentleman" of Concord both an admiration and an affinity. The value of finding and analyzing such a relationship is the evidence it offers for the value of tradition and the relationship of that tradition to poets and poetry, and the insight which such a study can afford readers to the writings of two great "intellectual" poets, one of the nineteenth century, one of the present; of two—as Borges himself might express it—"amanuenses" of the one great Spirit that connects all literature of the past and present and—if human beings continue to read—of the future.

Notes

1. Willis Barnstone, ed. *Borges at Eighty: Conversations* (Bloomington: Indiana University Press, 1982): 5.
2. Jorge Luis Borges, In collaboration with Esther Zemborain de Torres, *An Introduction to American Literature.* Trans. L. Clark Keating and Robert O. Evans (Lexington: University Press of Kentucky, 1973): 26.
3. Carlos Cortínez, "Otra Lectura de 'Emerson' de Borges," *Revista Chilena de Literatura* 19 (1982): 98.
4. Borges, *An Introduction to American Literature,* 25.
5. Cited by Ronald J. Christ, *The Narrow Act* (New York: New York University Press, 1969): 42.
6. Borges, *An Introduction to American Literature,* 26.
7. Borges, *An Introduction to American Literature,* 26.
8. *Borges: A Reader.* Edited by Emir Rodriguez Monegal and Alastair Reid. (New York: E. P. Dutton, 1981): 215.
9. Borges, *Doctor Brodie's Report.* Trans. Norman Thomas di Giovanni (New York: E. P. Dutton, 1972): 10.
10. Barnstone, *Borges at Eighty*, 12.
11. Monegal and Reid, *Borges: A Reader*, 24.
12. Christ, *The Narrow Act*, 11–12.
13. Borges, *An Introduction to American Literature*, 24.
14. Barnstone, *Borges at Eighty*, 67, 165.
15. Christ, *The Narrow Act*, 11–12.
16. Cortínez, "Otra Lectura de 'Emerson' de Borges," 95.
17. Perry Miller, ed. *Major Writers of America* (New York: Harcourt, Brace and World, Inc., 1966): 307.
18. Monegal and Reid, *Borges: A Reader*, 327.
19. Barnstone, *Borges at Eighty*, 14.
20. Jorge Luis Borges, *Other Inquisitions: 1937–1952* trans. Ruth L. C. Simms (Austin: University of Texas Press, 1964): 69.
21. Jorge Luis Borges, *DreamTigers*. Trans. Mildred Boyer and Harold Morland (Austin: University of Texas Press, 1964).
22. Monegal and Reid, *Borges: A Reader*, 163.
23. Barnstone, *Borges at Eighty*, 9.
24. Borges, *An Introduction to American Literature*, 25.
25. Christ, *The Narrow Act*, 131.
26. Barnstone, *Borges at Eighty*, 42.

Julie Jones (essay date 1986)

SOURCE: "Borges and Browning: A Dramatic Dialogue," in Borges the Poet, edited by Carlos Cortinez, The University of Arkansas Press, 1986, pp. 207–17.

[*In the following essay, Jones explores Borges's debt to Robert Browning,, especially, in his adaptation of the dramatic monologue.*]

In a rather backhanded tribute to Robert Browning, Jorge Luis Borges comments that "si hubiera sido un buen escritor de prosa, creo que no dudaríamos que Browning sería el precursor de la que llamamos literatura moderna."[1] In a writer who has repeatedly emphasized his preference for plot over character and his suspicions about the nonexistence of personality, this interest in the work of a poet who described himself as "more interested in individuals than abstract problems"[2] is curious, yet despite his claim in *Introducción a la literatura inglesa* of this widely accepted view of Browning, Borges seems drawn to a different reading. For him, Browning is "el gran poeta enigmático,"[3] and, with Dickens, one of "dos grandes artífices góticos."[4] In the introduction to English literature, Borges summarizes a poem he must have especially liked, "How It Strikes a Contemporary": "el protagonista puede ser Cervantes o un misterioso espía de Dios o el arquetipo platónico del poeta,"[5] and among **"Los precursores de Kafka,"** he numbers another of Browning's poems, "Fears and Scruples," in which the speaker defends a stubbornly enigmatic friend who, it is hinted in the last line, may be God. Borges appears particularly interested in *The Ring and the Book*, with its deployment of multiple narratives on the part of the different characters, each of whom presents his own version of the same murder.[6] Browning's development of point of view, along with his ambiguity and what Borges sees as a quality of irreality are probably the basis for his argument that Browning be considered a precursor to James and Kafka and, through them, to much modern literature. Considering his own bent for the exotic, Borges must have been intrigued by the perspectives Browning opens on distant times and places, although he does not mention it. Although Borges' reading of Browning is quirky enough—he has nothing to say about the enormous energy or about the determined optimism that so offended T. S. Eliot—he is not alone in his evaluation of Browning's influence on modern literature. Ezra Pound, for example, claimed Browning as his literary father and pushed him tirelessly. In an essay on the relation between Browning and the Anglo-American Modernists, G. Robert Stange points out three primary reasons for Browning's prestige: his attempt to render spoken speech in verse; his use of an elliptical method with startling jumps and juxtapositions that put the onus of interpretation on the reader; and his elaboration of the dramatic monologue, a form with obvious importance for the literature of perspective developed by James, Conrad, Proust, Joyce, Woolf and Faulkner.[7] Like so much modern literature, the dramatic monologue insists on the fragmentary, the incomplete; it opens up new areas of experience and conveys them through a single, and therefore limited, perspective.

The use of a conversational tone and an elliptical approach is widespread throughout twentieth-century poetry, but the dramatic monologue, perhaps the dominant form now in Anglo-American poetry, has never really caught on in Hispanic verse. Borges, however, uses the form rather frequently. That he does so may be the result of his intellectual formation in a library composed of English books; still, this fondness for a form that has traditionally been a vehicle for the presentation of character is odd. It is best seen by focusing on Borges' adaptation of the dramatic monologue, as it was developed by Browning, to suit his own ends.

In 1947, Ina Beth Sessions listed the characteristics of the "perfect dramatic monologue": "that literary form which has the definite characteristics of speaker, audience, occasion, revelation of character, interplay between speaker and audience, dramatic action, and action which takes place in the present."[8] The problem with this schema is that it excludes many of Browning's best monologues and is totally inadequate for dealing with such modern examples as "The Love Song of J. Alfred Prufrock" or Pound's "The Tomb at Akr Çaar," in which a soul addresses its mummified body. Although development of character is central to the majority of Browning's monologues, there are notable exceptions—"Saul," "Rabbi Ben Ezra," "Fears and Scruples," "How It Strikes a Contemporary." Sessions' description is useful as an index of features that often are presented in the form, but it should not be taken as prescriptive. In his seminal study, *The Poetry of Experience*, Robert Langbaum argues that it is more important to consider effect rather than mechanics. For him, the essential effect is to give "facts from within,"[9] but he offsets this contention by observing that "there is at work in [the monologue] a consciousness . . . beyond what the speaker can lay claim to. This consciousness is the mark of the poet's projection into the poem."[10] Ultimately, Park Honan's definition may offer the most useful rule of thumb: "a single discourse by one whose presence in the poem is indicated by the poet but who is not the poet himself."[11]

Before examining the dramatic monologue in Borges, it should be helpful to take a brief look at one of Browning's more representative monologues. In his introduction to English literature, Borges mentions "An Epistle of Karshish," in which "un médico árabe refiere la resurrección de Lázaro y la extraña indiferencia de su vida ulterior, como si se tratara de un caso clínico."[12] The entire poem takes the form of an epistle written from Karshish to his mentor, Abib. Karshish writes at some length about his journey into Judea, including details about the political situation and his medical discoveries. Finally, he gets around to the real reason for his writing—his encounter with Lazarus. Even though he dismisses Lazarus as a "case of mania—subinduced / By epilepsy,"[13] it is evident that he is rationalizing an experience that haunts him, and at the end of the letter, having apologized repeatedly for "this long and tedious case" and actually written his good-byes, he suddenly bursts out:

> The very God! think, Abib; dost thou think?
> So, the All-Great, were the All-Loving too—
> The madman saith He said so: it is strange.

"An Epistle of Karshish" is representative of the Browning monologue as it takes up a character at a specific point in time, at a moment of personal as well as historical crisis. It is thick with detail which establishes time and place and, more importantly, delineates character (a reference to the herb borage, for example, not only demonstrates Karshish's attempt to circumvent his discovery, it also reveals the scientist's practiced eye). The protagonist addresses a particular person, but the communication is really a pretext for a "dialogue between self and soul" in which, while attempting to come to grips with a disturbing incident, he sums up his entire life. The letter is an expression of self *and* an exploration: what if Lazarus is right? The poem is open-ended; the outcome of the struggle, unresolved. An ironic tension is established between the speaker, who has an incomplete understanding of a firsthand experience, and the reader, whose knowledge is much greater, but who is separated from the event by two millenia.

It is not difficult to see why the poem appeals to Borges. In its oblique approach to a great historical moment, it brings to mind his speculations about why the thief asked to be saved in **"Lucas XXIII"** and why Judas betrayed Christ in **"Tres versiones de Judas."** Browning's ironic manipulation of point of view in the monologue looks ahead to **"La busca de Averroes,"** Borges' narrative about the Arab translator of Aristotle, a man of high intelligence, who is prevented by his belief in Islam, on which his strength is founded, from accomplishing the task he has set himself, defining comedy and tragedy. Although repeatedly exposed to clues about the nature of the theater, he is doomed to ignore them. The story is told from the third person (except for an intrusion by Borges at the end to remind us that he is as ignorant of Averroes as Averroes is of drama), but the perspective is so carefully limited and so free of analysis that it is almost internal,[14] and its effect is close to that of the dramatic monologue: it gives the facts "from within."

However, rather than discussing possible analogues in his fiction, it is preferable to examine what Borges does with the dramatic monologue in his poetry. Among the speakers are his ancestor Francisco Laprida; Alexander Selkirk; Hengist, the Jutish king of Kent; God; Heraclytus; a Chinese library guard; Tamerlan, an English madman; Browning himself; Ulysses; an unknown Saxon warrior; an unknown inquisitor; an unknown conquistador; the Altamira painter; the Caliph Omar; Alonso Quijano; and Descartes. For the most part, these are short poems; a number are sonnets. There is neither room to develop nor an intention of developing the kind of psychological complexity that is Browning's peculiar characteristic. Instead, Borges tends to offer just a glimpse of the other.

"Hengist Cyning"[15] is a fine example of the use of the dramatic monologue to open a perspective on the distant past by showing, instead of explaining, a way of thinking that is distinctly not modern. The poem opens with an epitaph that substantiates the claims made by the voice of the dead ruler, Hengist the first Jutish king of Kent, whose monologue makes up the body of the poem. Hengist is concerned with clearing up a misunderstanding about his life. The British accuse him of betrayal because he killed his king but what Hengist wants clarified is that the real betrayal lay in the selling of his strength and courage. By turning on the British Vortigen, he reaffirms his personal worth: "yo *fui* Hengist el mercenario" (v. 7, italics mine); and *now* he speaks as king. His speech is laconic, as austere as the epitaph engraved on stone, and appropriate for a Northern warrior king. His reference to the murder is understated and curiously touching: "Le quité la luz y la vida" (v. 16). In an economy based on limited good, the only way to attain "luz y vida" is to deprive someone else of these things (the following verse is, "Me place el reino que gané"). In any event, the murder needs no more justification than the comment that "la fuerza y el coraje no sufren / que las vendan los hombres" (vv. 12–13). That he should lay waste the British cities and enslave the subjugated populace is simply taken for granted. Like many dramatic monologues ("My Last Duchess" is a good, if far more complex, example), the poem is a gratuitous assertion of self. The real brunt of the message is: This is what I am, "Yo he sido fiel a mi valentía" (v. 27). To whom is Hengist speaking? A chance passerby at the grave? Future generations? The sole possible audience is Borges, sensitive to these cries from the past, and through him, the reader on whom he now confers a privileged insight into the workings of an archaic sensibility.

Borges has always been interested in what Browning calls that "moment, one and infinite,"[16] when a man recognizes his destiny. Hengist turned on Vortigen because he realized that he was meant to rule rather than be ruled. The body of the poem deals with the upshot of that discovery. **"El advenimiento"**[17] focuses on the moment itself, when the anonymous painter of the Altamira cave saw the herd of buffalo he later painted (like **"Hengist Cyning,"** the narration here takes place centuries after the event and is addressed to the void—or the ears of the poet):

> Son los bisontes, dije. La palabra
> No había pasado nunca por mis labios,
> Pero sentí que tal era su nombre.
> Era como si nunca hubiera visto,
> Como si hubiera estado ciego y muerto
> Antes de los bisontes de la aurora.
> Surgían de la aurora. Eran la aurora.
> No quise que los otros profanaran
> Aquel pesado río de bruteza
> Divina, de ignorancia, de soberbia.
> Pisotearon un perro del camino;
> Lo mismo hubieran hecho con un hombre.
> Después los trazaría en la caverna
> Con ocre y bermellón.
>
> (vv. 23–37)

Like many of Borges' poems, **"El advenimiento"** arises from an intellectual question: how did the Altamira caves come to be painted? Borges answers the question with an impression that is vivid because it is rendered from within. The speaker is neither described nor analyzed. He simply tells us what, not why, he thought, and we instinctively feel—yes, it must have been like that. Through his use of the monologue, Borges allows a very distant, hazy event to become real. For the speaker, the critical moment comes when he sees the herd; the painting, which has had such a great impact on twentieth-century art, is an afterthought. The real genius, Borges suggests—and this notion obviously has wider application—lies in seeing.

In the last verses of the poem, Borges dissolves the image he has created:

> . . . Nunca
> Dijo mi boca el nombre de Altamira.
> Fueron muchas mis formas y mis muertes.
>
> (vv. 38–40)

Rodríguez-Monegal writes that for Borges, "All men who perform the same basic and ritual act are the same man."[18] As an artist, the speaker has more in common with other artists than he does with his other, nonartist self, the primitive man who must traffic with his tribe, hunt for food, sleep, make love. Since Borges conveys to the reader *only* what is relevant to the epiphanic moment, it is possible for this individual to be subsumed into the species. This type of transformation does not much interest Browning. For the most part, he builds up portraits of the whole man, full of troublesome details that cannot be wished away, even when he concentrates, say, on a man's art, as in "Fra Lippo Lippi" and "Andrea del Sarto."

Borges uses the monologue to explore situation rather than character: how did the cave paintings come about? what is the reason for an apparent act of treason? Silvia Molloy comments that in Borges' fiction, character and situation usually coincide.[19] In general, this is true of the poetry as well. As a form, the dramatic monologue is suited to this kind of overlapping since it involves the presentation of character *in situ.* Eliot, too, uses the monologue in a way similar to Borges—if "Prufrock" is a rounded portrait of a shattered man, "The Journey of the Magi" and "The Wasteland" (a series of monologues uttered by Tiresias in different times and places) are more concerned with situation.

Like **"El advenimiento," "Poema conjectural"**[20] is an example of a monologue concerned with what Mary Kinzie calls "hidden history," the point when the individual merges with the archetype.[21] The poem takes place at a specific historical moment. The prefatory note explains: "El doctor Francisco Laprida, asasinado el día 22 de setiembre de 1829 por los montoneros de Aldao, piensa antes de morir." The action is dramatic, but the narrative is secondary to Laprida's discourse. He is even now being hunted down. Although he accepts his approaching death "sin esperanza ni temor," (v. 11), he is confused and bitter about the *kind* of death being doled out to him since it represents a denial of the grounds of his existence, his "Yo, que estudié las leyes y los cánones, / yo, Francisco Narciso de Laprida" (vv. 6–7). He is lost, not because he is about to die, but because his ending makes no sense in terms of his life. The representative of civilization is being done in by the forces of barbarism.

In the second stanza, Laprida reaches for an analogy that may help him understand his peculiar fate. "Aquel capitán del Purgatorio," to whom he refers, Buonconte da Montefeltro, falls into the group of the Late Repentant. In 1289, he commanded the Aretines in an unsuccessful attempt against the Florentines at Campaldino. Following the defeat, he was hunted down; his throat was cut, and his body carried away by the Arno. According to Dante, at the moment of his death, he repented his life of violence and called out the name of Mary, thus saving his soul. The manner of Buonconte's death coincides with Laprida's, but more important is Laprida's identification with a figure who reaches understanding just before he dies, and the fact that Laprida looks to the universal, embodied in literature, to come to terms with his individual situation; that is, the particular has meaning only in relation to the general. In the remainder of the stanza, Laprida returns to the narrative of his flight. His killers are drawing closer. Earlier he heard shots; now he hears hooves. The outer hunt parallels the inner search; time is running out for both. The situation is similar to that in **"El milagro secreto."**

At the beginning of the third stanza, Laprida thinks back to his life, much in the terms he used earlier, but the fourth verse signals a change:

pero me endiosa el pecho inexplicable
un júbilo secreto. Al fin me encuentro
con mi destino sudamericano.

(vv. 25–27)

The analogy in the previous stanza opens the way for a revelation, a recognition not of Christian divinity, but of the collective unconscious of his race. Seen in this fresh light, Laprida's death is a confirmation, not a denial of self.[22] At this critical juncture, Laprida discovers his "insospechado rostro eterno" (v. 37); he becomes one with the archetype—not only of the gaucho, but of warriors over the centuries, including Dante's Aretine captain, whose death he reenacts.

In the last stanza, it only remains to consummate his fate. Laprida, like Buonconte, narrates his own death. This point of view produces a disturbing close-up effect: "Pisan mis pies la sombra de las lanzas" (v. 39):

Ya el primer golpe,
ya el duro hierro que me raja el pecho,
el íntimo cuchillo en la garganta.

(vv. 42–44)

In the poem, we find a number of elements typical of the dramatic monologue. The protagonist is forced to formulate his thoughts at a moment of dramatic intensity. Through his discourse, he arrives at a revelation and subsequent understanding. Although the language is pure Borges, it is not beyond the reach of an educated forebear who is, in any event, not speaking out loud.

Through the prefatory note and the title, as well as the language, Borges reminds the reader of his shaping presence in the poem. The "conjectural" establishes the same relationship between creator and creation as does the last paragraph in **"La busca de Averroes."** The tension thus set up between past and present, between reality and literature, is associated with the odd notion that only through recourse to letters does Laprida recognize that he is destined to be a man of action. The world of literature provides access to the universal. Yet even though he is, so to speak, disseminated through history, Laprida remains simultaneously fixed for the reader in the memorable gesture of his death, just as the Altamira painter is fixed in the moment he sees the herd.

In her study of his oscillations between the impersonal and the personal, Molloy points to Borges' use of gesture which, she argues, is much like Stevenson's: it gives shape to character, idea or emotion by means of an act or an attitude that captures our attention.[23] Even though he sweeps a character away, Borges often leaves us with something akin to the Cheshire cat's furious grin, a gesture that stays with us. The monologue provides Borges with a ready source of irony—the character who announces his "yo" most tenaciously finds that the only appropriate term is "nosotros," but it also offers a means of making the experience vivid—the character's own perspective. Because in **"El advenimiento"** we see the herd through the protagonist's eyes, join him imaginatively at the crack through which he peers, both he and the herd, in short, the entire situation, are sharply etched in our minds. Similarly, for an instant, we also find ourselves with Laprida at his death just because our angle of vision is exactly his. It is for this reason that Langbaum describes the dramatic monologue as a "poetry of sympathy."[24] Actually, the disparity between Langbaum's insistence that the monologue give the "facts from within" and his contention that there is a greater consciousness at work in the poem is only apparent, as these poems demonstrate. Borges manipulates point of view here to provide additional tension between the particular and the universal, the individual and the archetype. There is a great pathos to these creations that seem to be so bright and are suddenly sent up in smoke.

It is precisely because Borges does not take advantage of the speaker's perspective that **"Browning resuelve ser poeta,"**[25] a poem inevitably in this discussion, is less successful than many of his other dramatic monologues. The title suggests that the poem will focus on a specific occasion—the point when Browning decided to become a poet—but the great moment eludes the poem. The speaker's remark, "descubro que he elegido / la más curiosa de las profesiones humanas" (vv. 2–3) is undercut by the next comment—"salvo que todas, a su modo, lo son" (v. 4), which reveals a diffidence characteristic of Borges, but quite alien to Browning. The poem turns on a playful series of allusions that continually remind the reader of the author's presence in the poem. For example, the reference to Browning's use of colloquial language:

haré que las comunes palabras—
naipes marcados del tahur, moneda de la plebe—
rindan la magia que fue suya
cuando Thor era el numen e el estrépito

(vv. 5–12)

does double duty since the two metaphors for common words point toward Borges' own work. "Los naipes del tahur" is the composition for which the Borges persona does not win an award in "El Aleph"; the coin is probably the "zahir." The poem is graceful and clever, but it lacks the tension that gives a number of other monologues strength. Here the speaker, Browning, is simply swallowed up by the central theme, which is the intertextuality of all literature. Other poems discussed involve identifiable circumstances even though their speakers may now be disembodied voices monologizing centuries after an event; nevertheless, there is an experience and an attitude to remember. The real location of **"Browning resuelve ser poeta"** is in the pages of universal literature, rather than the "rojos laberintos de Londres" (v. 1) that are dismissed in one verse, and it takes place not at some point in the 1820's, but over the centuries. What is missing here is the memorable gesture that would, as Stevenson suggests, capture our attention.

The true power of the dramatic monologue as Borges uses it lies in its ability to create tension between the temporal and the eternal, between the individual speaker and the archetype, and to offer us a privileged perspective on a situation or mode of thought that would otherwise be inaccessible. If his tribute to Browning falls short of this potential and is—to this reader's mind—less successful, the vivid images that so many of the other dramatic monologues leave testify to Borges' brilliant use of a traditional form.

Notes

1. Richard Burgin, *Conversaciones con Jorge Luis Borges* (New York: Holt, Rinehart and Winston, 1968): 48.
2. Jorge Luis Borges, *Introducción a la literatura inglesa* (Buenos Aires: Editorial Columba, 1965): 46. My translation.
3. María Esther Vásquez, "Entrevista a Borges," *Jorge Luis Borges*. Edited by Jaime Alazraki. (Madrid: Taurus, 1976): 71.
4. Jorge Luis Borges, *Obras completas III. Otras inquisiciones* (Buenos Aires: Emecé, 1957): 121.
5. Borges, *Introducción a la literatura inglesa*, 47.
6. Burgin, *Conversaciones*, 48–9.
7. G. Robert Stange, "Browning and Modern Poetry," in *Browning's Mind and Art*. Edited by Clarence Tracy. (New York: Barnes and Noble, 1968): 153.
8. Ina Beth Sessions, "The Dramatic Monologue," in *PMLA*, 62 (1947): 508.
9. Robert Langbaum, *The Poetry of Experience* (New York: W. W. Norton, 1963): 85.
10. Langbaum, *Poetry of Experience*, 94.
11. Park Honan, *Browning's Characters* (New Haven: Yale University Press, 1961): 122.
12. Borges, *Introducción a la literatura inglesa*, 47.
13. Robert Browning, *Poetical Works: 1833–1864*, edited by Ian Jack. (London: Oxford University Press, 1970): 594, vv. 79–80. The poem appears on pp. 594–602.
14. Mary Kinzie, "Recursive Prose," *Prose for Borges* (Evanston, Ill.: Northwestern University Press, 1974): 28.
15. Jorge Luis Borges, *Obra poética* (Madrid: Alianza Editorial, 1975): 213.
16. Browning, "By the Fireside," *Poetical Works*, 586, v. 181.
17. Borges, *Obra poética*, 409–10.
18. Emir Rodríguez-Monegal, "Borges: The Reader as Writer," *Prose for Borges*, 120.
19. Silvia Molloy, *Las letras de Borges* (Buenos Aires: Editorial Sudamericana, 1979): 76.
20. Borges, *Obra poética*, 129–30.
21. Kinzie, "Recursive Prose," 34.
22. The poem is, of course, an attempt to find consolation for a needless death—like W. B. Yeats' "An Irish Airman Foresees His Death" and "In Memory of Major Robert Gregory." Interesting in this connection is Jaime Alazraki's discussion of "El Sur," the story in which a librarian who lies dying of septicemia in a hospital in Buenos Aires dreams that he is killed defending his honor in a knife fight somewhere in the South. He sees the "death" as both a wasteful reminder of the country's barbarism and an effort to return to an epic past: "es un exceso y una privación, una destrucción y una forma de realización, una negación y un acto de afirmación." [Jaime Alazraki, *Versiones, Inversiones, Reversiones* (Madrid: Editorial Gredos, 1977): 40.]
23. Robert L. Stevenson cited in Molloy, 124. (I am paraphrasing in English.)
24. Langbaum, *Poetry of Experience*, 79.
25. Jorge Luis Borges, *The Gold of the Tigers: Selected Later Poems*, a bilingual edition, ed. and trans. Alastair Reid. (New York: E. P. Dutton, 1976): 52, 54.

María Kodama (essay date 1986)

SOURCE: "Oriental Influences in Borges' Poetry: The Nature of the Haiku and Western Literature," in *Borges the Poet*, edited by Carlos Cortinez, The University of Arkansas Press, 1986, pp. 170–81.

[*In the following essay, Kodama discusses Borges's use of the traditional Japanese poetic forms of* tanka *and* haiku.]

In the foreword to his ***Collected Writings*** (1969), and in other works, Borges has expressed many judgments on poetry and style which indicate the way he gradually assumed the essential poetic forms of the Japanese *tanka* and *haiku.* He attempted those two forms for the first time in ***El Oro de los Tigres*** (1972) and in ***La Cifra*** (1981). Borges began his prologue to the *Collected Writings* by claiming: "I have not rewritten the book. I have toned down its Baroque excesses, I have trimmed rough edges, I have blotted out sentimental verses and vagueness and, in the course of this labor sometimes pleasing and sometimes annoying, I have felt that the young man who in 1923 wrote those pages was essentially—what does essentially mean?—the elderly gentleman who now resigns himself to what he penned or emends it. We are both the same; we both disbelieve in success and in failure, in literary schools and in their dogmas; we both are true to Schopenhauer, to Stevenson and to Whitman. In my opinion, ***Fervor de Buenos Aires*** foreshadows all that came afterwards." He ends by saying: "In those days, I sought sunsets, outlying slums and unhappiness; now, mornings, downtown, and serenity."

These words express not only the writer's feelings on his work, and on himself, but reflect also an essential search, foreshadowed as he tells us, from the beginning. This search, or attempt, is the oldest in the world. It began with Homer, and will continue as long as men write. Its aim is to discover with the utmost formal rigor the center, eternity. This search has often been attempted in the East, particularly in Japan and in the West, and particularly in Borges.

In the West, literature begins with the epic, with poems which throughout Europe tell the tales of heroes in hundreds and hundreds of lines. A perfect expression is found in the famous beginning of Virgil's *Aeneid:* "Arma virumque cano." "*Arms and the man I sing,*" as Dryden translated. The mind accepts the word "arms" immediately; it refers, of course, to the deeds of man. In the West those poems throughout the centuries grow briefer and briefer until they reach the avant-garde schools, among them Ultraism. In the case of Spanish literature this generated some of the most important changes since the introduction of the Italian sonnet by Garcilaso, not so much by itself, but by the changes wrought by its impulse.

Borges' career began with a flirtation with Ultraism, and then followed in his own personal way, a way that led him, in a wide circle, to Japan. He, the maker, even as God Himself, sought what is essential to all poetry and especially to Japanese poetry. Japanese poetry tries to carve into a few precious lines of seventeen syllables the meeting of time and space in a single point. The maker, even as God Himself tries to abolish succession in space.

In his own way Borges has tried to express the same wish in the foreword to his *Historia de la Eternidad* (1936):

> I don't know how on earth I compared to 'stiff museum pieces' the archetypes of Plato and how I failed to understand, reading Schopenhauer and Scotus Erigena, that they are living, powerful and organic. Movement, the occupation of different *places* in different moments is inconceivable without time; so is immobility, the occupation of the same place in different points of time. How could I not perceive that eternity, sought and beloved by so many poets, is a splendid artifice, that sets us free, though for a moment, of the unbearable burden of successive things.

In *The Aleph* (1949) he also says:

> The Aleph's diameter must have been two or three inches, but Cosmic Space was therein, without diminution of size. Each object (the mirror's glass, for instance) was infinite objects, for I clearly saw it from all points in the universe . . . I saw the Aleph from all points; I saw the earth in the Aleph . . . I saw my face and entrails . . . and felt dizziness and wept because my eyes had seen that conjectural and secret object whose name men take in vain but which no man has looked on: the inconceivable universe. I felt infinite veneration, infinite pity . . . For the Kaballah, this letter the En-Sof, the limitless and pure God Head.

These ideological elements form converging aspects sympathetic to the intent of Japanese poetry, which must be examined in some detail in order to understand both its poetic patterns and their purpose.

As in the case of Western literature, Japanese literature begins by groping its way. The task of finding a precise date for the birth of regular forms in prose and verse is not an easy one. The earliest example is the *Kojiki*, a record of ancient matters, compiled *circa* A.D. 712. Afterwards came the *Nihon Shoki*, a chronicle of Japan, A.D. 720. In the year A.D. 751 there appeared a compilation of Chinese verses written in Japan, the *Kaifūsō: Fond Recollection of Poetry.* Therein are found texts dating from the last part of the seventh century. The Nara Period offers the first great anthology of poetry, the Manyōshū Collection of *A Myriad Leaves.* This compilation was undertaken towards the end of the eighth century. In the *Kojiki* and in the *Nihon Shoki* the length of the lines in the poems and in the songs varies from three to nine syllables though even in this early period we find the habit of repeating five and seven syllables. In the Manyōshū the poems have already a fixed number of lines and the forms are regular. The lines are invariably compounded of five and seven syllables passing from one to the other. An example is the poem in which Prince Arima is getting ready for a journey:

> Iwashiro no
> Hamamatsu ga e wo
> Hikimusubi
> Masakiku araba
> Mata kaerimimu.

On the beach of Iwashiro. I put the knot together. The branches of the pine. If my fate turns out well, I shall return to see them again. This particular form of thirty-one syllable poems in five lines of 5, 7, 5, 7, 7 each is the most frequent and the most lasting of the three forms evolved in the Manyōshū Period. In Japanese poetry it is called *tanka* or *waka.* The other two are the *sedoka* and the *choka.* The *choka* is a long poem with no limit to the number of lines. The longest of these poems attains one hundred and fifty lines. It passes, like the *tanka*, from 5 to 7 syllables ending in a line of 7 syllables. It could also be completed by one or two or more *hankas* or envoys written after the manner of *tanka* and summing up the subject of the whole poem. However, of all stanzas to be found in Japanese poetry, the most congenial to the Japanese mind seems to be the *tanka*, since it still survives, along with the *haiku* that is engendered by an evolution of the *tanka* towards a greater brevity and a greater conclusion.

During the Manyū Period, poetry tended toward a private lyricism. The *tanka*, however, underwent a considerable evolution, which ended in a new form, the *haiku.* A crucial point was the transition of the caesura or pause in the syntax. In the *Manyū* Period most *tankas* had their caesura after the second or the fourth line. The poem is thus divided into three units of 5, 7 (12) and 5, 7 (12) and 7 syllables. This pattern hinders the attempt to pass from a short line to a long one and is weakened by the last short unit.

A verse from Hitomaro Kashū provides an example:

Hayabito no
Na ni ou yogoe
Ichishiroku
Waga na wa noritsu
Tsuma to tanomase.

Clear and loud as the night call of a man of Haya, I told my name. Trust me as your wife. [The Haya, a southern Kyūshū tribe, famous for the clarity of their voices, were employed at the Imperial Palace as watchmen. A woman tells her name to signify her assent to a proposal of marriage.]

Towards the end of the Heian Period (794–1185) and in the Kamakura Period (1185–1603), the caesura comes after the first and the third line. The poem is thus divided into three longer units of 5, 12 and 14 syllables. As an example the poem of Narihira is given, from the novel *Ise Monogatari:*

Tsuki ya aranu//
Haru ya mukashi no
Haru naranu//
Waga mi hitotsu wa
Moto no mi nishite.

Can it be the moon has changed, can it be that the spring is not the spring of old times? Is it my body alone that is just the same? This division gave the poet a greater freedom. It favoured the evolution of the imayō style, where the 12-syllable line had a caesura after the seventh. Far more important is the fact that the second caesura is stronger than the first.

This latter style of *tanka* was divided into the two principal parts, the first three lines and the last two lines (17 syllables and 14 syllables). From this division came the form of linked verse, the *renga*, whose initial stanza comprises three lines, the second two lines, the third three lines, and so on. In due time, the initial stanza of the *renga* became independent and took the name of *haiku.* The curious fact that the season of the year was always recorded or hinted at in those first three verses may have favored the process. A mild surprise clung to it, a sudden enlightenment akin to the *satori* of Zen Buddhism. This is the origin of *haiku*, which was essentially in its beginning the old linked poem of the fourteenth century, ruled by the ideas and conventions peculiar to the *tanka.*

Bashō (1644–1694) fixed forever the road of the *haiku.* Bashō stated that the *haiku* should use the common speech of men avoiding, let it be understood, vulgarity. He abounded in images and words forbidden to the *tanka.* Sparrows instead of nightingales; snails instead of flowers. The poet should be "one with the crowd but his mind should always be pure." He should use "common language and somehow make it into a thing of beauty." He should feel pity for the frailness of all things created and feel keenly *Sabi*, a word that stands for solitude, for lonely sadness, and for the melancholy of nature. Above all, he should so express the nature of the particular as to define, through it, the essence of all creation. His seventeen syllables should capture a vision of the nature of the world.

The best example of this teaching is his famous *haiku*:

Furu ike ya
Kawazu tobikomu
Mizu no oto.

An old pond. A frog jumps in, sound of water. First, we have something changeless, the pond, then something quick and moving, the frog, and lastly the splashing water, which is the point where both meet.

In an examination of Borges' poem **"Un Patio"** from ***Fervor de Buenos Aires*** (1923), we find many elements in common, metrics apart.

With evening
the two or three colors of the patio grew weary.
The huge candor of the full moon
no longer enchants its usual firmament.
Patio: heaven's watercourse.

The patio is the slope
down which the sky flows into the house.
Serenely
eternity waits at the crossway of the stars.
It is lovely to live in the dark friendliness
of covered entrance way, arbor, and wellhead.

[*trans. Robert Fitzgerald*]

Unknowingly, this poem follows the indications of Bashō.

How could a South American poet, after so many centuries, attain the very essence of the *haiku?* A possible explanation may be found in the fact that the essence of poetry is timeless and universal and when a writer attains it, as in the case of the Greek tragic poets, the achievement has no ending. An altogether different clue may be given us by Borges' childhood. His paternal grandmother was English, knew her Bible by heart and was continually quoting from it. I have been told that she could recite chapter and verse for any sentence in the Holy Writ. After Grimm, Borges read and reread the *Arabian Nights* in an English version and then went on to a now forgotten book, *Fairy Tales from Old Japan* by Mitford, an American scholar. During the first World War, the works of Schopenhauer sent him to the study of Buddhism. Borges explored with eagerness the books of Hermann Oldenberg on the Buddha and his teaching. These many interests gave him an open mind, a hospitable mind, sensitive to the most different cultures. Thus unaware of his path, he followed the century-old road of Japanese poetry towards the discovery of the *haiku.* Things done unconsciously are done well, and writers should not watch too closely what they are writing. If they do, the dream betrays them.

In the early 1970s, Borges deliberately undertook the composition of *tankas* and crowned that attempt in the 1980s with the composition of *haikus.* The stanza has seventeen syllables; Borges wrote seventeen *haikus.* Some may be chosen and examined more closely. The form will not be taken into account, since seventeen Spanish or English syllables may not be heard as seventeen syllables by an Oriental ear and vice versa. Japanese verse is meant not only to be heard but to be seen; the *kanjis* make a pattern that should be pleasant and moving to the eye. This kind of picture is unfortunately lost in a Western translation.

The *haiku* may be defined as an ascetic art. The ascesis is by far the most important element and the most difficult to attain. Therein we find a fundamental difference between East and West. Ascesis, in the West, is a mean towards an end. We instinctively think of passing from pleasure to suffering; from happiness to sanctity. In the East, ascesis is an end in itself and therefore stands in no need of explanation or justification. Strangely enough, the rigor of ascesis is linked in the East to art. In the West, art passes from life to artifice, from the simple to the complex. The *haiku* is as near to life and nature as it can be and as far as it can be from literature and a high flown style. This ascesis is the reverse of vulgarity.

The chief contribution of Japan to world literature is a pure poetry of sensations, found only partially in Western letters. The great difference between the *haiku* and western poetry is this material, physical, immediate character. It is an exaltation of the flesh, not of the sexual. In the *haiku* we find blended in equal proportions, poetry and physical sensation, matter and mind, the creator and creation. The choice of subjects is significant; war, sex, poisonous plants, wild animals, sickness, earthquakes, that is to say all things dangerous or threatening to life, are left out. Man should forget those evils if he aspires to live a life of mental health. The art of *haiku* rejects ugliness, hatred, lying, sentimentality and vulgarity. Zen, on the other hand, accepts those evils, since they are part of the universe. The heat of a summer day, the smoothness of a stone, the whiteness of a crane are beyond all thought, emotion or beauty which the *haiku* tries to capture. Japanese literature, with particular regard to the *haiku,* is not a mystic one. The *haiku* is, of all artistic forms, perhaps the most ambitious. In seventeen syllables it grasps, or tries to grasp, reality. Intellectual and moral elements are ruled out.

The *haiku* has nothing in common with Good, Evil or Beauty. It is a kind of thinking through our senses; the *haiku* is not a symbol. It is not a picture with a meaning pinned on its back. When Bashō says that we should look for the pine in the pine and for the bamboo in the bamboo, he means that we should transcend ourselves and learn. To learn is to sink into the object until its inner nature is revealed to us and awakens our poetic impulse. Thus a falling leaf is not a token or symbol of autumn, or a part of autumn; it is autumn itself.

Here is a *haiku* by Borges and another by Kitō, Buson's disciple:

Hoy no me alegran
los almendros del huerto.
Son tu recuerdo.

The almond blossoms hold no cheer for me today; they are but your memory. Kitō wrote:

Yū-gasumi
Omoeba hedatsu
Mukashi kana.

The mists of evening when I think of them, far off are days of long ago. In the last poem the mist of evening reminds him of days past. The dim twilight is akin to the dim past. For Borges the almond blossoms bring back a happy, and perhaps recent past. The starting point of both pieces is nature. In another *haiku* Borges says:

Desde aquel día
no he movido las piezas
en el tablero.

Since that day I've not moved the pieces on the chessboard. And Shiki's *haiku* expressed a similar thought:

Kimi matsu ya
Mata kogarashi no
Ame ni naru.

Are you still waiting? Once more penetrating blasts turn into cold rain. Shiki looks back on a woman who may still be expecting him. Her (or his) loneliness may be hinted at by the penetrating blasts of wind and rain. Solitude is also the theme of the Borges *haiku.* The lonely chessboard stands for the lonely man. In this *haiku,* solitude is the solitude of the poet; in Shiki's *haiku* solitude is the solitude of the other.

In another *haiku*, Borges suggests:

Algo me han dicho
la tarde y la montaña.
Ya lo he perdido.

The evening and the mountain have told me something; I have already lost it.

Teishitsu (1610–1673) also composed a similar idea:

Kore wa kore wa
To bakari, hana no
Yoshino-yama.

My, oh my! No more could I say; viewing flowers on Mount Yoshino. Teishitsu is overwhelmed by a powerful beauty that he cannot describe; in Borges' case a revelation has been given him by a fleeting moment, a revelation that he is unable to express.

Further, Borges writes:

El hombre ha muerto.
La barba no lo sabe.
recen las uñas.

The man is dead. The beard is unaware of it. His nails keep growing. Which is similar to the composition by Bashō (1644–1649), who wrote:

Ie wa mina
Tsue ni shiraga no
Haka mairi.

All the family equipped with staves and greyhaired, visiting the graves. Death, in Borges' *haiku,* is not represented as pathetic or memorable, sorrowful or fatal, but rather as disgusting and strange, as a curious physical happening. In this particular *haiku* Borges fulfills a requisite we have already noted; that the stanza is a meeting point of something everlasting, death, and something going on for a while, such as the grim circumstance of the growing beard and nails. Death in Bashō's *haiku* is presented in a casually indirect way: the poet sees the family visiting graves and feels that those old men and women will soon be dead. The theme of death was forbidden to the writers of *haiku;* Bashō, a follower of Zen Buddhism, dared to use it.

The moon presents another image to Borges:

Bajo el alero
el espejo no copia
más que la luna.

Under the eaves the mirror holds a single image. The moon.

This is complemented by an earlier *haiku* by Kikaku (1661–1707) who composed:

Meigetsu ya!
Tatami no ue ni
Matsu no kage.

A brilliant full moon! On the matting of my floor shadows of pines fall. Kikaku sets a picture before us. The shadows of the pines can be seen because the moon is in the sky. In both poems solitude is signified by the full moon, absence is the real subject of both, and a fleeting point of time is held by the words. An image of eternity in the Japanese poem is in the full moon; eternity in Borges' *haiku* is reflected in a quiet mirror.

The sense of loneliness may also be found in two other *haikus* by Borges:

Bajo la luna
la sombra que se alarga
es una sola.

Under the moon the growing shadow is but a single one.

La luna nueva.
Ella también la mira
desde otra puerta.

The new moon. She too is gazing on her from another door.

Let us now compare a Western *haiku* and an Oriental one. First here is one by Borges:

¿Es un imperio
esa luz que se apaga
o una luciérnaga?

This dying flash is it an empire or a firefly? Compare it to a *haiku* by Bashō:

Natsu-kusa ya!
Tsuwamono-domo ga
Yume no ato.

You summer grasses! Glorious dreams of great warriors now only ruins. The subject of both poems is commonplace: the mortality of all things. We should recall, by the way, Seneca's memorable sentence: *Una nox fuit inter urbem maximam et nullam,* in which the last word speaks of the destruction of the entire city. The two *haikus* quoted express the futility of all human endeavours.

Next we might look at this *haiku* by Borges:

La vieja mano
sigue trazando versos
para el olvido.

This old hand goes on writing verses for oblivion. A *haiku* by Jōsō is complementary:

No mo yama mo
Yuki ni torarete
Nani mo nashi.

Both plains and mountains have been captured by the snow. There is nothing left. Jōsō (1662–1704) was one of the ten special disciples of bashō and a follower of Zen Buddhism. He tells us that nothing lasts. Even the mountains and their strength are blotted out by the most immaterial things such as snow. In Borges' *haiku*, the *haiku* itself is written for final and relentless oblivion.

Two other *haikus* are presented for comparison. Borges writes:

La vasta noche
no es ahora otra cosa
que una fragancia.

The endless night is now but a fragrance. And the poet Mokudō (1665–1723) wrote:

Haru-kaze ya!
Mugi no naka yuku
Mizu no oto.

A gentle spring breeze! Through green barley plants rushes the sound of water. Perhaps this last *haiku* by Borges is one of his best. The poem refers to a single instant where the unseen night reveals herself to the poet. The last line of Mokudō's *haiku* had been used already by his teacher Bashō in his most famous poem. Nobody thought of repetition as plagiarism; nobody thought in terms of personal vanity. The *haiku* is a splendid habit of a whole country, not of an individual. It is considered that poetry in Japan is a living thing, and every person from a laborer to the Emperor is a poet.

In examining these poems it is necessary to ask if there is a certain virtue common to all poetry in all ages and lands. The answer may be sought in Borges' foreword to ***El Oro de los Tigres***, that: "to a true poet every single moment of his life, every deed or dream should be felt by him as poetic, since essentially it *is* poetic" . . . "Beauty is common in this world." In the foreword to ***El Otro, El Mismo*** Borges tells us that "the fate of a writer is very strange. At the beginning he is Baroque, insolently Baroque; after long years he may attain, if the stars are auspicious, not simplicity, which is meaningless, but a shy and secret complexity." This is the way of the *haiku.* The brief *haiku* is the apex of a vast pyramid.

Jaime Alazraki (essay date 1988)

SOURCE: "Enumerations as Evocations: On the Use of a Device in Borges' Late Poetry," in *Borges and the Kabbalah: And Other Essays on His Fiction and Poetry*, Cambridge University Press, 1988, pp. 116–23.

[*In the following essay, Alazraki discusses Borges' use of the device of enumeration in his poetry.*]

Enumerations in literature are as old as the Old Testament, but in modern times they have achieved the status of an established rhetorical device only since the writings of Walt Whitman. Such are the conclusions of Detlev W. Schumann and Leo Spitzer, two critics who have studied enumerations in contemporary poetry. Spitzer summarized his findings in a well known essay entitled "Chaotic Enumerations in Modern Poetry."[1] There he says: "All seems to indicate that we owe chaotic enumerations as a poetic device to Whitman."[2] In a different essay devoted to Whitman, Spitzer defines the device as "consisting of lumping together things spiritual and physical, as the raw material of our rich, but unordered modern civilization which is made to resemble an oriental bazaar. . . ."[3] If enumerations have been, until Whitman, one of the most effective means of describing the perfection of the created world in praise of its Creator, it was Whitman's task to render that same perfection and unity into attributes of our chaotic modern world."[4] Whitman did not invent the device, but he used it with such intensity and skill that his poetry became a showcase of the rich possibilities offered by the device for poets who succeeded him. In Spanish America, Darío and Neruda were deeply influenced by Whitman and his enumerative style. So was Borges, who wrote about Whitman and on enumerations as early as 1929.

In a short note entitled "The Other Whitman," he argued that Europeans misread Whitman: "They turned him into the forerunner of many provincial inventors of free verse. The French aped the most vulnerable part of his diction: the complaisant geographic, historic, and circumstantial enumerations strung by Whitman to fulfill Emerson's prophecy about a poet worthy of America."[5] Borges viewed enumerations and free verse—at that time—as foundations of European avant-garde poetry. "Those imitations," he concluded caustically, "were and are the whole of today's French poetry."[6] He then added, on the subject of enumerations, "many of them didn't even realize that enumeration is one of the oldest poetic devices—think of the Psalms in the Scriptures, and of the first chorus of *The Persians*, and the Homeric catalogue of the ships—and that its intrinsic merit it not its length but its delicate verbal balance. Walt Whitman didn't ignore that."[7]

Almost fifty years later, in a footnote to his latest collection of poems, ***La cifra***, Borges restated the same notion. Referring to the poem **"Aquél,"** he wrote, "this composition, like almost all the others, abuses chaotic enumerations. Of this figure, in which Walt Whitman abounded with so much felicity, I can only say that it should impress us as chaos, as disorder, and be, at the same time, a cosmos, an order."[8] There are three elements here that need to be emphasized. The first is that Borges adopts in 1981 the term coined, or rather divulged, by Spitzer as it was used earlier by Schumann. Raimundo Lida translated Spitzer's article into Spanish and it was published in Buenos Aires in 1945. It is presumable that Borges read it, but he didn't have to, since the term has become part of our literary jargon and we use it familiarly, unaware of our debt to either Schumann or Spitzer. What matters is that this is the first reference Borges makes to the device under the name of "chaotic enumerations."

The second point is that Borges emphasizes the idea of order in the guise of chaos underlying the effectiveness of chaotic enumerations in Whitman. This is the very core of Spitzer's definition: "Whitman's catalogues," he says, "present a mass of heterogeneous things integrated, however, in a majestic and grand vision of All-One."[9]

The third and last point is Borges' explicit recognition that his last collection, ***La cifra***, abuses chaotic enumerations. He is right. Although enumerations appear already in his early collections, and reappear throughout his entire poetic work, the device is considerably more frequent in his latest book. Following is an attempt to track the course of enumerations in Borges' poetry, and an effort to define the implications of the device in the development of his art.

For a writer who has been an early reader and admirer of Whitman, who has written several essays on him, who has acknowledged his debt to Whitman in numerous texts, early and late, and who has (more recently) translated *Leaves of Grass* into Spanish, it is not at all surprising to find in Borges' own poetry the use and abuse of enumerations. They appear as early as 1925 in his collection ***Luna de enfrente***, in such poems as **"Los Llanos," "Dualidá en una despedida," "Al coronel Francisco Borges," "La promisión en alta mar," "Mi vida entera,"** and **"Versos de catorce."** With the exception of **"Mi vida entera"** (**"My Whole Life"**), these poems use enumerations either partially or for the rhythmic element performed by a repeated word or anaphora. What sets **"My Whole Life"** aside from the others in his early poetry is the use of enumerations in a manner that will become characteristic of his later work. Note the poem in a translation by W. S. Merwin:

> Here once again the memorable lips, unique and like yours.
> I am this groping intensity that is a soul.
> I have got near to happiness and have stood in the shadow
> of suffering.
> I have crossed the sea.
> I have known many lands; I have seen one woman and two
> or three men.
> I have loved a girl who was fair and proud, and bore a
> Spanish quietness.
> I have seen the city's edge, an endless sprawl where the
> sun goes down tirelessly, over and over.
> I have relished many words.
> I believe deeply that this is all, and that I will neither see
> nor accomplish new things.
> I believe that my days and my nights, in their poverty and
> their riches, are the equal of God's and of all men's.[10]

With the years, the list will become longer, the lines shorter, the voice deeper, the tone calmer, but the effort to survey his whole life through enumerations will remain the same.

But what exactly do enumerations enumerate in poetry? In the case of Whitman, they list the diversity or even chaos of a country, time, or people, in order to cluster that diversity into a unity: the poem renders that oriental bazaar of our unordered civilization—in the words of Spitzer—into "the powerful Ego, the 'I' of the poet, who has extricated himself from the chaos."[11] This is not the use Borges makes of enumerations. In his second essay on Whitman, he comments on this use of enumerations reminiscent of the holy texts found in most religions: "Pantheism," he writes, "has disseminated a variety of phrases which declare that God is several contradictory or (even better) miscellaneous things." He then brings up examples from the *Gita*, Heraclitus, Plotinus, and the Sufi poet Attar, and concludes: "Whitman renovated that device. He did not use it, as others had, to define the divinity or to play with the 'sympathies and differences' of words; he wanted to identify himself, in a sort of ferocious tenderness, with all men."[12] Borges himself has employed this particular type of enumeration, proper to pantheism, in his fiction, in the description of divine visions or theophanies in stories like "The Aleph," "The Zahir," and "The God's Script," but not in his poetry.

There is another use of enumerations. It is best summarized by Whitman himself toward the end of his essay "A Backward Glance Over Traveled Roads" when he writes, "*Leaves of Grass* indeed has mainly been the outcropping of my own emotional and personal nature—an attempt from first to last, to put a *Person*, a human being (myself, in the latter half of the 19th Cent., in America) freely, fully and truly *on record*."[13] But for Whitman to put a human being on record was to write about Humanity and Nature, History and Politics, America and Sex, or, as he says elsewhere, "to sing the land, the people and the circumstances of the United States, to express their autochtonous song and to define their material and political success."[14]

Borges shares this task of poetry ("to articulate in poetic form my own physical, emotional, moral, intellectual and aesthetic Personality," in Whitman's words), but in a much more modest and restricted way. Compared to the cosmic world of Whitman, Borges' poetry is an intimate environment inhabited by sunsets and cityscapes, streets and outskirts, authors and books, branches of his family tree, Argentine heroes and counter-heroes, obsessions and mythologies, metaphysical and literary reflections, Old English and Germanic sagas, time, blindness, memory, oblivion, old age, love, friendship and death. There is no need to reconcile these two different perceptions of poetry belonging to Whitman and Borges, the question is rather how to explain the latter's admiration for the former.

In the preface to ***Elogio de la sombra*** he wrote, "I once strove after the vast breath of the psalms and of Walt Whitman."[15] And in his poem **"Buenos Aires,"** from the same collection, he writes: "Buenos Aires is a tall house in the South of the city, where my wife and I translated Whitman whose great echo, I hope, reverberates in this page."[16]

And again in the preface to ***El otro el mismo*** he insisted, "In some of these poems, Whitman's influence will be—I hope—noticed."[17] That Whitmanesque "vast breath" is present, paradoxically, in poems where enumerations convey intimate evocations of the poet's personal past, as in his early poem **"My Whole Life,"** written in 1925. Another example, chronologically, of this type of intimate evocation is the second of the **"Two English Poems"** written in 1934. Like the previous one, this too is a sort of family album in which the most significant experiences and events of the poet's personal life are recorded: desperate sunsets, lean streets, ragged suburbs, a lonely moon, his grandfather killed on the frontier of Buenos Aires, his great-grandfather heading a charge of three hundred men in Peru, the memory of a yellow rose, books, explanations, theories, the poet's loneliness, darkness, and his heart. The poem can be read, indeed, as a microcosm of his entire poetic work; most of his major themes and motifs are spun in this early cocoon.

What needs to be pointed out, though, is that this poem typifies the kind of enumerations that will be predominant in later poetry. There is no chaos here, in the sense used by Spitzer, as an expression of modern world disorder. There is a random survey of experiences we call chaotic enumerations, but the chaos refers mainly to the nature of the presentation rather than to the disorder of the representation (be that a country, a civilization, or the world). Borges too strives "to put a person on record," but not, as in Whitman's case, in the crucial latter half of the nineteenth century, during the rise of America as a world power, but in a very familiar time and in a place that is perceived more in personal than in historical terms.

Enumerations in which the specified material belongs to a strictly intimate space and a highly personal time may be illustrated by this passage:

> Stars, bread, libraries of East and West,
> Playing cards, chessboards, galleries, skylights, cellars,
> A human body to walk with on the earth,
> Fingernails, growing at nighttime and in death,
> Shadows for forgetting, mirrors busily multiplying,
> Cascades in music, gentlest of all time's shapes,
> Borders of Brazil, Uruguay, horses and mornings,
> A bronze weight, a copy of the Grettir Saga,
> Algebra and fire, the charge at Junín in your blood,
> Days more crowded than Balzac, scent of the honeysuckle,
> Love and the imminence of love and intolerable remembering,
> Dreams like buried treasure, generous luck,
> And memory itself . . . All this was given to you . . .[18]

This scrutiny of things past and present comes from **"Matthew XXV:30"** written in 1963. It is a recasting, slightly modified, of the enumeration put forth in the second **"English Poem"** of 1934, which in turn rewrites the earlier inventory recorded in **"My Whole Life"** of 1925. They are not the same poem: each one has a different intent and a different tone suitable to that intent. In the first, the emphasis is on the admission that, as the poem declares, "this is all, and I will neither see nor accomplish new things," a lucid anticipation, in 1925, of Borges' basic approach to writing as rewriting. The second is a love poem, and in it the poet's life is inscribed through its most memorable assets to be offered, as a trophy, to the beloved one: "I am trying to bribe you with uncertainty, with danger, with defeat."[19] The third poem recounts those same items, concluding: "You have used up the years and they have used up you / And still, and still, you have not written the poem."[20]

The evocation of those chosen moments or things or people will be repeated throughout Borges' entire poetic work, although never in quite the same way. Specifically it will appear in the poems **"Somebody," "Elegy,"** and **"Another Poem of Gifts."** In some cases, the poem enumerates not the things that life gave the poet but those it didn't—poems about gifts not received, like **"Limits,"** expanded into **"An Elegy of the Impossible Memory,"** and tried once again in **"Things That Might Have Been."** In other poems, there are just inventories of things dear to the poet's memory, like **"The Things,"** reenacted in **"Things,"** and repeated once again in **"Inventory."** In poems like **"The Threatened One"** and **"To the Sad One,"** personal things and interests are listed together. There are also poems whose enumerations are intended to give not a portrayal of the poet but of somebody else, or of animals, places, countries, cultures, books, or questions, such as **"Descartes," "The Righteous Ones," "The Orient," "Israel," "Buenos Aires," "Iceland," "The Islam," "England," "A Thousand and One Nights,"** and **"Insomnia."** Finally, in a poem like **"John I:4"** the enumeration foregoes the particulars and concentrates on the abstract side of gifts from life.

But the more interesting and the more relevant to this study are those instances of enumeration addressed to a survey of the poet's life. In addition to those already mentioned, the following should be added: **"I," "I Am," "Talismans," "The Thing I Am," "A Saturday," "The Causes," "The Maker," "Yesterdays,"** and **"Fame."** What pertains to the first three poems applies to these also; each has its own focus, its own inflection and tone. Yet all share the condition of enumeration as a means of evoking the poet's past and reflecting upon his present. The theme is recast, again and again, each time to strike a different chord, a different poem. The method was essentially set forth in that early poem of 1925; time completed it, skill refined it. The early hesitant and elementary lyrics evolved into the perfection and complexity of Borges' later poetry in which we hear the same intrinsic melody, but the music now has the balance, the harmony and serenity that befit a master.

A final and concluding remark. Borges' penchant for summaries is proverbial. He has insisted that "to write vast books is a laborious nonsense" and suggested that "a better course is to pretend that those books already exist and then offer a summary, a commentary."[21] Such a tendency applies to his poetry as well. The poems mentioned as examples of enumerations are summaries of the poet's major themes and motifs, indexes of his poetic production, or metonymies of his main subjects. His ancestors' battles and deaths, splendidly sung in numerous poems, are now resolved in a single and slim line: "I am the memory of a sword." His entire poetic endeavor is compressed into a single verse: "I have woven a certain hendecasyllable," and the plots and counter-plots of his fiction are encapsulated in a terse line from the poem **"Fame"**: "I have only retold ancient stories." There is no need for more. Borges, the master of metonymy, understands that having constructed a literary world of his own, an artful intimation suffices.

I also believe that this type of enumeration expresses his long held notion that "memory is best fulfilled through oblivion." Everything must be forgotten so that a few words remain. But those few words, in turn, condense and contain everything—personal Alephs, indeed. Oblivion thus becomes the ultimate realization of memory: "Viviré de olvidarme": "I shall live out of forgetting about myself," he says. What is left is an echo, a trace, a single line, the wake of a long journey that the poem proceeds to compile.

Notes

1. Leo Spitzer, *Lingüística e historia literaria* (Madrid: Gredos, 1961): 245–291. Second edition.
2. Spitzer, *Lingüística*, 258.
3. Leo Spitzer, "Explication de Text." Applied to Walt Whitman's poem "Out of the Cradle Endlessly Rocking." Included in *Essays on English and American Literature* (Princeton University Press, 1962): 23.
4. Spitzer, *Lingüística*, 261.
5. Jorge Luis Borges, "El otro Whitman." Included in *Discusión* (Buenos Aires: Emecé, 1957): 52. My own translation.
6. Borges, "El otro Whitman," 52.
7. Borges, "El otro Whitman," 52.
8. Jorge Luis Borges, *La cifra* (Buenos Aires: Emecé, 1981): 105.
9. Spitzer, *Lingüística*, 258.
10. Jorge Luis Borges, *Selected Poems 1923–1967*. Edited by Norman Thomas di Giovanni. (New York: Delacorte Press, 1972): 43.
11. Spitzer, "Explication de Text," 22.
12. Jorge Luis Borges, "Note on Walt Whitman." Included in *OI*, 73–4.
13. Walt Whitman, "A Backward Glance o'er Travel'd Roads." Included in *Leaves of Grass, Authoritative Texts, Prefaces, Whitman on His Art, Criticism* (New York: A Norton Critical Edition, 1973): 573–4.
14. Whitman, "Backward Glance," 574.
15. Borges, *ES*, 11.
16. Borges, *ES*, 128.
17. Borges, *OM*, 11.
18. Borges, *SP*, 93.
19. Borges, *OM*, 18.
20. Borges, *SP*, 93.
21. Borges, *F*, 11.

Jaime Alazraki (essay date 1988)

SOURCE: "Outside and Inside the Mirror in Borges' Poetry," in *Borges and the Kabbalah: And Other Essays on His Fiction and Poetry*, Cambridge University Press, 1988, pp. 107–15.

[*In the following essay, Alazraki discusses the significance of mirrors in Borges's poetry.*]

In the Preface to his fifth book of poetry—***In Praise of Darkness***—Borges writes: "To the mirrors, mazes, and swords which my resigned reader already foresees, two new themes have been added: old age and ethics."[1] Mirrors are a constant in Borges' poetry, but long before becoming a major theme or motif in his works, mirrors had been for Borges an obsession that goes back to his childhood years. To his friends he has told that as a child he feared that the images reflected on his bedroom mirror would stay there even after darkness had effaced them. For the boy, the images inhabiting mirrors were like the ghosts haunting the castle of a gothic novel—constantly lurking and threatening through ominous darkness.

In the brief piece entitled "The Draped Mirrors" from ***Dreamtigers*** he reminisces upon those fears: "As a child, I felt before large mirrors that same horror of a spectral duplication or multiplication of reality. Their infallible and continuous functioning, their pursuit of my actions, their cosmic pantomime, were uncanny then, whenever it began to grow dark. One of my persistent prayers to God and my guardian angel was that I not dream about mirrors. I know I watched them with misgivings. Sometimes I feared they might begin to deviate from reality; other times I was afraid of seeing there my own face, disfigured by strange calamities" (***DT*** [***Dreamtigers***], 27).

One of the earliest references to mirrors appears in the essay "After the Images" originally published in the journal *Proa* in 1924 and later included in his first book of essays, *Inquisiciones* (1925). There he says: "It is no longer enough to say, as most poets have, that mirrors look like water . . . We must overcome such games . . . There ought to be shown a person entering into the crystal and continuing in his illusory country, feeling the shame of not being but a simulacrum that night obliterates and daylight permits" (***I***, 29). This first use of mirrors as the country of simulacra appears also in his first poems. **"La Recoleta,"** from *Fervor of Buenos Aires* (1923), opens with a series of images in which mirrors are just a simile, the vehicle of a comparison which is repeated with the frequency of a linguistic tic. In that poem he says that when "the soul goes out."

> Space, time and death also go out,
> As when light is no more,
> And the simulacrum of mirrors fade . . .
>
> (*OP* [*Obra Poetica, 1923–1964*], 20)

In his first volume of poetry and in the next—***Moon Across the Way*** (1925)—mirrors are referred to merely on account of their reflective function. The city is "false and crowded / like a garden copied on a mirror." In **"El jardin botánico,"** "each tree is movingly lost / and their lives are confined and rugged / like mirrors that deepen different rooms." In **"Ausencia,"** the reflection on the mirror represents the reflected object: "I shall raise life in its immensity / which even now is your mirror: / stone over stone I shall rebuild it." In other poems, some qualities associated with mirrors are mentioned: the silence of mirrors in **"Atardeceres"**; their capacity for repetition in **"El Paseo de Julio,"** for multiplication in **"Mateo, XXV, 30,"** and for memory in **"El reloj de arena."**

These random references meet in the poem **"Mirrors"** included in ***Dreamtigers*** (1960). In many ways this poem is a recapitulation of most of the previous motifs. Borges recalls his early fears of mirrors and asks: "What whim of fate / made me so fearful of a glancing mirror." The poem is an attempt to answer that question. A first explanation is its generative power: "They prolong this hollow, unstable world / in their dizzying spider's web." Here Borges reiterates an idea advanced earlier on **"Tlón, Uqbar, Orbis Tertius."** Facing a spying mirror, Bioy Casares "recalled that one of the heresiarchs of Uqbar had declared that mirrors and copulation are abominable, because they increase the number of men" (*L* [*Luna de enfrente*], 3). And in the poem he writes:

> I see them as infinite, elemental
> Executors of an ancient pact,
> To multiply the world like the act
> Of begetting. Sleepless, Bringing doom.
>
> (*DT*, 60)

A second answer to the same question defines mirrors as "a mute theater" of reflections where "everything happens and nothing is recorded," and where the Other breaks in:

> Claudius, king of an afternoon, a dreaming king,
> Did not feel he was a dream until the day
> When an actor showed the world his crime
> In a tableau, silently in mime.
>
> (*DT*, 61)

This last stanza brings to mind that memorable idea formulated in the essay **"Partial Enchantments of the *Quixote*,"** where Borges wrote:

> Why does it make us uneasy to know that the map is within the map and the thousand and one nights are within the book of *A Thousand and One Nights?* Why does it disquiet us to know that Don Quixote is a reader of the *Quixote*, and Hamlet is a spectator of *Hamlet?* I believe I have found the answer: those inversions suggest that if the characters in a story can be readers or spectators, then we, their readers or spectators, can be fictitious.
>
> (*OI* [*Otras Inquisiciones*], 48)

In a similar fashion, the poem **"Mirrors"** concludes:

> God has created nighttime, which he arms
> With dreams, and mirrors, to make clear
> To man he is a reflection and a mere
> Vanity. Therefore these alarms.
>
> (*DT*, 61)

Here we get much closer to the ultimate meaning of mirrors in Borges' poetry. That illusory reality that mirrors produce becomes in turn a profound mirror of our own universe since our image of the world is just a fabrication of the human mind. The world as we know it is that illusory image produced on the mirror of culture, "that artificial universe in which we live as members of a social group."[2] Mirrors, like the map within the map, like Don Quixote reader of the *Quixote*, and like Hamlet spectator of *Hamlet*, suggest that our intellectual version of reality is not different from that "ungraspable architecture / reared by every dawn from the gleam / of a mirror, by darkness from a dream."

Mirrors and dreams have for Borges an interchangeable value. In the poem **"Spinoza,"** for instance, the lens grinder "dreams up a clear labyrinth— / undisturbed by fame, that reflection / of dreams in the dream of another / mirror . . .", and more explicitly in the poem **"Sarmiento"** where dreaming is tantamount to "looking at a magic crystal." Borges has pointed out that "according to the doctrine of the Idealists, the verbs *to live* and *to dream* are strictly synonyms" (*L*, 164). A more transcendental significance of mirrors in Borges' poetry should emerge, thus, from a syllogistic transposition of the terms *life, dream* and *mirror.* If *life* is a *dream* Somebody is dreaming, and dreams are, as stated in the poem **"The Dream,"** "reflections of the shadow / that daylight deforms in its *mirrors*," life is, consequently, not less illusory than the images reflected on the surface of the mirrors. In the poem **"The Golem,"** the dummy is the dream of a Rabbi who in turn is the dream of a god who in turn is the dream of another god and so on *ad infinitum* as suggested in **"The Circular Ruins."** Yet, it should be noted that the Rabbi's golem is described as "a simulacrum," as "a distressing son" and as "a symbol," and that all these terms have been used before in relation to mirrors. In the Rabbi's lamentations as he gazes on his imperfect son—"To an infinite series why was it for me / to add another symbol? To the vain / hank that is spun out in Eternity / another cause and effect, another pain?"—there is an unequivocal echo of the "multiplying and abdominable power of mirrors." On the other hand, in the poem **"Everness"** the universe is but the mirror of a total memory: God. God, in another poem entitled **"He,"** "is each of the creatures of His strange world: / the stubborn roots of the profound / cedar and the mutations of the moon." God is, in addition, "the eyes that examine / a reflection (man) and the mirror's eyes." Also Emmanuel Swedenborg knew, according to the poem so entitled, "like the Greek, that the days / of time are Eternity's mirrors."

The notion that the whole of Creation is but a reflection of a Divine power is more clearly defined in the short stories. In "The Aleph," for example, Borges writes that "for the Kabbalah, the Aleph stands for the *En Soph*, the pure and boundless godhead; it is also said that it takes the shape of a man pointing to both heaven and earth, in order to show that the lower world is the map and mirror of the higher." And, in a more condensed manner, in "The Theologians": "In the *Zohar* it is written that the higher world is a reflection of the lower," and once again in "the Zahir": "The Kabbalists understood that man is a microcosm, a symbolic mirror of the universe; according to Tennyson, everything would be." The pertinence of these quotations to our subject lies in the value conceded to reality as a reflection and the notion that such reflections contain a secret order inaccessible to men. Our reality, says Borges (our reality as codified by culture), is made of mirror images, appearances that reflect vaguely the Other, or, more precisely, as the sect of the Histrionics sustains in "The Theologians":

> To demonstrate that the earth influences heaven they invoked Matthew, and I Corinthians 13:12 ("for now we see through a glass, darkly") to demonstrate that everything we see is false. Perhaps contaminated by the Monotones, they imagined that all men are two men and that the real one is *the other*, the one in heaven. They also imagined that our acts project an inverted reflection, in such a way that if we are awake, the other sleeps, if we fornicate, the other is chaste, if we steal, the other is generous. When we die, we shall join *the other* and be him. (***L***, 123)

Borges' short stories and poems are full of characters and people searching for *the other*, for the source of the inverted reflection. Laprida, in **"Conjectural Poem,"** "who longed to be someone else" finds *the other* "in one night's mirror" when he can finally "comprehend his unsuspected true face." The idea of this life as a composite of reflections whose source is *the other* appears even more clearly in the poem devoted to López Merino's suicide included in the collection ***In Praise of Darkness*** (1969). There he says:

> The mirror awaits him.
> He will smooth back his hair, adjust his tie (as fits a
> young poet, he was always a bit of a dandy), and
> try to imagine that the other man—the one in the
> mirror—performs the actions and that he, the
> double,
> repeats them . . .
>
> (***PD*** [***In Praise of Darkness***], 41–3)

Even about himself Borges has written in the poem **"Junín"**: "I am myself but I am also the other, the dead one" (***SP*** [***Siete Poemas***], 211).

Mirrors are thus defined as the residence of the other. Life outside the mirror, by contrast, surfaces as a reflection, as a dream, and as a theater. Sometimes the reader witnesses a dialogue between the simulacrum outside the mirror and the other inside the glass. Among those poems, none has dramatized in such a definite manner that old dialogue between the two Borgeses that reverberates throughout his work as **"El centinela"** (**"The Sentry"**) included in ***El oro de los tigres*** (1972):

> Light comes in and I remember: he's there.
> He begins by telling me his name which is (clearly) mine.
> I come back to a slavery that has lasted more than seven times
> ten years.
>
> He imposes his memory on me.
> He imposes the everyday miseries, the human condition on me.
> I am his old male nurse; he forces me to wash his feet.
> He lies in wait for me in mirrors, in the mahogony, in store
> windows.
>
> One or two women have rejected him and I must share his grief.
> Now he is dictating this poem to me, which I don't like.
> He requires me to undertake the hazy apprenticeship of stubborn
> Anglo-Saxon.
>
> He has converted me to the idolatrous cult of military dead men,
> with whom I could perhaps not exchange a single word.
> On the last step of the staircase I feel that he is by my side.
>
> He is in my steps, in my voice.
> I hate him thoroughly.
> I notice with pleasure that he can barely see.
> I am in a circular cell and the infinite wall gets tighter.
> Neither of us fools the other, but we both lie.
> We know each other too well, inseparable brother.
> You drink water from my cup and you devour my bread.
> The door of suicide is open, but the theologians affirm that in
> the ulterior shadow of the other kingdom, I will be there,
> waiting for myself.[3]

The reader notices without much effort that **"The Sentry"** is a reenactment of the piece **"Borges and Myself"** from ***Dreamtigers.*** Both texts are part of an exchange between Borges the writer and Borges the man, between "a man who lives and lets himself live" and "the other who weaves his tales and poems," between one condemned to his inexorable destiny as writer and one who from the depth of a mirror paces equally inexorably toward his "secret center." In both texts the voice comes from an intimate Borges who watches the other as though one were the audience in a theater and the other an actor on stage, but whereas in the prose the exchange takes place between Borges the writer and the other who simply lives, in the poem the exchange is much less symmetric. The confrontation is not between the writer and the man. There is no confrontation, but rather reflections voiced by a person who has reached seventy and contemplates, in the manner of Kohelet, his life and the miseries of the human condition. This Borges, profoundly intimate, looks at the other as a sentry and examines this sentry's visible and public life as a fiction or a theatrical representation. To define life as a dream presupposes the notion that with death we shall wake up from that dream; to define the world as a stage implies the idea of a spectator who will applaud or boo when the show is over. Likewise, there is an obverse of the mirror that reproduces and multiplies, that dreams and gesticulates, and there is reverse from whose depths the other—the awake one and the spectator—watches us. The ultimate meaning of mirrors in Borges' poetry lies in that reverse, dwelling of the other, house of the self. **"Ars Poetica"** has masterfully expressed this meaning:

> At times in the evening a face
> Looks at us out of the depths of a mirror;
> Art should be like that mirror
> Which reveals to us our own face.
>
> (***SP***, 143)

Of the various significations that mirrors propose throughout Borges' poetry this is, beyond any doubt, the most transcending and the richest in suggestions. In a strict sense, we are dealing with the mirror of poetry as a road of access to the other, with literature as a bridge between the visible side of the mirror and the other side which poets of all times have always tried to reach. There is a mirror that "melts away, just like a bright silvery mist" so that the poet, like Lewis Carroll's Alice, may go through the glass and jump into the other side—the looking-glass room of fantasy; and to such a mirror Borges refers in the poem devoted to Edgar Allan Poe:

> As if on the wrong side of the mirror,
> He yielded, solitary, to his rich
> Fate of fabricating nightmares . . .
>
> (***SP***, 173)

But the mirror that in the last analysis Borges vindicates as a vehicle of art is the one "which reveals to us our own face." In the context of ***Dreamtiger***'s Epilogue, it is clear that the face he alludes to is a symbolic face which, like a cipher, encodes the destiny of the writer. It is this writer who "shortly before his death discovers that that patient labyrinth of lines (his writings) traces the image of his face" (***DT***, 93).

The poem **"Oedipus and the Riddle"** also adheres to this same meaning. Borges had already reviewed the myth of Oedipus and the Sphinx in *The Book of Imaginary Beings.* There he explains:

> It is told that the Sphinx depopulated the Theban countryside asking riddles and making a meal of any man who could not give the answer. Of Oedipus the Sphinx asked: "What has four legs, two legs, and three legs, and the more legs it has the weaker it is?" Oedipus answered that it was a man who as an infant crawls on all four, when he grows up walks on two legs, and in old age leans on a staff. (*BIB*, 211–12)

With these materials Borges makes his poem:

> At dawn four-footed, at midday erect,
> And wandering on three legs in the deserted
> Spaces of afternoon, thus the eternal
> Sphinx had envisioned her changing brother
> Man, and with afternoon there came a person
> Deciphering, appalled at the monstrous other
> Presence in the mirror, the reflection
> Of his decay and of his destiny.
> We are Oedipus; in some eternal way
> We are the long and threefold beast as well—
> All that we will be, all that we have been.
> It would annihilate us all to see
> The huge shape of our being; mercifully
> God offers us issue and oblivion.
>
> (***SP***, 191)

In the monstrous image of the Sphinx, Oedipus recognizes his own destiny and that of all man, and Borges adds: "It would annihilate us all to see / the huge shape of our being." But the poet inevitably looks for "the shape of his being," and his written work is but the mirror where he will see his face, and in it the total image of his fate. But such a moment, similar to a revelation, comes "shortly before death." One of Borges' most personal and intense poems, **"In Praise of Darkness,"** celebrates old age and darkness as forms of happiness; in the last lines he returns to the same idea presented in **"Oedipus and the Riddle"** but now in order to tell us that if art is "the imminence of a revelation that is not yet produced" (*OI*, 4) it is so because that last line to be traced by a hand stronger than any destiny (Death) is still missing:

> From south and east and west and north,
> roads coming together have led me
> to my secret center.
> These roads were footsteps and echoes,
> women, men, agonies, rebirths,
> days and nights,
> daydreams and dreams,
> each single moment of my yesterdays
> and the world's yesterdays,
> the firm sword of the Dane and the moon
> of the Persian,
> the deeds of the dead,
> shared love, words,
> Emerson, and snow, and so many things.
> Now I can forget them. I reach my center,
> my algebra and my key,
> my mirror.
> Soon I shall know who I am.
>
> (***PD***, 125–7)

Only with death the patient labyrinth of lines that represents the writer's work is completed; only with death the labryinth yields its key and reveals its center; and only with death it becomes possible to cross and jump into the mirror and join the other, a way of saying that only then a revelation finally occurs as the outer image from this side of the mirror encounters its counterpart on the other side, looks at the shape of his being, and discovers who he is.

Notes

1. J. L. Borges, *In Praise of Darkness* (Tr. by Norman Thomas di Giovanni). New York, Dutton, 1974, p. 10.
2. Claude Lévi-Strauss, *Arte, lenguaje, etnología* (Entrevistas de Georges Charbonnier), México, Siglo Veintiuno, 1968, pp. 131–132.
3. I thank my friend and colleague Willis Barnstone for having produced under rather unfavorable conditions this English translation of "El centinela."

Jaime Alazraki (essay date 1988)

SOURCE: "Language as a Musical Organism: Borges' Later Poetry," in *Borges and the Kabbalah: And Other Essays on His Fiction and Poetry*, Cambridge University Press, 1988, pp. 124–36.

[*In the following essay, Alazraki examines Borges's later poetry, and praises its ability to convey "verbal music."*]

From his early poems of the twenties to his later collection ***Historia de la noche*** (***A History of the Night,*** 1977), Borges' poetry has traveled a long way. It first moved from a nostalgic rediscovery of his birthplace, Buenos Aires, to a cult of his ancestors and an intimate history of his country: heroes, anti-heroes, counter-heroes. He then found that metaphysical subjects, literary artifacts, and religious myths were not unworthy material for poetry: **"The Cyclical Night," "Poem Written in a Copy of Beowulf,"** and **"The Golem"** are samples which illustrate this later period. His perception of poetry in those years could be defined, in T. S. Eliot's dictum, "not as a turning loose of emotions, but as an escape from emotion: not as the expression of personality, but as an escape from personality." A reflective and ruminative poetry. His ruminations were not about the fortunes or misfortunes of the heart, or existential angst, or the conundrum of life, but about the monuments of the imagination, and particularly those of literature: intellect as passion, culture as the true adventure, knowledge as invention. A rather selfless poetry, a poetry in which the most powerful presence of the self is found in its absence.

A grandson and great-grandson of military heroes, Borges turned his poetry into an epic exploration by evoking everything poetry can possibly evoke other than his own personal drama. In his more recent poetry this drama is defined as a lack of personal drama. Borges muses relentlessly and painfully about his life devoid of heroic violence: "Soy . . . el que no fue una espada en la guerra" (I am that who did not wield a sword in battle) "¿Yo, que padecí la vergüenza / de no haber sido aquel Fransisco Borges que murió en 1874" (I, who suffered the shame / of not having been that Francisco Borges who died in 1874) (***RP*** [***La rosa profunda***], 83).

> Estoy ciego. He cumplido los setenta;
> No soy el oriental Francisco Borges
> Que murió con dos balas en el pecho,
> Entre las agonías de los hombres,
> En el hedor de un hospital de sangre . . .
>
> (***RP***, 107)

> I am blind, and I have lived out seventy years.
> I am not Francisco Borges the Uruguayan
> who died with a brace of bullets in his breast
> among the final agonies of men
> in the death-stench of a hospital of blood . . .
>
> (***GT*** [***The Gold of Tigers***], 79)

> Soy también la memoria de una espada
>
> (***RP***, 13)

> I am also the memory of a sword
>
> (***GT***, 49)

Since he is denied a sword, he turns poetry into a sword; since epic action has been ruled out of his life, he converts poetry into an epic exercise:

> Déjame, espada, usar contigo el arte;
> Yo, que no he merecido manejarte.
>
> (***RP***, 45)

> Let me, sword, render you in art;
> I, who did not deserve to wield you.

How did he accomplish this? By effacing himself from his own poetry, by speaking of everybody but forgetting about himself. Borges has said of Bernard Shaw that "he is the only writer of our time who has imagined and presented heroes to his readers," and he explains further:

> On the whole, modern writers tend to reveal men's weaknesses and seem to delight in their unhappiness; in Shaw's case, however, we have characters who are heroic and whom one can admire. Contemporary literature since Dostoevsky—and even earlier—since Byron—seems to delight in man's guilt and weaknesses. In Shaw's work the greatest human virtues are extolled. For example, that a man can forget his own fate, that a man may not value his own happiness, that he may say like our Almafuerte: "I am not interested in my own life," because he is interested in something beyond personal circumstances.[2]

Here we find a first explanation of the seemingly impersonal quality of his poetry; yet what Borges defends is not impersonality but an epic sense of life. The poet disregards his own tribulations to become the singer of virtues, values, people, and literary works dear to him. Haunted by the memories of his ancestors' "romantic death," Borges celebrates the courage of heroes and knife fighters ready to die in defense of a cause or belief more precious than their own life. Since he is denied an epic destiny on the battlefield, he will turn literature into his own battlefield by refusing to speak about himself, by lending his voice to others. This epic attitude has been deliberate, and it stems from his family background as well as from the fact that, as he put it, "my father's library has been the capital event in my life":[3] books as events, intellection as life, past as present, literature as passion.

Until 1964. That year Borges published a sonnet entitled **"1964"** with which he inaugurated a new theme in his poetry. To what he has called his "habits"—"Buenos Aires, the cult of my ancestors, the study of old Germanic languages, the contradiction of time"[4]—he now adds his broodings over what can be called a vocation for unhappiness. The sonnet opens with the line "Ya no seré feliz. Tal vez no importa" (I shall no longer be happy. Perhaps it doesn't matter) (***OM*** [***El otro, el mismo***], 175), a motif that appears and reappears in his last four collections between 1969 and 1976,[5] and culminates in the 1976 sonnet **"Remordimiento" ("Remorse")**, included in ***La moneda de hierro*** (***The Iron Coin***):

He cometido el peor de los pecados
Que un hombre puede cometer. No he sido
Feliz. Que los glaciares del olvido
Me arrastren y me pierdan, despiadados.
Mis padres me engendraron para el juego
Arriesgado y hermoso de la vida,
Para la tierra, el agua, el aire, el fuego.
Los defruadé. No fui feliz. Cumplida
No fue su joven voluntad. Mi mente
Se aplicó a las simétricas porfías
Del arte, que entreteje naderías.
Me legaron su valor. No fui valiente.
No me abandona. Siempre está a mi lado
La sombra de haber sido un desdichado.

(***MH [La moneda de hierro***], 89)

I have committed the worst sin of all
That a man can commit. I have not been
Happy. Let the glaciers of oblivion
Drag me and mercilessly let me fall.
My parents bred and bore me for a higher
Faith in the human game of nights and days:
For earth, for air, for water, and for fire.
I let them down. I wasn't happy. My ways
Have not fulfilled their youthful hope. I gave
My mind to the symmetric stubbornness
Of art, and all its webs of pettiness.
They willed me bravery. I wasn't brave.
It never leaves my side, since I began:
This shadow of having been a brooding man.

(***MEP***, 607)

I have dealt with and elaborated on this subject,[6] and I won't repeat myself. It will suffice to say that Borges' treatment of this intimate side of his life has little to do with romantic confessionalism, or with yielding to the same weakness he earlier condemned in modern literature. If he now breaks the silence about himself and tells us about his unhappiness, he does so without self-pity, without tears or pathos, simply by acknowledging it as a fact, or rather, as a sin. The poem represents the acceptance of that sin as guilt, and throughout the poem he assumes this sin of unhappiness with the same poise and endurance with which epic heroes accept defeat. He breaks the diffidence of his previous poetry without outcries, almost restating his early selflessness, since his misfortune, his having been unhappy, is not a torment one mourns over but a sin one must accept quietly or even expiate, or perhaps sublimate in the silence of a verse. "One destiny," he wrote in "The Life of Tadeo Isidoro Cruz," "is no better than another, but every man must obey the one he carries within him" (*A*, 85). Such is the spirit of his own acceptance: a heroic stamina that welcomes triumph and adversity with equal courage.

His later collection of poems—***Historia de la noche***—adds yet new paths into the elusive territory of his intimacy. The accomplished writer, the celebrated poet, the man who welcomes love and death with equal resignation and joy, feels now that decorum could also be an expression of vanity, that modesty in the face of death is but another form of pettiness blocking total reconciliation. The circle of life closes in, unhappiness no longer matters, and a mundane virtue matters even less. Borges seeks oblivion, but since oblivion is a privilege denied to his memory, he backtracks through its meanders, paths, and deep chambers:

A veces me da miedo la memoria.
En sus cóncavas grutas y palacios
(Dijo San Agustin) hay tantas cosas.
El infierno y el cielo están en ellas.

(***HN*** [***Historia de la noche***], 87)

Sometimes I fear memory.
In its concave grottoes and palaces
(Said Saint Augustine) there are so many things.
Hell and Heaven lie there.

There is no way out of memory but death:

Soy el que sabe que no es más que un eco,
El que quiere morir enteramente.

(***HN***, 120)

I am he who knows he is but an echo,
The one who wants to die completely.

Two elements set ***Historia de la noche*** apart from his previous collections: a restrained celebration of love, and a serene acceptance of everything life brings, for better or for worse, including the imminence of death. Not that the old motifs or "habits" are missing here; they are present but in a different way. They are part of his indefatigable memory, and as such they inevitably reappear: tigers, mirrors, books, dreams, time, ancestors, friends, authors, knives, cities, and countries. The manner in which these motifs enter into the poem has changed. **"El tigre" ("The**

Tiger"), for example, is an evocation of the animal that fascinates Borges as an obsession of his childhood, for its beauty, and because it brings reverberations of Blake, Hugo, and Share Kahn. Yet the last line reads: "We thought it was bloody and beautiful. Norah, a girl, said: It is made for love" (***HN***, 35). This last line makes the difference, and gives the poem an unexpected twist. The recalled anecdote—a visit to the Palermo Zoo—was an old strand in his memory, but only now has its true momentum been recaptured, only now does the tiger's face of love surface and overshadow all previous faces to mirror the author's own. In no other book of poems has Borges allowed him self to deal with love with such freedom and with a distance which ultimately is the condition of love's magic. **"Un escolio" ("A Scholium")** offers a second example of this new theme. Borges returns to the world of Homer, and here too, as in previous poems, he chooses Ulysses' homecoming to Ithaca as one of the four stories that, he believes, comprise everything literature could ever tell. It appears in the brief prose piece "Los cuatro ciclos" ("The Four Cycles") from ***The Gold of the Tigers***, where Borges comments: "Four are the stories. During the time left to us, we'll keep telling them, transformed" (***OT*** [El oro de los tigres], 130). The story first appears in one of his most successful early poems, **"Ars Poetica,"** as a metaphor for art:

> They say that Ulysses, sated with marvels,
> Wept tears of love at the sight of his Ithaca,
> Green and humble. Art is that Ithaca
> Of green eternity, not of marvels.
>
> (***SP***, 143)

Four years later, in the collection ***El otro, el mismo*** (***The Self and the Other,*** 1964), Borges turned the episode into a sonnet, **"Odyssey, Book Twenty-Three,"** but the emphasis is now on the unpredictability of fate. In **"A Scholium,"** on the other hand, the story becomes a love poem. Borges chooses the moment when the queen "saw herself in his eyes, when she felt in her love that she was met by Ulysses' love" (***HN***, 47). In each of the four versions of the story, one witnesses a switch of emphasis and preference: in the first, the focus is on the notion that literature is "the history of the diverse intonations of a few metaphors" (***OI***, 8); in the second, Ulysses' return to Ithaca is seen as a metaphor for art; the third captures the idea that "any life, no matter how long or complex it may be, is made up essentially of a *single moment*—the moment in which a man finds out, once and for all, who he is" (***A***, 83); and in the fourth, the accent is on love as an inviolable common secret. But the last version reveals also that the old metaphor has become Borges' own metaphor, because what the last poem underlines is the nature of love as a secret bond, as an unwritten pact expressing itself through its own code: "Penelope does not dare to recognize him, and to test him she alludes to a secret they alone share: their common thalamus that no mortal can move, because the olive tree from which it was carved ties it down to earth" (***HN***, 47). Borges chooses allusion as the language of love, but allusion also as the literary language he prefers. In the same prose poem, he adds: "Homer did not ignore that things should be said in an indirect manner. Neither did the Greeks, whose natural language was myth." What we have here, therefore, is a double metaphor. Penelope resorts to allusion to communicate with Ulysses; Borges, in turn, alludes to Homer's story to communicate his own perception of love. The thalamus as the metaphor for Penelope's love becomes the metaphor Borges conjures up to convey his own feelings about love. It is worth pausing on this aspect of his art. Not only because this example dramatizes an all too well known device of his writing—the Chinese box structure to which he subjects much of his fiction and poetry—but because this last volume of poems further refines that device to the point of perfection. In the epilogue to ***Historia de la noche***, he offers a possible definition of this literary artifice:

> Any event—an observation, a farewell, an encounter, one of those curious arabesques in which chance delights—can stir esthetic emotions. The poet's task is to project that emotion, which was intimate, in a fable or in a cadence. The material at his disposal, language, is, as Stevenson remarks, absurdly inadequate. What can we do with worn out words—with Francis Bacon's *Idola Fori*—, and with a few rhetorical artifices found in the manuals? On first sight, nothing or very little. And yet, a page by Stevenson himself or a line by Seneca is sufficient to prove that the undertaking is not always impossible.
>
> (***HN***, 139)

Borges, who in his early writings held that "unreality is the necessary condition of art," knows only too well that literature, and art in general, as Paul Klee once said, "is different from external life, and it must be organized differently." What Borges restates in the epilogue is his old belief that "since Homer all valid metaphors have been written down," and the writer's task is not to write new ones but to rewrite the old ones, or rather to translate them into his own language, time, and circumstance, very much in the way the nineteenth-century symbolist writer, Pierre Menard, undertook the rewriting of the *Quixote*. The creative act lies, then, not so much in the invention of new fables as in their transformation into vehicles of new content, in the conversion of an old language into a new one. Borges retells Ulysses' story of his return to Ithaca, but in each of his four versions a new perception has been conveyed.

The same principle can be applied to his other "fables." He keeps repeating them, as he himself has acknowledged, but it is a repetition of the materials, not of their substance. There is no escape from that "absurdly inadequate" tool—language—yet with those same trite words the poet shapes the uniqueness of his emotion. **"Gunnar Thorgilsson"** offers a third example of this outlook on literature which sees in the new a derivation from the old: Iceland, which appears and reappears in Borges' poetry, is evoked once more, but now the focus is not on the ship or the sword of the sagas, but on the wake and the wound of love. The poem concludes simply: "I want to remember that kiss / You gave me in Iceland" (***HN***, 59). **"El enamo-**

rado" (**"The Lover"**) and **"La espera"** (**"The Waiting"**) are also love poems in which Borges tersely reviews some of his literary habits—moons, roses, numbers, seas, time, tigers, swords—but they are now shadows which vanish to uncover the only presence that truly counts:

> Debo fingir que hay otros. Es mentira.
> Sólo tú eres. Tú, mi desventura
> Y mi ventura, inagotable y pura.
>
> (*HN*, 95)

> I should feign that there are others. It's a lie.
> Only you exist. You, my misfortune
> And my fortune, inexhaustible and pure.

If literature is, as Borges once wrote, "essentially a syntactic fact," it is clear that his latest volume of poetry should be assessed not for whatever is new at the level of theme (love being the thematic novelty), but by how he succeeds in bestowing on old subjects a new intensity and a rekindled poetic strength. The reader of his last collection can find here the vertex of his new achievement.

Those of us who have been closely following Borges' poetry of the last ten years have witnessed several changes in his voice. His earliest poems strove to convey a conversational tone. They were a dialogue with the familiar city, its myths and landscapes, sometimes bearing Whitmanesque overtones. To emphasize that intimate and nostalgic accent, he often used free verse, local words, and Argentine slang. Then when he "went from myths of the outlying slums of the city to games with time and infinity" (*A*, 152), he opted for more traditional meters and stanzaic forms. This alone conferred a certain stilted inflection on his poetic voice. Rhymes were strong and at times even a bit hammering (Scholem was made to rhyme with Golem). He brought the hendecasyllable and the sonnet to new heights, stimulated undoubtedly by his advanced blindness. In spite of this sculptural perfection, there was still a declamatory falsetto in his voice that was particularly apparent when he read (or rather recited) aloud his own poetry. It goes without saying that this stiffness, however slight, disappeared in his best poems. In 1969, five years after his previous collection ***El otro, el mismo,*** he published ***In Praise of Darkness.*** With this volume Borges freed his verse from any linguistic slag. The sonnet, the form he has been using most frequently since, bordered on perfection: these sonnets are masterfully carved, with chiseled smoothness and a quiet flow that turns them into verbal music.

Poetry as music has always been to Borges a crystallizing point at which language succeeds in bringing forth its melodic core. This is not a music produced by sound; the poem turns words into a transparent surface which reveals a certain cadence, a harmony buried under the opacities of language, much in the same manner as music rescues a privileged order of sound and silence from a chaotic mass of sounds. In the prologue to the collection ***El otro, el mismo***, he has explained this understanding of poetry:

> On occasion, I have been tempted into trying to adapt to Spanish the music of English or of German: had I been able to carry out that perhaps impossible adventure, I would be a great poet, like Garcilaso, who gave us the music of Italy, or like the anonymous Sevillian poet who gave us the music of Rome, or like Dario, who gave us that of Verlaine and Hugo. I never went beyond rough drafts, woven of words of few syllables, which very wisely I destroyed. (*SP*, 279)

My contention is that Borges, whose "destiny"—as he put it—"is in the Spanish language" (*GT*, 31), has found in his most recent poetry not the music of English or German or of any other poet, but his own voice, and through it a music the Spanish language did not know before him. Not that Spanish did not produce great poets. It certainly did, and each of them represents an effort to strike a different chord of that musical instrument language becomes at the best moments of its poetry. One has only to think of Jorge Guillén as a definite virtuoso of that instrument, as a poet whose voice has given to Spanish some of the most luminous and joyous movements of its hidden music. Like Borges, Jorge Guillén has sought through his work to touch that musical kernel contained in language very much the way brandy is contained in the residual marc. For Borges, as for Guillén, poetry is a form of linguistic distillation.[7]

In ***Historia de la noche,*** there is hardly a subject or motif that has not been dealt with in his previous collections, love being the exception. **"Ni siquiera soy polvo"** (**"I Am Not Even Dust"**), which deals with the trinity Cervantes-Alonso-Don-Quixote as a dream-within-a-dream-within-a-dream, is a variation on a theme previously treated in **"Parable of Cervantes and Don Quixote"** (***Dreamtigers***) and in **"Alonso Quijano Dreams"** (***The Unending Rose***). **"The Mirror"** returns to his old obsession with mirrors first recorded in the short piece **"The Draped Mirrors"** (***Dreamtigers***), and then meticulously explored in the thirteen quatrains of **"The Mirrors"** (***El otro, el mismo***). The same could be said of **"Lions"** vis à vis **"The Other Tiger," "Dreamtigers,"** and **"The Gold of the Tigers."** Or **"Iceland"** as a new avatar of **"To Iceland"** (***The Gold of the Tigers***). Or **"Milonga del forastero,"** which is a sort of Platonic summation of all his other *milongas.* But precisely because Borges returns to his old subjects (he once stated: "A poet does not write about what he wants but about what he can"), the subject matters less than the voice. Furthermore: the voice is the subject.

In this last collection Borges further refines a device first developed in **"Another Poem of Gifts"**: the poem as a long list, listing as a poetic exercise. **"Metaphors of the Arabian Nights," "Lions," "Things That Might Have Been," "The Lover,"** and **"The Causes"** follow this pattern. The device accentuates the magic character of poetry as a voice speaking in the dark, words reaching out for meanings that are beyond words. What is left is a music that speaks from its innumerable variations, but the variations are not repetitions. They are, as in the art of the fugue, new versions of the same tune, and in each variation the theme is further explored, condensed, and simplified, until it becomes so transparent that one sees the bottom, the poet's deepest voice, a face free of masks, a certain essence that more than saying, sings. It is as if Borges had put behind him his old habits as themes to focus on the tones and inflections of his own voice; and what that voice expresses is a serenity, a calm not heard in the Spanish language since Juan de la Cruz or Luis de León. Borges must have felt that he was nearing that shore of harmony glimpsed by the mystical poets. In the last poem of the collection, **"A History of the Night,"** he wrote referring to the night: "Luis de León saw it in the country / of his staggered soul." Yet the soul that surfaces from Borges' last poems is not one pierced by divine emotion, but a fulfilled and resigned soul that can see life as a river of "invulnerable water," an earthy soul anchored in life and yet unfearful of death, one that can look upon life from a timeless island against whose shores time breaks and recedes like sea waves:

"Adán es tu ceniza"

La espada morirá como el racimo.
El cristal no es más frágil que la roca.
Las cosas son su porvenir de polvo.
El hierro es el orín. La voz, el eco.
Adán, el joven padre, es tu ceniza.
El último jardín será el primero.
El ruiseñor y Píndaro son voces.
La aurora es el reflejo del ocaso.
El micenio, la máscara del oro.
El alto muro, la ultrajada ruina.
Urquiza, lo que dejan los puñales.
El rostro que se mira en el espejo
No es el de ayer. La noche lo ha gastado.
El delicado tiempo nos modela.

Qué dicha ser el agua invulnerable
Que corre en la parábola de Heraclito
O el intrincado fuego, pero ahora,
En este largo día que no pasa,
Me siento duradero y desvalido.

(***HN*** 131)

"Adam Is Your Ash"

The sword will die like the vine.
Crystal is no weaker than rock.
Things are their own future in dust.
Iron is rust, the voice an echo.
Adam, the young father, is your ash.
The last garden will be the first.
The nightingale and Pindar are voices.
Dawn is the reflection of sunset.
The Mycenaean is the gold mask.
The high wall, the plundered ruin.
Urquiza, what daggers leave behind.
The face looking at itself in the mirror
Is not yesterday's. Night has wasted it.
Delicate time is shaping us.

What joy to be the invulnerable water
Flowing in Heraclitus's parable
Or intricate fire, but now, midway
Through this long day that does not end,
I feel enduring and helpless.

(trans. Willis Barnstone)

A restatement of his famous line "Time is the substance I am made of. It is a river that carries me away, but I am the river" (*OI*, 197). Now, however, the same idea flows without the lapidary sententiousness of the essay; simply, with ease and resolution, unconcerned with rejections or acceptances, free of outcomes or outcries, a meditative voice reconciled with life, accepting its gifts and losses with the same acquiescent gesture.

In the poem **"The Causes,"** Borges goes through an inventory of mementoes from history, literature, and life. The list encompasses some of the most memorable moments of his own poetry and becomes a sort of miniature of his poetic *oeuvre*. The poem closes with two equally compressed lines: "All those things were needed / so that our hands could meet" (***HN***, 128), a masterful coda that renders his tight survey of motifs into a love poem. This is the surface, however impeccable, of the text, its outer meaning. But what the text also says, between the lines, is that its laconic eloquence, terse to the point of diaphaneity, is sustained by sixty long years of poetic creation, the understated notion being: all those poems were needed so that this one could be written. The idea appears at the end of one of his most relaxed and subtly personal short stories, "Averroes' Search" (1947): "I felt, on the last page, that my narration was a symbol of the man I was as I wrote it and that, in order to compose that narration, I had to be that man and, in order to be that man, I had to compose that narration, and so on to infinity" (*L [Labryrinths*], 155). Literature, as well as life, as an inexorable concatenation of causes and effects; each poem as a stepping stone toward the poem; the poem as a symbol of the poet: in order to write this poem I had to write all the others; in order to write this poem I had to be the man I was. But this last poem does not form a circle with the others, it is rather the answer to the others, a sort of prism that reintegrates the dispersed shades of his poetry into one text, and this text gleams like a single beam of white light with a radiant simplicity that none of the individual texts had. With ***Historia de la noche*** Borges' poetry has found an equilibrium that undoubtedly conveys his own inner serenity; but this serenity, being a linguistic externalization, is also a song through which the Spanish language voices a music unheard before: an austere, poised, dignified, and quiet music:

Soy el que no conoce otro consuelo
Que recordar el tiempo de la dicha.
Soy a veces la dicha inmerecida.
Soy el que sabe que no es más que un eco,
El que quiere morir enteramente.

(***HN***, 119–20)

I am one who knows no other consolation
Than remembering the time of joy,
I am at times unmerited joy,

I am one who knows he is only an echo,
One who wants to die totally.

(trans. Willis Barnstone)

The young poet who once delighted in the exhilaration of his own performance has been left far behind. The voice we hear now is that of a consummate musician who has achieved total mastery over his medium. The music we hear now is that of the Spanish language attuned to its own registers, and that of a poet skillfully true to his own perceptions.

Notes

1. Jorge Luis Borges, *La rosa profunda* (Buenos Aires: Emecé, 1975), p. 53; *The Gold of the Tigers; Selected Later Poems*, trans. A. Reid (New York: E. P. Dutton, 1977), p. 63. When English translations have been available, I have indicated the source; when unavailable, I have provided my own.
2. Rita Guibert, *Seven Voices* (New York: Vintage, 1973), p. 98.
3. J. L. B., Epilogue to *Historia de la noche,* p. 140.
4. J. L. B., *Selected Poems*, p. 278.
5. They are *Elogio de la sombra (In Praise of Darkness),* 1969; *El oro de los tigres (The Gold of the Tigers)* 1972; *La rosa profunda* (The Unending Rose), 1975; and *La moneda de hierro* (The Iron Coin), 1976.
6. In my essay "Borges o el dificil oficio de la intimidad: reflexiones sobre su poesía más reciente", *Revista Iberoamericana* XLIII, 100–101 (julio-diciembre 1977), pp. 449–463.
7. Borges has written on this subject:

   Pater wrote that all arts aspire to the condition of music, perhaps because in music meaning is form, since we are unable to recount a melody the way we can recount the plot of a story. Poetry, if we accept this statement, would be a hybrid art—the reduction of a set of abstract symbols, language, to musical ends. Dictionaries are to blame for this erroneous idea, for, as we seem to forget, they are artificial repositories, evolved long after the languages they explain. The roots of language are irrational and of a magical nature. The Dane who uttered the name of Thor or the Saxon who uttered the name of Thunor did not know whether these words stood for the gods of thunder or for the noise that follows the lightning. Poetry tries to recapture that ancient magic. Without set rules, it works in a hesitant, daring manner, as if advancing in darkness.

   (*SP*, 279–80).

Marcelo Abadi (essay date 1989)

SOURCE: "Spinoza in Borges' Looking-Glass," translated by Leila Yael, Borges Studies on Line. J. L. Borges Center for Studies & Documentation. January 13, 2000. Retrieved March 30, 2000, from http://www.hum.au.dk/romansk/borges/bsol/abadi.htm.

[*In the following essay, Abadi discusses the influence of the philosopher Spinoza on Borge's poetry, focusing on his sonnets "Spinoza," and "Baruch Spinoza."*]

In the same tongue in which Spinoza refuted the Jewish authorities who brought about his expulsion from the Amsterdam Synagogue, three centuries later an Argentinean writer, long since blind, dictated a sonnet entitled **"Baruch Spinoza"**. Some years earlier he had dictated another sonnet, called, simply, **"Spinoza"**. The poet—Jorge Luis Borges, of course—is one of the most prominent writers in any tongue. He produced no famous novel, no successful play, he created no character comparable to Don Quixote, or Hamlet, or even Father Brown. But in his poems, stories and essays our century can detect a voice that stirs the dormant wonder which, according to the Greeks, lies at the source of the love of knowledge and wisdom.

Borges claimed to be "simply a man of letters"[1]; in private he had described himself as a "puzzled literary man". Yet, though he never purported to be a philosopher, the stuff of his creation is often philosophical: the riddles on which the mind dwells while pondering problems such as the reality of the external world, the identity of the self, the nature of time.

The Vienna Circle held metaphysics to be a branch of fantastical literature. Borges shared this view, referring ironically but also appreciatively to metaphysics and enumerating among the masters of the genre authors such as Plato, Leibniz, Kant . . . and Spinoza, whose invention of an infinite substance with infinite attributes he considered a superb fiction.

Borges, admitting that he appraised philosophical ideas according to their aesthetic value or inasmuch as their content were singular or marvellous, never led his readers to expect a style of rigorous demonstration or sustained coherence, which is not to be found in his writings. Nevertheless, one should not hasten to conclude that he was indifferent to truth; he felt there is ultimately a close solidarity between beauty, truth and good. And if he did express deep-rooted scepticism, it was scepticism that spurred his vigilant quest.

But Spinoza deemed his own philosophy to be the true one. In his system there was no place for doubt, not even the provisory doubt of Descartes.

What, then, was the message that three centuries after his death the Dutch philosopher conveyed to the Argentinean man of letters? How is the doctrine of Spinoza to be read in the works of Borges?

In *A Borges Dictionary*,[2] the entry on Spinoza calls attention to echoes of his geometrical method of deduction of reality in **"Death and the Compass"** (a rigorous detective story where the name of the philosopher appears as a clue) or, too, in **"Tlön, Uqbar Orbis Tertius",** where a fictitious planet is developed, foreshadowed by a pronouncement to the effect that copulation and mirrors are abominable because they multiply the visible universe. And, of course, Spinoza's name appears in this story also, though the narrator points out that in Tlön only thought—not thought and extension—would be conceivable as a divine attribute (which is indeed a recurrent idea of Borges'). We should, however, not overestimate these allusions. Borges' imagination is certainly less akin to Spinoza's doctrine than to Berkeley, Hume, Schopenhauer, Bradley or Mauthner, whose influence is often acknowledged by the author himself and by critics. We would rather underline the fact that in hardly any of Borges' numerous works written in collaboration—some of which are quite philosophical—does Spinoza's name appear. On the other hand, Borges did write two poems on Spinoza but none on the other philosophers mentioned. It would seem that there is something secret, or at least private, about the relationship.

And surely this is not due solely to the fact that Spinoza was deeply admired by Borges' father—a professor of psychology, at times a writer—who initiated his son into literature and metaphysics and, most certainly, into freethinking, in a sometimes ostensibly religious country.

It is therefore only natural to focus on Borges' poems on Spinoza, follow their development and attempt to understand the differences between them, as we listen to the age-old dialogue between poetry and philosophy.

The first sonnet, "Spinoza", is to be found in a collection of poems called ***El otro, el mismo*** (***The other, the same***), which appeared in 1964. It is a beautiful poem, and Borges, who often pretended to forget his own writings, enjoyed reciting it to whomever asked him about it. More than ten years later, he was requested to contribute to a volume on Spinoza which the Jewish Museum of Buenos Aires was preparing in commemoration of the tricentenary of the philosopher's death.[3] Borges composed a new sonnet: this time the name was **"Baruch Spinoza."**

In the prologue to ***El otro, el mismo***, Borges made fun of his "habit of writing the same page twice over, with minimal changes", generally resulting, in his own opinion, in a somewhat inferior second version. And in the prologue to ***La moneda de hierro*** (***The Iron Coin***), where the second sonnet on Spinoza was included, he refers to it as a probable worsening of the first poem. So that when, years later, in answer to a journalist's query as to his favourite compositions, he mentioned **"Everness"** and "one on Spinoza,"[4] it is tempting to conclude that he was referring to the first sonnet of the two. Which is quite possible, but perhaps unfair.

I should imagine that Borges laid value on the fact that—surprisingly enough—the first sonnet expresses Spinoza's doctrine more accurately than the second, which is a looser rendering and certainly a more fictionalized interpretation of Spinoza's endeavour. I say surprisingly enough, because the second sonnet was composed after a period in which Borges undertook a thorough study of Spinoza's works, read about them (particularly in Alain and Russell), and resolved to write a book which was to be entitled *Clave de Spinoza* or *Clave de Baruch Spinoza* ("Key to Spinoza", or "Key to Baruch Spinoza"). This project even appears as having been accomplished, in the playfully bogus biography of himself to be found in the *Enciclopedia Sudamericana* of the year 2074 which he "quotes" in the Epilogue of his ***Obras completas***[5] (***Collected Works***). In Mexico, conversing with Ruffinelli, he avowed, "I am preparing a book on Spinoza's philosophy, because I have never understood him. He has always attracted me, less than Berkeley, less than Schopenhauer, but I cannot understand Spinoza."[6]

Now, is it true that Borges could not grasp Spinoza's philosophy? Did he understand it after resuming his studies of it? And was the book—that cipher of Spinoza more than once announced but never written—finally condensed into the fourteen lines of the second sonnet?

Let us turn to the first one. It is known that after his expulsion from the Synagogue, Spinoza had to leave Amsterdam for a sort of exile in exile, never renouncing his convictions nor embracing a new faith. In order to safeguard his proud independence, he refused, to the end of his relatively short life, chairs, pensions and honours. He preferred to make a living by polishing lenses, and this is how the first lines of the sonnet portray him:

> Las traslúcidas manos del judío
> Labran en la penumbra los cristales.
>
> [The Jew's translucent hands
> Polish the crystal lenses in the half-light.]

The lenses symbolize Spinoza's days and works; one might say they also illustrate—more definitely so in the last verses of the sonnet—a central trait in Modern philosophy, which never ceased to conceive of the human mind as a mirror upon whose fidelity depends the accuracy of whatever knowledge of reality may be achieved.[7]

But Modern rationalism and empiricism both had to contend with the prejudices of the revealed religions in order to ensure the constructing of science. And the struggle was not always bloodless: it often led to isolation and silence, persecution and burning at the stake. Small wonder, then, that a sinister theme should emerge immediately in the sonnet in the shape of fear and monotony:

> Y la tarde que muere es miedo y frío.
> (Las tardes a las tardes son iguales.)
>
> [And the dying dusk is fear and chill.
> (The twilight hours are all alike.)]

However, neither fear nor monotony perturb the thinker:

> Las manos y el espacio de jacinto
> Que palidece en el confín del Ghetto

Casi no existen para el hombre quieto
Que está soñando un claro laberinto.

[The hands and the hyacinth air
That pales towards the confines of the Ghetto
Barely exist for the quiet man
Who is dreaming up a clear labyrinth.]

Most singular, this labyrinth dreamt up by Spinoza. In the sad dusk it is a light, perhaps the way. It is clear as the hand-polished crystal the dreamer transforms into lenses or as the text the poet was to evolve centuries later out of his own brave darkness.

A "clear labyrinth": I wonder whether the expression is strictly an oxymoron. Actually, Borges' labyrinths do not always cause despair; some there are, infinite and formless, where a man may lose his way and die; others, like the world at times, are the scene of solitude and boredom, but, then again, the scene of deeds of valour guided by love, and there are yet those that constitute a secret order towards which nostalgia is drawn and hope will strive. In 1984, from Knossos, Borges writes, "It is our precious duty to imagine that there is a labyrinth and a thread. We shall never come upon the thread. We may grasp at it and lose it in an act of faith, in a cadence, in dream, in the words we call philosophy, or in plain and simple happiness."[8]

In the first tercet on Spinoza we learn that

No lo turba la fama, ese reflejo
De sueños en el sueño de otro espejo,
Ni el temeroso amor de las doncellas.

[He is not disturbed by fame, that reflection
Of dreams within the dream of another mirror,
Nor by the timorous love of maidens.]

How could Borges fail to admire the outcast for whom his father, Jorge Guillermo Borges, had felt such devotion, the exiled philosopher who had committed himself to the passion of understanding, while declining honours and braving insecurity?

Spinoza had cast off vanity and illusion, if ever he had been burdened by them, and had scaled the heights of the unadorned essence of his calling. Now,

Libre de la metáfora y del mito

[Free from metaphor and myth],

for he has no craving to dazzle with rhetorical devices, and has banished from knowledge the finalism that remits man to belief in supernatural beings,

Labra un arduo cristal: el infinito
Mapa de Aquél que es todas Sus Estrellas.

[He grinds an arduous crystal: the infinite
Map of the One who is all His stars.]

The dusk has died away. Suddenly in the darkness a refulgent crystal, like the vertiginous Aleph, shines with the radiance of all the stars. Infinity has been tamed by a memorable creation, a map of the universe which is also the map of God.

Why this equation? Because for Spinoza there is only one substance: God or Nature. Whether or not this scandalous identification was the reason for his excommunication, it is the notorious starting point of the *Ethica ordine geometrico demonstrata*, which, for obvious reasons, was published only after his death.

Descartes, whom Spinoza had studied and commentated, moves from the self and its ignorance to eventually apprehend the existence of God and to attain knowledge of the world. Spinoza, on the other hand, starts from the 'cause of itself' (*causa sui*), which is God. And Spinoza's divinity is not the personal and transcendent creator God of revealed religion, nor is it a being superior to ourselves and outside the order of nature, nor yet a Being who shows indignation, feels compassion, works miracles or causes His son to die for our salvation. *Deus sive natura*, says Spinoza: God, that is Nature. God is the only reality; outside God there is nothing. But, then, Nature is the only substance and outside Nature there is nothing. This explains why, from the time his doctrine came to be known, Spinoza has been considered by some to be an inspired pantheist, the philosopher "drunk with God" that Novalis evokes, whereas others see him as the "prince of atheists", the stubborn naturalist who acknowledges none other than the physical order. At any rate, in Spinozism, science has no need to refer to any supernatural order whatsoever, man is not a fracture in Being and may attain salvation through philosophy, and, furthermore, the State should not be subordinate to religion.[9]

In Borges' story La escritura de Dios (The Writing of God), the magus Tzinacán, the narrator and protagonist, when relating his ecstasy, defines it as "union with divinity, with the universe" and adds, in parentheses, "I don't know that these words differ". Does Tzinacán's (Borges') thought coincide here with that of the *Ethics?* Yes and no. Yes, because he proclaims the identicality of God and Nature. No, because these equatable realities are in fact mere words: "I don't know that these words differ."[10] And Borges well knows that words do not touch the hardcore of reality, that no language is the map of the world, the cipher of the universe or of a life.

This melancholy conviction, which fissures the edifice of classical rationalism, pervades the second sonnet, the one entitled **"Baruch Spinoza."** Shortly prior to composing it, as we have said, Borges had applied himself to a diligent study of Spinoza's works, which was to prelude a book on the philosopher. One of the conclusions this study had led to—presaged, no doubt, by his inveterate repudiation of all systematic thinking—was expressed in an interview some years later.[11] On this occasion Borges averred that the geometrical form of the *Ethics*, far from being essential to Spinoza's doctrine, was not even appropriate to its exposition. He affirmed that Spinoza "had not originally conceived the book in this manner . . . Only later did he endow it with this absurd machinery" Moreover, "he chose this mechanism mistakenly". Borges deplored this, since he believed that the content of the *Ethics* could have been expounded without recourse to such a mechanism, just as Spinoza had expressed it in letters to his friends, which were "most readable and lovely."[12]

The author of the *Ethics* had intended this work to be impersonal: alone the voice of reason, with the characteristic timbre it had acquired from Galileo and Descartes, was to be audible in its development; no affectivity whatsoever should resound, however indirectly. But Borges—whose own poetry, while often purporting to be objective, springs from subterraneous emotion—discovered, behind the screen of axioms, demonstrations and corollaries, a poignant figure: the sad, tenacious, intrepid Baruch. And the sonnet **"Baruch Spinoza"** begins by presenting him faced with the infinite task that he has assigned himself or that has singled him out among all the men of his times:

Bruma de oro, el occidente alumbra
La ventana. El asiduo manuscrito.
Aguarda, ya cargado de infinito.
Alguien construye a Dios en la penumbra.

[A golden haze, the west glows
Through the window. The assiduous manuscript
Awaits, already laden with infinity.
Someone is constructing God in the fading light.]

It is the same time of evening, probably in the same surroundings suggested in the sonnet **"Spinoza".** But the crystal transparency of the lenses is not evoked; only a window glows in the last rays of the setting sun. And there, alone, sits Baruch constraining himself to write out infinity.

The greatness of Spinoza's task is already apparent; so, too, is his glorious, inevitable failure. Clearly, the aim outlined in the first sonnet was far from modest, or even attainable: the philosopher had set himself no less than to facetting a diamond that would reflect God, or to drawing an infinite map of the universe. But in **"Baruch Spinoza"** ambition is directed, perhaps by its own logic, towards another, higher order of endeavour: this God, this universe, is to be carved out of the coarse stuff of language, none the more polished for all its geometrical form.

Un hombre engendra a Dios. Es un judío
De tristes ojos y piel cetrina;
Lo lleva el tiempo como lleva el río
Una hoja en el agua que declina.

[A man is begetting God. He is a Jew
With sad eyes and sallow skin;
Time bears him along as a river bears
A leaf on the downward flow.]

A toy in the river of time—a plaything, like the autumn leaf or the sheet of paper reverberant with the incipient poem—Spinoza does not bemoan, as does the Heine of another of Borges' poems,[13] the "fate of being a man and being a Jew". The one lay prostrate, recalling the "delicate melodies" he had instrumented; the other obstinately crafted a"delicate geometry". The third quatrain of this Elizabethan sonnet goes on to say:

No importa. El hechicero insiste y labra
A Dios con geometría delicada;
Desde su enfermedad, desde su nada,
Sigue erigiendo a Dios con la palabra.

[No matter. The wizard persists and fashions
God with delicate geometry;
Out of his infirmity, out of his nothingness,
He continues to erect God with the word.]

Galileo had observed that the world is a book written in mathematical characters. Borges' metaphysician, having learnt to read—and to write—these characters, could legitimately nourish more ambitious or more feasible projects than those devised by the alchemist, or by the Prague Rabbi who engendered the Golem, the senseless mannequin barely good for sweeping out the Synagogue.[14] And yet, the terms used by Borges evoke magic, the Kabbala, dreams, perchance literary creation.

Borges belittled the geometrical form of demonstration of the *Ethics*, showing scanty regard for its mathematical, Cartesian inspiration. The analytical geometry discovered by Descartes is reduced to a "delicate geometry", which in turn refers back to a verbal art. Spinoza is creating God out of the word, as the poet creates the text. This word, Borges says, is uttered by the philosopher "out of his infirmity". And perhaps nothing is farther from this idea than the view Spinoza held of himself and man in the world. While Novalis will consider life as an "infirmity of the spirit", while Pascal was dismayed by "the eternal silence of the infinite spaces", man according to Spinoza participates fully in being; no room is left for any sense of helplessness in the heliocentric universe proposed by Modern science.[15]

It is true that Descartes took an interest in magic in his youth, and true, too, that as a young man Spinoza studied the Kabbala, the mystics and the poets and was also contemporary with Pascal. But of all this there remains in the *Ethics* much less than what these last lines we have quoted might suggest. On the other hand, in the Fifth Part and referring to God, we do find the none too theistic idea expressed in the final couplet of the sonnet:

El más pródigo amor le fue otorgado,
El amor que no espera ser amado.

[Love most prodigal was granted him,
The love that never expects to be loved.]

It was not Spinoza's intention to forge a God, but to discover, deduce, an order which is the order of the unique reality or that of its only two attributes known to us: extension and thought.[16]

His conception of the unity of nature is not the same as the one born of Renaissance enthusiasm, but rather the revigorating gesture that asserts scientific optimism while rationally satisfying all man's longings and while requiring a society in which man may reveal himself freely.

Spinoza's God, as Borges recalled in another text, "abhors no one and loves no one."[17] How then would Spinoza expect His love? Are not his declarations to this effect, above all, a way of underscoring the completely impersonal nature of this God of the *Ethics*?

Perhaps what Borges in turn exhalts, at the close of this sonnet, is a norm akin to the one he finds and values in Robert L. Stevenson, which proclaims that man must be just, whether God be just or not and whether God exist or not.[18] Likewise the poet must "work at the incorruptible verse,"[19] though the material at hand be perishable.

Spinoza as portrayed in the second sonnet is stripped of his geometrical armour; his formulations are not the inexorable deduction of reality: reason is an art of the word and there is nothing to warrant any deep correspondence between this art and the world.

Nevertheless, in 1979, on being asked to name his favourite historical character, Borges unhesitatingly answered, "Spinoza, who committed his life to abstract thought."[20] It is evident then that in composing **"Baruch Spinoza"** it was not his intention to present the philosopher as a mythmaker who fabulizes a God promptly to be vaunted as the only and uncreated reality.

Neither should this sonnet be read as formal tribute rendered in deference to a distant thinker nor yet as a mere critique of a conceptual system. Rather does the poem mark the author's encounter, in the labyrinth of the world and of ideas, with an old fellow-adventurer, an ally, a friend.

Despite his claims to the contrary, I believe that Borges had always understood the architecture of the edifice erected by Spinoza, but never deemed it inhabitable by man, conducive to attaining indubitable knowledge, or to experiencing a kind of eternity, to salvation.

He was sensitive to the philosopher's deep yearnings, but disbelieved the algorithmic spells summoned up to satisfy them. The studies he undertook prior to composing the second poem annotated led him to demythologise the mathemathical apparatus of the *Ethics*, to view its author, ultimately, as "simply a man of letters" and to strengthen his own misgivings. They did not, however, undermine the admiration his father had passed on to him; they only altered the affective quality of this sentiment, guiding it more closely to the thinker, the laborious, mystical freethinker, than towards the systematic result of his thought. Thus, one might say that the first sonnet is truly, and not only by virtue of its title, the poetical exposition of a quasi classical Spinoza by Borges, while the second is, no less truly, the evocation of an intimate, lovable Baruch by Jorge Luis.

In later years, Borges was to insist on his incapacity to apprehend Spinoza's doctrine.[21] Or else he would say that he could understand it, but that this doctrine constitutes a religion, not a system, and that its author should be considered a saint.[22]

Albeit, to the end of his life in 1986, Borges was wont to answer questions on Spinoza (after he became blind, answering questions was one of the ways he most used to avoid writing, or, perhaps, in order to write) with a strong feeling of admiration. I suppose he felt that the finest creation of the *Ethics* was its very author. The *Ethics* may prove not to attain Truth, or the Absolute, but it mirrors the gaze that seeks them regardless of menaces, disdaining fame and riches. Baruch, not God, is construed by the architecture of the *Ethics*. And history teaches us that he existed and lived up to his ideas.

Most certainly, Borges admired the audacity of Spinoza's philosophical intention (invention) and adhered to many of its religious,[23] ethical and social implications. But, above all, he perceived in the thinker's life the acceptance of a cogent intellectual passion and saw perhaps in that life an image of his own existence, entirely committed to an unquestioned literary destiny.

Notes

1. Carlos Cortínez (ed.), *Simply a Man of Letters*, Orono, 1982
2. *A Borges Dictionary*, by Evelyn Fishburn and Psiche Burns. Will soon appear in England, the United States and Argentina.
3. Museo Judío de Buenos Aires, *Homenaje a Baruch Spinoza*, Buenos Aires,1976. The poem by Borges is on page 7.
4. *La Prensa*, Buenos Aires, April 8, 1984.
5. J. L. Borges, *Obras completas*, Buenos Aires,1981 (from now on cited as *O.C.*), p.1143.
6. Cf. *Plural*, Mexico, August 1974, number 35.
7. Cf. R. Rorty, *Philosophy and the Mirror of Nature*, Princeton, 1979.
8. "El hilo de la fábula", in *Los conjurados*, Madrid, 1985, p.61.
9. F. Alquié, *Servitude et liberté selon Spinoza*, Les cours de Sorbonne: Paris, 1959, p.72.
10. in *O.C.*, p.598.
11. *La Opinión*, Buenos Aires, August 31, 1980.
12. For a recent discussion of the idea of geometrical order as a rhetorical device, cf. Herman de Dijn, "Conceptions of Philosophical Method in Spinoza: Logica and Mos Geometricus", in *The Review of Metaphysics*, Washington D. C.,September 1986, vol. XL,No.1, issue 157.

13. "París,1856", in *O.C.*, p.914.
14. Cf. "El alquimista" (*O.C.*, p.925) and "El Golem" (*O.C.*), p.885.
15. Cf. F. Alquié, *Nature et vérité dans la philosophie de Spinoza*, Les cours de Sorbonne: Paris,1958, pp.118, 119, *passim.*
16. I believe that latterly Borges (see for ex. "Nihon", in *La cifra*, Buenos Aires, 1981, p.101) committed an interesting mistake: that of considering the knowable attributes of substance according to Spinoza to be space and time rather than space and thought as they in fact are. A slip of the memory or perhaps an attempt to make the existence of finite beings more comprehensible?
17. "El primer Wells" (*O.C.*, p.698). In a suggestive article brought to my attention by P .F.Moreau, J. Damade quotes this essay from *Otras inquisiciones*, and compares the indifference of Spinoza's God to the indifference Borges shows towards the creatures of his own making. Cf. J. Damade, "Le Dieu indifférent et le voyageur immobile", in *Europe*, Paris, May 1982, pp. 126–130.
18. Cf. Borges' prologue to the translation—by himself and R. Alifano—of. Stevenson's fables: *Fábulas*, Buenos Aires, 1983, p.11.
19. "El hacedor", in *La cifra*, p.50.
20. *Argencard*, Buenos Aires, May, 1982.
21. See "Nihon", in *La cifra*, p.101.
22. Cf. "Spinoza, une figure pathétique", in *Europe*, Paris, May 1982, pp.73–76.
23. Borges, of course, utterly disbelieved in divine punishment or reward and, more generally, in God, the personal God of the Bible. Sometimes he was tempted by a sort of pantheism. He recalled Bernard Shaw's expression, "God is in the making". "Why not [believe], Borges asked, in a God who may be evolving through stones, through plants, through beasts, through men (. . .), through the days to come (. . .)"? Cf. Carlos Cortínez (ed.), *Borges the poet*, Fayetteville, 1986, p.24.

Howard Giskin (essay date 1990)

SOURCE: "The Mystical Experience in Borges: A Problem of Perception," in *Hispanofila*, Vol. 98, No. 2, January, 1990, pp. 71–85.

[*In the following essay, Giskin explores the role and significance of mythical experience in Borges's work.*]

A reader of Borges is likely to notice that his work, especially his short stories, is not always easily accessible. This is due not to any deliberate desire for obscurity, but rather his persistent allusion to mythical themes such as the search for self and ultimate knowledge. A journey, metaphorical or actual, frequently ends in epiphany in which a character discovers his true place in the universe.[1] The mystical experience in Borges includes four characteristics which are common to all epiphany, as cited by William James in *The Varieties of Religious Experience:* (1) *Ineffability:* Mystical union defies expression. It must be directly experienced and perceived, yet cannot be communicated to others. (2) *Noetic experience:* The mystic feels that tremendous knowledge has been imparted to him. (3) Transiency: The mystical interlude is very brief. (4) *Passivity:* The mystic feels his own will to be in complete abeyance to that of some superior power (292–93) [2]

One frequently finds in Borges instances in which characters see with absolute clarity the interrelationship of all things in the universe and the interrelationship of the universe with oneself. This act of knowing is ineffable, exceeding the limits of language. The mystical experience in Borges, as for all mystics, is a momentary transcendence of sense perception and intellect. For him, the problem of perception is central. His wideranging knowledge of philosophy and theology has imbued him with deep skepticism. He doubts that we can trust either what the mind or the senses tell us about the universe. Amid this chaos of endlessly differing perceptions, there appear frequently in Borges instances of mystical experience in which an individual instantaneously, and *sub specie aeternitatis*, intuits the true nature of things. It is at precisely these moments of epiphany that the human subject experiences the fundamental underlying unity of the universe. In the story "El Aleph," Borges descends into a dark cellar where he has been told he shall behold the Aleph (The Aleph is a form of infinity concentrated in one point): "¿Cómo transmitir a los otros el infinito Aleph, que mi temerosa memoria apenas abarca? . . . Por lo demás, el problema central es irresoluble: la enumeración, siquiera parcial, de un conjunto infinito. En ese instante gigantesco, he visto millones de actos deleitables y atroces; ninguno me asombra como el hecho de que todos ocupan el mismo punto, sin superposición y sin transparencia. Lo que vieron mis ojos fue simultáneo: Lo que transcribiré, sucesivo, porque el lenguage lo es . . . El diámetro de Aleph sería de dos o tres centímetros, pero el espacio cósmico estaba ahí, sin disminución del tamaño" ("El Aleph" 163–4).

This epiphany is at the core of Borges' literary mysticism. Borges attempts to describe, using the limited and imperfect tool of language, an infinite experience, an experience which, by its very nature, overflows the narrow boundaries of language. For Borges epiphany is an experience of *multum in parvo*, multiplicity in unity; all things are revealed as they truly are and in their true relationships. Everything is seen as fundamentally One, while nevertheless manifested as individual and seemingly unrelated entities. Borges quotes Plotinus in "Historia de la eternidad": "Dice Plotino con notorio fervor: 'Toda cosa en el cielo inteligible también es cielo, y allí la tierra es cielo, como también lo son los animales, las plantas, los varones y el mar . . . todos están en todas partes, y todo es todo. Cada cosa es todas las cosas'" (15). The epiphany in Borges involves a revelation of the numen, which can burst forth and flood the mind, resulting in an overwhelming intellectual illumination. As a result of this experience the individual feels himself inseparably one with the entire universe. His sense of identity extends to include all the cosmos.[3]

The mystical experience is Borges' answer to the uncertainty of the rational mind. Borges expresses his doubt of the mind and senses in many of his works. Throughout his writings he entertains the possibility that the universe, as we perceive it through reason and the senses, is not as it really is. Who, then, creates this illusion of reality? Humans, according to Borges, create their own realities. The planet Tlön is a metaphor for this creation. On Tlön, the very act of perceiving an object changes it ("Tlön, Uqbar, Orbis Tertius," 27). This unusual state of affairs bears a similarity to Heisenberg's Uncertainty Principle, which says that the observer, by the mere act of observing, alters that which he observes.[4] This is significant since Borges himself does not accept the traditional Cartesian subject/object duality. The subject as observer can no longer be said to have access to reality as it is. In the mystical experience the subject/object distinction breaks down and becomes meaningless. In epiphany subject and object fuse, allowing a knowing of an entirely different order to take place.

For Borges, it is futile to search for the final laws of the universe. He contends that the actual workings of the universe remain hidden behind a veil of appearance, which the rational intellect cannot penetrate. The best the intellect can do is to create provisory schemas. Is the universe governed by chaos? Humans will do their best to disprove this hypothesis by attempting to impose order by way of the mind. For Borges, all perception is, by its very nature, selective. In every act of perception there is perhaps an infinity of unperceived or ignored material ("La postulación de la realidad" 69). Mystical intuition differs radically from normal perception in that nothing is ignored or selected, but rather the whole is seen in its infinite complexity *sub specie aeternitatis* and instantaneously. Our world is simplified to fit our conceptions of the way we think it should be, which is most often not the way it actually is. Our normal perception is filtered through a haze of attitudes, desires, emotions, and habits, which distort our vision of reality. But can truth ever be attained when the mind, as Borges notes, sees selectively, picking and choosing only what pleases it? Borges does not believe that reason can arrive at the true nature of things. Any attempt to do so will necessarily end in failure: ". . . notoriamente no hay clasificación del universo que no sea arbitraria y conjectural. La razón es simple: no sabemos qué cosa es el universo" ("El idioma analítico de John Wilkins" 105). He suggests, however, that the impossibility of comprehending the divine scheme of the universe should not dissuade us from creating human schemes, although we must admit that they are merely provisional (105).

Stressing the provisional relationship of language and reality, Borges, in the same work, quotes Chesterton: "Esperanzas y utopías aparte, acaso lo más lúcido que sobre el lenguaje se ha escrito son estas palabras de Chesterton: 'El hombre sabe que hay en el alma tintes más desconcertantes, mas innumerables y más anónimos que los colores de una selva otoñal . . . Cree, sin embargo, que esos tintes, en todas sus fusiones y conversiones, son representables con precisión por un mecanismo arbitrario de gruñidos y de chillidos. Cree que del interior de un bolsista salen realmente ruidos que significan todos los misterios de la memoria y todas las agonías del anhelo'" (106). Language is at best an imperfect tool with which to describe and investigate reality. Language can be used to describe, analyze, name, and even create, but words are not reality itself. Words are a part of reality, not the whole of reality. There will necessarily be many things that language cannot contain. Language talks about reality, but it is not reality.

Borges notes that Pythagoras wrote nothing, believing only the spoken word a vehicle of truth. For Borges, the written word is a petrification of an essentially fluid reality which is constantly changing, like Heraclitus' river (**"La poesía"** 102). Plato, he tells us, narrates an Egyptian fable against writing in which books are likened to painted figures which appear alive, but do not answer questions asked of them ("Del culto de los libros" 111). All language is a freezing and making static of a fundamentally dynamic reality. Language is an instrument, and its objectification through the written word gives the illusion that truth can be captured and recorded. Language, however, can never reveal truth in its entirety. For Borges, existence not language is the fundamental mystery. Language can never fully reveal reality because language is sequential. To describe anything fully, even the most insignificant object, an endless list of attributes would result. ("Sobre el Vathek de William Beckford" 133) There is no limit, for example, to what can be said about a simple object such as a pencil, because our description of it could continue forever. It is clear that, for Borges, language does not exhaust the expression of reality. The mystical experience is, for him, a way of attaining intimate contact with reality, and without the limitations of language. He acknowledges the impossibility of ever fully capturing the numen in language, but as a poet he must try. In **"La luna,"** he speaks of his desire to embrace through poetry that which is beyond words:

> Siempre se pierde lo esencial. Es una
> Ley de toda palabra sobre el numen.
> No la sabrá eludir este resumen
> De mi largo comerico con la luna . . .
>
> Cuando, en Ginebra o Zurich, la fortuna
> Quiso que yo también fuera poeta,
> Me impuse, como todos, la secreta
> Obligación de definir la luna . . .
>
> Pensaba que el poeta es aquel hombre
> Que, como el rojo Adán del Paraíso,
> Impone a cada cosa su preciso
> Y verdadero y no sabido nombre . . .
>
> (71–74)

The poet, as Borges suggests, through his superior vision and art points to that which lies behind things. He wishes to give a thing its true and unknown name, but he knows that this is impossible, because its true name is unspeakable. The essential reality is always lost when we attempt to cage and ossify the living, changing numen in words. Spirit or numen, like Heraclitus' river, is in a state of perpetual flux. The poet attempts the impossible: to capture living spirit with the pen. The moon cannot be defined. "Moon" is merely a pale reflection of the moon, not the moon itself. And yet it is the poet's duty to search for the true names of all things, an endless search, to be sure.

The second element of the epiphany in Borges is noetic experience in which the individual gains direct and instantaneous insight into the nature of reality.[5] Mystical knowledge is thus contrasted to rational knowing, which can be only partial and imperfect. A frequent accompaniment of the mystical experience is a sense of absolute vision into the nature of things. One has the feeling that reality is for the first time seen in its primal, unconditioned, and indescribable splendor. In "La escritura de Dios," Borges narrates just such an illumination:

> Entonces ocurrió lo que no puedo olvidar ni comunicar. Ocurrió la unión con la divinidad, con el universo (no sé si estas palabras difieren). El éxtasis no repite sus símbolos; hay quien ha visto a Dios en un resplandor, hay quien lo ha percibido en una espada o en los círculos de una rosa. Yo vi una Rueda altísima, que no estaba delante de mis ojos, ni detrás, ni a los lados, sino en todas las partes, a un tiempo. Esa Rueda estaba hecha de agua, pero también de fuego, y era (aunque se veía el borde) infinita. Entretejidas, la formaban todas las cosas que serán, que son y que fueron, y yo era una de las hebras de esa trama total, y Pedro de Alvarado, que me dio tormenta, era otra. Ahí estaban las causas y los efectos y me bastaba ver esa Rueda para entenderlo todo, sin fin . . . Quien ha entrevisto el universo, quien ha entrevisto los ardientes designios del universo, no puede pensar en un hombre, en sus triviales dichas o desaventuras, aunque ese hombre sea él. Ese hombre *ha sido él* y ahora no le importa. ¿Qué le importa la suerte de aquel otro, qué le importa la nación de aquel otro, si él, ahora es nadie?
>
> (120–21)

Mystical union, regardless of tradition, represents an intuition of the here and now, as it is in the present moment. Paradoxically, as Zen argues, we are always in direct contact with Truth, but by some trick of thought or reason have forgotten this. The mystical experience is merely the lifting of the veil which clouds our vision. The priest Tzinacán, in "La escritura de Dios," experiences an incommunicable bliss of understanding, comprehending once and for all the ultimate designs of the universe. All things are well and seen in their proper places; the universe unfolds as it must. For Tzinacán, although left to die in a prison, the universe is infinitely hospitable. The possibility of illumination by an inflowing of the numen is everpresent. For Borges, spirit is a "presence" behind the objects and occurances of everyday reality, and this "presence" is potentially available to each and every one of us at every moment. The mystical experience is an opening to the everpresent numen. Everyday reality does not so much conceal the enigma of existence, but *is* that mystery itself; a tree, a rock, the sky, these constitute the sacred aspect of Being. In **"Una brújula"** all things point to a deeper unnamable presence:

> Todas las cosas son palabras del
> Idioma en que Alguien o Algo, noche y día,
> Escribe esa infinita algarabía
> Que es la historia del mundo . . .
>
> Detrás del nombre hay lo que no se nombra;
> Hoy he sentido gravitar su sombra
> En esta aguja azul, lúcida y leve
> Que hacia el confín de un mar tiende su empeño.
>
> (33)

Borges sees all things, but particularly simple objects, as revealing most easily that which lies behind everyday appearance. All things point to the ineffable, which cannot be directly seen or named, but rather felt as a shadow in our experience. In mystical traditions the normal waking state is referred to as a "dream." This dream state is one of illusion created by a clouded or "veiled" consciousness. Tzinacán realizes that his true identity is not that of priest or decipherer, but something far greater, the entire universe. Although imprisoned physically, he is now truly free (119). Finally at home in the universe, Tzinacán blesses even his bleak surroundings. The secret script of the tiger's skin, which he has tried in vain for years to decipher, now becomes clear to him (his god had confided the code to the living skin of the jaguars in remote antiquity). Simply to utter these words would bring infinite power, but he shall never say them because he no longer remembers the man "Tzinacán" (121). The priest's mystical experience is transient; although he may recall the mystical interlude for long afterwards, the mystical state does not last long. In "El Aleph," we do not know the exact length of time which elapses in the cellar while Borges views the Aleph, but we know it is short, "a single gigantic instant" (164–65). In "La escritura de Dios," the actual duration of the epiphany is short, although Tzinacán is permanently transformed by the experience (120–21).

In addition to the transient nature of the epiphany in Borges, the result of mystical illumination is a sense of being in the grasp of some higher controlling power.[6] The illuminated man experiences himself as a vehicle or receptacle of a higher power, and this power urges him to search for his true self. Throughout his work, Borges exhibits a concern for the problem of the identity of the individual. Cutting through the layers of false identity is of central concern for Borges, and the mystical experience is the final unveiling of true personhood, which is paradoxically a sense of being "no one." Both Buddhist and Hindu mysticism stress heavily the illusory nature of the ego or sense of self as agent. They deny the objective existence of any entity called the "self," which can be described as the subjective feeling of being a causal agent acting separately from, or on other entities (Trungpa 122–23). Tzinacán no longer remembers Tzinacán, because Tzinacán *as* Tzinacán does not exist. The illuminated Tzinicán loses his sense of himself as an independent agent or ego. It is precisely in this sense that he forgets who he is. He ceases to identify with his previous ego self, but rather with the cosmos as a whole. He does not think in terms of one man, the man he was, because he is literally no longer that man. He cannot now be concerned with what worries ordinary men. Mystics call this state of being unity consciousness (Wilber 142). Unity consciousness is what we are when we are not our professions, our thoughts, our possessions, our body, our names, nor anything else. Somewhat paradoxically, however, our identity becomes (in actuality, always was) everything that exists, the entire cosmos. In this mystical vein Walt Whitman writes in "Song of Myself": "I find I incorporate gneiss, coal, long-threaded moss, fruits, grains, esculent roots, / And I am stucco'd with quadrupeds and birds all over . . ." (sec. 31). Likewise, Tzinacán can no longer remember Tzinacán because he is the trees, the sun, the moon and the stars—they are him, and he is them. Buddhists call this "big mind," as opposed to the "little mind" of unenlightened awareness. Ordinary perception tells us that we are separate entities, but mystical union reveals that we are and always have been one with all of creation (Wilber 42). Tzinacán awakens from the dream which was his previous life, only to discover that he, as a separate self, does not exist. The man Tzinacán may die, but the cosmos is eternal, and Tzinacán is the cosmos.

In **"Yo,"** Borges contemplates his own shifting sense of self:

La calavera, el corazón secreto,
los caminos de sangre que no veo,
los túneles de sueño, ese Proteo,
las vísceras, la nuca, el esqueleto.
Soy esas cosas. Increíblemente
soy también la memoria de una espada
y de un solitario sol poniente
que se dispersa en oro, en sombra, en nada.
Soy el que ve las proas desde el puerto;
soy los contados libros, los contados
grabados por el tiempo fatigados;
soy el que envidia a los que ya se han muerto.
Más raro es ser el hombre que entrelaza
palabras en un cuarto de una casa.

(48)

Borges marvels at the elements that make up "Borges." "Borges" is his bodily parts, his memory, his perceptions, his hopes and desires, and most importantly his dreams, "los túneles de sueño, ese Proteo." Dreams are the subterranean key to identity for Borges. They cannot be grasped or seen, yet neither can many parts of the body, such as the heart or skull. "Borges" appears to be the sum of many seen and unseen qualities and attributes. "Soy esas cosas. Increíblemente . . ." "Borges" too is the memory of all that has happened to him, of what he has seen and done. He is the sum of perhaps an infinity of attributes, events, emotions. But stranger than to be all these things is to be the man called "Borges," an indivisible unity composed of a myriad of disparate elements, paradoxically and inexplicably whole, a microcosm of unity in diversity. That such a unity exists is at once a great mystery and a wonder to him. Is Borges merely the sum of all these things he names, a collection of attributes somehow tied together by a vague sense of "I-ness?" Who is Borges? Paradoxically, Borges knows that although he is somehow the "sum of all his parts," he is more than that also. He is not merely the one whom he sees in the mirror, nor even he who writes poetry, but something else altogether, an unnamable presence, a vague sense of Being behind "Borges." In **"Soy,"** Borges expresses the feeling that he is "no one":

Soy el que sabe que no es menos vano
que el vano observador que en el espejo
de silencio y cristal sigue el reflejo
o el cuerpo (da lo mismo) del hermano.
Soy, tácitos amigos, el que sabe
que no hay otra venganza que el olvido
ni otro perdón. Un dios ha concedido
al odio humano esta curiosa llave.
Soy el que pese a tan ilustres modos
de errar, no ha descifrado el laberinto
singular y plural, arduo y distinto,
del tiempo, que es de uno y es de todos.
Soy el que es nadie, el que no fue una espada
en la guerra. Soy eco, olvido, nada.

(62)

According to Buddhists, behind all self-identity is emptiness or *shunyata*.[7] To understand *shunyata* means to grasp reality in absence of duality and conceptualization (Trungpa 188). To experience oneself as "nothing" is to know the numinal emptiness behind external form and attributes. Borges sees the reflection of his body in the mirror, which he knows is not truly him. The body, he knows, is only a reflection of a deeper reality of what he is. By saying that he is "nothing," Borges is not making a nihilist proclamation, but rather an acknowledgement of the numenal emptiness which lies behind the illusion of selfhood. Mystical traditions uniformly teach that all persons, in fact all things, are part of a more inclusive reality and fundamentally unified. At this level of the psyche, we are literally one, because the (inherited) content of our psyches is the same. Mystics view the "personal" strata of the psyche as superficial because these are not a true representative of what we are. They postulate a level of psyche in which we are not merely one with all other members of his race, but one with all creation. In "Los teólogos" Borges implies the transcendental unity of all humans, when he suggests that a particular theological treatise appeared to have been written by all men or no one in particular because of its universality (38). At the end of this story, we discover that in the eyes of God, the two feuding theologians, Aurelian and John de Panonia, are the same man (45). From a Jungian point of view, the warring theologians project onto each other precisely the qualities and characteristics which they fail to recognize in themselves, their shadows ("The Shadow" 9). The theologians are the same man, because their conceptions of one another are projections of the other's shadow. Each objectifies evil in the form of the other.

This conception is consistent with mystical traditions, which insist that all qualities we see in others, both positive and negative, are qualities which we ourselves contain. Many mystics have held that our vision of the universe, the macrocosm, is entirely a reflection of the soul, or microcosm. The hater is the hated, and *vice-versa* to the extent that he fails to recognize the opposing quality in himself. The mystic sees all events as reflections of his inner nature. For the mystic, subject collapses into object; there is no distance between "I" and "other." There are many tales in world literature which attempt to illustrate the identity of all persons. In a footnote to "El acercamiento a Almotásim," Borges notes: "esa y otras ambiguas analogías pueden significar la identidad del buscado y buscador." He observes that in the *Mantig-al-Tayr (Colloquium of the Birds)* of the Persian mystic Attar, the searchers for the magnificent bird the Simurg discover that they are actually the Simurg and the Simurg is each one of them and all (45). In "La forma de la espada" Borges similarly suggests the identity of all men: "Lo que hace un hombre es como si lo hicieran todos los hombres. Por eso no es injusto que una desobediencia en un jardín contamine al género humano; por eso no es injusto que la crucifixión de un solo judío baste para salvarlo. Acaso Schopenhauer tiene razón; yo soy los otros, cualquier hombre es todos los hombres, Shakespeare es de algún modo el miserable John Vincent Moon" (138).

For Borges, the search for self involves deep reflection upon his own identity, and yet he remains "disidentified" with his own attributes and what others recognize as "Borges": "He olvidado mi nombre. No soy Borges . . . / soy el que sabe que no es más que un eco, / El que quiere morir enteramente. / Soy acaso el que eres en un sueño. / Soy la cosa que soy. Lo dijo Shakespeare . . ." (**"Borges"** 19–20). What is perhaps most interesting about this poem is Borges' lack of identification of his inner being with the man called "Borges." Again, who is Borges? He knows that his true identity has very little to do with "Borges." He is something mysterious, unnamed and unnamable behind the name and attributes. This sense of mystery is expressed throughout Borges' work by a continual search for self through an integration of the contents of his unconscious into his conscious self-image or persona, thus enlarging his vision of himself (Jung, "The Transcendent Function" 91). Indeed, the highest form of mysticism is a complete integration of the unconscious (including the collective unconscious) into consciousness. But this confrontation is not an easy task. The ego (persona, self-image) experiences terror, sometimes extreme, when delving into the unconscious regions of the psyche (Neumann 380). This is because the ego has no idea what it will find in the dark corners of the psyche. These hidden, forgotten, and repressed contents of the psyche are objectified and experienced as "monsters" or "demons" in the confrontation of the conscious and the unconscious. The ego is heroic because it confronts, explores, and finally conquers the uncharted world of the unconscious psyche. In mystical writings, the spiritual seeker is often portrayed as a warrior of the highest order, precisely because the battle with the self is the most difficult struggle one can face (*Dhammapada* 50).

Each new addition of a previously unconscious element results in the birth of a new self, but this birth is often painful. The encounter with the unconscious "always leads to an upheaval of the total personality and not only of consciousness" (Neumann 380). This fact explains Borges' fear of mirrors, which threaten to reveal his true "face," through a confrontation with himself. He imagines his true face to be hideous. In **"La pesadilla,"** he says that a nightmare of his is the idea of masks. He is afraid to remove the mask he wears for fear of seeing his true (atrocious) face (43). For the artist, however, this confrontation with the self is necessary. It is the source of creativity, for beneath the mask lies the numen. Borges' fear of plumbing his psychic depths is well-founded, since instead of integration "there is also the possibility that the ego will succumb to the attraction of the numinous and, as a Hasidic maxim puts it, 'will burst its shell.' This catastrophe can take the form of death in ecstasy, mystical death, but also of sickness, psychosis, or serious neurosis" (Neuman 397). In **"Los espejos"** Borges' fear of mirrors because of their revelatory nature is evident:

> Yo, que sentí el horror de los espejos
> No sólo ante el cristal impenetrable
> Donde acaba y empieza, inhabitable
> Un imposible espacio de reflejos . . .
>
> Infinitos los veo, elementales
> Ejecutores de un antiguo pacto,
> Multiplicar el mundo como el acto
> Generativo, insomnes y fatales.
>
> (63)

Mirrors are portals into an infinite and unlimited world, the world of the numen, of ecstasy, but also of nigthmares and insanity. The ego resists the "emptiness" of the numenological world. For the ego to become nothing is a kind of death. This is why to be "reborn" one must die, or properly speaking, one's ego must die. The descent into the depths of the unconscious is also a voyage to the source and unlimited fount of creativity. Paradoxically, the voyage ends with the realization that one is nothing but a vehicle for the transmission of something far greater than onself. Perhaps it is true, as Borges writes in "Los teólogos," that "cada hombre es un órgano que proyecta la divinidad para sentir el mundo" (42). In the final stages of mysticism (illumination) the ego is absorbed into the void, and the sense of "I" as separate entity dissolves. This is called death of the ego in mystical terms. Borges' fear of dissolution of his sense of self is reflected in **"Los espejos"**: "Dios ha creado las noches que se arman / De sueños y las formas del espejo / Para que el hombre sienta que es reflejo / Y vanidad. Por eso nos alarman" (65). Mirrors are a threat because they represent the awakened consciousness which incorporates ego into the void. When this happens, the "old" man exists no more, and the "new" man is born. Everything provides a numinous background; everything in the world becomes a symbol and a part of the numinous, and God is seen everywhere (Neumann 410).

It is evident that mysticism in Borges conforms to the four characteristics of the epiphany cited by William James: ineffability, noetic experience, transiency, and passivity. The epiphany in Borges is incapable of being fully expressed in language. During the mystical experience, an individual transcends the normal boundaries of perception and intellect, intuiting instantaneously the true nature of things and the unity of the universe. One bypasses the rational mind, gaining absolute clarity into the nature of things; the subject becomes one with the object, and a knowing of "communion" takes place. Such knowing is of an entirely different order than sequential reason, since all normal perception is necessarily selective and incomplete. The true nature of reality can never be revealed through language, since language objectifies and freezes reality. The numen, Borges believes, can never be captured in language, but it is the poet's duty to try. The epiphany in Borges includes a noetic experience in which the individual achieves direct and instantaneous insight into the nature of reality. Transience is another quality of the mystical experience in Borges, as evidenced in "El Aleph" and "La escritura de Dios." Finally, during the epiphany, the individual comes to feel that rather than doing anything, something *happens* to him. Another power, believed to be outside oneself, takes over. For Borges, this constitutes a sense of being "no one" or "nothing." He often ponders his own identity in his writings, thinking of himself as other than the attributes and qualities which constitute him. In Borges, being "no one" is synonymous with being everyone. His literary mysticism reveals the entire human race to be microcosmically contained in every individual. Ultimately, the distinction between "I" and "other" is blurred. Borges searches repeatedly for clues to his own identity, often reflecting upon his fear of self-revelation. He fears the discovery of his true identity (his "true face"), which he imagines beyond his capacity to endure. Nevertheless, he senses that behind the illusion of his personal identity lies not the face of a monster, but divinity.

Notes

1. The mystical roots of Borges' thought have not yet been fully investigated. Jaime Alazraki's important work *La prosa narrativa de Jorge Luis Borges* examines numerous elements of Borges' art, but does not directly treat mysticism. Gene H. Bell-Villada's *Borges and his Fiction: A Guide to his Mind and Art* contains a chapter entitled "El Aleph: The Visionary Experience," in which he elucidates selected aspects of Borges' mysticism without considering its overall role in his work. Alberto C. Pérez in *Realidad y suprarrealidad en los cuentos fantásticos de Jorge Luis Borges*, realizes that mysticism is central to Borges' thought, but does not examine sufficiently the importance of mystical themes which recur throughout Borges' poetry, essays, and stories. The only work which treats Borges' mysticism with any degree of thoroughness is Giovanna de Garayalde's *Jorge Luis Borges: Sources and Illumination.* De Garayalde argues that Borges was strongly influenced by Sufi (mystical Islamic) stories and parables. She successfully shows that many of Borges' techniques and themes have precedents in centuries-old Sufi stories.
2. Borges himself is a mystical thinker, and has acknowledged that he had several mystical experiences in his life. Quoting from a previous article "Sentirse en muerte," published in 1928 and concerning an experience during a stroll in Buenos Aires, he writes in "Nueva refutación del tiempo": "Me sentí muerto, me sentí percibidor abstracto del mundo; indefinido temor imbuido de ciencia que es la mejor claridad de la metafisica" (180). In an interview with Willis Barnestone and Jorge Oclander, Borges one commented that he has had two mystical experiences, but cannot tell them: "what happened is not to be put into words . . . I had the feeling of living not in but outside of time" (*Borges at Eighty: Conversations* 11).
3. Transpersonal psychologist Ken Wilber writes "the most fascinating aspect of such awesome and illuminating experiences . . . is that the individual comes to feel, beyond any shadow of a doubt, that he is fundamentally one with the entire universe, with all worlds, sacred or profane. His *sense of identity* expands far beyond the narrow confines of his mind and body and embraces the entire cosmos" (3).
4. "According to the Uncertainty Principle, we cannot measure accurately, at the same time, both the position and the momentum of a moving particle. The more precisely we determine one of these properties, the less we know about the other" (Zukav 133).
5. Epiphany does not confer knowledge in the traditional sense, but in silence rids one of delusion. It is only when the mind becomes quiet that mystical wisdom is received: about this all mystics agree. In his "Cántico espiritual," San Juan de la Cruz describes the infusion of mystical knowledge directly into the soul, bypassing the normal perceptual faculties. Divine communication takes place "en la noche serena": "Esta noche es la contemplación en que el alma desea ver estas cosas. Llámala noche, porque la contemplación es oscura, que por eso la llaman, por otro nombre, mística teología, que quiere decir sabiduría de Dios secreta o escondida, en la cual, sin ruido de palabras y sin ayuda de algún sentido corporal ni espiritual, como en silencio y quietud, a oscuras de todo lo sensitivo y natural, enseña Dios ocultísima y secretísimamente al alma sin ella saber cómo; lo cual algunos espirituales llaman entender no entendimiento" (39:12, 960).
6. Andrew M. Greely writes: "something besides the conscious self-controlling reality principle is operating" (17).
7. The "nothingness" which is characteristic of Borges' aesthetics is most similar to the concept of *shunyata*

or "emptiness" in Buddhistic thought, a non-conditioned mode of being in which everything is in a state of potentiality or possibility. *Shunyata* represents something which cannot be named, much less defined. It is the groundless ground of existence in which all things are paradoxically undifferentiated yet exactly what they are (cf. Nishitani and Streng).

Works cited

Alazraki, Jaime. *La prosa narrativa de Jorge Luis Borges.* Madrid: Editorial Gredos, 1974.

Bell-Villada, Gene H. *Borges and his Fiction: A Guide to his Mind and Art.* Chapel Hill: U of Carolina P, 1981,

Borges, Jorge Luis. "El acercamiento a Almotásim." *Ficciones.* Buenos Aires: Emecé, 1956.

———. "El aleph." *El aleph.* Buenos Aires: Emecé, 1957.

———. *Borges at Eighty: Conversations.* Bloomington: Indiana UP, 1982.

———. "Borges." *Historia de la noche.* Buenos Aires: Emecé, 1977.

———. "Del culto de los libros." *Otras inquisiciones.* Buenos Aires: Emecé, 1960.

———. "La escritura de Dios." *El aleph.* Buenos Aires: Emecé, 1957.

———. "Los espejos." *El otro, el mismo.* Buenos Aires: Emecé, 1969.

———. "La forma de la espada." *Ficciones.* Buenos Aires: Emecé, 1956.

———. "Historia de la eternidad." *Historia de la eternidad.* Buenos Aires: Emecé, 1953.

———. "El idioma analítico de John Wilkins." *Otras inquisiciones.* Buenos Aires. Emecé, 1960.

———. "La luna." *El otro, el mismo.* Buenos Aires: Emecé, 1969.

———. "La penúltima versión de la realidad." *Discusión.* Buenos Aires: Emecé, 1957.

———. "La pesadilla." *Siete noches.* México, D.F. Fondo de Cultura Económica, 1980.

———. "La poesía." *Siete noches.* México, D.F. Fondo de Cultura Económica, 1980.

———. "Soy." *The Gold of the Tigers: Selected Later Poems, A Bilingual Edition.* Trans. Alistair Reid. New York: Dutton, 1976.

———. "Sobre el *Vathek* de William Beckford." *Otras inquisiciones.* Buenos Aires: Emecé, 1960.

———. "Los teólogos." *El aleph.* Buenos Aires: Emecé, 1957.

———. "Tlön, Uqbar, Orbis Tertius." *Ficciones.* Buenos Aires: Emecé, 1956.

———. "Una brújula." *El otro, el mismo.* Buenos Aires: Emecé, 1969.

———. "Yo." *The Gold of the Tigers: Selected Later Poems, A Bilingual Edition.* Trans. Alistair Reid. New York: Dutton, 1976.

The Dhammapada. Trans. Juan Mascaro. New York: Penguin, 1978.

Garayalde, Giovanna de. *Jorge Luis Borges: Sources and Illumination.* London: Octagon, 1978.

Greely, Andrew M. *Ecstasy: A Way of Knowing.* Englewood Cliffs, N.J.: Prentice, 1974.

James, William. *The Varieties of Religious Experience.* New York: Mentor, 1958.

Jung, C. G. "The Transcendent Function." *The Structure and Dynamics of the Psyche.* Trans. R.C.F. Hull. Collected Works. 19 vols. Bollingen Series XX. Princeton: Princeton UP, 1969.

——— "The Shadow." *Aion: Researches into the Phenomenology of the Self.* Trans. R.C.F. Hull. Collected Works. 19 vols. Bollingen Series XX. Princeton: Princeton UP, 1975.

Neumann, Erich. "Mystical Man." *The Mystic Vision: Papers from the Eranos Yearbooks.* Bollingen Series XXX, 6. Princeton UP, 1968.

Nishitani, Keiji. *Religion and Nothingness.* Trans. Jan van Bragt. Berkeley: U of California P, 1982.

Pérez, Alberto C. *Realidad y suprarrealidad en los cuentos fantásticos de Jorge Luis Borges.* Miami: Ediciones Universal, 1971.

San Juan de la Cruz. *Obras completas.* Madrid: Editorial de Espiritualidad, 1957.

Streng, Frederick J. *Emptiness: A Depth Study of the Philosopher Naranjuna and his Interpretation of Ultimate Reality.* New York: Abingdon, 1967.

Trungpa, Chogyam. *Cutting Through Spiritual Materialism.* Boston: Shambala, 1973.

Whitman, Walt. "Song of Myself." *Leaves of Grass.* Eds. Bradley Scully and Harold W. Blodgett. New York: Norton, 1973.

Wilber, Ken. *No Boundary: Eastern and Western Approaches to Personal Growth.* Boston: Shambala, 1981.

Zukav, Gary. *The Dancing Wu Li Masters: An Overview of the New Physics.* New York: Morrow, 1979.

Martin S. Stabb (essay date 1991)

SOURCE: "The Making of a Writer," in *Borges Revisited,* Twayne Publishers, 1991, pp. 1–36.

[*In the following excerpt, Stabbs examines Borges's early poetry.*]

Borges became famous as a writer through his prose rather than through his poetry. Today he is usually thought of first as the creator of fictional labyrinths, then as the writer of erudite short essays, often on arcane subjects, and only last as a poet. Yet he began as a poet and has worked more or less continuously in this genre. Most important, he reveals more of himself in his verse than in any other kind of writing. The capriciousness and learned frivolity of much of his prose are rarely found in his poetry. By contrast, we see in it the other Borges—the sincere and ardent youth of the twenties or the contemplative and nostalgic writer of the sixties and seventies. For many this is an unknown Borges; perhaps it is the real Borges.

Borges's career as a poet and writer began when he was in his late teens. His travels in Europe and contact with the Spanish avant-garde have already been noted. Like most young literary rebels, the members of the circle with whom he first became associated, the *ultraístas,* craved innovation and were repelled by the tastes of their fathers. The poetic movement against which they were reacting was *modernismo,* a rich and complex style of writing that drew heavily on the French fin de sìecle poets: Valéry, Rimbaud, Leconte de Lisle, and others. Led by the Nicaraguan Rubén Darío, and in Argentina by Leopoldo Lugones, *modernismo* dominated Hispanic letters—in Spain as well as the New World—through the 1890s and well into the twentieth century. It would be impossible to characterize the movement adequately here. It is sufficient to say that on the formal level, the *modernistas* endeavored to revitalize the poetic lexicon by replacing the tired adjectives of romanticism with new and unusual ones; they experimented with long-forgotten metrical schemes as well as with innovative ones; and perhaps most interestingly, they sought to blend, confuse, and interchange the distinct sensory realms in their poetry. Following the French poets Baudelaire and Rimbaud, they attempted to establish "correspondences" between sound and color. Taking what the Parnassians had done in their poetry as a point of departure, they tried to create verbal statuary in which the precise tactile and visual terms replaced the romantic's overt egocentrism and emotive vocabulary. From Verlaine they acquired the notion that words possess an inherent musical quality which might be the very essence of poetry. The content of *modernista* poetry, like its form, differed substantially from the literature that preceded it. The newer poets preferred the artificial, whereas the romantics glorified the world of nature. They held to theories of detachment and objectivity, whereas the romantics exalted the ego and cultivated literary confessionalism. The poets of the 1890s shunned overt political or social involvement, whereas many of their predecessors had been activists and reformers. The *modernistas*, like the romantics, enjoyed decorating their poetry with the trappings of a distant age, but when they sought escape into the past their favorite periods were the Renaissance and the classical age in contrast to the romantic's love of the medieval. Finally, the typical *modernista* tried hard to avoid the romantic's penchant for the picturesque: hence he did not concern himself with the Indian, the *fatherland*, or local color. Instead he wrote of the court of Versailles or of the sensuous refinement of ancient Greece. Though the Spanish American *modernistas* imitated their European mentors to a great extent, their poetry—particularly the best pieces of the leading writers—had much originality.

It would be inaccurate to claim that Borges's poetry, even that of the early *ultraísta* period, was merely a reaction to *modernismo.* It is true that he wished to purge his poetry of certain specific *modernista* techniques and mannerisms, but like all good poets his objective was to affirm his own poetic values rather than to refute those of his predecessors. Borges admits that he never adhered to the position sketched out in his "Ultraist Manifesto" of 1921. The points he emphasized are nonetheless worth enumerating: the reduction of lyricism to metaphor; the combining of several images in one; and the elimination of adornments, sermonizing, and all forms of poetic filler. A corollary to his view that poetry must be purged of unnecessary embellishments was his conviction that rhyme and meter contributed little to the value of a poem.[1]

Borges was less explicit about the thematic materials that *ultraísmo* was to employ, but in general he favored contemporary rather than antique poetic furnishings. He even proclaimed that the poets of his generation preferred the beauties of a transatlantic liner or of a modern locomotive to the magnificence of Versailles or the cities of Renaissance Italy. This statement is only half-serious: what he meant was that the here and now—the immediate environment—is the logical point of departure for creating genuine lyricism and that the overuse of highly decorative trappings typical of *modernista* poetry detracted from true lyrical expression and impeded the poetic process.

At first glance, the forty-five short pieces of free verse in Borges's first collection, ***Fervor de Buenos Aires*** (***Fervor of Buenos Aires,*** 1923), seem to be little more than a group of vignettes describing familiar scenes in and around his native city. A few, however, present exotic scenes: **"Benarés"** describes the Indian city of the same name; **"Judería"** (**"Ghetto"**), the Jewish quarter of an unspecified but obviously European city. One poem, **"Rosas,"** takes as its point of departure the figure of Argentina's tyrannical nineteenth-century dictator. A limited number of poems are purely introspective and as such they do not describe any specific external reality. The poems vary from seven or eight lines to as many as fifty, with fifteen to twenty lines being about the average. In keeping with *ultraísta* precepts, neither regular meter, rhyme, nor regularized strophes are in evidence. The absence of traditional forms does not mean that these poems have no structure: like other writers of free verse, Borges does incorporate formal devices into his poetry. The effectiveness of these devices will be better appreciated after his poetry is examined in greater detail.

The mood of the ***Fervor de Buenos Aires*** is established in the opening lines of the first poem, **"Las calles"** (**"Streets"**):

> The streets of Buenos Aires
> have become the core of my being.

Not the energetic streets
troubled by haste and agitation,
but the gentle neighborhood street
softened by trees and twilight . . .

Las calles de Buenos Aires
ya son la entraña de mi alma.
No las calles enérgicas
molestadas de prisas y ajetreos,
sino la dulce calle de arrabal
enternecida de árboles y ocaso . . .

(*OP* [*Obra poetica, 1923–1964*] 64, 17)[2]

Despite the word *Fervor* in the collection's title, the reader soon becomes aware that this is a restrained fervor, a reflective passion directed toward an internalization of all that surrounds the poet. This goal is best achieved by selecting that portion of reality which is most easily assimilated: not the bustling downtown streets, but the passive, tree-shaded streets of the old suburbs. It may be a valid generalization to say that in much of his early poetry Borges sought out the passive and manageable facets of reality in order to facilitate the creation of his own internal world. A random sampling of the modifiers used in the ***Fervor*** bears out the point. For instance, he writes of "trees which barely mutter (their) being" ("árboles que balbucean apenas el ser"; ***OP*** 64, 23); of the "easy tranquillity of (the) benches" ("el fácil sosiego de los bancos"; ***OP*** 64, 26); of the "fragile new moon" ("la frágil luna nueva"; ***OP*** 64, 43); of "withered torches" ("macilentos faroles"; ***OP*** 64, 47); of "the obscure friendship of a vestibule" ("la amistad oscura de un zaguán"; ***OP*** 64, 30); of the ray of light which "subdues senile easy chairs" ("humilla las seniles butacas"; ***OP*** 64, 34) in an old parlor; and of "streets which, languidly submissive, accompany my solitude" ("calles que, laciamente sumisas, acompañan mi soledad"; ***OP*** 64, 57). Borges's frequent use of the late afternoon as a poetic setting may have a similar function. Aside from the obvious fact that the beauty of sunsets and the coming of night have always appealed to writers, the dulling of reality's edges at this time of day gives the poet a special advantage in his task of shaping the external world.

One cannot help wondering why the young Borges felt a need to infuse reality with these qualities of passivity and submissiveness. Perhaps his innate shyness coupled with the experience of foreign travel and subsequent return to the half-familiar, half-alien scenes of his childhood led him to view the world with trepidation and a sense of insecurity. His vocabulary throughout the ***Fervor*** is revealing. It clearly indicates that he is seeking tranquillity, familial solidarity, and a kind of serenity that can only be associated with parental protectiveness. Examples are abundant. In **"Las calles"** he speaks of the neighborhood streets as providing "a promise of happiness / for under their protection so many lives are joined in brotherly love" ("una promesa de ventura / pues a su amparo hermánanse tantas vidas"; ***OP*** 64, 17); in **"Cercanías" ("Environs")** he writes of "neighborhoods built of quietness and tranquillity" ("arrabales hechos de acallamiento y sosiego"; ***OP*** 64, 62); and in the beautifully understated final verses of **"Un patio"** he sums up the peace and serenity of the traditional Latin residence by exclaiming "How nice to live in the friendly darkness / of a vestibule, a climbing vine, of a cistern" ("Lindo es vivir en la amistad oscura / de un zaguán, de una parra y de un aljibe"; ***OP*** 64, 30).

Closely related to Borges's poetic transmutation of "hard" reality into a pliable, manageable reality is his recourse to a certain philosophical notion that comes to occupy a central position in all his work. In **"Caminata" ("Stroll")**, one of the less anthologized poems of ***Fervor*** he writes: "I am the only viewer of this street, / if I would stop looking at it, it would perish" ("Yo soy el único espectador de esta calle, / si dejara de verla se moriría"; ***OP*** 64, 58). In **"Benarés,"** superficially one of the least typical pieces in the collection, Borges describes in considerable detail a place he has never seen. He admits in the opening lines that the city is "False and dense / like a garden traced on a mirror" (Falsa y tupida / como un jardín calcado en un espejo"; ***OP*** 64, 53). Yet at the very end of the poem he seems amazed that the real Benares exists: "And to think / that while I toy with uncertain metaphors, / the city of which I sing persists" ("Y pensar / que mientras juego con inciertas metáforas, / la cuidad que canto persiste"; ***OP*** 64, 54). In a better known poem, inspired by the Recoleta cemetery, he observes that when life is extinguished "at the same time, space, time, and death are extinguished" ("juntamente se apagan el espacio, el tiempo, la muerte"; ***OP*** 64, 20). What Borges is driving at in these poems is made explicit in another piece, **"Amanecer" ("Daybreak")**. The poem is set in the dead of night, just before daylight appears: with "the threat of dawn" ("la amenaza del alba"), the poet exclaims,

I sensed the dreadful conjecture
of Schopenhauer and Berkeley
that declares the world
an activity of the mind,
a mere dream of beings,
without basis, purpose or volume.

Resentí la tremenda conjetura
de Schopenhauer y de Berkeley
que declara que el mundo
es una actividad de la mente,
un sueño de las almas,
sin base ni propósito ni volumen.

(*OP* 64, 47)

In the rest of the poem, Borges follows out the logic of Berkeleyan idealism. There is a brief moment, he writes, when "only a few nightowls maintain / and only in an ashen, sketched-out form / the vision of the streets / which later they will, with others, define" ("sólo algunos trasnochadores conservan / cenicienta y apenas bosquejada / la visión de las calles / que definirán después con los otros"; ***OP*** 64, 48). In this moment in which few or no mortals are maintaining the universe, "it would be easy for God / to destroy completely his works" ("le sería fácil a Dios / matar del todo su obra!"; ***OP***, 48). Berkeley, as a corollary to his idealism, posited God as the maintainer of the universe—if and when there were no human beings available to perceive and hence to guarantee its existence. But Borges injects another thought into the poem, and one that is alien to Berkeleyan philosophy. He suggests that there is some danger that God might choose to take advantage of this brief period when the universe hangs by a thread. The implication here is that a capricious, vindictive, or negligent God may actually wish to destroy the world. Rather than in Berkeley, the source for this notion is to be found in Gnosticism, a philosophical current that has shaped much of Borges's thought. **"Amanecer,"** at any rate, ends on an optimistic note: dawn comes, people awake, God has not chosen to destroy the world, and "annulled night / has remained only in the eyes of the blind" ("la noche abolida / se ha quedado en los ojos de los ciegos"; ***OP*** 64, 49).

Two of Borges's best-known essays, written years after the poetry of the ***Fervor***, are intriguingly titled "Historía de la eternidad" (A history of eternity, 1936) and "Nueva refutación del tiempo" (A new refutation of time, 1947). In both these pieces, as well as in many other essays, stories, and poems, Borges's preoccupation with time is most apparent. This very human desire to halt the flow of time persisted through the last years of Borges's career, as we shall note when the poetry of the seventies and eighties is examined. Certain words and phrases that crop up in ***Fervor*** illustrate this intense desire. The verb *remansar* (to dam up, to create a backwater or eddy) and its related adjective *remansado* are not particularly common terms in the Spanish poetic lexicon though they appear several times in the ***Fervor*** and occasionally in later collections. Borges writes of an "afternoon which had been damned up into a plaza" ("la tarde toda se había remansado en la plaza"; ***OP*** 64, 25); of a dark, old-fashioned bedroom where a mirror is "like a backwater in the shadows" ("como un remanso en la sombra"; ***OP*** 64, 62); of doomlike solitude "dammed-up around the town" ("La soledad . . . se ha remansado alrededor del pueblo"; ***OP*** 64, 67). The significance is obvious: if time is a river, then the poet is seeking the quiet backwaters where time's flow is halted. Though Borges's fascination with time has often been interpreted as an example of a purely intellectual exercise, the very personal sources of this interest should not be overlooked. The traumatic return to Buenos Aires as well as the essential inwardness of his personality clearly help account for the emphasis on this theme in his early work.

In addition to the *remanso* motif, the ***Fervor*** contains other fine examples of Borges's reaction to the rush of time. He begins the poem **"Vanilocuencia" ("Empty talk")** by stating "the city is inside me like a poem / which I have not succeeded in stopping with words." ("La ciudad está en mí como un poema / que no he logrado detener en palabras" ***OP*** 64, 32). Although words, especially in the form of poetry, seemingly "freeze" or "pin down" the flow of time, Borges is aware of the crushing fact that the objects of the world are "disdainful of verbal symbols" ("desdeñosas de símbolos verbales"; ***OP*** 64, 32) and that despite his poetry every morning he will awake to see a new and changed world. The futility of trying to check the flow of time by literary creations, by recalling the past, or by surrounding oneself with old things appears clearly in the ***Fervor*** and subsequently became a dominant theme in all of Borges's writing. His attitude is ambivalent and leads to a poetic tension for he knows that time—in the brutally real, everyday sense—flows on, that the world will change, that he will grow old, and that the past is forever gone. Yet he is reluctant to give in without a struggle, though he knows his efforts are futile. And so the rich and plastic descriptions of antique furniture, of old photographs, and of timeless streets are usually undermined by a word or phrase suggesting that their solidity and apparent timelessness are merely illusory. For example, the old daguerreotypes in **"Sala vacía" ("Empty Drawing Room")** are deceiving by "their false nearness" ("su falsa cercanía"), for under close examination they "slip away / like useless dates / of blurred anniversaries" ("se escurren / como fechas inútiles / de aniversarios borrosos"; ***OP*** 64, 33). Another possible way of deceiving oneself about time, of "refuting" time, as Borges would later say, is found in the realm of ritualistic activity. The point is well exemplified in **"El truco" ("The trick")**, a poem whose thematic material is a card game, but whose message is that in playing games—essentially participating in a ritual—"normal" time is displaced. He writes, "At the edges of the card table / ordinary life is halted" ("En los lindes de la mesa / el vivir común se detiene"; ***OP*** 64, 27). Within the confines of the table—a magical zone—an ancient, timeless struggle is again waged, and the "players in their present ardor / copy the tricks of a remote age" ("los jugadores en fervor presente / copian remotas bazas"; ***OP*** 64, 28). Borges concludes the poem with the thought that this kind of activity "just barely" immortalizes the dead comrades whose struggles are relived. For a brief moment in the heat of the game, past and present are fused. The mythical kings, queens, and princes whose faces decorate the "cardboard amulets" become comrades-in-arms of the twentieth-century Argentine country folk seated about the table.

Borges's poetry, if examined with an objective eye, reveals surprisingly sentimental, affectionate qualities. There are, for example, some touching love poems in ***Fervor***: among these **"Ausencia" ("Absence")**, **"Sábados" ("Saturdays")**, and **"Trofeo" ("Trophy")** are especially noteworthy. And when Borges writes of his favorite streets, of patios and suburban gardens, he adopts a tone of filial devotion that suggests the warmest of personal relationships. He displays a mood of frankness and sincerity which those who know his work only superficially do not usually associate with him. Indeed, some of the material in the first edition (omitted in later editions) is almost confessional in tone.[3] It seems as if the Borges of 1923 were at a crossroads. Had he been a man of different temperament, it is quite possible that he would have yielded to the temptation of creating a literature of unrestrained personal catharsis. Instead, he chose to deny the emotive side of life in his art. At least he promised that he would do this in his poetry. As he writes in one of the last poems of the ***Fer-***

vor: "I must enclose my twilight tears / within the hard diamond of a poem. / It matters not that one's soul may wander naked like the wind and alone . . ." ("He de encerrar el llanto de las tardes / en el duro diamante del poema. / Nada importa que el alma / ande sola y desnuda como el viento . . ."; ***OP*** 64, 64).

But Borges was not yet ready to sacrifice life and passion to art. Thus he states in the prologue to his second collection, ***Luna de enfrente*** (***Moon across the way,*** 1925), that "Our daily existence is a dialogue of death and life. . . . There is a great deal of nonlife in us, and chess, meetings, lectures, daily tasks are often mere representations of life, ways of being dead."[4] He states that he wishes to avoid these "mere representations" of life in his poetry, that he prefers to write of things that affect him emotionally, of "heavenly blue neighborhood garden walls," for example. It is understandable, then, that among the twenty-eight compositions of ***Luna de enfrente***, poems of deep personal involvement should predominate over pieces of a more detached and formalistic nature. A feeling of intimacy pervades the ***Luna***: a third of the poems are in the second-person familiar form and the bulk of the remainder are in the first person. By contrast, the earlier ***Fervor*** contains only a few pieces directed to the familiar "you" (*tú*), while the majority are in the relatively impersonal third person. A further indication of the greater degree of intimacy of ***Luna de enfrente*** is seen in Borges's tendency to personify such inanimate things as the pampa, city streets, and the city itself. Finally, a substantial number of the compositions in the 1925 collection are love poems, among which are such memorable pieces as the **"Antelación de amor"** (**"Anticipation of Love"**) and the **"Dualidá en una despedida"** (**"Duality on Saying Farewell"**).

Several typically Borgesian themes that appeared in ***Fervor*** are again seen in ***Luna de enfrente***. The same tendency to soften or undermine exterior reality is evident in Borges's frequent use of the hazy light of twilight or dawn. This technique is well illustrated in such pieces as **"Calle con almacén rosado"** (**"Street with a pink store"**), **"Dualidá en una despedida"**, **"Montevideo,"** and **"Ultimo sol en Villa Ortúzar"** (**"Sunset Over Villa Ortuzar"**). Of even greater interest in the ***Luna*** is the poet's preoccupation with time. In this collection Borges's emphasis is on the relationship between time and memory rather than on the simple desire to halt time's flow. More precisely, memory becomes the *remanso*, the quiet backwater in which time's onward rush is checked. This relationship is very clear in **"Montevideo,"** a poem in which Borges states that the more old-fashioned, less bustling Montevideo helps recreate the Buenos Aires of his early memories. Of the Uruguayan city he writes: "Like the memory of a frank friendship you are a clear and calm millpond in the twilight" ("Eres remansada y clara en la tarde como el recuerdo de una lisa amistad").[5] A somewhat similar verse appears in the magnificent **"Anticipation of Love,"** when the poet describes his beloved asleep as "calm and resplendent like a bit of happiness in memory's selection" ("quieta y resplandeciente como una dicha en la selección del recuerdo"; ***OP*** 64, 77). In these and other poems memory performs the important function of preserving past experience against the onslaught of time. But, Borges implies, memory is also a storehouse, a kind of infinite filing cabinet, the contents of which we cannot always control. We may indeed remember too much. In **"Los llanos"** (**"The plains"**) he writes, "It is sad that memory includes everything / and especially if memories are unpleasant" ("Es triste que el recuerdo incluya todo / y más aún si es bochornoso el recuerdo"; ***OP*** 64, 76). Perhaps these lines prefigure Borges's bizarre account—to be written some twenty years later—of **"Funes el memorioso,"** the man who remembered everything.

Some two years before Borges published ***Luna de enfrente*** he was asked to answer a series of questions for a magazine survey of young writers. In answer to a question about his age, he wrote "I have already wearied twenty-two years."[6] The choice of words here is significant, for there is the curious tone of the world-weary old man even in his work of the mid-1920s. This tone, contrasting markedly with the passionate lyricism of several pieces in the ***Luna de enfrente***, takes the form of the poet's proclaiming that he has already lived a good deal of his life and that he will do nothing new in the future. The theme is very clear in **"Mi vida entera"** (**"My Whole Life"**):

> I have crossed the sea.
> I have lived in many lands; I have seen one woman and two or three men
> . . . I have savored many words.
> I profoundly believe that this is all and that I will neither see nor do any new things.
>
> He atravesado el mar.
> He practicado muchas tierras; he visto una mujer y dos otros hombres.
> . . . He paladeado numerosas palabras.
> Creo profundamente que eso es todo y que ni veré ni ejecutaré cosas nuevas.
>
> (***OP*** 64, 98).

A somewhat similar tone is present in some of the poems describing the pampas: in **"Los llanos,"** for example, Borges tries to infuse the plains with a feeling of tiredness and resignation suggestive of his own mood. It is difficult to determine what lies behind this pose of bored world-weariness. Is Borges retreating from life or is he simply stating what has become a cornerstone of his esthetic edifice: that there is nothing new under the sun; that changes, progress, novelty, and history are simply a reshuffling of a limited number of preexisting elements? Perhaps this is the philosophy he intends to set forth in the cryptic line that ends his poem **"Manuscrito hallado en un libro de Joseph Conrad"** (**"Manuscript Found in a Book of Joseph Conrad"**): "River, the first river. Man, the first man" ("El río, el primer río. El hombre, el primer hombre"; ***OP*** 64, 88).

Although history may be nothing more than the recurrence or the reshuffling of what has always been, Borges is nonetheless fascinated by historical events and personalities. Several of the pieces in the ***Luna*** show this interest. The dramatic death of the nineteenth-century gaucho leader Quiroga is very effectively commemorated in **"El General Quiroga va en coche al muere"** (**"General Quiroga Rides to His Death in a Carriage"**); the death of his own ancestor, Colonel Francisco Borges, provides the subject matter of another piece; and **"Dulcia linquimus arva"** evokes the early days of settlement on the pampas. Of the three, the poem to Quiroga is the most interesting for several reasons. First, the night scene of Quiroga's coach rocking across the moonlit pampa has a dramatic, almost romantic, feeling of movement uncommon in much of Borges's poetry. Second, though he is here still more or less faithful to the free verse tenets of his youth, Borges sees fit to place the poem within a fairly regular structure—rhythmic lines of about fourteen syllables arranged in quatrains having considerable assonance. The effect of this form is striking; it suggests the beat of the horses' hooves and the rocking of the coach racing on toward its encounter with destiny:

The coach swayed back and forth rumbling the hills:
An emphatic, enormous funeral galley.
Four death-black horses in the darkness
Pulled six fearful and one watchful brave man

. . . . .

That sly, trouble-making Córdoba rabble
(thought Quiroga), what power have they over me?
Here am I firm in the stirrup of life
Like a stake driven deep in the heart of the pampa.
. . .

(El coche se hamacaba rezongando la altura:
un galerón enfático, enorme, funerario.
Cuatro tapaos con pinta de muerte en la negrura
tironeaban seis miedos y un valor desvelado.

. . . . .

Esa cordobesada bochinchera y ladina
[meditaba Quiroga] ¿qué ha de poder con mi alma?
Aquí estoy afianzado y metido en la vida
como la estaca pampa bien metida en la pampa;

(***OP*** 64, 80)

It is to Borges's credit as a poet that despite his mild adherence to the restrictive poetic tenets of *ultráismo* he sensed the rightness of a more traditional form for this particular poem.

In **"El General Quiroga va en coche al muere"** Borges provides an insight into the kind of historical characters and events that were to dominate much of his later work, especially his prose. What fascinates him are those moments in which an individual—soldier, bandit, or similar man of action—reaches a crucial point in his life, a dramatic juncture where a turn of fate, a sudden decision, or a dazzling revelation cause a man to follow one path rather than another. Such events are delicate points of balance that determine whether a man shall become a hero or traitor, a martyr or coward. Borges was especially intrigued by them since they often provided a glimpse of an alternative track for history. What would have been the course of Argentine history if Rosas had not killed Facundo or if (as in one of his later poems) King Charles of England had not been beheaded? **"General Quiroga Rides to His Death in a Carriage"** is also significant in that it reveals another important side of Borges's interests. Though he may have been a shy and retiring bibliophile, he did have an undeniable affection for men of action. Gunmen, pirates, *compadres* (a kind of Buenos Aires neighborhood tough), ancient warriors, and modern spies fill the pages of his poetry, essays, and fiction.

The last group of early poems Borges chose to publish as a collection, ***Cuaderno San Martín*** (***San Martin Notebook***, 1929), contains only twelve pieces, one of which, **"Arrabal en que pesa el campo"** (**"Suburb in which the country lies heavily"**), has been omitted from more recent editions. Two themes dominate these poems: nostalgia for the past, and death. Often the two blend in a mood of elegiac evocation. Thus in the most memorable poems of the book Borges writes of the "mythical" founding of Buenos Aires; of his beloved Palermo district as it was at the close of the nineteenth century; of his grandfather Isidoro Acevedo; of the final resting place of his ancestors, the Recoleta cemetary; and of the suicide of his friend and fellow poet Francisco López Merino.

What the poet preserves in his memory in a sense lives; only what is gone and forgotten is really dead. In **"Elegía de los portones"** (**"Elegy to gates"**), for example, Borges describes the act of forgetting as "a minuscule death" ("una muerte chica"; ***OP*** 64, 107). Yet he is perfectly aware that death—real death—is undeniable: he knows that his attempts to negate its reality through memory and through poetry will be frustrated. He is haunted by the song of the wandering slum-minstrel in the poem to the Chacarita cemetery: "Death is life already lived. / Life is approaching death." ("La muerte es vida vivida, / la vida es muerte que viene"). It even haunts him when he writes, in the same piece, that he doesn't believe in the cemetery's decrepitude and that "the fullness of only one rose is greater than all your tombstones" ("la plenitud de una sola rosa es más que tus mármoles"; ***OP*** 64, 122).

One of the most interesting pieces in the collection is on the death of Borges's ancestor, Isidoro Acevedo. Aside from its intrinsic value, this poem is noteworthy because in it Borges gives a clear hint of the kind of literature he would produce in the decade to follow. This "prefiguring"—to use one of his own favorite terms—of his future prose occurs in the description of Acevedo's last day. The old man lying on his deathbed in a state of feverish delirium plans a complete military compaign in his mind. Though Acevedo only mutters a few fragmentary phrases, Borges uses these as a point of departure to recreate the very concrete fantasy he assumes his moribund grandfather was in effect experiencing:

He dreamt of two armies
that were going into the shadows of battle;

he enumerated each commanding officer, the banners,
each unit

. . . . .

He surveyed the pampa
noted the rough country that the infantry might seize
and the smooth plain in which a cavalry strike would
be invincible.
He made a final survey,

he gathered together the thousands of faces that man
unknowingly knows after
many years:
bearded faces that are probably fading away in daguerreotypes,
faces that lived near his own in Puente Alsina and
Cepeda.

. . . . .

He gathered an army of Buenos Aires' ghosts

. . . . .

He died in the military service of his faith in the *patria.*

Soñó con dos ejércitos
que entraban en la sombra de una batalla;
enumeró los comandos, las banderas, las unidades.

. . . . .

Hizo leva de pampa:
vió terreno quebrado para que pudiera aferrarse la infantería
y llanura resuelta para que el tirón de la caballería fuera invencible.
Hizo una leva última,
congregó los miles de rostros que el hombre sabe sin
saber después de los años:
caras de barba que se estarán desvaneciendo en daguerrotipos,
caras que vivieron junto a la suya en el Puente Alsina
y Cepeda.

. . . . .

juntó un ejército de sombras porteñas

. . . . .

murió en milicia de su convicción por la patria.

(***OP*** 64, 113–14)

Those who are familiar with Borges's fiction may appreciate the similarity of this poem to such short stories as the "Ruinas circulares" ("The Circular Ruins"). There are only a few steps between describing the disturbing concreteness of dreams and suggesting that what we call the real world may actually be the product of some unknown being's dream.

Borges continued to write poetry after 1929, though his output of verse, particularly during the thirties and forties, was not very great. There may be some significance to the fact that between the summer of 1929 and the spring of 1931 he published nothing. This hiatus may have been due to the extremely unsettled political and economic conditions of the period: a similar pattern can be observed in the literary activity of other Argentine writers during the same two years. When Borges resumed publishing, he devoted himself chiefly to essays and literary criticism, genres in which he had been working steadily throughout the twenties. It was not until 1934 that he again began writing poetry. Oddly enough, he broke his poetic silence with two pieces composed in English. These were followed by **"Insomnio"** (**"Insomnia"**, 1936), **"La noche cíclica"** (**"The Cyclical Night,"** 1940), **"Del infierno y del cielo"** (**"Of heaven and hell"**, 1942), **"Poema conjectural"** (**"Conjectural poem,"** 1943), and **"Poema del cuarto elemento"** (**"Poem of the fourth element"**, 1944). Between March 1944 and April 1953 Borges wrote no poetry; at least he published none. Yet it was during this period that he produced his most celebrated stories and a number of important essays. The seven poems that Borges published between 1934 and 1944 are, at first glance, quite dissimilar in both form and content. The **"Two English Poems,"** for example, are amorous in theme and are cast in extremely free verse, so much so that they could be regarded as poetic prose:

I offer you my ancestors, my dead men; the ghosts
that living men have honoured in marble:
my father's father killed in the frontier of
Buenos Aires, two bullets through his lungs,
bearded and dead, wrapped by his soldiers in
the hide of a cow; my mother's grandfather
—just twenty-four—heading a charge of
three hundred men in Peru, now ghosts on vanished
horses."

(***OP*** 64, 142)

"Insomnio" is also written in free verse, but unlike the **"Two English Poems"** its lines are generally shorter and its appearance on the printed page is more traditional. **"La noche cíclica,"** in sharp contrast to most of the poetry Borges had published previously, is written in neat quatrains rhymed in the *cuarteto* pattern (abba). In the next two poems of this group, **"Del infierno y del cielo"** and **"Conjectural Poem,"** Borges reverted to a rather free unrhymed form, only to use the *cuarteto* again in 1944 in his **"Poema del cuarto elemento."** The significance of these formal shifts should not be overestimated: they only indicate that Borges would from this point on be bound neither by the orthodoxy of his free-verse *ultraísta* years nor by the orthodoxy of traditional forms.

Why Borges chose to write the **"Two English Poems"** in the language of his paternal grandmother is a matter neither he nor his commentators have discussed. Perhaps these compositions are merely a tour de force or perhaps they indicate a feeling of alienation from the not too pleasant surroundings of Buenos Aires in the early thirties. Certain details in the poems suggest the latter possibility. Borges reveals an ennui and desperation in these pieces that are clearly lacking in the earlier poetry. The opening lines of the first poem are indicative of this mood: "The useless dawn finds me in a deserted street corner." A bit later he speaks of the night as having left him "some hated friends to chat / with, music for dreams, and the smoking of / bitter ashes. The things that my hungry heart / has no use for." The piece ends on a note of great intensity summed up in some of Borges's finest lines. At daybreak, the poet says, "The shattering dawn finds me in a deserted street of my city." The "lazily and incessantly beautiful" woman to whom the poem is addressed is gone. The poet is left with only memories of the encounter and with a desperate longing: "I must get at you, somehow: I put away those / illustrious toys you have left me, I want your hidden look, your real smile—that lonely, / mocking smile your cool mirror knows" (***OP*** 64, 140–41). The same tone of desperation pervades the second English poem when the poet asks his beloved:

> What can I hold you with?
> I offer you lean streets, desperate sunsets, the
> moon of jagged suburbs.
> I offer you the bitterness of a man who has looked
> long and long at the lonely moon.

Throughout the remainder of the piece—as quotable as any Borges has written—he continues to enumerate what he can "offer." The last lines reinforce and climax the entire poem: "I can give you my loneliness, my darkness, the / hunger of my heart; I am trying to bribe you / with uncertainty, with danger, with defeat" (***OP*** 64, 142–43). The details of these give a picture of almost surrealistic disintegration: *lean* streets, *shattering dawn, jagged* suburbs. These are not typically Borgesian adjectives. And in **"Insomnio,"** a poem whose intent is admittedly quite different from that of the English pieces, the poet's restlessness is aggravated by visions of "shattered tenements" ("despedazado arrabal"), "leagues of obscene garbagestrewn pampa" ("leguas de pampa basurera y obscena", and similar scenes (***OP*** 64, 138).

The references to insomnia, to loneliness, to bitterness, and the use of adjectives suggestive of disintegration have little in common with the often ardent, though seldom desperate, poems of the earlier collections. The unusual character of his verse of the thirties points to the fact that he was undergoing a period of transition in his literary career. Borges seems, moreover, to have suffered some kind of personal crisis, aggravated, perhaps, by a political and economic environment distasteful to him. An examination of his prose of the mid-1930s supports this view. It is especially significant that the genesis of his distinctive fiction—a literature of evasion, his critics might say—comes precisely at this time.

Notes

1. Borges, "Ultraísmo," 466–71.
2. This poem does not appear in later editions of the *Obra poética.*
3. An interesting example of the poetry suppressed in later editions is "Llamarada." The piece is actually a prose poem, quite confessional, and even a bit erotic. Note the line, "deseando . . . perdernos en las culminaciones carnales."
4. Jorge Luis Borges, *Luna de enfrente* (Buenos Aires: Proa, 1925), 7.
5. Jorge Luis Borges, *Poemas: 1923–1958* (Buenos Aires: Emecé, 1958), 82. Although it appears in the original and in this 1958 collection, "Monterideo" is omitted from later editions of the *Obra poética.*
6. Jorge Luis Borges, "Contestación a la encuesta sobre la nueva generación literaria," *Nosotros* 168 (May 1923): 16–17.

Martin S. Stabb (essay date 1991)

SOURCE: "A Late Harvest," in *Borges Revisited*, Twayne Publishers, 1991, pp. 69–100.

[*In the following excerpt, Stabb offers a brief survey of Borges's later poetry.*]

Later Poetry

In 1964, Borges's publishers, the Buenos Aires firm of Emecé Editores, brought out a single volume ***Obra poética*** (***Poetic works***) that included, with some modifications, his three early collections and a group of mostly newer compositions under the subheading "El otro, el mismo" ("The other, himself").[1] This section of the volume also includes the poems of ***Dreamtigers***, though they are not identified as such. In addition, the collection retrieves a few poems from the forties and early fifties that had not appeared in earlier poetic collections. The 1979 ***Obra poética*** uses the same subtitle, "El otro, el mismo," for a section of the volume but adds a new prologue and a number of poems written in the late 1960s while it excludes the material from ***Dreamtigers.*** The same volume also includes a short collection of folkloric poetry, ***Para las seis cuerdas*** (***For the six strings***, 1965), ***In Praise of Darkness*** (1969), the poetry from ***The Gold of the Tigers*** (1972), ***La rosa profunda*** (***The profound rose***, 1976), and ***La moneda de hierro*** (***The iron coin,*** 1976). The ***Historia de la noche*** (***History of the night***) appeared late in 1977 and is not included in the 1979 ***Obra poética.*** Borges's last two collections of poetry, ***La cifra*** (***The cipher***) and ***Los conjurados*** (***The plotters***), were published in 1981 and 1985 respectively.

It was seen earlier that after the mid-1930s, following a decade of prolific work in the genre, Borges's poetic activity was apparently declining. Yet a few poems of these years must be briefly noted: **"La noche cíclica"** (**"The Cyclical Night"**), a philosophical piece on the idea of cyclical history; **"Del infierno y del cielo"** (**"Of heaven and hell"**), a poem that signals Borges's growing fascination with *otredad*, a theme that came into full flower in ***Dreamtigers***; and the dramatic **"Poema conjectural"** (**"Conjectural Poem"**), one of Borges's personal favorites. **"Mateo XXV, 30"** (**"Matthew XXV:30"**) is another piece that serves to introduce the later poetry and also to underscore the importance of poetry in Borges's life. In it he likens himself to the foolish virgins in the parable of the ten talents. Though he has been given everything, all the raw material a poet might desire, "Stars, bread, libraries of East and West / . . . a human body to walk with on the earth / . . . algebra and fire" ("Estrellas, pan, bibliotecas orientales y occidentales / . . . un cuerpo humano para andar por la tierra / . . . algebra y fuego"), a voice tells him "You have used up the years and they have used up you, / and still, you have not written the poem" ("Has gastado los años y te han gastado, / Y todavía no has escrito el poema").[2]

By the mid-1960s Borges seems to have regained considerable momentum as a poet. Both thematically and technically his work displays a richness not seen since the 1920s. Although he appears to have acquired new interests, such as ancient Norse and Anglo-Saxon culture, older preoccupations persist, such as his unceasing infatuation with his native city and the history of his family. Certainly history, viewed at times in the microcosm of a small but crucial event, and at other times in broad sweep, remained a central concern. Closely related to his interest in the specifics of history is his constant fascination with time. And perhaps at the very root of all these concerns is a notion that recurs almost obsessively in his poetry as well as in his prose: the idea of the world as a complex enigma, expressed at times in the form of a labyrinth, or as the dream-made-real of a capricious creator.

On the technical side, a few generalizations can be made regarding the poetry of this later period. One of these is that while Borges never abandoned free verse and experimental forms, he shows an increasing tendency to use traditional metric patterns, notably the sonnet (in both its English and Italianate forms) and the hendecasyllable, especially as used in rhymed *cuartetos* (quatrains). Borges frequently stated that his fondness for more structured verse stemmed, at least in part, from the fact that it was easier for a nearly blind person to write poetry in these forms because it required less dependence on a visual text.

The first separately published poetry collection of the sixties is, in a sense, an anomaly. ***Para las seis cuerdas*** consists of only eleven compositions, all cast as lyrics of *milongas*, an Argentine musical form of the recent past. These pieces are written in strongly accented octosyllabic verse, hardly Borges's favorite metrical vehicle. Yet their spirit and content could not be more Borgesian: they reflect, albeit in a ritualistic, stylized manner, the world of passion and violence that pervaded the Buenos Aires lower-class outer suburbs of a century ago. This is the same world that fascinated Borges in his earliest narratives such as **"Streetcorner Man,"** and that would continue to haunt him in his prose of the seventies: a vanished no-man's-land where the pampa impinges on the city; where weapons appear to have a life of their own; and where neighborhood *compadritos* settle old scores in almost balletic knife fights. Note, for example a fragment from the **"Milonga de Calandria"** (**"Milonga about Calandria"**): "He wasn't one of those technicians / Who'd use a trigger to bet his life / The game that he enjoyed / Was the dance that's done with a knife." ("No era un científico de esos / Que usan arma de gatillo; / Era su gusto jugarse / En el baile del cuchillo"; ***OP*** [***Obra poética, 1923–76***], 310). Although they can hardly be considered examples of Borges's most important poetry, the *milongas* of this collection provide an impressive example of how a sophisticated poet can take full advantage of a rich folkloric tradition. Moreover, those who are fond of ancient ballads or who enjoy Argentina's gauchesque poetry will find ***Para las seis cuerdas*** especially satisfying.

It is more difficult to generalize about the other poetry of the decade. Leaving aside the *milongas*, the sixty-odd poems of the period constitute an album of Borges's wanderings both spiritual and real. Prominent among his concerns are such things as the world of ancient Norsemen and Britons, comments on his favorite authors, his characteristic fascination with historical turning points, and the ever present evocation of old Buenos Aires. Many of these apparently disparate themes are, however, quite similar in underlying motif. For example, his near obsession with weapons, especially swords and daggers that seem to have a mystical autonomy, is glimpsed in the sonnet **"A una espada en York"** (**"To a sword in York"**) as well as in the prose poem **"El puñal"** (**"The dagger"**). In one case the setting is ancient Britain, in the other it is the Hispanic world of Spain and Argentina, yet in both pieces the weapons are underscored as "symbols and names" of heroic destinies. In **"El puñal,"** especially, the idea of the weapon as an independent living thing is clear:

> It is more than a metallic artifact . . .
> it is in a sense eternal, this dagger
> that killed a man in Tacuarembó
> and the daggers that killed Caesar.
> It desires to kill, it wants to shed fresh blood.
>
> Es más que una estructura de metales . . .
> es de algún modo eterno, el puñal
> que anoche mató a un hombre en Tacuarembó
> y los puñales que mataron a César.
> Qiuere matar, quiere derramar brusca sangre.
>
> (***OP***, 281)

The same motif dominates the free-verse **"Fragmento"** (**"Fragment"**) in which Borges evokes the sword of Beowulf, "una espada que será leal / Hasta una hora que ya sabe el Destino" ("a sword that will be loyal / Until that hour already known by Destiny"; ***OP***, 228). The theme is further evidenced in several pieces dealing with heroic deaths: the fine sonnet to the medieval Icelandic leader Snorri Sturluson and the poem to a nameless casualty of the American Civil War, **"Un soldado de Lee"** (**"A Soldier under Lee"**).

But not all the poetry of this period is centered on death or bloody weapons. A number of finely wrought sonnets present vignettes of favorite personages such as Emerson, Poe, Whitman, Cansinos-Assens, Heine, Swedenborg, Spinoza, and Jonathan Edwards. Finally, several poems may be described as purely lyrical in nature. Of these, two sonnets, one titled in English, **"Everness,"** and the other in German, **"Ewigkeit,"** are particularly striking. Both are structured around one of Borges's perennial concerns—the timeless realm of memory. The first piece begins with the affirmation "Sólo una cosa no hay. Es el olvido" ("Only one thing does not exist. It is forgetting"); almost the same verse appears in the first tercet of **"Ewigkeit"**: "I know that one thing does not exist. It is forgetting" ("Sé que una cosa no hay. Es el olvido"; ***OP***, 258–59). **"Everness"** is perhaps the more personal of these companion pieces, as it hints at a long-remembered love. The poet recalls a face "left" in the reflection of mirrors at twilight and then concludes in a lovely pair of tercets:

> And everything is part of that diverse
> Glass of memory, the universe;
> Whose arduous corridors are endless
> And whose doors close as you walk by
> Only on the other side of twilight
> Will you see Archetypes and Splendors.
>
> Y todo es una parte del diverso
> Cristal de esa memoria, el universo;
> no tiene fin sus arduos corredores
> Y las puertas se cierran a tu paso;
> Solo del otro lado del ocaso
> Verás los Arquetipos y Esplendores.
>
> (***OP***, 258)

Borges referred to his collection of 1969, ***In Praise of Darkness***, as his "fifth book of verse" and he notes in his prologue that while some prose "co-existed" with the poetry, he would prefer that the volume be read as a book of verse. The fact that half a dozen very short prose pieces are included leads Borges to make some interesting observations regarding the fine line that divides prose from poetry: "It is often said that free verse is no more than a typographical sham; I feel an error lurks in this assertion. Beyond its rhythm, the typographical appearance of free verse informs the reader that what lies in store for him is not information or reasoning but emotion."[3]

And indeed it is poetic emotion that awaits us in this collection. For example, the title piece, though placed at the end of the volume, represents one of Borges's most lyrical moments. Musing on his age and blindness, he observes:

> My friends are faceless
> women are as they were years back.
> one street corner is taken for another,
> on the pages of books there are no letters.
> All this should make me uneasy,
> but there's a restfulness about, a going back.
>
> Mis amigos no tienen cara,
> las mujeres son lo que fueron hace ya tantos años,
> las esquinas pueden ser otras,
> no hay letras en las páginas de los libros.
> Todo esto debería atemorizarme,
> pero es una dulzura, un regreso.
>
> (***PD***, 125)

Then, after recalling the multitude of his life's memories, he concludes: "Now I can forget them. I reach my center, / my algebra and my key, / my mirror. / Soon I shall know who I am" ("Ahora puedo olvidarlas. Llego a mi centro, / a mi álgebra y mí clave, / a mi espejo. / Pronto sabré quien soy"; ***PD***, 127). A number of other poems in this collection reveal similar lyrical richness coupled with strong personal references. **"Junio, 1968" ("June, 1968")**, for example, is another lovely free-verse piece in which the poet uses a third-person viewpoint to describe himself at the task of arranging books in his library. The scene is set in a "golden afternoon," and the subject, while lovingly handling each volume muses:

> . . . Alfonso Reyes surely will be pleased
> to share space close to Virgil
> [to arrange a library is to practice,
> in a quiet and modest way,
> the art of criticism.]
>
> . . . a Reyes no le desagradará ciertamente
> la cercanía de Virgilio,
> (ordenar bibliotecas es ejercer,
> de un modo silencioso y modesto,
> el arte de la crítica."
>
> (***PD***, 71)

The poem ends on a touching personal note with Borges again recognizing his blindness, the fact that he can no longer fully appreciate the books he is handling, and, most important, that he will never produce *the* book, "the book which . . . might justify him" ("el libro que lo justificará"; ***PD***, 71).

During the last decades of his life Borges did a considerable amount of traveling, and his poetry testifies to his odyssey. Not surprisingly, whether he writes of Cambridge, Israel, or Iowa, his reaction to these places is essentially internal rather than external. Yet the fact that he vaguely senses the reality of unfamiliar locales seems to activate his muse, producing some fine lyrical moments, filtered through a rich matrix of literary and personal recollection. Thus in the sonnet **"New England, 1967"** he writes:

> Any day now [we are told] snow will come
> and out on every street America
> awaits me, but as evening falls I feel
> the slowness of today and the brevity of yesterday.
> Buenos Aires, yours are the streets that I
> go on walking without a why or when.
>
> Pronto (nos dicen) llegará la nieve
> y América me espera en cada esquina,
> pero siento en la tarde que declina
> el hoy tan lento y el ayer tan breve.
> Buenos Aires, yo sigo caminando
> por tus esquinas, sin por qué ni cuándo.
>
> (***PD***, 27)

The opposite perspective is seen in **"Acevedo,"** a sonnet in which Borges celebrates a visit to his grandparents' property on the pampa and which brings to mind other similar regions he has known: "Plains are everywhere the same. I have seen / such land in Iowa, in our own south, in the Holy Land. . . . / That land is not lost. It is mine. I own / it in wistfulness, in oblivion" ("La llanura es ubicua. Los he visto / en Iowa, en el Sur, en tierra hebrea. . . . / No los perdí. Son míos. Los poseo / En el olvido, en un casual deseo"; ***PD***, 81).

With regard to meter, throughout the collection the sonnet vies with free verse, with the former often used for pieces stressing external description and the latter for more intimate, confessional lyrics. Although this is far from an invariable relationship, it does account for a goodly number of the collection's poems. Some support for this notion may be seen in the unusual coupled pieces on the famous Dürer engraving, **"Dos versiones de 'Ritter, Tod und Teufel'"** (**"Two Versions of 'Ritter, Tod und Teufel'"**). In the first version, a sonnet, the graphic work is described in firmly drawn "objective" terms; in the second, consisting of twenty-two unrhymed hendecasyllables, Borges writes of "the other path" suggested by the knight's journey, that is, his own path, his own mortality.

The many canonical themes that run through ***In Praise of Darkness*** and the familiar ghosts that haunt its pages cannot be adequately treated in this brief discussion. In addition to the motifs noted here, the rich sampling of Borgesian preoccupations found in the volume would include the metaphor of the labyrinth, Heraclitus's river of time, the *Rubaiyat*, and of course Buenos Aires with its *compadritos*, knife fights, and passions.

In his 1972 prologue to ***The Gold of the Tigers*** Borges wrote that "for anyone who has lived out seventy years . . . there is little to hope for except to go on plying familiar skills, with an occasional mild variation and with tedious repetitious."[4] This very modest assessment of the collection may be, to a degree, accurate, yet Borges certainly made a fine art of variation on familiar themes—itself the very essence of great literature, as he so often suggested. A good example is seen in the rich hendecasyllables of **"Cosas"** (**"Things"**), a rather long enumerative poem in which Borges lists, with much fondness, those things that have been forgotten, that become invisible under certain conditions, that exist unperceived, or that have only the most ephemeral life:

> The mirror which shows nobody's reflection
> after the house has long been left alone.
>
> . . . . .
>
> The momentary but symmetric rose
> which once, by chance, took substance in the shrouded
> mirrors of a boy's kaleidoscope
>
> . . . . .
>
> The colors of a Turner when the lights
> are turned out in the narrow gallery
>
> . . . . .
>
> The echo of the hoofbeats at the charge
> of Junín, which in some enduring mode
> never has ceased, is part of the webbed scheme.
>
> El espejo que que no repite a nadie
> Cuando la casa se ha quedado sola
>
> . . . . .
>
> La simétrica rosa momentánea
> Que el azar dio una vez a los ocultos
> Cristales del pueríl calidoscopio.
>
> . . . . .
>
> Los colores de Turner cuando apagan
> Las luces de la recta galería
>
> . . . . .
>
> El eco de los cascos de la carga
> De Junín, que de algún eterno modo
> No ha cesado y es parte de la trama.
>
> (***GT***, 19–21)

The piece ends with a reference familiar to readers of Borges: "El otro lado del tapiz. Las cosas / Que nadie mira salvo el Dios de Berkeley" ("The other side of the tapestry. The things / which no one sees, except for Berkeley's God"). The appeal to Berkeleyan idealism no longer seems to be a philosophical concern; rather the concept has become a trope suggesting that vast obverse of reality that is best perceived poetically.

A somewhat similar mood prevails in another piece on a familiar theme: the sonnet **"On His Blindness,"** wherein the poet is "unworthy" of direct perception of the real world yet may still savor the riches of literature. Formally the poem is a gem: few sonnets show a better relationship between octave and sestet, dramatically introduced by the verb "I am." Yet another magnificent reworking of an old theme is found in the free-verse composition **"El centinela"** (**"The Watcher"**). Here, as in several earlier texts, Borges is haunted by the ghostlike presence of his "otherness." The poem begins as daylight enters his room, bringing consciousness of the other Borges who not only "lurks" in the room's mirrors and other reflecting surfaces but who even "dictates to me now this poem, which I do not like" ("dicta ahora este poema, que no me gusta"; ***GT***, 29). This is the same being whom, he confesses, has been rejected by several women and who has forced him into the difficult study of the Anglo-Saxon language. The poem concludes with a bitter irony that reveals Borges in a decidedly grim mood: "We know each other too well, inseparable brother. / You drink the water from my cup and you wolf down my bread. / The door to suicide is open, but theologians assert that in the subsequent shadows of the other kingdom, there will be I, waiting for myself" ("Nos conocemos demasiado, inseparable hermano. / Bebes el agua de mi copa y devoras mi pan. / La puerta del suicidio está abierta, pero los teólogos afirman que en la sombra ulterior del otro reino, estaré yo, esperándome"; ***GT***, 29).

A number of pieces in the collection strike familiar chords for anyone who has read the earlier Borges. **"Hengist quiere hombres (449 A.D.)" "Hengist Wants Men, (A.D.**

449)", while celebrating Anglo-Saxon culture from the first Germanic invasions onward, affirms a tenuous line of historical determinism: the Jutish chieftan, Hengist, not only wanted men to capture Britain, but also was sowing the seeds for Shakespeare's literature, for Nelson's ships, and for Borges—the grandson of England's Fanny Haslam—to write his poetry. Several poems again evoke the world of Buenos Aires knife fighters, others sing of the gauchos, and a few stand out for their novelty. Among the latter we find a series of short poems cast in the form of the Japanese tanka, a topical piece on the first moon landing, a poem on the prehistoric cave art of Altamira. One of the most interesting of these atypical compositions is **"Tú"** (**"You"**), a poetic comment on the impersonality of contemporary life and death. The initial verse firmly asserts: "In all the world, one man has been born, one man has died" ("Un solo hombre ha nacido, un solo hombre ha muerto en la Tierra"; ***GT***, 25). To consider people as masses, he asserts, represents only the "impossible calculations" of statistics. This one individual is Ulysses, Cain, Abel, or Darwin on the bridge of the *Beagle.* He is a dead soldier at Hastings, Austerlitz, or Gettysburg. He is also an anonymous patient dying in a hospital, a Jew in a gas chamber; in short, he is you or I. The impressive final verse disproves the charge that Borges was an unfeeling intellectual lacking in human warmth: "One man alone has looked on the enormity of dawn. / One man alone has felt on his tongue the fresh quenching of water, the flavor of fruit and of flesh. / I speak of the unique, the single man, he who is always alone" ("Un solo hombre ha mirado la vasta aurora. / Un solo hombre ha sentido en el paladar la frescura del agua, el sabor de las frutas y de la carne. / Hablo del único, del uno, del que siempre está solo"; ***GT***, 25).

The mid-1970s was a period of considerable poetic production for Borges. Moreover, the three volumes of verse that were published between 1975 and 1977, ***La rosa profunda***, ***La moneda de hierro***, and ***Historia de la noche***, show little diminution of his lyric powers. The first collection, for example, presents several well-turned sonnets that have an almost Parnassian elegance: **"La pantera" ("The panther")**, **"Habla un busto de Jano" ("A bust of Janus speaks")**, or **"El bisonte" ("The buffalo")**. A striking experiment in this form is his Alexandrine sonnet, **"La cierva blanca" ("The white doe")**, a piece evidently inspired by a fleeting dream. He uses the same metrical scheme for another unusual poem in the second collection, **"El ingenuo" ("The simple soul")**. In this piece he confesses his wonderment at ordinary things rather than "marvels"—that a key can open a door, or that "the cruel sword can be beautiful / and that the rose has the fragrance of a rose" ("la espada cruel pueda ser hermosa, / Y que la rosa tenga el olor de la rosa"; ***OP***, 486). These collections are especially rich in intertextual echoes. For example, the sonnet **"Soy" ("I am")** ends on a note suggestive of the Baroque poetry of a Góngora or Sor Juana: "I am an echo, a forgetting, nothing" ("Soy eco, olvido, nada"; ***OP***, 434). And of course there are the innumerable intratexts—poems whose subjects elicit reverberations of Borges's own poetry or prose: ancient Norse warriors, mirrors, coins, and old-time knife fighters like Juan Muraña.

Although Borges's poetry of this period remains impressive in terms of its quality as well as quantity, it is colored by a growing preoccupation with death and general pessimism. Aside from the obvious—that he was growing older—a number of other factors may explain this mood: the ill health and subsequent death of his mother and the brief return of Perón along with the continuing failure of Argentine democracy are a few of these. The bare-boned eleven-line free-verse poem **"El suicida" ("The suicide")** is a particularly strong indicator of his frame of mind:

> I shall die and with me the sum
> Of the intolerable universe.
>
> . . . . .
>
> I am looking at the last sunset
> I hear the last bird.
> I bequeath nothingness to no one.
>
> . . . . .
>
> Moriré y conmigo la suma
> Del intolerable universo.
>
> . . . . .
>
> Estoy mirando el último poniente
> Oigo el último pájaro.
> Lego la nada a nadie.
>
> (***OP***, 430)

The theme of his blindness, which in earlier poems often functioned in a positive manner, now contributes to this autumnal gloom. Thus in the twopart composition **"El ciego" ("The blindman")** he speaks of his "insipid universe," of being "deprived of the diverse world," and finally of how now "I can only see to see nightmares" ("solo puedo ver para ver pesadillas"; ***OP***, 450). Yet a kind of sweet sadness pervades such pieces as the nostalgic **"All Our Yesterdays," "Elegía" ("Elegy")**, **"La clepsidra" ("The hourglass")**, and the enumerative poem **"Talismanes" ("Talismans")**. In the latter piece, after fondly recalling old friends, cherished objects, and pleasant experiences, he concludes in chilling tones: "Surely they are talismans, but they are useless against the shadow that I cannot name, against the shadow that I must not name" ("Ciertamente son talismanes, pero de nada sirven contra la sombra que no puedo nombrar, contra la sombra que no debo nombrar"; ***OP***, 459). A somewhat similar mood pervades the poems of his 1977 collection, ***Historia de la noche.*** Among a number of memorable lyrics at least one must be briefly noted. In the English-titled **"Things That Might Have Been"** he considers the possibility of such things as books that Dante might have written after finishing the *Divine Comedy*, of the course of ancient history had the beautiful Helen of Troy not existed, and of other literary or historical events that did not come to pass. He concludes this enumeration of "what might have been" when, in a striking final verse, he sadly thinks of "The son I never had" ("El hijo que no tuve").[5]

In the prologue to his penultimate book of verse, ***La cifra***, Borges discusses "verbal" poetry as opposed to "intellectual" poetry. To illustrate the two he cites first the hauntingly lyrical first strophe of Ricardo Jaimes Freyre's "Peregrina paloma imaginaria," and then the essentially intellectual verse of Luis de León's "Vivir quiero conmigo."[6] He states that his desire in this collection is to follow a middle course between these two extremes. How successful he is in achieving this objective is difficult to determine. What is clear, however, is that the collection is rich in opposing elements. At times its tone is serene and hopeful while at other times death, desperation, and nihilism hold sway. As to form, the sonnet gives way, with but one exception, to free verse, prose poems, or the unrhymed hendecasyllable. Thematically, a great deal of the collection is simply a reworking of well-known Borgesian motifs, and by comparison with his earlier poetry these pieces on Berkeleyan idealism, time, infinite regression, Buenos Aires, and so on are not especially impressive. One relatively new theme does appear in several pieces: the culture and especially the literature of Japan. In ***The Gold of the Tigers*** he had already experimented with the tanka form; here Borges presents, with considerable success, seventeen examples of the more familiar haiku. Several other pieces on such subjects as the game of go, and the Shinto religion are further indications of this interest.

On balance, however, the dominant mood of the collection is one of resigned weariness and melancholy, broken only occasionaly by a ray of sunshine. This is seen in any number of pieces. For example, in the title poem he writes of the moon, "Has agotado ya la inalterable / suma de veces que te da el destino. / Inútil abrir todas las ventanas / del mundo. Es tarde" ("You have already exhausted the unchangeable / sum of times destiny has given you. / It is useless to open all the windows / of the world. It is late").[7] An even more negative tone is evident in **"Al adquirir una Enciclopedia"** (**"On acquiring an encyclopedia"**) in which the poet contrasts his joy and wonderment at having this new possession "with eyes that no longer function" and hands that "fumble" through its illegible pages (***C*** [***La cifra***], 23). But perhaps the most desperate poem in the collection, and yet one that contains some lovely verses, is **"Eclesiastés 1,9"** (**"Ecclesiastes 1:9"**). He begins with a series of strong hendecasyllablic lines, introduced by the word "if," that mention simple everyday acts; he observes that *if* he does any of these things, he is only repeating what he has done before. Borges then states, in the crucial thirteenth verse: "No puedo ejectuar un acto nuevo, / tejo y torno a tejer la misma fábula, / repetido un repetido endecasílabo" ("I cannot perform a single new act, / I weave and re-weave the same tale, / I repeat a repeated hendecasyllable"). He goes on to confess that night after night he has the same nightmare and the same labyrinthine obsessions. The final verses are especially dramatic: "I am the weariness of an unmoving mirror / or the dust of a museum / I hope for only one untasted thing, / a gift, a bit of gold in the shadows, that maiden, death" ("Soy la fátiga de un espejo inmóvil / o el polvo de un museo. / Sólo una cosa no gustada espero, / una dádiva, un oro de la sombra, / esa virgen, la muerte"; ***C***, 27–28).

Borges's last collection of poetry, ***Los conjurados***, is signed 9 January 1985, a year and a half before his death. Like the previous volume, it is dedicated to María Kodama, the woman who was to become his bride just before his passing. Again, like ***La cifra***, the volume includes some fourteen short prose pieces, or about a third of its content. Some of these texts are reminiscent of the parables written years earlier in ***Dreamtigers***, and because some of the poems are in blank verse, the fine line between prose and poetry is not always easy to establish. There are, nonetheless, a goodly number of sonnets and even a few octosyllabic *milongas* in the collection.

In one of the shorter prose pieces, "Posesión del ayer" (Possession of yesterday), while pondering the notion that in a sense what we lose is often retained in a special way, Borges remarks, "Every poem, with time, becomes an elegy."[8] This observation certainly applies to many of the collection's pieces. One of the many cases in point is the lovely poem **"La joven noche"** (**"The young night"**). The tone here is one of gentle acceptance; the twilight of life reduces the world to pure essences, to Platonic ideas. Citing a favorite author Borges comments: "Goethe said it better: *nearby things became distant.* / There four words sum up all twilight. / In the garden the roses stop being roses / and wish to be the Rose" ("Mejor lo dijo Goethe: *Lo cercano se aleja.* / Esas cuatro palabras cifran todo el crepúsculo. / En el jardín las rosas dejan de ser las rosas / y quieren ser la Rosa"; *Co*, 29). A somewhat similar mood pervades poems such as **"Doomsday"** or **"Tríada"** (**"Triad"**). The latter, a fine example of free-verse innovation, is built upon three statements, each a bit longer than its predecessor and each describing the "alivio" (relief) felt immediately before death. The first two statements—or verses—speak of famous men such as Caesar or Charles I of England. The final segment, however, is expressed in personal terms as "The relief that you and I will feel at the moment preceding death, when fortune casts us free of the sad habit of being someone and of the weight of the universe" ("El alivio que tú y yo sentiremos en el instante que precede la muerte, cuando la suerte nos desate de la triste costumbre de ser algiuen y del peso del universo"; ***Co***, 20). The very fact that Borges, then eighty-five, was still exploring that fascinating no-man's-land between prose and poetry, was still writing fine sonnets, and was continuing to rework the rich metal of earlier texts suggests that even though death was close, he remained a poet of substantial talent and considerable vigor.

Notes

1. Borges's publisher, Editorial Emecé, however, published a later separate volume of poetry titled *El otro, el mismo* (Buenos Aires: Emecé, 1969).
2. Jorge Luis Borges, *Obra poética: 1923–76* (Madrid and Buenos Aires: Alianza-Emecé, 1979), 194–95. Succeeding references appear parenthetically in the

text as *OP.* Some of the later poetry has been translated in *Selected Poems 1923–67*, ed. with an introduction by Norman Thomas di Giovanni (New York: Delacorte Press, 1972). The translations in my text are, however, my own, though they occasionally parallel the published versions quite closely.

3. Jorge Luis Borges, *In Praise of Darkness*, trans. Norman Thomas di Giovanni (New York: Dutton, 1974), 10. Succeeding references appear parenthetically in the text as *PD*. In this case I have retained di Giovanni's translations.
4. Jorge Luis Borges, *The Gold of the Tigers: Selected Later Poems; Bilingual Edition*, trans. Alastair Reid (New York: Dutton, 1977), 7. Succeeding references appear parenthetically as *GT*. I have retained Reid's translations in my text.
5. Jorge Luis Borges, *Historia de la noche* (Buenos Aires: Emecé, 1977), 91.
6. Ricardo Jaimes Freyre (1868–1933) of Bolivia was an important poet of the *modernista* movement; Luis de León (1527–1591) was a major poet and theologian of Spain's Golden Age.
7. Jorge Luis Borges, *La cifra* (Madrid: Alianza, 1981), 12. Succeeding references appear parenthetically in the text as *C*.
8. Jorge Luis Borges, *Los conjurados* (Madrid: Alianza, 1985), 63. Succeeding references appear parenthetically in the text as *Co*.

Keith Polette (essay date 1993)

SOURCE: A review of *The Preface and John 1:14*, in *The Explicator*, Vol. 51, No. 3, Spring, 1993, pp. 151–53.

[*In the following essay, Polette finds similarities in the conception of God held by Borges and that of seventeenth-century Puritan minister, Edward Taylor.*]

The power of the imagination to unify opposites and thus reveal the interplay between the eternal and the temporal, or the Divine and the human, links Edward Taylor, a seventeenth-century Puritan colonial minister, to Jorge Luis Borges, a twentieth-century secular Argentine writer. Separated by time and language, Taylor and Borges become, in a sense, two human eyes in the face of God. The two writers offer poetic visions of two important acts of creation: Taylor re-visions the wonder of Genesis in his "Preface," and Borges sees with bright and broad eyes the poetry of St. John's Gospel. Both poets, via the imagination, reconcile and harmonize oppositional forces and ideas by discovering the sacred in the experience of the profane. They express their experience of this discovery in clear, common language and sing in simple human song of that which is more than human. It might be said that God, or the poets' conception of God, is "languaged alive" through each writer's pen.

Taylor describes a God who deliberately fashioned the world. The God he writes about is not the distant, judgmental God who presided darkly over the Puritan world, but a God who works and works hard. In the "Preface," Taylor writes,

> Upon what base was fixed the Lath wherein
> He turned the Globe, and rigged it so trim?
> Who blew the bellows of his Furnace Vast?
>
> (lines 3–5)

Here, Taylor envisions a different kind of God, not one who waved his hand, uttered some magic words, and pulled the universe from his Godly top hat. Taylor's God is a working God surrounded by wood and iron, soot and smoke, whose determined brow is smudged with grime, whose face drips with sweat, and whose hands are rough and calloused. Such a God grunts and groans in the act of hammering out the universe on the anvil of the imagination.

Moreover, Taylor has a vision of this same rough-handed God as a God who "Laced and Filleted the earth so fine" (9), and who "made the Sea its Selvedge" (11). This God, then, is also soft, gentle, and feminine and has an eye for beauty and intricate design. For Taylor to imagine that God is both male and female, that he/she resides in all human endeavors and is to be found not only in heaven, but in the objects of nature and of human construction shows evidence of twofold consciousness. Taylor sees God through the interplay of the masculine and the feminine, the sacred and profane, the temporal and the eternal, and the conscious and the unconscious.

Jorge Luis Borges expresses the same twofold consciousness in his poem **"John 1:14"** by showing the cross-fertilizing of the eternal with the temporal. In his poem, Borges suggests that God, being a mystery that human beings will never fully understand, still needs language to become a reality for humanity; he writes, "I who am the Was, the Is, and the Is To Come again condescend to the written word . . . which is no more than an emblem" (7–10). The "word which is no more than an emblem" becomes the linguistic thread that gently yokes the Divine to the human, or the eternal to the temporal.

Once made flesh through the word, God (through Borges, or through Borges's persona) speaks of those human things that he "knew" and valued: "memory, hope, fear, sleep, dreams, ignorance, flesh, the blind devotion of dogs" (22–26). He continues, "My eyes saw what they had never seen—night and its many stars" (29–30). Here the Divine describes the experience of immediate temporality in concrete language. Through such use of language, the Divine becomes known and knowable through self-reflexivity. This seems to echo the Zen notion that until enlightenment occurs the human mind is like a hand trying to grasp itself or an eye trying to see itself. Borges may be suggesting that God needs man in order to be God. Or, put another way, infinity without finity conjoined is ultimately formless and without emblematic meaning.

Borges understands what Taylor understood, that the experience of God is the experience of the imagination's power to penetrate finitude in order to discover infinitude. By such penetration followed by reflection and the creation of poetry, Taylor and Borges have granted the world its being by knowing that God can not only "turn this globe upon his lathe," but also feel "homesick" when thinking back upon "the smell of that carpenter's shop." Thus, Borges and Taylor experience the world in which a Divine presence signals that distinctions exist without divisions, that discordant opposites are reconciled, and that the unconscious and the conscious are harmonized.

Works cited

Borges, Jorge Luis. *In Praise of Darkness.* New York: Dutton, 1969.

Taylor, Edward. "The Preface." *The American Tradition in Literature.* Ed. George Perkins, Sculley Bradley, Richmond Croom Beatty, and E. Hudson Long. New York: McGraw-Hill, 1990.

Joseph Tyler (essay date 1993)

SOURCE: "Medieval Germanic Elements in the Poetry of Jorge Luis Borges," in *Readerly/Writerly Texts*, Vol. 1, No. 1, Fall-Winter, 1993, pp. 97–105.

[*In the following essay, Tyler demonstrates Borges's interest in medieval Germanic literature, and points to elements of it in his poetry.*]

> *Libros como el de Job*, LA DIVINA COMEDIA, Macbeth *(y, para mí, algunas de las sagas del Norte) prometen una larga inmortalidad . . .*
>
> Borges, "Sobre los clásicos."[1]

. . . In the preface to *Literaturas germánicas medievales* (1978), Borges states that the aim of his book is "to trace the origins of three literatures which emerged from a common root, and whose complex historical vicissitudes transformed and separated, as occurred also with the diverse languages in which they were written" ("Medieval Germanic Literatures" 7, hereafter referred to as *MGL*; my trans. Translations hereafter are my own). My aim here is to trace elements from those literatures in several poems included in his ***Obra poética*** and elsewhere.

Borges's initial interest for these literatures begins at home with the English origins of his father: "My father's English came from the fact that his mother, Frances Haslam, was born in Staffordshire of Northumbrian stock" ("An Autobiographical Essay" 136; Bantam, 1971). In his autobiographical essay, the Argentine poet talks about his attraction to the medieval Germanic literatures and to their poetic forms:

> I had always been attracted to the metaphor, and this leaning led me to the study of the simple Saxon kennings and overelaborate Norse ones. As far back as 1932, I had even written an essay about them. The quaint notion of using, as far as it could be done, metaphors instead of straightforward nouns, and of these metaphors being at once traditional and arbitrary, puzzled and appealed to me. I was later to surmise that the purpose of these figures lay not only in the pleasure given by the pomp and circumstance of compounding words but also in the demands of alliteration. Taken by themselves, the kennings are not especially witty, and calling a ship "a sea-stallion" and the open sea "the Whale's-road" is no great feat. The Norse skalds went a step further, calling the sea "the sea-stallion's-road," so what originally was an image became a laborious equation. In turn, my investigation of kennings led me to the study of Old English and Old Norse. (*The Aleph and Other Stories 178*)

Borges's experience with these medieval Germanic literatures led to his lecturing and teaching the subject in and out of the university. His research efforts in this field culminated in the publication of *Antiguas literaturas germánicas* (*Old Germanic Literatures*), an earlier version of *Literaturas germánicas medievales.*[3] The earlier text appeared in México in 1951, and it is in **"Mateo, XXV, 30,"** a poem published as part of his ***El Otro, el mismo*** in 1953, that we find the first traces or elements of these medieval Germanic literatures. This single reference to "La saga de Grettir" is the bridge that connects a simple title with a full composition, a poem entitled **"A Saxon"** (A.D. 449). This poem, with its indefinite and anonymous title, is symbolic for its generic value, for it transmits diachronically the metamorphosis or rudimentary individuals into men of letters, as the last two stanzas of the poem clearly testify. The poem ends with a long, chaotic enumeration of words which together compose one single sentence.

> He brought with him the elemental words
> Of a language that in time would flower
> In Shakespeare's harmonies: night, day,
> Water, fire, words for metals and colors,
>
> Hunger, thirst, bitterness, sleep, fighting
> Death, and other grave concerns of men;
> On broad meadows, and in tangled woodland
> The sons he bore brought England into being.
>
> (***Selected Poems, 1923–1967*** 107, hereafter referred to as ***SP***)

Later in other poems, Borges joins the many bards who sing of the moon with these meaningful lines:

> There's an iron forest where a huge wolf
> Lives whose strange fate is
> To knock the moon down and murder it
> When the last dawn reddens the sea.
> (This is well known in the prophetic North;
> Also, that on that day the ship made out
> Of all the fingernails of the dead will spread
> A poison on the world's wide-open seas.)
>
> (***A Personal Anthology***, 197)

These parenthetical lines derive from Scandinavian literature (*The Poetic Edda*) where one reads of Ragnarökr ("The Twilight of the Gods"), a poetic title for a short piece found in ***Dreamtigers*** (26). The original source for these referential lines appears within the text of the "Medieval Germanic Literatures" where Borges writes:

> This is the Twilight of the Gods (Ragnarökr). Fenrir, a wolf muzzled by a sword, breaks its millenial prison and devours Odin. The ship Naglfar sets sail, constructed with the fingernails of the dead. (In the *Snorra Edda* we read: "one must not allow someone to die with uncut fingernails, because he who forgets it hastens the construction of the ship Naglfar, feared by the gods and men.")
>
> (102)

Engrossed by this phenomenon of nails growing after death, Borges writes yet another piece simply entitled **"Toenails."** But what is treated mythically in the earlier example becomes simply another curiosity in the later work.

Gradually we move away from these peripheral elements and we approach a concentration of poems directly related to the central subjects of the medieval Germanic literatures. A poem functioning as an inaugural part of these cardinal themes is appropriately entitled **"Embarking on the Study of Anglo-Saxon Grammar."** Here again we find autobiographical data supporting a now commonly-held hypothesis about the poet's kinship to early skalds. In selecting the term *embarking* for the poem's title, the translator chose his words wisely, for it is a sort of voyage in time that the poet (anchored in his native Buenos Aires) chose to undertake. "I come back to the far shore of a vast river / Never reached by the Norsemen's long ships [*los dragones del viking* reads the original] / To the harsh and workwrought words / Which, with a tongue now dust, / I used in the days of Northumbria and Mercia / Before becoming Haslam or Borges" (***SP***, 139). Serious studies of these words, symbols of other symbols, will keep the poet researching, learning, and writing about his findings.

Proceeding along the same path, we come to Borges's sonnet **"Poem Written in a Copy of Beowulf."** Here Borges trades the internal rhyme of the former composition for the external rhyming scheme of the sonnet in its original version (abba abba cdd cdd). What may seem at first, if one pardons the oxymoron, a silent clamor for weaving and unweaving words—("At various times I have asked myself what reason / Moved me to study . . . / The Language of the blunt-tongued Anglo-Saxons")—ends up being a philosophical commentary comparing the bard's lexical toil with his weary existence: "I tell myself: It must be that the soul / Has some secret sufficient way of knowing / That it is immortal . . . / Beyond my anxiety and beyond this writing / The universe waits." He concludes, "inexhaustible, inviting" (***SP***, 155).

The third in this series of poems dealing with the medieval Germanic literatures, **"Hengest Cyning,"** has a Nordic flavor. Both poem and title contain a binary value; the composition starts with The King's epitaph:

> Beneath this stone lies the body of Hengist [sic]
> Who founded in these islands the first kingdom
> Of the royal house of Odin
> And glutted the screaming eagle's greed.
>
> (***SP***, 157)

Then he continues with the neo-fantastic element of the King's speech, supposedly after death, in defense of his own deeds:

> I know not what runes will be scraped on the stone
> But my words are these:
> Beneath the Heavens I was Hengist the mercenary.
> My might and my courage I marketed to Kings
> Whose lands lay west over the water
> Here at the edge of the sea
> "Called the Spear-Warrior";
> But a man's might and his courage can
> Not long bear being sold,
> And so after cutting down all through the North
> The foes of the Briton king,
> From him too I took light and life together.
> I like this kingdom that I seized with my sword;
> It has rivers for the net and the oar
> And long seasons of sun
> And soil for the plough and for husbandry
> And Britons for working the farms
> And cities of stone which we shall allow
> to crumble to ruin,
> Because there dwell the ghosts of the dead.
> But behind my back I know
> These Britons brand me traitor,
> Yet I have been true to my deeds and my daring
> And to other men's care never yielded my destiny
> And no one dared ever betray me.
>
> (***SP***, 157)

Composed of alternating long and short verses, the protracted text contrasts with the briefer portion of the composition in both size and content. Its tempo, nevertheless, is kept with internal rhyme and an occasional alliteration—"no sé que runas habrá marcado el hierro en la piedra / Hay ríos para el remo y para la red"—***Obra poética*** 234–235; italics added). The poem is not only interesting because of its contrasting elements, but also because of its narrative components. Especially appealing are those parts mentioning the geography, the toil of the Briton farmers, and the fateful decay of their cities. As a matter of fact in **"The Elegies,"** Borges mentions something to this effect at the same time that he quotes another scholar; thus in "The Ruin" he comments, "Stopford Brooke, in a dignified tone, says that the Saxons disdained city life, allowing the existing towns in England to fall into ruin and later composing elegies to deplore those ruins" (*MGL*, 24).

In his next poem titled simply **"Fragment,"** Borges's attention is focused upon a sword. Here things are deconstructed, so to speak, for the rhymer sings of one of the basic elements for settling discords: "A sword carved with runes . . . / A sword from the Baltic that will be celebrated in Northumbria, / A sword that poets will equate to ice and fire . . . / A sword to fit the hand of Beowulf" (***SP***, 159). There are fifteen rhythmic mentions of the word "sword," and the placement of the word creates for the reader a pattern of pulsating sounds that resemble a collective image of the blade. Needless to say, the poem abounds in "kenningar": a sword "That will stain with blood *the wolf's fangs* / And *the raven's ruthless beak.* / That will bring down *the forest of spears*" (***SP***, 159). Another title connecting with the same pattern is that of **"A una espada en York"** (**To a Sword in York**). And in ***La Rosa profunda*** there appears a sonnet titled **"Espadas"** (**"Swords"**), a sort of *arma virumque cano* that starts with a brief enumeration of famous blades. Borges himself, in a concluding note, explains that the weapons listed belonged to Sigurd, Roland, Charlemagne, and King Arthur.

Moving from the naming of the basic symbols of conflict to the praising of those who lexically celebrated victory and the spoils of war, the author dedicates his next poem **"To a Saxon Poet,"** a simple title designating two different compositions included in the collection I have been quoting from. Because of its vertical concatenation of apostrophes addressed to an anonymous bard who normally extolls heroes and heroic deeds, this poem resembles the previously discussed **"Fragment."** From the eulogy to the nameless Saxon poet, Borges shifts to **"Snorri Sturluson,"** a tragic figure depicted here in a sonnet and the subject of the writer's twice-told-tales. Let us briefly consider the first of these variants:

"Snorri Sturluson, (1179–1241)"

You, who bequeathed a mythology
Of ice and fire to filial recall,
Who chronicled the violent glory
Of your defiant Germanic stock
Discovered in amazement one night
Of swords that your untrustworthy flesh
Trembled. On that night without sequel
You realized you were a coward. . . .
In the darkness of Iceland the salt
Wind moves the mounting sea. Your home is
surrounded. You have drunk to the dregs
Unforgettable dishonor. On
Your head, your sickly face, falls the sword
As it fell so often in your book.

(***SP***, 163)

Yet in another, but shorter, version of this biographical piece, Borges mentions the name of Sturluson—famous as historian, archaeologist, builder of hot baths, genealogist, president of an Assembly, poet, double traitor, victim of beheading, and ghost—as the main source for his "Kenningar," an essay on poetic language published together with an article titled "Metaphor" in his *History of Eternity.* It should be added that we find a more unabridged biographical note about Sturluson within the frequently quoted "Medieval Germanic Literatures."

A final poem with an oxymoronic title **"The Generous Enemy"** is composed of nine elliptical verses, seven of which are subjunctive phrases expressing an eloquent greeting, emitted by Muirchertach, King of Dublin, cheering the exploits of the rival King Magnus Barford;[4] the final couplet, however, foretells King Magnus's final defeat and demise. The contradictory content of **"The Generous Enemy"** concurs with its title, and it seems to be a direct rendition of a piece taken from the *Anhang zur Heimskringla* by Hugo Gering, according to the final note provided by Borges at the poem's conclusion. The peculiarity of this text lies not only in its given form and content, but also in its almost total exclusion from other Borgesian writings such as the "Medieval Germanic Literatures." It is there that we find a brief mention of it, for it appears insignificantly important on a list of other minor compositions that preceded Snorri Sturluson's *Heimskringla.* There we read:

> Another historical work, valuable for the verses and compositions it cites, is called *Fagrskinna* (Beautiful Skin) because of the elegant binding of one of the two copies which were preserved in the seventeenth century, and then destroyed in a fire. Another similar compilation is called *Morkinskinna* (Rusty Skin), and includes biographies of Magnus Olafson, who was king of Norway and Denmark; of Harold Hardrada, Harold the Cruel, who fought in Italy, in Sicily and in the Orient; of Magnus Berfoett, Magnus Bare Foot, who fell in ambush in Dublin; and of Sigurd Jorsalafari (Sigurd the Pilgrim, Sigurd the Traveler to Jerusalem), who fought against the Spanish Arabs, and died insane.
>
> (*MGL*, 150–51)

Ultimately, I suggest that Borges's interest in medieval Germanic literature has numerous causes, but one in particular seems to lie slightly hidden within his autobiographical strata. Living in a world of created doubles (*ein doppelgänger*), Borges has conceived the character Juan Dahlmann and sets him in a conflict very much like Borges's own self in **"Borges and I."** In the poem, too, Borgas-poet-persona undergoes a kind of personality split while yearning to become one with his predecessors. It is important to recall here one of my preliminary citations when Borges recites, "I come back . . . / To the harsh and work-wrought words / I used in the days of Northumbria and Mercia / Before becoming Haslam or Borges" (***SP*** 139). It is in his *Historia de la Eternidad* that Borges expresses, in a footnote, a similar affinity. Speaking about Snorri Sturluson's epithet as traitor, he defensively states, "Traitor is a harsh word. Sturluson, perhaps, was merely an available fanatic, a man shockingly torn apart by consecutive and opposite loyalties. On the intellectual order, I know of two examples: that of Francisco Luis Bernárdez, and mine" (*Historia de la Eternidad* 49). Borges's earlier books of poetry, ***Fervor of Buenos Aires, Moon Across the Way***, and ***San Martin Copybook***, speak of his native Buenos Aires. His ***The Self and The Other*** talks about his other Fatherland, that of Northumbria and Mercia. Thus, poetically Borges comes to his very own forking paths choosing for the moment to relive the past of his *other.* Indeed, the ubiquity of medieval Germanic elements in Borges's poetry mirrors cogently the English side of his ancestry, which has often been interpreted as his *other self.*

Notes

1. Italics and emphasis added. Also, whenever I quote poetry, I provide the page number(s) rather than the line(s) to facilitate reference to translations.
2. Cf. my article "Borges y las literaturas germánicas medievales en *El libro de arena*," *Hispanic Journal*, II 1 (1980): 79–85.
3. Jorge Luis Borges with María Esther Vázquez, "Medieval Germanic Literatures," trans. Joseph Tyler (unpublished MS 1985).
4. Magnus III, King of Norway (1093–1103), was also called Magnus the Bare foot Norwegian, *Magnus Barford*, 24 August: 1103. He conquered the Orkney and the Hebrides, and was killed before Dublin during an invasion of Ireland, *The New Cyclopedia of Names*, Vol. III, eds. Clarence L. Barnhard, et al. (New York: Appleton-Century-Crofts, 1954) 2575.

Works cited

Borges, Jorge Luis. "An Autobiographical Essay." *The Aleph and Other Stories 1933–1969.*, Trans. Norman Thomas di Giovanni, with Borges. New York: Bantam, 1971.

———. *Dreamtigers.* Trans. Mildred Boyer and Harold Morland. Austin: U of Texas P, 1964.

———. *Historia de la Eternidad.* Buenos Aires: Emecé Editores, 1966.

———, and María Esther Vázquez. *Literaturas germánicas medievales.* Buenos Aires: Emecé Editores, 1978.

———. "Medieval Germanic Literatures." Trans. Joseph Tyler. (Unpublished.)

———. *Obra poética.* Buenos Aires: Emecé Editores, 1967.

———. *A Personal Anthology.* Ed. Anthony Kerrigan. New York: Grove, 1967.

———. *Selected Poems, 1923–1967.* Trans. Norman Thomas Di Giovanni. New York: Delacorte/Seymour Lawrence, 1972.

Alexander Coleman (essay date 1994)

SOURCE: "The Ghost of Whitman in Neruda and Borges," in *Walt Whitman of Mickle Street: A Centennial Collection*, edited by Geoffrey M. Sill, The University of Tennessee Press, 1994, pp. 257–69.

[*In the following essay, Coleman demonstrates the strong influence of Walt Whitman on the poetry of both Borges and the Chilean poet Pablo Neruda. Coleman focuses on the contrasting effects of this influence on the two poets.*]

In writing his lucid overview of the history of Walt Whitman's presence in Spanish America, Professor Fernando Alegría of Stanford University had to come to grips with a question that inevitably haunts Hispanists as they try convincingly to identify the "influence" of such a magisterial and protean poet as Walt Whitman in the poetry of Pablo Neruda and Jorge Luis Borges. Professor Alegría's bafflement before his task might well serve as a starting point for my own comments:

> To study Whitman in Spanish American poetry is to trace the wanderings of a ghost that is felt everywhere and seen in no place. His verses are quoted with doubtful accuracy by all kinds of critics; poets of practically all tendencies have been inspired by his message and have either written sonnets celebrating his genius or repeated his very words with a somewhat candid self-denial.
>
> (Qtd. in Gay Wilson Allen, *New Walt Whitman Handbook*, 534)

We have to start, therefore, with the fact that Whitman undergoes a sea change as he enters the imagination of poets in Spanish; not only is what they know of Whitman very much to the point, but what they do not know or choose to ignore in *their* visions of Whitman is even more to the point. Without having made an exhaustive survey of the matter, I would say that "Song of Myself," the "Calamus" poems, "Salut au Monde," "Song of the Open Road," "Crossing Brooklyn Ferry," and "When Lilacs Last in the Dooryard Bloom'd," with a few others, have attained almost canonical status in Spanish, whereas *Drum-Taps* and most of the prose—above all, *Democratic Vistas*—offer a figure of Whitman which, while not at all contradictory to the first canonical Whitman, does not quite jibe in all respects and thus is not perceived with the same intensity. For instance, in the essay entitled "Whitman, Poet of America," by the contemporary Mexican poet Octavio Paz, we find such sentences as the following:

> Whitman can sing with full confidence and innocence democracy on the march because the Utopia of America is confounded and is indistinguishable from American reality. The poetry of Whitman is a great prophetic dream, but it is a dream within another dream, a prophecy within another even more vast which feeds it. America dreams itself in Whitman's poetry because it itself is a dream. And it dreams itself as a concrete reality, almost physical, with its men, its rivers, its cities and its mountains. . . . Before and after Whitman we have had other poetic dreams. All of them—be they called Poe or Darío, Melville or Emily Dickinson—are, more precisely, attempts to escape the American nightmare.
>
> (*El Arco* 299–300; trans. by A. C.)

Well, this is one way of putting it. But I want to emphasize that, as we enter into the world of poetry in Spanish, I do not wish, nor do I feel competent, to compare such a comment as that of Octavio Paz with the multiple, contradictory, and ungraspable literary reality that is Walt Whitman. I merely want to tell you as clearly as I can *how he is seen by poets writing in Spanish.* For their purposes, their ways of seeing him may entail gross misreadings, or partial overlookings or abandonings, of aspects of Whitman, in poetry and in prose, which do not serve their creative purposes. I am merely saying that, in responding to Whitman as they read him and as they imagined him, they found their own voices, with Whitman possibly present as a subtext for their own most original utterances.

I have chosen to look at two of Whitman's most fervent admirers, Pablo Neruda of Chile, born in 1904, and Jorge Luis Borges of Argentina, born in 1899. Both are eminently worthy of consideration, because both are major poets who have openly confessed their allegiance and their debt to Whitman, and both have produced texts that express, in poetical terms, the overwhelming magisterium of the author of *Leaves of Grass.*

Having said that, we could not imagine two poets less similar to each other, two poets who have had such differing convictions over the years concerning the nature of poetry, the relation of word to object, and the relation of the poem to the self and the society which engendered the poem. I wish to emphasize the radically opposed natures of their achievements, including some amusing comments with which they expressed, sometimes in barbed terms, their mutual admiration mixed with the most openly argued views concerning each other's personal and poetic selves. Bits of literary gossip—i.e., Borges on Neruda, Neruda on Borges—are always to be taken with high seriousness, given the indisputable grandeur of the two poets' respective achievements. But since in many ways these achievements are irreconcilable, the simplest way to contrast the two is brashly to suggest that the only thing they had in common was their mutual admiration of Whitman; they were parallel lines in poetry, touching ever so slightly in various periods of their poetic development, whether early, middle, or late. The one constant between the two is Whitman—that is to say, *their* peculiar and at times idiosyncratic imagining of Whitman's achievement. They both started out enunciating keen dissatisfaction with the Spanish language, showing a determination to infuse into a fossilized poetic language a new vigor, new metaphors, a new view of the poet in the cosmos. Thus Whitman, generalized and mythic, is at the core of their revolt against both didactic poetry and the aestheticist excesses of *Modernismo.*

But almost as soon as that is said, we must recognize their divergence: Neruda began to write political poetry, while Borges wrote increasingly metaphysical poetry. In his major phase, the political poetry of the thirties and the forties, Neruda abandoned his earlier hermeticism to obey Tolstoy's final injunctions contained in *What is Art*?—that is, art should produce "a feeling of brotherhood and love of one's neighbor." Neruda glories in his poetic multiplicity, in his role as a civic poet of national and continental consciousness, a poet who intentionally simplifies his language to make it a mode of communication with the unawakened consciousness of all Latins. In this prophetic, bardic phase, Neruda's poetry is above all celebratory and hortatory, and he is a poet of optimism and plenitude, an agent of moral fervor—all this in order that the word touch and press itself upon those who have never been given a voice. Does this not echo Whitman's transcendental vision? It must be said, though, that such a poet—the role of such a poet—is not at all prevalent in the post-Whitmanian literary history of the United States, and such a voice is immensely difficult to transmit in a manner that sounds contemporary, in the same way that translations of Mayakovsky pose difficulties in English. The point is that Neruda's divergence from an Eliotic poetry of anguish gave him an audience that before had been quite unimaginable. The Mexican novelist Carlos Fuentes, who was a witness to Neruda's hypnotic power in mass readings of his poetry, often attended by thousands, expresses this matter in a revealing interview:

> This extraordinary fact could only occur in a culture such as that of Latin America, where a poet can still be a poet of the people. I don't think you have to be a poet of the people to be a good poet, of course. I think Mallarmé is a great poet. I'm just trying to explain this phenomenon of a writer who is really capable of giving voice to the voiceless. And of being repaid for this art with the grace of anonymity. Of being recited by people who do not know that the poet exists, or that the poems were written by a man called Pablo Neruda. This is unthinkable in the United States.
>
> (Mac Adam and Coleman 677)

For the moment, you will have to take it on faith that the poetry of Borges is a radically different proposition, in all its phases. As Neruda's most imposing poetry takes wing by being read aloud, Borges's poetry is not heard but overheard. As we shall see, he began as a poet inebriated with Whitman's vision of the possibilities of poetry in this age, but his evolution over the years is not toward a poetry of a striding multiplicity of selves, but toward a more private, delimiting voice which owes less to oratorical or acoustic sound with abundant accumulative images than to a single inner vision, a voice which comes across *both* in English or Spanish as reminding us of the meditative poetry of Eliot, Yeats, Donne, or Herbert. If I were to say one thing about the differences between the two to end this introduction, I might say that Neruda in his most political phase lives a poetry of touching, of communication, of diving into the world and being immersed in its processes; while Borges's voice veers away from society to the solitary expression of a rich inner vision. And let it be said that each poet reads and sounds differently in English. Borges's voice more nearly matches our verbal expectations, our unconscious contemporary expectation of the nature of poetry, while Neruda's discontent with his translators is not at all related to the incompetence or insensitivity of the various hands who have translated him, but rather to his deepest suspicions about the suitability of the English language as a medium for his neo-Whitmanian verse. In a memorable comment, he noted, "It seems to me that the English language, so different from Spanish and so much more direct, often expresses the meaning of my poetry but does not convey the atmosphere." He prefers above all his own poetry in Italian, "because there's a similarity of values between the two languages, Spanish and Italian." "English and French," he says, "do not correspond to Spanish, neither in vocalization, nor in placement, color or weight of the words. This means that the equilibrium of a Spanish poem . . . can find no equivalent in French or English. It's not a question of interpretive equivalents, no; the sense may be correct, indeed the accuracy of the translation . . . may be what destroys the poem" (Guibert 35–36). The same impression is not given by the poetry of Borges either in Spanish nor in English, above all because, at home in Buenos Aires, Borges's first language was English and the resultant tone of his mature poetry is much more subdued than Neruda's. I bring up these differences not to emphasize an interesting but irrelevant aside, but to remind you once again that the two men's allegiance to Whitman, *their* Whitman, is still more or less constant—both are translators of good portions of *Leaves of Grass.* Neruda, however, is an unquestioning celebrant of Whitman's mission as Neruda appropriated it; while Borges, a fervent adept at first, challenges both Whitman's vision and his language, all while constantly commenting upon his various and changing views of Whitman over a poetic career that spans, as does Neruda's, some six decades.

Where we touch their books, so do we touch each man, each poet in himself. There is an auspicious encounter between Neruda and Borges, which, though lying well within the realm of a literary anecdote, might help us distinguish between the invisible and unconscious impulses of the two authors as they began their respective lives as poets.

In June or early July 1927, Neruda, at the age of twenty-three, had been named Chilean honorary consul in Rangoon. On his way to his post via a circuitous route, he stopped off in Buenos Aires on his way to Portugal, from whence he would travel by steamer to Burma. By that date, Neruda had written one of his most famous texts of exacerbated love poetry—the "Twenty Love Songs and One Desperate Song." He had also by then written a few of the first poems now contained in *Residence on Earth,* including the "Galope Muerto" ("Dead Gallop"), with which the book still opens. Borges, on the other hand, was already a well-known figure in Buenos Aires, author of two volumes of poetry and two collections of critical essays. After arriving in Ceylon, Neruda took the time to recall to a friend his epic meeting with the young Borges, and his words give us a convenient point of departure for distinguishing the two poets and their poetry. Speaking of Borges, Neruda noted that

> he seems to be more preoccupied about problems of culture and society, which do not seduce me at all, which are not at all human. I like good wines, love, suffering, and books as consolation for the inevitable solitude. I even have a certain disdain for culture; as an interpretation of things, [I think that] a type of knowledge without antecedents, a physical absorption of the world seems to me better, in spite of and against ourselves. History [itself], the problems of "knowledge" as they call them, seems to be lacking some dimension. How [many of these problems] would fill up the vacuum? Every day I see fewer and fewer ideas around and more and more bodies, sun and sweat. I am exhausted.
>
> (Aguirre 46, trans. A. C.)

Naturally, this intuitive, even mysterious perception by Neruda of the young Borges might be read many ways, but for our own convenience, I would baldly state that here Neruda announces himself as a poet of the body, where the body will be both the perceiver and filter of all perception, and that the mind of the poet, the verbalizing faculty, should do nothing but submit to the sensual apparatus of the body as it moves through the world. Neruda's disdain for bookish culture, even though he was a voracious reader and tireless bibliophile, is striking, and we also note that the poet views "a physical absorption in the world" as greater material than an intellectual perception. For Borges, all of Neruda's evaluations are reversed, in ways we may now proceed to explore.

Absorption in the world is fundamental to Neruda. In a later interview, he makes this more precise:

> Just as the action of natural elements pulverizes our deepest feelings and transforms them into an intimate reflective substance . . . which we call literature, so also it is the writer's duty to contribute his own work to the development of the cultural heritage, by pulverizing, purifying and constantly transforming it. It is the same effect nutrition has on the blood, on the circulation. Culture has its roots in culture, but also in life and nature.
>
> (Guibert, 47)

This is the fundamental agency of the Whitmanian body which we must recognize in all Neruda, in spite of the radical transformations of style, tone, politics, and themes evident throughout his work. The body must be all men, the agent of all perception and suffering; as he says, "There's only one command [for the poet], and that is to penetrate life and make it prophetic: the poet should be a superstition, a mythic being" (Aguirre 60).

Neruda has no single poetic voice; as he says, "We are many." Thereby he affirms the absolute license of the unleashed poet to start each book anew, with new poetic duties and new audiences to be reached. We can see a touchingly adolescent, sentimental poet in him, then a poet of contemplation of infinite space, then a poet of disintegration and hallucinatory reality, available to us in his harrowing *Residence on Earth.* But there are more Nerudas. After his return from the East, serving during the Spanish Civil War as a Chilean diplomat in Spain, Neruda's poetry took a firm grip on material reality and politics. While in Spain in 1935, he translated the second, third, and thirtieth section of "Song of Myself" and also composed a fundamental manifesto for the new direction of this poetry, an essay entitled "Towards an Impure Poetry," in which Emerson's and Whitman's injunctions are reformulated into an anti-aesthetic aesthetic. In Ben Belitt's translation, the key passages are the following:

> Let [this] be the poetry we search for: worn with the hand's obligations, as by acids, steeped in sweat and in smoke, smelling of lilies and urine, spattered diversely by the trades that we live by, inside the law or beyond it.
>
> A poetry impure as the clothing we wear, [as impure] as our bodies, soupstained, soiled with our shameful behavior, our wrinkles and vigils and dreams, observations and prophecies, declarations of loathing and love, idylls and beasts, the shocks of encounter, political loyalties, denials and doubts, affirmations and taxes.
>
> ("On Impure Poetry" xxi)

After visiting the sacred city of the Inca empire in 1943, Neruda became an even broader poet, more conscious of his role in the celebration of a silent "dead" consciousness. The result of his 1943 visit was the stunning "Heights of Macchu Picchu"; in a prose note composed after his visit, this poet's change of focus, as he ever exchanges old clothes for new, is very apparent. He remembers the effect of those silent stones on his imagination, commenting:

> I could no longer segregate myself from those structures. I understood that if we walked on the same hereditary earth, we had something to do with those high endeavors of the American community, that we could not ignore them, that our neglect or silence was not only a crime but the prolonging of a defeat. . . . I thought many things after my visit to Cuzco. I thought about ancient American man. I saw his ancient struggles linked with present struggles.
>
> ("Translating Neruda," 144)

Neruda's communion reaches its culmination in the final passage of "The Heights of Macchu Picchu," where the poet begs the living and the dead to speak through him, just as Whitman had begged of the dead in canto 24 of "Song of Myself":

> Through me many long dumb voices,
> Voices of the interminable generations of prisoners and slaves,
> Voices of the diseas'd and despairing and of thieves and dwarfs,
> Voices of cycles of preparation and accretion. . . .
>
> (*LG*, 52)

Neruda's exhortation joyfully, heroically, takes on the same grand task:

> I come to speak through your dead mouth.
> All through the earth join all
> the silent wasted lips
> and speak from the depths to me all this long night
> as if I were anchored here with you,
> tell me everything, chain by chain,
> link by link, and step by step . . .
> Fasten your bodies to me like magnets.
> Hasten to my veins to my mouth.
> Speak through my words and my blood.
>
> ("Alturas de Macchu Picchu," 237–39)

Borges is so different from all that you have read up to now that it is hard to know where to begin. We might start by saying that his is an intensely playful and droll intelligence, one that sees himself looking at himself, a kind of intelligence where the mind-body problem in poetry is resolutely solved in favor of mind. Above all, he is often cruel and insouciant toward his earlier poetic selves and his earlier literary allegiances, a king of irascible high humor that is the polar opposite of the very uncritical but no less powerful poetic intelligence of Pablo Neruda. Borges's views on Whitman follow along the above inconstant lines. For instance, in 1970, he published in the *New Yorker* a "profile" under the title "An Autobiographical Essay," which is a mine of information about his earliest attempts at poetry, attempts in which Whitman plays a role, though not a happy one. Listen to the *tone* of the aging Borges as he assesses the qualities of his earliest poetry:

> It was also in Geneva (in 1918) that I first met Walt Whitman, through a German translation by Johannes Schlaf ("Als ich in Alabama meinen Morgengang machte"—"As I have walk'd in Alabama my morning walk"). Of course, I was struck by the absurdity of reading an American poet in German, so I ordered a copy of *Leaves of Grass* from London. I remember it still—bound in green. For a time, I thought of Whitman not only as a great poet, but as the *only* poet. In fact, I thought that all poets the world over had been merely leading up to Whitman until 1855, and that not to imitate him was a proof of ignorance. . . . [Later,] I saw my first poem into print. It was titled "Hymn to the Sea" and appeared in the magazine *Grecia*. . . . In the poem, I tried my hardest to be Walt Whitman:
>
> O sea! Oh myth! O Sun! O wide resting place!
> I know why I love you. I know that we are both very old,
> that we have known each other for centuries . . .
> O Protean, I have been born of you—
> both of us chained and wandering,
> both of us hungering for stars, both of us with hopes and disappointments. . . .

Here is Borges's comment: "Today, I hardly think of the sea, or even of myself, as hungering for the stars. Years after, when I came across Arnold Bennett's phrase 'the third-rate grandiose,' I understood at once what he meant" ("An Autobiographical Essay," 217, 220). As one sees from the tone and the humorous optics of old Borges looking at young Borges, the joke is not on Whitman, but on an immature imagination looking at Whitman with an uncritical, hagiographic point of view. Some six years later, Borges published in Buenos Aires a collection of verses, one poem of which, **"My Whole Life,"** is once again a Whitmanian exercise. But now the former grandiosity has been reduced to a more inviting poetic modesty:

> Here once again the memorable lips, unique and like yours.

> I am this groping intensity that is a soul.
> I have got near to happiness and have stood in the shadow of suffering.
> I have crossed the sea.
> I have known many lands; I have seen one woman and two or three men.
> I have loved a girl who was fair and proud, with a Spanish quietness.
> I have seen the city's edge, an endless sprawl where the sun goes down
> tirelessly, over and over.
> I have relished many words.
> I believe deeply that this is all, and that I will neither see nor accomplish
> new things.
> I believe that my days and my nights, in their poverty and their riches, are
> the equal of God's and of all men's.
>
> (***Selected Poems***, 43, trans. W. S. Merwin)

This is still an unsatisfactory poem, but the enumerations have a more modest and restricted sense. You still feel that he wants to encompass worlds with his poem, but the feeling in Borges is less cosmic and more humble; one feels that he is trying to carve out a voice for himself from amid the welter of voices that pulsate through "Song of Myself." Four years later, in 1929, Borges wrote **"The Other Whitman,"** a laudatory essay in which he suggested, allusively, one of the principal fascinations that Whitman exercises for Borges—Whitman's *twoness*, the distance between "Walter Whitman, Jr." and "Walt." Or, as Paul Zweig has put it, "his simultaneous personalities of adventurous word master and unsophisticated man of the people" (117).

We should be prepared for Borge's critical inconstancy before the phenomenon of Whitman, Borges's wavering allegiance to him. In the following instance, the interviewer, Richard Burgin, caught Borges in a rather grumpy mood about Whitman's world view:

> in Whitman everything is wonderful, you know? I don't think that anybody could really believe that everything is wonderful, no? Except in the sense of it being a wonder. Of course, you can do without that particular kind of miracle. No, in the case of Whitman, I think that he thought it was his duty as an American to be happy. And that he had to cheer up his readers. Of course he wanted to be unlike any other poet, but Whitman worked with a program, I should say; he began with a theory and then he went on to his work. I don't think of him as a spontaneous writer.
>
> (Burgin 141)

I would be remiss not to mention two final artifacts related to Borges and Whitman. The first is the former's translation of most of the original edition of *Leaves of Grass*, an effort announced as "in preparation" in a Buenos Aires literary magazine of 1927, but which actually was not published until 1969. Borges contributed a stunning prologue to his *Hojas de hierba*, in which he returns, maniacally, to the baffling duplicity, doubleness, or twoness of Whitman, and at the same time gives us a splendid appreciation of Whitman's achievement. Borges says:

> Those who pass from the glare and the vertigo of *Leaves of Grass* to the laborious reading of any of the pious biographies of Whitman always feel disappointed. In those gray and mediocre pages, they seek out the semidivine vagabond that these verses uncovered for them, and they are astonished not to find him. This, at least, has been my own experience and that of all my friends. One of the aims of this preface is to explain, or try to explain, that disconcerting discord. . . .
>
> He needed, as did Byron, a hero; but his hero had to be innumerable and ubiquitous, symbol of a populous democracy, like the omnipresent God of the Pantheists. That creature has a twofold nature; he is the modest journalist Walter Whitman, native of Long Island, a man whom some friend in a hurry might greet in the streets of Manhattan; and he is, at the same time, the other person that the first man wanted to be and was not, a man of adventure and love, indolent, courageous, carefree, a wanderer throughout America . . . there is almost no page on which the Whitman of his mere biography and the Whitman that he wanted to be and now is are not confounded in the imagination and affections of generations of men.
>
> (*Hojas de hierba* 18, 20–21; trans. A. C.)

During one of his last visits to the United States, Borges wrote a short poem, **"Camden 1892,"** which makes its quiet and painful point amid a grey, subdued rhetoric:

> The fragrance of coffee and newspapers.
> Sunday and its tedium. This morning,
> On the uninvestigated page, that vain
> Column of allegorical verses
> By a happy colleague. The old man lies
> Prostrate, pale, even white in his decent
> Room, the room of a poor man. Needlessly
> He glances at his face in the exhausted
> Mirror. He thinks, without surprise now,
> *That face is me*. One fumbling hand touches
> The tangled beard, the devastated mouth.
> The end is not far off. His voice declares:
> I am almost gone. But my verses scan
> Life and its splendor. I was Walt Whitman.
>
> (***Selected Poems***, 175, trans. Howard and Rennert)

Notes

1. Fernando Alegría, *Walt Whitman en Hispanoamérica*, as cited in Gay Wilson Allen, *New Walt Whitman Handbook* 534. The problematical task of translating from English to Spanish is complicated in Whitman's case by the fact that Whitman's most energetic translator in Spanish America at the beginning of the century, Alvaro Armando Vasseur, knew no English and used *Italian* translations from Whitman's English as the "base" language. The matter becomes even more grotesque, since the Italian translator was heavily influenced by Nietzsche's rhapsodic style in *Also Sprach Zarathustra*. A full history of this series of misreadings is to be found in Santí.

Works cited

Aguirre, Margarita. *Pablo Neruda/Héctor Eandi—Correspondencia durante* Residencia en la Tierra. Buenos Aires: Editorial Sudamericana, 1980.

Allen, Gay Wilson. *The New Walt Whitman Handbook.* New York: Hendricks House, 1962.

Borges, Jorge Luis. "An Autobiographical Essay." *The Aleph and Other Stories, 1933–1969.* Ed. and trans. Norman Thomas di Giovanni. New York: Dutton, 1978. 217–20.

———. "Camden 1892." *Selected Poems, 1923–1967.* Trans. Richard Howard and César Rennert. Ed. Norman Thomas di Giovanni. New York: Delacorte, 1972. 175.

———. "My Whole Life." *Selected Poems, 1923–1967.* Trans. W. S. Merwin. Ed. Norman Thomas di Giovanni. New York: Delacorte, 1972. 43.

Burgin, Richard. *Conversations with Jorge Luis Borges.* New York: Holt, Rinehart and Winston, 1969.

Felstiner, John. *Translating Neruda: The Way to Macchu Picchu.* Stanford, Calif.: Stanford UP, 1980.

Guibert, Rita. *Seven Voices: Seven Latin American Writers Talk to Rita Guibert.* New York: Knopf, 1973.

Mac Adam, Alfred, and Alexander Coleman. "An Interview with Carlos Fuentes." *Book Forum* 4 (1979): 677.

Neruda, Pablo. "Alturas de Macchu Picchu." Trans. John Felstiner. In his *Translating Neruda*, 203–39.

———. "Oda a Walt Whitman," *Obras Completas.* By Pablo Neruda. 3d ed. Buenos Aires: Editorial Losada, 1968. 1: 1357.

———. "On Impure Poetry." *Pablo Neruda, Five Decades: A Selection.* Ed. and trans. Ben Belitt. New York: Grove Press, 1974.

Paz, Octavio. *El arco y la lira.* 2d ed. Mexico City: Fondo de Cultura Económica, 1967.

Santí, Enrico Mario. "The Accidental Tourist: Walt Whitman in Latin America." *Do the Americas Have a Common Literature*? Ed. Gustavo Pérez Firmat. Durham, N.C.: Duke UP, 1990.

Whitman, Walt. *Hojas de hierba.* Ed. and trans. Jorge Luis Borges. Buenos Aires: Editorial Lumen, 1969.

———. *Leaves of Grass: Comprehensive Reader's Edition.* Ed. Harold W. Blodgett and Sculley Bradley. New York: New York UP, 1965. Abbreviated as *LG.*

Zweig, Paul. *Walt Whitman: The Making of the Poet.* New York: Basic, 1984.

Donald L. Shaw (essay date 1995)

SOURCE: "Manometre (1922–28) and Borge's First Publications in France," in *Romance Notes*, Vol. XXXVI, No. 1, Fall, 1995, pp. 27–34.

[*In the following essay, Shaw introduces two of Borges's earliest poems, including variants and a French translation of one, which were discovered in a little-known magazine published in Paris in the 1920s.*]

In his essay "Pour la préhistoire ultraïste de Borges" (*Cahiers L'Herne* 161) Guillermo de Torre writes: "Dans ses premières lignes autobiographiques—celles qu'il rédigea pour une *Exposición de la actual poesía argentina* (1927)—Borges écrit: 'Je suis porteño . . . Je suis né en 1900 . . . En 18 j'allais en Espagne. Là j'ai collaboré aux commencements de l'ultraïsme . . . ' Eclairons ce point-là: 'J'ai collaboré' et avec quelle fréquence et quelle intensité! A peine ouvre-t-on un quelconque numéro de cette tendance, *Grecia, Ultra, Tableros. . . .* qu'on y trouve quelques écrits de lui en prose ou en vers . . ." Gloria Videla extends the list to include *Cosmópolis, Cervantes* and *Reflector.* In the magazines mentioned in her book she also includes *Manomètre.* But since in her bibliography she mentions only the brief review which it carried of Guillermo de Torre's *Hélices* (1923), without either details or page-numbers, she may not have seen the original. Clearly, however, this little magazine deserves attention not only by Hispanists but also by students both of comparative literature and of cultural movements in Europe in the 1920s.

Manomètre began publication in Lyons in 1922, dying in 1928 after nine numbers. Its founder and contributing editor was a young doctor with literary pretensions, Emile Malaspine (1892–1953). He had served in the First World War as a medical auxiliary and been gassed in 1918. While recuperating in Switzerland during the following year he met Vicente Huidobro and almost certainly through him came into contact with other Spanish and Spanish American poets and with the little reviews in which they published. Thus he was presently able to contribute, like Borges, to the *Ultraista* magazine *Alfar,* published in Corunna between 1921 and 1927 and to *Proa* (1922 and 1924–26) in Buenos Aires. About the time he met Huidobro, Malespine also met Hans Arp, the French poet, painter and sculptor and possibly through him contacted Herwarth Walden, the editor of the immensely influential *Der Sturm* in Berlin (1910–1932) to which he would contribute along with Tristan Tzara. No doubt through other acquaintances Malespine would also publish in *Het Oversicht* (Antwerp), *Mertz* (Hanover), *Ma* (Vienna), and even *Zenit* (Zagreb-Belgrade), as well as sundry French magazines. His career illustrates how interconnected the small literary and artistic magazines of the day in Europe tended to be.

Manomètre engaged Malespine's main efforts in the 1920s outside his profession. It is not impossible that it was inspired by Huidobro's similar magazine *Creación* which began to appear a year earlier than its French counterpart. Both published items in several languages and accepted, in addition to poetry, illustrations of contemporary painting and architecture and articles on the arts in general, including the "new" music. A glance at the list of contributors to *Manomètre* is quite startling. They included acquaintances like Huidobro, Arp, and Guillermo de Torre; fellow editors of other little magazines (who could return the favor) like Walden, Julio J. Casal (the editor of *Alfar* between 1923 and 1926), and *Alfar's* next editor, Julio González del Valle; poets like Rogelio Buendía, Borges, and others best forgotten who were active with Huidobro and de Torre in Spanish *Ultraísta* magazines; and friends of friends like Tzara, Soupault, Mondrian and the Mexican Stridentist, Maples Arce. The list is remarkable until we recall that around the same time *Grecia* in Spain (whose editorial board included Buendía) was publishing contributions by (or translations of) Apollinaire, Marinetti, Cocteau, Tzara, Reverdy, Soupault and others of similar caliber.

Sadly, the first contribution in Spanish to *Manomètre*, "Poesía sin lógica" (*Manomètre* 1, pp. 11–13),[1] is unsigned. It purports to specify, very schematically, the difference between contemporary poetry and that of earlier periods. It contains nothing surprising to anyone who has read, for instance, the *Prisma* manifesto of 1921 signed by Guillermo de Torre, Guillermo Juan, Eduardo González Lanuza and Borges, which itself rehearses the basic doctrines of an already well-established "new" poetry, that of the European avant-garde. It is in fact a simplified explanation of what the *ultraístas*, in this case, took for granted, with certain concessions to a provincial French readership familiar with Spanish. The writer insists on the suppression of anecdotic content, rhyme and metre, while stressing the continuing importance of rhythm and musicality, with predictable references to Rémy de Gourmont and Verlaine. What links this short essay to Borges's views at this time is the insistence on imagery as the stuff of poetry, so that what is to be aimed at is "música de imágenes" without the necessity of logical or syntactical connections from line to line or stanza to stanza. "La sensación interna domina la sensación externa. (Cenestesia) . . . A la lengua lógica se substituye la lengua cenestésica . . . Un poema perfectamente lógico no es poético . . ." (p. 13). What makes this item interesting is that it was almost certainly written by Guillermo de Torre. If so, it represents one of his earliest attempts to explain the outlook of the group of poets to whom he belonged. The chief reason, apart from the content, which points towards de Torre as the author, is that the essay contains the phrase "Palabras en libertad" which subsequently became the title of a section in his only book of poetry, *Hélices* (1923). Poems by de Torre appear in the second, third and eighth numbers of *Manomètre*.[2] Clearly Malespine saw de Torre as a more promising poet than Borges, but had serious doubts already about *ultraísmo* and the avant-garde. Indeed, before long Malespine was issuing his own manifestos, in favor of what he called "Suridéalisme" (7, 109–11 and 9, 154–55). The second of these was merely a polemical article directed against a Parisian take-over of the name of his "movement". In the first, however, he develops his criticism of recent poetry as merely a pattern of rhythms and images (especially the latter) and calls for a return to ideas and to simpler poetic diction. Nonetheless, as we saw, he did publish another poem by de Torre.

The inclusion of items by Huidobro and Borges, not forgetting those by more minor figures like Maples Arce, Rogelio Buendía, Julio Casal, Roberto Ortelli and Julio González del Valle, is interesting chiefly because of the way they figure alongside others by Tzara,[3] Soupault,[4] Arp,[5] and Mondrian, who contributed a little essay on "Les arts et la beauté de nôtre ambiance tangible" (6, pp. 107–8). Huidobro's contribution is his poem "La Matelotte" from *Automne régulier* (1925). It is identical with the version contained in his ***Obras completas*** (I, 1976, pp. 344–45) save in one respect: line 6 here reads "Les bateaux traînent les vagues jusqu'à toucher le ciel" while the ***Obras completas*** text has "monter au ciel".

The two poems by Borges: **"Sábado"** (2, p. 12) and **"Atardecer"** (4, p. 71) are another matter. So far as I know, these were the first of his poems to be published in France and, in the case of the second, the first to be translated into any language. The second number of *Manomètre*, in which **"Sábado"** appeared, came out in October 1922. By this time Borges had returned to Buenos Aires from Spain and was preparing ***Fervor de Buenos Aires*** (1923) in which the poem figures under the title **"Sábados"** and was dedicated to his then *novia* Concepción Guerrero (Meneses 43–52). Shortly before the poem appeared in *Manomètre* a version had appeared in *Nosotros* (Buenos Aires) in September 1922. None of the three versions is identical to any of the others. The version in *Manomètre* reads as follows:

"Sábado"

Benjuí de tu presencia
que luego he de quemar en el recuerdo
y miradas felices
de ir orillando tu alma
Afuera hay un ocaso joya oscura
engastada en el tiempo
que levanta las calles humilladas
y una honda ciudad ciega
de hombres que no te vieron
La tarde calla o canta
Alguien descrucifica los anhelos
clavados en el piano
Siempre la multitud de tu hermosura
en claro esparcimiento sobre mi alma

The version in *Nosotros* published a month earlier, reads as follows (the variants are in italics):

"Sábado"

Benjuí de tu presencia
que *iré quemando luego* en el recuerdo
y miradas felices
de *bordear tu vivir.*
Afuera hay un ocaso joya oscura
engastada en el tiempo
que *redime* las calles humilladas
y una honda ciudad ciega
de hombres que no te vieron.
La tarde calla o canta.
Alguien descrucifica los *acordes*
clavados en el piano.

Siempre la multitud de tu *belleza*
en claro esparcimiento sobre mi alma.

(Scarano, 93–95)

Finally, the version published in ***Fervor de Buenos Aires*** was as follows:

"Sábados"

Para mi novia, Concepción Guerrero

Benjuí de tu presencia
que iré quemando luego en el recuerdo
y miradas felices
de bordear tu vivir.
Hay afuera un ocaso, alhaja oscura
engastada en el tiempo
que redime las calles humilladas
y una honda ciudad ciega
de hombres que no te vieron.
La tarde calla o canta.
Alguien descrucifica los anhelos
clavados en el piano.
Siempre la multitud de tu hermosura
en claro esparcimiento sobre mi alma.

Although it was published earlier, the *Nosotros* version seems to be a corrected version of the text in *Manomètre* since it is clearly closer to the ***Fervor*** text. Some points are interesting. We notice that in *Nosotros* Borges has discreetly restored punctuation. Secondly, he replaces "luego he de quemar" with "iré quemando luego" but, on the other hand, he substitutes "bordear tu vivir" for "ir orillando tu alma". This last substitution removes both an overstatement and an Argentinism. It refines the effect of line 4; but in addition the change deliberately introduces the only "verso agudo" in the poem as amended, altering the whole rhythmic effect of the opening. As we know, a major feature of Borges's early poetry about Buenos Aires was its tendency to humanize the city-scape. Here that tendency is intensified by the substitution of "redime", a verb more appropriate to humans, for the more banal "levanta". The change seems to have been made in order to emphasize Borges's sense of the contrast between the squalid streets and the beauty of the sunset. Interestingly, the two other changes made in the *Nosotros* version do not survive into the poem as it appeared in the first edition of ***Fervor***: "anhelos" becomes less metaphorically "acordes" in the allusion to a piano in the background, but "anhelos" is wisely restored in 1923. Similarly, Concepción's "hermosura" becomes "belleza" in the *Nosotros* version, losing the acoustic effect of the tonic accents on "multit*U*d" and "hermos*U*ra", but Borges again had wise second thoughts. In the version contained in ***Fervor*** the change from "joya" to "alhaja" in line 5 is presumably dictated by a desire to balance "afuera" earlier in the line; in this case the change is surely an improvement. It is not clear why the title is shifted from singular to plural in ***Fervor***, since the experience which the poem expresses seems to be related to a specific occasion. Perhaps the change is related to "la multitud de tu hermosura", in the sense that each Saturday evening of the kind evoked reveals one more facet of Concepción's manifold beauty.

The second Borges poem to be published in *Manomètre* was then entitled **"Atardecer."** Later, when it was incorporated into ***Fervor de Buenos Aires***, it lost its individual existence and title, becoming instead stanza three (lines 9–18) of **"Sábados"**, which was expanded to 28 lines. The only difference between the *Manomètre* version and the lines as they appear later in ***Fervor***, is that in the *Manomètre* text there is no punctuation other than a final period thoughtlessly added by Malespine at the end of his translation. In ***Fervor***, punctuation is restored. Since this is probably the first poem by Borges ever to be translated, I reproduce the original and the translation:

"Atardecer"

A despecho de tu desamor
tu hermosura
prodiga su milagro por el tiempo
Está en tí la ventura
como la primavera en la hoja nueva
Quedamente a tu vera
se desangra el silencio
Ya casi no soy nadie
soy tan solo un anhelo
que se pierde en la tarde
En tí está la delicia
como está la crueldad en las espadas

"Le Soir Tombe"

En dépit de ton désamour
ta beauté
par le temps son miracle prodigue
le bonheur est en toi comme
le printemps dans la feuille neuve
Quiétement à ton côté
le silence perd son sang
Déjà presque personne ne suis
Suis seulement un désir
qui se perd avant la nuit
Le délice est en toi
comme est la cruauté dans les épées.

Despite helpful work by Guillermo de Torre, Videla, Meneses, Linda Maier and others, if and when the much-heralded critical and annotated edition of the complete works of Borges ever appears (hopefully it will be begun before his centenary), much more research will be required on his early poetry, including that contained in manuscripts which are still coming to light, and in small journals of which *Manomètre* is a hitherto neglected example. It is to be hoped that the process of accumulating evidence, to which this note is a modest contribution, will continue, until we have really adequate and systematic documentation of this period of his career.

Notes

1. The pagination of this collection is as follows: No. I is paginated 1–16; thereafter the other eight numbers are paginated consecutively 1–155. To avoid misunderstanding I give both the number of the magazine and the pages as they appear in the collected edition.

I owe the discovery of *Manomètre* to the Curator of the Borges Collection at the University of Virginia's Alderman Library, Dr. J. B. Loewenstein, to whom I return grateful thanks.

2. To be precise: "Inauguración" (dated "Madrid 1922 [2, pp. 6–7]), "Ventilador" (from *Hélices* [3, pp. 40–41]), with a short introduction by Malespine, praising *Hélices* and declaring his friendship with de Torre, but already uttering a significant warning against "l'image outrancière" and de Torre's use of recherché language, and "Balneario" (dated "Ontaneda, septr 1924" [8, 132–33]).
3. "Herbiers des jeux et des calculs," from *De nos oiseaux* 1929 (3, p. 38); "Préalable" and "Précise" from *L'arbre des voyageurs*, 1932 (5, p. 87 and 8, p. 136); "Les écluses de la pensée", "Le nain dans son cornet", "Chaque ampoule contient mon système nerveux" and "Carnage abracadabrant", all four from *L'antitête: Monsieur Aa l'antiphilosophe*, 1933 (2, pp. 4–5 and 7, p. 118). All of these are fully documented in the first two volumes of Tzara's *Oeuvres complètes*, Paris, Flammarion, I, 1975 and II, 1977.
4. A note on Paul Eluard's *Répétitions* (2, pp. 10–11) and another on Tzara's *De nos oiseaux* (4, pp. 75–76).
5. "Die Schwallenhode" (2, p. 11) and four illustrations, one of which is accompanied by an untitled poem beginning: "die fahnenflüchtigen engel stürzen verhetzl herein" (8, p. 130).

Works cited

Huidobro, Vicente. *Obras completas.* Santiago de Chile: Andrés Bello, 1976.

Maier, Linda S. "Three 'New' Avant-garde Poems of Jorge Luis Borges." *Modern Language Notes* 102 (1987):223–32.

Manomètre: collection complète. Paris: Editions Jean-Michel Place, 1977.

Meneses, Carlos. *Jorge Luis Borges. Cartas de juventud.* Madrid: Orígenes, 1987.

Roux, D. de & Milleret, J. de (eds). *Jorge Luis Borges.* Paris: Cahiers L'Herne, 1964.

Scarano, Tommaso. *Variante a stampa nella poesia del primo Borges.* Pisa: Giardini Editori, 1987.

Tzara, Tristan. *Oeuvres complètes*, Paris: Flammarion, I, 1975 and II, 1977.

Videla, Gloria. *El ultraismo.* Madrid: Gredos, 1963.

Johnny Wink (essay date 1996)

SOURCE: "What to Make of an Even More Diminished Thing: A Borgesian Sonnet Considered in a Frosty Light,"in *Publication of the Arkansas Philological Association,*Vol. 22, No. 2, Fall, 1996, pp. 77–85.

[In the following essay, Wink praises Borges as a writer of sonnets.]

Some years ago I heard an otherwise bright young man announce in the student union at the University of Arkansas at Fayetteville a literary critical approach which promised to save time and which I have since come to think of as the arm's length theory of evaluative reading. He contended that he could hold a text before his eyes at arm's length and deem it worthy of reading or not based solely upon the shapes the words conspired to make on the page he was holding at bay. He was later prevailed upon to modify slightly this approach by agreeing that the number of permissible shapes might vary in direct proportion to the age of the poem.

The shape a poem assumes when it is a sonnet is no longer a permissible shape. My interlocutor had not quite the chronological surety of the fellow in the Viennese section of John Irving's *The Hotel New Hampshire*, a cocksure young Bohemian who knew to the moment and in what cafes artistic movements had begun and ended. And so he wasn't quite sure what to do with Robert Frost's "The Oven Bird." The sonnet's being irregularly rhymed was in its favor. However, it was still a sonnet, and it was not a hundred years old. My friend felt that it was clearly on the cusp.

I suspect that Robert Frost did, too. Although I have as of yet seen nothing in print about the matter, I feel certain that, whatever is the range of possible referents for "the diminished thing" of the poem's last line, it must include the sonnet form itself.

"The Oven Bird"

There is a singer everyone has heard,
Loud, a mid-summer and a mid-wood bird,
Who makes the solid tree trunks sound again.
He says that leaves are old and that for flowers
Mid-summer is to spring as one to ten.
He says the early petal-fall is past
When pear and cherry bloom went down in showers
On sunny days a moment overcast;
And comes that other fall we name the fall.
He says the highway dust is over all.
The bird would cease and be as other birds
But that he knows in singing not to sing.
The question that he frames in all but words
Is what to make of a diminished thing.

(119–20)

To be sure, the sonnet form had not in 1916 fallen into quite the disrepute it was later to encounter. E. A. Robinson won a couple of Pulitzer Prizes in the 1920's with a body of poetry liberally laced with sonnets, and Edna St. Vincent Millay's vogue was yet to come. However, Frost's poem deals not with utter exhaustion but, rather, diminution. When a marriage or a season or a poetic form hath in the Ram his halve cours yronne, what is to be done? That is the question the oven bird frames, according to our persona/paraphraser. I propose that one answer to the oven bird's question is "The Oven Bird" a weirdly-rhymed, but almost monotonously metrical, sonnet. And if the question is framed "in all but words," the answer is framed in nothing *but* words, the words that make up "The Oven Bird."

Mark Van Doren feels that the rhyme scheme of the poem is odd enough to disqualify it from categorization as a sonnet:

> All of the rhymes have been telling, for these pentameters chime in a strange, wayward fashion, promising a sonnet (the poem is fourteen lines) yet giving none. The rhyme now is expressive of the dreariness the bird suddenly feels, remembering the dust; though it is a dreariness he can overcome, for he keeps on talking.
>
> (76)

I see nothing in the poem's rhyming character expressive of dreariness. It's rather a startling omnium gatherum of schemes, featuring a couple of couplets, a duo of terza rima triplets, and a closing quatrain rhyming abab (although by the time we get to it, we have moved down the alphabet to fgfg). The couplets enclose the triplets and in so doing hint at the abba scheme of the Petrarchan octave.

Structure in a Petrarchan sonnet means an octave and a sestet; in a Shakespearean sonnet we expect three quatrains and a closing couplet. Frost's nifty little hybrid adds two and four and divides by two. "The Oven Bird" makes of the diminished thing of the sonnet form a tripartite arrangement. The first three lines announce the singer everyone has heard. The next seven translate his song into speech. The final four sum up what he has said. It's as if we're in the realm of the disjunctive presque-Petrarchan here: a septet is interrupted three-sevenths of the way through by another septet. The interrupted septet then resumes in line eleven and marches to its conclusion.

The meter of the poem is not quite so exciting, although its almost dreary regularity is perhaps as it should be, given the humdrum nature of the oven bird's report on the season. There is, however, one line which, metrically speaking, offers almost as much variety as do the rhyme scheme and the structure: "Loud, a mid-summer and a mid-wood bird . . ." To my way of hearing, this line features a trochee, a spondee, a pyrrhic, an iamb, and another spondee.

What to make of a diminished thing? A sonnet the deliciously grab bag nature of which makes the sonnet form, given all the possibilities here realized, feel like anything but a diminished thing.

The scene shifts. Now the one playing youth to my crabbed age is a current student of mine at Ouachita, an articulate and remarkably well-read fellow who for some reason views poetic forms with genuine suspicion.

"You mean Borges wrote a *sonnet*?" he queries, incredulity blistering his tongue. "*Jorge Luis* Borges?" I tell him yes, Borges wrote at least two sonnets about which I know and which I have read.

"Composición escrita en un ejemplar de la gesta de *Beowulf*"

A veces me pregunto qué razones
Me mueven a estudiar sin esperanza
De precisión, mientras mi noche avanza,
La lengua de los ásperos sajones.

Gastada por los años la memoria
Deja caer la en vano repetida
Palabra y es así como mi vida
Teje y desteje su cansada historia.

Será (me digo entonces) que de un modo
Secreto y suficiente el alma sabe
Que es inmortal y que su vasto y grave
Círculo abarca todo y puede todo.
Más allá de este afán y de este verso
Me aguarda inagotable el universo.

"Poem Written In A Copy of *Beowulf*"

At various times I have asked myself what reasons
moved me to study, while my night came down,
without particular hope of satisfaction,
the language of the blunt-tongued Anglo-Saxons.

Used up by the years, my memory
loses its grip on words that I have vainly
repeated and repeated. My life in the same way
weaves and unweaves its weary history.

Then I tell myself: it must be that the soul
has some secret, sufficient way of knowing
that it is immortal, that its vast, encompassing
circle can take in all, can accomplish all.
Beyond my anxiety, beyond this writing,
the universe waits, inexhaustible, inviting.

(Qtd. in Monegal 285–86)

On the face of it this poem appears to be a real *cri de coeur* a lyric from which has disappeared utterly the distance between author and persona. Indeed Borges *was* aging and going blind when in the late 1950s he undertook the study of Anglo-Saxon. **"Poem Written in a Copy of *Beowulf*"** was published in 1964. Even the title suggests the casual, a something jotted down in a margin in a moment of despair which turns, upon reflection, into another moment, this one of grand affirmation.

Yet there is nothing casual about the poem's structure. Like "The Oven Bird" Borges' poem blends elements of earlier sonnet forms. The feel of it is essentially Petrarchan, for it features a crisp turn in line nine, along with a rhyme scheme in the octave which is *almost* Petrarchan: abbacddc. The hint of the Shakespearean comes in with the change of rhymes in the second quatrain of the octave and, again, in the closing couplet. The allusion to sonnet-writing is for me even slyer than Frost's.

The persona convinces himself in the sonnet's octave that the soul is immortal ("it must be") and that "its vast, encompassing / circle can take in all, can accomplish all." One of the things the soul can accomplish is the composition of yet another powerful expression of our condition in the form of a sonnet, that form which, like the poem's persona, is weary of time but which has accomplished much and which can accomplish more, despite the ravages of age. Two projects are saved in the poem's octave: the persona will continue to study the language of the blunt-tongued Anglo-Saxons and the sonnet will conclude itself, understanding that beyond all anxiety and writing awaits a universe which can neither exhaust nor be exhausted by forms and which invites all manner of moods and styles to behold it.

The universe of Borges' poem proves more receptive than those who object to sonnets and other poetic forms on the grounds that something has happened in our century to prevent powerful expression from occurring within the precincts of preordained verbal structures. A colleague of Jack Butler at the College of Santa Fe has assured Jack that poetic forms are still permissible (how kind of him!), but that nothing really important is going to happen in them. In *Writing Poetry: Where Poems Come From and How to Write Them*, David Kirby teams up with Galway Kinnell to produce a profoundly baffling passage:

> Following World War I, it is the general consensus that the ignorant armies were victorious. Writers of the modern era can have no illusions about the disappearance of the world's grace, says Kinnell which is why "for modern poets—for everyone after Yeats—rhyme and meter amount to little more than mechanical aids for writing. . . . In rhyme and meter one has to be concerned with how to say something, perhaps *anything* which fulfills the formal requirements. It is hard to move into the open that way."
>
> (16)

What have World War I and the supposed disappearance of the world's grace got to do with poetic form? If global catastrophe renders formal possibilities in poetry impossible, why didn't the Black Death stop Petrarch in his tracks? How is it that Yeats could move into the open with rhyme and meter but nobody after him can? If nobody after him has been able to move into the open in rhyme and meter, have I hallucinated the great sonnet by Borges discussed above? I've never been present at a more powerful moving into the open than the one which takes place in the sestet of the Borges poem and which is accompanied by the stately drumbeat of loose iambics and the splendid ticking of terminal rhymes: modo/sabe/grave/todo/verso/universo.

In a true Petrarchan sonnet, written to celebrate the invention of the sonnet form, Borges declares the resources of the sonnet to be as limitless as the sequestrations of night and the revelations of day.

"Un poeta del siglo XIII"

Vuelve a mirar los arduos borradores
De aquel primer soneto innominado,
La página arbitraria en que ha mezclado
Tercetos y cuartetos pecadores.

Lima con lenta pluma sus rigores
Y se detiene. Acaso le ha llegado
Del porvenir y de su horror sagrado
Un rumor de remotos ruiseñores.

¿Habrá sentido que no estaba solo
Y que el arcano, el increíble Apolo
Le habrá revelado un arquetipo,

Un ávido cristal que apresaría
Cuánto la noche cierra o abre el día:
Dédalo, laberinto, enigma, Edipo?

"A Poet Of The Thirteenth Century"

Think of him laboring in the Tuscan halls
on the first sonnet (that word still unsaid),
the undistinguished pages, filled with sad
triplets and quatrains, without heads or tails.

Slowly he shapes it; yet the impulse fails.
He stops, perhaps at a strange slight music shed
from time coming and its holy dread,
a murmuring of far-off nightingales.

Did he sense that others were to follow,
that the arcane, incredible Apollo
had revealed an archetypal thing,

a whirlpool mirror that would draw and hold
all that night could hide or day unfold:
Daedalus, labyrinth, riddle, Oedipus King?

(Qtd. in Monegal 277)

In Frost and Borges, one finds blooming—having bloomed—figures of capable imagination, poets able to hold up to experience that exquisite "whirlpool mirror that would draw and hold / all that night could hide or day unfold, . . ." and to make of the amalgam of experience and carefully-wrought mirror such gems as "The Oven Bird" and **"Composición escrita en un ejemplar de la gesta de *Beowulf*."**

Works cited

Borges, Jorge Luis. *Borges: A Reader.* Ed. Emir Rodriguez Monegal and Alastair Reid. New York: E.P. Dutton, 1981.

Frost, Robert. *The Poetry of Robert Frost.* Ed. Edward Connery Lathem. New York: Holt, Rinehart and Winston, 1969.

Kirby, David. *Writing Poetry: Where Poems Come From and How to Write Them.* Boston: The Writer, Inc., 1989.

Van Doren, Mark. *Introduction to Poetry.* New York: The Dryden Press, 1951.

Richard Sanger (essay date 1997)

SOURCE: "'Todos queriamos ser heroes de anecdotas triviales': Words, Action and Anecdote in Borges' Poetry," in *Bulletin of Hispanic Studies,*Vol. LXXIV, No. 1, January, 1997, pp. 73–93.

[*In the following essay, Sanger considers the function of "self-enacting discourse" in Borges's poetry.*]

In his speech on the topic of arms and letters in Chapters 37 and 38 of the first part of Cervantes' novel, Don Quixote, as a knight errant, naturally upholds the superiority of arms over letters, arguing that the soldier's goal of peace is nobler, and that his life entails greater sacrifices and requires physical, as well as mental, strength. However, when he ends his speech reiterating his desire to 'hacerme famoso y conocido por el valor de mi brazo y filos de mi espada', we are told of the impact his words have had on the barber, the priest and the others assembled at the inn: 'En los que escuchado le habían sobrevino nueva lástima de ver que hombre que, al parecer, tenía buen entendimiento y buen discurso en todas las cosas que trataba, le hubiese perdido tan rematadamente en tratándole de su negra y pizmienta caballería.'[1] The phrase points up one of the great ironies of the novel: that, though Don Quixote has chosen to devote himself to arms and the world of action, his real talent lies in words, especially words that advocate or describe action.

When Pierre Menard sets out to write *Don Quixote* in Jorge Luis Borges' well-known story ["Pierre Menard, autor del *Quijote*"], it is no accident that one of the three fragments he completes is precisely Chapter 38. Borges' narrator, of course, understands why Don Quixote should argue in favour of arms; the surprise is that, three centuries later, 'el don Quijote de Pierre Menard—hombre contemporáneo de *La trahison des clercs* y de Bertrand Russell—reincida en estas nebulosas sofisterías!'. Four possible explanations are put forward:

> Madame Bachelier ha visto en ellas [nebulosas sofisterías] una admirable y típica subordinación del autor a la psicología del héroe; otros (nada perspicazmente) una *transcripción* del Quijote; la baronesa de Bacourt, la influencia de Nietzsche. A esa tercera interpretación (que juzgo irrefutable) no sé si me atreveré a añadir una cuarta, que condice muy bien con la casi divina modestia de Pierre Menard: su hábito resignado o irónico de propagar ideas que eran el estricto reverso de las preferidas por él.[2]

The question is left hanging: Does Pierre Menard really favour arms? Could it be that Cervantes' novel secretly sides with letters? And what, we may wonder, about Borges himself?

In Borges' poetry, the debate between the life of action and that of letters is one of the most constant themes, and the answer he develops is not always as equivocal as in **'Pierre Menard, autor del Quijote'.** Like a wiser Don Quixote, Borges the poet devotes himself to words that represent and, in their own way, become action. Of course, he phrases the question in a slightly different way from Don Quixote. For the knight errant and for his creator, who, we should remember, was a soldier long before he became a novelist, the life of letters included the study and practice of law: a 'letrado' was a lawyer, and the aim of 'letras' (or 'learning' in J. M. Cohen's translation), as Don Quixote states, is 'poner en su punto la justicia distributiva y dar a cada uno lo que es suyo, y entender y hacer que las buenas leyes se guarden'.[3] This means that, although such letters have a very real influence on the real world, they are not the most glamorous of careers. As a means of securing justice, if somewhat less effective, Don Quixote's free-lance vigilantism, with the lofty aim to 'desfazer tuertos y enderezar agravios', has the incomparable advantage of rewarding one with renown—especially when those you defeat are forced to go mumble your name and wondrous deeds before the lady you serve.

For Borges, in contrast, the life of 'letras' usually means the life of a writer—a career concerned not with justice but one, as he often reminds us, that promises everlasting renown. Borges' idea of what the life of action might be in his day is less specific. The most logical choice would have perhaps been something like the life of another famous Argentinian from a well-to-do family, Che Guevara: a combination of idealism, romance and altruism. But, leaving aside the politics, Borges never really seems to consider the life of action as a possibility in his own day: unlike Don Quixote, he is unwilling to believe that the heroisms of an earlier time can be repeated in the present. In **'Página para recordar al coronel Suárez, vencedor en Junín'**, a poem written in the last years of the first Peronist regime, Borges contrasts the battle his great-grandfather fought against the Spaniards with the predicament of his own time:

> Su bisnieto escribe estos versos y una tácita voz
> desde lo antiguo de la sangre le llega:
> —Qué importa mi batalla de Junín si es una gloriosa
> memoria,
> una fecha que se aprende para un examen o un lugar
> en el atlas.
> La batalla es eterna y puede prescindir de la pompa
> de visibles ejércitos con clarines;
> Junín son dos civiles que en una esquina maldicen a
> un tirano,
> o un hombre oscuro que se muere en la cárcel.[4]

Though, as the illustrious ancestor reminds his great-grandson, the battle is eternal or, to put it another way, the struggle continues, Borges the poet preferred to fight it in its older and grander variants. The figures who exemplify the life of action for him are all from the past and enveloped in a bookish mist—either the Saxons and Danes of the sagas, gauchos like Juan Muraña or his own military forbears who fought in the Wars of Independence or on the Argentinian outback.

If, unlike the knight errant, Borges does not consider the soldier's life as a career option, this does not mean he renounces the idea of action. Instead, alongside the description of heroic military feats undertaken by historical figures, Borges does something else—he presents the life of letters, or significant moments in it, as a life of action. This he does by portraying speech as an action that occurs in a certain context, and by using that context to give words the force of the 'magical symbols' they once were, as he writes in the prologue to ***La rosa profunda*** (420). Quevedo's composition of a memorable verse thus becomes as important as the beheading of Charles the First or the battle of Junín. By showing words he has composed for these figures as actions in certain contexts, Borges is advancing a general argument in favour of his own particular guild (the Men of Letters) against Don Quixote's claim that the life of action is superior. He is also making his own words into something more than words, into action.

I

The narrative form that Borges uses in order to make his argument is one that he denigrated at the start of his poetic career: the anecdote. This has not often been considered the chief glory and strength of modern poetry. Lorca, when he wanted to downplay the poem's popularity, spoke dismissively of 'La casada infiel' as 'pura anécdota andaluza' and such detractors of contemporary poetry as A. S. Byatt continue to use the term with disapproval, most damningly in conjunction with the adjective 'prosey'. The pejorative connotations of the term arise mainly from the claim that all anecdotes make: namely, that the events recounted actually occurred. This claim to historical veracity is the ostensible *raison d'être* of all anecdotes and present in what Heinz Grothe, in the only monograph on the subject, calls 'the first scientific definition of the anecdote', that of Dalitzsch:

> Anekdote ist die einen Einzelmenschen behandelnde, kurze Geschichte ohne Nebenhandlung, in der durch individuelle Züge des Handelns und Sprechens die Characteristik einer Persönlichkeit oder Kennzeichnung einer gemeinsamen, womoglich allgemeinmenschlichen Eigenschaft einer Gruppe von Menschen geboten wird. Dabei ist wesentlich, dass diese Geschichte entweder tatsächlich auf einer historische Begebenheit zurückgeht oder wenigstens den Anspruch erhebt, für historisch genommen zu werden in Bezug auf das zu charakterisierende Individuum.[5]
>
> (The anecdote is a brief tale without a subplot which has a single protagonist and which, through the particular details of the action and speech, reveals the characteristics of a person or the general qualities of a group of people. Therefore it is essential that this story is either actually based on historical fact or at least claims to be historical fact as far as the individual in question is concerned.)

Anecdotes are merely anecdotal because they recount actual events that somehow fall short of the magical transformations we require of art. True but trivial, they are more journalism than literature, raw material rather than polished work.

The most obvious way the anecdote lays claim to historical veracity is by dealing with figures and national traits that are known to its audience; it does not create new characters. In direct oral communication, this means that the raconteur, aware of the make-up of his audience, will often speak of mutual acquaintances. In published texts and on radio and television broadcasts, one has no such assurance and the whole realm of mutual acquaintances and figures from one's private life is eliminated. The subject of the anecdote becomes either the famous or the raconteur himself. The fact that collections of published anecdotes, such as the *Oxford Book of Literary Anecdotes*, are usually ordered by the name of the subject attests to the importance of the reader's ability to recognize the subject.

Of course, a story that concerns a historical figure is not necessarily true. The real test of an anecdote is a poetic one: if not historically verifiable or even accurate, it need only be symbolically true. Grothe writes:

> Der Urstoff einer Anekdote kann weit zurückreichen. Ob er 'wirklich wahr' ist, also tatsächlich geschehen, oder ob er 'erdacht' worden ist, das ist eigentlich unwichtig: wesentlich ist, dass das besondere Geschehnis, so wie es geschildert wird, hatte geschehen können.[6]
>
> (The basis of an anecdote may lie deep in the past. It is basically unimportant whether it is 'really true', i.e. actually happened, or whether it was 'invented': what is essential is that the particular event as it is represented could have happened.)

In his 'Nota sobre Walt Whitman', Borges makes the same point rather more forcefully:

> Un hecho falso puede ser esencialmente cierto. Es fama que Enrique I de Inglaterra no volvió a sonreír después de la muerte de su hijo; el hecho, quizá falso, puede ser verdadero como símbolo del abatimiento del rey.[7]

This test of poetic or symbolic truth is what governs the elaboration of anecdotes in poetry; this is particularly true of poems which present a historical situation that cannot be verified, say, the thoughts of Whitman as he looks at himself in the mirror for the last time.

Because the anecdote purports to recount an actual event, involving real figures, it is natural to see it as the record of that event—that is, as an instance of narrative in which language plays a role analogous to the sculptor's marble, merely representing the action of the story. It is narrative at its simplest, a story that tells us something that actually occurred, recounted by an apparently trustworthy and objective narrator whose motives are more or less transparent—or, at least, do not form the main intrigue of the story. Even the self-aggrandizing personal anecdote, the what-Winston-Churchill-said-to-me-when-I-met-him tale, lays claim to being the record of an event.

Things, however, are not quite this simple. In defining the anecdote as 'something unpublished; a secret history', Dr. Johnson followed etymology and Greek and Latin usage. Whatever else it may be, the anecdote is first and foremost an oral form and, though Grothe has no qualms about treating it as a 'literary genre' (introduced into German literature by an Italian and gaining great popularity in the eighteenth century), we should. No one *writes* anecdotes; we tell them, record them or write them *down.* In other words, there is something inherently oral about the anecdote, and the transition from the spoken to the written form involves a modification and loss of these qualities. For this reason, whenever poets have sought to bring poetry closer to the 'language of men', as Wordsworth did, the anecdote has been a natural form for them to choose.

There is a further sense in which the anecdote is an oral phenomenon: it is a form that is enormously concerned with direct speech and its context. As any collection of them will illustrate, the most typical anecdote involves someone recounting what someone else said in certain circumstances. For this reason, it can be seen as the most basic instance of narrative—the simplest possible combination of description and dialogue, of what Plato called diegesis and mimesis. In some cases, this use of direct speech has been taken to be the defining characteristic of the anecdote: Grothe quotes an anonymous eighteenth-century editor who claimed that the anecdote always contained 'eine charakterisierende Herzens-oder Geistsäusserung' (a characteristic utterance of the heart or spirit).[8] There are, of course, exceptions to this rule, anecdotes that end in actions or gestures rather than words; nonetheless, these gestures and actions themselves can often be interpreted as speech acts of one sort or another. Even the 'resourcefulness' anecdote, the what-so-and-so-did-when-such-and-such-happened story, often carries a symbolic meaning that resembles verbal exchanges.

The anecdote, then, represents action—yes, but the action that it represents most often is speech. To return to Dr. Johnson's definition, it is unpublished utterance: what is unpublished, though, is not the circumstantial detail of the framing narrative but the direct speech which this circumscribes. In other words, the anecdote is speech, originally perhaps something like the scattered *bon mots* of orators, and the framing narratives, or circumstances, simply come attached, like the bibliographical references of a published work. In fact, the editor of the proceedings of a recent colloquium on the subject defines the anecdote as 'un apophtègme en action', and cites Chamfort's *Caractères et anecdotes* as illustrating particularly well 'ce passage d'une forme aphoristique à une forme narrative'.[9] A great many anecdotes simply supply the context for memorable or epigrammatic speech.

The context, however, is essential. From a certain perspective, it is possible to claim that all poems that situate speech in a certain context are anecdotal. Telling us who said what and where and when, such poems bind their words to particular circumstances which we, through lack of empathy or understanding, may be unwilling to identify with or look beyond.[10] The combination of direct speech and circumstance or 'framing narrative' that characterizes anecdotal poems also stands behind other forms of poetry. When information regarding these circumstances is incorporated into a character's speech and the framing narrative is discarded, the result is a dramatic monologue. If the framing narrative is discarded completely and no information incorporated into the speech, the result is an occasional poem—a work which, while not recounting an anecdote, refers implicitly to one, most often in its title.

II

There is no development that characterizes Borges' mature poetry (that is, the works that followed ***Cuaderno de San Martín*** [1929]) more than his adoption and continual use of the anecdote. As a young *ultraísta,* he denounced the 'anecdotismo gárrulo' of his contemporaries and championed metaphor as the 'elemento primordial' of poetry;[11] as an aging poet, however, it was the anecdote that his imagination repeatedly resorted to. Following Borges' own theoretical preoccupations, however, most critics have concentrated on metaphor as the barometer by which to measure the changes in his poetry. Thus Guillermo Sucre traces the poet's evolution from the extravagances of *ultraísmo* to the sobriety of a poetry that is 'pobre e inmortal'.[12] The official source of this view is Borges' 1950 essay, 'Lametáfora', which recants on *ultraísta* claims and advocates the simple and eternal similes while criticizing the Islandic *kenningar* and the baroque conceits of Góngora. In the well-known story, 'La busca de Averroes', it is worth noting, the same theme surfaces: Borges has the character Averroes defend the use of a cliché (the blind camel of destiny) against the argument that 'cinco siglos de admiración la habían gastado'.[13]

The absolute predominance that the *ultraístas* gave to metaphor had other consequences. Since they assumed that metaphor was solely the creation of individual genius and not also popular speech, the diction and sentiment of their work tended to remain self-consciously literary. The poems of Borges' first book, ***Fervor de Buenos Aires*** (1923), are wistfully descriptive evocations of the Argentinian capital. The gently ironic lines the later Borges addresses to a minor poet of the Anthology might almost serve to describe the poet of that early volume:

> Dieron a otros gloria interminable los dioses,
> inscripciones y exergos y monumentos y puntuales
> historiadores;

de ti sólo sabemos, oscuro amigo,
que oíste al ruiseñor, una tarde.

(190)

If it is hard to find one poem in the collection that does not place the poet in the city streets at dusk, it is harder still to see how such work could ever be considered avant-garde. The poems are simply too intent on nostalgically reconstituting the city of the poet's birth.

The delicacy of these early poems contrasts sharply with the robust polemic of the essays that accompanied them. In an article entitled 'Ultraísmo', published in *Nosotros* in 1921, Borges vigorously attacked the two dominant poetic schools of the period:

> Antes de comenzar la explicación de la novísima estética, conviene desentrañar la hechura del rubenianismo y anecdotismo vigentes, que los poetas ultraístas nos proponemos llevar de calles y abolir. Y no hablo del clasicismo, pues el concepto que de la lírica tuvieron la mayoría de los clásicos—esto es, la urdidura de narraciones versificadas y embanderadas de imágenes, o el sonoro desarrollo dialéctico de cualquier intención ascética o jactancioso rendimiento amatorio—no campea hoy en parte alguna.[14]

The most interesting part of this manifesto, however, are not the jabs that Borges takes at the Parnassian followers of Rubén Darío; it is his criticism of 'el anecdotismo vigente' and the so-called 'sencillistas' who propagated it:

> Por cierto, muchos poetas jóvenes que asemějanse inicialmente a los ultraístas en su tedio común ante la cerrazón rubeniana, han hecho bando aparte, intentando rejuvenecer la lírica mediante las anécdotas rimadas y el desaliño experto. Me refiero a los sencillistas, que tienden a buscar poesía en lo común y corriente y a tachar de su vocabulario toda palabra prestigiosa. Pero éstos se equivocan también. Desplazar el lenguaje cotidiano hacia la literatura, es un error. Sabido es que en la conversacion hilvanamos de cualquier modo los vocablos y distribuimos los guarismos verbales con generosa vaguedad [. . .] El miedo a la retórica—miedo justificado y legítimo—empuja los sencillistas a otra clase de retórica vergonzante, tan postiza y deliberada como la jerigonza académica, o las palabrejas en lunfardo que se desparraman por cualquier obra nacional para crear el ambiente. Además, hay otro error más grave que su estética. Ni la escritura apresurada y jadeante de algunas fragmentarias percepciones ni los gironcillos autobiográficos arrancados a la totalidad de los estados de conciencia y malamente copiados, merecen ser poesía. Con esa voluntad logrera de aprovechar el menor ápice vital, con esa comenzón continua de encuadernar el universo y encajonarlo en una estantería, sólo se llega a un sempiterno espionaje del alma propia, que tal vez resquebraja e histrioniza al hombre que lo ejerce.[15]

The poets are reprimanded for their use of everyday language and for their autobiographical subject-matter; it is noteworthy that the two are seen to go hand in hand. And the autobiographical impulse is what leads them, 'with the miserly desire to profit from the tiniest fraction of life', to pass off such personal anecdotes as poetry.

There are, we may note, several difficulties that Borges fails to consider here. Firstly, if one writes autobiography in anything other than a low anecdotal style, there is a danger that the author's self-importance will sabotage the whole venture. Julius Caesar and Charles de Gaulle attempted to solve the problem by composing their memoirs in the third person. (Affecting just the 'shameful' plain-speaking rhetoric Borges criticizes, present-day politicians hire ghost writers to compose their memoirs in the first person, as if that were a guarantee of their sincerity.) When Wordsworth describes childhood card games as 'strife too humble to be named in verse' or Seamus Heaney likens himself to 'a fleet god' running through the tunnels of the London Underground, we may start to wonder just who the author thinks he is.[16] Likewise, if an author decides to write his autobiography in a form that is not anecdotal, the suggestion that he or she perceives an overall and perhaps divinely-inspired pattern or destiny to their lives can be similarly disconcerting.

For Borges, the answer to this dilemma is simple: not to write autobiographical verse. Or, rather, since all verse is inescapably autobiographical, not to write verse that is autobiographical in the traditional manner. This is how that 1921 *ultraísta* manifesto ends:

> Un resumen final. La poesía lírica no ha hecho otra cosa hasta ahora que bambolearse entre la cacería de efectos auditivos o visuales, y el prurito de querer expresar la personalidad de su autor. El primero de ambos empeños atañe a la pintura o a la música, y el segundo se asienta en un error psicológico, ya que la personalidad, el yo, es sólo una ancha denominación colectiva que abarca la pluralidad de todos los estados de conciencia. Cualquier estado nuevo que se agregue a los otros llega a formar parte esencial del yo, y a expresarlo: lo mismo lo *individual* que lo *ajeno.* Cualquier acontecimiento, cualquier percepción, cualquier idea, nos expresa con igual virtud; vale decir, puede añadirse a nosotros [. . .] Superando esa inútil terquedad en fijar verbalmente un yo vagabundo que se transforma en cada instante, el ultraísmo tiende a la meta primicial de toda poesía, esto es, a la transmutación de la realidad palpable del mundo en realidad interior y emocional.[17]

In other words, there is a part of the self that is unbounded by time and space and has the potential to be anyone. As Borges writes in a famous story from *Ficciones*, 'Acaso Schopenhauer tiene razón: yo soy los otros, cualquier hombre es todos los hombres, Shakespeare es de algún modo el miserable John Vincent Moon'.[18] The same idea is restated in the prologue to Borges' last book, *Los conjurados*: 'No hay poeta, por mediocre que sea, que no haya escrito el mejor verso de la literatura, pero también los más desdichados.'[19] In writing about Walt Whitman or Robert Browning, the poet is being just as autobiographical as if he were writing about his own life—he is writing about his own life, his own imaginative life. In this sense, this 1921 essay foreshadows all of Borges' later doublings and disguises of the self, while providing a rationale for the kind of anecdote he would eventually use.

The criticism of the anecdote found in these early declarations echoes criticisms made by other avant-garde groups in Spain and France at the time. It also contrasts sharply with the practice of the mature Borges. Beginning with the collections entitled ***El hacedor*** (1960) and ***El otro, el mismo*** (1964), some of whose contents were composed as early as 1943, we find poem after poem presenting us with short anecdotal situations: historical figures (writers, soldiers, philosophers) go for walks, dream up lines of verse, read newspapers and—most frequently—die. In Sucre's words, this later poetry 'sigue el fluir de una meditación que no desdeña lo cotidiano, lo anecdótico'.[20] In the prologue to ***Elogio de la sombra*** (1969), Borges seems to admit as much, suggesting slyly that these developments are due to his readers' demands:

> No soy poseedor de una estética. El tiempo me ha enseñado algunas astucias: [. . .] preferir las palabras habituales a las palabras asombrosas; intercalar en un relato rasgos circunstanciales, exigidos ahora por el lector . . .
>
> (315)

These 'circumstantial details, which readers now demand' are in large part the framing narratives of the anecdote: when and where and to whom such a thing was said. The prologue to ***Los conjurados*** reiterates the claim in very similar terms:

> En este libro hay muchos sueños. Aclaro que fueron dones de la noche o, más precisamente, del alba, no ficciones deliberadas. Apenas si me he atrevido a agregar uno que otro rasgo circunstancial, de los que exige nuestro tiempo, a partir de Defoe.[21]

Given the often abstract nature of Borges' thought, such details are perhaps welcome. If his poetry is at times overly cerebral (his conquistador proclaims 'Yo soy el Arquetipo' [483]), such details help mitigate the tendency towards abstraction.[22]

This adoption of the anecdote does not, however, have the consequences one might expect. In his book on the Generation of 1927, Tony Geist comments on an *ultraísta* manifesto (that of *Prisma* 1921) in the following manner:

> Borges et al. intiman aquí, sin llegar a enunciarlo, uno de los postulados básicos del ultraísmo. Para conseguir esta independencia de la metáfora, que produce en el poema 'la contextura . . . de los marconigramas', es imprescindible la supresión de la anécdota. De la realidad exterior, que rehuye el poeta, procede la anécdota, la historia vulgar que sujeta la metáfora y facilita su comprensión y traducción. Sólo la figura liberada de todo nexo con el mundo extrapoético puede crear un poema 'despojado de todas sus vísceras anecdóticas y sentimentales, podado de toda su secular hojarasca retórica y de su sofística finalidad pragmática'.[23]

This connection to exterior reality, as we have seen, is made through its claim to historical veracity and its use of historical figures, and by the fact that it is primarily an oral form. That is, the anecdote uses both the personalities and the language of the streets.

Borges' anecdotes do not, however, tend to bring the reader any closer to what Geist calls exterior reality; nor do they concern the 'historias vulgares' of contemporary life. And only very rarely are they autobiographical in any traditional sense. Instead, the great majority of them concern the historical and literary figures of a bookish past. This tends to confirm the least generous estimates of his poetry: that it consists mainly of outmoded and ceremonious exercises in which the dust of libraries supplants the fire of original inspiration. Hence, the relentless parade of names, the patriotic odes (**'Oda compuesta en 1960'**, **'Oda escrita en 1966'**), the eulogies (of England, France, the German language, wine and chess) and the elegies, the sonnets and the tightly-rhymed quatrains. The value of the poems, one might then argue, consists mainly in the insights they provide into the mind of their creator: they are seen as exhibits in the arcane field of Borges studies, the literary allusions and esoteric references to be deciphered by initiates who share the enthusiasms of their author and know the precise significance of such references in their master's universe.

There are, thankfully, other ways of looking at Borges' poetry. If, as he argued in that 1921 *ultraísta* manifesto, the self is nothing more than 'a collective noun designating the sum of all states of consciousness', including those imagined, then the poet's imaginary experience of other writers' lives and works constitutes a part of his own identity. Sixty-two years later, the answer Borges gave to a question at a conference both explains this reliance on such literary and historical figures (which I have suggested is characteristic of the published anecdote) and illuminates his notion of the self:

Question: *Señor Borges, it seems that some authors end up hating their characters a bit, like Unamuno maybe with Augusto Pérez. Is there a Borgesian character that you don't like that much now, or for which you lack any affection at all?*

Borges: But I've never created a character. It's always me, subtly disguised. No, I can't invent anyone—I'm not Dickens, I'm not Balzac—I can't invent people. I'm always myself, the same self in different times or places, but always, irreparably, incurably, myself.[24]

And that self is what you imagine it to be.

The first collection of Borges' mature poetry, ***El hacedor***, begins with a quatrain in which the poet savours the irony of his fellow creator, God, in placing a blind man amidst so many books:

> Nadie rebaje a lágrima o reproche
> Esta declaracion de la maestría
> De Dios, que con magnífica ironía
> Me dio a la vez los libros y la noche.
>
> (119)

If what follows is unabashedly literary in subject matter ('Yo, que me figuraba el Paraíso / Bajo la especie de una biblioteca'), it is because the poet's reading material forms a part of his experience that he assumes is much more interesting than the banal details of his daily life. At the end of his 1977 ***Obra poética***, in the epilogue to ***Historia de la noche***, Borges is still in his library, foreseeing our objections:

> De cuantos libros he publicado, el más íntimo es éste. Abunda en referencias librescas; también abundó en ellas Montaigne, inventor de la intimidad. Cabe decir lo mismo de Robert Burton, cuya inagotable *Anatomy of Melancholy*—una de las obras más personales de la literatura—es una suerte de centón que no se concibe sin largos anaqueles. Como ciertas ciudades, como ciertas personas, una parte muy grata de mi destino fueron los libros. ¿Me será permitido repetir que la biblioteca de mi padre ha sido el hecho capital de mi vida? La verdad es que nunca he salido de ella, como no salió nunca de la suya Alonso Quijano. (558)

Borges' argument is the same as Cervantes': literature and literary models condition our perception of reality, and therefore are part of it. The use of literary allusions to defend one's use of literary allusions, referring to Montaigne, and *then* Burton, is almost self-parody. It is also an example of words doing and saying at the same time—what one might call 'self-enacting discourse', that carries out what it describes. The paragraph both makes a verifiable statement about the world (are Montaigne's essays and Burton's *Anatomy* full of literary allusions?) and, like Austin's performative, does something (alluding to Montaigne and Burton) that can only be done in words. In a library full of words saying things, Borges is performing little tricks, making them do things.

III

One of the authors most often alluded to by Borges is Emerson and the sonnet that bears his name as its title (237) is typical of Borges' procedures. It presents a picture of the New England writer at a certain point in time and space, something like a vignette from an imaginary biography. Both the title and the demonstrative of the poem's first verse, '*Ese* alto caballero americano', show the author assuming that the reader will recognize his subject; it is also assumed that we will recognize the significance of the poem's other literary reference, the volume of Montaigne that Emerson closes. The poem's first eight lines sketch, in a fashion that recalls the evocative mode of Borges' early work, a picture of Emerson abandoning his reading and walking out towards the sunset:

> Ese alto caballero americano
> Cierra el volumen de Montaigne y sale
> En busca de otro goce que no vale
> Menos, la tarde que ya exalta el llano.
> Hacia el hondo poniente y su declive,
> Hacia el confín que ese poniente dora,
> Camina por los campos como ahora
> Por la memoria de quien esto escribe.

The last six lines then transcribe his thoughts in first-person direct speech. (Though this thematic division follows the Italian model of two quatrains and two tercets, the poem is actually a modified Shakespearean sonnet, rhymed ABBA CDDC EFFE GG, a form often used by Borges). Thus we move from an exterior vision that places the poem's subject in context to direct speech presenting his thoughts—the one to be weighed against the other.

Mere evocation, however, is not the poem's goal; if we look closely at the details of the first eight lines, we can see that Emerson is portrayed at a moment in his life that, more than defining, may be described as epiphanic. It is the point that Borges has defined on more than one occasion:

> Cualquier destino, por largo y complicado que sea, consta en realidad *de un solo momento:* el momento en que el hombre sabe para siempre quien es.[25]
>
> Un hombre se propone la tarea de dibujar el mundo. A lo largo de los años puebla un espacio con imágenes de provincias, de reinos, de montañas, de bahías, de naves, de islas, de peces, de habitaciones, de instrumentos, de astros, de caballos y de personas. Poco antes de morir, descubre que ese paciente laberinto de líneas traza la imagen de su cara.
>
> (170)

This revelation of the self, then, occurs just before death. If we reread the first two quatrains allegorically, it is clear that Emerson is dying. Montaigne, the subject of one of Emerson's best-known essays, is just the kind of author one reads for consolation at the end of one's life; to be closing the book on him and then walking into the sunset is, in figurative terms, to die twice—to die the death of the East Coast intellectual and the very Western death of a man of action.

But there is also another sense in which Borges' Emerson closes the book on Montaigne. In this final moment, able to see the (apparently limitless) limits of his achievements, he discovers who he is and yet, unlike the great French stoic, is unwilling to accept the picture he sees:

> Piensa: Leí los libros esenciales
> Y otros compuse que el oscuro olvido
> No ha de borrar. Un dios me ha concedido
> Lo que es dado saber a los mortales.
> Por todo el continente anda mi nombre;
> No he vivido. Quisiera ser otro hombre.

The paradox of the last line, Emerson's dissatisfaction with his life despite his great renown, may refer to some detail of the real Emerson's life or thought.[26] The more likely cause, though, is that Emerson regrets having devoted his life to literature and philosophy.[27] He has not lived—that is, he has not lived the life of action. In closing the book on Montaigne, Emerson is closing the book on books.

Practically all the anecdotal poems that Borges wrote about historical figures end with similar epiphanic moments. In fact, an inordinate number of them concern writers who, like Emerson, are about to die. After reading them, one is left with the feeling that Borges is using the other figures to contemplate vicariously his own death: Snorri Sturluson, Whitman and Heine, among others, are shown facing their own deaths in evocative sonnets. The revelations they experience often consist of paradoxes similar to that of **'Emerson'**: Snorri, the author of bloody sagas glorifying the bravery of his countrymen, realizes that he is a coward; Whitman realizes that he, the aging man of flesh and blood, is no longer the Walt Whitman of the poems that will survive him; and Heine, in contrast, is told by the poet that his poems will not save him from death. In other poems, the epiphany presented is one of artistic creation: Quevedo thinks of a memorable line, Petrarch invents the sonnet, and Cervantes (over and over again) dreams of Don Quixote.

In a sense, these poems might be more accurately described as vignettes. They have none of the accidental, fortuitous or surprising qualities that usually colour anecdotes about the famous. Nor do they portray their subjects in society, speaking with other people, as most such anecdotes do. Instead, they use atmospheric details to construct portraits that attempt to grasp, in solitude, an essential part of their subjects' characters—most often, that final picture of themselves that they apprehend just before death. Although they implicitly claim to be historically true, we as readers have no way of verifying their accuracy and, more significantly, realize that neither has Borges—what counts then is their poetic (or symbolic) truth. We judge them as fabrications to place beside our own imaginary pictures of their subjects. And, in doing so, we judge the justice of Borges' imagination.

Nonetheless, the poems are also more than disinterested vignettes or portraits. In each case, the poet has his motives and the subject has something to *tell* him. If we take the model of the meeting-the-famous anecdote, the poem then becomes the narration of the encounter between Borges' imagination and Emerson. The key point in these poems is the shift from the social niceties and exterior description of the subject to the presentation of the inner revelation he experiences, i.e. what he has to tell the narrator—and sometimes what the narrator has to tell him. At this point, the poem moves from representing action to presenting speech. In the sonnets, this shift usually occurs after the first two quatrains; this thematic division following the Italian model contrasts with the modified Shakespearean sonnet of three quatrains and a couplet, rhymed ABBA CDDC EFFE GG, that Borges often uses. The result is that the Italian form seems superimposed upon the Shakespearean model and the rigidity of the thematic division is mitigated formally. This shift in perspective casts the narrator, sometimes rather clumsily, into the role of an omniscient, mind-reading clairvoyant. As in other sonnets, the thoughts and words of the subject in **'Emerson'** are introduced by the verb 'pensar' placed at the start of the ninth verse. (In some poems, the verb 'saber' is used.) What follows the verb, however, is first-person speech. It is both the momentary revelation of the self that Borges often refers to, and something else: speech delivered with authority. In other words, Borges is borrowing the figure of Emerson to endow his own words with significance and power. In passing, we can note the verbal ambiguity that binds verses 7–9:

> Camina por los campos como ahora
> Por la memoria de quien esto escribe.
> Piensa: Leí los libros esenciales . . .

The obvious subject of the verb form 'piensa' is Emerson walking through the fields; there is, nonetheless, another third-person singular antecedent for the verb, the 'quien esto escribe' that immediately precedes 'piensa'. The grammatical subject of the verb, then, is both Emerson and Borges: they are both united in the rather grand intonations of the first person that follows.

In **'Emerson'**, we know from the title who the subject of the poem is and therefore are led to have certain expectations, which the poem both fulfils and frustrates. Employing a favourite Borges trick, the sonnet entitled **'Camden, 1892'** (239) reverses this procedure: it describes an apparently banal and everyday scene only to reveal its significance in the final verse. An old man turns away from the newspapers and his coffee to look at himself in the mirror:

> Piensa, ya sin asombro, que esa cara
> Es él. La distraída mano toca
> La turbia barba y la saqueada boca.
> No está lejos el fin. Su voz declara:
> Casi no soy, pero mis versos ritman
> La vida y su esplendor. Yo fui Walt Whitman.

These poems simulate or reproduce what might be called the chance-encounter-with-the-famous anecdote: we start off with mundane details, maybe something mildly intriguing, are introduced to a curious figure or activity, and then are flabbergasted to discover who or what it was. Unlike **'Emerson'**, **'Camden, 1892'** is able to present its subject in his casual wear and slippers. (Not that Whitman would have had it any other way.) The surprise, then, is how the everyday or apparently insignificant then becomes invested with meaning.

There are other differences. In **'Camden, 1892'**, the verb 'pensar' is used to introduce an indirect account of Whitman's last thoughts; it is only with the rather declamatory 'su voz declara' that we move into direct speech. Although the declaration is grandiose, we note that the speaker's mouth is 'saqueada'—'pillaged' or 'looted'. The poet has exhaled his wonderful poetry and is now all used up. The tedium and banality of his present contrast with the glorious declaration: 'Yo fui Walt Whitman.' 'I was Somebody' is not something one would normally say in everyday (non-theatrical) life, as those who can speak usually still *are*. Borges' Whitman has become his verses and the whole of the poem builds up to the final lapidary declaration which, like and unlike that of Ozymandias in Shelley's sonnet, asks us look upon his works and rejoice.

In both poems, we are presented with direct speech in the voice of the poems' subjects. Like an officious master of ceremonies, the narrator tells us (or doesn't) who this poem's subject will be, hints at how eminent he is and then bids him speak for himself. There is, it seems, nothing more important in these poems than the attempt Borges makes to endow a certain set of words with authority—the authority accorded to age and eminence. The words 'Yo fui Walt Whitman' become a performative, a verbal enactment of the poet's death.

But though the figures of these poets are borrowed and the words put in their mouths, the ultimate responsibility—and authority—rests with Borges. It is he who has concocted the situation and who reports the words; he, furthermore, edits them, thinks them worth reporting and suggests the significance they have. If **'Emerson'** hints at the tacit link between narrator and subject, other poems show the narrator moving to direct speech, addressing the subject of the poem. The sonnet about Heinrich Heine, **'París, 1856'** (240), ends with Borges shifting from this third-person clairvoyance to second-person address:

> Piensa en las delicadas melodías
> Cuyo instrumento fue, pero bien sabe
> Que el trino no es del árbol ni del ave
> Sino del tiempo y de sus vagos días.
> No han de salvarte, no, tus ruiseñores,
> Tus noches de oro y tus cantadas flores.

Here, it is not the famous writer who has something to tell the poet but rather the opposite. The encounter is closer to the typical anecdote: it rouses one of the characters to significant, if not terribly original or memorable, direct speech. In this sense, the poem is an event, an encounter between Borges and the shade of Heine—and not an attempt by Borges to squeeze some wisdom from a vignette. The narrator's mind-reading clairvoyance, what he knows about Heine and about time, is what presumably gives him the authority to dispatch the German poet in this fashion.

In all these poems, Borges' apparent omniscience, his ability to enter the minds of his characters, masks something else: the poet's absolute power and freedom to invent whatever he wants. When Borges pretends to be reporting the words or thoughts of another character, he is following a convention adopted to give those words power and significance; he is also disguising the fact that he has the power to determine exactly what those words will be. The use of a famous third person mitigates this power to some extent: if the sonnet is about Emerson, the poet is forced to consider what the reader's idea of Emerson might be, and to provide a convincing portrait of him. This, in turn, may lead to certain ethical concerns involved with the writing of history. Given that one is using the name of a real person, how 'true', in a symbolic sense, must one's portrait of him or her be? Can a writer simply manipulate events and personalities to suit his own ends? For the most part, Borges' philosophical idealism short-circuits such inquiries. Nothing exists outside the mind. We all have our own different Emersons, and they are part of ourselves.

If the clairvoyance of such poems as **'Emerson'** wears thin after a while, it is because we sense that Borges is not acknowledging the true source of the words—himself. **'Una rosa y Milton'** (213), one of Borges' best sonnets, is explicitly about the power the poet has to rescue, or invent, objects and events arbitrarily from history. Remembering the etymology of the word, we might even read the poem as a symbolic justification (and *modus operandi*) for Borges' 'anthology' of famous last words from the poets:

> De las generaciones de las rosas
> Que en el fondo del tiempo se han perdido
> Quiero que una se salve del olvido,
> Una sin marca o signo entre las cosas
> Que fueron. El destino me depara
> Este don de nombrar por vez primera
> Esa flor silenciosa, la postrera
> Rosa que Milton acercó a su cara,
> Sin verla. Oh tu bermeja o amarilla
> O blanca rosa de un jardín borrado,
> Deja mágicamente tu pasado
> Inmemorial y en este verso brilla,
> Oro, sangre o marfil o tenebrosa
> Como en sus manos, invisible rosa.

The subject-matter recalls a quandary formulated by Coleridge and cited by Borges in *Otras inquisiciones*: 'Si un hombre atravesara el Paraíso en un sueño, y le dieran una flor como prueba de que había estado allí, y si al despertar encontrara esa flor en su mano . . . ¿entonces, qué?'[28] Here, Borges, who always 'figuraba el Paraíso / Bajo la especie de una biblioteca' (120), retrieves a rose from the dusty past and bids it to open and glow, like a rose, in his verse.

Unlike the Heine sonnet, however, this poem retains the fortuitous quality that often characterizes oral anecdotes. It is not destiny, as the poet claims, but the arbitrary power of poetic creation that accords him the gift of naming the flower. The last rose Milton lifts to his face could just be any rose—in fact, as the last six lines make clear, it is just any rose. Borges tells us he doesn't know whether it is red, yellow or white, gold, blood or ivory. But neither did Milton know its colour: the significance of it being Milton is that he, like the author of the poem, is blind. The poem thus conjures up the flower only to make it disappear, 'tenebrosa / Como en sus manos, invisible rosa'. The poet makes us see and then makes us not see. The poem thus becomes an event—it doesn't recount one. The last six lines, as in so many of the other sonnets, contain direct speech that leads us inside the mind of the poem's subject, 'tenebrosa / Como en sus manos'. The words, however, are the narrator's. By addressing the flower, his words do what they say—they summon the rose into existence. Borges is drawing our attention to the particular actions that words—and men of letters—are capable of. At the same time, he is acknowledging the real source of his words, and the arbitrary power that he, as poet, possesses.

IV

In the poems examined so far, Borges has shown men of letters in moments when their speech has become tantamount to action. There is, however, another side to the coin—that of the men of action and their approach to words. The most impressive and idiosyncratic of Borges' poems dealing with the life of action is **'Poema conjetural'** (186—87). As a dramatic monologue, it does away with the shift from external to internal that characterized the sonnets; instead, it has to integrate an external vision of its speaker into his speech in a way that balances lyric revelation with narrative detail. The conjecture of the poem's title consists, in the first instance, of the poet's imagining the lawyer Francisco Laprida's description of his own death in battle. Besides the apparent impossibility of someone lucidly describing his own death, there exists the further unlikelihood that Laprida's thoughts before death would include the opening description of the battle:

Zumban las balas en la tarde última.
Hay viento y hay cenizas en el viento,
se dispersan el día y la batalla
deforme, y la victoria es de los otros.
Vencen los bárbaros, los gauchos vencen.

The poem's prefatory note tells us that these are his thoughts before death: 'El doctor Francisco Laprida, asesinado el día 22 de septiembre de 1829 por los montoneros de Aldao, piensa antes de morir:'. Nonetheless, being caught up in the fighting and fleeing, there is no reason why he should need to describe it—even to himself.

Of course, these anomalies are caused by the need to integrate an external perspective into Laprida's speech. Part of the problem is that the setting of the poem supplies the speaker with no obvious interlocutor. In Borges' short story-cum-dramatic monologue, **'Deutsches Requiem'**, a Nazi war criminal defiantly addresses the court that will sentence him to death: we accept his descriptions of himself and his work because we know it is part of an exculpatory explanation directed at others. In **'Poema conjetural'**, there is no such audience—if Francisco Laprida is talking to anyone, he is talking to himself. The poem is thus what Barbara Herrnstein Smith calls 'interior speech'.[29] But rather than the chaotic string of impressions such a term might lead us to expect, Laprida presents us with a beautifully constructed and rhetorically polished oration. There is nothing inherently 'interior' about the style of the poem; one might, in fact, question whether there is anything inherently 'interior' about any style of writing. There is likewise no attempt to emphasize the drama of the situation by making it affect the speaker's descriptive abilities: no enemy bullet is going to stop him from finding *le mot juste*. The entire poem, with its dramatic setting and descriptive felicities, is really just Laprida's last words, an elaborate equivalent of the direct speech that closes so many of Borges' sonnets.

The real reason Laprida has for describing himself to himself is revealed in his middle name, Narciso. This, nonetheless, is convincing enough: the narrator's narcissistic dwelling on the details of his defeat and death manages to fulfil, without undue clumsiness, the practical necessity of supplying us with enough circumstantial information to understand what is happening. In other words, the arrogant tone of Laprida's voice is the perfect vehicle for conveying the necessary self-description:

Yo, que estudié las leyes y los cánones,
yo, Francisco Narciso de Laprida,
cuya voz declar´daó la independencia
de estas crueles provincias, derrotado,
de sangre y de sudor manchado el rostro,
sin esperanza ni temor, perdido,
huyo hacia el Sur por arrabales últimos.

The whole poem is a self-dramatization, in which Laprida looks in the mirror and, with great aesthetic self-regard, describes himself dying. In fact, given the rapturous tones in which Laprida describes it, one is led to assume that he, like his creator, has often imagined the circumstances of his death. And, like the poem, this death is a composition.[30]

In discussing the young Borges' objections to the anecdotal poetry of his contemporaries, I noted that he failed to take into account the risks of writing autobiography in anything other than a low anecdotal style—namely, that the author's self-importance may sabotage the whole venture. 'I looked resplendent in my white uniform as I strode energetically up to the podium to receive the well-deserved medal from the President of the Republic' is a claim that one instinctively wants to dispute when made in the first person; in the third person, it is much easier to let pass. In **'Poema conjetural'**, the autobiographical arrogance of the first-person narrator is balanced by his fascination with the details of his defeat and death. The final effect, then, is that of a proud man taking a morbid, quasi-sexual delight in his submission to lowly reality:

Yo que anhelé ser otro, ser un hombre
de sentencias, de libros, de dictámenes,
a cielo abierto yaceré entre ciénagas;
pero me endiosa el pecho inexplicable
un júbilo secreto. Al fin me encuentro
con mi destino sudamericano.

It is this curious morbidity and his fatalism, rather than his pride, that make him most intriguing. He is, we discover, the opposite of Borges' Emerson—a soldier who dies in action but who wished to be a man of letters. In fact, as a trained lawyer, he is, in Cervantes' terms, a man of letters; his 'South American' destiny, however, requires that he forgo such cultured, literary aspirations and submit to a violent and ignominious death in a remote and swampy province.

The revelation Laprida experiences before death is, for readers of Borges, no surprise; here, it is spelled out with a kind of rhapsodic pedantry:

A esta ruinosa tarde me llevaba
el laberinto múltiple de pasos
que mis días tejieron desde un día
de la niñez. Al fin he descubierto
la recóndita clave de mis años,

la suerte de Francisco de Laprida,
la letra que faltaba, la perfecta
forma que supo Dios desde el principio.
En el espejo de esta noche alcanzo
mi insospechado rostro eterno. El círculo
se va a cerrar. Yo aguardo que así sea.

Even to his own considerable detriment, Laprida takes aesthetic pleasure in witnessing the completion of fate's design. The description he gives is practically a catalogue of all the different ways of representing death in Borges' work: 'los espejos, laberintos y espadas que ya prevé mi resignado lector', as he referred self-mockingly to them in the prologue to ***Elogio de la sombra*** (316).

Unlike many of the sonnets, however, **'Poema conjetural'** does not end with this revelation of self. Instead, Borges has his speaker describe the very end of his life in the same elegant unrhymed hendecasyllables:

Pisan mis pies la sombra de las lanzas
que me buscan. Las befas de mi muerte,
los jinetes, las crines, los caballos,
se ciernen sobre mí . . . Ya el primer golpe,
ya el duro hierro que me raja el pecho,
el íntimo cuchillo en la garganta.

There is no attempt at psychological realism, horror, exclamations and so forth; the death has all been composed and imagined beforehand, and the adjectives chosen. Borges is attempting to make words do the impossible: to send them into battle and through death. The dilemma recalls Ginés de Pasamonte's response when asked by Don Quixote whether he has finished his life story: '¿Cómo puede estar acabado [. . .] si aún no está acabada mi vida?'.[31] Laprida's words end only when the knife slits his throat.

In portraying the experience of a violent death, **'Poema conjetural'** works by understatement. The key to this is Laprida's morbid aestheticism and a kind of aristocratic bearing and fatalism that prevents him from doing anything unbecoming in the face of death. If we believe there is an actual death in the poem, it is because of the speaker's very composure and fascination with his death, and not any high-pitched attempts at conveying horror. For Francisco de Laprida, a man of action who wished to be one of letters, the poem is an attempt, perhaps his only attempt, to make that action into words. For this reason, it is perhaps not surprising that his words should be wordy and descriptive; that, though a dramatic monologue, the poem should be almost more concerned with description than speech. It is, to paraphrase Orwell's famous comment on Auden's 'Spain', not the poem of a man for whom death is just a word but, rather, the poem of a man who wishes to make his death into words. This means it is both the description of a man's death, and the dramatic monologue of someone trying to describe his death.

According to its own premises, **'Poema conjetural'** is spoken or 'thought' by a man of action. Ultimately, however, it is the poem of a man of letters—the poet whose conjecture the poem is. Like Emerson, Laprida wishes, or wished, for a fate that is not his own. Unlike Emerson, his wish is fulfilled: thanks to the conjecture, or intervention, of the poet, the action of his life and death do become words. Although the poem gives a rhapsodic description of Laprida's death in action, the real victors of the poem—and perhaps the cause of the speaker's 'júbilo secreto'—are the instrument of the conjecture that transforms his defeat into victory: words. In this sense, **'Poema conjetural'** makes the same argument in favour of the life of letters as the many sonnets concerned with the lives of famous poets. Even when they are romanticizing the soldier's life, the poet's words, like Don Quixote's, uphold his own vocation.

V

How does the mature Borges' use of the anecdote contrast with his early criticism of anecdotal poetry? By dealing primarily with historical and literary figures, his later poems avoid 'esa voluntad logrera de aprovechar el menor ápice vital' that afflicts autobiographical poets. Language and the imagination, he argues, can permit us to be (or to pretend we are) other people in other times. Why then use them to dwell on mundane details of our actual lives? Instead, by using other figures (and a certain amount of mundane detail to create dramatic tension, as in **'Poema conjetural'**), Borges is able to deal with what he views as truly significant themes. Francisco Laprida's dramatic monologue is simply a developed anecdote, a long series of last words uttered in exceptional circumstances. One can bolster this argument further with references to Borges' view of the self, and to the Kabbalah, as Borges no doubt would.

The other criticism of his early anecdotal contemporaries concerned their use of everyday, colloquial language: 'Desplazar el lenguaje cotidiano hacia la literatura es un error.' True to this axiom, the poems of his early books remained descriptive treatments of the streets of Buenos Aires, poems which attempted to use language to evoke certain moods and places in the same way an artist might use paint. With the introduction of the anecdote, this approach changed: his poetry started to concern itself with the context and power of speech. In sonnets such as **'Emerson'**, Borges uses a described context to endow flat statements with a sense of drama and authority: the aim is not to stop the reader dead in his tracks with an arresting image but, with a short narrative, to give certain words as much power as possible. Thus the very banal statement that ends **'Una mañana de 1649'** (276), the sonnet about Charles the First going to his beheading:

No lo infama el patíbulo. Los jueces
No son el Juez. Saluda levemente
Y sonríe. Lo ha hecho tantas veces.

The poem ends with the throw-away phrase that a harried mother might direct at a truant child. What makes it effective is the build-up and the story, the context that it is placed in.

Because of its emphasis on the act of speech, the anecdote permitted the mature Borges to examine, with the arrogance and insecurities of any writer, the contrast between the life of letters and the life of action. The real quandary for Borges, as for his Emerson, was: how can a life of letters become a life of action? As a young *ultraísta*, Borges attempted to transform the world with metaphor and ended up describing it, in a melancholy literary way. By presenting the figures of other writers in his later poetry, and placing words in their mouths, Borges was able to show their words as actions in their lives. In **'Una rosa y Milton'**, it is Borges himself whose words become an action—the action of summoning up the last rose Milton raised to his face. This desire to convert words into action is carried to the extreme in **'Poema conjetural'**: through the figure of Francisco Laprida, Borges was able to charge verbally into battle and beyond. Francisco Laprida's unfulfilled wish to be a man of letters makes his wordy death that much more plausible.

For the mature and late Borges, poetry is this attempt to make words into action:

> La palabra habría sido en el principio un símbolo mágico, que la usura del tiempo desgastaría. La misión del poeta sería restituir a la palabra, siquiera de un modo parcial, su primitiva y ahora oculta virtud. (420)

Unlikely as it may seem, this idea stands behind all Borges' occasional verse, his invocations and his eulogies and his odes. The anecdote, however, creates its own occasion; it provides him with another form to attempt this task, and a context in which to reflect upon it. Looking back on his youth in the prologue to ***El otro, el mismo*** (1964), he wrote:

> En su cenáculo de la calle Victoria, el escritor—llamémoslo así—Alberto Hidalgo señaló mi costumbre de escribir la misma página dos veces, con variaciones mínimas. Lamento haberle contestado que él era no menos] binario, salvo que en su caso particular la versión primera era de otro. Taleseran los deplorables modales de aquella época, que muchos miran con nostalgia. Todos queríamos ser héroes de anécdotas triviales.
>
> (173)

Speaking of repetition and anecdotes, Borges tells an anecdote of which he, however much he regrets it, is the hero. Saying becomes doing, the words action. The libraries and literary salons were perhaps as good an arena for heroism as the pampas and battlefields.

Notes

1. Miguel de Cervantes Saavedra, *El Ingenioso Hidalgo Don Quijote de la Mancha* (Barcelona: Juventud, 1971), 394.
2. Jorge Luis Borges, *Ficciones* (Madrid: Alianza/Emecé, 1971), 56.
3. Cervantes, *El Quijote*, 389.
4. Jorge Luis Borges, *Obra poética, 1923–1977* (Madrid: Alianza/Emecé, 1977), 193. Unless otherwise indicated, all poems, prologues and epilogues are quoted from this edition.
5. Heinz Grothe, *Anekdote* (Stuttgart: Metzler, 1971), 7. My translation.
6. *Ibid.*, 94–95. My translation.
7. Jorge Luis Borges, *Obras completas* (Buenos Aires: Emecé, 1974), 252–53.
8. Grothe, 6. My translation.
9. Alain Montandon, *L'anecdote (Actes du colloque de Clermont-Ferrand, 1988)* (Clermont-Ferrand: Université Blaise Pascal, 1990), vi.
10. It is instructive to look at the example of a poet who tried to eschew almost all external referents in his work. Writing about Mallarmé's occasional verse in the *Times Literary Supplement,* 27 January 1989, 75, Richard Sieburth points out:

    > Critics have occasionally deplored what they take to be the later Mallarmé's waste of time and talent on such futile fulfilments of epistolary obligation—mere distractions from his real work, mere excuses to go on deferring his ultimate book. It would be wrong, however, to dismiss the greater portion of Mallarmé's correspondence as the empty observance of the rituals of civility—just as it would be misleading to isolate his 'major' poetry (all fifty pages of it) from the hundreds of *vers de circonstances* that he so delighted in inscribing on fans, flyleafs, Easter eggs, or stones. Try as he might to eliminate all traces of chance or personal voice from the field of pure poetic language, most of Mallarmé's writing in fact tends to be profoundly occasional, that is, grounded in accidental social or public circumstance and, more often than not, ironically miming a desire for dialogue.

    In this light, one is tempted to see Mallarmé's occasional verse as the return of what he repressed from this 'major' work. The *tombeaux, éventails,* and other *vers de circonstances* carry out literally the act that anecdotal poems represent in their framing narratives: they place their utterances in the external world.
11. Gloria Videla, *El ultraísmo* (Madrid: Gredos, 1971), 201–03.
12. Guillermo Sucre, *Borges, el poeta* (México: UNAM, 1967), 50.
13. Jorge Luis Borges, *El Aleph* (Madrid: Alianza, 1971), 101.
14. Quoted in César Fernández Moreno, *Esquema de Borges* (Buenos Aires: Perrot, 1957), 50.
15. *Ibid.*, 50–51.
16. See William Wordsworth, *Prelude* in *The Oxford Authors: William Wordsworth*, ed. Stephen Gill (Oxford:

Oxford Univ. Press, 1984), Book 1, 1, 540; Seamus Heaney, *Station Island* (London: Faber, 1984), 13.

17. In Fernández Moreno, 55–56.
18. Borges, *Ficciones*, 138.
19. Jorge Luis Borges, *Los conjurados* (Madrid: Alianza, 1985), 13.
20. Sucre, 55.
21. Borges, *Los conjurados*, 14.
22. In the prologue to *La cifra*, Borges appears to recognize this:

    Mi suerte es lo que suele denominarse poesía intelectual. La palabra es casi un oxímoron; el intelecto (la vigilia) piensa por medio de abstracciones, la poesía (el sueño), por medio de imágenes, de mitos o de fábulas. La poesía intelectual debe entretejer gratamente esos dos procesos.

    See Jorge Luis Borges, *La cifra* (Madrid: Alianza, 1981), 11.
23. Anthony Leo Geist, *La poética de la generación del 1927 y las revistas literarias* (Madrid: Guadarrama, 1980), 53.
24. Carlos Cortínez, ed., *Borges the Poet* (Fayetteville: Univ. of Arkansas Press, 1986), 57.
25. Jorge Luis Borges, *Prosa completa* (Barcelona: Bruguera, 1980), II, 44.
26. In fact, the poem probably alludes to Emerson's epigram: 'The scholar is enchanted by the magic of words on the page until he ends up leading a life as thin and dry as the paper they are printed on.' I quote, paraphrasing, from memory since I have been unable to locate the sentence, either in Emerson's work or the context in which I first read it.
27. These last lines echo, in less harsh terms, the effect of an earlier poem, 'El poeta declara su nombradía', which, after cataloguing an apocryphal Arabian poet's enormous success, ends with the wish, 'Ojalá yo hubiera nacido muerto' (167).
28. Jorge Luis Borges, *Prosa completa* (Barcelona: Bruguera, 1980), II, 139.
29. Barbara Herrnstein Smith, *On the Margins of Discourse* (Chicago: Univ. of Chicago Press, 1980), 205.
30. In *Poetry of Experience* (New York: Norton, 1957), Robert Langbaum discusses 'the self-descriptive convention' in Shakespeare 'whereby the good characters speak of themselves frankly as good and the wicked as wicked'; this, he argues, is 'the entirely adequate expression of an absolutist world-view' (162). One might claim that Laprida's own self-description derives from a similarly absolute view of the world, as both the mention of 'barbarians' at the start of the poem and the description of the 'ruinosa tarde' suggest.
31. Cervantes, *El Quijote*, 209.

Beret E. Strong (essay date 1997)

SOURCE: "Borges and Girondo: Who Led the Vanguardia?" in *The Poetic Avant-Garde: The Groups of Borges, Auden, and Breton*, Northwestern University Press, 1997, pp. 71–97.

[*In the following excerpt, Strong contrasts the relationship of Borges and his fellow Argentine writer Oliviero Girondo to the Spanish modernist movement known as Ultraísmo.*]

Borges and Girondo: Who Led the Vanguardia?

In the 1920s, the Argentine vanguardia valued Borges's lyric poems more highly than Girondo's prose poems. Aside from their mutual commitment to the use of metaphor and to a couple of new literary journals, the two poets had little in common. In important ways Borges was as conservative and traditional as Girondo was radical and avant-garde. That Borges's early work was at that time more highly valued than Girondo's is partly because of the literary establishment's conservatism and the vanguardia's unwillingness to risk upsetting that establishment. Where Girondo was critical of the wealthy, state institutions, the Catholic Church, and the sexual mores of his day, Borges avoided topical issues. He changed course several times in his early years, while Girondo—like Breton—remained committed to the philosophy of the vanguardia. Though both were products of the same cultural atmosphere and had experienced European avant-gardism firsthand, they grew farther and farther apart over the decades. Girondo produced his most radical book, *En la masmédula* (In the uttermarrow, 1954) at a time when Borges was fast becoming a literary and political conservative.

In recent years, critics have echoed the values of the vanguardia by privileging Borges—who helped promote Argentine literature's image of itself as serious and traditional—over Girondo, who mocked and rebelled against this notion of the national literature. Moreover, their treatments of Girondo emphasize his role as the enfant terrible of the vanguardia; he becomes a colorful illustration of avant-garde outrageousness. That he is the *only* such illustration often goes unmentioned. Ironically, Girondo legitimates the vanguardia's status as an avant-garde, while Borges legitimates a decidedly un-avant-garde national literature-in-formation. Through the repetitive action of generations of critical texts, the vanguardia has in many ways become synonymous with Borges, whose poetry and essays stand in an ironically antithetical relationship to the movement's rhetoric. Umberto Eco (1983) writes, "It is not the ability to speak that establishes power, it is the ability to speak to the extent that this ability becomes rigid in an order, a system of rules, the given language" (240–41). The official critical myth also emphasizes the Boedo-Florida conflict and fails to examine with care the differences between the movement's two leaders. Coupled with the rigidity of the movement's reiterated myth-of-self, these critical choices distort the history of the vanguardia.

The literary establishment's attention to Borges during the 1920s and 1930s is consistent with its promotion of projects of cultural nationalism, such as the consolidation of a canon and the building of national literary institutions. To put it bluntly, Borges was a better instrument of cultural propaganda than Girondo, who consequently received less credit for his important role in the movement. The many differences between the poets should present a challenge to critics who start from the erroneous premise that the vanguardia's work was poetically and theoretically consistent. I suspect, though, that an important reason why critics have elided the contrasts between Girondo and Borges is that such an analysis would contribute to the dismantling of the official myth of a unified avant-garde.

Because Borges's oeuvre has been internationally acclaimed while Girondo is known primarily to literary Hispanists, there has also been a tendency in recent years to emphasize Borges in these histories. But as early as 1930 Borges was historicized as the official vanguardia leader, even though having a conservative leader runs afoul of avant-garde ideology. The privileging of Borges over Girondo in later years was increasingly influenced by questions of value and Borges's international fame. Fame, of course, builds on fame. But while Borges was certainly the superior writer when he turned his hand to fiction, Girondo's early poetry is significantly more interesting and innovative than Borges's from an avant-garde point of view. Neither poet produces during these early years an especially memorable body of poetry; Borges evokes a subtle and appealing lyricism, but Girondo's work would have the greater impact on later generations of Argentine poets. Girondo is perhaps the less fortunately born in the sense that he is less suited to his place of birth and would have done better had he been born in Europe. As it is, he turns to Europe for inspiration and support. . . .

In its historical series on the vanguardia, the Centro Editor de América Latina devotes most of two essays to the movement's official history, especially martinfierrismo and the Boedo-Florida conflict. Girondo and Borges are treated separately from each other. When the poets are mentioned together, the emphasis is usually on finding some degree of commonality. About their first books, Carlos Mastronardi (1980/1986) writes: "Se trata de obras nada semejantes entre sí, pero que responden con pareja eficacia a las apetencias de remozamiento que . . . empieza[n] a manifestarse con creciente intensidad" (1). (The works have nothing in common but they respond equally effectively to the appetite for rejuvenation that . . . is beginning to show itself with increasing intensity.) Masiello makes much the same gesture, but treats their poetry separately.[1] Leland (1986) points to the poets' shared "concern for the resonances of the image" without mentioning the differences between them (36). Sarlo Sabajanes emphasizes the diversity of the vanguardia group, only to make her own gesture of erasure of their differences:

> Se ha hablado mucho de la falta de coherencia interna del grupo que hizo la revista *Martín Fierro*. . . . Lo cierto es que . . . el martinfierrismo trasciende a *Martín Fierro*, supera las fronteras, existentes pero invariablemente laxas, de la revista y se conforma en signo constituyente de un grupo coetáneo y generacional.[2]

> (Much has been said about the lack of internal coherence of the group behind the journal *Martín Fierro*. . . . What is certain is that . . . martinfierrismo transcends *Martín Fierro*, overcomes the existing but invariably lax borders of the journal, and becomes the constituent sign of a contemporary and generational group.)

A number of histories of the movement—such as Iturburu's *La revolución martinfierrista*, María Raquel Llagostera's prologue to the anthology *Boedo y Florida*, and Teodosio Fernández's (1987) *La poesía hispánoamericana en el siglo XX* (28–33)—follow the pattern of discussing the vanguardia's central polemic—Boedo versus Florida—without examining the differences dividing the leading vanguardia poets themselves.

Compared to Borges and Girondo, the central Auden poets were quite similar, though when they disbanded at the end of the 1930s, a clamor of voices—including those of the poets themselves—argued that the poets had never had much in common. This refutation was based on hindsight and a collective sense of a failed mission. But the Argentine vanguardia has been historicized as a successful and important movement, which it in fact was. It seems odd that the vanguardia's cohesiveness and integrity have gone unchallenged except by a handful of critics such as Beatriz Sarlo. Given the institutional drive to divide literary history into movements, undermining the vanguardia's integrity would force a revision of Argentine literary history as written. All historical revisionism involves a loss of previously accepted meaning, which can in turn threaten the institutional ideology that erected the history in the first place.

The differences between Borges and Girondo suggest that poetic and personal differences are often less important than the company poets keep and the publications in which their signatures appear. Borges's choice of journals, for example, largely accounts for why he was identified with Florida instead of Boedo. Had he made different publishing choices and had different friends, he might have been able to write the same poems and publish some of them in Boedo's journals.[3] In an important sense, however, Borges was destined for Florida long before the conflict between the groups arose. He had laid the groundwork for an aesthetics-realism opposition when he brought ultraism to Buenos Aires and helped gather together a new generation of aesthetics-oriented writers. Borges was allied with Florida for reasons extending beyond his texts to the social circumstances of his life. And though avant-garde movements like to believe that their every new move is made with the freshness of total autonomy, Borges in 1924 was already largely determined by the Borges of 1921 who helped create *Prisma* and whose family was socially connected to the cultural elite.

When it came to marketing and self-promotion, the young Borges was a traditionalist. If the primary journal of the vanguardia, *Martín Fierro*, occasionally lapsed into the taboo rhetoric of popular advertising, its leading poet did not. Borges paid three hundred pesos to publish three hundred copies of ***Fervor de Buenos Aires*** (***Fervor of Buenos Aires***) (1923) and refused to promote it for the public. Though he later wrote, "I never thought of sending copies to the booksellers or out for review" (Alazraki 1987, 34), he devised a publicity strategy aimed directly at important literary figures. He talked *Nosotros* editor Alfredo Bianchi into slipping copies of the book into the coat pockets of the journal's visitors and staff (Alazraki 1987, 34). When he returned from Europe a year later, Borges found he had a reputation as a poet. He describes this first book as "essentially romantic," a reflection of his desire to write "poems beyond the here and now, free of local color and contemporary circumstances" (Alazraki 1987, 84–85). The antithesis of the early Auden, pylon poet and lover of modernity and machinery, Borges here empties the city streets that Darío filled with people some twenty years earlier.[4]

The effect of Borges's unwillingness to participate in modern marketing techniques is mitigated by his prolific output of literary and theoretical texts during the 1920s and his willingness—shared by Breton—to publish and republish his early essays. Most of the essays in *El tamaño de mi esperanza* ("The dimension of my hope") (1926), for example, had already appeared in *La Prensa, Nosotros, Inicial, Proa*, and *Valoraciones*. Borges participated simultaneously in mainstream and avant-garde publishing. In comparison, the Auden poets published more in the mainstream, while the surrealists stuck more closely to their own publications. All three groups, however, published books with major presses and wrote from time to time for major journals. Their postures vis-à-vis the market were different, however. Where Borges appears to have been reluctant, the Auden poets were unabashed in their self-promotion. The surrealists were most inventive in their strategies; they wanted both to insult the market and to make it do their bidding.

Like the martinfierristas, Borges tended to say one thing and do another when it came to getting his work into print. To *Nosotros*'s 1923 survey of the new literary generation, Borges gave antimodern responses. Asked his age, he responds "Ya he cansado veintidós años." (I've already exhausted twenty-two years.) He professes a commitment to ultraism, classical syntax, and sentences "complejas como ejércitos" (as complex as armies). About older literary masters he admires, he says: "Mis entusiasmos son ortodoxos. Entre los santos de mi devoción cuento a Capdevila, a Banchs, y señaladamente a nuestro Quevedo, Lugones."[5] (My enthusiasms are orthodox. Among the saints of my devotion I count Capdevila, Banchs, and most of all, our Quevedo, Lugones.) To admire postmodern poets—the nearest literary ancestor—is not only anti-avant-garde behavior, but is also a less self-differentiating choice than most young poets tend to make.

A number of critics have accepted uncritically Borges's canonization choices, echoing and reinforcing his opinions. José Miguel Oviedo's comments reflect Borges's changing point of view. Of Borges's first three books of poems, he writes:

> With them, Borges wanted to create a new poetic tradition, specifically Argentine, which . . . was a *challenge to tradition* and the Hispanic legacy, a *gesture of radical independence*. The argentinisms and neologisms of his early poetry (which have been erased or revised in later editions) were a *defiant sign of his literary stance of that decade.*
>
> (in Cortínez 1986, 124–25; my emphasis)

Only in his earliest essays did Borges make such claims, though Oviedo—echoing the early manifesto-writing Borges—represents him as having succeeded at them. Borges was no revolutionary, and in later life he disagreed with Oviedo's point of view: "I can now only regret my early ultraist excesses. After nearly half a century, I find myself still striving to live down that awkward period of my life" (Alazraki 1987, 35). If Oviedo were to consider fully Burges's admissions of debt to older poets and how his attitude toward his early work changed, he would find it difficult to call the poetry a product of "radical independence." Borges realized that his early claims were exaggerated, for though he distinguished himself through the use of argentinisms and neologisms, he brought neither device to Argentine literature. It is widely known that modernist poets invented criollo and Greek- and Latin-based neologisms. "Luna ciudadana" (Citizen moon) shows that by 1909 Lugones had set the standard for linguistic exploration: "Mientras cruza el tranvía una pobre comarca / De suburbio y de vagas chimeneas . . . / *Fulano*, en versátil aerostación de ideas, / Alivia su consuetudinario / Itinerario" (Lugones 1961, 110). (While the streetcar crosses a poor area / Of suburbs and vague chimneys . . . / *John Doe*, in a versatile air station of ideas, / Lightens his usual / Itinerary.)

Critics have supported Borges's efforts to remove the bulk of his early work from the Borges canon. The international literary community's portrait of "Borges" is that of a great short story writer and mediocre poet of conservative political and traditional literary values. Most of the time "Borges" is the older fiction-writing Borges, the one who became known in Europe and North America only after he shared the Formentor Prize with Samuel Beckett in 1961. This Borges is a product consumed on northern soil whose literary works date mainly from stories written in the late 1930s, 1940s, and 1950s, and whose philosophical point of view is generally taken from *Otras inquisiciones* (1952) and interviews conducted late in life. In his biography of Borges, Emir Rodríguez Monegal has contributed to the notion that the early Borges was somehow not the real article by calling him "Georgia" for the first three decades of his life. In 1930, "Georgia" magically turned into "Borges," though we are never told how he finally earned the right to wear the long pants of the adult writer.[6] Borges's abundant output in the early years is not unusual among important avant-garde figures. Auden, Spender, and Day Lewis were prolific poets, essayists, critics, and journalists, and Breton and Aragon each published several important texts in their early years. Though militantly avant-garde writers such as Breton were vociferous in their opposition to the professionalization of writers, such voluminous output certainly suggests that Breton *was* a professional writer. Flooding a literary market he claimed to disdain is a contradictory choice. It is the Dada paradox all over again: How does a movement create the public it needs to sustain itself without pursuing traditional avenues of self-promotion and consecration? No movement has satisfactorily solved this problem that provided the raw material for many of surrealism's fiercest in-house battles.

The secondary erasures of critics—where they devalorize what Borges removed from his canon or did not allow to remain in general circulation—mask the poet's sometimes violent means of exercising power over the canonization process. Borges later explained that he suppressed a lot of work because he felt he had been carelessly prolific:

> This period, from 1921 to 1929, was one of great activity, but much of it was perhaps reckless and even pointless. I wrote and published no less than seven books—four of them essays and three of them verse. I also founded three magazines and contributed with fair frequency to nearly a dozen other periodicals . . . Three of the four essay collections—whose names are best forgotten—I have never allowed to be reprinted.
>
> (Alazraki 1987, 37–38)

Auden edited his work heavily and experimented with ordering his poems in ways that disturbed the chronology of their composition. Breton, too, revised himself, but he did not try to outmuscle the predilections of critics the way the other two did. Instead, he merely added a new text amending or adjusting his previous point of view to his extremely long list of publications. He was less focused on what his body of work would look like posthumously and more on what he wanted to say at a given moment. He exemplifies the radical avant-garde's obsession with the present.

Critics have by and large opted to reinforce Borges's choices by assessing the early poetry and essays as less valuable than the later fiction and by opting not to write about them much. In fact, the early work is considerably less valuable in that it is less universal and less interesting than the later work. But it is also important to note that the excision of some of it from his canon served Borges's desire to present a consistent face to the world. In contrast, Auden's carefully considered revisions were often overruled by critics who rejected editorial changes he made on his 1930s poems after the decade was over. There were two Audens, a number of critics argued, and the later one was inferior to the "social poet." This divided Auden became a convenience to those who wanted to treat "the early Auden" separately.

Borges's case is the other side of the coin. Where a rupture in a poet's work is difficult to deal with—as in the case of Auden in 1940 and Borges's Spanish ultraism days—critics have been surprisingly willing to opt for the cleaver. While the juvenalia of many writers is less interesting than more mature work, Borges, the object of hundreds of critical works, is no ordinary writer. Auden's juvenalia has received abundant attention, Borges's very little. Graciela Palau de Nemes has labeled Borges's early history—a history he largely rejected—"prehistory."[7] De Torre's article "Para la prehistoria ultraísta de Borges" (For Borges's ultraist prehistory) includes a discussion of *Prisma*'s 1921 debut, thus suggesting that Borgesian "history" began in 1922 or 1923.[8] In the face of lesser deviations, such as Borges the erratic vanguardia leader, critics sometimes go to considerable lengths to sew up the holes and inconsistencies in their portrait of the writer.

I am not aware of a work that plumbs the ideological implications of Borges's suppression of his early work, though Borges's own critique is interesting. He condemns for their excesses *Inquisiciones* (Inquisitions) (1925), *El tamaño de mi esperanza* (1926), and *El idioma de los argentinos* (The language of the Argentines) (1928), and claims to have written and destroyed three books before he published ***Fervor de Buenos Aires***s. *Los naipes del tahúr* (Tarot cards) he describes as literary and political essays. Another early work was approximately twenty free-verse poems "in praise of the Russian Revolution, the brotherhood of man, and pacifism. . . . This book I destroyed in Spain on the eve of our departure" (Alazraki 1987, 33). In his "Autobiographical Essay," however, Borges says he destroyed the book of poems because he failed to find a publisher for it (Rodríguez Monegal 1978, 165). Borges describes his early experiences with literary journals in an agentless way that absolves him of responsibility for seeking a publisher: "Three or four of [the poems] *found their way* into magazines—**'Bolshevik Epic,' 'Trenches,' 'Russia'**" (Alazraki 1987, 33; my emphasis). About one of the books of essays he did publish, Borges writes,

> I was doing my best to write Latin in Spanish, and the book collapses under the sheer weight of its involutions and sententious judgments. The next of these failures was a kind of reaction. I went to the other extreme—I tried to be as Argentine as I could. I got hold of Segovia's dictionary of Argentinisms and worked in so many local words that many of my countrymen could hardly understand it. (Alazraki 1987, 38)

Borges's early ultraist poems are tinged with political and erotic language, language he later avoided in his work. The early work should be studied because its suppression raises the question, What is the critic's stake in starting a history well after that history has begun? Here the problem is an anomalous stage of Borges's development, one that doesn't fit the impersonal, nostalgic, Berkeleyan poetry he later writes. Like Auden, Borges often revised his discursive persona and creative work. Unfortunately, he and critics have erased too well some of the contradictions that characterize his first decade in the public eye. Of Borges's transition from ultraist poet to fiction writer in the early 1930s, Rodríguez Monegal offers such comments as "subtly, ironically, through his example, [Alfonso] Reyes would lead Georgie away from the baroque and teach him how to write the best Spanish prose of the century." But this statement is too simple an explanation of the transition (Rodriguez Monegal 1978, 213). Assigning an end date to ultraism presents yet another problem, for while ultraist poets continued to publish ultraist poems in the late 1920s, Borges became the single most powerful force in the dating of the movement. De Torre claims the movement was over in the spring of 1922, while Robert A. Ortelli argues that it was thriving in 1923, a proof being the publication of Borges's ***Fervor de Buenos Aires*** (Bastos 1974, 76). This illustrates the critic's tendency to identify movements with their leaders.

In rejecting poetic predecessors, the ultraists most often emphasized their objection to rhyme and to worn-out metaphors. In his early essays, Borges expresses some disdain for Lugones, the champion of rhyme, though he acknowledges him in the *Nosotros* survey as an important influence on the vanguardia. In *Leopoldo Lugones,* published decades later, Borges insists: "I affirm that the work of the 'Martín Fierro' and 'Proa' poets . . . is absolutely prefigured in a few pages of the *Lunario*" (qtd. in Running 1981, 149). In his eighties, Borges comments, "Todos—en aquel tiempo—no sólo lo imitábamos sino que hubiéramos querido ser Lugones" (Ferrari 1985, 210). (All of us—at that time—not only imitated him but would have liked to be Lugones.) Such inconsistencies help explain why Borges wanted to suppress his essays. The essays reveal, for example, that Borges, a determined writer of free verse, chose a critical battle—the rejection of rhyme as an important aspect of ultraist poetics—that he as a *poet* had already settled. Though heavily influenced by Lugones, Borges was even more influenced by Walt Whitman, at least on the question of free verse versus rhyme. Why then did he expend so much energy on an issue he had resolved for himself? Was it to defend the vanguardia movement's rebellion of choice[9] or, like *Martín Fierro*, to engage in avant-garde-style battles for the sake of creating polemics and attracting publicity? This is the kind of question that should be asked if we are to understand what is at stake in his selective canonical suppressions. We might come to view certain strategic choices as the erasure of embarrassing experiments with the power of trumped-up polemics.

Such polemics contrast with the traditional values the young Borges expressed about poetry: "El ultraísmo no es quizá otra cosa que la espléndida síntesis de la literatura antigua."[10] (Ultraism is perhaps nothing other than the splendid synthesis of ancient literature.) In fact, his earliest published poems, even those with topical references, are undeniably antimodern. **"Guardia roja" ("Red Guard")** appears to be about the Russian Revolution but, except for the title, it could describe a number of premodern wars:

El viento es la bandera que se enreda en las lanzas
La estepa es una inútil copia del alma
De las colas de los caballos cuelga el villorio encendido
y la estepa rendida
no acaba de morirse
Durante los combates
el milagro terrible del dolor estiró los instantes
ya grita el sol
Por el espacio trepan hordas de luces
En la ciudad lejana
donde los mediodías tañen los tensos viaductos
y de las cruces pende el Nazareno
como un cartel sobre los mundos
se embozarán los hombres
en los cuerpos desnudos.[11]

(The wind is the flag which tangles in the lances
The steppe is a useless copy of the soul
From the horses' tails hangs the burning jerkwater town
and the conquered steppe
does not finish dying
During the battles
the terrible miracle of pain stretched the moments
the sun already screams
Through space hordes of lights climb
In the distant city
where the middays strum the tense viaducts
and the Nazarene hangs from the crosses
like a handbill over the worlds
men will cover themselves
in naked corpses.)[12]

In contrast to early surrealism's valorization of the metaphor whose tenor and vehicle form the most striking and unlikely pair, ultraist metaphors tend to link the spiritual and the human with the physical, nonhuman world. Here the sun screams, human pain and the middays play the viaducts like a musical instrument, and the landscape mirrors the soul. There is no modern diction here; only a lack of punctuation and insistent assonance assert the poem's modernity. Senses are mixed up; the sun, usually represented by visual or tactile imagery, is here anthropomorphized into a screaming, dying soldier. The oxymoron, a quintessentially Borgesian trope, is represented by the "terrible miracle" of pain. The perspective is that of a human survivor, the distant village hanging from the tail of a running horse. There is Girondian hyperbole—men up to their eyes in corpses—and irreverence, Christ hanging like the poster for a local show. Both tendencies will be muted in poems Borges writes a mere handful of years later.

Like Whitman, Borges has a very personal relationship to poetry and often invokes the first person. In **"Himno del mar" ("Sea hymn")**, published in Spain, he sounds like Whitman:

Oh mar! oh mito! oh sol! oh largo lecho!
Y sé por qué te amo. Sé que somos muy viejos,
Que ambos nos conocemos desde siglos.
Sé que en tus aguas venerandas y rientes ardió la aurora de la Vida.
(En la ceniza de una tarde terciaria vibré por primera vez en tu seno)

(Meneses 1978, 58)

(O sea! O myth! O sun! O long seabed!
And I know why I love you. I know we are very old,

That we have known each other for centuries.
I know that in your venerable and laughing waters burned the dawn of
Life.
(In the ash of a terciary afternoon I vibrated for the first time in your
bosom)

The poem prefigures the Borges who at age twenty-five will write: "Creo que no veré, ni realizaré cosas nuevas" (I believe I will neither see nor accomplish new things).[13] This Borges looks into the past for timeless sources of poetry. Nestor Ibarra (1930)—not insignificantly a Borges scholar—argued in 1930, "Lo moderno no ha arraigado, no ha podido arraigar en la Argentina" (126). (The modern has not taken root, has not been able to take root in Argentina.) Girondo (1987) the rebel of the vanguardia, contradicts Ibarra's assessment. "Biarritz," from *Veinte poemas para ser leídos en el tranvía* (Twenty poems to be read on the streetcar) (1922), contains the following undeniably modern fragments:

Automóviles afónicos. Escaparates constelados de estrellas falsas. Mujeres que van a perder sus sonrisas al bacará.

Cuando la puerta se entreabre, entra un pedazo de "foxtrot."

(21)

(Hoarse automobiles. Shop windows constellated of false stars. Women who will lose their smiles at baccarat.

When the door opens, a piece of "foxtrot" comes in.)

While Girondo shares many of Borges's devices, his subject and diction create a portrait of modern urban decadence. He uses a form of telegraphese more commonly found in European poetry and his speaker avoids personal pathos and moral judgments. Because of the differences between Girondo and Borges and the analogous gap between the vanguardia's rhetoric and behavior, descriptions of the movement diverge widely. Critics who take at face value the vanguardia's statements tend to see radical innovation while others emphasize its (that is, Borges's) conservatism. Ultraism, according to Ibarra (1930), is a purely rhetorical school characterized by vagueness, temporal and spatial dimensions, a lack of argument, and idealism (104). But this description pertains to *Borges's* poetry, not to that of other ultraist poets, and certainly not to Girondo's prose poems. Rodríguez Monegal (1978) points out that Ibarra's work, while ostensibly about the ultraist movement, is really the first book-length treatment of Borges. As such, it conflates Borges and the vanguardia (239).

Borges was interested in German Expressionism, English poetry, and the comparatively tame experiments of ultraism, while Girondo participated in early Dadaist and surrealist *spectacles* in Paris. In poetry, Borges privileges the traditional; Girondo, the modern. Though he seeks a timeless national essence, however, Borges fails to escape the modern. **"Jactancia de quietud"** (**"Boasting of stillness"**) creates an "I"-"them" opposition where "they" are time pressed, market oriented, and modern. The speaker, in contrast, is a philosophical Whitmanesque Everyman who inhabits the countryside.

Seguro de mi vida y de mi muerte, miro los ambiciosos y quisiera
entenderlos.
Su día es ávido como un lazo en el aire.
Su noche es tregua de la ira en la espada, pronta en acometer.
Hablan de humanidad.
Mi humanidad está en sentir que somos voces de una misma penuria.

. . . . .

Mi nombre es alguien y cualquiera.
Su verso es un requirimiento de ajena admiración.
Yo solicito de mi verso que no me contradiga, y es mucho.

. . . . .

Paso con lentitud, como quien viene de tan lejos que no espera llegar.[14]
(Sure of my life and death, I look at the ambitious and would like to
understand them.
Their day is avid like a lasso in the air.
Their night is a respite from the sword's ire, ready to attack.
They speak of humanity.
My humanity is in feeling that we are voices of a shared poverty.

. . . . .

My name is anyone and whoever.
Their verse is a necessity of alien admiration.
I ask of my verse that it not contradict me, and that is a lot.

. . . . .

I pass slowly, like one who comes from so far he has no hope of
arriving.)

The voice of this poem is surprisingly mature for a poet in his mid-twenties. Rural, timeless, and in many ways transpersonal, the poem nevertheless bears the marks of avant-garde ideology. The "other" is portrayed as ambitious, hurried, perhaps insincere ("they" speak of humanity, but what have they said?). Most important, "they" are *poets*. The "alien admiration" that supports their verse might well be the plebeian tastes of a market supported by recent immigrants. Though gentleness replaces *Martín Fierro*—like rhetoric, the poem features an opponent against whom the speaker defines himself. For all of Borges's attempts to be timeless, we are still in the 1920s, one of Argentine literature's more binary decades.

One of Girondo's many "membretes" or memoranda, published only two years later, offers a very different view of argentinidad and nationalism:

> ¿Estupidez? ¿Ingenuidad? ¿Política? . . . "Seamos argentinos"—gritan algunos. . . . —Sin advertir la confusión que implica ese imperativo, sin reparar que la nacionalidad es algo tan fatal como la conformación de nuestro esqueleto.[15]

> (Stupidity? Ingenuousness? Politics? . . . "Let's be Argentines"—some shout. . . . Without understanding the confusion this imperative implies, without noticing that nationality is something as inevitable as the shape of our skeletons.)

Responding to a 1924 *Martín Fierro* survey on whether a specifically Argentine sensibility and mentality exist, Girondo answers yes, but he states that he sees no reason why writers should have to prove the existence of argentinidad by displaying it in their work.[16] This attitude places Girondo at the margins of the vanguardia's projects of cultural nationalism. Early efforts to place him at its center failed. One such effort, an unsigned essay in *Martín Fierro*, makes the weak argument that Girondo brings a new sort of criollismo to Argentine literature: "algo de franqueza gaucha mezclada con rudeza y desplante indígena"[17] (something of the gaucho's frankness mixed with indigenous coarseness and arrogance). Though much of *Veinte poemas* and all of *Calcomanías* were written in Europe and Girondo was apparently unconcerned about being labeled *extranjerizante,* his editors are still apologizing for him. In the prologue to *Veinte poemas para ser leídos en el tranvía, Calcomanías, Espantapájaros* (*Twenty poems to be read on the streetcar, Decals, Scarecrow*) (1987), Rodolfo Alonso argues that Girondo is "no menos nacional por más universal" (Girondo 1987, 1) (no less national for being more universal). This argument was hard to make in the 1920s, when the national and the universal were one of the era's major binary divisions. The fact that it was still being made in the 1980s reflects the strongly held Argentine belief that the nation's writers should concern themselves with national reality.

Girondo and Borges represent two views of cultural nationalism in the 1920s. Girondo believed that—being Argentines—it was impossible not to produce Argentine literature, while Borges felt a literary text was national only if its contents dealt with national themes and motifs (Borges 1974, 48, 57; Girondo 1987, 10). Borges later rejected his early view and the change of heart caused him to discard a number of his early poems. In an interview conducted when he was eighty-five, Borges says of ***Luna de enfrente*** (***Moon across the way***): "Cometí un error capital, que fue el de 'hacerme' el argentino" (Vázquez 1984, 51). (I committed a capital error, which was to 'make myself' Argentine.) Borges made Buenos Aires the focus of his early poetry. **"Las calles"** opens with "Las calles de Buenos Aires / ya son mi entraña."[18] (The streets of Buenos Aires / are already my innermost self.) Many of ***Fervor***'s poems are set in Buenos Aires: in the rich man's cemetery Recoleta, in the *arrabales* or suburbs, and at the Plaza San Martín. Borges (1974) imagines his own death in Buenos Aires, calling Recoleta "el lugar de mi ceniza" (18) (the site of my ashes). In the spirit of linguistic nationalism, Borges fashions a new spelling from Argentine dialect. In **"Atardeceres"** (**"Dusks"**) he omits the final "d" from "oscuridad" and in **"Calle con almacén rosado"** (**"Street with a pink store"**), he uses the "vos" form. Early essays betray an even more insistent commitment to his version of criollo spelling. In contrast, Girondo's nationalist gestures are much milder. In the 1922 prologue to *Veinte poemas*, he argues the importance of having faith in "our phonetics," only to undermine himself by saying that these phonetics are perhaps "badly educated."

If in the 1920s Borges is a Berkeleyan idealist, in later life he modifies his stand, making a statement in *Otras inquisiciones* that critics have taken to mean that he was a realist: "El mundo, desgraciadamente, es real; yo, desgraciadamente, soy Borges." (Borges 1974, 771). (The world, alas, is real; I, alas, am Borges.) But the early poem **"Amanecer"** (**"Dawn"**) describes daybreak as a threat to all life because, as Berkeley argued, if things exist only because they are perceived, there is little to guarantee the existence of the world when everyone sleeps. The poem's speaker, one of the few nocturnal *flâneurs* or street wanderers who keep the city alive each night, philosophizes about his experience:

> reviví la tremenda conjetura
> de Schopenhauer y de Berkeley
> que declara que el mundo
> es una actividad de la mente,
> un sueño de las almas,
> sin base ni propósito ni volumen.
>
> (Borges 1974, 38)

> (I felt again that tremendous conjecture
> of Schopenhauer and Berkeley
> which declares the world
> an activity of the mind,
> a dream of souls,
> without foundation or purpose or volume.)
>
> (trans. di Giovanni; Borges 1985, 25)

This excerpt, however, is not what Borges wrote in the early 1920s. It is the official version disseminated by translators to the English-speaking world and it is the edited version found in his ***Obras completas*** (***Complete works***). Borges originally wrote:

> realicé la tremenda conjetura
> de Schopenhauer y de Berkeley
> que arbitra ser la vida
> un ejercicio pertinaz de la mente,
> un populoso ensueño colectivo
> sin basamento ni finalidad ni volumen.
>
> (Borges 1923 a, n.p.)

> (I fulfilled the tremendous conjecture
> of Schopenhauer and of Berkeley
> that contrives to make life
> a tenacious exercise of the mind
> a populous collective dream
> with neither foundation nor finality nor volume.)

The differences between this and the later version are small but important. The early language is more erudite and therefore less accessible to some readers. The speaker is more arrogant about his experience—instead of merely reliving ("reviví") the idealist conjecture, he has caused it to happen or fulfilled it ("realicé"). The agent or speaker has a more active role and through the force of will and effort has saved the city almost single-handedly. Borges frequently explores the power of the poetic speaker. In the *Nosotros* ultraism manifesto, he argues that ultraism supports "la meta principal de toda poesía, esto es, a la transmutación de la realidad palpable del mundo en realidad interior y emocional"[19] (the principal goal of all poetry, which is the transmutation of the palpable reality of the world into inner, emotional reality). In ***Fervor***'s **"Caminata" ("Long walk")**, the speaker makes an even clearer statement about the power of a solitary night walker to keep the world alive in an idealist's world: "Yo soy el único espectador de esta calle, / si dejara de verla se moriría" (Borges 1923a, n.p.) (I am the only observer of this street, / if I stopped looking at it, it would die.)

Borges, who admired and tried to emulate what he perceived as the intellectual humility of Macedonio Fernández, later did his best to erase some of these early quasi-autobiographical traces. In the 1969 revision of the prologue to ***Fervor***, notes Pezzoni, Borges deletes a reference to himself as a "desconfiado y fervoroso escribidor" (fervorous and mistrustful writer). He is trying to cut the early Borges down to size.[20] Borges's early conception of the self is erratic. In "La nadería de la personalidad" (The nothingness of the personality), published in 1925, he agrees with Schopenhauer: "El yo no existe" (The self doesn't exist) and argues that the personality is a dream or illusion. A year later, he writes, "Toda literatura es autobiográfica, finalmente." (All literature is ultimately autobiographical.) Literature may be imaginary, archetypal, or personal, he writes, adding "Yo solicito el último." (I seek the last [of the three].)[21]

In early essays, Borges views the subject as a linguistic—but not transcendentally powerful—entity. He writes (1928) "El ser no es categoría poética ni metafísica, es gramatical" (126). (The self is neither a poetic nor a metaphysical category—it is grammatical.) This view is not borne out by his poetry, however, where speakers often function as interpreters of a world they create through metaphor. In **"Singladura" ("Day's run")**,

> El mar es una espada innumerable y una plenitud de pobreza.
>
> . . . . .
>
> El mar es solitario como un ciego.
> El mar es un huraño lenguaje que yo no alcanzo a descifrar.
>
> . . . . .
>
> En la cubierta, quietamente, yo comparto la tarde con mi hermana
> como un trozo de pan.[22]
>
> (The sea is a countless sword and a plenitude of poverty.
>
> . . . . .
>
> The sea is as solitary as a blind man.
> The sea is an unsociable language I cannot manage to decipher.
>
> . . . . .
>
> On deck, quietly, I share the afternoon with my sister like a piece
> of bread.)

Though the speaker calls attention to the failure of his meaning-making activities, he is nevertheless interpreting the sea through the lens of Borges's experience—a father going blind for congenital reasons, lunch with Norah, the habit of making text out of world. His litanic attempts to evoke the sea suggest that the poet triumphs over his subject, even as a diagnostician of its mystery.

Where Borges constructs the world, Girondo tears it—both subjects and objects—apart. A clear illustration of the subject's instability can be found in **"Espantapájaros" ("Scarecrow")** (1932):

> Yo no tengo una personalidad; yo soy un cocktail, un conglomerado, una manifestación de personalidades.
> En mí, la personalidad es una especie de forunculosis anímica en estado crónico de erupción; no pasa media hora sin que me nazca una nueva personalidad.
>
> (Girondo 1987, 66)
>
> (I don't have a personality; I am a cocktail, a conglomerate, a manifestation of personalities.
> In me, personality is a sort of psychic boil in a chronic state of eruption; not half an hour goes by without a new personality being born.)

Girondo and Borges share a love of the first person and its power. But Borges uses the spiritual power of the self to make things poetic, while Girondo makes poetry by destroying and dismembering synecdochally the world around him and the poetic subjects who people it. Borges's **"Otra vez la metáfora" ("Once again the metaphor")** contains the following statement: "Las cosas (pienso) no son intrínsecamente poéticas; para ascenderlas a poesía es preciso que las vinculemos a nuestro vivir, que nos acostumbremos a pensarlas con devoción" (Borges 1928, 56). (Things [I think] are not intrinsically poetic; to raise them to the level of poetry we must link them to our lives, so that we become accustomed to thinking of them with devotion.) Borges's project is thus antithetical to that of Girondo, who, Masiello (1986) argues,

> produce un sujeto violento, que viaja a través de la moderna civilización. Agresivo y descaradamente fuerte, su sujeto lírico es el terrorista máximo de la vanguardia, que proclama su poder por los abundantes lugares e imágenes que se atreve a poseer y destrozar.
>
> (114)
>
> (produces a violent subject who travels through modern civilization. Aggressive and impudently strong, his lyrical subject is the greatest terrorist of the avant-garde,

proclaiming his power through an abundance of places and images he dares to possess and destroy.)

While in *Inquisiciones* (1925), Borges offers a detailed discussion of types of metaphors, by 1928 he argues that the poet should *not* focus on creating new metaphors.[23] And whereas he began the decade rejecting the anecdotal in poetry, he ends it arguing that poetry should be anecdotal and that abstractions are unpoetic (Borges 1928, 127). The poem **"Arrabal"** (**"Suburb"**) reflects this evolution, changing markedly between 1921 and 1943. In the early version, Buenos Aires is a text created by the speaker:

. . . y sentí *Buenos Aires*
y literituricé en la hondura del alma
la viacrucis inmóvil
de la calle sufrida
y el caserío sosegado[24]

(. . . and I felt *Buenos Aires*
and made literature in the depths of the soul
from the immobile crossroads
of the suffering street
and the quiet hamlet)

In any hands but these, the man-as-city device would be unmistakably modern. But as we have seen, Borges specializes in the paradox of modern urban atavism. In the 1943 version—which became the standard version of the ***Obras completas***—Buenos Aires has metamorphosed from *text* to *world.* The speaker's role has thus changed substantially. No longer is the poet making literature of the city or creating the city in and through language. Instead, there is a simple, personal statement of belonging to a place:

. . . y sentí *Buenos Aires*
Esta ciudad que yo creí mi pasado
es mi porvenir, mi presente;
los años que he vivido en Europa son ilusorios,
yo estaba siempre (y estaré) en Buenos Aires.

(Borges 1974, 32)

(. . . and I felt *Buenos Aires*
This city that I believed to be my past
is my future, my present;
the years I have lived in Europe are illusory,
I always was (and will be) in Buenos Aires.)

Whereas for Borges the city is often closely identified with the poetic subject, Girondo consistently objectifies and makes it alien. In *Veinte poemas'* "Verona," for example, Girondo has a statue of the Virgin menstruate into a fountain:

La Virgen, sentada en una fuente, como sobre un "bidé," derrama un agua enrojecida por las bombitas de luz eléctrica que le han puesto en los pies.[25] (The Virgin, seated in a fountain as over a "bidet," leaks water reddened by the electric lamps they have put at her feet.)

Unlike Borges, Girondo (1987) makes baldly contemporary references. In "Croquis de arena" (Sketch in the sand), photographers sell the bodies of bathing women for eighty centavos apiece (14). Like the French symbolists who were one of his most important influences, Girondo enjoys shocking the conventional reader. In "Milonga," the dancers are crudely sexualized:

El bandoneón . . . imanta los pezones, los pubis y la punta de los
zapatos.
Machos que se quiebran en un corte ritual, la cabeza hundida entre los
hombros, la jeta hinchada de palabras soeces.
Hembras con las ancas nerviosas, un poquitito de espuma en las axilas,
y los ojos demasiado aceitados.
De pronto se oye un fracaso de cristales. Las mesas dan un corcovo
y pegan quatro patadas en el aire.

(Girondo 1987, 91)

(The accordion . . . magnetizes nipples, groins and shoetips.
Males who break in ritual twist and jerk, their heads sunk between
their shoulders, their mugs swollen with vile words.
Females with nervous rumps, a little sweat in their armpits and overly
greasy eyes.
Soon the noise of breaking glass is heard. The tables hump and buck,
kicking their four legs into the air.)

Whereas Borges renders the world sacred, Girondo, consistent with the Continental avant-garde, attacks cultural icons and institutions, here eliding the difference between people and furniture as both metamorphose into barnyard animals. Breton would have approved: Girondo personifies the inanimate, dehumanizes the animate, profanes the sacred, works to defy expectation, and turns the world upside down. Carnivalesque in the Bakhtinian sense, he overwhelms even Borges. In a 1925 review of *Calcomanías*, Borges applauds Girondo's work in a qualified way: "Es innegable que la eficacia de Girondo me asusta. . . . Girondo es un violento. Mira largamente las cosas. . . . Luego las estruja."[26] (It is undeniable that Girondo's effectiveness scares me. . . . Girondo is a violent person. He looks generously at things. . . . Then he crushes them.) J. Schwartz (1979) calls the anthropomorphization of things and the "cosificación" (thingification) of people in Girondo's poetry a "fusion of differences" (192–94). Girondo's modern city collapses the division between subject and object, revealing the alienation and sterility that result from a loss of individuality and separateness. Like Eliot, he indicts modernity even as he modernizes literary form.

The prologues to their first books illustrate well the differences between Borges, an exemplar of Argentine cultural identity, and Girondo, an affront to it. Borges is earnest, self-important, and serious. His project is the nationalization of Buenos Aires: "He rechazado los vehementes reclamos de quienes en Buenos Aires no advierten sino lo extranjerizo" (Borges 1923a, n.p.). (I have rejected the vehement claims of those in Buenos Aires who notice nothing but the foreign.) In the city he will uncover the sacred: "Aquí se oculta la divinidad." (Here the divine hides itself.) He represents himself as one who uses the "primordial" meanings of words, ending with an apparently humble apology that he, not the reader, is the author of these poems. The last two words of the prologue of ***Fervor de Buenos Aires*** are, however, "my verses." Borges could have used the definite article to depersonalize the work, but he does not. Not surprisingly, he removed this trace of authorial assertiveness from the 1969 reprint of the prologue.

Girondo's prologue to *Veinte poemas* opens with an attack on its audience: "¿Qué quieren ustedes!" (What do you want!) One finds poems, he says, thrown into the middle of the street, "poemas que uno recoge como quien junta puchos en la vereda" (poems one gathers up like scraps of trash from the sidewalk). Do we write to humiliate ourselves? Why publish "cuando hasta los mejores publican 1.071% más de lo que debieran publicar?" (when even the best publish 1,071% more than they ought to?) The argument he makes for publishing his book is surrealist: The everyday is an admirable manifestation of the absurd and cutting through logic is the only way to arrive at true adventure. In an even more surrealist act, he ends by celebrating the contradictions of these arguments. "No renuncio ni a mi derecho de renunciar, y tiro mis *Veinte poemas*, como una piedra, sonriendo ante la inutilidad de mi gesto" (Girondo 1987, 9–11). (I don't renounce even my right to renounce, and I throw my *Veinte poemas* like a stone, smiling at the futility of my gesture.) If Borges's prologue spiritualizes the nation, Girondo's evokes the nation-bashing of Tzara and Breton. It is not surprising then, given their cultural and historical moment, that Borges becomes the spokesperson of an avant-garde operating in a nationalist age while Girondo is the movement's unruly older brother.

Because the first edition of *Veinte poemas* was published in Paris, it came to Argentina as a European product. Both *Nosotros* and *La Nación,* which were part of the ideological apparatus Girondo attacked in his prologue, published reviews by European critics. Had the production and reception of *Veinte poemas* been a purely national affair—without the cachet of foreign critics and, in the words of Delfina Muschietti, the "mediating and neutralizing"[27] effect of their criticism on scandalous material—it is unlikely Girondo's early work would have been enthusiastically received. His second book, published in Madrid, was also favorably received by the bastions of consecrated culture. European critics, accustomed to the textually outrageous, reacted almost exclusively to the book's aesthetics, calling it "original" and "revealing" and describing it as full of "magnificent explosive images."[28] In contrast, Borges's early work was considered nostalgic (de Torre), dignified (Ramón Gómez de la Serna), and formally classic (Enrique Díez-Canedo) (repr. Alazraki 1976, 21–26, 29–31). Locally, the critical reaction to Girondo's first book was decidedly tepid. Reviews published in *La Nación* in 1923–24 have such titles as "La literatura nacional en el extranjero" and "La literatura sudamericana vista desde París." The emphasis is less on the works themselves than on what the European critics think about them. An angry article appearing in *Martín Fierro* in March 1924 called the newspapers and journals that failed to review *Veinte poemas* "cretinous," an epithet usually reserved for Boedo (20).

Girondo was not so lucky thereafter. *Espantapájaros* (1932) and *En la masmédula* (1954), each more radical than the last and both published in Buenos Aires, were given lukewarm receptions (Muschietti 1985, 160–61). *Espantapájaros* was greeted with silence from *La Nación* and *Sur*, the journal in important ways representative of the avant-garde generation in the 1930s. Arturo Capdevilla repeated in *Nosotros* an Argentine woman's comment that the book was "nasty" (Girondo 1987, prologue). *Espantapájaros* represents a significant rupture in Girondo's work. There are no more foreign travel sketches and few signs that the poetic speaker is upper class. We must ask whether Argentina's elite publications shunned the book in part because its contents reflected little cultural or economic privilege.

Girondo's relationship to the literary market became more unacceptable in high cultural circles as the years went by. He published *Veinte poemas* in two editions aimed at two audiences. The first edition sold for five pesos, the popular second edition—published by Martín Fierro Editorial in 1925—for only twenty centavos. The Parisian printing was a luxury edition, almost certainly paid for by Girondo, who chose to withhold many copies from sale. The majority of the Argentine audience, then, had to wait three years for Girondo's book to become available. In 1932, Girondo made a boldly ostentatious marketing gesture that scandalized the anticommercial cultural elite but was, ironically, aimed at that very elite. To sell *Espantapájaros,* he had a life-size papier-mâché scarecrow driven about for days in a funeral carriage drawn by six horses and accompanied by footmen dressed in the style of the late eighteenth-century French Directory.[29] The scarecrow was dressed in a top hat and monocle reminiscent of the French dandy. Young women hired for the occasion sold all five thousand copies of the unusually large edition from a locale Girondo rented in Buenos Aires's most fashionable neighborhood.[30] Major newspapers refused to cover the event.[31]

Girondo claimed that at age eighteen he had a "sagrado horror" (sacred horror) of publicity (qtd. in J. Schwartz 1987, 43). But he was already familiar with the audience-enlarging strategies of the Dadaists at the time he staged a play that required an actor to insult the audience by calling it "stupid." He also tried to produce a journal called *Comedia*, but the publisher "forgot" to distribute it.[32] By his own account, he then—like Borges—destroyed a lot of work until he published *Veinte poemas.* Because Buenos

Aires was not Paris, Girondo was caught in the avant-garde dilemma of wanting to confront a large audience with material it wouldn't tolerate.[33] He struggled to resolve the conflict between the privileges of his class and his desire to democratize the literary market. The title of his first book suggests that it be read in a streetcar, transportation for those who couldn't afford their own automobiles. A *Martín Fierro* article complaining about the lack of recognition by Argentine critics of *Veinte poemas* however, calls its title ironic. *Espantapájaros*'s subtitle, *Al alcance de todos* (Within everyone's reach) is somewhat ironic, as Girondo did not take the necessary steps to distribute his books to the masses, nor were they likely to find it to their taste.

In the 1920s, Girondo broke rank with his socioeconomic class by satirizing the aristocracy, though he did nothing to undermine the class system itself. He also defied the vanguardia, especially *Martín Fierro* and *Proa*, by declaring himself opposed to state-sanctioned prizes and to writers holding public office. Borges, in contrast, accepted with pleasure the Second Municipal Prize for prose in 1929. He later headed the National Library for the better part of two decades, a post Victoria Ocampo helped obtain for him.[34] Though critical of the upper classes, Girondo did not advance the cause of the Argentine poor. He was a satirist, not a populist or a revolutionary. Formally radical but socially and politically ambivalent, he vacillated between enjoying and denouncing the privileges of his class. He did more than any other Argentine vanguardia writer to force the relationships among literature, institutions, and the market to reveal themselves to the public eye, much as Dadaism forced the European public to confront the crisis of cultural value. In the 1920s, however, he was merely an apprentice in radicalism.

Girondo did not become the avant-garde's second most important poet until well after World War II when his work was "reevaluated." In her prologue to Girondo's *Espantapájaros y otros poemas* (Scarecrow and other poems), Delfina Muschietti dates this reevaluation from the 1960s. Only then did high culture receive him in its center, she says. For decades he was considered a destructive element to be counterposed to the constructive Borges, the lover and preserver of Argentine tradition.[35] Girondo was the cosmopolitan aficionado of speed and modern things who captured images with a mock camera eye and turned cities into postcards. Borges was a slow, nostalgic, willfully *porteño* writer with highly narrative syntax; Girondo was fast, international, and partial to fragmented, cubist images.[36]

Girondo's formal innovations were markedly less well accepted in Argentina than were those of Borges. His use of the prose poem, borrowed from the French symbolists, was new to Argentina and was thus a more radical choice than free verse. Evar Méndez's (1927) article "Doce poetas nuevos" (Twelve new poets) praises Borges even as it puts Girondo on the literary sidelines (17, 26; see also Muschietti 1985, 165–66). The conservative Argentine spirit, says Méndez, sees in Girondo "una amenaza terrible para la estabilidad del lirismo escrito" (a terrible threat to the stability of written lyricisim). Méndez, however, offers only a lukewarm defense of Girondo. Late in life, Borges criticizes Girondo for his market-oriented behavior, calling him the "más flojo" (laziest, weakest) member of the vanguardia (Muschietti 1985, 168). In an important sense, Girondo was too avant-garde for his movement. But if the movement was too conservative to foreground Girondo's poetry, it still found him essential.[37] On trips through Latin America and Spain, Girondo represented five Argentine and two Uruguayan journals, including those of the Argentine vanguardia.[38] Unlike Borges, he did not sign the manifesto he wrote, which—significantly—was also the vanguardia's most important document. The omission of this signature is meaningful in the context of how differently the movement treated the two poets.

Muschietti argues that Girondo's texts corrode the dominant social, literary, moral, and religious premises of Argentine culture. Girondo (1987) once said his aesthetic goal was to "abrir al arte las puertas de la vida" (prologue) (open the doors of life to art) and that "un libro debe construirse como un reloj, y venderse como un salchichón" (Girondo 1968, 146–47; see also 1987, prologue) (a book should be put together like a clock, and sold like a sausage). J. Schwartz (1979) likens Girondo's wealthy casino revelers in "Biarritz" to Eliot's Prufrock: they are mocked and rendered sterile and mechanistic (224). Though he rejects social norms and scandalizes the public, however, Girondo's early revolution is merely *aesthetic*.[39] His satirical attacks—on women, the church, and the lazy rich—neither change nor seriously threaten the norms and institutions that produce Argentine literature. That Girondo remains the *cas limite* of the vanguardia defines the movement's essential conservatism. His sexual rebellion is traditional and machismo-ridden: women are objectified, dismembered, or made crudely animalistic. Like the surrealists, Girondo believed that undermining conventional language will change reality. But, like them, he failed in his mission to revolutionize literary relationships. As Umberto Eco (1983) describes this problem, "Literature says something and, at the same time, it denies what it has said; it doesn't destroy signs, it makes them play and it plays them" (242). The *cas limite* of the Auden group is different. In a decade characterized by extremes, it is occupied by Louis MacNeice, the one who tried to occupy a middle ground. For the surrealists, the *cas limite* is in one sense Breton, whose monomaniacal relationship to the surrealist cause is unparalleled. In another sense, it is the poets who did not fit: Aragon, because he became a devoted communist, and others, who were, in Breton's eyes, followers of literature.

If the differences between Borges and Girondo were noted but not widely discussed during the 1920s, they have since become clear. As Enrique Molina notes, the independent Girondo opted out of the complacent vanguardia well before the end of the decade:

> Volvió la espalda a sus compañeros de generación, que tras proclamar una mistificade actitud iconoclástica,

acabaron por ubicarse dentro de las jerarquías tradicionales, pastando idílicamente en los prados de los suplementos dominicales. La efervescencia martinfierrista se diluyó en una mera discusión de aspectos formales. Ajenos a un auténtico inconformismo, la mayoría de los componentes del grupo terminaron en las más reaccionarias actitudes estéticas.[40]

(He turned his back on generational compatriots who, having proclaimed a falsely iconoclastic attitude, ended up situating themselves inside traditional hierarchies, grazing idyllically in the pastures of the Sunday supplements. The martinfierrist effervescence diluted itself in a mere discussion of formal issues. Unaware of authentic nonconformity, most of the group members ended up with the most reactionary aesthetic attitudes.)

Borges did in certain ways become the aesthetic reactionary described here, and he later saw in these early efforts to be avant-garde a good deal of posturing.

Literary historians tend not to discuss Borges and Girondo together largely because they had little in common philosophically and poetically. However, because they were the two most important leaders of the vanguardia—Borges offering an aesthetics, Girondo the movement's avant-garde gestures and publicity—this is a complex and perhaps strange choice. It is likely that Girondo was marginalized partly because he was too aware of issues of power and privilege to provide the vanguardia with a spokesperson uncritical of the movement's ideology and behavior. . . .

Notes

1. See, for example, the references to Borges and Girondo as the most important poets of the decade and as participants in the vogue of the Grand Tour of Europe (Masiello 1986, 23, 126).
2. Introduction to *Revista Martín Fierro* (1969), 11–12. See also Sarlo's "Síntesis y tensiones," in Altamirano and Sarlo (1980), 168–69.
3. As Bürger (1984), 51–52, points out, the art market privileges the signature over the work itself. Foucault's author-function, then, is in a sense more important than the literary or artistic work. Paradoxically, avant-garde movements tend to undermine somewhat the notion of individual artistic production, erasing differences among their members in order to present a united front.
4. Sylvia Molloy points this out in "*Flâneries* textuales: Borges, Benjamin y Baudelaire," in Lerner and Lerner (1984), 495.
5. "Nuestra encuesta sobre la nueva generación literaria," *Nosotros* 44, no. 168 (123): 16–17; repr. Ulla (1969), 254.
6. For the transition between "Georgie" and "Borges," see Rodríguez Monegal (1978), 232–33.
7. See, for example, Graciela Palau de Nemes, "Modernismo and Borges," in Cortínez (1986), 221.
8. This essay can be found in Flores (1984), 30ff.
9. The vanguardia was not in fact consistent about its condemnation of rhymed verse. Although no poet wrote an essay justifying the use of rhyme, some of the lesser vanguardia poets used it and *Martín Fierro* did not shy away from publishing rhymed poems, especially satirical ones.
10. Borges, "Al margen de la moderna lírica," *Grecia* (Sevilla) 39 (31 January 1920); qtd. in Pezzoni (1986), 70.
11. Meneses (1978), 71; from *Tableros* (Madrid) 1 (15 November 1921).
12. Unless otherwise noted, translations of poems from the Spanish are mine, sometimes in consultation with Ana Rosa Rapaport de Genijovich. Any errors, of course, are mine.
13. From *Luna de enfrente;* qtd. in Ibarra (1930), 43.
14. *Proa* 1, no. 1 (1924): 49.
15. Oliverio Girondo, "Membretes," *Martín Fierro* 3, no. 34 (1926); repr. *Revista Martín Fierro* (1969), 150.
16. "Contestaciones a la encuesta de 'Martín Fierro,'" *Martín Fierro* 1, nos. 5–6 (1924); repr. *Revista Martín Fierro* (1969), 42.
17. *Martín Fierro* 1, no. 2 (1924); repr. *Revista Martín Fierro* (1969), 21.
18. Borges (1974), 17. "Entraña" can be defined as heart, insides, entrails, disposition. Here it means the deeply personal and essential.
19. From *Nosotros* 39, no. 151 (1921); 471.
20. Pezzoni (1986), 91. Masiello (1986), 87, argues that the mature Borges has "personalized" literary history as a "precondition" of artistic excellence.
21. Borges, "La nadería de la personalidad," in Borges (1925), 93, 84; Borges (1926b), 152.
22. *Proa* 1, no. 1 (August 1924): 49–50.
23. "Examen de metáforas," in Borges (1925), 65–75.
24. The 1921 and 1943 excerpts from the poem are quoted in Pezzoni (1986), 79. I am grateful to Pezzoni for his analysis of the two versions. He calls the early version of the poem "formalist" and the late version a product of "lived experience."
25. Girondo (1987), 27. Many of the city poems of *Veinte poemas*, such as "Verona," "Sevillano," "Biarritz," "Venecia," and "Rio de Janeiro," were written in the cities they took as their subjects.
26. Jorge L. Borges, "Calcomanías," *Martín Fierro* 11, no. 18 (1925); repr. *Revista Martín Fierro* (1969), 91.
27. Delfina Muschietti uses these terms in her prologue to Girondo (1987).
28. The first of these descriptions is by Ramón Gómez de la Serna, "La vida en el tranvía," review of *Veinte poemas para ser leídos en el tranvía, El Sol* (Madrid) (4 May 1923). The second is by Jules Supervielle,

"*Veinte poemas* para Oliverio Girondo," *Revue de l'Amérique Latine* (Paris) (March 1924). Both critics were friends of Girondo's. The reviews were reprinted in *La Nación* and may also be found in J. Schwartz (1987), 326–29.

29. This is the story told by Norah Lange, who married Girondo some years later. See J. Schwartz (1987), 216, for her account.

30. See Running (1981), 129. Four years later, in 1936, the average edition was only 3,500 copies. Rivera (1985a), 582.

31. This refusal is reminiscent of the major French newspapers' refusal to write about surrealist *spectacles* in Paris in the aftermath of the Saint-Pol-Roux banquet. In early 1920s France, Girondo's display would have been considered an artistic act in its own right.

32. This account is from "Nahuelpan: Diez minutos con Oliverio Girondo, fuerte mentalidad agridulce," *Columba* 1, no. 3 (2 June 1925): n.p. It can be found in J. Schwartz (1987), 43.

33. Muschietti points to the central contradiction of Girondo's behavior: "Su rechazo del burgués como *celui qui ne comprend pas* más un aparente desdén por el mercado literario se contredicen con su intento por generar un nuevo público que, además de masivo, tuviero acceso a los criterios de ruptura estéticoideológicos y a una competencia especializada." (His rejection of the bourgeois as *celui qui ne comprend pas* plus an apparent disdain for the literary market contradict his intention to generate a new public that, in addition to being massive, would have access to [understanding] the criteria of an aesthetic-ideologic rupture and to a specialized competence.) Muschietti (1985), 162.

34. For one of Girondo's statements of opposition to the state's role in professionalizing the writer, see "Girondo no cree que en el exterior interese la literatura argentina," *Crítica* (15 May 1960), in J. Schwartz (1987), 48.

35. The description of Borges paraphrases a comment by Evar Méndez (1927), 26.

36. J. Schwartz's (1979) useful comparison is one of few that portrays Borges and Girondo as opposites (151).

37. As its publicist, his role was analogous to those played by Michael Roberts and John Lehmann of the *New Signatures* group in England.

38. *Martín Fierro* took much of the credit for its agent's successful mission. See "Oliverio Girondo en misión intelectual," *Martín Fierro* 1, no. 7 (July 1924); repr. J. Schwartz (1987), 173. Though avant-garde movements distribute power and roles in the way that best suits their needs and goals, they are rarely credited with such rational behavior. For example, Roberts and Lehmann, whose poetry was never so good as that of the core group of Auden poets, had important roles as editors and publicists.

39. In the 1940s and 1950s, as Girondo became more surrealist in practice, his philosophies were in some ways as revolutionary as those of the French surrealists. Girondo's later work has often been compared to the early poetry of Peru's César Vallejo, author of *Trilce* (1922), as a map of the discursive limits of poetry in Spanish.

40. Enrique Molina, "Hacia el fuego central o la poesía de Oliverio Girondo," in Girondo (1968), 12. Molina was a disciple of Girondo in the 1940s during the heyday of Argentine surrealism.

Works cited

Alazraki, Jaime, ed. 1976. *Jorge Luis Borges.* Madrid: Taurus Ediciones.

———. 1987. *Critical essays on Jorge Luis Borges.* Boston: G.K. Hall.

Bastos, Maria Luisa. 1974. *Borges ante la critica argentina, 1923–1960.* Buenos Aires: Ediciones Hispamerica.

Cortinez, Carlos, ed. 1986. *Borges the Poet.* Fayetville: U. of Arkansas Press.

Eco, Umberto. 1986. *Travels in Hyper Reality.* Trans. William Weaver. San Diego: Harcourt Brace Jovanovich.

Fernandez, Teodosio. 1987. *La poesia hispanoamericana en el sieglo XX.* Madrid: Taurus Ediciones.

Ferrari, Osvaldo. 1985. *Borges en dialogo; conversaciones de Jorge Luis Borges con Osvaldo Ferrari.* Buenos Aires: Ediciones Grijalbo.

Girando, Oliviero. 1987. *Espantapajaros y otros poemas.* Buenos Aires: Centro Editor de America Latina.

Ibara, Nestor. 1930. *La nueva posia argentina: ensayo critico sobre el ultraismo, 1921–1929.* Buenos Aires: Molinari e Hijos.

Leland, Christpher Towne. 1986. *The Last Happy Men: The Generation of 1922, Fiction and the Argentine Reality.* Syracuse: Syracuse University Press.

Llagostera, Maria Raquel. 1987. *Boedo y Florida.* Buenos Aires: Centro Editor de America Latina.

Lugones, Leopoldo. 1961. *Lunario sentimental.* Buenos Aires: Editorial Centurion.

Masiello, Francine. 1986. *Lenguaje e ideologia: las escuelas argentinas de vanguardia.* Beunos Aires: Hachette.

Mastronardi, Carlos. 1980/1986. "El movimiento de 'Martin Fierro.'" *Historia de la litreatura argentina: Los proyectos de la vanguardia.* Buenos Aires: Centro Edit or de America Latina.

Mendez, Evar. 1927. "Doce poetas nuevas." *Sintesis* I, no. 4 (September):15–33.

Muschietti, Delfina. 1985. "La fractura ideologica en los primeros textos de Oliviero Girondo." *Filologia* 20, no I:153–69.

Rodriguez Monegal, Emir. 1978. *Jorge Luis Borges: A Literary Biography.* New York: Dutton.

Running, Thorpe. 1981. *Borges' Ultraist Movement.* Lathrup Village, Mich: International Book Publishers.

Schwartz, Jorge. 1979. *Vanguardia y cosmopolitismo en la decada del veinte: Oliviero Girando y Oswald de Andrade.* Ph.D. diss., Universidade de Sao Paulo, Brazil. Ann Arbor: University Microfilms International.

———, ed. 1987. *Homenaje a Girondo.* Buenos Aires: Ediciones Corregidor.

Vazquez, Maria Esther. 1980. "Victoria Ocampo, una argentina universalista." *Revista Iberoamericana* 110–11 (January-June): 167–75.

Edward Hirsch (essay date 1998)

SOURCE: "Jorge Luis Borges," in *The Wilson Quarterly*, Vol. XXII, No. 4, Autumn, 1998, pp. 109–14.

[*In the following excerpt, Hirsch discusses Borge's love of reading and of languages, focusing on his conception of poetry as "a collaborative act between writer and the reader."*]

We tend to think of Jorge Luis Borges (1899–1986) exclusively in terms of fiction, as the author of luminous and mind-bending metaphysical parables that cross the boundaries between the short story and the essay. But Borges always identified himself first as a reader, then as a poet, finally as a prose writer. He found the borders between genres permeable and lived in the magic space, the imaginary world, created by books. "If I were asked to name the chief event in my life, I should say my father's library," he said in 1970. "In fact, sometimes I think I have never strayed outside that library."

Borges was so incited, so inflamed by what he read, so beholden to what he encountered, that it demanded from him an answer in kind, a creative response. He was an Argentine polyglot who learned English even before he learned Spanish (in a sense he grew up in the dual world of his father's library of unlimited English books and his mother's sensuous Hispanic garden). As a teenager in Geneva during World War I he also learned Latin and German, which he considered the language of the philosophers, and in old age he devoted himself to studying old Germanic languages. One could say that reading others spurred him into writing poetry, which was for him something so intimate, so essential, it could not be defined without oversimplifying it. "It would be like attempting to define the color yellow, love, the fall of leaves in autumn," he said. He loved Plato's characterization of poetry as "that light substance, winged and sacred."

One of the persistent motifs in Borges's work is that our egos persist, but that selfhood is a passing illusion, that we are all in the end one, that in reading Shakespeare we somehow become Shakespeare. "For many years I believed that literature, which is almost infinite, is one man," he said. "I want to give thanks," he wrote in **"Another Poem of Thanksgiving,"**

> For the fact that the poem is inexhaustible
> And becomes one with the sum of all created things
> And will never reach its last verse
> And varies according to its writers. . . .

Borges never viewed poetry in the way the New Critics did, as an object, a thing unto itself, but rather as a collaborative act between the writer and the reader. Reading requires complicity. He wrote:

> The taste of the apple (states Berkeley) lies in the contact of the fruit and the palate, not in the fruit itself; in a similar way (I would say), poetry lies in the meeting of poem and reader, not in the lines of symbols printed in the pages of a book. What is so essential is the aesthetic act, the thrill, the almost physical sensation that comes with each reading.

Borges's first book of poems, ***Fervor of Buenos Aires*** (1921), was inspired by his native city and written under the sign of a vanguard imagist sect called the *ultraístas*, a group of Spanish poets who believed in the supreme power of metaphor and the liberating music of free verse. "I feel that all during my lifetime I have been rewriting that one book," he said. He wrote poetry throughout the 1920s, but then it mysteriously deserted him as he went on to create a new kind of narrative prose, the astonishing work that registered his greatness: *Inquisitions* (1925), *Universal History of Infamy* (1935), *The Garden of Forking Paths* (1941), *Ficciones* (1944), and *A New Refutation of Time* (1987), among others. (The first English collections of Borges's writing, *Labyrinths* and *Ficciones*, appeared in 1962.)

Borges suffered from hereditarily weak eyesight and eventually became the sixth generation of his family to go blind. This was an especially tragic fate for the reader and writer who was also the director of Argentina's National Library. In **"Poem of the Gifts,"** written in the 1950s, he speaks of God's splendid irony in granting him at one time 800,000 books and total darkness. The conclusion of the poem underscores the tragedy of a man who had been denied access to what he most loved:

> Painfully probing the dark, I grope toward
> The void of the twilight with the point of my faltering
> Cane—I for whom Paradise was always a metaphor,
> An image of libraries.

The fabulist returned to poetry in the 1950s with a more direct and straightforward style, a beguiling and deceptive simplicity. He dictated his poems to classical meters and chanted them aloud at readings. He wrote about the flow of rivers and the nature of time, his ardor for Buenos

Aires, the cult of his ancestors, his study of Old Norse and Anglo-Saxon, the contradictions of temporal experience, the power of certain sunsets, certain dawns, the immanence of a revelation always about to arrive. His poems show how much he loved to read the narrative language of storytelling (of Rudyard Kipling, G. K. Chesterton, and Robert Louis Stevenson, of *Gilgamesh* and *Beowulf*), and the magical language of lyric poetry (of runes, riddles, and spells, of Walt Whitman at his most incantatory and Ralph Waldo Emerson at his most oracular), and the investigatory language of metaphysical speculation (from Spinoza to Kafka, from Schopenhauer to Berkeley, Swedenborg, and Unamuno). He was a rapturous writer, a literary alchemist who emerged as an explorer of labyrinths, an adventurer in the fantastic, a poet of mysterious intimacies who probed the infinite postponements and cycles of time, the shimmering mirrors of fiction and reality, the symbols of unreality, the illusions of identity, the disintegration of the self into the universe, into the realm of the Archetypes and the Splendors.

Mark Couture (essay date 1999)

SOURCE: "Empty Words: Vanity in the Writings of Jorge Luis Borges," in *Romance Notes*, Vol. XXIX, No. 3, Spring, 1999, pp. 265–71.

[*In the following essay, Couture discusses the centrality of "vanity" as a word and as a concept in Borges's writing.*]

Twisting an old Spanish saying, Bryce Echenique wrote that Borges "más sabía por viejo y sabía más todavía por diablo" (7). Alastair Reid, speaking of conversations with Borges about translation, said that Borges's modesty could be deadly. These remarks allude to one of Borges's greatest charms, something that attracts us more than his audacious, sophisticated metaphysical speculations: his coy sense of humor. I think that a great deal of the humor in Borges can be attributed to his sense of the vanity of literature, his own included. Borges, while aware of the beauty and power of words, also knew that words, at last, are just words, and as such are ultimately destined to fail us. Part of the subdued chuckle of recognition we experience as we read Borges comes from this awareness. Borges's writings have the uncanny knack of deflating our preconceived notions of the nature of language and literature. "Vanity," etymologically, means "emptiness." One of Borges's most effective *diabluras* is a deflation, a gentle reminder running through his texts of the illusory character of literature, a knowledge that literature is not life, nor are literary politics literature.

Perhaps it is inevitable that someone so bookish as Borges, who seemed to live for and through books, be supremely aware of literature's limitations. In fact, this is a principal theme of Borges's writing. Yet this insight into the vain emptiness of the literary undertaking is not without an accompanying blindness. Borges may have suffered not only from a literal blindness, but from a metaphorical blindness as well: what might be called a blindness to "real reality," to the hustle and hum above and beyond the pages of the books he spent his life reading. Certainly this was a common complaint about him from his contemporaries in the days before Borges was famous throughout the world.[1] Interestingly, Borges's prioritizing of literature over life, to put in banally, is precisely what first attracted North American academics to him.

What I propose here is a preliminary mapping of the uses and meanings of the words *vano* and *vanidad* in Borges's writings. Since the word occurs frequently in both Borges's poetry and prose, I aim to construct a sort of contextual glossary of the term in order to show how this simple word encapsulates a certain philosophy of language and literature: the notion that words, despite their occasional power and glory, inevitably let us down.

In **"La luna,"** a poem from ***El hacedor***, Borges writes, echoing his own "Aleph," of a man who undertakes the impossible task of writing an infinite book in which he plans to "cifrar el universo." He finishes the project, only to realize that he has forgotten to include the moon. The poem then becomes an inventory of literary moons. Near its end, the poem takes a seemingly autobiographical turn by switching to the first person, as the poet confesses that he too, years ago in Geneva, took upon himself the "secret obligation" to define the moon. As the poem draws to a close, the poet admits to the vanity of this task: "Ya no me atrevo a macular su pura / aparición con una imagen vana" (186).[2] The use of the verb *macular*, to stain or blemish, suggests a notion of literature as a sort of stain on silence; metaphors (*imágenes vanas*), even words themselves, are inadequate in the face of the quotidian moon in the night sky. The opposition of adjectives, *vana / pura*, relays the message that words fail us, even if the message can only be relayed through words.

The doubling technique, so prevalent in Borges, is often used to reflect on the shared vanity of the literary undertaking. By writing about the vanity of another's work, Borges alludes to the vanity of his own by establishing networks of correspondence between the poet whom Borges is writing about and himself. In **"Baltasar Gracián,"** a poem about the death of the great *preceptista* of the Spanish baroque, Borges registers his dissatisfaction with Gracián's writing using the notion of vanity. Since Gracián's soul is devoid of music (an allusion to Verlaine's "la musique avant toute chose"), in its place there is "sólo un vano / Herbario de metáforas y argucias . . ." (159). While certainly a severe critique of literature as artifice, the poem also implicitly doubles Borges and Gracián; it is a recognition that, to some extent, the failures of Gracián are those of Borges himself. The identification between Borges and Gracián is highlighted by the poem's use of *laberintos* in its first and last lines. In this relatively late poem, we see Borges looking back as much as his younger, "vanidosamente barroco," self as at Gracián.[3]

The poem's ending calls to mind one of Borges's most famous stories, "La muerte y la brújula." At the end of the story, the detective Erik Lönnrot is led to his death, having solved the puzzle that had been elaborated by Red Scharlach to trap him. Facing death at the hands of Scharlach, Lönnrot can think of nothing but another labyrinth, another riddle distracting him from the more immediate question of life and death. The same is true of Gracián in the poem: as he faces his own death he can think of nothing but puns, emblems, and labyrinths.

One of Borges's recurrent fascinations or terrors is the mirror, which, needless to say, is the quintessential symbol of vanity. The reference in **"Los espejos"** is typical:

> Dios ha creado las noches que se arman
> De sueños y las formas del espejo
> Para que el hombre sienta que es reflejo
> Y vanidad. Por eso nos alarman.
>
> (179)

The rhyme of *espejo* with *reflejo:* could anyone else get away with it? It would be interesting to know what the baroque young Borges would have made of it?[4]

One could go on enumerating the appearance of *vano, en vano, vanamente* and *vanidad* in Borges's poetry. One more example should suffice to highlight its importance. Borges writes in **"Composición escrita en un ejemplar de Beowulf"**:

> Gastada por los años la memoria
> Deja caer la en vano repetida
> Palabra y es así como mi vida
> Teje y desteje su cansada historia.
>
> (233)

Although one may find some solace in literature, the literary act, finally, is destined to be the repetition of hollow words. Repetition of turns of phrase and of ideas serves in the end to empty these ideas and turns of phrase of meaning. There is more than a note of stoic resignation in this stanza: literature may be a vain enterprise, but life itself is only expressed in textual terms: "mi vida / Teje y desteje su cansada historia."

The word *vanidad* and it variants also frequently make their way into Borges's prose, even into his most famous pieces. In **"Borges y yo,"** the short piece from ***El hacedor*** about the split between the literary personality and its humble alter ego, Borges writes about his tastes:

> Me gustan los relojes de arena, los mapas, la tipografía del siglo XVIII las etimologías, el sabor del café y la prosa de Stevenson; el otro comparte estas preferencias, pero de un modo vanidoso que las convierte en atributos de un actor.
>
> (69)

Once these "preferences" are given literary expression, they lose some of their inherent value: following the etymology of my key word, one could say that they are "emptied out." The literary act, the act of putting things into words, automatically cancels authenticity. There are things, tastes, preferences, and all the rest, as they say, is literature.

I cannot conclude without a cursory glance at some of the vain distractions we encounter when we take up Borges. First among these is the "vanity" of the artist who wants to be known to readers only through the texts that he considers to be his best: the vanity of an author who goes out of his way to eliminate all traces of his "youthful indiscretions." I've heard an anecdote about a youngish Borges making the rounds of Buenos Aires's bookstores, buying up all the copies of *Inquisiciones* that he could find in order to take them home and burn them. Marcos Barnatán writes about a visit of Borges and María Kodama to a bookstore in Mallorca, where Borges was shown a copy of Carlos Meneses's recently released compilation *Poesía juvenil de J. L. Borges*:

> Borges le dijo a María que rompiera el libro. A lo que ella respondió que en la portada había una buena foto de él. "Entonces conserve la portada y rompa el resto" sentenció Borges.
>
> (110)

And yet Borges did not go so far as to act as if he had never written the essays of *Inquisiciones El tamaño de mi esperanza* or *El idioma de los argentinos.* First of all, he would often refer to these early essays in his interviews, if only to critique their baroque excessiveness, the lack of the sort of concision that characterizes his later writings. Yet even in the most vehement of these repudiations there is a certain acknowledgement, a wink at the ghost of one's former self.

Another symptom of this artistic vanity is the incessant changing and polishing of his poems. Borges, like Cervantes, has the reputation in some circles of being a "bad" poet. I don't think this label is quite fair. While Borges's poems don't have the intensity of imagery of those of Neruda or Lezama, they do have a quiet, metaphysical intensity and a thematic complexity that can be overlooked in superficial readings. Borges's earliest poems are the extreme example of the vanity of this constant revision. The poems of the ***Fervor de Buenos Aires*** in the socalled ***Obras completas*** that Borges himself supervised in his lifetime often bear little resemblance to the poems originally published under the same title in 1923, even though the first sentence of the book's prologue reads, "No he reescrito el libro" (9). A hypothetical critical edition that charted all of the variants in Borges's poetry would be voluminous. In an interview Borges, quoting Keats regarding this ongoing propensity to revise, said, "it is myself that I remake." Is there not a certain vanity involved in this unwillingness to relinquish control over one's poems, in this on-going desire to remake one's former self?

The passage that first got me thinking about reading Borges through the prism of vanity is from one of his best stories,

"El Aleph." In the story, Carlos Daneri Argentino, an acquaintance of the narrator (a certain "Borges") writes a vast, all-encompassing poem called "La tierra." The poem is inspired by the aleph, a point containing all possible points seen at all possible times, which just happens to be found in Daneri's basement. In the course of events, "Borges" literally stumbles upon the point, seeing all of time and space. Through this act of mere perception he succeeds where Daneri had failed in his vast poem: he achieves a communion with the whole by merely resigning himself to being no one, by not writing.

"El Aleph" is full of sentences that use the word *vano*. The story begins with a brief reflection on change. The day that Beatriz dies, The Borges character looks up and notices that a cigarette advertisement has changed:

> Cambiará el universo, pero yo no, pensé con melancólica vanidad; alguna vez mi vana devoción la había exasperado; muerta yo podía consagrarme a su memoria, sin esperanza pero también sin humillación.
>
> (156)

A little further on, Borges describes the yearly dinners, held to commemorate Beatriz's death, as "melancólicas y vanamente eróticas." The recurrence of the word suggests that the notion of vanity has more than a little bearing on the idea of literature being developed in the story. Carlos Daneri Argentino's vast literary enterprise is vain in that it is doomed to failure.

At the end of a brilliant article, Enrico Mario Santí suggests that "El Aleph" be read *en clave*, that it is, among other things, a parody of Neruda's monumental *Canto general.* While Neruda's poem had not yet been published when Borges's story came out, news of a gargantuan, Whitmanesque poem by Neruda had long been discussed in Latin American intellectual circles.[5] Santí writes that "the point of the parody is to identify the object of the cult as the desire for totalization—what could otherwise be called an anxiety of literary legitimacy" (173–74). This desire or anxiety of legitimacy is certainly a symptom of the poet's vanity, for a certain vanity is essential for even the attempt to write such a work.

"La tierra," Daneri's endless poem, is a vain rhetorical exercise, as the perceptive "Borges" of the story points out early on, even before being aware of the existence of the aleph: "Tan ineptas me parecieron esas ideas, tan pomposa y tan *vana* su exposición, que inmediatamente las relacioné con la literatura" (158, emphasis added).[6] In this line, the notion of literature as an exercise in vanity couldn't be clearer, for it expands outward: not only is Daneri's poem a vain enterprise, but literature itself is too. Needless to say, I was disappointed when reading "El Aleph" in another edition, to find that the word *vana* had suddenly become *vasta.* But I guess that is a reflection of my own vanity, not that of Borges or the whole of literature.

Notes

1. Jaime Alazraki quotes Enrique Anderson Imbert: "Those of us who devotedly accompany him in his descents to buried temples suffer at times the suffocation of so much rarefied air. I doubt if we could endure to live there too long should Borges persist in inhabiting them forever. Perhaps we will kill ourselves or die as did his Babel's librarians" (3).
2. All page references to Borges's poems are to the *Obra poética (1923–67).*
3. The older Borges frequently refers to his younger self as a baroque writer, as in a 1981 interview with Antonio Carrizo:

   "Cuando era joven . . . yo quería ser Lugones, Quevedo, y escribir en un estilo barroco" (101). A principal defect of the baroque, according to Borges, is its inherent vanity. In the introduction to his anthology of Quevedo's poetry Borges writes that "el defecto esencial del barroco es de carácter ético; denuncia la vanidad del artista"

   (15).
4. Marcos-Ricardo Barnatán comments:

   "Borges asocia la idea del espejo a la de la vanidad y también a la mentira . . . La proliferación de espejos en la poesía del Borges maduro le obligó a reiterar sus rimas con la palabra reflejo, vicio que le imputaron los omnipotentes críticos, sin percatarse de que en la reincidencia borgiana nacía un nuevo concepto de la originalidad. Ya sólo Borges podría rimar espejo con reflejo, así como Góngora al abusar hizo exclusiva para sí la rima de plumas con espumas."

   (48–49).
5. Perhaps Borges objected to such lines in Neruda's long poem as "déjame a mí, poeta de nuestra pobre América, coronar tu cabeza con el laurel del pueblo" (4.29), or "Pablo Neruda, cronista de todas las cosas" (4.26).
6. This change is not included in Jaime Alazraki's register of variants in his *Prosa narrativa de Jorge Luis Borges.*

Works cited

Alazraki, Jaime. *La prosa narrativa de Jorge Luis Borges.* Madrid: Gredos, 1974.

———, Ed. *Critical Essays on Jorge Luis Borges.* Boston: G. K. Hall & Co., 1987.

Barnatán, Marcos-Ricar *Borges: Biografía total.* Madrid: Ediciones Temas de Hoy, 1995.

Borges, Jorge Luis. *El Aleph.* Madrid: Alianza, 1990.

———. *Fervor de Buenos Aires.* Buenos Aires: Emecé, 1969.

———. *El hacedor.* Madrid: Alianza, 1996.

———. *Obra poética (1923–1967).* Buenos Aires: Emecé, 1967.

Bryce Echenique, Alfredo. *Permiso para vivir.* Barcelona: Anagrama, 1993.

Carrizo, Antonio and Jorge Luis Borges. "Borges el memorioso." *CHA* 505/507 (1992): 99–112.

Neruda, Pablo. *Canto general.* Barcelona: Seix Barral, 1983.

Quevedo, Francisco de. *Antología poética.* Ed. Jorge Luis Borges. Madrid: Alianza, 1982.

Santí, Enrico Mario. "The Accidental Tourist: Walt Whitman in Latin America". *Do the Americas Have a Common Literature?* Ed. Gustavo Pérez Firmat. London & Durham: Duke UP, 1990. 156–76.

Norman Thomas diGiovani (essay date 1999)

SOURCE: "One Mind at Work," in *The Times Literary Supplement*, No. 5019, June 11, 1999, p. 14ff.

[*In the following essay, diGiovani discusses the process of collaborating with Borges in the translation of his poetry.*]

In November 1967, in Harvard Square, I walked into Schoenhof's Foreign Bookshop and asked for a copy of Jorge Luis Borges's collected poems. When the clerk brought me the book, he said, "You know Borges is speaking here next week." That was the first link in an invisible chain of cause and effect that brought me together with Borges in a working association that lasted for nearly five years. It was also the first link in a network that was soon to connect me with Buenos Aires in particular, with the River Plate in general, and with many dozen friends the world over.

I went home from Schoenhof's that day with a copy of Borges's ***Obra poética*** under my arm, and the following week I attended his public lecture in Memorial Hall. But the whole time, while I was reading the poems and listening to Borges and afterwards reading and studying the poetry further, I was transported to another realm. The words in the book and those spoken by the man on the stage were unmistakably one and the same, and I was struck by the gentle quality and humanity that each radiated. I had first come across it in lines of verse that Borges had written about his friend Elvira de Alvear, a Buenos Aires society woman whose life ended in madness. The poem, in the form of a bronze plaque, now adorns Elvira's tomb in the Recoleta cemetery.

> She once had everything but one by one
> Each thing abandoned her. We saw her armed
> With beauty. The morning and the hard light
> Of noon from their pinnacle revealed to her
> The glorious kingdoms of the world. Evening
> Wiped them away. . . .

During the autumn of 1967 and winter of 1968, all of Cambridge was buzzing about Borges's presence. But I was probably the only one who went home after that November lecture and wrote Borges a letter. In it, I asked if I could work with him on a volume of his poems in English translation. I told him that, a few years before, I had edited a selection of poems by Jorge Guillén, the Spanish poet who had lived and taught for years around Boston, and that my plan for Borges's poems was to produce something along similar lines. At this point, the hand of fate came heavily to intervene. Borges was notorious for never answering letters, and yet he answered mine, telling me to phone and to come and see him. I phoned. He asked me to come that very afternoon and to bring the poems I had done. "I haven't done any poems yet", I said in panic. "Come anyway", he said. That was the 3rd of December. I knocked at Borges's door, walked in, and was to stay for nearly five years.

On that first afternoon, we talked about a recent poem of his that I liked very much. It was on an Anglo-Saxon figure, Hengist Cyning, who founded the first Saxon kingdom in what is now England.

The extraordinary thing about that encounter, as I look back on it, was the fact of a poem about a Saxon king from the fifth century AD linking an older Argentine writer and a younger American, in Massachusetts, with the pair of us speaking in a flow of Spanish and English. The link, of course, was poetry and the music of words. I found out at the same time that Borges considered Guillén to be the finest poet then writing in the Spanish language. I also found out that Guillén's daughter, who was an old friend of mine, was accompanying Borges to a class he gave three times a week on contemporary Argentine writers. So when I had written my letter invoking Guillén's poems and his name, I could not have given myself a better recommendation.

Within a month, Borges and I had planned the whole book, which would become his ***Selected Poems, 1923–1967.*** Together we made a choice of 100 poems, I began to commission poet-translators to make the English versions, we secured the necessary rights from the Argentine publisher, and I sold the project to an American publisher. Our method was to make a literal rough draft of each piece that was to be in the selection, which I would use both to help the translators get started and later to criticize their drafts as they came in. Sometimes letters would pass back and forth several times between me and a particular poet before each of us was satisfied with the result. Only after that would I take the poem to Borges for a final reading. Nearly a dozen American and British poets participated, and Borges and I were gratified by the way such distinguished writers flocked to the project.

The winter of 1968 was an important time for Borges. Five of his books were then available in English (the first two had appeared in 1962); he was at Harvard, as the prestigious Charles Eliot Norton Professor of Poetry, to give six public lectures; and interest in his work in the United States was swelling to a crest. Through the poets involved in the ***Selected Poems***, word got out about what Borges and I were up to in our meetings. In the beginning, these took place two or three times a week; soon they increased, and I was forced to move near Cambridge so that we could work in daily sessions. Borges would exhort me in his typically self-effacing way, "When you write to the translators, tell them that in spite of my poems the translations must be good." Of course, that was just the sort of remark that made our collaborators redouble their efforts. Borges and I began to be asked to organize readings, using our new translations, at a number of Greater Boston universities; and, a few months later—with several of the translators reading—at the YM-YWHA, in New York.

Meanwhile, quite by chance, an unusual piece of information came my way. At the time we were working, Borges became the subject of a long interview with several pages of photographs, in *Life en español.* The woman conducting it, Rita Guibert, was a frequent visitor at Borges's flat. One day I heard her ask him whether he had ever worked with any of his other translators the way he was working with me. No, never, he said. I found his reply remarkable. The several editors and translators involved in every one of those first five books of Borges's had, at one time or another, been in contact with him, but none had ever consulted him about his or her translation. It was a wonder to me that so many had overlooked anything so obvious. Borges was the easiest of men to approach, he was unfailingly co-operative, and he also spoke very fine English. The greatest resource of all—the author himself, steeped in the English language and its literature—had gone untapped. Moreover, I came to find, Borges's English was better than that of his translations. Later on, he confessed to me that one translator had contacted him a few years before to say she could find no equivalent in English for the title of his prose piece called "El hacedor". "That was odd", Borges said, "because I thought up the title in English. It comes from the Scottish poet Dunbar. My Spanish title was a translation from the English right from the start." That title, of course, was "The Maker".

During this same period, I approached Borges about translating one of his short stories. We had been working on the poems for a couple of months by then, and I was curious to see whether we could apply the method we had evolved with the poetry to a longer work in prose. I warned him that I did not know enough about Argentina to translate any of his stories on my own, so would only try my hand at it if he would help. I said we could then credit the finished product as having been translated in collaboration with the author. Borges was stunned by the suggestion. "Of course, I'll help," he said, "but won't it hurt you to say that I took part?" I told him it would give the work more authority. "Yes, I see that," Borges said, "but in my country a translator would be far too jealous to share credit with the author."

The first story we translated together—it was "The Other Death"—turned into one of the happiest and most fortuitous experiences of my life. Altogether I worked on the tale for about a week, including the three afternoon sessions that I spent on it with Borges. When we finished, I saw that what we had achieved was truer to the original tone and meaning and complex intentions of the author than any other translation of his into English up until then. For his part, some time later, Borges told a class at Columbia University that

> When we attempt a translation, or re-creation, of my poems or prose in English, we don't think of ourselves as being two men, We think we are really one mind at work.

At the outset of taking on "The Other Death", on my own I had puzzled out and made a rough draft of the story. Since there were a number of elements in it so local that only an Argentine would understand them, and only an Argentine who spoke perfect English could have explained them, it was plain that I should not try to make perfect sentences in English of what I did not fully grasp. So I left gaps. I want to emphasize that my intention at this stage had been only to produce a makeshift draft that I could later go over with the author so as to get the meaning straight. Naturally, where simple sentences flowed out into solid English prose, I let them flow. When I completed my draft, I took it round to Borges. I read to him half a sentence or so in Spanish, followed by the equivalent portion of my rough-and-ready English version. Where the gaps fell, Borges would interrupt before I could explain my difficulty and he would say, "Now in this next bit you won't understand such-and-such", and he would launch into an elaborate description of River Plate rural life or history that would provide me with exactly what I lacked. It soon became clear that the affinities between the plains of Argentina and those of the United States, with their vast open stretches of range land for grazing cattle, were greater than one at first imagined. There had to be terms common to both countries to express the similarity of their frontier histories. And there were—if only one avoided the dictionary, whose word-for-word equivalents are often of little value.

We forged ahead, sentence by sentence, sometimes feeling that what I had was good enough as it stood, sometimes revising extensively. On occasion, Borges corrected me; on occasion, I asked him to clarify. Often, no sooner had I read out one of my sentences than I saw ways of improving it before he could make the suggestion himself. In some cases, he offered an alternative or variations that I would return home with to test on my own. We would keep trying to free the sentences of cumbersome or indirect locutions. Passive constructions might become active; negative, positive. A phrase like "marchaban desde el Sur"—they marched from the south—might become "on their march north". Our aim at this point was simply to get all of the Spanish into some kind of English, and in order to do so I needed a full understanding not only of the text but also of Borges's intentions. It did not matter to us yet that during the completion of this stage we might still be fairly literal or provisional. Often, in fact, we remained deliberately undecided about such details as finding the right word or phrase or shade of meaning.

After a session with Borges, I would return home and type out what we had gone over together, then set to work shaping and polishing the sentences and paragraphs, this time trying to supply the exact words. Now I would refer back to the Spanish only for checking rhythms and emphases. The concern would be with matters of tone and tension and style. To anyone who constructs a piece of prose and cares about style, this amounts to a slow and painstaking search for meanings to fit the sound patterns one keeps turning and turning in one's head. After finishing this stage—and it was far and away the most time-consuming part of the job—I read the not-quite-final draft to Borges for approval and a last test. This time we completely ignored the Spanish and only tinkered here or there with a word.

I still remember how much trouble that complicated first sentence of "The Other Death" gave me. It was the classic Borges opener, fulfilling his personal dictum that if you began with a long, involved sentence, by the time the reader got to the end of it he had made his way well into the story and would be hooked. I must have sat there for over an hour on that sentence alone, taking it apart and putting it together, testing it and retesting it for crucial balances and rhythms. What made the sentence so hard was its multiple clauses. Here it is:

> I have mislaid the letter, but a couple of years or so ago Gannon wrote to me from his ranch up in Gualeguaychú saying he would send me a translation, perhaps the first into Spanish, of Ralph Waldo Emerson's poem, "The Past", and adding in a PS that don Pedro Damián, whom I might recall, had a few nights earlier died of a lung ailment.

I am quite fond of that sentence, not only because it was the first prose of Borges's that I ever translated but also because to me it stands for the beginning—the first story itself, the method we invented there on the spot, and, gratifyingly, the contract it landed us from the *New Yorker* magazine. They invited us to súbmit to them any of Borges's work previously untranslated—stories, poems and essays, past and to come.

The long sentence quoted above, I hasten to point out, is not the version of it that appeared in print either in the magazine or in the volume it was subsequently destined for, in 1970, *The Aleph and Other Stories.* On two occasions since then, in quoting the sentence I have revised it. I mention this to indicate that a translation, like any other piece of writing, can always be improved.

On a number of occasions, Borges and I were able to make new translations of some of his finest tales—even ones translated three or more times previously into English. I have likened our achievement in these stories to the cleaning of old pictures. In our effort, we tried hard to restore the clarity, the sharpness and the colour of the originals. Once, when I read him the finished draft of his celebrated story "The Circular Ruins", Borges wept. "Caramba," he said, "I wish I could still write like that." These were the versions of his work that Borges had long awaited and that he now considered to be definitive.

Borges left Cambridge to return to Argentina in April 1968, and several months later I joined him in Buenos Aires. After I went to live in his country, where I stayed for nearly four years, those bits of any text I did not understand and left blank in my early drafts got fewer and fewer. But nothing changed with regard to the tacit assumptions and agreements that underlay the method that Borges and I had worked out for ourselves. We agreed, for example, that a translation should not sound like a translation, but should read as though it had been written directly in the language into which it is being made. While this may appear obvious, for a writer and translator as accomplished as Vladimir Nabokov, the opposite held true. He maintained that a translation should sound like a translation. But Borges and I wanted his translations to read like original works. He once confessed to me that, when earlier versions of his stories were read to him, he recognized the particular piece as his, but always thought he wrote better than that. In the preface to *The Aleph and Other Stories*, we stated:

> Perhaps the chief justification of this book is the translation itself, which we have undertaken in what may be a new way. Working closely together in daily sessions, we have tried to make these stories read as though they had been written in English. We do not consider English and Spanish as compounded of sets of easily interchangeable synonyms; they are two quite different ways of looking at the world, each with a nature of its own. English, for example, is far more physical than Spanish. We have therefore shunned the dictionary as much as possible and done our best to rethink every sentence in English words. This venture does not necessarily mean that we have willfully tampered with the original, though in certain cases we have supplied the American reader with those things—geographical, topographical, and historical—taken for granted by any Argentine.

Borges and I further agreed that in translating from Spanish into English, words with Anglo-Saxon roots are preferable to words of Latin origin. Often this means that the first word suggested by the Spanish should be avoided. On a number of occasions, Borges said he could never understand why his early translators would translate *habitación oscura* into "obscure habitation" when what he meant was "dark room". Of course, when choosing the first word suggested by the Spanish, there is the danger of falling into the trap of the false cognate, or false association. The translation of one Borges story is badly marred at a crucial point when the word *discutir*, "to argue", is translated as "to discuss". A professor of Spanish-American literature at an American university once criticized me in print for having translated Borges's words *mas notorio atributo* as "most obvious trait". He wanted the translation to read "most notorious attribute", not only ignoring the context of the phrase but also being caught out by the false cognate. "Notorio" in this instance meant simply "noteworthy", or "obvious", without the negative connotation the word carries in English.

Borges has a marvellous prose poem about Shakespeare called **"Everything and Nothing".** In the opening line, Borges described Shakespeare's words as "copiosas, fantásticas y agitadas". One translation of this reads, "copious, fantastic, and agitated"; a second, "copious, imaginative, and emotional". This is distinctly better and shows that the translator is not just translating the words but is thinking about their meaning in terms of Shakespeare. A third translation reads, "copious, fantastic, and stormy". A fourth, "multitudinous, and of a fantastical and agitated turn"—a solution both long-winded and stodgy. A fifth version—the one made by Borges and me—reads, "swarming, fanciful, and excited".

There were other factors working for us that underpinned our method. Foremost was Borges's command of English and his sense of English prose style. An anecdote will illustrate just how sensitive he was to English. In 1964, Borges fixed to his collected poems the following paragraph, taken from one of Robert Louis Stevenson's letters:

> I do not set up to be a poet. Only an all-round literary man: a man who talks, not one who sings. . . . Excuse this little apology; but I don't like to come before people who have a note of song and let it be supposed I do not know the difference.

As the Spanish-language editions of Borges's work were riddled with errors, I thought I had better look that quotation up in Volume Two of the edition Borges had cited. When I did, sure enough, I found an error—but not a printer's error. What I found was that Borges had tampered with the text. It was not, as in his version, "Excuse this little apology; but I don't like to come before people" etc. Rather, the correct text ran: "Excuse this little apology for my house; but I don't like to come before people", and so on. When I asked Borges why he had suppressed the words "for my house", he said it was because they sounded silly and thereby weakened the text. But he added that for our edition of his poetry I could print the epigraph any way I liked.

A few years later, in London, travelling with Borges—it is uncanny how this takes the shape of a Borges story—I bought the beautiful twenty-six-volume Vailima edition of Stevenson's works. Back in Buenos Aires, I don't know for what reason, I checked the source of the epigraph again; this edition had been published twenty-four years after the one Borges had used, and it had been newly edited as well. There I found that the quotation read: "Excuse this little apology for my muse . . .". Muse, not house. Now it made perfect sense. The original letter had been handwritten, and its editor had misread the word "muse" as "house". Borges, without having seen the original, had sensed the mistake.

Jay Parini (essay date 1999)

SOURCE: A review of *Selected Poems*, in *The Nation*, New York, Vol. 268, No. 30, May 31, 1999, pp. 25–8.

[*In the following review, Parini discusses the volume* Selected Poems of Borges *(1999), edited by Alexander Coleman.*]

With Pablo Neruda and Alejo Carpentier, Jorge Luis Borges set in motion the wave of astonishing writing that has given Latin American literature its high place in our time. Yet Borges stands alone, a planet unto himself, resisting categorization. Although literary fashions come and go, he is always there, endlessly rereadable by those who admire him, awaiting rediscovery by new generations of readers.

One tends to think of Borges as the writer of a dozen or so classic stories, such as "Pierre Menard, Author of the Quixote," "The Circular Ruins," "The Lottery in Babylon," "The Secret Miracle" and—my favorite—"Tlön, Uqbar, Orbis Tertius," where the author imagines a parallel universe. This idiosyncratic, mind-altering fiction was mostly written in the late thirties and forties (*Ficciones*, his central collection, appeared in 1944, gathering most of his best stories to date). Yet Borges was well-known as a poet long before he tried his hand at fiction.

Now a generous volume of his poetry has been published by Viking, edited by Alexander Coleman and translated by various hands, including Alastair Reid, Mark Strand, W. S. Merwin and Robert Fitzgerald. This follows *Collected Fictions*, which appeared last September in a matching edition, translated by Andrew Hurley. Next fall a third volume, containing Borges's essays, will appear, thus making available in English virtually all of his important work.

Reading the stories, poems and essays side by side, one sees that it makes no sense to think of him as a writer constrained by genre; if anything, his work as a whole interrogates, even ridicules, the very notion of genre. In the famous Prologue to *Ficciones,* he wrote: "The composition of vast books is a laborious and improverishing extravagance. To go on for five hundred pages developing an idea whose perfect oral exposition is possible in a few minutes! A better course of procedure is to pretend that these books already exist, and then to offer a résumé, a commentary." Thus, his stories were born of critical commentaries, much as his poetry is deeply involved in the fictions, as one discovers in reading through his ***Selected Poems***, where his abiding themes (the puzzle of identity, the illusory nature of the physical universe, the alluring yet maddening nature of love) and symbols (the mirror, the labyrinth, the tiger, the game, the double) are summoned and repossessed.

Even the sacred boundary between writer and reader is blurred, as in the introduction to Borges's first book of poems, where he wrote: "If in the following pages there is some successful verse or other, may the reader forgive me the audacity of having written it before him. We are all one; our inconsequential minds are much alike, and circumstances so influence us that it is something of an accident that you are the reader and I the writer—the unsure, ardent writer—of my verses."

The author of Borges's early poems does seem ardent, but there is little unsureness. In **"Truco,"** in which a card game becomes a metaphor for art, the poet seems astoundingly self-assured as he writes:

> A furtive slowing down
> keeps all words in check,
> and, as the vagaries of the game

repeat and repeat themselves,
the players of that evening
reenact ancient tricks:
An act that brings to life, but very faintly,
the generations of our forefathers
who bequeathed to the leisure of Buenos Aires
truco, with all its bids and its deceptions.

That first volume, published in 1923, was called ***Fervor de Buenos Aires***, and the title suggests the nature of the poems: feverish evocations of the city where Borges was raised and spent much of his life. The young poet soon became a key figure in a literary movement called Ultraísmo—a version of Surrealism—although its effects, in the poems, consist of little more than a residue of inventiveness in lines such as "Light roams the streets inventing dirty colors" or "The street's end opens like a wound on the sky." (There is also that Surrealist penchant for the prose poem, at which Borges excelled throughout his long writing life.)

Whitman was, as Borges often noted, his earliest model, but the poet of the twenties was obviously reading widely in English, French and Spanish poetry. He was already obsessed by "the enigma of Time," which in **"Year's End"** he regards as

the miracle
that, though the chances are infinite
and though we are
drops in Heraclitus' river,
allows something in us to endure,
never moving.

Late in life, Borges wrote: "The fate of a writer is strange. He begins his career by being a baroque writer, pompously baroque, and after many years, he might attain if the stars are favorable, not simplicity, which is nothing, but rather a modest and secret complexity."

The early poems do occasionally exhibit a touch of baroqueness, with their elaborate conceits and symbols, but nothing like in the major stories, where baroqueness occasionally overwhelms other effects. Having cast himself in Whitman's shadow, Borges as poet was saved from a certain kind of excess; in **"Boast of Quietness,"** there is a wonderful blend of Borgesian hermetics and Whitmanesque openness:

Time is living me.
More silent than my shadow, I pass through the loftily
covetous multitude.
They are indispensable, singular, worthy of tomorrow.
My name is someone and anyone.
I walk slowly, like one who comes from so far away
he doesn't expect to
arrive.

Borges spoke English from early childhood with his maternal grandmother, who was herself British, so his native language was always infused with Anglicisms. Indeed, the oddity and richness of his syntax in Spanish, even the way the phrases are gathered and pitched, owes something to his vast reading in English poetry. He adored the Old English poets, Milton and Shakespeare, the Romantics and (as any bookish British child reared in the Edwardian era would) Kipling and Stevenson. Aware that he would eventually inherit his father's blindness, he had memorized most of his favorite poems by middle age, when his eyesight finally dissolved. (In 1971, in Scotland, I heard him recite a long passage from *Beowulf* by heart—in Anglo-Saxon!)

He turned to fiction in the mid-thirties, not returning to poetry until the fifties and sixties, when his finest volumes—***The Maker*** and ***The Self and the Other***—were published. In the former, Borges sets in place a number of symbols and metaphors, which he then reworks in various ways, always deepening them. In the prose Epilogue to ***The Maker***, for example, he writes:

> A man sets himself the task of portraying the world. Over the years he fills a given surface with images of provinces and kingdoms, mountains, bays, ships, islands, fish, rooms, instruments, heavenly bodies, horses, and people. Shortly before he dies he discovers that this patient labyrinth of lines is a drawing of his own face.

In his next book, in **"Of Heaven and Hell,"** he repossesses and complicates the same analogy:

In the clear glass of a dream, I have glimpsed
the Heaven and Hell that lie in wait for us:
When Judgment Day sounds in the last trumpets
and planet and millennium both
disintegrate, and all at once, O Time,
all your ephemeral pyramids cease to be,
the colors and the lines that trace the past
will in the semidarkness form a face,
a sleeping face, faithful, still, unchangeable
(the face of the loved one, or, perhaps, your own)
and the sheer contemplation of that face—
never-changing, whole, beyond corruption—
will be, for the rejected, an Inferno,
and, for the elected, Paradise.

The greatest poetry is always motivated by a writer's sense of that terrible dislocation between the mind and the world; the poem itself rises in that gap, intrusive, begging for consideration, helpless and hopeless, trying to patch over the silence that is always (in theory) beyond improvement yet somehow unsatisfactory. Borges addresses this subject directly in **"The Other Tiger,"** my favorite in this volume. Here, Borges compares the "real" tiger, who exists "on the fringes of the Ganges," with the tiger created by the poet with his pen:

Evening spreads in my spirit and I keep thinking
that the tiger I am calling up in my poem
is a tiger made of symbols and of shadows,
a set of literary images,
scraps remembered from encyclopedias,
and not the deadly tiger, the fateful jewel
that in the sun or the deceptive moonlight
follows its paths, in Bengal or Sumatra,
of love, of indolence, of dying.

In the end, the poet seeks a "third tiger." "This one," he says,

will be a form in my dream like all the others,
a system, an arrangement of human language,
and not the flesh-and-bone tiger
that, out of reach of all mythologies,
paces the earth.

As ever in Borges, the fictive tiger is more real, more satisfying, than the tiger who paws the earth or curls, sleeping, in the folds of the cerebrum. The fiction flares, takes on memorable life, between the unspoken world and the unspoken mind.

The bulk of these poems appear in Alastair Reid's translations, and one can only be grateful to him for devoting his considerable poetic gifts to Borges (as he has, in years past, to Neruda and others). If anything, Reid seems to improve upon the Spanish. In the above passage, for instance, Borges writes about the third tiger becoming "un sistema de palabras/Humanas," or "a system of human words." Reid's phrase, "an arrangement of human language," interprets and extends what Borges has written in thrilling ways, faithful to the text yet substituting for the easy, more literal translation an equivalent that possesses a life itself as poetry in English.

In poem after poem of this period, Borges mixes desire and metaphysical speculations tinged with lamentations for "this dear world losing shape, fading away / into a pale uncertain ashy-gray / that feels like sleep, or else oblivion." In the beautiful **"Rain,"** he reflects on the elusive nature of memory and time, using the literal phenomenon of rain as a springboard for larger musings: "Quite suddenly the evening clears at last / as now outside the soft small rain is falling. / Falling or fallen." Soon memories of rain fetch recollections of lost time: "The evening's rain / brings me the voice, the dear voice of my father, / who comes back now, who never has been dead."

Although his finest poems appeared between 1955 and 1965, Borges returned again and again to the form, often finding that "modest and secret complexity" he longed for in poems such as **"Things," "Fragments from an Apocryphal Gospel," "In Praise of Darkness," "The Gold of the Tigers"** and **"The Unending Rose."** With remarkable consistency over a lifetime, the same themes and images sustained his attention, and one can hear the earliest Borges, with some adjustments, in the latest.

A fitting epilogue for his work, perhaps, can be found in **"The Suicide,"** a fierce, eloquent poem in which the poet eerily reconsiders his legacy, which is no more (or less) than the legacy of his readers:

Not a single star will be left in the night.
The night will not be left.
I will die and, with me,
the weight of the intolerable universe.
I shall erase the pyramids, the medal lions,
the continents and faces.
I shall erase the accumulated past.
I shall make dust of history, dust of dust.
Now I am looking on the final sunset.
I am hearing the last bird.
I bequeath nothingness to no one.

FURTHER READING

Bibliographies

Foster, David William. *Jorge Luis Borges: An Annotated Primary and Secondary Bibliography.* New York: Garland, 1984, 328 pp.

Scholarly in its depth and comprehensive in its range.

Loewenstein, C. Jared. *A Descriptive Catalogue of the Jorge Luis Borges Collection at the University of Virginia Library.* Charlottesville and London: University Press of Virginia, 1993, 254 pp.

Catalogs a major collection dedicated to providing "reliable information about the origins and development of" Borges's texts.

Biography

Woodall, James. *Borges: A Life.* New York: Basic Books, 1997, 333 pp.

Contains significant scholarly tools, including bibliography and catalogs of travels, awards, and films based on his works, as well as a lucid account of life and work.

Criticism

Menocal, Maria Rosa. *Writing in Dante's Cult of Truth: From Borges to Bocaccio.* Durham, N.C.: Duke University Press, 1991, 223 pp.

Adopting a Borgesian, non-linear aproach to literary history, views Dante and Borges in a relation of reciprocal influence.

Additional coverage of Borges's life and career is contained in the following sources published by the Gale Group: *Authors and Artists for Young Adults*, Vol. 26; *Contemporary Authors*, Vols. 21-24R; *Contemporary Authors New Revision Series*, Vols. 19, 33; *Contemporary Literary Criticism* Vols. 1, 2, 3, 4, 6, 8, 9, 10, 13, 19, 44, 48, 83; *Dictionary of Literary Biography*, Vol. 113; *Dictionary of Literary Biography Yearbook*, Vol. 86; *DISCovering Authors*; *DISCovering Authors: British*; *DISCovering Authors: Canadian*; *DISCovering Authors Modules: Most-Studied Authors* and *Multicultural*; *Hispanic Literature Criticism*, Vol. 1; *Hispanic Writers*; *Major 20th-Century Writers*; *Short Story Criticism*, Vol. 4; and *World Literature Criticism*, Vol. 1.

Gabriela Mistral
1889-1957

(Born Lucila Godoy y Alcayaga) Chilean poet, educator, and diplomat.

INTRODUCTION

During the first half of the twentieth century, throughout Latin America, Mistral achieved iconic status as mystic, mother, and teacher. She fashioned a poetry that expresses a betrayed and abandoned woman's angry longing for love and children. Mistral was dedicated to restoring meaning and identity to the economically and politically oppressed. Her vision of the anguish, the need, of a South American people pillaged and impoverished—spiritually as well as materially—by European exploitation and denigration was balanced by hope achieved through the Christian assumption of self-sacrifice in the service of liberating others from ignorance and suffering.

BIOGRAPHICAL INFORMATION

Of Spanish, Basque, and Indian descent, Mistral was born Lucila Godoy y Alcayaga on April 7, 1889, to an educated but poor family in Chile. In 1891, when she was two years old, her father, a schoolteacher and poet, abandoned the family, to return ten years later. At fifteen, Lucila began to teach school. During the next decade, she went from being an elementary school teacher to a secondary school professor to an inspector general of schools to principal of the *Liceo de Senoritas* from 1910 to 1922. In 1922, she served as an advisor on rural education to the Mexican Minister of Education. She also was a visiting professor at Middlebury College in Vermont, Barnard College in Manhattan, and the University of Puerto Rico. Following heartbreak, and the suicide of her beloved in the early 1900s, she began composing a series of melancholy "*Sonetos de la muerte*" ("Sonnets on Death"), which she entered in a Santiago writing contest in 1914 under the pseudonym Gabriela Mistral. She won the contest and national fame, and her celebrity spread quickly throughout the Americas. The cost of her first book, published in the United States in Spanish, was defrayed by a group of Spanish teachers who heard her poetry read at Columbia University. The concern in her verse for outcasts, downtrodden and impoverished people, and her active support of children, exemplified by her donation of the profits from her poetry to Basque orphans of the Spanish Civil War, brought her a reputation for humanitarianism and saintliness. She served as the Chilean delegate to the League of Nations, the Institute of Intellectual Cooperation, and the United Nations, and as consul for Chile to Italy, Spain, Portugal, Brazil, and the United States. In 1945, the Swedish Academy awarded her the Nobel Prize for Literature. She died of cancer in the United States in 1957.

MAJOR WORKS

In each of her four volumes of poetry *Desolation, Tenderness, Felling*, and *Wine Press*, Mistral's work reflects a melancholy acceptance of the suffering life entails, and of the sacrifice required to alleviate that pain. Her works also show a transition from romantic, expressionist self-involvement with internal anguish and despair to a teacher's and a stateswoman's efforts to inspire in her readers curiosity and knowledge about the natural world, love for its beauty, communion with the spirit, and humane concern for each other.

CRITICAL RECEPTION

The success of Mistral's poetry was immediate when the "*Sonetos del muerte*" won the Juegos Florales laurel crown and gold medal from the city of Santiago, Chile. In 1922, *Desolacion* was published in New York. American poet, Langston Hughes, in the preface to his translation of some of her poems, calls her language "simple and direct." H. J. Gullberg, when awarding Mistral the Nobel Prze for Literature, said, "... this poet offers us her potion, which has the savor of earth and which quenches the thirst of the heart." However, critics usually interpret Mistral's poetry as a direct expression of a personality they conceive to be similar to that of the Virgin Mary, and, in most critical discussions of her poetry, that personality is as much the subject of admiration and even devotion as the work itself.

PRINCIPAL WORKS

Sonetos de la muerte [*Sonnets on Death*] (poetry) 1914
Desolacion [*Desolation*] (poetry) 1922
Ternura (poetry) 1924
Tala (poetry) 1938
Lagar (poetry) 1954
Selected Poems of Gabriela Mistral [translations by Langston Hughes] (poetry) 1957
Poema de Chile [revisions by Doris Dana] 1967

CRITICISM

Clarence Finlayson (essay date 1941)

SOURCE: "Spanish-American Poet: The Life and Ideas of Gabriela Mistral," in *Commonweal*, Vol. 35, No. 7, December 5, 1941, pp. 160–63.

[*In the following essay, Finlayson introduces Mistral to North American readers as a poet of sadness, an advocate for the downtrodden, and as a Christian evangelist of Democracy.*]

In 1889 there was born in Vicuña, a small town in northern Chile, an infant who in the course of years was destined to be one of the most famous women of our time. Lucila Godoy was of humble parentage. Her family gained its living working in the fields, as did the majority of the neighbors in that agricultural region. Her earliest years were thus spent in the country. At the age of 15 she began her calling as a teacher in a small rural school. For several years, years which were decisive in her development, Lucila Godoy was dealing with children and with the very poorest children in her native land. When she was about 20 years old she went from elementary to secondary school teaching. She remained as a teacher and then as director of a school for 15 years. Throughout that period she visited many of the educational institutions in Chile, teaching at Traiguen, Antofagasta, Andes, Punta Areñas, Temuco and Santiago. Her idealistic and apostolic temperament exercised a strong influence on young people. But no one, or hardly anyone, knew then of her daily labor, heroic, hidden, and most fruitful for the invisible domains of the human soul.

When she was a teacher at Andes, a village near the mountains, she became known throughout her native land through a literary gathering that took place at Santiago, the capital, and was sponsored by the writers' society of that city. Carried away by her admiration for two European poets, Gabriel D'Annunzio and Frederic Mistral, she had submitted to the conference some remarkably beautiful poems entitled **"Soñetos de la Muerte"** (**"Sonnets on Death"**). She presented them under the pseudonym of Gabriela Mistral that was to be famous all over the world and bury her real name forever. They were published in Chile in 1922. Immediately there was the greatest enthusiasm for her poetic talents, seldom found in South America in so striking, so appealing, so profound a form. Her lyrical talent was recognized as among the very highest in all Spanish literature.

In Chile as in other Spanish-American countries it is the custom to give great writers commissions or consular posts in foreign lands in order to supply them with the necessary surroundings to develop their talents and thus brilliantly represent their country. It must be borne in mind that the Latin race has great esteem for literature. Especially in South America the leading poets attain a fame often wider and more popular than that of the most noted statesmen. Pablo Neruda, another of our greatest Chilean poets, has read his poems out of doors in public parks before thousands of people. In this way poetry takes on educative values, promoting esthetic sentiments.

In 1922 the Chilean Government gave Gabriela Mistral a commission to go to Mexico to study the founding and organization of libraries. The same year her complete poems were published in a volume entitled ***Desolación***. The first edition was published in New York under the auspices of the Spanish Institute, whose president, Federico de Onis, was professor of Spanish Literature at Columbia University.

In Mexico Gabriela Mistral became associated with the educational work of José Vasconcelos and took the greatest interest in the problem of the Indian. At times her desire to express the sadness found in those original inhabitants of our America appears in her poetry.

Her educational and poetical endeavors were so successful that in 1926 she was appointed the cultural representative of Spanish-America at the League of Nations at Geneva. In Europe she filled the post of Secretary of the Institute for Intellectual Cooperation with its residence in Paris at the Palais Royal. In 1928 she represented Chile and Ecuador at the International University Conference at Madrid. The year before she had been the delegate of the Teachers'

Association of Chile at Locarno. From then on Gabriela Mistral belonged to the consular service of Chile and has been Chilean consul at Madrid, Lisbon, Nice and elsewhere. At present she is Chilean consul at Nictheroy, Brazil. Changes in political parties in Chile, when new presidents come in and the whole diplomatic corps is supplanted, have not affected her. So great is her reputation that each successive government feels honored to have Gabriela as its representative abroad.

Her poetry and some of its qualities

Although her poetry is little known in the English language, it enjoys universal favor among our peoples. Some of her compositions have been translated into French, English, etc., but they have not reached the general public. From here on I shall endeavor to say something about several of her poems. In all of them there is a unique delicacy, gentle resignation and an inclination that is spontaneously ethical. Her principal influences are the Bible, Tagore, the Mexican poet, Amado Nervo, and the outstanding Spanish-American poet, Rubén Darío.

"Decalogue of the Artist," a kind of "Ars Poetica," is one of her most famous compositions. Its force is so great that this literary jewel might have appeared over the signature of Paul Claudel. Its religious character makes it particularly profound. Here are these ten commandments:

"Decalogue of the Artist"

1. Thou shalt love beauty which is the shadow of God over the universe.

2. There is no art that is atheistic. Even though thou dost not love the Creator, thou wilt affirm His existence by creating in His likeness.

3. Thou shalt not use Beauty as fodder for the feelings, but as the natural food of the soul.

4. It shall not serve as a pretext for luxury or vanity but only as a spiritual exercise.

5. Thou shalt not seek it in the market place nor put thy talents at the service of the vulgar, for Beauty is virginal and what is found in the market place is not beauty.

6. Beauty will rise from thine heart to thy poem and thou shalt first be cleansed.

7. Beauty shall also bear the name of Pity and will console the hearts of men.

8. Thou shalt bring forth thy work as a child is born, staunching the blood of thine heart.

9. Beauty shall not be for thee an opiate that lulls thee to sleep, but a generative wine which fires thee to action, for if thou dost fall from thy full stature of man or woman thou dost cease to be an artist.

10. After thine every creative act thou shalt emerge humbled, for thou shalt have fallen short of thine own vision and short of that wonderful vision of God which is nature.

The poetry of Gabriela Mistral has from time to time touched on profound metaphysical subjects. It is in accord with our temperament and character to regard nature as a mother that is always protecting us, as part of the breath of our daily life, moreover something to which we subconsciously ascribe life or personality. The Spanish-American poet is often imbued with cosmic ideas: the universe appears to him as an all-embracing whole, as a continuing and perennial echo of his own aspirations, as the vesture of his intimate and most profound sorrows.

European romanticism took hold in Latin America as a natural expression of our fatalistic, passionate temperament, chained down by nature. Chile lies between the ocean and the mountains and is virtually a long narrow shore, like an island always facing the Pacific. There is a constant sensation of imprisonment, yet a feeling of limitless space by which the vastness of the sea, always before our eyes, falsely appears to liberate us.

All this has given us a certain attitude of resignation and of pensiveness that is marked in our poetry. Even in the most ancient native literature of our America there throbs and breathes that resignation in the face of facts, of life, of the world. It is a pessimism that is never still, never satisfied. It is continually nourished by a hidden ancestral force. It is not the state of mind of which Chesterton spoke, which at the moment of inspiration and success delights in its own created work, its own work of art, and then intones a hymn of joy together with all creatures in the universe. No, our pessimism is a tranquil pessimism, fatalistic, rather of feeling than of thought. Nor is it for this reason the transcendental pessimism of a Leopardi, systematically transcendental, consciously conceived, having for its basis a reality sorrowful in itself. Our pessimism comes naturally; it is emotional, not metaphysical; corresponds to a sadness caused by our terrible and limited natural surroundings pressing down on us, confining us, limiting us.

In the most simple poems of Gabriela Mistral we find that tendency and that sadness. Take for example her poem:

"La Lluvia Lenta" ("The Slow Rain")[1]

Esta agua medrosa y triste,
como un niño que padece,
antes de tocar la tierra
desfallece

Quieto el árbol, quieto el viento,
¡y en el silencio estupendo,
este fino llanto amargo
cayendo!

El cielo es como un inmenso
corazón que se abre, amargo.
No llueve: es un sangrar lento
y largo.

Dentro del hogar, los hombres
no sienten esta amargura,
este envío de agua triste
de la altura.

Este largo y fatigante
descender de aguas vencidas,
hacia la tierra yacente
y transida.

Bajando está el agua inerte,
callada como un ensueño,
como las criaturas leves
de los sueños.

Llueve . . . y como un chacal trágico
la noche acecha en la sierra.
¿Qué va a surgir, en la sombra,
de la Tierra?

¿Dormireis, mientras afuera
cae, sufriendo, esta agua inerte,
esta agua letal, hermana
de la Muerte?

Gabriela Mistral often likes to explain poetically the mysteries of things. In one of her prose poems she says:

"Lo Feo" ("Ugliness")

You have not unraveled the enigma of ugliness. You do not know why the Lord and Master of the lilies of the field permits the snake in the fields and the toad in the well. He permits them. He allows them to cross over the dewy moss.

With ugliness matter is weeping; I have heard its moan. Look upon sorrow and embrace it. Love the spider and the beetle as sorrowful because they do not, as the rose does, possess the gift of felicity. Love them because they are a deluded aspiration for beauty, an unheard desire for perfection. They are like one of your days, wasted and wretched in spite of you. Love them because they do not remind us of God, nor do they make us think of His beloved countenance.

Have a lively sympathy for those that seek, so intensely with tremendous longing, the beauty that will not come. The spider, with its enormous belly, dreams of ideals in its delicate web, and the beetle exudes a moisture over its black loins in order to attain by a trick a fugitive brilliance.

In another prose poem, one of her most beautiful monologues, she gives Christian counsel on the humility we ought to have in our actions, in our life. It is no doubt one of her most moving compositions:

"A Un Sembrador" ("To a Sower")

Sow without looking upon the earth where the seed falls. You are lost if you turn to the countenances of the others. Your glance inviting their reply will strike them as an invitation to praise you and even if they agree you are right, they will refuse to make this reply out of pride. Give your word and follow eagerly without turning your head. When they see you have gone some distance, they will accept your seed; perhaps they will kiss it tenderly and carry it to their hearts.

Don't stamp your portrait on the metal of your doctrine. That will deprive you of the love of the selfish ones and the selfish are the world.

Speak to your brethren in the shadows of the late afternoon in order to obscure your countenance and disguise your voice to the point that it is indistinguishable from any other voice. Make yourself forgotten, make yourself forgotten. . . . Do as the branch that does not keep any trace of the fruit that it allows to fall to the ground.

Toward the most business-like, those who claim to be least interested in dreams, let them know the infinite value of a dream and refrain from aggrandizing him who dreamed it.

Do as the father did who forgave his enemy on surprising him in the act of embracing his son. Suffer yourself to be embraced in your marvelous vision of redemption. Regard it in silence and smile. . . .

Let the sacred joy of entering into thought be sufficient for you; let the solitary and divine savor of its infinite sweetness suffice for you. It is a mystery in which God and your soul are present. Shall you not surrender to that tremendous witness? Knowing once you have possessed it you will not forget.

God also maintains that modest silence because. He is the Humble One. He has poured forth His creatures and the beauty of things through hills and valleys, silently, with less noise than the grass makes in growing. Let the lovers of things come and regard them, get to know them, become enraptured with them, tenderly holding them close. Never give your vision a name. It is silent, silent and it smiles.

Many of these poems equal and even surpass the prose poems of Tagore. There is in South American poetry a deeper Christian sentiment, a more profound invocation to God, as Lord of the universe and Master of souls. There never flourishes in her poems the strain of pantheism that the Orientals bring to all their compositions.

Gabriela Mistral in all her poems conceals or manifests a universal maternal instinct for children, the poor and the unfortunate. That spiritual maternity comes from the purity of her ideal. Solitude in her interior life impels her that more profoundly toward communion with all her kind, with humanity, with all created beings, with God. And in God are joined and perfected all desires.

Her apostolate, aside from that of teaching, took her to Mexico where she concerned herself with the problem of the Indian. There she understood the soul of our America, its secret and real foundation; the Indian serves as the racial basis whence came, upon intermingling with the Spaniards, our Ibero-American race. Together with Vasconcelos she struggled to incorporate the Indian into the civilization of Spain.

In these terrible times the voice of Gabriela Mistral has allowed itself to be raised in favor of democracy. With her wide moral authority she has been speaking and writing on the need of defending liberty. She has recently expressed these sentiments clearly and finally, making an appeal to the conscience of youth to become Christian and repel the totalitarian dangers that menace South America from within. I had the honor of addressing her in a message that appeared in the Chilean review, *Hoy*, over a month ago, congratulating her on her courageous declarations. In that message I demonstrated that our whole tradition has always been converging toward liberty, toward social democracy. At this hour, I told her, we must join with the United States of America to protect our spiritual heritage. Gabriela Mistral regards America as the world of the future and desires continental solidarity in order to work and struggle for the formation of a society more like the Kingdom of God. In order to attain this destiny we must today disabuse ourselves of the fatalistic and economic conception of the modern world in order to transform it into an ordered conception of scientific and cultural disciplines based on more universal justice and more perfect love.

With these few words I have sought to present Gabriela Mistral to the American public. South America now produces great writers, has arrived at a certain cultural maturity that is beginning to take on universal lineaments. Especially in poetry we have given Spanish literature values of the first rank. Names such as those of Pablo Neruda, Leopoldo Lugones and others follow the splendid tradition of Rubén Darío, Herrera y Reissig, Amado Nervo; they are thrusting beyond our frontiers to be appreciated in Europe and other quarters of the globe. Gabriela Mistral is today the most prominent figure in our culture.

Notes

1. That tearful and sad water, like a suffering child, before reaching the earth languishes. Tranquil the tree, tranquil the wind and in the fearful silence that fine rain sorrowfully falling. The sky is like a huge heart that opens in sadness. It is not rain: it is a long slow bleeding. Inside the house men do not feel this sadness, that flood of sorrowful water from above. That long and tiring descent of conquered waters leaves the earth flattened and exhausted. The mass of water is falling, silently as a dream, as the fragile creatures of dreams. It rains . . . and like the tragic figure of a jackal, the night lies in wait on the mountain ridge. What will come forth in the darkness from the earth? Will you sleep on while outside there is falling sorrowfully that lifeless water, that lethal water, sister of death?

H. J. Gullberg (essay date 1945)

SOURCE: "Nobel Prize Citation," in *Selected Poems of Gabriela Mistral*, translated by Langston Hughes, Indiana University Press, 1957, pp. 13–16.

[*Gullberg addresses a tribute to Mistral in the following citation from the Swedish Academy, awarding her the Nobel Prize for Literature.*]

The tears of a mother once caused an entire language disdained by polite society to retrieve its nobility and come into its glory through the power of poetry. It is said that the first of two poets to bear the name of the wind of the Mediterranean, Mistral, while still a student, by having written his first verses in French, caused his mother to weep a flood of tears. She was an untutored peasant of Languedoc who did not understand such purity of language. It was then that her son decided to write henceforth in Provençal, his mother tongue. He wrote *Mireio* which recounts the love of a pretty little peasant woman for a poor artisan, a poem from which the perfume of the earth in flower rises. . . . In this way the old language of the troubadours became again the language of poetry. The Nobel Prize for Literature in 1904 brought this event to the attention of the entire world. Ten years later the poet of *Mireio* died.

The same year that World War II began, at the other end of the world among the flowers of Santiago de Chile, a new Mistral came to attention and was awarded the same Prize for her poems of love dedicated to death.

The story of Gabriela Mistral is so well known among the peoples of South America that in going from country to country she has become almost a legend. And now, from the crests of the Cordilleras of the Andes and across the vastnesses of the Atlantic, she has at last come to us that we might recognize her anew in this room, and here she is.

In a little village in the Valley of the Elqui River a few decades ago, a young school teacher was born who was called Lucila Godoy y Alcayaga. Godoy was her father's name, Alcayaga that of her mother, one or the other being of Basque origin. Her father, who was a teacher, improvised verses with facility. This talent in him seemed to be related to that restlessness and instability ascribed to poets. He deserted his family while his daughter, for whom he had made a little garden, was still an infant. Her pretty mother, who was to live a long time, has reported that she often came across her small daughter deep in conversation with the birds and flowers of the garden. According to one version of the story, she was dismissed from school. She was evidently considered not gifted enough to have hours of instruction wasted upon her. She learned through self-instruction, and eventually she became a teacher in the little village of Cantera. It was there, at the age of twenty, that her destiny was fulfilled. A railroad man worked in the same village, and a passionate love affair developed between them.

We know little of their story. We are cognizant only that he betrayed her. One day in November, 1909, putting a bullet through his temple, he killed himself. The young woman became disconsolate. Like Job, she cried aloud to the skies that had allowed this to happen. From that valley lost in the barren, burning mountains of Chile came a voice that men heard far and near. A banal tragedy of every day life lost its private character and became a part of world literature. It was then that Lucila Godoy y Alcayaga became Gabriela Mistral. The provincial little school teacher, this young colleague of Miss Lagerlöf of Marbacka, was to become the spiritual queen of all Latin America.

As these poems written as a memorial to death became connected with the name of a new poet, the somber and passionate verses of Gabriela Mistral began to spread throughout all South America. However, it was not until 1922 that she published in New York her greatest collection of poems, ***Desolacion, (Despair).*** These are the tears of a mother that fall upon a book and, in the fifteenth poem, tears that flow over the son of death, a son that never was born.

A son, a son, a son! I wanted a son of yours
and mine, in those distant days of burning bliss
when my bones would tremble at your least murmur
and my brow would glow with a radiant mist.

I said *a son*, as a tree in spring
lifts its branches yearning toward the skies,
a son with innocent mien and anxious mouth,
and wondering, wide and Christ-like eyes.

His arms like a garland entwine around my neck,
the fertile river of my life is within him pent,
and from the depths of my being over all the hills
a sweet perfume spreads its gentle scent.

We look as we pass at a mother big with child,
whose lips are trembling and whose eyes are a prayer.
When deep in love we walk through the crowd,
the wonder of a babe's sweet eyes makes us stare.
. . .

Gabriela Mistral shared her maternal love with the children whom she taught. It was for them that she wrote those simple songs and those rounds collected in Madrid in 1924 under the title, ***Tenura, (Tenderness).*** Once in her honor four thousand Mexican children sang her rounds. Gabriela Mistral became the poet of motherhood by adoption.

It was not until 1938 in Buenos Aires that, for the benefit of the young victims of the Spanish Civil War, her third great collection, ***Tala***, appeared—a title which might be translated as ***Devastation*** but which also means a children's game. In contrast with the pathetic mood of ***Desolacion, Tala*** exhales the cosmic calm that envelops the South American earth whose perfume reaches unto us. We find ourselves anew in the garden, hear anew her intimate conversations with nature and with things. Through a curious mixture of holy hymns and naïve songs for children, of poems about bread and wine, salt, wheat, water—this water that one might very well bend to the needs of thirsty men—sing the primitive needs of human life.

From her maternal hand this poet offers us her potion, which has the savor of earth and which quenches the thirst of the heart. It is a part of that source that flowed from the Isles of Greece for Sappho, and for Gabriela Mistral in the valley of the Elqui, the source of poetry that never dries up on the earth.

Gabriela Mistral, you have made a very long voyage in order to hear so short a speech. Within a few minutes I have related for the countrymen of Selma Lagerlöf, as if it were a story, the amazing journey that has taken you from the desk of a school mistress to the throne of poetry. It is to render homage to the riches of Spanish American literature that we address ourselves today especially to its queen, the poet of ***Desolacion***, who has become the great singer of mercy and motherhood. From the hands of her Royal Majesty, I beg you to receive the Nobel Prize for Literature which the Swedish Academy awards you.

Sidonia Carmen Rosenbaum (essay date 1945)

SOURCE: "Gabriela Mistral," in *Modern Women Poets of Spanish America*, Hispanic Institute in the United States, 1945, pp. 171–203.

[*In the following essay, Rosenbaum examines the appearance and development of such characteristic themes as passion, violence, asceticism, materialism, and pan-Americanism in Mistral's poetry.*]

The year that so tragically cut short the career of Delmira Agustini—1914—was to introduce to the Spanish American world of letters another poetess of first rank: the Chilean, Gabriela Mistral. Her best known poems, sprung, most of them, from a common fount of pain (the death, by suicide, of her lover), of ***Desolation***—as her first book is called—are simpler in form than the tortuous ones of Delmira. But they disclose cavernous depths, and their intensity sounds the very pith of human emotion, especially in those where—as in the somber ones that tell of the lover's self-inflicted death—she speaks of "the ineffable" with bland and almost disconcerting serenity and casualness.

1. Life and Works

Lucila Godoy Alcayaga—as she was called before she adopted that pseudonym which has now become so famous—was born in the little town of Vicuña, in the fertile and benign valley of Elqui, in 1889. Her father, don Jerónimo Godoy Villanueva, by profession a rural schoolmaster, by vocation a poet of somewhat mediocre talents, left his home—never to return—when Lucila was three years old. Yet, although she had been so early deprived of his "paternal counsel and care," she always harbored for him a deep filial affection born, perhaps, of a certain similarity of interests and a genuine admiration for that "extraordinary man" who "knew too many things" . . .[1]

Among the poems he dedicated to his daughter—and which she remembers "with sweetness and melancholy"—is the following (rather innocuous) cradle-song that might have inspired her to essay that type of composition which is one of her favorites, and in which she has proved so successful:

Duérmete, Lucila, que el mundo está en calma,
Ni el cordero brinca ni la oveja bala.
Duérmete, Lucila, que cuidan de vos
En tu cuna un ángel, en el cielo Dios.

Duérmete, Lucila, ojitos de cielo,
Mira que tu madre también tiene sueño.
Angel de la Guarda, házmela dormir
Para que a su madre no la haga sufrir.

Angel de la Guarda, cuídame a este lirio
Que mañana al alba rezará conmigo.
Duérmete, niñita, duérmete por Dios,
Que si no te duermes me enojo con vos.[2]

Her father's bent for "a walking knowledge of geography" left the child Lucila entirely under the care of her mother, doña Petronila Alcayaga, "a very handsome and delicate woman," with a "soft and pathetic voice" (to whom Gabriela dedicated some of her most tender pages), and of her maternal half-sister, Emelina Molina Alcayaga ("mi santa hermana Emelina"), who became a rural schoolteacher about the time Lucila was born. And so the teaching profession that was to become the guiding motive of her life, and the poetic gift that has made her unique in Spanish American letters, were already present, in one form or another, in her immediate family.

She spent the first twelve years of her life among peasants. And she has always maintained a close contact—and spiritual affinity—with these people of the soil. She likes to speak of her "rurality" and of her humble origin: "vengo de campesinos y soy uno de ellos". Her work abounds in rural allusions, and a certain earthiness pervades everything that springs from her pen. Without the benefit of "guidance," and entirely devoid of formal training, this quiet, sensitive and sad child early began to feed her eager mind with random reading. While looking over the scant resources she had at hand, she came upon some poems of her father's—"the first I ever read"—which fired her imagination and started her, at the age of fifteen, upon the literary road she has by now so long and well traversed. Her first compositions were in prose—a mellow prose, well grounded in the long-faltering but still prevalent romantic tradition, and surcharged with "poetic" phrases, with baroque imagery and with sadness. Her poems, which flowed from her dolorous soul almost simultaneously, follow the same stylistic, mental and emotional patterns. These early contributions of Lucila Godoy were published in the local press: *El Coquimbo* and *La Voz de Elqui.*

The sad, the grief-filled note—which in her early compositions seems overworked, and somewhat of a pose—becomes tonic, and characteristic of almost all her poems, for very early in life she knew pain to be "the only reality." In a letter written to a friend when she was about sixteen, she says: "There is something in my being which engenders bitterness; there is a secret hand which filters gall into my heart, even though happiness surrounds me." And the same thought recurs in her first articles and poems which speak of grief as the genial lyre which intones the most sublime of songs.

"Flores negras," written in 1905 for the album of "Lolo," is a typical adolescent poem of disillusionment, anguish, despair, and has little in it to forecast the advent of the great poetess of a decade later:

Yo no puedo cantar porque no brota
El verso ya de mi alma entristecida.
¿Quieres que vibre el harpa que está rota?
¿Quieres que cante el alma que está herida?

Ya no es el tiempo que el papel dejaba
Un reguero de esencias y de amor,
Cuando en mis pobres versos derramaba
Las hojas de la flor de mi ilusión.

Murió la inspiración, tan sólo el llanto
Lleva a mi alma la miel del sentimiento,
Y, si llega a entonar un triste canto,
Es aquel del sollozo y del lamento.

. . . . .

Yo que tan sólo sé llorar, no dejo
Sino flores marchitas en mi senda,
Y mis canciones, de dolor reflejo,
¿Podrán, dime, formarte alguna ofrenda?

Otoño, ruina, angustias y cenizas
Son los sueños que viven en mi mente.
¿Los juncos mil? Se los llevó la brisa,
¿La idea? Se agotó como una fuente.

Por eso pido que jamás repases,
Estas estrofas que son flores negras,
Sin perfume, sin vida, porque nacen
En el valle otoñal de mi alma enferma.[3]

Gabriela wisely eliminated these early puerile efforts (which were born "in the autumnal valley" of her "sick soul") from her books, and gave for publication only those that did not mar the general superior tone of her work.

But Gabriela Mistral is not exclusively a writer. She is, above all, a teacher[4]—"the rural teacher" personified. She was only fifteen when, entirely untaught, she began her didactic career which was to terminate some twenty years later when she was given a pension by the Chilean government in recognition of her work at home and abroad. She started as an assistant in a rural school in La Compañía (Coquimbo) and later became a teacher in several of the primary schools in near-by provinces and towns. About 1908 she sought admittance to the Normal School of La Serena. But the opposition was strong. Because of her writings and strange ways (she "smoked a great deal" and was, moreover, adjudged a girl "with pagan ideas"), she was considered somewhat of a radical. Some three years later, however, in spite of her continued lack of formal training—and through the intercession of her good friend, the future president of Chile, don Pedro Aguirre Cerda—she was considered eligible to teach in the secondary schools. In this capacity she served, with distinction, in the Liceos of Traiguén, Antofagasta and Los Andes. Seven years later she was made Director of the Liceo of Punta Arenas (1918–1920), and then of those of Temuco (1920–1921) and Santiago (1921–1922).

It was at the beginning of this spectacular rise, at Coquimbo, that Lucila met Romelio Ureta, the young man who was so tragically responsible for the flowering and crystallization of her great literary career. He was a handsome railroad employee. It is said that, through no fault of his own—to help "a friend in need"—he was prompted to "borrow" some of the company's funds with the intent of returning them. But it evolved into the familiar story: unable to replace the amount before the "borrowing" could be detected, and abandoned in his plight by his "friend," he sought escape in suicide—"shattering his temples like delicate glass." The echo of that shot—says Soiza Reilly[5]—was "Gabriela Mistral" . . .

In 1914, five years later, a poetic tournament was to take place in Santiago—undoubtedly to stimulate the somewhat stagnant Chilean poetic talent. Aspiring poets sent their contributions from all parts of the country. But the first prize was awarded to a timid rural school teacher for her powerful and stirring **"Sonnets of Death."** With characteristic modesty she refused to be present at the award. (But now she admits that she, silent and unnoticed, watched her triumph from an anonymous seat in the gallery).

Because of her talent in handling difficult rural teaching problems, and because of her literary work—which daily became more esteemed—her name had by now crossed the local, and even national, limits. And in 1922 she was invited to collaborate in the Rural Education Reform which José Vasconcelos was instituting in Mexico. She remained in that country for two years.

From then on, her career becomes international in character. In 1924 she sets out for her first trip abroad and visits the United States, France and Spain. Her government later sends her to Geneva as its representative to the Committee of Intellectual Cooperation of the League of Nations. In 1928 she forms part of the administrative council of the Cinematographic Educational Institute founded in Rome. Back from Europe, she comes again to the United States as visiting professor at Columbia University and at Vassar and Middlebury Colleges. She is later given, successively, the Chilean consulship in Naples, Madrid, Lisbon, and finally Nice. At present (1945) she is the cultural attachée of her country's embassy in Rio de Janeiro.

In 1937 she was sent by the Chilean government on a cultural mission to most of the countries of Spanish America where she was received with great acclaim and fervor. In 1945 she received the highest international recognition when she was awarded the Nobel Prize for Literature.

It was in 1914 that "Gabriela Mistral" came into being. Until then her compositions had always borne the signature that revealed her dual Basque ancestry: Lucila *Godoy Alcayaga.* There has been some disagreement as to the origin of the pseudonym of this "mestiza de vasca"—as she likes to call herself. Some, like Silva Castro,[6] attribute it to her admiration for the Provençal poet Frédéric Mistral whom she mentions among her favorites in her poem **"Mis libros"**; while others—including Figueroa[7]—more rightly state that it stems from the name sailors give to the strong wind that blows in the Mediterranean: *maestral, minstral* or *mistral.* Mañach,[8] saying that she synthesizes the spiritual and the material, sees that fusion in her pen-name: "*Gabriela:* angelic annunciation, presence of the spirit; and *Mistral*: warm breath of the earth" . . .

From the day that the poet Víctor Domingo Silva read her **"Sonnets of Death"** at the Juegos Florales in Gabriela's "absence," her name triumphantly resounded throughout the nation. Anthologies and other publications readily sought her collaboration. But as yet no book of hers had appeared.

In 1921, Professor Federico de Onís, of Columbia University, made her the subject of a lecture which he gave in the Instituto de las Españas. His audience, which was composed largely of North American teachers of Spanish, was so impressed by the depth and haunting beauty of her poems, with which Professor de Onís punctuated his critical exposition, that it was eager to become better acquainted with the work of this extraordinary woman—herself a teacher. When it was learned that they had never been published in book form, the idea of collecting these poems was born. Thus, her first book, ***Desolación***, was published in 1922, not in her native Chile, but in the United States where her admirers have since become legion, and where many of her poems have appeared in translation.

A year later, a second edition, with slight modifications and additions, appeared in Chile, with a new prologue by Pedro Prado. This was followed, in 1926, by another (with some variations and omissions) whose value was enhanced by a penetrating study of the poetess by the eminent Chilean critic *Alone* (Hernán Díaz Arrieta).

The New York edition of ***Desolación*** was to give rise to a somewhat steady flow of publications—although most of them were merely to reproduce, at least in part, compositions already included in the various editions of her first book. In 1923 she published an anthology, *Lecturas para mujeres*, which she compiled during her sojourn in Mexico. It contains, among countless compositions in prose and verse by outstanding writers of the world, many of her own. That same year the editorial house Cervantes of Barcelona published a selection of her poems in volume LXV of its series *Las mejores poesías (líricas) de los mejores poetas.* In 1924 her children's songs—most of which were already familiar to the readers of ***Desolación***—appeared, also in Barcelona, under the title ***Ternura.***

Her most recent book is another poetic collection: ***Tala*** (1938), which, like ***Desolación***, was also born "of a circumstance."[9] In 1941 there appeared an *Antología*—under the imprint of the Empresa Editora Zig-Zag of Santiago—which contains a generous selection, by the author, of the preferred poems of her two books: ***Desolación*** and ***Tala.***

Gabriela Mistral's prose is as important as her verse. It consists of numerous articles[10] published in the outstanding periodicals in the Spanish language. These have never appeared in book form. Written in a style that is vigorous, direct, succinct, passionate, they cover a wide and heterogeneous range, as do her interests: history, geography, sociology, literature, politics, life in general. But her main concern is, and has always been, Latin America. And it is its heart-beat that she sounds whether she is speaking of it in general, or of any one specific country: Puerto Rico, Ecuador, Mexico, her native Chile; whether she is describing the Andes, the pampas, the Mexican *maguey*, the Chilean mining lands; whether she is eulogizing its writers, its statesmen, its patriots; or commenting on its language, its peoples, its myths, its native crafts, its traditions, its heritage.

This Americanism of hers is lost—outwardly—in ***Desolación*** where, with the exception of a dreary and limited Chilean landscape, the only spectacle and climate seen and felt are those of her own bitter, ardent, bleeding soul. But in ***Tala***, America—Indoamerica—reappears in all its strength, its glory and its color.

Of the women poets whom we are studying, Gabriela Mistral is the most cosmopolitan, the best known internationally. She is the only one who, besides the general recognition as a poetess and writer, has attained that of being regarded as the spiritual mentor of the Spanish American world in a degree rarely equaled before by any man and never by a woman.

Jorge Mañach best defines this poetess in the title of his warm and penetrating essay: "Gabriela: alma y tierra."[11] For she is, indeed, a rare, an extraordinary example of the difficult and not always felicitous wedding of the spiritual and the material, of the abstract and the concrete, of "soul and earth" . . . In her work a perfect blending is achieved, however, not in the conceptual or stylistic sense which results in ideologic or formal antithesis, but in a manner which transcends the artistic. For it is born of a faithful reflection of her personality and manner. Her mind elaborates trenchant thoughts—of almost divine essence—which her pen clothes in the most natural, the most current, the most casual, the most soil-rooted, the most familiar of expressive garb. And this in Gabriela is not forced, nor rhetorical. For it springs directly from her need of close contact with the earth, with reality, with the material, even when expressing the conceptual and the abstract. Her thoughts, therefore, however winged and abstruse, are always earth-bound by her expression which, like her manner, is characterized by its directness, its lack of flourish or ostentation, its homespun quality.

But this corporeality is, as we have said, merely formal; for there is no one further removed from the material than she. Her tastes, in all ways, are ascetic; the mundane foibles and adornments, and all the wiles of feminine allure, hold no meaning for her. She is utterly lacking in that narcissism so characteristic of other women poets—notably Juana de Ibarbourou. When she speaks of herself—which is seldom—she is prone to stress her plainness (which only love can turn to beauty). She never expresses any delight in the materialistic, sensual side of life; no zest in its pleasures. And the thought of death, merely as a devastator of all that is ephemeral or deteriorative, does not haunt or perturb her. Her conception of love is never carnal, for she knows that the flesh is perishable and transitory. The soul alone harbors the all-essential. And the essence of the kiss is there, not on the lips. Therefore death, the disintegrator of all matter, is not—cannot be—the end of love. She is confident that, within the earth, the lover waits for her, unchanged in spirit, although bereft of flesh and of desires; and that when, the weary journey over, she finally takes her place beside him, they will know one another again, and talk for an eternity:

Sentirás que a tu lado cavan briosamente,
Que otra dormida llega a la quieta ciudad.
Esperaré que me bayan cubierto totalmente . . .
¡Y después hablaremos por una eternidad!

(**"Los sonetos de la muerte"**, II)[12]

Delmira Agustini was, stylistically, still dominated by the sumptuous—and ofttimes fatuous—elegance and ornateness of the Modernists. Gabriela Mistral, although she also underwent the modernist influence, is typical of the sober, realistic, more prosaic reaction. Her poems do not exhibit any of the princely and palatial attributes of the Rubendarian school: its pearls, its diamonds, rubies; its agates, emeralds and marbles; its gardens, fountains, parks; its roses, its swans, its doves. And, rather than the mythical Olympian fields, her feet tread the solid ground. They feel beneath them the earth, the soil, "the common clay." Instead of the intoxicating, sensuous waves of incense, of the voluptuous and exotic perfumes, she breathes the clear, pure, clean, natural rural air. And her eyes do not feast themselves on impossible, unattainable, celestial, super-human or glittering visions, but on "the gold and sweetness of wheat," on "sacred roads," on "the green handkerchief" of the trees. Her dictum—so felicitously realized in her life and in her work—has always been: "Give me simplicity, and . . . profundity."

Definite—although widely heterogeneous—influences have been ascribed to her work. She herself has, verbally and in writing, hailed many "masters": . . . el arte me fué revelado en la persona de un libro . . . de aquél que es mi Maestro y al que profeso una admiración fanática, un culto ciego . . .: Vargas Vila";[13] "Es agradecimiento todo en mi amor de Martí, agradecimiento del escritor que es el Maestro americano más ostensible en mi obra";[14] "Mis maestros en el arte para regir la vida: la Biblia, el Dante, Tagore y los rusos".[15] And in a poem, **"Mis libros"**,[16] she has given what one might call a sentimental bibliography: her favorite writers and books—all of which have been viewed as possible sources:

¡Biblia, mi noble Biblia, panorama estupendo,
En donde se quedaron mis ojos largamente,
Tienes sobre los Salmos como lavas hirvientes
Y en su río de fuego mi corazón enciendo.

. . . . .

Antes que tú me moriré: y mi espíritu
En su empeño tenaz,
Sentándose a las puertas de la muerte,
Allí te esperará.

. . . . .

Allí donde el sepulcro que se cierra
Abre una eternidad . . .
Todo cuanto los dos hemos callado
Lo tenemos que hablar!
Después de ti, tan sólo, me traspasó los huesos
Con su ancho alarido, el sumo Florentino.
A su voz todavía como un junco me inclino;
Por su rojez de infierno fantástica atravieso.

Y para refrescar en musgos con rocío
La boca requemada en las llamas dantescas,
Busqué las Florecillas de Asís, las siempre frescas
¡Y en esas felpas dulces se quedó el pecho mío!

. . . . .

Poema de Mistral, olor a surco abierto
Que huele en las mañanas, yo te aspiré embriagada!
Vi a Mireya exprimir la fruta ensangrentada
Del amor y correr por al atroz desierto.

Te recuerdo también, deshecha de dulzuras,
Verso de Amado Nervo, con pecho de paloma,
Que me hiciste más suave la línea de la loma,
Cuando yo te leía en mis mañanas puras.

Stylistic similarities and spiritual affinities have been established between this autochthonous Chilean poetess and the Spanish writers of the Golden Age—notably the mystics for their lyric fervor, their expressive vigor, and their verbal "concretion" of the spiritual—, Omar Kháyyám, Victor Hugo, Guerra Junqueiro, Walt Whitman, Rubén Darío, Unamuno, Amado Nervo, Juan Ramón Jiménez, Romain Rolland, Ada Negri . . . But in spite of all these palpable or implied sources of inspiration, her work—both prose and verse—has a marked and unmistakable stamp. For although, especially in the earlier stages, she may have come under the preponderant influence of one writer or another, the very fact that these have been so dissimilar—Vargas Vila, Martí, Tagore—has made her style (which she has gleaned and fashioned from such wide, diverse, and almost contradictory sources) a singular, distinct, and wholly personal one.

2. Analysis of "Desolación"

The title ***Desolación*** applies aptly only to a section of the book—"Dolor"—for not all the compositions included in it are the bitter fruit of that desolation into which the lover's death plunged her. There are poems which disclose a deeply religious nature; poems of rich Biblical flavor; poems that reveal the depth of an overpowering, but frustrated, maternal feeling; children's poems; poems that are inspired by her profession; and, finally, those that spring directly from that tragedy that made her feel that it was her tortured heart that bled its red into the sunsets . . . The book closes with a section of "Prose" which contains the "Teacher's Prayer," the "Poems of the Mothers," the "Motifs of the Clay," the "Poems of Ecstasy," and other lyrical non-poetic compositions including some children's tales such as "Why the reeds are hollow," "Why the roses have thorns," etc. At the end there is a "Voto" in which the author says: "God forgive this bitter book . . . In these hundred poems there lies bleeding a past in which the song became blood-drenched to relieve me" . . .

Love

Tu eres un vaso vaciado. Te volcó un grande amor y ya no te vuelves a colmar más . . .

In the pages of ***Desolación*** she recalls with nostalgic and live passion all the phases of that love which to her was never sensual gratification—never ecstasy, nor exhilaration, nor joy. For love, as she knew it, was "a bitter exercise." It was not merely that "stubborn, weary sheaf" that is the body, but a wind or breath of God that cuts deep into the "racemes" of the flesh. "*It's what is in the kiss*"—she says—"*not on the lips.*" And that is why she tells the lover not to touch her—expecting to find love in her arms, her mouth, her neck . . . For one day all this will vanish; her body will disintegrate, and she whom he kissed will lie—without lips—in the moist ground (**"Intima"**).

She looks upon love, one might say, as a religion—as something almost tragically serious; something one enters into everlastingly—not "until death do us part," but on to eternity. Death severs the mortal bonds, but love lives on to be resumed beyond this life in "the quiet city" . . . And because love holds so vital a meaning for her; because she fears she may some day lose that which she now considers an inalienable part of herself, she loves with passion, with an overbearing feeling of possession, of ownership—which is deemed more characteristic of man than of woman. In this she is the antithesis of Juana de Ibarbourou and other poetesses who, like her, are the quintessence of femininity in their "weakness," in their surrender, in their whims and irrationalities in love. Gabriela is demanding—domineering. She does not plead with the man to be faithful; she threatens him with heavenly wrath—and with vengeance—if he breaks the sacred tie that binds them. She makes God her conspirator in this, implying that He does not want the lover to live without her. This implication that his faithfulness is *demanded* by an exigent God is poignantly expressed in her powerful poem, **"Dios lo quiere"**:

Dios no quiere que tú tengas
Sol, si conmigo no marchas.
Dios no quiere que tú bebas
Si yo no tiemblo en tu agua.
No consiente que tú duermas
Sino en mi trenza ahuecada

(*D*,[17] 107)

From the day she saw "him" pass along the road—a light song upon his "careless mouth"—she felt the lash of love, and knew that, perhaps, henceforth her face would be bathed in tears; for since she (who had so long walked alone) saw him cross her path, God had clothed her in pain:

> Iba sola y no temía;
> Con hambre y sed no lloraba;
> Desde que lo vi cruzar,
> Mi Dios me vistió de llagas
>
> (*D*, 98)

She knew the torturing allure of love, its tyranny, and its inevitability. For once one comes under its spell, one cannot escape it—one has to hearken to it, harbor it, believe in it, although one may sense, as she did, that all that leads to death (**"Amo amor"**).

And because the love she felt was so overpowering, so intense, it was ineffable—she could not trust its utterance to the obscure words of man. Moreover, it came from so deep within that its "burning torrent" died before it reached the throat. The excruciating pain of that forced silence was more atrocious to bear, she thought, than death . . . (**"El amor que calla"**).

She who had been ashamed of her sad mouth, her broken voice, her rough, coarse knees, was transfigured and made beautiful by the lover's glance and by his kiss (**"Vergüenza"**). Yet she, a beggar now turned queen, lived in constant fear of his leaving her, and would ask—even in dreams—if he were still with her:

> Como soy reina y fuí mendiga, ahora
> Vivo en puro temblor de que me dejes,
> Y te pregunto, pálida, a cada hora:
> "¿Estás conmigo aún? ¡Ay! no te alejes!"
>
> Quisiera hacer las marchas sonriendo
> Y confiando, ahora que has venido;
> Pero hasta en el dormir estoy temiendo
> Y pregunto entre sueños: "¿No te has ido?"
>
> (*D*, 109)

Her love delved its way so deep, became so passionate, so desperate, that she was seized with a Medean jealousy which would not tolerate the least transgression on the lover's part. And even as the world had become more beautiful since love "pierced" them with its fragrance, so now "the earth would cast forth snakes"—she warned him—if his soul betrayed her soul. The kiss that he gave another would, inevitably, reach her ears; the caves would re-echo his perfidious words to her; and the clouds would mirror above her the face of her whom he loved. "Go forth like a thief to kiss her"—she said—"but when you lift up her head, you will find my tear-stained face." Even death could not free him from the dire retribution of her wrath: for ten years he would lie beneath the earth, with hands outstretched, to receive her scalding tears:

> Pero te va a brotar víboras
> La tierra si vendes mi alma;
>
> . . . . .
>
> Beso que tu boca entregue
> A mis oídos alcanza,
> Porque las grutas profundas
> Me devuelven tus palabras.
> El polvo de los senderos
> Guarda el olor de tus plantas
> Y oteándolo, como un ciervo,
> Te sigo por las montañas . . .
>
> A la que tú ames, las nubes
> La pintan sobre mi casa.
> Vé cual ladrón a besarla
> De la tierra en las entrañas;
> Mas, cuando el rostro le alces,
> Hallas mi cara con lágrimas
>
> (*D*, 107)

But her fears were founded in truth. And when she saw him pass by "with another" (**"Balada"**), she asked God what reason there was now for her to be upon the "pallid earth" (**"Extasis"**). In her maddening wrath against this other Judas ("me vendió el que besó mi mejilla"), she fervently prayed the Lord to snatch the faithless one from the clutches of those "fatal hands," or to sink him in "the long sleep" which He alone knows how to give (**"Sonetos de la muerte"**, III) . . .

When the lover himself broke "the tremendous pact" and died without having awaited God's signal; when he, voluntarily, stayed "the rosy bark of his living," she at first could not grasp the significance of that dire meaning. And forgetting that his "light foot" had now turned to ashes, she again went to their usual meeting-place:

> Yo me olvidé que se hizo
> Ceniza tu pie ligero,
> Y, como en los buenos tiempos,
> Salí a encontrate al sendero
>
> (*D*, 123)

Thoughts of him became an obsession, and she constantly saw his image: he touched her in the night-dew, bled in the sunsets, looked for her in the moonbeams:

> Me toca en el relente;
> Se sangra en los ocasos;
> Me busca con el rayo
> De luna, por los antros
>
> (*D*, 125)

Life became aimless and bitter—everything in her mouth acquired "a persistent taste of tears." And yet,—as she went along singing her "beautiful vengeance"—she had one consolation: no longer would his mouth know the shame of that kiss which "dripped concupiscence"; nor would the hand of any other woman dispute with her over his handful of bones! She longed to see him again—it mattered not where, she said, nor how:

. . . Volverlo a ver, no importa dónde,
En remansos de cielo, o en vórtice hervidor,
Bajo unas lunas plácidas o en cárdeno horror!

(*D*, 131)

—to wrap herself about his bleeding neck . . .

And although she was aware of the sin he perpetrated by taking his own life, she begged God to forgive him, calling Him "Father," for that word "tastes more of love."[18] He was her "all"—she told Him—in a passage vibrant with beauty and poignant simplicity: her glass of freshness, the honeycomb of her mouth, the lime of her bones, the sweet reason of her day, the chirping in her ear, the girdle of her dress! (**"El ruego"**). And she felt ashamed to live on in so cowardly a manner—for she neither went in search of him nor succeeded in forgetting (**"Coplas"**).

Yet gradually his image faded, and as she desperately, but vainly, "scratched" her wretched memory in an attempt to recover it, she felt that she was never more like a beggar than now—without the memory of him. For having his semblance was like having a child of his—like a fragrance emanating from her bones . . . But perhaps, she thought, it was not merely his image that she had lost, but her own soul on which she had once hewn his likeness like a wound (**"Coplas"**). Her "premature widowhood," as Rafael Estenger[19] aptly calls it, left her desolate—bereft of the two beings who would have made her life complete and rich: the husband and the potential son.

One of the qualities of Gabriela which distinguish her from most of the other women poets is her chastity. For she is one of the very few poetesses who view love soberly and purely. Perhaps the use of the words "esposo" and "hijo" lends a tone of propriety to her poems of love which are wholly lacking in that erotic abandon and carnal urge so characteristic of Delmira, for instance, for whom the body was "a divan of delight." And how different the connotation, in her poems, of the words *flesh, body, arms, hands, mouth, lips, tongue* . . . from that which they assume in the ardent and voluptuous verse of so many other poetesses.

Maternity

Una que amó, y cuyo amor pidió, al recibir el beso, la eternidad . . .

Her conception of love is, as we have said, profoundly religious and pure. Its purpose is not to appease desire, to satisfy carnal appetities, but soberly to give thought to the richest, the most precious, the most sacred heritage of woman: maternity.[20] That, as she says in the introduction to *Lecturas para mujeres*, is woman's only reason for being in this world:

Y sea profesionista, obrera, campesina o simple dama, su única razón de ser sobre el mundo es la maternidad, la material y la espiritual juntas, o la última en las mujeres que no tenemos hijos . . .

Sterility, therefore, is woman's greatest tragedy and shame:

La mujer que no mece un hijo en el regazo,
Cuyo calor y aroma alcance a sus entrañas,
Tiene una laxitud de mundo entre los brazos;
Todo su corazón congoja inmensa baña.

. . . . .

¡Y una mendiga grávida, cuyo seno florece
Cual la parva de Enero, de vergüenza la cubre!

(*D*, 18)

Yet woman is, instinctively, a mother. And she who was never to cradle a child in her own bosom; who was never to feel its "warmth and aroma" permeate the innermost fibers of her being; who was never to dissolve into tenderness for the fruit of her own womb, feels maternal towards all children.[21] That is why her profession has always been so sacred to her, for she feels that through it she fulfils, at least in part, the mission of all women: spiritual—if not physical—maternity. In her now famous "Teacher's prayer" she asks God to make her *more maternal than the mothers* so that she may "love and defend," as they do, those who are not flesh of her flesh . . .

The thought of her impotent motherhood recurs to torture her:

No espigará entre mis rodillas
Un niño rubio como mies

(*D*, 28)

Baldías del hijo, rompo
Mis rodillas desoladas

(*D*, 106)

but nowhere more tragically than in the first part of the **"Poema del hijo"**:[22]

¡Un hijo, un hijo, un hijo! Yo quise un hijo tuyo
Y mío, allá en los días del éxtasis ardiente,

. . . . .

Decía: ¡un hijo!, como el árbol conmovido
De primavera alarga sus yemas hacia el cielo.

Sus brazos en guirnalda a mi cuello trenzados;
El río de mi vida bajando hacia él, fecundo,
Y mis entrañas como perfume derramado
Ungiendo, en ese infante, las colinas del mundo.

Al cruzar una madre grávida, la miramos
Con los labios convulsos y los ojos de ruego,
Cuando en las multitudes con nuestro amor pasamos.
¡Y un niño de ojos dulces nos dejó como ciegos!

En las noches, insomne de dicha y de visiones,
La lujuria de fuego no descendió a mi lecho.
Para el que nacería vestido de canciones,
Yo extendía mi brazo, yo ahuecaba mi pecho . . .

El sol no parecíame, para bañarlo, intenso;
Mirándome, yo odié, por toscas, mis rodillas;

Mi corazón, confuso, temblaba al dón inmenso;
¡Y un llanto de humildad regaba mis mejillas!

(*D*, 138–139)

Yet, later, when the hope of maternity vanishes, she rationalizes that a child of hers might have had her "tired mouth," her "bitter heart," her "defeated voice"; that it might have been born with the lover's poisonous heart, his lips (which would have again abjured); that it might some day have said, with rancor, what she herself had inwardly said to her father: "Why has your flesh been fecund?" And so she blesses her fruitless womb, and is content to know that her hapless race has died within it . . .

But the maternal urge is so strong in her that she sees its reflection in every aspect of life, in all manifestations of nature. The earth itself is a woman with a child in her arms; the mountain, too, is a mother, and in the afternoons the fog plays about her shoulders and knees like a child; the tree is but a "sweet womb" that harbors nests; the open furrow, in its soft depths beneath the sun, is like an ardent cradle; the vine—like a newly-delivered mother—is fatigued from its abundant producing;[23] the rain is fearful and sad, like a suffering child. And even God is invested with maternal feelings as He sings His cradle-songs to that saintly "maestra rural" who gave herself so noiselessly to death:

Y en su Dios se ha dormido, como en cojín de luna;
Almohada de sus sienes, una constelación.[24]
Canta el Padre para ella sus canciones de cuna
¡Y la paz llueve largo sobre su corazón!

(*D*, 44)

She who saw her own dire love bring only bitterness and sorrow; she who had been often harsh and commanding, exigent and domineering, melts into maternal tenderness when he who "passed with another" and aroused her wrath and the desire for vengeance, lies defenseless, like a dolorous child—and no longer alluring—in the pallid sleep of death:

Te acostaré en la tierra soleada, con una
Dulcedumbre de madre para el hijo dormido,
Y la tierra ha de hacerse suavidades de cuna
Al recibir tu cuerpo de niño dolorido

(*D*, 118)

No book of hers has appeared without a section of cradle-songs. And although they never reach the intensity, the perfection and the depth of those poems in which she unveils the bleeding tragedy of her soul, they are, nonetheless, so tender and moving that another poetess, María Olimpia de Obaldía, herself a mother, asks her where she learned the rhythm of the cradle-song which she sings low, with the softness of moonlight:

¿Dónde aprendiste el ritmo de la canción de cuna
Que cantas quedamente, con suavidad de luna?

Death

Owing, undoubtedly, to the spiritual crisis which she had so recently suffered, she shows in ***Desolación*** a constant preoccupation with death; death which in her mind is so irrevocably linked with destiny—that "fatal mixture of blood and tears." It is the thought that *we have to die*, that we are but "flesh of the grave" that causes the Thinker in the initial poem of the book, **"El Pensador de Rodin,"** to twitch in bitter anguish. And no tree twisted by the sun in the plain—she tells us—, no lion of wounded flank, suffers the pain, the agony and the terror of this man who meditates on death:

Con el mentón caído sobre la mano ruda,
El Pensador se acuerda que es carne de la huesa,
Carne fatal, delante del destino desnuda,
Carne que odia la muerte, y tembló de belleza.

Y tembló de amor, toda su primavera ardiente,
Y ahora, al otoño, anégase de verdad y tristeza.
El "de morir tenemos" pasa sobre su frente,
En todo agudo bronce, cuando la noche empieza.

En la angustia, sus músculos se hienden, sufridores.
Cada surco en la carne se llena de terrores.
Se hiende, como la hoja de otoño, al Señor fuerte

Que le llama en los bronces . . . Y no hay árbol torcido
De sol en la llanura, ni león de flanco herido,
Crispados como este hombre que medita en la muerte

(*D*, 5)

Still, we all know that the "long weariness" of living will grow upon us some day, and that the soul will tell the body that it no longer wants to drag its weary mass along the rosy path that men, happy to live, traverse (**"Los sonetos de la muerte": II**). And that at the thought of our "orphanhood," of our solitude, as we go alone through the world, "all flesh, with anguish, asks to die" (**"In memoriam"**). These are the conflicting thoughts that burden her mind at nightfall . . .

The process of disintegration repeatedly comes to her mind when she thinks of that "disgregadora impura" which is death. That is why, perhaps, the flesh, as we have seen, holds no real meaning for her; for it is merely the guileful, perishable covering of that divine essence—that "breath of God"—we have within; a "weary, reticent sheaf" that crumbles when She of the Deep Eyes casts her dire, somber and withering glance upon it.

Always prone to be concrete, her descriptions of death are graphic and specific. Not content with the mere suggesting of its outward signs and symptoms, she seems to find a certain morbid delight in evoking, with precise detail, its lurid physical aspects:

Y la tremenda albura cayó sobre tu faz

(*D*, 26)

¿Quién te alcanzó en los ojos el estupor de Dios?

(*D*, 27)

. . . Todo
El estupor que blanquea las caras
En la agonía . . .

(*D*, 102)

Me olvidé de que te hicieron
Sordo para mi clamor.
Me olvidé de tu silencio
Y de tu cárdeno albor,

De tu inerte mano torpe
Ya para buscar mi mano;
¡De tus ojos dilatados
Del inquirir soberano!

(*D*, 124)

These descriptions become more harrowing and gory when applied—as in the case of the lover—to suicide:

¿Cómo quedan, Señor, durmiendo los suicidas?
?Un cuajo entre la boca, las dos sienes vaciadas,
Las lunas de los ojos albas y engrandecidas,
Hacia un ancla invisible las manos orientadas?

(*D*, 121)

She seems obsessed with the care and "adjusting" of the dead after the last agony—perhaps because she herself was not present when the lover's defenseless, desolate body most needed her tender care and ministration ("¿Qué tú, amortajadora descuidada / no cerraste sus párpados / ni ajustaste sus brazos en la caja!"):

¿Quién te juntó las manos? ¿Quién dió, rota la voz,
La oración de los muertos al borde de tu lecho?

(*D*, 27)

¿O Tú llegas después que los hombres se han ido,
Y les bajas el párpado sobre el ojo cegado,
Acomodas las vísceras sin dolor y sin ruido
Y entrecruzas las manos sobre el pecho callado?

(*D*, 121)

Religion

Her poems reveal a deep religiousness which, like all her other emotions—her love, her jealousy, her maternal feeling—is also strong and vehement. But her religion is not conventional, dogmatic or doctrinal. For as Nieto Caballero[25] says, "she carries her cathedral within."

Rather than to the Virgin, to whom Juana de Ibarbourou dedicates such tender and devout pages, Gabriela, in her Calvary, speaks to Christ—not the benign, the gentle Christ, the Shepherd, but to the tortured and bleeding One:

Cristo, el de las carnes en gajos abiertas;
Cristo, el de las venas vaciadas en ríos . . .

(*D*, 7)

or to a God of wrath and vengeance—He of the "terrible and strong" breast, Who knows how to mete out just punishment. Some of the poems are definite prayers or hymns (**"Al oído de Cristo"**, **"Himno al árbol"**, **"Plegaria por el nido"**, **"Hablando al Padre"**, **"Tribulación"**, **"Nocturno"**, **"El ruego"** . . .); others—in their themes, in their allusions, in their imagery—breathe and exhale the serene, the noble, the patriarchal air of that "stupendous panorama" which is the Bible.

In her prayers there is always the passionate note, and a forceful—and almost commanding—tone which could be considered irreverent were it not born of that vehemence and one-purposeness so characteristic of her in all things. This is seen, better than elsewhere, in **"El ruego"** where she threatens to *fatigue* His ear with prayers and with sobs for the rest of her life—or until He pardons him (whom she loved) for having shattered his temples:

Aquí me estoy, Señor, con la cara caída
Sobre el polvo, parlándote un crepúsculo entero,
O todos los crepúsculos a que alcance la vida,
Si tardas en decirme la palabra que espero.

Fatigaré tu oído de preces y sollozos,
Lamiendo, lebrel tímido, los bordes de tu manto,
Y ni pueden huírme tus ojos amorosos
Ni esquivar tu pie el riego caliente de mi llanto.

¡Di el perdón, dilo al fin!

(*D*, 136)

Nature

Although Gabriela Mistral is not what is conventionally known as a poet of nature—for her descriptions are seldom objective, seldom purely esthetic—there is in this book the constant presence of the soil that nurtured her, of the rustic scenes and labors, and of the various natural phenomena with which more than once she identifies herself.

The rural surroundings in which she passed the earlier part of her life left their lasting imprint on her soul and on her work, and the familiar landscapes are depicted, not merely as such, as we have already said, but more often to reflect a personal state of mind or emotion. Her "nature background," therefore, is somewhat limited; for she selects, for the most part, those aspects of it that best mirror and interpret her moods—especially when she was felled by the driving wind of tragedy. And succumbing to the so-called "pathetic fallacy," she is prone to infuse her own feelings into what would otherwise be "static" nature. Characteristic of these "nature-moods" are her descriptions of desolate and arid expanses:

En la tierra yerma,
Sobre aquel desierto
Mordido de sol . . .

En la estepa inmensa
En la estepa yerta
De desolación . . .

(*D*, 48)

solitary, suffering trees:

En el medio del llano,
Un árbol seco su blasfemia alarga;
Un árbol blanco, roto
Y mordido de llagas . . .

(*D*, 151)

Uno, torcido, tiende
Su brazo inmenso y de follaje trémulo
Hacia otro, y sus heridas
Como dos ojos son, llenos de ruego

(*D*, 153)

sobbing and howling winds:

El viento hace a mi casa su ronda de sollozos
Y de alarido . . .

(*D*, 149)

. . . el viento, vuelto
Mi desesperación, aúlla y pasa

(*D*, 151)

fearful, sad, plaintive, "vanquished" rain:

Esta agua medrosa y triste
. . . . .

Este fino llanto amargo
. . . . .

No llueve: es un sangrar lento
y largo.
. . . . .

Este largo y fatigante
Descender de aguas vencidas . . .

(*D*, 166)

mute, incessant snow:

Siempre ella, silenciosa . . .
. . . siempre su azahar sobre mi casa;
Siempre, como el destino, que ni mengua ni pasa . . .

(*D*, 150)

Her dolorous spirit, moreover, does not look to the hope or promise of dawn, but rather to the blackness of night in which to lose sight of the mantle of tears that clothes her. Night, therefore, lends its bleakness, its dourness, its tragedy, to these "tone poems" of hers. But they are more frequently infused with the burning red of the bleeding sunsets ("la hora de la tarde, la que pone / su sangre en las montañas") which are so colored, she sometimes thinks, by the gaping wounds that sorrow and pain left within her:

¿Seré yo la que baño
La cumbre de escarlata?

Llevo a mi corazón la mano, y siento
Que mi costado mana

(*D*, 164)

Y en cualquier país las tardes
Con sangre serán mis llagas

(*D*, 108)

Her descriptions—and comparisons—are rich in nature imagery (with which she constantly evokes spiritual analogies):

Estoy lo mismo que estanque colmado
Y te parezco un surtidor inerte

(*D*, 101)

Si tú me miras yo me vuelvo hermosa
Como la yerba a que bajó el rocío

(*D*, 110)

En esta hora, amarga como un sorbo de mares

(*D*, 114)

Cada surco en la carne se llena de terrores.
Se hiende, como la hoja de otoño, al Señor fuerte

(*D*, 5)

Eran sus barbas dos sendas de flores

(*D*, 15)

Pecho, el de mi Cristo,
Más que los ocasos,
Más, ensangrentado . . .

(*D*, 20)

Más espeso que el musgo oscuro
De las grutas, mis culpas son;
Es más terco, te lo aseguro,
Que tu peña, mi corazón!

(*D*, 30)

. . . En mis días,
Como la lluvia eterna de los Polos, gotea
La amargura . . .

(*D*, 139)

And the more active and vital aspects of rural life—the harvest, the vintage—are often pictured, especially in her imagery of such superb earthy and live quality:

Creo en mi corazón, el que en la siembra
Por el surco sin fin fué acrecentado

(*D*, 36)

Ruth, más callada que espiga vencida

(*D*, 16)

Ya en la mitad de mis días espigo
Esta verdad con frescura de flor.
La vida es oro y dulzura de trigo . . .

(*D*, 24)

No espigará entre mis rodillas
Un niño rubio como mies

(*D*, 28)

Pasó por él su fina, su delicada esteva,
Abriendo surcos donde alojar perfección

(*D*, 44)

Te acordaste del negro racimo,
Y lo diste al lagar carmesí;
Y aventaste las hojas del álamo
Con tu aliento en el aire sutil.
¡Y en el ancho lagar de la muerte
Aún no quieres mi pecho exprimir!

(*D*, 116)Apacenté los hijos ajenos, colmé el troje
Con los trigos divinos . . .

(*D*, 141)

Maternity is logically related to harvesting:

Y una mendiga grávida, cuyo seno florece
Cual la parva de Enero . . .

(*D*, 18)

Segar te ví en Enero los trigos de tu hijo . . .

(*D*, 17)

Sometimes nature is obdurate and remains insensible to her joy or to her sorrow:

Le he encontrado en el sendero.
No turbó su ensueño el agua
Ni se abrieron más las rosas

(*D*, 97)

Sin un ímpetu la tarde
Se apagó tras de los álamos.
Por mi corazón mendigo
Ella no se ha ensangrentado . . .

(*D*, 159)

But more often she—like God—is her conspirator in love: "The very earth will disown you / if your soul barter my soul" . . .[26]

La tierra se hace madrastra
Si tu alma vende a mi alma.
Llevan un escalofrío
De tribulación las aguas.

. . . . .

Pero te va a brotar víboras
La tierra si vendes mi alma . . .

. . . . .

Beso que tu boca entregue
A mis oídos alcanza,
Porque las grutas profundas
Me devuelven tus palabras.
El polvo de los senderos
Guarda el olor de tus plantas . . .

. . . . .

A la que tú ames las nubes
La pintan sobre mi casa . . .

(*D*, 106–107)

The image of the lover—after his death—is not only carried deep within (engraved upon her soul) but is reflected in the sunsets, in the moonbeams, the wind, the snow, and other sympathetic aspects of nature:

Me toca en el relente;
Se sangra en los ocasos;
Me busca con el rayo
De luna, por los antros.

. . . . .

Le he dicho que deseo
Morir, y él no lo quiere,
Por palparme en los vientos,
Por cubrirme en las nieves;

Por moverse en mis sueños,
Como a flor de semblante,
Por llamarme en el verde
Pañuelo de los árboles

(*D*, 125)

Style

There is never any gaiety in her poetry—nor lightness—for her emotions are always ardently passionate (in the love poems), intensely serious (in the "philosophic" or religious ones), or poignantly tender (in the maternal ones, or cradle-songs). Her tone, when not tragic, is preeminently sad. For life, love, nature—which, at some time or another, may smile at other poets—turn only a tear-stained face to her.

Pain, therefore,—the pain of life, the pain of love, the pain of death—bitter, burning, disconsolate or excruciating pain, is the constant companion of ***Desolación.*** And there are few poets who express it in richer detail, with more plasticity, or with greater violence than she. For she seems to find sensual—almost perverse—pleasure in depicting mental and physical anguish, agony, terror; in voicing the moans, the cries, the shrieks that such pain induces; in evoking the image of open, gaping, oozing wounds; of flesh rent into palpitating shreds; of veins emptying into rivers of blood . . .

Her vocabulary[27]—which, in general, is not uncommonly rich or varied—acquires then an extraordinary force and intensity, mainly through the repetitious, constant use of certain words suggestive of bodily suffering and pain: of burning, of piercing, of rending, of cutting, of cleaving, of bleeding.[28]

The following *verbs of violence* appear again and again in ***Desolación:*** *hender* (to cleave, to split), *romper* (to break, to cut asunder), *rasgar* (to rend, to claw, to lacerate), *morder* (to bite, to gnaw), *clavar* (to nail, to gore), *socarrar* (to singe, to scorch), *hurgar* (to stir, to poke, to dig—as a wound), *taladrar* (to bore, to perforate), *arañar* (to scratch, to claw), *tronchar* (to chop off, to break with violence), *trizar* (to break into fragments—as with a blow), *llagar* (to wound), *desgarrar* (to rend, to tear), *magullar* (to mangle), *azotar* (to whip, to lash). Equally abundant are the incisive and piercing instruments: *garfio* (hook), *hierro* (iron—instrument to wound with), *zarpa* (claw), *cuchillo* (knife), *puñal* (dagger), *clavo* (nail, iron spike). The words *llaga* (sore), *herida* (wound), and *sangre* (blood)—a logical result of all this flogging and cutting—abound, as does *entraña* (entrail) to designate the depth of her feeling, her pain, her passion . . . There is no dearth of examples, for almost every page contains lines like the following:

¡Garfios, hierros, zarpas, que sus carnes hiendan
Tal como se hienden quemadas gavillas;
Llamas que a su gajo caduco se prendan,
Llamas de suplicio: argollas, cuchillas!

(***D***, 8)

Pecho, el de mi Cristo,
Más que los ocasos,
Más, ensangrentado . . .
. . . . .

Costado de Cristo,
Otro labio abierto
Regando la vida:
Desde que te he visto
Rasgué mis heridas!

(***D***, 20)

Tengo ha veinte años en la carne hundido
—Y es caliente el puñal—
. . . . .

El que vino a clavarlo en mis entrañas
Tenga piedad!

(***D***, 22)

Los hierros que le abrieron el pecho . . .

(***D***, 43)

Mi Dios me visitió de llagas

(***D***, 98)

Rasga vasos de flor, hiende el hondo glaciar

(***D***, 99)

Y me clavo con un dejo
De salmuera en tu garganta

(***D***, 108)

Me socarró la boca . . .

(***D***, 114)

Por la mojada puerta de las hondas heridas

(***D***, 121)

. . . Sabía suya la entraña que llagaba

(***D***, 136)

She is prone to use words that *intensify* the feeling or expression—sometimes resorting to hyperbole:

. . . Socarradura larga
Que hace *aullar*!

(***D***, 23)

A la sombra de Dios *grita* lo que supiste . . .

(***D***, 27)

Fatigaré tu oído de preces y sollozos

(***D***, 136)

Cristo, el de las *carnes en gajos abiertas*;
Cristo, el de las *venas vaciadas en ríos* . . .

(***D***, 7)

Raza judía, *río de amargura* . . .
Y crece aún tu *selva de clamores* . . .

(***D***, 10)

Manos que *sangraron* con grafíos y en ríos

(***D***, 39)

People—and things—are *twisted, knifed, bitten* by the sun, by anguish, by sores, by thirst and hunger:

. . . árbol *torcido*
de sol . . .

(***D***, 5)

El sol caldeo su espalda *acuchilla*

(***D***, 14)

. . . desierto
Mordido de sol . . .

(***D***, 48)

Un árbol . . .
. . . *mordido* de llagas

(***D***, 151)

Retorcido de angustia y sol

(***D***, 155)

Te *muerden* la sed y el hambre

(***D***, 107)

And although her manner has an outward calmness—"the exterior serenity of a rock"—her actions and gestures, as expressed in her poetry, are indicative of a vehement, turbulent, tempestuous and volcanic nature:

Baldías del hijo, *rompo*
Mis rodillas desoladas

(***D***, 106)

Boca *atribulada* y *convulsa* . . .

(***D***, 127)

Deshechas las rodillas, *retorcida* la boca

(***D***, 140)

Araño en la ruin memoria;
Me *desgarro* y no te encuentro

(***D***, 143)

Yo *muerdo* un verso de locura

(***D***, 34)

Yet, in spite of all this verbal violence, there are few people more tender than this "maestra rural" whose eyes are hollowed deep to harbor more tears, and whose smile is but a way of weeping with kindness . . . That is what is so extraordinary about her poetry which has the rare power of disclosing, simultaneously, a vehemence which disconcerts, and a softness and tenderness which are not common—even in women.

3. Analysis of *Tala*

Tala, published in 1938, is the vintage of sixteen years of intense and errant living. This is a more complex book than the first, and reflects the spiritual vicissitudes which attended her for nearly two decades. Its mastery, its sureness of style and precise choice of words reveal the mature artist who has gone through the bitter exercise of attaining that much-prized "difficult simplicity."[29] The tragic love note, the morbid preoccupation with death, the vehemence—dominant in ***Desolación***—are now superseded by far more varied motifs, by a serenity that reveals an emotion more contained (whose key note is hope), and by an expression less tortured.

Yet, basically, this book is not so very different from the other (as one might suppose at a cursory glance). And Gabriela is the first to recognize it: "This book carries a small residue of ***Desolación***", she says in the notes, "and the book that follows it—if one is to follow—will also carry a residue of ***Tala.***" She then gives a homely, rural illustration of this process of "continuity" which applies to artistic endeavor as well as to nature: "It is thus in my valley of Elqui with the pressing of the grapes. Pulp upon pulp remains in the fissures of the wine-press. The peons of the vintage come upon them afterwards. The wine has already been made and that is left for the next round of the baskets."

In the **"Voto"** of ***Desolación***, where she spoke of that "bleeding past" which her poems disclosed, she expressed the hope that in the future, in a more clement spiritual clime, she would sing "words of hope" without looking again at her heart. And in the poem **"Palabras serenas,"** also of that first book, she had said:

Mudemos ya por el verso sonriente
Aquel listado de sangre con hiel

(***D***, 24)

For in the mid-course of her life she (who before had seemed to revel in the pleasurable cold—"gustoso frío"—of the knife of pain that cut her) "harvested" this truth: that life is the gold and sweetness of wheat; that hate is brief, while love is "immense"; that a brooklet can make us smile, even though our eyes be heavy with weeping; and that the mere singing of a lark makes us sometimes forget that "it is hard to die." And knowing that "the fruits of grief" are neither good nor beautiful, in ***Tala***, too, she strives to give us "the praise of happiness," as the "tremendous voyage" across the "thick fog" of sorrow (her mother's death) finally ends in the hope of the **"Locas letanías"**:

¡Recibe a mi madre, Cristo,
Dueño de ruta y de tránsito,
Nombre que ella va diciendo,
Sésamo que irá gritando,
Abra nuestra de los cielos,
Albatros no amortajado,
Gozo que llaman los valles.
¡Resucitado, Resucitado!

(***T***, 34)

If the crucial moment of the lover's death brought about the tortured pages which gave title to her first book, that of her mother's results in several poems of a calm, mystic flavor. And the maternal note—so strong, so passionate, so persistent in ***Desolacíon***—is more subtly, perhaps, but no less forcefully present in this book whose very birth reveals a maternal gesture of the highest order.[30]

Already in ***Desolación*** one saw her ascetic disregard for the material in her interpretation of love, of life, of death. But in ***Tala*** one can discern, with greater clarity, this process of "de-materialization" as she denudes herself of all mundane wants and fears, and emerges pure and serene in "the sweet air" of her hope and of her faith. She is spiritually richer now ("Tengo la dicha fiel / y la dicha perdida"), and she is reconciled to the duality of life which has the sensuous delights of the rose and the poignant prick of the thorn ("¡"Ay! qué amante es la rosa / y qué amada la espina"). She rests content in the knowledge that there are two angels that watch over her simultaneously—one that brings her happiness, and one that brings her pain:

No tengo sólo un Angel
Con ala estremecida:
Me mecen como al mar
Mecen las dos orillas
El Angel que da el gozo
Y el que da la agonía . . .

(***T***, 47)

And so not even the loss of deep spiritual joys can wring from her a "cry of agony," nor dampen her newly-found peace, for she now knows that "the eternal soul" suffers no loss:

Tuve la estrella viva en mi regazo,
Y entera ardí como un tendido ocaso.
Tuve también la gruta en que pendía
El sol, y donde no acababa el día.
Y no supe guardarlos . . .
. . . . .

Y los perdí, sin grito de agonía,
Que vengo de una tierra
En donde el alma eterna no perdía

(*T*, 38)

Some of her lines recall the mystic fervor of Saint Theresa (with whom she has more than once been compared), and of Saint John of the Cross[31]—both in concept and in style:

Algún día ha de venir
El Dios verdadero
A su hija robada, mofa
De hombre pregonero.
Me soplará entre la boca
Beso que le espero,
Miaja o resina ardiendo
Por la que me muero

(*T*, 41)

Acaba de llegar, Cristo, a mis brazos,
Peso divino, dolor que me entregan . . .

(*T*, 31)

"En los filos altos
Del alma he vivido:
Donde ella espejea
De luz y cuchillos,
En tremendo amor
Y en salvaje impetu,
En grande esperanza
Y en rasado hastío.
Y por las cimeras
Del alma fué herido."

"Y ahora me llega
Del mar de mi olvido
Ademán y seña
De mi Jesucristo,
Que, como en la fábula
El último vino,
Y en redes ni cáñamos
Ni lazos me ha herido."

"Y me `doy entero
Al dueño divino
Que me lleva como
Un viento o un río"

(*T*, 178)

While others seem to stem from that "popular"—folkloric—vein in which Spanish poetic tradition is so rich:

La mañanita
Pura y rasada
Quedó linda
De la venteada.

. . . . .

Y yo me alcé
Con lucerada;
Medio era noche,
Medio albada

(*T*, 54–55)

There is in ***Tala*** a keener mental subtlety, a more volatile and hermetic quality (notably in the sections "Alucinación" and "Historias de loca") than in the first book where plasticity and directness always made the meaning clear—perhaps because now some things are seen through the inventive and scintillating facets of the imagination and fantasy, or through the undulating maze of allegory.

But she has not lost touch with the earth. And like Antaeus she always seems to gain new vitality, new strength, new confidence from her contact with it. That is what lends such vigor and warmth and "substance" to her **"Materias,"** which sing of the simple, the elemental, the vital things: bread, salt, water, air—all of which seem so much a part of her and of her work:

Huele a mi madre cuando dió su leche,
Huele a tres valles por donde he pasado:
A Aconcagua, a Pátzcuaro, a Elqui,
Y a mis entrañas cuando yo canto.

Otros olores no hay en la estancia
Y por eso él así me ha llamado;
Y no hay nadie tampoco en la casa
Sino este pan abierto en un plato,
Que con su cuerpo me reconoce
Y con el mío you reconozco.

. . . . .

Pan de Coquimbo, pan de Oaxaca,
Pan de Santa Ana y de Santiago.

En mis infancias yo le sabía
Forma de sol, de pez o de halo,

. . . . .

Después le olvidé, hasta este día
En que los dos nos encontramos,
Yo con mi cuerpo de Sara vieja
Y él con el suyo de cinco años.

(**"Pan"**. *T*, 75–76)

Mano a mano nos tenemos,
Como Raquel, como Rebeca.
Yo volteo su cuerpo roto
Y ella voltea mi guedeja,
Y nos contamos las Antillas
O desvariamos las Provenzas

Ambas éramos de las olas
Y sus espejos de salmuera,
Y del mar libre nos trajeron

A una casa profunda y quieta;
Y el puñado de Sal y yo,
En beguinas o en prisioneras,
Las dos llorando, las dos cautivas,
Atravesamos por la puerta . . .

(**"Sal"**. *T*, 79–80)

Hay países que yo recuerdo
Como recuerdo mis infancias.
Son países de mar o río,
De pastales, de vegas y aguas.
. . . . .

Quiero volver a tierras niñas;
Llévenme a un blando país de aguas.
. . . . .

Tenga una fuente por mi madre
Y en la siesta salga a buscarla,
Y en jarras baje de una peña
Un agua dulce, aguda y áspera.

(**"Agua"**. *T*, 81–82)

En el llano y la llanada
De salvia y menta salvaje,
Encuentro como esperándome
El Aire.
. . . . .

Cuando camino de vuelta,
Por encinas y pinares,
Todavía me persigue
El Aire.
. . . . .

Al amanecer, me duermo
—Cuando mis cabellos caen—
Como la madre del hijo,
Rota del Aire . . .

(**"El Aire"**. *T*, 85–87)

There is nostalgia in her evoking of scenes—of games—of her childhood, and it is only through these basic, unchangeable, unfailing, tangible, *material* things that she can feel herself secure and firm in the billowy sea of doubt, of fear and of uncertainty . . .

The first section, "Muerte de mi madre", recalls, in substance, some of the well known pages of ***Desolación.*** But how different these poems (**"La fuga"**, **"Lápida filial"**, **"Locas letanías** . . .") from the **"Nocturno"**, **"Los sonetos de la muerte"**, **"Interrogaciones"**, **"La espera inútil"**, **"La obsesión"**. What had been passion and tragic despair is now more often serenity and hope. She has, for the most part, discarded the ardent, impassioned tone which tragedy awakens in youth. Life has mellowed her somewhat rude expostulations, and her prayers—no less fervent—reveal a comfort and a certainty in salvation that did not exist in the earlier book where she felt she had to *fatigue* the ear of Christ with her prayers for the redemption of the dead lover.

Her maternity now reaches unfathomed, unforeseen, prodigious depths, for it embraces all things—all people. And her protective "mother instinct" surges wild and passionate at the thought of her own mother wandering aimlessly and alone in the mystic pale of death; of Christ nailed piteously on the Cross. Her feelings for her mother, for the Father, are not "filial" then, but "maternal"[32] This dual parent-child, child-parent relationship which is more or less present in all forms of love, is expressed factually, in the poem **"Cascada en sequedal"** where she calls the water both "mother mine" and "child of mine":

¡Agua, madre mía,
E hija mía, el agua!

(*T*, 84)

But her maternal feeling is more conventionally, concretely and specifically expressed in her **"Canciones de cuna"**:

Duerme, mi sangre única
Que así te doblaste,
Vida mía, que se mece
En rama de sangre.

Musgo de unos sueños míos
Que te me cuajaste,
Duerme así, con tus sabores
De leche y de sangre.
. . . . .

Mi semillón soterado
Que te levantaste;
Estandarte en que se pára
Y cae mi sangre;
. . . . .

En la noche, si me pierde,
Lo trae mi sangre.
¡Y en la noche, si lo pierdo,
Lo hallo por su sangre!

(*T*, 197–198)

in the admirable poem, **"La cuenta-mundo,"** where the mother explains to her infant child the magic and the wonder of the air, the light, the larks, the mountain, the water, the animals, the butterflies, the fruit, the pine tree, the fire, the house, the earth . . .; and in the tender and nostalgic poem **"Niño mexicano"**:

Hace doce años dejé
A mi niño mexicano;
Pero despierta o dormida
Yo lo peino de mis manos . . .
¡Es una maternidad
Que no me cansa el regazo
Y es un éxtasis, que tengo
De la gran muerte librado!

(*T*, 117–118)

Tala is, undoubtedly, a more objective book than the first in that it often goes beyond herself for inspiration. ***Desolación*** had sung of life, of death, of nature, of motherhood—all in relation to her own emotions; all facets of her own self exegesis. But in this book we see her transcend the personal and disclose "the outer world"—and especially that part of it which has always been her main concern: America. Her Americanism, in its richest and warmest sense, is patent here, not only in the section properly called "América", but in all those poems which sing, in one form or another, of its landscapes, its places, its flora, its fauna, its people, its heritage, its destiny . . . There is an attempt—an ideal—to disregard and efface national boundaries and to fuse all into that "heart-shaped" beautiful land (land of the Incas and of the Mayas, of the Quichés, the Quechuans and Aymarans) which is her America; an ardent wish to see those "downtrodden racemes of sacred vine"—which are the Indians of old—restored to their pristine destiny; and a fervent promise to abide with and restore the greatness of their heritage:

Gentes quechuas y gentes mayas
Te juramos lo que jurábamos.
De ti rodamos hacia el Tiempo
Y subiremos a tu regazo;
De ti caímos en grumos de oro,
En vellón de oro desgajado,
Y a ti entraremos rectamente
Según dijeron Incas Magos.

¡Como racimos al lagar
Volveremos los que bajamos . . .

(***T***, 96–97)

And so in the part called "América" she essays two "hymns"[33] in almost epic manner: one to the tropical sun ("sol de los Incas, sol de los Mayas, maduro sol americano") and one to the Andes ("carne de piedra de América"). This natural union which the "ripe American sun" and the "stony flesh" of the Cordillera effect is what she hopes to see, in fact, in those lands which "speak the language of Saint Theresa, of Góngora and Azorín."

Not the least interesting and valuable part of the book are the "Notas" with which it ends. In them she gives "the reason" for ***Tala***, elaborates on some points of her ars poetica, explains and justifies the use of particular words[34] and rhyme schemes,[35] and comments on some of the poems. She also makes interesting and characteristic references to her preferred choice of certain words of distinct rural flavor[36] (for to her "el pueblo" is "la mejor criatura verbal que Dios crió") and ascribes the origin of some of the archaisms[37] which she is fond of using, to the popular speech of her own country, rather than to the Spanish classics—as has been so frequently stated. These notes are personal, and in the best Mistralian tradition: a meaty, wholesome prose written in a homely, conversational tone.

Notes

1. These biographical references, and those that follow, were drawn, mostly, from the two books on Gabriela: Virgilio Figueroa, *La divina Gabriela*, Santiago de Chile, 1933; and Raúl Silva Castro, *Estudios sobre Gabriela Mistral*, Santiago de Chile, 1935.
2. Figueroa, *op. cit.*, p. 42.
3. Figueroa, *op. cit.*, p. 61.
4. . . . la enseñanza es mi preocupación . . . la primaria se lleva mis preferencias." (*Ibid.*, p. 145.)
5. Juan José Soiza Reilly, *Mujeres de América,* Buenos Aires, [1934], p. 43.
6. *Op. cit.*, p. 3.
7. *Op. cit.*, p. 72.
8. Jorge Mañach, "Gabriela: Alma y tierra", in *Revista Hispánica Moderna*, New York, 1937, III, p. 108.
9. "Alguna circunstancia me arranca siempre el libro que yo había dejado para las Calendas por dejadez criolla. La primera vez el Maestro Onís y los profesores de español de Estados Unidos forzaron mi flojedad y publicaron *Desolación;* ahora entrego *Tala* por no tener otra cosa que dar a los niños españoles dispersados a los cuatro vientos del mundo".

   (*Tala*, p. 271).
10. "He vivido veinte años haciendo un periodismo fatigante con el que apenas puedo" . . .

    (Figueroa, *op. cit.*, p. 257).
11. *Loc. cit.*
12. Bécquer, in his Rima XXXVII, expresses an almost identical thought
13. Silva Castro, *op. cit.*, p. 5. In the light of such fervent admiration on her part, the

    "Master's" judgment of her—some years later—is somewhat severe: "La Mistral es un caso patológico. Para estudiarla hay que recurrir a los libros de medicina". (R. Maya, "Entrevista con Vargas Vila",

    Nosotros, Buenos Aires, 1924, XLVII, pp. 252–253).
14. G. Mistral, *La lengua de Martí*, La Habana, 1934, p. 41.
15. Silva Castro, *op. cit.*, p. 8.
16. Appears in the second edition of *Desolación,* Santiago de Chile, 1923, pp. 52–54.
17. In this study we will use "D" when quoting from *Desolación* (New York, 1922); "T" will be used for *Tala* (Buenos Aires, 1938).
18. *Te llamaré*
    Padre, porque
    La palabra me sabe a más amor . . .

    (*D*, 75)

    The Spanish dramatist of the Golden Age, Mira de Amescua, offers a similar distinction between the words "Señor" and "Padre":

    Señor,—dije mal "señor"
    Que en este nombre hay rigor
    Por la sucesión del hombre—
    Padre digo, porque es nombre
    De más dulzura y amor.

    (El esclavo del demonio).

19. "Gabriela Mistral, virgen y madre", in *Cuba Contemporánea*, La Habana, 1927, XLIX, p. 220.

20. . . . "la santidad de la vida comienza en la maternidad, la cual es, por lo tanto, sagrada". (D, 185).

21. One of her best poems, "El niño solo" (D, 19), expresses this sentiment:

Como escuchase un llanto, me paré en el repecho
y me acerqué a la puerta del rancho del camino.
Un niño de ojos dulces me miró desde el lecho
¡y una ternura inmensa me embriagó como un vino!

La madre se tardó, curvada en el barbecho;
el niño, al despertar, buscó el pezón de rosa
y rompió en llanto . . . Yo lo estreché contra el pecho,
y una canción de cuna me subió, temblorosa . . .
Por la ventana abierta la luna nos miraba.
El niño ya dormía, y la canción bañaba,
como otro resplandor, mi pecho enriquecido . . .

Y cuando la mujer, trémula, abrió la puerta,
me vería en el rostro tanta ventura cierta,
¡que me dejó el infante en los brazos dormido!

22. "My most deep-felt poem"—she once said—"is the 'Poema del hijo', lament of my useless existence".

23. She follows through the analogy in intellectual "production", and feels that her verse, like a child, is nurtured with her blood: "Como un hijo con cuajo de mi sangre se sustenta él". And in "The artist's decalogue" she gives as one of the precepts: "You shall give forth your work as one gives a child: drawing blood from your heart" . . .

24. These two lines are reminiscent of Delmira's: "El dios duerme, Julieta; su almohada es de estrellas" . . .

25. L. E. Nieto Caballero, "Gabriela Mistral", in *Repertorio Americano*, San José, Costa Rica, January 11, 1930.

26. "God wills it". Translation of "Dios lo quiere", by Katherine Garrison Chapin, in *Poetry*, Chicago, 1941, LIX, 123–125.

27. Silva Castro has made a special study of it in his *Estudios sobre Gabriela Mistral*, pp. 149–227.

28. Silva Castro speaks of her verbal and ideologic *sadism*, and of how "she seems to be seized with delirium when speaking of hooks and knives" . . . (*Retratos literarios*, Santiago de Chile, 1932, p. 157).

29. Gabriela once said: "Yo he sufrido mucho para llegar a cierta sencillez". (Figueroa, *op. cit.*, p. 138).

30. See p. 176, note 1.

31. In *Desolación*, also, there were passages which recalled the manner—and expression—of the author of *Cántico espiritual.* San Juan in his "Canciones entre el Alma y el Esposo" wrote:

Ni ya tengo otro oficio,
Que ya sólo en amar es mi ejercicio.

. . . . .

Después que me miraste:
Que gracia y hermosura en mi dejaste.

Gabriela, likewise, uses the words "oficio" and "ejercicio" in reference to love: and the loved one's glance, in her case, too, can transform plainness into beauty:

Ya no tengo otro oficio
Después del callado de amarte . . .

(*D*, 127)

Y amar (bien sabes de eso) es amargo ejercicio . . .

(*D*, 136)

Si tú me miras, yo me vuelvo hermosa . . .

(*D*, 110)

32. Pero a veces no vas al lado mío:
Te llevo en mí, en un peso angustioso
Y amoroso a la vez . . .

(*T*, 12)

Acaba de llegar, Cristo, a mis brazos
Peso divino, dolor que me entregan . . .

(*T*, 31)

33. It is time—she says, commenting upon them in the notes—that the "minor tone" which came as a violent reaction, and repugnance, to the pompous, bombastic, romantic "epic trumpet", and which is so appropriate for the singing of the intimate, simple aspects of life so dear to present-day writers in Spanish America, be discarded now in favor of the "major tone" which is needed to sing of that "formidable spectacle" which the American scene and heritage present.

34. [*Saudade*] . . ."encabezo una sección de este libro, rematado en el dulce suelo y el dulce aire portugueses, con esta palabra *Saudade.* Ya sé que dan por equivalente de ella el *soledades* castellano. La sustitución vale para España; en América el sustantivo *soledad* no se aplica sino en su sentido inmediato, único que allá le conocemos".

(*T*, 277).

[*Albricia*] "En el juego de las *Albricias* que yo jugaba en mis niñeces del valle de Elqui, sea porque los chilenos nos evaporamos la *s* final, sea porque las albricias eran siempre cosa en singular—un objeto escondido que se buscaba—la palabra se volvía una especie de sustantivo colectivo . . . El sentido de la palabra en la tierra mía es el de *suerte, hallazgo*, o *regalo.* Yo corrí tras la *albricia* en mi valle de Elqui, gritándola y viéndola en unidad. Puedo corregir en mi seso y en mi lengua lo aprendido en las edades feas—adolescencia, juventud, madurez—pero no puedo mudar de raíz las expresiones recibidas en la infancia. Aquí quedan, pues, esas albricias en singular".

(*T*, 279).

35. "Nocturno de la Consumación"—"Cuantos trabajan con la expresión rimada, más aún con la cabalmente rimada, saben que la rima, que escasea al comienzo a poco andar se viene sobre nosotros en una lluvia cerrada, entrometiéndose dentro del verso mismo, de tal manera que, en los poemas largos, ella se vuelve lo natural y no lo perseguido . . . En este momento, rechazar una rima interna llega a parecer . . . rebeldía artificiosa. Ahí he dejado varias de esas rimas internas y espontáneas. Rabie con ellas el de oído retórico, que el niño o Juan Pueblo, criaturas poéticas cabales, aceptan con gusto la infracción".

(*T*, 274–275).

"Beber"—"Falta la rima final, para algunos oídos. En el mío, desatento y basto, la palabra esdrújula no da rima precisa ni vaga. El salto del esdrújulo deja en el aire su cabriola como una trampa que engaña al amador del sonsonete. Este amador, persona colectiva que fué millón, disminuye a ojos vistas, y bien se puede servirlo a medias y también dejar de servirlo . . ." (

T, 277).

36. "Estos Recados llevan el tono más mío, el más frecuente, mi dejo rural con el que he vivido y con el que me voy a morir".

(*T*, 280).

37. "No sólo en la escritura sino también en mi habla, dejo, por complacencia, mucha expresión arcaica, sin poner más condición al arcaísmo que la de que sea fácil y llano. Muchos, digo, y no todos los arcaísmos que me acuden y que sacrifico en obsequio de la persona antiarcaica que va a leer. En América esta persona resulta siempre ser una capitalina. El campo americano—y en el campo yo me crié—sigue hablando su lengua nueva veteada de arcaísmos abundantes. La ciudad, lectora de libros doctos, cree que un tal repertorio arranca en mí de los clásicos añejos, y la muy urbana se equivoca" . . .

(*T*, 275)

Langston Hughes (essay date 1957)

SOURCE: An introduction to *Selected Poems of Gabriela Mistral*, translated by Langston Hughes, Indiana University Press, 1957, pp. 9–12.

[*In the following introduction to his translations of her poetry, Hughes pays tribute to Mistral as a poet and as a person.*]

She did not sign her poetry with her own name, Lucila Godoy y Alcayaga, because as a young teacher she feared, if it became known that she wrote such emotionally outspoken verses, she might lose her job. Instead she created for herself another name—taking from the archangel Gabriel her first name, and from a sea wind the second. When the poems that were quickly to make her famous, ***Sonetos de la Muerte***, were published in 1914, they were signed Gabriela Mistral.

She was born in 1889 in the Chilean village of Vicuña on the River Elqui in a valley where the sweetest of grapes grow. She grew up in the little town of Montegrande where her father was a schoolmaster, and she in turn became a teacher in rural schools, sometimes walking miles into the country to meet her classes. Her father made up verses for village fiestas and, as a young woman, his daughter composed little poems for texts to help children learn to read. She met a young man, Romelio Ureta, with whom she fell in love, but they were never married. For reasons unrelated to their friendship, Ureta committed suicide. Out of love for him and of her desolation at his death came the first of a series of poems soon to be read throughout all Latin America. These included ***Sonnets of Death***, **"Prayer"** and the **"Poem of the Son"**, in whose stark beauty and intensity her personal tragedy "lost its private character and became a part of world literature. It was then that Lucila Godoy y Alcayaga became Gabriela Mistral.

As her renown as a poet grew, so grew her reputation as a teacher of children. The young woman who had no children of her own took her work as an educator very seriously, and explored what was for Chile and the times the most progressive methods of enlightening young minds—visual aids, extracts from great literature, games sometimes in place of books. At first in country schools and coastal villages, then in Santiago de Chile she became an influence in educational circles, and soon was given a government post in the Department of Education at the capital. A group of teachers brought about the publication of her first book—happily for us, in the United States. Federico de Onis, Professor of Spanish Literature at Columbia University in New York, one day gave a talk about her and a reading of a few of her poems. This so inspired his students—most of whom were (or intended to be) teachers of Spanish—that they wanted to lay hands on more of her work. Then they learned that as yet no volume of her poems had been printed. Gabriela Mistral's first book, ***Desolacion***, was published by the Spanish Institute of Columbia University in 1922. It has since been reprinted in various editions in South America, each time containing more poems as well as revised versions of previous work, for Gabriela Mistral rewrote often.

In Madrid in 1924 ***Ternura*** was published. In Buenos Aires in 1938 appeared a third small volume, ***Tala***, the proceeds of whose sale went to the relief of the Basque orphans of the Spanish Civil War. In 1954 ***Lagar*** appeared in Chile, and there that same year a new edition of ***Deso-***

lacion was printed. In 1950 in Santiago the "Poemas de las Madres" (included in ***Desolacion***) had appeared separately in a beautiful limited edition with drawings by Andre Racz. By then in Spanish speaking countries Gabriela's name (and almost everyone in referring to the poet said simply *Gabriela*) had long been a household word. She had become one of the most popular poets of her tongue. Although her first publication was achieved in our country, in Continental Europe her poems were more widely translated than in England or the United States. Even after she was awarded the Nobel Prize for Literature, why so little of Gabriela was translated into English, I do not know. Much of her poetry is simple and direct in language, never high-flown or flowery, and much easier, I think, to translate than most poets writing in Spanish. Since her poetry is so intensely feminine, however, I hesitated to attempt translations myself, hoping that a woman would do so. None did, in terms of a book. So when Bernard Perry of the Indiana University Press requested that I do so, it intrigued me to try—for the simple reason that I liked the poems.

For the most part I have selected from the various books those poems relating to children, motherhood, and love, including the famous **"Poem of the Son"** and **"Prayer"** written during her period of complete desolation, after the man for whom she cared so greatly had died by his own hand.

I have no theories of translation. I simply try to transfer into English as much as I can of the literal content, emotion, and style of each poem. When I feel I can transfer only literal content, I do not attempt a translation. For that reason I have not translated the three ***Sonetos de la Muerte.*** They are very beautiful, but very difficult in their rhymed simplicity to put into an equivalent English form. To give their meaning without their word music would be to lose their meaning.

The music of Gabriela's poetry started around the world a decade or more before she left her native Chile in the early thirties to begin her own travels, first to Mexico, which had asked her assistance in the organization of rural schools and libraries, then to become Chile's delegate to the League of Nations Institute of Intellectual Cooperation. And in 1931 Gabriela Mistral came to the United States as an instructor in Spanish history and civilization at Middlebury and Barnard colleges. Later she represented her government in various diplomatic posts in South America and Europe, and was a member of the United Nations Subcommittee on the Status of Women. For two years, at President Aleman's invitation, she lived in Mexico as a "guest of the nationa." She was Chilean Consul in Brazil, Portugal, at Nice, and Los Angeles. Then after a year as Consul at Naples, in 1953 Gabriela Mistral came again to the United States and settled down in a charming house in Roslyn Harbor, Long Island, where she lived until her death. For twenty years before her death, Gabriela had been honored as Chile's only "life consul"—so appointed by a special enactment of the Chilean Congress—her consulate designated to be "wherever she finds a suitable climate for her health and a pleasant atmosphere to pursue her studies." In the end she chose Roslyn Harbor.

Early in the new year of 1957 Gabriela Mistral died. When the news reached Chile, President Ibañez decreed three days of national mourning. In the United Nations she was eulogized. And the press of the world paid her tribute. In an article at the center of a full page devoted to her memory in *The New York Times Book Review*, Mildred Adams wrote, "Gabriela's clarity and precision, her passion and that characteristic which can only be called her nobility of soul are accepted as ideals. She will not quickly vanish from the literary consciousness of those who value the Spanish tongue." And in *El Diario de Nueva York* Ramon Sender said, "There are poets who hide behind their verses. Others give themselves from their first poem, and so it was with Gabriela Mistral."

Margaret Bates (essay date 1961)

SOURCE: "Gabriela Mistral's *Poema de Chile*," in *The Americas*, Vol. XVII, No. 3, January, 1961, pp. 261–76.

[*In the following essay, Bates retraces the poetic journey through Chile Mistral undertook in her unfinished* Poema de Chile.]

The distinguished Chilean poet, Gabriela Mistral, winner of the Nobel Prize for literature in 1945, died in Hempstead, Long Island, on January 10, 1957, of cancer. In the numerous articles that appeared in newspapers and magazines after her death the factual mistakes about her life and writings were endless. Although her critics have not been careful to separate myths from facts, most of these errors can be corrected by referring to books or articles about her—but not the mistakes about her as yet unpublished ***Poema de Chile.*** For this reason I have assembled these notes about the ***Poema de Chile*** taken from conversations with Gabriela during the last four years of her life which she spent for the most part working on the ***Poema*** and on her ***Lagar*** poems. Part of the ***Lagar*** poems she published in 1954. The rest of her ***Lagar*** poems will be published posthumously by her literary heir, Doris Dana.[1] These will probably appear before the unfinished ***Poema de Chile*** because of the difficulties inherent in the preparation of the ***Poema*** for publication.

Let me quote two sentences, full of errors, from an article describing the ***Poema*** written by Carlos Santana:

> Gabriela Mistral alcanzó a completar antes de morir lo que pudiera ser su obra poética cumbre, **"Recado de Chile"**, pero la dejó escrito lápiz. . . . Según Miss Doris Dana, la abnegada amiga de Gabriela en los últimos años, la gran poetisa completó la corrección de los originales del **"Recado de Chile"** en los dos años fina-

> les de su vida, a pesar de que su salud estaba ya seriamente quebrantada y de que el trabajo, por lo mismo, le era difícil.[2]

The source of this information, Doris Dana, is authoritative. Santana must have misunderstood her. It is true that Gabriela spent the last years of her life correcting this poem but at the time of her death it was far from finished. The fact that he says it was written in pencil would be proof of this because a great deal of correcting intervened between the first rough draft that Gabriela always wrote in pencil and the final printed version. Only the "legendary" Gabriela wrote those perfect first drafts that needed no correction . . . in a moment of "inspiration." It was Gabriela's *modus operandi* in all her poetry, not only in the ***Poema***, to correct her rough draft until the corrections began to menace legibility; the corrected draft would then be copied on a typewriter, this in turn would be corrected. The correcting would continue on subsequent copies until Gabriela felt she could no longer improve upon the poem. At the time of Gabriela's death most of the ***Poema*** had been typed out and arranged alphabetically in loose leaf notebooks. A subject index referred to each part. This was just an interim arrangement to enable the person working with Gabriela to find the section she wanted.

Santana calls the ***Poema*** the ***Recado de Chile.*** Gabriela usually called it the ***Poema de Chile***, although sometimes, she would refer to it as the ***Recado de Chile*** or the ***Recado sobre Chile.*** In the ***Pequeña antología de Gabriela Mistral***[3] two fragments of it are published: **"Bío-Bío"**[4] and **"Selva austral."**[5] These she calls **"Trozos del poema *Viaje imaginario por Chile* (*Lagar*)."** Apparently this title was rejected. I never heard her use it. She says here it is from ***Lagar*** because in 1950 when the ***Pequeña antología*** . . . was published Gabriela intended to publish all the poetry she had written since ***Tala*** (1938) in ***Lagar.*** But in 1953, after an index had been made of most of her unpublished poetry, and after one typewritten copy of each of her poems had been placed in a loose-leaf notebook—hitherto they had been scattered—Gabriela realized for the first time that she had enough poems for two volumes. She therefore decided to publish the ***Poema de Chile*** separately. There was really material for more than two volumes but two volumes was Gabriela's estimate. Although the ***Poema*** is quite distinct from the rest of the poems of ***Lagar***, Gabriela had decided to publish them both together just for the sake of bulk. She had an aversion to publishing thin books. Her generosity of spirit would not countenance meanness. To her a thin book signified a lack of generosity.

By the time ***Lagar*** was published in Chile (December, 1954), less than half the poems that were originally destined for it had been corrected and were ready for publication. What was published was only the first volume. Gabriela always found correcting very onerous and often would say: "Tomorrow you have to make me correct this," and she would put crosses next to the lines or the words that didn't please her. Usually tomorrow took some time to arrive. Perhaps it is this distaste that made her very early decide not to collect her poetry and publish it in a book, a decision which another side of her nature easily melted: in Gabriela's code of honor as in that of Santa Teresa de Avila the first commandment was to be *agradecida:* to respond generously to the generosity of others. Often Gabriela had nothing else to give but her poetry. Gathering it together, correcting and eliminating was such hard work that she called it a *tala*, a chopping down of trees in a huge forest. The circumstance that moved her to make her first *tala* was a plea from some teachers of Spanish in the United States. They had read some of her poetry in newspapers and magazines and to express their admiration for the poetry of a fellow school teacher they offered to defray the cost of publication of a collection of her poetry.[6] This plea was rewarded by ***Desolación*** (1922). Sixteen years later her second *tala* resulted in ***Tala*** (1938). The proceeds from this book were to go to the Basque children left homeless as a result of the Spanish Civil War.[7] The result of her final *tala* sixteen years later was ***Lagar*** (1954) which she published in Chile in gratitude for the hero's welcome her country generously extended to her. This *tala* was the most difficult because her usually robust health was undermined already by cancer. Her time had run out and an immense unpruned poem, the ***Poema de Chile***, remained behind.

The ***Poema*** describes a journey Gabriela makes through Chile in the company of a little Chilean boy of Indian extraction (*mi niño atacameño*) and a baby fawn. It takes place after her death when her spirit returns to Chile for its last journey on earth. In the northern province of Atacama she adopts the little boy to whom she intends to show the wonders of his native Chile. To everybody but the boy and the fawn she is invisible.

This lyrical explanation of the world to a child recalls her **"La cuentamundo"** in ***Tala.*** Here a mother describes to a child the meaning of air, light, larks, mountains, water, animals, butterflies, fruit, pine trees, fire, the home, mother earth, the rainbow, strawberries, pineapples, Argentine wheat, and God's carriage. In **"La cuenta-mundo"** it is the child who appears without having come from anywhere:

> (Niño pequeño aparecido
> que no viniste y que llegaste
> te contaré lo que tenemos
> y tomarás de nuestra parte.)[8]

In the ***Poema de Chile***, which might be called *La Cuenta-Chile*, it is Gabriela. But the ***Poema*** is different in other respects: the narrator is not just any mother but Gabriela herself—it is full of autobiographical details; the personality of the boy is developed through dialogue; the humanization of nature has gone much further.

With the development of the boy's personality through dialogue Gabriela solves more than one problem. The boy stands for common sense, a very necessary foil for a gay, disembodied spirit. Gabriela's world, although he enjoys it when he allows himself to be seduced by it, is very strange to him. He's very glad that she is invisible to everybody else because he becomes uncomfortable when he thinks of what people will say about this queer companion.

> —Claro, tuviste el antojo
> de regresar así en fantasma
> para que no te conozcan
> las gentes alborotadas.
> Casi pasas las ciudades
> corriendo como azorada,
> y cuando tienes diez cerros
> paras, ríes, cuentas, cantas.
> —Tapa tu boca que tú
> no les pones mala cara
> y gritas cuando los Andes
> con veinte crestas doradas
> y rojas hacen señales
> como madres que llamaran.
> Yo te gano la profía
> indito frente taimada.
> ¿Cómo vas a convencer
> a una criada en sus sombras
> y de ellas catequizada?
>
> ("Flores")[9]

The boy constantly takes Gabriela to task and chides her for the disproportion between her lofty ideas and her actual state. When Gabriela talks to him about grace he wants to know how a poor thing in rags like her would know anything about grace:

> —¿Qué llama la gracia, mama,
> pobrecilla que no llevas
> sobre ti cosa que valga?
> —La gracia es cosa tan fina
> y tan dulce y tan callada
> que los que la llevan no
> pueden nunca declararla
> porque ellos mismos no saben
> que va en su voz o en su marcha
> o que está en un no sé qué
> de aire, de voz o mirada.
> Yo no la alcancé, chiquito,
> pero la vi, de pasada,
> en el mirar de los niños,
> de viejo o mujer doblada
> sobre su faena o ———[10]
> en el gesto de una montaña
>
> ("Flores")

Gabriela here, as in real life, is a nomad in a sedentary world. Her *patiloquismo*, the word she coined for this malady, has its compensation in discovering grace in her travels, grace which, she often lamented, had passed her by. However, in the ***Poema***, as a disembodied spirit she loses the gravity which in her life and in her other poetry worked against her attaining *gracia*.

This friendly bickering between Gabriela and the boy she called "chacota con el niño" and often complained of the strain it was to compose in this narrative genre in which she had little training. But this *chacota* she hoped would give the poem a *sabor criollo:* "Una conversación con un niño pobre no puede estar demasiado bien hablada . . . yo quiero suprimir el *bonitismo* en este ***Poema.***" Most attempts, she lamented, to attain a true *sabor criollo*, had failed and had turned out to be either vulgar or forced and unnatural.[11]

Gabriela's poetry from its very beginning is marked with a nearness to animate and inanimate things. Her personal vision of the world is unique in its penetration into man himself through the humanization of matter. Like St. Francis, Gabriela

> felt near to the beasts, the birds, and the flowers. For him it was a most natural thing to befriend a wild animal, to protect the life of a bee, to converse with a falcon. When he sang his glowing tributes to the sun, to water, to fire—to all inanimate things, he desired only to show his kinship with the earth. This he considers somehow divine because our Lord, Jesus Christ, deigned to live on it when He came to regenerate us by His blood and His grace.[12]

Man is intimately tied to the materiality of things, he penetrates them but is not lost in them. As the ***Poema*** developed this closeness to matter is intensified. Nature is humanized by Gabriela's fresh, colorful strokes: the mountains wave welcome to the travellers; the trees are inns that beckon them to approach; the metals blink. Everything moves as if it suddenly were endowed with human form. This religious closeness to nature with which Gabriela was born is remarkable because of its intensity. Palma Guillén de Nicolau, who accompanied Gabriela in Mexico, describes how surprised she was when she met Gabriela for the first time in 1923: ". . . cómo me sorprendía y me admiraba aquel sentimiento religioso que en ella despertaban las cosas y aquella oración que le subía a los labios con las desnudas palabras de Job o de David."[13] And it is to impart this feeling to the boy that she has descended. He must learn to love the land, to cultivate it. When they come to the *boldo* tree she tells him to cut some leaves:

> Corta, pónlas contra el pecho
> aunque son recias son santas
> te irán ellos respondiendo
> con tacto y bocanada.
>
> ("Boldos")

They both sleep beneath it:

> Aquí se duerme sin pena
> doblando la trebolada.
> Agradece, cara al cielo,
> sombra, cobijo y fragancia.
> ¡Qué mal duermen los hombres
> en el hondón de sus casas!
> Se desperdician las hierbas
> y la ancha noche estrellada.
>
> ("Boldos")

The beauty of the night is constantly extolled:

Tanto fervor tiene el cielo,
tanto ama, tanto regala,
que a veces me quiero más
la noche que las mañanas.

("Noche andina")

As they approach Lake Llanquihue the boy is told to approach this water which is quiet and secretive, only for swans:

Yo me sé un agua escondida
que no camina ni canta
y aunque es tan hermosa nadie
se la busca ni se la ama.
Es el agua de los cisnes,
verde, secreta, extasiada.
. . . . .

Es tu lago Llanquihue
la más dulce de tus aguas.
Parece que está adorando
sólo cuchichea, no habla.
Pero se tiene un respiro,
una hablilla, una monada.
No haber miedo de allegarse
recibirle la mirada.
Nadie te miró tan dulce
y con tan larga mirada.

("Cisnes")[14]

The section "Viento norte" is very similar to **"El aire"** of the marvelous *Materias* section of ***Tala***:

Porque yo me envicié en él
como quien se envicia en vino
trepando por los faldeos
siguiéndolo por el grito.
Yo no era más, era sólo
su antojo y su monojillo
y me gustaba este ser
su jugarrete[15] de niño
en donde estoy todavía
lo llamo a voces, mi niño.

("Viento norte")

Gira redondo en un niño
desnudo y voltijeante,
y me toma y arrebata
por su madre.

Mis costados coge enteros
por cosas de su donaire,
y mis ropas entregadas
por casales[16] . . .

("El aire," ***Tala*****)**

The wind has another toy: the palm tree:

Todos los aires la buscan
por su resonar de velas
que cantan y que murmuran
o rezongan comadreñas.

("Las palmas")

There are constant references in the poem to the moment Gabriela will take leave of her unenthusiastic disciple. In "Despedida," after describing the call of her Master she repeats her reasons for descending to earth:

Ya me voy porque me llama
un silbo que es de mi Dueño,
llama con una inefable
punzada de rayo recto.

Yo bajé para salvar
a mi niño atacameño
y por recorrer la Gea
que me crió contra el pecho
y acordarme volteándola
su trinidad de elementos.

("Despedida")

In "Las flores de Chile" she laments not being present for the boy's wedding:

—Qué pena mía no verte
con novia encocoradada,
y la iglesia ardiendo en luces
y oir gritos y campanas
—Cuando hablas así de loca,
mama mía, me atarantas.
Mejor te callas y tomas
las manzanillas cortadas.
—Gracias, sí, mi niño, pero
no me gustan de cortadas.
Se doblan sus cabecitas
y en poco, no valen nada.

("Las flores de Chile")

Another autobiographical detail[17]. . . . Gabriela did not like cut flowers for the reason she gives here.

In another reference to her departure she confesses the failure to impart her enthusiasm for earth's "trinity of elements":

Cuando mañana despiertas
no hallarás a la que hallabas
y habrá una tierra extendida
grande y muda como el alma.

("Flores")

The earth will be mute because there will be nobody to translate its language.

Although there are many parts entitled "Despedida," and many allusions to the final departure throughout the poem, this does not mean that the poem, even the first rough draft, was completed. If Gabriela had lived a decade longer this poem might not be ready for publication. Hardly a day passed without Gabriela's remembering some Chilean phenomena that had been overlooked. Because of her love for the underdog, simply because he was an underdog, she was especially repentant when what she had forgotten was some insignificant shrub, tree, fish, or bird. Her Chilean encyclopedia was not to restrict itself to fauna and flora, although these would predominate; there was also the history of Chile to be considered. There is even a part that begins: "Qué será Chile en el cielo?"

The poem is very uneven because some of it remains in rough draft, some parts have a few corrections and other parts have undergone quite a thorough pruning. A special difficulty presented itself with the ***Poema:*** instead of working with one rough draft, of correcting it and copying the corrections until it was finished, Gabriela would often begin a new version that would run roughly parallel to the other. It would be hard to say how many versions of "El mar" she wrote without referring to previous ones.

Nor did Gabriela have a clear outline in her head of the organization of the poem. Since it was a journey from northern Chile to southern Chile (there was even a moment when she considered south to north) the general plan of a travelogue could be followed but even this had many problems of transitions . . . to O'Higgins, to *garzas*, to palm trees, palm trees in general and specific types of palm trees, to insignificant fish and algae, to mention a few. The final decision after much meditation and consultation on the subject of organization was usually to wait until all the parts were finished and then put them together . . . perhaps this shouldn't be called a decision—it was the only thing to do.

In the ***Poema*** the sea represents eternity. In the presence of the sea, the true lover, all the others pale: Her Gaea, Mother Earth, is inferior because she sings the same old song over and over again. She can speak only with poplars and cedars and her silence is sullen. She spits the dust of the dead into the eyes of the traveller, makes his hair white and his face wooden—he is always burnt by the sun and out of breath on her highways. The hardy sailors who embark have chosen the better half: they will never know hunger or thirst; their eyes will shine as they did at birth. They will be regaled eternally by the sea's ever changing song, a song for heroes, the song of King David, Homer, and the archangels. They will be united with their loved ones who are dead:

Ya me cansé de la ruta
que me enseñó su jadeo
y su polvo innumerable
y su taimado silencio.

. . . . .

Ya bostezo de la Gea
que no canta como Homero,
menos como los Arcángeles,
menos como el Rey Hebreo.

. . . . .

A la tierra no me di
sólo me di al Violento
porque nunca él es el mismo
y nunca fué prisionero
y es cantador sin fatiga
con mi labios eternos.

. . . . .

Nunca a la Tierra me di
sólo le presté mi cuerpo.

. . . . .

No es cual la tierra mama
que repite el mismo cuento.

. . . . .

Me voy a embarcar un día
para otro gran viaje sin término,
sin costa, sin desembarco,
viaje sin puertos, eterno.
Mi boca tendrá el sabor
de un loco viaje sin puertos
y recobrarán mis ojos
el color de su nacimiento.

. . . . .

¿A qué me cuentan historias
de costas que no deseo
donde nunca fué feliz
y blanquearon mis cabellos
y vi morir a los míos
sólo por no haber su aliento.

Each of these quotes is from a different rough version of "El mar." Gabriela enjoyed writing about her husband, the sea, and laughed at the violence of this passion which caused her to be so unfaithful to the earth.

In "La Cuenta-Mundo" it is the rainbow, not the sea, that makes the bridge to eternity:

El puente del Arco Iris
se endereza y te hace señas . . .
Estaba sumida el puente
y asoma para que vuelva.
Te da el lomo, te da la mano,
como los puentes de cuerda . . .
¡Ay, no mires lo que miras
porque de golpe te acuerdas . . .!
¡Vuélvele la cara al puente;
deja que se rompa, deja . . .!

("El arco-iris," *Tala*)[18]

Intimations of immortality might make us impatient for this last trip but one has to wait for the "Carro del cielo" to descend and when it does:

Entonces sube sin miedo
de un solo salto a la rueda
¡cantando y llorando de gozo
con que te toma y que te lleva!

("Carro del cielo," *Tala*)[19]

At one point in the ***Poema*** Gabriela explains that she has descended to teach the boy also friendship for the dead.

Another autobiographical note in the ***Poema*** is the triumph of the country over the city. Gabriela flies quickly over Santiago—one can not hope to find a warm reception there, the natives will send their dogs at you—and shows nothing but disdain for the artificial life of the *citadinas* and their pride in this artificiality. The city gardens are full of proud flowers that are *aseñoreadas* and who refuse to *doncelear* with the *campesinas rasas.*

Casi pasas las ciudades
corriendo como azorda,
y cuando tienes diez cerros
paras, ríes, cuentas, cantas.

("Flores")

If one must travel he should keep off the highways:

Nada hay más triste, chiquito,
que rutas sin compañeros
parecen bostezos blancos,
jugarreta[20] de hombre ebrio.
Preguntadas no responden
al extraviado ni al ciego.
Parecen unas mujeres
que jugasen a perdernos.
Pero tú sabes de rutas,
mallicias y culebreos.
No las tomes, no las sigas
que suelen ser mataderos
Bien escogiste y tomaste
basquecillos y entreveros.

("Hallazgo")

Gabriela considered the years she spent as a child in Montegrande, very close to nature, the happiest of her life. The feeling that life close to the soil lifts man morally never left her. But man must be able to call the land his own. She was interested therefore in the passage of the Agrarian Reform Law[21] which she hoped would distribute the land more equitably and wipe away absenteeism. In the poem she constantly refers to this happy future when the poor boy accompanying her will own a parcel of land. She assures him that there is no greater joy than the cultivation of the land.

If one were to trace the genesis of the ***Poema***, like that of most of the poetry of Gabriela, it could be found in ***Desolación***, her first collection. As she matures her themes develop but do not change. A glance at the table of contents in her books—she always arranged her poems according to theme—show the same themes constantly recurring. Nor does her style change fundamentally: "Su manejo de idioma . . . es ya de mano maestra desde que empieza a escribir . . . Milagro igual no ocurre ni aun con Rubén Darío."[22] Therefore the differences between ***Desolación***, ***Tala***, and ***Lagar*** are difficult to describe. Some critics have considered ***Lagar*** closer to ***Desolación*** than to ***Tala*** especially because of those poems in ***Lagar*** that describe her desperation at the death of her nephew—whom she had been raising as her son—under very tragic circumstances:

Todavía los que llegan
me dicen mi nombre, me ven la cara;
pero yo que me ahogo me veo
árbol devorado y humoso,
cerrazón de noche, carbón consumado,
enebro denso, ciprés engañoso,
cierto a los ojos huído en la mano.
En una pura noche se hizo mi luto
en el dédalo de mi cuerpo
y me cubrió este resuello
noche y humo que llaman luto
que me envuelve y me ciega.

. . . . .

En lo que dura una noche
cayó mi sol, se fué mi día,
y mi carne se hizo humareda
que corta un niño con la mano.

(**"Luto,"** ***Lagar***)[23]

Of these poems Margot Arce says:

> Lo anecdótico tiene tanta importancia aquí como en los libros anteriores, aunque se recata tras un velo de alucinación y ensueño. La realidad biográfica está presente, pero siempre al borde del desvarió; siempre entre lo real y lo soñado . . . Por momentos parece haber traspasado el límite, no saberse muerta o viva; y comienza a dialogar con sus fantasmas. . . .[24]

In reading over these poems in ***Lagar*** the intensity of this "delirio," as Gabriela called it, reminded her of some of her early "gritos" in ***Desolación***: "It's just as violent as ***Desolación***, but at the same time it's not ***Desolación***; it's quite different." The detachment that Gabriela wished for so often came to her along this very bitter path. She had gone out so far that "arrows can't reach me."[25] But this wound made her see things as never before, or rather see through things as never before. This freer, less inhibited imagination of Gabriela had two sides: one pessimistic, the other optimistic. Most of ***Lagar*** is black with the pain caused by the sword's thrust.[26] The ***Poema de Chile***, or, to be more exact that part of it written or corrected after 1944[27] is bright in this new light as Gabriela, a happy, disembodied spirit, makes her last trip through Chile. It is remarkable how tame and sedate the "Cuenta-Mundo" is when placed beside the best parts of the ***Poema de Chile.***

Besides the difficulty Gabriela experienced with the dialogue in the ***Poema***, she complained of being bored by the monotony she imposed upon herself when she chose one form for the whole poem. For some reason she felt it should have formal unity as well as unity of content. Therefore she had to do some violence to her spirit when a part of the poem came to her already enveloped in a rhythm which was not that of the poem. Her last decision was to write the poem in traditional ballad meter, the *romance:* eight syllables to the line, no fixed stanzaic length, with even lines rhyming in *asonancia.* However a large part of the poem had already been written in a nine syllable line and Gabriela left it that way or corrected it sporadically.[28] The versions I saw her write usually had eight syllables and the corrections I saw her make were usually from a nine to an eight syllable line. The change from nine to eight syllables may have occurred between 1938 and 1945: the five parts that were added to the "Cuenta-

Mundo" in ***Ternura*** (1945) have eight syllables while the earlier parts in ***Tala*** (1938) have nine.[29]

But it must be remembered that Gabriela did not adhere strictly to isosyllabism. For instance, in twenty verses of nine syllables there might be one with eight or ten. An occasional break such as this in isosyllabism can not constitute free verse (Gabriela also wrote in free verse). For some reason quasi-isosyllabism is not recognized by most of Gabriela's critics, if critics they can be called. They wrote these occasional breaks off as carelessness. It was far from that. Gabriela distinguished very carefully between breaks of this kind which were dictated by a very fine ear and those that needed correction. Next to these latter she would put a mark to call her attention to the need of correction. This she also did when reading the poetry of others. But there were the critics—"pavorosos" Gerardo Diego calls them—[30] who had read carefully the *preceptivas* and *retóricas* written for ignorant students—any deviation was severely criticised by them. What was originally written to be perceptive for the neophyte only was taken to be perceptive also for genius, for those creative writers who were making the norms of the future. In the face of this unjust criticism Gabriela defended her deviations by referring to them as *prosaismos voluntarios*. These breaks are certainly not prosaic but Gabriela was not interested enough in criticism to bother very much about terminology. She even agreed with them about her ear: "Yes," she said, "it is *desatento y basto*," and she continued to make very good use of it.[31]

Notes

1. I should like to express my thanks here to Doris Dana for permission to quote excerpts from the *Poema de Chile.*
2. "Recado de Chile," *Diario las Américas* (Miami), January 15, 1957.
3. (Santiago, 1950). "Cuatro tiempos del huemul" (pp. 86–95) is also part of the *Poema de Chile* although it is not cited here as a fragment.
4. Pp. 96–100.
5. Pp. 101–109.
6. *Desolación* (New York, 1922), p. ii.
7. *Tala* (Buenos Aires, 1938), p. 271.
8. *Poesías completas de Gabriela Mistral,* ed. Margaret Bates (Madrid, Aguilar, 1958), p. 287. This I will refer to as *Poesías completas.*
9. Each part of the *Poema* has a title.
10. The manuscript has a blank space here. Gabriela often left spaces if the word didn't come to her immediately and went on.
11. Gabriela was repeating in 1955 something that she had said earlier—almost with the same words. In *Zig-Zag* (July 6, 1918) Gabriela had praised Carlos Acuña's *Vaso de arcilla:* "Creo que no hay nada más difícil que hacer poesía criolla. Es tan fácil caer en la grosería y en la insipidez." Raúl Silva Castro, "Producción de Gabriela Mistral de 1912 a 1918," *Anales de la Universidad de Chile*, año 115, no. 106 (1957), p. 248.
12. "Versicle of Peace" delivered by Gabriela Mistral on receiving the Serra Award of The Americas for 1950. (*The Americas,* VII, 3 [January, 1951], 282.)
13. I quote from the typescript of a lecture given by Palma Guillén de Nicolau at the Universidad Femenina, Mexico, D. F., April 30, 1957, p. 4. It has no title.
14. After Gabriela's death I discovered that she had published in *Sur* (November, 1939, pp. 17–18) a very inferior version entitled "Lago Llanquihue." It would seem to me to be a rough draft published in a weak moment at the insistence of some friend. Gabriela calls the water "tierna y vieja" but the tenderness is not as well expressed as in this excerpt I quote from the *Poema.*
15. Gabriela sometimes uses this word, as well as "jugarreta," with its New World meaning. The suffixation does not always give the word the pejorative sense of "mala pasada."
16. *Poesías completas*, p. 451. In this first edition there are many misprints. Here *casuales* should be read *casales.* In the second edition the misprints will be corrected.
17. Most of Gabriela's poetry is autobiographical. This does not cause difficulties in the *Poema de Chile* because the circumstances of the poem, that fact that she is talking to a child, keep her away from the psychological complexity of *Lagar,* for instance, which is written parallel chronologically to the *Poema.* Even "the right kind of reader" sometimes misinterprets some of the poems of *Lagar* because of the predominance of autobiography, autobiography of a very unique and original personality:

    "Encontrarse cara a cara por primera vez con un ser *tan peculiar* como Gabriela, con una personalidad tan cautivadora, es un acontecimiento que sigue siempre gravitando en nuestra vida."

    (Victoria Ocampo, "Gabriela Mistral y el premio Nobel," Testi-*monios; tercera serie* [Buenos Aires, 1946], p. 173.)

    According to Palma Guillén de Nicolau, an intimate friend, Gabriela's writings only give a fragmentary portrait of her:

    "Era uno de los seres a los que hay que conocer personalmente para darse cuenta de la multiplicidad de sus dones. Gabriela no se dijo entera a si misma en sus mejores poesías. Su obra no ha entregado sino muy fragmentariamente lo que ella fué."

    (Typescript of a lecture on Gabriela Mistral given April 26, 1957, at the Facultad de Derecho, Universidad Nacional de México, p. 9.)

    Gabriela's poetry poses a special problem for those critics who say, *and for very good reasons,* that one should not go beyond the text, that one should not read things into poetry by making use of information extrinsic to the poem. For most writers this is the best method because of the normalcy of the experiences described by them but if this method is used with Gabriela Mistral often something will be lacking in the understanding of the poem.

18. *Poesías completas*, pp. 291–292.
19. *Poesías completas*, p. 308.
20. See note 15.
21. Agrarian Reform only is mentioned in the *Poema*. But that was second best. Gabriela's ideal was common ownership of the land and equitable sharing of its fruits, a truly Christian community. And it wasn't in books that Gabriela had discovered this ideal. She had experienced the joy of such a society as a child in Montegrande. In this Andean valley division of the land was simply a formula; the land belonged to everybody. In this patriarchal setting generosity was expected and not applauded as something exceptional. Gabriela, as she grew older, realized more and more how rare this truly Christian communism of her childhood was, and how impossible it was to restore it. The hard-headed Sancho who accompanied her on her journey certainly would laugh at such fantastic ideas. The Agrarian Reform was something he could accept. Much to Gabriela's chagrin these ideas sometimes caused a "Communist Legend" to grow up around her ("Alone" [Hernán Díaz Arrieta] discusses this in: "Gabriela Mistral y el comunismo," *La tentación de morir* [Santiago, 1954], p. 100). The social justice she worked for was a Christian social justice. She was constantly looking for practical ways of solving the problem of the poor Chilean farmer working someone else's land, without training and without tools and proper equipment. Sometimes she would send seeds back to Chile, other times, technical publications. The best solution she saw in television as an educational instrument and one of diversion—this, she thought, might be powerful enough to cure the plague of alcoholism that resulted from the frustrations of a hard, sub-human, unrewarding life.
22. Dulce María Loynaz, "Gabriela y Lucila," *Poesías completas*, p. cxix.
23. *Poesías completas*, p. 712.
24. Margot Arce de Vázquez, *Gabriela Mistral, persona y poesía* (San Juan, Puerto Rico, 1958), pp. 93–94.
25. "La desasida," *Poesías completas,* p. 604: ". . . que de haber ido tan lejos / no me alcanzan las flechas."
26. In some of the poems of *Lagar* there is a feeling of peace and happiness as Gabriela sees again her loved ones who are separated from her by death. In *Tala* she had called to them in vain. One of her purposes in returning to earth in the *Poema* was to teach the boy the importance of the friendship of the dead. Separation by death does not cause her the anguish it did in *Tala.* Her belief in immortality had become stronger.
27. This is a surmise on my part. Gabriela's typescripts are seldom dated.
28. The poem "Lago Llanquihue" (see note 14) is an example of an intermediate version, I would surmise. It has a predominance of nine syllable verses (14 out of 26). There are 4 verses of eight syllables; 3 verses of nine or eight, 5 verses of ten.
29. The "Cuenta-Mundo" section (*Poesías completas*, pp. 287–313) consists of an introduction and 17 poems. In the five poems that were published for the first time in *Ternura*, 1945 ("La piña," "La fresa," "Trigo argentino," "Carro del cielo," "El arco iris") the eight syllable verse predominates. Already in *Tala* (1938) in "La tierra" (pp. 221–222) the "niño" has become "niño indio": "Niño indio, si estás cansado, / tú te acuestas sobre la Tierra. . . ."
30. "Imperfección y albricia," *Homenaje a Gabriela Mistral* (Madrid, 1946) p. 37. What intrigues Gerardo Diego is the "rhythmical elasticity" of Gabriela. He is exasperated at the pedantry of critics like Julio Saavedra Molina who call "imperfection" what to Diego is "necessary abnormality." But what is even more curious is

    ". . . de tales escrúpulos y casi remordimientos llega a contagiarse el propio poeta. Abundan en las confesiones de Gabriela Mistral alegatos de silvestre rudeza y excusas de autodidáctica, e incluso rubores de la nativa y no vencida limitación y bastedad. Ni ella ni sus aristarcos tienen razón" (pp. 38–39).

    This problem I have referred to in "Apropos An Article on Gabriela Mistral," *The Americas*, XIV, 2 (October, 1957), 145–151.
31. A proof of her sensitivity, in spite of all her confessions in regard to her ear, is her attitude to the reading of her own poetry. This has also been discussed in my "Apropos An Article . . ." (note 30). What I said there has since been corroborated by Dulce María Loynaz in "Gabriela y Lucila," *Poesías completas*, p. cxxxix. Dulce María Loynaz, realizing how difficult it was to read aloud the poetry of Gabriela, rehearsed beforehand with Gabriela: "Leía yo ante una Gabriela entredormida, bajos los párpados, inmóviles los músculos del rostro. Pero bastaba el salto de una coma, el titubeo de un acento, o simplemente que la inflexión no fuese la esperada por ella, para verla ya incorporada en el asiento, atajándome el verso con mano ligera como firme." Dulce María Loynaz read in Gabriela's place since Gabriela realized that "su voz no era la más indicada para ello . . ." (p. cxxxix). Those who have heard the recordings of Gabriela reading her own poetry would hardly agree.

Margot Arce de Vasquez (essay date 1964)

SOURCE: "Poetry," in *Gabriela Mistral: The Poet and Her Work*, translated by Helene Masslo Anderson, New York University Press, 1964, pp. 21–93.

[*In the following excerpt, Arce de Vasquez offers a broad survey of Mistral's poetry ranging from the beginning to the end of her career, and an in-depth explication of selected works.*]

Gabriela Mistral's poetry stands as a reaction to the Modernism of the Nicaraguan poet Rubén Darió (*rubendarismo*): a poetry without ornate form, without linguistic virtuosity, without evocations of gallant or aristocratic eras; it is the poetry of a rustic soul, as primitive and strong as the earth, of pure accents without the elegantly correct echoes of France. By comparison with Hispanic-American literature generally, which on so many occasions has been an imitator of European models, Gabriela's poetry possesses the merit of consummate originality, of a voice of its own, authentic and consciously realized. The affirmation within this poetry of the intimate "I," removed from everything foreign to it, makes it profoundly human, and it is this human quality that gives it its universal value.

Passion is its great central poetic theme; sorrowful passion similar in certain aspects—in its obsession with death, in its longing for eternity—to Unamuno's agony; the result of a tragic love experience. *Pathos* has saturated the ardent soul of the poet to such an extent that even her concepts, her reasons are transformed into vehement passion. The poet herself defines her lyric poetry as "a wound of love inflicted on us by things." It is an instinctive lyricism of flesh and blood, in which the subjective, bleeding experience is more important than form, rhythm, or ideas. It is a truly pure poetry because it goes directly to the innermost regions of the spirit and springs from a fiery and violent heart.

The second important poetic motif is *nature,* or rather, *creation,* because Gabriela sings to every creation: to man, animals, vegetables, and minerals; to active and inert materials; and to objects made by human hands. All beings have for her a concrete, palpable reality and, at the same time, a magic existence that surrounds them with a luminous aura. In a single moment she reveals the unity of the cosmos, her personal relationship with creatures, and that state of mystic, Franciscan rapture with which she gathers them all to her. . . .

Desolation (*Desolación*)

The publication of ***Desolation*** in 1922, Gabriela Mistral's first book of poems, is one of the important events in the modern history of Hispanic-American poetry. The new voice immediately reveals its originality as it stands out above the chorus of other feminine voices who, according to Federico de Onís, have achieved in that moment of post-modernism, "the full affirmation of their lyrical individuality."[1] Passion, strength, the strange mixture of tenderness and harshness, of delicacy and coarseness, give this voice a unique accent. Her words exercise an irresistible fascination on the reader, leaving in his mouth a bitter aftertaste of blood. After the publication of ***Desolation***, Gabriela's fame grew rapidly; a legend began to weave itself around her.

According to the *Introduction* (*Palabras preliminares*), the book was published thanks to the initiative of Federico de Onís, at that time director of the Hispanic Institute in the United States, and a group of North American Spanish teachers. It was their homage to the great literary and moral value of "a writer of the first rank, in whom the Spanish spirit speaks with new vigor and voice."[2] The publication only reaffirmed the prestige and popularity that Gabriela was enjoying even before the first edition of her works.

Desolation consists of a body of seventy-three poems, grouped under the headings "Life" (*Vida*), "School" (*Escuela*), "For Children" *Infantiles*, "Sorrow" (*Dolor*), and "Nature" (*Naturaleza*), a collection of poetic and poematic prose writings and four cradle songs. The prose writings would merit a separate study. Their themes are the same as those of the poetry: the ideal teacher, the artist and artistic creation, motherhood and children, living beings and materials, the ecstasy of love, the Passion of Christ, death, Beauty, and the Eternal. There are some stories for school, each with a moral, in which the protagonists are not animals, as in the fables, but roses, reeds, the root of the rose bush, the thistle, the pond. Her style recalls the parables of the New Testament. Seeking to avoid direct admonition, the author uses these lovely imaginative fictions to attempt to form the moral conscience of children. One would have to consult these pages written in prose to clarify Gabriela's religious, aesthetic, moral, pedagogical, and social ideas and to determine her literary sources, her readings (the Bible, Tagore, Oriental literature, the *Little Flowers* of San Francisco, Martí, folklore), and the peculiar nature of her sensitivity. Some of her social concerns are evident in the themes of poverty, the seduced woman, illegitimate children, abandoned children, work, class prejudices, self-righteousness, all profoundly tinged with a sense of human solidarity and true Christianity.

In the "Poems for Mothers" (*Poemas de las madres*) and "Poems of Ecstasy" (*Poemas del éxtasis*), both very beautiful, the poet achieves that fusion of the frankest realism—almost of verbal crudity—with the most delicate poetry: the chaste ardor of a sensuality spiritualized through maternal longing and the religious sense of life that is perhaps the most personal trait of her poetic vision of the world, the one that sets her apart from other American poetesses.

The **"Wish"** (**"Voto"**), found on the last page of the book, alludes to anecdotal and biographical elements—her bitterness, the painful past, the finding of hope—and to artistic creation as a catharsis. With the **"Wish"** she offers her work as if excising a piece of her heart, in order to break free from an already definitive past. She renounces subjectivism, "to stain the song with blood and so relieve oneself." "From the spiritual plateaus I will sing to console men, without ever looking at my heart again" (p. 243). These words are a prelude to the more objective lyricism, the abandonment of the romantic attitude, that is almost literally carried out in ***Felling*** (***Tala***).

The title ***Desolation*** is from the first poem of the section "Nature" (*Naturaleza*) and is thus titled because it describes a desolate landscape of mist and fog, a true mental landscape, the projection of a psychological state, which dominates the book and gives the keynote and emphasis to the leading poems.

Eighteen poems appear under the heading "Life" (*Vida*) without forming a unit. A reading of these allows us to enter the world of the poet as we observe her response to the challenge of external events—the killing of Jews in Poland, the death of Amado Nervo, the publication of a book by Alone; her reaction to things—Rodin's "Thinker," the cross of Bistolfi, the Book of Ruth; or to profounder, more subjective experiences—religious faith, love, art itself. The first pages reveal to us her personal accent, her harsh style filled with strong, plastic imagery and realistic, throbbing words, and her primary preoccupations, those that define and give unity to her vision of the world. Pain is an inescapable but redeeming reality; the union with Christ, the longing for motherhood, children, the anguish of creating, and that of dying, will reappear on the pages that follow and in all her later books as poetical constants, but with variations that the passage of time will impose upon them.

"To the Virgin of the Hill" (**"A la Virgen de la colina"**), **"Future"** (**"Futuro"**), and **"Serene Words"** (**"Palabras serenas"**) would be better suited to the sections "Sorrow" (*Dolor*) and "Nature" (*Naturaleza*). The first poem is a prayer to the Virgin, analogous to the **"Nocturne"** (**"Nocturno"**); the second, with prophetic overtones, communicates the same total desolation as in the **"Landscapes of Patagonia"** (**"Paisajes de la Patagonia"**). **"Serene Words"** repeats in verse the resolutions of the **"Wish"** (**"Voto"**) and could be placed in the background.

The reading of these first poems leaves us with an odd impression, like that of a strange, tormented landscape. All the Modernist refinement and subtleties vanish, charred to a crisp by this somber ardor. The words possess the plasticity of clay, and with marvellous ease they keep molding the emotions, the shades of feeling, the heart-rending impring that reality leaves on the poet's heart. From that heart the verses seem to spring in torrents, barely tempered by reason. They are romantic without rebelliousness or satanism, baroque, yet unpolished in form.

"Credo"

Creo en mi corazón que cuando canta
sumerje en el Dios hondo el flanco herido
para subir de la piscina viva
como recién nacido.

Creo en mi corazón el que yo exprimo
para teñir el lienzo de la vida
de rojez o palor, y que le ha hecho
veste encendida.

pp. 35–36.

"Creed"

I believe in my heart that when
The wounded heart sunk within the depth of God sings
It rises from the pond alive
As if new-born.

I believe in my heart what I wring from myself
To tinge life's canvas
With red or pallid hue, thus clothing it
In luminous garb.

And although the sign of death seems to hover over these poems, we can feel within them the hidden throb of life, of pleasure, of the fondness for palpable beauty, of the impetus to create with which they attempt to elude death's terrible reign. Gabriela's personal adherence to Christ, Christian acceptance of sorrow, love for one's neighbor, the certainty of possessing the gift of song, faith in oneself stand in opposition to the elegiac tone in poems like **"In the Ear of Christ"** (**"Al oído de Cristo"**), **"The Child Alone"** (**"El niño solo"**), **"The Strong Woman"** (**"La mujer fuerte"**), **"Creed"** (**"Credo"**). But let not the contradiction deceive us: one must seek the true root of this lyricism in the polarity pleasure-pain, maternity-sterility, hope-desolation, life-death that lends its tautness and heartbreak to the style, that contracts and swells the phrase, that anoints the words now with blood, now with honey. Desolation and tenderness, wine press and felling, the titles of the books, record directly or through symbols the agony of life inherent in this dialectic.

The poems grouped under the headings "School" (*Escuela*) and "For Children" (*Infantiles*) reveal Gabriela's deep interest in children and in the problems of pedagogy. To the strictly poetic values of those verses one must add the validity of their ideas and of the moral or religious lesson they attempt to communicate. The poet considers that the purpose of education is the spiritual formation of the student, the harmonious development of his personality and character. She takes great care to teach and emphasize the primary importance of religious, moral, and aesthetic values and to awaken the student's consciousness of duty, of his relationship to God and creatures, and of the full enjoyment of Beauty. She proposes for him a Christian ethic of love, pardon and service, of respect for all beings, and of confidence in God as a provident and loving father.

She demands of the teacher the virtues of a saint: virility, fortitude, purity, gentleness, sweetness, joyfulness, poverty, submission to pain and death, and inner peace, because she conceives of teaching as a calling and an apostleship, a divine task entrusted to men. With other illustrious teachers of the past, Gabriela believes in the educational power of beauty, and she clothes her teachings in beautiful descriptions, in the playful fantasy of stories, and in the symbolism of the parable. Upon reading these poems we can see that she found in teaching a way of satisfying maternal desires and an outlet for the springs of her stifled tenderness. It was also a way of perpetuating herself by living on in her disciples, as she reveals to us in **"The Shining Host"** (**"El corro luminoso"**):

En vano queréis
ahogar mi canción:
¡un millón de niños
la canta en un corro
debajo del sol!

En vano queréis
quebrarme la estrofa
de tribulación:
¡el coro la canta
debajo de Dios!

In vain you try
To smother my song:
A million children
In chorus sing it
Beneath the sun!

In vain you try
To break my verse
Of affliction:
The children sing it
Under God!

Without ever becoming superficial or oversentimentally tasteless, these poems are within the grasp of children's understanding and imagination. They awaken and refine their sensitivity with witty poetic fictions, with the nobility of elevated thoughts. Especially outstanding is **"Rounds"** (**"Rondas"**), grouped around the theme of universal harmony. It is a poem in eight parts that reaches its climax when Christ penetrates the chorus, transforming it into a mystical experience. The dance movements, the significance of small gestures, the rich plasticity of description, the beauty of the symbol and the images contain many possibilities for dramatic execution. **"Rounds"** could be made into a beautiful expressionistic ballet if an intelligent choreographer were to interpret it as a contrast with the medieval dances of death. Through its affirmation of life, love, and peace, the reader perceives the conception of the poem as an attempt to create a true anti-dance macabre:

"Los que no danzan"

Una nina que es inválida
dijo: "¿Cómo danzo yo?"
Le dijimos que pusiera
a danzar su corazón . . .

Luego dijo la quebrada:
"¿Cómo cantaría yo?"
Le dijimos que pusiera
a cantar su corazón . . .

Dijo el pobre cardo muerto:
"¿Cómo, cómo danzo yo?"
Le dijimos: "Pon al viento
a volar tu corazón . . ."

Dijo Dios desde la altura:
"¿Cómo bajo del azul?"
Le dijimos que bajara
a danzarnos en la luz.

Todo el valle está danzando
en un corro bajo el sol,
y al que no entra se le ha hecho
tierra, tierra el corazon.

p. 90.

"Those Who Do Not Dance"

A crippled child
Said: "How shall I dance?"
Let your heart dance
We said.

Then the invalid said:
"How shall I sing?"
Let your heart sing
We said.

Then spoke the poor dead
thistle,
"But I, how shall I dance?"
Let your heart fly to the wind
We said.

Then God spoke from above
"How shall I descend from the
blue?"
Come dance for us here in the
light
We said.

All the valley is dancing
Together under the sun,
And the heart of him who
joins us not
Is turned to dust, to dust.

In the two sections "Sorrow" (*Dolor*) and "Nature" (*Naturaleza*), we find the more impressive poems, those "in which there bleeds a painful past" (p. 243). They provide the internal unity of the book; they justify the title of the book, ***Desolation.*** The twenty-five poems that follow the first heading speak directly, in the romantic fashion, of love and of pain; the eleven of the second, although they describe landscapes of the furthest point of Chile, reflect as in a mirror intimate loneliness, the hunger for death after the failure of love. The two groups form an inseparable unit.

In "Sorrow" (*Dolor*), the poems are arranged in such a way that they seem to follow the thread of the chronological development of a story from its beginning until its tragic conclusion; the first poem is titled **"The Meeting"** (**"El encuentro"**), the last one, **"The Bones of the Dead"** (**"Los huesos de los muertos"**). But a careful reading will reveal the presence of another story of love. **"The Prayer"**

(**"El ruego"**) closes the cycle of the first story; the **"Nocturne"** (**"Norturno"**) expresses the crisis of the second, the more decisive one.

But, although the poems in "Sorrow" (*Dolor*) refer to two different experiences, their arrangement in an order that has nothing to do with the strict chronological sequence of events throws the reader off the track and makes him believe that Gabriela is dealing with one only love frustrated by the suicide of the loved one. The poems **"Sonnets of Death"** (**"Sonetos de la muerte"**), **"Questions"** (**"Interrogaciones"**), **"The Obsession"** (**"La obsesión"**), **"Songs"** (**"Coplas"**) of page 127, **"Eternal Candles"** (**"Ceras eternas"**), **"To See Him Again"** (**"Volverlo a ver"**), **"The Sentence"** (**"La condena"**), **"The Glass"** (**"El vaso"**), **"The Prayer"** (**"El ruego"**), and **"The Bones of the Dead"** (**"Los huesos de los muertos"**) seem to refer to that particular painful event. **"Silent Love"** (**"El amor que calla"**), **"Ecstasy"** (**"Extasis"**), **"Intimation"** (**"Intima"**), **"God Wills It"** (**"Dios lo quiere"**), **"Watchful"** (**"Desvelada"**), **"Shame"** (**"Vergüenza"**), **"Ballad"** (**"Balada"**), **"Affliction"** (**"Tribulación"**), **"Nocturne"** (**"Nocturno"**), and almost all the poems in the section "Nature" (*Naturaleza*) seem to allude to the second love experienced some years later. This was a profound, ardent experience that opened in the poet's heart a wound whose bleeding traces we can still perceive in ***Wine Press*** (***Lagar***), her last published book. In **"Poem of the Son"** (**"Poema del hijo"**) and **"Songs"** (**"Coplas"**) of page 142, the two stories are fused and interlaced.

There is a considerable anecdotal element in these poems, and we run the risk of attaching greater significance to the wealth of biographical allusions than to the pure artistic values. Yet as we read, we cannot help but be amazed at the transformation of living reality into beauty.

Few poets sang of love with more passion, with more wrathful words. How far from the subtleties, the delicate and modest sensitivity of an Elizabeth Barrett Browning or a Christina Rossetti! Here is a possessive, all-absorbing emotion with the force of surf or stormy wind. Here is tenderness smothered by jealousy. Vengeful and rebellious rancor darken the song and wrench from it disturbing resonances; the ecstasy of the flesh shudders with mortal foreboding.

The poems of "Sorrow" (*Dolor*) record the critical moments of the emotional experience[3] sometimes as psychological sensations, sometimes as projections on a rustic landscape that serves as its setting. The enamored one wanders through those valleys and gardens talking with nature's creatures in an intimate dialogue that recalls the accents of the Spouse in the Song of Songs. Her emotion overflows like an elemental, teluric force, in which the maternal—almost matriarchal—essence displaces the erotic. Behind the impassioned tremor we sense the heavy sensuality, the thirst for earthly happiness that makes the senses tremble, even though the spirit may be the victor in its struggle for purity and for perpetuating the transitory.

The poet conceives of love as a demanding, powerful, cunning divinity that enslaves us and against whom all resistance is futile. Ruled by its fatal power, she abandons herself to feeling with a jealous vehemence that has more of hate than of love. Every so often tenderness, fulfilled pleasure will soften her words: but the dominant note will always be "all or nothing," the vengeful fury of a new Medea who does not hesitate to destroy that which she loves as well as herself.

"Dios lo quiere"

I

La tierra se hace madrastra
si tu alma vende a mi alma.
Llevan un escalofrío
de tribulación las aguas.
El mundo fué más hermoso
desde que yo te fuí aliada,
cuando junto de un espino
nos quedamos sin palabras,
¡y el amor como el espino
nos traspasó de fragancia!

¡Pero te va a brotar víboras
la tierra si vendes mi alma!
baldías del hijo, rompo
mis rodillas desoladas!
Se apaga Cristo en mi pecho
¡y la puerta de mi casa
quiebra la mano al mendigo
y avienta a la atribulada!

II

Beso que tu boca entregue
a mis oídos alcanza
porque las grutas profundas
me devuelven tus palabras.
El polvo de los senderos
guarda el olor de tus plantas
y oteándolo, como un ciervo,
te sigo por las montañas . . .

A la que tú ames, las nubes
la pintan sobre mi casa.
Vé cual ladrón a besarla
de la tierra en las entrañas;
mas, cuando el rostro le alces,
hallas mi cara con lágrimas.
Dios no quiere que tú bebas
si yo no tiemblo en tu agua.
No consiente que tú duermas
sino en mi trenza ahuecada.

Si te vas, hasta en los musgos
del camino rompes mi alma;
te muerden la sed y el hambre
en todo valle o llanada
y en cualquier país las tardes
con sangre serán mis llagas.

Y destilo de tu lengua
aunque a otra mujer llamaras,

y me clavo como un dejo
de salmuera en tu garganta;
y odies, o cantes, o ansies,
¡por mí solamente clamas!

Si te vas y mueres lejos,
tendrás la mano ahuecada
diez años bajo la tierra
para recibir mis lágrimas,
sintiendo como te tiemblan
las carnes atribuladas,
¡hasta que te espolvoreen
mis huesos sobre la cara!

pp. 106–108.

The very earth will reject you
If your soul sells mine.
Within the waters there seethes
The chill of tribulation.
The world was more beautiful
From the time that I was yours,

When together beside a thorn tree
We stood without words,
And love like a thorn
Pierced us with its fragrance!

But snakes will spring from the earth
If you sell my soul;
Barren of child, I crush
My desolate knees.
Christ is stifled within me,
And the door of my house
Breaks the hand of the beggar
And chases the woman in pain.

The kiss you may give another
Rings within my ears
Because the deep caves
Are echoing your words.
The dust of the road
Retains the scent of your steps
And like a deer tracking
I follow you through the mountains . . .

The clouds will paint on my house
The other whom you may love.
Go like a thief to kiss her
In the bowels of the earth;
But when you lift her face
You will find mine tear-filled before you.

God will not let you drink
If I tremble not in the water.
He will not let you sleep
Lest cradled in my tresses.

If you leave you break my soul
On the very moss you tread;
Hunger and thirst will seize you
On every mountain and plain
And in every land the blood-filled days will be my wounds.

And my name slips from your tongue
Though you may call another,
And I will pierce your throat
As with the taste of brine;
And whether you hate, or sing, or long
For me alone you will clamor!

If you leave and distant die,
The hollow of your hand will wait
Ten years beneath the earth
To catch my falling tears,
Feeling the very trembling
Of my afflicted flesh,
Until my bones crumble
To dust upon your face!

The enamored one also speaks with God and attempts to enlist Him in her cause. When she underlines the spiritual rather than the physical nature of her emotion, she reveals its religious sense, the divine spark that illuminates it:

"Intima"

¡Es un viento de Dios que pasa hendiéndome
el gajo de las carnes volandero!

p. 105.

"Intimation"

It is a wind of God that passes piercing me
With the fleeting barb of the flesh!

and she warns her beloved that their union is an indissoluble pact, a decree of the Divinity.

It is not surprising that her song takes the form of prayer in its moments of fulfillment as well as in those of affliction. Like Unamuno, she wants to transcend the fleeting aspects of pleasure and worldly ties and conquer death. Her maternal longing and its antipode, the anguished certainty of dying, drive her to asceticism. In **"Intimation"** (***Intima***), she rejects experience of the flesh that imprisons love in its deathly chains:

Tú no beses mi boca.
Vendrá el instante lleno
de luz menguada, en que estaré sin labios
sobre un mojado suelo.

Y dirás: "La amé, pero no puedo
amarla más, ahora que no aspira
el olor de retamas de mi beso.

p. 104.

You, do not kiss my mouth,
There will come the moment filled
With dying light, in which I will be without lips
On a wet ground.

And you will say: "I loved her once, but can
No longer love her, now that she cannot breathe
The genista scent of my kiss.

In **"Poem of the Son"** (**"Poema del hijo"**), she escapes from lust in order to offer her child a pure bed and womb:

En las noches, insomne de dicha y de visiones,
la lujuria de fuego no descendió a mi lecho.
Para el que nacería vestido de canciones
yo extendía mi brazo, yo ahuecaba mi pecho.

p. 139.

In the nights, sleepless with joy and visions,
I did not take fiery lust to my bed.
For the one to be born clothed in songs
I opened my arms and breast instead.

Sorrow and death are the constant companions of this love, from its dawn to its sunset, and even in the brief moments of happiness they cast upon the poetry their somber shadows, subtle shadings that bind fear to pleasure, anguish to tenderness.

When we enter the inner region of ***Desolation*** for the first time, we are surprised to hear a new language of love. Though still resounding with old echoes, it is free from the refinements and exquisiteness that literary elegance and urbanity have been imposing on the expression of love from the days of the Provençal troubadours and Petrarch to the present. The new language free of prudery, reflects rustic realism, the frank manner with which people who live close to the soil refer to the events of life and to feelings: a natural simplicity that calls a spade a spade. The words are direct, concrete, a bit coarse. Their intensity, the ardor of the epithets, the strength of the images lend purposeful energy and great plasticity to the verses.

Gabriela is not guilty of that immodesty, audacity, and erotic excess of other women who have sung to love in our America. Her maternal instinct and her moral and religious sensibility compel her to be prudent. In her longing for spirituality and purity she responds, in a very Spanish way, to the problem of death.

She has struck some critics as excessive, wrathful. Hyperbole is, actually, one of the characteristic traits of her style. Yet there is no doubt that compared to the somewhat decadent preciosity of the Modernists, her voice has the vigor of elemental forces, because she draws emotion directly from the living waters of feeling, from the deep, inner truth of a soul that has not been weakened by the effeminacy of this century.

In 1918 Gabriela went to Punto Arenas on the Straits of Magellan to become director of the school for girls. For two years she stayed in that inhospitable region, in voluntary exile, fleeing from the places in which she had lived the terrible drama of her love. Pursued by cruel memories, desolate, her wounds still fresh, she vented her pain and hunger for death on the new landscape. The poems included in "Nature" (*Naturaleza*), and perhaps the **"Songs"** (**"Coplas"**) (p. 142) of "Sorrow" (*Dolor*), were written at this time. They faithfully transmit her brooding mood, that dark longing to immerse herself in despair and solitude.

The description of the landscape is now merely the means by which Gabriela reveals the anguish of her heart. The states at the southernmost tip of Chile have nothing in common with the fertile, luminous beauty of her native Elqui valley, with the fruitful abundance of its orchards, the transparency of its rivers, the warm fragrance of its breezes. Here there is only a white endless plain, howling winds, foggy skies, and a long night, filled with phantoms.

The poet feels alone and abandoned in these places, among people who do not speak her language.

Los barcos cuyas velas blanquean en el puerto
vienen de tierras donde no están los que son míos;
sus hombres de ojos claros no conocen mis ríos
y traen frutos pálidos, sin la luz de mis huertos.

Y la interrogación que sube a mi garganta
al mirarlos pasar, me desciende, vencida:
hablan extrañas lenguas y no la conmovida
lengua que en tierras de oro mi pobre madre canta.

Desolation, pp. 149–50.

The ships that fill the port with their sails of white
Come from lands where there are no boats of mine;
They do not know my rivers, these men whose light eyes shine
And they come bearing pale fruit without my orchards' light.

And the rising question that my throat demands
As I watch them pass, vanquished, now retreats:
They speak strange tongues, tongues not so sweet
As the one my mother sings in golden lands.

But at the same time, she initiates a tremendous dialogue with these beings, a dialogue shaken by fatal omens; and in the sadness of things and the thousand pained faces of nature about her, she keeps discovering the projections of her inner world, the faithful image of her own tragic mask.

The selection of poetic themes reveals the perfect identification between the moral and external landscapes; the images reveal her conception of sorrow as a bleeding passion similar to that of Christ, the fixed idea of death as the only, powerful wellspring of lyricism. The poet watches the snow falling upon the plain:

la nieve como el polvo en la huesa;
miro crecer la niebla como el agonizante.

Desolation, p. 150.

The snow like dust upon the tomb;
As one dying, I watch the swelling mist.

On the trunk of a dry tree, she notices how

"Arbol muerto"

sube de la herida un purpurino
musgo, como una estrofa ensangrentada.

p. 151.

"Dead Tree"

From the wound there rises a purple
Moss, like a blood-stained stanza.

As she listens to the tinkle of the rain she wonders if it is possible to sleep:

"La lluvia lenta"

mientras afuera
cae, sufriendo, esta agua inerte,
esta agua letal hermana
de la Muerte?

p. 167.

"The Slow Rain"

While outside
There suffering falls this inert water
This lethal water, sister
to Death?

And the constant presence of this hidden death gives the landscape its fearful beauty, so removed from the strength, majesty, sweetness, and light of the American scenes in ***Felling*** (***Tala***) and ***Wine Press*** (***Lagar***). . . .

TENDERNESS (*TERNURA*)

Gabriela's second book, ***Tenderness,***[4] of which there are already four editions, is a collection of all her children's poems up to 1945. The last edition reproduces those published in the three preceding editions, in the first two of ***Desolation,*** those from ***Felling*** (***Tala***), and a score of new poems. The book opens with a dedication to her mother and sister, Emelina, both of whom exercised so much influence on Gabriela's spiritual formation and on her choice of teaching as a career. ***Tenderness*** contains seven sections: "Lullabies" (*Canciones de cuna*), "Rounds" (*Rondas*), "The Raving Woman" (*La desvariadora*), "Tricks" (*Jugarretas*), "Story-World" (*Cuenta-Mundo*), "Almost for School" (*Casi escolares*), "Stories" (*Cuentos*), and a "Colophon by Way of Explanation" (*Colofon con cara de excusa*). The "Colofón," datelined Petropolis, Brazil, is of great interest for the critical evaluation of Mistral's children's poetry and very useful in sketching an intellectual and moral portrait of the poet. Most of this commentary is devoted to the presentation of a theory on the origin of cradle songs, the explanation of the scarcity of such songs in American lands, and the reasons for their present decline. She sees the most important factor as "the decline of physical motherhood, not only the reduction in the number of children but the refusal of many woman to bear children or to be the milking fig tree of stories. The woman who has never nursed, who does not feel the weight of her child against her body, who never puts anyone to sleep day or night, how can she possibly hum a *berceuse*" (p. 185)? The definition of the lullaby as "the dialogue that takes place each day and night between the mother and her soul, her child and the Gea, visible during the day and audible at night" (p. 184) strikes us as the best, the most precise, and the most profound of any we have heard.

The titles of the different sections correspond to those in former editions, with the exception of "Tricks" (*Jugarretas*), which in ***Felling*** (***Tala***) was called "Reward" (*Albricia*), and "Almost for School" (*Casi escolares*), which was called "For Children" (*Infantiles*) in ***Desolation.*** In both cases, the change indicates the desire to establish a more precise correlation between the title and the content and tone of the poems appearing under those titles. "The Raving Woman "(*La desvariadora*), which mostly contains new poems, is also a highly appropriate name because all these poems refer to fantasies and exaggerations born of the obsession with motherhood.

Some poems are not very suitably grouped. **"Mexican Child"** (**"Niño mexicano"**) is not truly a lullaby; in **"The Little Box of Olinalá"** (**"La cajita de Olinalá"**), there is no raving by a delighted mother; **"Little Red Riding Hood"** (**"Caperucita Roja"**) retells the well-known story, highlighting its ferocious aspect, and has nothing in common with the charming and original fantasies of **"Mother Pomegranate"** (**"La madre granada"**) and **"The Pine with Pine Cones"** (**"El piño de piñas"**); it seems to be the least pedagogical, the least suited to a child's sensibilities. **"Caress"** (**"Caricia"**), **"Sweetness"** (**"Dulzura"**), **"Little Worker"** (**"Obrerito"**) express pure filial tenderness without the didactic or moralizing purposes of the other poems in this same section.

The title, ***Tenderness***, is well suited to the general character of the book and to the principal emotion that is the source of its poetry. All the poems sing to the pleasure of motherhood, the miracle of having a child, the charm of little animals, the loving understanding between the earth and its creatures. After the tremendous passionate, sensual energy of ***Desolation***, this second work reveals to us the powerful vitality, the hunger for happiness, "thc spiritualization of voluptuousness which is tenderness,"[5] the other poles of the poet's spirit.

Gabriela pours forth into these poems her longing to transcend the ephemeral aspects of passion through motherhood, to seek the eternal in the transitory. It is significant that in **"Song of Death"** (**"Canción de la Muerte"**) she calls death the "Counter-mother of the world" (*Contra-Madre del Mundo*) (***Tenderness***, p. 54).

The themes of ***Tenderness*** duplicate almost all the major motifs of her poetry: maternal love, its pleasures, enchantments, fears, fantasies; the child, his games and legends; the earth (nature, landscape, heavens, constellations); matter (animals, vegetables, minerals, things made by man); toil; America, sleep, death, peace, cosmic harmony, Jesus Christ, God the Father. The poetic development of such rich, varied material keeps these poems free from monotony, trivia, foolishness, and the shoddy prosiness, too often found in this genre. Gabriela is not guilty of becoming artificially child-like, of abandoning the adult point of view, nor of using the silly language that adults presumptuously attribute to children. She makes use of that reserve of unspoiled childhood latent in the spirit of all great poets, and she has attempted (so she tells us in the Colofón) to follow the model of European children's folklore (Spanish, Provençal, Italian) and of general folklore itself, "in search of childlike language, attempting to fathom the clear, profound mystery of its expression." Above all, she has loved and respected the memory of children (p. 190), striving to fathom the secrets of their souls, their imaginative and creative energy, the intensity of their attention. She knows very well that "the singer or balladeer for little ones, the chanter of their dwarf-like cathedral, the master of their songs is not just created, but comes slowly along his starry way, and no one can hasten him along" (p. 189).

From the beginning of her literary career she had worked on this difficult genre, and perhaps no other American poet—except the Martí of *Ismaelillo*—has achieved more beautiful, authentic, and convincing results. All her children's poems have the same depth and intensity of conception and emotion as her adult poetry, qualities that admirably frame the very mischief, malice, playful grace of rhythm, and intent of the verses of childhood. Nothing is spontaneous in these poems: even the most fleeting glance discloses the artistic deliberation evident at each step. Gabriela's comments in "Colofón" indisputably corroborate this observation. The poet has stated for herself all the problems of this genre and has made a strenuous effort to solve them; she is fully aware of her successes and failures. Not the least of the difficulties involved is the struggle with language, the desire to overcome what she calls "verbal hybridization." "Speech," she affirms, "is, after the soul, our second possession and perhaps we have no other possession in this world. Let the one who experiments with it and knows he is experimenting rework it as he pleases" (pp. 189–90).

The result of this vigilance is the precedence of the intellectual note over the sentimental and instructive in these poems: that which is exclusively due to "art" is more evident here than in ***Desolation.*** By saying this we do not detract from the poetic values of ***Ternura.*** Quite the contrary. The Cuban Jorge Mañach has already made a decisive and just evaluation.

> This art of speaking to childhood is one which only those who have a very deep sense of the spiritual and the concrete can master. The fusion of tremulousness with plasticity, of the malice of beautiful expression with the innocence of the emotion—what a faultless achievement in the pages of ***Ternura***!
>
> [p. 8]

The wide publication of the lullabies, rounds, and games in this book is evidence of their success. Gabriela has followed the traditional Spanish rhythms closely, giving preference to the ballad form. Besides this form, there also appear the heptasyllabic and hexasyllabic short ballads, the unfinished *seguidilla*, short songs and rondelet-like refrains. There is an abundance of similar combinations based on the nine-syllable line, a meter that is very common in her poetry. The monotony and regularity of the rhyme in these forms is broken at times by a certain harshness and dissonance, by the sudden insertion of a long line or a shorter one, or by an unexpected change of rhyme. The repetition of phrases and lines and the parallelism of their internal structure creates an effect similar to the humming and rhythm of rounds. Gabriela's verse line, very rarely melodic, imparts a sensation of muffled, rending, insistent murmur. On occasions, however, it achieves a winged lightness, a heightened vivacity, and is filled with folkloric grace and freedom.

If we were to study these poems in the chronological order in which they were written, we would observe the change within them wrought by the passage of time. Those published in ***Desolation*** greatly resemble traditional lullabies and rounds. The very immediate influence of Spanish folklore is confirmed at every step. The musical forms do not offer any variety. Those found in the section "For Children" (*Infantiles*) seem to have been written for possible classroom use; and this is precisely the use to which they have been put. Almost all of them embody a moral teaching or attempt to develop in the student specific attitudes, inclinations, and sentiments: love for nature and country, respect for animals, attention to the miracles of creation, brotherly union, the encouragement of fantasy and of the aesthetic sense. We perceive traces of the Old Testament and of the *Little Flowers* of St. Francis. Franciscan love for all beings acts as a common denominator in all the poems.

The children's poems of ***Felling*** (***Tala***) are already completely different. The poet has freed herself from her models and attempts original subject matter and rhythms; she has rid herself completely of academic concerns. The lullabies, more elaborate, more correct, more interesting from the artistic point of view, have lost something of the freshness and naturalness of the first ones. The other poems, no longer concerned with pedagogy, gain in malice, in imaginative intoxication, in playfulness. **"The One-Armed"** (**"La manca"**), **"The Little Straw"** (**"La pajita"**), **"The Parrot"** (**"El papagayo"**) demonstrate the extent to which the poet has managed to approach the child's soul, to put us in his place and capture his way of seeing and feeling reality. The delicious stories **"Mother Pomegranate"** (**"La madre granada"**) and **"The Pine with Pine Cones"** (**"El piño de piñas"**), a series of somewhat ironic personifications and enchanting, suggestive images—some already very intellectualized—share a strong plasticity that could be compared to the absurd fantasies of Walt Disney.

But the more recent poems, those that incorporate the American theme into the children's genre, appear more terse in their treatment, somewhat forced, perhaps too literary. Some of their details remind us of Góngora and García Lorca. **"The Arrorró of Elqui"** (**"El arrorró elquino"**), **"Quechua Song"** (**"La canción quechua"**), **"Patagonian Lullaby"** (**"Arrullo patagón"**), **"The Round of the Ecuadorian Ceiba Tree"** (**"Ronda de la ceiba equatoriana"**) are examples of her effort to create American children's songs against a background of regional local color; her vocabulary in these poems is a mixture of regional and indigenous expressions, with allusions to the flora, the fauna, the beliefs, superstitions and the Indian culture of these lands.

Still more elaborate are the **"Song of Virgo"** (**"Canción de Virgo"**) and the **"Song of Taurus"** (**"Canción de Taurus"**), which create a series of myths of stellar motherhood. The poet seems to attribute a maternal sense to the entire universe, not only to the earth. It is curious that there is never any mention made of the father in these poems—an allusion that, on the other hand, is usually recurrent in folk lullabies. In these poems, the mother, or the thousand mothers, give themselves completely to the sweet task of lulling their children to sleep. In this intimate colloquy—actually almost a monologue—the mother tells her child about the world; she unburdens herself of her most secret worries, sorrows, and forebodings. In the rhythmic sway of the lullaby, there is a gradual tightening of the ties that bind the creative love of God—the only Father who has access to this closed circle—to the love of the earth for its little creatures. In several lullabies and rounds we witness this gradual expansion, like the widening of concentric circles, that starts with the mother's song and gradually grows until it embraces the totality of the cosmos and God himself, "the only love that moves the Sun and the other stars." Motherhood has a double significance for Gabriela: it is part of the divine because it is a joyous creation; it attains the eternal because it scoffs at death and spiritualizes the fleeting pleasures of the flesh.

> ¡es un viento de Dios que pasa hendiéndome
> el gajo de las carnes, volandero!
>
> It is a wind of God that passes, piercing me
> With the fleeting barb of the flesh! . . .

"Felling" (*Tala*)

The poetic world of ***Felling*** differs radically from that of ***Desolation.*** Going from one to other is like going from the Old Testament to the Gospels. Or it may be likened to entering the illuminating state of mysticism after leaving behind the asperities of asceticism. The entire atmosphere has changed; happiness modulates the style. In ***Felling*** there speaks the spirit that has controlled the flesh. Her voice retains its passionate rapture, but the structural rhythm now flows in peaceful measures, though it is still intense. At certain moments hope is raised to the high-pitched, joyous heights of ecstasy. The poem **"Grace"** (**"La Gracia"**), which strikes us as being the lyrical peak of her work and its culmination, captures the essence of this spiritual moment in words of intense conciseness. Some lines echo accents heard in Saint John of the Cross.

> Pareció lirio
> o pez-espada.
> Subió los aires
> hondeada,
> de cielo abierto
> devorada,
> y en un momento
> fué nonada.
> Quedé temblando
> en la quebrada.
> ¡Albricia mía!
> ¡arrebatada!

Felling, p. 55.

> It seemed a lily
> Or sword fish to me,
> It scaled the airs
> Pulling free,
> Devoured by the open sky
>
> Hungrily,
> And in a moment
> A mere speck to see.
> I stood trembling
> In the ravine,
> Oh, joy of mine!
> Torn from me!

The first section of ***Felling,*** "Death of My Mother" (*Muerte de mi Madre*), establishes the continuity between this book and its predecessor. **"The Flight"** (**"La fuga"**), the **"Nocturnes of Consummation"** (**"Nocturnos de la consumación"**), **"The Defeat"** (**"La derrota"**), and **"Old Weavers"** (**"Tejedores viejos"**) prolong the religious crisis already noted in the aforementioned **"Nocturne." "Mad Litanies"** (**"Locas letanías"**) and **"Nocturne of the Descent"** (**"Nocturno del descendimiento"**), on the other hand, manifest the return to hope, the true entry into a new moral climate. The second of these poems is reminiscent of some passages from "The Christ of Velázquez" (*El Cristo de Velázquez*) by Unamuno; the first sings with the joy of faith in resurrection. Pain at her mother's death has transformed itself into the certainty of a future life in the peace of Christ. We know that this change occurred following the reading of Henri Bergson's *Les deux sources de la religion et de la morale.* The chapter in which Bergson studies Christian mysticism moved the poet deeply and started her longing and searching for grace.

The second part, "Hallucination" (*Alucinación*), contains recollections, dreams, and visions like **"Paradise"** (**"Paraíso"**) and **"Midnight"** (**"La medianoche"**). **"Tales of the Madwoman"** (**"Historias de loca"**) merit special attention. Their dominant characteristic is fantasy; the first tale imagines the world as it was before the birth of death and records the terrible effects upon everything of this newly-born death. In the second poem, the nature of poetry is likened to a "flower of the air"; the third tells of the spiritual liberation of the soul as it divests itself of the body, that shadow that had always chained it to the law of time; the fourth relates a dream-like experience. These four poems gather together all the major themes of Gabriela Mistral's latest poetry: death, the absolute, poetry, dreams. They are not tales of a madwoman; on the contrary, they contain some of the poet's deepest, most elaborate thoughts.

The section called "Matter" (*Materias*) presents us with another kind of poetic experience: the rapture she feels as she looks at things that suddenly seem to reveal the hidden essence of their being. Beneath our gaze one day, bread, salt, water, air take on values they never had before. It is a rediscovery filled with surprises, a kind of mystical union with reality. For a moment the poet senses the divine presence in things and loses herself in fascinated contemplation.

Beneath the heading "America" (*América*) are joined together eulogies, landscapes, and memories of our continent; the tropical sun, the Andes, the hills and palm groves of Puerto Rico, the Panamanian dance *tamborito*; she sings to the Americas with the fervor of one in love. She sees the sun and the mountain range as unifying factors in the Americas and envisions the United States of the South both as a political reality and a cultural unit based on the restoration of the indigenous past to the present. Gabriela's Americanism goes beyond national frontiers and embraces in the same loving gesture the Mexican child, the sweet earth of Puerto Rico, the pagan spell of the *tamborito.*

The language in all these poems is enthusiastic and passionate. The two Hymns have the hyperbolic accents of a litany; the vision of Puerto Rico is captured with maternal tenderness; the description of the Mexican cornfield and of Mexican men has the power of a stone relief or the ritualistic rhythm of a Diego Rivera fresco.

Las mesas del maíz
quieren que yo me acuerde.
El corro está mirándome
fugaz y eternamente.
Los sentados son órganos,
Las sentadas magueyes.
Delante de mi pecho
La mazorcada tienden.
De la voz y los modos
gracia tolteca llueve.
La casta come lento,
como el venado bebe.
Dorados son el hombre,

el bocado, el aceite,
y en sesgo de ave pasan
las jícaras alegres.
Otra vez me tuvieron
éstos que aquí me tiene,
y el corro, de lo eterno,
parece que espejee . . .

. . . . .

El pecho del maíz
su fervor lo retiene.
El ojo del maíz,
tiene el abismo breve.
Su obsidiana se funde
como una contra-nieve.
El habla del maíz
en valva y valva envuelve.
Ley Vieja del maíz,
caída no perece,
y el hombre del maíz
se juega, no se pierde.

Felling, pp. 108–10.

The tables of corn
Want me to remember.
The group gazes at me
Fleetingly and eternal.
The seated men are organ
cactus,
The women maguey.
Before my breast
They spread the ears of corn.
Their voices and their manner
Bespeak their Toltec grace.
The clan eats slowly,
As the young deer drinks.

Golden are the men,
The food, the oil,
And like the graceful sweep
of birds
The happy chocolate cups are
passed.
Once before they held me
They who hold me now,
This group which seems to
shine,
With the light of eternity . . .

. . . . .

The breast of the corn
Retains its warmth.
The eye of the corn,
Bares a shallow abyss.
Its obsidian melts
As a counter-snow.
The tongue of the corn
In sheath upon sheath
enclosed.
Ancient law of the corn,
Which fallen, does not
perish,
And the man of the corn
Moves with it, never lost. . . .

Wine Press (*Lagar*)

Sixteen years after ***Felling,*** Gabriela published ***Wine Press***,[6] her swan song. This book was also a selection that discarded much of what she had written during those years, as well as a mirror of the times in which the poet lived and of her personal life and suffering. They were sixteen terrible years for human society as a whole as well as for the individual. During this period were World War II, the Korean War, the Cold War; denouncing was promoted and rewarded, persecutions, concentration camps, refinements of physical and psychological tortures; forced, mass exodus, insecurity, suspicion, fear, hysteria, thermonuclear bombs. Those years saw such an absolute undermining of values that peace became a "cursed word,"[7] and those who wanted peace became suspect and persecuted; values were so monstrously perverted that the attempt to avoid war took the form of a senseless race for arms that became more and more lethal. These were the years, still not over, of loathing and "nausea."

These years were critical on the personal and psychological level as well. For Gabriela they brought continuous travel, the suicide of her friends, Stefan Zweig and his wife, and that of Juan Miguel Godoy, the nephew she had raised and loved as a son and who had died under obscure circumstances in the flower of his eighteenth year. They were also the years of her Nobel Prize for literature, the slow decline of her health, her premonition of imminent death. In those years, from 1938 to 1954, she constantly changed her place of residence. She returned to America on her way back from Europe. She visited Brazil, Uruguay, Argentina, Chile, and her native Elqui valley, Peru, Ecuador, Panamá, Cuba, Mexico, the United States. On two other occasions she again went to Europe and spent time in Nice and Naples. In 1945, in Stockholm, she received the highest literary recognition of all. Now she could permit herself the luxury of living wherever she chose: the Chilean government was always eager to honor her with a diplomatic post; Mexico made her a gift of some land; she purchased houses in Santa Barbara, California, and in Petropolis, Brazil. Every so often it would seem that she had finally found repose: she would light the fireplace, build a library, collect records of folk music and folk poetry, cultivate a garden and orchard, form a circle of friends. But she never stayed for long; once again she would move from one place to another, spurred on by something within herself, something that she had perhaps inherited from her roving, vagabond father. Over and over she renewed her wandering as one possessed, restless, as if fleeing, always reliving memories, dreaming of her little village of Montegrande, her Italian sea, tropical palm groves, the cornfields of her Mexico. The longest sojourns were in Nice, Brazil, Veracruz, and the United States. She left Nice because of the war and Brazil because she was shattered by the overwhelming triple suicide. Her last years were spent in the United States, first in New York, then in Washington, Miami, Monrovia, Santa Barbara, and finally, in Roslyn Harbor, Long Island. In spite of her now serious illness, she summoned strength to attend the Convention of Writers on Martí in Cuba, the Lectures for Responsible Freedom at Columbia University, or to carry out her duties as a member of the Committee on Women's Rights of the United Nations.

All this left its trace in ***Wine Press. Wine Press*** is the internalization and poetic transfiguration of these events and experiences. The anecdotal element is as important here as in the former books, although it is hidden behind a veil of hallucination and dream. The biographical reality is present, but always on the border of fantasy; always oscillating between the real and the dreamed.

The title of the work repeats that image of the **"Nocturne"** (**"Nocturno"**) in ***Desolation:***

> ¡Y en el ancho lagar de la muerte
> aun no quieres mi pecho exprimir!

> And in the wide wine press of death
> You still will not drain my heart!

In the wine press of life and death, the poet has wrung from herself the bitter juice of these lines, and she has been left exhausted, as if emptied of herself. Now she no longer seeks death with that passionate rebellion of youth and unrequited love. She feels it "crossing the threshold"; she awaits it in silence, she wills it. At times she seems to have crossed the line and no longer knows whether she is dead or living; and she begins to converse with her ghosts.

The book is made up of a Prologue, an Epilogue, and thirteen sections. There is no prose included, nor are there any explanatory notes as there were in ***Desolation***, ***Tenderness***, and ***Felling.*** All of this supposes a stricter evaluation of the lyrical product, a greater security in her own creation, in the right to her own language. Through **"The Other One"** (**"La otra"**), the poem that serves as a prologue for Gabriela, we learn that she has left behind the ardor and sensuality of her young years;

> Una en mí mate;
> yo no la amaba.
>
> Era la flor llameando
> del cactus de montaña;
> era aridez y fuego;
> nunca se refrescaba.
>
> p. 9, lines 1–6.

> Let one in me be killed;
> I did not love her.
>
> She was the blazing flower
> Of the mountain cactus;
> She was barrenness and fire;
> She was never refreshed.

This poem now speaks to us of a different Gabriela, divested of matter, spiritualized, reconciled to death. **"The Other One"** presides over the work and renews in verse the "Vow" (*Voto*) of ***Desolation***:

> In these one hundred poems there lies bleeding a painful past, in which my song was stained with blood in order to offer me some respite. I leave it behind me like a dark ravine and up the more clement sides I climb towards the spiritual plateaus, where a broad light will finally fall on my days. From them I will sing words of hope, without looking at my heart again: I will sing as a man of mercy once wished to, to "console men." At thirty years of age, when I wrote *The Decalogue of the Artist* [*El decálogo del artista*], I stated this "Vow" [*Voto*].
>
> p. 243.

The strange poem that serves as an epilogue, **"Last Tree"** (**"Ultimo árbol"**), sings of the definitive dream in the fresh shade of a tamarind or cedar tree, inheritor of

lo que tuve
de ceniza y firmamento,
mi flanco lleno de hablas
y mi flanco de silencio;

Soledades que me dí,
soledades que me dieron,
y el diezmo que pagué al rayo
de mi Dios dulce y tremendo;

Mi juego de toma y daca
con las nubes y los vientos,
y lo que supe, temblando,
de manantiales secretos.

p. 188, lines 21–32.

What I had
Of ash and firmament
What I had of voice
And what I had of silence;

Solitudes I gave myself
Solitudes given to me,
And the tithe I paid to the
lightening bolt
Of my sweet and tremendous
God;

My game of give and take
With the clouds and winds,
And what I learned,
trembling,
From secret springs.

Here she is surrendering her spiritual and moral self, not only her body. She delineates her psychological traits in the firm brush strokes of this exact self-portrait. Gabriela loved trees "as one loves a man," a husband. Her treatment of them was that of one person to another; it was an exaltation and personification that went beyond simple love for creatures or rustic familiarity with living things of the soil. The self-portrait reveals the almost pantheistic face of the poet and her deification of nature. In addition, trees and animals were the sources for numerous affectionate names she gave people of whom she was fond, either in friendly conversation with them or in poetic treatment.

"Una mujer"

Cuando dice "pino de Alepo"
no dice árbol que dice un niño.
y cuando dice "regato"
y "espejo de oro," dice lo mismo.

p. 87, lines 5–8.

"A Woman"

When she says "pine of Aleppo"
She does not mean a tree she means a child.
And when she says "rivulet"
And "golden mirror," she means the same. . . .

[***Wine Press***] lacks tonal unity. The poems within the group "Tricks" (*Jugarretas*), almost all those in the section "Nature" (*Naturaleza*), and the "Rounds" (*Rondas*) reveal to us the playful, mocking, happy Gabriela who lived side by side with the one of the tragic mask: a Gabriela of clear, capricious, and imaginative laughter, capable of running through the fields, embracing the trees, flinging herself to the ground to inhale, avidly, its fragrances; an elemental and bacchic creature, strongly attracted by a search for earthly happiness, entranced with the beauty of the world.

"El reparto"

Y otras tomen mis sentidos.
Con su sed y con su hambre.

p. 14, lines 23–24.

"The Distribution"

And let others take my senses.
With their thirst and with their hunger.

In **"Eight Little Dogs"** (**"Ocho perritos"**) this aspect of happiness is shown as the desire for instinctive life, though joined to the divine order of the creation:

Y yo querría nacer con ellos.
¿ Por qué otra vez no sería?
Saltar unos bananales
una mañana de maravilla,
en can, en coyota, en venada;
mirar con grandes pupilas,
correr, parar, correr,
tumbarme
y gemir y saltar de alegría,
acribillada de sol y ladridos
hija de Dios, sierva oscura
y divina.

p. 36, lines 15–24.

And I would want to be born
with them.
Why could it not be again?
To jump through banana groves
One miraculous morning,
As a dog, coyote, or deer;
To gaze with large pupils,
To run and stop, run and fall
And whimper and jump for joy,
Pierced by sun and barks
A daughter of God, humble and
divine servant.

The first section, "Fantasy" (*Desvarío*), contains only two poems: **"The Distribution"** (**"El reparto"**) and **"Request for Blanca"** (**"Encargo a Blanca"**), both on a religious theme—the divestment and distribution of the bodily senses after death, a return in spirit to communicate with the living. Some incidental confessions have psychological interests:

"Encargo a Blanca"

Y otras tomen mis sentidos . . .
Y no llores si no te respondo
porque mi culpa fué la palabra.

p. 15, lines 13–14.

"Request for Blanca"

And do not weep if I do not answer
For my sin was the word.

The religious beliefs are not clear, nor do they follow a definite body of dogma. Poetically at least, she seems to deny the resurrection of the flesh:

"El reparto"

Acabe así, consumada
repartida como hogaza
y lanzada a sur o a norte
no seré nunca más una.

p. 14, lines 25–28.

"The Distribution"

Let me end thus, consummated
Doled out like bread
And flung to south or north
Never again to be one.

On the other hand, she alludes to the state of expiation of sins in the beyond (purgatory?):

Y no llores si no te respondo . . .

and to the communication between living and dead. She conceives of the beatific state as a pure vision, as all encompassing intelligence and knowledge:

"El reparto"

¿Ojos? ¿para qué preciso
arriba y llena de lumbres?

En mi patria he de llevar
todo el cuerpo hecho pupila,
espejo devolvedor,
ancha pupila sin párpados

Iré yo a campo traviesa
con los ojos en las manos
y las dos manos dichosas
deletreando lo no visto
nombrando lo adivinado.

p. 13, lines 1–16.

"The Distribution"

Eyes? Why do I need them
In the above, filled with
lights?
In my Country I am to wear
My whole body as an eye,
A reflecting mirror
A wide pupil without lids.

I will run across the country
With my eyes in my hands
And my two hands joyous,
Tracing the unseen
Naming what was guessed.

She calls paradise "my country" and the earth "my dwelling place." This stylistic trait was not found in former works. It consists of calling things by very personal, metaphorical names, written with a capital letter, at times modified by the first person possessive. It is as if, in this way, the poet were sentimentally and subjectively taking possession of things, attributing to them some extraordinary value and thus creating for herself her own universe.

It would be appropriate to add to this group the eight poems of the section "Religious Verses" (*Religiosas*). Three of them, **"Indian Noël"** (**"Noël indio"**), **"Christmas Pines"** (**"Pinos de Navidad"**), **"Christmas Star"** (**"Estrella de Navidad"**), objectively deal with the theme of the Incarnation and belong to the class of poems for children by virtue of their gay rhythm, graceful images, and their form of story, ballad, and lullaby. **"Indian Procession"** (**"Procesión India"**) expresses ideas and images analogous to the two hymns in ***Felling***. The popular worship of Saint Rose of Lima is evidence—as are the mountain range and the tropical sun—of the eternal spiritual community of the American peoples. The blessing of food in **"Lunch in the Sun"** (**"Almuerzo al sol"**) serves as a pretext for exalting the luminosity and plenitude of noon. With almost mathematical conciseness, in the style of Valéry, she evokes the table, the fruit, the gestures of the table companions, setting them all into the harmonious rhythm, the clean color, and the plastic imagery of a still life. The simple, daily act is thus clothed in profound, ritualistic beauty.

Bendícenos la jarra
que abaja el cuello gresco,
la fruta embelesada,
la mazorca riendo,
y el café de ojo oscuro
que está empinado, viéndonos.

Las grecas de los cuerpos
bendígalas su Dueño;
ahora el brazo en alto,
ahora el pecho,
y la mano de siembras,
y la mano de riegos.

pp. 133–34, lines 17–28.

We are blessed by the jug
That lowers its young neck,
The enchanting fruit,
The laughing corn,
And the dark-eyed coffee
Tipped, and gazing at us.

The graceful curves of
bodies
Let the Lord bless them;
Now the arm on high
Now the breast,
Now the hand that sows
And the hand that waters. . . .

The section entitled "War" shows us a Gabriela preoccupied with external events, no longer enclosed in the ivory tower. As in the case of the other Nobel laureate, Quasimodo, her verses capture the echoes of what is happening in the world, of the political and social problems of her time. World War II moves her to reflect upon the fate of Europe, to sing of the heroism of Finland, the lonely suffering of the wounded, the anguish of the persecuted and exiled. All the poems throb with the feeling of human solidarity in pain, with vehement protest against injustice, with the heroic sentiment of life; it is a moral conception of stoic strength modelled after Job and the Maccabees. Gabriela was incapable of considering political and social problems in the abstract. Being a woman, the essences moved her more than the historical situation. The human, private, personal case interested her above all. With her motherly tenderness and genuine charity, she would commit herself immediately, with great generosity and without reserve.

"The Trail" (**"La huella"**) is the best poem in this group. It is written in alternate lines of seven and five syllables, which are purposely grouped in three units: the flight, the identification with the pursued, and the discovery that the persecution extends to the ends of the earth and that it is impossible to stop it. The insistent rapidity of the rhythm, the continuous linking of enumerative series, and the precipitous, breathless rush of verbs communicate the impression of hasty flight, of anguish and relentless pursuit. The poet takes pity on the pursued, shields him, tries in vain to erase his tracks with the passionate gestures of a mother or lover:

¡Voy corriendo, corriendo
la vieja Tierra,
rompiendo con la mía
su pobre huella!
¡O me paro y la borran mis
locas trenzas,
o de bruces mi boca
lame la huella!

p. 24, lines 44–51.

I come running, running,
Across the old Earth,
Shattering with my steps
Your poor trail!
Else, I stop and my flying
locks erase it,
Or face down, my mouth
Licks away your trail!

The intensity of the feeling is revealed through the tenderness or force of some of the images:

Ni señales, ni nombre,
ni el país, ni la aldea;
solamente la concha
húmeda de su huella;
solamente esta sílaba
que recogió la arena
¡y la Tierra-Verónica
que me lo balbucea!

. . . . .

la huella, Dios mío,
la pintada huella:
el grito sin boca,
la huella, la huella!

. . . . .

su marca de hombre
ducle y tremenda.

pp. 23–24, lines 5–12; 31–34; 41–42.

Neither signs, nor name,
Nor the country nor the town;
Only the moist shell of your
trail;
Only this syllable
Captured by the sand
And stammered to me
By the Veronica-Land!

. . . . .

The trail, my God, the
painted trail:
The mouthless scream
The trail, the trail!

. . . . .

Its sign of a man
Tremendous and sweet.

Two other poems, **"The Prisoner's Woman"** (**"Mujer de prisionero"**) and **"Jewish Emigrant"** (**"Emigrada judía"**), included under the headings "Madwomen" (*Locas mujeres*) and "Wandering" (*Vagabundaje*), are also inspired by contemporary conditions. The first poem deals with a theme that was of great concern to Gabriela because of its moral implications and its repercussions on the family life of prisoners. On her travels she would often visit prisons to speak with the inmates and comfort them, reminding them that their guardian angel was with them in their loneliness. As often as she could, she initiated steps—difficult and even risky at times—to have them released or to alleviate their suffering. She felt drawn to them by the bond of sorrow and the humble Christian awareness that we are all sinners. The second poem describes the spiritual state of the emigrants. If we remember that she spent her life wandering, far from her country or the lands she loved, we will understand why this portrait of the Jewish emigrants seems more like her own self portrait:

Tan sólo llevo mi aliento
y mi sangre y mi ansiedad.
Una soy a mis espaldas
otra volteada al mar:

mi nuca hierve de adioses,
y mi pecho de ansiedad.

. . . . .

¡y aventada mi memoria
llegaré desnuda al mar!

pp. 170–171; lines 13–18; 29–30.

So alone I carry my courage
And my anguish and my blood.
One of me always looking
behind

The other thrust into the
sea:
My neck wracked by farewells
And my breast by fear.

. . . . .

And with my billowing memory
I will come naked into the
sea! . . .

In addition to the theme of the natural beauty of the Americas as a source of inspiration, we find in ***Wine Press*** the description of the palm groves of Cuba, the desert of Arizona, a Brazilian orchard, not formerly sung to, and the new themes of the poppy, the okote pine, the dry silkcotton tree, the Uruguayan corn tassel, the stone of Parahibuna, the pruning of trees, the rose bush and the almond tree. Here nature continues to be an inexhaustible mine of allusions, comparisons, images and, at times, a projection of the inner spiritual being. Her way of looking at it is very far from the romantic subjectivism and the mental landscapes of ***Desolation.*** In these poems, a profound, contemplative vision of strong religious roots predominates. They seem to soothe the spirit of the contemporary reader. In our century of urbanism, over-industrialization, and technology, of productivity without creativity, in a world that is increasingly anti-natural and unreal, the necessity for contact with nature is becoming a question of life or death. Man must return to his center, to live in a more natural and simple fashion, to re-incorporate himself into the rhythm of the cosmos, if he is to preserve the integrity of his person, his whole and true humanity. These verses console because they are the reflection of a human spirit that had always maintained an ardent relationship with the real and fundamental things in life: with God, the earth, sex, love, death; of a spirit uncontaminated by the destructive viruses of our materialistic, artificial, and skeptical civilization. The poet's childhood was spent in the country, among mountains, in direct, joyful, imaginative, free communication with plants and animals, with clouds and stars; her child's hands helped in the agricultural chores, in the kind of manual workmanship that does not breed dulling routine nor blunt the creative faculties. Her poems on nature are descriptions, eulogies of living things: behind the veil of their bright sensorial beauty, they reveal their true essence, their mystery. The poet personifies and spiritualizes these living beings; she gazes at them with warmth and reverence. She sees them not as isolated objects, not as food for sensual pleasure, but as living parts of an organism, phases of the harmony that sings the perennial psalm of praise to the Creator. She can say of the California poppy:

En la palma apenas duras
y recoges, de tomada,
como unos labios sorbidos
tus cuatro palabras rápidas,
cuando te rompen lo erguido
y denso de la alabanza.

p. 93, lines 13–18. . . .

In my palm you hardly last
And plucked, you withdraw
Your four words rapidly
Like tasted lips,
When they break your lofty
Full-bodied beauty.

For Gabriela work was a happy and creative activity that also had locked within it its mystery, its relationship to God and to the earth. She regarded tools with brotherly tenderness because they complement the hand of man, they help and accompany him in his labor and directly or indirectly they play a part in the decisive moments of his life. In the poem entitled **"Tools"** (**"Herramientas"**), she describes and humanizes them; she speaks and laughs with them; she makes requests of them; she attributes gestures of passion or of feminine tenderness to them:

"Herramientas"

Revueltas con los aperos,
trabados los pies de hierbas
trascienden a naranjo herido
o al respiro de la menta.
Cuando mozas brillan de ardores
y rotas son madres muertas.

Toque a toque la azada viva
me mira y recorre entera
y le digo que me dé
al caer la última tierra;
y con ternura de hermana
yo la suelto, ella me deja . . .

pp. 127–128, lines 13–18, 41–48.

"Tools"

Heaped among the farm tools,
The stalks of cuttings tied
They smell of wounded orange tree
Or of the breath of mint.
When maidens glow with ardor
And shattered are dead mothers.

Stroke by stroke the living hoe
Looks at me and vigorously toils
And I beg it to give me
The last bit of earth as it falls;
And with a sister's tenderness
I release her, she leaves me . . .

The praise of the **"Worker's Hands"** (**"Manos de obreros"**) evokes their "tremendous beauty," their silent understanding with the earth. They are the hands of farmers, fishermen, miners, weavers, marked with the painful imprints of time, work, and material; anonymous hands that toil for us, as wise in the weaving of children's clothing as in digging the grave:

> y mi huesa la harán justa
> aunque no vieron mi espalda.
>
> p. 130, lines 27–28.
>
> And they will fit my tomb to me
> Though they have not seen my measure.

Christ takes pity on them and when they rest from their labors

> las toma y retiene
> entre las suyas hasta el Alba.
>
> p. 130, lines 41–42.
>
> He takes them and holds them
> Between his own until Dawn.

In verses of classical pattern, with soberly restrained baroque words and images, the poet describes the pruning of a rose bush, an almond tree, and a tree in wintry slumber. The pruning is carried out not only with knowledge and ability but also with the participation of the spiritual powers and the emotions. It is an action that is both intellectual and moral; a true creation, like that of a poem or the education of a son. Of all the poems in ***Wine Press***, these are the most elaborately styled, the most cerebral and elegant. But they are also the least Mistralian in tone and form. . . .

When compared to the former books, ***Wine Press*** reveals its own individualities of language and style. It represents the results of an evolution that has progressively purified the lyricism of romantic overtones, infusing it with greater objectivity and simplicity. The effort to fit the language more closely to the poetic intent is more evident here than in the past. The poet has not lost any of her intuitive spontaneity, imaginative force, or intensity; however, she develops those materials with greater deliberation and care. In this way she evolves a language free of encumbrances, relieved of sensuality and sentimentalism. Her voice has the dry, crackling ardor of the Psalmists and the Prophets, without any pleasure in the sensory values of the word. The almost complete absence of color, of sonorous and melodic effects, and of descriptions of shape and movement is not capricious: the lineal elements supersede the musical and pictorial ones. The result is an asceticism that imparts severity and vigor to the language.

While the vocabulary retains archaic forms, peculiarly American expressions, and idioms of popular, regional origin, they are already fewer in number when compared to the lexicon of her prose writings and of her earlier poetry.

On the other hand, one notes an unusual abundance of references, of learned forms and Latinisms, some phonetic, some semantic. The most insistent references pertain, naturally, to American geography, to its fauna and, above all, to its flora. There are also astronomical, mythological, biblical, religious, and literary references. The direct observation of reality, rural childhood, the cosmic emotion, religious probing, the reading of the Bible and of the Graeco-Roman classics provide these allusions. Within the group of Latinisms and cultismos, scarce in her former work, there seems to exist a decided preference for words of antepenultimate stress (*alácrita, acérrimo, frenético, pávido, vívido*). This may perhaps be determined by the metric needs of the verse line or by the desire to produce certain sonorous effects. This kind of excessive correctness is heightened by a notable reduction in the number of regional and vernacular expressions. The *cultismos* are found especially in such poems as **"Finnish Champion"** (**"Campeón Finlandés"**), **"Fall of Europe"** (**"Caída de Europa"**), **"Sonnets of Pruning"** (**"Sonetos de la poda"**), **"Earthly Message"** (**"Recado terrestre"**). Because of the serious tone of these poems and the need to suit the lexicon to the theme and to the elegant metric form, the *cultismos* are quite appropriate.

The poet retains her preference for strong words of violent, unabashed realism—ardor, fervor, fire, to rend, wound, open, break, slice, scorch, flay, singe—because the tendency to emphasize remains a characteristic trait of her language. . . .

The peculiarities of syntax create a still more personal style. They are of even greater interest than the vocabulary, not so much for their novelty as for the author's technique of cumulative repetition. The outstanding characteristics of the syntax are a tendency toward multiple-clause sentences, enumerations in series of phrases of parallel structure, and repetitions of words, phrases, and lines. In this way the poet achieves effects of rapidity, emphasis, monotony, or intensity. The reader feels himself pulled along by a succession of things, allusions, images, as if he were obliged to follow the curve of a parabola.

The marked affectionate quality of the poetic language is heightened by the use of diminutives, possessives, datives, exclamatory sentences, interjections, rhetorical questions, and forms of address of the most intimate tenderness. There is a predominance of simply constructed affirmative sentences, of relative phrases that describe acts rather than qualities. All of this, in addition to the extraordinary wealth of verbs, imparts movement to the language; but frequently it is also responsible for its falling into the flowing, slack rhythm of prose.

There is a lack of fullness and melodic variety in the phrase. Its intonational curve is only slightly modulated and shaded, as in that of a prayer or confidence. There is created a general impression of monotony, of muted tones. One must exclude from this generalization the sections "Tricks" (*Jugarretas*) and "Rounds" (*Rondas*), where the imitation of folkloric melodies create charmingly light, vivacious, graceful effects.

The metric rhythm lacks variety. Most of the poems follow the pattern of the eight- or nine-syllable ballad, with the exception of the **"Sonnets of Pruning"** (**"Sonetos de la poda"**), the incomplete *seguidillas*, the couplets in which some of the "Rounds" (*Rondas*) and "Tricks" (*Jugarretas*) are written, the free hendecasyllable line in the solemn, heroic poems, and some anasyllabic combinations that put into play lines of five, six, seven, eight, nine, ten, eleven, twelve, and fourteen syllables. There are also little ballads of six- and seven-syllable lines. The free eleven-syllable lines and the anasyllabic combinations convey fullness and rhythmic majesty; the varieties of the ballad form create an impression of singsong; the *seguidillas* and couplets embody the agile movement of dance.

There is a certain uncertainty in the measure of the initial lines. At the beginning of the poem the poet seems to be seeking a rhythm without seeming to find it; after the fourth or fifth line, the testing stops and the rhythm flows surely, without vacillation. There is, likewise, a lack of complete control of the rhyme; there are combinations of perfectly rhymed assonants, changes of rhyme within the poem itself; the adopted model is not faithfully followed. The assonances or consonances are imperfect and they deviate from the established rules.[8] Again, as in the preceding works, unccented words (*si, que, sobre, tan*) occupy a position of rhyme or stand at the end of the line.

The poet is not concerned with melodic or rhythmic beauty; she does not attempt to produce pleasant or harmonious auditory effects. She tends to monorhyme, to a music of dissonantal harmonies. She does not have a good ear; her musical sensitivity is neither elegant nor refined. The line that is most natural to her suggests the sounds of nature, the low-voiced singing that accompanies absorption in work, the whispers and prayers of women, the murmur of someone who speaks to himself, not wishing to be heard. This music, however, is very well suited to the poetic themes because it intensifies the mournful, funereal tone of most of the poems.

The manipulation of the adjective, as a stylistic technique, is of extreme importance in ***Wine Press***. We should consider it more from the standpoint of the role of imagination in this work than as a mere element of the lexicon. There is an over-abundance of adjectives. They are even grouped in twos and threes. There is hardly a noun that does not carry with it its real or figurative modifier. The poet is not as interested in specifying the palpable qualities of things—color, form, sound, taste, smell, texture—as she is in indicating certain shadings that imply a personification ("muffled linen," "sickly light," "deceitful cypress," "feverish fruit") and that project her own mood on things. The repetition of "mad," "demented," "insensate," "drunk" as qualifiers for very diverse beings and things of nature conveys a sense of strong, passionate, disordered movement.[9]

The past participle is also used as an adjective to qualify the result of an action. Most of the participles—and they are very numerous—allude to actions that undo, break, destroy, or consume things: "burned," "consumed," "divided," "pierced," "crushed," "choked," "flung down," "devoured." Since they almost always describe moral activities, they shed light upon the true meaning of the work's title. The anguish of earthly existence drains man as the wine press extracts the juice from the cluster of grapes, leaving them crushed and spent. The participle denotes the state that results from the cessation of action; the moment things and living beings strip themselves of their dynamics, they decay into death.

The poet prefers personification and simile to other kinds of imagery. Everything, even the material and the inert, is animated, personified, animalized, or vegetableized; everything can be expressed in terms of something else. The characteristic trait of this poetic cosmos is this incessant activity, the fluidity, the fusion of boundaries until they are completely erased.

There is a simile at every step. "Tree," "albatross," and "gulls" are the ideal terms of comparison that appear most repeatedly. The first simile is suggested by the analogy between the form of the tree and the circulatory system, between the tree's shade and moral anguish, and by the tree-Cross relationship. The second and third similes are suggested by the soaring, powerful, zigzagging, flight of these sea birds; perhaps by the reading of Coleridge's "Ancient Mariner."

On occasion, there is a subtle, tender, delicate comparison:

"Encargo a Blanca"

Porque mi culpa fué la palabra.
Pero dame la tuya, la tuya
que era como paloma posada.

p. 15, lines 14–16.

"Request of Blanca"

Because my sin was the word.
But give me yours, yours
So like a dove alight.

Or there is the fitting comparison between a moral, psychic action nd unrelieved, domestic chore:

"La desásída"

Mi voluntad la recojo
como ropa abandonada.

p. 64, lines 35–36.

"The Forsaken One"

I gather together my will
Like clothing carelessly strewn.

On occasion one finds a very intellectual comparison, based on literary memories, like the one drawn between the doors and the Cassandra of Aeschylus' *Agamemnon*.

On many occasions the simile adopts a fixed mode of expression not evident in the other books. It may be a combination of (1) *a verb*, either in infinitive or conjugated form; (2) the preposition "in"; (3) a *noun* alone or modified by one or several adjectives:

cae en linda presa soltada.
she falls as beautiful prey set free.

en rápidas resinas se endurecía su habla.
her speech hardened as rapid resins.

arde en fucsias y dalias.
it burns as fuschias and dahlias.

entra en madre alborotada.
she enters as a mother alarmed.

In its final form, the comparative relationship is conveyed through the adverb, which describes the verbal action and fulfills its logical function of being a complement of manner.

All of the stylistic characteristics described above reveal to us the inner life of the poet, her conception of the world, the ethical-religious roots that nourish her song. The images clarify and define her vision of the cosmos. ***Wine Press*** transports us to a complex world governed by imagination and memory. Its poems evoke sensory or mental objects, recreating and beautifying them through a play on their relationship to the rest of reality as it is perceived by the senses, the intelligence, and the memory. We look out on a ghost-like, hallucinated multitude of beings in motion, in continuous flux. We witness the transformation and dissolution of apparitions: for a moment they reveal their faces to us, they gesture to us, only to disintegrate immediately, like mist and foam. This vision corresponds exactly to Gabriela's spiritual state, to the delirium that rent her as she stood polarized between the here and the beyond, and to her resigned acceptance of death as a necessary and desirable end to the game and dream that is life.

Notes

1. *Antología de la poesía española e hispanoamericana* (Anthology of Spanish and Hispanic American poetry) (Madrid: R.F.E., 1934), p. xviii.
2. *Desolación* (Desolation) (1st ed. New York: Hispanic Institute, 1922).
3. Let us glance at some titles: "The Meeting" (*El encuentro*), "Ecstasy" (*Extasis*), "Intimation" (*Intima*), "God Wills It" (*Dios lo quiere*), "Watchful" (*Desvelada*), "Affliction" (*Tribulación*), "Sonnets of Death" (*Sonetos de la muerte*), "The Useless Wait" (*La espera inútil*), "To See Him Again" (*Volverlo a ver*), etc.
4. Gabriela Mistral, *Ternura* (4th ed., Buenos Aires: Espasa-Calpe, 1945).
5. Jorge Mañach, *Gabriela: alma y tierra. En Gabriela Mistral, Vida y obra*, Bibliografía. Antología. (New York: Hispanic Institute, 1936), p. 7.
6. *Lagar* (Santiago, Chile: Ediciones of the Pacific, 1954). *Tala* was published in 1938.
7. This is what Gabriela called it in a now famous article.
8. There are rhymes of ú-a with é-o, í-o, ó-a, ié-o é-a with ó-o, í-a í-a with í-e
9. "Mad cascade," "drunken albatross," "insensate waves," "demented flame," "mad tresses," "mad breath."

Margot Arce de Vasquez (essay date 1964)

SOURCE: "Nocturne (*Nocturno*)," in *Gabriela Mistral: The Poet and Her Work*, translated by Helene Masslo Anderson, New York University Press, 1964, pp. 113–22.

[*In the following essay, Arce de Vasquez offers an explication of Mistral's* "Nocturne", *arguing that the poem traces a course from the bitterness of betrayed passion to resignation and an ascetic focus on the predominance of death.*]

An analysis of Gabriela Mistral's work will always present serious difficulties to anyone who attempts to study it rigorously. The one who undertakes such a task will not be able to ignore the intimate relationship between the themes of the poetry and the life of the poet. From the data contained in the published biographies, he will have to separate, very delicately, what is true from what is a product of the imaginative enthusiasm of her biographers. Even when reading Gabriela's own accounts of her life, he will have to tear away the mask of fiction she wore to shield herself from the impertinent or malevolent curiosity of the world. Perhaps in her mature years, when she was more serene, she attempted to temper, through ambiguity, the almost brutal frankness of her first book, ***Desolation.***

However, the biographical elements in her verses neither diminish the beauty of the fiction nor the quality and skill of the art with which she has transfigured reality. **"Nocturne"** (**"Nocturno"**) from ***Desolation*** can be used as an example.

¡Padre nuestro que estś en los cielos,
por qué te has olvidado de mí!
Te acordaste del fruto en febrero,
al llagarse su pulpa rubí.
¡Llevo abierto también mi costado,
y no quieres mirar hacia mí!

Te acordaste del negro racimo,
y lo diste al lagar carmesí;
y aventaste las hojas de álamo
con tu aliento, en el aire sutil.
¡Y en el ancho lagar de la muerte
aún no quieres mi pecho exprimir!

Caminando vi abrir las violetas;
el falerno del viento bebí,
y he bajado, amarillos, mis párpados,

por no ver más enero ni abril.
Y he apretado la boca, anegada
de la estrofa que no he de exprimir,
¡Has herido la nube de otoño
y no quieres volverte hacia mí!

Me vendió él que besó mi mejilla;
me negó por la túnica ruín.
Yo en mis versos el rostro con sangre,
como Tú sobre el paño, le dí
y en mi noche del Huerto, me han sido
Juan cobarde y el Angel hostil.

Ha venido el cansancio infinito
a clavarse en mis ojos, al fin:
el cansancio del día que muere
y el del alba que debe venir;
¡el cansancio del cielo de estaño
y el cansancio del cielo de añil!

Ahora suelto la mártir sandalia
y las trenzas pidiendo dormir.
y perdida en la noche, levanto
el clamor aprendido de Ti:
¡Padre nuestro que estás en los cielos,
por qué te has olvidado de mí!

Desolation, pp. 116–17.

Our Father who art in heaven,
Why hast Thou forsaken me!
Thou did'st remember the February fruit,
When torn was its pulp of ruby.
My side is pierced also
Yet Thou will'st not look at me!

Thou did'st remember the dark grape cluster
And did'st give it to the crimsoned press,
And Thou did'st fan the poplar leaves
With thy breath of gentleness.
Yet in the deep wine press of death
Thou still would'st not my heart express!

As I walked I saw violets open;
And I drank the wine of the wind,
And I have lowered my yellowed eyelids
Never more to see Winter or Spring.
And I have tightened my mouth to stifle
The verses I am never to sing.
Thou hast wounded the cloud of Autumn
And Thou will'st not turn toward me!

I was sold by the one who kissed my cheek;
He betrayed me for the tunic vile.
I gave him in my verses, my blood-stained face,
As Thine imprinted on her veil,
And in my night of the Orchard I have found
John reluctant and the Angel hostile.

And now an infinite fatigue
Has come to pierce my eyes:
The fatigue of the day that is dying
And of the dawn that will arise;
The fatigue of the sky of metal
The fatigue of indigo skies!

And now I loosen my martyred sandal
And my locks, for I am longing to sleep.
And lost in the night, I lift my voice
In the cry I have learned from Thee:
Our Father who art in heaven,
Why hast Thou forsaken me!

No other poem of hers is so faithful to the facts, or expresses more beautifully the spiritual turmoil caused within her by the betrayal of her beloved and his marriage to another. It is one of the most beautiful poems of ***Desolation***, one of the most Mistralian in theme and style. It records the disillusion of second love and it voices the anguish, the clamor for death. But art has so sublimated the personal element that the reader finds in **"Nocturne"** not the individual, usual case of a betrayal of love but the representation of all human sorrow in its most solitary, most inescapable moment.

The Title

The title has no musical connotation. It denotes the identity night-sorrow, of age-old use in world literature.

y perdida en la noche levanto
el clamor aprendido de Tí.

lines 35–36.

and lost in the night I lift my voice
in the cry I have learned from Thee.

In addition to this, however, her use of the image "and in my night of the Orchard" underlines the poet's identification with Christ. It is possible that Gabriela may also have been influenced by José Asunción Silva's "Nocturne," which she admired so much. Other nocturnes—**"The Defeat"** (**"La derrota"**), **"The Consummation"** (**"La consumación"**), and **"Old Weavers"** (**"Tejedores viejos"**) of ***Felling***—are very similar in mood to the poem here under discussion. They and the **"Nocturne"** form a link between one book and the other.

Metric Pattern

In addition to the similarity of mood, these poems share identical rhythmic patterns: stanzas of six ten-syllable lines, with assonance on the last syllable of the even lines. It is a monotonous rhythm, strengthened by repetitions and parallelisms of phrases and lines. Such a meter could easily degenerate into simple singsong if, as in the **"Nocturne,"** the lines were not interlaced with exclamations that rise like cries above the murmur of the psalmody. There is perfect compatibility between the metric form and the artistic intent: the **"Nocturne"** is a prayer fashioned on the pattern of the psalms. The first versicle from The Lord's Prayer and part of the first one from the Twenty-first Psalm—with a slight variation—open and close the poem in the style of a refrain:

¡Padre nuestro que estás en los cielos
por qué te has olvidado de mí!

lines 1–2.

Our Father who art in heaven
Why hast Thou forsaken me?

The refrain frames the prayer in the same way that the chants do the psalms. We now discover the true meaning of the poem's title: "nocturne" is the name given to each of the three parts of the matins prayer in the divine service. Unlike a monk, however, the poet does not rise to praise God at midnight; sleepless and grieved, she hurls her imprecation from the night of her abandonment and helplessness.

In the carefully constructed composition we distinguish two thought units, each of which contains three stanzas. The third stanza, which closes the first unit, is the longest of all: eight lines instead of the six required by the metric pattern. This variation marks the division between the two units.

The first unit develops the theme of divine forgetfulness by the serial enumeration of four parallel phrases, similar in content and syntactical structure. These cover the three initial stanzas. Each phrase includes its antithesis: Thou did'st remember all things; Thou will'st not remember me.

Te acordaste del fruto en febrero
. . . y no quieres mirar hacia mí.

Thou did'st remember the February fruit
. . . yet Thou will'st not look at me!

. . . . .

Te acordaste del negro racimo,
aventaste las hojas del álamo
. . . y aun no quieres mi pecho exprimir.

Thou did'st remember the black grape cluster,
Thou did'st fan the poplar leaves
. . . yet Thou would'st not my heart express.

. . . . .

Has herido la nube de otoño . . . y no quieres volverte hacia mí.

Thou hast wounded the cloud of autumn
and Thou will'st not turn toward me!

The reiteration of this reproach produces an effect of mounting intensity and reveals to us the poet's intention of dramatizing her absolute abandonment and exclusion, through the will of God, from the norm that governs all of creation.

Although He is called Father, the God of the **"Nocturne"** bears more resemblance to the powerful, terrible Jehovah of the Old Testament than to the one of the Christian revelation. The poet demands that His destructive force annihilate her in the same way that he ripens the fruit, wrings the juice from the cluster of grapes in the wine press, fans the dry leaves and dissolves the cloud of autumn. At the root of this conception—which has a considerable pagan element—there throbs the rebellious protest against pain, the thirst for annihilation. The poet feels that God has abandoned her and pictures him movingly as an implacable and hostile power.

With supreme artistry she has chosen for the series of contrasts four objects already approaching the terminal point of their seasonal cycle: fruit in February,[1] the black grape cluster, the dry leaf, the autumn cloud. The adjectives of color in the hues of ruby, crimson, and black evoke the image of blood. The poet claims that "her side is also pierced," in the same way that the fruit already shows the first signs of its approaching decomposition.

The first line of the third stanza interrupts the series with an impassioned evocation of the sensory beauty and intoxication of the world. For but a moment we glimpse the ardent pleasure of the senses, the impetus of the creative and positive forces of life and the spirit, only to return immediately to the obsessive insistence of the final antithesis:

Caminando vi abrir las violetas,
el falerno del viento bebí,
y he bajado, amarillos, mis párpados,
por no ver más enero ni abril;
y he apretado mi boca, anegada,
de la estrofa que no he de exprimir.
Has herido la nube de Otoño
y no quieres volverte hacia mí.

lines 12–20.

As I walked I saw violets open,
And I drank the wine of the wind,
And I have lowered my yellowed eyelids,
Never more to see Winter or Spring;
And I have tightened my mouth to stifle
The verses I am never to sing.
Thou hast wounded the cloud of Autumn
And Thou will'st not turn toward me!

The contrast between the autumnal images of ripening harvest and rain and the spring images of flowering and Dionysian vitality is very effectively drawn in this passage. But the poet closes her eyes to the tenderness of the violets and stifles the song that rushes to her lips.

The very Mistralian vocabulary of this first part is characterized by an intense realism that recalls the plastic style of the Spanish baroque writers: "to wound oneself," "the pierced side," "black cluster," "to wring," "I have stifled," "yellow eyelids," "fruit," "pulp," "wine press," "you fanned," "leaves," "wounded"; they are words that originate in rural, agricultural experiences. The vocabulary of the second part derives from the poet's intention to compare her personal sorrow with the passion of Christ. They are all strong, concrete, expressive words intended for descriptions of violence and death.

The fourth stanza, the first of the second thought-unit, describes the cause of the sorrow with forceful images: it is a true passion that almost literally repeats the passion of the Lord. We note the rapidity with which the facts are narrated, the abundance and expressive force of the verbs all in the preterite tense:

Me vendió el que besó mi mejilla,
me negó por la túnica ruín.
Yo en mis versos el rostro con sangre,
como Tú, sobre el paño, le dí,
y en mi noche del Huerto me han sido
Juan cobarde y el Angel hostil.

lines 21–26.

I was sold by the one who kissed my cheek,
He betrayed me for the tunic vile.
I gave him in my verses, my blood-stained face,
as Thine imprinted on her veil,
And in my night of the Orchard I have found
John reluctant and the Angel hostile.

It is a stanza brimming with biographical allusions, with keys that depict the experience and its consequences on her spirit. Taken together with the refrain that frames the poem, it becomes quite clear that the analogy with the passion of Christ is the point of departure for this poem. More precisely, all of the **"Nocturne"** is a variation, a kind of mental projection, only partially explicit, of the first lines of the Twenty-first Psalm, "My Lord, my Lord, why hast Thou forsaken me? Thou art far from my prayers, from the words of my cry." These words, spoken by the Lord upon the cross, enable us to see the unfathomable depths of nothingness to which the Savior descends, with full awareness and complete liberty, in order that men may be redeemed. The poet, also crucified, knows something of that abyss; from its depths she calls out to the Father with the same anguished and mighty cry. This first analogy contains the others within it: the image "my side is also pierced," of the first stanza; "my night of the Orchard"; "I was sold by the one who kissed my cheek"; "he betrayed me for the tunic vile"; "In my verses, my blood-stained face."

There is an extremely important detail that differentiates the second part of the poem from the first. The poet no longer speaks to the Father, the First Person of the Holy Trinity. She now turns to the Son and speaks to him in intimate conversation, as if she were reflecting on her personal situation and comparing it to the Passion. By virtue of this change, her human anguish is transfigured and sweetened in union with the Redeemer. The rebellious, almost defiant, imprecation is followed by the humble entreaty, free from bitterness, modulated and moderated by fatigue. The entire poem thus takes on a profoundly Christian sense. The stanza upon which we are commenting appears at the moment of maximum tension and lyricism.

The anticlimax immediately begins with the fifth stanza. Here the poet speaks to us of her fatigue, of that total exhaustion that follows all crises, acting as a psychological respite. In the first line, the image "to pierce my eyes, finally" still follows from the comparisons with the Passion. The exclamation "finally" indicates relief from the spiritual tension. One hears something like a deep sigh in the new series of four parallel constructed lines, with their comparisons of past and future, summer and winter:

el cansancio del día que muere
y el del alba que debe venir;
¡y el cansancio del cielo de estaño
y el cansancio del cielo de añil!

lines 29–32.

The fatigue of the day that is dying
And of the dawn that will arise;
And the fatigue of the sky of metal
And the fatigue of indigo skies!

We should view this stanza as the symmetric opposite of the third stanza of the first part. There, the poet felt the call of life, of beauty and of song, but by an effort of will she rejected it, in rebellious protest. Here, indifference invades her; nothing attracts her, nothing is capable of freeing her from her endless fatigue. She could say, inverting Kempis' phrase: Life, where is thy sting?

The metaphor "life—road" reappears in the first and third lines of the last stanza:

Ahora suelto la mártir sandalia
y las trenzas pidiendo dormir
y perdida en la noche levanto
el clamor aprendido de Tí.

lines 33–36.

And now I loosen my martyred sandal
And my locks, for I am longing to sleep
And lost in the night, I lift my voice
In the cry I have learned from Thee.

In the third stanza, as we have seen, the comparison made way for a tender and beautiful digression among rough images of consummation. Now it awakens in the poet a longing for rest, for lying peacefully in the sleep of death. She no longer invokes the inflexible law that consumes all things in time; she clamors at the doors of the Son's heart and surrenders, helpless, to his mercy. The lines, "and lost in the night, I life my voice / In the cry I have learned from thee," denote a closer bond with God, a confidence greater than the questions and reproaches of the first part of the poem.

The **"Nocturne"** summarizes the main themes of Gabriela Mistral's poetry: God, love, sorrow, death, the scorn of the world, the search for the eternal. As in any romantic form, she lays bare the subjective experience without reticence, without minimizing it; she expresses overwhelming emotions. Her sources are perhaps too human, too deeply felt, too sensual, and each line, as it springs forth, seems to leave a fresh imprint of tears and blood.

Yo en mis versos, el rostro con sangre
como Tú, sobre el paño, le dí.

I in my verses, with blood-stained face,
As Thine imprinted on her veil.

In the "Artist's Decalogue" (*Decálogo del Artista*), Gabriela had said: "You will bring forth your work as a son is brought forth: with the very blood of your heart. (Beauty) will rise from your heart to your song, having purified you first" (***Desolation***, p. 207). This process of purification and liberation is effected in the **"Nocturne,"** transmuting the acrimony into fatigue, the rebellious imprecation into trusting prayer, and clothing these feelings in beautiful, precise, moving language. In the poems that follow, in the section "Nature" (*Naturaleza*), the passion, purified by artistic catharsis, is freed from exaggerated sensuality. It flows into purer verse, more objective lyricism, still intense but as if diffused in fog, mist, in the desolate snows of the Antarctic. In Gabriela Mistral's poetry—as in that of all the fine poets of the Spanish language—realism is gradually transformed into idealism, and sensual pleasure into ascetism, into *memento mori*.

Notes

1. February in Chile is the height of summer.

Carmelo Virgilio (essay date 1985)

SOURCE: "Woman as Metaphorical System: An Analysis of Gabriela Mistral's Poem 'Fruta,'" in *Woman as Myth and Metaphor in Latin American Literature*, edited by Carmelo Virgillo and Naomi Lindstrom, University of Missouri Press, 1985, pp. 137–50.

[In the following essay, Virgilio advances a metaphorical understanding of Mistral's use of the conventional image of women and of women's roles in her poetry.]

"Fruta"

En el pasto blanco de sol,
suelto la fruta derramada.

De los Brasiles viene el oro,
en prietos mimbres donde canta
de los Brasiles, niño mío,
mandan la siesta arracimada.
Extiendo el rollo de la gloria;
rueda el color con la fragancia.

Gateando sigues las frutas,
como niñas que se desbandan,
y son los nísperos fundidos
y las duras piñas tatuadas . . .

Y todo huele a los Brasiles
pecho del mundo que lo amamanta,
que, a no tener el agua atlántica,
rebosaría de su falda . . .

Tócalas, bésalas, voltéalas
y les aprendes todas sus caras.
Soñarás, hijo, que tu madre
tiene facciones abrasadas,
que es la noche canasto negro
y que es frutal la Vía Láctea . . .

from *Cuenta-mundo*[1]

"Fruit"

Onto the sun-white grass
I free the spilled fruit.

That gold comes out of Brazilian lands
enclosed in dark wicker baskets where it sings
from out of Brazilian lands, my child,
they send the siesta in bunches.
I stretch out the roll of glory;
color rolls out with fragrance.

You go after the fruits on all fours,
like little girls they skitter off,
and they are melting-soft loquats
and hard tattooed pineapples . . .

And everything scents of Brazilian lands,
Bosom of the world that nurses it all,
that, if not for Atlantic waters,
would overflow its skirt . . .

Touch them, kiss them, turn them over and over
and you will learn all their faces.
You will dream, child, that your mother
has seared features,
that night is a black hamper
and that the Milky Way is a fruit tree . . .

Gabriela Mistral has all too often been taken to task for allegedly offering in her work too literal or mimetic a representation of woman. If this were true, one could understandably quarrel with the type of statement she would then be making about womanhood. Her insistent theme of maternity as female fulfillment would therefore take on unpleasant overtones befitting the Freudian dictum "biology as destiny."[2] However, in this paper I argue that Mistral's treatment of the maternal function should be separated from any possible implication about how real-world women are to realize their potential. After all, we shall be looking here at autonomous poetic texts and, moreover, at texts of a highly metaphorical nature—not at all at a set of directives concerning how women ought to feel or behave.

I propose to look instead at the larger poetic system wherein woman and maternity are simply elements, albeit prominent ones. This system in its scope goes far beyond the question of women's social role. In effect, it is so globally inclusive that, as we shall see, it seeks to take in the entire cosmos. At issue, then, is an immense spiritual quest whose goal is the generation of meaning and whose proof lies in the symbolic code or system developed by the poet. Within such a code, woman and procreation are present as meaning-bearing signs in a larger, all-encompassing poetic language.

While the above-mentioned issues can be traced throughout Mistral's lyric production, the short collection of poems *Cuenta-mundo* must be considered exemplary of the type of mythic coding that interests us here. As the title indicates, the idea of working out a language capable of "speaking" or figuring the world is strongly present. Furthermore, woman and female powers of procreation play a prominent role as terms through which this symbolic and metaphorical "speaking" is to become possible.

Though the collection deserves to be studied as a whole, since it constitutes a mythic reconstruction of the cosmos that is uniquely feminine in the lexical framework in which Roland Barthes places myth,[3] in this paper I shall limit my observations to only one poem, **"Fruta."** In it Mistral, transcending the familiar sexual connotations of fruit and asserting her favorite themes and sub-themes (namely solitude, maternity, and mysticism, with their variants, grief, love, nature, and death), explores the internal reality of an entity emblematic of woman's ambivalence. She invests fruit with new dimensions, making it a symbol of the lonely messianic role of the female, implying that grief and self-immolation are necessary for the creation and survival of mankind.[4] In addition, we propose to examine how the text discloses a probing into the primordial enigma surrounding procreativity and equates the latter with artistic creativity.

To begin with, let me refer briefly to the four-line enneasyllabic composition "La cuenta-mundo," which sets forth an overall scheme while it introduces the conceptual and most of the formal characteristics of **"Fruta"** and other poems:

Niño pequeño, aparecido
que no viniste y que llegaste,
te contaré lo que tenemos
y tomarás de nuestra parte.[5]

Little ghost child,
who never came and yet arrived,
I'll tell you about our world
and you will share it with us.

One notices at once how the text evokes a set of associations with the educative aspect of the maternal function, the transmission of knowledge from mother to child. The mother is, in this context, familiar with the world's workings and ready to pass this information on to her offspring. Also evident are other possible meanings of motherhood. The physical production of the child is here alluded to in a lament over barrenness ("Niño pequeño, aparecido, que no viniste"). This lament is then countered by an affirmation of the notion that, even in the absence of physical procreation, a child may be created through other means ("y que llegaste").

Given the prominence of this theme of mothering-without-mothering in Mistral's poems, it is safe to assume that the allusion is to the creative work viewed as a correlative of and substitute for physical motherhood. In this respect, the paradox expressed in the antithesis "que no viniste . . . y que llegaste" leaves one no alternative but to consider mother, child, and world as mere abstractions. Interpreted symbolically, they then transcend rigid temporal and spacial limitations to represent instead immanent elements of eternal truth. As a result of this transformation, Mistral loses in the text the earthly traits of the sterile woman and reacquires, in this new realm of artistic rebirth, the inalienable rights of her sex. This introductory quatrain and the poems that follow constitute a subtle invitation to return via the imagery of her verse to the poet's own childhood—a mythic world of innocence, illusion, and dream where objective, adult logic disappears and the subjective concept of primal universal order rules.[6] It posits the world we find in **"Fruta."**

Almost casually, a female persona using the lyrical "I" announces she is casting onto a sunny meadow the fruit presumably brought along:

En el pasto blanco de sol,
suelto la fruta derramada.[7]

Onto the sun-white grass
I free the spilled fruit.

Following the overall scheme that predominates in *Cuentamundo,* "fruta" becomes a word-symbol for the decomposition of the external world and the creation of a new *poetic* one wherein the more profound connotations of fruit can be examined. In this symbolic framework, *fruit,* understood as *offspring,* discloses woman's maternal mission: *freeing* the life she brought or *spilled* into the world. Underlying this message are further inferences prompted by the rhetorical context in which the verbs *soltar* (to free) and *derramar* (to spill) appear. The first suggestion is that the cleavage implicit in childbirth at some unspecified time in the past (past participle *derramada*) is predestined because the act of spilling is involuntary. The second is that a mother gives birth cognizant that the fruits of her love, once liberated from her dark womb into the light, are to be consciously freed like newborn animals scattered in a warm pasture.[8]

The second stanza contains the second and third movements:

De los Brasiles viene el oro,
en prietos mimbres donde canta
de los Brasiles, niño mío,
mandan la siesta arracimada.[9]

That gold comes out of Brazilian lands
enclosed in dark wicker baskets where it sings
from out of Brazilian lands, my child,
they send the siesta in bunches.

The most discernible variant in this second movement is the introduction of the third-person narrative voice and the addition of yet another poetic persona expressed by the directive vocative "niño mío." Both replace the first-person voice of the initial stanza, thus amplifying the poetic dimension. The impression immediately derived from these four lines is that of a cradle song, as the metric rhythm reproduces a swinging and rocking movement that matches the fruit's swaying journey from Brazil in dark wicker. Ultimately, the singing and rhythm insinuate the image, sound, and movement of a mother lulling her child to sleep.

The interior structure of this second movement derives from symbolism and imagery. The noun "Brasiles," or Brazilian lands, is of capital importance, for it gives rise to an intricate series of associations further revealing and reinforcing the central theme—woman's ambivalent, mysterious nature, which presupposes her ties with earthly and divine power. The figure of Brazil is commonly linked with the legendary, fathomless riches of those dark and secret recesses that have captivated humanity's imagination for centuries. Aside from this image, Brazil conveys an even deeper symbolism. It recalls the figure of the bare-breasted Amazon, the mythic hermaphrodite whose traits epitomize the strength this vast and complex land draws from the interplay of its many components. The text, by making Brazil—the source of the fruit—a symbol of pluralistic totality, endows womanhood with the traits of the Amazonic virago. Brazil as origin suggests further implications for the Amazonic myth: it becomes an extraordinary place whose integrity rests on the harmonious coexistence of opposites and implies the mythological paradise free of discord, discrimination, unrest, suffering, or conflict. The hermaphrodite, uniting dominant traits of male and female, symbolizes an ideal condition, largely unknown in our world.[10] Thus the text is transcending earthly reality and describing instead a mythic-mystic journey in a timeless, paceless context, with Brazil functioning as mother and paradise and perhaps even God.[11] Such interpretation is substantiated by the verb form "mandan" (they send) and by the plurality of the noun "Brasiles." Together, verb and noun suggest the anonymous and magnanimous will that chooses woman's deceptively fragile womb, the "prietos mimbres" (dark wicker baskets), for the purpose of delivering to earth forms of life conceived in it own precious image. The noun "oro," or gold, is thus used to mean life, reflecting its radiant, loving source. In the same framework, the metaphor "siesta arracimada" (siesta in bunches), understood as a reference to the prenatal condition of living beings in which it is still possible to exist in a perfect state of peace and unity, would call to mind the image of the ideal world whence all life originates and flows naturally from one generation to another.

In the third movement, represented by the last two lines of the second stanza—"Extiendo el rollo de la gloria; / rueda el color con la fragancia" ("I stretch out the roll of glory; / color rolls out with fragrance")[12]—the text reinstates the lyrical "I," which now figures again as the dominant poetic voice. The maternal persona behind it seems to be retracing her steps to elaborate on what she had stated in the first stanza. She no longer addresses herself to her would-be child but to the reader to remind one how the fruits fall out as a result of her unfolding or opening out their container—traditionally, a paper cone.

From a strictly logical standpoint, the conceptual and formal characteristics of the third movement would indicate that this couplet could have followed or been incorporated into the first stanza. In effect, the third movement continues and reinforces the imagery of the first one, for it infers the preestablished natural dictates of childbirth. Moreover, with the introduction of the image produced by the metaphor "rollo de la gloria," depicting the mother's womb-cornucopia, the complex levels of symbolism and imagery stratify. At this point, "siesta arracimada" of the second movement, previously understood as an allusion to the child being lulled to sleep, now suggests that this infant is a "frutita," a small fruit himself hanging in a bunch (hence the Spanish "arracimada"—a play on the words "racimo" and "rama") from his mother's breasts ("prietos mimbres"), seen as the branches of the dark tree of her body. With this new symbolic dimension, it is understood that as the mother is singing her child to sleep she pulls out her breast ("Extiendo el rollo") against which the sleeping child lies while nursing.

The third movement, with the reappearance of the first-person singular voice and the reiteration of the third, also completes a cycle wherein one witnesses the image of fruit becoming more and more abstract. What was "fruta" in the first stanza turns successively into "oro" and "siesta arracimada," ultimately achieving full transparency in the metaphor "rueda el color con la fragancia." This systematic disintegration of fruit as a one-dimensional entity into particles evoking optical, tactile, gustatory, and olfactory sensations can be attributed to the poet's effort to recreate the synesthetic totality of fruit with her breast and with her child. Subsequently, if one carries a step further the symbolism of fruit's container within its rhetorical framework—"rollo de la gloria"—a number of other images surface. "Rollo," first seen as the mother's womb-cornucopia and then as her breast, now denotes the female genealogical sphere as well as astrological completeness and even divine perfection.[13]

Structurally, the imagery integrates the superficially fragmentary nature of the first three movements. The strophic order represents the reconstruction of the feminine mission in anti-empirical, transcendental terms, rejecting any human systematization of the cosmic process. The text's view may be summarized as consisting of (1) *creation* ("en el pasto blanco de sol, / suelto la fruta derramada"); (2) *conception* ("De los Brasiles viene el oro"); (3) *gestation* and *sustenance* ("en prietos mimbres . . . mandan la siesta arracimada"). This new poetic logic not only explains the tying of the strophic knot ("suelto la fruta . . . Extiendo el rollo de la gloria") but also constitutes the end of a cycle and the return to the initial process of continuous creation.

The fourth movement reestablishes the multiple symbolic perspectives. On the first level of illusion the child is the object of the mother's scrutiny as he pursues on all fours the elusive fruits that she identifies for him: soft loquats and hard, tattooed pineapples. On the second symbolic level, the child is seen groping for his mother's hard breasts with their soft nipples.

Gateando sigues las frutas
como niñas que se desbandan,
y son los nísperos fundidos
y las duras piñas tatuadas . . .

You go after the fruits on all fours
like little girls they skitter off,
and they are melting-soft loquats
and hard tattooed pineapples . . .

The text, by making explicit the relationship between "frutas" and "niñas," both feminine nouns, attaches feminine characteristics to fruit. The lack of grammatical elision deliberately makes the child and fruits dependent on the same verb form, "sigues" of the main clause. By this means it is possible for the text to link the act of following and that of the fruits' dispersing, fruit and offspring, and finally, the poet's imaginary child and all living beings that abandon their matrix after creation. In the realm of this new logic, the lexical forms of the stanza can only be interpreted in highly polysymbolic terms. "Sigues" corresponds to the infant's effort to grope for the breasts as they separate from his mouth and from each other while the mother moves her torso. As a dual image, it also corresponds to the fruit following the same predestined path of all little girls whose mission demands that they cut their maternal bond—an idea made explicit by the Spanish "desbandarse."

Furthermore, one notices portrayed symbolically in the exotic, soft, molten loquat and hard, tattooed pineapple a tolerance for extremes that, by allowing softness and sweetness to coexist with durable and indelible strength, emphasizes the feminine, hermaphroditic nature of fruit. The suspension marks ending the stanza suggest that behind the aforementioned polarity of external and internal characteristics of fruit lie the opposite forces of feminine reality, the continuum of life, and, in an even broader sense, the concept of the self-renewing creative process.

The fourth stanza, representing movement five, melds the entire relationship between the fruit, breast, and child triplicity:

Y todo huele a los Brasiles
pecho del mundo que lo amamanta,
que, a no tener el agua atlántica,
rebosaría de su falda . . .

And everything scents of Brazilian lands
bosom of the world that nurses it all,
that, if not for Atlantic waters,
would overflow its skirt . . .

A new level of imagery is now attained with Brazil portrayed as a huge, enormous woman or even as a single breast. Yet, this quatrain could have more logically followed the second movement, forming the following chain: "De los Brasiles viene el oro," "de los Brasiles . . . / mandan la siesta arracimada," where "oro" and "siesta" can now be viewed as milk. The strophic dislocation therefore reflects the composition's own subjective cosmic vision, and one looks then for a different poetic logic resting on a symbolic plane: in the interior imagery of the first movement. Therein the earlier image of Brazil as a hermaphroditic Amazon is brought back to complement and highlight the image of feminine completeness of movement four.

The new plane of imagery representing woman as bosom *of the world* now establishes the female figure as a complex entity, and this is achieved by the integration of cosmic elements. Here, feminine ambivalence, expressed in the interaction of offspring and mother, mother and earth, earth and water, water and human flesh, dissolves the apparent ambiguity engendered by the relative pronoun "que" at the beginning of the third line. Brazil is now equated with both fruit and breast, all three over-running land boundaries to flow throughout the world, for the implication here is that Brazil's milk *is* her fruit.

In the two movements of the last stanza, the mother-fruit motif advances, along with the major and minor themes. The imperative is used to assert motherly and spiritual authority in an explicit way:

Tócalas, bésalas, voltéalas
y les aprendes todas sus caras.
Soñarás, hijo, que tu madre
tiene facciones abrasadas,
que es le noche canasto negro
y que es frutal la Vía Láctea . . .

Touch them, kiss them, turn them over and over
and you will learn all their faces.
You will dream, child, that your mother
has seared features,
that night is a black hamper
and that the Milky Way is a fruit tree.

The external structure of the stanza indicates that this is the only sextain representing a whole poetic unit. The first two lines are topical and form movement six, uniting with the last four, which in turn produce the composition's seventh and final movement. Between these last two movements is a continuity that brings to the foreground the integrity of the poem's message before concluding it. Thus, fruit, breast, milk, woman, mother and child, humanity and creation, earth and universe are irrevocably fused. Even the rhythm integrates diverse elements as it echoes the cadence of the earlier cradle song before sounding a slower, reflexive, concluding tempo, indicating that the child has fallen asleep.

In the first couplet, the imperative and the reiteration of the same grammatical ending reproduce the rhythm of the fruits or breasts turned over and over. Concomitantly, there emerges the maternal invitation to have her body explored, suggested by the addition of the metaphor "y les aprendes todas sus caras" in the second line. After all, fruit is meant to be touched, kissed, sucked, like a mother's breast. The visual, tactile, and gustatory sensations in the phrase "Tócalas, bésalas, voltéalas," coupled with the implications of the following parallel clause "y les aprendes todas sus caras," lead not only to the physical but also to the spiritual discovery of woman. At this symbolic level, one visualizes fruit and breasts submitting voluntarily to a predestined task intended to surprise and gratify both the mother's offspring and the world that partakes of Brazil's abundance. All discover with each touch, each kiss, each turn a new pleasure that will nourish and fortify.

In the closing movement, the poetic persona seems to be whispering to her child, whom she has finally lulled to sleep in the silence of the night. Here the verb form "soñarás," on which the parallel clauses "tu madre tiene facciones abrasadas," "es la noche canasto negro," and "es frutal la Vía Láctea" all depend, serves as a key word. First of all, the allusion to the oneiric experience of the child establishes a bond between the consciousness of the mother and the subconscious mind of the child. Furthermore, the future tense almost confirms that, in this state representing the meeting of two perceptions of human reality, the offspring will discover in dream what the mother as woman already senses. This intuitive capacity, so integral a part of the feminine character and so essential to creativity, is revealed by the structural function of the verb "soñar" in its symbolic form. It fuses the two movements by disclosing their intrinsic characteristics. Thus the *mother* created by the poet's imagination identifies spiritually with the other half of the artistic creation: the fruit child.

Having linked Brazil and fruit, mother and offspring, woman and creation, we now also understand woman's presence, essence, and ascendency. The key words "facciones abrasadas," "noche," "frutal," and "Vía Láctea" are employed to integrate externally and internally the structural aspects of the entire poem. The common link between these word-symbols is their relationship to the four basic cosmic elements: air, fire, earth, and water. They are also the cardinal points of woman that are used in the text to accentuate female completeness.[14] Thus woman becomes synonymous with mother nature and associated with complexity, contradiction, and mystery. Through the same symbols, the ritual (the innate and natural sacrifice of woman—the freeing of a nurtured child), which had remained implicit up to this point, surfaces in the last three lines, where it is ultimately substantiated by the reference to the mythic-mystic ascendency of the female figure. If one recalls the ocean voyage of fruit from a remote, bountiful, sunny Brazil and remembers the separation of fruit from its source to make the long trip in tight, dark, wicker hampers—a mission intended to please and nourish the world—it should not be difficult to grasp the symbolic level of the closing movement.

As before, the symbology of this final movement is pluralistic. The "facciones abrasadas" could intimate the mother-poet's point of origin: the sun, which symbolizes light, life, Heaven, and God, and the divine inspiration that guides the artist. On the other hand, the adjective "abrasadas" could also correspond to *abraded, seared*, or *burned*, referring to Brazil's parched soil and the mother's dried breast after she has weaned her child. Moreover, the choice of this particular adjective denotes pain and anguish as well as abuse. Night, mankind's silent reminder of the dark and mysterious infinity that surrounds us all, fulfills here a dual function: it is correlative to both "prietos mimbres" and "rollo de la gloria." Both are containers, the former to transport the child to a future he cannot, at this point, visualize—perhaps even his death—and the latter the child's physical and spiritual container, suggestive of the dark, peaceful womb. The last two symbols, "frutal" and "Vía Láctea," complete the poem's entire cycle. Both function as coordinates in the dualistic structure of the composition since they imply source of life and nourishment. They also bring together the two planes on which the composition is constructed: "frutal" as the telluric level, "Vía Láctea" as the nebulous, distant realm of the imagination—a child's vision of Heaven or paradise. The ensuing imagery portrays the fruit tree and the Milky Way suckling and then releasing their offspring—fruit and heavenly bodies—to float all alone in darkness and silence on their eternal mission: the former in their wicker hampers across the great ocean,[15] the latter abandoning their luminous source so that they might brighten the universe. From their distinct yet similar acts of cleavage, new fruit trees and new constellations will be formed whose children will then carry on the creative, lonely, sacrificial, self-fulfilling, and metaphorically maternal assignment.

Notes

1. Gabriela Mistral, *Poesías completas*, 3d ed. (Madrid: Aguilar, 1966). Henceforth, all references to Mistral's poetry will apply to this volume. The English translation of "Fruta" is mine.
2. For a thought-provoking discussion of this topic, see Robert Seidenberg, "Is Anatomy Destiny?," in *Marriage in Life and Literature* (New York: Philosophical Library, 1970), pp. 119–56.
3. Lisa Appignanesi indicates that the term *femininity* is one generally misunderstood because it is vague.

   > "As such it constitutes what Roland Barthes calls a 'myth': a statement which bears no *direct* relationship to the object it describes (woman) and evokes a range of suggestions which is culturally determined"
   >
   > (*Femininity and the Creative Imagination* [London: Vision, 1973], p. 2).

   The implication is that *feminine* is an adjective denoting not sociological characteristics, but rather constituent factors such as creativity, sensibility, suggestiveness, intuitiveness, etc.—traits that may be found in man as well as woman. Consequently, the artist can be said to possess all of those characteristics, regardless of sex. In this respect, *Cuenta-mundo* is more than just a woman's view of the world; it is instead a hymn to the spiritual nature of Creation and to all that is good, beautiful, and everlasting on earth.

4. Gabriela Mistral's view coincides, albeit fortuitously, with Erich Neumann's pronouncement that

   "woman experiences herself first and foremost as the source of life. Fashioned in the likeness of the Great Goddess, she is bound up with the all-generating life principle, which is creative nature and a culturecreating principle in one. . . . Abduction, rape, marriage or death, and separation are the great motifs underlying the Eleusinian (matriarchal) mysteries"

   (*The Great Mother*, 3d ed. [New York: Pantheon, 1963], p. 306).

5. *Poesías completas*, p. 287.
6. Thus, Mistral's transmutation supports the theories of such researchers as Otto Rank and Carl G. Jung, who

   "believe that artists try to recapture the spirit of childhood, when freedom and innocence accompanied security and nourishing love given by parents—a golden age. The attempt to recapture paradise lost is repeated in mythic patterns and images of the quest"

   (Grace Stewart, *A New Mythos: The Novel of the Artist as Heroine 1877–1977* [St. Albans, Vt.: Eden Press, 1979], p. 8).

   Mistral's eminent capacity for mythmaking is brought to the fore by Juan Villegas (in "La aventura mítica en 'La flor del aire' de Gabriela Mistral," *Revista Iberoamericana,* no. 95 (1976), pp. 217–32), who maintains that Mistral consistently structures her works according to certain myths and mythic images consonant with both her universal concerns and personal experience.

7. *Poesías completas*, p. 296.
8. The message conveyed by the imagery of this couplet corresponds admirably to the Spanish *dar a la luz:* to give birth. It is worth noting how a similar imagery representing infants as young animals put out to pasture emerges from *Lecturas para mujeres:*

   "Vosotras, madres, decís: ¡Los hombres lo han querido! ¡Los hombres se han vuelto fieras! ¿Y quiénes son los hombres? Miradlos, pues: son cosa diminuta que engorda y sonríe a la sombra de vuestro seno, como se agranda y dora el grano de uva a la sombra del parral.

   "De vosotras salieron; vosotras los cargásteis mientras no pudieron caminar; vosotras los trajisteis de la mano. Ahora os sentís extrañas a ellos; os asustáis de sus crímenes y exlamáis: ¡Los hombres! ¡Los hombres!—como gritarían las madres del rebaño devorado en la noche: ¡Los lobos! ¡Los lobos!"

   ("You, mothers, say: Men do this! Men have wanted it this way! Men have turned into wild beasts! And who are these men? Well, just look at them: they are diminutive things that fatten and smile in the shade of your bosoms, like grapes growing and brightening in the shade of the vine arbor.

   "They came out of you: you carried them while they were unable to walk; you led them by the hand. Now you feel as strangers before them; their crimes frighten you and you exclaim: 'Men! Men!'—as mother-sheep would cry: 'Wolves! Wolves!,' when their flock is devoured in the night")

   (*Lecturas para mujeres,* 3d ed. [San Salvador: Ministerio de Educación, Departmento Editorial, 1961], pp. 111–12).

9. *Poesías completas*, p. 296.
10. Juan Cirlot, *A Dictionary of Symbols* (London: Routledge and Kegan Paul, 1971), pp. 40–41.
11. Ibid.
12. *Poesías completas*, p. 296.
13. "Signs and Symbols," in *The Random House Dictionary of the English Language*, college ed., (New York: Random House, 1968), p. 1535. Also, see Neumann, *The Great Mother*, p. 141.
14. Cirlot, *A Dictionary of Symbols*, p. 4, appropriately claims that according to the most elemental cosmogonies, nature is depicted as a hermaphrodite: "Of the four Elements, air and fire are regarded as active and male: water and earth passive and female."
15. By giving the fruits' container a definitive shape, "prietos mimbres," the poet finalizes her conviction that woman is essentially a mother, whose symbol is the womb. As such she is preordained to shelter her children and then release them from her bond.

Nita M. Dewberry (essay date 1993)

SOURCE: "Sleep Images in Gabriela Mistral's 'Canciones de Cuna,'" in *CLA Journal*, Vol. 37, No. 9, 1993, pp. 94–103.

[*In the following essay, Dewberry discusses the imagery and associations surrounding sleep in Mistral's lullabies.*]

Lucila Godoy Alcayaga, a Chilean poet known by her pen name of Gabriela Mistral, wrote very subjective poetry and prose which expressed values essential to contemporary man. She gained popularity and literary fame to the extent of earning the highest literary award in the world, the Nobel Prize for Literature, presented to her in Sweden on November 15, 1945. She was both the first woman and the first Hispanic-American writer to receive this high, universal recognition.[1]

Mistral was born into a poor family on April 7, 1889, in the Chilean village of Vicuña on the River Elqui. As a child, she lived in the small town of Montegrande, where

her father was a schoolmaster and where she, in turn, became a teacher.[2] For Gabriela Mistral, teaching was a cause in which she worked with much enthusiasm, freedom, and creative spirit. It was evident that she loved the teaching profession. Fear of losing the profession she loved caused her to adopt the pseudonym of Gabriela Mistral. Both components of the name obviously contain spiritual values, and they reveal something of her conception of the world and of man: "Gabriela," for the archangel Gabriel, divine messenger of good news; "Mistral," for the poet Frederic Mistral, from Provence. Gabriela had great admiration for this poet and expressed special admiration of his work entitled *Mireille*. Thus, she adopted his name, Mistral.[3]

While a teacher in La Cantera in 1907, Gabriela first experienced love with an employee of the railroad company named Romelio Ureta, but their friendship was upset by frequent disagreements and finally ended. In 1909, Ureta committed suicide for reasons of personal honor that had nothing to do with his relationship with Gabriela Mistral. This event, however, left Gabriela Mistral very saddened, and on December 22, 1914, she completed ***Sonetos de la muerte***, dedicated to the memory of Ureta. With them she obtained literary recognition, winning a Gold Medal in the poetic Floral Games in Santiago.

A little after this first literary success, Mistral met a young poet from Santiago and fell in love again. But he too left her, in this case to marry a wealthy young lady. Because of this experience, Gabriela asked for a transfer to Punta Arenas in the extreme south of Chile. She remained there two years, secluded, in a desolate region. Soon, she began to write the moving and thoughtful poetry of ***Desolación.*** The very title of the book expresses her heartbreaking experience. In her disappointment, she turned her thoughts to children and wrote of them, transforming her frustrated longing for motherhood into the tenderness one observes in the section "Canciones de cuna" (Spanish for "lullabies").

This section, "Canciones," is filled with sleep images representing death, love, fear, escape, and contentment, all symbolizing the recent emotional experiences of Gabriela Mistral. Furthermore, here she shows her affection for the American lands and people. The anguish and loneliness she felt is recreated on almost every page of ***Desolación***, and especially in the "Canciones de cuna" one can see and feel her longing for companionship and love.

On January 10, 1957, Gabriela Mistral died of cancer in the United States, where she had been serving as Consul of Chile, and her remains were removed to Chile, Montegrande, in the Elqui Valley, where they now rest.

Sleep imagery appears in the section "Canciones de cuna" in ***Desolación*** to suggest specific emotions of happiness and pain experienced in life by the author. Here the predominant images are those of sleeping, being put to sleep, and rocking to sleep. This sleep imagery brings out the desolate and lonely feelings of the author and her desire to escape from her traumatic love experiences. An analysis of the psychological meanings of sleep in general allows us to see the specific meaning these images have in "Canciones de cuna." The feelings of contentment, love, desire to escape, fear, and death are symbolized in the sleep imagery of the *canciones* to show the stages of the author's emotional life that are portrayed in this section of the volume entitled ***Desolación.***

In the poem **"Apegado a mí,"** the very first poem of "Canciones," one sees fear represented through a want of companionship, a want of protection, and the fear of death symbolized through sleep images. The mother feels attached to the infant and wants him to sleep close to her, but it is also evident that although the mother wants to protect the infant, she needs the companionship and closeness of the child:

> Velloncito de mi carne,
> que en mi entraña yo tejí,
> velloncito friolento,
> ¡duérmete apegado a mí![4]

This desire for companionship during sleep is representative of her fears. Thus, in the *estribillo*—"duérmete apegado a mí!"—the mother wants the baby next to her, for she fears the unknown. Even among some cultures fear was a dominant reason for communal sleeping, since there was a strong fear of the night and its perils. Gabriela Mistral demonstrates this fear of sleep in **"Apegado a mí"** through night images of howling dogs, disturbingly heavy breathing, and trembling like a little blade of grass:

> La perdiz duerme en el trébol
> escuchándole latir:
> no te turben mis alientos,
> ¡duérmete apegado a mí!
>
> Hierbecita temblorosa
> asombrada de vivir,
> no te sueltes de mi pecho,
> ¡duérmete apegado a mí!
>
> (Mistral 147)

In the book *Sleep*, Gay Gaer Luce and Julius Segal state that the common fear of sleep derives from a belief that animals and men function only because each is inhabited by a smaller being: a little animal in animals and a little man in men. This little man inside the man is known as the soul. Life depends upon the presence of the soul. Therefore, without it, death ensues. Thus, sleep appears as a temporary absence of the soul and an experience close to death.

In the Fiji Islands of the Southwest Pacific and among other tribes, people went to great extremes not to awaken a sleeping man. It was believed that a man's soul was out wandering during sleep and in a sudden awakening it might not have time to get back.[5] This uncertainty leaves men with a fear of sleep which is by association a fear of

death, loneliness, and despair. This association between sleep and death is not really extinct in modern man and is seen throughout this poem, **"Apegado a mí,"** and especially in its last stanza:

> Yo que todo lo he perdido
> ahora tiemblo de dormir.
> No resbales de mi brazo:
> ¡duérmete apegado a mí.
>
> (Mistral 147)

This stanza makes it obvious that the mother fears losing her baby and herself to the unknown: sleep, the mysterious process not yet understood completely.

In the poem **"La madre triste,"** the mother is anxious and concerned about the world and its problems. Thus, she wants the child to escape these problems in sleep, an act that the mother herself cannot accomplish because of worry:

> Duerme, duerme, dueño mío,
> sin zozobra, sin temor,
> aunque no se duerma mi alma,
> aunque no descanse yo.
>
> (Mistral 153)

The poem ends by expressing the desire of letting the baby sleep in place of the mother so that he may be peaceful and content. The baby and the mother are seen as one entity:

> Duerma en ti la carne mía,
> mi zozobra, mi temblor.
> En ti ciérrense mis ojos:
> ¡duerma en ti mi corazón!
>
> (Mistral 153)

Again, the whole purpose of a *canción de cuna* is to put the baby to sleep. The mother feels that a baby must sleep, and the mother's feelings are imposed upon the baby, as in the poem **"La madre triste."**

Most mothers love their infants and want them to rest for the sake of their health. At the same time, the children get a chance to escape the world and its problems. All evil ceases as a mother sings a lullaby and a child falls asleep peacefully. Thus, in the poem **"Suavidades,"** the symbol of escape appears, but in this case in the form of peacefulness. The baby escapes peacefully from the wrongdoings of the world as seen in the first stanza:

> Cuando yo te estoy cantando,
> en la Tierra acaba el mal;
> todo es dulce por tus sienes:
> la barranca, el espinar.
>
> (Mistral 154)

The image of sleep is distinctly brought out in the second and last stanza of the poem. The child tries to fight off sleep; it does not want to be separated from his mother and the world. However, the mother escapes the cruelties of the world through the act of cuddling and caring for the child. The following quote from **"Suavidades"** expresses the contradiction of the baby's fight to maintain reality and the mother's wish to escape it:

> Cuando yo te estoy cantando,
> se me borra la crueldad:
> suaves son, como tus párpados,
> ¡la leona y el chacal!
>
> (Mistral 154)

The poem ends with the child fighting to stay in touch with reality by not sleeping. Nevertheless, he fights a losing battle against the mother's sweetly sung *canciones de cuna.*

The emotions of having fear and escaping are often produced because of love. In **"Apegado a mí"** the mother feels fear for the child and for herself because of love. Also, in **"Suavidades"** and **"La madre triste,"** the mother loves her child so deeply that she wants him and herself to escape the cruelties and evils of the world.

This emotion, love, is expressed in the poem **"Meciendo."** In this poem appears the image of the mother putting the infant lovingly and caringly to sleep. The title of the poem, **"Meciendo,"** emphasizes the preparation for sleep. The mother rocks the infant just like nature rocks all living things:

> El mar sus millares de olas
> mece, divino.
> Oyendo a los mares amantes
> mezo a mi niño.
>
> (Mistral 149)

The nurturing or rocking to sleep is vivid in this poem through the image and through the rhythm. The action expresses love and pleasure for both nature and man:

> El viento errabundo en la noche
> mece los trigos.
> Oyendo a los vientos amantes
> mezo a mi niño.
>
> (Mistral 149)

Being cradled can be very important to the infant in order to achieve sleep. Freud believed that compulsive bedtime rituals were universal. Furthermore, he believed that almost everyone performs them whether he or she is conscious of them or not. Without these rituals, man cannot function properly.[6] In addition, without these same rituals nature would become unbalanced. No one knows what causes these actions that keep nature and man balanced, as no one knows why the Creator continues to cradle (love) his worlds:

> Dios Padre sus miles de mundos
> mece sin ruido.
> Sintiendo su mano en la sombra
> mezo a mi niño.
>
> (Mistral 149)

This image of *mecer*, the cradling of the child, symbolizes a loving, caring expression of nature, the Creator, and man.

Death is symbolized through sleep in the poem **"La noche."** Images that had suggested death and love in the poems **"Apegado a mí"** and **"Meciendo,"** respectively, are united in this poem. Here the image of sleep reminds the reader of death and its effect upon the world which appears in the following stanza:

Porque duermas, hijo mío,
el ocaso no arde más:
no hay más brillo que el rocío,
más blancura que mi faz.

(Mistral 150)

Again, sleep seems to represent death: the death of the child which leaves the world in a state of silence, in stillness and unbalanced. Nothing exists except the sorrow and loneliness reminiscent of death:

Porque duermas, hijo mío,
el camino enmudeció;
nadie gime sino el río;
nadie existe sino yo.

(Mistral 15)

The suggestion of the idea of the soul leaving the body during sleep is apparent in the following stanza. In it everything is peaceful, tranquil, and without motion. A kind of supernatural force takes control:

Se anegó de niebla el llano.
Se encogió el suspiro azul.
Se ha posado como mano
sobre el mundo la quietud.

(Mistral 150)

The image of *mecer* appears again at the end of the poem as if to express a love and care for the baby and for the world. However, even though there is love and love of mankind, death does exist. Everyone must sleep just as everyone must die. Gabriela Mistral expresses in this poem her feelings of loving and caring for mankind during these periods of apparent death; it is as if she would like the world to escape and forget its cares, like a sleeping baby:

Yo no sólo fui meciendo
a mi niño en mi cantar:
a la Tierra iba durmiendo
al vaivén del acunar.

(Mistral 150)

In contrast to these earlier poems that contain the image of sleep as symbols of stillness and death, the poem **"Me tuviste"** expresses in the act of sleep the emotion of contentment and happiness. In the first stanza of the poem, the narrator is telling the loved one to sleep and to be content:

Duérmete, mi niño,
duérmete sonriendo,
que es la ronda de astros
quien te va meciendo.

(Mistral 151)

There is no feeling of fear, leading to loneliness and despair between the child and the mother, as in the poem **"Apegado a mí."** Instead, in **"Me tuviste,"** the two are together and content. The image of light also contributes to produce feelings of hope, since there is no darkness to create gloom:

Gozaste la luz
y fuiste feliz.
Todo bien tuviste
al tenerme a mí.

(Mistral 151)

The speaker, who can be a mother talking to a child or a lover talking to her loved one, directs the beloved to sleep peacefully. The world is content and there is love for mankind. This love and contentment is expressed in the following stanza, one in which the nurturing image of rocking or cradling appears again:

Duérmete, mi noño,
duérmete sonriendo,
que es la Tierra amante
quien te va meciendo.

(Mistral 151)

Hope and love are expressed throughout the poem. The color symbolism has also changed from the white of stillness suggested in "la noche" ("se anegó de niebla el llano") to the red of love in **"Me tuviste"** (Miraste la ardiente / rosa carmesí"). The mother responds to the child reaching out into the world when he reaches out to love her: "Estrechaste al mundo: / me estrechaste a mí." This image creates a parallelism between mother and nature nurturing each other once more.

The poem is again written as a lullaby. It is a preparation for sleep and for the nurturing love that the cradling action will provide. Sleep has no negative connotation in this poem, being showered with harmony, peace, and love. The poem ends by the speaker telling the baby to sleep well, reassured by God's love:

Duérmete, mi niño,
duérmete sonriendo,
que es Dios en la sombra
el que te va meciendo.

(Mistral 151)

The poems analyzed contain images of sleep that represent emotions as contradictory as love, contentment, escape, fear, and dread of death. Through Gabriela Mistral's poetry we can see psychological insights as to why and how the mother and infant react toward sleep the way they do. Their reactions respond to the universal feelings that psychologists believe are hidden behind man's attitudes toward sleep. The symbols chosen by Mistral represent the feelings many mothers have toward their infants and make the reader realize how well her poetry has captured the reality of everyday life as well as the psychological insights hidden behind the simple action of putting a baby to sleep.

Notes

1. Margot Arce de Vazquez, *Gabriela Mistral: The Poet and Her Work* (New York: New York UP, 1964) 7.
2. Arce de Vazquez 8.
3. Arce de Vazquez 6.
4. Gabriela Mistral, *Desolación* (Madrid: Espasa-Calpe, 1951) 147. Hereafter cited parenthetically in the text.
5. Gay Gaer Luce and Julius Segal, *Sleep* (New York: Coward-McCann, 1966) 26–27.
6. Luce and Segal 25.

Linda Maier (essay date 1993)

SOURCE: "The Crepuscular Landscape Motif in Two Poems by Gabriela Mistral," in *Hispanofila*, Vol. 109, September, 1993, pp. 49–56.

[*In the following essay, Maier analyzes two of Mistral's poems, both of which dwell on twilight images, for modernist and avant-garde elements; Maier calls her a "poet of transition."*]

Gabriela Mistral's rise to fame occurred during a transitional phase in Hispanic literature. In 1914, she achieved national recognition when she was awarded first prize in Chile's annual literary competition. Her celebrity spread abroad when in 1921, Professor Federico de Onís gave a lecture on Mistral's poetry to a group of North American teachers of Spanish who were so impressed that they promoted the publication of her first collection of poetry, ***Desolación*** (New York: Instituto de las Españas en los Estados Unidos, 1922). Thus, Mistral's work emerged in a period when the avant-garde had begun to compete for public attention and acclaim with the more established late *Modernistas.*[1]

In attempting to determine Mistral's position within the literary spectrum, a number of critics associate her with *Modernismo* (Aubrun, Dinamarca, Iglesias, Mañach, Rodríguez Luis) while it has also been suggested that her work displays the avant-garde reaction to it (Arce de Vásquez 21, Goic, Rosenbaum 178). Still others place her squarely between these two trends (Bellini 346, Corvalán 36–37, Forster 109, Franco 276, Mangini González 440). In order to settle this issue, the analysis of a familiar motif common to both *Modernista* and avant-garde poetry, that of the *crepúsculo*, in two poems of this period—**"Tarde,"** first published in 1914 in *Sucesos* (Valparaíso), and **"Desolación,"** the title poem of the 1922 collection[2]—may help to reveal the dominant features of Mistral's work.

The crepuscular landscape motif in Mistral's poetry is often mentioned, though few critics, with the exception of Cedomil Goic, have examined it closely. Mistral's twilight landscapes reflect her own emotional condition; through the pathetic fallacy device, Nature assumes the poet's pain and grief. As Raúl Silva Castro states, "La visión del paisaje en [Gabriela Mistral] . . . viene a ser un espejo en que fielmente se copia un tormento humano personalísimo"; furthermore, continues Silva Castro, "[e]l crepúsculo para la poetisa es rojo sobre todo, y le recuerda la sangre de su martirio y las heridas de su dolor" (*Estudios* 88, 146). Dusk introduces an atmosphere of melancholy and gloom which only becomes more oppressive when night falls:

> [Mistral's] dolorous spirit, moreover, does not look to the hope or promise of dawn, but rather to the blackness of night in which to lose sight of the mantle of tears that clothes her. Night, therefore, lends its bleakness, its dourness, its tragedy, to these "tone poems" of hers. But they are more frequently infused with the burning red of the bleeding sunsets . . . which are so colored, she sometimes thinks, by the gaping wounds that sorrow and pain left within her. . . .
>
> (Rosenbaum 190)

Ironically, since the sunset image figures so prominently in her work, Mistral herself views it as a trite image in her essay, "El país sin crepúsculo," included in *Materia*:

> El crepúsculo se ha vuelto como más rendido de cuantas alabanzas lleva en su ridícula bolsa de vidrios insensatos. Cada hombre que quiere ser poeta (y cada pobre diablo también), se ha probado el alma en sentir el crepúsculo.
>
> Por todo eso, el crepúsculo ha parado en más caduco, de fatiga, como los hombres demasiado alabados.
>
> Yo no le amo. Yo le odio su traición. . . .
>
> (147)

Notwithstanding her contempt for the crepuscular landscape theme, Mistral not only adopts it in one of her early poems, **"Tarde,"** but also treats it in the straightforward *Modernista* manner rather than undermining it in the parodic style of certain late *Modernistas* and avant-garde poets.[3] This poem contains all the typical *Modernista* elements: the twilight hour, pastoral setting, sheep bells tinkling in the distance, and a tone of sadness.

In structure, content, and technique **"Tarde"** sets a typical *Modernista* crepuscular tableau. Mistral employs a metric pattern popularized by Darío, the sonnet in Alexandrines. Though often faulted for the metrical defectiveness of her poems, here Mistral nearly achieves the formal perfection sought after by *Modernista* writers. The consonantal rhyme scheme conforms to the sonnet format: abab cdcd eef fgg.

Each line contains the expected caesura, which in certain lines (vv. 3, 7–8, for example) is arranged with slight poetic license.

Ostensibly, the poem describes a peaceful, rustic twilight scene, but it also expresses a powerful contrasting mood. As the sun sets, the sky changes colors (vv. 1–2), and a soft breeze blows with a muted rustling sound (v. 5). Shepherds lead their flocks down the hill to return them to their enclosure for the night (vv. 7–8), and the sheep bells ring as the stars begin to shine (vv. 13–14). This calm appears to soothe the human spirit (vv. 3–4) whose turmoil is nevertheless reflected in the sun's final, intense glow (vv. 10–11). However, as Mistral's later work makes evident, this serenity is illusory since it only precedes what may be termed the "dark night of the soul." The hour of twilight deceptively offers the promise of spiritual repose when in fact it brings only renewed anguish. Dusk is, as Mistral later explains, "la hora que dicen tímida, y que es la hora de la traición, en que la tierra de facciones íntegras se vuelve peligrosa, toda entera como un camino que se fundiera, vaga como un fondo marino . . ." ("El país sin crepúsculo" 147). The sun's clarity becomes murky at dusk.

This theme, that the twilight reflects intensified spiritual confusion, is reinforced by the poem's technical features, which alternate between established and unexpected literary devices. As the following textual analysis demonstrates, on the one hand, the poet seems to accept standard literary practice while on the other, certain elements, such as the use of harsh alliteration and intentional syntactical disorder, run counter to and disrupt it. In fact, the poem's stylistic dissonances, as outlined and explained below, parallel its message of human despair.

Classical and Biblical allusions and an ambiguous alliterative pattern create a false impression of tranquillity. Extratextual references to the Bible and Vergil (vv. 7–8) call to mind an edenic idyll. In keeping with the implied peacefulness of the scene, predominantly sonorous consonants add a pleasant quality. The poem opens on a subdued note, with explosive consonants muted by their voiced nature: "*M*uere el *d*ía con una *d*ulzura de *m*ujer" (emphasis added). In verse 2, the voiced aspirants and sibilants reproduce the afternoon hush: "y el *c*ele*s*te y el ro*s*a *v*an *c*ediendo al *v*ioleta." (Emphasis added.) This sibilance recurs throughout the poem which indeed closes with these soft sounds: "El cora*z*ón de bron*c*e *s*ollo*z*a en *las es*quila*s* / y l*as es*trell*as* mue*s*tran *sus* lágrim*as* tranquil*as*" (vv. 13–14). However, a key line that describes the easing of spiritual distress is marked by both sibilants and explosive consonants, thereby belying its apparently comforting statement: "El hervor del *e*s*p*íri*t*u *s*e *s*ien*t*e de*c*re*c*er: / *c*omo un *e*s*t*an*q*ue *p*leno, *c*ada *p*asión *s*e a*q*ui*e*ta." (Emphasis added.) Rather than diminishing at sunset, human misery intensifies.

Hyperbaton and enjambement further underscore this sense of spiritual agitation. The drastic syntactical alteration of the poem's opening lines signal the internal dissarray. The inversion of normal subject-verb word order (vv. 1–2 and 7–8) is a graphic expression of the imminent emotional upheaval and focuses attention on a key idea, death, which upsets the orderliness of life: "*Muere* el día . . ." (emphasis added). Likewise, the technique of enjambement periodically breaks the poem's smooth flow (vv. 6–7, 7–8, 10–12).

The poem's imagery and vocabulary further highlight the atmosphere of mourning prefigured by the sunset. The poem's two central metaphors present an opposition between time and eternity, death and immortality with the accent on the former. The day is compared to a dying woman dressed in silk (vv. 1, 5) while the earth is an angel with both face and wings (vv. 6–7). Word choice, however, stresses death and the trauma it causes. Terms related to death ("Muere," "ahogando"), sadness ("plañe," "solloza," "lágrimas"), and agitation ("hervor," "pasión," "mueve," "golpe," "caos," "arrebata," "fuerzas," "pulsación," "intenso") far outnumber those referring to peace and quiet ("dulzura," "espíritu," "decrecer," "se aquieta," "descendiendo," "se extingue," "tranquilas"). The progression of colors appearing in the twilight sky shifts from blue and pink (vv. 2, 8) to violet (v. 2) with the sun's final golden glow (v. 11) producing the poem's climax, and emotional nadir: the flaming red sunset (v. 12: "que hace arder todo el cielo . . .").

The troubling elements which intrude on the *Modernista* framework of **"Tarde"** do not subvert the crepuscular landscape motif, but rather serve to reinforce the notion of betrayal alluded to by Mistral in her 1927 essay. This essay envisions a mythical region of eternal daylight, "El país sin crepúsculo," undisturbed by the threat of death:

> Allá, donde el crepúsculo es vencido, están los hombres y las mujeres fieles, parecidas al cedro sin joroba, que porque no han visto anochecer ignoran la huida, y permanecen, permanecen. Tienen un perfil de agaves duros y sus cinco sentidos meridianos no han olido el olor de buitre de la muerte; y su ojo apacentado en la luz no se levanta y se baja a cada hora para espiar el horizonte.
>
> Tranquilos, en el mediodía blanco, ellos hacen su estrofa larga o la tendedura de su surco.
>
> (148)

In both Mistral's early poem and her later essay, the sunset betrays its promise of serenity and offers only suffering and pain. **"Tarde"** anticipates the even darker crepuscular landscape of **"Desolación."**

This poem introduces the final section of poetry, "Naturaleza," of Mistral's 1922 collection, heads the trio of poems designated "Paisajes de la Patagonia," and lends the book its title. However, despite its salient position within Mistral's poetic corpus, **"Desolación"** has not been the subject of detailed critical analysis. A notable *crepúsculo*, this poem therefore warrants close examination.

The structure of **"Desolación"** resembles that of **"Tarde."** Here again Mistral uses the *Modernista*-inspired Alexandrine with caesura; but rather than a sonnet, the poem consists of eight stanzas of four lines each with consonantal rhyme (abba cddc etc.). This poem may be divided into three parts which describe the following: 1) the desolate antarctic landscape where the poet watches the sun set (stanzas 1–2), 2) the poet's loneliness and separation from those she loved who have died and her alienation from the strangers around her (stanzas 3–5), 3) the falling snow and nightfall (stanzas 6–8).

The mood of **"Desolación"** is altogether grim and somber, though a series of oppositions is established which only serve to underline the dominant tone. Despite the snowy whiteness of the landscape and the twilight, a sense of gloom overshadows the scene and contrasts with the approaching darkness: "Y en la llanura blanca, de horizonte infinito, / miro morir inmensos ocasos dolorosos" (vv. 7–8). Dark images ("bruma," "noche," "sin la luz," "la huesa," "la niebla," "duelo") are silhouetted against the light background ("llanura blanca," "ocaso," "velas blanquean," "ojos claros," "frutos pálidos," "tierras de oro," "la nieve," "albura," "cielos," "mirada," "azahar"). Indeed, images of whiteness, light, and pallor outnumber those referring to darkness. The white snow is likened to a pale face pressed against the windowpanes of the poet's house (v. 27), the ever vigilant eye of God (vv. 29–30), and orange blossoms (v. 30), normally symbolic of marriage and happiness but here linked to death and sadness.

Vocabulary relating to death and suffering is prevalent throughout the poem, beginning with its title, **"Desolación."** The wind "sighs" and "howls" around the poet's house, muffling her own cries (vv. 5–6). The poet describes the sunset as a daily "death" (v. 8) and in a powerful image the snow appears "como el polvo en la huesa" (v. 21). Like a dying person (v. 22), she is unable to do anything except watch the snow pile up and the fog thicken. The atmosphere of mourning (v. 25) and bereavement (v. 10) occasioned by the crepuscular landscape inevitably infects the poet.

The tone is one of despair, as the title suggests, and fatalism. As in **"Tarde,"** hyperbaton and enjambement reflect the poet's inner turmoil. Choppy phrasing (vv. 1–2, 5–6, 11–12, 13–14, 17–18, 19–20, and 29–30) depicts the poet's emotional upset. The muddled word order of the poem's opening lines is likewise indicative of an emotional disturbance. The poet yearns for communion with both the living and the dead, but when she attempts communication, her expression is distorted and rendered ineffectual (vv. 17–18). The abundance of negatives (vv. 3, 14, 15, 16, 19, 23, 30) increases the mood of pessimism which the poet ultimately resigns herself to accept: "siempre, como el destino, que ni mengua ni pasa, / descenderá a cubrirme, terrible y extasiada."

The poet's frame of mind parallels the sun's descent into the dark abyss of silence and loneliness. Mistral opposes verbs of descent (vv. 18, 21, 28, 32) to those of ascent (vv. 12, 17, 22), and the former mirror not only the sun's gradual disappearance but also her downcast emotional attitude. In this desolate physical and mental landscape, the overpowering silence prevents the communion the poet desires. Vocabulary relating to silence (vv. 11, 18, 29) counters that referring to sound (vv. 5–6, 9, 17, 19, 20) and extinguishes it: "Y la interrogación que sube a mi garganta / . . . me desciende, vencida." Mistral's use of alliteration also expresses this sense of frustrated communication. The repetition of unvoiced explosive consonants is systematically neutralized by softer sounds. In stanza 2, for example, the hard *c* sounds are cancelled out by the lateral *m* and long *o* sounds: "El vient*o* hace a *m*i *c*asa su *r*onda de s*o*ll*o*z*o*s / y de alarid*o*, y *q*uiebra, *c*omo un *c*ristal, *m*i grito. / Y en la llanura blanca, de h*o*riz*o*nte infinit*o*, / *m*iro *m*orir in*m*ens*o*s *o*cas*o*s d*o*l*o*r*o*s*o*s." (Emphasis added.) Similarly, these lateral consonants and sibilants offset even the voiced explosive consonants, as in the poem's final stanza: "*S*iem*p*re ella, *s*ilencio*s*a, como la gran *m*irada / *d*e *D*ios *s*obre *m*í; *s*iem*p*re *s*u a*z*ahar *s*obre *m*i *c*a*s*a; / *s*iem*p*re, *c*omo el *d*es*t*ino, *q*ue ni *m*engua ni *p*a*s*a, / *d*es*c*en*d*erá a *c*ubrir*m*e, terrible y exta*s*iada." (Emphasis added.)

The emotional depression will recur infinitely at dusk. Word choice contrasts terms of limit (vv. 3, 23, 24, 26) with limitlessness (vv. 1, 4, 7, 8, 10, 12, 22, 24, 25, 28, 29, 30, 31), thereby indicating the eternal nature of the poet's spiritual anguish. Anaphora (vv. 6–7, 16–17, 23; vv. 8, 21–22, 25) also signals the inescapable reappearance of this condition; tellingly, Mistral repeats the word *siempre* in the poem's final stanzas (vv. 28–29, 31) and employs the verb *ser* rather than *estar*, thus denoting permanence, in the progressive tense: "¡siempre será su albura bajando de los cielos!"

From this analysis it may be concluded that Mistral's early crepuscular landscape poetry synthesizes both *Modernista* and avant-garde elements, consequently reflecting the transitional nature of her work. Both **"Tarde"** and **"Desolación"** present a static moment or fixed scene at the twilight hour, a convention especially favored by the *Modernistas* but also invoked by avantgarde poets for different purposes. In both poems Mistral displays a formal expertise not usually attributed to her. She adopts a metric pattern preferred by the *Modernistas*, and the stylistic techniques are calculated to convey the theme of spiritual torment; thus, both poems achieve, to a varying degree, the *Modernista* goal of formal perfection though neither presents a gratuitous message in the vein of art for art's sake. Between **"Tarde"** (1914) and **"Desolación"** (1922), Mistral moves from the colorful imagery of *Modernismo* to the black and white austerity of the avant-garde. However, unlike more progressive poets—such as Borges, Herrera y Reissig, Lugones, and Neruda, for example—Mistral does not introduce incongruous or urban elements into her crepuscular landscapes, and she does not intend to subvert tradition. As Jean Franco and others have suggested, Gabriela Mistral is truly a poet of transition:

> Tanto por su persona como por su poesía, Gabriela Mistral está en medio de dos épocas. Su formación

pertenece al siglo XIX. . . . Pero se vio obligada a vivir en un mundo moderno. . . . Pero aunque había nacido con el nuevo siglo aún no pertenecía a él, no era moderna en el sentido en que eran modernos un Neruda o un Vallejo, porque sus valores eran los del pasado. Ello no significa menospreciar su poesía, sino simplemente situarla en una tendencia distinta a la que había dado origen a los movimientos contemporáneos.

(276)

Notes

1. It is interesting to note that at about the same time *Desolación* appeared, the following books were published: *Poemas puros: Poemillas de la ciudad* by Dámaso Alonso (1921), *Bazar* and *Orto* (1922) by Francisco Luis Bernárdez, *Fervor de Buenos Aires* by Jorge Luis Borges (1923), *Imagen* by Gerardo Diego (1922), *Veinte poemas para ser leídos en el tranvía* by Oliverio Girondo (1922), *Saisons choisies* (1921) and *Finis Britanniae* (1923) by Vicente Huidobro, *Las horas doradas* by Leopoldo Lugones (1922), *Los aguiluchos* by Leopoldo Marechal (1922), *La canción de la fiesta* (1921) and *Crepusculario* (1923) by Pablo Neruda, *Presagios* by Pedro Salinas (1923), and *Trilce* by César Vallejo (1922).
2. These two poems are included in the following: "Tarde," in Raúl Silva Castro, *Producción de Gabriela Mistral de 1912 a 1918* (Santiago: Ediciones de los Anales de la Universidad de Chile, 1957) 42, 69, and "Desolación," in Gabriela Mistral, *Desolación* (New York: Instituto de las Españas en los Estados Unidos, 1922), 149–50.
3. See Kirkpatrick for an explanation of this subversive technique in Lugones and Herrera y Reissig. See also Maier for a similar view of Borges' early poetry.

Works Cited

Alegría, Fernando. *Genio y figura de Gabriela Mistral.* Buenos Aires: Editorial Universitaria de Buenos Aires, 1966.

Alvárez-Borland, Isabel. "Víctor Hugo, Gabriela Mistral, y *L'intertextualité.*" *Revista de Estudos Hispánicos* 18 (1984): 371–80.

Arce de Vázquez, Margot. *Gabriela Mistral: The Poet and Her Work.* Trans. Helene Masslo Anderson. New York: New York UP, 1964.

Aubrun, Charles V. "Gabriela Mistral, Rubén Darío y la invención poética." *Quaderni Ibero-Americani* 6 (1973–74): 142–46.

Bellini, Giuseppe. *Historia de la literatura hispano americana.* Madrid: Castalia, 1986.

Corvalán, Octavio. *Modernismo y Vanguardia.* New York: Las Américas, 1967.

Dinamarca, Salvador. "Gabriela Mistral y su obra poética." *Hispania* 41 (1958): 48–50.

Feito, Francisco E. "Del tiempo y la distancia en la *Desolación* de Gabriela Mistral." *Festschrift José Cid Pérez.* Eds. Alberto Gutiérrez de la Solana and Elio Alba-Buffill. New York: Senda Nueva de Ediciones, 1981. 205–09.

Forster, Merlin H. *Historia de la poesía hispanoamericana.* Clear Creek, Indiana: The American Hispanist, 1981.

Franco, Jean. *Historia de la literatura hispanoamericana a partir de la independencia.* Barcelona: Ariel, 1973.

Goic, Cedomil. "'Cima,' de Gabriela Mistral." *Revista Iberoamericana* 48 (1982): 59–72.

Iglesias, Augusto. *Gabriela Mistral y el Modernismo en Chile.* Santiago de Chile: Editorial Universitaria, 1950.

Jiménez Martos, Luis. "Gabriela Mistral y el paisaje de Chile." *Atlántida* 5 (1967): 299–302.

Kirkpatrick, Gwen. "Lugones and Herrera: Destruction and Subversion of *Modernismo.*" *Romance Quarterly* 33 (1986): 89–98.

Maier, Linda S. "Los rasgos modernistas en la poesía temprana de Borges." *Ensayos de literatura europea e hispanoamericana.* Ed. Félix Menchacatorre. San Sebastián: U. del País Vasco, 1990. 281–84.

Mañach, Jorge. "Gabriela y Juan Ramón o la poesía 'nobelable.'" *Cuadernos del Congreso por la Libertad de Cultura,* no. 40 (Jan.–Feb. 1960): 57–61.

Mangini González, Shirley. "Mitología y cosmología en Gabriela Mistral y Pablo Neruda." *Discurso Literario* 2 (1985): 439–55.

Marval, Carlota. "Gabriela Mistral: El tema de la muerte." *Arbor* 96 (1977): 73–78.

Mistral, Gabriela. *Desolación.* New York: Instituto de las Españas en los Estados Unidos, 1922.

———. "El país sin crepúsculo." *Materia: Prosa inédita.* Ed. Alfonso Calderón. Santiago de Chile: Editorial Universitaria, 1978. 147–49.

Monterde, Francisco. "Gabriela Mistral (1889–1957)." *Revista Iberoamericana* 22 (1957): 333–37.

Peralta Peralta, Jaime. "El paisaje original de Gabriela Mistral." *Cuadernos Hispanoamericanos* 53 (1963): 471–81.

Rodríguez, Mario. "El lenguaje del cuerpo en la poesía de la Mistral." *Revista Chilena de Literatura,* no. 23 (April 1984): 115–28.

Rodríguez Luis, Julio. "Relaciones entre Gabriela Mistral y Juan Ramón Jiménez." *La Torre,* Año 8, no. 32 (Oct.–Dec. 1960): 93–95.

Rosenbaum, Sidonia Carmen. *Modern Women Poets of Spanish America.* New York: Hispanic Institute in the United States, 1945.

Saavedra Molina, Julio. "Gabriela Mistral: Vida y obra." *Revista Hispánica Moderna* 3 (1936–37): 110–35.

Silva, Hernán. "La unidad poética de *Desolación.*" *Estudios Filológicos* 4 (1968): 152–75 and 5 (1969): 170–96.

Silva Castro, Raúl. *Estudios sobre Gabriela Mistral.* Santiago de Chile: Editorial Zig-Zag, 1935.

———. *Producción de Gabriela Mistral de 1912 a 1918.* Santiago: Ediciones de los Anales de la Universidad de Chile, 1957.

Maryalice Ryan-Kobler (essay date 1997)

SOURCE: "Beyond the Mother Icon: Rereading the Poetry of Gabriela Mistral," in *Revista Hispanica Moderna,* Vol. 50, No. 2, December, 1997, pp. 327–34.

[*In the following essay, Ryan-Kobler argues that Mistral's poetry contradicts the accepted, simplified image of Mistral as the saintly mother of Latin America.*]

The psychoanalyst and feminist Julia Kristeva posits that the speaking subject's unconscious drives persist in the linguistic, psychic and societal orders. These rhythmic drives, or the Semiotic, initially orient the infant towards the body of the mother. When the child passes through the mirror stage and the oedipus complex, this attachment is repressed. Here, the father intervenes, sundering the bond with the mother, but reconciling the child to the estranged mother through the Symbolic medium of language. Kristeva maintains that the maternal Semiotic is not totally repressed after this rupture with the mother, but rather courses the Symbolic order of language in the form of the tone, rhythm, and material properties of language. Other indices of these semiotic drives surface in the text as contradiction, nonsense, disruption, silence and absence. The Semiotic opposes all fixed, transcendental significations of the Symbolic which sustain the bulwarks of patriarchal order and power: God, father, state, order and property. (Kristeva, *Revolution in Poetic Language* 19–106)

Thus, in Kristevan theory, the symbolic and the semiotic are interwoven in language; the dialectic between them determines the discourse as narrative, theory or poetry. A purely semiotic mode of communication, for example, composed of tone, rhythm and sound, is music.

The *power* of the mother in the preverbal order of the Semiotic can not be underestimated. For that reason, it is repressed or forbidden in the Symbolic. Regression, or reunion with the forbidden maternal produces psychosis, and likewise bars the subject from participating in this order.

Discourses of maternity prevalent in the West (those of religion, science, and certain feminisms) obscure the visceral, primal quality of the semiotic. A pervasive silence surrounds the experience of raw pain as well as the *jouissance* of the semiotic maternal body, undermining its power in society and its affiliation with matrilinearism. Thus, the Symbolic overshadows the Semiotic, preventing it from challenging and undermining the Law of the Father.

Kristeva's icon of the Virgin Mother exemplifies the suppression of the maternal semiotic in the West. (Kristeva, "Stabat Mater" 49–55). The Virgin Mother is the pure vessel, the medium of the Word, or the name of the Father. Emphasis is placed on the Name of the Father who impregnates her, and is displaced from the semiotic body in the maternal processes of pregnancy and birth. This emphasis, according to Kristeva insures paternity and usurps any claims of matrilinear society on the God-child. The Virgin Mother has been domesticated, deprived of her *jouissance,* and as the "mater dolorosa" is only allowed to suffer. The Virgin is the representative of the repressed Semiotic, being only the "silent ear, milk and tears", metaphors of non-speech excluded from the Symbolic (Oliver 51). Unable to contain the semiotic, the Church controls it through the image of the Virgin Mother. By projecting the semiotic onto the symbol of the Virgin, it ceases to be a threat to the paternal order.

Nevertheless, the persistence of the cult of the Virgin affirms matrilinearism and bears witness to those unconscious, primal needs of identification with the mother. Moreover, the whole notion of the feminine is subsumed into the aseptic maternal contained in the icon. Maternity itself is attained in a virginal state. Women identify with the suffering Virgin, the "mater dolorosa", and in this way, dissociated from the semiotic, they remain participants in the realm of the Father without sacrificing their mothers.

Although men fully embrace language because they pass through the oedipal complex that threatens them with castration and forces them to identify with the Father of the Law, women never completely enter language since they identify with their mothers to some degree. For the woman artist this is crucial. The authorial self for the woman writer derives from identifying with their phallic position in the Symbolic. The lure of the maternal semiotic however puts them in danger of returning to that pre-oedipal identification with the mother that results in psychosis. Writing for the woman artist becomes a contest between the symbolic and the semiotic, between the protective phallic shield and the lure of the mother. When not identifying with the Symbolic, they are outside the Law, and according to Kristeva represent "visionaries, dancers who suffer as they speak" (quoted in Oliver, 112).

Longing for the mother and identity with her occurs through childbirth. Thus the process of pregnancy and birth safely renews identity with the mother. Longing for motherhood in the poems we will read, becomes a longing for the lost mother and the semiotic body.

Nearly forty years after her death in 1957, the persona of Gabriela Mistral (1889–1957) as spiritual mother of Latin

America overshadows her literary legacy. Critics have cast her as the hieratic mother icon. Indeed, the image of the saintly mother pervades Mistral's work. ***Poemas de las madres*** (1950) are dedicated to pregnant mothers. ***Ternura*** (1924) is totally dedicated to children's poems. The poet, speaking of her own intense, if frustrated desire to mother, prays in her prose poem **"La oración de la maestra"**: "Dame el ser más madre que las madres, para poder amar y defender / como ellas lo que no es carne de mi carne (9–10)".

Yet, the image of the mother is an ambiguous one in Mistral's work as I will show in this paper. The poem **"Electra en la niebla"**, discussed at length here, bears witness to the ambiguous mother image in the Mistral opus. I suggest that the reception of the texts of Gabriela Mistral mimics the drama of the symbolic versus the semiotic dramatized in Kristeva's Virgin Mother, foregrounding the mother icon of the Law and banishing her semiotic counterpart.

A critical conspiracy appears to have existed around Mistral's work that foregrounded the positive and traditional image of the mother, effectively silencing those passages and poems which reveal the conflicted, anguished treatment of the maternal. Mistral complied with critics and accepted her poetic persona.[1] Through a combination of literary artifice and personal diplomacy Mistral inserts herself into the literary order without inviting criticism or ostracism for exposing the raw underside of the maternal in her texts. She manipulates the masks of mother and teacher to both reveal and conceal herself. In several volumes of poems she disappears behind the masks of conformity, encoding her desire in comfortable stereotypes of the feminine. These poems stand as testaments of compliance and repression in the Symbolic. Nevertheless, through the literary artifice of myth and hermeticism, and sometimes alongside the stereotype, the poet crafts her texts to betray an unresolved conflict with the very image of the saintly mother, and ultimately defies the social order she appears to so carefully avoid offending.

Several poems from the poet's opus illustrate my thesis. **"La maestra rural"**, an early poem from ***Desolación*** (1922) has certainly forged the image of Mistral as exemplary mother-teacher. In **"Electra en la niebla"**, Mistral disguises herself in the folds of the ancient tale of matricide, revealing the writer's anguished relationship to the maternal, and her expulsion from the realm of the Father, undermining her own authorial position. Finally, in her hermetic work **"La Fuga"** from "Muerte de mi madre" (***Tala***, 1938) Mistral eroticizes the mother and regresses into her embrace.

I propose that beneath the masks of the writer, in the depths of her verses, lie the anguished psyche of the writer and the true complexity of her character. The pious mother and teacher is but a mask that Mistral uses to insert herself into the realm of the Father, the Symbolic. In the drama of her obsession with the mother we see another drama unfold: an unresolved sense of identity that exposes the deconstructive properties of her work. Here, she discloses her ambivalence, her rebellion to the Symbolic order, to the Name of the Father, and her desire to adhere to, or to return to the semiotic body.

The pious teacher and mother that emerges in the criticism of **"La maestra rural"** provides a classic example of the way Mistral has been read in the past. The image underscores all that is socially positive in this feminine figure. She is pure and modest, a servant of that God who gives anchor to the patriarchal order:

> La maestra era pura. "Los suaves hortelanos",
> decía, "de este predio, que es predio de Jesús,
> han de conservar puros los ojos y las manos,
> guardar claros sus óleos, para dar clara luz".
>
> (1–4)

Critics have read selectively, privileging positive markers of the feminine stereotype, and dismissing those signs of the anguished woman woven into the description:

> La maestra era alegre. ¡Pobre mujer herida!
> Su sonrisa fue un modo de llorar con bondad.
> Por sobre la sandalia rota y enrojecida,
> era ella la insigne flor de su santidad.
>
> (9–12)

The image of the mother-teacher here, is one of anguish, if not rage, as suggested by some critics. (González and Treese 35–38) The mother-teacher is a variant of Kristeva's Virgin Mother, the suffering "mater dolorosa", or the feminine that has survived in the social order, deprived of its raw energy.

In the same poem, Mistral addresses her alienation which she channels into a sense of superiority and a drive for perfection in her station in the rural society. Addressing the mother of one of her students who had unkindly gossiped about her she charges:

> Campesina, ¿recuerdas que alguna vez prendiste
> su nombre a un comentario brutal o baladí?
> Cien veces la miraste, ninguna vez la viste
> ¡y en el solar de tu hijo, de ella hay más que de ti!
>
> Pasó por él su fina, su delicada esteba,
> abriendo surcos donde alojar perfección
> La albada de virtudes de que lento se nieva
> es suya. Campesina, ¿no le pides perdón?
>
> (21–28)

Here, the poetic voice clings to her image as mother-teacher to overcome the pain of rejection or her marginalization by the villager who maligns her. While wearing the mask of virtue, she makes a stunning remark to the campesina, alleging that she, the teacher, is the true mother of the student: "y en el solar de tu hijo, de ella hay más que de ti"! (24). Again, we see the image of the saintly mother, the mask of conformity in dialectical relation to her sense of marginalization and alienation from the social order. The raw energy of the mother, the rage, resides just below the surface, producing an image of a pathetic "mater dolorosa". The dead mother in strophe six, awaiting her daughter from beyond the grave, is an important motif in Mistral's poetry, and describes the longing for the lost mother banished from the order of the Father but surfacing to reclaim what she has lost:

Daba sombra por una selva su encina hendida
el día en que la muerte la convidó a partir,
Pensando en que su madre la esperaba dormida
a La de Ojos Profundos se dio sin resistir.

(29–32)

The writer suggests here that reunion with the mother can only be attained in death. That is, the power of the mother is repressed, yet constantly beckons to the daughter, producing anguish because it must be resisted. Nevertheless, this primal relationship obscures all others, governs all others from beyond the grave, or at least undermines them, leaving the subject alienated from the world around her.

The struggle between the semiotic and the symbolic is less thinly disguised in the poet's later work. The matricidal **"Electra en la niebla"** dramatizes the poet's ambiguous relationship to the maternal. It demonstrates the constant lure of the forbidden semiotic, thus betraying a troubled alliance with the Father. **"Electra en la niebla"** recalls the ancient tale of Electra and her brother Orestes who killed Clytemnestra, their mother, to avenge the death of Agamemnon, their father. In the myth, Orestes was driven mad by the Furies as punishment for his unnatural act. For his part, Freud adopted Electra, the woman who kills her mother in order to avenge her father, as the female counterpart of the Oedipal complex, dramatizing in the socialization process the repression of the maternal, or semiotic, in favor of the symbolic.

In rewriting the myth, Mistral privileges Electra's role in her mother's death. Thus, it is Electra who approaches madness as Cytemnestra, her slain mother, surfaces from the semiotic to reclaim her daughter. Symbolically, as Electra abandons herself to the fog-like folds of the mother, she symbolically abandons the fatherland:

En la niebla marina voy perdida,
yo, Electra, tanteando mis vestidos
y el rostro que en horas fue mudado.
Será tal vez a causa de la niebla
que así me nombro por reconocerme.

(1–5)

The omnipresent fog is the mother surrounding her with her shroud: "La niebla tiene pliegues de sudario / dulce en el palpo, en la boca salobre". (87–88) Yet, this funereal fog also recalls the waters of pre-consciousness, of pre-birth when mother and child are an inseparable dyad.

Electra no longer has a sense of the world about her, the world of the paternal order. The town about her has disappeared, dissolving into the fog:

Esta niebla salada borra todo
lo que habla y endulza al pasajero
rutas, puentes, pueblos, árboles
No hay semblante que mire y reconozca
no más la niebla de mano insistente
que el rostro nos recorre y los costados. (43–48)
Ella es quien va pasando y no la niebla
Era una sola en un solo palacio
y ahora es niebla-albatrós, niebla-camino
niebla-mar, niebla-aldea, niebla-barco.

(112–115)

Electra identifies with the fog, and thus with the mother as she says: "O yo soy niebla que corre sin verse / o tú niebla que corre sin saberse" (101–102). She knows she must continue to resist her dead mother, or be swallowed up in her embrace and in her revenge: "pero marchar me rinde y necesito / romper la niebla o que me rompa ella" (108–109).

Her relationship to her brother is also a mirror image, suggesting again the regression to the Imaginary stage and transference to a loving Imaginary father (which precedes the stern Father of the Law in the Symbolic). The brother, thus, is the precursor of the Symbolic father, but at this point he simply replaces the mother of the mirror stage. Identity with the male precursor of the Symbolic may well be a vestige of the poetic subject's authorial role in that realm which is now undermined by the surfacing of the semiotic:[2]

por ser uno lo mismo quisimos
y cumplimos lo mismo y nos llamamos
Electra-Orestes, yo, tú Orestes-Electra.

(98–100)

In the presence of the fog, of the mother surrounding them, Electra advises her brother that they cannot continue to exist in the realm of the father. The mother's beckoning from beyond the grave is a call to self-immolation:

Porque ella—tú la oyes—ella llama,
y siempre va a llamar, y es preferible
morir los dos sin que nadie nos vea
de puñal, Orestes, y morir de propia muerte.

(80–83)

Union with the mother implies self-destruction, automatic exile from the realm of the Father. In the end, Electra succumbs, alone. It is significant that her authorial mirror image of the brother disappears. Either mad, or by one mythical account, rescued by Athena to reestablish the patriarchal order, he abandons her. She is left to wander endlessly in the mother, exiled from the fatherland:

No dejes que yo marche en esta noche
rumbo al desierto y tanteando en la niebla (70–71)
Orestes, hermano, te has dormido
caminando o de nada te acuerdas
que no respondes.

(119–121)

The writer abandons her authorial role in the Symbolic, and is submerged in the maternal semiotic. Thus, we see that Mistral, as Electra, both writes and, at the same time, undermines and rebels against that authorial role.

Finally, the hermetic work **"La fuga"** from "Muerte de mi Madre" (***Tala***, 1938) laments the death of the mother, and rewrites the myth of Orpheus and Eurydice. Here, a feminine Orpheus descends to the underworld to rescue her mother or mother-substitute ("madre mía"). The writer again abandons the fatherland, this time to wander infernal "paisajes cardenosos", seeking the mother figure. In this journey to recover the mother, participation in the Symbolic is sacrificed for return to the Semiotic:

Madre mía, en el sueño
ando por paisajes cardenosos:
un monte negro que se contornea
siempre, para alcanzar el otro monte
y en él que sigue estás tú vagamente,
pero siempre hay otro monte redondo
que circundar, para pagar el paso
al monte de tu gozo y de mi gozo.

(1–8)

The anguished voice joyfully anticipates ascending to the mountaintop, a landscape whose physical characteristics are associated with the body of the mother from the child's perspective. The relationship in the semiotic is preverbal, and hence, mother and daughter sense each other's presence; they do not see or speak with each other:

Vamos los dos sintiéndonos, sabiéndonos
mas no podemos vernos en los ojos
y no podemos trocarnos palabra.

(11–13)

Moreover, the poetic voice eroticizes the mother-daughter union by engaging the myth of Orpheus and Eurydice:

cual la Eurídice y el Orfeo solos
las dos cumpliendo un voto o un castigo,
ambas con pies y con acento rotos.

(14–16)

As in the ancient myth, the poetic voice enters the underworld to free Eurydice from death. Here the mother or the mother-lover substitutes for Eurydice.[3] Attempts to return her to life, to the realm of the Father fail.

The conflictive desire of the speaker for the forbidden maternal is demonstrated in the way the speaker carries her mother's remains secretly within her in violation of the Law of the Father. In a futile attempt to reconcile herself with the Father, she presents herself and her mother-lover before the gods, hoping to sanction this forbidden love:

Pero a veces no vas al lado mío:
te llevo en mí, en un peso angustioso
y amoroso a la vez, como pobre hijo
galeoto a su padre galeoto,
sin decir el secreto doloroso:
que yo te llevo hurtada a dioses crueles
y que vamos a un Dios que es de nosotros.

(17–24)

The illicit union with the mother, or mother-substitute is monstrous:

porque mi cuerpo es uno, el que me diste,
y tú eres un agua de cien ojos,
y eres un paisaje de mil brazos,
nunca mas lo que son los amorosos
y un pecho vivo sobre un pecho vivo
nudo de bronce ablandado en sollozo.

(31–36)

The mother seeks her with a hundred eyes, and possesses her with a thousand arms, reference to both the unnaturalness of the relationship as well as to its inevitability. It is an impossible love that is condemned to the infernal; outside the realm of the Father, it remains outside the Law.

The poem ends in a hellish vortex of madness as the poetic subject reenters the infernal, womb-like "vórtice rojo" of the mother. Thus she becomes an exile from the realm of the father:

hasta el momento de la sien ardiendo
del cascabel de la antigua demencia
y de la trampa en el vórtice rojo!

(50–52)

The poem celebrates the semiotic in a journey through hell. Return to the womb violates all the laws of the Symbolic, of language and society. Return to the mother undermines the very act of writing, and so describes a troubled relation to the Name of the Father. The poem depicts an act of rebellion against the Father, a rejection of a male authorial role and a search for identity with the mother in the Semiotic. Thus the poem becomes a protest against the loss of the mother, and a magnificent attempt to move the Semiotic into the realm of the Father, or simply to bequeath a testament of search for the mother.

In conclusion, the icon of Gabriela Mistral as spiritual mother of Latin America invites us to explore the richness and complexity of a poetry stamped with the image of the maternal but hiding all manner of ambiguity and contradiction within the folds of its verses. Not only is the maternal the earmark of Mistral's poetry, it also is key to her conflicted sense of identity, from her portrayal of herself as the "mater dolorosa" sanctioned by the realm of the Father, to her open rebellion and union with the mother in **"Electra en la niebla"** and **"La fuga"**. The conflicted and ambiguous relationship toward the maternal demonstrated in these poems gives life and definition to her work. No longer can Mistral be dismissed as simply a saintly icon of motherhood, for the underside of that icon teems with anguish, alienation and rebellion.

Notes

1. The reason for this compliance is open to speculation. Sylvia Molloy suggests that Mistral accepted

the *mater et magister* persona to hide what she terms the "unspeakable" in her life, her lesbianism. See Sylvia Molloy, "Female Textual Identities: The Strategies of Self-Figuration," *Women Writing in Latin America. An Anthology*, Eds. Sara Castro-Kláren, Sylvia Molloy, Beatriz Sarlo (Boulder, San Francisco, Oxford: Westview Press: 1991), 107–123.

2. I have divided the poetic voice in the poem into a feminine poetic voice (Electra) and the mirror image of an authorial male voice (the brother Orestes) to show the conflict that exists between the Symbolic (associated with the Word) and the Semiotic in the woman writer.
3. Notice that Eurydice and Orfeo are referred to with the feminine "las dos" and "ambas" in the next line.

Works Cited

González, Mike, and David Treese. *The Gathering of Voices.* London and New York: Verso, 1992.

Kristeva, Julia. *Revolution in Poetic Language.* trans. Margaret Waller. New York: Columbia University Press, 1984.

———. "Stabat Mater." *Tales of Love.* trans. Leon S. Roudiez. New York: Columbia University Press, 1987.

Mistral, Gabriela. *Desolación, Ternura, Tala, Lagar.* México: Editorial Porrúa, 1973.

———. "Electra en la niebla", In *Homenaje a Gabriela Mistral.* Santiago, Chile: *Orfeo: Revista de poesía y teoría poética*, 23–7 (1967): 118–120.

———. *Poemas de las madres.* Santiago de Chile: Pacífico, 1950.

———. *Ternura: canciones de niños.* Madrid: Saturnino Calleja, 1924.

Molloy, Silvia, "Feminine Textual Identities: The Strategies of Self-Figuration," *Women Writing in Latin America. An Anthology.* Eds. Sara Castro-Kláren, Sylvia Molloy, Beatriz Sarlo. Boulder, San Francisco, Oxford: Westview Press, 1991. 107–123.

Oliver, Kelly. *Rereading Kristeva. Unravelling the Double Bind.* Bloomington and Indianapolis: Indiana University Press, 1993.

FURTHER READING

Biographies

Agosin, Marjorie. "Remembering Gabriela," translated by Cola Franzen. *Sojurner* Vol. 15, No. 2, (October 1989), 15–16.

A prose-poem memoir-tribute links the poet's verse with the memoirist's recollections.

Fergusson, Erna. "Gabriel Mistral." *Inter-American Monthly* Vol. 1, No. 4 (August 1942), 26–27.

Offers a sketch of Mistral as a person and as the "embodiment of an era."

Furness, Edna Lue. "Gabriel Mistral Professor, Poet, Philosopher, and Philanthropist." *Arizona Quarterly* Vol. 13, No. 1 (Spring 1957), 118–23.

An obituary tribute focusing on Mistral's role as a teacher.

Gazarian Gautier, Marie-Lise. "Gabriel Mistral Remembered." *Review: Latin American Literature and Arts* Vol. 41, No. 7, 1989, 22–25.

A centennial tribute.

Rudd, Margaret T. "The Spanish Tragedy of Gabriela Mistral." *Romance Notes* Vol. 18, No. 1 (Fall 1977), 38–48.

An account of Mistral's troubles as consul to Madrid in 1933.

Criticism

Bates, Margaret. "The Definitive Edition of Gabriel Mistral's Poetry."*Revista Interamericana de Bibliografia* Vol. 16, No. 2 (April 1966), 411–15.

Studies the editorial process of selecting from variant readings in establishing definitive texts for Mistral's poetry.

Caimano, Sister Rose Aquin, O.P., Ph.D. *Mysticism in Gabriela Mistral*, New York: Pageant Press International, 1969, 328 pp.

In a study of mysticism and Mistral, Caimano concludes Mistral's aim in her poetry was not union with the Deity, but with herself and her fellow creatures.

Preston, Sister Mary Charles Ann, S.S.N.D., M.A. *A Study of Significant Variants in the Poetry of Gabriel Mistral*, Washington, D.C.: The Catholic University of America Press, 1964.

Studies the effect of various readings in Mistral's poetry on the sense and sensibility of the poems.

Additional coverage of Mistral's life and career is contained in the following sources published by the Gale Group: *Hispanic Literature Criticism*; *Major Twentieth-Century Writers*; and *Twentieth-Century Literary Criticism*, Vol. 2.

Philip Sidney
1554-1586

English courtier, statesman, soldier, playwright, essayist, poet, and prose writer.

INTRODUCTION

Known for his chivalry, statesmanship, extensive knowledge, and literary gifts, Sidney has earned the reputation as the quintessential Renaissance man. The estimation of Sidney as an ideal knight overshadowed his merits as a literary artist until early in the twentieth century, but since then he has been admired for his innovative and elegantly ornate poetic style, careful craftsmanship, and the force of emotion in his seemingly simple lines of poetry. The overriding concern in Sidney's verse is love, a theme that is given its most witty and rhetorically sophisticated expression in *Astrophel and Stella.* This sonnet sequence, the first of its kind in the English language, is generally regarded as Sidney's masterpiece and one of his great contributions to English literature; with it he overturned the conventions of the Petrachan sonnet and revolutionized the form. His other great literary contributions were the first statement of English poetics, *A Defence of Poetry* and the most recognized work of English prose fiction in the sixteenth century, *Arcadia.* The latter work, an elaborate romance, also contains poetry in a wide range of forms. Sidney is regarded by scholars to be one of the central literary figures of the Elizabethan period. His innovations in structure and style taught subsequent generations of poets how to use meter to reflect the rhythms of speech and began a tradition of complex love poetry that would be continued by John Donne and William Shakespeare.

BIOGRAPHICAL INFORMATION

Sidney was born November 30, 1554, at Penshurst, Kent, to an aristocratic family. His father, Sir Henry Sidney, was the Lord Deputy of Ireland, and his uncle Robert Dudley was Earl of Leicester. He was named after his godfather, Philip II of Spain. Sidney attended Shrewsbury School, where he met Fulke Greville, who would be his longtime friend and eventual biographer. He studied grammar, rhetoric, and religion at Christ's Church, Oxford, but left in 1571 without taking a degree. He then embarked on a grand tour of Europe, studying politics, languages, music, astronomy, geography, and military arts, and becoming acquainted with some of the most prominent statesman, artists, and scholars of his age. During his years abroad, Sidney became friends with the scholar Hubert Languet, whose ardent Protestantism had a lasting influence on him. The two men maintained a correspondence that offers interesting insights into Sidney's life and career.

When Sidney returned to England in 1575, he entered the court of Queen Elizabeth I. While at court he engaged in literary activities and associated with other writers and scholars, notably the poet Edmund Spenser, who dedicated *The Shepheardes Calender* to Sidney. Sidney was an excellent horseman and became renowned for his participation in tournaments and entertainments at court. But his main interest was in a career in public service. In 1577, at the age of twenty-two, he was sent as ambassador to the German emperor and the Prince of Orange. The ostensible purpose of the visit was to offer condolences to the princes on the deaths of their fathers, but Sidney's real task was to determine whether the princes would be in favor of forming a Protestant league. Such an association with other Protestant states in Europe, it was hoped, would protect England by counterbalancing the threatening power of Roman Catholic Spain. However, Sidney's career was cut short because the queen found Sidney too outspoken and zealous in his Protestantism.

Unable to secure a public post, Sidney turned to writing literature. In 1578 he composed a light drama, *The Lady of May,* for the queen. In 1580, Sidney opposed the queen's proposed marriage to the Duke of Anjou, the Roman Catholic heir to the French throne. Elizabeth showed her displeasure by having Sidney dismissed from court for a time. He moved to the estate of his sister, Mary Herbert, Countess of Pembroke, and wrote a long pastoral romance, *Arcadia,* which he dedicated to her. It may also have been during this time that he composed *The Defence of Poetry.* In 1581, Sidney met Penelope Devereux, who later married Lord Rich. Sidney fell in love with Lady Rich, and in 1582 composed a sequence of love sonnets, *Astrophel and Stella,* about his passion. While away from the London court, Sidney held office as a member of Parliament in Kent and continued to correspond with foreign statesmen and entertain important visitors.

Sidney was soon back in the queen's favor. He was knighted in 1583, the same year he married Frances Walsingham. Even after his return to public life, he continued to write literature. In 1584, he undertook major revisions of his *Arcadia* manuscript and began on a work translation of the Psalms. In 1585, Sidney was appointed governor of Flushing, in the Netherlands. He served as second-in-command to his uncle Leicester in the English expeditionary forces that were aiding the Dutch in their revolt against Catholic Spain. While participating in an ill-conceived ambush on a Spanish convoy at Zupten, Sidney was wounded in the leg. He developed gangrene and died a few weeks later. His death occasioned much mourning in the Netherlands and in England. His body was transported home and he was given a lavish funeral of a type usually reserved for royalty. Some of England's most distinguished writers were among the hundreds who composed elegies to honor him. It is said that Londoners who came to see Sidney's funeral progression cried out, "Farewell, the worthiest knight that lived."

MAJOR WORKS

Sidney's most important works all were published after he died, although during his life handwritten copies of his manuscripts circulated among his friends and relatives. It was typical of Elizabethan gentlemen to be nonchalant towards and even dismissive of their literary endeavors, and Sidney referred to many of his works as "mere trifles." His first literary effort, *The Lady of May*, a light court entertainment about a woman who cannot choose between two men who want to marry her—a rich shepherd of "smale Desertes and no faultes" and a woodsman of "manie Desertes and manie faultes"—was not left as a text but as a detailed transcription of the production. The piece includes prose speeches as well as singing and dancing. Sidney's work is distinguished from other light court dramas of the time by its literary touches, and prefigures the more sophisticated court masques of the seventeenth century. In addition to its central theme of the active versus the contemplative life, the piece also includes themes that were to become prominent in Sidney's later works, including the veneration of a lady by her lover and the use of language. A two-stanza poem "Supplication" is the only work Sidney wrote in praise of the queen. The work also is of political importance, as it seems to be Sidney's comment to the Elizabeth about her mistaken choice of suitor in the French Duke of Anjou.

Sidney did not finish his revisions to *Arcadia* before he died, and on his deathbed he requested that his manuscripts be destroyed. Shortly after his death, an edition containing his revisions was published. In 1909, original manuscripts of *Arcadia* were discovered. With that finding, the revised version has come to be known as the *New Arcadia* (or the *Revised Arcadia*) and the original, unrevised version the *Old Arcadia*. The latter is much shorter, less extravagant, and does not include many of the contrivances that mark the later edition. Also, the *Old Arcadia* is essentially a prose work although it does contain some poems, while the *New Arcadia* contains considerable sections of poetry interspersed with the prose. The plot in both is the same: two princes set off to find love in Arcadia, fall into love with two Arcadian princesses, and eventually, after a series of misunderstandings, marry them. There is disagreement among critics about which version is superior, and some commentators have dismissed most of the poetry in *Arcadia* as slight. However, others have remarked at the astonishing variety of forms and experimental spirit at work in the poetry of the *Arcadia*, and the poetic dialogue "Ye Goatherd Gods" is admired for its originality of meter and ornate amplification.

The central theme of almost all of Sidney's poetry is love, and this is the major concern in the pieces in *Certain Sonnets*. They were likely written around the same time as the *Arcadia*, and as in the poems of that work, they have an experimental quality. Sidney's theme of love was taken to its greatest heights in his masterpiece *Astrophel and Stella*, about a courtly lover who chronicles his passion for a lady. The 108 sonnets are fashioned after the Petrachan sonnet form (named for the Italian poet Petrach) and use Petrarchan conventions such as ornate style and the theme of veneration of a beloved woman. However, the beautiful simplicity, elegance, and rhythmic control of the poems set them apart from earlier sonnets and in fact revolutionized the form. The poems of *Astrophel and Stella* also are sexual in nature, as Astrophel implores his lady, using a number of rhetorical plays, to allow him to bed her. Stella accepts his Astrophel's advances on certain conditions, but Astrophel finally pleads for his release.

Another project that Sidney left uncompleted at his death was a translation of Biblical psalms into verse. These paraphrases have received little critical attention, as most readers find the stilted regularity and forced rhyme of the verses detract from their meaning. Some critics have seen them as important exercises in diction and meter that aided Sidney in his development as a poet. Apart from his own verses, Sidney also wrote one of the first (and still reputed to be among the best) statements of English poetics. *The*

Defence of Poetry introduced the critical ideas of Renaissance theorists to England and defends poetry against Puritan objections to imaginative literature.

CRITICAL RECEPTION

After Sidney's death, some of England most noted poets wrote elegies to honor his memory. Spenser's "Astrophel" laments his friend's passing, and *The Faerie Queene* contains verses praising Sidney. The effect of the outpourings of grief seems to have, in some measure at least, obscured Sidney's works by painting a portrait of a knight, military expert, and Protestant leader who is larger than life. Little commentary on Sidney's works appeared during his life or even in the years following his death, when his works were published and reissued in several editions. The idealized portrait of Sidney continued into the Victorian era, but again little sustained criticism of his work appeared. Notable among nineteenth-century responses are those by William Hazlitt, who found but little to recommend in Sidney's verses, and Charles Lamb, who took exception to Hazlitt's characterization and said the best of Sidney's sonnets "are among the very best of their sort." At the beginning of the twentieth century, reaction to Sidney was mixed: T. S. Eliot found the *Arcadia* "a monumental dullness," however, Virginia Woolf admired the realism and vigor of the verses. But critical commentaries were beginning to appear, including several biographies that sought to reveal the man behind the myth. By the middle of the twentieth century, Sidney's reputation enjoyed an upswing. Theodore Spencer's influential 1944 essay, "The Poetry of Sir Philip Sidney," noted the experimental nature of Sidney's early poetry and the variety of the forms he used. The 1950s to the early 1980s saw a huge increase in interest in Sidney's works. Critics explored the historical and political context of his writing, matters of prosody and style, the central theme of the life of action and responsibility versus that of contemplation and love, as well as the textual differences between the two versions of the *Arcadia*. Other studies have discussed the sexual nature of *Astrophel and Stella*, Sidney's self-conscious use and discussions of language, the use of irony, and the structure of the poems. Critics also have noted Sidney's use of classical meters and tropes and the influences of the Italian poets Petrarch and Sannazaro on his verses. Critical response to Sidney's poetry declined after the mid–1980s, but scholars do continue to contribute to the secondary literature. In the late twentieth and early twenty-first centuries, critics have been especially interested in Sidney's expressions of the limits of language and his attitudes toward sexuality.

PRINCIPAL WORKS

Poetry

The Countess of Pembroke's Arcadia [*New Arcadia*] (mixed-mode romance) 1590
Astrophel and Stella (sonnet sequence) 1591
Certain Sonnets 1598
The Psalms of David (translation; with Mary Sidney Herbert) 1823
The Countess of Pembroke's Arcadia [*Old Arcadia*] (mixed-mode romance) 1926
The Poems of Sir Philip Sidney 1962

Other Major Works

The Lady of May (mixed-mode drama) 1578
The Defence of Poetry [also published as *An Apology for Poetry*] (essay) 1595
The Correspondence of Sir Philip Sidney and Hubert Languet 1845
Miscellaneous Prose of Sir Philip Sidney 1973

CRITICISM

John Bailey (review date 1910)

SOURCE: "Sir Philip Sidney," in *Poets and Poetry: Being Articles Reprinted from the Literary Supplement of 'The Times'*, by John Bailey, Clarendon Press, 1911, pp. 28–36.

[*In the following review of John Drinkwater's edition of* The Poems of Sir Philip Sidney, *originally published in the* Times Literary Supplement *in 1910, Bailey contends that Sidney marks an important stage in the development of English poetry after Chaucer; and Sidney was the first practitioner of a new beauty of language and mastery of rhythm.*]

Of all the English poets none has a fame so independent of his poetry as Sidney. Other poets—Milton, for instance, and Marvell—have played as great or a greater part in the life of their country; but their lives had not the grace, nor their deaths the glory, of the life and death of Sidney. His life was mainly, at least in appearance, the most futile and barren that a man can choose, that of a courtier; yet he managed so to tread that trivial stage that his fellow-actors in the piece discovered to their surprise that there was a part in it for the wise man, the hero, and the saint. He died in one of the most inglorious of English military exploits; but he so died that he has buried its shame in the eternity of his nobleness. No one ever lived more loved or died more lamented. *Tu Marcellus eris*. That was the feeling of all England and of many high hearts outside England, when the news of Zutphen came. *Manibus date lilia plenis*. All the poets did that—Constable in a noble sonnet, Raleigh in a long 'epitaph' fuller of thought and matter and the sorrow of admiration than of poetry; and the greatest of them, the one who had paid Sidney perhaps the finest compliment even he ever received by calling himself 'the southern shepherd's boy', Spenser, who wished to be thought Sidney's scholar and pupil, poured out his grief again and again for his country's loss and his own.

O noble spirit! live there ever blest,
The world's late wonder, and the heaven's new joy;
Live ever there, and leave me here distrest
With mortal cares and cumbrous world's annoy;
But where thou dost that happiness enjoy
Bid me, O! bid me quickly come to thee,
That happy there I may thee always see.

'The world's late wonder, and the heaven's new joy'—that was not a mere phrase of compliment, as it so easily might have been; the words, coming from Spenser's mouth and applied to Sidney, meant exactly what they said, what the poet sincerely felt. And more than the poet, more even than that Elizabethan world which first wept over Sidney's death. It has been the feeling, in some degree, of all sensitive spirits from that day till now. For the service of the State, for the new hopes of literature, for a greater thing than either, human life itself, the picture and growth of it as a thing of beauty and perfection, the death of Sidney at the age of thirty-two was one of the tragedies of history. It is one of those events of which, after three hundred years, we are still unable to read without thinking of what might have been. Such force is there in a great name when it is the symbol of so many fair things as were joined together in Sidney; noble birth, a high part to play, and a great stage to play it on; this world and all the glory of it; gifts, great enough to make the memory of another man, and yet, in this case, only the setting of things much brighter and more precious; wisdom beyond the young years, virtue walking erect in very slippery places, a burning love of country shining bright in a world of intrigue; and, in an age still struggling out of barbarism, the divine gift of poetry.

Sidney's poetry, like everything else about him, is perhaps greater in a certain charm of presence and promise than in actual performance. But he is still of real, not merely of historical, importance. The business of English poetry after the death of Chaucer was to get back to his ease, his metrical power, his large and human naturalness, his beauty of speech and form; and it took about two hundred years to do it. In that long journey Surrey and Wyatt represent the first important stage and Sidney the second. The first may have been the more difficult; but that the second carried us a good deal further than the first may be seen at once by putting Surrey's best sonnets side by side with Sidney's. There is a certain strength in the Epitaph on Clere which Sidney never acquired; and Sidney himself never wrote a lovelier line than

Aye me! whilst life did last that league was tender.

But Sidney would have been scarcely more likely than Waller or Pope to let such a rugged verse as

Clere, of the Count of Cleremont, thou hight,

be circulated with his name attached to it. In the forty years or so that lie between them had come a new beauty of language and a new mastery of rhythm of which Sidney was the first example and of which he must retain the credit, however soon and however completely his achievements were eclipsed by Spenser and a greater even than Spenser. Between Chaucer and Sidney there is no English poetry either of such human and rational outlook upon life or of such fine workmanship as the ***Astrophel and Stella*** Sonnets. They still, it is true, abound in the forced fancies which were partly an inheritance from the Middle Age, and partly a new irrationality of that very Renaissance which claimed to bring, and did bring, a purifying fire of reason into so many fields of human activity. But irritated or wearied as we may easily be by such tiresome affectations as the 'roses gules' on the 'silver field' of Stella's face, we very soon become aware that that is not Sidney; it is only the fashion of his time, from which no man entirely escapes. The true Sidney, the Sidney who was a new and permanent star in our poetical heaven, is not in things of that sort, over-frequent as they are, but rather in such things as—

True that true beauty Virtue is indeed,
Whereof this beauty can be but a shade
Which elements with mortal mixture breed.
True, that on earth we are but pilgrims made,
And should in soul up to our country move;
True, and yet true that I must Stella love.

or the wonderful openings of his two most famous sonnets:—

With how sad steps, O Moon, thou climb'st the skies

and

Come, Sleep! O Sleep, the certain knot of peace,
The baiting-place of wit, the balm of woe,

where we are not surprised to find that we have foretastes of Shelley and Shakespeare; or such lines, fit to hold their place in any ripest poetry of all the world, as—

And yet amid all fears a hope there is

or

And Love doth hold my hand and makes me write

or

And Humbleness grows one with Majesty,

or that Shakespearian

Gone is the winter of my misery.

This is the poetry which Mr. Drinkwater makes more accessible by his handy little volume. He prefaces it with two introductions, a biographical and a critical; both competently and sensibly done, telling the plain reader all he need know about the man and the poet. On the thorny and controversial question of the relation in which the poet's sonnets stand to the facts of his life, the relation of Astrophel and Stella to Philip Sidney and Penelope Devereux, he takes, if we may dare to brave some distinguished critics enough to say so, the only line that is possible to a man who knows what poetry is. Dante and Beatrice, Petrarch and Laura, Sidney and Stella, Shelley and Emilia Viviani, Shakespeare and the mysterious youth—these are not fictions, still less are they facts. They are poetry, which is neither fiction nor fact but truth. To suppose that the convincing intensity of the *Vita Nuova* or the sonnets of Sidney or Shakespeare proves that they are newspaper biographies of their subjects is simply to show that the critic does not understand the nature of poetry. To suppose that the slightness, coldness, and bareness of the relations of the lovers in actual fact, so far as we know them, prove that the poems are mere fictions, is simply to make the same mistake from the opposite side. Great poets do not live in a vacuum; they have their eyes and hands on life, their own life and the lives of others. The poet finds in life the stuff of his work; but he never leaves it as he finds it. He touches nothing without transfiguring it, recreating it, giving it new birth; and only one who should have as great a genius for seeing prose in poetry as the poet has for seeing poetry in prose could rediscover the facts out of a reading of the poems. Sidney was in love 'with an ideal of his own', as Mr. Drinkwater says, and he chose to clothe Penelope Rich with it. How much of it actually belonged to her we can no more tell now than we can travel back from Michael Angelo's Lorenzo dei Medici to the actual Duke of Urbino.

It is unfortunate that Mr. Drinkwater's editing is not on a level with his two introductions. He has allowed far more misprints and mistakes to slip through than should be excused even in a popular reprint of this sort. To give one instance only, the word 'draught' in Sonnet 38 is puzzling enough to the ordinary reader without being misspelt 'drought', which simply renders it entirely unintelligible. Nor can he be congratulated upon his few notes. Such notes as that on the thirty-ninth sonnet, where he goes out of his way to mention Grosart's ridiculous notion that there is a play on 'sub rosa' in the words 'a rosy garland', and only puts it aside to suggest that the words refer to 'the light of imagination in the mind', are the very reverse of helpful. When the poet wrote 'rosy garland' he meant what he said and nothing else, just as he did when he wrote 'smooth pillows' or 'sweetest bed'.

But these are small matters, and the reason for this little book's existence is not notes, or even introductions, but Sidney himself. Those who buy it will do so because they want to have ***Astrophel and Stella*** to put in their pockets. And there will always be people who want to do that as long as English poetry has readers. For Sidney has some claim to be considered the first of our poets to use the English language in its permanent and final shape. Chaucer, who was born two hundred years before him, could anticipate it by flashes of genius, could help powerfully to create it; but he could not, in the nature of things, write it continuously. Spenser, who was born two years before him, may almost be said to have carefully avoided doing so. But in Sidney we come, not occasionally but constantly, upon poetry that could not be accused of any affectation of archaism if it were written to-day.

> I never drank of Aganippe well,
> Nor ever did in shade of Tempe sit,
> And Muses scorn with vulgar brains to dwell;
> Poor layman I, for sacred rites unfit.
> Some do I hear of poets' fury tell,
> But (God wot) wot not what they mean by it;
> And, this I swear by blackest brook of hell,
> I am no pick purse of another's wit.
> How falls it then that with so smooth an ease
> My thoughts I speak; and what I speak doth flow
> In verse, and that my verse best wits doth please?
> Guess we the cause! What, is it thus? Fie, no.
> Or so? Much less. How then? Sure thus it is,
> My lips are sweet, inspired with Stella's kiss.

There is not a word here which poets do not use to-day. Sidney attained at one stroke what was denied to the age of Chaucer and left unsought by the archaism of Spenser, the English that was coming and was to remain the mature and perfect language of English poetry. Of course he does not give the whole; the whole was to include, for instance, large contributions from Spenser, of whom so much was almost immediately rejected. But all Sidney gave has been kept. His English was the English of the seventeenth and eighteenth centuries, and it is still ours. That is seen even more clearly in some of the songs than in the sonnets. And it is good to have an excuse for reminding people that ***Astrophel and Stella*** is a book not only of sonnets but of songs. Take this, for example:—

> But when their tongues could not speak,
> Love itself did silence break;
> Love did set his lips asunder
> Thus to speak in love and wonder.
>
> 'Stella, sovereign of my joy,
> Fair triumpher of annoy:
> Stella, star of heavenly fire,
> Stella, loadstar of desire,
>
> 'Stella in whose shining eyes
> Are the lights of Cupid's skies:
> Whose beams when they once are darted,
> Love therewith is straight imparted.
>
> 'Stella, whose voice, when it speaks
> Senses all asunder breaks:
> Stella, whose voice when it singeth,
> Angels to acquaintance bringeth.

In poetic quality, pretty as it is, this seems to live on the surface of things when compared with the best sonnets; and of course the imaginative atmosphere belongs, in part at any rate, to a generation that was passing away. But the language does not; nor the ease and spontaneity of movement. They look on to Herrick and Waller, and even to Prior and Phillips.

But there is more in Sidney than merely technical achievement. He was a real poet. Whether if he had lived he would have been one of our great poets it is impossible now to say. Probably not. To be that demands more of a man than he—with his eyes fixed on great action in the field of politics and religion—would ever have given. Only Milton could greatly serve two masters; and he, besides being Milton, knew from the first which it was his peculiar call to serve; and after a brief desertion, for a special end, faithfully returned to his post. But what Sidney actually did in his few years, and in spite of his divided interests, is enough to give him a high place, a place among the poets who live in their own right, and not by grace of historical considerations. He was the perfect flower of that singular society in which, to use language which would not have seemed to it in the least priggish, it was the admitted aim of a gentleman to learn and practise both the intellectual and the moral virtues. Spenser described it as a man of letters and as an artist. Sidney was within it, was himself its model and hero. And he brought the lofty seriousness of its ideal, its unfaltering conviction that life is a thing with a meaning, into his poetry with such fine instinct as to make of a series of love sonnets a school not merely of art and language but of manners and of life. They are not written for edification, as so much of Spenser is, and their language is not primarily the language of edification. But take it at its most unrestrained phase, take it where in appearance the poet abandons himself most unreservedly to his passion, and is it, we ask, an unedifying effect that it produces even there? If a poet have as high a soul as Sophocles, said Goethe, he will produce a moral effect whatever he does. Here is what is, perhaps, Sidney's most passionate sonnet; we will leave it to give its own answer as to the effect it produces:—

> No more, my dear, no more these counsels try;
> O give my passions leave to run their race;
> Let Fortune lay on me her worst disgrace;
> Let folk o'ercharged with brain against me cry;
> Let clouds bedim my face, break in mine eye:
> Let me no steps but of lost labour trace;
> Let all the earth with scorn recount my case—
> But do not will me from my love to fly.
> I do not envy Aristotle's wit,
> Nor do aspire to Caesar's bleeding fame;
> Nor aught do care though some above me sit;
> Nor hope nor wish another course to frame,
> But that which once may win thy cruel heart;
> Thou art my wit and thou my virtue art.

Edwin A. Greenlaw (essay date 1913)

SOURCE: "Sidney's *Arcadia* as an Example of Elizabethan Allegory," in *Essential Articles for the Study of Sir Philip Sidney*, Archon Books, 1986, pp. 271–85.

[*In the following essay, originally published in* Anniversary Papers by Colleagues and Pupils of George Lyman Kittredge *in 1913, Greenlaw argues that by Elizabethan standards* Arcadia *is a heroic poem; Sidney provides the type of allegory his audience would have expected, and the work reflects political crises of sixteenth-century England.*]

By Sidney and his contemporaries, ***Arcadia*** was regarded as an heroic poem. Fraunce lists it with the Iliad, the Odyssey, and the Aeneid;[1] Harington cites it in his defense of the structure of *Orlando Furioso*;[2] Harvey says that if Homer be not at hand, ***Arcadia*** will do as well to supply examples of the perfect hero: "You may read his furious Iliads and cunning Odysses in the brave adventures of Pyrocles and Musidorus, where Pyrocles playeth the doughty fighter like Hector or Achilles, Musidorus the valiant Captaine, like Pandarus or Diomedes; both the famous errant knightes, like Aeneas or Ulysses."[3] And Meres, after a reference to the *Cyropaedia* as being an absolute heroical poem, this reference, by the way, being lifted bodily from Sidney's *Defense*, says that Sidney "writ his immortal poem, The Countess of Pembrokes Arcadia, in Prose, and yet our rarest Poet."[4] As to Sidney's own conception of heroic poetry, it is sufficient to note his reference to Orlando, Cyrus, and Aeneas as types of excellence presented by poets; his theory that it is not riming or versing that maketh a poet; his conception of the *Cyropaedia* as giving the "portraiture of a just empire"; his test of a poet by his power of "feigning notable images of virtues, vices, or what else, with that delightful teaching"; and the eloquent praise of heroic poetry as the highest of "kinds," even as the poet surpasses, in his power to teach, both historian and philosopher.[5]

This conception of ***Arcadia*** as being an heroic poem, together with the theories set down by Sidney in his *Defense*, makes it reasonable to infer that the book was thought to conform to the ideas of the time as to the province of this "kind." The Puritan attack on poetry intensified the view, inherited by the Renaissance from the mediaeval period, that the great epics should be regarded as allegories. But there is a difference between the interpretation of Virgil given, for example, by Alberti in 1468, and the conception held in the time of Tasso and Spenser. The earlier view was still mediaeval: the Aeneid was an allegory of Platonism and Christianity, which were held to be identical.[6] Of the sixteenth-century interpretations, that of Douglas, as might be expected from the author of the *Palice of Honour*, is still medieval. Stanyhurst regards Virgil as a profound philosopher, but says nothing of any theological motive.[7] But Sidney sees in Aeneas the portrait of the "excellent man"; "a virtuous man in all fortunes"; "no philosophers precepts can sooner make you an honest man than the reading of Virgil . . . there are many mysteries contained in poetry which were of purpose written darkly."[8] Nash inveighs against "the fantasticall dreames of those exiled Abbielubbers" as contained in the metrical romances, but counts poetry "a more hidden and divine kinde of Philosophy, enwrapped in blinde Fables and darke stories, wherin the principles of more excellent Arts and morrall precepts of manners, illustrated with divers examples of other Kingdomes and Countries are contained."[9] This theory of allegory is more fully explained by Harington:

"The ancient Poets have indeed wrapped as it were in their writings divers and sundry meanings; . . . for the litterall sence (as it were the utmost barke or ryne) they set downe in manner of an historie the acts and notable exploits; . . . then in the same fiction, as a second rine and somewhat more fine, as it were nearer to the pith and marrow, they place the Morall sence profitable for the active life of man; . . . maine times also under the selfesame words they comprehend some true understanding of naturall Philosophie, or sometimes of politike government, and now and then of divinity: and these same sences that comprehend so excellent knowledge we call the Allegorie, which Plutarch defineth to be when one thing is told, and by that another is understood."[10] In the passages just cited we have a view of allegory quite different from that illustrated by the *Romance of the Rose* or by *Piers Plowman*. The whole theory is excellently summed up by Spenser in his letter to Sir Walter Raleigh; in which he says that he has followed "all the antique Poets historicall; first Homere, who in the Persons of Agamemnon and Ulysses hath ensampled a good governour and a vertuous man, the one in his Ilias, the other in his Odysseis; then Virgil, whose like intention was to doe in the person of Aeneas; after him Ariosto comprised them both in Orlando; and lately Tasso dissevered them againe, and formed both parts in two persons, namely that part which they in Philosophy call Ethice, or vertues of a private man, coloured in his Rinaldo; the other named Politice in his Godfredo." Finally, we have, in a single sentence in the *Defense*, evidence of Sidney's acceptance of the view that an heroic poem may be written in prose, and that it should have allegorical significance: "For Xenophon, who did imitate so excellently as to give us *effigiem justi imperii* . . . under the name of Cyrus, . . . made therein an absolute heroical poem."[11]

We now need evidence that Sidney regarded his ***Arcadia*** seriously. According to the views usually expressed in recent criticism, the book was carelessly written, during a period of enforced retirement from court, for the delectation of the writer's sister; it was a mere toy of which its author was ashamed and which he wished never to be published; it has no serious significance.[12] There are three objections to these views. In the first place, it was a point of honor among gentlemen writers in that age to affect contempt for their literary works;[13] moreover, there may have been reasons why Sidney should have hesitated to print a book capable, in those suspicious times, of direct application.[14] In the second place, the testimony of Fulke Greville is that of an intimate friend; it is too earnest to be disregarded; and it exactly fits the character of Sidney as revealed in his conversations and his correspondence. Greville says that it was Sidney's aim "to turn the barren Philosophy precepts into pregnant Images of life." The story, he says, had a twofold character; on the one hand, it was to represent "the growth, state, and declination of Princes"; on the other, "to limn out such exact pictures" that a courtier might know in all ways how to conduct himself toward his Prince as well as in "all other moodes of private fortunes or misfortunes." We are to see, "in the scope of these dead images . . . that when Soveraign Princes, to play with their own visions, will put off publique action, which is the splendour of Majestie, and unactively charge the managing of their greatest affaires upon the second-hand faith, and diligence of Deputies, . . . even then they bury themselves, and their Estates in a cloud of contempt, and under it both encourage, and shaddow the conspiracies of ambitious subalternes to their false endes, I mean the ruin of States and Princes." He speaks of "this extraordinary frame of his own Common-wealth," and, at the end of his biography, insists once more that Sidney's aim "was not vanishing pleasure alone, but morall Images, and Examples . . . to guide every man through the confused Labyrinth of his own desires, and Life."[15] Finally, the discovery of an earlier ***Arcadia***, in manuscript form, by Mr. Dobell in 1907, showing as it does that Sidney was making a thorough and radical revision of his book, presents convincing proof that he regarded it seriously. Probably he was at work upon this revision even up to the time when he engaged in the expedition in which he met his death; at any rate, we have the evidence of Greville's letter to Walsingham to show that Sidney left in trust with his dearest friend his revision of his work, and "notwithstanding even that to be amended by a direction sett downe under his own hand how and why."[16] As to the fact recorded by Greville that, when dying, Sidney wanted his manuscript burned, it should be remembered that he had got only half through with his revision and no doubt felt the uselessness of preserving a mere fragment, while the solemnity of the hour of death made him feel the vanity of it all. In a similar mood, Chaucer wished all of his work that we value most highly to be destroyed.

My purpose thus far has been to establish, by a *priori* evidence, the grounds for assuming that ***Arcadia*** was regarded as an heroic poem; to show what characteristics this "kind" was supposed to have in the view of Sidney and his contemporaries; and to give reasons for thinking that the author regarded his work as a serious attempt to illustrate these theories. We now turn to the work itself for further evidence.

In the first place, the revision changed the earlier version from a pastoral romance, with the simplicity of a direct tale, into a complicated heroic "poem." The manuscript copies begin with an account of the oracle that sent Basilius into retirement, this fundamental circumstance being fully disclosed at the outset instead of being held in suspense.[17] Philanax attempts to dissuade the "Duke" in direct conversation and with possession of all the facts, instead of through a letter based on imperfect knowledge. Again, the long story of the Captivity, which in the revised form is structural, not an episode, is wholly wanting in the manuscripts. And most significant of all, the epic story of Pyrocles and Musidorus, vitally important as it is to the structure of the revised form, originally appeared in eclogues.[18] The effect of this radical change is to make the Pyrocles-Musidorus story the main plot, not the Basilius-pastoral motive, while the whole is now thrown into the form of an heroic "poem," which follows the rules of Aristotle, as Sidney understood them, with considerable accuracy.[19] In its revised form, the first book contains the story of how the two princes arrive in the kingdom of Basilius, and how they meet and fall in love with Philoclea and Pamela, being compelled to conduct their wooing in disguise because of the strange whim that has seized the king. The epic history of Pyrocles and Musidorus is reserved for the second book, which it dominates. It is in this epic history that Sidney presents the chief exposition of his "Ethice, or vertues of a private man." The method is most artful: Musidorus tells the first group of adventures; Philoclea and Pamela follow with explanations of the stories of Erona and Plangus, and Pyrocles finishes the account. But the narration is by no means continuous, being interrupted several times by incidents that either afford comic relief or remind us of the central plot, these interruptions having the effect of interludes.

The ten adventures that make up this epic history are by no means of the haphazard type of the conventional chivalric romance. They fall into two well-defined groups, in the first of which, it seems to me, the influence of the *Cyropaedia* is plain, while the second group finds its unity in the fact that the adventures deal with various sins against love and have a well-defined allegory. The adventures of the first group open with an account of the boyhood and education of the two heroes that parallels with some closeness the account of the education of Cyrus given by Xenophon. In each case there is stress on ethical training; on the study in their sports of the elements of war, and inuring of their bodies to hardship; this training occupying their time until, in all three cases, they are about sixteen years of age.[20] Then Pyrocles and Musidorus go to aid Evarchus against his enemies, this Evarchus being the uncle of Musidorus, just as Cyrus goes to the aid of his uncle Cyaxares.[21] Though Sidney's heroes are prevented by the shipwreck from reaching Evarchus, the parallelism with Xenophon still holds.[22] The strategy of Cyrus depends on his power to win various minor kings as allies, on his establishment of better conditions of government by casting out tyranny and righting wrongs, and on his habit of leaving his allies in independent control of their territories while uniting them into a federation. Illustrations are found in his treatment of the Armenians, the Hyrcanians, the wronged Gobryas, etc.[23] Just these methods are used by Pyrocles and Musidorus in the Phrygian episode, in which the wicked prince is overthrown, a new government established, the crown offered to Musidorus, who refuses it; in the Pontus episode, next following, in which precisely the same course is followed with the addition that an alliance between Phrygia and Pontus is arranged; and in the Leonatus-Plexirtus episode.[24] There are other evidences of the influence of Xenophon, such as the correspondence between the ethical and political thought in the two works; the deliberate balancing of Cyrus as a type of the good prince against Cyaxares, the type of effeminacy, envy, and tyranny, which finds a counterpart in the balance between Pyrocles and Musidorus and the various evil princes with whom they have to do; and studies of various admirable types of character. One of the most interesting of these last, from the point of view of our inquiry, is the parallel between Parthenia and Panthea; the two stories are not the same in details, but are closely similar in their beauty and pathos, while Xenophon, like Sidney, distributes his romantic story through a considerable portion of his work.[25] It is to be noted, finally, that Cyrus is praised for the same qualities of justice, personal bravery, and winning personality so well illustrated by the heroes of ***Arcadia***.[26]

The second group of adventures in the epic history seems at first sight more difficult to follow, especially as Sidney finds it necessary to give the histories of such characters as Plangus, Erona, etc., as additions to the main story. This involved method is similar to that used by Spenser, and the adventures themselves are like Spenser's in type and allegorical character. After establishing the various kingdoms on firm foundations, the two heroes become knights-errant. The change is marked by a sentence that is significant of the difference between ancient and Renaissance epic: "And therefore having well established those kingdomes . . . they determined in unknowne order . . . to seeke exercises of their vertue; thinking it not so worthy to be brought to heroycall effects by fortune, or necessitie, like Ulysses and Aeneas, as by ones owne choice and working."[27] The adventures are those of Erona and Antiphilus, of Pamphilus, of Anaxius, of Chremes, and of Adromena. Unity is gained through the fact that the misfortunes which the heroes now seek to correct proceed not from tyrannical or unjust government but from sins against love. Erona has blasphemed against Cupid, and is punished by her passion for Antiphilus; this man, as his name indicates, being guilty of sin against love in his unworthiness, in his cruelty toward Erona, and in his selfish desire to save his own life at the cost of hers.[28] The story of Pamphilus, the inconstant lover, is even more in the manner of Spenser.[29] The tone of this portion of the narrative is admirably kept in the interlude which interrupts Philoclea's story of Erona, in which Miso and her ill-favored daughter tell stories that are travesties of love.[30] As to the other adventures, Anaxius represents Pride; the Plangus story introduces unlawful love, which finds a climax in the story of Andromena, while Chremes is the Malbecco-Barabas-Shylock who would sacrifice wife or daughter for his property.[31] This allegorical treatment of sins against love is supplemented by the increasing stress on the guilty passion of Basilius and Gynecia for Zelmane-Pyrocles.[32] On the other hand, types of love showing tenderness and beauty are supplied by Palladius and Zelmane, the woman page;[33] while the entire story of Pyrocles and Musidorus is an example of the exaltation of friendship between men so constantly found in Renaissance literature.[34]

It is now possible to summarize this exposition of the virtues of the private man. Sidney has treated his education and his wisdom in dealing with public and private wrongs. He is actuated by the desire for glory, this glory being not personal but subordinated to the duty to right wrong and rescue the oppressed.[35] Love is the guide to all his actions, this love being manifested in his devotion to his friend and in his efforts to stamp out all unworthy and lustful love. The relation of this to the main situation is also clear; Pyrocles and Musidorus, great as is their valor and achievement, are made subject to love, even submitting to fantastic disguises (Zelmane, Dorus) in their obedience to its high behests. This course of development may seem to us somewhat anti-climactic, but to the spirit of the Renaissance it rings absolutely true.

We come now to Sidney's conception of the Prince. This subject is treated from different points of view. The epic of Pyrocles and Musidorus presents the ideal of his education and the character of his youth. This portion of the book also contains examples of what he should not be: not a follower of lust and pleasure, like the king of Iberia; not melancholy, suspicious, observing a "tode-like retyrednesse," like the king of Phrygia; not a creature of whim and caprice, rewarding without desert and punishing without reason, like the king of Pontus.[36] This last type is more fully delineated in Antiphilus, the base man suddenly exalted, who "made his kingdom a Tenniscourt, where his subjects should be the balles."[37] More direct methods are observable in the exposition of the Machiavellian theory of statecraft. There are three important studies of this subject, presenting Machiavellism under as many aspects. Plexirtus stands for the Machiavellian tyrant: he secured the crown by unjust means; kept it by the aid of foreign mercenaries who were established in citadels, the nests of tyrants and murderers of liberty; he disarmed his countrymen to prevent their return to the cause of his father; be blinded his father and sought the death of his brother Leonatus, following the precept that all who have any claim to the throne must be destroyed; he was crafty enough to hide his faults, thus not only deceiving his subjects but securing for his service good men like Tydeus and Telenor. Even after he was thrust from the throne, he was still able through hypocritical humility to win the confidence of Leonatus, only to seek to poison his brother and secure the throne again. When, finally, he was given a neighboring kingdom as a field in which he might practice his art with less inconvenience, he contrived the death of his faithful Tydeus and Telenor, fearing that their popularity would create faction against him.[38] The second example is found in the story of Clinias, who is the Iago of this Machiavellism as Plexirtus is its Richard III. Sophist, tragedian, hypocrite, he stimulates rebellion against Basilius while pretending to be innocent of wrong and indeed to have been anxious to restrain the mischief-makers. It is a picture of unmitigated baseness and cowardice.[39] The third portrait shows how a man of noble instincts, but more regardful of honor as Hotspur understood the term than possessing any solid qualities, swollen by a windy ambition, outwardly courteous and humane, may be a follower of Machiavelli. Amphialus follows the rules very closely: he accepts the results of his mother's plotting by holding the rightful claimants to the throne in captivity; he foments rebellion by appeals to the malcontents; he pretends to have at heart only the safety and best interests of the kingdom. In his strategy he follows the rules also: he pays attention to his citadel, his supplies, his selection of the men who are to be nearest him, making use even of their vices. In the jousts, characterized as they are by an outward courtesy, he is the seeker for renown in order to make an impression on others, as laid down in the twenty-first chapter of *Il Principe*.

Sidney shares the feeling of his time that a wise monarchy is the true form of government. His attack on oligarchy as being the cause of the worst of tyrannies prefaces the story of the wise Evarchus: "For they having the power of kings, but not the name of kings, used the authority as men do their farms."[40] Democracy is no less impossible. The story of the giants of Pontus suggests Spenser's allegorical method.[41] The two chief instances, however, of Sidney's distrust of the commons are found in the account of the rebellion against Basilius and in the depicting, near the end of the story, of the anarchy resulting from the supposed death of the king.[42] In the first of these Zelmane (Pyrocles) asks the rebels what they want, and the confused replies indicate Sidney's conviction that popular rule would bring anarchy.[43]

All these illustrations, however, are merely supplements to that which is the central theme in Sidney's treatment of the Prince: the contrast between Evarchus, the wise prince, and Basilius, king in name only. One of the most eloquent passages in the book is that in which the author paints, in Evarchus, his ideal monarch.[44] Coming to the throne when his kingdom was prostrated by tyranny, he was compelled at first to command respect by severity. After he was firmly established, "then shined forth indeede all love among them, when an awful feare, ingendred by justice, did make that love most lovely." He lived the life he wished his people to live, and lived it among them, not apart from them; he did not regard their persons and their property as instruments for his own pleasure, for "while by force he took nothing, by their love he had all."[45] "In Summe . . . I might as easily sette downe the whole Arte of government, as to lay before your eyes the picture of his proceedings." Contrasted with this ideal is the course of life pursued by Basilius. The significance of this central idea of the book is not that Sidney wished to portray an ideal life away from the conventionality of the court, but the disasters that come upon a nation when its sovereign, fearful of fate, retires to solitude in an effort to avoid it. Kalander's account of Arcadia: the solid qualities of its people, their love for Basilius, the respect in which the nation was held by neighboring peoples, the peace that encouraged happiness and invited the Muses, all this is sharply contrasted with the evils that follow. The letter of Philanax warns the king against superstition and points out the consequences of his retirement.[46] The rest of the main plot shows how these prophecies came true. The king is the prey to flatterers like Clinias and base upstarts like Dametas; the rebellion of the commons is due to the practices of those who seek to profit by the king's seeming cowardice; lust rules his own life; the people are torn by factions so that Cecropia and Amphialus bring about civil war; utter chaos results, and the larger duties of Basilius to aid Evarchus in repelling hostile nations are neglected. Philanax sums up the indictment when he tells Basilius that his whole duty, as a Prince and the father of a people, is "with the eye of wisdome, the hand of fortitude, and the hart of justice to set downe all private conceits in comparison of what for the publike is profitable."[47] Over against this is set, in the closing pages of the story, the nobility of Evarchus, strengthening his people against expected attack; seeking to form alliances among other nations against a common enemy; going to Arcadia to try to withdraw its prince from burying himself alive; and with calm justice dooming his own son to death in his effort to bring to an end the anarchy he found there.

Thus Fulke Greville spoke with full knowledge in saying that Sidney intended more than idle amusement in his story. Corroborative evidence is found in his account of the conversations between the two friends, and in Sidney's correspondence with Languet. Sidney, we are told, complained of the "neglect" of the Queen in her failure to use the Huguenots as a means of checking the increasing Spanish aggression; it was "an omission in that excellent Ladies Government" that Austria "gained the fame of action, trained up his owne Instruments martially, and got credit with his fellow-bordering Princes," a condition that came through a "remiss looking on"; a yet greater oversight was characteristic of England and France, because "while their Princes stood at gaze, as upon things far off, they still gave way for the Popish and Spanish invisible arts and counsels to undermine the greatness and freedom both of Secular and Ecclesiastical Princes." "In this survey of forrain Nations," we are told, "he observed a fatal passivenesse generally currant, by reason of strange inequalities between little humors and great fortunes in the present Princes reigning."[48] In this "fatal passiveness," due as it was to "little humors" of those who should be alert, we have the keynote to the interpretation of the story of Basilius. The testimony of the correspondence with Languet is not less explicit: Sidney expresses impatience with the delays and intrigues of Elizabeth and Burghley; "our princes," he says, "are enjoying too deep a slumber; nevertheless, while they indulge in this repose, I would have them beware that they fall not into that malady in which death itself goes hand in hand with its counterpart."[49] At the very time when he was working on his book, Sidney was in disgrace because he had addressed a letter to the Queen protesting against the proposed French marriage. It is this sloth, this foolish fear of fate, this wasting of time in amorous toying while factions were multiplying and plots against the throne grew ripe, that the Basilius story shows forth. Sidney does not hold up the pastoral life of Basilius as a model; he does not find in it an admirable withdrawal from the cares of life; it is no idyllic existence in the forest of Arden, but a criminal evading of responsibility that will bring ruin to any state.[50] Sidney's book, concrete application of the theories of the province of poetry laid down in his *Defense*, springing out of his interest in the problems of government, the object of his care during the ripest and most thoughtful years of his life, is less truly to be described as a pastoral romance than as an "historicall fiction," a prose counterpart of the *Faerie Queene*, having for its object "to fashion a gentleman or noble person in vertuous and gentle discipline," and to portray "a good governour and a vertuous man." That this intention was not vaguely moral, but was intended by Sidney to apply to political conditions in his own time and to the crisis that he saw was coming upon England, I shall seek to show more fully in another place.

Notes

1. *Arcadian Rhetorike*, 1588.
2. *Preface*, 1591.
3. *Pierces Supererogation*, 1593.
4. *Palladis Tamia*, 1598.
5. *Defense*, ed. Cook. pp. 8, 11, 17, 30, 31.
6. Villari, *Machiavelli*, I, 128.
7. Smith, *Elizabethan Critical Essays*, II, 137.
8. Sidney, *Defense*, ed. Cook, pp. 8, 17, 57. Webbe in 1586 expressed exactly the same view (*English Poetrie*, ed. Arber, p. 28).
9. *Anatomie of Absurditie*, in Smith, *Elizabethan Critical Essays*, I, 323, 328; *Works*, ed. McKerrow, I, 25ff.
10. *Preface*, in Smith, *Elizabethan Critical Essays*, II, 201–202.
11. *Defense*, ed. Cook, p. 11.
12. W. Stigant, in *Cambridge Essays*, 1858, pp. 110 ff., sees contemporary references in the romance, and accepts Fulke Greville's views; but recent opinion is fairly represented by M. Jusserand (*English Novel*, p. 245), who thinks Greville was exaggerating and that Sidney's main object was not politics, but love. Sir Sidney Lee (*Great Englishmen,* pp. 99, 100) is more than usually inaccurate, a specimen being his name "Synesia" for Gynecia, and his statement that she is a "lascivious old queen"!
13. Of many illustrations of this point, the passage in Puttenham's (?) *Arte of English Poesie* will serve:

    "I know very many notable Gentlemen in the Court that have written commendably, and suppressed it agayne, or els suffred it to be publisht without their own names to it; as if it were a discredit for a Gentleman to seeme learned and to shew himselfe amorous of any good Art"

    (Smith, II, 22).

    Compare Spenser's dedications for self-depreciation exactly similar to that contained in Sidney's letter to his sister; and note that Sidney speaks of his *Defense* as an "ink-wasting toy."
14. It will be remembered that the reason for Sidney's retirement was his bold letter to the Queen about the French marriage. That this brought him into great danger is indicated by Languet's letter, October, 1580, from which it is clear that Sidney realized the risk he ran, but wrote the letter because he was ordered to do so, presumably by Leicester (Peares, *Correspondence*, p. 187).

15. *Life of Sidney*, chaps. i, xviii.
16. Arber, *English Garner*, I, 488.
17. For a similar withholding of the fundamental situation, compare the revised *Arcadia* with the *Faerie Queene*, in which we should not know of the plan of the entire poem at all were it not for Spenser's explanation in his letter to Raleigh.
18. For this account of the manuscripts I am indebted to Mr. Dobell's article in the *Quarterly Review*, CCXI, 76–90.
19. Sidney was in Italy at the time when Aristotle was just coming to be regarded as a literary dictator. His letters to Languet speak of his anxiety to be able to read the works of the philosopher in the original (Pears, *Correspondence*, p. 28). In the *Defense* he shows acquaintance with Aristotelian theory, having gained his knowledge either directly or through the works of Scaliger. A convenient statement of Elizabethan understanding of these rules as applied to heroic poetry is in Harington: The fable should be grounded on history; the action should be limited in time to not more than a year; there should be nothing incredible; the "peripeteia" should be "the agnition of some unlooked-for fortune either good or bad" (Smith, II, 217). It is worthy of note that in this very connection Harington appeals to *Arcadia* as an authority, and that Sidney does indeed observe these rules in his pseudo-historical setting of Greek kingdoms, dynasties, and civil wars; in the limitation of the main action to a few months, while antecedent action is told indirectly; and in the elimination of the supernatural elements so common in the romances.
20. *Cyropaedia*, I, ii; *Arcadia*, II, vii.
21. *Cyropaedia*, I, v; II, i; *Arcadia*, II, vii.
22. Sidney's use of pirates, shipwrecks, etc., to diversify his narrative illustrates, as is well known, his indebtedness to the Greek romances (cf. Stigant, Cambridge Essays, 1858, p. 110). Stigant and others have held that he also adopted from Heliodorus the device of beginning in the midst of the action. But he might equally well have got it from the theory of epic poetry held in his time. Tasso thought Virgil and Heliodorus used the same method (Dunlop ed., Bohn, I, 30).
23. *Cyropaedia*, II, iv; IV, ii, vi.
24. *Arcadia*, II, viii–x.
25. The references in Xenophon are IV, vi; V, i; VI, i, iv; VII, i, iii.
26. Compare the "triumph" of Cyrus (*Cyropaedia*, III, iii) and that of Sidney's heroes (*Arcadia*, II, xxiii).
27. *Arcadia*, II, ix.
28. *Arcadia*, II, xii, xiii.
29. His character is given II, xviii; see especially his "jollie scoffing braverie," Cambridge ed., p. 268.
30. Ibid., II, xiv.
31. Ibid., II, xvii ff.
32. Ibid., II, xvi, xvii.
33. Ibid., II, xx–xxiii.
34. This motive is due in part to the admiration for Cicero. Of the many illustrations, the stories of Damon and Pythias and of Titus and Gysippus, as told by Elyot (*Boke of the Governour*, xi, xii) and others, may be cited. The climax of such stories is that a friend will seek to die for his friend if need be, and this motive is several times used by Sidney. There are also resemblances between Sidney's presentation of the various types of love and Spenser's, especially in *Faerie Queene*, IV.
35. This conception of honor is, of course, a subject constantly treated in Renaissance literature. Sidney begins with the idea that constitutes the theme of the *Cyropaedia*: "For to have been once brave is not sufficient for continuing to be so, unless a man constantly keep that object in view" (*Cyropaedia,* VII, v); on which compare Sidney: "High honor is not only gotten and borne by paine and danger, but must be nursed by the like, or els vanisheth as soone as it appeares to the world" (*Arcadia*, II, ix). But Cyrus has in view the definite purpose of building an empire; the knightly progress of Pyrocles and Musidorus is to seek through individual exploits not only to serve others but to exercise their virtues without regard to personal ambition. It is a theory of education, and is preparatory to the work of the Prince.
36. *Arcadia*, II, xix, viii, ix.
37. Ibid., II, xxix.
38. There are even verbal resemblances that prove the source of this exposition; these I have no space to give, but any one who will take the trouble to read the passage in Sidney will at once recognize how close is the parallel. Every one of the characteristics of Plexirtus is a concrete illustration of principles taken from Machiavelli or from the hostile summary of the theory by Gentillet. That Sidney was acquainted with Machiavelli appears in his correspondence with Languet. In one case (Pears, p. 53) he shows hostility to the central doctrines of this political philosophy.
39. *Arcadia*, II, xxvii ff.
40. *Arcadia*, II, vi. On this compare Elyot, I, ii, and *The Courtier*, Book IV.
41. *Arcadia*, II, ix. The giants represent a mistreated populace, useful to a wise prince, but a source of danger made greater through their ignorance.
42. *Arcadia*, II, xxv, xxvi. It should be stated that I have confined my investigation to that part of *Arcadia* which is indubitably Sidney's. The second passage (ed. Baker, pp. 564 ff.), though it comes in the portion revised by the Countess of Pembroke, bears the marks of having been written by Sir Philip.

43. The passage is too long to quote, but the suggestions for tariff reform, change of administration, public improvements, reduction of the high cost of living, the desire of each class for a reduction in all products other than its own, all remind one of the political campaign of 1912; while the blind confidence in a larger number of statutes as necessary to the welfare of the state is preëminently American. Less pleasant, because of its betrayal of Sidney's aristocratic contempt for the mob, though it is good fun, is his ridicule of the butchers, tailors, and millers, together with the account of the artist, ancestor of the modern war correspondent, who was to paint the battle of the Centaurs and rushed to the fray in search of local color. He got it.
44. *Arcadia*, II, vi.
45. Compare the object lesson, on the subject of riches, taught by Cyrus to Croesus, *Cyropaedia*, VIII, ii.
46. *Arcadia*, II, iv.
47. Ibid., III, xix. This is just what Sidney told the Queen in 1580.
48. *Life*, Caradoc Press Reprint, 1907, pp. 18 ff.
49. Pears, pp. 58–59.
50. Even the oracle which led Basilius to leave his duties in order, as he thought, to avoid the loss of his kingdom, finds a counterpart in Elizabeth's superstitious regard for nativities and portents. (Cf. Aikin, *Memoirs*, II, 27). As to the unpleasantness of that part of *Arcadia* which deals with the lust of Basilius and Gynecia, about which much has been written, we have merely a presentation of what the author believes will happen when princes lead slothful lives, with perhaps a reference to immoral and unnatural conditions at Elizabeth's court. Compare Spenser's stinging castigation of these conditions in *Colin Clout*, lines 664 ff., in which he shows the pettiness and selfish hollowness of the court, and makes a similar distinction between pure love as understood by the "shepherds" and the licentious talk of the courtiers on "love, and love, and love my dear." This gallantry, filled with "lewd speeches and licoentious deeds," profanes the mighty mysteries of Love. Compare also Languet's letter to Sidney, written soon after a visit to London: "To speak plainly, the habits of your court seemed to me somewhat less manly than I could have wished, and most of your noblemen appeared to me to seek for a reputation more by a kind of affected courtesy than by those virtues which are wholesome to the state" (Pears, p. 167). I have given other evidence of these conditions in my discussion of the relations between Spenser and Leicester (*Publications of the Modern Language Association*, September, 1910).

Theodore Spencer (essay date 1944)

SOURCE: "The Poetry of Sir Philip Sidney," in *ELH: A Journal of English Literary History*, Vol. 12, No. 4, December 1945, pp. 251–78.

[*In the following essay, Spencer emphasizes the importance of "art, imitation, and exercise" in Sidney's early poetry and views Sidney as breaking convention with* Astrophel and Stella.]

1

Although a large amount of literature has accumulated around the life and work of Sir Philip Sidney, it is somewhat remarkable that no thorough study of his poetry, *as* poetry, seems to exist. Courthope, in his *History of English Poetry*, describes Sidney's life rather than his writing, and though we frequently hear, in general terms, of the importance of Sidney's contribution to English poetry, most discussions of that contribution are concerned with its historical or autobiographical significance rather than its actual poetic value. Even the best of Sidney's critics and biographers, such as Miss Mona Wilson, tend to follow the example of Lamb, and to give us generous quotations rather than analysis and evaluation. Mr. Kenneth Myrick, in his careful analysis of Sidney as a literary craftsman, hardly discusses the poetry at all.

But Sidney's poetry deserves close attention, not only because of its historical importance, but also because it is a striking example, one of the most striking in existence, of the relation between form and content, convention and passion, experiment and accomplishment. Its historical importance, its value for Sidney's own generation were, to be sure, great, but it can have importance and value for other generations as well, generations in which, like Sidney's and our own, poetry needs awakening and guidance.

2

When, at the end of his noble *Defence of Poesie*, written in the early 1580's, Sidney makes a rapid survey of recent English poetry, he cannot find much to praise. He admires Chaucer's *Troilus*, though he does not mention *The Canterbury Tales*, he admires Surrey, though he does not mention Wyatt; he admires the *Mirror of Magistrates* and Spenser's recent *Shepheardes Calendar*. That is all; "besides these," he says, "I do not remember to have seen but few (to speak boldly) that have poetical sinews in them. For proof whereof," he continues, "let but most of the verses be put in prose, and then ask the meaning, and it will be found, that one verse did but beget another, without ordering at the first what should be at the last, which becomes a confused mass of words, with a tingling sound of rhyme, barely accompanied with reasons."

Sidney is even more specific in sonnet XV of ***Astrophel and Stella***, where he describes what seem to him (and to us) the three chief faults of his poetic contemporaries; they seek for meaningless pseudo-classical decoration, they rely too much on alliteration, and they too slavishly imitate Petrarch:

You that do search for every purling spring
Which from the ribs of old Parnassus flows,
And every flower, not sweet perhaps, which grows

> Near thereabouts, into your poesy wring;
> Ye that do dictionary's method bring
> Into your rhymes, running in rattling rows;
> You that poor Petrarch's long-deceaséd woes
> With new-born sighs and denizen'd wit do sing:
> You take wrong ways; those farfet helps be such
> As do bewray a want of inward touch,
> And sure, at length stol'n goods do come to light . . .

It was the "inward touch" which, as we shall see, Sidney most prized, and which, in his own best poetry, he so admirably reveals. But before it could be expressed English poetry needed to do some hard work; it needed leadership and practice. "Yet confess I always, that as the fertilest ground must be manured, so must the highest flying wit have a Dedalus to guide him. That Dedalus, they say both in this and in other, hath three wings to bear itself up into the air of due commendation: that is Art, Imitation and Exercise."

Those three words, Art, Imitation and Exercise, which he uses in their precise critical sense, sum up admirably the first part of Sidney's brief poetic career. From 1576 to 1580, by which latter date the first draft of the ***Arcadia*** was finished, Sidney practised his art by imitating every verse form he could think of, and by exercising every available linguistic and rhetorical device. He evidently realized that it was not enough to attack the Parnassian flowers, or weeds, of Gascoigne, the Petrarchanism of Thomas Watson, and the alliterative monotony that stumped on wooden feet through the contemporary anthologies; both he and his contemporaries—Spenser, Greville, Dyer and Harvey—were aware that something more positive must be accomplished. They were enthusiastic about the prospect. To them poetry itself was, in Sidney's words, "full of virtue-breeding delightfulness," and, like the Italian followers of Aristotle, Sidney extolled poetry as greater than either of its rivals, philosophy and history, for it combined the wisdom of the one with the concrete examples of the other.

The young men of the late 'seventies had an equal enthusiasm for the English language. Throughout the correspondence on poetry between Spenser and Gabriel Harvey there is a feeling of excitement for what Harvey calls "so good and sensible a tongue as ours is," and their discussion of details is more than irrelevant pedantry. The interest shown by Spenser and Harvey in such matters is an example of how the English vocabulary was being re-examined, with a loving as well as a pedantic concern. And Sidney himself claims that English is superior to any other modern language as a medium for either quantitative or rhyming technique; it is of all vulgar tongues, the "most fit to honour Poesie." The art of poetry and the native language in which it was to be expressed were both worthy of all the art and exercise which could be devoted to them. It is with this conviction that Sidney began his poetic career.

3

Sidney's earliest important poetic task was a metrical version of the first forty-three psalms. Although, as Miss Mona Wilson points out, "Donne professed to admire them, and Ruskin really did," other critics, including Miss Wilson herself, dismiss them as having little or no importance. It is true that their intrinsic merit is small, for they almost never rise from the ground of ordinariness, but the student of Sidney's poetry should not ignore them. For they are, in two respects, examples of "Art, Imitation and Exercise." They are experiments in metrics and, in a smaller degree, experiments in vocabulary. With the exception of psalms VII and XII, both of which are in terza rima, each psalm is translated in a different stanza form, and this in itself indicates, though in a mechanical way, Sidney's creative energy. There are stanzas which have only one rhyme throughout (XV), there are stanzas of various lengths, from three lines to ten, and there are stanzas in which short lines are contrasted in various ways with long ones. A number of the rhyme schemes are original with Sidney, and if only for this fact the psalms are worth notice. Furthermore several of the verse forms are early experiments in a kind of metrical music, as yet undeveloped and by no means yet enchanting, which Sidney was later to explore with much greater success: the music which is produced by a contrast between masculine and feminine rhymes. The device, of course, was nothing new in itself; the novelty consists in the deliberate self-consciousness and consistency with which Sidney employs it. In psalm VI, for example, the second and fourth rhymes are invariably feminine:

> But mercy, Lord, let mercy thine descend,
> For I am weak, and in my weakness languish;
> Lord help, for ev'n my bones their marrow spend
> With cruel anguish.

And there are a number of other examples where the same, rudimentary but effective, device occurs.

The vocabulary of the Psalms is simple, limited and commonplace. It is no way remarkable, which is why it is well worth observing. For much of Sidney's later success as a poet comes from his ability to express himself in the most ordinary and every-day words, words that have all affection and decoration stripped off them, that go straight to the center of meaning:

> Fool, said my Muse to me, look in thy heart and write.

And in translating the psalms, Sidney was almost forced to use simplicity; the original required it, and it was congenial to his nature.

> But ever, ever shall
> His counsels all
> Throughout all ages last.
> The thinkings of that mind
> No end shall find
> When times, Time shall be past.
>
> (XXXIII)

Such a stanza is, to be sure, unusual. Most of them are much more clumsy:

The Lord, the Lord my shepherd is,
And so can never I
Taste misery.
He rests me in green pastures his;
By waters still and sweet
He guides my feet.

But even in something as awkward as this, in which directness of expression has to be inverted and cramped into a preconceived pattern, there is metrical experiment and simplicity of diction.

4

When Sidney wrote the poems in the ***Arcadia*** (I am thinking of both versions), he was not only educating himself, he was educating a whole generation. They may be academic, like work done at a university, but universities can play an essential role in society. The poems in the ***Arcadia*** played that role for the poets of the sixteenth century. By them, to change the figure, a whole poetic landscape, hitherto unexplored, was revealed. It was not, to be sure, exactly natural; it was clustered with wax models, dressed in the hired costumes of shepherds and arranged in the langurous poses of conventional artifice; the water in its streams was pumped and the flowers in its fields were of paper. But it was a landscape which Englishmen had seen before, if at all, only in occasional glimpses, and it had one peculiarity which kept it from being merely a scene on the stage; at any moment a breath of fresh wind might strike it; the wax figures might come to life, the water might run by itself over the pebbles, and the flowers might suddenly be real.

The poems in the ***Arcadia*** represent an astonishing variety of forms. At least forty-five different metrical devices or stanzas are used; English, classical and Italian. There are couplets, six-line stanzas, and rhyme-royal; there are elegiacs, hexameters and hendecasyllabics; there are sonnets, canzone, sestinas and, above all, terza rima; no form seems to have been too foreign or too difficult for Sidney to attempt. It is—what Gabriel Harvey called it—a "gallant variety," an attempt to make available for English poetry the entire technical range of the craft; it is "Art, Exercise and Imitation" on the most comprehensive scale.

But with the exception of one or two poems the whole collection has been damned by nearly all modern critics as—to quote Miss Wilson—"a deservedly forgotten mass." This is not just. A great number of the poems, to be sure, are undistinguished in diction, monotonous in technique and boring in subject matter; they are exercises and nothing else. But there are others—more than is commonly recognized—which are something more than exercises, which are important not merely from the historical point of view, but which are examples of a kind of poetry that is as original as we look back on it now as it seemed to Sidney's own contemporaries.

The poets of Sidney's circle have been severely rebuked for wasting their time in trying to write English poetry in classical metres. Their "versifying," as they called it, has been regarded as an intrepid march up a hopelessly blind alley, and its results dismissed as both futile and barbarous. Yet those who have spoken of it in these terms have, I believe, looked at it from too absolute a point of view. For the experiments in classical meters, though rarely successful in themselves, were just what English poetry, in the 'seventies, most needed. After the accomplishment of Wyatt and Surrey, English poetry, though the work of Sackville is an exception, had apparently lost its ear. Technically speaking, it was in the doldrums. Its sense of rhythm had become half paralyzed, and the only meter it seemed to be aware of was the iambic. The blank verse of *Gorboduc* (1561), for example, is unenlivened by any metrical variation; the invariable iambs march five abreast implacably down the page. When Gascoigne uses anything but an iamb, which he rarely does, it happens by accident, not intention. The metrical disease known as poulter's measure, which was endemic in the 'sixties and 'seventies, aggravated the situation. Sidney himself uses it once—for purposes of parody—in the first poem in the revised ***Arcadia***; perhaps he puts it there to show what sort of poetry he was anxious to displace:

Her forehead jacinth-like, her checks of opal hue,
Her twinkling eyes bedeck'd with pearl, her lips as sapphire blue;
Her hair like crapal-stone; her mouth O heavenly wide,
Her skin like burnish'd gold, her hands like silver ore untried.

And the only device used to alleviate this tuneless monotony, the device of alliteration, had nothing to do with rhythm; it was merely another kind of clog put upon a way of writing that was badly clogged enough already. The general impression we get of most English poetry in the 'sixties and early 'seventies is that of dullness, flatness and cowardice; it is as if the writers did not dare to vary from the iambic foot for fear of losing their sense of rhythm altogether. This is true even of Sidney's translation of the psalms; hardly a single foot in all the poems varies from the iambic norm.

If English poetry were ever to have any music in it, if the rhythm of the lines were rightly to echo the rhythm of the thought, if there were ever to be any of that essential *drama* in English verse technique, by which a resolved conflict occurs between the basic metrical pattern and the necessary rhythm of the meaning—if all this were to happen, the situation which existed before 1576 had drastically to be changed. The practice of verse technique needed a violent wrench to get it out of its dusty rut. And this wrench, this virtual dislocation was, I suggest, largely accomplished by the experiments in classical meters. To a modern reader the prolonged discussion between Spenser and Harvey as to whether the second syllable of "carpenter" should be long or short, or whether "heaven" is a monosyllable or a disyllable, seems a waste of time, but actually it was not. What such discussions did was to make people *think* about words; in order to "versify," words had to be broken up, each syllable had to be weighed and considered, and new rhythmical combinations had to be found which were as far removed as possible from the unthinking jog-trot of the prevalent iambic habit.[1]

To take an example. One of the classical forms which Sidney uses in the ***Arcadia*** is what he calls "Asclepiadickes"—lesser Asclepiad Verses. As used by Sidney this requires a five foot line, with the following scansion:

> – ᴗ / – ᴗ ᴗ / – / – ᴗ ᴗ / – ᴗ ᴗ

Here there are no iambs at all; instead we have feet of three different kinds; a spondee, three dactyls and a monosyllable. The result is a rhythm which may, perhaps, be foreign to the character of the English language, yet which is interesting not merely as an experiment but also delightful as an accomplishment:

> O sweet / woods, the de / light / of soli / tariness[2]
> O how much I do like your solitariness,
> Where man's mind hath a freed consideration,
> Of goodness, to receive lovely direction.[3]

The "versifying" experiments re-inforced one very important matrical lesson, namely that the same kind of foot did not necessarily have to be repeated throughout the line. Perhaps the most valuable part of the lesson was the practice gained in employing the spondee. This heaviest of metrical feet is rare in Sidney's immediate predecessors (with the notable exception of Wyatt), but in the classical meters it has to be widely used, for a wide variety of effects. An ear trained by experiments with spondees was able to give the conventional iambic thump the variation, the weight, that it needed, and Sidney frequently transfers to his rhymed accentual poetry the spondaic experience he had learnt from his quantitative exercises:

> Earth, brook, flow'rs, pipe, lamb, dove
> Say all, and I with them,
> Absence is death, or worse, to them that love.
> Since stream, air, sand, mine eyes and ears conspire;
> What hope to quench, where each thing blows the fire.[4]

But this is only one detail. When Sidney came to write ***Astrophel and Stella*** he had at his command many other devices for varying the feet in a given line; he no longer beats out continuous iambs as he does in his translation of the psalms; he is various, dramatic and musical. And he was able to be these things more readily, there can be little doubt, because of his classical experiments.

How far from iambic monotony, for example, is the first line of Sonnet XX:

> Fly, fly, my friends, I have my death's wound, fly!

or the dramatic last line of LXXI:

> But ah, Desire still cries,—"Give me some food!"

or the spondees that begin XLIII:

> Fair eyes, sweet lips, dear heart, that foolish I . . .

or the cretics in LXXVIII:

> Beauty's plague, virtue's scourge, succor of lies.

or the effective emphasis on the word "plant" in LXXVII:

> That voice which makes the soul plant himself in the ears.

Few of Sidney's classical experiments are successful as complete poems; the asclepiads quoted above dry up as they progress, and the hexameter Echo verses, which begin so charmingly—

> Fair rocks, goodly rivers, sweet woods, when shall I see
> peace? Peace.
> Peace? What bars me my tongue, who is it that comes me
> so nigh? I.

—these degenerate, as was perhaps inevitable with so artificial a device, into mere mechanics. But there is one example of Sidney's versifying which is successful almost throughout, and, because it is little known, I quote it entire. It is written in what Sidney himself calls "Anacreon's kind of verses,"[5] the pattern being: ᴗ – ᴗ – ᴗ – –. It was first published in the 1598 folio of the ***Arcadia***, but was not, apparently, meant to be a part of that work.

> When to my deadlie pleasure,
> When to my lively torment,
> Lady, mine eyes remained
> Joined, alas, to your beams,
>
> With violence of heav'nly
> Beauty tied to virtue,
> Reason abasht retired,
> Gladly my senses yielded.
>
> Gladly my senses yielding,
> Thus to betray my heart's fort,
> Left me devoid of all life.
>
> They to the beamy suns went,
> Where by the death of all deaths,
> Find to what harm they hastned.
>
> Like to the silly Sylvan,
> Burn'd by the light he best lik'd,
> When with a fire he first met.
>
> Yet, yet, a life to their death,
> Lady, you have reserved,
> Lady, the life of all love.
>
> For though my sense be from me,
> And I be dead who want sense,
> Yet do we both live in you.

Turned anew by your means,
Unto the flower that aye turns,
As you, alas, my Sun bends.

Thus do I fall to rise thus,
Thus do I die to live thus,
Changed to a change, I change not.

Thus may I not be from you:
Thus be my senses on you:
Thus what I think is of you:
Thus what I seek is in you:
All what I am, it is you.

The poem starts slowly and somewhat laboriously, for the spondees at the end of each line are not always happily chosen, and the conceit which is the framework of the poem may seem at first to be too heavily ground out by the mind. But even in the first part of the poem there is a weight of both concept and rhythm, and without the conceit the poem could not develop, as it so movingly does, to the depth and haunting intensity of the last eight lines. At the end we have writing which is purely characteristic of Sidney at his best; the language is very simple, the verbal paradox ("changed to a change I change not") is the expression of a deeply embedded truth, and there is a cumulative intensity through repetition, combined with a control of rhythmic movement, which conveys, by its slow weightiness, the conviction of passion. There had been nothing quite like this in English poetry before, and there has been nothing quite like it since.

5

The ***Arcadia*** contains four or five times as many poems in Italian verse forms as it does poems in classical meters. There is a double sestina and a single sestina, there are seventeen sonnets, four poems in octaves, three canzone, and nine poems—the longest are among them—in terza rima. Once more a whole new range of expression is opened to English poetry.

When, in *The Defence of Poesie*, Sidney discusses the relative merits of quantitative and rhyming verse, he praises each for separate reasons: "Whether of these be the more excellent, would bear many speeches. The ancient (no doubt) more fit for music, both words and tune observing quantity, and more fit, lively to express divers passions by the low or lofty sound of the well-weighed syllable. The latter likewise with his rhyme striketh a certain music to the ear; and in fine, since it doth delight, though by another way, it obtaineth the same purpose, there being in either sweetness, and wanting in neither, majesty. Truly the English before any vulgar language, I know is fit for both sorts."

The lesson to be learnt from the Italian, as Sidney suggests, was different from that taught by the classics. The classical experiments were valuable chiefly as showing what variations could be made inside the individual line; the Italian gave practice in variations from one line to another. Both provided exercises in movement, but the movement in the Italian forms was of a broader kind. It was stanzaic, not linear; it could train the ear in a more elaborate melody and counterpoint.

Consequently Sidney set himself to experiment with rhyme as fully as possible. His enthusiasm for the resources of the English language had been already richly illustrated in his own practice by the time he wrote the *Defence*, and what he there says about the advantages of his native tongue were generalizations from his own experience. He is specific concerning one important detail. The Italian language, he observes, is handicapped by not having masculine rhymes; Italian rhymes are always either feminine rhymes or triple rhymes, which the Italians call "*Sdrucciola*: the example of the former is *Buono, Suono*; of the *Sdrucciola* is *Femina, Semina*. The French of the other side, hath both the male as *Bon, Son*; and the Female as *Plaise, Taise*. But the *Sdrucciola* he hath not: where the English hath all three, as *Due, Trew, Father, Rather, Motion, Potion.*"

This particular advantage of the English language Sidney deliberately exploited at least three times in the *Arcadia*, and the technical possibilities it reveals are so awakening to the ear that the result is worth examining in some detail. A good example is the long duet between Lalus and Dorus in the first book.

As far as its rhyming technique is concerned, the poem has six movements. It begins in terza rima with triple rhyme:

Come *Dorus*, come, let songs thy sorrows signify:
And if for want of use thy mind ashamed is,
That very shame with love's high title dignify.
No style is held for base, where love well named is.

This continues for some seventy lines, and then modulates into double rhyme:

Her peerless height my mind to high erection
Draws up; and if hope-failing end life's pleasure,
Of fairer death how can I make election?
Once my well-waiting eyes espied my treasure . . .

Then, in a third modulation, the rhyme becomes single:

This maid, thus made for joys, O Pan bemoan her,
That without love she spends her years of love:
So fair a field would well become an owner.
And if enchantment can a hard heart move,
Teach me what circle may acquaint her sprite,
Affections charms in my behalf to prove.

This continues for a few lines more, and then, the poem having, as it were, anchored on the monosyllabic rhyme, it rides there in a different rhythm. The fourth movement abandons terza rima for an internal chime of monosyllables:

Kala at length conclude my lingering lot:
Disdain me not, although I be not fair,

Who is an heir of many hundred sheep
Doth beauties keep, which never sun can burn.

The fifth movement consists of four five-line stanzas of five and three beat lines, rhyming *abccb*, the last line of one stanza being also the first line of the next:

Such force hath love above poor Nature's power,
That I grow like a shade,
Which being naught seems somewhat to the eyne,
While that one body shine,
Oh he is marred that is for others made.

And the poem concludes by returning, with a kind of technical leap, to the triple-rhyme terza rima with which it began:

Oh he is marred that is for others made,
Which thought doth mar my piping declaration,
Thinking how it hath marred my shepherd's trade.
Now my hoarse voice doth fail this occupation,
And others long to tell their love's condition. . . .

It is clear enough that this is not great poetry; the content is conventional, monotonous and dreary, and the demands of the rhyme-scheme are so exacting that only by accident is the phrasing ever felicitous. Furthermore, in spite of Sidney's enthusiasm, triple rhyme in English is something of a tour-de-force; it calls more attention to itself than any technical device should, and we too frequently ask ourselves, as we read, how the poet is going to pull it off instead of accepting it as a thing done. It is a means become too obviously an end.

But the exercise, for the healthy growth of English poetry, was extremely valuable: a pianist practises arpeggios which he will not duplicate when he plays an actual composition, yet he could not play the composition so well if he had not first practised the arpeggios. And Sidney's experiments with different kinds of rhyme are not always mere muscular exercises; sometimes, if only briefly, the modulation from one kind to another produces an extra rhythmical vibration which is musically effective—as in the following passage from the terza rima dialogue between Basilius and Plangus in the second book:

Thy wailing words do much my spirits move,
They uttered are in such a feeling fashion,
That sorrows work against my will I prove.
Methinks I am partaker of thy passion,
And in thy case do glass mine own debility . . .

But though Sidney's exercises in terza rima are highly interesting from the technical point of view, and though they were valuable for showing the poets of the sixteenth century what could be done with English rhyme, they are not his most successful imitations of Italian art. His real triumph is with the sestina, and the most beautiful of the poems in the ***Arcadia*** is the double sestina in book one which begins:

You goat-herd Gods, that love the grassy mountains.

The poem has been well described by Mr. Empson:

> Nowhere in English literature can [the] use of diffuseness as an alternative to, or peculiar brand of, ambiguity be seen more clearly than in those lovely sestines of Sidney, which are so curiously foreign to the normal modes or later developments of the language. . . . This form has no direction or momentum; it beats, however rich its orchestration, with a wailing and immovable monotony, for ever upon the same doors in vain. . . . Limited as this form may be, the capacity to accept a limitation so unflinchingly, the capacity even to conceive so large a form as a unit of sustained feeling, is one that has been lost since that age.[6]

The poem is admirably constructed. For ten stanzas the two shepherds Strephon and Klaius lament their desolation with increasing passion, the repetitions become weightier and weightier, sinking more and more deeply into grief; then the cause of their grief—their lady's absence—is revealed in the climactic eloquence of the eleventh and twelfth stanzas, and the poem ends in the three-line coda required by the sestina form, a coda which reiterates the permanence of their sorrow:

Our morning hymn is this, and song at evening.

A musical analogy, as so often with Sidney's poetry, is almost inevitable. The first ten stanzas swell with a slow and steady crescendo, and the language and the rhythm gradually acquire an extraordinary force:

Strephon:
I wish to fire the trees of all these forests;
I give the Sunne a last farewell each evening;
I curse the fidling finders out of Musicke:
With envie I doo hate the loftie mountaines;
And with despite despise the humble vallies:
I doo detest night, evening, day, and morning.

Klaius:
Curse to my selfe my prayer is, the morning:
My fire is more, then can be made with forrests;
My state more base, then are the basest vallies:
I wish no evenings more to see, each evening;
Shamed I have my selfe in sight of mountaines,
And stoppe mine eares, lest I growe mad with Musicke.

After this intensity comes the resolution or revelation, the statement which clarifies and relieves the despairing darkness by explaining its cause. The stanzas must be quoted in full, for only quotation can show how carefully they are made. In each the verb is held back till the beginning of the fifth line so as to produce the maximum rhetorical effect; it is an example of the precise and necessary craftsmanship which underlies all of Sidney's work, and which controls so authoritatively the movement of his verse. The metrical variations are also masterly.

Strephon:
For she, whose parts maintainde a perfect musique,[7]
Whose beautie shin'de more then the blushing morn-

ing,
Who much did passe in state the stately mountaines,
In straightness past the Cedars of the forrests.
Hath cast me wretch into eternall evening,
By taking her two Sunnes from these darke vallies.

KLAIUS:
For she, to whom compar'd, the Alpes are vallies,
She, whose lest word brings from the spheares their musique,
At whose approach the Sunne rose in the evening,
Who, where she went, bare in her forhead morning,
Is gone, is gone from these our spoyled forrests,
Turning to desarts our best pastur'de mountaines.

STREPHON:
These mountaines witnesse shall, so shall these vallies,

KLAIUS:
These forrests eke, made wretched by our musique,
Our morning hymne is this, and song at evening.

6

To find his own voice, to discover his own poetic idiom and his own rhythm, is the main business of a poet. It is not a simple matter, and the discovery occurs in various ways, ways which vary according to the character (both personal and poetic) of the poet and according to the character of the age which surrounds him. But there is one constant fact which is true of all poets and at all times; the discovery of oneself depends on an act of submission. For the poet, as for the human being, to lose one's life is to find it. In our time this fact has been widely recognized, though it has been expressed in widely differing terms. In a minor way it is what Pound means when he calls his poems "Personae"; it is what Housman discovered when he spoke through the mouth of the Shropshire Lad. It is the fact that lies behind the search of W. B. Yeats for the anti-mask—the discovery of the self by contemplation of its opposite; it is what T. S. Eliot expresses by his theory of the "objective co-relative" and by his requirements that poetry should be as "impersonal as possible."

In the sixteenth century this saving loss of personality, this discovery of self through submission to an "other," could be accomplished to a considerable extent through convention. Convention is to the poet in an age of belief what the *persona* is to the poet in an age of bewilderment. By submission to either the poet acquires authority; he feels that he is speaking for, is representing, something more important than himself—or, in the case of the *persona*, he is at least representing something different from his own naked and relatively insignificant ego; in both cases he has taken the first step toward universality.

But the submission to convention is by no means a passive process, even if the poet does it so naturally that he never thinks of doing anything else. The convention, whether it involve setting, as in the pastoral, or tone, as in the elegy, or technique, as in the sestina, must obviously be freshened by continual re-examination so that it is re-made every time it is used. This is what Sidney did with the double sestina which I have just quoted. The pastoral setting, the traditional tone of lament, the rigorous form of the verse have been revitalized not merely by Sidney's superb technique, but by the fact that he has put into them something more than the purely conventional emotion. In a way that does not often happen in the ***Arcadia*** the external conventions have here become a *persona*, an objective co-relative, for Sidney's own projected feelings.

Or, perhaps more accurately, the convention has stimulated, has even created, those feelings. Once the poet has set himself the task of writing an amorous complaint, that deep melancholy which lay beneath the surface glamor of Elizabethan existence and which was so characteristic of Sidney himself, begins to fill the conventional form with a more than conventional weight. It surges through the magical adagio of the lines; they have that depth of reverberation, like the sound of gongs beaten under water, which is sometimes characteristic of Sidney as of no other Elizabethan, not even Shakespeare.

The most famous of the poems in the ***Arcadia***, in fact the only one which is at all well-known, is the sonnet in book three beginning "My true love hath my heart and I have his." The theme of the poem, the exchange of hearts, is a common one, and in the sestet, at least, it is expressed in a commonplace fashion, but there are two things about it which make it memorable: the monosyllabic simplicity of the diction (only twelve words are not monosyllables), and the flawless movement of the rhetoric. The poem is a perfectly drawn circle, ending most contentedly where it began: "My true love hath my heart, and I have his." This particular movement is something new in English sonnet writing; it is one more example of the continual experimenting which make the poems in the ***Arcadia*** such a striking revelation of what could—and sometimes of what could not—be done with the English tongue.

7

I have spoken of the value of convention as a means of poetic release, and I do not want in any way to slight its importance; but convention is, after all, only a means to an end, the great and difficult end of direct and accurate expression. To catch, in the words of T. E. Hulme, "the exact curve of the thing," whether it be an external object, a thought, an emotion, or, more likely, a combination of all three, to make the glove of verbal expression skin-tight, this is what all poetry aims for. Only by finally achieving this honesty, this truth, can the poet discover his own idiom, his own rhythm, his own voice. Consequently all poets have, like Shakespeare, consistently attacked affectation (the spotted underside of convention), and none more vigorously than Sidney. In ***Astrophel and Stella*** Sidney tries deliberately to put convention aside, and to speak out for himself. He is by no means always successful, and one of the first things a critic must do in discussing this third and obviously most important part of his poetic work is to determine where and how the success does or does not occur. But Sidney's attempt, whether invariably successful or not, is the significant thing, his attempt to be himself, to find a richer and more exacting freedom than that given by the *persona* of convention, the attempt that was to be Sidney's legacy, not only to the generation of poets which immediately followed him, but to all poets since.

Sidney states his aim at the beginning of the sequence. The famous first sonnet of ***Astrophel and Stella*** is a manifesto of sincerity, an eloquent rejection of anything but the strictest devotion to honest feeling. It is also characteristic of Sidney at his mature best: the structure is perfect, the single movement rises to its climax through a flawless logical progression as well as through a rhythmical pulsation, the language is very simple, the images are strikingly exact, and—what is here first fully developed in Sidney's poetry and is to distinguish many of the finest sonnets in the sequence—the climax is presented dramatically:

> Loving in truth, and fain in verse my love to show,
> That she, dear she, might take some pleasure of my pain,
> Pleasure might cause her read, reading might make her know,
> Knowledge might pity win, and pity grace obtain,
> I sought fit words to paint the blackest face of woe,
> Studying inventions fine, her wits to entertain,
> Oft turning others' leaves, to see if thence would flow
> Some fresh and fruitful showers upon my sun-burnt brain.
>
> But words came halting forth, wanting invention's stay,
> Invention, Nature's child, fled step-dame Study's blows,
> And others' feet still seem'd but strangers in my way.
> Thus great with child to speak, and helpless in my throes,
> Biting my truant pen, beating myself for spite,
> "Fool!" said my Muse to me, "Look in thy heart and write."[8]

At least six other sonnets are on the same theme; Sidney rejects all decoration, all exaggeration, all borrowing; he will write only of Stella, for to copy nature is to copy her, and he will, he says,

> in pure simplicity
> Breath out the flames which burn within my heart,
> (XXVIII)
> Love only leading me into this art.

Who Stella was, and whether or not Sidney as a man felt a genuine passion for her, are puzzling questions, but not worth much conjecture. All that matters is that she was a symbol around which were mustered a set of important emotions, emotions which were multiplied and intensified, sometimes perhaps even induced, by Sidney's desire to express them. Everyone who writes poetry knows that once a subject matter is accepted, or an object of potential emotion set up in the mind, all sorts of previously unnoticed emotional iron-filings flow toward it as to a magnet, and new patterns are formed the shape of which had been unexpected until the act of composition has made them mysteriously appear. The conscious act of deliberation which focusses the mind on fulfilling the requirements of a given poetic form invokes hitherto subconscious relationships and intensifications which may produce a final result that is quite different, and much richer, than anything planned at the start. Such a process had already occurred, as we have seen, in Sidney's double sestina in the ***Arcadia***; the convention of the love sonnet, in spite of all that Sidney had to say against its artificiality, gave a further opportunity. A Laura, a Stella, a dark lady, has only a thin and shadowy "reality" as a biographical fact compared to her reality in the poetry ostensibly written about her. Whether Stella was Lady Rich or somebody else (she was in all probability Lady Rich) is of no importance to the student of Sidney's poetry. Her symbolic value is all that matters.

Sometimes this value is unhappily small, and we feel, as in sonnet LXXIV, that Stella—or in this instance Stella's kiss—is too trivial a matter to justify the weight of rhetoric that Sidney crowns it with. But even in so anticlimactic a sonnet as this one there are lines which exemplify Sidney's admirable simplicity and force:

> And this I swear by blackest brook of hell,
> I am no pickpurse of another's wit.

These qualities are common throughout the sequence, and many illustrations of them could be given, but they appear perhaps most clearly in the eighth of the interspersed songs, a love poem which has very few equals in the language, and which no one but Sidney could have written. It has not only force and simplicity, but also intensity and passion. It is a dialogue, a presentation in dramatic terms of that conflict between chaste and passionate love with which all sixteenth century art, both visual and verbal, was so much concerned, and to which Sidney's richest love poetry gave so full and deep an expression: "The argument cruel chastity, the prologue hope, the epilogue despair."[9]

The verse form is as simple as the diction; octosyllabic couplets with alternate masculine and feminine rhymes, a triumphant result of Sidney's earlier experimentation:

> In a grove most rich of shade,
> Where birds wanton music made,
> May, then young, his pied weeds showing
> New perfumes with flow'rs fresh growing,
>
> Astrophel with Stella sweet
> Did for mutual comfort meet,
> Both within themselves oppressed,
> But either in each other blessed.
>
> Him great harms had taught much care,
> Her fair neck a foul yoke bare;
> But her sight his cares did banish,
> In his sight her yoke did vanish.

For a time they are silent, till love makes Astrophel speak. He praises Stella's beauty in exquisite language, and presents as delicately as possible the arguments for the satisfaction of their love. When he is finished,

> There his hands (in their speech) fain
> Would have made tongue's language plain;
> But her hands his hands repelling,
> Gave repulse, all grace expelling.
>
> Then she spoke. Her speech was such
> As not ears but heart did touch,
> While such wise she love denied,
> As yet love she signified,

Her refusal is as gracious, as courtly, as simply expressed, as Astrophel's invitation, but what she says is no mere following of convention, it is universally right and true. She does not deny her passion, as a more conventionally minded poet would make her do; her passion is as genuine, as burning, as Astrophel's. But she will not submit to it lest the submission spoil her love by shame:

> "Astrophel," said she; "my love
> Cease in these effects to prove;
> Now be still, yet still believe me,
> Thy grief more than death would grieve me.
>
> If that any thought in me,
> Can taste comfort but of thee,
> Let me, fed with hellish anguish,
> Joyless, hopeless, endless, languish.
>
> If those eyes you praised be
> Half so dear as you to me,
> Let me home return, stark blinded
> Of those eyes, and blinder minded.
>
> If to secret of my heart,
> I do any wish impart
> Where thou art not foremost placed,
> Be both wish and I defaced.
>
> If more may be said, I say,
> All my bliss in thee I lay.
> If thou love, my love content thee,
> For all love, all faith, is meant thee.
>
> Trust me while I thee deny,
> In myself the smart I try;
> Tyrant Honor doth thus use thee—
> Stella's self might not refuse thee.
>
> Therefore, dear, this no more move,
> Lest (though I leave not thy love,
> Which too deep in me is framed)
> I should blush when thou art named."
>
> Therewithal away she went,
> Leaving him to passion, rent
> With what she had done and spoken,
> That therewith my song is broken.

It is interesting to compare this poem with "The Ecstasie" of Donne. Both are love poems, both are concerned with the conflict, or at any rate the balance, between physical and spiritual love, both use for the most part, simple and colloquial language, both—for what the fact is worth—are in octosyllabic couplets. But otherwise they are very different. Donne's performance is much more brilliant; the Platonic and the Aristotelian traditions, botany, physiology, cosmology and theology are all brought to bear on the situation; Donne's Briareus-like mind takes hold of virtually all the available knowledge of his time as material to weave into his texture. The result is a very fine poem, admirably planned and frequently superbly phrased. But it is a little inhuman; unlike the song of Sidney it does not bleed.

Sidney's poem is more elemental, more direct, than Donne's; compared to Donne's brilliant sophistication Sidney's straightforward and graceful strength seems almost archaic, like Greek sculpture of the sixth century B. C. or the painting of Duccio. Donne writes, as he and his lady look into one another's eyes:

> Our eye-beams twisted, and did thread
> Our eyes upon a single string . . .

Which is very clever. But when Sidney wants to express the same idea, though he uses paradox, he is much more simple:

> Wept they had, alas the while;
> But now tears themselves did smile,
> While their eyes by love directed
> Interchangeably reflected.

It is, in fact, a relief to turn back, after reading Donne, to Sidney, for in Sidney there is a baring of the heart rather than an exercise of the mind, and we feel that for the healthy life of English poetry it is the example of Sidney that is more central and more sound.

In ***Astrophel and Stella*** there is much more, of course, than simplicity and directness, though simplicity and directness are the foundations on which the other qualities are built. There is an occasional magic:

> A rosy garland and a weary head. . . .
>
> (XXXIX)
>
> Wise silence is best music unto bliss. . . .
>
> (LXX)
>
> —my soul which only doth to thee
> As his sole object of felicity
> With wings of love in air of wonder fly. . . .
>
> (LXXXVI)

And, perhaps more important, there is very frequently, as in the opening sonnet, drama. The thought is introduced by a dramatic question: "Come, let me write, and to what end?" (XXXIV) or it is put in the form of a quoted speech:

> Because I breath not love to every one,
> Nor do not use set colors for to wear,
> Nor nourish special locks of vowed hair,

Nor give each speech a full point of a groan,
The courtly nymphs acquainted with the moan
Of them who in their lips love's standard bear;
"What? He?" say they of me, "Now I dare swear
He cannot love. No, no; let him alone."

Or a sudden dramatic turn is given to the situation or the thought in the final couplet. Sonnet XVII, for example, is largely a fanciful one, it seems a typical piece of Renaissance mythological decoration. It tells how Cupid's bow and arrows were broken and how Nature made him new ones from Stella's eyebrows and eye-glances. Nothing could be more apparently artificial. And yet at the end Sidney rescues the sonnet from emptiness by bringing it back to life with dramatic simplicity. Cupid, he says, was delighted with his new weapons:

Oh how for joy he leaps, Oh how he crows!
And straight therewith, like wags new got to play,
Falls to shrewd turns; and I was in his way.

This quality of drama helps to give the impression of reality which we get from the best of the sonnets. They are not, said Lamb, "rich in words only . . . they are full, material and circumstantiated. Time and place appropriates every one of them. It is not a fever of passion wasting itself upon a thin diet of dainty words, but a transcendent passion pervading and illuminating action, pursuits, studies, feats of arms, the opinions of contemporaries and his judgment of them."

The drama lies not only in the external manner of presentation; it is also inherent in the conflict between virtue and desire which is so important an aspect of the subject matter. When the matter and the manner are both dramatic, Sidney is at his best (LXXI):

Who will in fairest book of Nature know
How virtue may best lodg'd in Beauty be,
Let him but learn of love to read in thee,
Stella, those fair lines which true goodness show.
There shall he find all vice's overthrow,
Not by rude force, but sweetest sovereignty
Of reason, from whose light those night birds fly,
That inward sun in thine eyes shineth so.
And not content to be perfection's heir,
Thyself dost strive all minds that way to move,
Who mark in thee, what is indeed most fair;
So while thy beauty drives my heart to love,
As fast thy virtue bends that love to good.
But ah, Desire still cries, "Give me some food!"

This sonnet illustrates another of Sidney's excellencies, his admirable control over movement, a control which had already been firmly practised in the poems in the ***Arcadia***. Each quatrain has its own idea, the second being a development of the first, and the third an extension and universalizing of the first and second, while the conclusion locks the whole together with its exclamatory and dramatic cry. This firmness of logical progression is always present in Sidney, but in a few of the finest sonnets he transcends it, and we have that slow, haunting, reverberating Sidneian music, a music both full and broad, which occurs in the double sestina in the ***Arcadia***, and which reappears with a deeper richness in the greatest of the sonnets in ***Astrophel and Stella***:

With how sad steps, O Moon, thou climb'st the skies!
How silently, and with how wan a face!
What, may it be that even in heavenly place
That busy Archer his sharp arrows tries?
Sure, if that long-with-love acquainted eyes
Can judge of love, thou feel'st a lover's case;
I read it in thy looks; thy languish'd grace,
To me that feel the like, thy states descries.
Then even of fellowship, O Moon, tell me,
Is constant love deem'd there but want of wit?
Are beauties there as proud as here they be?
Do they above love to be lov'd, and yet
Those lovers scorn whom that love doth possess?
Do they call virtue there, ungratefulness?

This same mastery of movement appears in another poem—not a sonnet—which shows once more how Sidney profited by the strictness of the early training he gave himself. The stanzas to the Nightingale are each divided into three sections which musically contrast lines of five beats with lines of three, and which, following an Italian model, invariably have feminine rhymes. The language is simple, and once or twice—as more frequently in the sonnets—has the succinctness of an epigram. The variations in the feet are also notable, and emphasize the theme, so common in Sidney, of the melancholy of unsuccessful love. And, as usual, the movement is ordered by a firm logical structure; it is a poem that could have been composed only by a master of technique, yet it is more than a merely technical success, for in spite of the somewhat literary conceit on which it is based, its lovely modulations convey real feeling.

The nightingale as soon as April bringeth
Unto her rested sense a perfect waking,
While late bare earth proud of new clothing springeth
Sings out her woes, a thorn her song-book making,
And mournfully bewailing,
Her throat in tunes expresseth
What grief her breast oppresseth
For Tereus' force on her chaste will prevailing.
O Philomela fair, O take some gladness,
That here is juster cause of plaintful sadness;
Thine earth now springs, mine fadeth;
Thy thorn without, my thorn my heart invadeth.
Alas, she hath no other cause of anguish
Than Tereus' love, on her by strong hand wroken,
Wherein she suffering, all her spirits languish
Full woman-like complains her will was broken.
But I who daily craving,
Cannot have to content me,
Have more cause to lament me,
Since wanting is more woe than too much having.
O Philomela fair, O take some gladness,
That here is juster cause of plaintful sadness:
Thine earth now springs, mine fadeth;
Thy thorn without, my thorn my heart invadeth.

Sidney wrote two love sonnets which were not printed as part of ***Astrophel and Stella***, but which were evidently planned to conclude the sequence. In them he at last resolves the long conflict between desire and virtue which, in the last half of the sequence at least, is expressed with such force and intensity and which seems to have been the cause of more than ordinary suffering. Desire is at last repudiated, and the love which "reacheth but to dust" is spurned in favor of love that is eternal. After the last one are printed the words, "Spendidis longum valedico nugis."

Both of these sonnets are very fine; among all of Sidney's work they offer the clearest justification for the claim put forward by one modern critic that Sidney rediscovered, for English poetry, the "grand style." The finest is perhaps the first, and less well-known of the two, though it is hard to choose between them. It is a triumphant example of Sidney's best qualities—his direct and forceful simplicity, his eloquent rhetoric, his emotional depth and truth, his control of movement, both within the single line and throughout the poem as a whole; and a discussion of Sidney's craft may appropriately end with its slow reverberant music sounding in our ears.

> Thou blind man's mark, thou fool's self-chosen snare,
> Fond fancy's scum, and dregs of scattered thought,
> Band of all evils, cradle of causeless care,
> Thou web of will, whose end is never wrought,
> Desire, desire! I have too dearly bought
> With price of mangled mind thy worthless ware;
> Too long, too long, asleep thou hast me brought,
> Who should my mind to higher things prepare.
>
> But yet in vain thou hast my ruin sought,
> In vain thou mad'st me to vain things aspire,
> In vain thou kindlest all thy smoky fire;
> For virtue hath this better lesson taught,
> Within myself to seek my only hire,
> Desiring nought but how to kill desire.

8

What Sidney accomplished in his own poetry and what he did for English poetry in general have both been somewhat overshadowed by the more ambitious and apparently more professional work of Spenser. The poems in the ***Arcadia*** have been neglected in favor of the contemporary poems in *The Shepheardes Calendar*, and the comprehensive width of *The Faerie Queene* has tended to relegate ***Astrophel and Stella*** to the position of minor poetry. For this Sidney himself is partly responsible, and for two reasons; in spite of his superb defence of the importance of poetry he subscribed too readily to the silly contemporary notion that no gentleman should be a professional writer, and, partly because of this notion, the content of his poetry was too narrowly limited to the subject of love. Even the most devoted admirer of Sidney finds it something of a chore to read through all the poems in the ***Arcadia*** because they are virtually all about the same thing; one lover after another—men and women, shepherds and kings—all rejoice or lament (chiefly the latter) about the condition of their affections. Spenser was wiser; more than half of the eclogues in the *Shepherd's Calendar* are concerned with other topics—with religion, politics, poetry and morality. And in the *Faerie Queene* he created an entire world, where love is only one among many other motivating passions. It is most unlikely that Sidney, if he had lived, would have written anything so extensive; he was too much in the center of active political life to have had the desire, or the time, for such a task. Spenser, fortunately, was only on the fringes of society.

But if we accept the limitations of Sidney's subject matter, and set his love poetry by that of Spenser, it is Spenser—if we except the "Epithalamion"—who suffers by the comparison. Spenser has justly been called a master of melody, his lines move with wonderful sweetness and grace, they carry the reader along with as little effort as that with which they were apparently composed. But, compared to Sidney, they are thin; their language, however musical, lacks weight. Spenser's style, compared to Sidney's, has two deficiencies: it is rarely pungent, and it is almost never dramatic. The reader is soothed, not challenged; enchanted, not awakened to a new reality.

This reality, this depth and pungency, we recognize as belonging not only to Sidney's awareness, but—as happens with all great poetry—as creative of a new awareness in ourselves. The art, exercise and imitation which Sidney so assiduously practised throughout the Psalms and the ***Arcadia***, resulted, in the best of the sonnets in ***Astrophel and Stella***, in poetry to which all lovers of honesty and directness must continually return. In this essential respect, it is Sidney—not Spenser—who is the most central of English poets in the generation that was soon to know Shakespeare.

Notes

1. The importance of "versifying" for the development of English poetic art is mentioned by G. D. Willcock, "Passing Pitefull Hexameters; a Study of Quantity and Accent in English Renaissance Verse," *Mod. Lang. Rev.*, 29 (1934). 1–19.
2. This line is a translation of Giovanni della Casa: "O dolce selva solitaria, amica." Mona Wilson, *Sir Philip Sidney*, p. 314.
3. Works, ed. Feuillerat, 2. 73. *Arcadia*, bk. 3.
4. *Works*, ed. Feuillerat, 1. 257, *Arcadia*, bk. 2.
5. E. Hamer, *The Metres of English Poetry*, p. 302: "a kind of iambic dimeter catalectic, not used in classical Latin, and not identical with any metre of Anacreon, but similar to the broken ionic dimeter of some of the fragments."
6. William Empson, *Seven Types of Ambiguity*, pp. 45 ff.
7. When quoting this poem I keep the old spelling, contrary to my practice elsewhere in this essay, because the difference in the spelling of this word is deliberate. When the art of music is meant, as in stanzas nine and ten, we have "Musicke"; elsewhere it is al-

ways "musique." This difference creates a noticeable difference of response in the reader.

8. In quoting from *Astrophel and Stella* I use the 1598 edition. M. Feuillerat in his Cambridge edition of Sidney's works, prints the text of Thomas Newman's first quarto of 1591. This is an egregious example of perverse devotion to the fatuous principle of following at all costs the earliest available text, a principle which has been set up for the guidance of modern scholars who lack the taste to know better. For the first quarto is a mass of nonsensical corruptions, and richly deserves Miss Wilson's description of it: "The general aspect of the text suggests that the purveyor of the manuscript was a serving man in the employ of one of Sidney's friends, who had made a scribbled copy, full of contradictions and misreadings, from which the printer set up as much as he could decipher, completing the lines with conjectures of his own, and leaving the punctuation to Snug the joiner." In fact the text was considered so shocking by Sidney's friends, as Miss Wilson points out, that "the unsold copies were impounded by the Stationer's Company." M. Feuillerat's edition of Sidney's works is likely to remain standard for a long time to come; it is therefore all the more wretched that he failed to see how mean a disservice he was doing his author by presenting his best work in a debauched and ridiculous form.

9. Thomas Nash, addresses to the reader, prefaced to Newman's first quarto of *Astrophel and Stella*.

James Appelgate (essay date 1955)

SOURCE: "Sidney's Classical Meters," in *Modern Language Notes*, April 1955, pp. 254–55.

[*In the following essay, Appelgate corrects Theodore Spencer's error in identifying the form of the poem "When to my deadlie pleasure."*]

The pseudo-quantitative English verses which enjoyed a brief fad in Elizabethan literary circles are generally an unlovely lot, and the late Professor Theodore Spencer was right to observe the relative merit among them of one of Sidney's efforts, a poem beginning, **"When to my deadlie pleasure,"** which appears among the ***Certaine Sonets*** of the 1598 folio.[1] Spencer, however, unaccountably mistook its form; he analyzes it according to the pseudo-Anacreontic pattern ˘ – ˘ – ˘ – –, remarking that "Sidney himself calls [this poem] 'Anacreon's kind of verses.'"[2] Sidney's identification, with notation of the pattern, is attached not to the poem which Spencer discusses but to one beginning, **"My Muse, what ailes this Ardoure?"** which appears in the Old ***Arcadia***.[3] **"When to my deadlie pleasure,"** on the other hand, is not given a metrical annotation by Sidney; and it is written in the pattern –˘˘ – ˘ – ˘ which is that of the Aristophanic line. Thus, Spencer's dissatisfaction with some of the final spondees in the poem may be explained by the fact that they are intended to be trochees. The Aristophanic line occurs as the first verse of the "lesser" Sapphic strophe, a distich used by Horace in *Odes*, I, 8.

In addition to being a kind of primrose among thorns, then, this poem is also one of the most esoteric of the experiments in classical meters. It may be observed generally that Sidney's poems of this sort exhibit considerably greater variety of experimentation than those of his contemporary "versifiers," who usually aimed at epic hexameters. Indeed, Sidney has only two poems, though relatively long ones, in the epic line: **"Lady reserved by the heavens"** (***Works***, II, 208–14 and IV, 77–86) and **"Faire rocks, goodly rivers"** (I, 352–53 and IV, 152–54). The others are written in lyric meters from Horace and Catullus. **"Unto no body my woman saith"** (II, 307) translates and imitates the elegiac distichs of Catullus, No. 70; its companion epigram, **"Faire seeke not to be feard"** is also in elegiacs, as are **"Fortune, Nature, Love"** (II, 208 and IV, 75–76) and **"Unto a caitife wretch"** (I, 357–59 and IV, 318–20). **"If mine eyes can speake"** (I, 143–44 and IV, 76–77) and **"O my thoughtes"** (IV, 401) are written in the greater Sapphic strophe.[4] The Phalacean hendecasyllable, which Sidney uses for **"Reason tell me thy mind"** (II, 236 and IV, 156–57), is a favorite line of Catullus (No. 42, for example); and Horace uses three times[5] the Asclepiadean line that Sidney adopts for **"O sweete woodes"** (II, 237–38 and IV, 157–58).

In the copy of the Old ***Arcadia*** that Feuillerat prints (vol. IV) the peeudo-quantitative poems are announced by name and by a notation of the meter; these identifications are all accurate, though the pattern notations for the elegiacs and the hexameters give no indication of variations which were allowable in classical practice and which Sidney in fact did admit into his.

Notes

1. *The Complete Works of Sir Philip Sidney*, ed. Albert Feuillerat (Cambridge, 1922–26), II, 316–17; Theodore Spencer, "The Poetry of Sir Philip Sidney," *ELH*, XII (1945), 251–78.

2. Spencer, *loc. cit.*, pp. 260–61.

3. *Works*, IV, 154–56; Feuillerat also prints this poem, without its identifying context, among the "Poems First Printed in the Folio of 1593," II, 234–35. Enid Hamer has a portion of the correct poem with her definition of the Anacreontic (which Spencer quotes), but does not include "When to my deadlie pleasure" among Sidney's pseudo-quantitative poems (*The Metres of English Poetry* [New York, 1930], p. 302).

4. Elegiac and Sapphic meters are of course common in both Catullus and Horace; the latter's *Rectius vives* (*Odes*, II, 10), for example, is written in Sapphics, though Sidney translates it into terza rima (*Works*, II, 307).

5. *Odes*, I, 1; III, 30; and IV, 8.

Jean Robertson (essay date 1960)

SOURCE: "Sir Philip Sidney and his Poetry," in *Elizabethan Poetry*, edited by John Russell Brown and Bernard Harris, Edward Arnold Publishers, 1960, pp. 111–129.

[*In the following essay, Robertson presents an overview of Sidney's poetry in relation to his life and his intentions.*]

Nothing that happened later in his life meant so much to Fulke Greville as Sidney had done. In the long postscript he had to make do with his friend's literary remains. So Sidney's biography was written, and by emphasizing the preceptual value of the ***Arcadia***, Greville tried to convey something of his 'searching and judicious spirit'; but his dissatisfaction kept breaking through the praise. With one of the flashes of insight that light up his fuliginous prose, he throws out that, unlike many writers whose works are better than themselves, the ***Arcadia*** both in form and matter was inferior to Sidney's unbounded spirit. 'His end was not writing even while he wrote'; his end was 'virtuous action'. On the other side, nothing delighted Sidney more than to escape from business to his books, and his 'idle times' were filled with reading and writing; he avoided the company of noblemen who despised literature. It is this pull between the active and contemplative life which makes Sidney perennially attractive to statesmen and soldiers, to poets and scholars alike. Nowhere is he more eloquent in *An Apology for Poetry* than in his praise of poetry as the companion of camps.

There was a truly remarkable absence of hostile contemporary comment, and unparalleled mourning after his death. He was, of course, much nicer than most Elizabethans; but then his parents, to whom he owed a great deal, were unusually honest and intelligent people. As a young man, he perhaps expected too much of other people. Languet wrote a timely letter about the necessity of putting one's friends' faults out of sight: 'unless you alter your opinion you will be always meeting with persons who will excite your wrath and give you cause for complaining'. This disillusioned French protestant thought it was much in the then troubled times if men did not actually betray their friends. He would not have approved of the furious letter Sidney wrote to his father's secretary, Molyneux, when he suspected that his private letters were being opened; nor did he approve of the quarrel with the Earl of Oxford. Sidney never became 'politic' in the sense that Burghley was; but he learned—at any rate in the last ten months of his life as Governor of Flushing—to manage and to work with men less idealistic than himself.

He was little more than a boy when he set off on his European travels, yet eminent statesmen and scholars immediately fell under his spell. The long score of works dedicated to him date from this time; on a later mission the leaders on opposite sides, Don John of Austria and William the Silent, were captivated—a marriage with the latter's sister was even mooted. These were personal triumphs and cannot be explained away as tributes to the nephew and heir of the Earl of Leicester and a very junior member of the English party which stood for a Protestant alliance with the German princes, sympathy for the Huguenots, intervention in the Netherlands against Spain coupled with an attack on the Spanish empire overseas, and an active colonization policy in the New World. These were the causes that Leicester, Walsingham, and Sir Henry Sidney urged on the Queen and Burghley, who cared little for the Protestant cause in Europe and had a deep distrust of the French and the Dutch: they were the causes with which Sidney identified himself on his return to England.

Languet had a more mature appreciation than Sidney of the many shifts in Burghley's foreign policy—even over the Queen's proposed marriage with Anjou, about which, probably at the instigation of Leicester, Sidney wrote a letter to the Queen urging the objections. Languet even understood the repeated delays in sending help to the Netherlands. It was scarcely necessary, though, to advise Sidney to be friendly to the Cecils. He had stayed with Burghley as a boy and won his friendship—though his father's suggestion of a match between him and Anne Cecil was not taken up. Sidney may have fretted at Elizabeth's vacillations, but he was never in doubt about her importance. She was, he wrote on 12 June 1575, shortly after his return home, a Meleager's brand to England, 'when it perishes farewell to all our quietness'. She might not have relished the further comment of this young man that she was 'somewhat advanced in years yet vigorous in health'. Sidney was not so fulsome as poets became in the 1590's in their flattery of the ageing Virgin Queen; but in contriving an entertainment like *The Lady of May* for her reception at Wanstead in 1578, and by taking part in the elaborate accession day tilts, he made his contribution to the cult. Moreover, his father, Sir Henry, served her well in Wales and Ireland, and was sometimes ill-rewarded for his faithfulness, and blunt in his criticisms of royal parsimony; and the beauty of his wife, Lady Mary, was destroyed by smallpox contracted through nursing the Queen. When the marriage between Sidney and Frances Walsingham was arranged without consulting her, Elizabeth went through the motions of displeasure with which she customarily greeted the marriages of her courtiers—but relented sufficiently to stand godmother to Sidney's daughter. Finally, she could not forgive him for being so careless as to get himself mortally wounded.

Sidney's letters of 1580–1 make it clear that it was not disgrace on account of his opposition to the Anjou match which kept him away from the Court, but poverty. What is the Queen going to do for him he asks Burghley (10 October 1581)? This and two further letters reveal that the money he so desperately needs is likely to come from impropriations of Papists' possessions. The scale of Sidney's requirements is indicated in the letter to Leicester of 28 December:

> Without it bee 3000^{li} never to troble yowrself in it, for my cace is not so desperate, that I woold gett clamor for less. Truly I lyke not their persons and much worse

> their religions, but I think my fortune very hard that my reward must be built uppon other mens punishmentes.

Sidney and Leicester were granted £3,000 from this source; but by 1583 Sidney was again in debt. In view of the large sums he needed and the very small sums an author could hope to obtain from selling his works to the stationers, there is no need to invoke his amateur status or supposed distaste for print to account for the fact that all his works remained in manuscript during his lifetime. ***Astrophel and Stella*** was clearly too private at the time it was written. The dedication to the Countess of Pembroke printed with the 1590 new ***Arcadia***, but written for the completed old ***Arcadia***, is couched in terms that suggest a preface to a book rather than a private letter; but Sidney changed his mind and started to recast the work and to add a great deal of new material. The new ***Arcadia*** was left unfinished at his death—and was probably not touched after 1584 (the date on the manuscript copy in the Cambridge University Library) when affairs of state increasingly engaged his attention. Sidney's defence of his uncle in reply to the libels in *Leicester's Commonwealth* (1584) was intended for the press, with its rather ridiculous challenge to the anonymous author: 'And from the date of this wryting, emprinted and published I will three monthes expect thyne answer'. But Sidney gave an excessive amount of space to his pride in being a Dudley, and a far more effective answer was provided by Gentili in his dedication of *De Legationibus Libri Tres* to Sidney. The only work which Sidney can be reproached for not having printed as it stood is *An Apology for Poetry*—the phraseology suggests that the author had readers in mind. He may have felt that he had been too slow in coming to the defence of poetry and that Lodge had adequately answered Gosson's attack in *The School of Abuse* in the year this work came out (1579); or, more likely, been too busy to arrange publication.

Enough has been said of Sidney's poverty to indicate that this 'Generall Maecenas of Learning' could not afford to support other poets. Patronage in this sense had to be left to his sister, the Countess of Pembroke; Sidney did pay for Abraham Fraunce's education at Cambridge and give four angels for a dedication to the translator, Richard Robinson, in 1570, but all he could usually offer was example and encouragement. Eleanor Rosenberg has suggested that Leicester delegated to Sidney the patronage of poetry; but this is to make patronage sound too organized. There was nothing tangible to delegate: Gosson's *School of Abuse* and Spenser's *Shepheardes Calender* were an unlucky and a lucky shot—not that Sidney seems to have taken great notice of *The Shepheardes Calender*. The letters of Harvey and Spenser written and published after it appeared have the rather unpleasant flavour of getting at Sidney.

The friendship of Sidney and Spenser is one of the might-have-beens of literary life. Spenser's long-delayed elegy *Astrophel* reveals that he was so out of touch as to suppose that the Stella of Sidney's poems was his wife. True, he speaks of his 'entire love and humble affection' to Sidney, but 'Patron of my young Muses' probably means no more than that he had chosen to dedicate *The Shepheardes Calender* to Sidney. The most that may be claimed is that W. L.'s commendatory verses to *The Faerie Queene* imply that Sidney encouraged him to write the poem. Dyer and Fulke Greville were Sidney's poet-friends; and it was to them that he bequeathed his books. Spenser's departure to Ireland in July 1580 may be the reason why the relationship never ripened; but a suspicion remains that a difference in social status, and perhaps the indiscretions of Gabriel Harvey, were factors. Whilst failing to mention specifically the poetry of his friends Dyer and Greville, at least Sidney put it on record in *An Apology for Poetry* that there was much poetry in *The Shepheardes Calender*—unless he was mistaken.

It is not clear when Sidney himself slipped into the name of poet. To read his correspondence with Languet is to follow the education of a statesman. He is to study enough astronomy to understand cosmography; but must not give too much time to it, nor to geometry (a noble study in itself) as he will so soon have to tear himself away from his literary labours. For the same reason, Greek had better be omitted. He must practise his Latin style for diplomatic correspondence; his French is nearly perfect and his Italian now sufficient; but it really was essential for an English diplomat to speak some German (Sidney promised to try though he thought it a beastly language). Next to the sacred scriptures, he should study the branch of moral philosophy which treats of justice and injustice; history he has made great progress with. Sidney replied regretfully that he would give up geometry, though he thought it would be of the greatest service in the art of war. He would content himself with only so much Greek as was necessary for the understanding of Aristotle, for, although translations appeared daily, the meaning was not declared plainly or aptly enough. If Sidney had started to write poetry, he kept remarkably quiet about it. Languet, with his hopes for the future of European protestantism centred on Sidney, might not have approved. Although the first version of the ***Arcadia*** was completed before Languet's death in 1581, Sidney does not once mention even the **'Ister Bank'** poem in which he celebrated his old tutor. (It should be noted that not all of his letters have survived.)

Sannazaro and Montemayor had both used the pastoral as a vehicle for semi-fictional autobiography; so it should be no surprise to find Spenser and Harvey masquerading as Colin Clout and Hobbinol in *The Shepheardes Calender*, and among the shepherds in the old ***Arcadia*** the melancholy Philisides, the pupil of Languet.[3] He is a stranger to Arcadia, and in response to earnest entreaty he describes his parentage, education, and travel abroad in words which offer an exact summary of Sidney's own career up to 1575. On his return, Philisides' 'course of tranquillity' was diverted by his falling in love with Mira, who rejected his suit.[4] In the new ***Arcadia*** (1590) Philisides has disappeared from the Eclogues; the first poem is sung by Amphialus to Philoclea (I. 394 f.) and the second is sent by Dorus to Pamela (I. 357). Life had marched on and Philisides is no longer the melancholy lover of Mira, who may or may not have been the Mira of Fulke Greville's sonnets.[5] Instead, Philisides appears at the annual joust held on the marriage anniversary of the Iberian Queen, running against an older man Lelius whilst the ladies watched from the windows—'among them there was one (they say) that was the *Star*, wherby his course was only directed'. It has been shown beyond all reasonable doubt that this episode shadows an accession day tilt at which Sidney tilted against Sir Henry Lee, the Queen's champion.[6] He did so in 1581, and a few months earlier in the same year Sidney was one of the challengers, and Lee appeared as an unknown knight, in a tournament called *The Four Foster Children of Desire* devised for the entertainment of the French commissioners who had come about the proposal for the Queen's marriage to Anjou. In Sonnet 41 of ***Astrophel and Stella*** the poet records that he has won the prize at a tilt

> Both by the judgement of the English eyes
> And of some sent from that sweet enemie *Fraunce*;

not because of his skill in horsemanship, nor because both from his father's and his mother's side he had inherited prowess at arms, but because '*Stella* lookt on'—the Star who looked on in the ***Arcadia.*** Her presence had the opposite effect in the tilt described in Sonnet 53.

Fiction and reality mingled in the pageantry of the Elizabethan court where the deliberate revival of chivalry gave Sidney a chance to exercise his ingenuity in devising the fashionable imprese for the shields of the knights in the tiltyard.[7] It was also part of this courtly life on the Italianate model that the knight should address sonnets to one of the ladies of the court, couched in emblematic language intended to be understood immediately by the lovers only, and to exercise the wit of others. Sidney chose Penelope Devereux, the wife of Lord Rich. In Sonnet 13 he refers to the Devereux arms 'argent a fesse gules in chief three torteaux':

> Cupid then smiles, for on his crest there lies
> Stellas fair haire, her face he makes his shield,
> Where roses gueuls are borne in silver field.

in Sonnet 65, to his own coat of arms 'Or a Pheon Azure':

> Since in thine armes, if learned fame truth hath spread,
> Thou [Cupid] bear'st the arrow, I the arrow head.

Half-seriously, Sidney argues in *An Apology for Poetry* that Plato cannot have banished poets from a republic in which community of women was allowed on account of their effeminate wantonness 'sith little should poeticall sonnets be hurtfull when a man might have what woman he listed'. The true Petrarchan code demanded that the poet should address his sonnets to a virtuous lady who was unable to return his affections. Secure in the knowledge of her unassailability, he was free to assail her with all his might. Sir John Harington understood the position perfectly:

> . . . To which purpose all that have written of this common place of love, and chiefly *Petrake* in his infinite sonets, in the midst of all his lamentation, still had this confort, that his love was placed on a worthie Ladie: and our English *Petrake Sir Philip Sidney*, or (as *Sir Walter Rawlegh* in his Epitaph worthely calleth him) the *Scipio* and the *Petrake* of our time, often conforteth him selfe in his sonets of *Stella*, though dispairing to attaine his desire, and (though that tyrant honor still refused) yet the nobilitie, the beautie, the worth, the graciousnesse, and those her other perfections, as made him both count her, and call her inestimably rich, makes him in the midst of those his mones, rejoyce even in his owne greatest losses.[8]

The epithet *inestimably rich* shows that Harington was in the secret; and this is confirmed by a copy in his own handwriting of the 1st Sonnet of ***Astrophel and Stella*** headed 'Sonnettes of Sr Philip Sidney to ye Lady Ritch'.

Before he died in August 1576, Walter Devereux had expressed the hope that his daughter Penelope would marry Philip Sidney; but, although there were some negotiations, Penelope's guardians, Burghley, Huntingdon, and Walsingham, evidently decided against the match. At any rate Penelope was married in late 1581—her subsequent lover and later husband, Mountjoy, afterwards declared that it was against her will—to the wealthy Lord Rich. Sidney provides the key to ***Astrophel and Stella*** in Sonnet 37 ('of my life I must a riddle tell') where the last line asserts that Stella 'Hath no misfortune, but that Rich she is'. This sonnet was not in the manuscript which Thomas Newman got hold of for printing the 1591 quarto; nor were eight stanzas of the 8th song (in which Stella seems to return Astrophel's love), stanzas 5–7 of the 10th song, nor the 11th song. If Sonnet 37 was omitted from copies circulated at Court as being too revealing, it was careless to include the other 'Rich' sonnets, 24 and 35. In 1598 the Countess of Pembroke restored Sonnet 37 and the missing songs.

If Penelope felt anything for Sidney, it was a passing episode. All that he permitted himself to say outside the sonnets was that 'over-mastred by some thoughts, I yeelded an inckie tribute unto them.' A letter from him to Walsingham dated 17 December 1581 (soon after Penelope's marriage to Lord Rich) implies that his marriage to Walsingham's daughter was already under discussion. The delay of the marriage to the spring of 1583 might have been occasioned by Sidney's passion for Penelope Rich or by his financial embarrassment; it could have been on the Walsingham side, for one John Wickerson wanted to marry Mistress Frances, and declared in February 1583 that the marriage had been consummated.[9] However convenient the match, Walsingham had a real affection and admiration for Sidney dating from the time when as ambassador in Paris he acted as the young traveller's guardian, and extending to the defrayment of his funeral expenses. For Sidney, it was not a brilliant marriage, but Walsingham agreed to pay his debts up to £1,500, and to provide board and lodging for the couple and their servants in his house. After Sidney's death, his widow married Penelope's brother, the Earl of Essex, and Lady Rich and Mountjoy maintained close relations with the Sidney family. The Essex-Sidney group was a very small and much intermarried one, and it was Lord Rich's misfortune to be an outsider.

Sidney's identity with Astrophel is complete in Sonnet 30 where one of the political questions concerns Sir Henry's Irish service:

> How *Ulster* likes of that same golden bit
> Wherewith my father made it once half tame.

Theories which require four actors, Sidney and Penelope, Astrophel and Stella, in this admittedly dramatic sonnet sequence, and which suppose that the references to poems which do not imitate '*Petrarchs* long deceased woes' are not to the sonnets before us, but to another imaginary set which Astrophel wrote, add unnecessary complication. The only poem in which the poet is a third person, the narrator of the dialogue of Astrophel with Stella, is the 8th song:

> Therewithall away she went,
> Leaving him so passion-rent
> With what she had done and spoken
> That therewith my song is broken.

In the Bodleian Library MS. Rawl. Poet. 85, f.36b, the last line reads 'That therewith his harte was broken'. The 1591 quartos obscured the nature of ***Astrophel and Stella*** as the first English canzoniere by printing the songs at the end, instead of interspersed as in 1598, where the story is clearer as some of the songs advance the action (Sonnet 73, for example, comments on the kiss which takes place in the second song). For a sonnet sequence tells a story. Nashe saw this at once; in ***Astrophel and Stella*** 'the tragicommody of love is performed by starlight . . . The argument cruell chastitie, the Prologue hope, the Epilogue dispaire'. This is the Petrarchan pattern, and Sidney embroiders it with all the conceits which were used by the Italian sonneteers and the Pléiade—the apostrophe to sleep, to lost liberty, to the sparrow and the lapdog allowed more favour than the poet by their mistress; the wind playing in her hair, the 'baiser', her resemblance to a house of splendour. Those who have studied Sidney's sources report that, though he may borrow an idea, a phrase, or a line, his development of it is nearly always original. He is creating within a living tradition rather than translating. Of course the sonnets claim that Astrophel does not 'flaunt in phrases fine' (3), does not employ stale Petrarchan antitheses ('living deaths', 'freesing fires' (6)), does not borrow from 'poor Petrarchs long deceased woes' for 'And sure at length stolne goods do come to light' (15), that he has foresworn the help of the muses (55), that he never had their help (74), that he has no wish to be considered a poet (90). All this is to convince Stella that his passion is real and he is obeying his muse's injunction to 'looke in thy heart and write' (1). Astrophel poses as a blunt, honest lover who can be trusted to mean what he says—also as a real man made of flesh and blood who is not going to be content to gaze at a woman on a pedestal for ever.[10]

Those who close their eyes to the fact that a story is being told and who persist in treating the sonnets as meditations on love or explorations of the lover's emotions not only ignore the nature of the sonnet cycle but also disregard the purpose of the Renaissance lyric—to persuade and to praise. The primary purpose of a sonnet was to 'get favour'. Sidney is, of course, only half-serious when he criticizes lyrics for failing in this respect:

> But truly many of such writings as come under the banner of unresistable love, if I were a Mistress, would never perswade mee they were in love.

Stella was not his only audience; several sonnets glance at the other audience of court wits which he expected to appraise his performance as a sonneteer, to assess the effectiveness of his pleading and his blazons. ***Astrophel and Stella*** is a semi-autobiographical, semi-fictional story of human passion, and Sidney expressly warns off 'curious' allegorical interpretations:

> When I say *Stella*, I do meane the same.
>
> (28)

Astrophel cannot be the human soul in search of God (represented by Stella) as some critics have suggested: Astrophel reproaches himself for his devotion to Stella with the old antithesis of Virtue/Reason versus Love (47, 52); and his friend tries to dissuade him from marring his mind with such a passion as love (14, 21). True, Bruno declared in the Dedication to Sidney of *Gli Eroici Furori* (1585) that the Petrarchan sonnets in his volume were to be interpreted allegorically: his lady's eyes were heavenly beauty, Cupid's arrows were the spiritual influences at work on the soul, and so on. This sort of use of Cupid imagery for devotional purposes became commonplace in the seventeenth century, but is quite foreign to Sidney's art. Bruno began his dedication with a tirade against the worship of some mistress instead of God; then he seems to have recollected, or someone reminded him, that he was addressing the author of ***Astrophel and Stella***, and so he exempts from his censure Queen Elizabeth and the ladies of the English court who are 'divine nymphs formed of celestial substance, like the divine Diana who reigns over them'. Bruno addresses a sonnet to these ladies

> E siete in terra quel ch'in ciel le stelle.[11]

This was taken as an allusion to the sonnets addressed to Stella by Florio in his dedication of Part II of the *Essays of Montaigne* (1603) to the Countess of Rutland (Sidney's daughter) and Lady Rich. Bruno's dedication is only valuable for the interpretation of ***Astrophel and Stella*** in so far as it shows that Sidney's sonnets were circulating fairly freely in 1585. Both the nature of a Petrarchan sonnet cycle, and the fact that neither Newman nor the Countess of Pembroke included them, argue against concluding the cycle with the sonnet against desire, **'Thou blindmans marke'**, and the sonnet against earthly love, **'Leave me, o Love which reachest but to dust'**, first printed in the 1598 folio with ***Certain Sonnets***.

Many of Sidney's arguments in *An Apology for Poetry* would be well known to his contemporaries, particularly to those who, like himself, had read the continental treatises by Scaliger, Minturno, and the rest. But Sidney's mixture of enthusiasm and urbanity, high seriousness and irony, has given us a host of fine quotable phrases from which a bright shadow falls over the shoulder of every Englishman who takes up his pen to write on the name and nature of poetry. Poetry for Sidney, as for many other writers starting with Plato, was the general term for the creative arts and literature: 'It is that fayning notable images of vertues, vices or what els, with that delightful teaching'. And so, though both Xenophon and Heliodorus wrote in prose, *Cyropaedia* and *Aethiopica* were heroical poems to Sidney. But as Plato had noted, the word *poetry* was generally kept for 'one species of poetry, that which has relation to music and rhythm'. Consequently, after the recognition that it is not rhyming and versing that makes a poet, for which Sidney could have cited Quintilian, Elyot, or Ronsard, he concedes that most poets have in fact chosen verse as their fittest raiment; and thereafter the discussion is confined to verse. Sidney substitutes the poet's own genius for Plato's divine inspiration. For him, the poet was both prophet and maker; no industry can make a poet, but the highest flying wit must have a Daedalus to guide him.

The three wings of his Daedalus are Art, Imitation, and Exercise: the rest of this chapter will be concerned with Sidney's attempts to become airborne. From that boyhood Sunday, 8 September 1566, when Master Philip ordered his servant William Marshall to give 12*d.* to a blind harper (perhaps the same one whose singing of the ballad of Percy and Douglas is praised so stirringly in *An Apology*), to the last gay gesture of having a poem he himself had composed called *La Cuisse Rompue* set to music and sung to him as he lay dying from his wound after Zutphen, Sidney delighted in music. He once wrote to his brother Robert 'you will not believe what a want I finde of it in my melancholie times'—the words of a listener rather than a performer. The pastoral tradition rather than musical knowledge is responsible for the choice of instruments—lyre, rebeck, lute, cittern—with which the various characters accompany their songs in the ***Arcadia***. In fact Sidney seldom provides his shepherds with the elaborate musical trappings used in the *Diana*—but then Montemayor really was a musician.

Some of the poems among the ***Certain Sonnets*** added to the 1598 edition of the ***Arcadia*** were written to be sung to extant tunes; and later some of Sidney's poems (whether or not they were written for the purpose) were set to music. Songs 2, 4, 8–11 of ***Astrophel and Stella*** are generally referred to as in trochaic metre. If these seven-syllable lines are read as a trochaic catalectic dimeter, one gets the sensation of rowing against the tide of the metre. But if the first syllable is taken as *anacrusis* or better still, as a foot which has lost its first syllable, the poems at once run more smoothly in accordance with the natural tendency of English towards iambic or rising metre. This is particularly clear in the exquisite 4th song where the refrain has four stresses and is obviously in rising metre, with inversion in the first foot of its first line:

'One | ly joy | now here | you are,
Fit | to heare | and ease | my care.
Let | my whispe | ring voyce | obtaine
Sweete | reward | for sharp | est paine:
Take me | to thee, | and thee | to me.'
'No, no, | no, no, | my Deare, | let be.'

King James VI warned poets to take heed that the number of feet in every line should be even, not odd.

In *An Apology* one of the arguments for the antiquity of poetry is that all ancient and primitive people had poets to make and sing songs. The modern poet, too, 'commeth unto you with words set in delightfull proportion, either accompanied with, or prepared for, the well inchaunting skill of Musicke'. No doubt Sidney was influenced by Ronsard's dictum that the chief end of the poet was to make fitting verses for music when he praises poetry as 'the onely fit speech for Musick (Musick I say, the most divine striker of the sences)'. The proper relation of words to music was manifest for Sidney in the psalms, which he recognized as songs written in metre. When Sternhold translated some of the psalms and had them published with the musical settings, he appears to have hoped that the courtiers of Edward VI would chant them instead of 'fayned rymes of vanitie'. There seems to be an echo of this somewhat forlorn hope in Sidney's remark about 'that Lyricall kind of Songs and Sonnets: which, Lord, if he gave us good mindes, how well it might be imployed, and with howe heavenly fruite, both private and publique, in singing the prayses of the immortall beauty, the immortall goodnes of that God who gyveth us hands to write and wits to conceive'. Whereas Sternhold, Hopkins, and most other English translators of the psalms had mainly used common or ballad metre (6/8 time), when Sidney made his translations he experimented with many different stanzaic forms, some of which are in direct imitation of metres in the Marot-Bèze psalter. It is reasonable to suppose that Sidney intended these psalms also to be sung to Claude Goudimel's musical settings. Both he and Sternhold may have been encouraged in their labours by the knowledge that Marot's psalms had once been the rage at the French court; but it is more likely that Sidney, being aware of the superiority of the French protestant psalter to the versions available for the reformed church in his own country, endeavoured to fill this want. Donne's poem *Upon the translation of the Psalmes by Sir Philip Sydney, and the Countesse of Pembroke his Sister*, which reads like a prefatory poem for a projected edition, claims that this is what the two authors had achieved.

We do not know whether Sidney met Ronsard in Paris in the summer of 1572; but he can hardly have avoided hearing something of de Baif's *Academie de Poésie et de Musique* founded in 1570 with the purpose of recapturing the divine effects the music of ancient Greece was purported to have had. The words for *la musique mesurée à l'antique* had in effect to be written in quantitative metres—a syllable of the same duration as each note. It is scarcely necessary to mention that no-one now takes the jesting allusion in the Spenser/Harvey letters to an 'areopagus' at

Leicester House to imply that Sidney and Dyer were trying to found an English equivalent of the French academies. Nor does this correspondence suggest that any concern with the requirements of music was behind the experiments of either Sidney and Dyer or Spenser and Harvey in 1579. Yet Sidney used the musical argument in a cancelled passage at the end of the 1st Eclogues of the old ***Arcadia***, which is found only in the Jesus and Queen's College Oxford MSS., where the shepherd Dicus defends quantitative and Lalus rhyming verse. The shepherds' arguments are summarized in *An Apology*, indicating that Sidney felt there was much to be said on either side—though he does not repeat Lalus's assertion (in flat contradiction of Ronsard) that music is the servant of poetry. Sidney, like Puttenham, though with some confusion of *rhyme* and *rhythm*, perceived that the choice was not between rhymed and quantitative verse, but between accentual-rhymed and quantitative-unrhymed verse. Having elected for quantitative verse, it became necessary to assign quantity to English syllables, some of which were seen to be long or short, but a great many more to be indifferent. Attempts to apply the Latin rule of position broke, as Harvey saw, on the chaotic state of contemporary spelling (Stanyhurst declared rather desperately that by spelling *passadge* so he had made the second syllable long). Harvey was somewhat sceptical about what Spenser told him in October 1579 of the 'lawes and rules of Quantities of English sillables for English verse' devised, as we learn later, by Mr. Drant, 'but enlarged with M. Sidneys own judgement'; and opposed to any rules about position or diphthongs which would alter the quantity given to any English syllable by common speech and general received custom. If the short 'Nota' written in the margin of the poem **'Fortune, Nature, Love'** in the St. John's College, Cambridge Manuscript of the old ***Arcadia*** is Sidney's version of Archdeacon Drant's rules, Harvey would neither have gained much enlightenment nor dissented, for the 'rules' amount to following the natural quantity of spoken English and ignoring misleading orthography.[12] This old ***Arcadia*** manuscript is the only one to give all the scansions for the eight quantitative poems. The markings were omitted in the printed editions of the revised ***Arcadia***, and it is doubtful whether the reader who did not happen to be aware that 'Phaleuciackes' implied the scansion marked below would immediately recognize the pattern:

> Reason, tell mee thy Mynde, yf here bee Reason

Presumably position between two consonants accounts for the second long syllable in the first *Reason* (Stanyhurst made himself miserable over *seasons*). *Mee* and *bee* are covered by the 'Nota' as short syllables disguised by false orthography; *yf* is presumably a particle 'used nowe long nowe short'; but *thy* one would expect to be long by analogy with *dye, hye* which are said in the 'Nota' to seem to have a diphthong sound. Sidney's efforts to provide the correct syllables drive him to much repetition and reliance on sentences of line length. He is not able to convey much meaning, and the quantities marked in the scansion are constantly being defeated by the natural stresses. The promise of opening lines ('My Muse what ailes this Ardoure?', 'O sweete woodes, the Delighte of Solitarynes') is seldom fulfilled. Campian was more successful than Sidney in writing quantitative verse because he chose unmistakably long syllables, avoided words of indifferent quantity and dependence on the rule of quantity by position, and, finally, chose words in which quantity and accent coincide. This selectiveness did, of course, very much reduce the number of words available and in practice meant the avoidance of most polysyllables.

Only one-fifth of the poems in the ***Arcadia*** are written in quantitative measures—the rest offer a great variety of verse forms, mainly Italian in derivation—sonnets, madrigals, terza rima, sestine. Here the technical interests is in the different stanzas and rhyme-schemes, or in such things as the imperfectly sustained triple rhymes of the dialogue of Lalus and Dorus (IV. 54 f.). Sidney even attempted, and triumphantly succeeded in, that complicated form the double sestina; here he shows the controlled handling of words he demanded of the poet 'not speaking . . . words as they chanceably fall from the mouth, but peyzing each sillable of each worde by just proportion according to the dignitie of the subject':

> You Gote-heard Gods, that love the grassie mountaines,
> You Nimphes that haunt the springs in pleasant vallies,
> You Satyrs joyde with free and quiet forrests,
> Vouchsafe your silent eares to playning musique,
> Which to my woes gives still an early morning:
> And drawes the dolor on till wery evening.[13]

The line-end words, *mountaines, vallies, forrests, musique, morning, evening*, are used in all the subsequent stanzas, but in a revolving order so arranged that the word at the end of the last line of a stanza is always the same as the word at the end of the first line of the next stanza. The full pattern is: *abcdef; faebdc; cfdabe; ecfbad; deacfb; bdfeca*; then repeat the whole series, ending with a tercet, *bdf*. This reliance on the same end-words makes for monotony of sound and subject matter. The effect is cumulative, and in English literature the poem is an exotic without progeny.

If the erratic insetting of the lines in the 1591 edition of ***Astrophel and Stella*** be ignored, and the 1598 grouping of the fourteen lines, 4–4–3–3, accepted, then Sidney's conception of sonnet structure was of an octet followed by the Petrarchan break at the sestet. Yet in 82 of the 108 sonnets the rhyme-scheme *cdc dee* could just as well be arranged *cdcd ee*, giving for the whole sonnet the Shakespearian pattern first stabilized by Surrey of three quatrains and a couplet.[14] But Sidney does not achieve the clarity or firmness of structure which is one of the pleasures of Shakespeare's sonnets—nor does he throw the weight on to the final couplet, but on to the final line. Even when a new sentence begins at the sestet, there is seldom a break or turn in the thought (often detectable in Spenser or Shakespeare where the sestet (or third quatrain) will begin with a 'Yet', 'But', 'Now'). Most of Sidney's sonnets are single movement poems. This is true also of the six sonnets in alexandrines, which Sidney handles with surprising grace and strength.

Whereas, outside a small group of enthusiasts concerned with the poverty of English metres, prosody probably excited as little interest among Elizabethan readers as it does today, the art of rhetoric was another matter, of serious concern to the orator, the preacher, the politician, the lover—to any man at any time concerned to persuade his fellow men to do or to believe something. Both Puttenham and Sidney accepted the Renaissance conception of the purpose of the lyric as to praise, to celebrate, and to plead. From these aims it followed that the lyric poet required as thorough a mastery of rhetorical figures as did the orator or the preacher. The fullest Elizabethan treatment of these figures is to be found in Puttenham's *The Art of English Poesy* (1589). Sidney deplored the excessive use of 'figures and flowers, extreamlie winter-starved' by versifiers, prose-printers, scholars, and some preachers. Yet the ***Arcadia*** and ***Astrophel and Stella*** have provided the happiest hunting ground for 'figures and flowers', starting with Abraham Fraunce's *The Arcadian Rhetoric* (1588) in which the English examples are taken from the unpublished old ***Arcadia*** and *The Faerie Queene*, and John Hoskins's *Directions for Speech and Style* (*c.* 1600), illustrated by reference to the ***Arcadia*** (1590). Sidney got the contemporary pleasure from recognizing figures; he praises Cicero's use of 'that figure of repetition' (though he warned his brother Robert against 'great study in Ciceronianism, the chief abuse of Oxford'), and the notable *prosopoeias* in the Psalms, 'the Beastes joyfulnes, and hills leaping'. Sonnet 31, with its transference of the poet's emotion to the moon, is largely carried by the personifications;[15] though the spacious and melancholy reverberations of the first quatrain are achieved quite as much by the initial inversion and the felicitous alternation of open *w* and soft *s* sounds, followed by the evocation of Cupid without actually naming him:

> With how sad steps, o Moone, thou climb'st the skies,
> How silently, and with how wanne a face!
> What, may it be that even in heav'nly place
> That busie archer his sharpe arrowes tries?

This, rightly esteemed as one of Sidney's finest sonnets, is only marred by the distortion of the true meaning, 'is ingratitude called virtue?', arising from the exigency of rhyme in the last line

> Doe they call *Vertue* there ungratefulnesse?

(Muir, however, defends the meaning of the line as Sidney wrote it.)

Sidney's unremitting use of figures must have been deliberate, and we miss some of the pleasure his contemporary readers enjoyed if we fail to recognize them in our turn. E. K. was less fatuous in 1579 than he sounds today as he exclaims in his notes to *The Shepheardes Calender* 'A pretye *Epanorthosis* or correction', 'A figure called *Fictio*', 'A patheticall *parenthesis*, to encrease a carefull *Hyperbaton*'. We can still recognize the linked chain of Sonnet 1, the *antitheton* of 'Fleshly vaile consumes, but a Sowle hathe his lyfe', *oxymoron* in 'absent presence', and even *epanorthosis* or *aposiopesis* in 'O teares! no teares, but rain'. Sidney's favourite figures were, it seems, *anadiplosis, anaphora, epizeuxis, ploce, prosonomasia*, and *traductio* (the tranlacer), and to recognize them is a useful exercise in the 'naming of parts', so long as it is not mistaken for a description of the whole. It is a relief to find how many difficult words turn out to refer to what it is sufficient for most of us to call a play on words: 'That all thy hurts in my harts wracke I reede' is a *prosonomasia*; 'Thus not ending the due prayse of her prayse' is a *synoeciosis*; 'My pype and songe made hym bothe song and Pipe forsweere' features *antimetabole* or the counterchange. If one can recognize proverbs, it is an advantage to know that their use was a recognized figure of speech, and a superadded glory to know that this figure was called *paroemia*.

Sonnet 27 can be analysed in terms of a *differing* or *dissentary* argument as defined in Ramist logic; but the poets did not need Ramus to tell them to put logic into their poetry. Thomas Wilson warned writers to have logic perfect before looking to profit from rhetoric. Sidney could truthfully claim to be 'a peece of a logician'; he was, moreover, a fervent Aristotelian, and it is not likely that he was much impressed by the Ramist attempts to simplify the teaching of logic and rhetoric—despite the dedication to him of de Banos' Life of Ramus, and his patronage of Abraham Fraunce and William Temple. In Ramist treatises the function of figures of speech is relegated from persuasion or proof to decoration for delight. Sidney approaches this position in his treatment of one figure—the simile. He objected to the way Lyly used similes from 'unnatural' history as part of his argument:

> Now for similitudes, in certaine printed discourses, I thinke all Herbarists, all stories of Beasts, Foules, and Fishes are rifled up, that they come in multitudes to waite upon any of our conceits; which certainly is as absurd a surfet to the eares as is possible: for the force of a similitude not being to proove anything to a contrary Disputer but onely to explane to a willing hearer.[16]

A rare instance of Sidney's 'euphuing of similes' may be found in *An Apology* where he reproaches the learned for attacking poetry:

> and will they now play the Hedgehog that, being received into the den, drave out his host? or rather the Vipers, that with theyr birth kill their Parents.

There are fine similes in ***Astrophel and Stella***, for example in Sonnet 11 comparing love to a child playing with an illuminated book; but Sidney is happiest in metaphor where he can give the reader the pleasure of discovery and recognition: 'Beware full sailes drowne not thy tottring barge'; 'and that unbitted thought | Doth fall to stray'; 'My mouth too tender is for thy hard bit'—or the elaborate horse and rider image of Sonnet 49. Even when, as in Sonnets 8 and 17 (which starts from Pontano's *De Venere et Amore* or *De Stella*) the conceit is suggested by another poet, the Cupid imagery is handled freshly and with ingenuity.[17] The most potent classical allusions are those in which the character alluded to is not named: 'the busie archer' of Sonnet 31; the unnamed presence of Orpheus in Sonnet 36, or of Narcissus in 82; the comparison of Astrophel to Prometheus in Sonnet 14:

> Alas, have I not paine enough, my friend,
> Upon whose breast a fiercer Gripe doth tire
> Then did on him who first stale downe the fire,
> While *Love* on me doth all his quiver spend?

In contrast to the elaborate and almost continuous poetic figures, and to the tireless metrical experiments, is the simplicity of Sidney's diction. It is not that he was indifferent to words; but that he had a patriotic pride in the fitness of English words for poetry. When a gloss is needed, it is for words like *myching* or *weltering*, now obsolete. Not that Sidney affected the obsolete. His inability (apparently forgetful of the precedent afforded by Theocritus) to allow Spenser's 'framing of his stile to an old rustick language' in *The Shepheardes Calender* makes it surprising to find even one poem in the ***Arcadia*** in an archaic style—the **'Ister Bank Song'** in celebration of Languet (IV. 237). Here are such words as *couthe, yclipped, ne, thilke, won'de, stowers, foen, mickle*. Sidney is credited by Hall with the introduction of the compound epithet:

> that new elegance
> Which sweet Phillisides fetch't of late from France,
> That well beseem'd his high-stil'd Arcady,
> Tho others marre it with much liberty
> In epithets to join two words in one.
>
> (Satire VI. 255–8)

This was a French sixteenth-century import from Greece; compare sommeil *charme-soucy*, dieux *chèvre-pieds*, and Sidney's *care-charming* sleep and *goat-herd* Gods. James VI disliked compound epithets and Dryden thought it a mistake to attempt them in English; but Sidney found that in a short poem like a sonnet a portmanteau-word will carry the same amount of meaning as a longer phrase: *wit-beaten, long-with-love-acquainted* eyes, *kiss-worthie* face. He sometimes forges a verb out of a noun; for example, 'How Holland hearts', 'Whom *Love* doth windlas so'. If he often preferred the colloquial and the direct, he was, like Daniel, 'well-languaged'.

Sidney did more than any other writer to make the continental experience and practice of poetry and criticism accessible to his countrymen while at the same time speaking in his own voice as an English poet. Had he lived into the next decade, he would surely have recognized that the fine poetry being written, much of it inspired by his example, gave the lie to his earlier diagnosis of 'want of merit' as the reason for the poor esteem into which poetry had fallen. As it was, in *An Apology* he picked out the winners—*Tottel's Miscellany* (he mentions only the Earl of Surrey's lyrics, probably because of his prominence on the title-page), *Gorbuduc* (it would be nice to think that he included Sackville's Induction in the meet furnishings of the *Mirror for Magistrates*), and *The Shepheardes Calender*. Spenser alone was writing poetry as fine as Sidney's best before 1586, and we must refuse to respect Astrophel's wish that there should not be

> Graved in mine Epitaph a Poets name.

Notes

3. He appears mainly in the Eclogues; see Sidney, *The Complete Works* (4 vols., 1912–26), edited by A. Feuillerat, IV, 67, 119, 151, 223, 229, 237, 312. Bryskett and Spenser both use this name for Sidney. Philisides became Astrophil (the correct form used by some contemporaries) under the influence of Stella.
4. *Works*, IV. 312.
5. Greville was referred to as Miraphilus by 1587; this, with the many verbal echoes of *Astrophel and Stella* in *Caelica*, suggests that his sonnets were written at the same time as Sidney's.
6. See Hanford and Watson; and Yates.
7. Sidney bought Ruscelli's *Imprese* in Venice; many devices will be found in the *Arcadia.*
8. Translation of Ariosto's *Orlando Furioso* (1591), Notes to Book XVI.
9. C Read, *Mr. Secretary Walsingham* (1925), III. 423, n. 2.
10. Anti-Petrarchan sentiment had already appeared in the sonnets of Wyatt and the Pléiade.
11. And you are to the earth as the stars are to the heavens.
12. The discussion of Dicus and Lalus in the Jesus and Queen's College Oxford MSS., and the 'Nota' in the St. John's College Cambridge MS., are printed by Ringler in *Philological Quarterly* (1950).
13. *Works*, I. 141; the poem was also in the old *Arcadia* (IV. 307). A convenient reprint will be found in F. Kermode, *English Pastoral Poetry* (1952).
14. For a useful analysis of Sidney's rhyme-schemes see Poirier, ed., pp. 32–4.
15. Other examples of Sidney's use of personification will be found in Sonnets 39, 74, 98, 103; and there is the universally sympathetic nature in the *Arcadia*—the pathetic fallacy' had, of course, been an ingredient of the pastoral since Theocritus.
16. Cf. *Astrophel and Stella*, Sonnet 3. Drayton Praised Sidney because he 'did first reduce I Our tongue from Lillies writing then in use, I Telling of stones, stars, plants, of fishes, flies, I Playing with words and idle similes'.
17. L. C. John, *Elizabethan Sonnet Sequences* (1938), credits du Bellay and Ronsard with introducing Al-

exandrian cupids from the Greek anthology; but they were commonplace in Italian Renaissance literature and art (see E. Wind, *Pagan Mysteries in the Renaissance*, 1958). Lever makes difficulties for himself and for Sidney's readers by insisting on treating Sidney's Love (*Amor*) and his Cupid as two different boys (pp. 68–9 and 85).

Robert L. Montgomery, Jr. (essay date 1961)

SOURCE: "Manner Over Matter," in *Symmetry and Sense: The Poetry of Sir Philip Sidney*, University of Texas Press, 1961, pp. 9–29.

[*In the following excerpt, Montgomery examines "symmetry" in the poetry of* The Lady of May, *the* Psalms, *and the* Arcadia, *and says that they reflect a strong experimental spirit that is not found in* Astrophel and Stella.]

It is common to assume that the *Lady of May* poems, the translations of the ***Psalms***, the ***Arcadia*** poems, ***Astrophel and Stella***, and the miscellaneous pieces in ***Certaine Sonets*** follow a steady chronology of composition from 1578 to approximately 1583. Theodore Spencer's essay on Sidney's poetic development assumes that order and establishes an ascending hierarchy of quality upon it.[1] Unfortunately, the problem is not so neat. *The Lady of May* is easily dated because it was performed for a visit of the queen at Wanstead, the Earl of Leicester's castle, but William Ringler's investigations indicate that many of the ***Arcadia*** poems overlap and extend beyond the composition of ***Astrophel and Stella***, and he is convinced that the translations of the ***Psalms*** should be dated in 1584. Finally, the poems in ***Certaine Sonets*** are of varying dates.[2] It is possible, therefore, that some of Spencer's observations need to be modified, especially those leading to the view that all the poetry supposed to precede ***Astrophel and Stella*** is experimental prelude. There are, Spencer acknowledges, fine poems and evidence of technical maturity in the "early" pieces, but only in the sequence does Sidney's talent display itself with full assurance.

In reality, a much more profound difference separates ***Astrophel and Stella*** from the *Lady of May* poems, the ***Psalms***, and the ***Arcadia*** poems. The latter three groups reflect a strong experimental spirit not found in the sequence, but it is more significant that this experimentation derives from a different creative principle. Furthermore, by no means all or even a majority of the ***Arcadia*** pieces betray the struggling apprentice or the green talent chiefly interested in technique at the expense of other things.

Those poems which are most striking for their ingenuity are scattered and, superficially at least, variable in type. Because they move beyond what is necessary for the conventional exercises of the novice, they are easily isolated, and we may wonder if they are uniformly the work of a novice at all. Occasionally Sidney appears anxious simply to master the intricacies of continental forms; occasionally, as in the ***Psalms***, the effort is to work in a variety of stanza forms and line lengths; sometimes the impulse is towards rigidly consistent rhythm; at least once Sidney tries his hand at a game similar in motive to pattern and acrostic poems. It is here in his most eccentric poem that we can begin to observe the quest for symmetry underlying all the other forms of experiment:

> [1]Vertue, [2]beawtie, and [3]speach, did [1]strike, [2]wound, [3]charme,
> My [1]harte, [2]eyes, [3]eares, with [1]wonder, [2]love, [3]delight:
> [1]First, [2]second, [3]last, did [1]binde, [2]enforce, and [3]arme,
> His [1]workes, [2]showes, [3]suites, with [1]wit, [2]grace, and vow's [3]might.
> (*Works*, II, 53)

It is unnecessary to reprint the remaining lines to see that one must read by the numbers: "Vertue . . . did strike . . . my harte . . . with wonder," and so on. The piece only just deserves the name of poetry, but apart from its slight artistic value, it manages to make sense. We may note further that each line is split almost exactly in half by the series of words, and this pattern extends through all fourteen lines. The result is monotonous symmetry indulged in for its own sake.

Sidney is never again so frivolous, but there are other poems in the ***Arcadia*** whose verbal tactics are quite as intricate. Consider, for example, the cluster of four poems near the beginning of Book 3. Each poem attempts to maintain one, two, or at the most three, rime sounds. One of the sonnets, "Since that the stormy rage of passions darcke," alternates "dark" and "light" as the rime words (a fairly common experiment).[3] The poem is not distinguished, but the necessity of maintaining the rime pushes Sidney to alter the sense of the two central images in repetition. There are also additional evidences of strong rhythmical pattern. Each quatrain is syntactically like the others, beginning with "since" and encompassing a subordinate clause, and, as in the last six lines, there is a profusion of word repetition:

> Since, as I say, both minde and sences darke
> Are hurt, not helpt, with piercing of the light:
> While that the light may shewe the horrors darke
> But cannot make resolved darkenes lighte:
> I like this place, whereat the least the darke
> May keepe my thoughtes, from thought of wonted light.
> (***Works***, II, 8)

Another sonnet in the group has only one rime sound, and most of the lines contribute heavy alliteration and strong rhythmical balance to the already obvious pattern:

> My mangled mind huge horrors still doe fright,
> With sense possest, and claim'd by reasons right:
> Betwixt which two in me I have this fight,
> Wher who so wynns, I put my selfe to flight.
> (***Works***, II, 9)

This may remind us of Dr. Johnson's remark about a woman's preaching, but the foremost organizing principle of these experiments deserves attention: they show an obvious, insistent pattern duplicated through several elements in the rhythm, as if Sidney's aim were to make all the resources of sound cooperate for a single balanced effect.

Exploring pattern in the same spirit but on a larger, more intricate scale, Sidney included two sestinas and a double sestina in the ***Arcadia***. The latter, **"You Gote-heard Gods,"** transcends technical exercise and will concern us in another context.[4] The sestinas, on the other hand, are a degree less ingenious and infinitely less accomplished. Their line-endings, which according to formula must not only be repeated but must also have a different order in each successive stanza, are all polysyllabic words concluding with a weak syllable, and Sidney takes pains to spread the monotonous, incessant beat by other means as well:

> Since wayling is a bud of causefull sorowe,
> Since sorow is the follower of evill fortune,
> Since no evill fortune equalls publique damage:
> Now Princes losse hath made our damage publique,
> Sorow, pay we to thee the rights of Nature,
> And inward griefe seale up with outward wailing.
>
> (***Works***, II, 138)

The list of the devices here is impressive. The first three lines commence with the same word (the rhetorical figure is anaphora)[5] and a periodic effect is managed through a carefully planned ordering of nouns, "wayling," "sorowe," "evill fortune," and "publique damage." In the next three lines these are arranged in reverse order. Further, the stanza is heavy with alliteration, assonance, consonance, and antithesis. The total effect is to highlight a strong rhythmical beat whose variations are muted. Needless to say, the discourse is obscure, but not through any great difficulty in the thought.

These examples outline the general directions of Sidney's experimental impulse. The tendency to hunt verbal ornament at the expense of other goals is plain, and so is the tendency for ornament to assume a more or less geometrical, balanced, and repeated shape. But whatever the deficiencies of such efforts, they are not eccentric for their times. Puttenham, in the remarks that follow, is merely the spokesman for much of the poetic bias of his age:

> Then also must the whole tale (if it tende to perswasion) beare his iust and reasonable measure, being rather with the largest than with the scarcest. . . . Sweetenes of speech, sentence, and amplification, are therefore necessarie to an excellent Orator and Poet, ne may in no wise be spared from any of them.[6]

The notion of the poet as orator leads naturally to the view that for both of them the best expression is the "largest" and implies that an idea must have full and measured verbal clothing "if it tende to perswasion." Puttenham is simply echoing one of the more common biases of his times, and those who held to this opinion—Ascham was one of the most influential[7]—helped to point a large portion of English lyric, as well as prose, style towards a heightened embellishment. If one examines the verse of Spenser, of the miscellanies, and of the sonnet sequences of the nineties, it is clear that one of its more persistent characteristics is the extreme exploitation of the audible patterns of language. The impulse seems to be to give lyric a clear and balanced rhythmical shape beyond the requirements of imitation, and this impulse has some importance when we consider the attempts of a variety of poets—Dyer, Campion, Sidney, to name a few—to impose classical rhythms on English verse.

Quite recently John Buxton has written that Sidney's exclusive motive for classical experiments was to fit verse to the requirements of musical notation. He cites a passage from the ***Arcadia***[8] which does not appear in any of its printed versions and comments: "Because of the quantitative effect of music when sung . . . Sidney, like de Baïf and his friends, thought it desirable to experiment with quantitative scansion on the Greek and Latin models."[9] Such experiments had been fashionable in France for some time. Du Bellay, Ronsard, and all the poets of the Pléiade had interested themselves in the musical performance of poetry, and Baïf in his *Académie de poésie et de musique* (1570) proposed detailed efforts to emulate in the vernacular the ancient identity of verse and music.[10] He and his colleagues toiled over quantitative verse to which musical notes could be adapted to match the metrical duration of the syllables. In England Campion was the most enthusiastic follower of this program, but as Catherine Ing demonstrates, he was successful only once.[11] There can be no doubt that Sidney was familiar with the French experiments or that he was aware of the widespread opinion that quantity was the common ground between the two arts of poetry and music. In the passage cited by Buxton[12] (a debate between two shepherds, Dicus and Lalus, as to the relative merits of "measured" and riming verse), Dicus, the exponent of quantitative verse, notes that words correspond to the "sounde" of music and measure to its "qualitie" in order that "for every sembref or minam it had his silable matched unto it, with a long foote or a short foote." The terminology is less than exact, but it is probable that "quality" means musical duration and "measure" syllabic duration, while the various components of the sound of words, volume, pitch, and pronunciation find their counterparts in melody and musical pitch. (Verse as read cannot imitate musical harmony; as sung by several voices it can, but this gets beyond the strictly rhythmic elements of language.) Unfortunately these remarks are not very illuminating. We cannot say that Dicus reflects Sidney's own views; the passage merely repeats a commonplace argument over the merits of two kinds of verse. Nor is it simply a question of assuming that when he wrote quantitative verse Sidney was largely concerned with exploring the musical properties of language. A good deal of his accentual verse is loosely designated as song. Nor is Sidney particular about what kind of music quantitative verse is especially adapted to. These uncertainties merely echo the general confusion of the age in its talk about the relations between poetry and music.[13]

Furthermore, the poems which Sidney wrote in imitation of classical forms are varied.[14] Two are in hexameters and are printed without any indication of the kind of music to be used in their performance. The same is true of his three Sapphics, and a song in the Aristophanic measure. In the absence of precise evidence one is at a loss to discuss their "musical" properties or propriety in any significant way. The same difficulty exists even when one attempts to evaluate their quantitative merits, for it is virtually impossible for an ear accustomed to the strong accentual basis of English rhythm to appreciate the duration of sound from syllable to syllable. We can roughly measure the relative duration of successive lines, but within the line we simply cannot eliminate the interference of speech stress. The only recourse is to see if the arrangement of stresses approximates the formal classical patterns.[15]

As an example the Sapphic concentrates on a form in which the rhythmical structure within the line is unbalanced, but the lines must, with minor variations, match each other, and the fourth line is always short.

— U — — — U U — U — —
— U — — — U U — U — —
— U — — — U U — U — —
— U U — —

Here is a stanza from one of Sidney's Sapphics:

If mine eyes can speake to doo harty errande,
Or mine eyes language she doo hap to judge of,
So that eyes message be of her receaved,
Hope we do live yet.

(***Works***, I, 143)

Accentually, as well as quantitatively, the rhythm is almost impossible in the initial trochees if we try to make them adjust to the conventional pattern. Furthermore, the spelling of "doo" (perhaps not Sidney's responsibility, but it is the same in the version from the old ***Arcadia***) when it should be a short or weak syllable is misleading, and it is scarcely easy to give the syllables of "errande," "judge of," or "receaved" equal duration or stress. Read aloud so as to fit the Sapphic pattern, the lines would be eccentric indeed.

Yet Sidney has attempted some sort of order in the poem. For one thing, the short fourth line constitutes a varied refrain throughout. Another, and more important, device is rhetorical repetition. "Eyes" occupies the same position through three successive lines. And the first three lines have feminine endings. Thus, if Sidney has failed to produce an imitation of a perfect Sapphic, he has at least given his piece a certain rhythmical order. What emerges is verse with a very heavy beat, with at least five strong stresses to each long line and three to the short (here the classical pattern is successfully imitated). Furthermore, the stresses tend to emphasize the first half of each line, giving the latter half a falling rhythm. Prominence is given the expressive properties of the eyes, and they prepare rhythmically for the assertive weight of "Hope we do live yet."

Thus, whatever Sidney's intentions may have been (and, to repeat, we cannot be certain of these), there emerges a kind of symmetry encompassing the stanza, not the individual line, and it is a symmetry largely managed by standard rhetorical maneuver. If anything, Sidney overdoes the strong beat, and the same difficulty mars his two hexameter poems, "Faire rocks, goodly rivers, sweet woods, when shall I see peace?" and "Lady reservd by the heav'ns to do pastors company honnor" (***Works***, I, 352; II, 208). The longer line and the general subjects of these pieces make them potentially more serious efforts. The first resolves itself into a lengthy lover's complaint which proceeds from point to point by means of an echo which twists the speaker's words by punning on them and continually turning his melancholy, idealistic worship of his mistress into a reproach of moral weakness. The echo device not only gives the verses a form of continuity, but also provides the major portion of whatever shape they have. And, since few of the lines seem to be true hexameters, Sidney once again depends upon the resources of formal rhetoric, this time to give the lines some internal organization in the midst of a general prosiness:

O I doo know what guest I doo meete: it is *Echo*.
T'is *Echo*.
Well mett *Echo*; aproch, and tell me thy will too.
I will too.

(***Works***, I, 352)

The intent is to produce dialogue in which the speaker has the largest share and Echo the smallest, and the quality of the discourse hovers between the accents of casual speech and the monotonous regularity of the echo device. The concluding lines will serve to illustrate:

Mockst thou those Diamonds, which onely be matcht by
the Godds? Odds.
Odds? what an odds is there, since them to the heav'ns I
preferre? Erre.
Tell yet againe, how name ye the goodly made evill?
A devill.
Devill? in hell where such Devill is, to that hell I doo
goe. Goe.

(***Works***, I, 353)

The word repetition here differs from other examples we have seen in that it does not always serve to balance the line. In the second line above Sidney uses internal rime for balance, but it is offset by the strong pause after "Odds." Whatever consistency there is stems from the echo device and from the generally strong stress with which the lines begin. We discover, then, an experiment in which Sidney seems hesitant to embrace the consequences of fully casual discourse and seeks a corrective, however slight, not so much in the forms of classical metrics as in the repetitive properties of formal rhetoric.

The second hexameter poem, **"Lady reservd by the heav'ns to do pastors company honnor,"** is equally committed to a discursive procedure and moves even farther in its dependence on oratorical devices. Zelmane, one of the two speakers (the poem is formally termed an eclogue), emphasizes devotion to his mistress in lines approaching the hyperbole of euphuism:

First shall fertill grounds not yeeld increase of a good seed:
First the rivers shall ceasse to repay their fludds to the *Occean*:
First may a trusty Greyhounde transforme himselfe to a Tigre:
First shall vertue be vice, and bewty be counted a blemishe,
Ere that I leave with song of praise her praise to solemnize,
Her praise, whence to the world all praise hath his only beginning.

(***Works***, II, 210)

We are here brought back to Puttenham's "sweetenes of speech, sentence, and amplification" as the order of poetry, and these are not reached by anything native to the classical hexameter. The noticeable rhythm of the lines—and a rhythmical principle at various levels is the most obvious motive for these experiments—may be traced directly to Sidney's familiarity with the mechanics of formal rhetoric: in this case, repetition within the line and through a group of lines, antithesis, and the period. Simply as attempts to get a kind of "music" out of the relative duration of syllables, these pieces are meager accomplishments; as instances of a search for the means to adjust heightened rhythmical patterns to various levels of discourse they hold more interest.

The most successful of the classical poems is the song, "When to my deadlie pleasure" (***Certaine Sonets***), composed in the Aristophanic measure (—U U — U— —). Once again the rhythmical structure owes less to the classical form of the line than it does to rhetoric, but for once Sidney is able to produce verses in which the stresses usually coincide with the formal metrical pattern of the type:

With violence of heav'nly
Beautie tied, to vertue,
Reason abasht retyred,
Gladly my senses yeelded.[16]

The conflict in the first line (*vi-* must have a stress) may be deliberate; at least it effectively stresses an important word. And the extraordinary number of polysyllables crammed into so limited a space produces a strong insistent beat which gains interest from the feminine endings. As in the Sapphics, the effect is to enhance the importance of the early syllables in the line stressing the clipped quality of the short, blunt statements. But at the end of the poem Sidney reverts to the pattern of rhetorical monotony and overstatement:

Thus may I not be from you:
Thus be my senses on you:
Thus what I thinke is of you:
Thus what I seeke is in you:
All what I am, it is you.

If the classical experiments remain formally uncertain, what can we say of their "musical" qualities? I would suggest that their "music" is not traceable to quantity any more than others of Sidney's poems are. The song above would be apt for performance by reason of its concentrated and continuous tempo, its symmetry of repetitious structure, and these are qualities we can discover again and again in short poems or songs which make no attempt to duplicate classical forms. Even in the perspective of burlesque Sidney's strategy is clear; it is merely heightened by the alliterative and assonantal symmetry of an "illnoysed song":

A Hatefull cure with hate to heale:
A blooddy helpe with blood to save:
A foolish thing with fooles to deale:
Let him be bold that bobs will have.

(***Works***, I, 325)

A fitting complement to this extreme example of shaped and symmetrical rhythm is the *Lady of May* poems, which otherwise deserve little comment. There are three songs placed in a brief pastoral narrative, and they are probably Sidney's earliest surviving lyrics. Balanced and obvious repetition is their most prominent, indeed almost their only, distinguishing characteristic. The first, entitled **"Supplication,"** is addressed to the Queen, and will stand for the others:

To one whose state is raised over all,
Whose face doth oft the bravest sort enchaunt,
Whose mind is such, as wisest minds appall,
Who in one selfe these diverse gifts can plant;
How dare I wretch seeke there my woes to rest,
Where eares be burnt, eyes dazled, harts opprest?

Your state is great, your greatnesse is our shield,
Your face hurts oft, but still it doth delight,
Your mind is wise, your wisedome makes you mild,
Such planted gifts enrich even beggers sight:
So dare I wretch, my bashfull feare subdue,
And feede mine eares, mine eyes, my hart in you.

(***Works***, II, 330)

The awkward mixed metaphors, stale diction, and unrelieved metrical regularity betray Sidney's apprenticeship, but the fulsome enumeration of the details of praise and deliberate word repetition in a balanced line and through series of lines are typical of his later work.

Like these early pieces, Sidney's translations of the ***Psalms*** concentrate chiefly on verbal formality as a means of fixing the structure of the poem. Differences of opinion over the dating of the translations and Sidney's lack of choice of subject matter make them awkward to criticize. The act of translation is a species of submission. Sidney used the task to try his hand at a variety of verse forms, though no doubt his devotional interests were equally engaged. In any case, they reveal both his strengths and weaknesses as a technician and demonstrate the continuity of the particular kind of ornament to which he clings in most of the ***Arcadia*** verse.

For Theodore Spencer the ***Psalms*** show Sidney able to join extreme simplicity of diction and a clear metrical beat.[17] The observation is undeniable, for he preserves both elements through all the different line lengths and stanza forms he attempts. But at the same time he holds to his familiar strategy of a discourse primarily ordered by stylized rhetoric, and founded in the addition of like details to one another. Occasionally the more obvious rhetorical devices give way to a free concentration on stanzaic pattern and definite, even excessive, riming effects. In any case, Sidney's impulse is toward equivalence, and the total effect of the translations is seldom that of artlessness.

Much like the ***Arcadia*** poems, the variety in Sidney's version of the ***Psalms*** is in line and stanza form. Most often he uses a short line, tetrameter, trimeter, or occasionally dimeter. No single poem employs a two-beat line exclusively. A few are in rime-royal and terza rima, one or two in alexandrines, and all are iambic. Many of the poems have different line lengths set in a regular pattern of variation. Nevertheless, Spencer's remarks on the diction and rhythm and the tendency to stylistic symmetry point to an underlying consistency of esthetic purpose.

One reason for concluding that the ***Psalms*** chiefly interested Sidney as exercises in technique is his failure to suit formal variety to the specific content and mood of the individual pieces. Such adaptations would still be possible had he used one or two forms only through the entire forty-three poems he translated. On grounds of their content alone there seems to be little excuse for the switch from a six-line stanza with a seven-syllable line in Psalm XVI to a four-line stanza with couplets of ten and eight syllables in Psalm XVII. Both poems, pleas for security and justice, are very much alike. Furthermore, Sidney frequently struggles to maintain line length and rime with dubious success, as in

> Thy work it is such men safe in to hemm.
>
> (Psalm V, st. vii, l. 7)

The verses are also full of inversions, in spite of the obvious pursuit of simple, homely statement:

> Arise, ô Lord, in wrath thy self up sett.
>
> (Psalm VII, st. 6, l. 1)

At least once an insistent stanzaic pattern becomes a serious obstacle. There is an important change in the direction of thought in the following stanza, yet nothing in the meter or arrangement of the lines cooperates with this shift:

> Even multitudes be they
> That to my Soul do say
> No help for you remaineth
> In God on whom you build
> Yet Lord thou art my shield
> In thee my glory raigneth.
>
> (Psalm III, st. 2)

The text lacks punctuation, but even if it did not, the total effect of the last three lines would be blurred, a muting of the contrast the Psalmist makes between the remarks of his enemies and his devotion to the Lord.

Elsewhere Sidney manages to confine sentence units strictly within stanzas or regular portions of stanzas. Even with allowances for a printer's alteration of text, the ***Psalms*** are ordinarily broken up into units containing entire statements: each stanza tends to be a complete and self-contained sentence. Such neatness also characterizes the sonnets in ***Astrophel and Stella***, but the sequence is far more sophisticated in letting its style translate finer shadings of thought and emotion. Exactness in fitting the discourse to a preconceived lyric pattern appears to be one of the major experimental aims of the ***Psalms***. Their identity with the sequence cannot be pursued too far.

In the realm of meter Sidney demonstrates a varying ability. Only one Psalm is completely regular (Psalm VIII), but in others the amount and purpose of the metrical variations fluctuates. In Psalm V the variations approach 25 per cent (nine variants in forty lines). Psalm VI has almost as high an incidence of irregularity (seven inversions in thirty-two lines), and here Sidney uses irregularity to good, if simple, effect. Compare the fifth and seventh stanzas:

> Loe I am tir'd while still I sigh and grone:
> My moistned bed proofes of my sorrow showeth:
> My bed (while I with black night moorn alone)
> With my teares floweth . . .
> Gett hence you evill, who in my ill rejoice,
> In all whose works vainenesse is ever raigning:
> For God hath heard the weeping sobbing voice
> Of my complayning.

The fifth stanza is not entirely regular: there is a possible first-foot trochee in line one, and the third foot of line two is certainly inverted by the trochaic phrase. But the variations in the seventh stanza are far more strategic. "Evill" may or may not be elided; if not it syncopates the line. "Who in" is trochaic, and in the following line "vainenesse" and "raigning" intensify the suggestion of falling rhythm, which contrasts with and prepares for the triumphant, regular beat of "For God hath heard the weeping sobbing voice."

In a sense, this use of variation (it epitomizes Sidney's best results throughout the translations) is oratorical. It is a formal strategy, altering the rhythm not for colloquial effect, but to heighten the persuasiveness of shifts in meaning or alterations in tone. There is little attempt to imitate the fluctuations of spontaneous mental and emotional responses. Occasions where such a texture might be fashioned are rendered with deliberate formality:

Then thinck I: Ah, what is this man:
    Whom that greate God remember can?
    And what the race of him descended,
    It should be ought of God attended.

(Psalm VIII, st. 4)

This level of ordered discourse is consistent with the character of the Psalms as rather stately expressions of man's relations with the Lord.

Another way in which Sidney relieves the strictness of his rhythms is occasional enjambment. In Psalm XVI it approaches the status of a consistent rule. At least it helps to soften the sing-song effect of the poem:

For I know the deadly grave
  On my soule noe pow'r shall have:
  For I know thou wilt defend
  Even the body of thine own
  Deare beloved holy one,
  From a fowle corrupting end.

These instances of departure from a strong, rather monotonous pattern are in no way remarkable in themselves. They are, perhaps, a reminder that Sidney is not committed merely to getting his accents and syllables in order, although this is clearly one of the main tasks of the translations.

Formally and in other ways the ***Psalms*** appear more primitive than the general run of poems in the ***Arcadia***. As I have suggested, some of this difference stems from the frequently inept inversions, the excessive use of intensive verbs (adding "do" to the main verb is a distinct mannerism through all the poems), and a greater use of the short line with strong rimes. Formal rhetoric is less consistent in the ***Psalms*** than in the ***Arcadia*** poems, but when it does appear, Sidney, like an orator, uses it for a full and balanced pattern of emphasis. If the ***Psalms*** are not always to be identified by their symmetry, they are often capable of it. In Psalm XXII, which Sidney makes an echo of the tormented outcry of Christ on the cross, the opening stresses heavy word repetition in a balanced rhythmical frame:

My God, my God, why hast thou me forsaken?
  Wo me, from me, why is thy presence taken?
  Soe farre from seeing, mine unhealthful eyes:
  So farre from hearing to my roaring cries.

O God, my God, I crie while day appeareth:
  But God thy eare, my cryeng never heareth.
  O God the night, is privie to my plaint
  Yet to my plaint, thou hast no audience lent.

One of the most important things about such a style is the deliberate way in which it simplifies the elements of discourse. "God," "me," "seeing," "hearing," and their surrogate images occupy the prominent places in each line and are balanced in pairs. The verse focuses rhythmically and steadily on the motifs and simple emotions suggested by these terms and by their positions. They swirl around in a circle more intensely heightened as the word repetition and rhythmical pattern continue. The nature of the ***Psalms*** allows Sidney to go a certain distance with this style, but he does not have the freedom he enjoys in compositions entirely his own. In the latter, especially in the ***Arcadia*** and the ***Certaine Sonets***, he is able to work with fully shaped poems. We have studied some examples of the most "experimental" (and perhaps the most tentative) of these, but, as I have suggested, the term may lose its value if it is used to describe all the pieces in which Sidney works with prominent and symmetrical orders of rhythm and rhetoric. In his songs we must begin to take Sidney more seriously because as we study them we shall begin to see that the formal symmetries he employs are not completely autonomous, although they may be redundant. In other words we shall begin to look at poems whose structures make sense in other terms, whose interest is not merely in the fulfillment of a technical plan.[18]

The songs discussed below are arranged in an order of increasing sophistication in their rhythm. No definite arrangement according to date of composition is feasible, although it may be that the best of them—those from the miscellaneous collection, ***Certaine Sonets***—postdate the others. Generally Sidney is most impressive in songs using a varied line length, although some of his finest work appears in the songs in ***Astrophel and Stella***, most of which are entirely regular. The majority of the ***Arcadia*** songs have a single line length and are patterned in restrictive, simple ways, much as the translations of the ***Psalms***. But unlike the ***Psalms*** their rhythms are not so severely conditioned by the chosen stanza form or an obvious attempt to master consistency of meter. One of the simplest of these reduces its subject to a series of easy contrasts in a line that appears rigidly balanced:

Wyth two strange fires of equall heate possest,
The one of Love, the other Jealousie,
Both still do worke, in neither finde I rest:
For both, alas, their strengthes together tie:
The one aloft doth holde, the other hie.
  Love wakes the jealous eye least thence it moves:
  The jealous eye, the more it lookes, it loves.

These fires increase: in these I dayly burne:
They feede on me, and with my wings do flie:
My lovely joyes to dolefull ashes turne:
Their flames mount up, my powers prostrate lie:
They live in force, I quite consumed die.
  One wonder yet farre passeth my conceate:
  The fuell small: how be the fires so great?

(***Works***, I, 310)

It is clear that the line, not the stanza, organizes the rhythm and provides a context for the pairs of opposing elements: love and jealousy, the fires and the self. In this fashion the poem moves forward, satisfying the order of contrast simply by repeating it, and the final couplet of the second stanza—in which Sidney attempts surprise by turning from what the speaker knows and can assert as fact to an unsolved paradox—fails to match the change in sense. Sidney preserves a regular meter when a departure might be in order. The usual cultivation of intensity through repetition outruns its usefulness.

Two brief songs, **"Get hence foule Griefe, the canker of the minde"** (***Works***, II, 50) and **"The love which is imprinted in my soule,"** (***Works***, II, 55) are fashioned around a few key words or personifications. Here again the tendencies of the rhythm and subject matter coincide in evenly shaped discourse. The first disposes such items as grief, complaint, cares, sighs, tears, thought, and hope in the grammar of imperatives, and moves forward by an obvious plan:

> Get hence foule Griefe, the canker of the minde:
> Farewell Complaint, the misers only pleasure:
> Away vayne Cares, by which few men do finde
> Their sought-for treasure.
> Ye helplesse Sighes, blowe out your breath to nought,
> Teares, drowne your selves, for woe (your cause) is wasted,
> Thought, thinke to ende, too long the frute of thought
> My minde hath tasted.

The last two stanzas complement these by welcoming the images of complaint transformed into joy. As before Sidney's chief concern is to fit his subject to a measurable pattern, to see it and express it in the geometry of completed form, although the rhythm has its judicious departures in slightly altered pauses and an inversion or two, and his habit of alternating feminine and masculine rimes (one of his more persistent devices in short lyrics) makes a pattern of light contrast between successive lines. There is even a kind of animation to the song, a vitality lacking in the translations of the ***Psalms*** and other labored exercises.

Of the longer "musical" pieces, the sestinas, a hymn or two, and some forcefully cadenced pastoral singing contests, as well as the songs in ***Astrophel and Stella***, something will be said in later chapters. On the level of rhythm these display the same impulses we are discussing here. And if we are to judge by these, Sidney's effort to produce the rounded, obtrusive lyric structure is plain. The ornament of the poem appears to be both skeleton and flesh. Order of all kinds, of syntax, rhythm, image, coincides on one level of symmetrical proportions, and in this respect Sidney's verse is the climax of a generation of poetic endeavor to control the tempo and the contours of lyric expression and to seek intensity through repetition and overstatement. *Tottel's Miscellany* is early evidence of these directions (one slipshod poem uses anaphora through thirty lines[19]), and the verse of Googe and Gascoigne,[20] different in other ways and often simple and direct, is nevertheless committed to severely shaped and amplified style. Judged by his lesser work Sidney has merely succeeded in polishing the devices of his forerunners.

But even in his songs he occasionally reaches a more sophisticated concept of structure. One or two of these, in ***Certaine Sonets***, are among the best the Elizabethans could produce and may serve to demonstrate what can be accomplished within the restrictions of verse produced to be sung, verse ostensibly committed to heavy verbal ornament. In these songs the subject remains simple, intellectually undeveloped, but the centers of interest are not therefore wholly in ornament. The framework of **"Ring out your belles,** let mourning shewes be spread" severely limits the range of the discourse, but the structure is subtly and quietly varied:

> Ring out your belles, let mourning shewes be spread,
> For love is dead:
> All Love is dead, infected
> With plague of deepe disdaine:
> Worth as nought worth rejected,
> And Faith faire scorne doth gaine.
> From so ungratefull fancie,
> From such a femall franzie,
> From them that use men thus,
> Good Lorde deliver us.
>
> (***Certaine Sonets***)

The form is the same through all four stanzas, with the final quatrain serving as a refrain. Bruce Pattison's remarks about the influence of musical considerations on the poet surely apply here, for the refrain, the obvious narrowness of the idea, the easy and graceful alliteration, all maintain the steady incantatory rhythm needed for the litany.[21] These qualities are familiar in poems whose sole task seems to be to present proportionate, repeated, and predictable form. But in other ways **"Ring out your belles"** is neither commonplace nor banal.

It has both local and extended balance: the meter of each line varies internally, but the pattern of one line may be repeated in another. Although lines one and two differ radically, their forms are repeated at the opening of the succeeding stanzas. But the variations are still important. They offer us hints of what Sidney was able to accomplish on a more extended and versatile scale in the sonnets, and they demonstrate his ability to use rhythmic form, however lightly, to beckon our attention away from its self-contained, circular, balanced shape even as it retains these qualities.

The first line itself is a warning that Sidney has modified his rather strained devotion to the neatly balanced line. The opening phrase, "Ring out your belles," probably calls for four strong, nearly equal stresses, although it might be construed as iambic, in which case there would be a sharp conflict between meter and spoken stress. The remainder of the line is more surely iambic. This colliding rhythm gives way to two simple iambs in the short second line, while the third line adds a foot and an initial spondee (or hovering accent: "love" demands more emphasis than the ordinary weak syllable by virtue of its position equivalent to "love" in the line before). What Sidney manages here is the apparently effortless task of a slight but very important shift in speech emphasis in two lines which superficially amount to nothing more than a commonplace rhetorical recurrence. In the fourth line Sidney reverts to consistent iambic structure, but the fifth opens with a trochee, possibly two, and has a weak final syllable. Probably the sixth line should be scanned iambically, but "faire" needs a strong spoken stress. This group of lines, regarded in isolation, is not only radically irregular in meter, but the irregularities are deliberate and effective. It is obvious that the verse aims at facilitating musical performance through its use of heavy stress, announcing to composer, musician, and vocalist alike the areas where their emphases should fall. Less obvious, perhaps, is the particular suitability of this small group of lines for reading aloud, for exclusively poetic performance. In the experiments we have considered previously Sidney's concern for the performing voice is always self-consciously oratorical, always intent on satisfying a concept of verbal shape, to which other matters may be sacrificed. In **"Ring out your belles"** we still have a strong and unmistakable verbal shape built on a principle of recurrence, but we have as well a metrical and vocal rhythm following the demands of *changing* emphasis in mood and subject matter.

The first line is emotionally strong, mingling insistence with mournfulness, after which the blunt statement of the second line is almost shocking; the change of rhythms is appropriate to the shift, as is the extreme contrast between the long and short lines. With the third line the emotion gets a second breath and proceeds to elaborate the discovery that love is dead; the second line had uttered this discovery with deceptive finality. The accent on "All" is necessary for the recovery of strength which is not fully apparent until we know that this line not only is longer than its predecessor but leads to enjambment as well. Emphasis in the fourth line comes through a different medium, the alliterated phrase "deepe disdaine," while in the fifth line the repetition of "worth" and the surprising accents offer still another approach. In the sixth line Sidney uses rhythmical counterpoint, alliteration, and assonance to assist the change to irony. Finally, the refrain, set off from the rest by heightened repetition (anaphora), has three rhythmically equivalent lines. A differently keyed emotion, approaching the litany, needs to be preserved unchanged, whereas the first six lines call for an accompaniment to subtle changes in feeling.

In moving from Sidney's merely "experimental" verse to such a poem as this, we move from poetry with all the signs of technical struggle and obvious effects to poetry which he is able to control on his own terms, but we do not change from ornamented to plain discourse. The emotion of **"Ring out your belles"** is public, formal, and impersonal. Its voice is flexible but scarcely spontaneous, even in appearance. Nor, it should be repeated, have we necessarily encountered an older or more practiced Sidney: we can only conclude that moments of ingenuity occasionally yield to fully conceived and executed poems. **"Ring out your belles"** may be of late composition, but it is probably no later than several others founded in rather clear and rigid structural proportion. We must remember, too, that in spite of the delicate rhythmical modifications in this song, it is like its less accomplished companion pieces in keeping to a strong, monotonous, overemphatic beat, which elsewhere Sidney employs with less discrimination. He is still rendering experience ceremonially, even effusively; and he conceives and executes it in terms of a symmetry which stamps almost all his verse except ***Astrophel and Stella***.

Notes

1. "The Poetry of Sir Philip Sidney," *ELH*, XII (1945), 251–278.
2. Ringler's findings are as yet unpublished, but he informs me that he dates the poems in *The Lady of May* in 1578; the "old" *Arcadia* poems, from late 1577 to late 1580, with all completed by the latter date except for a few revisions as late as 1584. He has "very strong evidence" for placing the composition of *Astrophel and Stella* in the summer of 1582. The ornateness of *The Lady of May* verses would suggest that Sidney's earlier verse is in that kind of style, but there is nothing to indicate that he abandoned it when he had reached a plainer, more perspicuous expression.
3. See also *Astrophel and Stella*, Sonnet 89. Janet G. [Espiner-] Scott, *Les sonnets élisabéthains,* pp. 40–41, cites R. Fiorentino's "Deh non ritorni à rimenarne il giorno" as an example of the type.
4. See below, Chap. 3, pp. 44–47.
5. Definitions of rhetorical figures are supplied in Appendix A.
6. *The Arte of English Poesie*, pp. 197–198.
7. "Of Imitation," *Elizabethan Critical Essays*, ed. G. Gregory Smith (London, 1904), I, 6.
8. The passage comes after the first eclogues; see *Works*, IV, 86. Buxton follows R. W. Zandvoort's inaccurate version (*Sidney's Arcadia, A Comparison of the Two Versions* [Amsterdam, 1929], pp. 11–12) which is drawn from the Queens College MS. of the *Arcadia*. Ringler's version is superior. See below, note 13.
9. *Sir Philip Sidney and the English Renaissance* (London, 1954), p. 116.
10. Frances A. Yates, *The French Academies of the Sixteenth Century* (London, 1947), pp. 36–42, provides a useful summary of this development. See her Appendix VIII for examples of the *vers mesurés* produced at Baïf's academy.
11. *Elizabethan Lyrics* (London, 1951), p. 117–118.
12. My excerpts are from the version printed by William Ringler from the St. John's College, Cambridge, MS. 308 (f. 40^{v}), *PQ*, XXIX (1950), p. 72.
13. See John Hollander, "The Music of Poetry," *Journal of Aesthetics and Art Criticism*, XV (1956), 232–244.
14. James Applegate, "Sidney's Classical Meters," *MLN*, LXX (1955), 254–255, provides the following list:

Hexameters: "Lady reservd by the heav'ns to do pastors company honnor" (*Works*, II, 208; IV, 77).

"Faire rocks, goodly rivers, sweet woods, when shall I see peace? Peace" (I, 352; IV, 152).

Elegiac distichs: "Faire seeke not to be feard, most lovely beloved by thy servants" (IV, 307; *Certaine Sonets*).

"Fortune, Nature, Love, long have contended about me" (II, 208; IV, 75).

"Unto a caitife wretch, whom long affliction holdeth" (I, 357; IV, 318).

"Unto no body my woman saith she had rather a wife be" (II, 307; *Certaine Sonets*).

Sapphics: "If mine eyes can speake to doo harty errande" (I, 143).

"O my thoughtes, sweete foode my onely owner" (IV, 401). This is a rimed sapphic.

"Get hence foule griefe, the canker of the minde" (II, 50; IV, 214). Also a rimed sapphic.

Phalacean hendecasyllable: "Reason, tell me thy mind, if here be reason" (II, 236; IV, 156).

Asclepiadean: "O sweet woods the delight of solitarines" (II, 237; IV, 157).

Aristophanic: "When to my deadlie pleasure" (II, 316; *Certaine Sonets*).

Anacreontic: "My muse what ail's this ardour" (II, 234; IV, 155).

15. An authoritative discussion of the theory behind these experiments is Gladys D. Willcock's "Passing Pitefull Hexameters," *MLR*, XXIX (1934), 1–19. She treats them as a serious and important effort to solve "the question of the interior structure of the line" (p. 1). As she remarks, there was much confusion before Puttenham (1589) because stress was not understood (although Sidney in the *Defence* [*Works*, III, 44] recognizes stress as fundamental to English rhythm), and she concludes that "when Elizabethans of this calibre [the allusion is to Webbe], and even of far better, talk about quantity and so on, they are speaking of something visible rather than audible" (p. 12). Yet Campion, when he attempted to adjust musical notation to the supposed quantity of the syllables in a poem, surely had audible duration in mind. See above note 12.

16. The horizontal dashes indicate quantitative pattern, the slanting lines, stress.

17. "The Poetry of Sir Philip Sidney," *ELH*, XII (1945), 254–255.

18. For a partial list of Sidney's songs which were given musical settings see Edmund H. Fellowes, *English Madrigal Verse, 1588–1632*, 2nd ed. (Oxford, 1947), index.

19. *Tottel's Miscellany*, No. 251; ed. Hyder E. Rollins, 2 vols. (Cambridge, Massachusetts, 1928), I, 196.

20. The most extreme example from Googe is "The oftener sene, the more I lust," *Eglogs, Epytaphes, & Sonettes* (1563), ed. Edward Arber (London, 1871), p. 96. Gascoigne's "The Steele Glasse" makes liberal use of the device.

21. *Music and Poetry of the English Renaissance* (London, 1948), p. 141 and esp. pp. 150–155.

S. K. Orgel (essay date 1963)

SOURCE: "Sidney's Experiment in Pastoral: *The Lady of May*," in *Essential Articles for the Study of Sir Philip Sidney*, Archon Books, 1986, pp. 61–71.

[*In the following essay, Orgel finds that Sidney's mixed-mode court masque about the contemplative life,* The Lady of May, *provides us with a "brief and excellent example of the way his mind worked."*]

Sidney's *The Lady of May* has gone largely unnoticed since its inclusion—apparently at the last moment, and in the interests of completeness—in the 1598 folio of his works. It had been commissioned by Leicester as an entertainment for Queen Elizabeth, and was presented before her at Wanstead, probably in 1578. It merits attention on a number of grounds, not the least of which is its obvious interest as a dramatic piece by the author of ***Arcadia*** and ***Astrophel and Stella***. It is characteristic of Sidney in its treatment of literary convention, its concern with examining and reassessing the underlying assumptions of pastoral; in the unique way, in short, that its creator thinks about literature. Every new form posed a set of new problems for Sidney: although he employed conventional modes, he took nothing for granted, and *The Lady of May* provides us with a brief and excellent example of the way his mind worked. In this entertainment, Sidney used the monarch in a functional way in the action of his drama. This device, which had been the central characteristic of the English court masque after 1513,[1] serves to define the genre even more than the formal dances, which were often but not inevitably present. Sidney, as usual, adds a new depth to the old device, but his use of it at all in such a context links him with Jonson and the Milton of *Comus* in treating the masque as primarily a literary form. The work has an additional point of interest which has also gone unnoticed for almost four centuries. It provides us, as we shall see, with an account of what must have been for Sidney and a few other alert observers (among whom no subsequent commentator may be numbered), a surprising fiasco.

> "Her most excellent Majestie walking in Wansteed Garden, as she passed downe into the grove, there came suddenly among the traine, one apparelled like an honest mans wife of the countrey, where crying out for justice, and desiring all the Lords and Gentlemen to speake a good word for her, she was brought to the presence of her Majestie, to whom upon her knees she offred a supplication, and used this speech."[2]

So begins *The Lady of May* in the 1598 folio, the basis of all our texts. The title is a modern invention appearing in none of the sixteenth- or seventeenth-century editions. Though running heads are used throughout the 1598 volume, there are none for this work, which concludes the book. And though the work starts on the verso of the last page of ***Astrophel and Stella***, there is no catchword for it on the recto. Typographically, in fact, it accosts us with the same abruptness which must have characterized the performance itself. What we possess is a text which is intended as a description of the actual production: no rewriting seems to have been done, and it remains as a unique record of an audacious experiment which went wrong.

From the outset, Sidney insists that the action of his drama has the same kind of reality as everything else at Wanstead. We are turned without warning from a country garden to the world of pastoral; turned, as it were, on a pivot; for, as in the masque, the centre is constant, the Queen cannot change. But deliberately, there is no artifice; no frame for the drama; no theatre; the actors bring their world with them and transform ours; they deny that they are "characters", treating their audience exactly as they treat each other; and we, as spectators, find we cannot tell them apart from ourselves. We need look no further than this to realize the extent to which *The Lady of May* is conceived in terms of the masque.

So the distraught suppliant makes her entreaty directly to the monarch standing before her. The catastrophe is a nuptial; the country-woman's daughter, the May Lady, has two suitors, a shepherd and a woodsman; and she cannot decide between them. The country people have taken sides, and the Lady's choice now has the aspect of a judgment on the relative merits of two ways of life, the contemplative and the active. It is the Queen who must settle the controversy, and the woman urges her to continue her walk; for "your owne way guides you to the place where they encomber her".

"And with that", the text continues, "she went away a good pace", leaving with the Queen a formal supplication. The ensuing poem is a traditional invocation with this difference: the muse, the inspiration of the work, is literally present. The poem must have been written out and handed to Elizabeth; presumably it was also read aloud for the benefit of the other spectators. In invokes and defines the monarch by first adducing a set of conventional attributes for her, and then qualifying these with another set. The Queen is, it says, exalted beyond the reach of ordinary people, but her greatness is also their comfort and protection. Though her countenance may be dangerous to look at,[3] it is also beautiful. Her mind is matchless in argument, but also wise and understanding. The point to be stressed here is that both sets of tropes, both the initial descriptions and what subsequently qualifies them, represent traditional attitudes toward the sovereign. The qualification does not weaken or deny the original metaphor, it only shows us another aspect of it; and the conventions, therefore, remain intact. The poem, in fact, examining a number of commonplaces about royalty, speaks wholly in terms of literary conventions, of stock tropes. It is an apt introduction to the work, in that its rhetorical method, a kind of dialectic of metaphor, is to be repeated in each of the several debates around which the drama is built; but we might also note that the masque itself is conceived as an examination of literary convention—of one of the basic assumptions of the traditional pastoral.

And yet the work *is* a pastoral. Let us remark from the outset, then, how characteristic it is of its author. Here, as everywhere in his writings, Sidney is above all a critic, and so we find this masque returning constantly to basic questions of its own form. *The Lady of May* is concerned with only a single aspect of the pastoral mode, the assumption that the contemplative life is intrinsically more virtuous than the active life. We may see the critique extended and deepened in the larger pastoral world of ***Arcadia***, that wild country where the retired life of the contemplative man is full of deception and misery, and the innocent lover, that indispensable figure of pastoral, is met with sudden and violent death. ***Arcadia*** is about what happens if we consider the real implications of pastoral romance, about the abrogation of responsibility in a world where nature is not friendly nor chance benign. Similarly, Sidney creates, in a Petrarchan sonnet sequence, a beloved who is literally unattainable, and a lover for whom the sense of loss and separation approaches the Calvinist sense of original sin. Both ***Arcadia*** and ***Astrophel and Stella*** are, obviously, serious in a way in which the Queen's entertainment at Wanstead cannot be. Nevertheless, the same intelligence is at work, the same sorts of questions are being asked; and the solutions, when they come, are arrived at only after all the traditional assumptions have been discarded. In *The Lady of May*, the validity of the conventional antithesis of pastoral—contemplation versus action—is to be questioned, thought through again from the beginning, debated and judged.

As the action proceeds now, the antithesis appears dramatically before us. Immediately after the supplication, "there was heard in the woods a confused noyse, and forthwith there came out six sheapheards with as many fosters haling and pulling, to whether side they should draw the Lady of May, who seemed to encline neither to the one nor the other side". We may wish to call this entry of rough country folk, juxtaposed with the rigid decorum of the opening poem, a dramatic antimasque; and certainly we can hardly imagine a more striking representation of the central conflict of the drama than a tug-of-war with the prize in the middle. We become aware at once, however, of the efficacy of the royal presence:

> "But the Queene comming to the place where she was seene of them, though they knew not her estate, yet something there was which made them startle aside and gaze at her."

Let us beware of calling this flattery: its name is convention. There is, simply, that in her countenance which they would fain call master. The validity of the debate—and indeed, the whole drama—here hinges on Authority, inherent in the nature of the monarch.

Two of the country people now attempt to explain the problem to the Queen, Lalus, "one of the substantiallest shepheards", and Maister Rombus, a pedant schoolmaster. Shepherds are traditionally the heroes of pastoral, and Lalus has been a successful enough shepherd to grow rich at the work. What enlightenment we may justly expect from him, however, is lost in the pretentious ignorance of his euphuism, and he soon yields his place to Rombus, who, he says, "can better disnounce the whole foundation of the matter".

Rombus is a scholar. If the shepherd is a conventional exemplar of the contemplative life, Rombus is the contemplative man in person. And yet, far from expounding the basic issues of the masque, his "learned Oration" only succeeds in adding burlesque Latinisms and bombast to the shepherd's periphrases. He barely reaches his subject, taken as he is with both his rhetoric and his accomplishments; and the true and tedious burden of his address turns out to be the local contempt for "the pulcritude of my virtues". If the contemplative man is without honour in his own country, then this pastoral land of Sidney's is a most unfamiliar one. In any traditional pastoral, Lalus and Rombus would in some way at least be at the centre of their world, would express at least some truth, embody some virtue which the work may ultimately assert. Here, on the contrary, we find that they cannot even express what the masque is about.

Both are dismissed by the clear, balanced, characteristically Sidneian prose of the May Lady, who proceeds to describe her two suitors, "the one a forrester named *Therion*, the other *Espilus* a shepheard". Espilus is rich, but Therion is lively; Therion "doth me many pleasures", but has a nasty temper, whereas Espilus, "though of a mild disposition", has done her neither any great service nor any wrong. "Now the question I am to ask you", she concludes, "is whether the many deserts and many faults of *Therion*, or the very small deserts and no faults of *Espilus* are to be preferred."

The Lady's prose is superseded by a more formal rhetoric as the two adversaries enter to speak for themselves. Therion challenges Espilus to a singing contest, the staple controversy of this most artificial form. The ideological conflict is now presented as verbal and musical as well. Since the argument must be discussed in some detail, I quote the poem in full:

Espilus

Tune up my voice, a higher note I yeeld,
To high conceipts the song must needes be high
More high then stars, more firme then flintie field
Are all my thoughts, on which I live or die:
Sweete soul, to whom I vowed am a slave,
Let not wild woods so great a treasure have.

Therion

The highest note comes oft from basest mind,
As shallow brookes do yeeld the greatest sound,
Seeke other thoughts thy life or death to find;
Thy stars be fal'n, plowed is thy flintie ground:
Sweete soule let not a wretch that serveth sheepe,
Among his flocke so sweete a treasure keepe.

Espilus

Two thousand sheepe I have as white as milke,
Though not so white as is thy lovely face,
The pasture rich, the wooll as soft as silke,
All this I give, let me possesse thy grace,
But still take heede least thou thy selfe submit
To one that hath no wealth, and wants his wit.

Therion

Two thousand deere in wildest woods I have,
Them I can take, but you I cannot hold:
He is not poore who can his freedome save,
Bound but to you, no wealth but you I would:
But take this beast, if beasts you feare to misse,
For of his beasts the greatest beast he is.

The singing match is also a formal debate. Therion, the man of action, has issued the challenge. Espilus begins, "as if he had been inspired with the muses", but the rebuttal always offers the stronger position in a debate, and Therion clearly knows what he is about. Rhetorically, this duet is set up in the same way as the earlier supplication: Espilus states his case through a series of metaphors; Therion shows that any trope is only a partial truth.

The shepherd opens in the Petrarchan manner: his love is higher than stars, firmer than earth; he is a slave to his mistress; she is a treasure. The world he adduces is severely limited, and "my thoughts, on which I live or die" turn out to be a set of perfectly conventional conceits. It is precisely the limitations of these metaphors—of this view of the world—that Therion, in his reply, exposes. High notes do *not* imply high thoughts, and neither are the stars so immutable nor the earth so solid as Espilus imagines. The forester has from the outset a much firmer grasp on the physical facts of this pastoral world than the shepherd has: Therion's conceits are related directly to apprehensible phenomena—the noise brooks make, falling stars, ploughed fields. Indeed, he even has a deeper understanding of the realities of Espilus' life than the shepherd appears to have. Therion uses Espilus' own characterization of himself as a "slave" to point out that his bondage is more real than he thinks: he is bound to his wealth, his flock. This is Espilus' "treasure", and his metaphor, says Therion, has thus equated his lady with his sheep.

And in his second turn, the shepherd goes on to make the comparison perfectly explicit:

"Two thousand sheep I have as white as milke,
Though not so white as is thy lovely face . . ."

The simile, happily, works out to the detriment of the sheep. But the limitations of Espilus' apprehension are now apparent. He boasts of his possessions and conceives of his mistress as one of them; "thy grace" is something he will add to his treasure. Finally we find that it is no longer the lover but the lady who is a slave, for he warns her against *submitting* to the wrong master, "one that hath no wealth".

To Therion, however, possession is a denial of humanity, and his reply, "Two thousand deere in wildest woods I have", is a statement not of his riches, but of his potentialities as a man. Instead of Espilus' wealth, he offers his own freedom and hers; one may keep beasts, "but you I cannot hold." His description of their marriage ("Bound but to you . . .") implies not her submission, but their mutual union; and the apostle of wealth, the shepherd, is ultimately seen as only a beast of the higher orders.

Throughout this exchange, the forester has continually undercut what is for the shepherd his only mode of thought, and hence of expression. It is clear that in every way Therion has the better of it. The argument, in fact, progresses with such ease that we may tend to credit the forester with an easy victory, and overlook its significance in the work as a whole. Surely it is unusual to find Espilus, the contemplative man, preaching the virtues of worldly wealth; we had thought it was only in the forest of Arden that shepherds were concerned with economics. But Sidney, like Shakespeare, is redefining the convention behind his work, examining and judging the values it implies. Therion has charged Espilus with using conventions he does not understand, with being unaware of the implications of his own metaphors. And the charge is directed as well at the audience at Wanstead, and at us. Essentially, this is the warning of a first-rate critic against abstracting literary devices from their contexts; and it is to become a warning against the dangers of asserting the traditional advantages of the contemplative life, without understanding the function the assertion served in the individual pastorals from which the tradition grew.

The case is discussed more fully in the debate which follows, a prose parallel to the singing match; "the speakers were Dorcas an olde shepheard, and Rixus a young foster, betweene whom the schoole-maister Rombus came in as moderator." Dorcas speaks for the contemplative view. He cites the legal profession—"the Templars"—as evidence that "templation" is "the most excellent", and sees in the shepherd the man best fitted to a life of contemplation. So, he continues, courtiers leave the court to sit in the country and write pastoral complaints about their mistresses. And here, for the first time, we see that the shepherd need not be a literal one: "So that with long lost labour finding their thoughts bare no other wooll but despaire, of yong courtiers they grew old shepheards." Their thoughts—contemplation—are their sheep; but in this work, even Dorcas is wary of metaphor. Unlike real sheep, he points out, these are unproductive.[4] And finally, the best Dorcas can say for them is that they are utterly harmless; his case rests on sentiment: "he that can open his mouth against such innocent soules, let him be hated as much as a filthy fox . . ."

This is not, even in itself, a very strong argument. But Rixus's rebuttal goes far beyond answering the shepherd's meagre claim. Dorcas's life has, he says,

> "some goodnesse in it, because it borrowed of the countrey quitenesse something like ours, but that is not all, for ours besides that quiet part, doth both strengthen the body, and raise up the mind with this gallant sort of activity. O sweet contentation to see the long life of the hurtlesse trees, to see how in streight growing up, though never so high, they hinder not their fellowes, they only enviously trouble, which are crookedly bent. What life is to be compared to ours where the very growing things are ensamples of goodnesse? we have no hopes, but we may quickly go about them, and going about them, we soone obtaine them . . ."

Again, simply by his position in the debate, the foster has the advantage. But more than that, we are aware that no case at all has been presented for the shepherd, and that it is Rixus, who, in this speech about the virtues of a life of action, is the one really concerned with the life of the mind. "This gallant sort of activity," he says, asserting its inherent nobility, "doth both strengthen the body and raise up the mind"; and his "ensamples of goodnesse" are drawn, like Therion's in the earlier debate, from the observable facts of the pastoral world. One would, I suppose, be hard put to find a *less* active "ensample" of the active life than "the hurtlesse trees", but the point is that the man of action is receptive to all experience; he is living as a part of nature, and everything in nature offers him an exemplary lesson; and consequently he, and only he, possesses the contemplative virtues as well. Indeed, we find that for Sidney there can be no dichotomy between contemplation and action: the one necessarily leads to the other. So, what we may call "original sin" in ***Arcadia*** is the renunciation of an active political life for a pastoral dream—which ultimately cannot be realized. We may compare with this the Elizabethan version of a classic invitation to give up the world, couched in the language of Espilus and rejected by the Renaissance prototype of wisdom:

> "Come, worthy Greek, Ulysses come.
> Possess these shores with me . . ."[5]

There can by this time, I take it, be no question about where the choice between Espilus and Therion must lie. The time for the judgment has come, and the May Lady submits her fate to the Queen, reminding her and us explicitly "that in judging me, you judge more than me in it". The answer should, then, be a statement about the nature of a whole convention, an apprehension of the kinds of values pastoral may validly assert. And since the case is so clear, we will find it amusing enough that Elizabeth should have picked wrongly, but astonishing that no one since then should have noticed the error.

> "It pleased her Majesty to judge that Espilus did the better diserve her: but what words, what reasons she used for it, this paper, which carrieth so base names, is not worthy to containe."

The omission of the reasoning is perhaps fortunate. Elizabeth, versed in the convention, picked Espilus because shepherds are the heroes of pastoral. But this is a most unconventional pastoral, and how wrong the Queen's choice was is apparent from the song of triumph which follows:

"*Silvanus* long in love, and long in vaine,
At length obtained the point of his desire,
When being askt, now that he did obtaine
His wished weale, what more he could require:
Nothing sayd he, for most I joy in this,
That Goddesse mine, my blessed being sees.

When Wanton *Pan* deceiv'd with Lions skin,
Came to the bed, where wound for kisse he got,
To wo and shame the wretch did enter in,
Till this he tooke for comfort of his lot,
Poore *Pan* (he sayd) although thou beaten be,
It is no shame, since *Hercules* was he.

Thus joyfully in chosen tunes rejoyce,
That such a one is witnesse of my hart,
Whose cleerest eyes I blisse, and sweetest voyce,
That see my good, and judgeth my desert:
Thus wofully I in wo this salve do find,
My foule mishap came yet from fairest mind."

"Espilus", we learn, "sang this song, tending to the greatnesse of his owne joy, and yet to the comfort of the other side, since they were overthrowne by a most worthy adversarie." But the song recounts how Silvanus, the archetypal fo(re)ster, *won* his love, and Pan, the archetypal shepherd, *lost* his, defeated moreover by Hercules, the archetypal man of action. Only the final couplet properly belongs to Espilus, who is clearly the loser.

We may muse a little on the mechanics of this fiasco. The judgment was obviously left entirely in the Queen's hands, and it is certainly possible that she was asked to deliver it on the spot. If she saw a text of the work beforehand and prepared her reply, it must have seemed somewhat impolitic for Sidney to tell the learned Eliza that she had missed the point. But why at least was the final song not revised?—or did the queen withhold her decision even from the author until the performance? And if so, did Espilus know Therion's victory song? Or—one final speculation—is the text we have, which was presumably owned by the Countess of Pembroke, simply an original script of the masque, with the Queen's decision indicated, but not including any alterations made for the actual performance?

At last, with a brief valediction, the masquers depart. No curtain closes, there is no theatre to leave; nothing has changed, and the Queen continues her walk through Wanstead garden. Sidney's problem had been to make a queen who was not a masquer the centre of his masque. His solution was to conceive his work as a series of addresses to the monarch, and its resolution as her reply—which is also her critique of the work. So rhetoric, not the traditional dance and spectacle, is the vehicle for the action of the drama; and the masque, then, is conceived entirely in literary terms. This looks forward to what Jonson tried to do with the form, to the assertion that if the masque was a spectacle, it was also a poem. Milton's *Comus* is even more obviously literary, and like *The Lady of May* it is highly rhetorical, centres around a debate and assumes—perhaps equally rashly—that its audience is capable of making the right choice between the contestants. Sidney's essay in the form is a worthy step on the way toward these. If it was a fiasco in production, its success, for those who care to look, is apparent on the page.

Notes

1. See Paul Reyher, *Les Masques Anglais*, Paris, 1909, pp. 18–28, 491–94.
2. The work is reprinted by Albert Feuillerat in *The Complete Works of Sir Philip Sidney*, Cambridge, II, 1922, pp. 329–38. Quotations in my text are from this edition.
3. Cf. p. 329: "I dare stay here no longer, for our men say in the countrey, the sight of you is infectious."
4. The disguised Musidorus, in *Arcadia*, II. 3, embodies the identical conceit in verse: "My sheepe are thoughts, which I both guide and serve . . ." Feuillerat, *Sidney*, I, 1912, pp. 163–64.
5. Samuel Daniel, *Ulysses and the Siren*.

David Kalstone (essay date 1965)

SOURCE: "The Arcadian Rhetoric" in *Sidney's Poetry* , Harvard University Press, 1965, pp. 60–101.

[*In the following essay, Kalstone examines the poetry of the* Arcadia, *and asserts that Sidney's work is more complex than the* Arcadia *of the Italian poet Sanazzaro.*]

Sidney's "gallant variety" of verses in the ***Arcadia*** divides itself into two groups: eclogues and occasional pieces.[1] The eclogues are to be found clustered between books of the romance, four sets of them joining the five books that make up the ***Arcadia***, and are thus distinguished from the occasional poems that are scattered singly through the text as part of the current of action. To the eclogues, Sidney allots a special function; there he draws most noticeably upon Sannazaro and the framework of the Italian *Arcadia*, presenting each set of eclogues as a dramatic unit on the model of the Italian pastoral.[2] The action of the romance halts; the Arcadian shepherds, who play virtually no role in the prose narrative, gather together; and the reader is suddenly transported into that timeless world in which sports, dancing, and poetic performance are the only valuable kinds of action. Sidney accepts Sannazaro's mise-en-scène as the natural refuge of the lover and as a landscape rich in inventions about love.

> But certainely, all the people of this countrie from high to lowe, is given to those sportes of the witte, so as you would wonder to heare how soone even children will beginne to versifie. Once, ordinary it is among the meanest sorte, to make Songes and Dialogues in meeter, either love whetting their braine, or long peace having begun it, example and emulation amending it.
>
> (***Complete Works of Philip Sidney***, I.27–28)

The ingenuity and variety of verse forms are striking, as they are in the Italian *Arcadia*. Here, in Sidney's eclogues, the experiments in Italian and classical meters for which he is noted are to be found.[3] But, given his view of love's corrosive effects upon the heroic life, Arcadian eclogues pose a further problem: to what extent can the exiled courtiers respond to the ideal landscape and richness of invention? how far can Arcadia temper their already painful experience of love?

1

Significantly, pastoral entertainment, which in Sannazaro's golden world is the order of the day, becomes in Sidney's Arcady a matter of interlude, of momentary felicity in performance. Before the First Eclogues the princesses, the queen Gynecia, and the disguised princes visit the scene chosen for the entertainment. We recognize the theater as Sannazaro's when we meet it in Sidney's stylized description:

> It was indeed a place of delight; for thorow the middest of it, there ran a sweete brooke, which did both hold the eye open with her azure streams, and yet seeke to close the eie with the purling noise it made upon the pibble stones it ran over: the field it self being set in some places with roses, and in al the rest constantly preserving a florishing greene; the Roses added such a ruddy shew unto it, as though the field were bashfull at his owne beautie: about it (as if it had bene to inclose a *Theater*) grew such a sort of trees, as eyther excellency of fruit, statelines of grouth, continuall greennes, or poeticall fancies have made at any time famous.
>
> (***Works***, I.118–119)

Having savored the perfections of the setting, pointing to its particular harmony as a theater and as a scene worthy of "poeticall fancies," Sidney suddenly prods the reader to a consciousness of his use of convention. In rush a fierce lion and a bear; the disguised princes are immediately put on their mettle to defend Philoclea and Pamela. Sidney does not mean us to be frightened; the effect is to amuse us by setting one romantic device, the intruding beasts, against another, the perfect setting. But the intrusion does remind us that for the courtly figures the landscape of Sannazaro has only an illusory beauty and happiness. It develops that the king's rebellious sister, Cecropia, has set the animals loose. While the king continues his personal caprices, she is preparing a revolution. In its gentle way the episode figures forth the dangers of pastoral retirement and the special values of vigilance. Before the eclogues begin, we are asked to be alert and critical of the seductions of the conventional Arcadian landscape. Again, when the spell of the First Eclogues has ended—a considerable spell that has kept shepherds and courtiers together far into the night—the opening of Book Two presses the reader to reevaluate the place of these pastimes in the lives of the heroes, the Arcadian princesses, and Basilius the king: "*In these pastorall* pastimes a great number of dayes were sent to follow their flying predecessours, while the cup of poison (which was deepely tasted of this noble companie) had left no sinewe of theirs without mortally searching into it" (*F*, I.145).

Sidney's ambiguous attitude toward pastoral performance (both its content and the literary form it takes) is one with his ambiguous attitude toward love. Such pleasures are apt to be brought to the bar of heroic responsibility and heroic virtue. Pastime, in the person of the Arcadian shepherds, only briefly assumes the foreground. Claiming precedence for music and love, they introduce the opening eclogues with a dance that "made a right picture of their chiefe god *Pan*, and his companions the *Satyres*." Their concluding couplet sets the tone of the eclogues: "As without breath, no pipe doth move, / No musike kindly without love." But pastoral diversion must ideally be judged against the life of action and right government. The participation of a king and princes in a pastoral celebration—their nobility tarnished somewhat by the fact of their retirement and their base disguises—sharply dramatizes Sidney's point of view. Like a later set of aristocrats in a later country paradise, that of Mansfield Park, the courtiers of Arcadia cannot join an entertainment with the innocence and impunity of shepherds.

Basilius, forgetful of his life as king to the point that he has come to live among the shepherds in their "desert places," becomes through this action both reprehensible and comic. As king of Arcadia, where even "the very shepheards have their fancies lifted to so high conceits," he has his choice of shepherd singers "either for goodnesse of voice, or pleasantnesse and wit." He encourages them by "great courtesie and liberalitie." But the grounds for criticizing his prolonged retirement to the forest lodges are clear. A loyal citizen, Kalander, defines the problem: "there is no cause to blame the Prince for somtimes hearing them; the blame-worthinesse is, that to heare them, he rather goes to solitarinesse, then makes them come to companie" (*F*, I.28). Poets are not to be banished from this commonwealth, as they are from Plato's ideal state. However, Basilius falls into the danger of solitariness, of only indulging his passions and his taste for passionate song. His behavior at the end of the First Eclogues is clownish rather than kingly: Zelmane, really Pyrocles in his Amazon guise, has just directed a song to the princess Philoclea with whom he is in love. Basilius, who has not penetrated the disguise and thinks Zelmane really a woman, imagining that the song was directed to him, falls to the ground in delight.

> What exclaiming praises *Basilius* gave to *Zelmanes* songe, any man may ghesse, that knowes love is better than a paire of spectacles to make every thing seeme greater, which is seene through it: . . . Yea, he fel prostrate on the ground, and thanked the Gods, they had preserved his life so long, as to heare the very musique they themselves used, in an earthly body.
>
> (***Works***, I.144)

Sidney's eclogues, then, are presented as a variety of court masque, at which the king does not always behave as well as he should. His disorder is surprising, a recognizable upsetting of convention; for Basilius and his queen, the princesses and the princely lovers (even though disguised) are expected to maintain the courtly decorum that aristocrats do in a masque.

Though they participate in the pastoral revels, Pyrocles and Musidorus are not absorbed into the shepherds' world as easily as Sannazaro's hero is accommodated to Arcadia. Even in a moment of relaxation, at an entertainment, Sidney does not slacken his dramatic reins. The princes share the shepherds' skill in song; love haunts their minds and "waketh in invention"; and like the shepherds they think of song as "a more large expressing" of the passions (***Works***, I.127). On the other hand, the princes style themselves as lovers with "the impediments of honor, and the torments of conscience." These qualifications determine the special nature of their poetry, as they attempt to translate the experience shared with the shepherds into attitudes and language more appropriate to their life of honor. They do not talk of the simple satisfactions of fulfilled desire, but of the hazards of desire and of that hoped-for state of virtuous love that informs the mind. So Musidorus, now the shepherd Dorus, about to join in the First Eclogues, rationalizes his delight in his new state: "more proud of this estate, then of any kingdom: so manifest it is, that the highest point outward things can bring one unto, is the contentment of the mind: with which, no estate; without which, all estates be miserable" (***Works***, I.116). But he registers as well the dangers they must undergo:

> O heaven and earth . . . to what a passe are our mindes brought, that from the right line of vertue, are wryed to these crooked shifts? But o Love, it is thou that doost it: thou changest name upon name; thou disguisest our bodies, and disfigurest our mindes. But in deed thou hast reason, for though the wayes be foule, the journeys end is most faire and honourable.
>
> (***Works***, I.117)

In the eyes of Pyrocles and Musidorus, the pastoral state largely symbolizes "foule wayes"; it is a state to which they have been reduced and from which they may eventually be redeemed by the virtues of love.

It is necessary to point out the sharp distinction between courtiers and shepherds, a distinction not operative in Sannazaro's pastoral, in order to explain the interest of some otherwise dull poems, long pastorals, in the first two sets of eclogues. Cast as singing contests in either *terza rima* (the standard form of the Italian eclogue) or hexameters, these poems represent a strange breed of pastoral indeed—more "dramatic incidents" than "musical compositions," to adopt Ringler's useful distinction.[4] In the most significant of them, courtly speakers oppose Arcadian shepherds, using the form of the singing contest to present opposed views of love and to emphasize the rigorous immunity of the princes to simple pastoral happiness. The poems are exploratory in more than their attempt to hew English lines to the shapes of Latin hexameter and Italian triple rhyme. They express discomfort with aspects of the pastoral convention. They pose voices and attitudes against one another; they project courtly figures who self-consciously redefine the role of pastoral lover. Awkward as they are, the poems show Sidney's critical mind attempting to dramatize some "questions of love" and maintaining the hostility to *otium* displayed in *The Lady of May*.

In the poem that stands at the head of the First Eclogues, Lalus, a rustic, challenges Dorus, the disguised Musidorus. Their *terza rima* exchanges set up a clear, in fact schematic, contrast between the real shepherd and the disguised hero. The two speakers even invoke different muses: Lalus calls on Pan and favors plain speech; Dorus makes a "high attempt" and addresses a Muse whom he asks to "historifie" his mistress' praise. Lalus loves a country maid, Kala; Dorus cannot identify his mistress "whose name to name were high presumption." Kala can be described with homely simplicity and comic awkwardness:

> A heape of sweetes she is, where nothing spilled is;
> Who though she be no *Bee*, yet full of honie is:
> A *Lillie* field, with plowe of *Rose* which tilled is.
> Milde as a Lambe, more daintie than a Conie is:
> Her eyes my eyesight is, her conversation
> More gladde to me, then to a miser monie is.
>
> (***Arc.***, 7:28–33)

Dorus' mistress defies description and can only be praised with elaborate (but not very readable) hyperbole:

> O happie Gods, which by inward assumption
> Enjoy her soule, in bodie's faire possession,
> And keep it joynde, fearing your seate's consumption.
> How oft with raine of teares skies make confession,
> Their dwellers rapt with sight of her perfection
> From heav'nly throne to her heav'n use digression?
>
> (***Arc.***, 7:40–45)

Lalus is advised against love by a prattling father; Dorus, philosopher that he is, is warned by a personified and hightoned Reason against reaching "beyond humanitie" in his love. The poem experiments with the *sdrucciola* (triple rhyme), but even in these experiments Sidney distinguishes his two speakers from one another: the real shepherd, as in the passage above, speaks in a base style depending on monosyllables (particularly the postponed verb, "is") for rhymes; Dorus, in keeping with the exalted state of his love, draws his rhymes from a ponderous Latin vocabulary ("consumption," "assumption," "confession," "digression").

It is easier to point out the intention of this poem—its attempt to contrast vocabularies of love—than it is to claim its success as a pastoral poem. In its intricate form the poem invites comparison with Sannazaro; metrically it follows the Italian's second eclogue very closely.[5] But Sidney's poem is much more abstract than Sannazaro's, and, as we might expect, the only hints of pastoral richness enter in the rustic's speech. Lalus, like the shepherd Espilus in *The Lady of May*, is intended as a figure of fun, boasting of his wealth in "many hundred sheep." Still he has a native sense of the fullness of pastoral love that is completely denied Dorus:

> . . . my sheep your foode shall breed,
> Their wooll your weede, I will you Musique yeeld
> In flowrie fielde; and as the day begins

With twenty ginnes we will the small birds take,
And pastimes make, as Nature things hath made.
But when in shade we meet of mirtle bowes,
Then Love allowes, our pleasures to enrich,
The thought of which doth passe all worldly pelfe.

(***Arc.***, 7:123–130)

Dorus, who feels the "inward bondage" of heroic lovers, scorns this kind of felicity. In his reply he transforms Lalus' offerings one by one into an inner landscape of despair. He dramatizes the strength of his desires, the distance between him and his virtuous love, and the necessary degree of separation from pastoral happiness:

My foode is teares; my tunes waymenting yeeld:
Despaire my fielde; the flowers spirits' warrs:
My day newe cares; my ginnes my daily sight,
In which do light small birds of thoughts orethrowne:
My pastimes none: time passeth on my fall:
Nature made all, but me of dolours made:
I finde no shade, but where my Sunne doth burne:
No place to turne; without, within it fryes:
Nor helpe by life or death who living dyes.

(***Arc.***, 7:138–146)

Insofar as there is any strength or vitality at all in Dorus' poetry, it appears in lines like these, which express the destructive power of love. Dorus' despair in lines 135–146 rings true. It succeeds poetically because of the sense of ceremony in Sidney's use of the *frottola*, a verse form he adapts from Sannazaro. Lacking end rhymes, the lines are connected by a chain of interior rhymes that provide only muted accents; a word at the center of each line echoes the concluding word of the preceding line. The pattern emphasizes the short clauses that make up the ritual denial of pastoral joys, while continuing the flow of lament with as little break as possible. Sidney parallels exactly the items that signify Lalus' simplicities of desire (music, fields, flowers) in creating Dorus' inner landscape. This landscape symbolizes Dorus' separation from simplicity, a separation enforced by his sense of "thoughts orethrowne," his "pastimes none." What Sidney is trying to find for his lovers of high conscience is a ceremony marking their despair, their separateness from the familiar ceremonial felicity of the Arcadian setting inherited from Sannazaro.

From this point of view, another of the eclogues (***Arc.***, 13) deserves attention.[6] Here the two princes, "desiring in a secret maner to speake of their cases" so that the princesses may understand who they really are, rather self-consciously discuss pastoral disguise and pastoral song. The exchange, potentially a witty one, is twisted out of shape in an effort to produce English quantitative verse. (Significantly these "dignified" attempts at domesticating Latin meters are reserved for the princes, denied to shepherds.) Each prince—Musidorus dressed as a shepherd, Pyrocles as an Amazon—points out the advantages of the other's state. Pyrocles-Zelmane envies the directness of lament available to the shepherd Dorus; Dorus replies that his suffering does not diminish "when trees daunce to the pype, and swift streames stay by the musicke." Dorus is jealous of the heroic appearance of Zelmane, who can openly act out her virtue; Zelmane counters that heroic virtue is dwarfed by the powerful effects of love. If heroic virtue cannot lighten the pains of love,

Then do I thinke in deed, that better it is to be private
In sorrows torments, then, tyed to the pompes of a pallace,
Nurse inwarde maladyes, which have not scope to be breath'd out.

(***Arc.***, 13:102–104)

And so pastoral lament is to be preferred, its virtue being that it is "not limited to a whispringe note, the Lament of a Courtier."

To express the immediate destructive power of love, the princes must find emblems for that power in the pastoral landscape around them:

And when I meete these trees, in the earth's faire lyvery clothed,
Ease I do feele (such ease as falls to one wholy diseased)
For that I finde in them parte of my estate represented.
Lawrell shews what I seeke, by the Mirre is show'd how I seeke it,
Olive paintes me the peace that I must aspire to by conquest:
Mirtle makes my request, my request is crown'd with a willowe.
Cyprus promiseth helpe, but a helpe where comes no recomforte.
Sweete Juniper saith this, thoh I burne, yet I burne in a sweete fire.
Ewe doth make me be thinke what kind of bow the boy holdeth
Which shootes strongly without any noyse and deadly without smarte.
Firr trees great and greene, fixt on a hye hill but a barrein,
Lyke to my noble thoughtes, still new, well plac'd, to me fruteles.

(***Arc.***, 13:113–124)

The verse, characterized by abstract pastoral equations, continues, using the trees of the forest one by one to "tell" the lover's sorrows. Awkward by any standards, the poem is interesting for the amount of maneuvering it goes through, for its deliberate discussion of what constitutes high lament. The poetic strand seized is that of pastoral melancholy, a strain familiar enough in Sannazaro and in his Petrarchan models. But Sidney expresses the desolate qualities of pastoral exile almost abstractly. Like Dorus' complaint in the opening eclogue - though in less skillful verse - the poem inventories the lover's sorrows relentlessly, using items of the pastoral landscape as emblems. The habit of listing (carried here to an absurd extreme), of assigning an emotional equivalent to every pastoral landmark ("Despaire my fielde; the flowers spirits' warrs"), gives to Sidney's pastoral love poems their peculiarly insistent quality, their sense of inescapable pain. A lyric like

Dorus' "My sheepe are thoughts" enlists the same responses - a hyperconsciousness of how the pastoral mode can be made to symbolize the sufferings of the courtly lover: "My sheepehooke is wanne hope, which all upholdes: / My weedes, Desire, cut out in endlesse foldes" (***Arc.***, 17).

The effect such poems give is one of an unyielding spareness. And Sidney rarely dramatizes the other side of pastoral experience: the richness for the Petrarchan lover in his new life of isolation or the satisfaction felt by Sannazaro's lovers in becoming part of the world of Arcadian imagination. We may remember Petrarch's pastoral lines, the vision to be balanced against the lover's desolate mountain wanderings:

I' l'ho più volte (or chi fia che m'il creda?)
ne l'acqua chiara e sopra l'erba verde
veduto viva, e nel troncon d'un faggio,
e'n bianca nube sì fatta che Leda
avria ben detto che sua figlia perde,
come stella che'l sol copre col raggio.

(*Rime*, 129)

The only characters in Sidney's eclogues who sense the richness of pastoral love denied to Dorus and Zelmane are the shepherds. They have the Third Eclogues to themselves and act out a rustic wedding completed by an epithalamium.[7] Sidney admires their simplicity but, ultimately treating them with comic irony, reminds us that they are incapable of the higher ranges of feeling that characterize his heroes. The best known lyric from the ***Arcadia***, "My true love hath my hart, and I have his," celebrates simple felicity in love. One of the surprises for the reader of the ***Arcadia*** is the frame in which Sidney places this song about the exchange of hearts. Dorus devises a plan to deceive Miso, wife of the king's clownish servant Dametas. He angers her by imagining a scene in which Dametas is found dallying with a beautiful shepherdess. The frail beauty of the fictional shepherdess' song, **"My true love hath my hart,"** lasts for a moment and is ironically qualified by its connection with the deception of the gross Miso and her boorish husband.

2

Of the unrelenting spare quality of Sidney's pastoral laments there is no better example than the double sestina, **"Yee Gote-heard Gods."** It makes a virtue of the unflinching abstraction that characterizes the laments of Pyrocles and Musidorus. Although the double sestina is not sung by the Greek princes, it too is designed to illuminate their situation. Sidney assigns the poem to Strephon and Klaius, two mysterious shepherds who play roles of varying importance in the different versions of the romance. As originally presented in the unrevised ***Arcadia***, they appear in the Fourth Eclogues: "two gentlemen they were, bothe in Love with one Mayde in that Contry named *Urania* thought a Shepherdes Daughter, but in deede of farr greater byrthe" (***Works***, IV.307). Like Musidorus they have disguised themselves as shepherds in order to serve a lady, and the double sestina they sing is filled with a sense, shared by the Arcadian heroes, of the destructive power of love.[8] In the revised version of 1590, Strephon and Klaius assume more prominent roles. They open the romance and, rescuing Musidorus from a shipwreck, introduce the hero into Arcadia. They are no longer described as gentlemen in disguise, but as shepherds capable of the highest ranges of feeling. The only shepherds not native to Arcadia, they are clearly to be distinguished from the rustics of the eclogues. They have come to the seacoast to mourn the departure of Urania for the island of "Cithera." In Klaius' praise of her we get a measure of what has been lost to the shepherds:

But in deede as wee can better consider the sunnes beautie, by marking how he guildes these waters, and mountaines then by looking upon his owne face, too glorious for our weake eyes: so it may be our conceits (not able to beare her sun-stayning excellencie) will better way it by her workes upon some meaner subject employed. And alas, who can better witness that then we, whose experience is grounded upon feeling? hath not the onely love of her made us (being silly ignorant shepheards) raise up our thoughts above the ordinary levell of the worlde, so as great clearkes do not disdaine our conference? hath not the desire to seeme worthie in her eyes made us when others were sleeping, to sit vewing the course of heavens? when others were running at base, to runne over learned writings? when other marke their sheepe, we to marke our selves? hath not shee throwne reason upon our desires, and, as it were given eyes unto *Cupid?* hath in any, but in her, love-fellowship maintained friendship betweene rivals, and beautie taught the beholders chastitie?

(***Works***, I.7–8)

Urania embodies love, Neoplatonic felicity; through her, passion is purified. Klaius' lament implies that, with her departure, Arcadia has fallen back upon the mercies of a blind Cupid, back into what Musidorus termed the "foule wayes" of love. The lost harmony for which these shepherds mourn means to them what the sense of wholeness in love means to Pyrocles and Musidorus. We cannot be sure of the way in which Sidney might have worked out the roles of Strephon and Klaius in a fully revised ***Arcadia***, but it is clear from the two existing versions that their experience parallels the heroes' separateness from the felicitous Arcadian setting; for that reason they are allowed to sound the opening notes of the ***Arcadia***. We hear their particular tone in the verse of the double sestina, which, for purposes of analysis, is quoted in full:

STREPHON:
Yee Gote-heard Gods, that love the grassie mountaines,
Yee Nimphes which haunt the springs in pleasant vallies,
Ye Satyrs joyde with free and quiet forrests,
Vouchsafe your silent eares to playning musique,
Which to my woes gives still an early morning:
And drawes the dolor on till wery evening.

KLAIUS:
O *Mercurie*, foregoer to the evening,

O heavenlie huntresse of the savage mountaines,
O lovelie starre, entitled of the morning,
While that my voice doth fill these wofull vallies,
Vouchsafe your silent eares to plaining musique,
Which oft hath *Echo* tir'd in secrete forrests.

S: I that was once free-burges of the forrests,
Where shade from Sunne, and sporte I sought in evening,
I that was once esteem'd for pleasant musique,
Am banisht now among the monstrous mountaines
Of huge despaire, and foule affliction's vallies,
Am growne a shrich-owle to my selfe each morning.

K: I that was once delighted every morning,
Hunting the wilde inhabiters of forrests,
I that was once the musique of these vallies,
So darkened am, that all my day is evening,
Hart-broken so, that molehilles seeme high mountaines,
And fill the vales with cries in steed of musique.

S: Long since alas, my deadly Swannish musique
Hath made it selfe a crier of the morning,
And hath with wailing strength clim'd highest mountaines:
Long since my thoughts more desert be then forrests:
Long since I see my joyes come to their evening,
And state throwen downe to over-troden vallies.

K: Long since the happie dwellers of these vallies,
Have praide me leave my strange exclaiming musique,
Which troubles their daye's worke, and joyes of evening:
Long since I hate the night, more hate the morning:
Long since my thoughts chase me like beasts in forrests,
And make me wish my selfe layd under mountaines.

S: Me seemes I see the high and stately mountaines,
Transforme themselves to lowe dejected vallies:
Me seemes I heare in these ill-changed forrests,
The Nightingales doo learne of Owles their musique:
Me seemes I feele the comfort of the morning
Turnde to the mortall serene of an evening.

K: Me seemes I see a filthie clowdie evening,
As soon as Sunne begins to clime the mountaines:
Me seemes I feele a noysome sent, the morning
When I doo smell the flowers of these vallies:
Me seemes I heare, when I doo heare sweete musique,
The dreadful cries of murdred men in forrests.

S: I wish to fire the trees of all these forrests;
I give the Sunne a last farewell each evening;
I curse the fidling finders out of Musicke:
With envie I doo hate the loftie mountaines;
And with despite despise the humble vallies:
I doo detest night, evening, day, and morning.

K: Curse to my selfe my prayer is, the morning:
My fire is more, then can be made with forrests;
My state more base, then are the basest vallies:
I wish no evenings more to see, each evening;
Shamed I hate my selfe in sight of mountaines,
And stoppe mine eares, lest I growe mad with Musicke.

S: For she, whose parts maintainde a perfect musique,
Whose beawties shin'de more then the blushing morning,
Who much did passe in state the stately mountaines,
In straightnes past the Cedars of the forrests,
Hath cast me, wretch, into eternall evening,
By taking her two Sunnes from these darke vallies.

K: For she, with whom compar'd, the Alpes are vallies,
She, whose lest word brings from the spheares their musique,
At whose approach the Sunne rase in the evening,
Who, where she went, bare in her forhead morning,
Is gone, is gone from these our spoyled forrests,
Turning to desarts our best pastur'de mountaines.

S: These mountaines witnesse shall, so shall these vallies,

K: These forrests eke, made wretched by our musique.
Our morning hymne this is, and song at evening.

(***Arc.***, 71)

Lovers like these have haunted literature at least since Petrarch's poet entered his enclosed valley that symbolized the confines of the lover's state. The reader recognizes Petrarch's figure reborn in Sannazaro's double sestina:

Lasso, ch'io non so ben l'ora nè 'l giorno,
che fui rinchiuso in questa alpestra valle;
nè mi ricordo mai correr per campi
libero o sciolto . . .

These once-free shepherds who find the pastoral world no more than a prison reappear in Sidney's poem:

I that was once free-burges of the forrests,
. . . . .
Am banisht now among the monstrous mountaines
Of huge despaire, and foule affliction's vallies.

It was Sannazaro, as we have seen, who realized that the very form of the double sestina could signify the unavoidable pains of love in the pastoral world. His terminations—*rime, pianto, giorno, campi, sassi, valle*—mark the limits of the lovers' experience. In the repetitions and returns of these words, Logisto and Elpino come against the confines of place (fields, rocks, valley), of time (the recurring days), and of their own endless laments (songs and complaints). The world of Strephon and Klaius in Sidney's poem is defined by similarly recurring words. As William Empson's excellent reading puts it:

> [The poem] beats, however rich its orchestration, with a wailing and immovable monotony, for ever upon the same doors in vain. *Mountaines, vallies, forrests; musique, evening, morning*; it is at these words only that Klaius and Strephon pause in their cries; these words circumscribe their world; these are the bones of their situation; and in tracing their lovelorn pastoral tedium through thirteen repetitions . . . we seem to extract all the meaning possible from these notions.[9]

Sidney's handling of these repetitions is much more adventurous than Sannazaro's, more original and complicated, more sensitive to proliferating meanings. Empson summarizes the associations that each of the six terminating words has gathered by the time the poem has made its returns. To take one as an illustration:

> *Mountaines* are haunts of Pan for lust and Diana for chastity, to both of these the lovers appeal; they suggest being shut in, or banishment; impossibility and impotence, or difficulty and achievement; greatness that may be envied or may be felt as your own (so as to make you feel helpless, or feel powerful); they give you the peace, or the despair, of the grave; they are the distant things behind which the sun rises and sets, the too near things which shut in your valley; deserted wastes, and the ample pastures to which you drive up the cattle for the summer.[10]

Yet it is necessary to understand not only the range of emotions included, but also the way in which these associations gather in time, the way they are disposed in the muted crescendo of the poem. This is what really distinguishes Sidney's poem from Sannazaro's and makes it such a splendid example of the individual talent working with tradition. Sidney has seen the possibilities in Sannazaro's organization of the sestina as a dialogue, employing pairs of stanzas, statement and response. But in Sidney's poem the shifts in attitude from one pair of stanzas to the next mark the stages in a magnificent crescendo that is absent in its Italian model. The poem moves from an opening memory of past joys through a violent climax of despair in the stanzas beginning, "I wish to fire the trees of all these forrests"; it closes with a brief coda of recollected harmony. Strephon and Klaius move away from the ordinary experience of pastoral joys, transforming them ever more rapidly into symbols of desire and suffering. There is no better example of the abstract quality of Sidney's pastoral than the continuing reminders in this poem that objects in the pastoral world are merely emblems for the flailing imagination of the despairing lovers. In Sannazaro's poem, the reader accepts fields, rocks, and valleys as emblems of the lovers' imprisonment simply because they recur twelve times, used in their literal meanings, and in their repeated cycles create a sense of confinement. But Sidney makes their symbolic value explicit almost from the outset, identifying his landscape as "monstrous mountaines / Of huge despaire, and foule affliction's vallies." From then on, these landmarks of time and place shift rapidly, assuming in each stanza a different metaphorical role—sometimes simply equated with mental states ("my thoughts more desert be then forrests"); sometimes caught in the act of being changed by the singer's tortured mind ("Me seems I see the high and stately mountaines, / Transforme themselves to lowe dejected vallies").

These nightmares are all the more convincing because they develop before the reader's eyes. The opening pair of stanzas sets a tone of ceremony and concord, which serves as a measure for the departures that follow. Strephon calls upon the gods of the earth—"Gote-heard Gods," nymphs, and satyrs—and Klaius, the gods of the heavens—Mercury, Diana, and Venus. Between them their invocations sanctify both the pastoral landscape, with its welcoming "grassie mountaines," "pleasant vallies," and "free and quiet forrests," and the comforting order of time, with the evening heralded by Mercury, the moon represented by Diana, and the morning led in by Venus. Here we have only a hint of the inner state of the lovers that separates them from the harmony around them. Nature in its innocence and variety contains the contraries of "pleasant vallies" and "savage mountaines," Diana and "Gote-heard Gods"; only the lovers' discord invites the tedium of a day measured by woes from "early morning" to "wery evening."

In the second pair of stanzas we move to the lovers themselves, to their recollections, with Strephon's "I that was once free-burges of the forrests" and Klaius' "I that was once delighted every morning." The shift is interesting. Not only does it introduce a different relationship between speaker and landscape, but it brings the six key words into differing kinetic relationships. "Mountaines" and "forrests," in the first section part of the same orderly exterior landscape, are here opposed to one another. This second pair of stanzas poises the lovers' former state as free hunters and musicians in tune with these valleys against their present inward feelings of banishment and darkness. With the only enjambment of the poem, we move decisively from the free outer landscape of the past, the hunters' forests, to the confining inner landscape of the present: "Am banisht now among the monstrous mountaines / Of huge despaire, and foule affliction's vallies." Mountains now symbolize despair and are monstrous rather than grassy. Strephon's once pleasant music now makes him a "shrich-owle" to himself each morning. Stable elements in the landscape lose their sure value so that molehills seem mountains to Klaius; they are replaced in his mind, as music is by cries.

This pair of stanzas, like every pair but the fifth, maintains a rigid grammatical parallelism: "I that was once (line 1) . . . I that was once (line 3)." Shifts of grammatical structure occur between pairs, but not within them. These structural repetitions, operating independently of the recurring key words, measure the pace of the poem and preserve the ceremonial quality of the opening invocations. Like the simple and occasionally colloquial diction, these effects control and mute the growing violence of the poem, a violence that begins to be felt in surreal phrases like "Am growne a shrich-owle to my selfe each morning."

As the poem progresses, then, elements of landscape take their places metaphorically as part of the inner world of fancy and lose their status as solid objects. Recollection continues in the third pair of stanzas with much less sense of the normal round of pastoral life that the shepherds have left behind. We hear briefly of "happie dwellers of these vallies," of "their daye's worke, and joyes of evening." But Strephon's "deadly Swannish musique" has "with wailing strength clim'd highest mountaines," and he finds his "state throwen downe to over-troden vallies." The metamorphosis of "forrests" in these two stanzas shows most graphically how recurring key words lead us into new areas of experience. For both Strephon and Klaius, the word becomes part of the lover's characterization of his thoughts, but the repetition introduces complexity rather than simplicity. Strephon declares, "Long since my thoughts more desert be then forrests," and Klaius responds, "Long since my thoughts chase me like beasts in forrests." Meanings proliferate. Thoughts are wastelands not rich and growing like forests; if we remember the "hurtlesse trees" of *The Lady of May*, we understand the state from which the lover has fallen. Thoughts are also active and pursue Klaius inescapably like savage beasts. Here Sidney not only characterizes a mental state, but refers ironically to the physical freedom of the earlier section of the poem: "I that was once delighted every morning, / Hunting the wilde inhabiters of forrests." The hunter becomes the hunted, the forest a place of danger.

The double sestina grows more energetic as it becomes more despairing. At the center of the poem, the cycle of rhymes beginning once more, the narration moves into the present tense. The juxtaposition of "sweete musique" and "murdred men in forrests" announces a climax of special ferocity. Now (lines 49–60) the feeling that the opening benevolent landscape has become, to the mind, a prison reaches its height. The verbs are active—not simply the seeing, feeling, and hearing of the previous set of stanzas, but gestures of violence toward the pastoral world: "I wish to fire the trees of all these forrests"; "I curse the fidling finders out of Musicke." Rhythm is accelerated, and each line is a completed sentence and action, contrasting with the longer sentences of earlier stanzas. Forests, evening, music, mountains, valleys, morning: each of these fixed points becomes in Strephon's verses a time or place to be destroyed. At the climax, Sidney breaks the rigid parallelism enforced upon every preceding pair of stanzas. Strephon's speech displays more violence than Klaius': "I wish to fire; I curse; I doo hate." Klaius' answer recognizes that violent gestures are futile, recoil, and cannot satisfy: "My fire is more, then can be made with forrests." He turns the violence upon himself: "I wish no evenings more to see, each evening." He catalogues his humiliations ("My state more base, then are the basest vallies") and concludes with a fierce recognition of his isolation even from the ceremonies of the poem: "And stoppe mine eares, lest I growe mad with Musicke."

At this point Sidney turns dramatically to introduce the cause of the shepherds' savage despair, the departure of Urania. It is a brilliant stroke, taking advantage of the sestina form in which the last word of a stanza is repeated to conclude the opening line of the next. The form poises Klaius' height of distress, "lest I growe mad with Musicke," against the wholesome power of Urania, "she, whose parts maintainde a perfect musique." In the metamorphosis of one word's meaning, in the swift traverse of emotional territory from music that maddens to music that signifies perfection, effect and cause are brought together and the progress of the poem recalled for us. The last pair of stanzas is a coda of recollected harmony; Urania embodies the order with which the poem began. Her departure spoils the forests and turns mountains to deserts. After the poem's note of despair, the reader is ready to believe that Urania does induce in her beholders liberty and awe, that she illuminates nature so as to make it seem ceremonious. Yet it is difficult to agree with Theodore Spencer that this ending relieves the despair of the poem.[11] Rather, the expansiveness of these last lines would seem to confirm it, emphasizing the gap between felicitous past and present distress. Each repeating word reminds us of the beauty of a world the shepherds have renounced, and the very structure of these last stanzas reminds us of the contrast: each stanza begins with a four-line praise of Urania but returns, with the main verbs that have been postponed to the fifth line, to the singers' distress, to the "eternall evening," the "spoyled forrests," the deserts and dark valleys of the body of the poem. We never learn why Urania has left Arcadia, but it appears to be a condition of Sidney's poetic interest that the fallen state is the present state, that the vision of wholeness and innocence has been shattered for these lovers.

One of Sidney's metaphors for Urania's power is that she "in straightnes past the Cedars of the forrests." It recalls the innocence and singleness of the forester's life in *The Lady of May*: "O sweet contentation to see the long life of the hurtlesse trees." In love, as well as in the active life, he is able to envision a state of perfection. But it is striking that he should describe this contentment in love from a distance, as a remote vision. He sees its perfections in memory, but imagination cannot effectively relieve the vivid sufferings and unresolved desires of the present. He lingers over, indeed fiercely celebrates, the consequences of this fallen state. This special feeling on Sidney's part is, I believe, the reason for the poem's distinctive power, its growing intensity. He did not find such strength in Sannazaro or in any of his predecessors in the double sestina.

To see this poem alongside the double sestina of Sannazaro is instructive. Both poems register a sense of hopeless imprisonment and banishment in nature. But halfway through his poem, Sannazaro introduces a voice heard by Elpino, which promises him (for no good reason) more fortunate days. He falls back upon the powers of poetry and announces that, like Orpheus, he will make woods and rocks dance and doves sing every day. This is enough to resolve the immediate problems of desire, and Elpino shifts to a more comfortable poetic mode in the second half of the poem without any apparent dramatic justification. Sidney accepts no such resolution; he sustains his sense of dramatic propriety so that when, in the last two stanzas, a shift in tone occurs, it comes as a felt necessity, as a tribute to the order that no longer exists. Orphic powers do not suffice: "And stoppe mine eares, lest I growe mad with Musicke."

What is sacrificed by Sidney, of course, is the high Arcadian mode, the celebration of harmony in love that exists as part of Petrarch's vision and dominates Sannazaro's. Sidney chooses to emphasize the dark melancholic vein in the pastoral lament. We may remember that, when Petrarch speaks of pastoral exile, it is to balance the rich possibilities of imagination in solitude against the pains of deprivation and desire. Petrarchan love is a continuous process of weighing and experiencing these two sets of feelings; it brings into play both the richness and the barrenness of pastoral. In Sannazaro's *Arcadia*, the rewards of imagination and the influx of poetic powers harmonize and obscure the lover's suffering. What we remember most from Sidney is the forceful imagery, the nightmare quality of "the dreadfull cries of murdred men in forrests," "the mortall serene of an evening," and "the Nightingales doo learne of Owles their musique."

Sidney's poem must be taken, I think, as a criticism of the easy resolutions of Sannazaro's *Arcadia*, and it should give us some indication of why the pastoral sections of the English romance strike a reader so often as un-Arcadian. The same poetic sensibility that lies behind Astrophel's sudden cry, "'But, ah,' Desire still cries, 'give me some food,'" is at work in the poet's dealing with the operatic lovers of Sannazaro's world.

3

The double sestina differs from Sidney's shorter poems in degree rather than in kind; its strength in organizing repetitions, the recurring words and grammatical structures, is in fact the strength of the occasional poems of the ***Arcadia***, though none of them is as impressive as Strephon and Klaius' massive eclogue. What Empson says of the double sestina can be applied to the songs and sonnets of the romance: "It is seldom that the meaning of a poet's words is built up so flatly and steadily in the course of using them. And limited as this form may be, the capacity to accept a limitation so unflinchingly, the capacity even to conceive so large a form as a unit of sustained feeling, is one that has been lost since that age."[12] The remark about sustained feeling and largeness of form is, of course, applicable only to the double sestina. But the notion of severe limitation of poetic resources is a generally fruitful one for considering Sidney's poems. What Empson terms "flatness" results from Sidney's low-keyed vocabulary, his use of monosyllables, and his reliance on rhythm, grammar, and devices of repetition rather than on highly allusive metaphor. As if the double sestina did not have enough of its own built-in repetitions, Sidney introduces further repeating schemes—anaphora and the rigidly parallel stanzas—not demanded by the form. It is true, of course, that in the double sestina he also draws upon powerful imagery, upon the vivid and haunting quality of certain expressions in combination with the strict formalities of the verse. The other Arcadian poems rely less on imagery; it is no wonder that critics of form like Roman Jakobson can cite them as splendid examples of the "poetry of grammar."[13]

For Sidney's contemporaries they constituted a poetry of rhetoric as well. That curious manual, *The Arcadian Rhetorike* of Abraham Fraunce, quotes from the double sestina at the conclusion of a catalogue of rhetorical figures, "sith all [its] grace and delicacie proceedeth from the figures aforenamed."[14] Fraunce has been discussing the repetition of words and sounds, figures belonging properly to the training of the orator[15]—yet he is concerned with the vitality of these rhetorical patterns in poetry. He takes delight in pointing out the combination of strictly poetic devices of repetition with the recognized rhetorical devices; rhyme, stanza, and meter assume places beside epizeuxis, anadiplosis, anaphora, and the other exotic capitals of the rhetorician's world. There is a strong emphasis, in other words, on the way in which the very structure of verse takes on the force of persuasive figures. *The Arcadian Rhetorike* collects its examples from Homer, Virgil, Petrarch, and Tasso, but draws most noticeably upon Sidney's ***Arcadia***, using poems still unpublished when Fraunce's book appeared in 1588. Compiled by a member of the Sidney circle, this handbook of poetic persuasion ranks high the elaborate symmetry of form that we have come to recognize as a feature of Sidney's verse in the ***Arcadia***.[16]

To the modern reader, indeed to the post-Shakespearean reader, the occasional poems of the ***Arcadia*** must seem bare—depending for their effect as they do, far more on rhetorical urgency than on metaphorical complexity. These poems, found in the body of the romance rather than among the eclogues, lament the overthrow of reason by love; they are spoken by the courtly figures of the romance who are caught in the strong toils of desire. In most of these verses Sidney places patterns of repetition at the service of wit, of the neat assurance that the experience of love, however chaotic for his characters, has been accepted as inevitable. Such lovers are masters of their griefs; if they do not often achieve Petrarch's lyric visions of perfection in love, they can at least measure the effects of love upon their own minds and register the dilemmas of their fallen states. Here is Pyrocles-Zelmane, loved by those he does not love and loving a princess who does not love him:

> Loved I am, and yet complaine of Love:
> As loving not, accus'd, in Love I die.
> When pittie most I crave, I cruell prove:
> Still seeking Love, love found as much I flie.
>
> (***Arc.*** 20)

The tone of dignity, fostered by balanced lines and recurrent words, lends an appearance of ordered judgment to an otherwise irrational and painful situation: that of the pursuer pursued. Repetitions confirm the speaker's frustration (loved, he complains of love); by the end of these four lines, the word seems empty of any hope it may have held for him. Yet the epigrammatic form offers us assurance that this is what courtiers must expect when they give way to their passions.

Patterned rhetorical devices are used in other ways to characterize the lover's experience: for example, to express succinctly the recoil of the passions. Gynecia at one point takes "a right measure of her present mind." She speaks of the way love and jealousy "their strengthes together tie": "Love wakes the jealous eye least thence it moves: / The jealous eye, the more it lookes, it loves" (*F*, I.310). The couplet describes an unbreakable circle of desire and affection. The two actors, personified love and the jealous eye, act upon each other: love, which begins in independent action as subject and actor of the first line, ends entwined with jealousy; as predicate of the second line, "loves" becomes the intensified action of the jealous eye that Love had awakened.

The singleness of effect that characterizes the short lyrics of the ***Arcadia*** can best be discussed by examining a complete poem. The following verses are written on a sandy bank near a stream, one of the resorts of the ever-complaining Zelmane-Pyrocles:

> Over these brookes trusting to ease mine eyes,
> (Mine eyes even great in labour with their teares)
> I layde my face; my face wherein there lyes
> Clusters of clowdes, which no Sunne ever cleares.
> In watry glasse my watrie eyes I see:
> Sorrowes ill easde, where sorrowes painted be.
>
> My thoughts imprisonde in my secreat woes,
> With flamie breathe doo issue oft in sound:
> The sound to this strange aier no sooner goes,
> But that it dooth with *Echoe's* force rebound
> And make me heare the plaints I would refraine:
> Thus outward helps my inward griefes maintaine.
>
> Now in this sande I would discharge my minde,
> And cast from me part of my burdnous cares:
> And in the sandes my paynes foretolde I finde,
> And see therein how well the writer fares.
> Since streame, aier, sand, mine eyes and eares conspire:
> What hope to quench, where each thing blowes the fire?
>
> (*Arc*. 21)

These lines make their impression through the cumulative power of repeating figures and stanzas; the poem is diffuse rather than concentrated in its local effects. Verbs are not heavily charged with metaphorical meaning, and Sidney often uses the weaker auxiliary forms ("doo issue," "would refraine"). Nor are his few metaphors particularly striking. The poem is stretched to a simple and well-defined framework. In each of the three stanzas, the lover looks to some aspect of nature around him for "ease." But in the stream he sees his own reflection and tears; in the air he hears his complaint echoed; and in the sand he sees the verses he has just written, the poem we have just read. The poem's form emphasizes once more the unbreakable circle of desire. The last couplet recapitulates its orderly progress ("streame, aier, sand") and reminds us that the poem's logic is emblematic of the inescapable suffering of Pyrocles. In the background of the poem, the four elements are in play: the lover's fire unsolaced by the water, air, or earth around him.[17] They serve as a subdued reminder of the perfect natural order from which, as in the double sestina, the lover has separated himself. Behind the poem lies the assumption that sometime in the past the speaker might have been able to find comfort in recognizing the order of nature ("trusting to ease mine eyes"). In his present fallen state, he is relentlessly cut off even from Sannazaro's consolation, nature's harmony reflected in a well-sung lament.

At least in theme and in the related rigor of its structure, the poem resembles the double sestina; but of course its tone is lighter, less tragic. Because it is less spectacular, less rich, we can see more of Sidney's poetic scaffolding. A skillful single tone of address disciplines the poem; individual figures are marshaled quietly and assuredly toward a limited and well-defined end. The first stanza is built upon recurrent phrases: "to ease mine eyes, / (Mine eyes even great in labour"; "my face; my face wherein there lyes / Clusters of clowdes." Fraunce cites this stanza in *The Arcadian Rhetorike* as an example of the figure anadiplosis.[18] These repetitions gently draw our attention away from the gesture of seeking consolation ("trusting to ease mine eyes . . . I layde my face . . .") to the speaker's inner disorder, which, ironically, prevents him from being comforted. Instead of the natural clouds mirrored in the stream, he sees his own face. In Sidney's ***Arcadia*** there are no "outward helps" for the relaxed will. The carefully balanced couplet that concludes the stanza neatly summarizes the dilemma: "In watry glasse my watrie eyes I see: / Sorrowes ill easde, where sorrowes painted be." The caesura in each line is heavily marked after the fourth syllable, and in each line the divided halves mirror one another in imitation of the action of the stanza. The elegant concluding turn restores bite to the conventional conceit of lovers reminded of their tearful state by brooks and streams.

Rhetorical turns, less frequent, organize the rest of the poem. The second stanza takes up the repeated "sound" of lines 8 and 9 in the rhyming "rebound" of line 10, all these effects pointing up the "echoes" around which the stanza is built. The summarizing couplet of the stanza again opposes "outward helps" to "inward griefes." It would be foolish to overstress the skill of this poem, one of many such small and quiet successes in the ***Arcadia***. Much of the reader's pleasure comes from piecing out its ground plan and discovering the energy of mind that Sidney applied to rhetorical schemes in poetry. Such patterns suggest an inescapable logic of the emotions, conveyed in a manner both worldly and decorous, which invigorates the conventional conceits and dramatic situations of pastoral love poetry. The poems, spoken by voices acquainted with the arts of persuasion, wryly and reasonably show us what happens when reason is overcome.

Most of the short pieces of the ***Arcadia*** are sonnets, and Sidney manages to adapt the sonnet form to his own insistent Arcadian rhetoric. The sonnets of the first two books of the romance follow the form used by Surrey—the form later to be Shakespeare's—ABAB/CDCD/EFEF/GG. Surrey makes of this open form a line-by-line accounting. The sestet of his sonnet in praise of Geraldine illustrates the point:

> Honsdon did first present her to mine yien:
> Bright is her hewe, and Geraldine she hight.
> Hampton me taught to wishe her first for mine:
> And Windsor, alas, dothe chase me from her sight.
> Her beauty of kind her vertues from above.
> Happy is he, that can obtaine her love.[19]

Another sonnet, "How each thing save the lover in spring reviveth to pleasure," again catalogues his experience line by line:

> When Windsor walles susteyned my wearied arme,
> My hande my chin, to ease my restlesse hed:
> The pleasant plot revested green with warme,
> The blossomd bowes with lusty Ver yspred,
> The flowred meades, the wedded birdes so late
> Mine eyes discover: and to my mynde resorte
> The ioly woes, the hatelesse shorte debate,
> The rakehell lyfe that longes to loves disporte.[20]

Neither Surrey nor Sidney (in these Arcadian sonnets) has a very clear notion of the sestet as a unit of development, with power to move the sonnet forward or change its course. It required Shakespeare's mastery of the open Surrey form to realize that possibility. But Sidney does see in the loose rhyme scheme opportunities for more than Surrey's descriptive catalogues. He chooses the repeating quatrains as his unit of expression. Here is a lament sung by the disguised Pyrocles:

> In vaine, mine Eyes, you labour to amende
> With flowing teares your fault of hasty sight:
> Since to my hart her shape you so did sende;
> That her I see, though you did lose your light.
>
> In vaine, my Hart, now you with sight are burnd,
> With sighes you seeke to coole your hotte desire:
> Since sighes (into mine inward fornace turnd)
> For bellowes serve to kindle more the fire.
>
> Reason, in vaine (now you have lost my hart)
> My head you seeke, as to your strongest forte:
> Since there mine eyes have played so false a parte,
> That to your strength your foes have sure resorte.
> And since in vaine I find were all my strife,
> To this strange death I vainely yeeld my life.
>
> (***Arc.***, 14)

This sonnet does not differ in pattern from the longer lyric, **"Over these brookes trusting to ease mine eyes."** In effect it falls into three stanzas, each roughly parallel in content and form, followed by a summarizing couplet. Here is a poem in which the mind measures its fall. Sidney's material is the psychology of love: hasty sight admits the lady's image to Pyrocles' heart, and reason despite itself is overthrown. Each stanza addresses a different faculty ("In vaine, mine Eyes"; "In vaine, my Hart"; "Reason, in vaine"). In the final couplet, the "I" of the poem makes his appearance to assess the accumulated frustration.

Like **"Over these brookes,"** this sonnet describes in its progress a circle. The lover in his audit turns from eyes and vain tears to the heart where the true, the inner, vision of his mistress can be found. In the second stanza we learn that the heart's "vision" brings, instead of Platonic illumination, desire and sighs. Pyrocles' concern is not with his mistress' perfection, but with his own loss of control. In the third quatrain, reason, which once ruled his heart; retreats to the head, its "strongest forte," only to discover the traitor eyes in command. Reason can find no place then in the lover's world. One falls from grace because of the action of the senses, and the process is made a continuous one in this sonnet.

To accent the orderly progress of personified faculties (eyes-heart; heart; reason-heart-eyes), Sidney employs a set of tight grammatical parallels. Each stanza falls into the pattern "In vaine . . . since" (with an inversion in line 9 postponing the appearance of "in vaine"). The words are resumed deliberately in the couplet: "And since in vaine I find were all my strife / To this strange death I vainely yeeld my life." The repetition is particularly effective as part of the witty and concise couplet that, in both lines, marks the caesura after the fourth syllable; the rhyming half of each line is a clause beginning with "I." It is the expectation set up by the recurring "vain" ticking away through the poem and now repeated in the coda that is responsible for the real bite of the poem. "Vainely," interposed between the familiar Petrarchan contraries of life and death in love, gives an unexpected fillip to that opposition. For "vain" connotes throughout the entire poem—as it does in line 13—the speaker's fruitless attempts to resist passion; now at the end of the sonnet he recognizes, with wry wit, that accepting passion is also vain and self-defeating, hence a "strange death." This shift of attitude tests our alertness and, of course, succeeds because it mocks expectations prepared by the rigid parallelism that precedes it.

To realize how important the rhetorical structure of this poem is, we need only survey its conceits. Sighs as bellows to fan the fires of love, living death, love as a combat of reason and passion: these are well-worn conceits with subdued and merely local importance. The rhetorical structure does not serve a dominant metaphor, as it frequently does in the sonnets of Petrarch and Shakespeare. What sting the poem conveys comes from a rhetorical surprise, the repeated "vainely" of its last line.

The Arcadian laments are designed to strike off a single impression. If a reader were confronted with a mixed bag of sonnets from the ***Arcadia*** and ***Astrophel and Stella*** and had no clues from the content of the poem, in most cases he could identify the Arcadian poems from their intentionally static quality. Of eighteen sonnets in the romance, fourteen are organized on the scheme of closely related quatrains, involving repeated figures or words, and a summarizing couplet. Sometimes the quatrains, to obtain a more subdued effect, repeat their rhymes, as in the case of a sonnet in Book Three, "Aurora now thou shewst thy blushing light" (***Arc***. 56). The rhyme scheme, ABAB/ABAB/ABAB/CC, heightens the impression of monotonous and inescapable pain that the poem urges upon the reader. Sidney achieves something of the effect of the double sestina by using only four rhyme words in the quatrains (*light, bait, right,* and *wait*), employing a different meaning for each word as it is repeated in each stanza. The couplet repeats the word *show*, first using it as a verb and then as a noun.

Sidney carries the technique of close repetition to an extreme in two poems of Book Three. One of them employs a series of fourteen words rhyming with *bright* (***Arc***. 42). Another, a lament of Zelmane's welcoming the cave as refuge for her "stormy rage of passions darcke" (***Arc***. 39), uses only *light* and *dark* as its rhymes. The poem consists of the familiar series of parallel stanzas deploying its rhymes ABAB/BABA/ABAB/AB and postponing the main clause until the final couplet has been reached: "I like this place, wheare at the least the darke / May keepe my thoughtes, from thought of wonted light." This sonnet, though it lacks the excitement of much of Sidney's other verse, is an interesting and revealing exercise. In it we glimpse the bare bones of the sonnet as used schematically in the ***Arcadia***; it appears intentional that repeating structures assume a symbolic value of their own. Here the dilemma of the heroic lover—his yearnings for "reasons light" or for the purity of "beauties light," which are blocked by "passions darcke"—is signified by the ceaseless alternation between *light* and *dark* in the rhymes of the poem.

Yet it would be unfair to overstress the uniform conception of the Arcadian sonnets. Especially in Book Three, Sidney sets the sonnet to tasks different from those already described. For the first time he gives independent attention to the sestet,[21] allowing it to convey a shift of meaning or interest. Although it is impossible to date these sonnets in relation to one another or to the sonnets in ***Astrophel and Stella***, the poems that open Book Three represent a more adventurous view of the possibilities of the sonnet than one finds in the poems of the earlier books.[22] They seem to represent new discoveries about the form for Sidney. A modest example is Philoclea's impatient sonnet, an address to time in the hope that she will soon be united with Pyrocles:

> O stealing time the subject of delaie,
> (Delay, the racke of unrefrain'd desire)
> What strange dessein hast thou my hopes to staie,
> My hopes which do but to mine owne aspire?
>
> Mine owne? o word on whose sweete sound doth pray
> My greedy soule, with gripe of inward fire:
> Thy title great, I justlie chalenge may,
> Since in such phrase his faith he did attire.
>
> O time, become the chariot of my joyes:
> As thou drawest on, so let my blisse draw neere.
> Each moment lost, part of my hap destroyes:
>
> Thou art the father of occasion deare:
> Joyne with thy sonne, to ease my long annoys.
> In speedie helpe, thanke worthie frends appeare.
>
> (***Arc***., 53)

This sonnet reveals the pressure of a mind in motion in a way that sets it apart from the earlier static sonnets of lamentation. Something has happened between the irritation of the opening of the octet ("O stealing time the subject of delaie") and the assured wish that opens the sestet ("O time, become the chariot of my joyes"). Philoclea, beginning with a series of cautious repetitions ("delaie / Delay"; "my hopes . . . / My hopes"; "mine owne . . . / Mine owne?"), takes on confidence in the second quatrain, reminding herself of her lover's faith. The joyful cajolery of the sestet is the result. The shift in tone from octet to sestet allows us to see time from two angles, first as the "subject of delaie," then with the anticipation of "chariot of my joyes." Sidney uses the sonnet in this case as something more than a series of repeating quatrains.

One of the later sonnets in Book Three moves even further from Sidney's version of the Surrey sonnet. This sonnet rhymes ABBA/ABBA/CDE/CDE, adopting the interlocking Italian form. It is also the first of the *Arcadia*'s sonnets to rely completely upon feminine rhymes. More important, it treats love and desire in more complex fashion than some of the earlier poems do. The speaker is Basilius, deceived into thinking he has spent a night of pleasure with Zelmane, when actually he has been with his own wife Gynecia:

> O Night, the ease of care, the pledge of pleasure,
> Desire's best meane, harvest of hartes affected,
> The seate of peace, the throne which is erected
> Of humane life to be the quiet measure,
>
> Be victor still of *Phoebus*' golden treasure:
> Who hath our sight with too much sight infected,
> Whose light is cause we have our lives neglected
> Turning all nature's course to selfe displeasure.
>
> These stately starrs in their now shining faces,
> With sinlesse sleepe, and silence, wisdome's mother,
> Witnesse his wrong which by thy helpe is eased:
>
> Thou arte therefore of these our desart places
> The sure refuge, by thee and by no other
> My soule is bliste, sence joyde, and fortune raysed.
>
> (***Arc***., 69)

The sonnet would be remarkable if only for its masterly invocation of Night, which later becomes almost a formula in Elizabethan poetry: the successive alliterative epithets for sleep and night convey in somnolent rhythms a sense of welcome repose. What is remarkable in Sidney's treatment is the manner in which the second quatrain qualifies the experience of the first. Night is not only the "ease of care," but "Desire's best meane." He can characterize it as part of the natural order, "harvest of hartes affected," in the sense that night satisfies desire, the inevitable product of the day. But desire also breaks nature's course, causing "lives neglected" and "selfe displeasure." The poem while offering respite keeps the speaker aware of "desart places," of which Strephon and Klaius constantly remind us. The rhetorical trick of the poem is to blame the day and Phoebus for the speaker's guilt; but that guilt remains, in the intrusive and striking "desart places," part of Basilius' sense of his situation. For such balance of the worlds of peace and desire in Sidney's poetry, we look usually to the more complicated verse of ***Astrophel and Stella***.

But it is true that the dominant poetic mode of the ***Arcadia*** is the static, plangent lament spoken by characters of high breeding, mourning over desire. Though the later poems of the ***Arcadia*** reveal new freedom and complexity in Sidney's handling of the resources of the sonnet, the range of the Arcadian sonnets is narrow, their function in the romance a limited one. Tragic lament is only one way to register the chaos of desire in a long work that has other ways of gaining the same effect—comic disguises, dramatic adventures, and maneuvers of plot. One of the great changes we shall see in ***Astrophel and Stella*** is that more pressure is put on the verse; love's complications are revealed not in a mosaic of poetry and plotted prose, but in the turnings of individual poems and a sequence of sonnets.

4

The love poems of the ***Arcadia*** refer the reader implicitly to the standards of the heroic world; they dramatize the lover's abdication of reason and the attempt to find order in love. It remains to ask what resolution, if any, Sidney effects between the destructive passion expressed in these lyrics and the behavior originally demanded of Pyrocles and Musidorus by their heroic education. We know that such a resolution does not occur in the poetry of the ***Arcadia***, and now we must refer to the prose for a further definition of Sidney's position.

One clue to Sidney's attitude toward the relation of love and duty lies in the series of tales in Book Two. These can be understood as an extended comment on the central action in Arcadia. Almost every one of the episodes deals with lust or an excess of love. Most important, these tales link private excess with public destruction in the same way that, in the Arcadian section, Basilius' lust is part of the lack of control that leads to the Arcadian rebellion and makes possible Cecropia's plots against the state. For example, Erona, the queen of Lycia, having ordered the images of Cupid pulled down, is suddenly seized with love for Antiphilus, a commoner. He marries her and, as king, becomes a prey to flatterers, making "his kingdome a Teniscourt" (***Works***, I.330). His eventual scorn of Erona and pursuit of Artaxia, the queen of Armenia, leads to his own death and to Erona's imprisonment. In a parallel tale, the king of Iberia marries a townsman's wife, Andromana, former mistress of his son Plangus. She directs her efforts toward forcing the uxorious king to banish his son and to give her effectual rule over Iberia. She tries also to seduce Pyrocles and Musidorus and, failing, makes every effort to take revenge on them.

It is one of the many calculated ironies of the carefully constructed second book of the ***Arcadia*** that the principal royal families involved are related to one another[23] and that the violence, both public and private, works itself out in the deaths of the innocent heirs, Palladius and Zelmane. Palladius, the son of Andromana and the king of Iberia, loses his life at the hands of Andromana's own soldiers while helping Pyrocles and Musidorus to flee the country. Zelmane, disguised as a page, dies of grief from the accumulated treacheries of her father Plexirtus and from unrequited love for Pyrocles.

Sidney's most moving dramatization of the public violence that can spring from personal passions comes in his description of a crucial battle in Amphialus' defense of Cecropia's castle. Amphialus has led his troops into a dangerous position after several skirmishes that were destructive for both the Basilian forces and his own. He has lost any sense of responsibility toward his followers in the hope that he can win glory for himself and hence gain the love of Philoclea. His love for her, the reader knows, will never be returned.

> And now the often-changing Fortune began also to chaunge the hewe of the battailes. For at the first, though it were terrible, yet Terror was deckt so bravelie with rich furniture, guilte swords, shining armours, pleasant pensils, that the eye with delight had scarce leasure to be afraide: But now all universally defiled with dust, bloud, broken armours, mangled bodies, tooke away the maske, and sette foorth Horror in his owne horrible manner. But neither could danger be dreadfull to *Amphialus*-his undismayable courage, nor yet seem ougly to him, whose truely-affected minde, did still paint it over with the beautie of *Philoclea*.
>
> (***Works***, I.392–393)

It is all there: the very real courage of Amphialus, the power of love to paint over the scene with glories, but also the waste of riches, the violence that misdirected action and excess of love can bring. With a slow turn of the kaleidoscope, the whole scene takes on a new and horrible complexion; his vision clouded by passion, Amphialus misuses his own instinct for heroism and martial virtue.

If the central action in Arcadia has anything in common with the heroic flashbacks of Book Two, it is a recognition of the degree to which feelings of love threaten or undermine the heroic life. Yet Sidney seems of two minds in his presentation of the princes' stay in Arcadia. Love, when disciplined, understood, and directed, can be the strongest ally of the heroic life. The Arcadian episode with its leisure for love can be important; the trials of love can be for Pyrocles and Musidorus part of the larger experience of learning to judge and act. Ideally, as Strephon and Klaius know, love can lead to thoughts "above the ordinary levell of the worlde" by beginning with "experience . . . grounded upon feeling." But in a fallen world—and of this condition Sidney keeps reminding us—even the most innocent love has its admixture of passion. This is the plight of Sidney's Astrophel, and it is also the situation of Pyrocles and Musidorus.

If there is any criticism to be made of the ending of the *Arcadia*, it must be made with the full realization that Sidney did not have the opportunity to revise his romance beyond Book Three. Even so, one wonders what sort of resolution would have been possible. What seems to be missing is the kind of climactic episode that one finds particularly in Book One of *The Faerie Queene*. If the princes have indeed had an education in the passions and been finally led back to the heroic world, one would like a demonstration of the harmony of the worlds of heroism and love, an episode that exemplifies the new fullness of knowledge in action.

However, this harmony of love and action is one of which Sidney himself was never certain. When at the end of the *Arcadia* Euarchus restores order, he judges that the princes, in abducting the princesses and in leaving the heroic world to adopt disguises, have abandoned the high standard of reason in action that is the ideal basis of Sidney's romance. Euarchus himself demonstrates the noble standards of the heroic world by refusing to withdraw his decision, even under the emotional stress of learning that the condemned heroes are his own son and nephew.

> If rightly I have judged, then rightly I have judged myne own children. Unlesse the name of a child, should have force to change the never changing justice. No no *Pyrocles* and *Musidorus* I prefer you much before my life, but I prefer Justice as far before you, while you did like your selves, my body should willingly have ben your shield, but I cannot keep you from the effects of your own doing.
>
> (*F*, II.201)

However, the awakening of Basilius dispels the tragic atmosphere, and the princes are free to go with their loves into the world of governors and heroes. Harmony comes as a result of comic accident.

For Sidney, then, there does not seem to be a final resolution of action and love. A description of both worlds—the world of responsible action and the world of pastoral love—is necessary for an adequate presentation of experience. There is no question of choosing "the quiet, retired life of the shepherd" as opposed to "chivalric and honorable achievement."[24] At the center of both worlds is imperfect man, attempting to exercise the obligations of reason. Sidney's heroic world offers the model of reasonable activity; his pastoral world presents in the vicissitudes of love a heightened example of the unavoidable obstacles to heroic striving.

Notes

1. The quoted phrase is Gabriel Harvey's, from *Marginalia*, ed. G. C. Moore Smith (Stratford-upon-Avon: Shakespeare Head Press, 1913), p. 226.

2. A theatrical analogy is relevant since, in the unrevised *Arcadia*, the five books are actually referred to as "actes" and the eclogues treated as theatrical interludes or entertainments. The division between eclogues to be read and eclogues to be performed was not a very firm one in the sixteenth century. One of the sources of Italian pastoral drama was the recited eclogue, the *ecloga rappresentativa,* of which an early example is Castiglione's *Tirsi* performed by Castiglione himself with Cesare Gonzaga in 1506. The term eclogue was used as late as 1572 by critics to describe Tasso's *Aminta*, very definitely a theatrical production. See W. W. Greg, *Pastoral Poetry and Pastoral Drama* (London, 1906), pp. 177ff for *Aminta,* and *passim* for an account of the relation of Italian pastoral poetry to pastoral drama.

3. It is noteworthy that the experiments occur primarily in the eclogues, while the poems in the body of the romance are sonnets or variants of the sonnet form. This is not a rigid practice, however, since in the revised version, many of the experimental eclogues are shifted into the body of the romance.

4. Ringler, *Poems*, p. xxxiv.

5. For a detailed analysis of the meter of this poem, see Theodore Spencer, "The Poetry of Sir Philip Sidney," *ELH*, XII (1945), 262–263. The eclogue moves in *terzine* from sections in triple rhyme to feminine endings and finally masculine rhymes. It continues with *frottola* and a *barzelletta*, both used in the Sannazaro poem.

6. This poem is not in the 1590 *Arcadia* but does appear in the folio of 1593.

7. *Arc.* 63. The work resembles Spenser's "Epithalamion" in some ways, particularly in its orderly progression by stanzas with refrain, each stanza introducing new tributes from Muses, Earth, Nymphs, etc. Characteristically, half of Sidney's poem is devoted to banishing possible dangers of love, particularly jealousy and "foule Cupid, syre to lawlesse lust."

8. In another poem (*Arc.* 72) Strephon and Klaius introduce the emblem of fishing for the "fish Torpedo faire" as equivalent to the lover's experience. "The catcher now is caught," lamed by his own desires.

9. Empson, *Seven Types of Ambiguity* (New York, 1931), pp. 45ff.

10. *Ibid.*, p. 48.

11. Spencer, p. 265.

12. Empson, p. 50. "Flatly" is Empson's revision of 1947. The 1931 edition, which I cite throughout, reads "patiently."

13. Roman Jakobson, "Poetry of Grammar and Grammar of Poetry," *Poetics*, Polska Akademia NAUK, Instytut Badan Literackich (Warsaw, 1961). Unpublished illustrations to this paper include a discussion of Sidney, *Arc*. 20.
14. Abraham Fraunce, *The Arcadian Rhetorike*, ed. Ethel Seaton (Oxford, 1950), p. 53.
15. George Puttenham terms such figures "sententious," in *The Arte of English Poesie*, ed. Gladys D. Willcock and Alice Walker (Cambridge, Eng., 1936), p. 196. Fraunce distinguishes "figures"—repeated patterns in several words—from "tropes" or "turnings" of single words from their "naturall signification" (p. 3). In the latter category are such devices as metaphor and synecdoche; in the former, such rhetorical patterns as anaphora, anadiplosis, and epistrophe.
16. See Robert L. Montgomery, *Symmetry and Sense: The Poetry of Sir Philip Sidney* (Austin, 1961).
17. This conceit is a congenial one for Sidney. See *Certaine Sonets*, 3.
18. Fraunce, pp. 36–37; "*Anadiplosis*, redubling, or reduplication is when the same sound is repeated in the ende of the sentence going before, and in the beginning of the sentence following after."
19. Quoted from *Tottel's Miscellany*, ed. Hyder Rollins (Cambridge, Mass., 1928), I, 9.
20. *Ibid*., I, 10–11.
21. *Arc*. 47. The sonnet "Do not disdaine" is the first in the book to divide the sestet into tercets in its rhyme scheme.
22. See *Arc*. 60, for instance. The sonnet experiments with handling three subjects and three verbs simultaneously.
23. The principal relationships are: Plexirtus is the half-brother of Andromana; her husband is the uncle of Artaxia, who marries Plexirtus.
24. See Hallett Smith, *Elizabethan Poetry: A Study in Conventions, Meaning, and Expression* (Cambridge, Mass., 1952), p. 11.

A. C. Hamilton (essay date 1969)

SOURCE: "Sidney's *Astrophel and Stella* as a Sonnet Sequence," in *ELH: A Journal of English Literary History*, Vol. 36, No. 1, March 1969, pp. 59–87.

[*In the following essay, Hamilton seeks to show that the 108 sonnets in* Astrophel and Stella *may be read as a single, long poem on the theme "loving in truth."*]

I

My purpose in this article is to show how Sidney's ***Astrophel and Stella*** may be read as a single, long poem rather than as a miscellany of 108 separate sonnets. Some awareness of the structure of the work, which accounts for our sense of its wholeness and its total impact upon the reader, has persisted ever since Nashe spoke of it, in the preface to the first quarto edition, as "the tragicommody of love . . . performed by starlight. . . . The argument cruell chastitie, the Prologue hope, the Epilogue dispaire." Though efforts to read the poem in terms of narrative, whether real or fictional, may seem misleading, unsatisfactory, or simply wrong, the effort to do so must be allowed. Any careful reader gathers that the sonnets form a sequence, however that term may be understood. I want to demonstrate why and how the sonnets are organized into a sequence with a unifying structure. What Erskine has claimed for Spenser's *Amoretti*, I shall claim for Sidney's poem: "Taking the sonnets as a whole, the critic must find in them the truest sequence of this decade. There is a progression in the story and in the poet's moods, from the beginning to the end, and each sonnet has its inevitable place. The series is really but one poem in which each sonnet is a stanza, and each stanza, as in the *Epithalamion*, a lyric unit."[1]

In asking whether any collection of sonnets composes a sequence, however, one must allow that each individual sonnet resists external ordering. Whether as a moment of meditation, outburst of passion, or merely an exercise in praise or witty compliment, it stands complete within itself, neither deriving from the preceding sonnet nor preparing for the next. By its form it is detached and closed; and through its rhyme scheme, it points inward. Even when a number of sonnets treat a common theme, they center upon it: each repeats, rather than develops, the theme. Further, any sonnet by Sidney seeks to exhaust itself in its final phrase. Like the punch line of a joke, the concluding point of wit is the occasion for all that comes before it, and nothing is left over.

Sonnet 9 illustrates the sonnet's discrete nature:

> Queene *Vertue's* court, which some call *Stella's* face,
> Prepar'd by Nature's chiefest furniture,
> Hath his front built of Alablaster pure;
> Gold is the covering of that stately place.
> The doore by which sometimes comes forth her Grace,
> Red Porphir is, which locke of pearle makes sure:
> Whose porches rich (which name of cheekes endure)
> Marble mixt red and white do enterlace.
> The windowes now through which this heav'nly guest
> Looks over the world, and can find nothing such,
> Which dare claime from those lights the name of best,
> Of touch they are that without touch doth touch,
> Which *Cupid's* selfe from Beautie's myne did draw:
> Of touch they are, and poore I am their straw.[2]

Here the set, rigid allegorical description turns from the heavenly guest who looks from the windows of Stella's eyes to the mansion filled with nature's choicest furniture in order to explode in the final phrase: the lover himself as the straw man attracted and burned by her light. The point of wit in the sonnet—almost its formal cause—lies in the shock of moving from the formal opening, "Queene *Ver-*

tue's court," to the plain, colloquial ending, "poore I am their straw." It cannot be claimed that our appreciation and understanding of this sonnet depend upon any other sonnet in the collection. Instead of being in any manner peculiar to Sidney, the language, conventions, and imagery are taken from a common stock of poetic counters shared by all sonneteers. Further, these are static: they do not develop or gain any larger or particular meaning through their repeated use. Each sonnet makes a fresh beginning, and a collection of them appears like stars against a black sky rather than related points on a narrative line.

By its nature the sonnet seeks an individual and isolated excellence in form and content. In its prescribed length and set rhyme scheme, it calls attention to itself as a technical tour de force and celebrates its own triumph of poetic craftsmanship. While a critical term such as "Shakespearean comedy" may refer to anything from a certain kind of character to a vision of reality, "Shakespearean sonnet" signifies a certain rhyme scheme. The brilliance of any sonnet lies entirely upon the surface. We are not better readers of the sonnet quoted above if we study the convention of the blazon from Geoffrey de Vinsauf through to the Italian and French poets of the fifteenth and sixteenth centuries, or if we speculate upon the identity of Stella. A sonnet shines brilliantly for the moment that it is read, only to fade entirely before the next sonnet. A reader has some justification for concluding that after he has read one love sonnet, he has read them all. The Renaissance love sonnet is a poem truly anonymous: it seeks a kind of poetic excellence achieved by Petrarch, and in this sense all aspire to become one sonnet.

With each sonnet exerting a strong centrifugal pull, a collection may not possess more than the adventitious unity of having been written by one poet and published together. No reader of Daniel's "Care-charmer sleep, son of the sable night" feels that he is the poorer for not having read the other forty-nine sonnets to Delia, nor does he bother to ask whether this sonnet appears early or late in the collection. It comes as a shock to any reader of Lodge's *Phillis* to stumble upon "I would in rich and golden-colored rain," falling as golden rain itself after so much drizzle. We read Donne's *Songs and Sonets* in any order without confusion, and most of us are not disturbed by the clear disorder of Shakespeare's sonnets.

A structure may be imposed in order to pull sonnets together into some larger unity. Religious sonnets may be structured by liturgical prayer or Church doctrine, as even the titles of Donne's *La Corona* and Herbert's *Temple* indicate, or by a tradition of formal meditation, as in Donne's *Holy Sonnets*. Doctrine and dogma limit the area in which such sonnets move, and the subject itself imposes a unity of mood. In contrast, the subject of love poetry requires, as Puttenham notes, "a forme of Poesie variable, inconstant, affected, curious, and most witty of any others" (*Arte*, I. xxii). That great original, Petrarch, offers his collection as *Rime Sparse*, scattered rhymes, or *Rerum vulgarium fragmenta*, pieces of matters written in the vernacular. He imposes a general order by arranging the 366 poems to indicate an over-all theme, his change from love of Laura to love of God through love of her. Yet this theme does not control our reading of any particular sonnet. The opening sonnet of repentance and the concluding hymn to the Virgin offer only a larger perspective upon love rather than an interpretation of any one poem. With its large, but simple, division into two parts, and its mingling of poetic forms and change of subject in order to gain variety, the *Canzoniere* remains a collection of discrete poems rather than one long poem. Only by the efforts of the commentators did the separate poems gain the continuous context through which the whole work could be read as an anatomy of love, biography, or romance. For this reason prose commentary on love sonnets, whether by the allegorical interpreters of Petrarch and his imitators or by the poet himself, as earlier in Dante's *Vita Nuova* and later in Bruno's *Eroici furori*, became a special literary genre in the Renaissance.[3] Such commentary may be genuinely needed when the poems are allegorical in intent or obscure through the welter of conflicting doctrines of love, but it may be attached to any collection. For all its completeness, a love sonnet appears as a fragment of some larger whole. Even by its concentration upon some moment of love, it assumes much that has not been told, what must have come before and what may come after. Its subject, more than any other, arouses our curiosity. No ordinary reader can refrain from offering a deeply personal response and no scholar can refrain from trading the most flimsy gossip.

Sidney does not impose any external structure or framework upon his collection unless it is biography. Despite his claim that right poets "borrow nothing of what is, hath been, or shall be," certain sonnets contain clear references to what is, or had been, in his own life, and these may be linked to provide a continuous narrative in terms of which all the sonnets may be read. C. S. Lewis has persuasively stated the case against such biographical reading:

> The first thing to grasp about the sonnet sequence is that it is not a way of telling a story. It is a form which exists for the sake of prolonged lyrical meditation, chiefly on love but relieved from time to time by excursions into public affairs, literary criticism, compliment, or what you will. External events—a quarrel, a parting, an illness, a stolen kiss—are every now and then mentioned to provide themes for the meditation . . . the sonnet sequence does not exist to tell a real, or even a feigned, story.[4]

William A. Ringler, Jr., replies that Sidney's sonnet sequence "tells of the love of a young courtier for a married woman" (p. xliv) whom he identifies as Sidney himself and Lady Rich. He may fairly claim that "we cannot avoid the biography" (p. 440); yet it need not follow, as he insists, that "the substance of his poem was autobiographical" (p. 447). On the other hand, while Lewis may fairly claim that a sonnet sequence is not a way of telling a story, Sidney's sequence does in fact tell a story. If that story is not taken as real—Sidney's affair with Lady Rich—it may be taken as feigned—Astrophel's love for Stella.

Each sonnet "belongs" to the poem in the sense that it treats Astrophel's love for Stella at some stage from their first meeting to their final separation. Together the sonnets record the stages of courtship from his first grief when he falls in love, to his joy when his love is shared, until his final despair when she rejects his love. Gabriel Harvey's comment that Chaucer's *Troilus and Criseyde* was "one of Astrophil's cordials"[5] suggests that Sidney tells a similar story of "the double sorwe of Astrophel. . . . In lovynge, how his aventures fellen / Fro wo to wele, and after out of joie." Sidney's remark in the *Apology*, that Chaucer in his misty time "did excellently in his *Troilus and Criseyde*" while "we in this clear age walk so stumblingly after him," may refer to his own deliberate imitation of Chaucer's poem.

Through this feigned story, Sidney provides an anatomy of love by analyzing all possible phases of the love between man and woman. Fulke Greville knew that Sidney's purpose in the ***Arcadia*** was "to limn out such exact pictures, of every posture in the minde, that any man being forced, in the straines of this life, to pass through any straights, or latitudes of good, or ill fortune might (as in a glasse) see how to set a good countenance upon all the discountenances of adversitie, and a stay upon the exorbitant smiling of chance."[6] Similarly, it may be said that Sidney's purpose in ***Astrophel and Stella*** is to limn out exact pictures of every posture of the mind of a man in love, from the first resistance to the birth of love, to full submission to love's fulfillment, to final reconciliation to its death. All the stages of loving and of being loved—from loving in hope and anguish, loving in expectation and joy, loving in absence, loving another, to loving in despair—are so set down that any man might (as in a glass) see how to set a good countenance upon all the discountenances of adversity in love, and a stay upon the exorbitant smiling of chance. The reader may find in Sidney that anatomy of love found in Petrarch by his commentators and noted by Harington: "in those his sweet mourning sonets . . . he [Petrarch] seemes to have comprehended all the passions that all men of that humour have felt."[7] Sidney is the English Petrarch because his poem has the comprehensive scope of a love epic.

If Sidney's poem is read as a real or feigned story, or even as an anatomy of love, it is still read in terms of something else, some imposed, external structure or framework. Do the sonnets have any internal structure, with a beginning, middle, and end, by which they are brought into the unity of a single poem?

Clearly sonnet 1 provides a beginning, as Aristotle spells out the term: it depends on nothing before it, and it leads to something else. It announces the program for a collection of sonnets through which "the deare She" may be moved to grant Astrophel her favor, and it proceeds to isolate the only source of his poetic inspiration, her image in his heart. Even by its twelve-syllable line, it is set off as a formal prologue to the rest. Equally clearly, sonnet 108 provides the ending. Though earlier readers, such as Grosart, wished to append ***Certain Sonnets*** 31 and 32 with their renunciation of earthly in favor of heavenly love, any pat, moral ending to ***Astrophel and Stella*** is utterly false to the whole poem. Its end is found in Astrophel's failure to resolve his agony and joy in loving. Inflicted with a double sorrow, and in a mood of quiet desperation, he leaves love for the world of action. The epilogue, as Nashe said, is despair. But the question remains: how do the intervening sonnets compose a middle?

Surprisingly, modern critics agree in dividing ***Astrophel and Stella*** into a definite three-part structure while they disagree entirely upon the division of its parts. In treating Sidney as the "English Petrarke," R. B. Young argues that the poem's structure is "one of analysis and synthesis, with the Petrarchan convention as its subject matter."[8] The divisions of the poem at sonnet 43 and song iii (after 83) are "marked by various formal devices . . . involving definite shifts of tone" (p. 40). He finds that sonnet 43 concludes the first division because it repeats the kind of allegory found at the beginning, only now the lover takes refuge in Stella's heart and experiences "poore *Petrarch's* long deceased woes" (pp. 54–55). Yet unless the reader takes the Petrarchan conventions as seriously as does Young—and he takes them more seriously than does Sidney—he would not notice any break at sonnet 43. In the immediate context, sonnet 40 invokes Stella who looks down upon the lover "from the height of Vertue's throne"; in 41, she looks down upon him from the lists and her beams guide his lance true; in 42, she looks down from her heaven and he praises her eyes as stars "Whose beames be joyes"; 43 extends the praise from her fair eyes to include her sweet lips and dear heart; and 44 addresses her heart in particular.

Ringler discovers "a clearly discernible three-part structure" (p. 423) quite different from Young's. He argues that Sidney grouped his sonnets "to mark definite stages in the progress of Astrophil's courtship" (p. xlv), and finds these stages at sonnet 51 and song viii. In the first fifty-one sonnets, Astrophel employs sophistical arguments to justify his thraldom to love, but then comes a shift in his attitude: "The mask is dropped in the 52nd sonnet, which marks the beginning of the second part of the sequence, where Virtue and Love argue for the possession of Stella" (p. xlvii). Yet this sonnet deserves such stress only if we allow that the sonnets are "ostensibly autobiographical" (p. xliv), and if we then interpret sonnet 52 as the point where Sidney claims Lady Rich's body. Otherwise it is read as an elaborate legal metaphor whose witty point is that Love lays legal claim to possess Stella's body. In sonnet 46 he had justified his desire; no disguise is thrown off at sonnet 52, and in the later sonnets he continues his suit.

John Buxton places the first break at sonnet 32 because Morpheus' claim that he steals Stella's image "recalls, as it must be intended to recall, the Muses' earlier advice"[9] in sonnet 1 to "looke in thy heart and write." Yet Morpheus does not offer advice upon how to write a sonnet, but explains how he brings life-like dreams of Stella to her lover. Further, this sonnet is part of an immediate sequence that uses the conventional metaphor of the lover in darkness: Astrophel communes with the moon in 31, dreams in 32, and finds himself "wrapt in a most infernal night" in 33. Morpheus' theft of Stella's image from the dreaming lover occasions sonnet 33 with its awakened memory of how Stella was stolen from him. There is no division here within the poem.

Neil Rudenstine groups sonnets according to themes, such as the grounds of Astrophel's love, the conflict within his love, and the treatment of style.[10] The difficulty with such grouping is that such themes may occur throughout the sequence. He finds a division at sonnet 40 because here Astrophel appeals directly to Stella in intimate terms. Even in this sonnet, however, he notes a retreat from the frank, personal appeal of the opening lines to the conventional Petrarchan posture of the close (pp. 235–36).

Since critics have placed the end of the first section of Sidney's poem variously at sonnets 32, 40, 43, and 51, one may fairly conclude that it does not possess "a clearly discernible three-part structure." Consequently, it may seem best to read the poem as a prolonged lyrical meditation without any structure, as does Lewis who, apparently, would read the sonnets in any order. Alternatively, with R. L. Montgomery, one may trace a general theme, such as the conflict between reason and passion, which may be found in any collection of love sonnets.[11] If one should persist in seeking a structure, as I intend to do, the first excuse is that elsewhere Sidney is keenly aware of poetic structure. He organizes the ***Old Arcadia*** into five acts; he patterns the Eclogues into a developing argument; and he carefully balances the opening and concluding pairs of poems in ***Certain Sonnets***. Furthermore, in the *Apology* he stresses poetic structure, both in larger terms when he discusses the "*Idea* or fore-conceit" by which he claims that a poet should be judged, and in particular terms when he seeks out English poems which he may praise for their "poetical sinews." I believe that Ringler is correct when he argues that "Sidney's work is more carefully structured than that of any other Elizabethan sonnet collection" (p. xlvi). My chief quarrel with his divisions, and those of the other critics, is that they are not simple and self-evident.

Any division of the poem into distinct parts is useful only as it remains simple. Ideally, it should be as simple as the division of the ***Old Arcadia*** into five acts, or *The Faerie Queene* and *Paradise Lost* into separate books. It should be evident to any careful reader and not depend upon special knowledge of Petrarchan conventions, Sidney's life, or distribution of poetic themes. I propose the simplest three-part division possible for a collection of 108 sonnets. I suggest that the poem is divided into three nearly equal parts which mark definite stages in its argument: sonnets 1–35, 36–72, and 72–108. By recognizing these divisions, we may read ***Astrophel and Stella*** as a sonnet sequence, that is, as one long poem with a unifying structure.

I must assume that Sidney arranged the sonnets in their present order, and therefore I find Pollard's arguments convincing:

> . . . the general sequence of the Sonnets is justified against its attackers by the consensus of all the manuscripts, by the failure of commentators to find any single group which has been broken up and can be reconstructed, and by the readiness with which the present order yields itself to a connected narrative.[12]

Apart from the expurgated sonnet 37, the Quartos agree with the order of the sonnets in the authoritative 1598 text, where they are numbered for the first time. Yet the best "evidence" is simply the sense that the present order yields.

The eleven songs raise special problems in their relation to the sonnets, in their two kinds, and in their order. Sidney presents his whole poem as "Songs and Sonnets," much as the ***Arcadia*** mingles prose and verse, and he distinguishes carefully between the two forms. In a general way, he follows Petrarch's division between the *sonetto*, or little song, and the *canzone* or big song. The sonnet severely controls the lover's emotions in order to express logically a witty idea in fourteen lines. Often it remains so lightly "witty" that it becomes darkened with repressed emotions. Sidney is one of the few poets who can casually ask, "Deare, why make you more of a dog then me?" (59), or lightly address the lecherous sparrow and himself in "Good brother *Philip*, I have borne you long" (83), or gaily play with the theme, "I on my horse, and *Love* on me doth trie / Our virgule horsmanships" (49), without giving way to sarcasm, cynicism, and humiliation. But at those points where emotion cannot be contained within the sonnet form, he breaks into song. This function of the song is expressed quite properly at the opening of Song i: ". . . now my breast orecharg'd to Musicke lendeth," and in its refrain: "To you, to you, all song of praise is due." Only in the harmony of song may the heightened vehemence of the lover's passion be expressed and controlled.

Ringler notes the distinction between the six songs in trochaic meters which "narrate the more important events of the sequence" and the five in conventional iambic meters which are "little more than fillers" (p. xlv). In the first quartos all the songs are grouped together after the sonnets, while in the 1598 edition some of them are distributed. I believe that all the trochaic songs are properly placed, except possibly song ii, but none of the iambic songs, except possibly song v.[13] Obviously, no understanding of the structure of the poem may depend upon their present order. Further, it would appear that there should be twelve songs to correspond to the total number of 12 × 9 sonnets. It soon becomes clear that, though the poem was carefully planned, it remains unfinished. Like all of Sidney's works, it must be judged by what he was trying to do, rather than what he accomplished, "for any understanding knoweth the skill of the artificer standeth in that *Idea* or fore-conceit of the work, and not in the work itself."

II

The structure of ***Astrophel and Stella*** derives from the program outlined in the opening sonnet:

> Loving in truth, and faine in verse my love to show,
> That the deare She might take some pleasure of my paine:
> Pleasure might cause her reade, reading might make her know,
> Knowledge might pitie winne, and pitie grace obtaine,
> I sought fit words to paint the blackest face of woe.

Here Stella's role is carefully spelled out: the pleasure that she will take in reading of his pain may bring knowledge of his plight, such knowledge may arouse her pity, and through pity she may offer him her favor. Astrophel's role is to write sonnets upon his woe that will effectively move her to such action, and he spells out carefully the means by which he may write once he turns from the inventions of other poets to find inspiration within himself. Stella's role is limited to ours as audience and readers, while Astrophel himself holds the stage both as lover and as poet. Or more correctly, he endeavors "her wits to entertaine" by presenting the image of a man "Loving in truth." That much becomes clear even from the dynamic clash of verbs, almost two to a line. These begin smoothly enough with "Loving . . . Studying . . . turning," then mount to the intensity of "Biting my trewand pen, beating my selfe for spite," to end with the simple, double imperative: "looke . . . write." Clearly his sonnets will be dominated, not by the high song of praise or the low sighs of lamentation, but by the voice of a man who is "great with child to speake." He will not be content, as most love poets seem to be, to please his mistress by praising her or arouse her pity by showing his grief: he will entertain her wits in order to move her to love him.

Since Astrophel, the poet-lover, provides the subject of his verse, sonnets 1–6 define his poetic method and the nature of his love. Sonnets 1 and 2 are carefully balanced: the first describes the stages by which Stella may be brought to love him; the second describes similar stages of knowledge, feeling, and action by which he has been brought to love her. Her paradoxical state is that she should take pleasure in his pain: his is that he should "call it praise to suffer Tyrannie" and believe all is well "While with a feeling skill I paint my hell." The theme of sonnet 2 is the most significant event in the act of loving, the *innamoramento*. Astrophel's moment of falling in love is not the sudden ecstasy of Marlowe's "Who ever lov'd, that lov'd not at first sight?", which lifts the lover out of himself into a timeless world, but a reluctant yielding that "did in mine of time proceed." Astrophel literally "falls in love": he falls within himself, divided against himself. It is not Stella, but himself, whom he must convince about his love.

Sonnet 3 elaborates the "inventions fine" of 1 into four schools of love poetry, which Astrophel sets apart from his own method of copying Love and Beauty in Stella's face. The easy "phrases fine" of other poets contrast with the "fit words" which he so painfully seeks in 1. He mocks them for their extravagance: for example, that a poet need call upon all the Muses simply to record his fancies. He opposes what they read in poetic manuals to what he reads in Stella's face. Simply expressed, he turns from Art to Nature. Then from Love which Nature writes in Stella's face, Astrophel turns in sonnet 4 to vain love in himself. The consequence of his falling in love is seen as a clash between love and virtue. Since the conflict lies within him, rather than between him and Stella, virtue is seen first within him rather than her. What this sonnet calls the "bate betweene my will and wit" is illustrated in sonnet 5. Against the set pattern of the previous sonnets, in which the octave is followed by a quatrain and couplet or by two triplets, this sonnet consists of two quatrains, a triplet, a couplet, and a final line that is divided into two parts in order to play "ought to" and "should" against the climax in "must." Wit tells Astrophel all that should be, in thirteen lines making irrefutably clear what Will demolishes in less than one line. The hammering repetition of "It is most true" and "True" is silenced by the unanswerable truth of fact. Sonnet 5 brings into the poem concepts of love in courtly love, neoplatonic doctrine, and Christian faith; significantly, there is no resolution: the positions of wit and will remain irreconcilable throughout the poem.

Sonnet 6 rounds out the opening group of sonnets—it uses the twelve-syllable line of 1—by treating the poet as lover. The extravagant posturings of other lovers are contrasted with his simple feelings, and their indirections and artifice with his "trembling voice." Mockery of others includes self-mockery, of course, even as he employs the extravagance he mocks in such phrases as "powdred with golden raine." His earlier professions of love—"Loving in truth" (1), "I loved, but . . ." (2), "*Vertue*, thou thy selfe shalt be in love" (4), and "I must *Stella* love" (5)—culminate in a simple confession: "I do *Stella* love."

The next six sonnets are divided into two groups of three: the first treats Stella and the second, Astrophel. The three central conceits in any collection of Petrarchan love sonnets are Beauty, Love, and Virtue, in that order: the lady's beauty arouses love which her virtue then opposes. Accordingly, Stella's beauty is treated in 7, her relation to love in 8, and her virtue in 9. As exercises in conventional themes, these sonnets use the three methods outlined in sonnet 6: oxymoron, mythology, and personification, in that order. The confident and sophisticated handling of these poetic devices constitutes a witty answer to the "trembling voice" which is all the poet-lover claims in sonnet 6.

Since Stella is the star, sonnet 7 describes her beauty through her eyes, whose beams shine as stars from a black sky. The conventional conceit becomes literal if we recognize that Lady Rich's eyes were in fact black. Unlike those poets, mocked in 6, who merely state a paradox, such as "heav'nly beames, infusing hellish paine," Sidney argues his in order to reach the logical conclusion that

Stella's bright beams are dressed in black because black is Love's mourning weed which honors her lovers' deaths. This mention of Love leads in 8 to the story of how Love responded to Stella's bright beauty, only to learn that, since she is a star, her light gives no heat; and so he fled to the lover's heart which now he kindles with love. The light from her eyes in 7 is extended to include her fair skin. The mythology is more than decorative, which is the point of Sidney's mockery of the device in sonnet 6: the story of the runaway Cupid is given a topical turn in the reference to Turkish invasions and England's state of peace. Further, it makes a witty analogy between "that Turkish hardned hart" and Stella's coldness, both causing Cupid to flee, in contrast to the lover's heart which burns Cupid. In sonnet 9, Love, aroused by Beauty, conflicts with Virtue. While Stella's beauty is the work of Nature (7) and the love that responds to her beauty is born in Greece (8), her virtue, whose setting is her beauty, is a "heav'nly guest." Sonnet 9 becomes a fitting climax to the praise of Stella's beauty seen in her eyes: her eyes which are Nature's chief work (7) but provide light without heat that "needs in nature grow" (8) are praised as windows through which Virtue gazes upon the lover. Further, it illustrates the witty and functional use of personification whose abuse is mocked in sonnet 9. To modify the point about this sonnet made earlier: while our understanding of it does not depend upon any other sonnet, it gains significance through its context. The formal praise of Stella's beauty belongs at just this point of the sequence. Ideally, the meaning of any Sidney sonnet, like the meaning of a word, is given by its context. Without some awareness of the nature of the context of this sonnet, and of its function within that context, readers may be led to reject it because of its abstractness and formality.

In these three sonnets of praise, the lover himself provides only the concluding point of wit: he bleeds, he is warmed by Love, he is drawn to Stella by Love and burned. In sonnets 10–12, though Stella's eyes are mentioned, the subject is Astrophel as he confronts her beauty, his love for her, and her virtue.

The witty play of reason upon sensual love, which characterizes Sidney's handling of the love sonnet, is treated in sonnet 10. Reason should move upward in stages by climbing the Muses' hill, reaching for Nature's best fruit, seeking heaven, and finally seeing into heaven. These are the stages through which the Renaissance poet moved from the lower poetic forms toward heroic and divine poetry. In Sidney's use of the lyric, however, Reason chooses instead to move downward to earthly matters of love and sense, and "still / Wouldst brabling be with sence and love in me." ("Brabling" conveys accurately the low, familiar level to which Reason has been reduced.) Finally Reason is led to defend sensual love by proving "good reason her to love." Such sensual love is illustrated in sonnet 11: Love is content to look upon Stella's outward beauty until reason urges: "foole, seekst not to get into her hart." Here Reason replies to Love and sense by offering "good reason her to love" for more than her outward beauty. But sonnet 12 shows why Cupid cannot get into her heart:

> . . . her heart is such a Cittadell,
> So fortified with wit, stor'd with disdaine,
> That to win it, is all the skill and paine.

As in the previous group, Stella's beauty is extended from her eyes (10), to her eyes, cheek, and breast (11), to the catalogue of her beauty in 12.

The first twelve sonnets provide a comprehensive introduction to the whole poem by relating Astrophel and Stella to the three counters of any Renaissance love poem. Her beauty incites his highest praise; his love for her causes his fall from an earlier state of innocence into a hell of unsatisfied desire; and her virtue keeps her free. Because of her virtue, she cannot call her lover's bluff. Hence, though he is bound by love, he remains free to yield himself entirely to her without fear of utter personal annihilation to which his words commit him. Her virtue is his security. Any Petrarchan poet would rather be frustrated in his desire to satisfy his love than frustrated in his desire to write about his agony of frustration. Hence the lover and his lady must exist upon different planes of existence, their positions fixed forever. Because of this, sonneteers soon discover the principle of perpetual motion: once having mastered the technical problems of the form, they may go on forever, and usually do.

Sidney introduces certain stresses that finally must destroy this fixed Petrarchan position. The symbolism that he adopts, of Stella as the star and Astrophel as the lover of the star, is too extreme to maintain. The praise of her "clear voyce" in sonnet 12, for example, prepares a role for her quite different from that of the distant and disdainful mistress. Even his act of writing sonnets assumes that, despite her virtue, she may be moved to offer him her favor. Her heart, "fortified with wit, stor'd with disdaine" (12), is clearly vulnerable to witty persuasion. Obviously, she will not remain forever impregnable. Yet the major stress upon any fixed relationship is Sidney's image of a man "Loving in truth." The direct, speaking voice, the intimate, cajoling tone, and the easy, familiar manner suggest the straight-forward, down-to-earth, insistent lover who will not long remain content with the degrading and embarrassing preliminaries of courtship. His love moves down to physical satisfaction rather than up to intellectual and spiritual consolation. He is seen as the poet in conflict with competing poetic styles, the dreamer in conflict with reality, the lover in conflict with himself, the courtier in conflict with society, the man in conflict with the flesh, and more particularly as Philip Sidney in conflict with his own ambitions: these facets of Astrophel are too various and competing to allow any fixed relationship to Stella. Dramatic changes are inevitable.

In sonnets 14–35, Sidney conveys the experience of a man loving in truth by placing Astrophel in a social context. Having been wounded by love, he becomes increasingly at odds with society until he remains alone in physical and spiritual darkness. In sonnet 14, he allows that Desire "Doth plunge my wel-form'd soule even in the mire / Of sinfull thoughts, which do in ruine end"; yet he defends his sinful state. The agony of loving is displayed with sharper awareness than before. In place of the earlier debate between Reason, Virtue, and Love, now the contest is directly internal and deeply personal. Linked sonnets show him poisoned (16), pierced with Love's arrows (17), bankrupt (18), fallen (19), mortally wounded through Love's ambush (20), and marred in mind and fortune as one "whom *Love* doth windlas [i. e., ambush] so" (21). Appropriately, with Stella's dramatic entrance at sonnet 20, her heavenly eye delivers the death wound that sets him apart from all others. As a result, he is pensive (23), jealous (24), frustrated (25), abstracted (27), enslaved (29), and withdrawn from the pressing political life around him (30). By the end of this sequence, his fall seems complete.

Within this general organization, the sonnets are linked in various ways. One sonnet may prompt the next. In sonnet 15, for example, he tells those poets who seek inspiration from Parnassus, Dictionaries, or Petrarch that they "bewray a want of inward tuch." For unless the poet is (in the words of the *Apology*) "lifted up with the vigor of his own invention," he will be led to seek every spring at Parnassus, his alliteration will remain mechanical, and his imitation of Petrarch will not be absorbed. Astrophel offers advice to such poets, rather than to himself as he did in sonnet 1: "*Stella* behold, and then begin to endite." Then in sonnet 16 he reveals what happened to him when he "beheld / *Stella*." Again, in sonnet 21 he asks his friend, "Hath this world ought so faire as *Stella* is?" and answers that question in sonnet 22 where he explains why the sun burns other ladies but only kisses Stella. (Here the connection is strengthened by the same concluding rhyme.) Sonnets are connected most simply by catalogue: Astrophel addresses his friends (20), his special friend (21), curious wits (23), rich fools (24), the wisest scholar (25), dusty wits (26), idle gossips (27), curious readers (28), and busy wits (30). Or they may be subtly organized by apparently casual linking. For example, sonnet 29 presents an elaborate and extravagant fiction of Cupid as a foreign aggressor who has conquered Stella's body, which is the coast upon which the lover looks. Sonnet 30 turns abruptly from this fiction to fact, the topical matter of Turkish aggression. Yet the question "Whether the Turkish new-moone minded be / To fill his hornes this yeare on Christian coast" does not concern Astrophel, for he thinks only of Stella. Then sonnet 31 shows him communing instead with the lover's moon. Or sonnets may be linked by chance association of words. In sonnet 23, the curious wits are dismissed as fools because they do not realize that Astrophel's thoughts dwell upon Stella's heart. Then sonnet 24 treats the filthy heart of the rich fool who possesses Stella. However, I suspect that such linking is allowed because the vision of Stella handled, enjoyed, and her beauty blotted with foul abuse is designed to clash violently with the triumphant victory of Stella's beauty over the sun in sonnet 22.

By sonnet 30 Astrophel is isolated from society and its concerns: he dismisses all the chief political questions of the day which exercise busy wits. As modern readers we may be distracted by trying to fix the seven international events alluded to. Clearly the sonnet is meant to shock: in his high social position, as the son of Sir Henry, and because of the important political role for which he was being groomed, Sidney should be deeply engaged in the vital issues that affect his country. This sonnet is his farewell to the world before he becomes further overwhelmed by love. In this personal context, speaking directly of himself, he addresses Stella for the first time: he dismisses the world's affairs "for still I thinke of you." His meditation upon her is illustrated in the famous sonnet 30. Its companion is sonnet 31, the colloquial address, "ev'n of fellowship, O Moone, tell me" being repeated in the address to Morpheus: "Vouchsafe of all acquaintance this to tell." Now in the darkened state of sleep, he projects Stella's image in his heart, the "Ivorie, Rubies, pearle and gold" which "shew her skin, lips, teeth and head so well." Suddenly in the next sonnet, this highly conventional image of Stella is juxtaposed to her real self as Lady Rich. As noted earlier, Morpheus' theft of Stella's image from the dreaming lover prompts the awakened memory of how Stella was in fact stolen from him. (Such a connection, which is typical of the turning-points in the poem, is too significant not to have been planned, yet too profound simply to have been planned.) The biographical reference, however closely it should be pressed, has been generally allowed. In his lament: "I . . . could not see my blisse," Sidney may be making a pun on the name, Devereux, from *heureux*=happiness, bliss, as does Spenser in his *Prothalamion*.[14] What matters though, is that he has forsaken life for a mere fiction: worse off than ever Pygmalion was, he is left with Stella's image while another enjoys her person. With this loss of his "heav'nly day," he is left "wrapt in a most infernall night." His isolation is complete.

This sudden irruption of biographical matter, which forces the distinction between the poet's golden world and Nature's brazen one, leads him to reappraise his roles as lover and poet. In sonnets 34 and 35 he asks the two fundamental questions about words, the first in relation to himself as a lover: "How can words ease?" and the second in relation to himself as a poet: "What may words say?"

At the outset Astrophel had assumed that by expressing his grief in verse, he would lead Stella to pity him; in 34, in an intensely private quarrel, he asks how expressing his grief may affect himself:

> Come let me write, "And to what end?" To ease
> A burthned hart. "How can words ease, which are
> The glasses of thy dayly vexing care?"
> Oft cruell fights well pictured forth do please.

Solace through utterance—the control of grief by imposing poetic form upon it—was a traditional function of verse. It is expressed by Donne in "The Triple Fool":

> I thought, if I could draw my pains
> Through rhyme's vexation, I should them allay:
> Grief brought to numbers cannot be so fierce;
> For he tames it, that fetters it in verse.

However, Sidney rejects one inference from this function of poetry (which Donne draws), that verse should remain private because publishing it only releases and renews grief:

> "Art not asham'd to publish thy disease?"
> Nay, that may breed my fame, it is so rare:
> "But will not wise men thinke thy words fond ware?"
> Then be they close, and so none shall displease.
> "What idler thing, then speake and not be hard?"
> What harder thing then smart, and not to speake?

Sonnet 34 makes abundantly clear that Astrophel cannot remain content with his present role as poet and lover.

At the beginning he had assumed also that he would show himself as a man "Loving in truth"; in 35 he recognizes that his truth must seem like flattery:

> What may words say, or what may words not say,
> Where truth it selfe must speake like flatterie?
> Within what bounds can one his liking stay,
> Where Nature doth with infinite agree?

Because of Stella's perfection, words lose their meaning. As a poet, he is reduced to that absurd posture, which he mocks in the ***Arcadia***, of uttering "those immoderate praises which the foolish lover ever thinks short of his mistress although they reach far beyond the heavens." His dilemma over language leads him to take full and final stock of his present position: not only is his language unable to praise her truthfully, but his love can know no bounds, no counsel can restrain his desire, and he has no hope of ever enjoying her. It leads him further to catalogue "*Stella's* great powrs" which confuse his mind in 34: her Chastity, Honor, and Fame, to which he adds the biographical fact—a climactc one—of who she is:

> Honour is honour'd, that thou doest possesse
> Him as thy slave, and now long needy Fame
> Doth even grow rich, naming my *Stella's* name.

The sonnet does not narrow down to a final point of wit but expands to the large claim: "It is a praise to praise, when thou art praisde." As a definition of the lyric as a poem of praise, it stands at the end of the first part of the poem.

III

The second part of the poem begins with sonnet 36, which records Stella's fresh assault upon Astrophel by her singing. For the first time he addresses her by name:

> Stella, whence doth this new assault arise,
> A conquerd, yelden, ransackt heart to winne?
> Whereto long since, through my long battred eyes,
> Whole armies of thy beauties entred in.
> And there long since, *Love* thy Lieutenant lies,
> My forces razde, thy banners raisd within:
> Of conquest, do not these effects suffice,
> But wilt new warre upon thine owne begin?
> With so sweete voice, and by sweete Nature so,
> In sweetest strength, so sweetly skild withall,
> In all sweete stratagems sweete Arte can show,
> That not my soule, which at thy foot did fall,
> Long since forc'd by thy beames, but stone nor tree
> By Sence's priviledge, can scape from thee.[15]

Until now she has remained the star: remote, bright in her beauty, assaulting him only with the bright beams from her eyes. Now she assaults him by the sound of her voice. Her eyes have been praised as Nature's chief work (sonnet 7; compare also sonnets 3, 9 and 17), but her voice adds Art to Nature and the harmony of their combined powers overwhelms him. Now when he sleeps, as in sonnet 38, her image "not onely shines but sings." Three songs analyze the combined effect of her eyes and voice: song iii relates how men's ears and eyes are charmed when "*Stella* singeth" and "*Stella* shineth"; song vi debates the precedence of her voice and face; and its companion, song vii, praises her eyes as "life-giving lights" but laments the effect of "her soule-invading voice." As the second highest sense, hearing is associated with the soul: traditionally, it is more directly linked with the soul than is the sight. In song i, Sidney praises Stella "Who hath the voyce, which soule from sences sunders," and in sonnet 77 he praises "That voyce, which makes the soule plant himselfe in the eares." The point of Astrophel's complaint in sonnet 36 depends on the distinction between the eyes which assault the body and the voice which assaults the soul. He sees no need for this second assault by her voice upon his soul, for his soul has been long since overwhelmed by her eyes.

This fresh assault by her voice creates an entirely new relationship between them. Her voice implies, of course, that she is an immediate, physical presence: she is present as one whom he hears and who hears him. As such, she cannot be treated in the conventional manner of the opening section but only in immediate and dramatic terms. Since the ear is the sense through which love affects the soul, Stella's voice arouses irrepressible desires. Or in terms of the poem's central image: being in her presence, her eyes offer him both light and heat through which he burns. Now when he extols her eyes, as in sonnet 42, he declares their malignant effect upon him: when he sees her "My life forgets to nourish languisht sprites." (Sonnet 53 illustrates this effect.) In three sonnets (40, 42, and 45) he is led to refer to himself as love's "wracke."

In this section the sonnets reveal the direct exposure to experience, both in loving and writing sonnets about loving. The immediate pressure of the moment is seen in the pointing to a specific time:

> This night while sleepe begins with heavy wings
>
> (38)
>
> Having this day my horse, my hand, my launce
>
> (41)

or dramatically, as in sonnet 47:

I may, I must, I can, I will, I do
Leave following that, which it is gaine to misse.
Let her go. Soft, but here she comes. Go to,
Unkind, I love you not: O me, that eye
Doth make my heart give to my tongue the lie.

He counter-assaults by a verbal assault upon her. His tone varies from humble supplication to witty, even sarcastic, attack. It is at once both personal and public, solemn and gay, self-effacing and insistent. Only in this section does he appeal directly to her for grace, as in sonnet 40: "O do not let thy Temple be destroyd," rather than indirectly by entertaining her wits. His plan is given in sonnet 61: "I *Stella's* eyes assayll, invade her eares." His visual assault upon her is seen in his shifting disguises: he changes from being the humble suppliant to the demanding lover. His verbal assault is heard in the shifts of tone. His tone becomes ever more strident, insistent, and even threatening. He addresses her in familiar terms as "my deare" (45) or simply "Deare" (46), or sarcastically in "Deare, why make you more of a dog then me?" (59), or almost insolently as "my young Dove" from whom he "crav'd the thing which ever she denies" (63). Though he opens sonnet 48 with the humble appeal, "Soule's joy, bend not those morning starres from me," he does so in order to conclude with the witty address: "Deare Killer."

As Astrophel shifts his disguise, Stella appears in various roles: from the distant star which he worships to the woman whom he desires. Sonnet 37 registers the clash between what she should be as Stella and what she is as Lady Rich:

Rich in the treasure of deserv'd renowne,
Rich in the riches of a royall hart,
Rich in those gifts which give th'eternall crowne;
Who though most rich in these and everie part,
Which make the patents of true worldly blisse,
Hath no misfortune, but that Rich she is.

The argument turns upon the sudden shift from the preposition "in" to the simple connective "is," and therefore from the worth bestowed upon her by the poet to the misfortune of bearing her husband's name. The surprise in the final line is not in the reference to Lady Rich but in a witty technical point. The catalogue of what Stella is "Rich in" should lead to personification: one who is rich in all good fortune should be called Rich. And so it does: she is Rich. But this literary identification is cut across by the historical fact: it is her misfortune that she is Rich.

The double awareness of what Stella is and who she is dominates this section of the poem. Astrophel may supplicate her humbly in sonnet 42, "O eyes, which do the Spheares of beautie move" or appeal to her as his "Soule's joy" in 48; but more often he mocks her as a perverse woman who denies him favors that she allows her dog (59), or pities him in his absence but disdains him in his presence (60), or most perversely allows his love while denying that he may love her (61, 62).

The connections between the sonnets reflect Astrophel's immediate involvement in the experience of loving, and writing directly about it. Links and associations between separate sonnets or within groups of sonnets become part of the immediate drama rather than thematic connections that reveal some larger argument. For example, in sonnet 44 he is led to wonder why she hears his grief yet fails to pity him: "what cause is there so overthwart, / That Noblenesse it selfe makes thus unkind?" He speculates that she is unkind, that is, unnatural, not because she is of "Tygre's kind" but because of her "heav'nly nature." In 47 he addresses her directly: "Go to, / Unkind, I love you not." Though he makes a passing reference to her being unkind in sonnet 57, it is not until sonnet 62 that he returns to this theme: "Late tyr'd with wo, even ready for to pine / With rage of *Love*, I cald my Love unkind." Though she responds with kindness on this occasion, he returns to the theme in 65: "Love by sure proofe I may call thee unkind." In these sonnets Stella's being unkind is not a unifying theme, however, but only one topic that Astrophel uses in his verbal assault upon her.

Though the connections between the sonnets are often close, they tend to be casual for they arise from an immediate experience. In sonnet 39 he woos sleep, apparently in vain, for 40 begins: "As good to write as for to lie and grone." The links between sonnets 40 to 44 have been noticed earlier. The praise of her eyes in 42 for their beauty, joy, and virtue is distributed in 43 in praise of her "Faire eyes, sweet lips, deare heart." In 47 he invokes his virtue to defend him against Stella's beauty: "Vertue awake, Beautie but beautie is," only to collapse when she enters. Sonnet 48, in which he addresses her eyes "Where Vertue is made strong by Beautie's might," depends upon 47 if we are to understand that the virtue is his, and why he claims now that her beauty strengthens it. The passing reference in 47 to himself as one "Whose necke becomes such yoke of tyranny" is expanded in 49 where he sees himself subject to love's tyranny.

Sonnets 50 to 58 illustrate the nature of the connections found in this section. In 50 he complains of the weak proportion of his words to express Stella's figure. In 51 he is confronted by the "unsuted speech" of the courtly gossiper who hinders his meditation upon Stella. In 52 the lover's suit of Stella is again stayed, this time by the quarrel between Virtue and Love. In 53 his martial race is stayed when Stella's glance causes his heart to quake. In 54 he defends those lovers "who quake to say they love." (His defence of "Dumb Swannes" extends the topical reference in 53 by playing upon the analogy between Sidnei and *cygni*.) In 55 he is determined to forsake all speech and cry Stella's name, for "So sweete sounds straight mine eare and heart do hit, / That I well find no eloquence like it." A break in the sequence comes at 56 where he pleads with her to "heare with patience my desire," but 57 records how "She heard my plaints," and the sonnet returns to 55 to show now the sweet effect upon him of her singing his grief. Sonnet 58 is a companion to 57, and so shares the same "b" rhyme. Yet it would be misleading to point to such connections, here or elsewhere in this section, as significant in themselves. They follow from the various aspects of Astrophel as the poet, lover, courtier, and knight as he adjusts his suit of Stella to meet their new relationship.

Their relationship, as it involves hearing as well as sight, not only overwhelms him as a lover but frustrates his role as a poet. His original plan had been that the pleasure she would take in reading his sonnets would arouse her pity; now she takes pleasure in his pain, but no more than that. In sonnet 44 she hears his complaints but fails to pity him because the perfection of her beauty is such that "the sobs of mine annoyes / Are metamorphosd straight to tunes of joyes." In 45 when she does not pity him even though she pities an unhappy lover in a fable that she has read, he is tempted to abandon his role of "Loving in truth" in order to substitute the more moving fiction of himself: "I am not I, pitie the tale of me." Donne's argument against having his poems made public and sung is that it "frees again / Grief, which verse did restrain": to Sidney's greater grief, when Stella not only hears his verse but sings it, he himself is led to take pleasure in his pain:

> A prety case! I hoped her to bring
> To feele my griefes, and she with face and voice
> So sweets my paines, that my paines me rejoyce.
>
> (57)

Again in 58 he laments that when Stella reads his verse, her voice and face are such that "most ravishing delight / Even those sad words even in sad me did breed." Frustrated as both poet and lover, he is forced to abandon his passive role.

Paradoxically, the limited success of Astrophel's courtship precipitates a crisis for him both as poet and as lover. In his opening program, he had assumed that Stella would be an ideal reader who would take pleasure in reading of his pain, and knowing his pain would pity him, and through love would offer him her favor. Unfortunately, she is not properly programmed: she turns out to be an increasingly perverse woman, balking at each step of his literary ladder. First she takes pleasure in his pain but no more; then she pities him but only in his absence (60); but worst of all, she accepts his love but rejects his desire. At 59, when she prefers her dog to him, he makes the veiled threat that he will stop loving her:

> Alas, if you graunt only such delight
> To witlesse things, then *Love* I hope (since wit
> Becomes a clog) will soone ease me of it.

In her perversity, she responds for the first time with "fierce *Love* and lovely hate" (60). Her sophistry in accepting his love but rejecting his desire (61, 62) is countered in 63 by having grammar's virtue outweigh hers. Her double negative in rejecting him is interpreted as her yielding.[16] At this stage the sonnets read as an intermittent commentary upon a developing intimacy. In his joy that she loves him, he seeks to claim that sonnets should record his "height of delight / In well raisde notes" and not be "bound prentise to annoy" (70). His crisis as a poet is that sonnets are so bound, and he concludes rightly that "Wise silence is best musicke unto blisse." Love's consent demands action, not words. His crisis as a lover is simply that he wants to satisfy his desire by action.

Sonnets 71 and 72 form the second major turning-point in the structure of the poem. As such, they are as carefully written as the allegorical cores of Spenser's *Faerie Queene*, and they serve much the same function. At the moment of his mounting joy, Astrophel reaches the crucial stage of love: through love for Stella, he may move up to some higher love or down to lust. In 71 he imitates Petrarch in order to test Petrarch's transcendent vision of Laura: he finds it wanting in human terms, and abandons it.[17] The 12th and 13th lines summarize the neoplatonic doctrine which has been present from the opening sonnets: "So while thy beautie drawes the heart to love, / As fast thy Vertue bends that love to good." Yet "what should be" is countered in the final line by "what is": "'But ah,' Desire still cries, 'give me some food.'" Sonnet 72 tells why Desire "because thou wouldst have all, / Now banisht art," and allows only half a line for Astrophel's rebuttal: "but yet alas how shall?" That final question is rhetorical yet puzzled, as though he were left paralyzed. Its tone contrasts sharply with the witty banter and cajolery of the previous sonnets with their verbal assault upon her, and particularly with the naughty ending of 68, the arch, gloating anticipation of 69, the sententious ending of 70, and the naked cry of 71. Unable to distinguish desire from love, or to forsake it, or to spiritualize it, he yields to it. The rest of the poem shows what happens when desire "wouldst have all."

IV

The concluding section of the poem begins at the moment Astrophel steals a kiss. This moment is described dramatically in song ii, analyzed in sonnet 73, and commented upon in an extended sequence. The simple movement of the three parts of the poem is from sight to hearing to touch. Sight awakens love; hearing arouses desire; and now touch seeks to satisfy desire. To the lust of the eye and the lust of the ear is added the lust of the flesh. This final section includes all the events of the "affair" between the lovers.

Pietro Bembo offers the most direct commentary upon the direction of Astrophel's love. In Castiglione's *Courtier*, he explains that when the lover sees a beautiful woman, his eyes will snatch the image of her beauty and carry it into his heart. There his soul "beginneth to beholde it with pleasure, and feeleth within her selfe the influence that stirreth her." If he represses the heat of lust, he will see beauty as "an heavenly shining beame" and satisfy his desire with "the vertue of seeing."[18] Accordingly, Bembo exhorts the lover to

> . . . lay aside therefore the blinde judgement of the sense, and enjoy with his eyes the brightnesse, the comelinesse, the loving sparkels, laughters, gestures, and all the other pleasant furnitures of beautie: espe-

> cially with hearing the sweetnesse of her voice, the tunablenesse of her wordes, the melody of her singing.
>
> (p. 313)

Yet he cautions him to be satisfied with "the sight and the hearing . . . the lookes of her eyes, the image of her countenance, and the voice of her wordes, that pearce into the lovers hart" (p. 314). He allows the reasonable lover to proceed as far as the kiss; yet he warns that, for the sensual lover, the kiss will be the knitting of bodies.

In sonnet 81, Astrophel allows that the kiss "even soules together ties / By linkes of *Love*"; what he goes on to say confirms Bembo's fears:

> But my heart burnes, I cannot silent be.
> Then since (deare life) you faine would have me peace,
> And I, mad with delight, want wit to cease,
> Stop you my mouth with still still kissing me.

Twelve poems, from song ii to sonnet 83 (most of them on the kiss) compose the erotic center of the poem. This sequence moves from the simple lyricism of the song, to the dramatic action of 73, the mock encomium of 75 (with its bawdy ending which suggests that Edward was willing to risk syphilis for the sake of his whore), the naughtiness of 76, the coy wittiness of 77, the invitation to adultery in 78, and the three traditional "baiser" sonnets, 79–81. It reaches an erotic climax in sonnet 82 in the image of plucking fruit from the guarded tree. (The nymph in Drummond's poem who is assured that she may kiss the old toothless man, Dorus, because "Y'ar sure he shall not your soft cherrie bite" may be more assured than Stella: Astrophel has bitten before, and promises not to bite again "even by the same delight.") The harshly cynical sonnet 83 is Astrophel's farewell to the kiss. By sonnet 85 and song x, he anticipates the full banquet of sense.

The affair itself to which the kiss leads may be reconstructed only if the songs are rearranged. The sonnets prepare for their meeting: he journeys to her (84) and anticipates the satisfaction of his desire (85); two songs describe their subsequent meeting in the garden which leads to his rejection (song viii) and despair (song ix); and two concluding sonnets describe his anguish at the event (86) and then hers (87). Twelve sonnets (88–99) register his state when absent from her. That absence may be simple physical separation, banishment, or the consequence of some action by which he has harmed her (93, with its effects carefully treated in 94–95). Four sonnets tell how he is entertained by other women in his absence (88, 91, 97, 106); four sonnets recall her beauty in sorrow (100), in sickness (101–102), and as he had seen her before his absence (103); and four poems describe his efforts to see her by a window (104, song xi, 105–106). The variety of these themes suggests poetical enlarging: he heightens his grief by all possible means, for "Sorrow onely then hath glory, / When tis excellently sory" (song ix).

Such "disorder" is found only if we are looking for a story simply told. The sonnets, apart from the songs, are the most carefully structured and arranged in the entire sequence. For example, sonnet 87 notes Stella's sadness at their parting:

> I saw that teares did in her eyes appeare;
> I saw that sighes her sweetest lips did part,
> And her sad words my sadded sence did heare.

Yet at her tears, sighs, and words, he "swam in joy, such love in her was seene." In sonnet 100, these three terms are expanded into two quatrains and a triplet in order to make the same claim that "Such teares, sighs, plaints, no sorrow is, but joy." The later sonnet is both more comprehensive in its reference and more powerful because the intervening sonnets have demonstrated his anguish, "the hell where my soule fries," which she pities. Her grief corresponds to his sickness through grief (94) and leads to the two sonnets on her sickness.

The two concluding sonnets resolve the entire poem. The demands of "living" and "loving" have been held in tension from the opening sonnet. Loving Stella had required Astrophel to withdraw from life and commit all his powers to her. Now he begs for the return of those powers in order to undertake effectively some action in the world, though he asks this only in order that she should not be shamed in him. Love is still maintained even as it yields to the demands of life. As it should, poetry leads to action.

The final sonnet turns from Astrophel's public figure to his private self. Its image of his breast as "that darke fornace" which contains his oppressed heart sums up the imagery of the entire poem. Immediately, it consolidates the earlier images of his anguish when he is separated from her: of his brain "darke with misty vapors" (94), the darkness of his thoughts (96), and his "mazde powers" (99). His imprisoned state through unfulfilled desire suggests Donne's image in the *Ecstasy*:

> So must pure lovers' souls descend
> To affections, and to faculties,
> Which sense may reach and apprehend,
> Else a great Prince in prison lies.

Yet Astrophel's agony arises from his sense of loss, and the image of the dark furnace reinterprets his earlier memory of how he first lost her: "wrapt in a most infernall night, / I find how heav'nly day wretch I did misse" (33). The "iron doores" that confine him may refer to the "iron lawes of duty" (87), as Ringler suggests (p. 491). Stella tells Astrophel that she leaves him because of "Tyran honour" (song viii), and it is the absence of honor

> . . . that empty sound
> Call'd *Honor*, which became
> The tyran of the minde,
> And so torments our Nature without ground

that defines the golden age in Tasso's *Aminta*.[19] Astrophel's state of despair suggests the hell to which desire has brought him. The image of her light that shines into his darkness returns to the poem's central image, the lover in darkness gazing up at the heavenly light of his star. The final sonnet focusses upon this image with full intensity. It is astonishing, yet consistent with the whole poem, that Astrophel should persist in his love without repenting, recanting, or turning from it. This final sonnet earns him the claim that he makes in the poem's opening phrase: "Loving in truth."

Notes

1. J. Erskine, *The Elizabethan Lyric* (New York, 1903), pp. 153–54.
2. I cite William A. Ringler's edition, *The Poems of Sir Philip Sidney* (Oxford, 1962) throughout. Despite my great respect for this edition, I cannot accept the spelling, "Astrophil." For the sake of the Greek root and the play upon Philip, that spelling of the name by itself may be allowed (p. 458); but for the sake of assonance, the only spelling, when coupled with Stella, can be "Astrophel." No one can *say* "Astrophil and Stella."
3. See John Charles Nelson, *Renaissance Theory of Love* (New York, 1958), pp. 15–66.
4. C. S. Lewis, *English Literature in the Sixteenth Century Excluding Drama* (Oxford, 1954), pp. 327–28.
5. *Gabriel Harvey's Marginalia*, ed. G. C. Moore Smith (Stratford-upon-Avon, 1913), p. 228.
6. Fulke Greville, *Life of Sir Philip Sidney*, ed. Nowell Smith (Oxford, 1907), p. 16.
7. *Orlando Furioso in English Heroical Verse*, by John Harington (London, 1591), p. 30.
8. Richard B. Young, "English Petrarke: A Study of Sidney's *Astrophel and Stella*," in *Three Studies in the Renaissance: Sidney, Jonson, Milton* (New Haven, 1958), p. 88.
9. John Buxton, *Elizabethan Taste* (London, 1963), p. 283.
10. Neil L. Rudenstine, *Sidney's Poetic Development* (Cambridge, Mass., 1967), pp. 183–221.
11. Robert L. Montgomery, Jr., *Symmetry and Sense: The Poetry of Sir Philip Sidney* (Austin, 1961).
12. Alfred W. Pollard, ed., *Astrophel and Stella* (London, 1888), p. xxxviii.
13. See Ann Romayne Howe, "*Astrophel and Stella*: 'Why and How,'" *SP*, 61 (1964), pp. 164–67. I agree with her ordering of the songs: song i after 28, song iii before 36, song iv before 63, and songs vi and vii between 56 and 58.
14. See Grosart's note in the *Variorum Spenser: The Minor Poems*, II. 504.
15. For the placing of song iii before sonnet 36, see note 13. If the song belongs anywhere in the sequence, it belongs here, especially as it introduces a new division of the poem. Placed before 36, the song explains the Orpheus image in lines 13–14, in particular, the reference to "tree" which has no explanation within the metaphor of the sonnet.
16. For the placing of song iv before sonnet 63, see note 13. I interpret the final refrain of this song to signify her yielding to him. I am surprised that it could be taken otherwise; yet Rudenstine refers to Astrophel's display of frustration and anger in his closing words (p. 258).
17. See the excellent analysis of this sonnet in J. W. Lever, *The Elizabethan Love Sonnet* (London, 1956), pp. 58–62, and also in David Kalstone, *Sidney's Poetry: Contexts and Interpretations* (Cambridge, Mass., 1965), pp. 118–22. Kalstone notes that the sonnet is "a rare example of what appears to be a direct response to a poem by Petrarch" (p. 117). In his analysis of the sequence, he argues that "*Astrophel and Stella* reaches a climax in sonnets 69–72" (p. 172).
18. Castiglione, *Courtier* (Everyman ed.), p. 313.
19. I cite Daniel's translation, "A Pastoral," in *Works*, ed. Grosart, I. 260.

Richard Lanham (essay date 1972)

SOURCE: "*Astrophel and Stella*: Pure and Impure Persuasion," in *English Literary Renaissance*, Vol. 2, No. 1., Winter 1972, pp. 100–15.

[*In the following essay, Lanham contends that the essential cause of the poem sequence* Astrophel and Stella *is sexual frustration.*]

The first sonnet in Sir Philip Sidney's sequence confronts the difficulty of writing poetry with a stale and borrowed rhetoric, the need to seek a fresh source of inspiration in real feeling and, presumably, in an unaffected praise and relationship to his mistress. Style becomes not only means but theme, and this at the earliest possible moment. Sidney betrays, too, that acute self-consciousness wherever we touch him, in life or art. Both poet and poetry assert themselves as of thematic consequence. The first line of the poem opens that dichotomy between words and deeds we come upon so often in the ***Old Arcadia***, and the sonnet as a whole would seem to pledge an effort to close it, to make sure that the "Loving in truth" is the kind of love the verse finally reveals. Thus we have a plea for spontaneous response in a world of stale rhetoric: "The famous first sonnet of ***Astrophel and Stella*** is a manifesto of sincerity, an eloquent rejection of anything but the strictest devotion to honest feeling."[1] Pursuing this train of thought, J. W. Lever finds the subject of ***Astrophil and Stella*** in Sidney's attempt to remain true to his own feelings when they no longer fit the tradition through which he must express them. "The principal theme of ***Astrophel and Stella*** appears, then, as a study of the inner conflicts that romance precipitates in the personality of a contemporary man."[2] The "driving force" of the sequence thus becomes "the expression of a complex personality." From here, but a step leads to C. S. Lewis' description of ***Astrophil and Stella*** as a "prolonged lyrical meditation."[3] The poet's internal struggle stands center stage, then, not his praise of Stella, and he struggles with the intractability of language as well as with the force of love. The anatomy of the struggle has been laid out for us by Richard B. Young's brilliant essay on the poem.[4] He traces with great acuity Sidney's adoption of one role after another in his effort to find, or devise, one true to his feelings and acceptable to a larger world of moral and social demands.[5] These views, which represent a consensus of the most recent critical thinking on the poem, find their center to be that heart into which Astrophil bids himself look at the end of the first sonnet. Sidney is imitating himself as poet and Petrarchan rhetor, and we are invited to share the often ironic scrutiny under which he puts himself or his various *personae*. Insincerity and stale rhetoric, extravagant Petrarchan compliment generally, which Sir Sidney Lee and others complained of, are now seen as the object of the poet's derisory humor, as carefully controlled by the dramatic context. Affectation becomes an important part of the story Sidney seeks to tell. The discrepancy between words and deeds, between real feeling and the rhetorical masks devised to conceal and distort it, emerges as a central theme in the poem, and the poem's relation to the ***Old Arcadia***, which Sidney had written just before, becomes a good deal clearer. And if we think of the heroic assertion of the ***New Arcadia*** which followed, perhaps we may legitimately find it a natural development from the heroic possibility which haunts the sonnets. Sidney is free to praise the heroic life precisely because he has inquired so closely into its cost, into the self-control which it demands.

All this agreement I find both attractive and persuasive. Yet the conception of ***Astrophil and Stella*** which makes it possible seems to ignore a substantial element in the sequence as a whole. Let us return to the first sonnet:

> Loving in truth, and faine in verse my love to show,
> That the deare She might take some pleasure of my paine:
> Pleasure might cause her reade, reading might make her know,
> Knowledge might pitie winne, and pitie grace obtaine,
> I sought fit words to paint the blackest face of woe,
> Studying inventions fine, her wits to entertaine:
> Oft turning others' leaves, to see if thence would flow
>
> Some fresh and fruitfull showers upon my sunne-burn'd braine.
> But words came halting forth, wanting Invention's stay,
> Invention, Nature's child, fled step-dame Studie's blowes,
> And others' feete still seem'd but strangers in my way.
> Thus great with child to speake, and helplesse in my throwes,
> Biting my trewand pen, beating my selfe for spite,
> 'Foole,' said my Muse to me, 'looke in thy heart and write.'[6]

The superbly dramatic last line has distracted attention from the considerably more important first four. The opening *gradatio* is, after all, both the blueprint for, and the *raison d'être* of, the entire sequence. Sincere Astrophil indeed wants to be. Love in truth, he does. And a sincere rhetoric he indeed wishes to create. But all this is as prologue to the swelling theme. He wants to obtain "grace." He wants to bed the girl. The essential cause of the sequence is sexual frustration. He is fain in verse his love to show because Stella will not allow him to show it in a more satisfactory manner. He tells himself in sonnet 70 that "Sonets be not bound prentise to annoy," that his muse can show the "height of delight." But she cannot, of course. The ironic couplet overturns the specious reasoning of the preceding twelve lines: "I give you here my hand for truth of this, / Wise silence is best musicke unto blisse." To attain that bliss, other kinds of music are tried. A great many kinds play their part, as many roles as Astrophil affects, as many conceits as he presses into service, as many oscillations and vacillations between *laus* and *vituperatio* as he wearily traces. Yet all are essentially not poetic but rhetorical; they all aim to persuade. Unless we simply agree to ignore the opening four lines of sonnet 1, the whole sequence is applied poetry. It has an ulterior motive. We find this inadmissible, no doubt. We are free, thus, to ignore it. Sidney seems to have felt differently. His purpose is to persuade the lady, and he begins his sincerity at home by confessing that this is so. For the critic, such a motive must for several reasons be regretted. It is not noble; coming from the pattern of nobility, it is troublesome. Still worse, plain desire, unlike spiritualized love, is not very talk-aboutable. Nor is it distinctive, as we should like Sidney, if he cannot be noble, at least to be. But this is how the sequence begins, and this is how it proceeds. The force of desire suffuses Sidney's dramatization of himself as Astrophil. He uses the word again and again in the sequence, as well as in the famous 31 of ***Certain Sonnets*** ("Desire, desire I have too dearely bought, / With price of mangled mind thy worthlesse ware"). The reader may feel that Sidney mounts the Platonic ladder to Love, but he himself makes no such brag:

> Desire, though thou my old companion art
> And oft so clings to my pure Love, that I
> One from the other scarcely can descrie,
> While each doth blow the fier of my hart:
> Now from thy fellowship I needs must part . . .
>
> (72)

He must refine his desire into Virtue's gold, he tells himself. But, once again, he is whistling in the dark:

> But thou Desire, because thou wouldst have all,
> Now banisht art, but yet alas how shall?

The texts which make "Love" mean predominantly, if not exclusively, "desire" recur so often that the point hardly needs arguing. Desire cries, at the end of 71, "give me some food." The rhyme is Virtue's "good," and there is no doubt as to which wins the contest. Stella in 68 is the "life of my desire." In 58, he is willing to grant Stella's self to Virtue, if he can have her body. In the 8th song, which Young sees as the center of the sequence, what is at stake is the physical act of love, whatever psychic superstructures Sidney's muse might, had he been successful, have afterwards built upon it.

Astrophil can be seen, then, in a posture very different from that of the secular meditator, harrower of the hell within. He looks in his heart, bites his truant pen, to find persuasive devices. Critics today are practiced passing well on a poetry of meditation, and find in it its own justification for being and then some. I do not think such an attitude altogether fits ***Astrophil and Stella***. A very practical purpose haunts Sidney's presentation of self. Such a direction, we should remember, was a very legitimate one for the sonnet-sequence to take. Once it shook free from the narrative obligations which fiction then assumed from the nascent Menippean form (the prose narrative bridges between the poems gradually expanding until they swamped the poetry) the sonnet-sequence might legitimately look out-ward or inward. Outward, it saw the mistress and consummation. It became applied poetry. Or it could look inward, harrow the soul of the poet, and make of love occasions for meditative introspection, so many burial urns for a Thomas Browne. The poetry here was pure, not applied, and a consummation, since it chased away the muse, was devoutly not to be wished.

Astrophil and Stella takes the outward path, desires consummation consummately throughout. Shakespeare makes of the sonnet-sequence a real meditative vehicle; Sidney does not. Shakespeare can do so because he loves both a man and a woman, and the woman he has long possessed. His itches are cosmic, neural, not young, fiery, adolescent. He can also do so because he expresses what the poverty of my style forces me to call a more capacious soul than Sidney's. When Shakespeare looks within himself, he finds an allegorical landscape as large as life. I, and I seem to be alone in this, do not find the heart into which Sidney looks one of any extraordinary richness. His themes are few, his scale hardly vast. On the one side we have desire. On the other, ambition, a bankrupt proverbial wisdom, and some chattering court wits who do not know (how, honestly, could they be expected to?) what is passing in the depths of Astrophil's soul. If love is largely desire, the personality in which it wreaks such havoc is very largely a conventional one. The dramatic power of the sequence, in fact, seems to come from precisely this simplified confrontation between desire and convention. Astrophil's personality comes to be resonant, symbolic, largely because it depicts so clearly, with such powerful drama, the impact of desire on a convention manifestly inadequate to cope with it. Thus dwelling on the richness or the modernity of Astrophil's (or Sidney's) personality, as Lever does, leads up the wrong track. It makes Sidney into a proto-Shakespeare and this is precisely what he was not. There is little deep thinking, aside from the large confrontation we have just described, in ***Astrophil and Stella***, unless it be in the reflections about language we shall subsequently discuss. The "philosophy," upon closer examination, turns out to be largely "argument." ***Astrophil and Stella*** is a great poem, but not a great philosophical one.

Kenneth Burke, in one of the most brilliant sections of *A Rhetoric of Motives*, isolates a concept which he calls "pure persuasion."

> With talk of "pure persuasion," the factor of degree can readily confuse us. Thus, we may think of social or literary courtship as pure persuasion, when we contrast it with a direct bid for sexual favors, or with commercial advertising. Similarly, education in contrast with debating might be called pure persuasion. And scientific or religious insemination may seem "pure" when compared with the injection of the doctrinal seed through political ideologies. But all these modes of expression are "impure," and seek advantage, as compared with the absolute, and therefore nonexistent, limit we speak of. Yet, though what we mean by pure persuasion in the absolute sense exists nowhere, it can be present as a motivational ingredient in any rhetoric, no matter how intensely advantage-seeking such rhetoric may be. . . . At this stage we need only note that the indication of pure persuasion in any activity is in an element of "standoffishness," or perhaps better, *self-interference*, as judged by the tests of acquisition. Thus, while not essentially sacrificial, it *looks* sacrificial when matched against the acquisitive.
>
> Pure persuasion involves the saying of something, not for an extra-verbal advantage to be got by the saying, but because of a satisfaction intrinsic to the saying. It summons because it likes the feel of a summons. It would be nonplused if the summons were answered.[7]

In such a Categorization, we would have to classify the persuasion in Shakespeare's sonnets as "pure," that of Sidney's "impure." His is the direct bid for sexual favors that Shakespeare's is not. And yet where would we rank the persuasion of this sonnet?

> With what sharpe checkes I in my selfe am shent,
> When into Reason's audite I do go:
> And by just counts my selfe a banckrout know
> Of all those goods, which heav'n to me hath lent:
> Unable quite to pay even Nature's rent,
> Which unto it by birthright I do ow:
> And which is worse, no good excuse can show,
> But that my wealth I have most idly spent.
> My youth doth waste, my knowledge brings forth toyes,
> My wit doth strive those passions to defend,
> Which for reward spoile it with vaine annoyes.
> I see my course to lose my selfe doth bend:
> I see and yet no greater sorow take,
> Then that I lose no more for *Stella's* sake.
>
> (18)

This is not the least strong of those sonnets which develop the central theme of passion and reason, self-division's cause. We see the poet writhing in the dichotomy, torn in two directions. Yet is he really? Which attitude does he mean us to take seriously, the regret of the first twelve lines or the very different regret of the last two? Both! we say, schooled on fertile tensions. This is true of course, but two kinds of persuasion seem to be operating. For the first twelve lines, Sidney's sonnet does not seem to be asking for anything at all. Quite the reverse. He regrets what he has lost. Then, in the ironic reverse of the couplet, he regrets that he has not lost more, that he has not more to lose, for Stella's sake. Yet, though he means this, we cannot believe that he means it in the same way as he means the first twelve lines. He would not, that is, welcome a suggestion from Stella as to further vain sacrifices which he might make in her behalf. The last two lines, then, are pure persuasion. He would welcome *more* self-division, more self-interference, than he has. We have to do with sacrifice for the sake of sacrifice, no verbal advantage aimed at. With this in mind, we might again inquire about the status of the first twelve lines. Might those sacrifices, too, be pure? Clearly they cannot be, since they are forced upon the poet. Yet he would not avoid making them; he would make use of them. The "pure persuasion" of the couplet is an attempt to move the whole sonnet into this category, to say to Stella, "See what I lose for you, even myself I will lose, and want only to lose more." Yet the attempt fails and is supposed to fail. The sacrifices of the first twelve lines are severe and severely felt, and worth it only if Stella relents. Thus Astrophil presents his unwilled sorrow as willed, tries to master his frustration by a trick, to transcend it with wit, to use it. This transcendence is what we admire in the sonnet and what Stella is supposed to admire. And, at the same time, she is to see that the victory is temporary, illusory. The attempt at "pure" persuasion is finally "impure," aimed at gaining Stella's consent. So, too, in 59, where Astrophil starts out purely, as wishing to be dog-substitute for Stella. He begins, "Deare, why make you more of a dog than me?" and ends up by implying, through the coy humor of his posturing ("If he be faire, yet but a dog can be . . . / He barks, my songs thine owne voyce oft doth prove") that Stella, if she does not say "yes," will be a bitch.

If we think of each of the sonnets as preserving, under the guise of a "pure" sacrifice, an "impure" plea for succor; if we think of each of them as moving up the *gradatio* of sonnet I; might it not then be possible to consider all the self-divisions of the sonnets as, however deeply (or shallowly, for that matter) felt, introduced into this sequence for particularly rhetorical purposes? Sidney divides himself because of the poetic—and hence finally rhetorical—gain to be got by putting himself back together as a gift to Stella. Might it not be that the meditation, viewed in light of the intention of the first four lines, becomes meditative mannerism in the service of a rhetorical purpose? Otherwise, it seems difficult to explain the continual repudiation of meditation's fruits in the couplet. If the meditations are primarily meditations, they are unusually meagre. So Astrophil is willing, eager, to repudiate them at the appearance, or even suggestion, of Stella. Look at sonnet 47:

What, have I thus betrayed my libertie?
Can those blacke beames such burning markes engrave
In my free side? or am I borne a slave,
Whose necke becomes such yoke of tyranny?
Or want I sense to feele my miserie?
Or sprite, disdaine of such disdaine to have?
Who for long faith, tho dayly helpe I crave,
May get no almes but scorne of beggerie.
Vertue awake, Beautie but beautie is,
I may, I must, I can, I will, I do
Leave following that, which it is gaine to misse.
Let her go. Soft, but here she comes. Go to,
Unkind, I love you not: O me, that eye
Doth make my heart give to my tongue the lie.

What it seems to say is that Astrophil can find no resource in his own complexities of character, in the wisdom of meditation. The resources of philosophy are bankrupt when faced with a flesh and blood Stella who scatters them like ghosts at dawn. The sonnet thus dramatizes the failure of introspection. It, and the many like it, might be more clearly conceived as *progymnasmata* rather than philosophic introspections, rhetorical efforts which press the failure of philosophy into service as a final, clinching argument. Sidney looks in his heart and declaims.

What I have been saying is that posturing, once admitted, admits no natural limitation. If Astrophil, or perhaps we should say Sidney, is "acting a role" at one point, he might be acting a role at any point. How do we judge? We cannot. All roles are equally dramatic and assumed, ludic, all arguments and feelings equally agonistic. All are directed toward changing Stella's mind because the desire Astrophil feels for her is simply of another order of magnitude from any arguments whatsoever. That is real, the rest "rhetoric." Pascal provides the gloss: "*Les passions sont les seuls orateurs qui persuadent toujours.*"

By referring to Astrophil and not to Sidney, I have dodged the problem of who is talking in ***Astrophil and Stella***. It was a pretext. There is no Astrophil in the poem except as a name. It is Sidney who speaks, when he speaks in the "biographical" sonnets, 18, for example, or 24 and 37, or 49 and 53, or 33 and probably, too, in the 8th song. When he postures, it is Sidney who postures and not Astrophil. Sidney did not title the work. Obviously he could not call it (for the manuscript circulation which is all he knew anything about or would have condoned) "Philip and Penelope." He was not trying to hide the truth so much as follow a convention which masked the truth under flimsy pretext. Young tries, as a formalist should, to see a consistent *persona*, the obvious biography lending "concrete context" (p. 15), but it is uphill work. Certainly he is right to see the "life," the verve of Sidney's self-portrayal coming not from its biographical veracity but from "his ability to see himself . . . as an actor in a variety of situations to which his thought, his feeling, and his manner of expression are adapted" (p. 23). But in a poem so full of posturing, so full of *personae*, to begin with, what need is there to reify a master *persona*? What does it add? Why not let the poem be backlighted by biography as Sidney intended? Perhaps the objection advanced by formalist theory may be allayed by remembering that ***Astrophil and Stella*** is an illegitimate type to begin with, applied poetry. Its nature as a vehicle of direct courtship makes it biographical from the beginning. Sidney takes as theme, after all, the relation of desire to the literary language available to describe and, presumably, control it. Everything we know about ***Astrophil and Stella*** militates against considering it as a finished poem, pure persuasion. He wrote it as an immediate effort to cope with an immediate crisis in feeling. The identities of both hero and heroine were clear. The original small manuscript audience was probably expected to fill in a good deal more biographical information than we now possess. It could supply, above all, the crucial tone, the spirit in which to read, a tone we must re-synthesize from the sonnets themselves. A substantial part of the manuscript audience must have known Sidney and thus had a standard, which the poem does not altogether supply by itself, against which to judge the posturing, the role-playing. I am not saying that the sequence cannot survive extraction from its biographical matrix. It can and has. But why extract it when it obviously gains from being left as the anomalous artifact, half art and half life, which it was? It is because it is applied poetry, poetry which aims directly at *making something happen*, that it adopts the rhetorical strategy it does.

Ringler, in his commentary, considers that "the legitimate critical procedure is not to ignore the biography but to find out what kind of biography it is" (p. 440). Yet, although he sorts out the biographical information in the poem with patient assiduity, he never answers his own question. What kind of biography is it? The principle of selection seems to me to be not what is needed to create concrete biographical or narrative context, but what is needed to reinforce Sidney's rhetorical purpose. He turns life to use as he turns imaginative life to use. Both try to persuade. He looks in his heart some of the time. At other times, he looks at the world and draws his strategy from there. The principle of choice is rhetorical effectiveness. In 45, for example, the poet looks at the scene in great hall or closet and learns his lesson from it. If fabled or dramatic lovers move Stella, he will become one. Sometimes, as in 101, the event (the sickness of Stella) provides a simple take-off point for a still simpler sonnet. The real world becomes not concrete detail but a great storage chest of rhetorical argumentation, the Mother of Inventions. Or look at the famous biographical aside, "Rich fooles there be":

> Rich fooles there be, whose base and filthy hart
> Lies hatching still the goods wherein they flow:
> And damning their owne selves to *Tantal's* smart,
> Wealth breeding want, more blist, more wretched grow.
> Yet to those fooles heav'n such wit doth impart,
> As what their hands do hold, their heads do know,
> And knowing, love, and loving, lay apart
> As sacred things, far from all daunger's show.
> But that rich foole, who by blind Fortune's lot
> The richest gemme of Love and life enjoyes,
> And can with foule abuse such beauties blot;
> Let him, deprived of sweet but unfelt joyes,
> (Exil'd for ay from those high treasures, which
> He knowes not) grow in only follie rich.
>
> (24)

Not much concrete detail is supplied about Lord Rich. Only what is needed for the rhetorical purpose of the poem, the contrast between blind Lord Rich and Sidney, who can see only too well. Lord Rich will grow rich in folly, Sidney in knowledge. Sidney inflates himself by damning Lord Rich, then discards him as a biographical prop.

The same criterion of rhetorical effectiveness should apply to Sidney's own presence in the poem. Critical opinion has ranged widely in this matter. The generation of Sir Sidney Lee found affectation everywhere and the "real" Sidney (i.e., "real feeling") but little. Theodore Spencer, whose *ELH* article in 1945 really started the current revaluation of Sidney, maintained precisely the opposite: "In ***Astrophel and Stella*** Sidney tries deliberately to put convention aside, and to speak out for himself" (p. 268). And David Kalstone recognizes the artifice but sees it as a series of masks: "The mastery of persons is what makes the sonnets of ***Astrophel and Stella*** a more flexible medium for writing about love than the sonnets of the ***Arcadia***" (p. 151). A rhetorical perspective finds common ground in all these viewpoints. Sidney certainly searches for his own voice, cries for food as directly as man can. He plays roles. But he also takes up stale affectation without the built-in ironic scrutiny. Young finds the irony pervasive. A recent article by Ann Howe takes issue and finds some of the ironically-defended poems (the early ones after I, for example) simply inept.[8] I see no reason why Sidney's rhetorical strategy could not call for convention at one time, ironic counterpoint at another. The concern for consistency stems from considering the sequence as wholly a literary artifact, from ignoring its persuasive purpose. In the *baiser* group, for example, a great deal is made of a kiss. The modern reader may find it tedious. Yet Sidney is simply seizing an occasion for persuasive poetry. The occasion did not lend itself to ironic improvement, so irony was left alone. Sidney was a conventional Petrarchan sonneteer playing with a trifle.

I cannot think it useful to number and categorize the roles Sidney plays. In a rhetorical structure such as he has created, *any* role could fit. And if we cannot find an artistic pattern in the roles, we cannot find a master *persona*, a standard to judge affectation in terms of the poem itself. Instead, we see Sidney casting about, using for his compulsive purpose whatever comes to hand. Great critics have disputed whether ***Astrophil and Stella*** tells a story, and if so what kind. This is a non-problem. The work chronicles a series of attempts to persuade. This is narrative of a sort, but of a peculiarly rhetorical sort. It stands halfway between life and literature and draws indiscriminately from both. Its protagonist is first fictional, then the real and historical Sir Philip Sidney. Both "story" ("real life") and consistent artistic metamorphosis of this ("*persona*," "pure poetry") enter in only as they serve a predominantly rhetorical purpose. ***Astrophil and Stella***'s mixture of fact and fancy makes perfect sense in its own terms. Only under the wrong formal expectations does it seem inconsistent.

Perhaps this is the moment to confront another famous and irrelevant problem—Sidney's sincerity. Sidney sincerely wants to persuade. His desire is sincerity itself. This he is obliged to tell us and, in the first four lines of 1, he does. All that comes after serves this purpose. He makes poetry out of his effort to find a "voice," to be sincere, but he makes poetry out of a good many other occasions and feelings and problems, too. We can quarrel with the end in view. Seduction, however fancy the language, may be wrong. But this has nothing to do with Sidney's "sincerity" in trying to bring it about. We can say that real love is sincere love and neither has anything to do with sex. Sidney would simply disagree, and we should have to kiss both Astrophil and Stella good-bye. We can say that, granted the end and the conception of love, Sidney was not justified in pretending to feelings he did not possess. He would reply that the force of desire to change—and fabricate—one's feelings was part of the story he was telling. ***Astrophil and Stella*** was about "sincerity." The only argument about the sincerity of ***Astrophil and Stella*** that might avail would be that he had not warned us about his rhetorical purpose. But he not only does this in the first four lines, he does it again and again. The force of desire is continually before our eyes. None of the charges will stand. Sincerity, except as a theme, is irrelevant to ***Astrophil and Stella,*** one of the non-problems that have plagued the poem.

Structure is just such another. The common denominator of critical examination and speculation of all the major sonnet-sequences, not just Sidney's, is a radical temptation to think, first, that the order of the sonnets *is* crucial and, second, that the traditional order is unsatisfactory. No other kind of poem quite so much draws out the critics' impulse to tinker and fiddle. Not that the impulse, much maligned, cannot be praised. Every professional reader of a sonnet-sequence is zealous, and rightly so, for a literary structure. He finds instead a rhetorical one, where order is considerably less important. He then makes it more important by taking as *the* arrangement what is only *an* arrangement, and thus keeps faith with his text and author. Or he takes the dilemma by the horns and rearranges. He has then kept faith with his sense of literary form, one which he thinks (again rightly) that Sidney, Spenser, Shakespeare would share with him. He does only what exigent circumstance, and perhaps sloth, prevented their doing for themselves. What of the explanations for their not doing it themselves? Common ignorance defends my speculation as well as the next man's: they did not think order was crucial. Some groupings, yes. Such smaller groupings constituted a rhetorical gesture as it were. But the overall order, and even the order within the groupings, was not crucial. The sonnets were discrete entities. Sidney's aimed outward, at persuading Stella. Shakespeare's turned inward, posturing for *les yeux internes*. But each was a discrete attempt at integration (of one kind or another). One might play off or depart from another, or a group from a single incident, but all were not conceived as a whole.[9]

In ***Astrophil and Stella*** the case seems especially clear. The sonnets are weapons, discrete weapons, each conceived in the hope that it would be the last. The form as a whole had no persuasive function, could have none since it was built up *seriatim*, over time. For the same reason, it could have no *ending* in the literary sense of the word. It could simply stop, confess defeat. The beginning was indeed crucial, but it was a rhetorical not a literary beginning. It set up a vital context for the rhetoric to follow. This done, Sidney could let time and chance take care of the "structure" and there is every indication that he did so. The well-known desire to place 31 and 32 from ***Certain Sonnets*** at the end of ***Astrophil and Stella*** represents the desire for a literary ending rather than a rhetorical cessation. Sidney's predicament has got, somehow, to be solved. Or at least *we* must be brought to a position of rest. All of this comes from foisting an alien formal expectation on the poem.

The structures which we find, then, are our own. So long as we admit this, they are not necessarily any the less useful. They are exercises in what Murray Krieger calls "contextualism," and even when they manage to say very little of value about the sonnets, they can be valuable forcing-houses for critical theory. By looking at the sequence as a potential collection of many structures, an infinite series of contexts, we can make of it an incredibly rich form.[10] I see no reason why this kind of rearrangement should not be vigorously pursued. Lewis scoffs that "if you arrange things to make a story, then of course a story will result from your re-arrangement" (p. 328). But you can rearrange a sequence into many shapes besides a story, and whatever *your* shape, it will create more meanings for others than your own perspective allows you to see. This blindness to potential meaning the artist himself shares. And is not the kind of tentative rearrangement scholars like to work out for the sonnet-sequence really of the same kind as their effort to weave larger discrete works into a coherent pattern, into what we call literary history? Both are, to a large degree, aleatory, but none the worse for it.

If ***Astrophil and Stella*** is, in essence, a rhetorical artifact, it is also *about* rhetoric, and to this second concern we must now turn. The ground has been well explored by Young. He remarks of 74 ("I never dranke of *Aganippe* well") that "by going beyond the question of the particular illusion, the conventional manner, to illusion itself, this sonnet makes explicit an issue implicit in the others" (p. 9). He carries the observation an important step further: "What I have been trying to show is that there is an analogy between the technical problems presented by the literary convention and the dramatic problems presented by the love story, and that it is not an accidental one." There seems to be more than an analogy. Sidney wants to make of his love and his love-poetry one thing. Stella then becomes his muse, and her charms the sum of all that poets ever writ:

Let daintie wits crie on the Sisters nine,
That bravely maskt, their fancies may be told:
Or *Pindare's* Apes, flaunt they in phrases fine,
Enam'ling with pied flowers their thoughts of gold:
Or else let them in statelier glorie shine,
Ennobling new found Tropes with problemes old:
Or with strange similies enrich each line,
Of herbes or beastes, which *Inde* or *Afrike* hold.
For me in sooth, no Muse but one I know:
Phrases and Problemes from my reach do grow,
And strange things cost too deare for my poore sprites.
How then? even thus: in *Stella's* face I reed,
What Love and Beautie be, then all my deed
But Copying is, what in her Nature writes.

(3)

The logical goal of such a blending would be the obliteration of any distinction between matter and manner, between words and feelings. Stella then becomes a touchstone for the quality of experience both literary (as in 15) and everyday. And Sidney wishes to disclaim any desire for experience or meaning she cannot represent. Sonnet 28 might be better attended than it has been:

You that with allegorie's curious frame,
Of other's children changelings use to make,
With me those paines for God's sake do not take:
I list not dig so deepe for brasen fame.
When I say '*Stella*', I do meane the same
Princesse of Beautie, for whose only sake
The raines of *Love* I love, though never slake,
And joy therein, though Nations count it shame.
I beg no subject to use eloquence,
Nor in hid wayes to guide Philosophie:
Looke at my hands for no such quintessence;
But know that I in pure simplicitie,
Breathe out the flames which burne within my heart,
Love onely reading unto me this art.

The disclaimer to any larger meaning than expressing his love may be more important than his eloquent plea that he forswears eloquence. Words are to be forced into absolute coincidence with his desire, to do it full and final justice. Such full expression will be the most persuasive rhetoric of all.

This is one strand of Sidney's thinking about language. It must be like Stella herself, unique, uniquely expressive. But he introduces a complementary strand. Language can play the common drab: "What may words say, or what may words not say, / Where truth it selfe must speake like flatterie?" (35). Such language all the poets use. With them, words force feeling and not vice-versa. Does Sidney realize that this may happen to him, too? He would seem to in those sonnets where he imitates Petrarch or someone else in forswearing imitation, and thus for the knowing reader ironically acknowledges his final enslavements to words and the conventional uses of them. He might also be thought to touch on the point obliquely in 45 where he builds, on the contrast between Stella's cruelty to him and her tears at a fable, a couplet which ends, "I am not I, pitie the tale of me." This, in a sense, is what he does in the whole sequence. Sidney's *use* of his reflections on the powers of language works, then, both sides of the street. When he is direct, we are—and Stella is—to think this the real language, that coincident with real deeds, real feelings. When he is oblique and ironical, we are to think him using, while at the same time he sees through and derides, the stale clichés of the rest of the cosmos.

Rhetorically, this double strategy promises well. But if we try to tease from it a coherent set of reflections on language and the ways in which language both enriches and sets bounds to human experience, we may be less successful. Look, for example, at one of the most striking sonnets in the sequence, 34:

Come let me write, 'And to what end?' To ease
A burthned hart. 'How can words ease, which are
The glasses of thy dayly vexing care?'
Oft cruell fights well pictured forth do please.
'Art not asham'd to publish thy disease?'
Nay, that may breed my fame, it is so rare:
'But will not wise men thinke thy words fond ware?'
Then be they close, and so none shall displease.
'What idler thing, then speake and not be hard?'
What harder thing then smart, and not to speak?
Peace, foolish wit, with wit my wit is mard.
Thus write I while I doubt to write, and wreake
My harmes on Ink's poore losse, perhaps some find
Stella's great powrs, that so confuse my mind.

It is a very good poem indeed. Sidney's characteristic excellences, the perfectly paced, directly colloquial voice, which controls an elaborate word-play, the stichomythic interlocutor, the intense, self-conscious reflection upon what he is and what he is doing, the powerful closing: all show through. And yet, if we are considering Sidney as a philosopher of language (or of anything else) must we not come in the end to agree with the last line? He is confused. Even the syntax, he points out to us, starts to crumble in the couplet. Let me anticipate the objections. Poets can be confused and no worse for it. There is Yeats. They can, too, write beautiful poems about their confusion. But there is a larger issue involved. Style, thinking about language, is no small theme in ***Astrophil and Stella***. Is the reader not entitled to know where he stands, what conception of language is really operating in the poem? And what relationship the deceptions of language really bear to human experience? Sonnet 34 never tells us what the relation between strong feeling and the compulsion to express it really is. No more does the sequence as a whole. Sidney raises the point but does not resolve it. It may be, in the larger sense probably is, beyond resolution. But surely a consistent set even of implications would enrich the poem. Again one must invoke the poem's essentially rhetorical strategy to explain the deficiency. Sidney's thinking about language is a tool (the doubleedged sword of rhetoric), like his thinking about everything else, to be *used* not pondered.

So too it is with the proverbial popular wisdom. Sidney confronts it. He sees that it will not do. It is manifestly inadequate to cope with experience, as anyone can see when he simply juxtaposes the two, as in 5. But we cannot say that he transcends it. He confronts desire, he confronts the ambivalent, lying heart of language, but he goes beyond neither. Nor does he coherently relate them one to another. These are fantastic objections, of course. Look what he does do. He makes of his own desire the great poetic representation of Desire in English. But because his purpose remains rhetorical throughout, he can neither anatomize desire, as Shakespeare does in sonnet 129, nor follow it through consummation into middle age, as Shakespeare does in 138. He cannot yoke desire and the censor in a brilliant philosophical pun, as Shakespeare's dazzling 135 does. Nor, of course, does Sidney attempt any of these Shakespearean purposes. Neither meditative nor philosophic, ***Astrophil and Stella*** begins and ends in the begging mode.

Notes

1. Theodore Spencer, "The Poetry of Sir Philip Sidney," *ELH*, XII, 4 (Dec. 1945), 251–78.
2. *The Elizabethan Sonnet-Sequence*, 2nd ed. (London, 1966), p. 74.
3. *English Literature in the Sixteenth Century* (Oxford, 1954), p. 327.
4. *English Petrarke: A Study of Sidney's Astrophel and Stella*, in *Three Studies in the Renaissance: Sidney, Jonson, Milton* (New Haven, 1958).
5. The two more recent studies of the poem develop the implications of this analysis. David Kalstone (*Sidney's Poetry* [Cambridge, Mass., 1965]), in his readings, is usually close to the implications of Young's study. Neil L. Rudenstine (*Sidney's Poetic Development* [Cambridge, Mass., 1967]), in a study proclaimedly derivative from Kalstone's, often ends up glossing Young at two removes.
6. *The Poems of Sir Philip Sidney*, ed. William A. Ringler Jr. (Oxford, 1962). All subsequent references are to this text.
7. (Los Angeles, 1969), pp. 268–69.
8. Ann Romayne Howe, "*Astrophel and Stella*: 'Why and How'," *SP*, LXI (1964), 150–69.
9. For the opposite case, most interesting and carefully argued, see A. C. Hamilton's fine recent article, "Sidney's *Astrophel and Stella* as a Sonnet Sequence," *ELH*, XXXVI, 1 (March 1969), 59–87. Ephim A. Fogel, too, most interestingly argues for a new biographical reading and a new, five-act, structure in "The Mythical Sorrows of Astrophil," *Studies in Honour of Margaret Schlauch* (Warsaw, 1960), 133–53.
10. Stephen Booth, in *An Essay on Shakespeare's Sonnets* (New Haven, 1969), has shown brilliantly how this may be done.

Alan Sinfield (essay date 1974)

SOURCE: "Sexual Puns in *Astrophel and Stella*," in *Essays in Criticism*, Vol. XXIV, No. 4, October 1974, pp. 341–355.

[In the following essay, Sinfield asserts that viewing Astrophel as the elegant but naïve courtier is misleading, since sexual double entendres are an important feature of Sidney's verbal skill.]

How far are Astrophil's feelings for Stella in Sidney's sequence sexual? The non-specialist reader at least tends to be blinded by the radiance of the prevalent image of Sidney as an urbane and elegant courtier throwing off Petrarchan conceits, and is unprepared to perceive much sexual passion in Astrophil. Perhaps we have not entirely recovered from romantic attitudes like the Reverend Alexander Grosart's in his edition of the ***Complete Poems*** (3 vols., 1877). Grosart insisted that the sonnets are not in their proper order, observing 'It is of the last importance to remember this; for upon the dates of these Sonnets and Poems is contingent our verdict of shame or praise'—he wanted to place the more obviously passionate sonnets before the marriage of Penelope Devereux so that Sidney (whom he identified with Astrophil) should not be seen making amorous advances to a married woman! (I, xlix). The decline of Victorian inhibitions did not greatly affect our notion of Sidney because it was off-set by the growing habit of contrasting sonneteers with Metaphysical poets. This gave modern critics almost as much incentive as their forbears for characterizing Sidney as largely simple, idealistic and traditional in both language and attitude. Even in recent critical studies and annotated editions, most of which have a lot to offer, commentators have been slow to appreciate, or to help the reader appreciate, the sexual inferences in the poems. I suggest that Astrophil's consciousness of the sexual nature of his passion for Stella is more extensive and more important than is usually implied.

It is generally assumed that Astrophil discovers a powerful sexual component in his love for Stella somewhere about the middle of the sequence; certainly the issue becomes relatively overt at that point. Thus in sonnet 52 he wittily proposes that the quarrel between virtue and love could be resolved by granting virtue 'that *Stella's* selfe; yet thus, / That *Vertue* but that body graunt to us' (quotations are from Ringler's Oxford edition). Then in sonnet 61 Stella at last gives a clear response to Astrophil's persistent importunings: clearly she thinks his passion is unacceptably sensual for she tells him that 'her chast mind hates this love in me' and that he can best show his devotion through chastity. But he pretends not to understand the point she is making:

O Doctor *Cupid*, thou for me reply,
Driv'n else to graunt by Angel's sophistrie,
That I love not, without I leave to love.

In fact the verbal dexterity is Astrophil's and he compounds it by imputing 'sophistrie' to Stella, for in his ridding concluding line he cleverly confuses her distinction between chaste and unchaste love. Many critics consider crucial sonnet 71 where, it is often said, Astrophil openly recognizes the sexual character of his passion. After appearing to praise Stella's virtue and beauty for thirteen lines he abruptly declares, '"But ah," Desire still cries, "give me some food"'.

Indeed, after sonnet 71 Astrophil's physical desire is very plain, especially in the sonnets about Stella's kiss and in the Fourth and Eighth Songs. We might notice particularly Astrophil's remark that Stella's jealous husband is so devilish that it is a pity he is without horns (i.e. has not been cuckolded—78); the neatly suggestive image of the kiss as 'Breakfast of *Love*'—implying that more substantial meals might follow in due course (79); Astrophil's apology for kissing Stella too vigorously (82); and his warning to her sparrow in 83 that it is taking advantage of the intimate privileges it has been allowed—in this sonnet we see both Astrophil's sensitivity (albeit humourously expressed) to Stella's distribution of her sexual favours and his awareness that such a warning could apply equally well to his own defiance of her insistence on chaste love. After this, the Fourth Song is a frank seduction piece where Stella resists only by 'force of hands' and a threat to end the relationship; the Eighth Song is apparently a more subtle attempt at the same thing, but it provokes Stella's outright and final refusal.

This much is now largely uncontroversial, though it has perhaps been underplayed. I want to make two further claims: that sexual *double entendre* is an important feature of Sidney's verbal skill and, following this, that Astrophil's love for Stella is sexual right from the beginning of the sequence. If these propositions are accepted they will add to the vigour and subtlety of the early sonnets especially (which have often been thought relatively artificial and empty) and increase our respect for Sidney's linguistic and emotional range. Astrophil's sexual desire is not something which develops rather surprisingly after sixty or so conventional Petrarchan exercises, but an important disruptive force in a relationship which is presented in a coherent, comprehensive and sustained way.

Despite the twentieth century rehabilitation of the sexual pun, it must be approached with caution. Because it involves language operating at the margins of the ordinary rules of comprehensibility this, even more than most, is a matter of interpretative tact and sensitivity. I would like to suggest five criteria which the thoughtful reader might keep in mind. First, the interpretations proposed should use senses demonstrably current in the language; second, in their immediate context they should be consistent with each other and with other levels of meaning; third, (in other than short poems) they should be appropriate to the theme and its treatment in the work as a whole; fourth, they should make the poetry appear better—more subtle, dense and interesting; and fifth, they should be compatible with the known practice of the poet and his contemporaries in that kind of poem.

A couple of blatant sexual puns are usually recognized in ***Astrophil and Stella***. One is at the end of 68 where Astrophil, observing Stella's goodness and her wish to make him similarly virtuous, remarks, 'O thinke I then, what paradise of joy / It is, so faire a Vertue to enjoy'. The pun on 'enjoy' actually affords three meanings: 'how splendid it must be to be so good'; 'how splendid it would be to have sexual intercourse with such a virtuous person'; and, with an ironic touch of the frustration and resentment that we also see, for instance, in 59 and 60, 'how gratifying it must be for you to be able to gain satisfaction by insisting on your honour (while I am suffering'). The other is in the sestet of 76 (a sonnet that one critic has rather surprisingly advanced as evidence that Astrophil is a romantic lover). Stella's approach is like a beautiful dawn, but this amiable sentiment is roughly undercut in the sestet by a clear allusion to male sexual arousal:

> But lo, while I do speake, it groweth noone with me,
> Her flamie glistring lights increase with time and place;
> My heart cries 'ah', it burnes, mine eyes now dazled be;
> No wind, no shade can coole, what helpe then in my case,
> But with short breath, long lookes, staid feet and walking hed,
> Pray that my sunne go downe with meeker beames to bed.

Astrophil is speaking about sexual excitement and fulfilment, as Barnaby Barnes knew when he imitated the sonnet initially 'The moonlight of her Chastity reproved me' but then dawn and 'Her Morning's blush' followed, and now it is practically mid-day. In the last line he asks her eyes to continue to approve his aroused state, 'Still smiling at my dial, next eleven!' (the image is of a sun-dial; *Parthenophil and Parthenophe*, XXIII, Sidney Lee, *Elizabeth Sonnets*, I, 182; cf. *Romeo and Juliet*, II. iv. 108).

In the first twenty-five sonnets of the sequence the leading motif is the mental debate between Astrophil's virtue or reason on the one hand and love, sense or will on the other. But the issue must be a very fine one unless Astrophil's passion is supposed to be physical. The obvious implication is that he has a sexual relationship in mind when, for instance, he tells reason to 'Leave sense, and those which sense's objects be: / Deale thou with powers of thoughts, leave love to will' (10). It seems that the main reason why critics do not perceive Astrophil's love as sexual from the first is the self-justification he attempts, particularly in sonnet 14:

> If that be sinne which in fixt hearts doth breed
> A loathing of all loose unchastitie,
> Then Love is sinne, and let me sinfull be.

But it is very doubtful whether Astrophil means here that he regards the notion of a sexual consummation with Stella with horror; his argument, I think, is rather more equivocal. He more probably means that his love is chaste in the same way that Shakespeare's Lucrece, though married, was chaste; she had reserved herself for one man and her rape was thus 'The story of sweet chastity's decay, / The impious breach of holy wedlock vow' (11. 808–9). Astrophil's love makes him reject the idea of sexual experience with anyone other than Stella—it is '*loose* unchastitie' that he loathes. Hero advances the same argument, in similar words and from the same kind of motive, in Chapman's continuation of *Hero and Leander*: 'We break chaste vows when we live loosely ever, / But bound as we are, we live loosely never' (III, 362–3).

This interpretation fits best the tendency of the surrounding sonnets, but in case it should seem an improbable assertion in the face of Astrophil's vehemence, we should notice that he has in effect already in this sonnet admitted the sensual basis of his passion.

> Alas have I not paine enough my friend,
> Upon whose breast a fiercer Gripe doth tire
> Then did on him who first stale downe the fire,
> While *Love* on me doth all his quiver spend,
> But with your Rubarb words yow must contend
> To grieve me worse, in saying that Desire
> Doth plunge my wel-form'd soule even in the mire
> Of sinfull thoughts, which do in ruine end?

The way this accusation is reported undermines the answer offered at the end of the sonnet. The 'Gripe', as well as being a 'grip' and a 'pain', is a vulture since Astrophil alludes to the punishment of Prometheus. (Actually, Prometheus was preyed upon by an eagle whereas Tityus for the attempted rape of Leto was similarly assaulted by a vulture. One is tempted to find the substitution significant but it was quite a common error.) Astrophil's comparison of his sufferings to those of the Greek demi-god would seem to confer heroic stature upon him, but we should remember that he has not done anything to benefit mankind, that it was Prometheus's liver that the eagle or vulture attacked and that the liver was thought the seat of sexual desire (thus Shakespeare's Tarquin visits Lucrece 'To quench the coal which in his liver glows', I 47). If it does occur to us that Astrophil is therefore really confessing to sexual lust and that his plight is something less than god-like, this is confirmed by his own term 'Rubarb words', for rhubarb was a purgative which would cleanse the liver—no doubt the friend's intention. Thus the imagery sinks from the titanic to the emetic and the passionately sexual nature of Astrophil's condition is established.

This implicit confession gives Astrophil's loathing of 'loose unchastitie' a disingenuous appearance and makes it likely that he has in mind merely the restriction of his attentions to Stella alone. Of course, this does not counter the friend's objection; as in sonnet 61, Astrophil plays with the terms of the accusation and only pretends to answer it. The notion that he is already dominated ('gripped') by sexual desire is not challenged in sonnet 14, therefore; indeed, it is strengthened by the deceptively self-righteous tone with which he parades] a reply that is partial in both senses of the word.

If we are not misled by sonnet 14 we may be more ready to see a sexual element in the most complicated pun in the sequence, that at the end of sonnet 9. 'Of touch they are that without touch doth touch': Stella's eyes are made of glossy black stone (touch) and they affect (touch) Astrophil without physical contact (touch). But this could mean that he is affected sexually—several senses of 'touch', including 'stirring the sexual parts', are evident in this speech from Jonson's *Every Man in his Humour*:

> Indeed, beauty stands a woman in no stead, unless it procure her touching. But, sister, whether it touch you or no, it touches your beauties; and, I am sure, they will abide the touch; an' they do not, a plague of all ceruse, say I: and it touches me too in part, though not in the—[*sc.* (w)hole].

(IV. vi. 100–5, ed. J. W. Lever, London, 1972.) Astrophil too is touched 'in part', even though Stella by no means encourages such sensations or the contact that might enhance them. In the same phrases we have his consciousness of her beauty, the emotional and sexual response this arouses in him and her aloof reserve. This combination, which will prove ruinous for Astrophil, is there from the start.

Sonnet 18 has been justly admired for the coherence of its imagery and the subtlety of its analysis of Astrophil's predicament. In the first quatrain he exclaims that when he goes into 'Reason's audite' he receives 'sharpe checkes' and knows himself by just account to be bankrupt 'Of all those goods, which heav'n to me hath lent'. He has wasted his talents; but what, then, does the second quatrain mean? Is it merely repetitious?

> Unable quite to pay even Nature's rent,
> Which unto it by birthright I do ow
> And which is worse, no good excuse can show,
> But that my wealth I have most idly spent.

Above all, what is 'Nature's rent'? I believe it is the getting of children, firstly because of a passage in the ***Arcadia***:

> Nature above all things requireth this,
> That we our kind doo labour to maintaine;
> Which drawne-out line both hold all humane blisse.
> Thy father justly may of thee complaine,
> If thou doo not repay his deeds for thee,
> In granting unto him a grandsire's gaine.
> Thy common-wealth may rightly grieved be,
> Which must by this immortall be preserved,
> If thus thou murther thy posteritie.
> His very being he hath not deserved,
> Who for a selfe-conceipt will that forbeare,
> Whereby that being aye must be conserved.

(Ringler, pp. 105–6). Here Geron, whose whole theme is the desirability of marriage, insists that for all kinds of noble reason we hold from nature the responsibility to procreate. Secondly, Shakespeare's fourth sonnet, the only one which shows considerable detailed borrowings from Sidney, uses just the same theme and imagery, and in a clearly sexual sense.

> Unthrifty loveliness, why dost thou spend
> Upon thyself thy beauty's legacy?
> Nature's bequest gives nothing, but doth lend,
> And, being frank, she lends to those are free.

'Spend' means to expend sexually, to discharge seminally; the beautiful youth chooses not to engender children in response to Nature's generosity, but this will bring him no profit

> For having traffic with thyself alone,
> Thou of thyself thy sweet self dost deceive.
> Then how when nature calls thee to he gone,
> What acceptable audit canst thou leave?

In Eric Partridge's *Shakespeare's Bawdy* we find sexual meanings for all the terms in this image cluster, including 'rent', which is copulation or, more probably, semen-expenditure paid as rent by a man to the woman legally his. Nature's rent, then, must be the rearing of children to replace oneself and one's partner: Astrophil is saying that he is debarring himself from the possibility of sexual intercourse in wedlock and the generation of offspring by his devotion to Stella who is unavailable for these purposes. Like Shakespeare's Antony, he has 'Forborne the getting of a lawful race' (III, xiii. 107). His (semen) wealth is 'idly spent', perhaps in nocturnal emissions. This area of meaning is taken up in the last lines of the sonnet, and, I think, confirms this interpretation:

> I see my course to lose my selfe doth bend:
> I see and yet no greater sorow take,
> Then that I lose no more for *Stella's* sake.

The loss is not only the general sacrifice Astrophil is making; it is also the loss of semen (Partridge again) and the last two lines therefore mean that Astrophil would be happy if he could make his sexual expenditure on Stella's behalf even greater—that is, if he could achieve a complete union with her! This vigorous and witty implication adds an important dimension to the simple emotion of the more obvious meaning, and shows how sophisticated is Astrophil's appreciation in sonnet 18 of the cost of his commitment to Stella. The issue is greater than a failure to develop his general talents: he is also depriving himself of the opportunity to continue his line, and is not even obtaining the consolation of sexual fulfilment. Without these implications the sonnet is very competent but not very interesting; with them it is an acutely personal assessment of Astrophil's situation and a telling prediction of the frustration he is to suffer. He already sees Stella as a physical attraction sufficiently serious to inhibit him from more legitimate modes of sexual expression and has even envisaged the long-term consequences of such a passion.

One place where we might expect Astrophil to think of sex is in relation to Stella's husband. In sonnet 24 he punningly compares Lord Rich to a miser; the sestet at first sight simply shows Astrophil's high estimation of Stella, but it is composed almost entirely of terms which feature in *Shakespeare's Bawdy*:

> But that rich foole, who by blind Fortune's lot
> The richest gemme of Love and life enjoyes,
> And can with foule abuse such beauties blot;
> Let him, deprived of sweet but unfelt joyes,
> (Exil'd for ay from those high treasures, which
> He knowes not) grow in only follie rich.

Lord Rich will presumably grow in folly primarily by becoming a cuckold (as in 78); it therefore appears that he 'enjoyes' (sexually) the 'richest gemme' and 'those high treasures', that is Stella's most intimate parts; the 'joyes' which he fails to appreciate are those of love-making. This imagery recurs in similar senses in Song Ten, which I discuss below; in the ***Old Arcadia*** Pamela is saved only by intruders from the loss of her virginity, 'her dearest jewel' (ed. Jean Robertson, Oxford, 1973, p. 306). And the 'foule abuse', somewhat ironically surely, is infidelity.

The sonnet works, then, on two levels. In part it is an attack on the crudeness of Lord Rich, against which is set Astrophil's more refined appreciation of Stella as very precious. But at the same time, in the sexual puns and the joke of the last line, Astrophil also emerges as coarse and materialistic. His valuation is physically based and differs from Rich's mainly in that Astrophil, if he had the good fortune to possess such a delectable object, would keep it safe. Jealousy of Stella's husband's marital rights does not bring out the best in Astrophil; the punning language draws attention to the simultaneous presence of idealistic and physical elements in his passion. The result is that more vigour and astringency than are usually acknowledged appear in his love, in the earlier sonnets as much as later on.

At first sight sonnet 22 simply offers a witty account of a journey in hot sun during which only Stella's complexion was unaffected by the heat:

> In highest way of heav'n the Sunne did ride,
> Progressing then from faire twinnes' gold'n place:
> Having no scarfe of clowds before his face,
> But shining forth of heate in his chiefe pride.

Riding is and was a very common image for the sexual act and the sun has traditionally sexual connotations—for instance in *The Faerie Queene*: '*Phoebus* fresh, as bridegrome to his mate, Came dauncing forth, shaking his deawle haire' (I, v, 2; the idea derives from Psalm XIX—T. W. Baldwin, *On the Literary Genetics of Shakspere's Poems and Sonnets,* 1950, pp. 5–6). Nevertheless, we probably notice nothing special until we come to the fourth line quoted. There the sun is in the full heat of sexual ardour and ready to assault any passing female. Partridge quotes *Othello*: 'As salt as wolves in pride' (III, iii, 408) and we may also think of *Lucreca*:

> While Lust is in his pride, no exclamation
> Can curb his heat or rein his rash desire,
> Till, like a jade, Self-will himself doth tire.

(ll. 705–7). The sun has an assignation:

> When some faire Ladies, by hard promise tied,
> On horsebacke met him in his furious race,
> Yet each prepar'd, with fanne's wel-shading grace,
> From that foe's wounds their tender skinnes to hide.

Compare sonnet 64 where Astrophil pleads, 'O give my passions leave to run their race'. The ladies are on horseback and by implication ready for sexual advances, but apparently they wish (coyly perhaps) to preserve themselves from the 'wounds' of sexual penetration.

Stella, however, doesn't need to be wary, for she is inherently inviolable (perhaps that is why she alone is unmounted):

> *Stella* alone with face unarmed marcht,
> Either to do like him, which open shone,
> Or carelesse of the wealth because her owne.

Stella is unperturbed by the sun's audacious behaviour 'open' is surely used in a way that is similar to Donne's in Holy Sonnet XVIII, where it means 'ready for sexual experience':

> And let myne amorous soule court thy mild Dove,
> Who is most trew, and pleasing to thee, then
> When she' is embrac'd and open to most men.

(ed. Grierson). Astrophil concludes by suggesting that the sun had more respect for Stella than for the other ladies:

> Yet were the hid and meaner beauties parcht,
> Her daintiest bare went free; the cause was this,
> The Sunne which others burn'd, did her but kisse.

The burning and parching suffered by the others may mean either that they experienced full sexual intercourse or that they contracted venereal disease (Partridge).

What makes sonnet 22 so witty is the fact that the sexual level of meaning depends entirely on metaphorical puns until the last phrase, for whereas the rest of the sonnet is often literally about going for a ride in the sun but only figuratively about sexual activity, the last phrase is the reverse, for the sun *kisses* only figuratively—the literal meaning of the verb is sexual. Thus the strategy of the sonnet is to provoke in the reader a growing suspicion that a sexual implication is present and then suddenly confirm it in the very last word so that we are thrown back to reconsider the whole poem at a different level.

The puns in the sonnets previously considered arise directly out of Astrophil's predicament as lover of Stella, but sonnet 22 is notable because the sexual hints in it are unprovoked. Since there is no special or intrinsic reason why Stella walking in the sun should make Astrophil think of sex, we must conclude that he does so simply because his mind is preoccupied with it at the time. The sonnet reveals the extent to which his thoughts are running on Stella as a sexual object. We might think of the assault imputed to the sun as some kind of projection of his own frustration. He is very aware of Stella's attractions but also (as we see in the reticence he attributes to the sun) of the fact that she is not to be wooed.

The use of the *double entendre* in these sonnets at the start of the sequence to indicate Astrophil's strong aware ness of Stella's sexual attractions is significant in three related ways. First, it contains in one group of words complex ideas and feelings that are simultaneous in his mind—they are aroused by a single experience (such as seeing Stella walking in the sun) and receive a single expression. Second, the tensions between meanings that are sometimes quite contrary (often chaste and unchaste love) reflect the central ambiguity in Astrophil's attitude and the principal dilemma that increasingly confronts him: the divergent meanings, held precariously together, enact the split in his response between his desires and his conscience. And third, the *double entendre* conveys his shame-faced alarm at the sensations and emotions he is experiencing: he is as yet reluctant to face his condition without the protective shield of an alternative innocent meaning. This last point is supported by the contexts in which the puns occur—his attempt at self-defence in sonnet 14, his recognition of the proper channels for his sexuality in 18, the violence of his attack on Lord Rich in 24 and the unprovoked associations he reveals in 22. Also, it is notable that as Astrophil is increasingly open about his desires, moving towards the crisis of the sequence in the Eighth Song, the *double entendre* is used far less and is reserved for blatantly direct meanings like those already mentioned in 68 and 76. His sexual importunity is acknowledged and only his most uncompromising sexual intentions need the safety-valve of an inoffensive alternative meaning.

This last point can be illustrated and the most glaring remaining instance of sexual punning will be illuminated if we consider the Tenth Song, where the rejected Astrophil asks when he will next see Stella. He wonders whether he may then be not 'debard from beautie's treasure', and he can't just mean looking at her because he would be doing that already. In the meantime he sends his Thought to visit her, telling it to treat her with the highest degree of intimacy—a degree which in person he has never been allowed:

> There unseene thou maist be bold,
> Those faire wonders to behold,
> Which in them my hopes do cary,
>
> Thought see thou no place forbeare,
> Enter bravely every where,
> Seaze on all to her belonging.

This is not the language of a respectful admirer of beauty; Astrophil is more or less undressing Stella in his mind. His approach is directly sensual—the nearest he ever comes to 'To his Coy Mistress':

> Thinke of my most Princely power,
> When I blessed shall devower,
> With my greedy licorous sences,
> Beauty, musicke, sweetnesse, love
> While she doth against me prove
> Her strong darts, but weake defences.
>
> Thinke, thinke of those dalyings,
> When with Dovelike murmurings,
> With glad moning passed anguish,

We change eyes, and hart for hart,
Each to other do imparte,
Joying till joy make us languish.

Perhaps this partly means that they would have great pleasure in each other's company, but the 'glad moning' and the joy which is followed by languishing are surely meant to suggest sexual intercourse. It is all too much for Astrophil:

O my thought my thoughts surcease,
Thy delights my woes increase,
My life melts with too much thinking;
Thinke no more but die in me,
Till thou shalt revived be,
At her lips my Nectar drinking.

Though at one level this final stanza means that Astrophil is made unbearably unhappy, it is also describing the ecstasy of sexual release. To 'melt' is to experience an orgasm—this is what it means in the ***Old Arcadia*** when Basilius spends the night enthusiastically with his wife, Gynecia, thinking her to be Cleophila, a fiction Gynecia is obliged to maintain: he 'did melt in as much gladness as she was oppressed with divers ungrateful burdens' (p. 227). To 'die' is of course the same thing. Astrophil's thought has been so successful in its visit to Stella that he is unable to contain himself: 'die in me' denotes a solitary orgasm. Max Putzel in his edition (Anchor, 1967) attributes 'obviously bawdy intention' to a doubtful manuscript version of this stanza, but it doesn't seem to me very different. There is a close analogy—perhaps even a source—in an erotic sonnet by one of the Pléiade, Jean-Antoine de Baïf, 'O doux plaisir plein de doux pensement'.[1] Here embracing and the uniting of soul with soul and body with body evoke the exclamation, 'O douce mort', as the poet's soul flows into his lady ('De moy dans toy s'ecoulant'); he becomes a lifeless mass ('masse morte'), but then her kiss returns his soul and restores his life ('Puis vient ta bouche en ma bouche la rendre, / Me ranimant tous mem membres perclus'). Astrophil imagines just such a scene, demonstrating both his great longing for Stella and his readiness to use the thought of her for solitary sexual stimulation.

If the sense of Song Ten does suggest that Astrophil is indulging rather pathetically in a barren sexual fantasy, it demonstrates powerfully his failure to adjust realistically to his rejection by Stella. There is very little prospect that he will ever be permitted to revive his powers by drinking nectar from her lips, let alone enjoy dovelike murmurings and glad moanings. It seems to me that his state in this song is almost hysterical; his romantic idealism has disintegrated under the strain of his disappointment and he is resorting to a vengeful brutalisation (comparable to that in the Fifth Song) of what remains of his relationship with Stella. If we compare the song with the earlier sonnets I have discussed we must be struck by the greater directness, indeed coarseness, with which Astrophil here behaves and uses words. The double meanings are employed to veil (very thinly in my opinion) a quite offensive conversion of Stella to a mere object of sexual fantasy, and the possibility of reading the song as idealistically sentimental and love-lorn only strengthens our sense of the confusion to which Astrophil's passion has reduced him.

Like the detection of Christ-figures, the discovery of sexual double meanings risks a response of boredom or hostility. However, I have tried to show that the criteria I proposed are to a considerable extent satisfied. All the meanings advanced here can be found in nearly contemporary writings, including Sidney's own and the sonnets and love poetry of other people; they are consistent both with their immediate context and with the sequence as a whole; and I think they do make the poetry better. I have concentrated upon the parts of ***Astrophil and Stella*** which have directly sexual implications not previously noted, but the interpretations I have proposed affect very many of the sonnets, adding qualifying and often ironical implications; indeed, they modify the whole way we think about Sidney. If correct, they must mean that the traditional image of the elegant but naive courtier is not only inadequate but misleading.

Note

1. *Les Amours de Jean-Antoine de Baïf* (1552), ed. Mathieu Augé-Chiquet (Geneva, 1972), XX, p. 147. Sidney must have known de Baïf's work on quantitative metres.

G. F. Waller (essay date 1974)

SOURCE: "This Matching of Contraries: Calvinism and Courtly Philosophy in the Sidney *Psalms*," in *English Studies*, Vol. 55, No. 1, February 1974, pp. 22–31.

[*In the following essay, Waller argues that the Sidney Psalter not only contains poetry that may be compared with that of the Metaphysical poets, but also is a reflection of important aspects in the literary and social ethos of the whole Sidney circle.*]

I

Since the publication of J. C. R. Rathmell's edition of the Sidney ***Psalms*** in 1963, there has been little evidence of the revaluation he hoped would follow. 'When recognition is accorded to the Sidney Psalter', wrote Dr. Rathmell, 'the history of the metaphysical revival of our own time will have to be rewritten'. He observed further that the work was 'virtually unknown even in academic circles . . . although it contains . . . some of the greatest poetry of the Elizabethan period'.[1] Dr. Rathmell's remarks obviously pointed towards a new assessment of the Psalms as a vehicle for translation and poetic meditation in the Renaissance, but what scholarly notice has been accorded the Sidney translations remains brief and largely written prior to his admirable edition.[2] The aim of the present paper is to examine certain aspects of the Sidney ***Psalms***, in order to illuminate important inherent qualities and also to show

how they reflect a crucial tension within the literary and social ideals of the Sidney circle.

Translation, however faithful to the word or spirit of the original, need not be mechanical, and it is to the credit of the Sidney Psalter that it first brought the whole of the Psalms into the mainstream of English lyric poetry. But in doing so, both Sir Philip Sidney and his sister, the Countess of Pembroke, embodied in their work an important tension that reverberates throughout the whole Sidneian ethos and, indeed, is found in Sidney's other literary works. Briefly, it is a tension between the moral and theological drives of Calvinist piety and the aesthetic doctrines of courtly philosophy, doctrines which ultimately rest on anti-Calvinist principles. I hope to show how the Psalms reflect and heighten this important tension.

The Countess probably took up her brother's incomplete manuscript in the early 1590's at the height of her influence as a patroness and minor practitioner of poetry.[3] Although the existence of any kind of English Areopagus at Wilton has long been dismissed, the Countess in particular and the writers who gathered informally about her in the last decade of the century did have certain literary and religious aims in common. They were implicitly dedicated to continuing the Sidneian spirit in English life and literature—and they were also united by a common Calvinist piety. Indeed what I am calling the Sidneian spirit is as much tempered by Calvin as by Castiglione. Although Sidney was widely hailed as embodying Castiglione's ideal, as for instance by Nashe, he was also admired for his firm piety, his dedicating his life to 'above all things the honour of his maker'. In the person and ideals of Sidney, the sophisticated aestheticism of the Italianate courtly ideal is heavily modified by practical Protestant piety. In Greville's significantly phrased description, which juxtaposes the dual elements of the Sidneian ideal, Sidney 'sweetly yoked fame and conscience together in a large heart'.[4] Indeed, the consistent modification in England of the doctrines of courtesy by the moral drive of Calvinism is an important subject for scholarly investigation.[5]

The sources of the Sidney ***Psalms*** have been well plotted by Dr. Rathmell and Professor William A. Ringler. Sidney used Marot's and Beza's French versifications, Wyatt's earlier English experiments, and naturally enough, Coverdale's Prayer Book Psalter, and the Geneva and Bishop's Bibles.[6] He undoubtedly, as my own readings of the Psalms make clear, consulted Calvin's and Beza's commentaries. More importantly, Sidney brought into the initial work on the translations his own meditations on the nature of lyric poetry in general and, specifically, on the Psalms as poetry. 'The holy *Davids* Psalms are', he writes, 'a divine *Poeme* . . . ', particularly, 'his handling his prophecie, which is meerly Poeticall'. The art of the Psalms is 'a heavenly poesie, wherin almost he sheweth himselfe a passionate lover of that unspeakable and everlasting bewtie, to be seene by the eyes of the mind, onely cleared by faith'.[7]

Perhaps even more significant are the philosophical assumptions Sidney—and, implicitly his sister—brought to the work. Introducing his translation of Calvin's Psalms, Arthur Golding stressed that the Psalms' importance lay in their 'earnest and devout lifting up of the mind' rather than their doctrines. Beza similarly suggests that while the 'holy Ghost . . . set them foorth by his secretaries, David and others', nevertheless unlike other parts of Scripture, they teach what we should say to God, not what God says to us.[8] From the slight but important hints here of an aesthetic rather than a doctrinal approach to the Psalms, it is not too big a step to Sidney's skilful matching of the Calvinist emphasis on man's helpless depravity with a neo-Platonic emphasis on man's will to aspire towards the divine through poetry. 'Our erected wit maketh us know what perfection is', Sidney argues, 'and yet our infected wil keepeth us from reaching unto it'. And yet the function of poetry is 'to lead and draw us to as high a perfection, as our degenerate soules made worse by their clay-lodgings, can be capable of . . . of lifte the minde from the dungeon of the bodie, to the enjoying his own divine essence'.[9] In the shimmering dialectic of the *Defence*, Sidney manages to encompass both man's depravity and his nobility. I am suggesting that in the Psalms, too, there is a similar duality, derived from, on the one hand, Sidney's embodiment of courtly, neo-Platonic ideals of man's nobility and self-transforming potential, and on the other, his deeply ingrained Calvinist piety. A similar tension is found in the Psalms translated by the Countess. Together, they reveal a fascinating and hitherto unexplored complexity in the intellectual history of the Sidney circle, a tension between Courtier and Christian, between Castiglione and Calvin.

II

The elements in the Sidney ***Psalms*** that I am seeking to isolate can conveniently be considered under four categories. There are, first, Psalms which in themselves give strong support to certain key doctrines of Calvinism; second, Psalms which were given specifically Calvinist interpretations by what is held by modern editors to be the Sidneys' main doctrinal source, the Geneva Bible; third, Psalms where, sometimes taking a suggestion from Beza or Calvin, sometimes independently, the Sidneys add a special Calvinist emphasis; fourth—and most significantly—Pslams where the Calvinist emphasis is firmly rejected and a deliberately courtly, even ultimately Pelagian, position is taken up. These differences are, I believe, not merely the result of intellectual confusion. The answer is more complex. In some cases, they reflect contrasting intellectual drives in the original Psalms that more dogmatic translations smooth over and, equally importantly, they bring out certain important preoccupations of the translators themselves. To illustrate these contentions, I shall look in turn at the four categories just outlined.

The first group is easily dealt with. Calvin and his followers found ready support for their particular theological emphasis in many Psalms. God's close providential control over time (19); the mystery of evil and death in God's pattern of universal justice (49); the dependence of Israel, as

God's chosen people, on his mercy (73); God's covenant with his elect (89), are all faithfully rendered by the Sidneys. In Psalm 143.2 the Countess brings out the point of the gloss in the Geneva Bible 'y[t] in Gods sight all men are sinners':

For Lord what living wight
Lives synnlesse in thy sight?

An equally succinct, though poetically more pleasing, note is found in her rendering of 127.1–2:

The house Jehova builds not,
We vainly strive to build it:
The towne Jehova guards not,
We vainly watch to guard it.

The brevity of these four lines constrasts more than favourably with Beza's prose paraphrase—an art designed, he says, to set 'the full sence and meaning of the holy ghoste in other words'[10]—which runs to some 300 words! As further examples of the Sidneys' renderings in this first group, 38 (man's depravity) and 61 (God's just punishment of man's sins) might be cited.

Then, second, there are those Psalms which lent themselves to the importation of Calvinist emphases, which are indeed usually stressed in the Geneva Bible. Here, however, the evidence is more complicated and suggests that some qualification is needed of Professor Ringler's claim that 'in everything affecting the meaning and interpretation of his own [version'], Sidney 'gave precedence to the Geneva' translation.[11] In the case of Psalm 8, as I shall later suggest, Sidney's divergence from Geneva and the Calvinist interpretations in general is total. But, as well, there are occasions where Sidney, and later his sister, draw heavily on other Calvinist translations or commentaries. There are, certainly, many occasions where Ringler's claim for the precedence of the Geneva version does hold. His comments, of course, apply only to those Psalms translated by Sidney; examples of the Countess' following Geneva are at 59.10 where Geneva has 'My merciful God will prevent me' and her versification is:

Thou ever me with thy free grace
Prevented hast.

94.10 also follows a Genevan expansion of the original Hebrew. 'He that chastiseth the nations, shall he not correct? he that teacheth me knowledge, shall he not know?' is the Geneva rendering. The last clause is added by the Biblical translation to complete the analogy which Coverdale's Prayer Book version, among others, leaves obscure, and the Countess follows suit:

Who checks the world, shall he not reprove?
Shall knowledge lack, Who all doth knowledge lend?

An interesting instance is at 147.20, 'He hathe not dealt so with everie nacion, neither have they knowen his judgements' (Geneva). Mary Sidney emphasises the Calvinist note of election particularly strongly:

No Nation els hath found him half soe kind,
For to his light, what other is not blynd?

Here she is echoing not the text but rather the dogmatic fervour of the Geneva marginal gloss which stresses that 'the cause of this difference is Gods fre mercie, which hathe . . . appointed the reprobate to eternal damnation'.

Other examples of this second category could be multiplied: Sidney's strong emphasis on election at 4.3, which echoes both Beza's and Calvin's glosses; imputed rather than inherent righteousness in 32.1; the total depravity of mankind and the vainness of works of supererogation in 14.1–2, where man

. . . and all his mates
Do workes, which earth corrupt, and Heaven hates:
Not one that good remaineth.

Beza's paraphrase is similarly emphatic: 'all doe make them selves abhominable, & not one of them doth lead his life aright'.

In the first and second categories, then, my argument extends or modifies certain observations already made by Ringler and Rathmell. But in the third category, something different is occurring. There are certain occasions when the poet's enthusiasm for a vigorous phrase emphasises an appropriate, but otherwise only implicit Calvinist reading, as for example, the Countess of Pembroke's ringing conclusion to 58:

The good with gladness this reveng shall see,
And bath his feete in bloud of wicked one
While all shall say: the just rewarded be,
There is a God that carves to each his own.

However strong and appropriate the last line, none of the Calvinist translations or glosses make much of it. Beza's paraphrase comes closest in words if not in tone: '. . . surely ther is a God in the earth, that doth also give every man his own'. The Geneva and Prayer Book versions are a tame 'there is a God that judgeth the earth', although once again the marginal gloss stresses the doctrinal note that Mary Sidney makes explicit when it states that 'seing God governeth all by his providence, he must nedes put difference betwene the godlie, and the wicked'. Similarly, Sidney's conclusion to 33 has a strong Calvinist emphasis on man's nothingness before God, a note not particularly stressed by Coverdale, Geneva, Beza or Calvin:

O lett thy mercy greate
On us be sette;
We have no plea, but trust.

An element of doctrinal stiffening is also introduced into 76.1–2. Geneva has

1. God is knowen in Judah: his Name is great is Israel

2. For in Shalem is his Tabernacle, and his dwelling in Zion.

The Prayer Book's version is similar, but the Geneva gloss adds that God's power is seen 'in prefering his people and destroying his enemies', a note of exclusiveness taken up by Mary Sidney:

Only to Juda God his will doth signify;
Only in Jacob is his name notorious;
His restfull tent doth only Salem dignify;
On Syon only stands his dwelling glorious.

Oddly enough, Calvin overlooks the exclusiveness implicit in the Hebrew; but Beza brings it out. God, he paraphrases, 'is only knowne in Judea . . . and he doth there only declare him selfe. . . .'[12]

An interesting example of the Countess' procedure in selecting different commentaries or glosses to back up a Calvinist stress is 62.11:

All powre is Gods, his own word showes,
Once said by him, twice heard by me:
Yet from thee, Lord, all mercy flowes,
And each manns work is paid by thee.

These lines were the subject of some controversy. Coverdale's version, though vague, is close to Mary Sidney's, and for once it may have been preferred over the Geneva translation, which states that God spoke an indefinite number of times, 'once or twice . . .', and Beza glosses this reading as signifying 'both with wordes and by the ende of the thinges'. Calvin, however, strongly rejects any such implication of divine hesitancy. His translation, which leads straight to the Sidney version, is 'once hath God spoken it, I have heard it twice, that power belongeth unto God'. His further comment is that 'once or twice' is too indefinite to be applied to God, since 'God eateth not his word when he hath once spoken it: it is our dutie to think leyzurely & advisedly uppon what soever is proceeded out of his mouth'.

A further particularly interesting example, indicating not merely a judicious selection among commentators, but a degree of meditational independence by the translator is found in 103.14:

Our potter he
Knowes how his vessells we
In earthly matter lodg'd this fickle forme.

The image of God as a potter and man as his clay, derived from Romans 9.21, is of course a favourite Calvinist commonplace:

If thou and thousands perish, it is nothing to him; hee cares no more for the destruction of the whole world, than thou doest for the throwing away of a little dust. . . . Therefore do not thou dispute with God, and aske, why are so many damned . . . shall the clay say to him that fashions it, what makest thou?[13]

But neither Geneva nor any of the commentators bring out the rhetorical possibilities of the image as explicitly as does Mary Sidney. Calvin's translation is 'he knoweth whereof wee bee made, he remembred that we are but duste'. Beza's paraphrase is closer without being explicit: 'for he knoweth that we are but earthen vessels, he knoweth that our substance is made of the earth'. In bringing out the doctrinal implications of the image, Mary Sidney is not only going back to the root meaning of the Hebrew, but she is enriching the meaning of her translation by bringing in a New Testament reference to which the Psalm obviously points forward. The example reinforces Dr. Rathmell's comment on her poetic practice that, at best she 'meditates on the text before her, and the force of her version derives from her sense of personal involvement'.[14]

III

So far, in analysing the first three of my four categories, I have shown how the Sidney translations reinforce certain insistent Calvinist notes in the Psalms, and in particular how Calvin's and Beza's commentaries, and occasionally various glosses, suggested to the Sidney's, as much as the text of the Geneva version, certain points of emphasis or development. But in my fourth category, something different is happening. I will now present evidence for the other pole of the tension I perceive in the Sidneian spirit as a whole. In what Louis Martz has called the Sidneys' 'attempt to bring the art of the Elizabethan lyric into the service of the psalmody',[15] I believe they imported not only the rhetorical vigour and flexibility of the court lyric, but also some of the sophisticated courtly philosophy that the secular lyric served to express. The Countess's expansion of 104.9, 'He appointed the moone for certeine seasons: the sunne knoweth his going downe' (Geneva), is an obvious example on a superficial level:

Thou makest the Empresse of the night,
Hold constant course with the most constant face:
Thou makest the sunne the Chariot-man of light,
Well know the start and stop of dayly race.

The elaboration comes straight from the conventional figures of the Elizabethan lyric. But there are more profound and revealing examples. The opening of 81 is a case in point. The Geneva translation reads:

1. Sing joyfully unto God our strength: singe loude unto the God of Jaakob.

2. Take the song and bring forth the timbrel, the pleasant harp with the viol.

The marginal gloss to the Psalm describes it as for 'solemne feasts & assemblies of the people, to whom for a time these ceremonies were ordeined, but now under the Gospel are abolished'. The same firm distrust of frivolity and ceremony is found in Calvin's and Beza's commentaries. God, says Calvin, is not to be 'worshipped . . . with idlenesse', and Beza emphasizes that godly celebration must be 'voyde of all wantonnesse, so that your joy may tend to the glory of God'. In the Countess of Pembroke's version, however, a joyful, musical, even frivolous, note is sounded:

> All gladness, gladdest hartes can hold,
> In meriest notes that mirth can yeld . . .
> Muster hither musicks joyes,
> Lute, and lyre, and tabretts noise:
> Lett noe instrument be wanting,
> Chasing grief, and pleasure planting.

The emphasis is on wholehearted celebration, a rich assemblage of music, colour and spectacle—again, the Countess is meditating on the poetic potential in the Psalm, and the poem is taking on an independent life beyond the stern boundaries of Reformed piety. Courtliness has triumphed over Calvinism.

The Countess's delight in ornamentation is also illustrated by an interesting elaboration of 45.13–14:

> This Queene that can a King her father call,
> Doth only shee in upper garment shine?
> Naie under clothes, and what she weareth all,
> Golde is the stuffe the fasshion Arte divine;

The translation is alive with the swirl of robes, the celebration of what might well pass for a courtly marriage ceremony of a costly-bedecked Elizabeth lady and an ideal *uomo universale* of the Renaissance:

> Fairer art thou than sonnes of mortal race.
> Because high God hath blessed thee for ay,
> Thie lipps, as springs, doe flowe with speaking grace.

The Psalm is unambiguously a celebration of the nobility and even the divine potential of man. It is instructive to note that it caused Calvinist commentators some difficulty. Beza asserts that the 'whole Psalme is altogether allegoricall', and devotes five earnest pages to unravelling its significance for the duties and rights of kings. Calvin is worried about the misapplication of such costly finery to church decoration and the sober service of God. He glosses it as an allegory of the church—a reading which is not denied by Mary Sidney's translation but which is, certainly on the most direct level, startlingly at odds with the tone of sensual celebration. Rather than being bogged down by doctrinal constraints, she has gone back to the original, and in her expansion, greatly added to the force of her version.

Where, I believe, this courtly strain I perceive in certain of the translations to be most evident and most at odds with Calvinism is in Sidney's version of Psalm 8, especially vv. 4–6:

> Ah, what is this man
> Whom that greate God remember can?
> And what the race of him descended,
> It should be ought of God attended?
> For thou in lesse than Angells state
> Thou planted hast this earthly mate;
> Yet hast thou made ev 'n hym an owner
> Of glorious crown, and crowning honor.

Predictably, this apparent paean of man also gives the Calvinists some trouble. Beza describes the Psalm as a thanksgiving to God for man's creation in Adam and redemption in Christ, and stresses that the Psalm underlines that 'man by his owne fault did fall' from his first high dignity. But the Psalm, on any fair reading, speaks of more than man's fallen state. Psalm 144.3, verbally similar in some respects, certainly lends itself to such a reading, and both the Geneva gloss and the Calvinist commentators make most of its unambiguous assertion of man's depravity. But Psalm 8 is another matter. Interestingly, it is quoted by Pico della Mirandola near the beginning of his *Oration on the Dignity of Man*, as a tribute to man's excellence and as the starting-point for his glorification of man's infinite powers of self-transformation. From Calvin to Pico almost encompasses the whole spectrum of Renaissance thought on the nature of man, and the stress on man's autonomy which underlies Pico's *Oration*, or is found in Bruno's celebration of man as magus, is both faithful to the tone of Psalm in question and anti-pathetic to the Calvinist doctrine of man's depravity.[16] Hence Calvinist commentators have a great deal of difficulty with the Psalm. The Geneva gloss on 8.14 is unconvincingly in line with that on 144.3, that God had no need to come 'so low as to man, which is but dust'. It is especially uneasy on the Psalm's stress on the 'crowning' of man which is glossed as only 'touching his first creation'. Calvin is in even greater difficulties. First of all, he disapproves of the Psalm's rhetorical extravagance—God, he comments on 8.3, has no great need of great rhetoricians, but merely of distinct speech. He then argues that the Psalm stresses the miseries of man, 'this miserable and vyle creature' and comments 'it is a woonder that the creator of Heaven . . . submitteth himselfe so lowe, as too vowtsafe too take uppon him the cares of mankind'. Such a conjunction of divine grace and what Calvin sees as the depravity of man evidently worries him. He describes it in the phrase I have taken as the title of my paper—'this matching of contraries'. The affinity between Calvin and the Renaissance neo-Platonists so brilliantly perceived some years ago by Professor Roy. W. Battenhouse is not evident here, where what Calvin sees as a neo-Pelagian misinterpretation of the Psalm is a distinct possibility.[17]

Sidney's version, certainly, has the appropriate wonder that man as a fallen creature should be elevated by God, but at the same time there is an almost hellenistic note of glorification that obviously appealed to the sophisticated courtly nature of the Elizabethan aristocrat. He turns the Psalmist's wonderment at the privilege of man into a celebration of man's possibilities, 'attended' by God, an 'owner' of regal status and 'crowning honor'. There is no sense of imputed glory, no acknowledgement of man's fallen nature. Man emerges, by implication, as a free and wondrous being, as capable on his own level of existence as his creator of 'freely raunging within the Zodiach of his owne wit'.[18] Courtly philosophy here is neatly combined with the celebration of man's creative autonomy to balance the Calvinist view of man as a sinful and limited being. Uniquely, the contraries coexist.

IV

I have argued in this paper that the Sidney Psalter not only, in Dr. Rathmell's words, 'contains poetry which bears comparison with the finest metaphysical verse',[19] but more, is a reflection of important aspects in the literary and social ethos of the whole Sidney circle. The Sidney translations draw out from the Psalms conflicting, even contradictory, attitudes to man's nature and place in the universe, and, as well, connect, as I hope to show in further studies, with similar tensions in Sidney's other works. To perceive in the Sidney Psalter the strands I have isolated is to be given an insight into an important aspect of the late Elizabethan mind.

Notes

1. J. C. A. Rathmell, 'Hopkins, Ruskin and the Sidney Psalter', *London Magazine*, VI (1959), 51; *The Psalms of Sir Philip Sidney and the Countess of Pembroke*, ed. J. C. A. Rathmell (New York, 1963).
2. e.g. L. B. Campbell, *Divine Poetry and Drama in Sixteenth-Century England* (Cambridge, 1959), pp. 50–4; Louis L. Martz, *The Poetry of Meditation* (New Haven, 1954), pp. 273–8; Robert L. Montgomery, *Symmetry and Sense* (Austin, 1961), pp. 20–6; *The Poems of Sir Philip Sidney*, ed. William Ringler (London, 1962), pp. l-li, 500–16. All references to the Sidney *Psalms* are from the Rathmell edition, quoted hereafter in the notes as *Psalms*. Citations from the text will give only Psalm number and line and will be incorporated into the text.
3. *Psalms*, p. xxvi; cf. Ringler, p. 501. See my '"This Matching of Contraries": Bruno, Calvin, and the Sidney Circle', *Neophilologus*, LVI (1972), 331–43; and 'Mary Sidney's *Dialogue*', *AN&Q*, IX (1972), 100–2.
4. See e.g. Thomas Nashe, *Works*, ed. Ronald B. McKerrow (Oxford, 1958), I, 7; Fulke Greville, *Life of Sir Philip Sidney*, introd. Nowell Smith (London, 1907), pp. 35, 40.
5. The present paper is part of a full-scale study on the subject now in the process of completion.
6. Ringler, p. 505; *Psalms*, pp. xiv, xix.
7. Sir Philip Sidney, *The Defence of Poesie*, in *Prose Works*, ed. Albert Feuillerat (Cambridge, 1963), III, 6–7.
8. *The Psalms of David . . . with M. John Calvins Commentaries*, trans. Arthur Golding (1571), Epistle Dedicatory; Theodore Beza, *The Psalms of David*, trans. Anthony Gilbie (1580), sig. iii[r]. Citations from both the text and commentaries in these works will give only the Psalm and verse and will be incorporated into the text. Similarly, citations from the text and glosses of the Geneva Bible (1560) will refer only to book, chapter, and verse, and will omit page references.
9. Sidney, *Defence*, pp. 9, 11.
10. Beza, Epistle Dedicatory.
11. Ringler, p. 506.
12. See also in this connection Psalms 98.2, 130.4.
13. John Preston, *Life Eternall* (1627), p. 127; cf. also *Isaiah* 64.8, *Jeremiah* 18.4.
14. *Psalms*, p. xx.
15. Martz, p. 273.
16. Pico della Mirandola, 'Oration on the Dignity of Man', in *The Philosophy of the Renaissance*, eds. H. Randall, E. Cassirer, and P. Kristeller (Chicago, 1948), pp. 225– 227; cf. Giordano Bruno, *De Magna, Opera Latine Conscripta* (Stuttgart, 1962), III 410ff. See also Frances A. Yates, *Giordano Bruno and the Hermetic Tradition* (London 1964), chs. 11–15.
17. See Roy W. Battenhouse, 'The Doctrine of Man in Calvin and Renaissance Platonism', *JHI* ix (1948), 447–71.
18. Sidney, *Defence*, p. 8.
19. 'Hopkins, Ruskin and the Sidney Psalter', p. 51.

Mariann S. Regan (essay date 1977)

SOURCE: "Astrophel: Full of Desire, Emptie of Wit," in *English Language Notes*, Vol. 14, No. 4, June 1977, pp. 251–56.

[*In the following essay, Regan maintains that Astrophel sometimes assumes the role of the conventional "foolish poet" of earlier love lyrics in order to convince readers he is a true lover.*]

Scholars have long attributed the dramatic vigor of ***Astrophel and Stella*** to Astrophel's variety of roles. However, no one has yet distinguished the "foolish poet" as one of these roles, nor has anyone noted that this role is a convention available to Sidney from earlier love lyrics, where many a poet-lover before Astrophel plays the "foolish poet" to persuade readers that he is a true lover. For often in Renaissance love lyrics the protean poet-lover will include among his many changes a pretense that he has lost control of his words, his language, his tongue—the "poet" part of himself. And when his "poet" has been thrown into confusion, his "lover" is shown thereby to be all the more sincere.

This "foolish poet" convention resembles the "inexpressibility" trope noted by Curtius, in which a speaker laments that his subject is beyond his powers of expression.[1] In both the "inexpressibility" trope and the "foolish poet" convention the poet-lover does not have full mastery of his words; however, with the trope he exalts the lady's divine beauties and with the convention he shows more immediately the extent of his *own* passion, good faith, and lover's reverence. This "foolish poet" who cannot command his words appears throughout the Renaissance love lyric in two forms, talkative and reticent, which are contraries to the same purpose. In his talkative form he seems to let his words run wild: he cannot stop boasting, inventing, threatening. Even while he is fitting his words into prescribed meters and rhymes, he can make these words seem to strain against their confines. In Bernart de Ventadorn's *canso* 40, the poet-lover repeatedly scolds his tongue: "Lenga, per que potz tan parlar?" (18) [Tongue, why do you talk so much?].[2] His wayward tongue proves his strong feeling, for he is impetuous, doomed ("mal escharnitz") without the lady, a man born for loving. He can hardly tame his words in this loquacious *canso*: his syntax is involuted, his sentiments tangled; his words outnumber those in each of the other *cansos*. His indictment of his loose tongue applies to these gabby poetic operations: "Ara folei de trop gabar" (43) [Now I play the fool with too much bragging].

Such rapt lovers often say more than they should. Petrarch's poet-lover, in retracting one of several rebellious charges against Laura's cruelty, apologizes, "Dolor, perché mi meni / fuor di camin a dir quel ch'i' non voglio?" (lxxi, 46–47) [Grief, why do you lead me / out of the way to say what I don't want to say?].[3] Ronsard's poet-lover describes himself to Marie as an endless fountain of words:

> Mais quand je suis tout seul aupres de mon plaisir,
> Ma langue interpretant le plus de mon desir,
> Alors de caqueter mon ardeur ne fait cesse:
> Je ne fais qu'inventer, que conter, que parler:
> Car pour estre cent ans aupres de ma maistresse,
> Cent ans me sont trop courts, & ne m'en puis aller.[4]
>
> [But when I am all alone near my beloved, / My tongue translating my greatest desires, / I never stop chattering passionately: / I do nothing but invent, relate, and talk: / For if I were near my mistress for a hundred years, / A hundred years would be too brief, and I could not leave.]

Perhaps this kind of antic wordiness, this free rein of the tongue, can even help provoke those rhetorical ingenuities so typical of poet-lovers: insofar as they are verbose, forever new, paradoxical, or even incomprehensible, so they are demonstrating the barely contained energy of their love. They are trying to play all the pageants at once, and their words speed up accordingly. If they use a "maggot ostentation" (*Love's Labor's Lost* V.ii.409), it is all to a purpose, to show that they love fiercely and from the heart.

The wordy "foolish poet," then, cannot turn off the faucet of his words; on the other hand, in his second form the "foolish poet" cannot turn this faucet on. He is tongue-tied, halting, quaking, speechless. Bernart's poet-lover in *canso* 17 is in this plight: "Qu'ela no sap lo mal qu'eu trai / ni eu no·lh aus clamar merce" (11–12) [For she does not know the pain that I suffer / nor do I dare to cry out to her for mercy]. His tongue is bound ("entrelia") before his lady, as is the ungrateful tongue of Petrarch's poet-lover, who rebukes it for desertion in a crisis:

> ché quando piú 'l tuo aiuto mi bisogna
> per dimandar mercede, allor ti stai
> sempre piú fredda, e se parole fai,
> son imperfette, e quasi d'uom che sogna.
>
> (xl)
>
> [For when I need your aid the most / To ask for mercy, then you remain / Still more cold, and if you do make words, / They are imperfect, like those of a man who is dreaming.]

Ronsard's poet-lover has no more cooperative a tongue: while "my feeble tongue" was gathering courage to speak to Cassandre, he once laments, a Centaur galloped up and carried her away (*Les Oeuvres*, I, 271). All this trembling silence, of course, is supposed to be testimony to the poet-lover's sincerity. As Petrarch's speaker puts it, "chi pò dir com'egli arde, è 'n picciol foco" (clxx) [Whoever can say how much he is burning, is in a small fire]. Shakespeare's poet-lover, himself quite familiar with the "tongue-tied Muse" (Sonner 85), exhorts his beloved, "O, learn to read what silent love hath writ" (Sonnet 23). Silence will speak eloquently of love. And just as the talkative "foolish poet" still managed to obey the rules of prosody, so the reticent "foolish poet" must express his wordlessness in words.

Just as he can play the naïf or plain speaker,[5] Sidney's Astrophel can use this "foolish poet" convention to create the impression that he "loves in truth." For example, as Astrophel advances ever closer to his desired possession of Stella, his words seem more and more to run away from him, and to spill out in tangled profusion. The plot of the sequence reaches its climax when Stella promises "conditionly / This realme of blisse" (69),[6] her gift of grace, and Astrophel, deciding to break the "vertuous course" that she has imposed upon him, rides to her house to claim full enjoyment of her (84, 85), only to be thoroughly and finally refused: "Alas, whence came this change of lookes?" (86). Two versions of this rebuff are given, in the Fourth and Eighth Songs placed between sonnets 85 and 87. It is near this high point of the action that Astrophel as "foolish poet" becomes markedly clumsy, verbose, preoccupied, seemingly heedless of his earlier care to find "fit words" (1) for his song, to express his struggling thoughts in poetic form (50). Now he seems to abandon himself to his enthusiasm with a reckless energy, let the words fall wherever they might:

> I, I, ô I may say, that she is mine.
>
> (69)
>
> Sweet kisse, thy sweets I faine would sweetly endite,
> Which even of sweetnesse sweetest sweetner art:
>
> (79)

Lines like these seem designed to be wild, as though written by a poet-lover so flustered and impatient that he does not bother to trim the mad excesses of his language. He is "full of desire, emptie of wit" (82). His comic, stumbling verbosity is in full play as he rides to Stella's house for the showdown:

Highway since you my chiefe *Pernassus* be,
And that my Muse to some eares not unsweet,
Tempers her words to trampling horses feet,
More oft then to a chamber melodie;
Now blessed you, beare onward blessed me
To her, where I my heart safeliest shall meet.
My Muse and I must you of dutie greet
With thankes and wishes, wishing thankfully.
Be you still faire, honourd by publike heed,
By no encrochment wrongd, nor time forgot:
Nor blam'd for bloud, nor sham'd for sinfull deed.
And that you know, I envy you no lot
Of highest wish, I wish you so much blisse,
Hundred of yeares you *Stella's* feet may kisse.

(84)

Astrophel is by no means the earnest and careful seeker of words here. He lavishes compliments and good wishes with a nervous excess, as though he were trying rather ineptly to ingratiate himself with the highway. But the highway, as we know, is not his first concern, and in this sense all the words of the poem are gratuitous. He is merely passing the time of the poem on his journey to Stella: filling out his eighth line with a pointless repetition, filling out his sestet with an absurd list of hypothetical future "events" for the highway, filling out the whole sonnet with vacuous blessings and wishings and thankings. He is "tossing words about pointlessly"[7] because the words are in his way, a task to be got over: the last hyperbole, a supposed wish for the highway, is there simply to betray his own unstated enormous desires. While he waits to see Stella, he lets his words run on without check. The same structure obtains in Sonnet 79, a frenetic catalogue relieved by Stella's arrival in mid-line 13: "but lo, lo, where she is, / Cease we to praise, now pray we for a kisse." The wordy "foolish poet" drops the reins of language, showing the "lover" to be beside himself with passion.

Astrophel's passion is never to be fulfilled. Controlled or uncontrolled, witty or preoccupied, he cannot brandish enough words to change Stella's "No" to "Yes." He receives his most favorable response, however, not when he is talkative but when he takes on his contrary tongue-tied shape: "They love indeed, who quake to say they love" (54). Perhaps such a humble "foolish poet" can be even more appealing to a lady than can the "foolish poet" with tumbling, eager, unstoppered words. At least, Stella in the Eighth Song seems to like the poet-lover's reticence, for she responds much more fully to Astrophel in the Eighth Song than in the Fourth Song, the other version of the same encounter. In the Fourth Song, Stella never emerges from her protective cover of "No"'s:

Your faire mother is a bed,
Candles out, and curtaines spread:
She thinkes you do letters write:
Write, but first let me endite:
Take me to thee, and thee to me.
'No, no, no, no, my Deare, let be.'

In this song Astrophel is not the "foolish poet" but the tactician with words, with his insistent carpe diem casuistry, his word-plays like "endite," his stealthy *reasons* for loving, his rhetoric to deceive a maid; Stella pulls back from him. By contrast, Astrophel in the Eighth Song is not clever. He begins with a diminutive catalogue:

'*Stella* soveraigne of my joy,
Faire triumpher of annoy,
Stella starre of heavenly fier,
Stella loadstar of desier.'

He continues in this ingenuous, rather bashful manner for three more stanzas without added complication, and when he approaches his actual request words almost fail him:

'Graunt, ô graunt, but speech alas,
Failes me fearing on to passe,
Graunt, ô me, what am I saying?
But no fault there is in praying.

'Graunt, ô deere, on knees I pray,
(Knees on ground he then did stay)
That not I, but since I love you,
Time and place for me may move you.'

Some scholars have noted the sense of formality and ritual in Astrophel's speech, and in these lines the parallelism of the three "Graunt" phrases (Young, p. 79; Rudenstine, p. 260). Yet the speaker here finds no security in his words, and in the three matched phrases themselves the grand "Graunt ô graunt" construction quickly degenerates to the bathetic "ô me" and "ô deere." Nichols even finds the kneeling pose "humorous" (p. 95). For this Astrophel loves so intensely that his words will not cooperate with his heart. And when he does recover his tongue, it is to defer to nature, praying that "not I . . . may move you," that is, disclaiming all credit for the powers of his rhetoric. He pleads with a subdued eloquence for a love that befits the "season":

'Love makes earth the water drink,
Love to earth makes water sinke;
And if dumbe things be so witty,
Shall a heavenly grace want pitty?'

His sense of occasion is certainly larger than the view of "Niggard Time" offered in the Fourth Song: he is making his wit subservient to time and place, not trying to exploit time and place through his wit. He is himself a "dumbe thing" who finds best expression through speaking less. By playing the "foolish poet," he can convince even the experts that this is "genuine naiveté" (Rudenstine, p. 263), the real Astrophel behind the roles. It is not Astrophel's fluency with "fit words" but his timidity with simple words that has at last succeeded in painting his "blackest face of woe," eliciting here the warmest response that Stella will ever give him. She protests a "deep" and faithful love for him in this song, "blisse" with him and "smart" without him; it is only "Tyran honour" that forces her to refuse his suit.

Sidney believed that a love lyric, above all, should seem to be written by one who was indeed in love, and he deplored those formulaic poems "under the banner of unresistible love" whose speakers seemed to feel no passion, "so coldly they apply fiery speeches." Thus in order to apply Astrophel's fiery speeches warmly and with *energia*, Sidney lets him play the "foolish poet" who has lost the fully controlled use of his words.

> I am not I, pitie the tale of me.
>
> (45)

Notes

1. Ernst R. Curtius, *European Literature and the Latin Middle Ages* (New York 1963), pp. 159–162.
2. Bernart quotations are from *The Songs of Bernart de Ventadorn*, ed. and trans. Stephen G. Nichols, Jr., et al. (Chapel Hill, 1965).
3. Quotations from Petrarch's *Canzoniere* are from *Le Rime Sparse e i Trionfi*, ed. Ezio Chiorboli (Bari, 1930); my translations.
4. *Amours de Marie*, in *Les Oeuvres de Pierre de Ronsard*, ed. Isidore Silver (Chicago, 1966), II, 62; my translations.
5. See Richard B. Young, *English Petrarke*, in *Three Studies in the Renaissance* (New Haven, 1958), p. 27 et passim; Neil L. Rudenstine, *Sidney's Poetic Development* (Cambridge, 1967), p. 204 et passim; and Robert L. Montgomery, Jr., *Symmetry and Sense* (New York, 1961), Chapter 5 et passim.
6. Quotations from *Astrophel and Stella* are from *The Poems of Sir Philip Sidney*, ed. William A. Ringler, Jr. (Oxford, 1962). References are to sonnet number.
7. J.G. Nichols, *The Poetry of Sir Philip Sidney* (Liverpool, 1974), p. 26.

Myron Turner (essay date 1977)

SOURCE: "When Rooted Moisture Failes: Sidney's Pastoral Elegy (OA 75) and the Radical Humour," in *English Language Notes*, Vol. 15, No. 1, September 1977, pp. 7–10.

[*In the following essay, Turner discusses the "rooted moisture" mentioned in elegy 75 in the* Old Arcadia, *and says the concept, which is derived from the Greek philosopher Aristotle, describes the "natural humidity" that is the basis of natural life.*]

In the **"Fourth Eclogues"** of the ***Old Arcadia***, the shepherd Agelastus leads his companions "in bewailing" the "general loss" of Basilius to the Arcadians.[1] Ringler points out that this elegy (OA 75) and Spenser's November ecloque "are the earliest examples of formal pastoral elegy in English."[2] Unlike Spenser's Colin, however, Agelastus maintains the naturalistic decorum of the classical form and is brought, finally, to bewail the helplessness of mankind before the natural processes which end in death:

> O Phisicke's power, which (some say) hath refrayned
> Approach of death, alas thou helpest meagerly,
> When once one is for *Atropos* distrained.
> Great be Physitions' brags, but aid is beggerly,
> When rooted moisture failes, or groweth drie,
> They leave off al, and say, death comes too eager-
> lie.
> They are but words therefore which men do buy,
> Of any since God *æsculapius* ceased.
>
> (109–116)

Both Ringler and Robertson gloss the "rooted moisture" of "When rooted moisture failes" as "vital spirits."[3] Rooted moisture is something quite different from vital spirits, however, and the process by which it fails and dries up is more fundamental to the despairing naturalism of Agelastus's invention.

In a small treatise on self-knowledge, Sidney's friend du Plessis Mornay defines what he calls "natural humidity":

> Euen as wee behold the flame of a lampe, to be nourished & maintained by some clammie drines which is in it: in like manner the bodie of any creature, hauing life and vnderstanding, hath som especial good humiditie, fat and ayrie, which commeth of the seede and essentiall beginning of the body, & disperseth it self throgh all the parts, wherein is carried this viuifying & celestiall heate, holding together & still nourishing this heate, which humiditie once consumed, immediately that heate is quenched.

Citing Aristotle as his authority, Mornay further explains that death occurs "when the heat natural is extinct: that is to say, when the primitiue & original humiditie (pure and intire) is consumed."[4] La Primaudaye, in his *French Academie*, calls this airy moisture by its more common name, radical humour, "because it is as it were the roote of life." He makes the same basic points as Mornay but explains, in addition, that "although this radical humidity be nourished by the ordinary food which the body daily receiueth," such nourishment "is not so pure nor so fit, nor so natural as the radicall humour it selfe neither can [it] wholy restore that which diminisheth and consumeth thereof, it must needes be that life would faile in processe of time." "By this meanes," therefore, "it commeth to passe, that the radicall humiditie and natural heat faile and perish both together. Whereby we may easily understand why mens bodies abide not alwaies in their strength, but faile & waxe olde."[5] Thus, the failure of "rooted moisture" explains the process of aging and natural death. Agelastus, unaware that Basilius has apparently been poisoned, bewails his loss in terms of an accepted medical concept first named and fully defined by Avicenna but having its origins in ancient Greece and most especially with Aristotle.[6] Aristotle, for instance, is the source for Mornay's assertion that radical humidity is "fat and ayrie." Aristotle argues that longevity depends upon the power of the body's innate moisture to remain moist; hence it must be "fatty," because "fatty things are not liable to decay" as they "contain air" which "does not become corrupt."[7]

To grasp the wider relationship of "rooted moisture" to Agelastus's imagery, one must be aware that the sixteenth century inherited from the ancient world what one writer calls "the constant confusion of air and water vapor" which fostered the Stoic concept of *pneuma*, or *spiritus*, as a hot breath.[8] This gives an added dimension to the notion that the radical humidity possesses the nature of air. In Aristotle, the vaporous heat of the *pneuma* is the generative principle of the male seed; this heat, he says, is "analogous to the element which belongs to the stars."[9] Here is the most obvious source for that "celestiall heate" which Mornay calls "viuifying" and La Primaudaye "quickening," the heat which comes with the radical humour from the seed. Discussions of radical humidity inevitably advert to the seed, the origin of life, which is moist and airy and warm. If, in the Galenic medical tradition, the three-fold *spiritus*—natural, vital, and animal—are nourished by respiration, one must also remember that *pneuma*, the warm vapor of breath and spirit, is in the seed itself.

With these few points in mind, let us briefly look at Agelastus's images. From the very first the art of Agelastus is an art of "doleful tunes" that breathes out spirit and depletes the moisture of life with exhausting "sorrowe." He looks to the trees to "receave" into their "porous barkes"

> The straunge resounde of these my causefull cries:
> And let my breath upon your braunches cleave,
> My breath distinguish'd into wordes of woe.
>
> (ll. 7–10)

Agelastus holds up before his imagination an image in which he pours the moist breath of life back into the vegetable nature with which it shares a common root: for "rooted moisture" is not merely metaphor but, rather, points to the belief that radical humidity is a moisture man shares with the plants and which is the basis of vegetative life.[10] If on the one hand he desires to pour himself back into nature, on the other he would have all of nature, like himself, breathe out its life and weep itself dry: this he seeks in the "weeping Myrrhe" (l. 13), in the hyacinthine "Ai" (l. 29), in the diurnal rain of "wofull teares" from "dimmy clowedes" (ll. 67–70), and in having "all the Sea" Earth's "teares accounted be" (l. 20). He would have all of nature participate in "death's detested crime" (l. 90), which is, of course, a crime only against human consciousness, the mind which can enhance nature yet has not even the powers of self-renewal of the "filthy snake" (ll. 82–87).

In the third stanza, "breath distinguish'd into wordes of woe" becomes the Echo, breath reaching out towards celestial answers, seeking to find the iteration of itself not on earth but somewhere in the farthest reaches of its progressive self-attenuation, as it rises, "One *Echo* to another cast" (l. 34). The unanswered Echo, the doleful tune that mounts aloft but finds no sound to repeat its being becomes, beyond the final attenuation of breath, not even air, but what is no longer air, the annihilation of naturalistic reality: "Death is our home, life is but a delusion" (l. 123). The poem leaves us with the failure of breath to have risen above the fatty moisture at the source of life, the failure of breath to have become Spirit. "Upon thy face let coaly Ravens swarme" (l. 19), says Agelastus to Earth. The Echo that mounts aloft can look forward only to becoming the earthbound wings of extinguished heat, the dead coals of an innate flame that has been consumed.

Notes

1. *The Countess of Pembroke's Arcadia* (*The Old Arcadia*), ed. jean Robertson (Oxford, 1973), p. 344. Ringler—*The Poems of Sir Philip Sidney*, ed. William Ringler, Jr. (Oxford, 1962)—attributes this elegy to Dicus (p. 419). In the present essay, I use Ringler's text of the poems and his notation and numbering; I use Robertson for prose passages.
2. Ringler, p. 419.
3. ———, p. 421; Robertson, p. 477.
4. Philip du Plessis Mornay, *The True Knowledge of a Mans Owne Selfe*, trans. Anthony Munday (London, 1602), pp. 40–43.
5. *The French Academie* (London, 1618), pp. 537–538 (i.e. sig.Zz4^r-Zz4^v, misnumbered in this edition as 547–548).
6. The concept of radical moisture has been treated by Thomas S. Hall, *Ideas of Life and Matter*, vol. 1 (Chicago, 1969), *passim* and in "Life, Death and the Radical Moisture: A Study of Thematic Pattern in Medieval Medical Theory," *Clio Medica*, 6 (1971), 3–23. I am indebted to Professor Hall for his having sent me a copy of his own essay, which was not otherwise immediately available to me, and for having at the same time sent me a copy of Michael McVaugh's study, "The 'Humidum Radicale' in Thirteenth-Century Medicine," *Traditio*, XXX (1974), 259–283.
7. *Parv. Nat.* 466a 23–25; my translation is that of W.S. Hett, *Aristotle: On the Soul, Parva naturalia, On Breath*, Loeb Classical Library (London, 1964).
8. S. Sambursky, *Physics of the Stoics* (London, 1959), p. 3.
9. *Generation of Animals*, trans. A.L. Peck, Loeb Classical Library (London, 1964), 736b 35–39.
10. *The Middle English Dictionary*, for instance, defines "radical moisture" as a "moisture of the root." One finds that the radical humour is the organic basis of growth, reproduction, and nutrition, commonly referred to as the "three powers" of the vegetative soul.

Gary L. Litt (essay date 1978)

SOURCE: "Characterization and Rhetoric in Sidney's "Ye

Goatherd Gods," in *Studies in the Literary Imagination*, Vol. 11, No. 1, Spring, 1978, pp. 115–24.

[*In the following essay, Litt asserts that Sidney uses imagery, syntax, diction, grammar, and metaphor to differentiate the characters and experience of the two shepherds in the* Old Arcadia *poem, "Ye Goatherd Gods."*]

Sidney's **"Ye Goatherd Gods"** is a masterful demonstration of formal and verbal artifice. The poem is virtually unmatched in rhetorical intricacy and complex manipulation of mood and environment, and deserves the praise and careful attention Empson, Kalstone, Ransom, and others have given it.[1] However, the depth, charm, and accomplishment of the poem is even more considerable upon recognition of the complex characterization of the shepherds—an aspect of the work which has generally been ignored. This characterization is a culminating effect of the poem, for Sidney not only masters an unnatural and difficult form, but also presents a mini-drama in which there is subtle differentiation of Klaius and Strephon, a definite pattern of emotional and psychological movement, and an attempt to examine several Renaissance rhetorical and philosophical stances through the characters, styles, and thoughts of the shepherds.

For many years, despite my great admiration for **"Ye Goatherd Gods,"** and Sidney's rhetorical brilliance in the poem, I was bothered by certain passages. Occasional lines and phrases seemed flat, awkward, or harsh; they gave the jarring sense of poetic wrong notes. I could not believe that a poet who could reach such peaks of verbal felicity in the poem would have Klaius mumbling his heartbrokenness in stale, unwieldy metaphors of molehills and mountains (l. 23). Furthermore, I was disturbed by certain grammatical and syntactical problems as Sidney allowed molehills to "fill the vales with cries instead of music" (l. 24), or as a shepherd bumbled his way through a line such as, "Curse to myself my prayer is, the morning" (l. 55). It would be easy to attribute such awakwardness to the difficulties of the form, but finally it occurred to me that Sidney might be giving the shepherds different rhetorical idioms in order to establish certain character distinctions between Strephon and Klaius.[2] At first the idea seemed far-fetched, but, in fact, upon careful examination, the most bothersome passages seemed to be those spoken by Klaius.[3]

In **"Ye Goatherd Gods"** Sidney uses imagery, diction, syntax, grammar, and metaphor to differentiate the shepherds in order to present two "types" of Renaissance character and style. These types provide a base against which the shepherds' emotional frustration at the loss of Urania can be measured and through which Sidney can explore the capacity of imagination, language, literary patterns, memory, and the pastoral setting to manage and compensate for archetypal loss—loss of love, life, harmony, justice, Eden.

The characterization of the shepherds is coordinated with brilliant structural development in the poem. Sidney slowly evinces the characters of Klaius and Strephon during the first eight stanzas. Yet, even while the two shepherds are being carefully distinguished, we see the dramatic psychological movement towards fragmentation and disintegration of those characters. Stanzas nine and ten present a violent alteration of the shepherds' personalities; this change of character is manifested in their alien thought processes and is emphasized by the breakdown of the syntactical and verbal parallelism of the poem. Finally, in stanzas eleven and twelve the remembrance of Urania returns some order and harmony to the world and their identities, though the memory alone cannot dispell their melancholy or the chaos of a fallen world. Furthermore, and this is more speculative, in the final stanzas Sidney may be forcing on us an examination of the two approaches to experience represented by Klaius (active, plain, passionate, natural) and Strephon (contemplative, rhetorical, melancholy, civilized), and, in my opinion, offering a judgment slightly favoring Klaius, who has a more direct, selfless approach to life.

Stanzas one and two establish the mood, the context of the lament, the environment (and words) for the sestina variation. Subtle differences already appear in the ways the shepherds respond to the environment and display their grief. Strephon speaks in a quiet, reflective mood as he calls up a scene of natural beauty and harmony in the invocation to his deities. Then in lines four through six, he gently modulates into an awareness of grief. Strephon is a creature of memory and carefully orchestrated moods. He savors contrasts and intensifies his grief by dwelling on them. His is a complex, multiple-perspectived view which is less immediate than that of Klaius, more aware of the past, the self-conscious present, and their relationship to the future. Klaius, on the other hand, responds impulsively, passionately. He seldom calculates for effect, shows little "literary" concern, displays slight awareness of anything but his present grief. The structural patterns of his laments emerge out of imitation of Strephon's lead. A creature of the present, he lives in a transformed environment of "woeful" valleys and "savage" mountains with little thought that there was ever another. He is mastered by his grief, which colors his perception of his environment.

These initial differences of response partially evolve out of the Renaissance character type each persona represents. Though both Strephon and Klaius are shepherds, the poem makes it clear that Strephon is a "literary" shepherd (such as Colin Clout?), having little to do with the actual mechanics of herding, and that Klaius, "every morning" is "hunting the wild inhabiters of forests" (ll. 19–20). In actuality, we are dealing with the ancient archetypes of shepherd and hunter, and the Renaissance reader would anticipate, more readily than we do, differences of perspective, interest, and personality. We see the first of many of these differences in the invocation of each "shepherd." Strephon invokes one class of shepherd deities—goatherd gods (pans?), nymphs, and satyrs. Quietly absorbed by his immediate environment, Strephon turns to its attendant spirits and merrymakers. There is something low-keyed, unified, perhaps consciously literary in his choice. Moreover, beginning at such a level, he can rise more climactically to the summit of his grief. The group itself has numerous social, literary and, if it is not too early to raise this spectre, sexual associations.

Klaius, on the other hand, begins his invocation by intently praying to the Olympians—Mercury, Diana, Venus. For Klaius, however, they are not mere literary abstractions as Strephon's nymphs and satyrs must be, for in Klaius' concrete way, he is really addressing part of his environment, the planets Mercury and Venus, and the moon. It is this visual reality which appeals to Klaius, for if we look at the intellectual reality of his choice of deities (something Strephon would be aware of) we find a slight obtuseness, or, perhaps more accurately, a lack of calculation as to literary and intellectual implications. Addressing Mercury, the shepherd deity, is quite appropriate. But there is strain in linking Diana and Venus, chastity and sexual fertility, in this trinity, to complain about the loss of the virtuous Urania's love and presence. We can see what effect Klaius is after—he wants a deity for shepherds, for hunters, and for lovers; but here, as so often in the poem, Klaius reaches after an effect to follow and match Strephon's lead and is only partially successful because of his lack of calculation and rhetorical orientation. As a result, we are often left with an impression of relative roughness, occasionally even crudity, compared to Strephon's sophisticated and considered use of language and materials.

The shepherds' rhetoric in these two stanzas does not differ radically; yet, there are differences. Strephon has finer musical modulation:"Ye goatherd gods, that love the grassy mountains" (l. 1); and he uses more alliteration, placing it in closely linked and intertwined patterns, including internal rhyme: "Which to my woes give *still* an early morning, / And draws the dolor on *till* weary evening" (ll. 5–6). Throughout the poem Klaius uses less alliteration and fewer figures than Strephon. (Sidney, in this matter of alliteration, as in others, allows only enough discrepancy between the two characters to indicate a difference of usage.) In addition, in line eleven Klaius perhaps displays a certain limitation of imagination or inspiration, being forced to repeat one of Strephon's lines in its entirety: "Vouchsafe your silent ears to plaining music."

Stanzas three and four intensify the development of character by considering the individual shepherd's relationship to society and by a glimpse into the psychology of each persona. The two stanzas also establish the verbal and syntactical parallelism of response suggested in the first two stanzas; this will dominate the form until stanzas nine and ten, when such parallelism is broken to suggest emotional chaos.

In stanza three, Strephon begins with a recognition of his social relationship. He is a "free burgess," citizen of the forests. He is linked to the community; his reference to sports (l. 14) and his musical reputation, "I, that was once esteemed for pleasant music" (l. 15), further underline a social orientation. Banishment, even self-imposed (l. 16), brings great pain for Strephon, but it also gives him the raw materials out of which he creates his mood, contrasts, songs.

Klaius is less socially oriented; he is a loner, a hunter who daily stalks the forest with autonomy and self-confidence. He has innumerable heirs from Natty Bumpo to Mellors. Klaius is his own world. He shows his independence, and, perhaps, egoism, in his variation on the theme of music. Strephon laments that he was "once esteemed" for music (l. 15). Klaius' parallel response begins, "I, that was once the music of these valleys . . ." (l. 21). Because of its curious ambiguity, there are several ways to interpret this statement, but all tend to emphasize Klaius' assertive independence. In terms of Klaius' music the passage suggests that he sees himself the only judge of its quality. Peer judgment and approval are unimportant to him; he *is* the music. In his isolation as hunter we can quite understand this perspective, but the ambiguity of the phrase suggests that Klaius sees himself as the essential harmonizing element of his environment. Like Wallace Stevens' jar, Klaius brings order and harmony to the wilds, perhaps to the world at large. However, this curious phrase about Klaius' music might be less a philosophical or psychological riddle than an example of his rhetorical ineptness, for, if we pursue the meaning of this passage, we find Klaius mixing his metaphors (and senses) as his music turns into darkness (l. 22). This mixed metaphor is even more apparent since we have just seen Strephon delicately thread his way through a sentence fraught with syntactical and psychological complexities and yet keep his metaphor intact as he ends up not a poet-songster but a "screech owl" (l. 18). Klaius' syntactical and referential difficulties are further emphasized as he has molehills filling the vales with cries in lines twenty-three and twenty-four. By the end of stanza four, rather clear-cut distinctions exist between Strephon and Klaius in terms of their use of language, and the two are also beginning to diverge psychologically.

Klaius' rhetorical problems are not meant to condemn him, and, in fact, he is not anti-rhetorical or unrhetorical. He is simply not intellectually or verbally as facile as Strephon. Though he is a long way from the plain style, within the context of Strephon's rhetorical practice, Klaius seems to partake of elements of plain-style philosophy. His plainer, rougher idiom is appropriate for a hunter and might be seen as more sincere and direct. The plainer poet often gives the impression of being a little nearer to the truth, so Klaius' roughness is not necessarily a disadvantage in the poem. He is using a different idiom, speaking out of a different psychology and experience. Let us look a little closer at that psychology, and Strephon's, as the two figures emerge out of these early stanzas.

Stanzas one through four have deftly sketched the fundamental characters and psychologies of Strephon and Klaius through a combination of traditional character associations, responses to their environment, and rhetorical usage.

Stanzas five and six begin to demonstrate how the behavior and thinking of the lovers, under the strain of grief, slowly become distorted and how Strephon and Klaius subtly meditate self-destruction in what might be seen as a traditional response to grief—a potential channel and sublimation which in this instance is not successful as relief.

Strephon's death meditations begin with the eminently poetic evocation of the swan song: "Long since, alas, my deadly swannish music / Hath made itself a crier of the morning" (ll. 25–26). His life has become disjointed, and his focus, as we might suspect from an artist and "intellectual," is on his song and mind; the one has become a "deadly" honk, the other a barren desert. Stanza five reeks of despair, desolation, death. There are no more rational and ritualistic (artistic) channels left for Strephon's impulses of grief, and we can soon expect radical changes. We are nearly at the limits of the capacity of metaphor, ritual, language, tradition, perhaps art in general, to contain and structure grief. Strephon's mind, after one last attempt at verbal ordering, will break dangerously free of its conventional controls and will move into an orgy of transformations in stanza nine.

Klaius' life has also become disjointed and death oriented, but he lacks the conventional techniques for channeling his grief. Unlike Strephon, he does not dwell on the internal and psychological effects of his anguish on his music or self. His sorrow is intense and plain; his death-wish is expressed in terms which emerge out of his immediate experiences with the environment. In fact, nearly all he says in this stanza is in direct response to an external environment. His songs alienate the people; he hates night and day (expressed in plain terms with a simple repetition in line thirty-four of "hate"). In his unnatural "passive" condition his thoughts chase him like beasts, as he draws the material for his simile from a simple reversal of his normal hunting activity. We, of course, see an image of Acteon and his fate in line thirty-five, but Sidney's point is, I believe, that Klaius does not see the correspondence, for he is writing out of his own experience, not literary tradition and associations. Finally, the stanza ends with a direct and simple death-wish; the active and proud Klaius would like to be "laid under mountains" (l. 36).

The shepherds are delicately poised on the edge of emotional chaos in stanzas seven and eight. We see their tortured imaginations begin radically to transform their perceptions of the environment, but the potential anarchy is controlled by the imposition of rigid form. Strephon introduces a rhetorical pattern which, when followed by Klaius, presents an exchange with balance, parallel syntax, and regular repetition. These stanzas are, in fact, the most balanced and symmetrical in the poem, and the illusion of control they suggest simply makes the emotional explosion in stanzas nine and ten more dramatic. There is immense emotional strain in stanzas seven and eight as the shepherds wind themselves up like springs, yet each shepherd continues to develop his distinctive character within the tight rhetorical structure and tense psychological one. These stanzas capture, as well as any earlier ones, the contrast of rhetoric, diction, imagery; the separate ways of perceiving and responding to the world; and the diverse wells of experience from which they draw their view of the world.

The rigorous parallelism in stanzas seven and eight gives an artificial sense of control which contrasts sharply with what is happening to the shepherds: the pain of each is transforming the world and, shortly, will alter their characters. In Strephon the transformation of the world is massive and outside of himself: mountains disintegrate to valleys, and nightingales learn screeching from the somber owls. Nature is in chaos. Strephon, aware of the process of change, locates himself in time at the poised moment of metamorphosis. There is an Ovidian sense of image and unrealness. Furthermore, throughout the poem, Strephon, more mind-and-imagination oriented, presents drastic shifts and contrasts—psychological, emotional, and physical. In stanza three he painted an internal, psychological landscape where he is "up" in "monstrous mountains" of despair and then "down" in "affliction's valleys." Such dramatic contrasts occur in nearly all his stanzas and are Strephon's characteristic way of perceiving and transforming his experiences. Stanzas three and five develop broad emotional and psychological contrasts of past and present. In stanza seven, Strephon's internal chaos and sense of violent contrasts are projected upon his external environment. For Strephon, the habit of metaphor and the perception of contrasts and comparisons become diseases; his mind loses the capacity to distinguish reality from literary and intellectual structuring.

On the other hand, Klaius, who functions more in terms of simile ("thoughts chase me like beasts") than metaphor, and who deals more in immediate sense response than in radical contrasts, can seem less dramatic in his encounters with experience and environment—though in no sense is he less intent or unimaginative. When Klaius' grief prompts imaginative transformation of his environment, as in stanza eight, we see him focus on the senses and on the moment and kind of sense transformation that occurs. He sees a "filthy cloudy evening," not the sun, or he feels "a noisesome scent, the morning," as in lines forty-five and forty-six; here, as is so often the case, we have Klaius' typical awkwardness. His senses, meaning, and syntax get strangely twisted as he struggles valiantly with his grief and language.

The weight of grief and pain has become too much to be handled by rhetorical structuring, ritual and repetition, literary traditions, or the imagination projecting on the environment, so in stanzas nine and ten there is nowhere for the mind and emotions to turn but to a purging through a temporary fury and insanity. Grief transforms the shepherds' personalities and intensifies their characteristic rhetoric. Each shepherd's speech abstracts essential aspects of his rhetorical style (e. g., Strephon: alliteration, parallelism; Klaius: simple repetition, syntactical strain) to express an inversion of character. Strephon becomes active, violent, as he strikes out to destroy and curse an environment which previously he had used reflectively for art. He abnegates his immediate world, "I wish to fire the trees of all those forests" (l. 49), his life, "I give the sun a last farewell each evening" (l. 50), and his society, "I curse the fiddling finders-out of music" (l. 51); he becomes elemental and direct as he "hates," "despises," and "detests" the environment which he had imaginatively manipulated earlier in the poem.

Klaius' personality also shifts at this moment of emotional chaos. His identity has been defined in terms of his relationships with his environment, but now he turns destructively in upon himself and creates (after the earlier fashion of Strephon) an internal, surrealistic hell. His environment provides the demons for his inferno as all the things he loved, including himself, move him towards madness.

Besides the emotions expressed and the personality inversions in these stanzas, another primary measure of the chaos is the near loss of parallelism between stanzas. In addition, for Strephon there is an intense use of harsh alliteration and fierce diction "curse, hate, despise, detest." Yet he does not give up his heavy use of adjectives (over-all Strephon uses twice as many adjectives in the poem as Klaius). Klaius' emotional state is also mirrored in an intensification of two grammatical problems already mentioned, syntactical strain and awkwardness of meaning. These problems are especially apparent in lines one, four, and five of stanza ten:

> Curse to myself my prayer is, the morning;
> My fire is more than can be made with forests,
> My state more base than are the basest valleys,
> I wish no evenings more to see, each evening;
> Shamed, I hate myself in sight of mountains
> And stop mine ears, lest I grow mad with music.

Stanzas nine and ten have brought the shepherds to emotional chaos and near madness; stanzas eleven and twelve give the reason for their grief, and at the mention of "she" (Urania) a certain amount of order and harmony returns to their thought and language. We should not miss the fact that Sidney creates suspense by postponing the reason for the grief until the end of the poem. We are perhaps meant to wonder what intense experience has disrupted *both* these shepherds' worlds, and remembering the "April" eclogue of *The Shepherd's Calendar*, we could as easily entertain thoughts of lament and elegy in stanzas one through ten, as thoughts of an absent loved one. And, in fact, we are perhaps doing Sidney and the poem a disservice in not seeing in Urania various allegorical possibilities which broaden the sweep and deepen the emotions of the poem. There are innumerable precedents (not the least of which is Spenser) for attaching larger moral, political, and philosophical meanings to Urania.[4] The emotional depth and complexity of the poem certainly warrant and encourage it.

The order and harmony which "she," even in memory, brings to the shattered emotions and disrupted world of the shepherds is first reflected in a halting return to the pattern of balance and parallel structure established earlier in the poem. Each shepherd begins his stanza, "For she . . .," and each has a line beginning with "who," but there is not the studied balance of the earlier stanzas; there are mostly off-key echoes between the stanzas of sounds, words, and syntactical patterns. For, in a sense, as in stanzas nine and ten, the shepherds are going their own ways—only this time, ways appropriate to their normal personalities and, as usual, in the context of their rhetorical identities.

There is deft, probing characterization in these last stanzas, as Sidney crystalizes the essential styles and characters and evaluates the relative merits of the two approaches to experience. I believe it is Klaius, the rhetorically plodding, bumbling "hunter," who, with simple honesty and selfless generosity, ultimately wins our greater respect. Strephon's response to Urania seems excessively physical and self-centered. He is absorbed by her harmonious "parts," her "beauty," her stateliness. He misses her physical presence. Furthermore, he seeks to blame someone for his grief, and the stanza paints a picture of her beauty only to focus more powerfully on *his* grief and what *he* has lost. The argument, in fact, is a nicely handled, though potentially bitter, accusation: "For she . . . whose beauty . . . hath cast me, wretch, into eternal evening. . . . By taking her two suns. . . ." (ll. 61–66). Strephon is self-absorbed; it would be difficult not to compare him to Astrophel, who possesses a good many of the same psychological and rhetorical qualities. This comparison will perhaps underline the fact that Strephon's responses are quite natural and understandable within the traditions of the Petrarchan personae and the decorative style; however, when we see Klaius respond more simply, abstractly, and generously to Urania, Sidney has perhaps finally given Klaius and the plainer style their due. Sidney's point would be, of course, that each style and approach has it place and advantages.

Klaius' response to Urania is focused not so much on his grief as upon her absence and the price the world pays for it. Furthermore, he is less concerned with her as a touchable, lovely woman than as a presence who brings beauty and harmony to the environment. We are reminded of Klaius' invocation, for Urania is approached more like a Diana or Venus than like a corruptible nymph: she is worshipped by Klaius with awe and distance. His descriptions of her beauty and effect are general, at times even obscure. Strephon's comparison of Urania to the mountains is pointed and accomplished with its *adnominatio* and alliteration, "who much did pass in state the stately mountains" (l. 63). Klaius' comparison is inapt and vague in its referents, "For she, to whom compared, the Alps are valleys" (l. 67).

However, Klaius' plainness, with its seemingly more heartfelt responses and language, begins to work in his favor. Soon the qualities of generalness and roughness only accentuate Klaius' depth of personal loss which finally emerges so plainly eloquent with his simple statement that Urania, "Is gone, is gone" (l. 71). It is perhaps unnecessary to mention the contrast of Strephon's "me" to Klaius' "our" as a final expression of Klaius' broader, more magnanimous orientation. Yet, by the end of the poem it is no easy matter to assess the respective intellectual, personal, and stylistic merits of the shepherds. One of the great strengths of the poem is that Sidney, the epitome of the Renaissance self-conscious, literary artist, can eventually be so generous to Klaius—but then Astrophel is really a combination of the finer, more sensitive aspects of both these personae.

Notes

1. William Empson, *Seven Types of Ambiguity* (Cleveland: Meridian, 1955), pp. 42–46. David Kalstone, *Sidney's Poetry* (New York: Norton, 1970), pp. 71–84, and "The Transformation of Arcadia," *Comparative Literature* 15 (1963), 234–249. John C. Ransom, *The New Criticism* (Norfolk, Conn.: New Directions, 1941), pp. 108–114. A. C. Hamilton, "Sidney's *Arcadia* as Prose Fiction: Its Relation to Its Sources," *ELR*, 2:ii (1972), 29–60.
2. Having arrived at a satisfying interpretation of the poem, I was granted the mixed blessing of discovering Alastair Fowler's *Conceitful Thought* (Edinburgh: Edinburgh Univ. Press. 1975). Fowler also concludes that Sidney "developed the distinction between Strephon and Klaius most delicately" (p. 44). I am pleased to have such reliable verification of an idea, but overall, our interpretations diverge considerably. Fowler's evocation of intellectual contexts—Isaiah, Theocritus, Ovid, Pico, Plolinus, *Anticlaudianus*, Lucretius, Conti—though interesting, tends to overburden the poem and its characterization. We need not dig so deeply for the materials out of which the characterizations emerge. Furthermore, by missing Sidney's key structural tactic, the chaotic disintegration and *reversal* of character in stanzas nine and ten, Fowler inaccurately distinguishes the personalities of the shepherds. Surely Klaius the hunter does not have "little empathy with the forest" (p. 46). However, rather than carry on a carping battle with Mr. Fowler, I would like to salute the usefulness of his effort and offer my own conceptions of Sidney's presentation and development of character in the poem.
3. This does not mean that Klaius' language is any less effective and striking, in its own way, than Strephon's.
4. See Fowler, pp. 52–58.

Daniel Traister (essay date 1982)

SOURCE: "Sidney's Purposeful Humor: *Astrophil and Stella* 59 and 83," in *ELH: A Journal of English Literary History*, Vol. 49, No. 4, Winter 1982, pp. 751–64.

[*In the following essay, Traister offers a close analysis of two sonnets, and concludes Sidney forces readers to reconsider experiences and approach the sonnets with the knowledge of their new implications.*]

Sidney's words, as Rosalie L. Colie has remarked, "can at once, in triumph, assert and deny the truth of what they say."[1] They give to Astrophil a verbal dexterity—or ambidexterity—that is one of his many attractions. Few characters in the literature of the English Renaissance are as engaging as the protean Astrophil who speaks to us from the sonnets and songs of Sidney's sequence. Capable of virtuoso emotional somersaults, of a gentle self-mockery in which most readers find Sidney's lightly ironic view of himself, and of an urbane wit which flashes sonnet after sonnet, song after song, Astrophil has proven irresistible to almost all audiences. Stella alone seems unimpressed. Most of his other readers find it difficult not to feel, when the sequence has ended, that Astrophil has failed to reach a goal we should very much like to have seen him reach. Much of this success is due to the witty geniality of his voice.

Astrophil and Stella succeeds as a whole for much the same reason. Most of its readers in recent years have found it witty: lightly melancholy, to be sure, but essentially comic in structure and meaning. Humorous and urbane, the young aristocrat who is its author neither overburdens his work with lumbering seriousness nor violates the canons of *sprezzatura*. In fact, the delicately comedic balance of, first, what most readers regard as Sidney's own most intimate concerns, and, second, his ironic detachment from the tale and its fictional protagonist, has seemed a major source of the poetry's delight.

Yet Sidney's conception of comedy is not very funny. Typical of his age, he believes that comedy is ultimately a didactic mode, "an imitation," as he writes, "of the common errors of our life" represented "in the most ridiculous and scornful sort that may be, so as it is impossible that any beholder can be content to be such a one."[2] For Sidney, comedy is a *negative exemplum*:[3] a "foil" that by showing us "the filthiness of evil" increases our capacity "to perceive the beauty of virtue" (*Apology*, 117, and notes, 188). Later in the *Apology*, Sidney remarks that the "end" of comical episodes in tragedies should "be not upon such scornful matters as stirreth laughter only, but, mixed with it, that delightful teaching which is the end of Poesy" (136–37). He has already differentiated laughter—which "hath only a scornful tickling"—from the more significant comic effect, delight—"Delight hath a joy in it, either permanent or present"—which facilitates teaching (136). If Sidney's statement of poetic theory in the *Apology* is an accurate guide to his poetic practice,[4] then the wit to which readers of his sequence respond may be (at least in some part) a seductive tool used to attract interest in ends not in themselves especially humorous—didactic ends, "that delightful teaching which is the end of Poesy."

Lip service to the validity of this hypothesis is general—but, it seems to me, the implications of such a theory for our reading of Sidney's sequence are not seriously pursued. In this paper, I consider two sonnets often cited in comment on the humor of ***Astrophil and Stella***[5] in an effort to suggest the direction that such pursuit should take. The first of these is Sonnet 59:

Deare, why make you more of a dog then me?
If he do love, I burne, I burne in love:
If he waite well, I never thence would move:
If he be faire, yet but a dog can be.
Litle he is, so litle worth is he;
He barks, my songs thine owne voyce oft doth prove:
Bid'n, perhaps he fetcheth thee a glove,
But I unbid, fetch even my soule to thee.
Yet while I languish, him that bosome clips,
That lap doth lap, nay lets, in spite of spite,
This sowre-breath'd mate tast of those sugred lips.
Alas, if you graunt only such delight
To witlesse things, then *Love* I hope (since wit
Becomes a clog) will soone ease me of it.

The second is the closely related Sonnet 83:

Good brother *Philip*, I have borne you long,
I was content you should in favour creepe,
While craftily you seem'd your cut to keepe,
As though that faire soft hand did you great wrong.
I bare (with Envie) yet I bare your song,
When in her necke you did *Love* ditties peepe;
Nay, more foole I, oft suffered you to sleepe
In Lillies' neast, where *Love's* selfe lies along.
What, doth high place ambitious thoughts augment?
Is sawcinesse reward of curtesie?
Cannot such grace your silly selfe content,
But you must needs with those lips billing be?
And through those lips drinke Nectar from that toong;
Leave that sir *Phip*, least off your necke be wroong.

These poems are obviously humorous: witty and urbane in precisely the ways that have made Astrophil and Sidney's sequence attractive to readers for centuries. But they are also didactic. The Renaissance, after all, knew "no neat separation of the comic from the didactic," Scoular reminds us; "wit and piety were combined in a way that affronts a stricter decorum."[6] Their didacticism emerges from a reader's amusement as he responds to their humorousness. As laughter proves inadequate to the complex experiences the sonnets record, the reader is forced to reconsider those experiences and the implications of his first response to them. Such reconsideration is designed to teach him his own susceptibility to the errors the sonnets represent and that he must be wary of the deceptive attractiveness of such errors now that he is better able to recognize them.[7]

This sort of flat-footed moralizing seems quite distant from the witty urbanity usually—and rightly—ascribed to Sidney. Yet the very casualness with which the didactic point awaits a reader beneath the amusing surface of both sonnets is a tribute to the poetic skill of the moralist (highly valued in the *Apology*). Sidney is as graceful here as in the exordium to his *Apology* where, for a moment, we think we are about to be told about horsemanship in a particularly engaging manner before being easily wheeled around to face the real subject of the discourse. Sonnets 59 and 83 wheel us around from amused laughter to more sober reflection just as gently, and just as relentlessly.

In both sonnets, Astrophil laments his relations with his love, contrasting his own distance from her with the favored state of her pets—her lap dog in Sonnet 59, her sparrow "Philip" in Sonnet 83. Both beasts possess what Richard B. Young has delicately called certain "sensual advantages" over Astrophil.[8] Of Stella's dog, Astrophil complains, "while I languish, him that bosome clips, / That lap doth lap, nay lets, in spite of spite, / This sowre-breath'd mate tast of those sugred lips." Phip, Stella's sparrow, peeps "*Love* ditties" in Stella's "necke," he "sleep[s] / In Lillies' neast," that is, on Stella's breasts (cf. Spenser, *Amoretti* 64), and he kisses Stella. Sidney's language defines the beasts' "sensual advantages" in terms bearing explicit sexual denotations.[9] Ignoring for the moment what this language suggests about Stella's sexual preferences, clearly one locus of the humor in both sonnets is their witty disparagement of Astrophil. Both he and the pets are interested in the same thing, but the animals succeed while the man does not. Such inversion of hierarchy is one of the most common causes of laughter.

Almost simultaneously, however, the sonnets suggest that hierarchy is not inverted to quite the degree it first seems. For both sonnets put more emphasis on Astrophil's near identity with Stella's pets than on his human superiority over them.

In Sonnet 59, of course, Astrophil tries to convince Stella that he *is* superior to her lap dog. The dog merely loves; Astrophil "burnes" in love. If Stella only gave him the opportunity, he would "waite" for, or upon, her with a more steadfast devotion. He is bigger and better-looking than any dog that "but a dog can be," and his songs are more enjoyable than the dog's barking. The dog must be "bid'n" to fetch Stella but a glove; dog-like but better than a dog, Astrophil fetches her, "unbid," his "soule." By mentioning her dog's "sowre" breath, Astrophil reminds Stella how much sweeter his own is. Yet inherent in these comparisons is not Astrophil's superiority but rather the assumption that dog and man are comparable—not an apple and an orange, but two apples. It is no idle ambiguity that, in line 11, the dog who is Stella's "mate" may be understood as Astrophil's mate as well.

In Sonnet 83, in fact, the beast—here Philip Sparrow—has become Astrophil's "brother." Astro*phil* and *Phil*ip share part of a name, and the author behind Astrophil shares all of a name, and a knighthood, too, with "sir *Phip*."[10] Joined with Astrophil in contention for Stella's favors, Phip is so successful that he merits Astrophil's "envie." He has enough of a relationship with Astrophil to "reward" his "curtesie" with "sawcinesse."[11] Hierarchy is amusingly inverted when Stella's pets pursue Stella with greater success than Astrophil; also amusing, Astrophil's language assumes kinship with bestial inferiors who, taking advantage of their new equality by getting "saucy" with patronizing Astrophil, deny hierarchy altogether.

That the beasts and Astrophil are comparable results from no raising of the beasts to a human level, however. Rather, Astrophil's humanity has decayed—metamorphosed—to make such comparisons possible. Love, of course, was frequently thought in this period to cause degenerative metamorphosis;[12] whatever its cause, metamorphosis is not a subject for gay, casual humor. Tuve, who speaks of the gaiety of Sonnet 59 (above, n.5), knows that metamorphosis can be "an image of man's betrayal of his spiritual allegiances to the intemperance of his other natural desires."[13] The reader who laughs at the situation these sonnets represent is laughing at the collapse of a human being into bestiality.

I state the matter more baldly than my reader may easily accept. Yet Astrophil's bestialization is more than merely "implicit" in the comparison his language initiates between himself and Stella's lap dog. Dogs have a large and (as usual) ambiguous range of conventional attributes. That the least favorable of these adhere, not to Stella's dog, but to Astrophil, forces a reader to regard Astrophil as less than her dog. For instance, her dog fetches Stella's glove while Astrophil boasts that he fetches her his soul. But her glove belongs to Stella, whereas Astrophil's soul is properly God's. It is not his to give away idolatrously to an earthly goddess. In doing its animal duty by subordinating itself to Stella's humanity, the dog—if in pursuing her it can be said to "hunt" at all—joins in a hunt which recognizes hierarchy and order and is hence a hunt for virtue.[14] But Astrophil seeks to replace the dog as the object of Stella's "clips" and to lie in her "lap"—and he *does* mean "country matters": he wants to be like those dogs that Edward Topsell regards as "emblems of vile, cursed, rayling, and filthy men" whose "publique and shamelesse copulation" associates them with low sexuality.[15] Astrophil hunts Venus, carnality, and cupidinous self-satisfaction. Choosing to be a dog in the wrong hunt (like Proteus in *Two Gentlemen of Verona*),[16] he displays that failure of reason to which "real" dogs were thought prone.[17] In short, trying to convince Stella of his superiority by comparing himself to a dog, Astrophil inadvertently shows himself to be like a dog—of the worst sort.

Astrophil does not recognize his own collapse into bestiality. As a result, he articulates it only obliquely, largely unaware of what he is telling Stella and us. Indeed, symptomatic of his collapse is a decay of the rational power necessary to understand and combat it. Nonetheless, Astrophil feels the effects of this collapse. In Sonnet 59, the artfully rigorous comparisons between Astrophil and Stella's lap dog are, from one point of view, gaily humorous. From another, however, they reflect Astrophil's pathetically desperate effort to attract Stella's attention. The strident extravagance of the poem's wit turns that wit back on itself, making it seem strained rather than natural. This strain reflects Astrophil's strain as he struggles with his tone, trying to moderate his desperation, in the course of composing this plea. His growing bestialization explains the sonnet's strange atmosphere, one in which playfulness becomes intricately intertwined with a cry anticipating the witlessness towards which Astrophil feels himself sliding: "Alas, if you graunt only such delight / To witlesse things, then *Love* I hope (since wit / Becomes a clog) will soone ease me of it." The "manly lover," as John Buxton calls him,[18] turns, before his own and the reader's eyes, into something much less than a man, something unmanned. The sonnet, apparently a wittily sardonic expression of Astrophil's jealousy, points far beyond this relatively simple emotion to realms of tension, insecurity, and desperation paralleled in the period only in certain of Shakespeare's sonnets.

Similarly in Sonnet 83, Astrophil again loses control. Linked here to a bird noted for its lecherousness,[19] he seems again to exhibit less human love than bestial lust. Threatening Phip with death in the last line, Astrophil reveals how bestial his passion has made him, demonstrating a capacity for a kind of violence appropriate to beasts rather than men. Thus he calls his human nature into question. Since the object of his wrath is a mere sparrow, Astrophil's threat is a grotesquely exaggerated response to Phip's "billing" with Stella that also questions his human rationality. Since injury to Phip would obviously injure Stella, whose loved creature he is, Astrophil's threat finally conveys his surprising indifference to Stella's emotional and sentimental concerns. In a context which offers many reasons for a reader to view Astrophil in bestial terms, such indifference encourages additional doubt about the nature of the emotion for Stella that Astrophil professes. He displays what looks like, not human love, but bestial lust directed at mere physical possession of the desired one, desired not as person but as object. Apart from such possession, he is otherwise unconcerned with a complete human being whose interests, affections, or desires matter in any way. It is curiously revealing that Stella is really of no consequence at all in this sonnet. Man and bird compete over her, but she comes into view only in fragments: a hand, a neck, breasts, lip, or tongue. The sonnet gives a reader no reason to think that Astrophil regards her as anything more than an object with whose physicality he is preoccupied, an object he does not even conceive as a whole.

Indeed, the attitude toward Stella which both sonnets imply is very unsettling. A reader should not take too literally the implications in the sonnets' language that Stella's behavior with her pets is overtly sexual. She may "bill" with Phip and "clip" and "lap" her little dog, but we need not visualize these actions too explicitly (see above, n. 9). Yet some unavoidable suspicion about the effect of this erotically charged language emerges from the fact that Sidney is drawing in both of these sonnets on two poems by Catullus, where sexual imagery often asks to be read as more than subtle innuendo.[20]

In the first of these poems, Catullus' speaker contrasts the intimate relationship of Lesbia and her pet sparrow with his own isolation from her. The language of this poem is erotically informed: the sparrow, with which Lesbia plays "in sinu tenere" (Catullus 2.2), offers her "soliacolum sui doloris" (2.7) in an almost certainly sexual sense and functions much like a surrogate phallus.[21] In the second poem, usually read in conjunction with the first, Catullus' speaker laments the death of Lesbia's sparrow because of the tears its loss has caused her.

Both of Catullus' poems give rise to a tradition—followed in Latin by Ovid and Statius; in English by Skelton, Gascoigne, Drummond of Hawthornden, Herrick, and William Cartwright; and by others in these and additional languages[22]—in which, after the death of a loved one's or friend's pet (not necessarily a sparrow), the poet attempts to console his friend or lover by praising the pet. He envisions for it a lovely tomb and a cheerful afterlife, or creates for it a fit epitaph. Such concern for an animal presupposes, indeed demonstrates, the poet's much greater regard or love for the dead beast's owner. The specifically sensual-sexual attributes of the phallic sparrow are not essential to the tradition, though they suggest a variant within its limits that a poet (such as Skelton) may wish to explore. The rhetorical flourishes through which the poet elaborates his praise for the dead pet, bewails its loss, fashions its poetic urn, and, above all, suggests his regard for its owner: these are essentials in this tradition. Quite self-consciously, Sidney inverts them all, implying at the same time a comparison between Stella and Lesbia that, in view of the sexual profligacy of the latter, is by no means flattering to the former.

Such implications point again to ambiguities in Astrophil's feelings about Stella, but more immediately significant is Sidney's inversion of the Catullan tradition. Phip, of course, is not dead in Sonnet 83, which is closer to Catullus 2 than 3. But for the reader aware of the tradition to which *both* of Catullus' poems are antecedent and to which Sonnet 83 is clearly related, the threat in the final line to strangle Phip, while funny, is also a shock. A deformation of expected social patterns (and, obviously, of the conventions of love relationships), the threat also deforms hitherto conventional literary patterns that the informed reader anticipates. By undermining the conventional expression of the poet's normal solicitude for both pet and owner, the threat—considered purely as a literary gesture—reinforces a reader's sense of Astrophil's utter indifference to Stella.

Moreover, as flat statement, unadorned and unelaborated, the threat is almost a plain style antithesis to the ornate amplification in praise of the pet a truly conventional poem would at this point have reached. Indeed, the plain style of the threat reverses the ornate style of the sonnet's opening. From the courtly salutation of the first line, a form of the trope prosopopoeia disguising momentarily the fact that the addressee is just a sparrow, to the blunt threat with which the sonnet ends, Astrophil has taken his reader down a steep stylistic descent, inverting the rhetorical amplification that the tradition of such poems leads their readers to expect. This rhetorical inversion parallels the sonnet's inversion of conventional praise for the pet and its owner.

Astrophil's descending rhetorical levels also parallel a reader's sense of the decay of his capacity to feel. As he becomes increasingly similar to the animal his poem concerns, he loses his full courtly humanity, ideally capable of elevated feeling dressed appropriately in elevated speech. The plain style may be a vehicle for "truth" (some such notion seems to be at the basis of Astrophil's poetic theory, as is frequently noticed). But its use, as here, to assert cruelty perverts the proper uses of the style. It contravenes the stylistic expectations aroused by the traditions from which the sonnet emerges, and represents a descent from the stylistic levels on which Astrophil could have chosen to address his loved one and all she holds precious. After all, the plain style is not the only vehicle for truth. As a courtier, Astrophil might decorously have adopted that "eloquence" which Henry Peacham told his complete gentleman is "a principal means of correcting ill manners, reforming laws, humbling aspiring minds, and upholding all virtue."[23] And though early in the sequence (in Sonnet 6, for instance) Astrophil had claimed the plain style as the particularly appropriate vehicle for the expression of the depth and truth of his feelings about Stella, this use of bluntness in Sonnet 83 for the purpose of threat is hardly consonant with what, earlier, he had had in mind.[24]

There is little need to belabor the obvious ways in which Sonnet 59 similarly inverts the Catullan tradition (to which, lacking any reference to a pet's death, it is admittedly less clearly related than the later sonnet; but see n. 22). Far from praising Stella's dog, Astrophil urges his superiority to it. He bewails its success, not its failures or loss, and does not praise its owner but instead, as Young notes (27), criticizes her "witlessness" in caring for her dog as she does. The enjambement on the last three lines yields a tortuously prosaic conclusion that, like the stylistic descent of Sonnet 83, is very different from the sort of rhetorical display such poems usually attempt.

Many sonnets throughout ***Astrophil and Stella*** question the precise meaning and value Astrophil gives to and finds in his "love," exploring ambiguities inherent in his (usually very complicated) attitudes towards Stella. These two humorous sonnets are among the most effective. Their Catullan echoes question Stella's nature by tainting her with Lesbia's sexual athleticism. They cast doubt on the nature of the love for Stella that Astrophil professes by demonstrating how indifferent he is to her as a person. By comparing Astrophil to beasts, in contexts which equate bestiality primarily with violence and sexual lust, the sonnets trace Astrophil's divergence from norms of courtly behavior in which human nature is most richly articulated and suggest the degree to which his metamorphic love has altered his humanity for the worse.[25]

Most significantly for our present purpose, these sonnets indicate Sidney's ability to mix within a basically comic mode serious moral concerns about Astrophil's decline from normatively "human" behavior patterns.[26] A multiplicity of conflicting attitudes is characteristic not only of Astrophil's feelings about Stella but also of Sidney's continuously shifting—and even shifty—presentation of the story his sequence relates. These various attitudes and the resultant multiple viewpoints are highly functional. The sonnets' humorousness, for instance, may offer something like "comic relief" from the didactic moral concerns they also display. Their humor helps also to "implicate" the reader in the action of the sequence. Throughout most of ***Astrophil and Stella***, the reader sympathizes with Astrophil's love-quest and wants him to succeed in it. But the reader who smiles over Astrophil's difficulties with two beasts, seeing only comic impediments to Astrophil's attainment of Stella, becomes entangled in the most doubtful aspects of his quest. Smiling at comic impedimenta, he must unexpectedly come to grips with Astrophil's unstated, ambiguous comparison of Stella to Lesbia, and his indifference to her; with the evidence these sonnets offer of lust, not love; and with the divergence from ideals of human behavior—and to a great degree from humanity itself—that Astrophil exhibits.

Sonnets can be reread instantly, as soon as their first jarring inconsistency is felt. They educate their reader in bits and pieces rather than, as Fish demonstrates of *Paradise Lost*, over a long journey through print.[27] As soon as the reader recognizes that smiles alone are insufficient to the experience of Sonnets 59 and 83, the inadequacy of his initial response forces him to reconsider the sonnets' significance(s) and the import of that first response. Such reconsideration, I think, makes clear that what he is reading "negatively exemplifies" first, what love is not (it is not simply physical lust), and second, how not to love (proper love does not reduce the lover to acting confusedly, irrationally, and bestially).[28] Insofar as the reader's amusement demonstrates how prone he himself is to mistake as "love" something that is so clearly something else, he must reconsider too his conception of what love is. Increasing awareness of the ambiguities inherent in Stella's portrayal may also lead to reexamination of the reader's notion of love's proper object. His laughter, originally genial as it indulgently contemplates Astrophil's plight, turns gradually critical—if not altogether censorious—as Astrophil's situation becomes more clearly the moral quicksand we have seen it to be; and it becomes corrective as the reader's indulgence of Astrophil, seen as less than fully justified, demands self-criticism.

The humor of these sonnets is necessary to provoke such reconsideration. It also makes the process considerably more pleasant and vital than a sermon or abstract philosophical argument (*Apology*, 104–09). The laughter such humor arouses sneaks past the slothful "infected will" to the knowledge of "perfection" possessed by man's "erected wit" (101), by which standard its inadequacy is plain. The reconsideration consequently demanded begins the active engagement of the reader necessary for the process—basic to Sidney's defense of poetry (112–15)—of *moving* men "to take that goodness in hand, which without delight they would fly as from a stranger," and teaching them, albeit indirectly, to "know that goodness whereunto they are moved" (103).[29]

Notes

1. *Paradoxia Epidemica: The Renaissance Tradition of Paradox* (Princeton: Princeton University Press, 1966), p. 95.

2. *An Apology for Poetry*, ed. Geoffrey Shepherd (1965; rpt. New York: Barnes and Noble, 1973), p. 117.

3. Geoffrey Fenton provides a contemporary explanation of the negative exemplum in *Certaine Tragicall Discourses* (London: Thomas Marshe, 1567), ☆3r. Generally, see A. D. S. Fowler, "Protestant Attitudes to Poetry, 1560–1590," Diss. Oxford 1957, pp. 309–11, 443–71. On the negative exemplum in Sidney, see D. W. Robertson, Jr., "Sidney's Metaphor of the Ulcer," *MLN*, 56 (1941), 56–61; Andrew D. Weiner, "'Erected Wit' and 'Infected Will': A Study of Sir Philip Sidney's *Old Arcadia*," *DAI*, 31 (1970–71), 736A (Princeton); Russell Morton Brown, Jr., "'Through All Maskes My Wo': Poet and Persona in *Astrophil and Stella*," Diss. SUNY-Binghamton 1972, p. 226; James J. Scanlon, "Sidney's *Astrophil and Stella*: 'See What it Is To Love' Sensually!" *SEL*, 16 (1976), 66 et passim; and Alan Sinfield, "Sidney and Astrophil," *SEL*, 20 (1980), 38–41.

4. Sinfield, "Sidney and Astrophil," 28.

5. See, e.g., Rosemond Tuve, *Elizabethan and Metaphysical Imagery: Renaissance Poetic and Twentieth-Century Critics* (1947; rpt. Chicago: Phoenix Books, 1961), p. 321; Richard B. Young, "English Petrarke: A Study of Sidney's *Astrophel and Stella*," in *Three Studies in the Renaissance: Sidney, Jonson, Milton* (1958; rpt. Hamden, CT: Archon Books, 1969), pp. 27–28, 60; David Kalstone, *Sidney's Poetry: Contexts and Interpretations* (Cambridge: Harvard University Press, 1965), p. 160; A. C. Hamilton, "Sidney's *Astrophel and Stella* as a Sonnet Sequence," *ELH*, 36 (1969), 68; and J. G. Nichols, *The Poetry of Sir Philip Sidney: An Interpretation in the Context of his Life and Times* (Liverpool: University Press, 1974), pp. 147–48. All quotations from Sidney's poetry are from the edition by William A. Ringler, Jr. (Oxford: Clarendon, 1962).

6. Kitty W. Scoular [Datta], *Natural Magic: Studies in the Presentation of Nature in English Poetry from Spenser to Marvell* (Oxford: Clarendon, 1965), p. 81.

7. I am indebted for this approach to Stanley E. Fish, *Surprised by Sin: The Reader in* Paradise Lost (New York: St. Martin's, 1967). I have also found useful his essay, "Affective Stylistics," now the appendix to *Self-Consuming Artifacts: The Experience of Seventeenth-Century Literature* (Berkeley: University of California Press, 1973) and reprinted again in his *Is There a Text in This Class? The Authority of Interpretive Communities* (Cambridge: Harvard University Press, 1980), as well as related studies by Stephen Booth, Paul J. Alpers, Lowry Nelson, Jr., and Wolfgang Iser.

8. "English Petrarke," p. 27.

9. On the erotic potentialities of Sidney's language (not frequently enough emphasized), see Dorothy Jones, "Sidney's Erotic Pen: An Interpretation of One of the *Arcadia* Poems," *JEGP*, 73 (1974), 32–47. An obvious instance of sexual wordplay in *AS* occurs in Sonnet 69; see also Alan Sinfield, "Sexual Puns in *Astrophil and Stella*," *EIC*, 24 (1974), 341–55. *Lap* in *AS* 59 indicates some of the difficulties a reader faces in judging the erotic force of a word at any given point in an Elizabethan text. Though *lap* as "vagina" is well established (*OED* 2b), its implications in *AS* 59 need not be sexual at all. Lap dogs were thought to ease the pains in a lady's bowels, taking such pains upon themselves through proximity. This notion is at least as old as Pliny (*The History of the World: Commonly Called The Natural History*, trans. Philemon Holland, sel. Paul Turner [1962; rpt. New York: McGraw-Hill, 1964], pp. 315–16); it is repeated as late as the seventeenth century on a sheet of Richard Napier's medical prescriptions: "Apply a puppy dog all night tille[?] it aswageth the swelling of the spleene" (Bodleian MS. Ashmole 1488, Part II, fol. 3v). In any event, poets may use obscene or perverse erotic details for profoundly antierotic motives, a point reiterated by Dustin H. Griffin, *Satires Against Man: The Poems of Rochester* (Berkeley: University of California Press, 1973), pp. 81–86 et passim.

10. Identity of names reinforces conventional recourse to autobiographical readings at this point: see, e.g., James Finn Cotter, "The 'Baiser' Group in Sidney's *Astrophil and Stella*," *TSLL*, 12 (1970), 400. But Sidney often uses autobiographical details to "flesh out" the verisimilitude of his characters, as is suggested by Jerome Mazzaro (*Transformations in the Renaissance English Lyric* [Ithaca: Cornell University Press, 1970], p. 104) and others. See most recently Sinfield, "Sidney and Astrophil," 25–41. In any case, Dyce notes that "*Philip*, or *Phip*, was a familiar name given to a sparrow from its note being supposed to resemble that sound" (*The Poetical Works of John Skelton*, ed. Alexander Dyce [London: Thomas Rodd, 1843], II, 121).

11. Compare the effect when, in *OA*, Pyrocles disconcertingly speaks to the lion that has been chasing Philoclea as his "competitor" and finds that it merits his "disdain" (*The Countess of Pembroke's Arcadia* [*The Old Arcadia*], ed. Jean Robertson [Oxford: Clarendon, 1973], p. 47). Such an attitude is among the sources of humor in both the *Arcadia* and *AS* 83.

12. As well as the obvious places in Spenser and Shakespeare, see, e.g., Geoffrey Fenton, *Monophylo* (London: William Seres, 1572), Y1r, or Geoffrey Whitney, "Homines voluptatibus transformantur," in *A Choice of Emblemes* (Leiden: Christopher Plantin, 1586), p. 82. Metamorphic love could also be ennobling, of course. But Sidney's images do not tend that way.

13. *Allegorical Imagery: Some Mediaeval Books and Their Posterity* (Princeton: Princeton University Press, 1966), p. 33. Irving Massey's study of literary metamorphosis, *The Gaping Pig: Literature and Metamorphosis* (Berkeley: University of California Press, 1976), which is concerned largely with modern works, similarly asserts at its outset that "metamorphosis is a morbid subject"; it considers its subject, however, from a point of view very different from mine. In the Renaissance, of course, metamorphosis can be positive, a sign of man's protean capacity to change himself, or—with specific regard to love—a sign of the ennobling transformation or new unity with his beloved that the lover experiences. But when, in an "ordinary," not particularly "literary" context, we meet the word "metamorphosis" as we meet it in Francis Clement's *The Petie Schole* (London: Thomas Vautrollier, 1587), C4v—"common playes," he writes there, "metamorphize, trāsfigure, deforme, peruert and alter the harts" of their audiences—we get an insight into its common, negative associations in the period. For an unusually rich view of the interpretive range available to Renaissance writers in just one metamorphic myth, see Leonard Barkan's excellent study, "Diana and Actaeon: The Myth as Synthesis," *ELR*, 10 (1980), 317–59.

14. The dog is involved in both types of the two hunts, the one for Venus and earthly love, the other for virtue and Christ's love, an image which retains its force well into the Renaissance; see, e.g., George Gascoigne, *Complete Works*, ed. John W. Cunliffe (Cambridge: Cambridge University Press, 1907–1910), I, 386.

15. *The Historie of Fovre-footed Beastes* (London: William Jaggard, 1607), p. 143. The erotic associations of dogs—specifically of lap dogs—remain important well beyond the sixteenth century. "Lap-d—s!" writes Robert Gould in *Love Given O're: or, A Satyr Against the Pride, Lust, and Inconstancy, & c. of Woman* (London: Andrew Green, 1682), p. 5,

"to whom they [women] are more kind and free, / Than they themselves to their own Husbands be. / How curst is Man! when Bruits his Rivals prove, / Ev'n in the sacred bus'ness of his Love."

See also Richard Ames, *The Folly of Love; or, An Essay Upon Satyr Against Woman* (London: E. Hawkins, 1691), p. 8. Both poems may be found in *Satires on Women*, intro. Felicity A. Nussbaum, Augustan Reprint Society, no. 180 (Los Angeles: William Andrews Clark Memorial Library, 1976), Belinda's lap dog Shock awakens her "with his Tongue" in *The Rape of the Lock* (I.115–16) in 1714, and the theme of the erotic dog retains vitality through the eighteenth century; see Donald Posner, "The Lady and Her Dog," in his *Watteau: A Lady at her Toilet*, Art in Context (New York: Viking, 1973), pp. 77–83.

16. I.i.63–69. Citations to Shakespeare are to *The Riverside Shakespeare*, ed. G. Blakemore Evans (Boston: Houghton, 1974).

17. Associated with drunkenness and "the irrational antics of topers" (H. W. Janson, *Apes and Ape Lore in*

the Middle Ages and the Renaissance, Studies of the Warburg Institute, 20 [London: Warburg Institute, 1952], p. 246; cf. *Othello*, II.iii.48–51), dogs are connected with the failure of human rationality that *AS* 59 represents. Dogs are also associated with ungoverned passionate desire, not only by bestiaries such as Topsell's (above, n. 15) but also by mythographical interpretations of the Actaeon story (e.g., Whitney, *A Choice of Emblemes*, p. 15, or *Twelfth Night*, I.i.18–22); Walter R. Davis demonstrates Sidney's knowledge of this tradition in "Actaeon in Arcadia," *SEL*, 2 (1962), 102–05 et passim. The association of dogs with hydrophobia and hence madness—which, like inebriation and unbridled love, are types of the failure of human rationality—needs no reference. On dogs generally, see Guy de Tervarent, *Attributs et symboles dans l'art profane, 1450–1600: Dictionnaire d'un langue perdu*, Travaux d'humanisme et renaissance, 29 (Geneva: Droz, 1958), s.v. *chien* (cols. 93–96); Beryl Rowland, *Blind Beasts: Chaucer's Animal World* (Kent, OH: Kent State University Press, 1971), pp. 153–65; William Empson, *The Structure of Complex Words*, 2nd ed. (1952; rpt. Ann Arbor: Ann Arbor Paperbacks, 1967), pp. 158–84; and Posner (n. 15, above).

18. *Elizabethan Taste* (New York: St. Martin's, 1964), p. 275.

19. See *OA* 10.79, and Ringler's note, p. 482. Generally, see Tervarent, *Attributs et symboles*, s.v. *passereau* (col. 299), and George Reeves Throop, "The Bird of Venus," *Washington University Studies, Humanistic Series: Heller Memorial Volume*, 9, no. 2 (April 1922), 275–91.

20. Catullus 2 ("Passer, deliciae meae puellae") and 3 ("Lugete, o Veneres Cupidinesque"), in *Carmina*, ed. R. A. B. Mynors (Oxford: Clarendon, 1958), pp. 1–3. Sidney's interest in Catullus is well known: see James A. S. McPeek, *Catullus in Strange and Distant Britain*, Harvard Studies in Comparative Literature, 15 (Cambridge: Harvard University Press, 1939), pp. 45, 240–41. He is the first poet to have translated Catullus into English (*CS* 13); a later translation, from Montemayor's *Diana*, echoes the theme of this Catullan poem (*CS* 28.33–40), and suggests that Catullan themes frequently interested Sidney. The Catullan sparrow reappears in Sidney, in conjunction with Urania, in *OP* 4. The use to which Sidney puts the sparrow in this poem contrasts quite markedly with the use of the sparrow in *AS* 83. Urania's eroticism seems innocent alongside Stella's, and her sparrow avoids any hint of phallic possibilities (see Fish, n. 21, below).

21. "In sinu tenere" may mean either "to her breast" or "in her lap": see Catullus, *The Poems*, ed. Kenneth Quinn (New York: St. Martin's, 1970), p. 92, and Quinn's earlier study, *The Catullan Revolution* (Melbourne: University Press, 1959), p. 98. The translation by Reney Myers and Robert J. Ormsby places the sparrow forth-rightly "between her thighs" (*The Complete Poems for American Readers* [New York: Dutton Paperback, 1970], p. 3). Playing with this pet, in her lap or between her thighs, and engaged in "fingertip" (Quinn ed., *Poems*, p. 92) relations with it and, presumably, with the proximate portions of her own body as well, Lesbia can be imagined engaging in a highly stylized form of masturbation. Fish remarks on the "phallic possibilities of the sparrow in the tradition of Catullus and Ovid" in *John Skelton's Poetry, YSE,* 157 (New Haven: Yale University Press, 1965), p. 102; Greek antecedents are suggested, and winged phalloi illustrated, by William Arrowsmith, "Aristophanes' Birds: The Fantasy Politics of Eros," *Arion,* n.s. 1 (1973–74), 119–67, esp. pp. 164–67. At least one of Sidney's contemporaries uses an image of a bird (not a sparrow) in a context explicitly masturbatory (Thomas Nashe, *The choise of valentines,* ll. 239–44, in *Works*, ed. Ronald B. McKerrow, rev. F. P. Wilson [1958; rpt. Oxford: Blackwell, 1966], III, 412–13).

22. Writing on Herrick's *Hesperides* 256, J. Max Patrick notes that the relevant genre includes poems on more than sparrows alone. Ovid, of course, laments Melior's parrot (*Amores* II.vi); Marvell's "Nymph Complaining for the Death of a Faun" is also part of the genre. See Patrick's edition of *The Complete Poetry of Robert Herrick* (1963; rpt. New York: Norton, 1968), p. 144; he is preceded in this point by McPeek, *Catullus in Strange and Distant Britain,* pp. 69–71. The point is important, for it explains why both McPeek (p. 296, n. 17) and I treat *AS* 59 as well as *AS* 83 as part of this tradition.

23. *The Complete Gentleman, The Truth of Our Times, and The Art of Living in London*, ed. Virgil B. Heltzel, Folger Documents of Tudor and Stuart Civilization (Ithaca: Cornell University Press, 1962), p. 18.

24. Such a reading of *AS* 83 supports, from another point of view, Neil L. Rudenstine's observation that "rhetoric and all the uses of language have a strong symbolic character for Sidney." He adds: "the formal and colloquial [styles] are set against one another; control, aspiration, and reason are set against their opposites." To find, as in this sonnet, both styles together indicates "extreme tension and self-division" (*Sidney's Poetic Development* [Cambridge: Harvard University Press, 1967], pp. 176, 178–79, 180). Cf. Jonathan Smith on *The Winter's Tale,* I.ii.128–46, in "The Language of Leontes," *SQ*, 19 (1968), 317–18. Tension and self-division are only to be expected in a sonnet that questions, as Sonnet 83 does, its speaker's feelings and human capacities.

25. In the most extensively developed bestial imagery in *AS,* Sidney compares Astrophil to the horse in order to reinforce this point. The image is considered in detail in Arvilla Kerns Taylor's fine study, "The Manège of Love and Authority: Studies in Sidney and Shakespeare," Diss. Texas 1969, *DAI*, 30 (1969–

70), 3025–26A. I am grateful to Maurice L. Shapiro of Tulane University for drawing my attention to this work.

26. Sidney's ability to work with mixed modes is gaining increased attention: see, e.g., Stephen J. Greenblatt, "Sidney's *Arcadia* and the Mixed Mode," *SP*, 70 (1973), 269–78.

27. But Fish's assumption that the initial reading produces the only significant response is questionable in any case: see Joseph H. Summers, "Stanley Fish's Reading of Seventeenth-Century Literature," *MLQ*, 35 (1974), 405; and David Newton-De Molina, rev. of *Self-Consuming Artifacts, Anglia*, 94 (1976), 531–33.

28. See Scanlon, "Sidney's *Astrophil and Stella*," which argues that Bembo's discourse in Castiglione's *Cortegiano* (Book 4) offers the standard against which Astrophil's behavior is to be negatively judged. Sinfield ("Sidney and Astrophil," p. 34) remarks that "Sidney is involved in the same protestant re-evaluation and redirection of love poetry" that Spenser's *Amoretti* exhibit, through "charting. . . . Astrophil's fall from reason and virtue into sensuality and eventual desperation."

29. An important essay on the *Apology* by Lawrence C. Wolfley discusses in considerable detail the significance to Sidney's poetic theory of his notions concerning poetry's ability to move men to virtuous action ("Sidney's Visual-Didactic Poetic: Some Complexities and Limitations," *JMRS*, 6 [1976], 217–41; Wolfley is by no means in agreement, however, with the assumption of this essay that Sidney's practice accords with his theory [241]). See also Tuve, *Elizabethan and Metaphysical Imagery,* chap. 14, esp. pp. 399 ff.

Maurice Evans (essay date 1984)

SOURCE: "Divided Aims in the *Revised Arcadia,*" in *Sir Philip Sidney and the Interpretation of Renaissance Culture: A Poet in His Time and Ours*, Croom Helm, 1984, pp. 34–43.

[*In the following essay, Evans contends that the* Revised Arcadia *is Sidney's attempt to put his theory of poetry into practice, but that his aims often are at odds as his mimetic genius clashes with and is stifled by a didactic purpose.*]

The ***Revised Arcadia*** is the most capacious of Sidney's literary works, and the one which expresses the widest range of his needs and interests. This paper explores some of the problems to which his peculiar eclecticism gave rise. It is a commonplace that the Renaissance ideal of man involved versatility and excellence in many different fields, but in the case of Sidney, the diversity is extreme. He was an idealist with more than a dash of romantic heroism in his nature, as his behaviour at Zutphen reveals, yet at the same time he had a ruthless and not always compassionate perception of human weakness. He loved heroism but did not believe in heroes. He was charmed by the glamour of old-time chivalry and yet was an earnest student of *realpolitik*: he was interested in people as they are, but he wanted to make them different. His imagination kindled at the old tale of Percy, yet his own theory of poetry was uncompromisingly didactic. He wanted to write: he wanted to do: and it is particularly in Poesy, in the ***Revised Arcadia***, that all these incompatibles come most nearly into direct collision.

If we can trust the impression of his language, which becomes incandescent whenever he refers to it, Sidney's deepest pleasure in poetry came from the release of the imagination which it offered . . . 'With a tale forsooth he cometh to you, with a tale which holds children from play, and old men from the chimneycorner. . . .' (*Defence*, 92.9–11) or the familiar description of the Golden World which only the poet can deliver, with its 'forms such as never were in nature, as the Heroes, Demigods, Cyclops, Chimeras, Furies, and such like' (*Defence*, 78.26–27). There is no trace of the moral or didactic here, only an intense delight in the liberation of the imagination from the constraints of the real world which, by his definition, only poetry can give. The emphasis throughout the *Defence* is always upon the 'delight' which poetry arouses, and the fiction which is the source of its power to move us. And yet most readers would agree, I think, that Sidney's greatest writing is mimetic, and that his lasting appeal stems primarily from his ability to describe accurately and unsentimentally a whole range of human weaknesses. The imaginative release into the pastoral world of the ***Old Arcadia*** leaves less of an impression than the ironic perception of human folly which Sidney gives us; and there can be no doubt that ***Astrophil and Stella*** is one of the fullest and subtlest studies of conscious self-deception in the language.

In the ***Old Arcadia*** he kept the two strains separate by exhibiting his main characters in situations where they showed themselves as men rather than as heroes, and channelling most of the idyllicism into the songs and pastoral eclogues; but the ***Revised Arcadia*** is a different matter. In the 1580s, the disappointment of his ambition to become a great and influential figure in public affairs seems to have driven Sidney to turn to literature as a kind of surrogate action. The *Defence* holds it up as the most powerful form of moral and political rhetoric, of all activities the one most profitable and necessary to the state and the individual. Poetry is to be valued as a practical force, the means of harnessing the imaginative delights of fiction to the direct improvement of society. It is that 'delightful teaching,' he says, 'which must be the right describing note to know a poet by' (*Defence*, 81.37–82.1) and the bland phrase 'delightful teaching,' which insists on a stronger fusion of profit and delight than its original in Horace, is the meeting place for the complex oppositions between the imaginative and the practical, the mimetic and the didactic which exist in Sidney's own nature.

The ***Revised Arcadia*** is Sidney's attempt to put his theory of poetry into practise. It is more explicitly didactic than anything he had written before; its heroes are more simply heroic, and the third book, which contains most of the wholly new material, seems to be constructed as a demonstration of the virtues appropriate to the old topos of 'Doing and Suffering.' His theory of fiction, and the delightful escape it offers from the foolish world of reality into the golden world of the poet's imagination, does not, on the surface at least, seem to provide much of the basis for a programme of practical moral reform. The argument of the *Defence*, however, derives in part from the tradition of euhemerism, still very much alive in Sidney's day, which offered him a conception of Heroic poetry most congenial to his desires. Euhemerism is, of course, the time-honoured theory concerning the nature of myth, in terms of which the gods of pagan mythology were interpreted as historical figures—heroes, rulers, conquerors, civilizers—who, for their services to mankind, were first revered and then eventually set up as gods or demigods for posterity to worship. The chief agent in this process of elevation was the Heroic poet, and such poets, therefore, are mythmakers who establish the moral myths which guide mankind, and who celebrate through the actions and conquests of their mythical heroes the virtues and vices to be emulated or avoided. For this reason, the poets were, in Puttenham's words, 'the first priests, the first prophets, the first legislators and politicians in the world.'[1] All of these were rôles which held a strong attraction for Sidney. Moreover the tradition was a main source of the moral interpretation of classic epic and heroic romance, and also, of the moral allegory attached to Greek myth which provided the matter for so much Renaissance iconography. This appealed to Sidney's humanism and at the same time offered a moral outlet for the imagination. In this world of moral mythology, didacticism and unlicensed imagination go hand in hand: the chimeras, furies and heroes which so delighted Sidney carried moral meanings as a matter of course. The poet as mythmaker can have it both ways.

The euhemeristic tradition provided Sidney with a variety of myths and mythical settings for his purposes in the ***Revised Arcadia***, the most obvious of which is the myth of the Golden Age, which forms the basis of the pastoral vision. The ***New Arcadia*** abandons the brisk narrative opening of the ***Old*** and instead establishes the action more firmly within the pastoral, with the idealized shepherds, Strephon and Claius. The pastoral mode, with its long tradition of moral significance derived from its association with the Golden Age and from the Christian overtones of unfallen Eden acquired later, offered Sidney an ideal moral landscape which fused very easily with his vision of the golden world created by the poet's imagination:

> There were hills which garnished their proud heights with stately trees; humble valleys whose base estate seemed comforted with refreshing of silver rivers; meadows enamelled with all sorts of eye-pleasing flowers; thickets, which, being lined with most pleasant shade, were witnessed so to by the cheerful deposition of many well-tuned birds; each pasture stored with sheep feeding with sober security, while pretty lambs with bleating oratory craved the dams' comfort; here a shepherd's boy piping as though he should never be old; there a young shepherdess knitting and withal singing, and it seemed that her voice comforted her hands to work and her hands kept time to her voice's music.[2]

This is very similar to Sidney's account in the *Defence* of the rich tapestry in which the poet can set forth the earth, but it carries also a strong symbolism of ideal order and unfallen innocence; and it can be used, as the Renaissance habitually used it, as a norm against which less ideal scenes can be judged and satirised. Sidney expands his moral field in this way by reminding us that Urania has left Arcadia, and by moving on at once to the description of the shipwreck and the account of the false pastoral idyll of Basilius' country court. This transition into a less than idyllic world enables him to draw on a different range of myths, namely those of the Herculean-type hero whose task is to conquer the ills of a fallen world and restore, if not the Golden, at least the Silver Age. In terms of this he has literary and moral sanction for the creation of heroes of the type of Cyrus, Aeneas or Ulysses in whom is 'each thing to be followed,' and their opposites such as Tantalus or Atreus, in whom there is 'nothing that is not to be shunned.' He already had promising heroes to draw on from the ***Old Arcadia*** who only needed a little moral stiffening and a wider canvas to fulfill their Herculean roles. Within the framework of Romance, Sidney was able to combine the pastoral and the heroic modes, and use them to provide the appropriate myths for the moral vision and the will to make it prevail. They furnish the constituents of this formula, 'delightful teaching.'

The theory of poetry argued in the *Defence* worked out very well within its limits, but for Sidney it eventually turned into something of a strait jacket. It released his imaginative and didactic impulses and allowed them to yoke together, but it largely denied those mimetic abilities of his genius which found their fullest expression in ***Astrophil and Stella***, and which had little place within the conventions and myths of the pastoral or the heroic world. Even the ironic presentation of Musidorus and Pyrocles in love is literary and stereotyped in comparison with the verisimilitude of Astrophil. Nor had Sidney the bridge of allegory which Spenser was able to construct between the real world and that of the Romance which was his medium. The logic of moral myth leads towards allegory, but Sidney's gift was not in that direction: his medium for moral persuasion was necessarily a literal one, the example; and he consistently turns what are potentially allegorical figures into individual people. Anaxius, for instance, is basically the traditional figure of Disdain, but Sidney makes a real person of him. Moreover the world which he describes draws increasingly nearer to the society of his own time, in spite of its classic and pastoral dress. Fiction, as he actually practised it in the ***Arcadia*** is not the free flight of the imagination, as it is defined in the *Defence*, but something closer to our own understanding of the term in relation, say, to the nineteenth century novel: it is mimetic and related to life, with rules and demands of its own. Yet he was saddled with a didactic theory which demanded the creation of characters in black and white, whose prime function was to demonstrate all the virtues and vices, the graces, skills and corruptions to which the reader must be exposed for his own good. By Book III Sidney may have discovered the difference between reading into the *Aeneid* whatever moral meanings one may wish to find there and actually composing a poem designed to express those moral meanings. In such a situation, mimesis and rhetoric contradict each other: the characters labour under their moral loads or are fragmented by having to demonstrate forms of excellence which are incompatible with each other. It is difficult to reconcile the Pyrocles in the rôle of practical politician or effective orator with the Pyrocles whose heroic courage can win a battle single-handed; and the Amphialus who knows how to provision an army or allocate responsibility according to the nature of his officers or exploit the different motives of his possible supporters is not the Amphialus who jousts with all comers on his island. Convention and reality, example and fact have become confused: the qualities being exemplified belong to different genres, even to different civilizations. This creates no problem in *The Faerie Queene*, where everything is kept at an equal distance from reality; but it matters greatly in the ***New Arcadia***, even though Sidney does his best to minimize the collisions between incompatible elements of his story by the use of an elaborate rhetoric which engrosses the attention in each particular instance and tends to isolate one sequence from another. But this itself fights against the coherence of the structure and the momentum of the action which Sidney is also attempting to achieve.

Sidney's handling of his heroes in particular shows the problems he had created for himself. He believed in the value of the heroic ideal, but he was too much of a realist to believe in heroes as a fact, and he places them firmly within the confines of fiction. Creating them must have been a similar task to that of Milton in creating an Adam before the Fall. Inevitably he turns to heroic literature for his models, and shows great resourcefulness in inventing situations where his characters can demonstrate their qualities; but by the end of Book II, the adventures are becoming stereotyped as they move from the conquest of kings to that of giants and eventually monsters; and by the end of Book III, when most other aspects of human prowess have been exhausted, he is driven for the sake of variety to the verge of 'camp' in the long unfinished fight between Anaxius and Pyrocles in woman's dress. Perhaps the very flippancy of what he found himself doing was a reason why he stopped. Amphialus, indeed, is Sidney's inevitable rebellion against his own technique of moral exemplification: he is the flawed hero, neither an Aeneas nor an Atreus, and the power and realism of his character bursts through the fabric of convention with an almost tragic intensity. He is the clearest evidence that Sidney was not content with the framework which he had chosen and was, in fact, torn between two different modes of moral teaching, the mythical and the dramatic. His treatment of heroines is more successful, partly, perhaps, because he believed that heroism is compatible with a greater degree of human weakness in a woman than he would allow in a man; partly because he had a stronger tradition of female idealism to build on. He succeeds best of all, however, with villains because, presumably, they come closer to real life than heroes—though even here it is not always easy to tell whether he is drawing on life or on the books of characters. Certainly he seems more at home with vice than with virtue; and the fine distinctions which he establishes between vices and follies, and the enormous gallery of pictures, from the boorishness of Dametas to the total egotism of Cecropia, rival even those of Ben Jonson. Here, mimesis and moral example unite in the common truth of the Fall.

Behind this confusion of literary intentions there is, as one would expect, a confusion of philosophies of which Sidney himself, together with many other Renaissance writers, may not have been aware: it is between the fashionable Platonism of the sixteenth century and the interpretations by the Renaissance commentators of the newly discovered *Poetics* of Aristotle. In an earlier paper, Professor Heninger has drawn attention to Sidney's interest in the new empiricism and his sympathy with the mimetic theory of art; and this is obviously true though not, I think, the whole story. Sidney seems to me on many occasions to be trying to follow both Plato and Aristotle at once, without fully recognizing the difference—like a man standing astride Plato's two horses which pull in different directions to use a simile which he himself would have understood very well. The theory of poetry in the *Defence* is a Platonic one, based on the assumption that the divine spark within the human soul, even after the Fall, will kindle to the impression of divinity outside itself. The inspired poet with his erected wit can perceive the divine ideas and embody them in images of ideal truth whose purity can strike, pierce and possess the sight of the soul, so that we are moved to love it whether we will or not. This is deceptively close to the moralised interpretations of Aristotle by the commentators, and the didacticism they attributed to the *Poetics*, reading into it elements of both Plato and Horace. The essential difference, however, lies in the fact that Platonism, as Sidney interpreted it, exerts its didactic pressure at the unconscious level: we are moved by the truths of poetry without knowing why, and often against our will; and it is only after we have been moved that the speaking picture defines for us the reason, so that men may 'know that goodness whereunto they are moved.' Catharsis, on the other hand, is normally understood by the Renaissance critics as a conscious and rational process: we seek to emulate those characters we admire and prudently flee the courses which end in tragedy. Sidney does not seem to distinguish between the two didactic modes, and draws on both traditions indiscriminately. There can be no doubt, however, that he fully understood the implications of Aristotle's Mimesis in relation to plot, character, and structure. In its close control of supporting detail and its stricter definition of motive, the ***New Arcadia*** shows the unmistakable influence of what Aristotle had said about probability and necessity: the plot proceeds from the nature of the characters and in turn defines them; and the main action moves forward with its own inevitable inner logic. Mimesis in this sense does not mix happily with any brand of overt didacticism.

The consequences of Sidney's divided aims can be seen in his very uncertain control of the 'speaking pictures' which form the basis of his 'delightful teaching.' They are explicitly didactic in intention, and their very name suggests a static tableau which is hostile to the verisimilitude of a dramatic story; yet, as Professor Heninger has suggested, the emphasis on the visual derives from Aristotle's Mimesis and is reinforced by Horace's tag 'ut pictura poesis,' in consequence of which the association of poetry and painting dominated poetic theory for the next two hundred years. Sidney himself in the *Defence* relates his 'speaking pictures' to mimesis and endows them with the Horatian function, to teach and delight, although, as we have seen, their method of teaching is basically Platonic; and with a pedigree as mixed as this some confusion is inevitable. At times he takes material which is mimetic and dramatic by nature and tries to make it perform the functions of emblem or hieroglyph; or alternatively, he attempts to fit pictures which are frankly emblematic into a mimetic context. He is most successful when he keeps the two strains separate from each other and uses his pictures as emblems. The brilliant picture embodying the nature of democracy, as Sidney understood it (p. 383), is a good example; or the little vignette describing Pamela at Prayer:

> But this prayer sent to heaven from so heavenly a creature, with such a fervent grace as if devotion had borrowed her body to make of itself a most beautiful representation; with her eyes so lifted to the skyward that one would have thought they had begun to fly thitherward to take their place among their fellow stars; her naked hands raising up their whole length and, as it were, kissing one another, as if the right had been the picture of Zeal, and the left of Humbleness, which both united themselves to make their suits more acceptable: lastly, all her senses being rather tokens than instruments of her inward motions.
>
> (p. 464)

This is explicitly a picture and an emblem: her appearance has been made a 'token' of what is to be expressed. Sidney has taken Pamela out of her narrative context and turned her into an illustration for a book of devotions. He is, of course, drawing on the familiar tradition of memory images: the picture of Pamela with her hands raised in the traditional posture of prayer stays in the memory, and will serve as a perpetual reminder that the constituents of true prayer are zeal and humility.

Sidney is less certain in his control, however, when he uses speaking pictures to arouse our feelings at moments of high drama, such as the scourging of Philoclea, for example (pp. 551–2), or the tragic death of Parthenia:

> . . . her roundy sweetly swelling lips a little trembling, as though they kissed their neighbour death; in her cheeks the whiteness striving by little and little to get upon the rosiness of them; her neck, a neck indeed of alabaster, displaying the wound, which with most dainty blood laboured to drown his own beauties, so here was a river of purest red, there an island of perfectest white, each giving lustre to the other. . . .
>
> (p. 528)

The moment is one of great tragedy but it does not come over in this way. The dying Parthenia is lost under the facade of ornament; the pain is distanced, and instead of pity and fear we have the sort of pleasing pathos to be found in a play such as Ford's *The Broken Heart*. This is a typical example of how Sidney handles tragic situation, and it is not easy to be sure of his intention. He may have been striving for a genuinely tragic effect but have failed to realize that speaking pictures are better at defining for the mind than embodying for the feelings: he may not have recognized that poetry is not in fact speaking picture, that words do not work like dramatic images, and that verbal descriptions produce different effects from real pictures. He may even have misunderstood Aristotle's conception of the tragic pleasure, which he himself calls 'delightful terribleness.' He agrees with Aristotle that Mimesis by its very nature gives pleasure, no matter what is being imitated; but in practice he seems never quite to trust this, and tends to embellish his tragic moments with a display of fine and witty rhetoric to ensure that the reader is adequately pleasured. His descriptions of battles, for example, anticipate those of Nashe, in the way they wrap up the ugly facts in conceited language and humour which at times borders on hilarity, as in the very funny account of Pyrocles' slaughter of the rebels.

There are signs, however, that Sidney was aware of the problems of communication and was constantly exploring and developing his techniques. If I may consider a final example, the great account in Book III of the first battle between Amphialus and the forces of Philanax shows Sidney attempting to separate the pictorial from the speaking dimensions of his speaking picture, the mimetic from the emblematic. The sequence begins with the simple, unaffected, purely mimetic account of the death of the young Agenor '. . . of all that army the most beautiful . . . full of jollity in conversation and lately grown a lover,' who puts his lance in rest 'as careful of comely carrying it as if the mark had been but a ring and the lookers on ladies.' It is a deeply moving passage which could almost come out of the *Iliad*. In the battle which follows, the weapons themselves seem to take over the field . . . 'Some lances, according to the metal they met, . . . did stain themselves in blood . . . But their office was quickly inherited, either by (the prince of weapons) the sword, or by some heavy mace or biting axe which, hunting still the weakest chase, sought ever to light there where smallest resistance might worse prevent mischief.' This is bordering on allegory, but the contrast it makes between the inhuman, impersonal quality of the weapons and the frailty and vulnerability of the human beings turns the pity of the first sequence into fear, and lifts the whole passage to the level of genuine tragedy.

Having first moved us, Sidney goes on to show us why we are moved in the final sequence which defines in a great set-piece the unnaturalness of war. This is the famous battle symphony, in which the clashing of armour and the groans of the dying provide the orchestration for 'that ill-agreeing music,' and the logic of all normal relations is put into reverse: the horses lay upon their lords instead of carrying them; the earth instead of burying men is buried by them, and the legs, having been cut off from their bodies, 'being discharged of their heavy burden, were grown heavier' (pp. 468–9). There is a complete change of key here from an emotional to an intellectual level, which could have led from one kind of tragedy to another, from one of character to one of ideas. In fact this does not happen; as is so often the case, Sidney is trying too hard: the extended and witty paradoxes, the puns on dispossessed and disinherited, the half jokes about the legs and fingers are ultimately too flippant for the moral point he is making; and what comes through is an impression of the brilliance and virtuosity of Sidney's own technique, as if he cared more for his picture than for what it was saying.

It is possible that this was the effect which Sidney intended, and that his elaborate rhetoric throughout the ***Arcadia*** is a deliberate means of distancing the often horrific actions from the reader, so as not to fright the ladies who read it. Certainly this is the overall effect of the work: ***The Arcadia***, to our profit and pleasure is a Romance, not an earnest moral treatise. Whether he would or could have redressed the moral balance if he had finished it, we cannot tell; but there is no point in speculating on this, any more than on Sir Thomas Browne's questions about what song the syrens sang, or what name Achilles assumed when he hid himself among women—though to the latter question Sidney might well have had an answer. The name would, of course, have been Zelmane.

Notes

1. George Puttenham, *The Art of English Poesie*, in G. Gregory Smith (ed.), *Elizabethan Critical Essays* (London, 1904), II, p. 6.

2. Maurice Evans (ed. and introduction), *The Countess of Pembroke's Arcadia* (Harmondsworth, 1977), pp. 69–70. Quotations from the *Arcadia* in the present essay are taken from this edition and incorporated into the text.

Paul Allen Miller (essay date 1991)

SOURCE: "Sidney, Petrarch, and Ovid, or Imitation as Subversion," in *ELH: A Journal of English Literary History*, Vol. 58, No. 3, Autumn, 1991, pp. 499–522.

[*In the following essay, Miller argues that* Astrophel and Stella *falls into the larger Petrarchan-Ovidian tradition, but Sidney uses the model to construct a lyric subjectivity that is uniquely his own.*]

Despite Sidney's repeated denials, the fact that he practiced extensive classical and Petrarchan imitation in ***Astrophil and Stella*** has been well established.[1] What remains to be asked is why and to what effect was this imitation employed? What was to be gained or lost by the poet? And how did his use of imitation affect the construction of the lyric subject whose voice dominates the collection? These questions cannot be answered simply by citing prevailing literary fashion or the spirit of the age. Such a strategy merely avoids the issue by moving to a higher level of abstraction. A real answer, even if only a partial one, will require a close analysis both of Sidney's imitative practice and of the historical and personal conditions which made that practice both possible and necessary. This essay will begin the effort to provide such an answer.

To start, it should be noted that the sonnet sequence, as developed by Petrarch and practiced by Sidney, offered occasion for the creation of a more complex and highly self-reflexive lyric subjectivity than any seen in the poetry of the Middle Ages. The rigidly hierarchical social system of feudalism left little room for the virtually autonomous ego, which the sonnets of a Sidney, a Shakespeare, or a Donne require. The lyric consciousness of medieval poetry is often impersonal, presented not through the signed manuscript or printed collection, but by the traveling jongleur. It is rapidly assimilated to the values and assumptions of its audience and acquires an exemplary value, rather than presenting the idiosyncratic and highly interiorized lyric subjectivity representative of the modern genre.[2] With the coming of the Renaissance, however, the status of the subject was open to change. No longer were individuals exclusively seen as occupying a fixed position within an unchanging hierarchy, but they could now begin to be defined in something close to modern, bourgeois terms: that is, as complex individuals whose communal status was determined by their actions and attributes, not by a mere accident of birth or the immutable will of God.[3]

Thus there was the chance for Sidney and others to create and fill a new ideological space for the poetic and personal ego. It was in this context that ***Astrophil and Stella*** was written and England's first, modern, lyric subjectivity was produced. The space which it both found and made was not created from a vacuum, but was produced from an opening made possible by a series of discrete historical conflicts. It was, consequently, a contested space. For while on the one hand, it was becoming more possible to view the individual as an entity separate from his or her position in society, on the other, the official ideology and political structure of the period were still largely dominated by the corporate values of the feudal past. Thus, as social relations became increasingly fluid—as the growth of mercantile capitalism undermined the stable property tenure and exchanges in kind upon which feudalism rested—they also became more stratified in their communal representations. Likewise, as the traditional role of the nobility receded, the symbolic distinctions between them, the bourgeoisie, the peasants, and petty craftsmen increased. Hence, what was once a functional if inegalitarian division of labor became more and more irrational, creating a situation in which, while the system's utility declined, the assertions of its necessity were multiplied.[4]

What was at stake in this crisis of confidence among the feudal elite is made clear by Elizabeth's intervention in the famous tennis court incident between Sidney and the Earl of Oxford. When Sidney (a mere gentleman) challenged Oxford to a duel, the queen, as Fulke Greville records,

> who saw that by the loss or disgrace of either, she could gain nothing, presently undertakes Sir *Philip*; and (like an excellent Monarch) lays before him the difference in degree between Earls, and Gentlemen; the respect inferiors ought to their superiors; and the necessity in princes to maintain their own creations, as degrees descending between the people's licentiousness, and the annoynted Soveraignty of Crowns: how the Gentlemans neglect of Nobility taught the Peasant to insult upon both.[5]

Greville's text simultaneously reveals the persistence of feudal ideology in the Elizabethan period, its importance to the crown, and the anxieties surrounding its continued existence. It is precisely these tensions and the way they manifest themselves in Sidney's use of classical and Petrarchan imitation that this study will examine.

I

Before looking at the poetry itself, it will be useful to gain a more precise understanding of Sidney's own position vis-à-vis Elizabethan society as a whole. It is, as we shall see, no less conflicted than the historical situation at large. In terms of religion, Sidney was a Calvinist and a strong advocate of a Protestant league. Nonetheless, far from rejecting the vanity of court life, he was a prominent participant in jousts, masques and other activities open only to recognized members of the gentry and nobility, and whose purpose was to preserve the hegemony of royal rule and feudal ideology.[6]

On his father's side, Sidney was from a gentle family long associated with the Tudor court. Through his mother, he was related to the Dudleys and was the nephew of the Earls of Leicester and Warwick. As the eldest son of an established family, he did not need poetic patronage from his feudal superiors, but was himself an important patron. Hence Sidney, unlike Spenser, Shakespeare and others, did not need poetry to empower his voice; nor was he required to use flattery to assure his material well-being. Indeed, his social status was such that it served to legitimate the very poetic forms he practiced, so that he himself became an object of imitation.[7]

This is not to say that Sidney's poetic discourse was unfettered by the constraints of his time; nor was Sidney immune to the economic and political crisis that gripped the Elizabethan feudal elite, as it struggled to adjust its ideology of public display and conspicuous consumption to the realities of increasingly expensive foreign luxury goods, and a merchant caste grown prosperous from Puritan frugality and from catering to the desires of the nobility. In fact, Sidney, like many of his peers, died deeply in debt. He was, however, never in the position of needing to seek remuneration for his poetry. He simply lived beyond his means, borrowed to maintain the lifestyle required of an aspiring courtier, and until his death awaited an appointment from the queen that would set his affairs aright. Thus while Sidney was dependent upon political patronage from the crown, poetry for him was neither a form of social empowerment nor a means of material support. Rather, it was practiced by him during those periods when he was out of favor at court and between public employments, and appears to have served primarily as a medium for the aesthetic sublimation of frustrated personal and political desires.[8]

Finally, though Sidney's class position was sufficiently elevated to free him from the necessity of seeking patronage, it was nonetheless ambiguous (he was merely a gentleman). Indeed, his knighthood came about as something of an accident, for when he was chosen to stand proxy for the Protestant Count Casimir's induction as a Knight of the Garter, protocol required that he be knighted first.[9] He also had close affinities with the growing bureaucracy of educated civil servants drawn primarily from the commons. Alan Sinfield sums up the situation well:

> The question of Sidney's class location is complicated by the fact that with the decline in the traditional roles of the feudal aristocracy . . . the nobility and gentry were redefining their importance to society in terms of public service. At the same time, the developing Tudor bureaucracy was recruiting relatively lowerclass men of talent who were thus gaining preferment to the higher gentry and aristocracy. So there was an uneven and mobile overlap of classes, roles and aspirations, and within this Sidney's family was placed quite ambivalently: he was at a point of structural confusion.[10]

Sidney, however, generally identified himself with the upper strata of the nobility and avidly supported the revival of chivalry at court. But when Leicester married late in life and had a son, Sidney, who until that time was the presumed heir of his estate, was left with little chance of moving significantly farther up the ladder of aristocratic advancement, and appeared at the next tournament wearing the impresa "SPERAVI" to show that his hopes had been dashed. It will also be recalled that during the poet's feud with the Earl of Oxford, the queen forbade Sidney's request for a duel on the grounds of his insufficient social status. Sidney thus stood astride several diverging currents of the Elizabethan ideological and social flux, and his poetry often reveals his alienation and an unconscious desire to escape the system he worked to maintain.[11]

Indeed, Sidney's work regularly betrays the contradictory pressures of his position: his ideology of chivalry, his class consciousness, his commitment to humanist learning, and the dictates of Calvinist theology. It is not surprising, therefore, that like the humanists who preceded him, Sidney often uses imitation as a means of imparting a certain stability to an ego otherwise in danger either of being absorbed into one of the period's competing discourses, or of simply being torn asunder. As Margaret McGowan writes, imitation gave the poets of the Renaissance "a kind of preordained stamp of achievement," a transhistorical claim to legitimacy within a closed and rigidly hierarchized society that still recognized primarily the prerogatives of birth and office, and not those of what liberal culture terms "the individual."[12] Thus imitation and its sanction of legitimacy provide Sidney with a way of mediating between contradictory historical and ideological tendencies, while nonetheless preserving the apparent coherence of his poetic ego. That coherence or stability, however, is largely a surface effect, for the poetry itself is often, in spite of its best intentions, subversive in both personal and political terms. And it is generally most subversive when the rhetoric of imitation is most clearly in view, subtly undermining both Sidney's subject position in Elizabethan society and the ideology which created it. Thus, to borrow Julia Kristeva's terminology, I will argue that Sidney's use of imitation in ***Astrophil and Stella***'s "phenotext" (the "apparent-text") serves as a shield that in turn allows for a freer play of the desires emerging from the "genotext" (the "generative-" or "pre-text") of his ideology and subconscious.[13]

II

> Astrophil's dazzlingly ingenious attempts to convince himself that love for Stella is actually a form of virtue or heroic activity are less and less successful as the sequence proceeds, and the unsparingly physical nature of his love becomes apparent.
>
> (Duncan-Jones, 75)

In light of Sidney's contradictory position within society, it is not surprising to find that his own relatively conservative theorization of the goals of poetry in the *Defence of Poesy* is not always consonant with his actual practice (Duncan-Jones, 63). For Sidney in the *Defence* expounds a vision of poetry as an ideological bulwark, defending the existing social structure against a threatened disintegration. The creation of such a poetry promised to be no easy task, for Elizabethan society was a volatile mix of feudalism, absolute monarchy, mercantile capitalism, and Protestant ideology, whose submerged contradictions would eventually explode into full-scale civil war. As Terry Eagleton writes:

> The poetry which Sidney defends is, of course, an institution inseparable from explicit ideological values—the values of a courtly classical humanism. . . . Literature for Sidney is a potent ideological instrument for inculcating those virtues appropriate to the hegemonic class of which he is a spokesman; it is for this reason above all that it must be protected from the criticisms of an assertive bourgeois puritanism. Sidney's text marks a moment of ideological buoyancy, an achieved synthesis of courtly and puritan elements; but the incipient pressures which call forth an *apology* for poetry will erupt soon afterwards, in the economically unstable, religiously fraught 1590s.[14]

According to the *Defence*, the ideal poet does not present the reader with difficulties, ambiguities or projections of subjectivity not immediately assimilable to recognized norms, but calls forth ideal images of virtue which inspire emulation.[15] His poetic ego is not unique or self-questioning, but paradigmatic for the society at large. "If the poet do his part aright, he will show you in Tantalus, Atreus, and such like, nothing that is not to be shunned; in Cyrus, Aeneas, Ulysses, each thing to be followed." The poet "nameth Cyrus and Aeneas no other way than to show what men of their fames, fortunes, and estates should do" (119, 137). He presents ideal forms: nature's "world is brazen, the poets only deliver a golden." The purpose of poetry is edification. It is the poet's task "not only to make a Cyrus, which had been but a particular excellency, as Nature might have done, but to bestow a Cyrus upon the world to make many Cyruses" (108–9).

The distinctly political function of the poet is made clearer by Sidney in the exemplary tale of the Roman general Menenius Agrippa who, when the Roman people had risen up against the senatorial oligarchy, addressed the plebeians and made them see the justice of the existing social relations. By telling the tale of the revolt of the other organs against the stomach—at which they were disgruntled because it got the best food—the general made the commons see that, like the stomach, the oligarchy was necessary to the continuing health of the political organism, whereupon "a perfect reconcilement ensued." The poet then, like Agrippa, is to teach his audience those virtues which promote social peace and preserve existing social relations. He may also, like the prophet Nathan, exercise a limited critical function by instructing a monarch who has "forsaken God," but only in such a manner as would allow that monarch to "see his own filthiness," not in such a way as to undermine his or the institution's authority (126–27).[16]

The poet's task, then, is to reproduce the sort of subjects necessary to the continuing health of England's late-feudal social formation. He is to produce not one Cyrus, but many. Yet the real question, for our purposes, is whether he should produce not only many Cyruses but also many Astrophils. The answer according to Fulke Greville is no, for while Greville lavishes a good deal of time in his biography of Sidney on explicating the ***Arcadia***'s power to promote virtue, he never so much as acknowledges ***Astrophil and Stella***'s existence. In addition, his praise of the ***Arcadia*** is only provisional, for he claims that Sidney in later life discovered the "vanitie of these shadowes, how daintily soever limned, as seeing that even beauty itself, in all earthly complexions was more apt to allure men to evill, than to fashion any goodness in them."[17] This is a position which casts a darkening eye on Astrophil's praise of Stella's charms and would appear to be at odds with Sidney's position in the *Defence*, where the claim is that the poet's golden world should move men to goodness. Even in the *Defence*, however, there is a certain ambivalence, in that Sidney acknowledges that a spectator, though moved to pity and tears by watching a well-made tragedy, may then proceed to commit abominations of every sort imaginable (123–25, 130). In addition, Thomas Moffet recorded that Sidney on his deathbed rejected ***Astrophil and Stella*** and demanded that it be destroyed: "Enraged at the eyes which had at one time admired Stella's so very different from those given by God. . . . He blushed at even the mention of his Anacreontics and once again begged his brother . . . that not any of this sort of poems should come forth into the light." The ambiguous status of ***Astrophil and Stella*** is also made clear by Giordano Bruno in the opening of his 1585 dedication of *De gli Eroici Furori* to Sidney: "Truly (most noble knight) it is the mark of a low, beastly, and filthy mind to be always studying and gazing at and giving one's most careful thought to the beauty of a female body."[18]

The most damning piece of evidence against ***Astrophil and Stella***, however, comes from the *Defence* itself, when Sidney addresses the fashion of sonnet writing, which had recently gripped the nation. Of this fashion, he says, "How well might it be employed, and with how heavenly fruit, both private and public, in singing the praises of the immortal beauty, the immortal goodness of that God which giveth us hands to write and wits to conceive" (152, see also 137–38). Yet this is clearly not the sort of conceiving Astrophil has in mind. In Sonnet 71, he begins by telling the reader in typical neo-Platonic fashion that Stella's beauty is the best home of virtue, and that in being drawn to Stella one is drawn to virtue. The last line of the poem, however, undercuts the earlier idealizing tone, returning us to the material world of sensuality and lust: "'But ah,' Desire still cries, 'give me some food.'" In the next sonnet, Astrophil tries to reform but, as the last couplet shows, is unsuccessful: "Thou Desire, because thou wouldst have all, / Now banisht art, but yet alas how shall?" The end of the sequence leaves the conflict unresolved: Stella, the unmovable star, will not yield, and Astrophil, the star-lover, will not accept a passive platonic love. Thus, unlike the end of the *Canzoniere*, the final poems of ***Astrophil and Stella*** achieve no ultimate sublimation of desire into divine transcendence, but rather leave the reader with one last Petrarchan paradox and no hope of resolution: "So strangely (alas) thy works in me prevaile, / That in my woes for thee thou art my joy / And in my joyes for thee my only annoy."[19]

The scene of writing, then, for Sidney is a scene of profound, internalized conflict, and it is this fact more than any external cause which may have led Sidney to believe that poetry needed a "defence." It could also be said that it is this same set of conflicting ideological currents that makes the construction of Astrophil's poetic subjectivity possible. For the ideological contradictions of the period, exacerbated by Sidney's anomalous social position, opened a space for the molding of a new form of poetic subjectivity, one that was not immediately assimilable either to existing social norms or to Sidney's own theorization of its goals. Sidney's work could be said to represent a prime example of that phenomenon Paul de Man labels "blindness and insight," for what makes ***Astrophil and Stella*** most interesting is precisely the way in which it diverges from and contradicts Sidney's own theorization of its aims. Yet, as with the cases de Man examines, Sidney's conflicting moments never meld to produce an informing dialectic because they never exist at the same discursive level at the same time.[20]

Before we examine selected examples of Sidney's use of imitation in ***Astrophil and Stella***, however, one objection to the position thus far developed must be considered. This objection, put forward by Thomas Roche, argues that ***Astrophil and Stella*** does indeed present a picture greatly at variance with Sidney's professed goals, but that this contradiction is deliberate and that his intention is to teach virtue by negative example. Sidney's poetics, however, leave little scope for such a position. Astrophil is neither wholly unattractive nor wholly virtuous, and he is certainly never condemned within the confines of the collection. This is hardly in keeping with the *Defence*'s strictures on shunning ethical ambiguity. Likewise, Roche's thesis can offer no explanation of Sidney's later rejection of the sequence, nor of Greville's choice to pass over what many now consider Sidney's greatest work.[21]

The refutation of Roche's contention allows me to bring up one more aspect of the sequence which I have deliberately avoided until now: its autobiographical element. That Sidney expected the reader to make the identification, at least in part, between Astro*phil* and *Phil*ip Sidney, as well as between Stella and Penelope Rich, formerly Devereux, seems beyond dispute. It would be pointless to rehearse all the arguments yet again, because they are as old as the sequence itself. Let it suffice to note that there are any number of allusions to Sidney's personal life in the poems, including the fact that Astrophil's coat of arms is the same as Sidney's, while there is an entire series of sonnets which pun on the implications of Penelope Rich's last name. This is not to say that ***Astrophil and Stella*** is a simple biographical recording of actual events. It is, rather, a construct in which various levels of discourse interact with one another to produce the picture of a dialogically complex subjectivity, which is of necessity textual. Nonetheless, it can be stated without fear of contradiction that many readers of the collection would have recognized traces of the author's identity within that construct, and it is hard to imagine that Sidney would have used an image so easily identifiable with himself as a method to instill virtue through negative example. Indeed, if the term "used" can be employed at all, it would appear that Sidney "used" ***Astrophil and Stella*** as a vehicle for self-exploration and self-construction, at least as much as he ever "used" it to teach virtue by positive, negative or any other sort of example.[22]

III

> The most intriguing example of the preservation of the image of Sidney's sexual "spot" is contained in Aubrey's *Brief Lives* where Sidney's death is laid not at the door of his wound but at the door of his refusal, over the best medical advise, "to forbeare his carnall

knowledge of" his wife Frances when his wound needed healing "upon which occasion there were some roguish verses made."[23]

With the collection's authorial and social context now more firmly established, let us return to the poems themselves. Of primary interest here will be an examination of how Sidney's use of Ovidian and Petrarchan imitation plays upon the tensions inherent in both his personal position and the society at large, so as to create a complex and multilayered lyric subjectivity ultimately alien to the Elizabethan social order. This investigation will require both a close reading of Sidney's actual imitative practice and an understanding of the multiple readings his subtexts imply.

Thus we might first observe that ***Astrophil and Stella***, like Petrarch's *Canzoniere*, is a consciously organized sonnet sequence, possessing both a diachronic development and a synchronic series of recurring thematic motifs. Among their other functions, these motifs serve to prevent the establishment of a single, univocal narrative capable of controlling the collection's interpretation, while also encouraging a multiplicity of possible readings by supplying a variety of contexts in which the individual poems can be read. The most common of these motifs is that of the Ovidian, warlike Cupid whose locus classicus is the opening line of *Amores* 1.9: "Militat omnis amans, et habet sua castra Cupido [Every lover is a soldier and Cupid has his fort]." That Sidney knew both the image and its origin is shown by his use of paraphrase of this line in the First Eclogues of the ***New Arcadia***, where the shepherd Thyrsis tells how his father tried to dissuade him from his love for Kala by saying, "Thou art no soldier fit for Cupid's garrison" (185). Likewise, Cupid appears throughout ***Astrophil and Stella*** in full Ovidian guise, with his torches and arrows, his siege machinery, and his capacity to render the poet an elegiac *servus amoris*.[24] J .G. Nichols has labeled these thematic images Petrarchan, but they are more properly termed Ovidian, inasmuch as Petrarch derived them directly from Ovid, and Sidney was familiar with the works of both Petrarch and the Roman love elegists. Moreover, as will be seen shortly, his use of these motifs frequently has a distinctly Ovidian tone. All the same, it is often difficult to identify with precision the exact source of a particular motif in ***Astrophil and Stella***. What is clear, though, is that Sidney appropriates the conventions of a recognized tradition which has already been canonized as possessing transhistorical value, and that he uses these conventions to construct a collection and a lyric subjectivity uniquely his own.[25]

A measure of how tight the articulations are between the Petrarchan and Ovidian aspects of this canonical discourse can be seen in another passage from the First Eclogues of the ***New Arcadia***. Here we find the shepherd Lamon recounting the tale of Strephon's and Claius's love for Urania, in the course of which the rustic singer evokes the image of Cupid as triumphing general behind whose chariot his victims follow: "Cupid the wag, that lately conquer'd had / Wise counsellors, stout captains, puissant kings, / And tied them to lead his triumph bad, / Glutted with them, now plays with meanest things" (201). The source of this image could be Petrarch, Ovid, or most likely, both. Ringler observes that "Cupid is so described in Petrarch's *Trionfo d'Amore*," which is certainly true.[26] But Cupid is also so described in *Amores* 1.2 and is associated by Ovid with triumphal processions in at least three more passages from the *Amores* (1.7.35–43, 2.9, and 2.12). Sidney would have been familiar with both of these sources and would have known from where Petrarch had derived this idea. Furthermore, the image as it appears in the ***Arcadia*** is so condensed that it would be difficult to assign priority to either text. What is clear, though, is that the image as Sidney received it already bore the stamp of transhistorical legitimacy and did not need to be defended. Moreover, it is illuminating to note that when a similar image of Stella's legs as Cupid's triumphal chariot appears in ***Astrophil and Stella*** 29, along with the other imagery that normally accompanies the *Cupido militans*, Ringler fails to identify any source whatsoever.

Stella's heart, finding what power *Love* brings,
To keepe it selfe in life and liberty,
Doth willing graunt, that in the frontiers he
Use all to helpe his other conquerings:
And thus her heart escapes, but thus her eyes
Serve him with shot, her lips his heralds arre:
Her breasts his tents, legs his triumphall carre:
Her flesh his food, her skin his armour brave,
And I, but for because my prospect lies
Upon that coast, am giv'n up for a slave.

(5–14)

The ironic context of "her breasts his tents, her legs his triumphall carre" would seem clearly to be more Ovidian than Petrarchan. Indeed, far from an idealization of the beloved, the poem presents a reduction to the material more reminiscent of Rabelais and Ovid than of Petrarch.

This reduction to the material is a rhetorical move which appears frequently in the sequence.[27] Hence in Sonnet 100, after a typically Petrarchan first quatrain comparing Stella's blushing cheeks to roses backed by lilies and thus highlighting their status as ideal objects, the poet switches in the second to a distinctly culinary terminology for describing her breasts:

O honied sighs, which from that breast do rise,
Whose pants do make unspilling creame to flow,
Wing'd with whose breaths, so pleasing *Zephires* blow,
As can refresh the hell where my soul fries.
O plaints conserv'd in such sugred phraise,
That eloquence it selfe envies your praise.

(5–10)

On this level, Sidney seems to be describing a pastry more than his beloved, and the waves of her panting breasts, maternally filled with flowing cream, have a distinctly erotic and material rather than idealizing cast. The result is analogous to the phenomenon of "grotesque degradation" described by M. M. Bakhtin in *Rabelais*, wherein established political and metaphysical hierarchies are brought down to an equal plane by contact with the material bodily stratum.[28] In the case of Sidney, however, it is not so much Stella who is brought down as Astrophil and the conventions of Petrarchan rhetoric.

Sidney, then, produces a synthetic work which, though difficult to trace to a single model, is easily recognizable as part of the larger Petrarchan-Ovidian tradition. And his use of that tradition serves throughout the collection both to provide thematic unity and to produce a complex set of dialogical relations between the individual poems. This intratextual cross-talk, moreover, subverts any attempt to establish a narrative capable of dictating the context in which the individual poems should be read and is part and parcel of the Petrarchan tradition. As Marion Campbell observes:

> No consistent psychological or narrative structure can be identified in *Astrophil and Stella* because the poem (like Petrarch's *Canzoniere*) dramatizes the process of creating a self and of narrating that self's history without those processes ever crystallising into the product of a self created or a story told. That is why the form of the poem is best seen as dynamic rather than static, metamorphosing as we read into an endless variety of forms, fragmenting and reforming, never achieving fixity. The poem offers us structuring elements in abundance, but these are included within its overall design rather than becoming the total explanation of it.[29]

Sidney's collection presents us not with an externalized, finished poetic self, but a dialogical self-in-the-making, founded upon a recognized tradition. It is a multifaceted self, which is never completely totalizable. The textual corollary of this phenomenon is that, while the poems often participate in complex intratextual networks linking them one to the other, the precise identity of those networks is constantly in flux. The ideological corollary is that ***Astrophil and Stella*** presents its audience with an open-ended, self-questioning lyric consciousness whose ultimate implications (if not actions) are subversive of the established order, especially when paired with the witty sexuality and materialism of the Ovidian tradition.[30]

That Sidney clearly understood the sexual implications of the Ovidian elements in the sonnet tradition can be seen in the following passage from the ***Arcadia***. Moving in order from the top of her body to the bottom, Pyrocles disguised as the Amazon Zelmane spontaneously composes a blazon on Philoclea as he/she watches her bathe. The passage cited begins just below the navel:

> Her belly then glad sight doth fill
> Justly entitled Cupid's hill:
> A hill most fit for such a master,
> A spotless mine of alabaster
>
> . . . . .
>
> In that sweet seat the boy doth sport:
> Loth, I must leave his chief resort.
> For such a use the world has gotten,
> The best things still must be forgotten.
>   Yet never shall my song omit
> Her thighs, for Ovid's song more fit.
>
> (289)

"Belly" here probably refers to that same lower region named by the Latin term *uterus*, which is also often translated "belly." "Cupid's hill" is a transparent reference to the *mons veneris*, and the sexual connotation of the image of the mine is clear. Philoclea's genitalia are passed over as "the best things," after which the thighs that surround them are described as "for Ovid's song more fit." This omission not only directly associates Ovid with what lies between her thighs, but also follows a pattern established in *Amores* 1.5, one of the earliest examples of the blazon form. The phrase "the best things" appears, moreover, as a euphemism for female genitalia in a mocking blazon of Dametas's daughter Mopsa. Ringler notes that it probably derives from *Metamorphoses* 1.502, in which Apollo is described gazing at Daphne and wondering "si qua latent meliora [if still better things lie hidden]."[31]

Reminiscences of *Amores* 1.5 are not, however, confined to the ***Arcadia,*** as can be seen in ***Astrophil and Stella*** 77, an idealizing blazon the last line of which also employs this same not so subtle euphemism for the female pudenda.[32]

> Those lookes, whose beames be joy, whose motion is delight,
> That face, whose lecture shewes what perfect beautie is:
> That presence, which doth give darke hearts a living light:
> That grace, which *Venus* weepes that she herself doth misse
>
> . . . . .
>
>   That voyce, which makes the soule plant himselfe in the eares:
> That conversation sweet, where such high comforts be,
> As consterd in true speech, the name of heav'n it beares,
> Makes me in my best thoughts and quietst judgement see,
> That in no more but these I might be fully blest:
> Yet ah, my Mayd'n Muse doth blush to tell the best.
>
> (1–4, 9–14)

In addition, lest it be thought that Sidney was unlikely to use such subtlety when addressing a subject so common, Sonnet 76 confirms this meaning. Here the poet begins with a standard comparison of his mistress' eyes to the sun, but as the sonnet moves toward its finish, those flaming orbs have warmed his desire to such an intensity that only one form of relief can be imagined: "No wind, no shade can coole, what helpe then in my case, / But with short breath, long lookes, staid feet and walking hed, / Pray that my sunne go downe with meeker beames to bed" (12–14).[33]

These are hardly the sole examples of Sidney's use of transparently sexual references beneath the cloak of classical imitation. Elsewhere in the ***Arcadia***, Amor's arrow, a standard piece of equipment for the Petrarchan-Ovidian *Cupido militans*, is clearly treated as an allegorical representation of the phallus. When the sisters Pamela and Philoclea are lying naked in their bed "cherishing one another with dear though chaste embracements, with sweet though cold kisses, it might seem that love was come to play him there without dart, or that, weary of his own fires, he was there to refresh himself between their sweet breathing lips" (245). The kisses are "chaste" because they are between sisters and neither woman possesses the "dart" required to fire their passion (though there are clearly erotic connotations to the entire situation). This passage, in turn, provides a crucial gloss on Sonnet 17 of ***Astrophil and Stella***, where, in another Ovidian context, Sidney puns on the sexual connotations of Cupid's dart as "pricking," again bringing its phallic dimensions to the fore:

His mother deare *Cupid* offended late,
   Because that *Mars*, grown slacker in her love,
   With pricking shot he did not throughly move
To keepe the pace of their first loving state.
The boy refusde for feare of *Marse's* hate,
   Who threatned stripes, if he his wrath did prove:
   But she in chafe him from her lap did shove,
Brake bow, brake shafts, while *Cupid* weeping sate:
   Till that his grandame *Nature* pittying it,
Of *Stella's* browes made him two better bowes,
And in her eyes of arrowes infinit.
O how for joy he leapes, o how he crowes,
   And straight therewith, like wags new got to play,
   Fals to shrewd turnes, and I was in his way.[34]

In Lacanian terms, Astrophil in this poem suffers a symbolic castration as the "pricking" phallus of Amor passes from its more appropriate owner to Stella's eyes. For it is Stella in the sequence who is to be the dominant, because refusing, partner, and it is her voice that represents the law. Ironically, then, it is she and not Astrophil who assumes the name of the father; it is she who has the power to castrate and control.

Sidney's subversion of the idealizing strains of the Petrarchan tradition through punning on its more erotic aspects was not, however, a purely personal act. Whether intended or not, it also had public and political implications. Elizabeth had deliberately established the conventions of Petrarchan poetry as the lingua franca of courtly politics, because its idealizing tendencies and its conventions of the lover "serving" his mistress were calked upon the same feudal relations she had to invoke to maintain her rule as a single woman. She too had assumed the name of the father. Thus it became the fashion to treat the Virgin Queen as the unattainable mistress at the top of the feudal pyramid surrounded by her adoring subjects/suitors. When Sidney takes this tradition and produces a sonnet sequence in which many of the same rhetorical tropes are used in a fashion which emphasizes their sexual and material aspects, he casts himself not only as an Ovidian poet but also as an ideological rebel.[35] For in Elizabeth's construction of the Petrarchan relationship, it was necessary that the lovers remain ideal, that they eschew too lusty a pursuit of the real object of their desire (be it power, Elizabeth herself, or some combination thereof). All the same, it is difficult to tell where Astrophil/Sidney consciously stood in all of this. As Ann Rosalind Jones and Peter Stallybrass note, "The logic of [Astrophil's] poems coincides with policial rhetoric in ways that raise the question of whether the lover poet is in control of the situation—or whether he is constructed by it."[36]

Nonetheless, it is important to recognize that Sidney's frequent use of the reduction to the material has a distinctly antihierarchical effect. It is noteworthy in this regard to recall the image of Cupid's triumph, for it will be remembered that behind Cupid's chariot come not only commoners but also "wise counsellors, stout captains, [and] puissant kings." The reduction of idealizing love to material lust has the effect of leveling out class distinctions: "How to the woods love runs as well as rides to the palace; / Neither he bears reverence to a prince, nor pity to a beggar" (***Arcadia***, 191). Yet this disregard for rank affect Sidney's relation not only to the queen or to the likes of the Earl of Oxford, but also his relation to the broad masses of those who were his social inferiors. This hardly seems likely to have been Sidney's intention, given his generally degrading portrayal of the commons in works like the ***Arcadia***; rather, it would appear to be the unintended effect of his use of classical imitation, wherein the voice of the other, the unconscious, and of history is allowed to seep in and overturn the hierarchy of values which in other places Sidney claims to defend. Consequently, the equalizing, transhistorical effect of imitation in Sidney functions so as to subvert the very social hierarchy he has pledged to defend. This schizophrenic quality of Sidney's verse is perhaps best captured in Sonnet 5, where reason and restraint are identified with the staid rule of monarchy and the free flow of passion with rebellion:

It is most true, that eyes are form'd to serve
The inward light: and that the heavenly part
Ought to be king, from whose rules who do swerve,
Rebels to Nature, strive for their owne smart,

   It is most true, what we call *Cupid's* dart,
An image is, which for ourselves we carve;
And, fooles, adore in temple of our hart,
Till that good God make Church and Churchman starve.

. . . . .

True, and yet true that I must Stella love.

(1–8, 14)

If we recall the identification of Cupid's dart with the phallus, this poem seems to allude directly to the subversive nature of Astrophil's idolatry of the phallus, both as his own sexual organ and in its symbolic castration and transference to Stella. The production of such a reading seems unlikely to have been this Calvinist's conscious intent, but its consonance with the larger imagistic patterns of his poetry cannot be denied.

There is, finally, a sequence of poems in which the intersection of public and private interests, the imagery of the *Cupido militans*, and the degradation of personal, political and metaphysical hierarchies reaches critical mass. These are the jousting Sonnets 41, 49, and 53. They all deal with Astrophil's participation in various tournaments and with the affect Stella has on his performance in them. The importance of these poems is crucial because of the central role such tournaments played in both Elizabethan ideology and in Sidney's own identity as a knight. The tournament and combat on horseback were the central symbols of chivalry and thus of the feudal order it supported. Indeed, the word chivalry itself is derived from the French term for horse, *cheval*, for without a *cheval* there would be no *chevaliers*. Likewise, tournaments and jousting matches since the time of Henry VII had assumed theatrical proportions and were staged as celebrations of royal power and the system of values on which it rested.[37] It is no accident, then, that the *Defence* opens with a discourse from Sidney's riding master in Vienna, and while Sidney insinuates that his master's claim that horsemanship is the foundation of all good policy is overblown, he equates his master's enthusiasm for horses with his own for poetry (Duncan-Jones, 63–64).

The three tournament sonnets follow a definite progression. The link between 41 and 53, as two contrasting treatments of a theme sounded in *Amores* 3.2, has already been noted by Germaine Warkentin, but the mediating role played by 49 and its Petrarchan allusions has not.[38] Sonnet 41 is conventional. Astrophil has just won the prize at a tournament and the onlookers want to know if it was gained through skill, strength, dexterity, chance or breeding. The answer, Sidney says, is none of these; Astrophil won because Stella deigned to look at him: "The true cause is, / Stella lookt on, and from her heavenly face / Sent forth beames, which made so faire my race" (12–14). This is a conventional idealizing sonnet that offers no hint of a grotesque degradation or reduction to the material.

The next poem is not so charitable. Here in a variation on the *servus amoris* theme from Latin love elegy, Sidney employs an image of Cupid riding the lover that recurs several times throughout Petrarch.[39] Yet in a twist that I believe is unique to Sidney—and a testament to his social status, since only knights rode in tournaments—Cupid rides him as he rides his horse:

> I on my horse, and Love on me doth trie
> Our horsemanships, while by strange worke I prove
> A horseman to my horse, a horse to Love;
> And now man's wrongs in me, poore beast, descrie.
>
> . . . . .
>
> He sits me fast, how ever I do sturre:
> And now hath made me to his hand so right,
> That in the Manage myselfe takes delight.
>
> (1–4, 12–14)

The lover here is dehumanized and, as in the elegiac and Petrarchan tradition, delights in his subjection. Yet while from a person of lower rank this avowal of subjection would merely reinforce the assumptions of feudalism's hegemonic discourse, in the person of a knight exercising his duties as a symbolic defender of existing social relations, the trope of the *servus amoris* takes on a more subversive meaning. It calls into question the social position occupied by the *chevalier* by showing him to be little more than a *cheval*; not only is he no better than other men, but he is also less than a man. Thus, whereas in Sonnet 41 love's idealizing qualities exalt Astrophil to a position of superiority relative to his fellows, in Sonnet 49 he is at best no better than most.

The logical consequences of this subversion of the idealized desire found in Sonnet 41 are then drawn in Sonnet 53, where once again Astrophil is competing in a tournament. This time, however, rather than winning because Stella casts her eyes upon him, he loses because he is so engrossed in her that he forgets to fight:

> In Martiall sports I had my cunning tride,
> And yet to breake more staves did me addresse:
> While with the people's shouts I must confesse,
> Youth, lucke, and praise, even fild my veines with pride.
> When *Cupid*, having me his slave descride
> In *Marse's* liverie, prauncing in the presse:
> "What now sir foole," said he, "I would no lesse,
> Looke here, I say." I look'd, and *Stella* spide.
> Who hard by made a window send forth light.
> My heart then quak'd, then dazled were my eyes,
> One hand forgott to rule, th'other to fight.
> Nor trumpets' sound I heard, nor friendly cries;
> My Foe came on, and beat the aire for me,
> Till that her blush taught me my shame to see.

The witty exterior of this poem should not distract from its more disturbing depths. The poet-knight is humiliated and unmanned because of his fixation on his beloved. At the same time, in an iconographical sense, the vertical hierarchy, in which he on his horse occupies an exalted position, is brought low, and he becomes one with those who live close to the ground (the *humiliores*). The Ovidian irony here functions as a defense mechanism that allows otherwise unacceptable thoughts and desires to find expression in a socially approved form.

On an even deeper and more personal level, there is a negotiation in this series of poems concerning Sidney's fundamental self-identity, a negotiation which reveals the profound interdependence between his public role and private self-image.[40] For there is a real sense in which Sidney's given name, Philip, points to his role as knight per se, inasmuch as his proper name is Greek for "Horse-Lover" (*Philippos*). That Sidney was sensitive to the implications of such speaking names and to the root meaning of the *phil* prefix of his own name can be seen in the very title of the collection ***Astrophil and Stella*** ("Star-Lover" and "Star") and in his use of the name Philisides ("Star-Lover" but also Philip Sidney) for a character meant to recall himself in the ***Arcadia***. Likewise, the king of Arcadia is named Basilius ("King"), his wife Gynecia ("Feminine"), his most faithful servant Philanax ("King-Lover"), a philandering knight Pamphilus ("All-Lover"), and among many others, the lower class and mean-spirited lover of the otherwise virtuous Queen Erona ("Desiring-Woman"), Antiphilus ("Opposed-to-Loving").[41]

If this reading of the relation between Sidney's given name, his knighthood, and his attention to matters of horsemanship both in ***Astrophil and Stella*** and in other works is correct, it would also provide another more profound gloss on the *Defence*'s opening excursus on Sidney's riding master, John Pietro Pugliano, who had taught the impressionable young man that "soldiers were the noblest estate of mankind, and horsemen the noblest of soldiers . . . they were the masters of war and ornaments of peace; speedy goers and strong abiders; triumphers both in camps and courts . . . that no earthly thing bred such wonder to a prince as a good horseman" (102). In this light, for Sir *Philippos* (or as Cupid calls him, in a vicious alliteration with Sir Phil, "sir foole") to be unhorsed is to experience not merely a degradation of social status but a dissociation of identity. This dissociation, in turn, both opens up possibilities for a deeper, more internalized elaboration of the speaking subject than was possible within the traditional feudal model, and exposes Sidney to the dangers of an infinite self-regression, which only the witty irony of these poems' Ovidian surface prevents from collapsing into an inarticulate gaze into the abyss. ***Astrophil and Stella***, then, works on two levels: both on a highly stylized and externalized level of literary presentation and imitation, and on a more profound, allegorical, virtually psychoanalytic level of self-investigation. Imitation thus functions not simply as an ornament of style, but as the legitimating element which insures the surface coherence of and provides the transhistorical legitimation for the poet's often complex and internalized lyric subjectivity. At the same time, it allows otherwise politically or theologically heterodox sentiments to find expression in a socially acceptable form.

For Sidney, as a noble amateur, the fact of his being a poet was not central to his social self-definition. It was rather a "supplement" to that self-definition, a necessary addition which served as a means of exploring, expressing, and ultimately negotiating the basic ideological and personal conflicts constitutive of his subject position in society vis-à-vis the demands of court, religion, and Eros itself. Sidney's poetry is at once separate from his personal identity and profoundly implicated in its constitution. It is—in his own words—a "toy," a glittering plaything.[42] Nonetheless, it is a toy which allows him to explore psychic regions that a more "serious" endeavor might not dare to plumb. Thus the same gap which necessarily marks the distance between the formalized world of Elizabethan court life and the psychic depths of its individual players could be said to be reproduced in Sidney's poetry in the form of the gap between the witty Ovidian exterior of the poems and the potentially disturbing sexual/political issues which the use of imitation allows to find expression. In this light, Sidney's death-bed denial of his "Anacreontics," even if not historically true (the report is never directly corroborated), is nevertheless a profoundly accurate depiction of these poems' ambivalent status vis-à-vis the social, political, and personal subject position of their creator.

Notes

1. See among others Thomas Roche, Jr., "*Astrophil and Stella*: A Radical Reading," *Sir Philip Sidney: An Anthology of Modern Criticism*, ed. Dennis Kay (Oxford: Oxford Univ. Press, 1987), 196–97; Michel Poirier, *Sir Philip Sidney: Astrophel et Stella* (Paris: Aubier, 1957), 21–25; V.L. Saulnier, *Du Bellay* (Paris: Aubier Editions Montaigne, 1951), 155; Janet G. Scott, *Les Sonnets Elisabéthains* (Paris: H. Champion, 1929), 44–45; Anne Lake Prescott, *French Poets and the English Renaissance* (New Haven: Yale Univ. Press, 1978), 252, n. 38; and William A. Ringler, Jr., *The Poems of Sir Philip Sidney* (Oxford: Oxford Univ. Press, 1962), 459–61, 470, and 480. All citations of Sidney's verse will be taken from this edition. See also Richard B. Young, "English Petrarke: A Study of Sidney's *Astrophel and Stella*," *Three Studies in the Renaissance*, Yale Studies in English (New Haven: Yale Univ. Press, 1958), 7, 17, 26–27 and 41–42; Germaine Warkentin, "Sidney and the Supple Muse," in Kay, 175–76; and Robert Montgomery, *Symmetry and Sense: The Poetry of Sir Philip Sidney* (Austin: Univ. of Texas Press, 1961), 64 and 79.

2. Germaine Warkentin, "The Meeting of the Muses: Sidney and the Mid-Tudor Poets," *Sir Philip Sidney and the Interpretation of Renaissance Culture: The Poet in His Time and Ours*, ed. Gary F. Waller and Michael D. Moore (London: Croom Helm, 1984), 19–20; Robert Durling, *Petrarch's Lyric Poetry* (Cambridge, MA: Harvard Univ. Press, 1976), 9–10 and 26; Thomas M. Greene, *The Light in Troy: Imitation and Discovery in Renaissance Poetry* (New Haven: Yale Univ. Press, 1982), 124; Gary F. Waller, "The Rewriting of Petrarch: Sidney and the Languages of Sixteenth-Century Poetry," in Waller and Moore, 75; Francis Barker, *The Tremulous Private Body* (London: Methuen, 1984), 31; Janet Coleman, *Medieval Readers and Writers, 1350–1400* (New York: Columbia Univ. Press, 1981), 45; Paul Zumthor, *Essai de Poétique Médiévale* (Paris: Editions du Seuil, 1972) 37–42, 64 and 69; and H. J. Chaytor, *From Script to Print: An Introduction to Medieval Vernacular Literature* (Cambridge: Heffer's, 1945), 11, 115 and 128. This is a highly abbreviated discussion of a series of issues which I have dealt with in greater detail in my "Lyric Texts and Lyric Consciousness" (Ph.D. diss., Univ. of Texas, 1989), chapters I and 4, as well as sections 1 and 2 of chapter 6.

3. Terry Eagleton, *William Shakespeare* (London: Basil Blackwell, 1986) 22–23, 98, and 100; J. Huizinga,

The Waning of the Middle Ages (New York: St. Martin's Press, 1924), 19; Stephen Greenblatt, *Renaissance Self-Fashioning* (Chicago: Univ. of Chicago Press, 1980), 88; Barker, 10; Wayne Rebhorn, *Lions and Foxes: Machiavelli's Confidence Men* (Ithaca: Cornell Univ. Press, 1988), 26–27; Pico della Mirandola, "Oration on the Dignity of Man," *The Renaissance Philosophy of Man*, trans. Elizabeth Livermore Forbes, ed. Ernst Cassirer, Paul Oskar Kristeller, John Herman Randall, Jr., (Chicago: Univ. of Chicago Press, 1948), 217–19 and 224–25; and Juan Luis Vives, "A Fable About Man," trans. Nancy Lenkeith, in Cassirer, Kristellar and Randall, 389–90.

4. Barker, 11 and 31–32; Greenblatt, 166–67; Coleman, 48 and 62; Zumthor, 34; Huizinga, 17; Perry Anderson, *Lineages of the Absolutist State* (London: New Left Books, 1974), 19, 23, 39, and 125–26; E. M. W. Tillyard, *The Elizabethan World Picture* (New York: Vintage Books, 1959), 11–12, 63 and 88–89; Alan Sinfield, "Power and Ideology: An Outline Theory and Sidney's *Arcadia*," *Essential Articles for the Study of Sir Philip Sidney*, ed. Arthur F. Kinney (Hamden, CN: Archon Books, 1986), 394; and Lawrence Stone, *The Crisis of the Aristocracy* (London: Oxford Univ. Press, 1967), 8–11, 16–21, 37, 71, 75, 97, 117 and 131. See also Terry Eagleton's excellent observations on these phenomena in *Criticism and Ideology* (London: New Left Books 1978), 60.

5. Fulke Greville, *The Life of the Renowned Sir Philip Sidney (1652)*, intro. Warren W. Wooden (New York: Scholars' Facsimiles and Reprints, 1984), 79; A. C. Hamilton, *Sir Philip Sidney: A Study of His Life and Works* (Cambridge: Cambridge Univ. Press, 1977), 3–4; Maureen Quilligan, "Sidney and His Queen," *The Historical Renaissance*, ed. Heather Dubrow and Richard Strier (Chicago: Univ. of Chicago Press, 1988), 173–74.

6. Andrew D. Weiner, *Sir Philip Sidney and the Poetics of Protestantism* (Minneapolis: Univ. of Minnesota Press, 1978), 18–28; Alan Hager, "The Exemplary Image: Fabrication of Sir Philip Sidney's Biographical Image and the Sidney Reader," in Kay, 48–49; Greville, 25–34; Hamilton, *Sir Philip Sidney*, 19; and Ringler, xxv-vii.

7. Mona Wilson, *Sir Philip Sidney* (London: Duckworth, 1931), 17–31; Hamilton, *Sir Philip Sidney*, 1–3; Katherine Duncan-Jones, "Philip Sidney's Toys," in Kay, 62; further references are cited in the text as Duncan-Jones; Ringler, xvi; J. G. Nichols, *The Poetry of Sir Philip Sidney: An Interpretation in the Context of his Life and Times* (Liverpool: Liverpool Univ. Press, 1974), 10–11; Jan van Dorsten, "Literary Patronage in Elizabethan England: The Early Phase," *Patronage in the Renaissance*, ed. Guy Fitch Lytle and Stephen Orgel (Princeton: Princeton Univ. Press, 1981), 191–92 and 199–200; John Buxton, *Sir Philip Sidney and the English Renaissance*, 2nd ed. (London: MacMillan, 1987), 3, 29–31, 185, and 205; Sinfield, "Power and Ideology," 406; Werner L. Gundersheimer, "Patronage in the Renaissance: An Exploratory Approach," in Lytle and Orgel, 3 and 12; Arthur F. Marotti, "'Love is not Love': Elizabethan Sonnet Sequences and the Social Order," *ELH* 49 (1982): 397, 409–13, and 418; Quilligan, 182; Roche, 185; Warkentin, "Sidney and the Supple Muse," 182; and Ann Rosalind Jones and Peter Stallybrass, "The Politics of *Astrophil and Stella*," *Studies in English Literature* 24 (1984): 63–64.

8. He never published his works. The very thought would have been a profound degradation of his status. Murray Roston, *Sixteenth Century English Literature* (New York: Schocken Books, 1982), 97; Ringler, lx; Marotti, 413 and 417; Hamilton, *Sir Philip Sidney*, 3 and 28; Stone, 86–88, 249, 254 and 266; and Quilligan, 189.

9. Duncan-Jones, 62; and Hager, 49–50.

10. Sinfield, "Power and Ideology," 402; see also 404.

11. Hamilton, *Sir Philip Sidney*, 3; Sinfield, "Power and Ideology," 401–2; and Margaret W. Ferguson, *Trials of Desire: Renaissance Defenses of Poetry* (New Haven: Yale Univ. Press, 1983) 16–17, and 168.

12. Margaret McGowan, *Ideal Forms in the Age of Ronsard* (Berkeley: Univ. of California Press, 1985), 6; see also Greene, 195; Waller, "The Rewriting of Petrarch,"76, and "'This Matching of Contraries': Calvinism and Courtly Philosophy in the Sidney Psalms," in Kinney, 412; and Maurice Evans, ed., *Sir Philip Sidney: The Countess of Pembroke's Arcadia* (London: Penguin Books, 1977), 31. All further citations will be taken from this volume.

13. Julia Kristeva, *La Révolution du Langage Poétique* (Paris: Éditions du Seuil, 1974), 83–85; and Fredric Jameson, "The Ideology of the Text," *Situations of Theory*, vol. 1 of *The Ideologies of Theory*, Theory and History of Literature, vol. 48 (Minneapolis: Univ. of Minnesota Press, 1988), 20.

14. Eagleton, *Criticism and Ideology*, 19; Alan Sinfield, "The Cultural Politics of the *Defense of Poetry*," in Waller and Moore, 124, and "Power and Ideology," 394.

15. Evans, 23; Hamilton, *Sir Philip Sidney*, 117; Duncan-Jones, 62–63; and Ronald Levao, *Renaissance Minds and Their Fictions: Cusanus, Sidney, Shakespeare* (Berkeley: Univ. of California Press, 1985), 143. All citations of the *Defence* will be from Robert Kimbrough, ed., *Sir Philip Sidney: Selected Prose and Poetry* (New York: Holt, Rinehart and Winston, Inc., 1969). Page numbers will be given in the text.

16. Ferguson, 160. For a futher expansion on this same theme, see the *Arcadia*'s description of how the princes Pyrocles and Musidorus were raised with

"the delight of tales being converted to the knowledge of all the stories of worthy princes, both to move them to do nobly and teach them how to do nobly; the beauty of virtue still being set before their eyes, and that taught them with far more diligent care than grammatical rules"

(258).

See also Weiner, 47–49.

17. Greville, 19–20; see also 12–18; and Duncan-Jones, 75. On the *Arcadia*, see Hager: "It will be noted that for all his supposed political acumen, the *Arcadia* unfolds a series of sexual intrigues only occasionally relieved by 'heroic" or 'political' matter" (47).

18. Moffet quoted by Sinfield, "Power and Ideology," 402; Bruno quoted by Buxton, 163.

19. Robert Montgomery, "Astrophil's Stella and Stella's Astrophil," in Waller and Moore, 48; Ringler, xliv.

20. Paul De Man, "The Rhetoric of Blindness: Jacques Derrida's Reading of Rousseau," *Blindness and Insight: Essays in the Rhetoric of Contemporary Criticism*, Theory and History of Literature, vol. 7 (Minneapolis: Univ. of Minnesota Press, 1983), 102–3; Colin Williamson, "Structure and Syntax in Astrophil and Stella," in Kay, 242; and Marotti, 399.

21. Roche, 187–88, 193–94, 198–99 and 201. This is not the first attempt to recuperate a Christian reading from *Astrophil and Stella*; see Buxton's comments on an earlier example of this type of reading, 164. See also Levao, 180.

22. Levao, 180–81; and Nichols, 87. For Astrophil as Sidney and Stella as Penelope Rich see Nichols, 86–87; Ringler, 435–47; Roche, 194; Hamilton, *Sir Philip Sidney*, 80–81 and 194; Marotti, 401 and 403; Quilligan, 185–86; and Robert Kimbrough, *Sir Philip Sidney* (New York: Twayne, 1971), 122–23. For the puns on the name Rich, see Sonnets 24, 35, and 37. There are other less obvious candidates as well.

23. Hager, 57.

24. These are all recurrent images in Ovid. The following is a brief list of passages in which one or more of these motifs appears in either the *Amores (A)* or the *Ars Amatoria (AA)*. *A*: 1.1, 1.2, 1.3.5, 1.6.29–34 and 57–58, 1.7.35–43, 1.9, 1.11.11–12, 1.15.27–28, 2.9, 2.12, 2.18.11–12; *AA:* 2.233–38, 3.577–90. See R. O. A. M. Lyne, *The Latin Love Poets from Catullus to Horace* (Oxford: Oxford Univ. Press, 1980), 71–81, on the generality of these themes in Latin love elegy. All citations of Ovid are drawn from *P. Ovidi Nasonis Amores, Medicamina Faciei Femineae, Ars Amatoria, Remedia Amoris*, ed. E. J. Kenney (Oxford: Oxford Univ. Press, 1965). For Sidney's use of these motifs see Marion Campbell, "Unending Desire: Sidney's Reinvention of Petrarchan Form in *Astrophil and Stella,*" in Waller and Moore, 92; Waller, "The Rewriting of Petrarch," 75; Nichols, 112, 115–16 and 136; Montgomery, *Symmetry and Sense*, 101 and 118–19; Young, 88; Hamilton, *Sir Philip Sidney*, 91, 196, n. 1, and "Sidney's *Astrophel and Stella* as a Sonnet Sequence," in Kinney, 193–221; Roche, 194, 221, and 225; and Ringler, xlvi and 439–40.

25. Nichols, 17–19. For more on Sidney's sources, the topoi of love elegy and their connections with the Petrarchan tradition, see Hamilton, *Sir Philip Sidney*, 10; Warkentin, "The Meeting of the Muses," 18; Clifford Endres, *Johannes Secundus: The Latin Love Elegy in the Renaissance* (Hamden, CN: Archon Books, 1981) 71–72; Ringler, xxxv-vi; Young, 29; and Poirier, 19–20.

26. Ringler, 495.

27. Roche, 200.

28. M. M. Bakhtin, *Rabelais and His World*, trans. Hélène Iswolsky (Boston: M. I. T. Press, 1968), 18–21.

29. Campbell, 93; see also 87; Levao, 293; Montgomery, *Symmetry and Sense*, 982–99; and Hamilton, *Sir Philip Sidney*, 183–84.

30. Montgomery, *Symmetry and Sense*, 103–4; and "Astrophil's Stella and Stella's Astrophil," 46; Levao, 162.

31. Ringler, 384. There is no small irony in the fact that this is the same episode which inspires much of Petrarch's laurel imagery. See also *Amores*, 1.5:

> "When she stood before my eyes with her garment cast aside, there was no part of her entire body which needed to be changed. What shoulders, what arms I saw and touched! How apt were her breasts for squeezing! How flat was her stomach beneath her well-formed breasts! What shapely sides! How young her thigh! But why give details? I saw nothing that was not praiseworthy, and I pressed her naked body to mine. Who doesn't know the rest?"

32. See also Ringler's notes to Sonnets 72 and 74, where he notes allusions to this same passage from the *Metamorphoses*.

33. See Roche, 199–200 and 204–5, for a similar reading of song 1; see also Ringler's enigmatic note on Sonnet 77.

34. On Elizabethan poetry's widespread use of subversive punning see Quilligan, 183–85. The sexual sense of the word prick is widely attested in the 1590s and can be seen as early as 1540 (*OED*).

35. Hager, 50 and 52; Quilligan, 175; Jones and Stallybrass, 53 and 64–65; Nichols, 12; Leonard Forster, *The Icy Fire: Five Studies in European Petrarchism* (Cambridge: Cambridge Univ. Press, 1969), 127, 139 and 145; Montgomery, *Symmetry and Sense,* 57; and Marotti, 397–99. On a similar phenomenon in the *Arcadia*, see Jones and Stallybrass, 57, citing Richard C. McCoy, *Sir Philip Sidney, Rebellion in Arcadia* (New Brunswick, NJ: Rutgers Univ. Press, 1979), 73.

36. Jones and Stallybrass, 55.

37. Gordon Kipling, "Henry VII and the Origins of Tudor Patronage," in Lytle and Orgel, 151, 160–62, and 164; Hager, 48–49; Nichols, 86 and 116; see also *Arcadia*, 153–169, 234 and 247–48, inter alia.

38. Warkentin, "Sidney and the Supple Muse," 182–83.
39. Ringler, 476.
40. On the interdependence of public and private roles in *Astrophil and Stella* see Levao, 196; and Jones and Stallybrass, 54, 57, and 67.
41. There is, in fact, no exact parallel in the Greek for *Erona*, but it is clearly derived from the same root as *eros*, since it is the queen's uncontrollable sexual desire for a member of the commons which is at the origin of her many trials and tribulations. There are then two possibilities, either Sidney's Greek grammar was a bit rusty and he thought the feminine, nominative, present participle of the verb *epao* was *erona* rather than *erosa* (a reasonable assumption given that the masculine nominative is *eron* and *a* is a common feminine ending), or he simply decided for reasons of euphony that Erona was a more appropriate English name than Erosa. A third possibility would see Erona as a conflation of the Greek *eros* and the Latinate *erroneous*.
42. The term "toy" is used in Sonnet 18, line 9. I am using "supplement" here in the Derridean sense. See Jacques Derrida, *Of Grammatology*, trans. Gayatri Chakravorty Spivak (Baltimore: The Johns Hopkins Univ. Press, 1976): 144–45.

Sally Minogue (essay date 1996)

SOURCE: "A Woman's Touch: Astrophil, Stella, and 'Queen Vertue's Court,'" in *ELH: A Journal of English Literary History*, Vol. 63, No. 3, 1996, pp. 555–70.

[*In the following essay, Minogue looks at sonnets 9 and 83 from* Astrophel and Stella *and suggests a reading of them that dramatizes the relationship between Queen Elizabeth and Sidney in which there are elements of playful and not-so-playful sexual subjection.*]

When Sidney, in 1581, presented to his Queen the New Year's gift of a jewel in the shape of a diamond-bedecked whip, how did she take it? Not, we presume, lying down, since in this relationship it had already been made clear to Sidney who had the whip-hand. To be in a position to exchange New Year's gifts with the Queen was itself a mark of favor (one used by Steven May as a means of confirming who was an actual courtier to Elizabeth rather than a court hanger-on).[1] Sidney was in that position in both 1580 and 1581; but those dates punctuate a period when at least some commentators see him as having been banished from Court because of pressing too strongly the case against Elizabeth's possible marriage to Alençon.[2] Given that in 1579 John Stubbs had had his writing hand amputated for an over-fierce public attack on the Alençon suit (a medievally brutish form of retributive censorship), Sidney must have known when he was preparing the Alençon letter that his favored position was at the very least at risk, if not his own person; at that point he clearly thought the risk worth taking.[3] The long period of rustication which followed the delivery of the letter (according to most authorities, late in 1579), was perhaps signalled by his being pushed down to the very end of the New Year's gift rolls in 1580, and it evidently led him to reflect more fully on the Queen's authority.[4] Sidney's 1581 gift looks like a sign of his recognition of Elizabeth's absolute power over him, a witty, coded self-abasement, an acceptance that such power was the necessary accompaniment of a royal favor which he was pleased to have, against the odds, sustained or retrieved.[5] The teasing nature of such a gift does however imply a closeness of relationship with Elizabeth not typically attributed to Sidney; its symbolic nature is in keeping with the fashion of the time, but there is a self-conscious and personal dimension which does fit with what we know of Sidney's wit.[6] Here I shall look at two of the sonnets from ***Astrophil and Stella***, 9 and 83, and suggest a reading of them as poetic versions of the jeweled whip, dramatizing both the public monarch-courtier relationship between Elizabeth and Sidney and a possible private relationship where at least the rhetoric of sexual subjection is used at once playfully and not-so-playfully. In sonnet 9, I will suggest, Sidney prostrates himself; in sonnet 83, he gives the Queen a speaking part and foretells his own possible political fate. The diamond sparkle of his wit, somewhat darker in the second poem, does not disguise, indeed it deliberately highlights, that he is under the whip.

Of particular interest to me in these readings is that, even while they seem to fall in with some of the current patterns of Renaissance criticism, they also cut against new orthodoxies insofar as they place Elizabeth as a woman firmly at the center of Sidney's poetic practice, and they also posit a Sidney showing signs through these sonnets of the frustration which resulted from his required submissiveness, a frustration which seems to have hardened later into positive dissent. My argument is conducted in terms not of discourse, but of materiality; it is realist and empiricist; in this I seek to add my voice to those which are now beginning to question the politics of new historicism. M. D. Jardine has convincingly demonstrated the potentially politically reactionary nature of certain versions of new historicism, arguing that:

> it is now more important than ever that critics on the left argue strenuously for the presence of competing sets of values and practices, before human struggle to overthrow systems which kept them from power is removed from our record of the past.[7]

While I recognize the ironies involved in attempting to answer this call by emphasizing the radical dimension of a period of monarchy, and identifying the "human struggle to overthrow systems which kept them from power" in the sullen dissent of at least a sort of aristocrat, I nonetheless believe it important to describe and identify correctly the contributions to change made by a female sovereign on the one hand, and by the courtier-poet who had perhaps the greatest influence on the English poetic tradition on the other.

The various historical, critical, and (new and old) historical-critical accounts of Sidney's relationship with Elizabeth during the crucial period 1580–82, and of the writing (and reading) of Sidney's sonnet sequence ***Astrophil and Stella***, contain tensions, uncertainties, and flat contradictions which may be more than the product of the problematic nature of historical inquiry. Sidney's relationship with his Queen seems itself to have been shot through with like ambiguities. While some argue that Wilton was an alternative Court and center of culture, it may also be seen as his retreat in times of disfavor. Sidney may be seen as powerless except for his potential inheritances from his uncles, or as having a sense of aristocratic and cultural power and position sufficient to allow him to forfeit royal patronage in favor of being himself a patron. As far as the poems themselves were concerned, there is no clear agreement about whether ***Astrophil and Stella*** circulated amongst the Court elite, or was private to Sidney himself, and so without an audience until after his death (and so no agreement about whether Elizabeth might have read any of the sonnets, and so whether they can now be read as contemporary appeals to Elizabeth's favor). With some of these issues it is impossible to determine what was the case, though this has not stopped critics from doing so, usually without cognizance that there might be a question mark.[8] For new historicists of the post-structuralist camp, the question mark has been elevated into the signifier *sine qua non*;[9] while new historicists of the cultural materialist stamp allow a little more room for maneuver, and indeed a little more room for actual history, though for most of them the dominant ideology is still in the end dominant, leaving no real possibility of change in the existing power relations.[10]

I shall argue that, while Sidney was himself torn between various ways of seeing and presenting himself, between early 1580 and at least the end of 1581, he recognized the need for submission to the Queen before all else.[11] He spends most of 1580 at Wilton, languishing in the Queen's disfavor; in a letter to Leicester in the August of 1580 he laments his loss of voice with the Queen, while also bemoaning his poverty; he submits with the New Year's gift in 1581; around July of that year he loses the heirdom to Leicester through the birth of Leicester's direct heir; in November of that year Penelope Rich marries and Alençon arrives again to pursue his suit, linking the defeat of Sidney's personal and political hopes; arguably, in the November Accession Day tilts, he appears wearing the crossed-through SPERAVI, signalling his public awareness of his lost hopes; and finally in late 1581 he is offered the prospect of some money from Elizabeth, but through a problematic avenue, the income from the forfeited goods of Papists-and still no position. This looks, presented thus baldly, like a very public and also a very private humiliation-shortly after which he probably begins writing ***Astrophil and Stella***. The sonnets I shall examine reflect the bitternesses and tensions Sidney had experienced, but also reflect the inevitability of submission. In the light of the historical circumstances it is difficult to deny the presence of England's brightest female star behind the Stella to whom Sidney subjects himself in this sequence. Yet ultimately, the way in which he spent the last few years of his life, and the manner of his death, suggest that he kicked against the Queen's supremacy, knowingly at the cost of his ambition and, as it happened, his life. Writing was one alternative form of power for him: the courtly love format which he uses so flexibly enabled him to express the complexity of his submission to a monarch who was also a woman, and gave him the imaginative control as author to compensate for the political control he lacked as courtier. At the same time, in at least the poems I shall examine, Elizabeth is accorded her actual identity as a fleshly woman, through sometimes explicitly sexual language, and this I see as extending rather than diminishing her power.

There is ample evidence in sonnet 9 of reference to someone more powerful, and indeed richer, than the supposed model of Stella, Penelope Rich. The first and third words of the sonnet are "Queen" and "court," and they sandwich the personified "Vertue," which we can read explicitly as Elizabeth's virginity, raised into something larger than itself (as indeed by this time it was, her childbearing capacities weighing clearly upon her advisers', and others', attitudes to the proposed match with Alençon), or as a more generalized goodness or good, which here might be construed ethically or politically. Elizabeth had to be "good"; but she was also good for her country. "Which *some* call Stella's face" seems deliberately to distance the author from those "some" (suggesting he has in mind another, Elizabeth). The cold images of virginity which multiply—alabaster, pearl, marble, "without touch"—mix paradoxically with the images of elaborate riches. The gold, porphir, and "locke of pearl" are precious petrifications of parts of the body (hair, lips, teeth). The Grace which "sometimes comes forth" from the pearl-locked mouth is that all too unreliable monarch's favor. Sidney/Astrophil, for all his power as writer of these lines, is indeed a "poore I" in comparison. He is touched (emotionally, sexually, personally) by a woman, but without actually being touched; and though himself touched (affected), cannot touch back (physically, as well as in terms of influence).

If Sidney were writing only to Penelope Rich, or to some fictional Stella, or in a generalized way to a poetically conventional woman, it could be said that the element of power which the woman in the poem has over him would be outweighed both by his power as writer of the poetic fiction, and by the particular way in which in this poem the fleshliness of the woman is turned into stone and she is withdrawn even from the humanizing power of touch. One is reminded of Midas. But if it is Elizabeth who is addressed here, it is Astrophil who is petrified rather than Stella. The valuable metal and stone cease to be emblems; they are rather the natural accoutrements of a female monarch. That is not to say that they are not also used emblematically; but they are used by Sidney with a nice sense of the ironic interplay between what they actually are and what, poetically and politically, they represent. The alabaster, gold, prophyry and marble might be the materials which actually *are* part of "Queen Vertue's court," with her privy chamber locked away behind those rich, promising porches, impenetrable except to her favorites. She can look out of its windows, but they may not look in, without her permission. There are a number of interesting references to windows in the documentary evidence surrounding Elizabeth; certainly Essex's 1591 letter to Elizabeth comes to mind, where he says that "no cause but a great action of your own may draw me out of your sight, for the two windows of your privy chamber shall be the poles of my sphere".[12]

Immediately one sees the sexual reading available here, as one can also in sonnet 9; both are made possible only because Elizabeth was a woman, and moreover one who used her sexual powers as part of her royal ones. But the sexual reading is interdependent with that in which access to the royal person means power, and where denial of that access renders the supplicant powerless. Essex is at the time of writing still in favor, indeed in touch; but even so his letter goes on to imagine a time when favor might be denied, and to predict his unwavering, indeed requisite, subjection in such a case. Sidney does not need to imagine it: the queen "without touch doth touch".

That Sidney's is the first sonnet sequence in English is often remarked, as is its influence, post-publication, on English poetry. The connection of such love poetry with political patronage is now seen as almost as well established, to the point where we are asked to recognize that "'love is not love'" in Elizabethan "love" poetry.[13] Elizabeth's profound influence on court culture goes without saying. There are a number of interpretations of Sidney's sonnets which put these factors together and offer "patronage" readings of the poems, or of the sequence as a whole. But I want to suggest that sonnet 9 is not just a patronage—or more properly, clientage—poem, it is also, and first, a love poem. For if love is not love in such poems, what is? Patronage readings such as Marotti's, and John Barrell's of Shakespeare's sonnets, attempt, as they would have it, to foreground a particular sense of "love" and to thereby privilege a political reading; but in their actual practice they render the foregrounded reading as somehow free-floating, disconnected from what would once have been called the primary sense and reading.[14] Yet the very notion of foregrounding or privileging a sense depends on some concept of hierarchy in the first place, a hierarchy thus being displaced. Indeed Barrell makes this clear:

> I have tried to defamiliarise the word—to specify out of all of its possible and various and compound meanings one which most clearly represents it as a part of the discourse of patronage, and most clearly removes it from the meanings we most readily attach to the word today.[15]

"Defamiliarise" and "the meanings we most readily attach" clearly suggest a commonly recognized primary meaning, though of course Barrell would argue that this is historically and culturally specific. But can we really be so confident that there was no similar sense of "love" in the sixteenth century? Is it not the case that the coded client/patron appeals are dependent on a prior understanding of the common use of the word "love"? If Marotti, Barrell, and many others who take the same critical line, are suggesting that sixteenth-century readers, unlike late twentieth-century readers (excluding literary critics), of these poems would see the patronage reading as primary, on the surface of the poem, then any notion of a code disappears. If we preserve the notion of a code-one which seems to be inherent in discussions of Renaissance culture, old and new historicist alike-then we have to see the metaphorical or hidden sense of the poem, and of the word "love," as dependent upon a prior sense.[16]

What that sense is I and all my contemporary readers are familiar with; Sidney also seems to have been familiar with it, when he remarks disparagingly of English "love" poetry:

> But truly many of such writings as come under the banner of unresistible love, if I were a mistress, would never persuade me they were in love: so coldly they apply fiery speeches.[17]

As this makes clear, the rhetoric of love was no guarantee of the actuality or the sincerity of the emotion; but that it was that emotion which was in question does not itself seem to be questioned by Sidney here. Jonathan Crewe reads Marotti as seeing the code of love rhetoric as being a sort of Elizabethan courtier back-slang, but back-slang is itself dependent on awareness of generally accepted meanings, since it works by reversing them.[18] With a word as important and extensive in its senses as "love," it looks as though even those in on the code might—indeed must—have sustained some usage of the word "love" in its non-patronage sense.[19]

The interpretation of the import of the word "love" in Elizabethan poetry is made less rather than more complicated by the fact that the chief patron of the period was a woman. Marotti recognizes early in his argument that Elizabeth's unmarried state, and therefore, *a fortiori*, her being biologically a woman, "preserved her symbolic *and real* value in both domestic and international transactions."[20] However, he is reluctant to see the amorous language "specifically encouraged" by her in her courtiers' addresses to her as anything other than a metaphorizing of "ambition and vicissitudes."[21] Yet we know that Elizabeth numbered amongst those courtiers a succession of men, ambiguously termed her "favorites", whose relations with her are marked by an intimacy of access and of language. Is there no distinction between the amorous language they use, and that used as a formal code? Marotti appears to think not, since he cites Essex's vocabulary in that mode as showing that "he utilized the same politically-invested language of love" as Sir Christopher Hatton's.[22] Yet Marotti pours contempt on Hatton's fulsome writing to her "in the idiom of a Petrarchan lover separated from his mistress," suggesting that his are "fanciful words for an astute politician."[23] Well, if Marotti is right, they are far from fanciful if what they actually express is encoded ambition; but Marotti's own words here give the lie to his thesis for his seeing Hatton's Petrarchan rhetoric as fanciful shows that the rhetoric at least depends on a prior reading, of love as—well, love. Marotti's apparent embarrassment arises from words which, even if they are metaphorical, still inescapably hold their primary meaning. And his embarrassment, echoed elsewhere in various historians' and critics' patent discomfort at the thought of an ageing Elizabeth flirting, if even in a coded way, with her young men, betrays an anxiety about seeing Elizabeth as a sexual being at all. Wallace MacCaffrey, for example, nudges coyly:

> On the lips of Dudley and Hatton, contemporaries of the queen, the language of knightly homage, the conventional praise of feminine beauty, tripped forth lightly, but when the devotee was a young man of twenty and the lady had rounded fifty, the fiction was harder to sustain.[24]

Crewe, writing from a very different perspective, and trying to hide his prejudices behind an arch knowingness, nonetheless falls into the same stereotyping, sympathizing with "the painful indecorum of [Sidney's] having to court, for obviously political reasons, an ugly old rich woman, becoming the Miss Havisham of the English world by the 1580s."[25] MacCaffrey's very recent account doesn't even allow Elizabeth a personal response from her equals in age; and neither male interpreter can stomach the possibility that a younger man could have feelings towards a considerably older woman which were other than self-interested.

The haste to read the amorous addresses to Elizabeth as expressive of *exclusively* political desire effectively robs her of her power as a woman. Not surprisingly it has taken a woman, Philippa Berry, to show the process whereby Renaissance scholars were able

> to displace the fundamental problem of the queen's gender. Perceived as both more and less than a woman, because a woman supposedly purged of sexual desire, she is either asserted or implied to reinforce rather than disturb the political and religious hierarchies of the patriarchy.[26]

Berry is arguing from a feminist perspective, and her interest at this stage of her argument is in revealing the way in which Elizabeth's relations with other women have thus been left out of account by Renaissance scholarship; but her closely argued view that Elizabeth's presence on the English throne "was a radical event" also allows us the freedom to give Elizabeth's sexuality a key place in her monarchy.[27] This in no way, in my view, weakens her power and its radical nature, but rather adds to those. It is quite evident from the length and nature of Elizabeth's reign, and in particular her manipulation of her (supposed) chastity, that she used, and was not used by, her sexual powers as part of her political powers. But to argue therefore that her sexual feelings and the sexual feelings of others about her never themselves came into play is reductive and unrealistic.

Elizabeth's own writings are inevitably short of evidence on this matter; she was an ever-cautious monarch. The tender intimacy of address which marks her correspondence with those she favored has an air of vulnerability which perhaps derives from its very disparity with her position, but it is counter-balanced by her fury when she was displeased. The only work we have of hers which seems to speak imaginatively of love is "I grieve and dare not show my discontent," generally seen as expressing her state of conflict on the failure of the Alençon suit.[28] Though it draws on some of the standard images and paradoxes of the love poetry of the time, it is impressive in its honesty in declaring feelings intended to be hidden by a public behavior that is itself revealed as a sham in the poem. There is a rhythmic shift in the second stanza, where the second and fourth lines adopt an eleventh syllable to produce an ending which in these circumstances of authorship it is perhaps not derogatory to call feminine. The unsettling produced by this small shift (regularity is restored in the final stanza) and the desire for an improbable escape from the ever-present "care" expressed in the wistful "Some gentler passion slide into my mind" again suggest a vulnerability which is particularly moving given the authorship. Since Elizabeth precisely addresses the conflict between personal feeling and public behavior here, her use of "love" would seem to be apolitical, since it is contrasted with "seem to hate," the latter which she is "forced" to do by the needs of the political situation. (The suggestion that the poem was actually addressed to the errant Essex would carry the same reading, though in that case the grief would seem more personal and more credible.)[29]

But if Elizabeth herself is unable to be more explicit than this rather generalized poem about her personal emotions and desires (and the frankness is even so such that it is difficult to imagine what, if any, audience she had in mind, other than herself), those who addressed her, in however coded a form, could be very explicit. If we accept the possibility that the Queen might have been central to Sidney's imagination when he composed some of the ***Astrophil and Stella*** sonnets (as Marotti's argument entails, and which Crewe sees almost as an old hat cover story to protect the real imaginative inspiration of the poems, Sidney's sister Mary Herbert), those poems which admit of a clearly sexual reading, among others, are particularly interesting.[30] Firstly, they show that at least the erotic sense of "love" is in play as well as a politically metaphorizing sense of it, and that therefore that sense of "love" can co-exist with its own metaphor. Such a double reading is hardly surprising in Renaissance poetry (and certainly not in Sidney's poetry, which yields many examples of what Daniel Traister calls his "ambidexterity"), yet it is one which those who want to insist that "love is not love" want to deny.[31] Secondly, these poems specifically associate this eroticism with Elizabeth in a way that is not just "ostensible" (Marotti's word) or "hollow" (Crewe in summarizing Marotti and other new historicists).[32] To return to sonnet 9, and to the word "touch"; it is used four times, three of them in the same line, as though the repetitions of the word could replace the missing actuality. From the myriad senses of "touch" available to Sidney, "magnet" is that most often used in the reading of his complex metaphor; but it seems more likely that he is referring to touchpowder, with himself as the straw about to be ignited. This reading fits with the use of "touch" as a euphemism for sexual contact, and accords with the excitability of the writing in the latter part of the poem.[33] It would be in keeping with the highly paradoxical nature of the whole poem and of the image of the woman's blowing both hot and cold that the sense of "touch" as touchstone, index of value, both materially and morally, is invoked. Does not this mixture of apparently contradictory meanings exactly fit the Elizabeth who drew suitors and favorites with the promise of her chastity (the promise being that they would be victorious over it) and kept them desiring while she remained desirable? There is of course a bitter side to such a relationship, and that is hinted at but not fully expressed in the self-denigrating images ("nothing such," "poore I," "straw"); and it is difficult not to be reminded of Freud's toothed vagina in the image of the door of red porphyry which is locked with pearl. But the somewhat unpleasant combination of sensuality and petrification, the sense of inflamedness with no mutual conflagration, is perhaps retrieved by the author's complete obeisance in the poem. He admires, desires, accepts; for it is the "Queene" who is at the head of the poem, and he, the "straw," at its, and her, foot.

If we move to sonnet 83 we see Sidney's bitterness much more fully in play—and as many commentators have noted, Sidney tends to "play" when he is most serious. Sonnet 83 has received relatively little attention, and where it has, the notion that the poem is addressed to Penelope Rich's sparrow "Philip" seems to be generally accepted. In fact much more noticeable is the self-referential element involved through the use of the name "Philip" and the playful diminutive "Sir Phip."[34] As soon as one sees the poem as therefore an address to the self, either from the self, or in the persona and voice of another, it becomes extremely interesting. For here the author's view of himself is overt, in a way seldom allowed in this most layered of sonnet sequences. In a letter to his uncle Leicester in 1580, during the period of his rustication, Sidney comments bitterly on the fact that if he returns to court, necessarily therefore in finery, the queen will assume from his silk doublet that all is well with him; he argues that anyway he has a cold and has lost his voice, "which is the only cawse keeps me from court since my only service is speech and that is stopped."[35] I am not the only one to see the double meanings here; but while Sidney was then writing in a position where he may still have had hope of regaining his queen's favor, as he seems wholeheartedly to have set out to do in his ironic submissiveness from the beginning to the end of 1581, sonnet 83 is likely to have been written from a position of hopelessness. The stopping of speech is here envisaged both in the comparing himself to a dumb creature, the sparrow, and in, finally, the threat of his neck being wrung. The sexual echoes of "billing" and indeed of "speech" itself reverberate here. My suggestion is that here Sidney is dramatizing Elizabeth's role in the sequence and in his own life by allowing her characteristic voice and view to speak in the poem. Sidney above all others would enjoy the irony of controlling the speech of his sovereign, at the very point when his voice can least be heard. The control is entirely literary—even to the point of again placing himself as the victim at the end of the poem, but here a victim not just of desire but of that final power of the monarch, the power of life and death.

A sort of ghastly wit pervades the poem, accompanying a sense of threat. One has encountered that sense of threat before, in Elizabeth's poems and letters, just as one has encountered those sometimes sinisterly playful *tendresses* and diminutives. It is impossible to establish Sidney's direct knowledge of those texts, but it is certain that he was fully acquainted with Elizabeth's style. The familiarity of "Good brother Philip" and "sir Phip" recalls "My Wat" of Elizabeth's "Ah silly pug" (which phrase itself finds an echo in "your silly selfe" in sonnet 83), and the tone of both poems is remarkably similar, characterized most clearly by affectionate impatience. (Accepting that May is right in pinning Elizabeth's poem to Ralegh to 1587, I am not attributing a direct influence, but noting the similarity of tone and language which suggests Sidney's knowledge of Elizabeth and ability to coin her style.)[36] Sidney's poem has the sharper edge, however; while Elizabeth's is offering reassurance after a quarrel, sonnet 83 promises a quick despatch after a period of indulgence. The final line of both poems recalls a much earlier poem of Elizabeth's, "The doubt of future foes," where, after expressing uncertainty and vulnerability of the same kind, and in the same formal antitheses, as found in "On Monsieur's Departure," she issues a clear and shockingly graphic warning to her enemies in the final couplet:

> Our rusty sword with rest, shall first his edge employ
> To poll their tops that seek such change and gape for joy.[37]

The crudity of "poll their tops" (the words and the threat) and the horrid ambiguity of "gape for joy" (which suggests the foolish gaping to a future different from that provided by Elizabeth, equivalent to the physical gaping of the mouth in the polled head) leave us in no doubt about the monarch's acceptance of necessary responsibility in executing her enemies where necessary. We are reminded of the bloody retribution to Stubbs. Sidney needed no reminding, and his sonnet 83 seems to reflect literarily what he might have feared his fate to be literally. Perhaps the setting it down in words might have absolved him of his fear; and perhaps he was aware of Elizabeth's view, explicit in the poem to Ralegh, "The less afraid the better shalt thou speed."

It is interesting to consider the possibility that Elizabeth read sonnet 83, and that Sidney wrote it knowing she might read it. If so, it is a daring expression of knowledge of the sovereign, while remaining a document of utter submission in its self-knowledge and its awareness of impotence. Add to this the erotic dimension of the poem (fully explicated by Traister who takes the "sparrow" reading) and it strikes as an act at once of arrogant folly and of self-abasement. If we do/can read the poem as expressing Elizabeth's view (filtered through Sidney's) of her relations with the courtier-poet, even as it wields a monarch's power ("Lest off your neck be wrung") it also suggests at least a period of remarkable indulgence. The octet refers to a period of considerable intimacy ("I was content you should in favor creep") dependent on the author's recognition of his position ("While craftily you seemed your cut to keepe"); there is even the suggestion of sexual intimacy ("oft suffered you to sleep In Lilies' nest, where love's self lies along"—and "love" here can be taken in both ways, sexual and political). But the sestet, following the convention, signals an abrupt change of tone: "What, doth high place ambitious thoughts augment? Is sawcinesse reward of curtesie?". Elizabeth was notoriously furious with those who overstepped the bounds of their favor; and this might be a direct reference to Sidney's injudicious letter advising avoidance of the marriage to Alençon. True impatience cuts through in "Cannot such grace your silly selfe content, But you must needs with those lips billing be?" This is the tone of one who knows the value of "grace" to one who is still caught up with "billing." Of course, all billing would cease, sexual, poetic, political, or otherwise, if the threat of the final line were carried out.

In mid-1581, the birth of a baby ended at least part of Sidney's aristocratic hopes, and later that year Alençon was back in England, his suit still encouraged by Elizabeth. Both events must have underlined Sidney's sense of his own impotence, where once he had promised to be so potent. His humiliation, partly at his own hands, culminated in December 1581 with his havering over accepting monies from the Queen (which he had begged) issuing from the revenues of the forfeited estates of recusant Catholics. Conscience, poverty and self-aggrandizement jostle on the page, and these letters do not make entirely comfortable reading.[38] Yet in 1582 Sidney was at work on a different sort of writing, cheerfully dramatizing pursuit and self-abasement in ***Astrophil and Stella***. Sonnet 83 can be seen as the literary equivalent of Sidney's appearing, perhaps at the 1581 November Accession Day tilts, with his insignia SPERAVI crossed through.[39] That public and theatrical self-irony, probably in front of Alençon, whose presence would further underscore his crossed-through hopes, personal and political, somehow turned a humiliation into a victory. ***Astrophil and Stella*** seems to me to do the same, telling a story of vicissitude and despair with a wit and poetic bravado which have given it a lasting glamor. That the fate Sidney made for himself, turning away from a slow death by submission to what no doubt seemed an endless one by septicaemia, was translated from its squalid reality into a glorious story is a final, literary, irony he would have, grimly, enjoyed. But his touchy Queen had the last political word, delaying his grandiose funeral to a time when it suited her (to distract the public from the execution of Mary Queen of Scots)—and then refusing to pay the expenses. In the meantime, ***Astrophil and Stella*** retains *its* power as a canonized work, but one which is falsified if we do not see the breadth and complication of Sidney's relationship with Elizabeth as reflected in it. That Elizabeth was a source—*the* source—of cash and status is part of his poetic self-abasement, as I have tried to argue in the discussion of sonnet 9; but the sense of his personal engagement with his feelings about her, and of his submissiveness to her, are most clearly expressed in the sexual dimension of the sequence, as I have argued in discussing sonnet 83. Anger about both is central to the passion of the sequence.

To argue that "love is not love" in Elizabethan sonnet sequences, and specifically in Sidney's, is to deny the power of Elizabeth's being a woman, and thus the radical nature of her period of power. It is also to deny her influence *as a woman* on some of the major literary productions of the era. Finally it is to deny Sidney his many-levelled self-awareness in at least some poems in the sequence. The best we can do as critics and as readers of history is to see the complex picture as fully as possible, given that we cannot possibly recoup a full understanding of what the contemporary history of Sidney and Elizabeth was. To insist that "love is not love" is to falsify that complexity, just as surely as it would be to insist that love is *only* love; it is one of the powers of literary production that, in the case of ***Astrophil and Stella***, both may be true.

Notes

1. Steven May, *The Elizabethan Courtier Poets: The Poems and Their Contexts* (Columbia: Univ. of Missouri Press, 1991), 22. May uses presence on the New Year gift rolls as a necessary rather than a sufficient condition for courtier status.
2. Dorothy Connell, *Sir Philip Sidney: The Maker's Mind* (Oxford: Clarendon Press, 1977), 107; F. J. Levy, "Sidney Reconsidered," in *Essential Articles for the Study of Sir Philip Sidney*, ed. Arthur F. Kinney (Hamden, CT: Shoe String Press, 1986), 5; for a counter-view see May, 98.
3. On Stubbs, see *John Stubbs's "Gaping Gulf" with Letters and Other Relevant Documents*, ed. Lloyd E. Berry (Charlottesville: Univ. Press of Virginia, 1968).
4. Katherine Duncan-Jones interprets this push to the end of the gift rolls as a possible sign of disapproval, *Sir Philip Sidney* (London: Penguin, 1991), 169, quoting *Progresses of Queen Elizabeth*, ed. J. G. Nichols, 1823.
5. William Ringler interprets it as signalling submission specifically over the Alençon suit (*The Poems of Sir Philip Sidney*, ed. William A. Ringler Jr. [Oxford: Clarendon Press, 1962], 440). Duncan-Jones interprets it as a sign of a more extensive submission, as I do, and she provides convincing evidence of this, 192–93. Neither commentator sees the more intimate, perhaps sexual, element in the representative gift which I am here suggesting. All references to *Astrophil and Stella* are from Ringler's edition.
6. See Alan Hager, "The Exemplary Mirage: Fabrication of Sir Philip Sidney's Biographical Image and

the Sidney Reader," in Kinney, especially 23–24, for an interesting analysis of Sidney's "reflexive irony." See also Duncan-Jones's description of "his readiness to quip even in the most stressful circumstances" (290).

7. M. D. Jardine, "New Historicism for Old: New Conservatism for Old?: The Politics of Patronage in the Renaissance," *The Yearbook of English Studies* 21(1991), 293–94.

8. Even the question of circulation, which might seem to be answerable by reference to historical record, attracts contradictory, confident, assertions. See Ringler, and May who follows him, for the view that the sonnets were entirely private to Sidney; most other critics adopt the generalized view of a small elite manuscript circulation. Others again would see the question as irrelevant. There is no direct evidence of circulation prior to the 1591 publication.

9. For example, Gary F. Waller, "The Rewriting of Petrarch: Sidney and the Languages of Sixteenth-Century Poetry," in *Sir Philip Sidney and the Interpretation of Renaissance Culture*, ed. Gary F. Waller and Michael D. Moore (London: Croom Helm, 1984).

10. For example, Laura Stevenson, *Praise and Paradox: Merchants and Craftsmen in Elizabethan Popular Literature* (Cambridge: Cambridge Univ. Press, 1984).

11. Levy provides a persuasive account of Sidney as torn between allegiance to God and allegiance to the Queen.

12. *Lives and Letters of the Devereux*, ed. Walter B. Devereux, 2 vols. (London: John Murray, 1857), 1:249–50.

13. Arthur Marotti, "'Love is not Love': Elizabethan Sonnet Sequences and the Social Order," *ELH* 49 (1982): 396–428.

14. John Barrell, *Poetry, Language and Politics* (Manchester: Manchester Univ. Press, 1988), 18–43.

15. Barrell, 23–24.

16. See Jonathan Crewe, *Hidden Designs: The Critical Profession and Renaissance Literature* (London: Methuen, 1986), 76–88, for an interesting and amusing discussion of the levels of "encryptment" in Sidney's sonnets.

17. From *The Defence of Poesy*, in *Miscellaneous Prose of Sir Philip Sidney*, ed. Katherine Duncan-Jones and J. van Dorsten (Oxford: Oxford Univ. Press, 1973), 117.

18. Crewe, 76.

19. See Quentin Skinner, "Meaning and Understanding in the History of Ideas," *History and Theory* 8 (1969): 3–53, for an authoritative account of the falsifications produced in the historical analysis of texts by anachronistically attributing concepts to authors; ironically, the new historicists who started out by issuing similar caveats have ended by falling into the very trap they warned against. Skinner places a premium on establishing authorial intention, whilst reminding us of the problems involved in doing so. David Norbrook, *Poetry and Politics in the English Renaissance* (London: Routledge and Kegan Paul, 1984), notes the reluctance of materialist and post-structuralist critics to acknowledge any role for intention, and warns that "to ignore the intention is effectively to depoliticise" (8).

20. Marotti, 398; italics in original.

21. ———, 398.

22. ———, 398.

23. ———, 398, 399.

24. Wallace MacCaffrey, *Elizabeth I* (London: Edward Arnold, 1993), 396.

25. Crewe, 80.

26. Philippa Berry, *Of Chastity and Power: Elizabethan Literature and the Unmarried Queen* (London: Routledge, 1989), 65.

27. Berry, 61.

28. In *Elizabeth I*, ed. Lacey Baldwin Smith (St. Louis: Forum Press, 1980), 57–58.

29. Suggested in a footnote to the poem, *The Norton Anthology of English Literature*, 6th edition, ed. M. H. Abrams, 2 vols. (London: Norton, 1993), 1:998.

30. Alan Sinfield, "Sexual Puns in *Astrophil and Stella*," *Essays in Criticism* 24 (1974), has argued convincingly for the presence of sexual puns throughout Sideny's sonnet sequence, and notes that "sexual *double entendre* is an important feature of Sidney's verbal skill" (6).

31. Daniel Traister, "Sidney's Purposeful Humor: *Astrophil and Stella* 59 and 83," *ELH* 49 (1982), 751.

32. Marotti, 406; Crewe, 75.

33. Sinfield notes this euphemistic reading, 346–47.

34. Duncan-Jones mentions this self-referential reading, 242.

35. *The Prose Works of Sir Philip Sidney*, ed. Albert Feuillerat, 4 vols. (Cambridge: Cambridge Univ. Press, 1962), 3:129.

36. For the text of Elizabeth's poem and May's dating discussion see May, 317–19.

37. *The New Oxford Book of Sixteenth Century Verse*, ed. Emrys Jones (Oxford: Oxford Univ. Press, 1991), 183–84.

38. See especially the letters of December, 1581, to Sir Christopher Hatton and to the Earl of Leicester respectively, in Feuillerat, 139 and 140.

39. Duncan-Jones argues effectively for this date, though she also mentions counter-arguments, 194–95 and 218.

FURTHER READING

Bibliography

Stump. Donald, Jerome Dee, and C. Stuart Hunter. *Sir Philip Sidney: An Annotated Bibliography of Texts and Criticism, (1554–1984).* New York: G. K. Hall, 1994, 834 pp.

Comprehensive bibliography detailing editions and translations of Sidney's work as well as secondary sources and other works pertaining to Sidney.

Biographies

Hamilton, A. C. *Sir Philip Sidney: A Study of His Life and Works*. Cambridge, England: Cambridge University Press, 1977, 224 pp.

Comprehensive study of Sidney relating his literary works to his life and the age in which he lived.

Howell, Roger. *Sir Philip Sidney: The Shepherd Knight*. Boston: Little, Brown & Co., 1968, 317 pp.

Popular biography that places Sidney in his historical-political context.

Kimbrough, Robert. *Sir Philip Sidney*. New York: Twayne Publishers, 1971, 162 pp.

Introductory study of Sidney's life and works.

Criticism

Brooks, Cleanth and Robert Penn Warren. *Understanding Poetry: An Anthology for College Students*. New York: Henry Holt & Co., 1938, 341–45.

Offers a discussion of the poem "Ring out your belles" as an example of a litany.

Cooper, Sherod M., Jr. *The Sonnets of Astrophel and Stella: A Stylistic Study*. The Hague and Paris: Mouton, 1968, 183 pp.

Comprehensive study of Sidney's sonnet sequence, concluding that Sidney used elements of English and French poetic traditions to shape his masterpiece.

Farby, Frank. "Sidney's Poetry and Italian Song-Form." *Sir Philip Sidney: A Study of His Life and Works*. Cambridge, England: Cambridge University Press, 1977, 224 pp.

Discusses the influence of Italian song forms on Sidney's use of rhyme.

Friedrich, Walter George. "The Stella of Astrophel." In *English Literary History* Vol. 3 (June 1936): 114–39.

Seeks to prove that the poems do not indicate an affair between Sidney and Lady Rich.

Galm, John Arnold. *Sidney's Arcadian Poems*. Salzburg: Institut für Englische Sprache und Literatur, Universität Salzburg, 1973, 229 pp.

Compares Sidney's poetry in *Arcadia* to that of Sannazaro, Montemayor, and Gascoigne.

Gibson, Wendy. "Sidney's Two Riddles." *Notes and Queries* Vol. 24 (December 1977): 520–21.

Concludes that "a pregnant woman" is the answer to the two riddles Sidney puts forth in his poem "And are you there old Pas?"

Hamilton, A. C. "The 'mine of time': Time and Love in Sidney's *Astrophel and Stella*." *Mosaic* Vol. 13, No. 1 (1979): 81–91.

Argues that the Petrarchan theme of "time and love" is not a major motif in the poems.

Jones, Ann Rosalind and Peter Stallybrass. "The Politics of *Astrophil and Stella*." *Studies in English Literature, 1500–1900* Vol. 24, Winter 1984, 53–68.

Suggests that the poems "function as a complex displacement of the ideological pressures of the court."

Kalstone, David. *Sidney's Poetry: Contexts and Interpretations*. Cambridge, Mass.: Harvard University Press, 1965, 203 pp.

Detailed study of the poetry stressing its intellectual context and noting Sidney's indebtedness to the Italian poets Petrarca and Sannazarro.

——— "Sir Philip Sidney and 'Poore *Petrarchs* Long Deceased Woes.'" *Journal of English and Germanic Philology* Vol. 63 (January 1964): 21–32.

Sees Sidney's work as a prologue to the poetry of William Shakespeare and John Donne.

Levy, Charles Samuel. "Sidneian Indirection: The Ethical Irony of *Astrophil and Stella*." *Sir Philip Sidney and the Interpretation of Renaissance Culture: The Poet in His Time and in Ours: A Collection of Critical and Scholarly Essays*, edited by Gary F. Waller and Michael D. Moore. Totowa, N.J.: Barnes & Noble, 1984, 55–56.

From "the perspective afforded by feminist criticism," contends that Astrophil "fails systematically to take Stella seriously as a moral and emotional being."

Montgomery, Robert Langford. *Symmetry and Sense: The Poetry of Sir Philip Sidney*. Austin, Tex.: University of Texas Press, 1961, 141 pp.

Seeks to locate and describe the ornate and plain styles in Sidney's poems and to suggest where each begins and ends.

Montrose, Louis Adrian. "Celebration and Insinuation: Sir Philip Sidney and the Motives of Elizabethan Courtship." *Renaissance Drama* Vol. 8 (1977): 3–35.

Reading of *The Lady of May* as Sidney's political message to Elizabeth about his role as a courtier-statesman.

Nichols, John Gordon. *The Poetry of Sir Philip Sidney: An Interpretation in the Context of His Life and Times*. Liverpool, England: Liverpool University Press, 1974, 181 pp.

Explores Sidney's life and work in its historical context, concentrating on *Astrophel and Stella* and touching on the *Arcadia* and *Certain Sonnets*.

Pettet, E. C. "Sidney and the Cult of Romantic Love." *English* Vol. 6, Summer 1947, 232–40.
Notes similarities and differences between Sidney's work and that of Chaucer and those in the romantic tradition of the medieval period.

Quitslund, Jon A. "Sidney's Presence in Lyric Verse of the Later English Renaissance." *Sir Philip Sidney and the Interpretation of Renaissance Culture: The Poet in His Time and In Ours: A Collection of Critical and Scholarly Essays*, edited by Gary F. Waller and Michael D. Moore. Totowa, N.J.: Barnes & Noble, 1984, 110–23.
Compares the influence of Sidney's poetry on writers such as Greville, Donne, Shakespeare, and Herbert.

Roche, Thomas P., Jr. "*Astrophil and Stella*: A Radical Reading." *Spenser Studies* Vol. 3 (1982): 139–9.
See Astrophil as an obsessive and selfish lover, not as the heroic figure of so many critical studies.

Rudenstine, Neil L. *Sidney's Poetic Development*. Cambridge, Mass.: Harvard University Press, 1967, 115–30; 277–83.
Views the poems in *Certain Sonnets* as a unified whole containing all the essential elements for poetry of serious love, including plot, varied moods and tones, and a controlling poetic voice.

Sinfield, Alan. "Astrophil's Self-Deception." *Essays in Criticism* Vol. 28 (January 1978): 1–18.
Argues that Sidney has the reader identifying with Astrophil while recognizing that his most basic flaw is his own self-deception.

Stillman, Robert E. "Poetry and Justice in Sidney's 'Ye goat-herd gods.'" *Studies in English Literature, 1500–1900* Vol. 22 (Winter 1982): 39–50.
Uncovers Sidney's sources for the poem and claims the work is meant to "reconcile the two most important trends in the history of pastoral romance."

Stratton, Clarence. "The Italian Lyrics of Sidney's *Arcadia*." *Sewanee Review* Vol. 25 (July 1917): 305–26.
Examines Sidney's masterful use of variety of Italian verse forms.

Thompson, John. "Sir Philip and the Forsaken Lamb." In *The Founding of English Metre*. New York: Columbia University Press, 1961, 139–55.
Claims that in Sidney's poetry "the metrical system of modern English reaches perfection for the first time."

Young, Richard B. "English Petrarke: A Study of Sidney's *Astrophel and Stella*." *Three Studies in the Renaissance: Sidney, Jonson, Milton*. Yale Studies in English, 138. New Haven, Conn.: Yale University Press, 1958, 1–88.
Argues that the structure of the work is one of "analysis and synthesis," and that its subject matter is the Petrarchan convention.

Additional coverage of Sidney's life and career is contained in the following sources published by the Gale Group: *Concise Dictionary of British Literary Biography Before 1660; Dictionary of Literary Biography* Vol. 167; *DISCovering Authors; DISCovering Authors: British; DISCovering Authors: Canadian;* and *DISCovering Authors Modules: Most-studied Authors* and *Poets*.

Paul Verlaine
1844-1896

(Full name Paul Marie Verlaine; also wrote under the pseudonym Pablo de Herlagñez) French poet, essayist, autobiographer, and short-story writer. For further discussion of Verlaine's career, see *PC*, Vol. 2.

INTRODUCTION

The following entry presents criticism of Verlaine from 1971 to 1998. For further information on Verlaine's poetry, see *PC*, Vol. 2.

Admired for the fluidity and impressionistic imagery of his verse, Verlaine succeeded in liberating the musicality of the French language from the restrictions of its classical, formal structure. Influenced by the French painter Antoine Watteau, Verlaine was fascinated by the visual aspects of form and color and attempted to capture in his poems the symbolic elements of language by transposing emotion into subtle suggestions. As a member of the French Symbolists, who believed that the function of poetry was to evoke and not to describe, Verlaine created poetry that was both aesthetic and intuitive. Although his verse has often been overshadowed by his scandalous bohemian lifestyle, Verlaine's literary achievement was integral to the development of French poetry.

BIOGRAPHICAL INFORMATION

Born in Metz, France, to deeply religious middle-class parents, Verlaine spent his youth in a guarded and conventional atmosphere until he became a student at the Lycée Bonaparte (now Condorcet). While he never excelled in his studies, Verlaine did enjoy some success in rhetoric and Latin. But despite winning a number of prizes in these areas, Verlaine was not a respected student, and he barely managed to obtain the baccalaureate. Upon graduation Verlaine enrolled in law school, but because of his heavy drinking and patronage of prostitutes he was quickly withdrawn from his academic pursuits. His father was able to secure a clerical position for him at a local insurance company, a position that allowed him time to frequent the Café du Gaz, then the rendezvous of the literary and artistic community, and to develop his literary talents. Around 1866, Verlaine began to associate with a group of young poets known as La Parnasse, or the Parnassians, which had adopted the doctrine of "art for art's sake." While Verlaine's poetic style was taking shape and setting precedents, his personal life was slowly dissipating due to his increasing consumption of absinthe, a liqueur flavored with wormwood. Despite his growing addiction and sometimes violent temperament, Verlaine's family encouraged him to marry, believing it could stabilize his raucous life. Verlaine sought out a young girl, Mathilde Mauté, who was sixteen in 1869, the year of their engagement. In 1871 Verlaine received a letter from a young poet named Arthur Rimbaud. Verlaine urged Rimbaud, a precocious and unpredictable seventeen-year-old genius, to visit him in Paris. Verlaine abandoned his wife, home, and employment to travel throughout Europe with Rimbaud. Their journey was punctuated by drunken quarrels, until Verlaine shot and wounded Rimbaud during an argument in 1873. Verlaine was arrested and sentenced to serve two years at Mons, a Belgian prison. While in prison, Verlaine turned from atheism to a fervent acceptance of the Roman Catholic faith in which he had been raised, which influenced much of his poetry of that period. After his release from Mons, Verlaine traveled to England to become a teacher of French, Latin, and drawing. In 1878 Verlaine moved to Ardennes, France, with one of his former students, Lucien Létinois, whom he called his *fils adoptif* (adoptive son).

Létinois died of typhoid in 1886. For the remainder of his life, Verlaine lived in poverty and reverted to alcoholism. After a number of hospital stays that allowed him to recuperate from his excesses, Verlaine died in humble lodgings in 1896.

MAJOR WORKS

Verlaine made his literary debut with the publication of *Poèmes saturniens* in 1866. While the volume was true to the Parnassian ideals of detached severity, impeccable form, and stoic objectivity, and was well-received by Verlaine's fellow poets, it took twenty years to sell five hundred copies, leaving Verlaine virtually unknown to general readers following its publication. In 1870, Verlaine began to move away from the tenets of the Parnassians with the publication of *Fêtes galantes*. In this collection he used visual and spatial imagery to create poetry that has been described as "impressionistic music." According to many critics, this volume first revealed Verlaine's poetic talents in their pure form and later established him as a precursor to the Symbolist movement. Verlaine's next volume, *La bonne chanson* (1870), contains verse inspired by his young wife. After he abandoned her and took up with Rimbaud, Verlaine published *Romances sans paroles* (1874), a collection of verse strongly influenced by his affair. Verlaine's masterful use of ambiguities, the smoothness and economy of his verse, and his usage of "half-light," or vague but deeply suggestive visual imagery, led Arthur Symons to call the book "Verlaine's masterpiece of sheer poetry." Following his time in prison, Verlaine wrote and published *Sagesse* (1881), a volume of poetry detailing his religious conversion. Later, he produced a trilogy exemplifying his religious genesis: *Amour* (1881) was to represent religious perseverance, *Parallèlement* (1889) moral relapse, and *Bonheur* (1891) repentance and consolation. In all three volumes, Verlaine continued to develop his personal voice and to progress toward simple and graceful accentuations. Although Verlaine published poetry in the later part of his life, including the tragic and brutal *Chansons pour elle* (1891), most critics contend that his best and most original work can be found in his earlier volumes. In the 1980s Verlaine's erotic poetry, which had been excluded from volumes of his complete works, was finally collected and published together under the title *Royal Tastes: Erotic Writings*. This volume includes the complete texts of *Les Amies* (1867), *Femmes* (1890), and *Hombres* (1891), also known as the *Trilogie érotique*, and is believed by many to help explain the dual nature of Verlaine's life and verse. Physically abusive, alcoholic, and sexually promiscuous with both women and men in his personal life, Verlaine also composed some of the most admired religious and spiritual verse in literary history. In the *Trilogie érotique* Verlaine wrote in great detail about his sexual excesses and debauchery, and many critics believe it was through these works that he attempted to reconcile his contradictory impulses.

CRITICAL RECEPTION

While many critics consider Verlaine to have been one of the harbingers of the French Symbolists due to the impressionistic and evocative nature of his poetry, he denied belonging to any particular poetic movement. Instead of labeling himself a Decadent or Symbolist, Verlaine preferred to call himself a "degenerate," indicating his individualistic and anarchic tendencies. Much attention has been given to Verlaine's use of familiar language in a musical and visual manner and his ability to evoke rather than demand a response from his readers. Verlaine's well-documented personal life has often overshadowed discussion of the merits of his numerous volumes of verse and his poetic genius. In Verlaine's work, as in his life, there was a constant struggle between the soul and the senses; between debauchery and repentance. This prompted critics to call him everything from a "propagator of moral cowardice" to "a victim of his own genius." Despite the many attacks on his character, Verlaine is considered a consummate poet whose extraordinary talents for fluid verse, figurative and suggestive language, and impressionistic imagery have assumed legendary stature. It was Verlaine, most critics agree, who was responsible for releasing French poetry from its technical severity and for bringing out the musicality inherent in the French language.

PRINCIPAL WORKS

Poetry

Poèmes saturniens 1866
Les Amies [as Pablo de Herlagñez] 1868
Fêtes galantes 1870
La bonne chanson 1870
Romances sans paroles 1874
Sagesse 1881
Jadis et naguère 1884
Amour 1888
Parallèlement 1889
Dedicaces 1890
Bonheur 1891
Chansons pour elle 1891
Femmes 1891
Hombres 1891
Liturgies intimes 1892
Elégies 1893
Odes en son honeur 1893
Dans les limbes 1894
Poems of Paul Verlaine 1895
Chair 1896
Invectives 1896
Royal Tastes: Erotic Writings 1984

Other Major Works

Les poètes maudits (essays) 1884
Les Uns et les autres (one-act play in Jadis et naguère) 1884
Mes hôpitaux (essays) 1891
Mes prisons (essays) 1892
Confessions: Notes autobiographiques (autobiography) 1895
Oeuvres complètes. 5 vols. (short stories, essays, autobiography) 1899–1903
Oeuvres posthumes. 3 vols. (essays and letters) 1911–1929

CRITICISM

A. E. Carter (essay date 1971)

SOURCE: "The Summing-Up," in *Paul Verlaine*, Twayne Publishers, Inc., 1971, pp. 117–22.

[*In the following essay, Carter provides an overview of Verlaine's poetic life.*]

A short life, less than fifty-two years; yet its output was considerable. From ***Poèmes saturniens*** until his death, Verlaine averaged one volume of poetry every eighteen months, plus a fair quantity of prose. Only the most prolific giants like Hugo have done better. What is its value?

Like all literary work, it must be judged by a double standard: what it meant to its age and what it means nowadays. Verlaine's contemporaries thought of him as an innovator: he had added new techniques to poetry and helped free it from traditional rules. Critics of the period were forever stressing this point. Their articles almost give the impression that before Verlaine verse was so fettered with regulations that little of any value was written.[1] Yet his much-advertised novelties were hardly extensive—experiments of one kind or another with the prosody of the time. It was strict: whatever political and social changes France went through after the Renaissance, the rules of versification remained constant. The language has no tonic accent, and certain techniques were therefore judged necessary to distinguish poetry from prose: a rigid scheme of alternate masculine and feminine rhymes, and a steady, pulsing beat, obtained by lines in equal numbers of syllables. Four, six, eight, and ten were common, but the standard measure was twelve: the famous alexandrine, skewered on a median caesura like a butterfly on a pin. Here are a few examples chosen at random over a period of two hundred and fifty years:

> . . . France, mère des arts, / des armes et des lois
> . . .
> . . . Rendre le ciel jaloux / de sa vive couleur . . .
> . . . Beauté, mon beau souci, / de qui l'âme incertaine
> . . .
> . . . Je le ferais encor, / si j'avais à le faire . . .
> . . . Je commence à rougir / de mon oisiveté . . .
> . . . Périssent tes serments / et ton Dieu que j'abhorre!
> . . .
> . . . Elle a vécu, Myrto, / la jeune Tarentine . . .

From mid-sixteenth century until the dawn of the nineteenth, in short, most French poets used the same prosodic machinery to express themselves.—Surely one of the strangest examples of literary conservatism on record.

The Romantics claimed emancipation. But though they lived at a time when traditional values had been challenged or over-thrown, they used their opportunity timidly. Victor Hugo was the most revolutionary of them all: he liked to boast that he had put a red cap of liberty on the dictionary and "dislocated" the alexandrine:

> . . . J'ai mis un bonnet rouge au vieux dictionnaire
> . . .
> . . . J'ai disloqué ce grand niais d'alexandrin . . .[2]

By which he meant that he had enlarged the vocabulary and placed the caesura elsewhere than at the sixth syllable, a proceeding known as *enjambement sur la césure*. This was not much. He was also fond of *rejet*—overflow of sense and rhythm from one line to the next:

> Mais c'est affreux d'avoir à se mettre cela
> Dans le tête . . .[3]

Baudelaire too liked stylistic tricks of this kind; examples of both may be found in his work, and they interested Verlaine as we know from the essay he wrote on his predecessor. When he wanted authority to justify his own tinkering with Classical machinery, he found it in Hugo and Baudelaire. In this sense his verse is a further development in the direction of twentieth-century *vers libre*.

He also liked to compose in lines of five, seven, nine, eleven, and thirteen syllables:

> . . . Une aube affaiblie . . .
> . . . C'est l'extase langoureuse . . .
> . . . Tournez, tournez, bons chevaux de bois . . .
> . . . Dans un palais, soie et or, dans Ecbatane . . .
> . . . Il faut, voyez-vous, nous pardonner les choses
> . . .

It was the *impair* he recommended in **"Art poétique,"** "vaguer and more soluble in the air, with nothing in it of heaviness and pose." But how much importance did he really attach to the formula? He later advised his disciples "not to take **'Art poétique'** too seriously, it's only a song"[4]; and much of his best verse, with less of heaviness or pose than anything else he wrote (most of the 'Ariettes oubliées' in ***Romances sans paroles***, for example) is not always composed in *impair*.[5]

He also liked to rhyme weakly or adequately instead of richly, according to another precept enunciated in **"Art**

poétique": "You'd do well, as you spend your efforts, to make Rhyme behave: if we don't watch it, where will it lead?"

> Vous ferez bien, en train d'énergie,
> De rendre un peu la Rime assagie:
> Si l'on n'y veille, elle ira jusqu'où?

For the benefit of those not familiar with these minutiae, a rhyme between "fidèle" and "nouvelle," where only one syllable echoes the other, is "weak"; "tige"and "vertige" (final vowels supported by identical consonants) are "adequate"; and "destinée" and "matinée," where each word has two sounds of equal value, are "rich." A great deal of noise was made over this point even before Verlaine's time, and I doubt very much whether any poet worthy of the name paid it much attention. Victor Hugo even turned the matter to ridicule with an extreme example of rich rhyme—where *every* syllable echoes the other:

> Gall, amant de la reine, alla, tour magnanime,
> Galamment de l'arène à la tour Magne, à Nîmes.[6]

If poets used only rich rhymes, they would not write much; most of Racine's rhymes are adequate at best and often weak; and the Romantics, in the long run, did as they pleased, using whatever rhymes came to hand—weak, adequate, or rich. So did Verlaine. Weak rhymes were part of his recipe for blurring the contours of meaning and creating a vague and dreamy impression: a specious theory which, again, he did not always practice. The rhymes of some of his most suggestive verse are frequently adequate. And while a few of the experiments he made with half-rhyme and assonance are mildly interesting—

> Les variations normales
> De l'esprit autant que du coeur
> En somme témoignent peu mal
> En dépit de tel qui s'épeure . . .

—at his most revolutionary in this respect he was clearly being facetious:

> J'opine
> Pour les deux en même temps . . . ni ne
> Dis mot . . .[7]

On this point as well he did not wish to be taken too seriously, and when his disciples began carrying **"Art poétique"** to its logical extreme and discarding rhyme completely, he was filled with misgivings: "The poem in question is *carefully* rhymed. . . . Use weak rhymes or assonance if you will, but use one or the other: French verse is impossible otherwise."[8]

More important was his treatment of the caesura. In numerous cases he ignored the sixth-syllable rule:

> L'inflexion des voix chères qui se sont tues.
> Laisse-la trompeter à son aise, la gueuse!
> De la douceur, de la douceur, de la douceur!
> Amour qui ruisselais de flammes et de lait . . .
> Il faut m'aimer! Je suis l'universel Baiser . . .
> Ces passions qu'eux seuls nomment encore amours . . .

Occasionally he even bridged it with a single word:

> Et la tigresse épouvantable d'Hyrcanie . . .
> D'une joie extraordinaire: votre voix . . .

Most striking of all, however, was the way he used *rejet* from one line to the next. The effect of rapt ecstasy throughout **"Mon Rêve familier," "Mon Dieu m'a dit,"** and later poems like **"Parsifal"** is one result:

> Car elle me comprend, et mon coeur, transparent
> Pour elle seule, hélas! cesse d'être un problème
> Pour elle seule, et les moiteurs de mon front blême
> . . .

> Je ris, je pleure, et c'est comme un appel aux armes
> D'un clairon pour des champs de bataille où je vois
> Des anges bleus et blancs portés sur des pavois . . .

> Parsifal a vaincu les Filles, leur gentil
> Babil et la luxure amusante—et sa pente
> Vers la Chair de garçon vierge que cela tente
> D'aimer les seins légers et ce gentil babil . . .

It is not too much to say that in this respect he was the most accomplished of French poets. None of the others ever used the technique with such consummate art—certainly not Hugo, not even Baudelaire.

There is little more to say of him as an innovator. He owed his reputation in that respect less to any real changes he introduced than to the fact that he was dealing with so rigid a structure that the least alteration appeared revolutionary. And here too the admiration of his disciples somewhat disconcerted him. "I'm having trouble with my Decadents," he wrote Dr. Jullien in 1888: "I'm very much inclined to drop gently all those brats, who are decidedly compromising."[9] Three years later he expressed his disapproval in even stronger terms: "To have poetry you've got to have rhythm. Nowadays people are writing lines of a thousand feet! It's no longer verse, it's prose and sometimes mere gibberish!"[10] He drew back from the new schools in consternation: refused to write for their manifestoes, refused to admit that he even knew what Symbolism was. "Symbolism? I don't understand. Must be a German word, eh? What the devil can it mean?"[11] A coolness resulted: the young men were offended and began looking elsewhere for a master. "He's too much under Baudelaire's influence," Jean Moréas declared in 1891, adding that he had nothing further to teach contemporary poetry, and that far from being an initiator, he was the end of a line, the last word of a dead tradition.[12]

Verlaine, indeed, was not the sort of man to found a school—even when tempted to it by the flattering imitations of other poets. He had taste enough to see that the imitations were usually mediocre. When Ghil, Kahn, Viélé-Griffin, Samain, Moréas himself tried to write like Verlaine they labored infelicitously: the attentuated effects of ***Fêtes galantes*** and ***Romances sans paroles*** explain much of the epicene posturing and masturbatory languour of Symbolism and Decadence. But he can scarcely be held accountable for these aberrations. He had no desire for disciples and, despite **"Art poétique,"** his talent was too spontaneous to bother with rules and regulations. *"I've formulated no theory,"* he declared in 1890, underlining the words to make his intention clear. "Perhaps that sounds naive, but naiveté seems to me one of a poet's most precious qualities." And again: "Let me dream if I want, weep when I like, sing when the idea comes to me."[13] It was a good definition of his work. Whenever he adopted a program or paid lip service to some esthetic creed or other, he labored in vain. His poetry (as he told Mallarmé) was "an effort to render sensation"[14]; and sensation is wholly personal, all the more so when the writer is a Verlaine, tied to a world of memory and illusion: childhood and his mother's affection, the Metz years, the long holidays with Elisa Dujardin at Lécluze. Throughout his existence, this sinking fund of regret and recollection dominated him; now subconsciously, now openly: each of his sentimental escapades was less an effort to relive the past than to impose it on the present, remarking life according to the data memory supplied. Mathilde, Rimbaud, Létinois, Cazals: each was expected to perform the same role—shielding him from reality, allowing him to inhabit a dream world of his own invention. Which meant carrying out the functions his mother had once assumed. Small wonder that in the long run they all lost patience. Hence the sexual and emotional failure of his life and (paradoxically) hence the success of his art. He was capricious, unstable, uncontrollable, forever on the sensual *qui-vive*, a man impossible in any normal context. But poetry is hardly a normal context, and when he began to write the very qualities that prevented rational adjustment gave his verse its peculiar beauty. He could never transcend himself: his inspiration obeyed nervous impressions, not the summons of conscious will. He had to wait until conditions were right; but when they were, when no preconceived idea or self-conscious theorizing intervened between him and sensation, he commanded one of the most seductive styles in the history of poetry. True enough, his key was minor and his tone low. But these are limitations, not defects, and we could easily make out a case in their favor. Subdued harmonies are often the most alluring of all. They speak to us more urgently and more intimately than other music, and for that reason we listen to them longest.

Notes

1. "He broke the cruel shackles of versification," "he opened a window," he sought "novelty, and an art that would be a combination of poetry, painting and music . . . a concert in color or a painting in music—a deliberate confusion of genres, a sort of Tenth Muse": opinions expressed by Moréas, Rachilde, etc.; quoted by Martino in *Verlaine*, 188, 193, 201, 189. Mallarmé's opinion was: "The father, the true father of all the young poets, is Verlaine, the magnificent Verlaine, whose attitude, as a man, I find as splendid as his attitude as a writer. Because it is the only possible one at a time when the poet must live outside the law: accept all suffering with so much pride and such a splendid swagger." Conversation with Jules Huret in 1891, reprinted in the Pléiade Mallarmé, p. 870.
2. "Réponse à un acte d'accusation," *Les Contemplations*, 1856.
3. Quoted by Verlaine himself in an essay on Barbey d'Aurevilly, 1865. *CML*, I, 1422.
4. Pléiade, p. 1074.
5. Of the nine pieces in *Ariettes oubliées,* four are in *impair* (I, II, IV, VIII), and in another IX, *pair* and *impair* alternate.
6. Ernest Raynaud, *Poetae minores* (Garnier Frères, 1931), p. 324. He quotes two other lines of the same kind, dealing with the poets who interest us:

   Les Rimbaud et les Verlaine,
Les reins beaux, ailés vers l'aine.
7. "Vers en assonances," *Chair*, Pléiade, p. 891; and "A la seule," *Invectives*, p. 958.
8. *CML*, I, 1265, letter to Ernest Raynaud of September 30, 1887.
9. *CML*, I, 1297.
10. To Jules Huret, *CML*, II, 1761.
11. *Ibid.*, p. 1760.
12. Quoted by Huret in his *Enquête*, p. 80.
13. Pléiade, 1074, and Martino, *op. cit.*, p. 188.
14. "J'ose espérer . . . que vous y reconnaîtrez, sinon le talent, du moins un effort vers . . . la Sensation rendue," letter of November 22, 1866. *CML*, I, 929.

Stella Revard (essay date 1971)

SOURCE: "Verlaine and Yeats's A Dialogue of Self and Soul," in *Papers on Language and Literature*, Vol. 7, No. 3, Summer, 1971, pp. 272–78.

[*In the following essay, Revard explores the influence of Verlaine and the French Symbolists on William Butler Yeats's* "A Dialogue of Self and Soul."]

It is usually recognized that Yeats was interested in the French Symbolist poets during his London residence in the 1890s and that this interest was stimulated by his friend, Arthur Symons, then at work on his book, *The Symbolist Movement in Literature*. Yet, because Yeats could read little French and because of the complexity and obscurity of these particular poets, direct influence is usually denied. Yeats, however, has recorded in his autobiography his fascination with the French Symbolists, noting that Symons read Mallarmé and Verlaine to him, both in French and in the translations Symons was working on.[1]

Yeats, himself involved in working out a symbolist system, admired the poetic principles of Mallarmé and the subtleties of his verse. To Verlaine Yeats was attracted in quite a different way, for the French poet's lyric simplicity, his complete absorption in the poetic moment. It is not unlikely that Yeats would have shared Symons's opinion that Verlaine's language made a "passive flawless medium for the deeper consciousness of things."[2] In Verlaine, it may be that Yeats saw the way in which to achieve penetration into the symbolic significance of experience without sacrificing the simplicity, directness, and literalism of pure lyric.

Verlaine occupied for Yeats a special place among the French Symbolist poets. Yeats was undoubtedly first attracted to Verlaine by the musical qualities of his verse, for Verlaine began as an impressionistic poet intent on portraying in poetry the subtleties of visual and tonal experience.[3] In his **"Art poétique,"** written in 1874, he had prescribed music before everything as the prime ingredient of poetry.[4] Words in poetry should, by the nuances of their rhythm and by shadings of their muted colors, convey an impressionistic surface as delicate as air and as subtle as veiled light so that the verse produced thereby should move upward in a kind of joyous liberation of spirit.

> De la musique encore et toujours!
> Que ton vers soit la chose envolée
> Qu'on sent qui fuit d'une âme en allée
> Vers d'autres cieux à d'autres amours.[5]

Verlaine, however, was among the first of the French Symbolists to criticize pure impressionism. As the biographer and critic Antoine Adam has reported, he felt that a poet must do more than record impressions: "He must penetrate beyond, into the mysterious core of things, he must, by way of appearances, pierce through to reality which is spirit." The poet undertakes to "apprehend within himself the tragedy of man" and depict the "heartbreaks, hopes for freedom, and the failures that comprise the pathos of our fate." He is to define and "discover the mysterious correspondence between the secret life of the soul and that of things." Such, Verlaine felt, was to be the true work and meaning of symbolism.[6]

It was only after his conversion to Catholicism in 1874 that Verlaine felt able finally to capture in poetry the essence of man, which he thought the poet must seek to distill. In his volume ***Sagesse***, he celebrates the humility of spirit, the delight experienced by the sinner as he acknowledges his essential humanity, is accepted by Christ, and reaffirms himself in virtue.[7]

Such, undoubtedly, was the doctrine of poetry which Verlaine was expounding upon during his lecture tour to England in November 1893 when he met the young Yeats.[8] Verlaine has insisted, Yeats records, "that the poet hide nothing of himself," though he must speak it all with "a care of that dignity which should manifest itself, if not in the perfection of form, in all events with an invisible, insensible, but effectual endeavor after that lofty and severe quality, I was about to say, this virtue." Yeats felt that the image that Verlaine presented, both through himself as he appeared on the lecture stage at Oxford, and through his doctrine and practice of poetry, was that of essential man. He strove, said Yeats, "to be his ordinary self as much as possible, not a scholar or even a reader, that was certainly his pose."[9] What Yeats, however, probably saw in Verlaine was not the severity and humility of the Christian convert, whose life of degraded Bohemianism and alcoholic abandon was, particularly at that period, often at odds with the doctrine he expounded in ***Sagesse***.[10] Instead Yeats thought Verlaine a poet at peace with self, a kind of reincarnation of the medieval poet Villon, whose simple lyricism Yeats admired: "It was this feeling for his own personality, his delight in singing his own life, even more than that life itself which made the generation I belong to compare him to Villon" (270–71).[11]

The impact, however, of the doctrine of personality which Verlaine spoke of was delayed, for, as Yeats recounts, he did not then understand "the meaning his [Verlaine's] words should have for [him]" (271). Yeats says that he was absorbed in "nothing but states of mind, lyrical moments, intellectual essences." He had not yet come to revaluate, as Verlaine had, the symbolist movement, to question its loss "in personality, in . . . delight in the whole man—blood, imagination, intellect, running together." Nor was he yet to dissent from the "new delight," held by the French Symbolists, apart from Verlaine, "in essences, in states of mind, in pure imagination, in all that comes to us most easily in elaborate music" (266). During his search for aesthetic systems in the 1890s, Yeats says that he "had not learned what sweetness, what rhythmic movement there is in those who have become the joy that is themselves." He does affirm that he had begun as a poet "with the thought of putting [his] very self into poetry." But while searching for the pure aesthetic experience, he had "cut away the nonessential"; thus he had come at last to care for "nothing but impersonal beauty." His imagination, says Yeats, "became full of decorative landscape and of still life"; trying to make his art "deliberately beautiful," he found he was following the opposite of himself (271).

Yeats's rediscovery of the whole personality and his rejection of those Symbolists who denied its value occur at precisely the same moment. The deliberate search for beauty, which was the aim of many of the Symbolists, seemed to Yeats a mistake, for it resulted in abstractions and overrefinement.[12] Moreover he found that as a poet he most achieved beauty as his result in his poetry when he "was not seeking [it] at all, but merely to lighten the mind of some burden of love or bitterness thrown upon it by the events of life" (272). There were, thought Yeats, two ways before literature—"upward into ever-growing subtlety, with Verhaeren, with Mallarmé, with Maeterlinck, until at last, it may be, a new agreement among refined and studious men gives birth to a new passion, and what seems literature becomes religion; or downward, taking the soul with us until all is simplified and solidified again" (266–77).

For Yeats it was the second way which prevailed: "We are only permitted to desire life." Poetry was finally to seem to him a by-product of life, personified as "that exacting mistress who can awake our lips into song with her kisses." Even with life, however, we must be cautious "not to give her all, we must deceive her a little. . . . Our deceit will give us style, mastery, that dignity, that lofty and severe quality Verlaine spoke of" (272).

After 1900, as Yeats began in his poetry to cast aside his elaborate coat of embroideries, to delight in the selfhood of the poet, to declare there was "more enterprise / In walking naked," he was arguing in his essays that poetry must be grounded in the intense vision of life. He had come to see that Verlaine as poet was a singer not of abstract beauty, as he had first appeared to him, but of the simple delight of life and self; he had come to view Verlaine the man, the irrepressibly gay old vagabond, as a representation of the union of intellectual insight with an acceptance of full, passionate life. In Verlaine, the forces of intellect and emotion were one.

At this time in Yeats's poetry, moreover, the passionate figure of the vagabond—the fool, crazy Jane, Tom O'Roughley—appears side by side with the earlier figure of the ethereal lover-poet or the intellectual seeker, Michael Robartes. Not, however, until the later poetry does Yeats attempt to unite in one figure—and it is to be in his representation of himself as poet—the tattered vagabond body of man with the aspiring intellect. This is the union which he understood finally Verlaine to have meant. So understanding, he proposes, "we should ascend out of the common interest, the thoughts of the newspapers, of the market place, of the men of science only so far as we can carry the normal passionate, reasoning self, the personality as a whole. We must find some place upon the tree of Life for the Phoenix nest" (272).

Most clearly perhaps it is in "A Dialogue of Self and Soul" that Yeats achieves the reunion of intellect and passion.[13] In part 1 of that poem the Soul proposes the hard ascent of intellect out of body; it urges that the Self set all its mind upon the "breathless starlit air," and "fix every wandering thought upon / That quarter where all thought is done." Finally, it says, the Self is to achieve that high darkness where the soul becomes indistinguishable from the darkness. The Self, however, lingers over life, symbolized by the consecrated blade wrapped in "that flowing, silken, old embroidery," things which it sees as "emblems of the day against the tower / Emblematic of the night." The Soul brands that pursuit of self as debilitating, for as the imagination becomes bound to the earth, the intellect wanders unable to be liberated from "the crime of death and birth."

> The man is stricken deaf and dumb and blind,
> For intellect no longer knows
> *Is* from the *Ought*, or *Knower* from the *Known*.

The resolution, which the Self proposes in part 2 of the poem, recalls the proposal which in his *Essays*, twenty years earlier, Yeats had made for poetry, the reuniting of the man, who is not to refine himself upward with the soul but is to distill imagination downward with the body, to become again whole man, "blood, imagination, intellect running together." To do so, one must accept the essential imperfectibility of life, not to compromise with life but to rejoice in it and to be content with one's own humanity. "A living man," says the Self, "is blind," impure because the very sources of life are impure; forced to "endure that toil of growing up," placed finally in the focus of society, the man becomes defiled and disfigured by the "mirror of malicious eyes" so that he no longer knows himself or his true shape. Yet to struggle against this fact is only to distort himself far more; the true self will only survive in turning back to life and not in turning away from it.

> I am content to live it all again
> And yet again, if it be life to pitch
> Into the frog-spawn of a blind man's ditch,
> A blind man battering blind men.

Having confessed the miseries and indignities of life, the Self, as it seeks to achieve integrity, cannot try to escape. Instead, with the kind of dignity which Verlaine so highly extolled, the Self acknowledges follies and pretensions alike and comes to peace with what it has become. With that final and total acceptance comes the surge of transcendent joy.

> I am content to follow to its source
> Every event in action or in thought;
> Measure the lot; forgive myself the lot!
> When such as I cast out remorse
> So great a sweetness flows into the breast
> We must laugh and we must sing,
> We are blest by everything,
> Everything we look upon is blest.

The response to life which Yeats records here is the dramatization of a principle which he had learned earlier, one which he credits to the example and the words of Verlaine as teacher. Yeats celebrates his discovery, in "A Dialogue of Self and Soul," of the sweetness "there is in those who have become the joy that is themselves." Like Verlaine he finds that the poet must appear in simplicity and honesty in his own poetic creation.

Notes

1. William Butler Yeats, *The Autobiography of William Butler Yeats* (Garden City, N.Y., 1958), p. 213. Yeats remarks that he would never know "how much [his] practice and [his] theory owe to passages that he [Symons] read [him] from . . . Verlaine and Mallarmé." Later, however, he was to disclaim that the Symbolists had had great impact upon him. Writing to C. M. Bowra in 1934 (in response to Bowra's having posted him a copy of his essay on the symbolist poets), Yeats says: "I don't think I was really much influenced by French Symbolists. My development was different, but that development was of such a nature that I felt I could not explain it, or even that

it might make everybody hostile. When Symons talked to me about the Symbolistes, or read me passages from his translations from Mallarmé, I seized upon everything that at all resembled my own thought; here at last was something I could talk about. . . . There was however one book which influenced me very greatly, it has just been edited by Le Galienne [*sic*], it was the younger Hallam's essay on Tennyson. It was only the first half of the essay which influenced me, and in that he defined what he called 'aesthetic poetry'. By 'aesthetic poetry' he meant exactly what the French mean by 'pure poetry'. It may interest you that an English critic was probably the first to make that definition." See C. M. Bowra, *Memories 1898–1939* (Cambridge, Mass., 1967), pp. 240–41.

2. Arthur Symons, *The Symbolist Movement in Literature* (New York, 1919), pp. 214–15.
3. On October 15, 1892, Yeats wrote in *United Ireland*: "In France a man may do anything he pleases, he may spend years in prison even, like Verlaine, and the more advanced of the young men will speak well of him if he have but loved his art sincerely, and they will worship his name as they worship Verlaine's life if he have but made beautiful things and added to the world's store of memorable experiences. . . . *Poetry is an end in itself; it has nothing to do with life* [my italics], nothing to do with anything but the music of cadences, and beauty of phrase" (quoted from Norman Jeffares, *W. B. Yeats, Man and Poet* [London, 1962], pp. 91–92).
4. There is some dispute about dating the "Art Poétique": Verlaine dates it in 1874, but the poem did not appear until 1882, when Verlaine was formulating his system. There is even some hesitancy about according the poem the status of a true "art of poetry." Eléonore Zimmermann, in *Magies de Verlaine* (Paris, 1967), p. 113, remarks that it is at variance with the stated "system," and Jacques Robichez, in his edition of the *Oeuvres Poétiques de Verlaine* (Paris, 1969), pp. 637–38, argues that it is too whimsical to have been intended as a serious statement of principle. Verlaine himself said, "Don't take my 'Art Poétique' literally—it is only a song" (Antoine Adam, *The Art of Paul Verlaine*, trans. Carl Morse [New York, 1963], p. 106).
5. Robichez, p. 261; this edition is the one I use throughout my text.
6. Adam, p. 103.
7. Ibid., pp. 34–35; pp. 108–09. *Sagesse VI* (Robichez, p. 192) is perhaps the best example of Verlaine's song of the repentant sinner. There he says farewell to the bleeding heart he possessed yesterday and welcomes the heart that flames with love. Dismissing alike joy and sorrow, the good and the bad of his former life, he announces the immense sense of peace come to the soul sufficient to itself.

   O vous, comme un qui boite au loin, Chagrins et Joies,
   Toe, coeur saignant d'heir qui flambes aujourd'hui,
   C'est vrai pourtant que c'est fini, que tout a fui
   De nos sens, aussi bien les ombres que les proies.

   Vieux bonheurs, vieux malheurs, comme une file d'oies
   Sur la route en poussière où tous les pieds ont lui,
   Bon voyage! Et le Rire, et, plus, vielle que lui,
   Toi, Tristesse, noyée au vieux noir que tu bries,

   Et le reste!—Un doux vide, un grand renoncement,
   Quelqu'un en nous qui sent la paix immensément,
   Une candeur d'une fraîcheur délicieuse. . . .

   Et voyez! notre coeur qui saignait sous l'orgueil,
   Il flambe dans l'amour, et s'en va faire accueil
   A la vie, en faveur d'une mort précieuse!
8. Adam, p. 56.
9. William Butler Yeats, "The Cutting of an Agate," *Essays and Introductions* (New York, 1961), p. 270; future references are to this edition and are cited by page numbers in my text.
10. Yeats, in his *Autobiography* (pp. 228–29), recording a later meeting in Paris with Verlaine in 1896, within a few months of Verlaine's death, remarks upon Verlaine's alternation between "the two halves of his nature with so little apparent resistance that he seemed like a bad child, though to read his sacred poems is to remember perhaps that the Holy Infant shared His first home with the beasts." The contradictions which Yeats observed in the joining of the spiritual opposites in the person of Verlaine are evident also in Yeats's poetic figure of Crazy Jane. If we understand the manger as a submerged image in "Crazy Jane Talks with the Bishop," Jane's reply to the Bishop's exhortation, "Live in a heavenly mansion, / Not in some foul sty," becomes a kind of plea for the union of seeming opposites, the divine and the animal instincts of man: "Fair and foul are near of kin, / And fair needs foul." Yeats surely is seeking in this poem to effect a union of the spiritual and physical impulses of man, remarking that the highest essence of love sought to manifest itself in the bestial stable: the "uncontrollable mystery" (as Yeats had phrased it in "The Magi") "upon the bestial floor."
11. Both Verlaine's vagrancy and his lyricism are implicit, of course, in this comparison with Villon. Paul Valéry (quoted in Verlaine, *Selected Poems*, trans. C. F. MacIntyre [Berkeley and Los Angeles, 1948], p. xiv) remarks in his essay "Villon et Verlaine" upon the two poets: "How could one imagine that this vagrant—so brutal in appearance and speech, sordid and yet perturbing and pathetic—could be the writer of the most delicate music in our poetry."
12. Bernard Levine, in *The Dissolving Image* (Detroit, 1970), p. 15, has commented on how Yeats differs

from the French Symbolists in his approach to the place of self in the creative experience: "Yeats did not subscribe to the 'pure art' as practiced by Mallarmé and Valéry, but he did want an art that was purified of everything that did not lead to a realization of Self and to an awareness of 'spiritual reality.' Yeats thought of creative power and artistic discipline as a means of discovering the energy of 'pure life.'"

13. *The Collected Poems of W. B. Yeats* (New York, 1955), pp. 230–31.

Hallam Walker (essay date 1972)

SOURCE: "Visual and Spatial Imagery in Verlaine's *Fêtes galantes*," in *PMLA*, Vol. 87, No. 5, October, 1972, pp. 1007–015.

[*In the following essay, Walker argues that the visual and spatial imagery in* Fêtes galantes *make that volume distinctive from Verlaine's other works of poetry.*]

Despite their display of certain characteristics, such as delicate suggestion and musicality, inherent in all his poetry, the poems in Paul Verlaine's ***Fêtes galantes*** stand apart from the main body of his works in two ways. First, they employ visual and spatial effects to an extent unusual in the rest of his poems, and second, as a total composition of twenty-two poems they possess a thematic unity based largely upon the relationships between recurrent ideas and spatial effects. Before elucidating these aspects of ***Fêtes galantes***, I wish to review briefly the general impressions produced by these poems and some typical critical efforts to deal with them.[1] Upon that criticism a new approach can be built.

Most observations on ***Fêtes galantes*** stress the atmosphere of dream which mingles hints of despair with sensual delights, all in stylized Rococo settings à la Watteau. The surface lightness of these poems is underscored by a shadow of doom, and a cold wind moves through the empty spaces of dream (*Œuvres poétiques*, p. 106). Jacques Borel terms the eighteenth-century settings of the pieces Verlaine's personal "monde du songe et de la mort" (*Œuvres poétiques,* p. 102), perceiving that the poet discovered the world of Watteau's paintings as a configuration of a realm existing within his own spirit. The poet's soul dwells for a while in a world that is embodied in the Rococo style yet somehow transmuted by his presence and the peculiar order he imposes. "Ce décor, c'est le rêve de l'âme" (*Œuvres poétiques*, p. 101). The phantoms which inhabit the gardens are part of Verlaine, and the final bleak emptiness is intensely his own.

The principle of personal projection within an established art form is very important. The poems are not merely imitations of Watteau paintings but rather the result of Verlaine's discovery of existing forms congenial to his visions. The value of the eighteenth-century decor is that it remains always itself, with strict limits and conventions, and simultaneously lends itself to being infused with the poet's spiritual presence. The relationship between landscape and soul is announced immediately in the first line of the initial poem, **"Clair de lune,"** "Votre âme est un paysage choisi."[2] In an analysis of the poem Marcel Schaettel says, "Certes, son 'Clair de lune' est bien un tableau et un spectacle, mais c'est aussi une âme à l'intérieur de laquelle le poète a pénétré, et ces 'grands jets d'eau sveltes parmi les marbres,' qui 'sanglotent d'extase' sont un des aspects essentiels de cette âme étrange, frivole et mélancolique, superficielle en apparence et cependant tourmentée par le spleen et l'idéal."[3]

The esthetic scheme of ***Fêtes galantes*** is certainly based upon the tensions between keen feelings and the settings into which they are projected. Jean-Pierre Richard sees Verlaine seeking "un instant à la fois très vague et très aigu."[4] An equivocal state of suspension is always sensed, for the poet is neither wholly immersed in his dream nor solidly fixed in reality. This general effect of absence mixed with presence, of intense detachment, is often described by critics in impressionistic terms. I believe that some precise sources for this effect can be identified, particularly in the visual and spatial images of the poems under consideration here. Before examining this imagery, however, we must note some criticism concerned with the musicality of Verlaine's works.

Octave Nadal, writing of Verlaine's vagueness, sees him seeking "songe sensation sentiment pur qui n'ont ni limites ni contours, ni existence formelle."[5] Despite an awareness of contour, Nadal says that Verlaine works "le plus volontiers dans la durée; le spatial semble être beaucoup moins son domaine" (*Paul Verlaine*, p. 88). He observes that the early works of ***Poèmes saturniens*** show elements of pictorial impressionism but that the ultimate choice by the poet was the use of musicality for the desired vagueness. Parnassian concern with plastic imagery is soon replaced by Verlaine's exploration and development of musicality to add a new poetic dimension. The whole matter of musical effects as the key to understanding of the special nature of this poet's creations is here broached, and much interesting work has been done along these lines.[6] "Le spatial" is often neglected for "la durée" in critical concerns, however.

The article by Alfred J. Wright, "Verlaine and Debussy: ***Fêtes galantes***," may be noted because of its direct juxtaposition of poetic and musical creations, with an assumption of similar esthetic aims in the two arts.[7] Wright shows that the composer often used techniques different from those of poetry to achieve similar effects, and it is helpful to see that many compositions in the mode of the "fêtes galantes" achieve a vagueness by means unlike those used by Verlaine. I single out this study because it keeps distinct the natures and resources of the two arts, avoiding the implication that one really can explain the other.

Attempts to explain the qualities of Verlaine's poetry (or of Watteau's paintings) largely by generalities borrowed from music can do little beyond suggesting a certain atmosphere in the works studied.[8] Without close analysis of analogous modulations of time and tone with their subtle irregularities in the several art forms, this critical technique is limited in its success. Some attention has been given to another means of understanding ***Fêtes galantes***, also with limited results, and this is the study of paintings by Watteau and Lancret as direct sources of inspiration for Verlaine.

Since the time of publication of ***Fêtes galantes***, when it was generally assumed that the Goncourts's study of eighteenth-century art provided subjects or inspiration for Verlaine, there has been considerable effort to equate poems and paintings according to subject matter. Jacques-Henry Bornecque has put an end to such speculations by bringing forth the facts of Verlaine's slight knowledge of the actual paintings and his familiarity with later engravings, a feeble source of color and atmosphere.[9] The common body of knowledge about Rococo style and "fêtes galantes" is well treated in his first chapter, showing how much Verlaine drew from contemporary poetry on such subjects. Bornecque's conclusion is, in brief, that it is pointless to try to fix exact pictorial sources for the poems. A few engravings are reflected in certain poems, but it is more vital to see that Verlaine had sensed and absorbed an essence of Rococo tone from various sources and that he shaped it to his own ends.

To proceed by analogies between the arts which treat a like subject matter is basically to study just these analogies, and little light is cast upon the themes and structures of the poems as literary art. The observation of similarities between poems and paintings can be followed, however, by analysis of the principles of form in one art which suggest that a similar phenomenon may be at work in the other. Thus, the essential musicality of Verlaine's poems probably emerges best in studies such as that by Guy Michaud rather than in comparisons with Debussy's music.[10] He examines the patterns of vowels and consonants along a time line, applying as seem appropriate some aspects of musical form to the poetry. Now, the sequence of patterns of things *seen* in ***Fêtes galantes*** lends itself to this sort of analysis. We can profitably seek out some of the principles of visual and spatial imagery in Watteau's paintings and inquire how they may apply to the sequential verbal creations of Verlaine's ***Fêtes galantes***, those poetic landscapes with figures. The current study is intended to increase understanding of some of the form which produces Verlaine's characteristic vagueness and which also is a definite framework for the expression of some important and unifying themes in the group of poems.

Our approach to the matter supposes, of course, that Verlaine had a great visual sensitivity; that such was the case is the strong conclusion reached by Eléonore Zimmerman in her *Magies de Verlaine*. She documents his keen visual awareness throughout his life and writings, noting the frequent verbal renderings of things perceived by the eye. An important point is made that the imprecise images of the poems start with sharp observations of the external world; "le vague de Verlaine, comme de tout grand artiste, est créé à partir de notations précises" (p. 281). Sharpness of vision is equaled by the ability to capture the characteristic gesture or tone in a few words. Both the intentional blur and the intensity of focus on detail are techniques of painting which have their parallels in Verlaine's poetic imagery, and, in ***Fêtes galantes***, the relationships between the visually vague and the precise are of especially great importance.

Transposing the general effect of vagueness into temporal terms we may say that Verlaine's poems give an impression of suspension in time, of the fleeting moment which achieves its immortality, caught in the art work like the fly in amber. The world of the Rococo parks is at once past and present, and this duality in time is an essential part of Verlaine's technique. Momentary poses or words are in a sense frozen so they may be in both their past and our present. This temporal phenomenon is scarcely dynamic, however, and creates little in the way of tensions, which are certainly to be sensed in his poems. Viewing these works in terms of the psychological or emotional imagery, we find it easier to identify the vague quality than to explain the intensity of feeling implicit in the stylized situations of love. The conventional desires and despairs of the lovers are given in detail in the poems, yet Verlaine makes us feel that for him the trite conventions suggest some more subtle aspects of love. The depths of meaning hinted at call for study, but our present task is to elucidate the artistic form. Let us just observe that the overall esthetic scheme of the work involves many ways of shifting back and forth between the precise and the imprecise, the acute and the anodyne. In **"Art poétique"** the poet expresses his predilection for "la chanson grise où l'Indécis au Précis se joint." Applying the principle of juxtaposition of the vague and the precise to the visual and spatial imagery of ***Fêtes galantes***, I believe we find a vital form which undergirds the entire work.

By employing shifts between sharp and indistinct focus Verlaine creates the marked sense of instability and uncertainty which basically keys our impressions of the poems. It is this principle of shifting which is of particular interest because it furnishes us with a definite structural form to use in analyzing the works, a task which tends to bog down in the "vague" when criticism concentrates only upon the hazy zone where one thing becomes another. Since the fluctuations of spatial structures seem to be tied in subtle ways to the intellectual and emotional variations within ***Fêtes galantes***, this can serve as a future means of approach to a study of the relationships between form and content.

I conclude from examination of Verlaine's poems and Watteau's paintings that the poet understood, despite limited pictorial sources, an essential part of Watteau's techniques with two-dimensional visual images, and that he furthermore found ways to use analogous verbal techniques. In simple terms we may call the images found in

Watteau those of "detachment" and "merging" to indicate the relationships between the human figures and the backgrounds in the paintings. The figures either stand isolated from the background in quite sharp focus, or else they tend to flow into the background and disappear. In a given painting both effects may occur, but one tendency will usually predominate and give the basic tone of the work. An excellent and well-known example of the effect of merging is found in "L'Embarquement pour l'île de Cythère," while "Gilles" shows the effect of detachment.[11] One's reactions to a painting are influenced by the handling of the virtual space depicted on the canvas, and the reactions are primary. In like fashion in ***Fêtes galantes*** Verlaine rapidly gives the reader visual imagery characterized by either sharp or dissolving focus in depth. On this basis much of the poem is apprehended.

Although detailed commentary on all of the poems is beyond the scope of this study, I shall examine each one for the spatial effects described above. The individual works are strongly marked by them, while as a whole the collection displays a unifying pattern based on the shifts between merging and detachment. The placement of the individual poems in the ensemble assumes great importance in this light, for the overall scheme of alternations and reinforcements of effects is a carefully composed sinuous line dependent upon a certain sequence of imagery.

Apparent in the first poem, **"Clair de lune,"** is the strong impression of fusion induced by the moonlight. We have already noticed the merging of ideas of "votre âme" and "paysage," and a scene briefly peopled by hazy figures dominates the first stanza. Ambiguity of appearance and feeling is stressed; "ils n'ont pas l'air de croire à leur bonheur." They and their song blend into the visual images, "se mêle au clair de lune," as Verlaine employs the characteristic verb "mêler." Emphasis upon fading back into the vague background is evident in the final stanza in which the birds, invisible and silent, dream among the dim trees. The human figures slip away to leave only the play of the waters which now contain the disembodied emotions, "sangloter d'extase." The focus at the last is upon "les grands jets d'eau sveltes parmi les marbres," while we lose all sight of the dancing maskers. There is no mistaking the tone or the significance of Verlaine's placing this poem at the head of his suite of ***Fêtes***; visual and spatial effects are far more numerous than those of sound (singing and sobbing), and the impression of figures merging into background serves as the keynote of the work as a whole.

In the next three poems we discover a shift toward a clear focus upon the figures so dimly glimpsed in the first work. **"Pantomime," "Sur l'herbe,"** and **"L'Allée"** show us the cast of characters, first called "masques et bergamasques" in **"Clair de lune,"** to be figures from the Italian commedia dell'arte. These stylized players, such as Arlequin, Colombine, and Pierrot, possess a clarity of delineation which will be as great as any in the world of the ***Fêtes***, but we must note that they are by their very nature insubstantial, having reality only as stock literary types. Verlaine catches each one in characteristic gesture.

The choice of the title **"Pantomime"** is interesting because of the stress upon the visual as opposed to the suggestion of sound in the original ideas for a title, "En aparté" and "A-parté" (Bornecque, p. 154). Verlaine evidently wished to direct our attention to the silent miming so clearly visualized; "Pierrot qui n'a rien d'un Clitandre / Vide un flacon sans plus attendre," or "Ce faquin d'Arlequin . . . pirouette quatre fois." Only the final stanza moves slightly toward the effect of merging of figure into scene; "Colombine rêve, surprise / De sentir un cœur dans la brise / Et d'entendre en son cœur des voix." Here, of course, it is feeling which blends with the setting and its mood, while the general effect remains that of distinct pictures of the characters, each framed in a portrait stanza.

Title is again important in the third poem, for **"Sur l'herbe"** makes us see an elegant gathering of ladies and their admirers in a park-like decor. We may mentally supply a Watteau landscape, yet there is truly no description of background other than a final reference to the moon. Instead, all emphasis is upon the neat portraits of abbé, marquis, and feminine characters, all achieved through snatches of their conversation. The poem is thus a clever companion piece for **"Pantomime."**

We may note here that a certain correspondence between states of feeling and visual imagery has already been established by Verlaine. The implied significance of the visual effects in terms of the psychological and the spiritual must be touched upon briefly, if far from deeply. Let us say for now that sharpness of focus seems indicative of a tendency to remain on the surface emotionally and physically, with shallowness of feeling evident in the neatly drawn figures. The depths of love are not to be realized when all remains in a superficial mode and individual detachment is dominant. **"Clair de lune,"** on the other hand, suggests that "extase" lies only in the fusion of sensual experience with the beauty of the setting. We are struck especially by the constant mood of solitude, either physical or psychological, which is present in both types of poems; Verlaine is creating variations on this theme with visual images, for different sorts of spiritual solitude are suggested by the figures' merging with the backgrounds and by their standing detached, even in group scenes. The poet composes a suggestive total pattern by such means, and it will be helpful to plot the line of development he traces, shifting back and forth in his focus visually and psychologically. The whole sequence of ***Fêtes galantes*** must be surveyed rapidly before we attempt to see the total pattern.

The fourth poem **"L'Allée"** continues the formation of the pattern by offering a detailed description of a single figure sharply separated from the background. Verlaine directs our gaze to certain aspects of the woman, framing each detail by punctuation, a practice not used in works of the character of **"Clair de lune"** in which all is flow and merging.[12] The superficial and shallow beauty is indicated by words like "façons" and "afféteries" to typify the manner of the woman. We see her "fardée" and with an "éclat un peu niais de l'œil." The painted, doll-like figure stands alone in a sort of mindless sensual beauty; she seems to mark one extreme of visual imagery used to convey graphically Verlaine's modulations between the sensual and the spiritual. In the following poem the movement is toward effects of fusion, both visual and sentimental.

"A la promenade" is built with an easy flow of images which tend to merge the characters, their feelings, and the natural setting at the start. This is followed by a more distinct visualization of the lovers' gestures and looks, which then become conventional flirtation. The most important aspect of the spatial imagery in this work is the direction of motion of focus, with our eyes being led from hazy background to distinct foreground. "Le ciel si pâle et les arbres si grêles / Semblent sourire à nos costumes clairs" are the opening lines. In the second stanza an attenuated light "nous parvient bleue et mourante à dessein." The spiritual collaboration of nature in the love scene is suggested by visual images qualified by affective touches. From "ciel pâle" which is the deepest background the poem moves to a sharp focus upon the expression of eye and mouth at the end. We compare this technique with that of **"Clair de lune"** and note the skillful variations on use of visual imagery in depth.

The next poem, **"Dans la grotte,"** achieves an almost theatrical illusion with the stylized, précieux posing of the lovers against the background of an artificial grotto, dear to Rococo taste in landscaping. As every detail of the protestation of eternal love is conventional and literary, we see only two figures frozen in fixed attitudes and cut off from any natural background. Verlaine has elected to insert here in the ***Fêtes*** a small gem of pastiche which swiftly pulls us back from our impression of the fusion of love and nature in **"L'Allée."** Such rapid shifts of mode continue in **"Les Ingénus"** which again stresses images of merging, with a natural setting playing a key role.

The use of the imperfect tense is noteworthy in **"Les Ingénus,"** for with the title, it suggests a departed experience of youth which remains as a disturbing memory; "notre âme, depuis ce temps, tremble et s'étonne." The hints of sensual love are given through the agency of nature when terrain and wind cause skirts to lift or when an insect causes exposure of "nuques blanches." The scene fades into evening and the past as Verlaine introduces the temporal dimension into what has been a spatial pattern; the line "Le soir tombait, un soir équivoque d'automne" sounds a familiar note of visual vagueness, but this time it is not written in the present tense.

"Cortège" then follows with sharp visual effects much like those of **"L'Allée,"** adding further suggestions of sensuality in a similar context. A beautiful woman passes "par les escaliers" (the only background stated) accompanied by a "singe" and a "négrillon" who are described as minutely as she. They cast lascivious glances at her charms while she remains remote and unobtainable, and the whole scene thus becomes a rather grotesque parody of the lover pining for his lady. Her "animaux familiers" are visualized both through details of description and through characteristic gestures, a technique observed in Verlaine's **"Pantomime."** The movement in the poem is across one plane of foreground with everything in the same clear focus.

The ninth piece in ***Fêtes galantes***, **"Les Coquillages,"** at once echoes **"Dans la grotte,"** repeating these words in the second line, and shifts away from its rigidly posed formality and pastiche. Using images linking physical passions and beauties with the colors and forms of the shells in the grotto, the poet suggests the merging of the lovers into the setting. The highly contrived imagery which culminates in the sexually suggestive last line tends to create a brittle effect, however, and we find that the fragility of the shells surpasses any reality in the passion. The work is interesting in the terms of our study because of its purely ideational variations on the theme of relationships between figures and setting.

Verlaine has now conducted us almost to the midpoint of the ***Fêtes***, following a zigzag path which produces a sense of fluidity in space, time, and thought. The visual imagery has reflected the ambiguities and shifts of focus in the sentimental lives of the inhabitants of the Rococo setting. There is the suggestion that nothing has permanence except the fleeting moment of sensual joy and that this permanence is achieved only through a fusion with the lasting beauty of the landscape, or rather its artistic rendering. So far, the summit of love has not been attained, but in **"En patinant"** Verlaine approaches it at a pivotal point in the development of his suite of poems.

The unusual length of this poem, sixteen stanzas, strikes our attention after the preceding brief works, as does the variety of scenes evoked. These characteristics seem to mark some sort of departure because the narrator speaks to his love not about one moment together but rather about the temper of their past meetings in each season of the year. The poem thus reinforces the theme of love's joy recalled in association with settings. The tone of the lovemaking is set first by summer's "émoi" or by the more delicate perfumes of spring's flowers. "Les cinq sens / Se mettent alors de la fête, / Mais seuls, tout seuls, bien seuls et sans / Que la crise monte à la tête." These lines follow three stanzas which present the effects of the settings, swiftly pulling the figures back from dissolving sentimentally and visually into the background. The cerebral approach to passion is far from a fusion with nature's mood, and detachment is the rule. There is no moonlight here but rather a clear light; "Ce fut le temps, sous de clairs ciels / (Vous en souvenez-vous, Madame?) / Des baisers superficiels / Et les sentiments à fleur de l'âme." Such phrasing stresses the idea that all remains on the surface, and it is interesting to note that an early title for the work was "Sur la glace" (Bornecque, p. 124). **"En patinant"** is a title which preserves some of this sense yet adds the idea of motion.

Verlaine seems to deal in this central work with the established pattern of alternating merging and detachment in space; the seasonal backgrounds wait ready to absorb the figures from the foreground, toward which they regularly step and remain in clear focus. Nature aids and abets each scene of love, although there is no real assimilation of the characters into nature until the very end, and even this has a superficial tone. After summer's mood of abandon ("un bien ridicule vertigo"), autumn finds the lovers disciplined and controlled. The movement from one scene to another is particularly to be noted in **"En patinant,"** since this movement produces a strong sense of continuity which heretofore has been supplied by the reader in his progress from poem to poem. With a shift into the present tense the final two stanzas show the couple gliding over the ice to disappear from view into a flower-filled chamber. "Et bientôt Fanchon / Nous fleurira—quoi qu'on caquette!" The verb "fleurir" brings us full circle back to the flowery scene of spring and effectively suggests a merging at last into a natural cycle. We retain a strong impression, nevertheless, of the figures as "irréprochable amant" and "digne aimée" which are the stereotypes inhabiting the world of the ***Fêtes***. The visual images connected with such figures suffice to typify them as distinct and detached. Wonderfully ambiguous in this way, **"En patinant"** exploits the principal spatial effects and succeeds in combining them in one poem. The superficial and the merging, bearing the connotations we have noted before, are together in one work to an extent that Verlaine will not attempt in the poems to follow. Resuming a vacillating and shifting pattern of spatial imagery, the total movement in the rest of the suite will lead ever farther away from the suggestion of fusion with and fulfillment in nature found in **"En patinant."** The function of this work in the middle of the ***Fêtes*** is that of a psychological and formal dividing point in the overall pattern.

The title of the next poem, **"Fantoches,"** signals a return to the figures from the Italian comedy encountered in **"Pantomime."** The scene is lit by the moon but the illumination is not that of **"Clair de lune"** since we see "Scaramouche et Pulcinella" silhouetted "noirs sur la lune." The doctor and his daughter (Colombine of poems two and nineteen) pose detached and sharply visualized in the portrait stanzas, while the natural setting is limited to references to "herbe brune" and "charmille." A nightingale plays a mediating role between the "fantoches" and the moonlit background, making its presence known through its singing, first "langoureux" then noisy when the song "clame la détresse à tue-tête." The theatrical effect of the composition is striking and clearly the intent of this poem about characters who are only puppets. The superficial quality of **"Fantoches"** is so marked that we must conclude that Verlaine placed it here in his ***Fêtes*** to stress this very effect.

"Cythère" comes next, followed by four other poems with consistent images of merging, and it seems as if the poet wished to balance **"Fantoches"** against this movement. In a group of succeeding poems, numbers seventeen through twenty, the tendency will be to resume strongly the spatial effects of sharp detachment, so that we perceive the zigzag pattern of motion back and forth in visual depth and focus is now composed of more pronounced swings and pauses. The almost alternate shifting of focus from one poem to the next in the first half of the collection is not the model for the second half. Let us see how the entire composition is carried through by Verlaine.

"Cythère" has images like "abrite doucement" and "l'odeur des roses . . . se mêle aux parfums qu'elle a mis." Nature's mood blends with that of the lovers throughout most of the poem, while at the end there is a witty and ironic touch which undoes a bit the idyllic atmosphere; "Et, l'Amour comblant tout, hormis / La Faim, sorbets et confitures / Nous préservent des courbatures." The title brings to mind Watteau's painting, but instead of showing the lovers moving off into a hazy setting of natural beauty, Verlaine's final focus is all upon foreground detail. The next poem, **"En bateau,"** seems to combine effects of detachment and fusion into background in a new way, although the material used is by now quite familiar to us.

We recognize here the group of figures encountered in **"Sur l'herbe,"** this time on a moonlight boating party. The technique of depiction through speeches and visual images is coupled with a setting reminiscent of **"Clair de lune."** As the "abbé" and "ce vicomte déréglé" talk and gesticulate, the whole group moves off into the dim moonlight which is stressed at the beginning and end of the work; "L'étoile du berger tremblote / Dans l'eau noire" and "la lune se lève / Et l'esquif en sa course brève / File gaîment sur l'eau qui rêve." The personification of the water recalls that in **"Clair de lune,"** serving to remind us again of the means often used by Verlaine to suggest emotion, embodiment of feeling in the natural background rather than in the human figures. The total effect is one of strong merging.

"Le Faune" is the fourteenth of the ***Fêtes galantes***, which now shows us two shadowy characters appearing upon the "boulingrins" for "ces instants sereins" before "cette heure dont la fuite / Tournoie au son des tambourins." The ephemeral and hazy atmosphere of this meeting of lovers is emphasized by these final lines. The statue of the faun mocks them with his laughing expression "présageant sans doute une suite mauvaise." A moment of love is suspended in space and time, just on the brink of swirling away to the sound of the music, and amidst all the fading scene the most definite image is that of the ironic face of the faun. The last poem of the suite, **"Colloque sentimental,"** will seem like a ghostly repetition of this fleeting tryst of "mélancoliques pèlerins."

The next work is a companion piece to **"Le Faune,"** sharing not only the principle of merging of figures into vague setting but also the same sort of final images to create such an effect. **"Mandoline"** does not stress music, despite its title, for there is only a subtle suggestion of musical accompaniment. At the start the characters are called "donneurs de sérénades" and "belles écouteuses," but then the images become visual and we proceed from a slight reference to background ("les ramures chanteuses") to a depiction of "Tircis" and other conventional figures from pastoral. The focus in the third stanza moves to fix upon details of dress, but this is seen clearly only in passing as the characters shift into "molles ombres bleues." The final stanza shows these shadows dissolving, dancing away into the night, this time to the music of the mandolin. The ending is an excellent example of Verlaine's procedure in mingling emotions, sound, characters, and natural setting, all on a basis of visual perceptions.

Leurs courtes vestes de soie,
Leurs longues robes à queue,
Leur élégance, leur joie,
Et leurs molles ombres bleues
Tourbillonnent dans l'extase
D'une lune rose et grise,
Et la mandoline jase
Parmi les frissons de brise.

The adjectives of color are to be noted, as is the identification of "extase" with the moonlight. A keynote from **"Clair de lune"** continues to sound.

"A Clymène" is characterized by the mingling of senses and states of feeling, a technique highly evocative of the Baudelairean synesthesia and its poetic forms. The stanzas in praise of the beauty include visual images, but they are merely part of the total impression of Clymène's charms. The residual picture we possess of the typical object of devotion, so often portrayed in these poems, permits us to visualize her, indeed makes us do so. The very conventional nature of the language of the "irréprochable amant" signals that we are in the superficial plane of the world of the ***Fêtes***; the atmosphere of posed pastiche such as that of **"Dans la grotte"** is handled with more subtlety, however, and there is a slight movement toward the fusion of senses seen in **"Mandoline."**

The logic of the arrangement of the ***Fêtes galantes*** has been based thus far upon a constant shifting of visual and spatial focus, with attendant intellectual and emotional effects. The poet has so prepared the way that he now can profit from a foregoing stock of images and refer to them merely by the tone of the poem. We see the fixed and superficial pose of the lover in the stylized love letter of the piece **"Lettre,"** and we also recognize in it the suggestion of the mode of detachment. **"Lettre"** is of interest as well in its foreshadowing of the end of the whole suite, when the ghosts of the lovers return. The letter writer declares his intention of dying and joining his love in a phantom embrace; "Mon ombre se fondra à jamais en votre ombre." The trite phrasing ("En attendant, je suis, très chère, ton valet") underscores the brittle superficiality here, yet we apprehend the principle of fusion of the lovers into a hazy space and time as one of the keys to Verlaine's "paysage de l'âme." In a detached and ironic mode the poet is actually presenting the same theme so often observed in his poems characterized by imagery of merging. Some more somber variations on this theme and mode are to be seen in the next two works.

"Les Indolents" resembles **"Le Faune"** in that the lovers are mockingly observed by "deux silvains hilaires," statues of grinning demigods of the woods. Through the medium of these statues we hear the empty and conventional words of passion uttered by the man, who suggests a dramatic death for love to the lady amused by his pretensions. In visual terms the focus is wholly upon foreground figures, a technique consistently associated with irony of tone and theme. The idea of death, even though treated ironically here, persists and comes to dominate the last poems of the ***Fêtes***.

"Colombine" is a reprise of the earlier images of characters from the commedia dell'arte and the "fantoches," but now the treatment assumes a tone of dark fatality. Pierrot, Arlequin, and the others become a procession of "dupes" led by a perverse enchantress, "l'implacable enfant." The familiar cast of **"Pantomime"** is shown again, each in typical gesture, so that we visualize the scene down to details such as the "yeux luisants" and "rose au chapeau." Despite the singing and dancing reminiscent of **"Clair de lune,"** the "troupeau de dupes" moves off toward some "mornes ou cruels désastres" in a "fatidique cours," led by lust for Colombine. The movement of the figures is a procession across a sharply depicted foreground without any suggestion of fading into the natural setting.

"L'Amour par terre" is a logical continuation of the theme of love cast down seen in the two preceding poems; "le vent de l'autre nuit a jeté bas l'Amour." The destruction of the statue of Eros by the forces of nature foreshadows for the poem's narrator his own "avenir solitaire et fatal." The empty pedestal is shown to us with the repeated lament "c'est triste," while words such as "tout seul" and "solitaire" stress heavily the impression of objects and characters standing isolated in the garden damaged by the storm. The last stanza is particularly effective in its visual images of detachment. The narrator appeals to his companion who is amusing her "œil frivole" with a purple and gold butterfly, a sharply visualized detail placed against a background which is no longer the typical Rococo garden but rather a "dolent tableau" of "débris dont l'allée est jonchée." The storm seems to have destroyed all hope of ever again merging into the world composed of natural beauty, moonlight, and love. The narrator senses this, but his beloved remains heedlessly indifferent.

Gloom and darkness, and the impossibility of recapturing the joys of love, are pervasive in the two final works, which also have an interesting modification of the imagery dealing with fusion of figures and setting. Accompanying the loss of love is a resigned despair which seems to linger on forever, haunting the world of ***Fêtes*** now inhabited by the phantoms of the lovers. **"En sourdine"** is characterized by very strong images of merging, but it is now into darkness and death that all dissolves. In a "demi-jour" invaded by black shadows there is deep silence; "pénétrons bien notre amour / De ce silence profond." The second stanza is almost a summation of the whole scheme of fusion of figures and setting, both visually and spiritually:

Fondons nos âmes, nos cœurs
Et non sens extasiés,
Parmi les vagues langueurs
Des pins et des arbousiers.

With use of branches, trees, wind, russet grass, and oaks, Verlaine stresses the background scene, while the verbs "pénétrons" and "fondons" are in dominant positions. The last stanza leaves no doubt about the tone of dark despair which permeates:

Et quand, solennel, le soir
Des chênes noirs tombera
Voix de notre désespoir,
Le rossignol chantera.

The two lovers seem at last assimilated into the scene, but their final appearance in **"Colloque sentimental"** makes it evident that they exist now only as disembodied spirits haunting neglected gardens. The cold wind of death has swept through the moonlit land of the ***Fêtes galantes***.

With the cruel transformation by time of both setting and characters in **"Colloque sentimental,"** this final poem lays heavy stress on the fugitive nature of the dreams of love in an enchanted world. The promised bliss still seems to elude the lovers who turn back in memory in search of it; "deux spectres ont évoqué le passé." The dark sky, the ruined park, the "avoines folles" which fill the former gardens, all stand in sharp contrast with the gentle beauty visualized in the earlier poems. The couple, cut off now from the visible world, is as vague as "deux formes," and we recognize them only by their voices. To the lover's reiteration of the old pleas the beloved replies that "l'espoir a fui, vaincu, vers le ciel noir." Emptiness of setting, "le vieux parc solitaire et glacé," and the dissolution of the human figures constitute the last image of visual fusion in the ***Fêtes***. This ending seems like a grim joke after the idylls suggested before, but it is hardly unexpected. Time has elapsed despite the brilliant evocation of the world of the past; the inhabitants have faded into death while the park has reverted to weeds. Night swallows all; "la nuit seule entendit leurs paroles."

In his ***Fêtes galantes*** Verlaine creates a suite of poems unified and articulated to a great extent through the use of visual and spatial imagery. The subtly varied stress, first upon sharp foreground figures and then upon fusion into dim setting, produces a rhythmic pattern in time as one poem follows another. If we sense an unsteadying zigzag motion in reading the suite, it is because of the gentle modulations or swift changes of focus called for to visualize things. In effect, the poet's handling of visual and spatial aspects of his work is of prime importance in his creation of a musicality. It is truly through visualization that we first feel the rhythms and modes which have an ultimately musical effect in the ***Fêtes***, both individually and as a total composition.

Synchronous harmonies or the effects of chords are, of course, part of Verlaine's poetic musicality, and these we have not tried to analyze. The essential form of these poems appears to be keyed to things seen as detached or merged (with their attendant accretions of meaning) which are arranged in a particular time sequence. The use of such means of expression is only part of Verlaine's great poetic capability, and an oversimplified explanation of his techniques is not intended. This study of verbally expressed visual patterns in space, which are also musical patterns in time, should suggest lines for future investigation. The pictorial in poetry surely finds one of its great masters in Verlaine, whose skill in handling essential artistic form is evident in ***Fêtes galantes***.

Notes

1. For the text of the poems my source is the Pléiade edition of Verlaine's *Œuvres poétiques complètes,* ed. Y.-G. Le Dantec and Jacques Borel (Paris: Gallimard, 1962).

2. Eléonore M. Zimmermann, *Magies de Verlaine* (Paris: José Corti, 1967), examines the meaning of "paysage" for Verlaine in Ch. x.

3. "Images formelles dans *Clair de lune* de Verlaine," *Revue des Sciences Humaines*, Fasc. 130 (April-June 1968), pp. 259–66.

4. *Poésie et profondeur* (Paris: Seuil, 1955), p. 166.

5. *Paul Verlaine* (Paris: Mercure de France, 1961), p. 94.

6. A selection of critical studies concerned with the relationships between Verlaine's poetry and music should include the following: Antoine Adam, *Verlaine, l'homme et l'œuvre* (Paris: Hatier-Bovin, 1953); Albert Béguin, *Poésie de la présence* (Neuchâtel: La Baconnière, 1957); Pierre Fortassier, "Verlaine, la musique et les musiciens," *Cahiers de l'Association Internationale des Etudes Françaises,* 12 (June 1960), 143–59; V. P. Underwood, "Sources théâtrales de Verlaine," *Revue d'Histoire Littéraire de la France*, 57 (April-June 1957), 196–203.

7. *French Review*, 40 (April 1967), 627–35.

8. An interesting use, or abuse, of musical terms by art historians is found in Pierre d'Espezel and François Fosca, *Histoire de la peinture* (Paris: Somogy, 1958), p. 130; they write of Watteau's paintings, "Le véritable sujet d'un tableau de Watteau est une nuance de sensibilité que le langage serait incapable de préciser. Au lieu de leurs titres vagues, ses œuvres devraient être désignés par des indications de nuances musicales: dolce, allegretto, appassionato, etc."

9. *Etudes verlainiennes: Lumières sur les* Fêtes galantes *de Paul Verlaine* (Paris: Nizet, 1959), passim.

10. *L'œuvre et ses techniques* (Paris: Nizet, 1957), pp. 71–84.

11. For paintings by Watteau and other artists, see François Fosca, *The Eighteenth Century: Watteau to Tiepolo* (New York: Skira, 1952), esp. the chapter "Watteau's Dreamworld."

12. Bornecque notes that Verlaine originally wrote this poem without interior punctuation, p. 156.

Philip Stephan (essay date 1974)

SOURCE: "1884–85: Verlaine's Influence and Les Deliquescences d're Floupette," in *Paul Verlaine and the Decadence, 1882–90*, Manchester University Press, 1974, pp. 81–98.

[*In the following essay, Stephan examines Verlaine's influence on the movement of young Decadent poets.*]

As Verlaine receives favourable treatment in critical articles, verse appearing in magazines reveals his influence on younger poets. The earliest instance we have been able to find is Guy-Valvor's (Georges André Vayssière) 'Raquettes et volants', which appeared in *Lutèce* on 7–14 September 1883. Guy-Valvor describes two girls playing badminton: oblivious to love, they are unaware that one day they will be the rackets and their lovers, 'les pauvres coeurs torturés', the shuttlecocks they hit back and forth. It is obvious that his poem copies Verlaine's **'La Chanson des ingénues'**:[1] both contrast the frivolity of young girls with their amorous maturity when they have grown into women, both use similar language and identical form. While in Verlaine's poem it is the girls who feel their hearts beat harder, '. . . / A des pensers clandestins, / En nous sachant les amantes / Futures des libertins', in Guy-Valvor's it is the poet-observer who is so moved: 'Sous l'enfant trouvant la femme, / Mon coeur se sentait frémir / A voir ces jeunes coquettes, / . . . / Se renvoyer le volant.' One stanza of 'Raquettes et volants' could serve as a summary of Verlaine's poem, as well:

> Mais elles, insouciantes,
> De l'amour encor lointain,
> Avec leurs grâces riantes
> Eblouissaient le jardin.

In both the girls wear white, airy dresses and shepherdess hats, in both they have blue eyes. The stanza

> Quand les blanches mousselines
> S'envolaient en plis bouffants,
> Les brises semblaient câlines
> Ravir les belles enfants!

recalls Verlaine's lines 'Et nos robes—si légères— / Sont d'une extrême blancheur', and the third line, with *câlines* seemingly out of place ('Les brises *câlines* semblaient . . .') recalls the difficult *vont charmant* construction which opens **'Clair de lune'** (p. 107). Turns of a phrase suggest Verlaine's very language: '[le volant] . . . / Par leurs prodiges d'adresse / Contrarié sans pitié', to choose from many possible examples, echoes the *préciosité* of much of the language of ***Fêtes galantes***.[2] Guy-Valvor need not have gone to Verlaine for the eighteenth century theme (although his equating an historical period with a subject for erotic revery is Verlainean), which was popular during the 1880's quite independently of ***Fêtes galantes***. As for the heptasyllabic line, Guy-Valvor's other poems are in alexandrines or other *vers pair* rhythms, and *vers impairs* in fact begin to appear only as such imitations of Verlaine become prevalent. Apparently **'Art poétique'** introduced a metre which Verlaine himself probably took from Baudelaire.

A year later Georges Khnopff has a dozen poems entitled 'XVIIIe siècle' in *La Jeune Belgique*,[3] a magazine which otherwise did not usually reflect decadent trends. In one ('III', pp. 436–7) Pierrot, with his flask of claret and his *pâté*, the word group *ce faquin d'Arlequin*, and the presence of Cassandre suggest Verlaine's **'Pantomime'**; the line 'La brise ride les bassins' recalls 'Et le vent doux ride l'humble bassin' of 'A la promenade' (p. 109). Another poem ('IX', p. 439) has numerous verbal similarities of this order, most of which echo **'Clair de lune'**—a further indication that Khnopff probably imitated Verlaine is the mingling of gaiety with melancholy, and the sad hearts hidden by carnival masks, which characterise ***Fêtes galantes***:

> La belle Colombine . . .
> . . . songe
> Que toute joie, au loin, n'est que mensonge
> Et que tous ces railleurs élégants et fantasques
> Déguisant leur ennui sous le blanc de leurs masques
> Et le satin brodé de leurs basquines roses
> Raffinent la tristesse adorable des choses.
>
> [p. 439]

It should be borne in mind that devices which remind us of Verlaine's verse were often in fact clichés of the period which he himself got from Victor Hugo, the Parnassians, or Baudelaire. This is true of the verbal music and the metric variations which became more and more common in poetry during the season 1883–84. The increasing popularity of the impressionist style must have been due to the Goncourts' prose rather than to Verlaine. Traits which are peculiar to Verlaine, and thus exclude his predecessors as possible sources, are echoes of his diction, his distinctive mood of dream and melancholy, his vagueness, and his taste for pale, muted colours. Such distinctions can be made in Emile Michelet's 'In votis':

> Ce serait par un soir doux et calme d'été,
> A l'heure où les lueurs et les rumeurs dernières
> S'éteignaient mollement dans la sérénité.
>
> . . . . .
>
> Elle aurait dix-huit ans et des mines câlines,
> Et me raconterait des riens, niaise un peu,
> D'une voix douce comme un choeur de mandolines,
> Blonde et blanche dans son peignoir de satin bleu.
>
> [*Lutèce*, 15–22 March 1884]

Although the opening line is an obvious echo of 'Donc, ce sera par un clair jour d'été' in ***La Bonne Chanson*** (p. 153), the various assonances and alliterations of the second line were in common use before Verlaine's poems began appearing in *La Nouvelle Rive Gauche.* In the last stanza, to the contrary, the conditional tense, the inversion of *niaise* and *un peu*, the simile based on aural *correspondances,* and the pairing of colours which are close to each other in hue or value ('Blonde et blanche') are most likely derived from Verlaine. Equally reminiscent of him is Charles Vignier's 'Dans le [*sic*] rose':

> Errants au pays falots
> Mes rêves, berceuses yoles,
> Ont arboré pour falots
> Deux yeux bleus, deux lucioles.
>
> [*Lutèce*, 27 April–4 May 1884]

As with Guy-Valvor's poem, the *vers impair* of seven syllables can be attributed only to Verlaine, and the vocables *falots* and *berceuses* are also typical of his verse. Additional poems by Vignier ('Paysage' and 'Vision', *Lutèce*, 18–25 May 1884; 'Retour de Cythère' and 'Tristesses', 1–7 September 1884) bear out the judgement of reviewers who commented on the Verlainean tenor of his collection of verse *Le Centon* in 1887.

A facetious, but revealing, commentary on the extent of Verlaine's influence is made by a parody which appeared in *Lutèce* in the fall of 1884:

> Las! la fleur qui fleure, effleure
> L'ultime heure, la meilleure,
> Et pleure;—oh! combien subtils
> Les sanglots en les pistils.[4]

Jean Laurent's poem does not seem too different from some of Vignier's serious verse; apparently, in the year since Guy-Valvor's poem appearred, ceratin of Verlaine's mannerisms had become platitudes of minor decadent verse! An accompanying letter has an epigraph from Verlaine consisting simply of two lines of suspension points, thus suggesting that a few poems were so honoured *ad nauseam*, and perhaps poking fun at the ineffableness of Verlaine's verse:

> Monsieur le Directeur,
>
> La très niaise humanitairerie musagète se meurt. D'aucuns pionniers, humbles mais fiers, installent audacieusement la poésie enfin vraie, celle du transcendantalement intime vertige (Obliquitas somnorum). Il faut les suivre, sinon les imiter. (Interroga virtutem tuam.) J'ai travaillé dans ce sens. Je vous envoie une de mes meilleures oeuvres. Son insertion dans *Lutèce* sera l'irréfragable sanction de mon enrôlement définitif. J'ose attendre.
>
> Salut dans l'art,
>
> Jean-Charles Laurent

As in this letter, the decadents' sometimes pompous literary theories and their Latinate prose style were common targets for parody. More interesting is the reference to *d'aucuns pionniers*, which implies that Verlaine and others had been accepted as guides.

At the end of 1884 and the beginning of 1885 the Belgian periodical *La Basoche* published two poems showing Verlaine's influence: 'Lune d'avril', by Adolphe Ribaux:

> La lune de printemps, sur les amandiers roses,
> Sur le vert chèvrefeuille et les pruniers en fleur,
> Glisse, comme un baiser, sa laiteuse pâleur,
> Et dans l'air musical flotte l'âme des choses.
>
> [1, 2 December 1884, p. 82]

and 'Sur la plage', by Jacques Madeleine:

> Blanches ailes des barques frêles,
> Vois ces taches d'un ton plus clair
> Sur le vert sombre de la mer:
> Sont-ce des voiles ou des ailes?
>
> [11, 3 January 1885, p. 120]

This highly impressionistic first stanza (dated, appropriately enough, at Etretat on the Channel coast) could have been imitated from Verlaine, or it could be cognate with Verlaine's landscapes. The date of the poem, the polish of its impressionism, and perhaps the interrogation in the fourth line, argue for Verlaine as the source. Almost certainly derived from Verlaine are the dream-like quality of the tercets and their apostrophe to an unreal, inaccessible woman. They duplicate the tone of love poems like **'En Sourdine'** (p. 120) and **'Circonspection'** (p. 329):

> Rêveuse qui les suit des yeux,
> Veux-tu regarder tous les deux
> La même voile, au loin qui tremble?
>
> La seule extase sans rancoeurs,
> Le plus délicat des bonheurs,
> C'est encor, de rêver ensemble.

Verlaine's influence is also apparent in the verse of his friend Jean Moréas, some of whose poems appeared in *Lutèce* ('Rythme boîteux' and 'Les Bonnes Souvenances', 29 June–6 July 1884; 'Remembrances', 10–17 August 1884), and whose first collection, *Les Syrtes*, came out at the end of the year. Reviewing the volume in *La Revue Contemporaine*, Gabriel Sarrazin praised it ('Ceci est un exquis volume de vers, et qui nous a complètement séduit'),[5] but with major reservations. Some poems, he says, are resonant and meaningless, others repeat, perhaps unintentionally, some of Baudelaire's mystic poems: 'Bref, *Les Syrtes* ne dégagent pas une pensée poétique vraiment originale, et en outre, l'art—si remarquable—de l'auteur va se perdre et s'enliser parfois dans le byzantisme [synonym for decadence].' Then—at least, implicitly—he compares Moréas to Verlaine: 'Son vers est le plus musical de l'heure actuelle et la suavité de sa mélodie métrique dépasse celle de M. Verlaine lui-même. . . . Puis la plastique de M. Moréas rivalise sa musique; en lui, comme en M. Verlaine, fusionnent avec science un peintre et un lyrique. . . .' In *La Basoche* a reviewer states bluntly: 'Jean Moréas est de ceux qui prennent pour devise les vers de Paul Verlaine: "Car nous voulons la nuance encore, / Pas la couleur, rien que la nuance",'[6] thus indicating not only

Moréas' debt to Verlaine but also the importance which **'Art poétique'** was beginning to have for the younger generation.

At the end of 1884 Léon Vanier published ***Jadis et naguère*** in an edition of 500 copies printed by Léo Trézenik, presumably on the same hand press he used for *Lutèce*. This was Verlaine's first collection of verse since his return to Paris, and it contained poems from all stages of his career, as well as **'Art poétique'**; it could therefore serve as an anthology for those who were just now beginning to read his poetry. In his review for *La Revue Contemporaine* Sarrazin is distinctly uncharitable; while granting 'l'adorable et musicale suavité' of some poems he states '. . . peut-être l'oeuvre entière de M. Verlaine relèverait-elle plus de la psychologe que de l'esthétique. . . . Pour le moment' nous nous contenterons de recommander à ceux qui se croient obligés d'aimer qu'on dépasse les limites permises de l'énervement et de la déliquescence de la pensée certaines pièces à cet égard très réussies, dans ***Jadis et naguère***, et de vrais modèles du genre: 'Sonnet boîteux', 'A Albert Mérat', 'Langueur', 'Madrigal', etc.'[7] It is significant that Sarrazin devotes most of his remarks to the decadence of Verlaine's poems.

What distinguishes the year 1885 from the preceding one is a growing awareness, both in little magazines and in the *grande presse*, of the existence of a decadent school of poetry, with Verlaine and Mallarmé at its head. Thus in an article by Paul Grandet in *Le Cri du Peuple* (quoted in *Lutèce*) we notice the matter-of-fact way in which Grandet describes Verlaine as the leader of the new poetry:

> De la poésie! mais cela n'est pas de la poésie, s'écrieront ceux pour qui M. Paul Verlaine est un grand homme et aux yeux desquels M. Laurent Tailhade (???!) est assez près d'égaler Victor Hugo. Sans doute, ce n'est pas de la poésie telle qu'ils la comprennent; assemblage de mots sans signification précise; petit jeu de patience à l'usage des fils de famille; idées: néant; rimes riches. . . .[8]

Writing in *Les Débats*, Paul Bourget observes that French literature is becoming increasingly like that of northern Europe, and that the place to look for the works of promising new poets is in the newspapers and magazines where they publish. Neither realism, nor pictorial verse, nor even Victor Hugo influence these young writers any longer; the only modern writer whom they revere as a master is Baudelaire, and then it is not the etcher of *Tableaux parisiens* but the mystic poet whom they esteem. He goes on to describe the influence of Verlaine:

> De tous les poètes de talent qui firent partie du groupe du *Parnasse*, un seul paraît avoir fait école parmi cette jeunesse, M. Paul Verlaine. Cet écrivain étrange, et dont le grand public ignore jusqu'au nom, a essayé de réproduire avec ses vers les naunces qui font le domaine propre de la musique, tout l'indéterminé de la sensation et du sentiment. Parfois il a échoué dans cette tentative presque impossible, parfois il a réussi à composer des poèmes d'une originalité délicieuse, comme celui-ci tiré de ses *Fêtes galantes*, et qui fait tenir en deux strophes tout un infini de rêveries: [quotes 'Le Faune', p. 115].
>
> Inégal et heurté, parfois exquis et parfois insaisissable, M. Paul Verlaine a une popularité de cénacle qui est un des signes les plus particuliers de cette époque. Il est aimé les par mêmes jeunes gens qui, du premier jour se sont reconnus dans les romans traduits de ce douleureux Dostoïewski! . . . de ces jeunes gens qui se passionnent pour la peinture de M. Gustave Moreau, pour les dessins de M. Odilon Redon, pour tout ce qui est suggestion, demiteinte, recherche de l'au-delà, clair-obscur d'âme. Après la débauche de réalisme à laquelle se sont livrés les écrivains de 1870, voici venir l'inévitable réaction; après l'idolâtrie de la vie, le culte du rêve. *A Rebours*, ce roman de M. Huysmans, où se trouvaient analysées les sensations d'un homme uniquement épris d'artifice, n'est pas loin d'être un livre de stricte exactitude . . .[9]

Bourget states Verlaine's ascendancy over younger writers in stronger terms than 'Jean Mario' did two years previously; for Bourget, Verlaine has 'fait école parmi cette jeunesse' and he enjoys 'une popularité de cénacle'. While heretofore decadence was seen as characterising a few obscure but worthy authors, for Bourget, as for subsequent observers, it is a widespread style among the young generation. Finally Bourget describes decadence not as a curious literary style but in aesthetic terms: dark introspection, Dostoievskian intricacy, and highly imaginative paintings. Although Bourget acknowledges the public's ignorance of Verlaine, he gives the impression of Verlaine presiding over substantial numbers of literate youth, a youth imbued with a coherent *esthétique.* The picture is not yet that of a school of poets, but it is closer to it than previous treatments of Verlaine as an unjustly neglected author only now beginning to receive his due.

Beside an edited version of Bourget's article in the 19–26 April issue of *Lutèce* appeared Trézenik's regular 'Chronique lutécienne' column, devoted to 'Les Décadents de l'allitérature': 'Ils ont longtemps porté les cheveux longs "à la Musset". Aujourd'hui les ciseaux de la décadence ont passé par là. Ils s'enorgueillissent d'une tête rase et se vantent d'un menton glabre "à la Baudelaire".'[10] After indicating Verlaine's influence on the decadents, he predicts that they will go on to new excesses: already Verlaine is insufficiently obscure, and the day is not far off when Mallarmé will be too clear and Poictevin too bourgeois. Trézenik's article is a practical, facetious counterpart of Bourget's; with the good-humoured mockery which was his trademark, he shows what decadent literature will be like when Bourget's aesthetics have been put into practice by the minor writers who, by and large, composed the decadent movement.

The publication in *Lutèce* of two of Jules Laforgue's *Complaintes* in March (8–15 March) and in June the first instalment of the second series of Verlaine's **'Poètes maudits'**, on Marceline Desbordes-Valmore (7–14 June), was illustrative of a new tone. Laforgue, who was to die prematurely of tuberculosis after composing a few slim volumes of ironic, pungently moribund verse, was an epitome of decadence; thanks to T. S. Eliot's and Ezra Pound's adoption in English of his techniques, he is also a principal link between decadence and contemporary poetry. When we see four of Verlaine's **'Limbes'** literally beside Laforgue's 'Complainte de mon Sacré-Coeur', as we do in the issue of 19–26 July 1885, we can appreciate how much poetic sensibility had changed in less than three years.

During the spring of 1885 *Lutèce* published facetious comments under the rubric 'Lettre d'un bourgeois', which purported to show the reactions of the typical conservative bourgeois to the new poetry, although, in a double-edged sort of way, the letters also indicated weakness of decadent verse. With reference to Mallarmé's 'Prose pour des Esseintes', recently published in *La Revue Indépendante*, one such letter complains that the writer is sick of 'Des Esseintisme' and its quest for the unusual at any cost (1–8 March 1885), and another observes, 'Et bien, en vérité, toute cette école actuelle, tous ces bons petits jeunes qui ne font qu'éclore à la littérature, sont des—oh! je vous en prie, M. Mostrailles, accordez-moi d'imprimer ce mot, qui rend si bien ma pensée—sont des emmerdeurs.'[11] The same writer protests that the decadents' philosophical pessimism is a German import unworthy of young Frenchmen.

The outstanding event of 1885, which brought the various confused notions of the new poetry into sharp focus, was the publication in May and June of *Les Déliquescences* of Adoré Floupette.[12] This was simply a collection of silly poems parodying the decadent manner, but even parody illustrated the decadent style, and, as with *A Rebours* the previous year, the furor attracted the attention of the general public and of the *grande presse*. Of course, it also brought fame to Etienne Arsenal and Bleucoton, as Mallarmé and Verlaine were dubbed in the book.

Like several other documents the importance of which in the history of decadence outweighs their intrinsic literary worth, *Les Déliquescences* appeared first in *Lutèce*. On 1–8 February there were two poems, obvious parodies of Mallarmé's style, over the signature of Etienne Arsenal: 'Le Petunia sauveur' and 'Cantique avant de se coucher'. The issue of 19–26 published under the title of 'Les Déliquescences' three 'Fragments d'une symphonie en vert mineur': 'Andante', 'Scherzo', and 'Pizzicati'. The issue of 3–10 May carried four more poems: 'Platonisme', 'Pour être conspué', 'Madrigal', and 'Rhythme claudicant". On 2 May these poems, and ten more, were published in a small brochure on luxury paper, one of Vanier's limited editions for bibliophiles.[13] In keeping with the parody, the title page gave 'Lion Vanné' as the publisher and Byzantium as the place of publication. This edition was so promptly bought up that a second one of 1,500 copies, augmented with a preface by Marius Tapora, pharmacist second-class, was published the following month. (The preface appeared in *Lutèce* for 14–12 June.) Even this edition was sold out in a fortnight, and copies soon became collector's items. 'Adoré Floupette' was the pseudonym of two *Lutece* contributors, Henri Beauclair and Gabriel Vicaire, both very minor poets who continued to publish conventional verse long after the *Déliquescences* affair. Ironically, the poems of *Les Déliquescences* are their best-known work, and, just as ironically, what began as another joke for the amusement of staff and readers mushroomed into the publication which brought more notoriety to the decadents than their serious literary efforts.

The 'Préface' describes the life of Adoré Floupette, his literary evolution from romantic to decadent, and how Tapora finds him in Paris. The two men go to a café, the *Panier fleuri*, where a decadent meeting is taking place, and where Floupette gets wonderfully drunk. In the course of the evening Bleucoton-Verlaine is positively identified by an allusion to one of his poems. The next day Floupette and Tapora visit Floupette's mentor, M. Poulard des Roses; Floupette recites Mallarmé's 'La Mort de la pénultième', and Tapora, too, decides to become a decadent. With much effort and goodwill he succeeds in understanding some of the decadent poets, but not all: if Bleucoton is comprehensible, Arsenal continues to elude him.

After the introduction, or 'Liminaire', which continues the satirical tone of the 'Préface', there follow the eighteen poems, some of them nonsense, others parodies of individual styles, and all of them exaggerations of decadent vocabulary and versification: 'Les Enervées de Jumiège', 'Platonisme', 'Pour etre conspué', 'Suavitas', 'Avant d'entrer', 'Idylle symbolique'; four poems comprising the movements of 'Symphonie en vert mineur: variations sur un thème vert pomme', 'Madrigal', 'Rhythme claudicant', 'Pour avoir péché', 'Le Sonnet libertin', 'Catique avant de se coucher', 'Remords', 'Bal décadent', and 'Décadent'.

The response from the philistine press was so prompt and voluminous that suddenly articles on Verlaine and the new poets were no longer a rarity. We shall, therefore, comment only on a few of the more representative ones. Gabriel Mermeix, writing in *Le XIXe Siecle* on 17 May, seems, to the merriment of the decadents, to have taken the whole thing seriously. In *Gil Blas* ('Le Décadent', 17 May 1885), Paul Arène merely questions the decadents' originality, pointing out that young poets have always sought novel effects. The *Revue Contemporaine* describes the decadent school, recognises the *Déliquescences* as a timely parody, and suggests that the parody hurts the minor followers more than it does the two leaders, Verlaine and Mallarmé.[14] Before undertaking to discuss 'Les Poètes impressionnistes et Adoré Floupette' the *Bibliothèque Universelle et Revue Suisse* felt obliged to explain, 'La langue des vers change si vite en France, à notre époque, qu'il suffit de la délaisser pendant quelques mois pour n'y plus rien comprendre du tout.'[15] It then approaches *Les Déliquescences* by way of Banville, Maurice Vaucaire (*Arc-en-ciel*, Lemerre 1885, in verse; prolific author of comedies and novels), and Mallarmé, after whom 'il n'y a plus qu'à tirer l'échelle' (p. 389). Sutter Laumann ('*Les Déliquescences*', *La Justice* 19 July 1885) ridicules the *Déliquescences*, and he seems to have originated the theory that decadent poetry could be composed simply by choosing words at random, in a dictionary or a hat, and arranging them according to the number of syllables. In *Le Figaro* (22 September 1885) Labruyère draws a humorous portrait of the typical decadent. Paul Armon, after some delay, discusses 'Les Poètes maudits', or decadents, in *La France Libre* for 3 October 1885.

In June appeared two articles which addressed themselves to the general question of philosophical pessimism among the youth of the country, rather than specifically to *Les Déliquescences*. Both seek to determine the causes and to describe the effects of the mood which prevailed among the young generation.

In *La Revue Bleue* for 6 June 1885 Dionys Ordinaire treats the question in a light, sarcastic, and mocking tone; while correctly identifying the phenomenon of pessimism, he refuses to take it seriously: 'Il souffle d'Allemagne, depuis quelques années, sur notre jeunesse française, un vent aigre et malsain qui nous apporte une épidémie nouvelle, inconnue à notre vieille Gaule: celle du pessimisme.'[16] He proceeds to describe, always in bantering terms, the effects of this malady and to discuss its Teutonic origin. The disease is all the more redoubtable in that the French, *outranciers* by nature, tend to overdo new ideas. Thus Teutonic pessimism has taken root in France, even among young men who have not read the German philosophers. These youths reject all the gifts of Mother Nature and long for death and even for complete annihilation of being. Such is the case of a few young writers who act like wits and wish to shock the bourgeoisie. Every school has its antecedents, and those of the pessimists are '. . . les moroses comme Stendhal, comme Mérimée, comme Flaubert, l'écrivain le plus surfait de notre siécle' (p. 707), and the '. . . poètes désespérés: Musset, le chantre de l'hystérisme; Baudelaire, l'esprit le plus gâté, le plus méchamment raffiné de notre temps, un solide écrivain toutefois; Richepin, l'auteur des *Blasphèmes*' (p. 708). Their psychologist is Bourget, and although Ordinaire dislikes him, he correctly describes his style: 'Ce style est métaphorique, plaqué de couleurs, précieux jusqu'à l'obscurité, plein de soleils couchants et de clairs de lune, imité, assez habilement d'ailleurs, de Taine, de Flaubert, des Goncourt, de ceux qu'on appelle coloristes parce qu'ils confondent la plume et le pinceau' (p. 708). Ordinaire compares Bourget's *L'Irréparable* to *Les Liaisons dangereuses* for its crass immorality, a comparison which he feels Bourget and his followers would welcome, since they are the decadents (and here is Ordinaire's first use of the term) of their century, as Crébillon *fils* and Laclos were of theirs. Expanding on this notion, he states:

> Ce mot de *décadent* sonne dans les pages de M. Bourget avec une fanfare si éclatante qu'il a piqué ma curiosité. Je me suis informé, et c'est ainsi que j'ai appris, non sans stupeur, que la maladie du pessimisme n'a pas atteint seulement quelques excentriques, mais qu'elle fait rage et infecte une notable partie de notre jeunesse.
>
> [p. 709]

Ordinaire ridicules the decadents for their unwarranted despair and contrasts them with the generous youth of previous times. As for himself, he sees cause only for optimism in the challenges that lie ahead, concluding:

> Pour moi, quand tous les autres motifs d'exister me manqueraient, quand je me sentirais menacé de choir en désespérance, je regarderais, si j'étais jeune comme vous, du côté de l'Allemagne, par la trouée des Vosges, et ce n'est pas Shopenhauer [*sic*] que je verrais.
>
> [p. 710]

(This patriotic note is less gratuitous than might be supposed: it was common to trace the pessimism of the younger generation to the defeat of 1870 and profess astonishment that such a Teutonic philosophy should have taken root in France. Fifteen and seventeen years after the defeat, anti-Prussian sentiment was again rising. Articles and cartoons in *Le Chat Noir* were so virulently anti-Prussian that French authorities seized the 13 January 1883 issue at the request of the German ambassador.)

The following week the same magazine published an article by the distinguished critic, Jules Lemaitre: 'La Jeunesse sous le Second Empire et sous la Troisième République'. A propos of a new edition of *Poésies de Jacques Richard*, a minor poet who flaunted his hostility to the Second Empire, Lemaitre dwells at length on the enthusiasm and generosity of the generation which was finishing its studies around 1860. At the same time, however, another literature was growing up, '. . . celle de la seconde moitié du siècle, une littérature d'observation morose et de recherche plastique . . . qui est devenue l'expression la plus exacte de notre tristesse et de notre détraquement. Flaubert écrivait son premier roman et Taine ses premiers livres de critique. Les Goncourt suivaient. . . .'[17] In contrast to that enthusiastic generation, today's youth is profoundly pessimistic, at least that portion of it which is engaged in creative writing. Perhaps this pessimism is justifiable, considering both the defeat of 1870 and recent political events: both the empire and the republic have failed them. Lemaitre now examines the literary expression of this pessimism, developing a point he first made in his article on J.-K. Huysmans a few months before: as literature shifts its emphasis from content to style it inevitably becomes sordid and amoral. His thesis is of real interest to us, because he does go to the heart of the decadent aesthetic:

> Et à mesure que, par une philosophie superbe et courte, les romanciers s'enfermaient dans la réalité fatale et brutale, ils attribuaient au style plus d'importance qu'on n'avait jamais fait. D'ordinaire, ce qui intéresse dans l'oeuvre d'art, c'est à la fois l'object exprimé et l'expression de cet object; mais, quand l'objet est vil, on est bien sûr que ce qu'on aime dans l'oeuvre d'art, c'est l'art tout seul. Voilà pourquoi le 'naturalisme,' loin d'être, comme quelques-uns le croient, un art grossier, est un art aristocratique, un art de mandarins égoistes, le comble de l'art. Et l'on voit aussi comment le naturalisme, et la poésie parnassienne, et l'impressionnisme s'appellent et s'engendrent. Quand

on renonce à ce qui avait été presque le tout de la littérature classique et de la littérature romanesque, à la peinture de la vie morale et à l'idéalisation de l'homme, que reste-t-il que la sensation, l'impression pittoresque et sensuelle? L'art nouveau se réduit peut-être à cette recherche inventive de la sensation rare. Mais cette recherche implique ou amène une indifférence absolue à l'égard de tout, morale, raison, science. De plus, la sensation toute seule est un abîme de tristesse; le désir qui l'appelle et qu'à son tour elle provoque est de sa nature inassouvissable.

[pp. 742–3]

The decadents themselves would have agreed with his characterisation of them: 'Ils sont ravis de se sentir décadents; ils se complaisent dans leur névrose et savourent leur déliquescence; et leur âme jouit profondément d'être pareille à un cadavre aux nuances changeantes et très fines qui se vide lentement' (p. 743). In conclusion he asks whether, in the final analysis, pessimism is an organic sickness of society or simply a literary style, and he replies that only time will tell.

Finally we come to Paul Bourde's article in *Le Temps* for 6 August 1885, in which he surveys the decadent phenomenon with stinging sarcasm:

D'après les oeuvres de l'école, et Floupette nous venant en aide, voici comment nous nous représentons le parfait décadent. Le trait caractéristique de sa physionomie morale est une aversion déclarée pour la foule considérée comme souverainement stupide et plate. Le poète s'isole pour chercher le précieux, le rare, l'exquis, Sitôt qu'un sentiment est à la veille d'être partagé par un certain nombre de ses semblables, il s'empresse de s'en défaire, à la façon des jolies femmes qui abandonnent une toilette dès qu'on la copie.

He mentions the decadents' Parnassian origins, he calls Verlaine and Mallarmé the two columns of the school, and he lists Moréas, Laurent Tailhade, Charles Vignier, and Charles Morice as members. He discusses their aversion to the natural, their religious attitudes, metric innovations, vocabulary, use of *correspondances* and analogy, and so on. In conclusion Bourde points out that decadence offers nothing new, since it is just a continuation and exaggeration of ideas already put forth by the Jeunes-France of Romanticism: 'Le romantisme épuisé a donné cette dernière petite fleur, une fleur de fin de saison, maladive et bizarre. C'est sûrement une décadence, mais seulement celle d'une école qui se meurt.'

Jean Moréas' rebuttal in *Le XIXe Siècle* for II August was 'Les Décadents', the first of his manifestoes defining the successive goals of current poetry.[18] He begins by quoting Vigny to the effect that 'les esprits paresseux et routiniers' find anything new ridiculous and barbarous, and he counters with his own sarcasm Bourde's attacks on the personal life of the decadents. He adduces the examples of Baudelaire and Poe to justify the decadent cult of art for art's sake and their use of symbolism and suggestion, Littré in defence of their neologisms. He concludes with another quotation from Vigny, urging the poet to remain well ahead of his public.

To the glee of the decadents, Bourde's name lent itself to a pun, since *bourde* in French means lie, 'poor excuse; frivolous tale'. L.-G. Mostrailles (Léo Trézenik) in *Lutèce* replies in an article entitled 'Bourde's bourdes'.[19] using the English possessive to emphasise the double meaning. With delightful wit Trézenik merely contests the passage in which Bourde '. . . accuse la rédaction de *Lutèce* . . . de se "pâmer" sur les élucubrations de M. Mallarmé', citing several articles in *Lutèce* which had criticised Mallarmé's obscurity, and he demands a retraction from the editor of *Le Temps*; Bourde's reply was to quote Verlaine's laudatory remarks on Mallarmé in his 'Poètes maudits' article.[20]

In his regular 'Chronique lutécienne' Trézenik congratulates himself on having obtained from the *grande presse* more publicity than it would ever have deigned to bestow on a more serious literary effort, confesses that the whole thing was not a parody but a joke made up by Beauclair and Vicaire, and accuses the whole press, particularly Mermeix and Bourde, of having fallen for it. Finally, he explains that *décadent* is a misnomer:

Il n'y a pas plus *décadence* aujourd'hui qu'il n'y eut décadence alors qu'à l'Art classique s'essaya à succéder le romantisme, alors qu'Hugo détrona Ponsard, alors qu'on acclama, en 1830, les *Burgraves* [*sic*] au détriment de *Lucrèce*. Il y a une simple transformation. Il y a tendance de la jeune littérature à faire *neuf*, et pour cela à faire *autre*. Les étiquettes ne signifient si bien rien que les prétendus décadents ont déjà été affublés de l'épithète de *néoromantiques*, parce que 'romantisme,' au fond, au temps de sa gloire et de son audace, ne voulait que dire *changement*. Et c'est encore faire du romantisme, aujourd'hui, mais du *néoromantisme* que de s'essayer à sortir, littérairement, de la routine et de l'ornière.[21]

In basing their appeal on the examples of established writers of the past and on the naturalness of constant, evolutionary change in literature, Moréas and Trézenik display good common sense and reduce the polemic to its just proportions; indeed, most decadent criticism is more sensible and down-to-earth than either the attacks of conservative critics or the practices of decadent writing which stirred up controversy in the first place!

The last article we shall consider was published outside France. From May to November Vittorio Pica published a series of articles in *La Gazzetta Letteraria* of Turin, entitled 'I moderni bizantini'—Francis Poictevin, Huysmans, and Verlaine.[22] The first article, on Poictevin, observes the flowering in France of *opere bizantine*, whose roots are to be found in the strange and pessimistic works of Edgar Poe and of Arthur Schopenhauer, and which, too refined for the general public, are intended for 'un pubblico ristretto di artisti et di iniziati, capaci d'intenderne et gustarne le squisite bellezze' (2 May 1885, p. 137). The essay on Huysmans is devoted largely to *A Rebours* and its analysis of Des Esseintes' literary and ecclesiastical tastes. The Verlaine article is remarkable: consisting of twenty newspaper-size columns, it made an unusually complete and intelligent study of his verse. A résumé would simply repeat what is now generally known, but we should mention Pica's detailed history of the *Parnasse*, his mention of ***Amour*** and *Les Poetes maudits*, and his references to the articles of 'Jean Mario' and Desprez. Pica emphasises decadence in Verlaine's poetry ('Langueur' is quoted in its entirety) and discusses the liberating influence of his metrics on French versification. Three years later Félix Fénéon translated the article for *La Cravache*.[23] Even in France Pica's insights would have been precocious for the period; his familiarity with current French literature must have been due to his contacts with Paris, for in the spring of 1885 he was foreign correspondent for *La Revue Contemporaine*. Otherwise, 'I moderni bizantini' anticipates by five years or more the spread of Verlaine's fame and that of decadence beyond the borders of France and Belgium.

Léo Trézenik came closer to the truth than anyone else when he observed that their joke had obtained for the decadents more publicity from large-circulation periodicals than their serious writing ever had. The decadents did not childishly seek publicity for its own sake; rather, reviewers in the *grande presse* had consistently overlooked their verse, so that when the clamour surrounding. *A Rebours* and *Les Déliquescences* brought their names and discussions of their verse—even hostile ones!—before the literate public, they made the most of the opportunity. Obviously people can only buy books that they have heard about, and now they were hearing about Verlaine, Mallarmé, Moréas, and the others. If the poetry esteemed by des Esseintes and parodied by Beauclair and Vicaire had really been inconsequential or a hoax, it would have gone no further; but because some poetry of real worth did exist behind the façade parodied by *Les Déliquescences* and ridiculed by a Bourde, sensitive readers who had first looked at it out of curiosity came to appreciate it for its real value. In this way, the nonsense and buffoonery of *Les Déliquescences* served a worthy purpose.

Les Déliquescences did not create a school of poetry where none had existed before, any more than *Les Poètes maudits* transformed minor poetasters into major poets; what the parody did achieve was to indicate the existence of a group of poets with common ideals and to name specific individuals among them. In their café discussions and social gatherings the decadents were probably more aware of comprising a 'school' than they had been two or three years previously. Lethève states that the press campaign against *Les Déliquescences* obliged the poets to group together and to define their goals.[24] Perhaps the fact that Jean Moréas was moved to compose his first manifesto by press treatments of *Les Déliquescences,* and not by those of *A Rebours* the previous spring, indicates that their sense of community had increased during the intervening year.

As for Verlaine, his position after *Les Déliquescences* can be appreciated in terms of his publications. Although he would never succeed in living from his pen, by the end of 1885 his poems were appearing frequently in magazines, and, what is more, henceforth Vanier would publish his earlier works, as well as his current ones, at his own expense, not Verlaine's! In 1886 ***Fêtes galantes*** was reissued in an edition of 600 copies, in 1887 ***Romances sans paroles***; the new volumes ***Amour*** (1888, 651 copies) and ***Parallèlement*** (1889, 600 copies) were followed in 1889 by a second edition of ***Sagesse*** in 1,100 copies; in 1891 Vanier brought out the first ***Choix de poésies*** in an edition of 1,500 copies. During the 1890's Verlain published at least one new volume of verse each year, in addition to placing poems in magazines.

Notes

1. *Oeuvres poétiques complètes*, Y.-G. Le Dantec and Jacques Borel, eds. (Gallimard, 1962), p. 75. Further references to poems by Verlaine will be identified in the text by title and page number in this edition.
2. For the text of the poem and additional information on Guy-Valvor, see our article 'Paul Verlaine and Guy-Valvor', *Romance Notes*, XI, 1 (autumn, 1969), 41–5.
3. III (1883–84), 435–40.
4. Jean-Charles Laurent, 'Les Fleurs blêmes', 28 September–5 October 1884. Laurent was actually Louis Marsolleau, a contributor to *Le Chat Noir*. See Noël Richard, *A L'Aube du symbolisme* (Nizet, 1961), pp. 171–2.
5. 'Poésie: *Les Syrtes*', I, 2 (25 February 1885), 290.
6. 'Chronique de l'art et du livre: les nouveaux-nés', I, 4 (February 1885), 169–70.
7. 'Poésie: *Jadis et naguère*', I, 1 (25 January 1885), 131–2.
8. 'Paul Verlaine et J.-B. Clément', 15–22 March 1885.
9. Quoted in 'La Poésie contemporaine', *Lutèce*, 19–26 April 1885.
10. *Ibid.*
11. 5–12 July 1885. See also 'Lettre d'un bourgeois' in the issue of 10–17 May.
12. Since few copies of the *Déliquescences* are available, it is useful to note where, besides *Lutèce*, extracts can be found. André Barre, *Le Symbolisme* (Jouve, 1912), gives the 'Liminaire' (pp. 149–50), followed by a description of all eighteen poems, with a few brief quotations (pp. 150–54). Richard, *A l'Aube du symbolisme*, quotes the 'Préface' *in toto* (pp. 281–315). G. L. van Roosbroeck, *The Legend of the Decadents* (New York: Columbia University Press, 1927), gives the complete texts of 'Les Décadents', 'Platonisme', 'Scherzo', and 'Remords', as well as brief passages from other poems. Adolphe Van Bever and Paul Léautaud, *Poétes d'aujourd'hui* (Mercure de France, 1947), III, pp. 396–9, give the texts of 'Les Enervés de Jumiège', 'Platonisme', 'Suavitas', and 'Idylle symbolique'. Finally, Albert Schinz, *Nine-*

teenth Century French Readings (New York: Holt, 1939), II, pp. 777–9, gives the texts of 'Cantique avant de se coucher', 'Décadents', and 'Scherzo'.

13. Here are the two original editions of *Les Déliquescences:* (*a*) 2 May 1885, 110 copies. This contains only the 'Liminaire' and the eighteen poems, and was printed by Trézenik on the press of *Lutèce.* Ten copies only carried the names of Vicaire and Beauclair on the cover. (*b*) 20 June, 1,500 copies. 'La Vie d'Adoré Floupette' by Marius Tapora is found on pages v-xlvii, 'Liminaire' and 'Déliquescences' occupy pages 49–80. This edition is incorrectly listed in *Journal de la librairie* (1885, second series, p. 492) as having appeared on 1 August; the first edition is not listed at all. In this edition Léon Vanier is correctly identified in the *achevé d'imprimer*, although elsewhere (i.e. on the title and first pages) he is still called Lion Vanné.

    There have been two reprints: (*c*) Crès edition, 15 May 1911, 635 copies. No. 1 of the collection 'Les Maîtres du livre', (*d*) Jonquières edition, 20 April 1923, 825 copies. See Richard, *A L'Aube du symbolisme*, pp. 174, 188 and 281.
14. 'Poésie: *Les Déliquescences*', II, 2 (25 June 1885), 266–7.
15. 'Chronique parisienne': 'Les Poètes impressionnistes et Adoré Floupette', XXVII, 80 (August 1885), 388.
16. 'La Jeune Génération', *Revue Politique et Littéraire* (*Revue Bleue*), XXXV, 23 (6 June 1885), 706. Further references to this article will be given in the text by page number.
17. *Ibid.*, XXXV, 24 (13 June 1885), 740. Further references to this article will be given in the text by page number.
18. Also in *Les Premières Armes du symbolisme* (Vanier, 1889), pp. 25–30.
19. *Lutèce*, 16–23 August 1885.
20. Bourde's confusion is understandable. Even today Guy Michaud lists *Lutèce* for November 1883 as the first publication of 'Don du poème' and 'Sainte', without indicating that they appeared as quotations in Verlaine's 'Poètes maudits' article (*Mallarmé*, Hâtier-Boivin, 1953, p. 187). These were, as a matter of fact, the only poems of Mallarmé to appear in *Lutèce*. Trézenik's hostility to Mallarmé's verse seems all the more incongruous in view of his efforts to promote Verlaine's, Corbière's, and Laforgue's.
21. 16–23 August 1885.
22. *Gazzetta Letteraria, Artistica e Scientifica,* IX, 18, 30, 46, 47, 48 (2 May, 25 July, 14, 21 and 28 November 1885), 137–9, 233–5, 361–2, 369–71, 378–9.
23. *La Cravache Parisienne*, 3 November 1888. See Jacques Lethève, *Impressionnistes et symbolistes devant la presse* (Colin, 1959), p. 282, n. 38.
24. See *ibid.*, p. 179.

Russell S. King (essay date 1975)

SOURCE: "Verlaine's Verbal Sensation," in *Studies in Philology*, Vol. 72, No. 2, April, 1975, pp. 226–36.

[*In the following essay, King examines the importance of grammar and verb choice to the meaning of Verlaine's poetry.*]

Recent studies of Verlaine's impressionistic style have been primarily "stylo-technical" rather than stylo-linguistic. Such studies, including notably Octave Nadal's "L'Impressionnisme Verlainien" and Alain Baudot's "Poésie et Musique chez Verlaine," have taken as their point of departure Verlaine's **"Art Poétique."**[1] Intent on examining the "musicality" of Verlaine's poetry, they demonstrate the contribution of diverse technical features including versification, uneven line-length, enjambement and sound patterns. Valuable though these analyses are to an understanding of Verlaine's poetic technique, they only incidentally isolate and explain certain linguistic choices which characterize Verlaine's impressionistic poetry. Jean-Pierre Richard has described Verlaine's poetry as that of "le pur sentir."[2] Though most critics readily agree, they fail to amplify this description by showing how sense and sensation in some measure control linguistic choices and thereby become significant structures within the language of the poem.

There is a close relationship between the nature of the senses and the function of the verb within the sentence. Despite the "names" of the five senses being nouns—*sight, hearing, smell, taste* and *touch* in English and *vue, ouïe, odorat, goût* and *toucher* in French—they are in fact abstract, nominalized forms of their equivalent verbs. Sensory perception remains an abstract concept until it is actualized through the verb, which links the "je" or person experiencing the sensation and the object which provokes it. Just as the verb links subject and object within the sentence, so do the senses link the person and the world:

PERSON-SUBJECT	SENSE-VERB	WORLD-OBJECT
	see	
	hear	
I	smell	the water.
	taste	
	touch	

This schema is useful too for demonstrating the shifting focus of the different poetic trends in nineteenth-century French poetry:

PERIOD	FOCUS	PREFERRED PARTS OF SPEECH
Romantic	"je-moi"	nouns and adjectives
Parnassian	the object	nouns and adjectives
Verlaine	senses	verbs and adverbs.

The object of this present essay is to examine the nature and stylistic implications of the centrality of the verb in Verlaine's poetry. Particular reference will be made to the poem, **"Le piano que baise une main frêle,"** in the "Ariettes Oubliées" of ***Romances sans paroles***, Verlaine's most characteristic and, probably, most original collection of poems, though frequent mention will be made of other characteristic poems from the same collection, ***Poèmes saturniens*** and ***Sagesse***.

Le piano que baise une main frêle
Luit dans le soir rose et gris vaguement,
Tandis qu'avec un très léger bruit d'aile

Un air bien vieux, bien faible et bien charmant
Rôde discret, épeuré quasiment,
Par le boudoir, longtemps parfumé d'Elle.

Qu'est-ce que c'est que ce berceau soudain
Qui lentement dorlote mon pauvre être?
Que voudrais-tu de moi, doux chant badin?

Qu'as-tu voulu, fin refrain incertain
Qui vas tantôt mourir vers la fenêtre
Ouverte un peu sur le petit jardin?

The importance of the verb lies not only in the choices and its frequency, but also, indirectly, in the consistent erosion of the two other areas of focus, the person and the world. Therefore the poem can be broken down in this way:

THE PERSON	THE VERBS	THE WORLD
mon pauvre être	baise	le piano
moi	luit	une main
	rôde	le soir
	épeuré	un bruit
	parfumé	un air
	dorlote	le boudoir
	voudrais	Elle
	as voulu	ce berceau
	vas mourir	chant
	ouverte	refrain
		la fenêtre
		le jardin.

If the reader accepts, in a general manner, currently accepted criteria for isolating the stylistic fact, he soon discovers that in Verlaine's poetry the "deviations from the norm," the elements which arrest the reader's attention, for the most part concern choices and forms of verbs. Certainly the most arresting linguistic features in **"Le piano que baise"** are precisely the choices of verbs:

Le piano que *baise* une main . . .
un air . . . *rôde* . . . par le boudoir . . .
un air . . . *épeuré* quasiment . . .
ce berceau . . . qui lentement *dorlote* mon pauvre être.
refrain incertain qui vas tantôt *mourir* . . .

Part of the "surprise" of these verbs lies in their metaphoric value as personification. The human presence is therefore introduced not directly through nouns and pronouns as much as through sensations and feeling implied by the verbs. It is precisely these verbal choices which underline the sense experience: touch in the "hand *kissing* the piano," sight in the "piano *shining* vaguely," sound in the "tune *prowling* through the boudoir," and smell in the "boudoir for long *perfumed* by Her."

It would appear that the importance of the verb is further enhanced by the unusual (in poetry) frequency of adverbs:

luit *vaguement*
rôde *discret*
épeuré *quasiment*
longtemps parfumé
lentement dorlote
tantôt mourir
ouverte *un peu*

In one way these adverbs serve a similar function to the adjectives like *vague, pâle* and *incertain* in contributing to the imprecision and suggestiveness of the linguistic reference. But also they extend the size and importance of the verbal unit, as opposed to the nominal and phrasal elements of the poem. Moreover the verb, along with certain adverbs of time, permits the mingling of tenses, and therefore a blurring of past, present and future. In this poem there is a mingling or interplay among all three:

PAST	PRESENT	FUTURE
un air bien vieux	baise	que voudrais-tu
longtemps parfumé d'Elle	luit	qui vas tantôt mourir.
Qu'as-tu voulu	rôde	
	dorlote	

This imprecision in time, the merging of present sensation with hazy memory of the past does not however detract from the significance of the verbs which communicate these notions, but further underlines their central function in Verlaine's impressionistic style.

Verlaine's preference for verbs as the central medium for conveying feeling and sensation is frequently illustrated by arresting choices and forms, for example, the pun in

Il *pleure* dans mon coeur
Comme il *pleut* sur la ville,

or displacement and choice in

Dans l'herbe noire
Les Kobolds *vont*.
Le vent profond
Pleure, on veut croire.

Quoi donc *se sent*?
L'avoine *siffle*.
Un buisson *gifle*
L'oeil au passant.

("Charleroi")

Elsewhere, verbs tend to be reflexive or intransitive:

Le son du cor *s'affige* vers les bois . . .
La bise *se rue* à travers . . .
Mon coeur qui *s'écoeure* . . .

Où *se dorlote* un paysage lent.
La cloche . . . doucement *tinte*.

The effect of these reflexive and intransitive forms is to make the verb less like a linking verb between two other more important units (subject and object of the sentence or clause) and to make it the principal point of focus.

Much of the poet's skill is expended on the use of verbal forms. In addition to unusual choices and reflexives, he had some predilection for unusual past participial forms:

automne *attiédi*
une âme *en allée*
au vent *crispé*
une aube *affaiblie*
ville gothique *éteinte*

Such participles serve, like adjectives and adverbs, to modify and obscure. But because of their strange form and choice they divert attention in some measure from the noun to which they are attached to themselves. They signify the feeling or sensation which is the poet's principal concern: not the autumn itself but the feeling of warmth, not the dawn but its pale light. It would appear then that there is a fusion of what may well have been the poet's skill in manipulating verbs effectively and expressively, and the function of the verb as the significant conveyor of feeling and sensation.

The Dissolution of the "Je Moi"

In **"Le piano que baise"** the "subject" is referred to explicitly on only two occasions—*mon pauvre être* and *moi*—and cannot possibly be considered the central point of focus. No information is provided as to his nature or identity, nor is he present in the first two tercets, although it is clearly he who *sees* and *hears* the piano in the pale evening light.

The "dissolution" and concealment of the poet's identity and presence are illustrated in two characteristic ways in this poem. The "je-moi," when it does occur, is expressed in an oblique case, rather than in the more active nominative case. J.-P. Richard emphasizes the poet's passivity and examines the tension between the person "qui accueille la sensation" and the thing "qui la produit." Despite the number of poems which begin with the nominative "je," like *Je devine, à travers un murmure* and *J'ai peur d'un baiser*, the usual pattern is to suggest a landscape, to introduce sound, and this reinforcement of the senses of sight and hearing induces a state of reverie in which there is a fusion of the external world and interior feeling and sensation. The poet does not appear to perceive *actively*, but receives *passively* through the senses. He is like the autumn leaf in **"Chanson d'automne."** This pattern of sight-sound-reverie is illustrated in **"Soleils couchants"**:

Une aube affaiblie
Verse par les champs
La mélancolie
Des soleils couchants.

La mélancolie
Berce de doux chants
Mon coeur qui s'oublie.

Here, as in **"Le piano que baise,"** where the poet uses *mon pauvre être* instead of *me, mon coeur* is used to achieve a kind of expressive but metonymic distancing, which further diminishes the presence of the person. In these two poems the reader is not aware of an active personality merely using a landscape as a means of conveying personal melancholy; rather, a special landscape subsumes a passive, almost absent person.

The second device illustrated by **"Le piano"** in dissolving the clear identity of the subject is the use of questions. The poem concludes with a sequence of three questions:

Qu'est-ce que c'est que ce berceau . . .?
Que voudrais-tu . . .?
Qu'as-tu voulu . . .?

They are rhetorical only in that no answer is provided or expected, but they do not presuppose a particular reply. In this way the poet avoids providing answers of fact and information—though, in **"Le piano,"** a link between the poet's past and the tune he now hears is obviously implied. Many of Verlaine's most celebrated poems contain, or conclude with, similar non-rhetorical questions:

Quelle est cette langueur
Qui pénètre mon coeur?
O bruit doux de la pluie
Par terre et sur les toits!

("Il pleure dans mon coeur")

Qu'as-tu fait, ô toi que voilà
Pleurant sans cesse,
Dis, qu'as-tu fait, toi que voilà,
De ta jeunesse?

("Le ciel est, par-dessus le toit")

These two examples both imply that there is some past reason for the present state of melancholy. But psychological, explanatory detail is suggested without being elaborated, thereby keeping the focus on the present mood rather than the past cause.

It is precisely in this aspect of causality that Verlaine's poetry differs most from that of his romantic predecessors. Simply by suggesting, often through unanswered questions, that there exists a reason for his present mood, but by refusing to give detail, the poet places the emphasis on effect. Thus, in these two following examples,

Je me souviens
Des jours anciens
Et je pleure.

("Chanson d'automne")

Il pleure sans raison
Dans ce coeur qui s'écoeure.
Quoi! nulle trahison?
Ce deuil est sans raison.

("Il pleure dans mon coeur")

the romantic poet would either have provided a "picture" of the past or would have attempted to fill in some of the facts or experiences from the past contributing to the present. Thus, for the romantic poet, poetry becomes a vehicle for projecting his own identity. A more detailed analysis of past experience and present emotion, with a greater emphasis on causality and psychology, inevitably contributes to a fuller portrayal of the subject's identity. But Verlaine resolutely rejects the romantic pattern and focus. The subject's identity is concealed behind the effect rather than the cause, for, it would seem, causality—which implies logic, intelligence and facts—would provide those precise details which would allow a more "real" recognizable personality to emerge.

Yet another way in which the subject's identity is obscured is through a shift in language registers. **"Le piano"** reflects this shift less clearly than a poem like **"La bise se rue"** (in ***Sagesse***): after the description of the landscape, the introduction of "sound," the language abruptly becomes more familiar and humorous. This is surprising, for it coincides with the first explicit appearance of the subject. One might expect the tone to be more serious, befitting the feeling of despair and hope. In **"Le piano"** the three questions expressed in a more familiar language with little that is unusual in the lexical choices—with the exception of *fin refrain incertain* and *doux chant badin*—introduce a certain verbal playfulness. Humor, unlike irony, always serves to divert attention away from the person.

The Dissolution of the "World-Object"

In **"Le piano"** the outside world appears to play a more significant part than the "je-moi" of the poet. But Verlaine is not a realist or a Parnassian. Alain Baudot has rightly drawn a distinction between the early "representative" poetry of Verlaine and the later "suggestive" less visible, less tangible world.

Verlaine achieves what he describes as "imprecision" of the contours in his ***"Art Poétique"*** through the use of adjectives. Almost all the nouns are qualified, not to provide more precise detail, but to blur the edges and make the object less clear:

> une main *frêle*
> le soir *rose et gris*
> un *très léger* bruit d'aile
> un air *bien vieux, bien faible et bien charmant*
> fin refrain *incertain*
> le *petit* jardin.

Many such adjectives occur in the bulk of Verlaine's impressionistic poetry (*pâle, blême, blafard, vague, délicat, étrange, inconnu*) which serve to erode the outlines and modify the precise contour. In ***"Le piano"*** the only two nouns that are not closely qualified by adjectives are *le piano* at the beginning and *vers la fenêtre* near the end. But, even here, the piano is "blurred" by the adverb *vaguement* modifying the verb. Likewise, in the second instance, the eye focuses not on the window itself, but on some less determined area "in the direction of the window."

There is yet another manner in which the sharp outline is blurred. This relates more to the function of the senses. It has already been suggested that a frequent pattern in Verlaine's poetry is to progress from something *seen* to something *heard*, and, with the consequent interaction and fusion of the two senses, to a vague state of reverie and reminiscence. This pattern is seen in **"Le piano"**: in the first two lines the words (the piano, a hand, shining, and the color of the light) contribute to the picture that is *seen*. The *seen* piano then becomes something less tangible, a *heard* tune: *un air bien vieux*, a *doux chant badin*, a *fin refrain incertain*. Indeed, one of the reasons for the importance of music for the poet seems to be precisely that it is some vague emanation from the real world which comes to "cradle" or "soothe" the poet. Interestingly, the same pattern of sight, sound and reverie is apparent in almost all the most celebrated "musical" poems of Verlaine: **"Soleils couchants," "Il pleure dans mon coeur," "Le ciel est, par-dessus le toit,"** and **"La bise se rue à travers."**

It is impossible to determine whether this "dissolution" of the subject and object, of personal identity and representation of the real world, causes, or results from, the enhanced function of the verb in Verlaine's poetic universe. Just as the verb cannot exist without subject and (usually) object, so sensation cannot exist without a person receiving it and a world or object producing it. However, for the verb and sensation to predominate, subject and object, that is, person and world, must be modified, reduced, blurred, and sometimes even suspended. Verlaine's poetic universe is not the romantic vehicle for projecting his own self and identity, nor is it the Parnassian re-creation in words of the precise physical, visible world; rather, it occupies a vague, indeterminate space somewhere between the two. Verlaine's poetry of sensation seeks to recreate, largely through the verb, that territory between the romantic "je" and the Parnassian "chose."

Notes

1. Octave Nadal, "L'Impressionnisme Verlainien," *Mercure de France* (May, 1952), pp. 59–74. Alain Baudot, "Poésie et Musique chez Verlaine," *Etudes Françaises* (February, 1968), pp. 31–54. See also Maurice Got, "'Art Poétique': Verlaine et la technique impressionniste," *La Table Ronde*, CLIX (March, 1961), pp. 128–36.
2. Jean-Pierre Richard, "Fadeur de Verlaine," in *Poésie et Profondeur* (Paris, 1955).

Richard P. Whitmore (essay date 1976)

SOURCE: A review of "Pantomime", in *The Explicator*, Vol. 34, No. , May, 1976, p. 71.

[*In the following essay, Whitmore discusses the irony of Verlaine's character studies in the poem* "Pantomime."]

In **"Pantomime,"** the second of Paul Verlaine's ***Fêtes galantes*** (1869), we are shown four sharply etched vignettes of stock characters from the *commedia dell'arte,* each performing in a miniature scene. In general, commentators treat these skits as if they were appropriate for their respective personages. But what is particularly revealing and yet requires detailed explication is the distinct irony behind Verlaine's choices. For here what each player does contrasts markedly with the traditional personality evolved for his role by the Italian comedy, especially as it had developed in France.

Divergency is a keynote of **"Pantomime,"** objectified by the clean and separate focus in which each scene is presented. Normally, the members of a *commedia* troupe improvised in concert. Yet here Cassandre is clearly off in the distance "au fond de l'avenue" (line 4), and the others also seem to execute their turns apart, almost simultaneously, in different sections of the rococo park in which the ***Fêtes galantes*** are set.

The disjunction of the scenes is further emphasized by the poem's form. Not only is each three-line stanza a separate, complete sentence, but each also begins by naming its particular focal personage. The full stops of the syntax are reinforced by the rhyme scheme. The first two lines of each verse are bound together with rich feminine rhymes, all the more remarkable for being built twice on proper names—"tandre," "tendre" (lines 1–2, very rich), "ombine," "ombine" (lines 7–8, also very rich), and "rise," "rise" (lines 10–11)—varied once by a pair of sufficient rhymes—"nue," "nue" (lines 4–5). In contrast, the final lines are masculine and do not rhyme at all with the others of their own stanzas. They rhyme only with the concluding line of the next verse and, even then, are either weak—"ois," "oix" (lines 9 and 12, no pronounced consonant) or sufficient—"té," "té" (lines 3 and 6). Each stanza is thus like a short film strip, its frames closely joined within, only to run out suddenly. Each clip is then followed by a different one, internally cohesive, too, but tangentially linked at best with no more than one of the other three.

But these personages are not only detached from one another by the form and the rhyme. They are also divorced from their own traditional, characteristic identities by their actions. The very first line, "Pierrot, qui n'a rien d'un Clitandre," establishes the tone of paradox which permeates the work. It is startling to hear that Pierrot has no resemblance to the lover Clitandre. True, Pierrot may be awkward and his love unsuccessful, but tender feelings dominate his life too. He and Clitandre are both devoted to something other than their bellies and Pierrot should be the antithesis of a simple glutton.

Yet in **"Pantomime"** Verlaine has Pierrot downing a stoup of wine, and then cutting into a rich meat pie (lines 2–3). The phrase "sans plus attendre" (line 2), emphasizing the close sequence of these actions, offers a further meaning—that of expecting nothing more, nothing better. Where is the Parisian Pierrot here, especially the Pierrot the whole capital had flocked to see in Deburau's brilliant mimes at the Théâtre des Funambules throughout the 1830's and '40's? Singularly emaciated in his white costume and make-up, Deburau had defined the figure as a *naïf,* always seeking what he could not attain, never satisfied with the ready-to-hand or down-to-earth. A Pierrot who is "pratique," as Verlaine terms his in line 3, is a self-contradiction.

Cassandre, too, is playing a false role. Typically a whining and scolding old miser, he seems here to show unselfish pity, weeping over "son neveu déshérité" (line 6). Most significantly, however, he sheds a "larme méconnue" (line 5), that is, one not recognized at its true worth. While "méconnue" normally indicates unappreciated merit, it may also designate what is overprized. The true value of a Cassandre's tear is nil. What is one nephew more among a skinflint's numerous disinherited kin? A secondary meaning of "méconnue" suggests that the tear may be disavowed, repudiated. Clearly, the actions of these figures cannot unquestioningly be taken at face value.

In the *commedia*, Harlequin, though often faced with obstacles, is always the wooer. His resourcefulness is used to please his Columbine. But what Verlaine underscores in his Arlequin is egotism, not tenderness or devotion. Here, he is from the first a knave, "ce faquin d'Arlequin" (line 7). He may take Colombine away, but the verb "combine" as used here is part of the familiar language with much the flavor of "pulls off the job" in English. The level of discourse equates Verlaine's Arlequin with a self-serving cozener. Furthermore, his concluding quadruple pirouette (line 9) brings the focus exclusively onto himself. Colombine is at the most a pretext for his celebration of his own skills.

Then what of Colombine? While the first three figures in **"Pantomime"** are superficial in their emotions, she shows depth. She senses a heart's presence in the breeze and is attentive to unnamed voices in her heart (lines 11–12). She seems to be a trusting ingénue, astonished ("surprise") at her discovery of deep feeling (line 10). But her naivety and sincerity here contrast with the fuller personality of the *commedia* figure. There she is often a clever young beauty whose schemes lead men a merry dance. Indeed, Verlaine, in **"Colombine,"** the next to the last of these ***Fêtes galantes***, evokes her as a "belle enfant / Méchante" (lines 17–18) whose "yeux pervers" (line 19) lead even Arlequin toward "mornes ou cruels / Désastres" (lines 29–30).

While none of these characters is true to his traditional identity, each is well suited to the dissimulation omnipresent in the world of the ***Fétes galantes***. Here, expediency reigns, "la vie opportune" as the first poem, **"Clair de lune,"** puts it. Here, role-playing is the way of life for all, aristocrats or entertainers alike. By introducing characters at variance with their normal personalities, **"Pantomime"** informs the whole ***Fêtes galantes***' tone of sadness. The "vie opportune" carries a risk. One may feign so many roles that only that of illusionist will remain. Then, like

Colombine, one may well be astonished at the possibility of perceiving authentic voices in one's heart.

Robert Storey (essay date 1979)

SOURCE: "Verlaine's Pierrots," in *Romance Notes*, Vol. 20, No. 2, Winter, 1979, pp. 223–30.

[*In the following essay, Storey explores the Pierrot figure in Verlaine's poetry.*]

Ce n'est plus le rêveur lunaire du vieil air
Qui riait aux aïeux dans les dessus de porte;
Sa gaîté, comme sa chandelle, hélas! est morte,
Et son spectre aujourd'hui nous hante, mince et clair.
Et voici que parmi l'effroi d'un long éclair
Sa pâle blouse a l'air, au vent froid qui l'emporte,
D'un linceul, et sa bouche est béante, de sorte
Qu'il semble hurler sous les morsures du ver.
Avec le bruit d'un vol d'oiseaux de nuit qui passe,
Ses manches blanches font vaguement par l'espace
Des signes fous auxquels personne ne répond.
Ses yeux sont deux grands trous où rampe du phosphore
Et la farine rend plus effroyable encore
Sa face exsangue au nez pointu de moribond.[1]

The sleeves of his blouse rippling like a shroud in the wind, his mouth gaping in mute and inexplicable anguish, the "holes" of his eyes gleaming with a phosphorescent fire—the unearthly specter of Verlaine's early sonnet has reached, for at least one of its admirers, "a stage of decomposition for which neither precedent can be found nor sequel imagined."[2] But **"Pierrot"** is by no means a poem without precedent; it is likely, moreover, that it was inspired by a single curious source. Although the Pierrot of spiritual *angoisse* was a familiar of the 80's and 90's (Verlaine's poem was published in 1882—but written in 1868), he was a godchild of the popular Parisian pantomime. "Ce personnage pâle comme la lune, mystérieux comme le silence, souple et muet comme le serpent, droit et long comme une potence"—so Baudelaire had described the Pierrot of the great Baptiste Deburau.[3] Indeed, long before Michel Carné was to romanticize this mime's career in *Les Enfants du Paradis*, Deburau was fetching darkly Faustian epithets from a number of his impressive contemporaries. "C'est Satan naïf et bouffon," declared Charles Nodier;[4] "C'est le Misanthrope de Molière," wrote Jules Janin;[5] and Gautier observed that "Pierrot, pâle, grêle, vêtu d'habits blafards, toujours affamé et toujours battu, [représente] l'esclave antique, le prolétaire moderne, le paria, l'être passif et déshérité qui assiste, morne et sournois, aux orgies et aux folies de ses maîtres."[6] Deburau's stage genius was, on the surface, utterly without pretension ("le Deburau de M. Janin n'est pas moi," he complained to George Sand; "il ne m'a pas compris"),[7] but it was, however unconsciously invoked and expressed, of an intoxicantingly malevolent kind. "La bouteille dont il montrait en souriant l'étiquette *laudanum* quand Cassandre avait fini de la boire, le dos du rasoir qu'il lui passait sur le cou," writes Deburau's biographer, "étaient des jeux auxquels il ne fallait pas donner l'occasion de devenir sérieux en mettant à l'épreuve sa patience, sa réserve, son sang-froid."[8] When, in 1836, the mime's discipline gave way beneath the jeers of a street-boy and he clubbed the urchin a fatal blow with his cane, his stage role assumed, inadvertently, an even more sinister air.

In a forgotten novella by Henri Rivière, published in 1860, this air provides the motive for Romantic melodrama—for a tale of madness, murder, and revenge. Rivière's story, *Pierrot*, describes the unhappy career of Charles Servieux, a young man who is witness to a disturbing pantomime at the Théâtre des Funambules just after recovering from two fits of insanity. The audacity and sinister gaiety of Deburau's *jeu* make an immediate and lasting impression, and Servieux comes to be obsessed by the idea of Pierrot as "l'ange déchu": "C'est ainsi que se dessina lentement dans mon cerveau un génie du mal, grandiose et mélancolique, d'une irrésistible séduction, cynique et bouffon par instants, afin qu'il se relevât plus haut après être tombé."[9] Servieux gives flesh to this vision by himself assuming the white blouse and mask, and not long after having picked out his Colombine from a company of poor *saltimbanques*, he is performing before an enthralled public on the stage of the Funambules. The young soubrette begins to play more true to type than Servieux would have wished: she soon abandons her pallid lover—now importunate both on and off the boards—for the company's Harlequin. And when the jealous Pierrot can no longer brook her unfaithfulness, he decapitates his rival in the full face of his audience during one of his own little macabre productions. Servieux dies of a fever shortly after his crime, having recovered, in his final hours, from his long delirium.

A single scene from this wonderfully improbable piece is worth summarizing in more detail. Soon after resolving to incarnate his conception of Pierrot *satanique*, Servieux goes on a retreat to Brittany. There, in a little house that is bordered on one side by a wall of "hautes montagnes boisées" and that gives out on the other "sur un torrent que grossissent les pluies d'hiver, et sur une plaine sans végétation," he passes his nights in perfecting his mute art. One evening, after imagining himself dismissing a host of wretched suppliants, one begging a few francs to make restitution for a petty crime, another to save her starving child, still another to escape total destitution on her hospital deathbed, Servieux pushes himself back from his table (which is heaped high with imagined wealth) to judge the effect of his diabolic performance:

> Ce soir-là, il y avait au ciel un orage splendide. J'avais en face de moi une glace où je me voyais. Je ne pensais plus aux misères humaines qui continuaient à passer, et je me regardai moins en acteur qu'en spectateur de cette scène lugubre. Ma taille me parut grandie. Ma main blanche, aux doigts effilés, continuait, d'un mouvement facile, à jouer avec la masse d'or qui était là présente, bien qu'elle n'existât pas. J'avais sur les lèvres un fatal sourire. Mes yeux enfoncés brillaient

d'un éclat insupportable; pas une écaille de ma farine n'était tombée. Au moment où je me regardais le plus attentivement et avec une sorte d'admiration pleine d'horreur, un éclair d'une largeur surprenante, pareil à une bande de feu, illumina mes fenêtres, et il me semble que tous les petits diables de la plaine qui, selon les superstitions bretonnes, hantent les pierres druidiques, noirs, aux ongles crochus, m'applaudissaient en riant, accroupis derrière mes carreaux. Je me fis peur et me dressai sur mes pieds; mais, au même moment, le roulement de tonnerre qui suivait l'éclair ébranla la maison tout entière; les vitres se brisèrent en mille éclats, et une lourde rafale de vent et de pluie éteignit les candélabres.[10]

In this final tableau we encounter Verlaine's "spectre"—that Pierrot who "aujourd'hui nous hante, mince et clair."[11] But even more interesting than Verlaine's probable use of this "source" is what seems to be his extreme condensation of Rivière's chief themes to compose a densely allusive portrait. Servieux himself admits that his Pierrot is condemned "fatalement" to "faire le mal"; but it is only after his crime that he realizes he is, in fact, doubly cursed: his inevitable mission is also quite literally a fatal one. So we may account, in part, for the preternatural moribundity in Verlaine's prophetic vision. And Servieux's madness, his ineluctable estrangement from men (and his Colombine)—these, too, find expression in one line of the sonnet, in those "signes fous auxquels personne ne répond."

Verlaine's poem is not, of course, simply a *réconstruction:* his reassembling the materials of Rivière's conte has an expressive as well as a rhetorical design. The young *poète saturnien* would naturally have been drawn to Servieux, as to a brother in *malheur*. Verlaine's fatal addiction to alcohol (a failing to which Servieux succumbs) and his homosexuality had, by 1862, thrust themselves on *le petit*; and however casually they were regarded by the author of *Confessions*,[12] they were probably met, by the younger man, with disquiet and self-disgust. Shame at his physical ugliness, at his visage of an "orang-outang," could only have exacerbated these feelings. Rivière's hero is not ugly: he is "un beau jeune homme au front vaste, avec de longs cheveux bruns bouclés et rejetés en arrière, au nez d'aigle, à la bouche spirituelle."[13] But this Christ-like beauty is little more than an emblem of Servieux's beauty of soul—and such beauty the precocious disciple of Baudelaire certainly *did* have, with all that was attendant upon it: sensitivity shading into weakness, self-reproach, dread and guilt; idealism decaying into arrogance, contempt, monomania, and cruelty. And unlike the Parnassian Pierrot glimpsed vaguely among the ***Fêtes galantes***, who leaps over bushes with flealike alacrity and, "pratique," slices into meat pies, the Pierrot of the sonnet has pushed through the impassable to emerge on the darker side of his spirit. He has crossed what the narrator of Rivière's tale calls—familiarly—"cette limite si faible qui sépare parfois le génie de la folie":[14] the *poète saint* of "Don Quichotte" has become a *poète maudit*.

When, in 1886–87, the poet again turned to Pierrot, it was not as a youthful analyst of the soul but, *parallèlement,* as an aging celebrant of the body. And once more he was drawing upon Pierrots of obvious precedent. Huysmans and Hennique had published their *Pierrot sceptique* in 1881, its black-frocked *railleur* inspired by a troupe of Pierrots from the "pays du spleen";[15] and two years later, Sarah Bernhardt had pulled on the clown's *casaque* to animate, at the Trocadéro, Richepin's all too fleshy *Pierrot assassin*. In both of these pantos the Pierrot of spiritual *faiblesse* gives way to a creature of appetite—but it would probably be a mistake to see in Verlaine's later portraits the *zanni* of these productions. The "Pierrot gamin" of ***Parallèlement***, of *Motif de pantomime* in the *Mémoires d'un veuf*, is neither dandiacally mordant (like Jules Laforgue's) nor neurotically macabre (like Paul Margueritte's). In the first four panels of *Motif de pantomime*, he is an "enfant chétif": "Douze ans, palôt, grandelet, maigrichon." His "jeu principal" is to walk along the gutters, gently squeezing the mud over his shoes. His other diversions are equally puerile: he trips up a "gâte-sauce" peddling his wares through the street and surreptitiously samples his gravy; he filches the curé's surplice and skullcap and decks himself out for the mardigras; he courts Colombine with pralines and prunes—until Harlequin sends him packing. "N'importe," Verlaine generously concludes in his "Epilogue": "il a joui, ri, souri. Et puis nul souci." An *enfant* who loiters outside obligation, responsibility, and law, this later Pierrot plays the fool with the irrepressible abandon of a street-waif.

But in this he is not alone. The Pierrots of the artist Adolphe Willette stand clearly behind Verlaine's *gamin*. In Willette's illustrations and *histoires sans paroles*, cartoons and watercolors that he produced by the score in the '80s and '90s, innumerable Pierrots of child-like insouciance *flânent* the streets of Paris. In a sketch of 1885, for example, later reproduced in *Feu Pierrot, 1857–19?*, a young Pierrot with a guitar slung on his back abducts a winged child from a park. They both get tipsy on wine, and Pierrot leaves the boy sitting dazed beneath a streetlamp to dance under three indulgently smiling moons. When, several panels later, they are reunited, the child skips into Pierrot's arms to kiss him passionately on the lips; but suddenly a dark figure steps into the sunlight and plunges a knife into the clown's back, leaving him dead and bleeding on the pavement.[16]

Except for his bathetically melodramatic demise—rare in Willette's *histoires pierrotiques*—the Pierrot that we meet here is nearly indistinguishable from Verlaine's. The latter, it is true, is still a schoolboy, packing a booksatchel instead of a guitar, but his endearing *méchanceté*, his naïve egoism, his obliviousness to bourgeois exactitude (he roams the streets in "gros souliers aux cordons sans cesse dénoués"), all suggest, in embryo, the careless bohemian of Willette. And both, of course, recall Verlaine's versified portrait of the "Pierrot gamin":

Bien qu'un rien plus haut qu'un mètre,
Le mignon drôle sait mettre
Dans ses yeux l'éclair d'acier

Qui sied au subtil génie
De sa malice infinie
De poète-grimacier.

Lèvres rouge-de-blessure
Où sommeille la luxure,
Face pâle aux rictus fins,
Longue, très accentuée,
Qu'on dirait habituée
À contempler toutes fins,

Corps fluet et non pas maigre,
Voix de fille et non pas aigre,
Corps d'éphèbe en tout petit,
Voix de tête, corps en fête,
Créature toujours prête
À soûler chaque appétit.

(p. 520)

But, though obvious, the similarities here are superficial: this Pierrot has an aggressiveness that evaporates the nostalgia of *Motif de pantomime*—and, with it, Willette's sentimentality. The image of the poet as impenitent libertine, vagabond, and spiritual *naïf* has been pushed to the edge of parody, and what emerges is clearly a grotesque, a "Caricature, . . . / La grimace et le symbole / De notre simplicité!" Perrot *gamin* is thus both a jeer and a deliriously mad declaration of self-abandonment. Now "l'âme / Vile, haute, noble, infâme / De nos innocents esprits," he offers an oddly poignant reply to the austere angst of the earlier Pierrot-specter. By tripling his "riche amertume," by exaggerating his gaiety, the poet as *zanni* has become one with his grimacing mask and, through a kind of frenzied, comic intoxication, has lost himself in order to gratify all the more gluttonously his forbidden appetites.

A mirror and a mask: Pierrot functions as both for the poet. To look upon the one was to see the other, the reflection within the disguise, and vice-versa. That Verlaine, like Hamlet, could both conceal and reveal himself within an antic disposition goes far towards explaining Pierrot's immense appeal to the artists of the late nineteenth century. Mediating as he does between public truth and private fantasy, comedy and pathos, the Self and the Other, he offers one small but effective key to this *parade sauvage*. "Je pourrais risquer sous cet avatar d'intermittentes apparitions," said Mallarmé of his nephew's Pierrot, "et, pour le plaisir de quelques délicats, être 'le monsieur en habit noir qui, à l'improviste, tire du fourreau ce glaive blanc.'"[17] To draw Pierrot out of Hamlet, a giddy clown out of a wraith-like victim of conscience: this was also Verlaine's wish—and accomplishment.

Notes

1. Paul Verlaine, "Pierrot," *Œuvres poétiques complètes* (Bibliothèque de la Pléiade; Paris: Gallimard, 1962), pp. 320–21. All citations from Verlaine's poems will be from this edition with page references in parentheses in the text.
2. A. G. Lehmann, "Pierrot and fin de siècle," in Ian Fletcher, ed., *Romantic Mythologies* (London: Routledge & Kegan Paul, 1967), p. 216. The present essay is, in part, an answer to Mr. Lehmann's article, which is riddled, inexplicably, with errors and inaccuracies. He misleadingly implies, for example, that Verlaine's sonnet is part of the "the mature writing of *Jadis et naguère*" (p. 221), and, working from this misapprehension, he suggests that it is a more technically accomplished restatement of *Grotesques* (1866) in the *Poèmes saturniens*. (Little more than two years separate the dates of the two poems.) My own researches have revealed that Mr. Lehmann's "prehistory" of Pierrot is distressingly unreliable.
3. Charles Baudelaire, "De l'essence du rire et généralement du comique dans les arts plastiques," *Le Portefeuille,* July 8, 1855; in *Œuvres complètes,* ed. Marcel A. Ruff (Paris: Editions du Seuil, 1968), p. 376.
4. In an article in the *Pandore*, July 19, 1828; cited in Louis Péricaud, *Le Théâtre des Funambules, ses mimes, ses acteurs et ses pantomimes, depuis sa fondation jusqu'à sa démolition* (Paris: Sapin, 1897), p. 78.
5. *Deburau, Histoire du théâtre à quatre sous pour faire suite à l'histoire du théâtre français* (1832; rpt. in 1 vol., Paris: Librairie des Bibliophiles, 1881), pp. 155–56.
6. *Histoire de l'art dramatique en France depuis vingt-cinq ans*, V (Paris: Magnin, Blanchard et compagnie, 1859), 24.
7. In George Sand, *Histoire de ma vie* (Paris: Lévy Frères, 1856), VIII, 248.
8. Tristan Rémy, *Jean-Gaspard Deburau* (Paris: L'Arche [Le Théâtre et les Jours], 1954), p. 143.
9. Henri Rivière, *Pierrot/Caïn* (Paris: Hachette, 1860), p. 27.
10. Ibid., p. 32.
11. Mr. Lehmann remarks that Rivière's conte is "one of the more naïve testimonies to the Funambules vogue" (p. 223), but he does not note its influence upon Verlaine—probably because he has not read the tale. According to his footnote, the "central figure, Pierre," is "a neurotic retired sea-captain" who imitates "Debureau's [sic] career fairly closely." Servieux is never referred to as "Pierre" in Rivière's story; although he suffers a near-drowning at sea, he is not a retired sea-captain, nor does he imitate Deburau's career, in any of its details.
12. Verlaine notes in his *Confessions* that, with the onset of puberty, "mes 'chutes' se bornèrent à des enfantillages sensuels, oui, mais sans rien d'absolument 'vilain'—en un mot, à des jeunes garçonneries partagées au lieu de rester . . . solitaires" (*Œuvres en prose complètes* [Paris: Bibliothèque de la Pléiade, 1972], p. 484).
13. Rivière, p. 4.
14. *Ibid.*, p. 71.

15. The troupe was the Hanlon-Lees, from England. See Huysmans' account of one of their performances in his *Croquis parisiens: Œuvres complètes de J.-K. Huysmans*, VIII (Paris: Crès, 1929), 21 ff.
16. In Adolphe Willette, *Feu Pierrot, 1857–19?* (Paris: H. Floury, 1919), pp. 90–91.
17. Mallarmé's remark was in response to a performance of Paul Margueritte's *Pierrot assassin de sa femme* (1881) (see Paul Margueritte, *Le Printemps tourmenté* [Paris: Flammarion, 1925], pp. 26–27).

Enid Rhodes Peschel (essay date 1981)

SOURCE: "Introduction: Verlaine: Soulscapes of Quiet and Disquiet," in *Four French Symbolist Poets: Baudelaire, Rimbaud, Verlaine, Mallarmé*, translated by Enid Rhodes Peschel, Ohio University Press, 1981, pp. 33–46.

[*In the following essay, Peschel presents an overview of Verlaine's life and career.*]

It's beautiful eyes behind veils,
It's the full noon's trembling light,
It's the blue jumble of bright
Stars in a tepid autumn sky!

Verlaine, **"Art of Poetry"**

Rimbaud used to say about Verlaine, "He's a charming child, violent and dangerous when he's drunk."[1] These clashing qualities permeate Verlaine's troubled and tormented life and poetry. On the one hand, there is charm—gentle, attractive and captivating; and there are the innocent strengths and lovable weaknesses one associates with childhood—like purity, spontaneity, vulnerability and naïveté.[2] On the other hand, however, there are anger, passion and viciousness, and a depression so devastating that it seeks relief in drunkenness. The tale of the contradictions in Verlaine's life is like a prelude that prepares one to understand, to accept—and to listen for—the contradictions in his poetry. For beneath the musical charm of his melodies, an anger and an anguish seep, or rend their way through.

Paul Verlaine was born in Metz on March 30, 1844. His father, Nicolas-Auguste, an adjutant battalion captain, was forty-six. His mother, Élisa, was thirty-five. She had had three miscarriages before Paul was born. He would be their only child.

In 1851, Captain Verlaine resigned his military commission and moved his family to Paris. Paul grew up adored by his mother and by his cousin whose name, like his mother's, was Élisa. Élisa Moncomble, an orphan eight years older than Paul, was being reared by Paul's mother.

When Verlaine was nine, he began attending boarding schools. Although he was a good student at first, by the time of his *baccalauréat* he had dropped to the bottom of the class.

At eighteen or nineteen, he began drinking. Around this time, in 1863, his first poem was published and he became friends with other writers in Paris, including Théodore de Banville, Villiers de l'Isle-Adam, Louis-Xavier de Ricard, Léon Valade, Albert Mérat, Catulle Mendès, Charles Cros and Sully Prudhomme.

During the next few years, two events deeply upset Verlaine: his father's death in 1865 (Captain Verlaine had been quite sick since 1862), and his cousin Élisa's unexpected death in February 1867, after a difficult childbirth. When Verlaine arrived for her funeral in Lécluse, where she had been living with her husband, the funeral procession was just leaving her house. Verlaine got so drunk for three days after this that he scandalized his entire family and the town. This pattern of grief followed by obstreperous drunkenness would recur.

Verlaine's first book, ***Poèmes saturniens*** (***Saturnine Poems***), was published in 1866. The press, Verlaine would later say, accorded it "a fine *succès d'hostilité*."[3] Although strongly influenced by the Parnassians, the book shows that Verlaine was already beginning to find his own voice. Thus, landscapes in several of these poems are already soulscapes. For example, **"Nevermore,"** which takes its title from Poe's "The Raven," blends ideas of love and loss, harmony and discord, happiness and nostalgic sadness, health and sickness, perfumed flowers and their inevitable demise: the beginning of love, therefore, and its end. And the melodious **"Autumn Song"** is a sad and sensuous merging with nature, with evil and with death.

Verlaine's next book, ***Fêtes galantes*** (***Gallant Festivals***), "whose title belies the deep sadness often found in the verses," as Diana Festa-McCormick notes,[4] appeared three years later, in 1869. This lyrical and disturbing medley of poems inspired by love and its loss takes its inspiration from the gallant festivals depicted in eighteenth-century painting (one thinks, for example, of Watteau's "The Embarcation for Cythera"). In the poems, maskers and figures from French pantomime and Italian comedy, phantoms and phantomlike people act out the gallantries that live and die beneath the moon's bewitching, but often less than beneficent, gaze.

Off and on around this time, Verlaine was drinking. Twice in July 1869, he tried to kill his mother. His relatives thought that married life might calm him down, and they proposed one of his cousins for his mate. Instead, Verlaine asked his friend Charles de Sivry if he could marry Sivry's half-sister, the sixteen-year-old Mathilde Mauté de Fleurville. Verlaine courted Mathilde with poems that he composed for her (e.g. "Before you depart, / Pale morning star . . ." and "The moon shines white . . ."). These lyrics would go into his next book, ***La Bonne Chanson*** (***The Good Song***), which was printed in 1870 but not distributed until 1872, because of the Franco-Prussian War.

On August 11, 1870, when Mathilde was seventeen (she was a year and a half older than Rimbaud) and Verlaine was twenty-six, they were married. At first, they lived in their own apartment and Verlaine was a clerk in the Hôtel de Ville (Town Hall). But a few months later, Verlaine participated in the Paris Commune of 1871; and when the Commune was overthrown, he lost his job. Since they could no longer afford their own apartment, Verlaine and his pregnant wife moved in with her parents at 14, rue Nicolet in August 1871. Rimbaud would arrive there one month later. . . .

On July 7, 1872, Mathilde was feeling ill. Her husband said that he would go out to find Dr. Cros. Verlaine did go out . . . and found Rimbaud. And on that day the poets began their travels together that would terminate one year later with two pistol shots in Brussels. During all this time of cruelty and callousness towards Mathilde, of drunkenness and of impassioned seeking for a "new love" with Rimbaud, Verlaine was writing one of his most beautiful and lyrical, and original, collections of poetry, ***Romances sans paroles*** ([Sentimental] ***Songs without Words***). It would be published in 1874, when the poet was in prison.

After the events in Brussels on July 10, 1873, Verlaine spent a year and a half in prison. There, he wrote many memorable and moving poems, including "My God said to me . . .," "Hope shines like a blade of straw . . .," "A great dark drowsiness . . ." (composed on August 8, 1873, the day on which he was sentenced), **"Kaleidoscope," "Art of Poetry,"** and his vision of Rimbaud and of their "crime of love," "**Crimen amoris**." In *Mes Prisons* (*My Prisons*), Verlaine evokes the atmosphere of "The sky is, above the roof . . .": "Above the front wall my window (I had a window, a real one! provided, the idea! with bars that were side by side . . . and I used to see, it was in August, the top swaying, with its voluptuously shivering leaves, of some tall poplar of a nearby boulevard or square. At the same time faraway noises, softened, would reach me, of a festival . . ." (p. 1131). These poems would be included in his next two books: ***Sagesse*** (***Wisdom***), published at Verlaine's expense, in 1881; and ***Jadis et naguère*** (***Long Ago and A Short While Ago***), published by Vanier in 1885.

In the spring of 1874, when Verlaine was in prison, Mathilde received an official separation from him and custody of their child. The court also ordered Verlaine to pay 100 francs per month for child support. The poet was distraught. In June he reconverted to Catholicism, the religion of his youth, and in August he received communion. ***Sagesse*** is imbued with religious inspiration and symbols, sometimes explicit and sometimes extremely delicate and subtle. Verlaine's faith—and this is scarcely surprising to anyone who knows his life—is not simple, nor is it exuberantly joyous. Instead, it is a constant struggle, a full acceptance of man's fallen state, sufferings and weaknesses with all of which, the poet believes, Christ empathizes and, through the crucifixion, embodies. Thus, "God" tells the "pitiable friend" in "My God said to me . . .": "Haven't I sobbed your utmost anguish, and haven't / I sweated the sweat of your nighttimes, pitiable friend / Who seeks for me where I am?"

Upon his release from prison in January 1875, Verlaine was expelled from Belgium. In late February, in Stuttgart, he saw Rimbaud for the last time. For some months after that, he corresponded with his former lover. But Rimbaud was now importuning him for money. On December 12, 1875, Verlaine sent Rimbaud a final letter: he said that he would not send him any money and also that he did not want Rimbaud to have his address. But he added that Rimbaud could write to him at Ernest Delahaye's. And over the years, when Verlaine no longer heard from Rimbaud, he would continue to ask Delahaye about the man whose poetry he would begin to reveal to the public in 1883 and 1884, in *Les Poètes maudits* (*The Accursèd Poets*), ten and more years after their liaison had ended.

From 1875 to 1879, Verlaine found teaching jobs: first in England—at a grammar school in Stickney (Lincolnshire), where he taught French and drawing, and then at a secondary school in Bournemouth. He taught French, English and history in France, from October 1877 to June 1879, at the Institution Notre-Dame de Rethel. The students and staff there thought him strange. "He kept his arms crossed on his chest, his hands spread out. The ecclesiastical staff thought this layman was overdoing it, and the students, with their lively sense of ridiculous, called him Jesus Christ."[5] Verlaine was drinking again and was finally dismissed from the school.

One of his pupils in Rethel was a nineteen-year-old peasant named Lucien Létinois. Verlaine became closely attached to him, and they traveled to England together. When they returned to France, Verlaine bought a farm in Juniville and lived on it with Lucien and Lucien's parents. Farming, however, proved a financial disaster for them, and so in 1882, Verlaine tried to get his job back at the Hôtel de Ville, from which he had been dismissed after the Paris Commune of 1871. But records of his trial, prison term and impending divorce arrived, and he was denied reinstatement in April 1883. It was a devastating blow. So was another event that occurred that month. For on April 7, Lucien died suddenly of typhoid fever. From this time on, although Verlaine's literary fame and acclaim were increasing, his style of living was becoming more and more degraded and desperate.

In September 1883, Verlaine moved with his mother onto a farm in Coulommes. Not only was farming a failure for him once more, but this time he led such a debt-plagued, drunken and degenerate life that he horrified the inhabitants of the environs. He spent a month in jail from April 13 to May 13, 1885, for having nearly strangled his mother when he was in a drunken rage. The month of his release from jail, Mathilde obtained her official divorce from him.

Destitute, Verlaine returned to Paris, and his mother moved into the building where he was living. He was suffering at this time from hydrarthrosis of the knee. Often he could not even get out of bed. When his mother died in January 1886, his hydrarthrosis prevented him from attending her funeral.

Four days after Verlaine's mother died, Mathilde's family insisted on getting money from him for his son, Georges, because Verlaine had never paid the child support required by the separation decree. "When the sheriff arrived, Verlaine handed over to him the bundle of twenty thousand francs worth of bonds that his mother had left, and which had been concealed under a mattress. A gesture at once noble and insane. For when he had paid Madame Verlaine's burial expenses and settled his bills, the poor man was left with exactly eight hundred francs."[6]

From 1886 until his death almost ten years later, Verlaine was constantly in and out of hospitals. . . . Often he was in great pain. In September 1887, he nearly died of hunger, and he contemplated suicide.

But his literary fame was growing. In 1888, the Decadents considered him a leader, but he soon disassociated himself from their doctrines. Every Wednesday, his admirers came to his room. Among them were Villiers de l'Isle—Adam, Maurice Barrès, Jean Moréas and Paterne Berrichon (who would later marry Rimbaud's youngest sister, Isabelle). In 1888, Verlaine's collection ***Amour*** **(*Love*)** was published, and in 1889, ***Parallèlment*** **(*In a Parallel Direction*)**.

All this time, Verlaine was drinking a lot. He frequented homosexual prostitutes (his collection ***Hombres*** **[*Men*]** was published posthumously). "I'm a feminine gender [un féminin], which would explain a great many things," Verlaine wrote F. A. Cazals on August 26, 1889.[7] Verlaine also frequented female prostitutes. . . .

In 1891, Verlaine was living at 15, rue Descartes, in a hotel frequented by prostitutes and pimps. Over the next years, he would be earning money both from his books, which were selling well, and from the lectures he was invited to give (e.g. in Nancy, London, Oxford, Manchester, Holland and Belgium). But whenever he had some money, he spent it wildly, inviting his friends on drunken sprees. . . .

Respect for Verlaine's poetry kept growing. He was elected "Prince of Poets" in 1894, succeeding Leconte de Lisle. The poet who would succeed him would be Mallarmé.

Just before Verlaine died, on January 8, 1896, he lived in some kind of quiet with Eugénie Krantz. At his graveside, speeches were given by several literary luminaries of the day, including François Coppée, Maurice Barrès, Gustave Kahn, Catulle Mendès, Jean Moréas and Stéphane Mallarmé.

"Your soul is a selected landscape," Verlaine begins **"Moonlight,"** the first of the lovely and unsettling, happy and sad, populated and lonely poems of his ***Fêtes galantes***. This poem, which sets the ambiguous scene for that entire book, is emblematic of much of Verlaine's other poetry as well:

Your soul is a selected landscape that maskers
And bergamasche go about beguiling
Playing the lute and dancing and quasi
Sad beneath their fantastical disguises.

While singing in the minor mood
Triumphant love and life that is opportune,
They do not seem to believe in their good fortune
And their song mingles with the moonlight,

With the calm moonlight sad and beautiful,
That makes the birds dream in the trees
And the fountains weep with ecstasy,
The great svelte fountains amid the marble statues.

Here, a landscape and a soulscape are equated. Perceptions in Verlaine's poetry are paramount, for just as a person's soul reflects or incorporates a "selected landscape," so a landscape will reflect or incorporate the person perceiving it. The soul in the first stanza is another person's soul (a woman's soul, perhaps, or perhaps *your* soul, the reader's soul, as you enter this world of gallant festivals). But that soul also reflects, in some profound and important ways, the poet's soul, for it is he who is depicting its inner depths. In that soul, the site of a masked ball, people are actors and dancers, "maskers and bergamasche." Their masks, which both conceal what they are and reveal what they might like to be or what they play at being, suggest theater and artifice, charm and disguise, enchantment and deceit. Are these phantomlike figures only acting the roles of lovers, or do they—or can they—love in reality? The word "bergamasche" is richly suggestive. While Verlaine seems to imply dancers by it, the word actually means some fast dances (or the music for those dances) similar to the tarantella, the rapid, whirling southern Italian dance for couples. "Bergamasche" therefore evoke exoticism, eroticism, and a whirling, swirling frenzy: the kind of dizzy, intoxicating and disequilibriating motion in which Verlaine so often delights (e.g. see **"Mandolin"** and **"Brussels: Merry-Go-Round"**).

Subtly now, indications of malaise are insinuated. The actors, dancers and musicians "go about beguiling" the soul they inhabit, enchanting, captivating and charming it for good—but perhaps for evil. Suddenly a chill ripples through. For the end of the first stanza reveals that amid all the charm and gaiety of the masked ball, the gallant figures are "quasi / Sad beneath their fantastical disguises." Words about seeming, that by their nature question the existence and very essence of what is seen and what is said, are one of the hallmarks of Verlaine's poetry. For him, things rarely *are*; instead, they *seem to be*, which means that they almost always suggest the lurking presence of something else, of something alien perhaps, or even opposite. These figures, clothed in their "disguises," seem sad, almost sad. What are they disguising? Are they really sad, or is that the poet's projection of himself onto the scene? In any case, a note of melancholy is sounded here. Too, the word "fantastical" insinuates a disturbing tone, for while it means fantastic—of the mind or the imagination—it also may imply something strange, or weird or grotesque.

In the second stanza, the poet continues his impressionistic medley of sights that are both precise and hazy, and of sounds that are simultaneously soothing and unsettling. Now the nature of everything evoked is questioned, for although the figures sing what would seem to be victorious, favorable and timely ("Triumphant love and life that is opportune"), still they sing these "in the minor mood," suggesting the melancholy and plaintive sounds associated with the minor key. Once again, a motif of seeming questions everything. Phrased now in a negative way ("They do not seem to believe in their good fortune"), the words cast doubt not only on the singers' feelings, but also on the nature of their fortune.

Finally, their song mingles with the moonlight: the microcosm of this soul inhabited by people and a landscape mingles fully with the macrocosm—with the universe, with "the calm moonlight sad and beautiful." The word "calm," like motifs of seeming, is a key word for Verlaine, a word that almost invariably veils an underlying malaise or frenzy, at times even a feeling of despair. "Calm" is often a mask or veil that Verlaine uses to cover, or to try to cover, a face of anguish. "Calm in the twilight that / The high branches make above, / With this profound silence let's / Completely imbue our love," he begins **"With Muted Strings,"** another of the ***Fêtes galantes*** which, like several poems in that collection, proceeds from ostensible calm to a cry of anguish: "And when the solemn evening / Falls from the black oaks, / Voice of our hopelessness, / The nightingale will sing."

The moonlight in **"Moonlight"** is at once "sad and beautiful": beauty for Verlaine implies the presence of sadness. So, too, does his notion of "ecstasy," for the very intensity of this emotional rapture leads inevitably to its loss (see, for example, **"Mandolin," "With Muted Strings"** and **"Sentimental Colloquy"**). In **"Moonlight,"** where "the fountains weep with ecstasy," the trancelike state is so overpowering that the joy expresses itself in tears: tears of rapture that recall sorrow and pain.

This brief examination of **"Moonlight"** suggests that Verlaine's poetry, which might appear calm or simple on the surface, is actually much more complex, extremely rich in underlying tensions and implications. Even such an apparently carefree piece as **"Streets"** (a poem inspired by Verlaine's and Rimbaud's stay in London) contains an inner anguish, despite its exclamatory refrain sounded five times, "Let's dance the jig!" For, from the poet's evocation of the woman's "mischievous eyes," to his exclaiming that the way she had of "making a poor lover grieve" was "really . . . charming indeed!", to his recalling in the last stanza that the times and talks they had had together were the "best" of his "possessions," certain impressions of pain and of melancholy have filtered through. When the refrain is sounded a final time after the last stanza, the poet's call to dance the jig seems like an attempt to shake off, by means of this fast, gay and springy dance, the loneliness, nostalgia and sadness that have been welling within him. "The desired lightness of motion and emotion is there; but almost inadvertently, the presence of thought, tinged by regret, has been insinuated. 'Let's dance the jig' contains at the end an echo of remembrance more than an invitation to joy," writes Henri Peyre.[8]

The incessant interplay between quiet and disquiet continues throughout Verlaine's poetry, contributing to its uniqueness and its melancholy beauty, and to its powers to enchant and to disturb. Thus, **"Crimen amoris,"** one of Verlaine's most fascinating and ambitious poems, modulates from a swirling and violently agitated vision into a melodious and peaceful soulscape at the end. It is almost as though for Verlaine the excess of one emotion calls for, and must be balanced by, its opposite. But for the reader well-attuned to the ceaseless struggles going on in Verlaine's tortured psyche, the calm vision at the end of **"Crimen amoris"** contains echoes of the agitations that preceded and—we know from Verlaine's life—would follow.

"Crimen amoris" is Verlaine's one-hundred-line vision of Rimbaud as a sixteen-year-old prophet, an "evil" angel, a "Satan," who also, in certain ways, resembles Jesus. It is written in lines of eleven syllables, a rhythm that is somewhat jarring to the French reader reared on classical alexandrines. But just because of the line's unevenness and its sense of imbalance, the *vers impair* is so well suited to this poem and to Verlaine's equivocal nature.

The "crime" takes place in Persia, in Ecbatana (the ancient name of Hamadan in present-day Iran). The location adds exotic, mythical and religious dimensions to the tale. As the poem opens, "Beautiful demons, adolescent Satans," celebrate "the festival of the Seven Sins." Their glorification of sensuous and sensual pleasures ("ô how beautiful / It is! All desires beamed in brutal fires") is, of course, a rebellion against the church. Their festival, as described lyrically, excitedly—delightedly—by the poet, is melodious, amorous, luxurious, and filled with "Goodness." Verlaine's words capture its splendor, rapture, fierceness and excitement, its tender erotic ecstasies that bring on tears, its cosmic proportions and powers of enchantment:

> Dances to the rhythms of epithalamiums
> Were swooning in long sobs quite tenderly
> And beautiful choirs of men's and women's voices
> Were rolling in, palpitating like waves of the sea,
>
> And the Goodness that issued from these things was
> so potent
> And so charming that the countryside
> Around adorned itself with roses
> And night appeared in diamond.

In stanza 5, Rimbaud, "the handsomest of all those evil angels," appears. Because he is deeply distressed, the other Satans try to cheer him. Finally, in stanzas 10–14, he addresses them, proclaiming a "gospel of blasphemy" that is at the same time a "metaphysical rebellion."[9] "'Oh! I will be the one who will create God!'" he begins his scandalous and prophetic pronouncements. He then delineates his dream of abolishing the concept of sin, for sins, he says, will henceforth be rejoined to virtues. And he announces that he will sacrifice himself—make himself sacred thereby—for the sake of others, and for the sake of "universal Love": "'through me now hell / Whose lair is here sacrifices itself to universal love!'" This, therefore, is his **"Crime of Love"** his vision of a new and revolutionary Love, of a total and completely unrestricted Love, of a Love that is universal, all-embracing, erotic, emotional and spiritual. But this Love is also a rebellion that implies, among other things, Verlaine's and Rimbaud's homosexual love. It is a physical and metaphysical revolt against the teachings of Catholicism, and so is a "crime" in the eyes of society and the church. The title is, therefore, an indictment against Rimbaud (and Verlaine). But it may also be interpreted as an indictment against the church and state that condemn a complete and free and universal Love.

The sacrifice, flame-licked, tortured, but exalted, begins in stanzas 15–18, with repeated intimations that death and destruction are imminent as the other Satans follow their visionary prophet:

> And the dying Satans were singing in the flames . . .
>
> . . . .
>
> And he, with his arms crossed in a haughty air,
> With his eyes on the sky where the licking fire climbs along,
> He recites in a whisper a kind of prayer,
> That will die in the gaiety of the song.

Suddenly, the song ends, for "Someone had not accepted the sacrifice." Everything is then destroyed, and all becomes "but a vain and vanished dream . . ." (stanza 21). But does that dream really disappear?

The four last stanzas are lyrical and calm, a gentle song after the exploding visions in the twenty-one that preceded. Yet calmness in Verlaine's poetry is so often a veil cast over an inner agitation that one cannot but wish to look more closely here. In stanza 22, the entire ambiance is veiled, wavering, almost palpitating; something seems to be rising from just below the surface. One senses a soul behind the scene. The plain is "evangelical," "severe and peaceful." The word "severe" might indicate an underlying strain. The tree branches, "vague like veils," suggest angels—or ghosts. They also "look like wings waving about," intimating angels' wings perhaps, or perhaps wings of birds that wish to fly—to flee.

In the next stanza, all seems calm. "The gentle owls float vaguely in the air / Quite embalmed with mystery and with prayer." But the word "embalmed" (as we pointed out at the end of Rimbaud's "Drunken Boat") suggests, along with sweet scents, intimations of death. "At times a wave that leaps hurls a flash of lightning." This sentence at the end of the stanza startles: its fire is reminiscent of the flames of the Satanic festival.

In stanza 24, a "soft shape" rises from the hills "Like a love defined unclearly still, / And the mists that from the ravines ascend / Seem an effort towards some reconciled end." In the context of Verlaine's other poetry, the word "seem" is somewhat troubling. While here it seeks to define nature in terms of the divine, still the word does raise a question, for it is certainly possible that the mists might not *be* "an effort towards some reconciled end."

The last stanza is clearly an invocation to Christ—a "heart," and a "soul," and a "word" (the Word), and a "virginal love":

> And all that like a heart and like a soul,
> And like a word, and with a virginal love,
> Adores, expands in an ecstasy and beseeches
> The merciful God who will keep us from evil.

The word "ecstasy" is used here in its religious sense, but for Verlaine, as we saw earlier, the notion of ecstasy leads almost invariably to feelings of loss, or pain or sadness. Two other words clearly inject some uneasiness into the apparently serene soulscape of this last stanza: "beseeches" ("réclame") and "evil" ("[le] mal"). The word "beseeches" stresses urgency and need. It means "to ask for earnestly," "to implore" and "to beg for." This is a heartfelt and a pressing prayer. One senses at this point the poet's profoundest longings for peace and for a pure love: for a "virginal love" that would counter the "crime of love," and for a "virginal love" that would be free from sexuality. The poet's calling upon God to help him in his distress is typical of Verlaine's religious poetry. It is also significant, I believe, that he does not beseech a "God who will lead us to good" but rather a "God who will keep us from evil." This is, in the closing quiet of **"Crimen amoris,"** a muffled cry of anguish. The fact that Verlaine ends his poem on the word "evil" suggests that "evil" will continue to torment—and to attract—him. In fact, judging from the length of the poem, and from the beauty and power of the description of the Satanic festival, that "evil" undoubtedly continued to allure Verlaine, even as he wrote the poem and sought to condemn the **"Crime of Love."**

Verlaine's poems mediate ceaselessly, therefore, between gaiety and sadness, hope and fear, quiet and disquiet. It is as though just below their melodious and apparently simple surfaces, a silent scream is waiting to be released. In his poetry, as Festa-McCormick notes, "The tragic shows through the surface, as it shows through the surface in certain impressionist paintings or in Watteau's so melancholy picture ["The Embarkation for Cythera"] in which the voyagers seem sadly satiated or disenchanted with the pleasure for which they are embarking."[10] Verlaine's moods and language, his mysterious music "with muted strings," his choice of rhythms, rhymes and words that continually question the scene's—and therefore the soul's—serenity, combine to create a state of uneasy calm, a vision of happiness or pleasure that may be undermined at any moment. One can sense in Verlaine's poetry, as in his life, both control and loss of control. For his soulscapes are permeated with a kind of restless repose and with tremors of the ephemeral or other-worldly which seek to convey calm or hope or joy, but which almost invariably insinuate hidden presences of pain or sorrow, as well. And always in Verlaine's poetry there is "Music before anything else. . . ." Never overpowering or thunderous in its orchestration, his music, lute-like, or like the music of other stringed instruments, is melodious, lyrical and seductive, an integral part of his poetry of moods and sensations. Through its sounds and its rhythms, his poetry filters into you, caresses you, possesses you, lulls you and disturbs you, subtly. You are taken into its beauty and its uneasiness, almost unawares. Verlaine's malaise, through his music, becomes your own disquietude. And his poetry, that "One wants to think caressing . . . both delights / And distresses simultaneously."[11]

Notes

1. According to their mutual friend Ernest Delahaye, in *Delahaye témoin de Rimbaud*, p. 187, n. 52.
2. For an excellent study of naïveté in Verlaine's art, see James R. Lawler, *The Language of French Symbolism* (note 1 above), pp. 21–70.
3. *Les Poètes maudits*, in *Oeuvres complètes de Paul Verlaine*, Vol. IV (Paris: Vanier, 1910), p. 79.
4. "Verlaine: Meditation within Shimmering Sketches," in *French Symbolist Poetry: Sou'wester*, p. 93.
5. Antoine Adam, *The Art of Paul Verlaine*, trans. Carl Morse (New York: New York University Press, 1963), p. 39.
6. *Ibid.*, p. 47.
7. In Henri Peyre, *Rimbaud vu par Verlaine*, p. 186.
8. "Verlaine: Symbolism and Popular Poetry" in *French Symbolist Poetry: Sou'wester* (note 28 above), p. 24.
9. Henri Peyre, *Rimbaud vu par Verlaine* (note 20 above), pp. 172–73.
10. Diana Festa-McCormick, "Y a-t-il un impressionnisme littéraire: Le cas Verlaine," *Nineteenth-Century French Studies*, Vol. II, Nos. 3 & 4 (Spring-Summer 1974), 152–53.
11. See Verlaine's sonnet beginning "The hunting horn grieves towards the forest. . . ."

Carol de Dobay Rifelj (essay date 1982)

SOURCE: "Familiar and Unfamiliar: Verlaine's Poetic Diction," in *Romance Quarterly*, Vol. 29, No. 4, 1982, pp. 365–77.

[*In the following essay, de Dobay Rifelj explores neoclassical diction in Verlaine's poetry.*]

In order for a figure to exist, a comparison must be possible between one form of expression and another which could have been used instead. As Gérard Genette notes, "l'existence et le caractère de la figure sont absolument déterminés par l'existence et le caractère des signes réels en posant leur équivalence sémantique."[1] This is the case not only with conventional tropes, but also with diction: only if another signifier is possible: *je m'ennuie* for *je m'emmerde, catin* for *putain*, does there come into existence a different kind of figure, a figure of register. On the next level of signification, *coursier* for horse carries the message "I am poetry" just as much as does *voile* for ship. But it stands only for a certain kind of poetry. In Verlaine's time, such usage was the norm: French poetry had a highly restricted set of conventions for poetic diction, distinguishing between high or "elevated" and low diction; between the sublime and the *médiocre* or *burlesque*; between noble and common, or "roturier." The first terms of these sets are obviously highly valorized. Those 19th century poets, including Hugo, Rimbaud, Corbière, and Verlaine, who breached this code—using colloquial or familiar words and even vulgar and slang expressions—were clearly setting their poetry against the accepted, almost sacred canon. In doing so, they implicitly recognized that the language of this canon was now too familiar, in the sense of commonplace, and they were led to new delimitations of acceptable diction.

Theoreticians from Aristotle on have linked a specialized vocabulary like that of French neoclassical verse to the use of metaphor. But in Verlaine, the use of familiar diction does not lead to a lessening of the importance of figure; in a sense, it allows for even greater, or at least different, possibilities of figural language. If conventionally "poetic" words and their opposite can be shown to be marked registers in poetic texts, it is because their existence permits a kind of movement that can be called tropological; the use of familiar diction calls attention to the surface of the work, preventing its language from being simply referential. Its very "earthiness" prevents it from being "down-to-earth" in the sense of being stabilized or giving the reader a more direct link to the outside world. Rather, it plays on the estrangement implied by its identification as an element of a specific register. As metaphor has been considered the breaking of the semantic rules of a language, register-shifts constitute a breaching of its pragmatic rules.[2] And this breach is one aspect of the figural dimension of language.

Whether the gap between such terms and their conventional counterparts is called parody or humor or opposition to poetic tradition, the reader must attempt to integrate it into some kind of structure. By examining the role of informal or colloquial diction in the figural structure of Verlaine's poems, we can see the different ways in which they exploit its possible stylistic motivations. Incorporating such language into coherent interpretations of the texts does not prove to be simple, however, and such an analysis reveals the complexity of a poet whose works have often been seen as direct, univocal, and even simplistic.

Given the entrenchment of neo-classical diction, it is not surprising that Verlaine's use of familiar language has had a varied critical response, ranging from hailing him as a revolutionary to condemning his later works, (in which such language is more prevalent), as vulgar or "prosaic." One critic tries to excuse his use of low language by referring to his low life:

> Avec Verlaine, nous avons affaire à un pauvre brave type, qui sort du bistrot ou de l'hôpital, trainant la patte, et qui nous raconte des choses très simples, ou très délicates, ou très élevées, dans la langue de tous les jours. Alors que les Parnassiens, en redingote et haut de forme, sont juchés tout en haut d'un trépied, Verlaine est sur l'asphalte du trottoir parisien.[3]

But Claude Cuénot, in his study of Verlaine's style, is much less indulgent: "Une étude complète du vocabulaire argotique de Verlaine aurait une importance lexicographique, mais ne comporterait guère d'intérêt esthétique, puisque la poésie est absente."[4] "Unpoetic" words, then, cannot constitute a poem. Verlaine himself seems to support this view when he writes:

> Tu n'es plus bon à rien de propre, ta parole
> Est morte de l'argot et du ricanement,
> Et d'avoir rabâché les bourdes du moment.
> Ta mémoire, de tant d'obscénités bondée,
> Ne saurait accueillir la plus petite idée . . .
>
> ***Sagesse*** I, iv

Verlaine said that he wrote these lines about Rimbaud, but added, "Après coup je me suis aperçu que cela pourrait s'appliquer à 'poor myself.'" He had introduced language of varying degrees of familiarity during the whole of his poetic career, and especially so after ***Sagesse***, where these lines appear. And indeed, he does so in this very passage: *tu n'es plus bon à . . ., la plus petite idée* and *rabâché* are certainly casual, familiar expressions. His word, then, rather than being destroyed by slang, receives a new impulse forward.

In order to make sense of such discourse, in order to make poetry of it rather than rejecting it out of hand, the reader must try to "naturalize" it, that is, to justify its use within the context of the poem. This naturalization can operate in various ways, on various levels. First, familiar language can be integrated by assigning the text to a "low" genre, where such diction would be the norm rather than an intrusion. On another level, it can be naturalized as appropriate to the poem's subject-matter: the signified might be "low" life (i.e. a popular subject) or "modern life," calling forth signifiers which mirror the level of the signified. Many examples of such motivation can be found in Verlaine. In texts which escape such categorizations, familiar diction must be incorporated at another level. **"Art poétique"** provides an example of a text whose self-referentiality leads to taking its unconventional language as signifying a rejection of conventional poetry. Other texts seem unmotivated even at this level and present a challenge to readability itself. In all these texts we must examine to what extent Verlaine's work justifies the naturalizations imposed on it by the urge to legibility and to what extent it defies any such analysis.

"Monsieur Prudhomme" is an example of a poem whose satirical quality helps to motivate the use of "low" language, satire being a genre characterized by the low style.

> Il est grave: il est maire et père de famille
> Son faux col engloutit son oreille. Ses yeux
> Dans un rêve sans fin flottent, insoucieux,
> Et le printemps en fleur sur ses pantoufles brille.
>
> Que lui fait l'astre d'or, que lui fait la charmille
> Où l'oiseau chante à l'ombre, et que lui font les cieux,
> Et les prés verts et les gazons silencieux?
> Monsieur Prudhomme songe à marier sa fille
>
> Avec monsieur Machin, un jeune homme cossu.
> Il est juste-milieu, botaniste et pansu.
> Quant aux faiseurs de vers, ces vauriens,
> ces maroufles,
>
> Ces fainéants barbus, mal peignés, il les a
> Plus en horreur que son éternel coryza,
> Et le printemps en fleur brille sur ses pantoufles.

The title already makes it status clear: Joseph Prudhomme, the main character in Henri Monnier's novels, was the archetypical bourgeois. The lampoon begins with the very first line, with the words "il est grave" and the stock expression "père de famille" heightened by the homonym *maire/mère*. M. Prudhomme is deaf, his ears "engulfed" in his collar (the word *faux* is also relevant here), as well as blind to the beauties of nature—spring is reduced to the level of his slippers. The rest of the poem confirms this description of his anti-esthetic, anti-poetic sentiments. Even the insults he addresses to poets are consummately bourgeois in the attitude they reveal (poets are unshaven, unkempt, and lazy), and in diction—*maroufles* or *vauriens* are perfectly acceptable terms. It is curious to note, however, that in order to form a contrast with his insensitivity, a conventionally poetic diction is used: not only is the subject nature and flowers, but the periphrase *l'astre d'or* for the sun is eminently neo-classical. It seems that when Verlaine wants to signal "poetry," he needs the easily recognizable "poetic" expression to do so.

Features of other registers conflict with this diction, like *coryza* and *cossu. Machin* is "très trivial" (Littré) and doubly comical here, recalling the word *machine* and indicating that the prospective fiancé is so conventionally bourgeois as to have lost all identity. The succession of adjectives in line 10 is funny, too, the physical epithet *pansu* following two nouns used as adjectives. *Botaniste* in this series indicates the only interest nature might have for him.

If the use of a conventionally poetic signifier is itself a sign, whose message is "I am poetry;" than slang expressions, used here to ridicule the de-humanized characters should be a sign of opposition to this language, and often they do have this role. But, in this text, where poets are referred to explicitly, and a traditionally "poetic" subject, the flowered spring, appears twice and ends the poem, where *rêve sans fin* is contrasted with M. Prudhomme's thoughts of a profitable marriage for his daughter, the traditional diction is valorized and paradoxically opposed to the characters who would be likely to approve only such language, who would surely say of this text: that isn't poetry.

Even in a text that would be considered more conventionally lyrical, one might consider "low" diction to be motivated by subject-matter. An example of such a poem is **"L'Auberge."**

> Murs blancs, toit rouge, c'est l'Auberge fraîche au bord
> Du grand chemin poudreux où le pied brûle et saigne,
> L'auberge gaie avec le *Bonheur* pour enseigne.
> Vin bleu, pain tendre, et pas besoin de passe-port.
>
> Ici l'on fume, ici l'on chante, ici l'on dort.
> L'hôte est un vieux soldat, et l'hôtesse, qui peigne
> Et lave dix marmots roses et pleins de teigne,
> Parle d'amour, de joie et d'aise, et n'a pas tort!
>
> La salle au noir plafond de poutres, aux images
> Violentes, *Maleck Adel et les Rois Mages,*
> Vous accueille d'un bon parfum de soupe aux choux.
>
> Entendez-vous? C'est la marmite qu'accompagne
> L'horloge du tic-tac allègre de son pouls.
> Et la fenêtre s'ouvre au loin sur la campagne.

Here the popular milieu calls forth many elements usually excluded from poetry: *vin bleu* (cheap wine), cabbage soup, and so on. The pictures of the wise men and Maleck Adel, the hero of a popular novel, would be typical in such an inn. In its homely and banal elements, the text resembles the poetry of Coppée or the Parnassian poets who treated rural subjects or even the descriptive poetry of Delille; and it is analogous to the realist/naturalist novel and its portrayal of lower-class life.

Since everything about this milieu is valorized and opposed to the dusty, painful road, familiar words in reported speech should be neither pejorative nor startling: the casual tone they create is in harmony with the place described, where one can obviously be at ease. But what differs in Verlaine's treatment of the subject is, in fact, the intrusion of familiar diction in the language of the poem. It contains elements from the speech one might expect to hear in a country inn: shortened forms like the elliptical first and fourth lines, including "pas besoin de passe-port" and familiar expressions—*n'a pas tort, entendez-vous, marmots* ("kids"), and *teigne* ("scabby").

These expressions play a role in the figural structure of the text as well, which is built on a correspondence between inside and outside. It is a poem concerned with signs, or language. "Ici l'on fume" and so forth, of course, imitate the messages on signs in shop windows, i.e. linked with the life inside the inn. Thus they recall the sign in the first stanza: "Happiness" is or should be the inn's name, since that is what is to be found within. And of what does this happiness consist? Of *talking* about happiness and comfort and love. So it is removed to yet another level, as the designatum of the inhabitants' conversation. The images or prints on the other hand are metaphors for the life outside; and they are called violent to underline the contrast. Thus, in the last line, the opening window is yet another "image" of the exterior world, framed by the window sill. The language of the poem functions as an imitation (another metaphor) or as another sign of the language of the environment.

In such a context, the speaker is placed in an ambivalent position: he is allowed, even invited within, but an inn is only a temporary lodging, a contingency of his travels. His link with it is an arbitrary one, as the phrase "pas besoin de passe-port" shows; he is just an observer. The poem has been compared to a genre painting; and indeed, it is like a print hung on the wall of a city person's apartment, with a title like "The Pleasures of the Simple Life." But the "simple life" has turned out to be another signifier, or another metaphor; and the language of the text, rather than grounding it in a correspondence between subject and register-level, serves to de-stabilize the depiction of a world that seemed attractive in its stability.

In other poems, the link between the signified and the "low" register level of the signifier can be naturalized in different ways, serving a variety of stylistic functions. In the sixteenth poem of ***La Bonne Chanson***, "low" language is linked with imagery of lowness and contrasted with "paradise," the presence of the loved one. In ***Sagesse*** III, xix, (**"Parisien, mon frère"**) it is the country-side which is opposed to the city. The two speakers in **"Qu'en dis-tu, voyageur"** (I,iii) are distinguished by the levels of language they use. **"Sonnet boiteux,"** from ***Jadis et naguère***, uses low diction to denigrate the city it describes; and in conjunction with repetitions, unfamiliar sounds and unusually long verses, it creates an effect of irritation and frustration. In **"Nocturne parisien"** (***Poèmes saturniens***), familiar diction sets modern Paris apart from the conventional subjects of Romantic and Parnassian poetry, as well as from the diction characteristic of such verse.

In a letter to Delahaye, Verlaine himself spoke of "ma poétique de plus en plus moderniste" (26 October 1872). There is an element of "modernism" in much of his poetry, from the ***Poèmes saturniens*** onward, in the sense of portraying 19th-century life as Baudelaire did, especially in his *Tableaux parisiens*, where the latter had himself introduced a certain amount of familiar discourse. Much of Verlaine's verse, and particularly **"Croquis parisien,"** which echoes Baudelaire's title, recalls this section of *Les Fleurs du mal.* Dedicated to François Coppée, whose sentimental verse treated emotional moments in ordinary banal lives, usually in Parisian settings, it thematizes the opposition between the contemporary and the past:

> La lune plaquait ses teintes de zinc
> Par angles obtus
> Des bouts de fumée en forme de cinq
> Sortaient drus et noirs des hauts toits pointus.
>
> Le ciel était gris. La bise pleurait
> Ainsi qu'un basson.
> Au loin, un matou frileux et discret
> Miaulait d'étrange et grêle façon.
>
> [Le long des maisons, escarpe et putain
> Se coulaient sans bruit,

Guettant le joueur au pas argentin
Et l'adolescent qui mord à tout fruit.]

Moi, j'allais, rêvant du divin Platon
Et de Phidias,
Et de Salamine et de Marathon,
Sout l'oeil clignotant des bleus becs de gaz.

Although the third stanza was omitted in ***Poèmes saturniens***, this poem was the target of several critical attacks. It was said to be "impressionistic," cacophonous, its images supposedly impossible to understand. Jules Lemaître wrote, "Il y a dans tout cela bien des mots mis au hasard.—Justement. Ils ont le sens qu'a voulu le poète, et ils ne l'ont que pour lui."[6] He criticized especially the first stanza, which contains elements like *zinc* and *par angles obtus* which Robichez calls "inédits" (p. 513). Indeed, the use of artistic terminology, unusual images, elements from modern life, and familiar expressions, in their novelty, constitute a metaphor for modern life itself. In other words, new forms of expression are to traditional poetry as the new age is to the old.

Like the artist's vocabulary, *angles obtus* is an unexpected lexical item, an intrusion from mathematical terminology. Elements normally considered low are included in the poem—gas jets, the meowing tomcat. Colloquial expressions like *bouts de fumée* and *moi, j'allais* also stand out in this manner, while giving the impression of a casual, conversational style. In the eliminated stanza, *escarpe*, a slang word for thief, and *putain*, which Littré calls a "terme grossier at malhonnête" are even stronger and are surely at least part of the reason for the stanza's suppression. The poem's rhythm contributes to its conversational tone: the five-syllable second line of each stanza throws off its regularity. And the short, declarative sentences, without the inverted syntax characteristic of traditional poetry, tend to negate their division into verses. The rhymes are all masculine, another unusual procedure; and the false rhymes—*zinc/cinq* and *Phidias/gaz*—reinforce this effect. These devices heighten the contrast set up between 19th-century Paris and ancient Greece. The sculptor Phidias is opposed to the aquafortists and sketchers of modern times, the battles of Salamis and Marathon to those between the prostitute and her clients, the thief and his victims; and, by implication, Plato's city state to the modern city of Paris. The winking gas-jets are the guiding lights of a new age; and their mention in the last line of the poem brings us back to the everyday world.

The familiar expressions in such a poem, then, can be naturalized as appropriate to their subject, Parisian street-life, a subject or field that is itself unusual. But also, the thematization of the modern, explicitly in opposition to the classical world, is paralleled in its language: the "divine" Plato is no more as the word *divin* is no longer in everyday use. And the poem's protagonist does not ponder his philosophy; he is dreaming as he travels through the city. A conversational language and tone, then, are doubly appropriate to the text.

It is interesting to note that the artistic vocabulary employed here refers primarily to etching, as the title of the section in which it appears, "Eauxfortes," would lead one to expect. *Plaquer, teintes, angles*, and *en forme de* refer to art work in general, while *zinc* and even *argentin* recall the metal engraving plates, and *mordre* is the expression used for the corrosive action of the acid's inscription in the metal.[7] The line "Des bouts de fumée en forme de cinq" makes explicit the link between such inscription and writing: written figures are analogous to engraved figures (or shapes); and this analogy is itself a figure, in yet another sense of the word. It is not the city which the poem describes (or which is inscribed in the poem), but rather, a sketch, an etching of the city. The text, then, is the representation of a representation. The scene is similarly presented as a series of unrelated impressions; and the line "Moi, j'allais . . ." underlines the speaker's detachment from what he sees. In his preoccupation with ancient Greece, he makes no attempt to comprehend what he sees and hears around him. But the final line makes clear the specular relation between him and his surroundings: he is himself observed by the gas jets: he is part of the picture. This integration by means of the eye incorporates the world of Greece as well, as the analogies between it and modern Paris show. And yet, the final line does not accomplish altogether a metaphoric totalization of the disparate images in the text. Plato and the famous Greek battles are known to the speaker and to us only through books, or, as here, through his dreams. The scene is that of a sketch; and even the rain is likened to music, rather than being a natural sound. So this written text cannot be said to describe the real world, but only another text; it is the metaphor of a metaphor, opening on to the possibility of a limitless play of relations characteristic of figural language.

As poems like **"Monsieur Prudhomme," "L'Auberge,"** and **"Croquis parisien"** show, even texts whose familiar diction would seem to be motivated by genre or subject-matter can be seen to resist the totalization imposed upon them by the process of naturalization. Such resistance can be seen even more clearly in **"Art poétique,"** which calls for analysis at another level: as a metalinguistic text, it has often been taken as a description of Verlaine's poetics. It exhibits a characteristic trait of the *ars poetica* genre: the tending toward the limit of performative, toward what Austin in *How to Do Things with Words* called the coincidence of action and utterance. Of course, there is no explicit performative "I hereby poeticize correctly" but the poem itself comes to represent such an utterance, and its theory/illustration model can bring into play a certain amount of self-referential discourse.

In this text, there are moments of theoretical statement simply followed by illustration. The second stanza, for instance, can be taken as a reading of the third, where the juxtaposition of the "indécis" and the precise is demonstrated. The reference to beautiful eyes, presumably clear and bright (on the level of the signified), is followed by *derrière des voiles*, which blurs the effect of the first part of the line as veils might do eyes. The word *tremblant* annuls the effect of *grand jour* (broad daylight) in the same way, as does *attiédi* for *ciels d'automne*. Similarly, the last line incorporates the contrast between *fouillis* and *clair*, while *bleu* gives the impression of their fusion, since it contradicts the whiteness of *claires étoiles*.

There are several examples of what could be called "méprises" in the text as well. *Soluble en l'air* contradicts the meaning of soluble, which refers to a liquid; *assassine* is used as an adjective; and not only is the jewel said to be forged, but it conflicts with "d'un sou." *Vent crispé* is another example: *crispé* means "dont la surface est un peu crispée par le souffle de quelque vent" (Littré); and there is an added resonance of the English "crisp air." But there are always instances of "méprises" in the choice of words; for the confusion of words, the taking of one for the other, is just another way of designating figural language. *Bijou d'un sou*, for example, can be called an oxymoron; *vent crispé* a kind of hypallage.

The last two stanzas present themselves as a summa of the precepts set forth in the poem. It incorporates vague expressions like *la chose, d'autres*, and plural nouns. There is a "méprise" in *la bonne aventure*, which here has the sense of "adventure" as well as its usual meaning of "fortune" (telling); it can also be taken as a metonymy for "fortune teller" or gypsy. That its epithet is *éparse* is another instance of a turning away from normal usage. Only *aventure/littérature* is a rich rhyme. But there are moments where precept and illustration coincide more directly. First, with reference to the rhythm: "préfère l'Impair" is part of a 9-syllable line. Second, there is an instance of onomotopoeia in which the coincidence of sound and sense parallels the precept enunciated: "sans rien en *lui qui pèse* ou *qui pose*." The stanza on rhyme, a critique of Parnassian verse and its extremely rich and rare rhymes and the funny, tricky rhyme of Banville, incorporates a mixture of internal rhyme and alliteration in *f* and *s* to a degree that has been called cacophonous. The two interior lines—where *ou* is repeated six times and echoes the rhyme in the preceding stanza—are difficult to read aloud, and their exaggerated rhyme has a comic effect. And the phrase "sans *quelque* méprise" itself illustrates imprecision.

But perhaps the clearest example of self-referentiality is the line "Prends l'éloquence et tords-lui son cou": the expression is itself the antithesis of eloquence, both as signified and as signifier, since the use of "*tords-lui*" and *son* rather than *le* are markers of a more casual style. This "neck-wringing" takes place throughout the poem in the conversational rhythm and the use of familiar expressions. *Fouillis* is a colloquial expression, and this status underlines its contrast with *claires étoiles*. *Grise*, while obviously representing the indécis/précis distinction, carries with it a resonance of its familiar meaning, "tipsy." Other elements from conversational speech include the *tutoiement*; "*c'est des* beaux yeux," *tu feras bien*, and *elle ira jusqu'où*, where the omission of the interrogative inversion is reinforced by its position as the rhyming word. Elements from situational registers usually avoided in poetry can be found here, too: *assagie* carries a connotation of childishness; and *ail de basse cuisine* is highly unusual in poetry. The use of familiar speech and elements from everyday life serve to create a contrast with the title, which would have led one to expect an elevated style like that of Boileau. And in this contrast itself resides the "message" of the *art poétique*. There is a reversal of the hierarchy: "la pointe" or eloquence, which should have been "elevated" is "basse" here. And it is music, which is "before everything else," which lets verse fly away and the soul go off to "other skies."

But, curiously enough, there are parts in the poem which are self-contradictory rather than self-referential. *Cou/ jusqu'où* is an example of the exaggerated rhyme censured. Though impure laughter is to be avoided, "cet ail de basse cuisine" is used to refer to it. And the most curious instance of this procedure occurs in the fourth stanza, where *nuance* is repeated three times, contrasted with color to render it even clearer and creating an internal rhyme like that decried in the seventh stanza. The harping tone created by all this is reinforced by the demanding "nous voulons"; and *pas, rien que* and *seul* are also pleonastic. All this thwarts the nuance so expressly called-for. This circumventing of the theory/illustration model can be seen again in the relation of the lyrical last two stanzas to the rest of the poem. The didactic tone—though at times a comic one—of the first section is absent here; the imperatives have become much more gentle subjunctives; there are no traces of familiar vocabulary; (in fact, *vont fleurant* is an obsolete, literary construction); the garlic has been transmuted into much more delicate seasonings. This poem, then, might seem to repeat the pattern of a text like Hugo's *Réponse à un acte d'accusation:* polemical passages using familiar discourse followed by a relapse into the elevated style. In that case the last two stanzas would represent ideal poetry, while the preceding explanations could be dismissed as didactic theorizing. But this poem cannot be called a simple statement of Verlaine's poetics—nor a "simple" statement" at all. Verlaine himself said of it: "Puis—car n'allez pas prendre au pied de la lettre *L'Art poétique* de ***Jadis et naguère***, qui n'est qu'une chanson, après tout, JE N'AURAI PAS FAIT DE THEORIE" (Préface aux ***Poèmes saturniens***).

The last line, relapsing into the casual mode, forestalls an interpretation which would divide the poem into a theoretical first part followed by a contradictory application. The *Petit Robert* gives as one meaning of the word *littérature:* "ce qui est artificiel, peu sincère," and uses this line as the example. But there was no such meaning of the word at the time: it is this poem itself which turns *littérature* into a pejorative word. The use of familiar discourse in this poem, then, because it is a "song" and in its deviation from conventional diction constitutes a sign denoting a rejection of traditional "literature." Verlaine has taken Boileau's title for a poem that, in its shiftings of style and tone, is distinctly anti-classical. The text's awareness of itself as language, as indicated by the title, leads to its disruption as simple assertion. Each time it seems to refer to something outside itself, beautiful eyes, for instance, it refers instead to its own language: here, the words "beaux yeux" and what follows. The signs become the referents; and the poem itself refers to this referring, or deferring. This *va-et-vient* between the surface of the text and its referent puts into action the figural movement of the text, a circular motion indicated by the imagery of joining and the figure of the sun. It seems to be a text about poetry; but it can only be "about," and turning about, itself.

Other texts likewise play on the reader's recognition of the stylistic incongruity of familiar language and invite interpretations which can take it into account. **"Paysage,"** from the section called "A la manière de plusieurs," parodies the dixains of Coppée, turning around the familiar Romantic topos of a day in the country with a lover and using familiar expressions and constructions to push Coppée's platitude to the extreme. Poems like **"Charleroi," "Jean de Nivelle"** (***Romances sans paroles***), and **"Images d'un sou"** (***Jadis et naguère***), combine elements from different milieux and several registers to produce a humorous tone or the disorienting effects prized so greatly later on by the decadents. Another text in which familiar language is at odds with rather than justified by its context is **"Un Pouacre,"** where insults, slang, and repugnant details produce a comic effect in their juxtaposition with the cliché of seeing the spectre of one's past, the figure of remorse.

Sometimes it seems that such contradictions in tone and level are impossible to incorporate at any level whatever. An example of such an instance is **"Nouvelles Variations sur le Point du Jour"** (***Parallèlement***) where a description of Paris calls up familiar language with no contrasting elevated moments.

Le Point du Jour, le Point blanc de Paris,
Le seul point blanc, grâce à tant de bâtisse
Et neuve et laide et que je t'en ratisse,
Le point du Jour, aurore des paris!

Le bonneteau fleurit "dessur" la berge,
La bonne tôt s'y déprave, tant pis
Pour elle et tant mieux pour le birbe gris
Qui lui du moins la croit encore vierge.

Il a raison, le vieux, car voyez donc
Comme est joli toujours le paysage:
Paris au loin, triste et gai, fol et sage,
Et le Trocadéro, ce cas, au fond . . .

Puis la verdure et le ciel et les types
Et la rivière obscène et molle, avec
Des gens trop beaux, leur cigare à leur bec:
Epatants ces metteurs-au-vent de tripes!

The diction ranges from casual ("Il a raison le vieux," *voyez donc*) to slang (*birbe*, "old man," *type, bec épatants, je t'en ratisse*) to vulgar expressions like *metteurs-au-vent de tripes*, (murderers, who disembowel their victims), and especially *ce cas*. This last word has two slang senses: "excrement" and "penis" and whichever applies in this case is highly improper in poetry. This poem appears in the section of ***Parallèlement*** called "Lunes," which has the same slang meaning as *mooning* does in English. Robichez finds such usage an "aveulissement du language" (p. 697). Since there is no opposition of such language to a different milieu, it cannot be naturalized in the same way as in the earlier poems. It seems that the language of the poem is taking over, responding to the impulses of sound and figure rather than logic. Word play is evident, as in the phrase "Sur le point de" in the title. **"Point du Jour de Paris"** calls forth "aurore de paris;" and it is related to the gambling imagery in the text, *paris, bonneteau*, and *je t'en ratisse*, meaning to "take" someone in a card game. As in a card game, the relations between the words are purely arbitrary or metonymic; they have only their sound in common. Thus *le bonneteau* becomes "la bonne tôt . . ."; *Paris* calls up *paris; tant, t'en*. The name of the quarter, "Point du Jour" has no relation to its referent either, since it is situated at the west of Paris. Verlaine had noted this fact earlier in the poem **"Aube à l'envers,"** evidently referred-to indirectly in the title **"Nouvelles variations."** The manuscript of the later poem shows an alternative title, "Couchants," which makes this explicit and which contains another twist because of the meaning of *coucher*, "to sleep with." *Grâce à* rather than *par la faute de* is another shift from what would be expected; as *épatants* seems an unlikely epithet for "metteurs-au-vent de tripes." *Car* has lost its function of drawing a conclusion from evidence: the countryside has no obvious connection with the maid's virginity. Besides, we have already been told she is corrupted and that the old man is in fact wrong. The poem seems carried along by its words as by the river it describes: the accumulation of disparate nouns and contradictory adjectives joined by *et's, puis*, and *avec*, the repetitions of the first stanza, all seem purely gratuitous. There is no consciousness ordering experience, no totalizing power. Attempts to link the white color of the dawn to the virginity of the maid or to her apron in a metaphoric process are futile: only metonymic relations of sound and contiguity seem to apply. The use of vulgar diction contributes to this contravention of the traditional mode of poetry, indeed of language in general. The only element joining this fragmented assemblage together is the poem's rhythmic structure, its rhyme, and its disposition into stanzas on a printed page. **"Variations"** could lead one to expect a theme in which the variations would be grounded. But the point of **"Le Point du Jour"** is its pointlessness: that where there should be a theme there is a hole or rather, a river, carrying the unordered detritus of the life in the city.

"Nouvelles Variations" is only an extreme example of a process seen in the poems discussed earlier: familiar discourse can play an important role in the texts where it appears, but it is an intrusion into conventional poetry and it does not let itself be dismissed with easy generalizations. It reminds us of its otherness, and as such, improper language becomes *im-propre*, figural, standing for a message not carried by its surface signification. In taking its place in the figural structure of the text, it escapes our attempts to account for it fully. The texts in which Verlaine uses familiar discourse, then, are far from lacking "poetry;" they are not to be excused by referring to his low life: from ***Les Poèmes saturniens*** on, they exploit important stylistic resources and take their place among the innovations in poetic language during the course of the 19th century. It is through the practice of such poets as Verlaine that the use of familiar language, slang, technical words, and so on have come to be more predictable in poetry. Because of the resistance these texts oppose to the reader's efforts to incorporate them into seamless, totalizing interpretations, they show Verlaine to be a much more complex, innovative, and interesting poet than the "naïf" versifier he is often taken to be.

Notes

1. *Figures* (Paris: Seuil, 1966), p. 210.
2. Charles Morris defines pragmatics as "that portion of semiotic which deals with the origin, uses, and effects of signs within the behavior in which they occur." *Signs, Language, and Behavior* (New York: Prentice-Hall, 1946), p. 219. See also his *Foundations of the Theory of Signs*, International Encyclopedia of Unified Science, I, 2 (Chicago: Univ. of Chicago Press, 1938).
3. Charles Bruneau, *Verlaine: Choix de poésies* (Paris: Centre de Documentation universitaire, 1950), p. 24.
4. Claude Cuénot, *Le Style de Verlaine* (Paris: Centre de Documentation universitaire, 1963), p. 137.
5. Paul Verlaine, *Oeuvres poétiques*, ed. Jacques Robichez (Paris: Garnier, 1964), p. 600. Poems quoted are from this edition or, when so noted, from the Y.-G. le Dantec Pléiade edition of the *Oeuvres poétiques complètes*, revised by Jacques Borel (Paris: Gallimard, 1962).
6. Quoted in Jacques-Henry Bornecque, *Les Poèmes saturniens de Paul Verlaine* (Paris: Nizet, 1952), p. 166.
7. I am endebted to Stephen Spector for this last remark.

Robert Greer Cohn (essay date 1986)

SOURCE: "Rescuing a Sonnet of Verlaine: 'L'Espoir Luit . . .'," in *Romanic Review*, Vol. 77, No. 2, March, 1986, pp. 125–30.

[*In the following essay, Cohn provides a close reading of Verlaine's sonnet* "L'espoir luit. . . ."]

L'espoir luit comme un brin de paille dans l'étable,
Que crains-tu de la guêpe ivre de son vol fou?
Vois, le soleil toujours poudroie à quelque trou.
Que ne t'endormais-tu, le coude sur la table?

Pauvre âme pâle, au moins cette eau du puits glacé,
Bois-la. Puis dors après. Allons, tu vois, je reste.
Et je dorloterai les rêves de ta sieste,
Et tu chantonneras comme un enfant bercé.

Midi sonne. De grâce, éloignez-vous madame.
Il dort. C'est étonnant comme les pas de femme
Résonnent au cerveau des pauvres malheureux.

Midi sonne. J'ai fait arroser dans la chambre.
Va, dors! L'espoir luit comme un caillou dans un creux.
Ah! quand refleuriront les roses de septembre!

This touching, humming, summery poem from Verlaine's ***Sagesse*** has been familiar to many of us since adolescence, when we came upon it in textbook anthologies or whatever. Does it really need another elucidation? Probably not, but "*on a touché au vers*", in modern criticism like that of Michel Serres, who has offered a Lucretian reading of it in his usual genetic way. Well, one may agree with fusions of science and art in such approaches generally, but there is a terribly important question of emphasis, dosage, tone. I think Serres, who is usually stylish and interesting, hit extremely wide of the mark in this instance, and his misreading points to a great deal that is wrong in contemporary criticism.

The poem does imply a descent toward the origins of life in nature, womb, infancy, but the accent is not on numbers, *pace* Serres, or even the multiple, or his familiar "bruit de fond" (and "acousphènes") and the like, which are rather too cold for art and certainly Verlaine's.

I'd say the poem steeps "baptismally" in utter humility and humble rural beginnings, with Christian undertones—at least subtle ones—befitting Verlaine's complete abjection and spiritual rebirth, after his prison experience, expressed notably in ***Sagesse***. We recall the simplicity and childlike faith of **"Le ciel est, par-dessus le toit"** from the same collection, or **"Je suis venu, calme orphelin"**.

The nativity scene in a stable—*sermo humilis*—is to the point of the straw shining in the farm-shed here. The constant theme of Verlaine's yearning for the peace, the lost paradise, in the mother or her presence—he had a remarkably intense relation with her, we know—has an important clear overtone in Mary, the fountain of feminine grace which pervades, nostalgically, the sonnet, and has to do, for example, with the drinking of water from the well. The roses at the end of the poem are, as in traditional symbolism, Hers, "full of grace". The whole of ***Sagesse*** is permeated with Her presence: "Je ne veux plus aimer que ma mère Marie". (II,II).

Midi sonne, in a Catholic country, is well understood—this end-of-cycle moment of repose, of reconciliation, of Being—from a comparison with Claudel's finest poem, "La Vierge à midi", at which calming instant he weeps with her "grand pardon", her generous maternal gift of self: "Parce que vous êtes là pour toujours, simplement parce que vous existez . . ."

The sheer Being is the whole point as in Verlaine's **"Le ciel est, pardessus le toit"** (the comma brings out the isolated purity of the *est*); "Mon Dieu, mon Dieu, la vie est là" . . .

Claudel, of course, owed an immense debt to this Verlaine, and said so. Don't we all.

Hope which shines in the lowly stable like a wisp of straw, then, is the miracle of faith (in life, in love, in Being going on, which is woman's essence to a needy male) rising out of despair, *de profundis*, and out of the most ordinary everyday experience or wild, random ("fou") nature in the raw countryside. True life "flows from the source", like mother milk or a glass of water from the well.

Serres sees the wasp buzzing erratically as an originary chaos from which number will arise, then the subtler rhythms of art, in a developmental scheme. But true art like Verlaine's doesn't follow linear patterns of progression: it tends to be circular, like the whole and fluid patterns of the metaphoric dimension, the visionary and imaginative realm, altogether. The tone is primarily that of static "epiphany" in the Joycean sense: the divinely maternal, the sensuous, earthy, childish, primitive, rural, natural. As in Plato's *Symposium* or D. H. Lawrence's view of feminine temperament, there is little split between high and low, past and future . . .[1]

So Serres' emphasis on number in connection with *Midi sonne*—the advent of the alexandrine with the stroke of twelve—misses the simple peaceful tone, maternal in that sense, reconciliatory with Her and the world in this still end-of-cycle moment (as in Valéry's "midi le juste" in the contemplative air of *Le Cimetière Marin*).

. . . . .

Serres raises a major question when he sees number as being prior to language. This is an entirely arbitrary and one-sided scientific view. I see no reason to settle for anything other than an undecidable here, as Mallarmé did with his polar pair of music and letters, stemming from a vibrant mystery including them both. I see no grounds for accepting original "structures" (I do not quite like the word) which are more analytic than synthetic, more numerical than pre-linguistic.

I quote from "The Structure of Ancient Wisdom" by Harvey Wheeler (J. Social Biol. Struct. 1982 5, 223–32):

> "Although Giorgio de Santillana thinks that numbers came before letters (de Santillana, 1961) and Mary Danielli holds that mandalic ideograms predated both (Danielli, 1974), it is generally assumed that naming and counting have almost equally remote symbolic and notational origins. The earliest Sumerian texts show that skills in these two idioms were taught in roughly coordinated sequences . . ."

Wheeler gives many examples, including one from Leibnitz. But it is really a matter of common sense to throw up one's hands in a sort of "fifty-fifty" gesture in all such problematic cases (heredity-environment, freedom-necessity, order-disorder . . .) where a dialectic goes off into infinite regress, chicken-and-egg, to deep mystery rather than any specific historical documentation. Since Mallarmé and his "fiction" epistemology, we tend to keep such matters open, problematic . . .

. . . . .

Serres is likewise unconvincing on the notion of a progression from an even to an uneven rhythm. He sees a neat scheme of evolution from the regular *bercement* to the last line which features a *sept* and a rose pattern which he claims to be pentagonal and an eleven-syllable line following an "Ah". This is far-fetched and forced. A *bercement* is regular but it is not at all monotonous; it is, rather, incantational, magic, as artistic as anything—one thinks of wonderful "Berceuses" like Stravinsky's in *The Firebird*. On the other hand, advanced music is very regular, as well as not. No, there is a circle, or spiral, here, not a scientist's line of progress.

So Mallarmé in his *Tombeau d'Anatole* saw a maternal *bercement* as the matrix of his poet's rhythm; before him, Baudelaire, in *La Chevelure*, wrote:

> Et mon esprit subtil que le roulis caresse
> Saura vous retrouver, ô féconde paresse,
> Infinis bercements du loisir embaumé!

There is here, as in the Mallarmé text (or his two *Eventail* poems), a notion not so much of poetic *evolution*, but rather a paradoxical, ironic (oxymoronic) play, interchangeably between up and down, fecundity and laziness, etc.

Similarly, the "pas de femme" of our sonnet have nothing to do with an advance from rhythm to music; they are a pure lovely phenomenon in themselves, as Mallarmé knew in *Le Nénuphar Blanc:* "Subtil secret des pieds qui vont, viennent . . .", with a fiercely tender erotic undertone, as in Valéry's canny *Les Pas*, accompanying a basically maternal tone: mother-sounds bringing comfort, or retreating in the night . . . The whole poem, as Henri Peyre comments, seems to be addressed by a mother to a sick child. But the poet's own viewpoint is intermingled: it is out of his own suffering self that this *pietà* is imagined. So there is a good deal of narcissistic feeling, self-accusation and self-pity, as so often in "le pauvre Lélian". The epiphany of a sacrificial child is really his. To whom—a third party?—is addressed "De grâce, éloignez-vous, madame?" That is unimportant: it gives the familiar feeling of a caring woman tip-toeing or walking out from a room as a child falls asleep . . .

A similar unsureness is in the last line: who says it? Small matter: the feeling is of the elegiac poet, as so often in Verlaine, yearning for a lost innocence in his sinning older years, which is the tone of "septembre" in part, the autumn of life as of the year. And the rose, *pace* Serres, is not a "pentagon", really, or not here; it is *the* symbol of woman and specifically the Virgin Mother. It ends the poem on another *round* note, that of plenitude and reconciled "womb" of Eden, (or beyond) as in Dante; the roundness of the *o* on the page has to do with this, as in Baudelaire's *Le Balcon*, addressed to a maternal muse; it begins with *O* and ends with a plunging into the globality of sky and ocean. Similarly, *La Chevelure*, likewise addressed, begins "O boucles" and ends with images of "l'azur du ciel immense et rond", "océan", and "oasis". Note all the o's as in Verlaine's roses.

Much of what Serres said can be *included* in an adequate commentary;[2] but the tone could hardly have been farther from the intimate musicality and intuitive art of Verlaine, which includes all sorts of drowzy echoes (dort-dorloter, arrose-rose, résonnent-sonne) and down-home visual effects, and altogether a great deal that is longingly personal, sentimental in a high sense, intensely human, desperately nostalgic, sinning and singing, freshly childlike under the prison dirt.

A more intimate look at details tells us:

In line 1: the image suggests a reminiscence of a nativity scene, pertinent to a Christian rebirth, and it is also what any sensitive child might see that is out of the way for his wayward glance alone. Little, he typically bends down to the little gleam in the hollow, below. Here, the light is coming down, like a blessing, through a chink in the stable wall, singles out an insignificant blade of straw, seen by "me", who am maybe if not a favorite son, at least a comforted one. Later, in Rimbaud, the light, with the impartiality it has in Vermeer (e.g., on a loaf of bread), touches a *pissotière* gnat with glory; and "la lumière donne sur une merde".

2: Verlaine instills in us pity for the vulnerable fearing "child", himself, together with the balm of the soothingly maternal voice, which protects from all outside the circle of her love.

3: her on-going presence, like the river of Proust's mother's voice reading to him and following him far through life, is in "toujours" as it is in Baudelaire's "Longtemps! toujours" (*La Chevelure*) and Claudel's "là pour toujours". Her affection is mingled with the sun's, a tender "Father's".

4: the injunction to sleep extends the soothing note out from a hypothetical bed into the surroundings; the whole peasant scene is safe, at peace with the world, having said grace perhaps at table or just at home in the simple rural scene. One easily sees Verlaine in that posture, perhaps because of *Le Coin de Table* where he appears with Rimbaud leaning on his elbow. It is crisp, concrete, alive as a Van Gogh portrait, that touch.

5: The modesty of the glass of water "au moins" adds to our affectionate concern; perhaps the child is sick, can take no more than that. He is pale and poor, a near-ghostly "âme".

6–8: *dors-dorloter* is incantatory, right for cradling a "child". And the summery humming of *chantonner* is right for this near-nothing simplicity, almost as natural as the wasp's.

9: *Midi* is well coupled with *grâce*, suggestively, at this calming point at mid-day, a good time to fall asleep, at middling home in the cosmos. Catholic bells then take us to the core, lull, promise. The incantatory appeasement is partly in *sonne-étonnant-résonnent-sonne* (as it was in *autumn-monotone* of another langorous poem).

10: In *dort*, the light of summer (*or*) filters into sleep; the *pas de femme* were discussed in our earlier pages. It *is* astonishing what they do to penetrate to an early core and reassure. Baudelaire's *Le Beau Navire* lingers over the effect on our instincts of a woman's walking.

11: *cerveau*: just as the "tête sonore" of *Green* resonates with kisses, this modern and understatedly concrete "brain" communicates very directly with the abdomen of plunging sensation. Indeed, like the "tête sonore (qui roule)", it is a loose-hanging, in this sense, as the soft head of a young elephant in *Le Beau Navire*. And it is sonorous as the image in *Le Bateau Ivre:* "plus sourd que les cerveaux d'enfants".

12: *arroser* continues the tone of solicitude, summer refreshment, and chimes with *roses; sonne* seems "sunny" and "filial" appropriately, to us English or German readers and perhaps to this bummer-around-England and visitor to Germany.

13: the *caillou* has the comforting gleam and something of the round sufficiency of the "golden ball" of childhood myth (*The Frog Prince*), which anthropologists like Robert Bly connect with the radiant integrity of our quondam innocence. The *creux* may suggest a place of rebirth and at-homeness, the womb, whence the reintegrated self may emerge clean and fresh. Such was the "trou chaud qui souffle la vie" in Rimbaud's poem about desperate children, *Les Effarés*.

14: Baudelaire's two masterpieces chanting the maternal calm in Jeanne Duval's hair or "blotti dans tes genoux"—*La Chevelure* and *Le Balcon*—both end with a question mark. So does Verlaine's sonnet. The greater the bliss, the more anguishing the thought of losing it, and it is partly faced in this way, offering a more open and vibrant ending, consonant with the undecidables of modern art (Rimbaud's defeated closes are a more radical expression of this mood). Moreover, the *septembre* and the absence of the roses further the elegiac, wistfully hopeful note, very typical of Verlaine.

And yet, the plenitude of what is hoped-for is in the *rondeur* of the *roses*, as it is in Dante and, as in him, *la boucle est bouclée,* at least suggestively: the hope of the beginning ("L'espoir") is restated. What progress is there then? We are obviously in an ultimately circular poetic universe, where Eden is lost and can be regained only at severe cost: winter, it is hinted, lies not far off ahead. We are not sure at all. Yet the promise is there, or far-out there, at least. Death seems less threatening in childlike faiths of this sort:

Qui cherche, parcourant le solitaire bond
Tantôt extérieur de notre vagabond—
Verlaine? Il est caché parmi l'herbe, Verlaine

A ne surprendre que naïvement d'accord
La lèvre sans y boire ou tarir son haleine
Un peu profond ruisseau calomnié la mort.

(Mallarmé)

Notes

1. The quiet tetrapolar pattern of this epiphany—like a *croisée*—is at play here as in typical Symbolist poetry (e.g. Mallarmé's *Les Fenêtres*).
2. For example, one can see the floating between odd and even as in "Midi sonne", thanks to the uncertainty of the mute *e* (Verlaine's *Art Poétique* itself plumps for the *flottement:* "l'indécis au précis se joint"); but one can find these aesthetic generalities at work in any good poem. That is not the gravamen of the sonnet at all.

Bernhard Frank (essay date 1988)

SOURCE: A review of "Wooden Steeds," in *The Explicator*, Vol. 46, No. 2, Winter, 1988, pp. 29–31.

[*In the following essay, Frank provides a brief explication of Verlaine's* "Chevaux de bois."]

"Chevaux de Bois"

Tournez, tournez, bons chevaux de bois,
Tournez cent tours, tournez mille tours,
Tournez souvent et tournez toujours,
Tournez, tournez au son des hautbois.

Le gros soldat, laz plus grosse bonne
Sont sur vos dos comme dans leur chambre;
Car, en ce jour, au bois de la Cambre,
Les maîtres sont tous deux en personne.

Tournez, tournez, chevaux de leur coeur,
Tandis qu'autour de tous vos tournois
Clignotte l'oeil du filou sournois,
Tournez au son de piston vainqueur.

C'est ravissant comme ça vous soûle
D'aller ainsi dans ce cirque bête!
Bien dans le ventre et mal dans la tête,
Du mal en masse et du bien en foule.

Tournez, tournez, sans qu'il soit besoin
D'user jamais de nuls éperons,
Pour commander à vos galops ronds,
Tournez, tournez, sans espoir de foin.

Et dépêchez, chevaux de leur âme,
Déjà, voici que la nuit qui tombe
Va réunir pigeon et colombe,
Loin de la foire et loin de madame.

Tournez, tournez! le ciel en velours
D'astres en or se vêt lentement.
Voici partir l'amante et l'amant.
Tournez au son joyeux des tambours.

—Paul Verlaine

"Wooden Steeds"

Go round, go round, fine steeds of wood,
A hundred, thousand times go round,
Go round again and round for good,
And round about to the oboe sound.

The hefty soldier and heftiest maid
(For today her masters also wander
On a lark in the part at Cambre)
On your backs, as though in private, ride.

Go round, go round, steeds of their heart,
While all around your merry-go-round
Pickpockets wink their sly retort,
Go round to the conquering cornet sound.

Amazing how to turn like that,
In vicious cycle, intoxicates you!
Fine for the belly but hard on the head,
A lot of ill and a lot of good.

Go round, go round, without the need
Of using spurs on either side
To help govern your circular ride,
Go round, go round and forget the feed.

And steeds of their soul, come now, come,
Already here the falling night
The pigeon and the dove unites,
Far from the fair and far from Madame.

Go round, go round! The velvet sky
Slowly puts its gold stars on.
Here lover, beloved, say good-bye.
Go round to the sound of the merry drums.

—Translated by Bernhard Frank[1]

"Wooden Steeds" (***"Chevaux de Bois"***) was inspired by the St. Gilles fair in Brussels when Verlaine, accompanied by the younger poet, Rimbaud, was visiting there in August, 1872. It appeared first in ***Romances Sans Paroles***, 1874 and later, in revised (and modified) form, in the first edition of ***Sagesse***. To understand why it has been called "technically one of the most brilliant poems [Verlaine] was ever to write,"[2] we must look at the subtle yet precise manner in which the poet replicates the motion of the carousel horses.

To establish the circular movement Verlaine opens the first and last line of all the odd-numbered quatrains with the word "*tournez*" ("go round"). In this fashion, the carousel completes a cycle at the end of every other stanza.

Yet the poet goes further. He succeeds in regulating the *speed* of the turns. Thus, in the opening stanza "*tournez*" appears twice in every line, providing the extra energy needed to overcome inertia. In the first and last lines of later odd-numbered stanzas, the word appears either once or twice-in-a-row, with the repetition giving an additional impetus.

In the final stanza, the second and third lines are end-stopped, halting the motion long enough for the lovers to get off the carousel. It resumes its turning, albeit a bit sluggishly—with only one "*tournez*" in the last line—now that the passion has gone out of it. Or has the passion gone out of the circus-crier/narrator who has been egging it on?

"Wooden Steeds," it has been pointed out, alternates stanzas of masculine and feminine rhymes.[3] The effect of this alternation is reenforced by another device: written in *vers impairs* of nine syllables, the stanzas also approximate, alternately, the English trochaic and iambic meters. Consequently, all the odd-numbered stanzas are imbued with a driving energy, while the even-numbered ones slacken markedly. Thus has Verlaine given us, in a splendid technical feat, not only the circularity and speed of the carousel, but also the see-saw motion of its steeds.

Notes

1. *Offering: Selected Poems of Rainer Maria Rilke and Paul Verlaine* (Buffalo: Goldengrove Press, 1986), p. 8.
2. Lawrence and Elizabeth Hanson, *Verlaine: Fool of God* (New York: Random House, 1957), p. 175.
3. E.g., Georges Zayed, *La Formation Littéraire de Verlaine* (Geneva: Librairie E. Droz, 1962), p. 363.

Laurence M. Porter (essay date 1990)

SOURCE: "Verlaine's Subversion of Language," in *The Crisis of French Symbolism*, Cornell University Press, 1990, pp. 76–112.

[*In the following essay, Porter questions the "musicality" of Verlaine's poetry and discusses his use of language, which makes the reader consider reality in new ways.*]

Verlaine has been neglected in recent years. The brevity of his poems; their songlike, informal diction; their paucity of metaphor and allusion; and their lack of those intellectual themes that are commonly held to characterize true "Symbolism"—from the beginning, all these features have tempted critics to judge his verse agreeable but minor. His alcoholism and the poetic decline of his final fifteen years, which he spent as a sodden derelict, have reinforced the trend to slight or to dismiss his work. Until recently even critics who have looked closely at his poems have tended to obscure our sense of the evolution of Verlaine's poetry by treating it in terms of what they perceive to be general, overarching tendencies such as "fadeur" (insipidity) or "naiveté,"[1] to say nothing of the all too familiar "musicality." A fine recent collection of French essays is disparagingly titled *La Petite Musique de Verlaine*.[2] Once one has described Verlaine's "music" by counting syllables and noting repetitions of sounds, there seems to be little more to say.[3] Like Lamartine, he has been damned with faint praise.

If one seriously addresses the question of Verlaine's musicality, it seems intuitively obvious that repetition and regularity are more "musical" than their absence. In actual music composed before the modern era, a high percentage of the measures occur more than once—only one-third or one-quarter of the total may be different—whereas in a literary work few if any sentences are repeated. Zola need use the same sentence only half a dozen times in a long novel such as *La Bête humaine* before critics start comparing it to a Wagnerian leitmotif. A modest amount of repetition in literature, then, has the same effect as the considerable amount of repetition in music. The phrases that echo frequently in a poem such as Verlaine's **"Soleils couchants"** attract all the more attention because they do not belong to a conventional pattern of recurrence in a fixed form such as the rondeau or the ballade.

No one, however, has yet done a statistical study to determine whether Verlaine deploys obvious forms of repetition—rich rhyme, internal rhyme, anaphora, epiphora, refrains, reduplication of single words, alliteration, and assonance—more frequently than less "musical" poets. Baudelaire and Mallarmé, in fact, seem to use more rich rhymes than does Verlaine; Baudelaire more often repeats lines. Nor has anyone done an empirical study to determine whether poems identified as "musical" by naive and by sophisticated audiences actually contain more repetitive devices than do other poems. No one, in short, has rigorously characterized "musicality" in language in linguistic terms. And no one who wishes to ascribe "musicality" to the verse of Verlaine and the other Symbolists has come to terms with the fact that all these poets were lamentably illiterate and incompetent as composers, as performers, and even as passive listeners to music.[4] While awaiting the outcome of the empirical and statistical studies of the future, we can best treat the problem of literary "musicality" by recognizing that "musicality" serves merely as a metaphor for the relative prominence of phonemic and verbal repetition; for allusions to, evocations of, and descriptions of things musical; for the foregrounding of rhythm, which is the essence of music; for vagueness of denotation; and for the suppression of overt narrative progression. (These last two traits often figure together in descriptions of that critical artifact called "literary impressionism.") Taken all together, these features do not help to distinguish Verlaine's poetry from that of many of his contemporaries.

One can obtain a more fruitful definition of Verlaine's "musicality" by observing what I consider to be a primary rule in literary criticism: once you have singled out a certain motif or a feature for analysis, seek its polar opposite. It is not the motif of "musicality" alone but the structure formed by thesis (here, "musicality"), antithesis (whatever for Verlaine may seem opposed to "musicality"), and the relationship between them which characterizes the creative individuality of the poet. This structure defines his imagination (in linguistic terms, his poetic "competence") and its expression (in linguistic terms, his poetic "performance") in a way that one isolated element such as "musicality," shared by many poets, could not possibly do.

Mistrusting the act of communication, each of the major French Symbolist poets focuses his principal suspicion on one particular, discrete point along the axis of communication. What Verlaine's good early verse does is to call into question the signifying capacities of the verbal medium itself. He fears lest the very ground of his utterances be meaningless or at least vitiated by the way it is ordinarily treated. The problem is not merely that he finds words inadequate to treat transcendent subjects (Mallarmé's difficulty) but rather that he finds words unreliable, period. Since he still wishes to write poetry, he has no recourse other than to exalt the "je ne sais quoi," the "imprécis," and to expatiate upon the topos of inexpressibility.

Antoine Adam, a noted critic of Verlaine, does not take the poet's antilinguistic stance too seriously. He invokes the testimony of Edmond Lepelletier, who saw Verlaine daily at the time of his early publications and claimed that lyrical expressions of love and sadness in the ***Poèmes saturniens*** and the ***Fêtes galantes*** were mere poses in a person interested primarily in dogmatic poetics. He cites two lines from **"Aspiration"** (1861) to suggest that the critique of love language in ensuing collections may derive as much from misogyny as mistrust of communication: "Loin de tout ce qui vit, loin des hommes, encor / Plus loin des femmes" (p. 15: Far from all that lives, far from men, and yet / Farther from women). Referring specifically to the ***Fêtes galantes***, Adam claims: "This poetry of an all-embracing melancholy dimension is, however, meant to be a game. . . . The poet amuses himself. . . . Baudelaire's sober doctrine [in Verlaine's **"A Clymène"**] becomes a pretext for subtle combinations of hues and fragrances. The enjambments that set off the ironical charge of a phrase, and the rhymes—profuse, unusual, employed in a hundred original ways—these are part of the fun."[5]

But in an interpretation similar to my own, Jacques-Henry Bornecque, who studied this crucial collection in much more detail, maintains that it traces a sequence of moods declining toward pessimism and despair. Verlaine contaminates with his own sadness the playful Regency world (1715–23) into which he had hoped to escape. His other writings of the same period include many macabre pieces that express his disgust with his contemporaries. Bornecque observes, "In those verse or prose pieces that are not 'fêtes galantes,' Verlaine does not disguise his feelings: he gives free rein to his peevishness as to his anguish, regularly and obviously swinging between aggressive bitterness and the despairing detachment which is the ebb tide of the former."[6] He cites many examples, notably the sinister short story "Le Poteau," which reveals a certain affinity with Baudelaire's "Vin de l'assassin." The death of Verlaine's beloved Elisa Moncomble four days before the composition of the first two "Fêtes galantes" seems decisive. Bornecque characterizes the collection as the work of a convalescent—a convalescent, one could add, with nothing to live for.

Sensitive though he is to Verlaine's moods, Bornecque overlooks the poet's mistrust of language, so characteristic of the Symbolist crisis. Unlike the other major French Symbolist poets, Verlaine focuses this mistrust on the linguistic medium itself, instead of on the acts of conceiving and communicating a message. He subverts the notion of the essential "humanness" of language by playfully (and of course figuratively) replacing human speakers with nonhuman ones. And by making utterances flatly contradict the situations to which they refer, Verlaine challenges our assumption that language provides reliable information. Many instances can be found in the prose works, particularly the *Mémoires d'un veuf.* There "Bons bourgeois" describes a family quarrel: after an exchange of insults, "la parole est à la vaisselle maintenant" (now the crockery [which the family members start throwing at each other] does the talking). Afterward the lady of the house excuses herself to her visiting country relative by saying "CELA N'ARRIVE JAMAIS" (that never happens). "Ma Fille" cancels its own language when after an idealized description the narrator announces, "Heureusement qu'elle n'a jamais existé et ne naîtra probablement plus!" (Fortunately she never lived and probably will not be born in the future!). In another story, Pierre Duchâtelet has a conversation with his wife in which he lies to conceal his imminent departure for a ten-day mission to a battle zone; on his return he finds a letter saying simply, "Monsieur—Adieu pour toujours" (Sir: Farewell forever). And if we read allegorically, considering the hand as the writer's instrument (cf. George Sand's "L'Orgue du Titan"), we could even say that artistic self-expression destroys its subject and is itself doomed to a sudden death. Such an interpretation illuminates Verlaine's tale "La Main du Major Muller" (from *Histoires comme ça*), where the preserved hand that had to be amputated after a duel comes to life, poisons its owner, and then quickly rots.

The most compelling corroborative evidence for Verlaine's dour linguistic self-consciousness, however, comes from the master article of all his literary criticism (and one that should be much better known): his response to another great Symbolist poet, Baudelaire. This piece appeared in the November 16, 1865, issue of *L'Art.* Of three individual lines cited as models, two treat nonverbal communication: "Le regard singulier d'une femme galante" (the odd glance of a promiscuous woman) and "Un soir l'âme du vin chantait dans les bouteilles" (One evening the soul of the wine was singing inside the bottles). From the five wine poems, in other words, the one line that Verlaine cites is one that gives a voice to a nonhuman entity. And from the "Tableaux parisiens" section, likewise, Verlaine singles out this passage:

> Et, voisin des clochers, écouter en rêvant
> Leurs hymnes solennels emportés par le vent
>
> . . . . .
>
> Je verrai l'atelier qui chante et qui bavarde.

(And, next to the bell towers, to listen dreamily / To their solemn hymns carried off by the wind / . . . / I shall see the workshop singing and chattering.)

After beginning the essay with the declaration that "le public est un enfant mal élevé qu'il s'agit de corriger" (the public is a badly brought up child: you have to chastise it), Verlaine gives as examples of appropriate behaviors instances of silencing: the poem **"Semper eadem"** with its repeated "Taisez-vous!" (Quiet!) and elsewhere the command to the beloved, "Sois charmante, et tais-toi" (Be charming, and be still). Far more is at stake here than mere playfulness.[7]

Whereas narrative and drama represent what is meaningful to at least several people or to a collective culture, the lyric represents what is meaningful to only one person. Poetry is half a conversation, a soliloquy or apostrophe to a being that is nonhuman, absent, or dead, and therefore incapable of responding in words. When we say "Rose, thou art sick," we don't expect an answer. In those instances where the interlocutor is not suppressed, poetry becomes "dramatic lyric" that shades into theater. In the lyric situation, where the single speaking voice is the norm, Verlaine sometimes imposes one of two marked choices. Either he uses free direct discourse—a conversation that does not identify the speakers—to multiply the sources of meaningfulness to the point where each interferes with the other and they blur; or else he introduces nonverbal elements so as to subvert meaningfulness at its source; or he does both at once, as in the paradigmatic **"Sur l'herbe"** of the ***Fêtes galantes***.

When Verlaine does depict the normal one-sided conversation, he undermines its meaningfulness as much as he can without sacrificing coherence. He tries to express his radical skepticism regarding the power of words to signify by undermining their status and seeming to replace them with something else. For him this something else is musicality: not a flight into a balmy vagueness, but the cutting edge of his satiric attack on the verbal ground of our relationships. By using uncommon "rhythmes impairs" (five-, seven-, nine-, eleven-, or thirteen-syllable lines) instead of the octosyllables, decasyllables, or alexandrines that were to dominate French poetry through the 1920s, Verlaine again makes a "marked choice"; he selects a form of expression that violates our expectations through the absence or the excess of a certain quality. He foregrounds the supreme musicality of rhythm at the expense of the other elements of poetry. Since the essence of music lies in rhythm more than in melody, harmony, intensity, or timbre, a poetry that calls attention to its rhythm makes that element a rival of the verbal poetry rather than its adjunct. Similarly, from the ***Fêtes galantes*** on, internal rhyme and assonance become more common in Verlaine's poetry, constituting a marked choice of sound repetition in excess of what one would ordinarily expect and thus suggesting, once again, an antiverbal musicality. More obviously, of course, words seem to become ancillary in Verlaine's texts when he uses them to denote, connote, or describe music and the visual arts.[8] He subverts language by using words to evoke indefinable states of vagueness and confusion; to designate situations in which the words themselves are trivial, insincere, or absurd; and to characterize acts whereby words cancel themselves or serve to impose silence. To produce a mere catalogue of such devices would be a facile and not very enlightening exercise. But as it happens, examining them in context can illuminate the structure of individual collections of verse and clarify the trajectory of Verlaine's entire career.

The section titled "Melancholia" in Verlaine's first collection of verse, the ***Poèmes saturniens*** (1867), presents the dilemma of the breakdown of signification thematically, by depicting the lyric self's nostalgia for a past time when love language was still meaningful. Distancing himself from his nostalgia in the last section of the ***Poèmes saturniens***, the lyric self shifts to a parody of love language from **"La Chanson des ingénues"** on; such parody persists to the end of the ***Fêtes galantes*** (1869). As the historical Verlaine strives to return to a conventional life, ***La Bonne Chanson*** (1870) transiently adopts a conventional, affirmative poeticizing. The ***Romances sans paroles*** (1872) revert to undermining signification, but they show rather than tell. A supreme discursive *prise de conscience* affirming vagueness and musicality as the highest poetic goals appears in **"L'Art poétique"** of 1874 (published only when ***Jadis et naguère*** appeared in 1882). This statement itself, however, is subverted by verbal excess, for there is a fundamental paradox in specifying how to be allusive.

Verlaine's Symbolist crisis, then, as I would define it, lasted from 1866 to 1874. After his conversion in prison, he seems to have become dedicated to betraying his earlier self. He reverts to a wholly conventional prosodic practice and to a thematic questioning, typical of Romanticism, of the codes and contexts of traditional beliefs rather than a questioning of the efficacy of the communicative process itself. Some thirty-two poems from his earlier years, previously unpublished in collections, appear in the later collections (notably in ***Jadis et naguère***, which contains twenty-seven of them) but without exception they lack the critical bite of those already published—the reason Verlaine had set them aside in the first place. A few pieces in ***Parallèlement*** (1889), composed probably between 1884 and 1889, again present a lyric self alienated from love and his own words and sinking into a preoccupation with mere physicality. But these poems appear superficial; they degenerate into self-parody; and they convey none of the fundamental questioning of signification characteristic of Verlaine's "Symbolist" period. Verlaine's 1890 article "Critique des

Poèmes saturniens"[9] rejected everything he had written before ***Sagesse*** in 1881—in other words, nearly everything most critics still find important:

> L'âge mûr a, peut avoir ses revanches et l'art aussi, sur les enfantillages de la jeunesse, ses nobles revanches, traite des objets plus et mieux en rapport, religion, patrie, et la science, et soi-même bien considérée sous toutes formes, ce que j'appellerai de l'élégie sérieuse, en haine de ce mot, psychologie. Je m'y suis efforcé quant à moi et j'aurai laissé mon oeuvre personnelle en quatre parties bien définies, ***Sagesse, Amour, Parallèlement***—et ***Bonheur*** [1891]. . . . Puis, car n'allez pas prendre au pied de la lettre mon **'Art poétique'** de ***Jadis et Naguère***, qui n'est qu'une chanson, après tout,—JE N'AURAI PAS FAIT DE THEORIE.
>
> [pp. 1073–74]

> (The age of maturity, and art as well, can take its revenge, its noble revenge, on the childishness of youth; it treats subjects closer and more appropriate to itself, religion, the fatherland, science, and itself examined carefully in every form, what I shall term the serious elegy, out of hatred for that word, psychology. As for me, I have striven to do so and I shall have left my personal work in four distinct parts, ***Wisdom, Love, In Parallel***—and ***Happiness***. . . . Moreover, for don't take literally my **"Art of Poetry"** in ***Formerly and Not So Long Ago***, which is only a song, after all—I SHALL HAVE CREATED NO THEORIES.)

With that disclaimer, Verlaine's self-betrayal was consummated. It had begun with the distribution of a "prière d'insérer" (publicity flier) for ***Sagesse*** in 1881, describing him as "sincèrement et franchement revenu aux sentiments de la foi la plus orthodoxe" (p. 1111: having sincerely and openly returned to the most orthodox sentiments of religious faith), including support of attempts to restore the monarchy.

Written from the time he was fourteen, Verlaine's earliest surviving poems reflect his admiration for the grandiosity of Victor Hugo. But from 1861 on (when he was seventeen) he initiates a thematic critique of poeticism in the manner of Musset and the late Romantics such as Corbière and Laforgue. **"Fadaises"** presents a series of conventional lover's homages in rhyming couplets (in French this sort of versification is called "rimes plates," "plates" also designating what is trite and inexpressive), with a surprise ending revealing that all of these compliments have been addressed to Lady Death.[10] The title (**"Insipidities"**) already dismisses the import of the verses that follow; the *pointe* of the conclusion dismisses life itself: "Et le désir me talonne et me mord, / Car je vous aime, ô Madame la Mort!" (p. 16: And desire spurs me on and bites me, / For I love you, O Mistress Death!). To equate love with death is a typically Romantic gesture. If the title works in conjunction with this equation to undermine the conventionality of the earlier verses, then Verlaine has done little new. But if the title can be held to dismiss the concluding Romantic cliché, as well as those clichés that the Romantic cliché is dismissing (with the implied topos of *vanitas vanitatum*), then Verlaine's world-weariness extends to and contaminates the verbal medium itself. Whether it actually does so, however, we cannot tell for certain from the text alone. But in the context of Romantic practice this poem stands out because Romantic poems do not usually appear under titles that make their protests, as well as the targets of those protests, seem frivolous from the outset. They do not do so, that is, until the ironic poetry of Corbière and Laforgue.

Additional albeit equally ambiguous evidence that Verlaine early adopted a skeptical attitude toward Romanticism appears in the early poem that most specifically comments on poetic creation, the **"Vers dorés"** of 1866 (p. 22). There he claims that poetry should be impersonal: "maint poète / A trop étroits les reins ou les poumons trop gras" (many a poet / Has loins too narrow or lungs too fat); only those who "se recueillent dans un égoïsme de marbre" (commune with themselves within an egoism of marble) are great. At first this statement seems simply to belong to the "second Romanticism" of Gautier or De Lisle, standing in opposition to the earlier belief that "Gefühl ist alles." But like the title of **"Fadaises,"** the term "égoïsme" again renders suspect Verlaine's homage to the "Neoclassic Stoic."

After the prologue, the first section of the ***Poèmes saturniens***, titled **"Melancholia,"** expresses a nostalgic faith in the charms of past love: "Et qu'il bruit avec un murmure charmant / Le premier *oui* qui sort des lèvres bien-aimées!" (**"Nevermore,"** p. 61: And how it rustles with a charming murmur / The first *yes* that leaves beloved lips!).[11] But this vision must not become too precise: in **"Mon Rêve familier"** the idealized woman speaks with the voice of the beloved dead "qui se sont tues" (who have fallen silent), but of her name the poet remembers only that it is "doux et sonore / Comme ceux des aimés que la vie exila" (p. 64: sweet and resonant / Like the names of loved ones whom life exiled). In the present time of narration, however—or more accurately, of lyricization—artistic self-consciousness begins to intrude. A poem such as **"Lassitude,"** for example, seems initially only to echo the Baudelairean taste for the illusion of love when it asks the beloved: "fais-moi des serments que tu rompras demain" (make me promises that you will break tomorrow; see, e.g., Baudelaire's "L'Amour du mensonge"). But Baudelaire never really loses faith in art, and Verlaine does. His epigraph from Luis de Góngora, "a batallas de amor campos de pluma" (for battles of love, fields of feathers), suggests by juxtaposition that not only the content of professions of love but perhaps even their verbal vehicle is false. The double meaning of *pluma*, feathers for lying on or writing with, implies that the falsity of the beloved's specious assurances may extend to and contaminate the verbal medium itself, where the cradling regularity of the verses reflects the sensuous pleasure of the caresses that the woman lavishes on the lyric self. Such a possibility, farfetched as it may initially seem, emerges blatantly in the poem **"L'Angoisse"** in the same section.

> Nature, rien de toi ne m'émeut, ni les champs
> Nourriciers, ni l'écho vermeil des pastorales

Siciliennes, ni les pompes aurorales,
Ni la solennité dolente des couchants.

Je ris de l'Art, je ris de l'Homme aussi, des chants,
Des vers, des temples grecs et des tours en spirales
Qu'étirent dans le ciel vide les cathédrales,
Et je vois du même oeil les bons et les méchants.

Je ne crois pas en Dieu, j'abjure et je renie
Toute pensée, et quant à la vieille ironie
L'Amour, je voudrais bien qu'on ne m'en parlât plus.

Lasse de vivre, ayant peur de mourir, pareille
Au brick perdu jouet du flux et du reflux,
Mon âme pour d'affreux naufrages appareille.

[p. 65]

(Nature, nothing in you moves me, neither the nurturant fields, / Nor the crimson echo of Sicilian pastorals, / nor the splendor of dawn, / Nor the plaintive ceremony of the sunsets. // I laugh at Art, I laugh at Man as well, at songs, / Poetry, Greek temples and the spiraling towers / That the cathedrals stretch forth into the sky, / And I see the virtuous and wicked as the same. // I don't believe in God, I abjure and forswear / All thought, and as for that old irony, / Love, I'd rather you not speak to me of it at all. // Wearied of living, afraid of dying, like / The lost brig, a plaything of the ocean's ebb and flow, / My soul is being rigged for fearsome shipwrecks.)

The poet rejects art, the very activity that defines him, and its products of music and verse. He surrenders himself to the rocking, delusive movement of the alexandrine verses like a lost ship. This "musicality," this hypnotic empty signifier, is reinforced by the pervasive additional regularity of verbal parallelisms. The first stanza is built around four successive clauses beginning in "ni"; the second begins by repeating "je ris de" and then lists four items each of which is preceded by "des"; the last verse of this stanza pairs "les bons et les méchants." The third stanza deploys a fourfold anaphora of "je" associated with what the poet abjures. More verbal parallels in lines 9 ("j'abjure et je renie."), 12 ("lasse de vivre, ayant peur de mourir"), and 13 ("du flux et du reflux")—the last with an internal rhyme—create a countercurrent of soothing regularity beneath the explicit textual meanings of the negation of nature, art, God, and love. Ultimately, of course, such denials and a passive yielding to rhythmic flux lead to the same thing: the ultimate disaster for which the lyric self prepares in the last line; the loss of a personal identity, which can be expressed and maintained only through words.

Generally, then, during the course of the **"Melancholia"** section of the ***Poèmes saturniens*** the poet affirms that words once had a transcendent meaning that they now have lost: they expressed the eternity of love (see **"Le Rossignol,"** pp. 73–74). As **"Lassitude"** reveals, the poet prefers this willfully recreated illusion to the reality of sexual fulfillment in the present. But the illusion can be sustained not by specific words themselves but only by the *idea* of words, just as the name of the beloved in **"Nevermore"** can be preserved only as a general impression. Finally, in **"L'Angoisse"** the despairing poet will reject all talk about love—remembered, potential, or allusive—to surrender himself to the rocking rhythm of the hemistiches. Thus the self comes to be suspended between life and death, as it is more specifically in the concluding lines of **"Chanson d'automne"**:

Et je m'en vais
Au vent mauvais
Qui m'emporte
Deça, delà,
Pareil à la
Feuille morte.

[p. 73]

(And I go off / On the evil wind / That carries me / Here and there / Like the / Dead leaf.)

For the historical Verlaine, alcoholism achieved a similar compromise between suicide and survival, preserving him as much as possible in a blurry, dreamy swoon that did not threaten immediate self-annihilation but offered the one advantage of that state—relief from pain. Such a narcissistic retreat into the self effaces the disappointments of the exterior world. And the incursions of the other arts into Verlaine's poetry obscure the meretricious words with which one attempts to communicate with that world. Not only is this poetry opposed to commitment—expressing "l'amer à la bouteille" rather than "la bouteille à la mer"—it also is anti-impressionist. For real impressionism opens itself to sensory experience; it does not exploit such experience as a narcotic.

The following section of the ***Poèmes saturniens***, titled "Eaux-fortes" (engravings), moves away from the verbal toward the visual. But at the same time the relative impersonality of these descriptive poems added to the frequent marked choice of "rythmes impairs" makes them more nearly "musical" than the ordinary poem, in a context that allows us to recognize such musicality as antiverbal. **"Croquis parisien"** has one five-syllable line amid three decasyllabic lines in each stanza; **"Cauchemar"** has lines of seven and three syllables; **"Marine"** has five-syllable lines. These are the first three of five poems in this section. When Verlaine returns to conventional versification in the last two, he preserves the titles that suggest works of visual art: **"Effet de nuit"** and **"Grotesques."** And as if to offset the return to rhythmical conventions, he treats subjects that make explicit his feelings of alienation: outcasts rejected by the elements and menaced with imminent death.

To the "musicality" of a marked choice of an unusual rhythm (pentasyllables again), the first of the "Paysages tristes," **"Soleils couchants,"** adds the "musicality" of an exceptional amount of repetition. In sixteen lines there are only four rhymes—two in each group of eight lines. Line 3 is the same as line 5; 11 is the same as 16. The expression "soleils couchants" appears four times as well as in the title, while the word "défilent" occupies the first three of five syllables in lines 13 and 14.

Moreover, the flux of transition subverts the stability essential to allow representation, and this poem is liminal on many levels. Both dawn and sunset, passages between darkness and light, are evoked. The poem's beach stands between sea and land, as its dream stands between waking and sleeping and its phantoms between life and death. Furthermore, these diverse states interpenetrate. The poem literally begins with a weak dawn light that suggests a sunset; in the last eight lines this natural setting, in turn, becomes the stage for "d'étranges rêves" associated only by simile with the setting suns. The event of the title, "setting suns," has been twice displaced, first to dawn and then to dream. The apparent history of the poem's composition thus moves backward: instead of the title serving as the pretext for the poem, the poem becomes, as it were, the pretext for the title. This multiplication of perspectives makes any particular sequence of associations appear arbitrary. The constellation of associations comes to seem rather like a musical theme that could equally well be played cancrizans (backward) or inverted. Verlaine is well aware of his poems' resistance to interpretation, as we can see in the sardonic self-glossing of stanzas 8 through 10 of **"Nuit du Walpurgis classique,"** the fourth poem in "Paysages tristes":

> —Ces spectres agités, sont-ce donc la pensée
> Du poète ivre, ou son regret, ou son remords,
> Ces spectres agités en tourbe cadencée,
> Ou bien tout simplement des morts?
>
> Sont-ce donc ton remords, ô rêvasseur qu'invite
> L'horreur, ou ton regret, ou ta pensée,—hein?—tous
> Ces spectres qu'un vertige irrésistible agite,
> Ou bien des morts qui seraient fous?—
>
> N'importe! ils vont toujours, les fébriles fantômes.
>
> [p. 72]

> (These agitated ghosts, now are they the thoughts / Of the drunken poet, or his regrets, or his remorse, / These ghosts stirred up in a rhythmical rabble, / Or are they quite simply the dead? // Now are they your remorse, day-dreamer courted / By horror, or your regrets, or your thoughts, eh? All / These ghosts agitated by an irresistible vertigo, / Or else might they be dead people gone mad? // No matter! They're moving still, the feverish phantoms.)

The tenor of the poem, visionary Romantic disorder, is negated by its triply Apollonian vehicle: the orderly alexandrines, the allusion to classical ancient Greece in Goethe's *Faust*, part II, and the regular French (rather than unkempt English) gardens of Le Nôtre, "correct, ridicule, et charmant" (proper, ridiculous, and charming). These words conclude and define the poem while repeating the last line and a half of stanza 1. The implied author retains a bit of playfulness by breaking the frame rather than affirming it, for example in the first stanza, when an excess of regularity creates dislocation because the vision is described as "un rhythmique [*sic*] sabbat, rhythmique, extrêmement / Rhythmique" (p. 71: A rhythmical Sabbath, rhythmical, extremely / Rhythmical). The word "extremely" forces the word "rhythmical" beyond the end of the line in an enjambment that disrupts rhythm. And again, at the beginning of stanzas 6 and 7, the word "s'entrelacent" (embrace) applied to the dancing specters literally obliges one stanza to carry over a sentence from the previous one. Thus, contrary to the classical norm, according to which each stanza contains one neat, complete sentence, these stanzas run over into each other, swept up in the grotesque, promiscuous dance of the dead.

It would be tempting to assume that Verlaine's mockery of conventional prosody in his Walpurgis Night functions to enhance by contrast his unconventional prosody, and that the latter's "musicality" offers us a haven of nonreferential innocence by challenging the false primacy of words. But Verlaine will not allow this impression to stand. The ensuing Saturnian poems will assail the innocence—both verbal and nonverbal—associated with love language and then insinuate this now-debased language into the "musical" world of purity so as to threaten the reassuring connotations of the orderly repetitions of "musicality" itself. The first move in Verlaine's parodic enterprise can be observed in **"La Chanson des ingénues"** of the section "Caprices." From the outset, these ingénues are faced with extinction because they inhabit "les romans qu'on lit peu" (novels that are seldom read). Are they actual young women or sentences ("la phrase," of feminine grammatical gender in French) in the text? The second stanza, beginning "Nous allons entrelacées" (p. 75), introduces a series of sentences that Verlaine has "interlaced" into one monstrously long sentence by replacing periods with semicolons for the remaining seven stanzas of the poem. The portrait of the ingénues also becomes textually "interlaced" with other suspect depictions of innocence, for the first phrase with which they characterize themselves—"Et le jour n'est pas plus pur / Que le fond de nos pensées" (And the daylight is no purer / Than the depths of our thoughts)—parodies Hippolyte's equivocal protestation to his father in Racine's *Phèdre* (IV, 2). The assaults of suitors are repulsed by "les plis ironiques / De nos jupons détournés" (the ironic folds / Of our averted skirts). These folds, ostensibly protective owing to the extra density of material that they interpose between female and male, also suggest both the folds of the female sexual organs and partially hidden thoughts. Such "pensers clandestins" emerge in the last two lines, where the ingénues imagine themselves as the future lovers of libertines. These young women were initially interchangeable from one novel to another. Now they have proven interchangeable in the roles of innocence and experience as well. They are unmasked as empty signs whose meaning is not innate or even fixed, but arbitrary and unstable.

"Sérénade" and **"Nevermore,"** near the end of the collection, intimately link the lulling reassurance of "musicality" to the falsity of words. **"Sérénade"** stresses rhythm by employing the unusual alternation of ten- and five-syllable lines we have already observed in **"Croquis parisien."** The poem recalls the Baudelairean quasi-pantoum (see "Harmonie du soir," where the second and fourth lines of each stanza become the first and third lines of the next), except that it uses stanzas rather than lines to achieve its lulling effect: the first of seven quatrains is also the fourth, and the second reappears as the seventh. The poem displays many other Baudelairean motifs: the beloved's onyx eyes, the Lethe of her breast, the Styx of her dark hair, her "parfum opulent." But Verlaine condenses Baudelaire's alternatives of adoration and sadistic assault into single lines: the poem as "chanson" is both "cruelle et câline" (cruel and cajoling); the woman is "Mon Ange!—ma Gouge!" (My Angel!—my Whore!) Such laconism appears flippant, as if Verlaine were suggesting that he could easily replicate Baudelaire's tricks. The anticlimactic platitude of the poet's supreme appeal for contact—"Ouvre ton âme et ton oreille au son / De ma mandoline" (open your soul and your ear to the sound / Of my mandolin)—plus the humbleness of his instrument add up to a pungent satire of lyrical conventions and a devaluation of lyricism itself, both in the modern sense of an emotional effusion and in the medieval sense of a poem designed to be accompanied by music. Above all, Verlaine writes a gay mockery of heterosexual romance.

"Nevermore" again adopts a Baudelairean device by repeating the first line of a five-line stanza at its end. Given an appropriate context, repetition above and beyond the ordinary in the lyric usually creates a reassuring world of regularity and stability. In Verlaine's poem the motif of repetition introduced by the versification reflects the psychic condition of the subject: the lyric self's aging heart will attempt to rebuild and readorn the past monuments of its hymns. But the fundamental falsity of existence has now extended its domain to encompass prayer as well as love: "Brûle un encens ranci sur tes autels d'or faux. . . . Pousse à Dieu ton cantique. . . . Entonne, orgue enroué, des Te Deum splendides" (Burn a rancid incense on your altars of false gold. . . . Heave your canticle to God. . . . Thunder forth, hoarse organ, splendid Te Deums). Other voices join the poet's in chorus in a pseudo-elegiac movement, but only to mingle the ludicrous with the noble: "Sonnez, grelots; sonnez, clochettes; sonnez, cloches!" (Ring, sleigh bells; ring, hand bells; ring, bells!). And at the end, the almost breathless recital of Baudelairean motifs in condensed form—an impatient and halfhearted reenactment—robs them of the tragic grandeur they had in the original: "Le ver est dans le fruit, le réveil dans le rêve, / Et le remords est dans l'amour: telle est la loi" (The worm is in the fruit, awaking in the dream, / And remorse is in love: such is the law). Finally, the title **"Nevermore,"** connoting the irretrievable uniqueness of an experience, is undercut from the beginning, for not only does it echo the refrain of Poe's "Raven," it has also been previously used in the ***Poèmes saturniens*** themselves.

The concluding poems just before the Epilogue are, in the manner of Parnassianism, intrinsically false. The notes to the Pléiade edition misleadingly claim that Verlaine tried to profit from the current vogue of Leconte de Lisle (considered, as recently as the early years of the twentieth century, to be the second greatest poet of nineteenth-century France, after Victor Hugo) and that he was untrue to himself by imitating Leconte de Lisle; but the Epilogue clearly shows that Verlaine's homage of imitation is once again ironic. He mocks the specious sublimity of the Parnassian pantheon and neo-Hellenism by casting himself in the role of one of "les suprêmes Poètes / Qui vénérons les Dieux et qui n'y croyons pas" (we supreme Poets / Who venerate the gods and don't believe in them). The following lines that reject inspiration in favor of effort are obviously ironic and parody the movement of "l'Art pour l'Art" (headed by Théophile Gautier) as well as the Parnassian school of Leconte de Lisle: "A nous qui ciselons les mots comme des coupes / Et qui faisons les vers émus très froidement." (Here's to us who chisel words like goblets / And write emotional verse quite in cold blood.) The truculence of Verlaine's parody, sharp as that of the young Rimbaud, has long been underestimated.

Verlaine's sense of the absurdity of language culminates in the ***Fêtes galantes***. More radically than before he attacks the notion that language is the proud, unmatched achievement of humanity. He deprives humans of speech and bestows it on nonhuman entities. By means of cacophony, he further assails the assumption that what is poetic is what is harmonious. By having the names of musical notes invade the poems, he refutes the belief that only what is verbal signifies. Finally, his satire of love language in this collection undermines the conventional association of intensity with originality by stressing the conventional rhetorical nature of expressions of intense love feelings.[12]

According to J. S. Chaussivert in his fine study of the ***Fêtes galantes***,[13] the twenty-two poems in this collection are arranged in a cyclothymic movement, a mood swing rising to and then falling away from a manic episode. The first two poems express a certain sadness and hesitation before the lyric self embarks on the adventure of the festival. The latter, Chaussivert continues, affords an opportunity for what Mikhail Bakhtin calls "carnival," episodic, ritualized, socially sanctioned transgression. The very title conveys this notion insofar as "galant" refers to flirtation and sex outside of marriage. (In classical French parlance, a "femme sensible" has had one lover; a "femme galante" has or has had several.) For Chaussivert, the poem **"En bateau"** sums up the irresponsible mood that colors the entire collection:

> C'est l'instant, Messieurs, ou jamais,
> D'être audacieux, et je mets
> Mes deux mains partout désormais!
>
> [p. 115]
>
> (This is the time, Sirs, if ever there was one, / To be audacious, and I'm going to put / My two hands everywhere from now on!)

Poems 3 through 19 depict this "phase where flirtatious playfulness fully unfolds,"[14] while the last three are impregnated with a postorgiastic melancholy.

Beneath the mounting and ebbing excitement of the festival, however, the ***Fêtes galantes*** follows a different trajectory, a steady devaluation of the word which is unaffected by the climax of the carnival mood. First, in **"Clair de lune"** and **"Pantomime,"** Verlaine invokes a silence that supplants conversation. Then music invades and disrupts the fragmented conversation of **"Sur l'herbe."** Intensifying these shifts in the discourse of an unchanging set of characters in *style direct libre* (a sequence of conversational remarks whose speakers are unidentified), the more radical kaleidoscopic shifts of characters in **"Fantoches"** and **"En bateau"** totally destroy narrative coherence. **"Mandoline"** then simultaneously dehumanizes the lovers and strips them of significant discourse while attributing such discourse to things.[15] Next, **"Lettre," "Les Indolents,"** and **"Colombine"** show rather than tell (as **"Mandoline"** had done) that the language of lovers is a set of empty signifiers. But although these poems leave declarations of passion unanswered, or reject or banish them, they do so in a lighthearted vein. Beneath the superficial frivolity of the concluding poems, **"L'Amour par terre"** and **"Colloque sentimental,"** however, the tone turns serious; and the lyric self, having been introduced as a personified observer, now becomes implicated in the failure of the language of love.[16]

The title ***Fêtes galantes*** itself calls into question the primacy of words by evoking Watteau's painting of the same name. And the tone of the frolicking masquers in the first poem, **"Clair de lune,"** clashes with their message: "l'amour vainqueur et la vie opportune" (conquering love and a life of opportunity). For they celebrate love "in a minor key." They themselves are "quasi tristes," as is the moonlight in which they gambol. That moonlight mingles with their songs in the second stanza and then supersedes human words in the third with its omnipotent nonverbal message: "Qui fait rêver les oiseaux dans les arbres / Et sangloter d'extase les jets d'eau" (p. 107: Which makes the birds dream in the trees / And the fountains sob with ecstasy). The birds become silent and immobilized; the inanimate fountains take on inarticulate human feelings in response to the moon's message. To be sure, in ordinary poetic prosopopoeia and apostrophe a real-life verbal exchange between two living, waking, neighboring human beings becomes an exchange between only one such human being and an addressee who could not actually respond. But one side of a conversation nevertheless remains. By the end of **"Clair de lune,"** however, the singing humans have been swept from the stage, and nature is left to commune wordlessly with itself.

The second poem, **"Pantomime,"** removes words from people altogether, except for the unspecified voices that Colombine hears in her heart. Each of the four stanzas presents a discrete character, totally cut off from the others in the present time of lyricization. People recapture words in the third poem, **"Sur l'herbe,"** but in a contextfree *style direct libre* that recalls Apollinaire's "Lundi rue Christine." We cannot say precisely how many speakers are involved or who is saying what. At least four persons must be present because the text mentions "Mesdames" and "Messieurs" in direct address. Three individuals are specified: an abbé, a marquis, and the dancer La Camargo. Dashes reveal that at least two are talking. But Verlaine is not particular about the distribution of their lines. A variant of the initial verse had no dash at mid-line to indicate a change of speaker, whereas one appears in the definitive version. Lines 7 through 11 suggest at least three male speakers, although theoretically any of them could be women. The free-floating conversation consists of insults and bantering flattery. We cannot tell whether the final five syllables ("Hé! bonsoir, la Lune!") constitute a facetious address to a celestial body or a comic sexual reference to an earthly one. ("Je vois la lune" in familiar parlance means "I see somebody's bare ass.") As if all these features did not make the poem sufficiently incoherent, a series of musical notes invades it twice. Even as music the two series remain ambiguous. Both begin with an ascending major triad but finish unresolved, one ending on the double dominant, the other on the dominant. And as the added emphasis in the text cited below indicates, in the middle stanza the musical notes homophonically invade their immediate context. Their innate musicality elicits a further "musical" response in the form of the marked repetitions of assonance and alliteration. The musical term "croche" (eighth note) is embedded here as well. And the stability of individual signifiers is further weakened by homonyms of the rhyme—*si* and *l'une*—inserted in stanzas 2 and 3:

L'abbé divague.—Et toi, marquis,
Tu mets de travers ta perruque.
—Ce vieux vin de Chypre est exquis
Moins, Camargo, que votre nuque.

—Ma flamme . . . *Do, mi, sol, la si.*
*L'a*bbé, ta noirceur se dévoile!
—Que je meure, Mesdames, *si*
Je ne vous dé*croche* une étoile!

—Je voudrais être petit chien!
—Embras*sons* nos bergères *l'une*
Après l'autre.—Messieurs, eh bien?
—*Do, mi, sol.*—Hé! bonsoir, *la Lune.*

(The Abbé is rambling.—And you, Marquis, / You put your wig on crooked. /—This old wine from Cyprus is exquisite, / Less, Camargo, than your nape. //—My love . . . Do, mi, so, la si. / Abbé, your evil scheme is exposed! /—I hope to die, ladies, if / I don't bring down a star for you! // I'd like to be a little dog! /—Let's kiss our shepherdesses one / After the other.—Well, gentlemen? /—Do, mi, so—Hi there! Good evening, Moon.)

Less radical, **"A la promenade"** exploits the semantic connotations of embedded homophony to underline the tone of pleasurable insincerity imposed on love language:

Trompeurs exquis et coquettes char*mantes,*
Coeurs tendres, mais affranchis du ser*ment,*
Nous devisions délicieuse*ment* . . .

[p. 109; emphasis added]

(Exquisite deceivers and charming coquettes, / Tender hearts, but freed from our vows, / We chatted deliciously . . .)

Both rhymes in this stanza end in a syllable that is a form of the verb *mentir*, to lie. This stanza, the middle one of five, is framed by notations of nonverbal communication far more significant than words, which thus are once again depreciated. The first stanza describes the indulgent, complicitous "smile" of the landscape; the last ends by conjuring up the provocative pout of a flirtatious mouth. Because words have been repressed, the suggestiveness of the sexual challenge in such details is all the broader. But predictably "La moue assez clé*mente* de la bouche" (the rather lenient pout of the mouth) again contains a homonym of the verb *mentir*.

"Dans la grotte" further devalues words by superimposing banality on insincerity. The poem consists entirely of a tissue of clichés descending to what even in this context is an anticlimax, and the third line of each quatrain, an alexandrine among octosyllables, presents the objective correlative of the rhetorical excess that pervades the poem. In the first stanza the lover announces, "Là! je me tue à vos genoux!" (There! I'll kill myself at your knees!). The fearsome Hyrcanian tiger seems a lamb next to his cruel Clymène. But he moderates his outburst in the second stanza. His sword, which has felled so many heroes, *will* end his life. Not only has the act been safely postponed to an indefinite future but metonymy separates the potential suicide from the instrument of his death (he now says "my sword will kill me" rather than "I shall kill myself). This substitution of the instrument for the agent implies that the lover is now at some distance from the act and also that he has a choice of possible ways to do himself in—or indeed he might choose not to kill himself at all. And so, as we could have predicted, in the third stanza the hero prudently concludes he does not need a sword; did not love pierce his heart with sharp arrows the moment the beloved woman's eye shone on him? The equivocal device of a rhetorical question, whose vehicle expresses uncertainty while its tenor conveys certitude, brings the poem full circle from despair to flirtation.

Obsession with sexuality forms the fixed center around which Verlaine's badinage and verbal artifice circle in the next three poems. **"Les Ingénus," "Cortège,"** and **"Les Coquillages"** first offer exciting glimpses of the woman's body: "Parfois luisaient des bas de jambes . . . c'étaient des éclairs soudains de nuques blanches" (Sometimes bare ankles twinkled . . . white napes suddenly flashed). These voyeuristic thrills are associated with specious words. In **"Cortège"** such glimpses become more overtly sexual, but they are not offered from the viewpoint of a poetic "nous"; instead, they are attributed to the lyric self's dissociated, projected primitivism and animality in the form of a monkey and of a "négrillon." The female object's going up- and downstairs in this poem represents sexual intercourse with an archetypal symbolism of regular movement and increasing breathlessness as one "mounts" the stairway. As in a series of dreams where the inadmissible repressed moves gradually toward direct expression, in this series of poems the lyric self at last becomes a "je." In **"Les Coquillages"** as in **"Dans la grotte"** the setting is again a cavern, but now the sexual symbolism—the lyric self enters the cave as a penis enters a vagina—is no longer masked by the reversal whereby the poet figure overtly imagines piercing himself with his sword rather than penetrating the desired woman. And the specious rhetoric of female "cruelty" (rejection) has disappeared. The cavern "où nous nous aimâmes" (where we once loved) is studded with shells. Each suggests part of the woman's complexion or body; one, particularly disturbing, suggests her vagina and thus reduplicates the entire rupestral setting. As the next poem, **"En patinant,"** implies with its scornful concluding cacophony "—quoi qu'on caquette!" (p. 113: whatever they may cackle!), only nature remains meaningful, and culture in the form of words may be dismissed entirely.

Here, midway into the collection, Verlaine moves beyond disparagement, mockery, cliché, hyperbole, and erasure to more radical ways of subverting words. Cacophony, the intimate enemy of lyric, gains reinforcement from structural incoherence, the enemy of context already apparent in **"Sur l'herbe."** Each of the nine stanzas of **"Fantoches"** and **"En bateau"** introduces a different set of characters. Such composition by juxtaposition becomes pictorial rather than narrative or syntactical. **"Fantoches"** attributes no words to its human characters, only gestures and body movements. A nonhuman being assumes the task of verbal communication: on behalf of a lovesick Spanish pirate, "un langoureux rossignol / Clame la *dé*tresse à *tue*tête" (p. 114: a languorous nightingale / Yells out distress at the top of its lungs). Any musical delights the mention of the dreamy nightingale might lead us to anticipate are promptly canceled by the excessive loudness and harshness of its song, described with six stop consonants within eight syllables. Similarly, in **"Le Faune"** inhuman noises shatter the momentary serenity surrounding the silent humans. The sinister laughter of a terra-cotta faun ushers them in, and the clattering of tambourines making noise without players escorts them out.

The sounds of nature become agreeable in the next poem, **"Mandoline,"** only further to devalue faithless love and its empty words by contrast. Maids and swains "échangent des propos fades / Sous les ramures chanteuses" (exchange trite remarks / Beneath the singing branches). While the trees sing, the promiscuous multiplicity of the human messages voids them of meaning. Damis "pour mainte / Cruelle fait maint vers tendre" (writes many a tender verse for many a cruel lady). The characters, portrayed as "donneurs de sérénades" and as "écouteuses," have no functions other than these idle diversions (p. 115). They are stock characters from pastoral, so familiar—like the "éternel [i.e., predictable and boring] Clitandre"—that they pall. Insubstantial as these phantoms already are, they will be further reduced: to their clothes, to their mood, and finally to their limp shadows, which whirl until they in turn are absorbed into the moonlight. The last word applicable to human speech in this poem, "jase," refers to the empty background chatter of the mandolin. Not only the signifying power of the speakers' words but even the speakers themselves have been erased.

The major transition of the ***Fêtes galantes*** occurs when the next poem, **"A Clymène,"** shifts from presenting lovers in general, as the previous pieces have done, to dramatizing the lyric self as lover. This self thus becomes directly involved in the failure of love language to signify. When the phrase "romances sans paroles" (borrowed, of course, from the title of Mendelssohn's musical composition) denotes the effect that the beloved woman has on the poet, words have been altogether deleted from the love relationship. Described as an "étrange / Vision," the woman's very voice is metaphorically robbed of sound as well as of words. The stripping away of its capacity for rational communication is represented by the violent enjambment that shatters the phrase placed in opposition to "voix."

The six concluding poems in the ***Fêtes galantes*** call into question the signifying abilities of words even more thoroughly and explicitly than any of the preceding poems. Through incongruous juxtaposition, through a diaphoric alternation of mutually incompatible tones,[17] **"Lettre"** presents a devastating critique of lovers' language which anticipates Roland Barthes or Nathalie Sarraute's satire of literary criticism in *Les Fruits d'or*. The verses in rhyming couplets (which in and of themselves suggest banality) begin by protesting the lover's total physical dependence on the presence of the beloved: "Je languis et me meurs, comme c'est ma coûtume / En pareil cas" (I'm languishing and dying, as my habit is / In such a case). The platitudinous iterative of the last three words promptly undercuts the melodramatic singulative. Undaunted by, and apparently unaware of, the breakdown of the illusion of devotion he is attempting to create, this unreliable narrator/lover continues with a pseudo-Platonic turn:

> enfin, mon corps faisant place à mon âme,
> Je deviendrai fantôme à mon tour aussi, moi,
> . . . . .
>
> Mon ombre se fondra pour jamais en votre ombre.
>
> [p. 117]
>
> (Finally, my body giving way to my soul, / I too will become a ghost in my turn, . . . / My shade will melt into yours forever.)

But this lofty assertion of selfless love is vitiated by the prosaic self-emphasizing disjunctive pronoun of the second line cited (*moi*); and in the line immediately following, the respectful distance of the "vous" is canceled by the presumptuous "tu" appearing in the flattest of homage clichés: "En attendant, je suis, très chère, ton valet" (Meanwhile, dearest, I am your humble servant). The typography itself emphasizes this presumption and triteness by isolating the line. The total effect is like that of the dialogue in a French classical play when the discourse of the master is interwoven with that of the servant, the master typically representing the superego and idealistic love, the servant embodying the id and the domination of bodily, materialistic impulses.

The third group of typographically distinct lines deploys the deliberate anticlimax (or, to use the more evocative French term, "rechute dans la banalité") of inquiring prosaically about the beloved's pets and friends (the conjunction implying their shared animality), particularly

> cette Silvanie
> Dont j'eusse aimé l'oeil noir si le tien n'était bleu,
> Et qui parfois me fit des signes, palsambleu!
>
> [p. 117]
>
> (That Sylvania, / Whose dark eyes I would have liked if yours had not been blue, / And who sometimes signaled to me, my word!)

By successfully tempting the poet to contemplate infidelity, Silvanie's nonverbal communication retrospectively nullifies all the exalted protestations of passionate fidelity that he had broadcast in his letter.

The fourth block of lines returns to the tone of exalted homage. The lyric self, more amorous than Caesar or Mark Anthony with Cleopatra, claims that he plans to conquer the whole world so as to lay its treasures at the beloved's feet as an unworthy token of his devotion. (That the woman as object of devotion is compared to a promiscuous historical figure, however, implicitly transforms her from a guiding star to a "femme galante" who is no better than she should be.) But then the last three lines intervene, impatiently breaking off the rhyming couplets in the middle of a pair. After repeating the mundane "très chère" of the isolated line, they blatantly dismiss as trivial and otiose all that has gone before,

> Car voilà trop causer,
> Et le temps que l'on perd à lire une missive
> N'aura jamais valu la peine qu'on l'écrive.
>
> [p. 117]
>
> (For that's too much chat, / And the time you lose reading a missive / Will never have been worth the trouble to write it.)

What we have learned from reading this poem, according to the lyric self, is that we should not have wasted our time on it in the first place. Rather than guide us to unknown heights of love, it has cast us down. By situating his metalanguage in final position, Verlaine has canceled his statement *en bloc*.

In the demonic world of the ***Fêtes galantes***, the ultimate realities are lust and death. Such an interpretation may sound melodramatic, but it is borne out by the text of **"Le Monstre,"** a poem composed at the same time as the poems in this collection:

> et les victimes dans la gueule
> Du monstre s'agitaient et se plaignaient, et seule
> La gueule, se fermant soudain, leur répondait
> Par un grand mouvement de mâchoires.
>
> [p. 128]
>
> (And the victims in the maw / Of the monster struggled and lamented, and only / The maw, suddenly closing, answered them / With a great movement of its jaws.)

In this Dantesque inner circle of Hell, the only response to words is annihilation. Words themselves, however, are false lust and false death, since they postpone both the gratification of lust and the consummation of death. In **"Dans la grotte,"** for example, the despairing homage of a promise of suicide functions to defer death; in **"Les Indolents"** the male's proposition of a suicide pact delays the fulfillment of lust until his practical lady friend interrupts: "Mais taisonsnous, si bon vous semble" (But let's stop talking, if you like). The implied author's mocking "Hi! hi! hi!" of conclusion then echoes the earlier laughter of the lady and of the watching fauns who serve as wordless advocates—so to speak—for the claims of nature against antinature.

Even the absence of words, however, does not guarantee sincerity in Verlaine's eyes. The false promises of a flash of exposed flesh are enough to dupe **"Les Ingénus." "Colombine"** accords a more extensive treatment to the motif of the unreliability of nonverbal communication. The heroine of that poem, "une belle enfant méchante" (a beautiful, wicked child), leads her flock of gulls on to no one knows where. The etymological sense of "enfant"—"without speech"—is clearly relevant in this poem. The level of communication has already been reduced to nonsense when the antics of the clowns who try to impress Colombine are summed up by a series of musical notes: "Do, mi, sol, mi, fa." But it degenerates further to an exchange among metaphorical animals. The tacit sexual promises made by Colombine's provocative clothes and seductive body are contradicted by her perverse feline eyes, which transmit the tacit command "A bas / Les pattes!" (Down, boy!).

The ominous title of the following poem, **"L'Amour par terre,"** announces at once the overthrow of the ideal of love. And it concludes with an unheard, unanswered question addressed to the lyric self's distracted female companion, who is engrossed in following the flight of a butterfly, itself an emblem of her inconstant attention. The twofold frustration of desire and art symbolized in the poem leaves her unaffected. She does not see the fallen statue of Cupid or the phallic pedestal standing sadly alone beside it, a pedestal on which the lyric self can scarcely decipher the sculptor's name. The topos of *exegi monumentum* has been superseded by that of *disjecta membra poetae*. And in each of the last three quatrains the lyric self's "c'est triste" contrasts jarringly with the playful, heedless mood of his insouciant female companion.

A rhetorical framework of six imperatives in **"En sourdine,"** the next-to-last poem, strains for a possible moment of happiness in love: "Pénétrons . . . Fondons . . . Ferme . . . Croise . . . Chasse . . . Laissonsnous persuader" (Let us imbue . . . melt together . . . close your eyes . . . fold your arms . . . banish every plan . . . allow ourselves to be persuaded). But in the final analysis the best these lovers have to hope for is the successful accomplishment of a speech act—in other words, that they will be persuaded. Paradoxically, they can achieve even that tenuous, imaginary triumph only by completely forswearing all verbal communication and, indeed, all purpose whatsoever ("tout dessein"). The couple's relationship survives only in the deep silence of a dark wood; there it is the gentle breeze rather than their own words that will "persuade" them to abandon themselves to languor; and when night falls, it must be the nightingale's song rather than their own voices that will convey their despair.

The final poem of the ***Fêtes galantes***, **"Colloque sentimental,"** deploys an oxymoronic title to oppose feeling with debate. In French, moreover, the first word can convey an ironic nuance, suggesting a conversation whose participants exaggerate the importance of what is being discussed. The verbal exchange occurs between two specters in the icy wasteland of a deserted park. Four times in succession, one of them tries to evoke the love and ecstasy that they shared in the past, only to be flatly refuted by the other with retorts such as "Non" and "C'est possible." Translating Baudelairean spleen into dialogue, this conclusion creates a verbal exchange at cross-purposes, like those in the theater of the absurd. By offering no scope for expansion or development, the eight isolated couplets of this poem reveal that there is no hope of escaping back into the past or forward into a happier future. Further, in the framework of the conversation, the partial repetitions of the first couplet in the third and the second in the last, instead of creating the reassuring effect of the stability of repetition, underscore the poem's drift toward entropy. "Two shapes" reappear as "two ghosts"; "you can hardly hear their words" in the last line becomes "and only the night heard their words" as the void engulfs them.[18] As a country-and-western song says, "If love can never be forever, what's forever for?" Discourse and love perish together.[19] Verlaine's greatest originality and achievement in the ***Poèmes saturniens*** and the ***Fêtes galantes*** was to combine the conventional Romantic motif of loss of faith in the permanence of love with the Symbolist's crisis of doubt regarding the transcendental permanence of any signified.

From this perspective ***La Bonne Chanson*** (1870), published the year after the ***Fêtes galantes***, seems retrogressive.[20] In the two earlier collections the poet, lacking faith in love, had also lacked faith in language. ***La Bonne Chanson***, in contrast, represents a transient episode during which love and language are glorified together. The certitude of being loved restores and enhances the imagined value of all the ways in which the lyric self can communicate with the beloved. During this phase words, rather than being experienced as a source or token of spiritual impoverishment, become pregnant with promise. The eighth poem of the collection, **"Une Sainte en son auréole,"** for example, celebrates

> Tout ce que contient la parole
> Humaine de grâce et d'amour;
>
> . . . . .

Des aspects nacrés, blancs et roses,
Un doux accord patricien:
Je vois, j'entends toutes ces choses
Dans son nom Carlovingien.

[p. 147]

(Everything that human speech contains of grace and love; . . . Pearly prospects, white and pink, / A sweet patrician harmony: / I see, I hear all of these things, / In her Carlovingian name.)

One detail in the text, however, makes this apparent triumph of signification seem suspect, transient, and unstable: an enjambment dissociates "parole" from "humaine" and introduces the latter term as if it expressed a limitation.

As the earlier collections have done, ***La Bonne Chanson*** establishes throughout a dichotomy of sincerity/insincerity, but places the lyric self squarely in the camp of sincerity, representing him as

témoignant sincèrement,
Sans fausse note et sans fadaise,
Du doux mal qu'on souffre en aimant.

[II, p. 143][21]

(sincerely bearing witness, / Without a false note or insipidity, / To the sweet sickness one suffers from in loving.) And again he exclaims:

ah! c'en est fait
Surtout de l'ironie et des lèvres pincées
Et des mots où l'esprit sans l'âme triomphait.

[IV, p. 144]

(ah! It's done with, / Especially the irony and the pursed lips / And words where wit used to triumph without soul.)

Bathed in the aura of a harmony of shared sentiments, the lovers will find that communication is assured: "elle m'écoutera sans déplaisir sans doute; / Et vraiment je ne veux pas d'autre Paradis" (IV, p. 144: No doubt she will listen to me without displeasure; / And truly I want no other Paradise.) When the poet finds himself flooded by the vertiginous impressions of the howling noise, acrid odors, and rushing movement of a railway carriage, he no longer feels, as he did before, that his being is dissolving,

Puisque le Nom si beau, si noble et si sonore
Se mêle, pur pivot de tout ce tournoiement,
Au rhythme [*sic*] du wagon brutal, suavement.

[VII, p. 146]

(Because the Name, so lovely, so noble and so resonant / Mingles, the pure hub of all this turning, / Sweetly, with the rhythm of the rough carriage.)

The untitled tenth poem refutes **"Lettre"** in the ***Fêtes galantes.*** Like its precursor, it is written in alexandrine rhyming couplets and divided into five blocks of lines. But in this poem the lyric self receives a letter rather than sends one. His tone remains consistent, and he is deeply moved. Even when at first glance his conversation with the loved one seems banal, the poet can read her expressions of love beneath the surface of the words (XIII). Her words and gestures are all-powerful (XV); the characteristic description of nonverbal communication, even here, represents an element of antilogocentrism that never entirely disappeared from Verlaine's poetry. The last five poems depict the poet and his fiancée united against the world. The couple is posited as a core of meaning (XVII, XVIII); the wedding day is eagerly anticipated (XIX), and the poet experiences exhilaration at the prospect of his union with his Ideal (XX, XXI). The beloved, in short, has become a signifier whose signified is the transformation of the poet: "tous mes espoirs ont enfin leur tour" (XXI, p. 155: all my hopes finally have their day). For the historical Verlaine, however, this attempt to metamorphose appears to have been an act of desperation. "So," observes Jacques Borel, "it seems that Verlaine must have rushed into marriage, so to speak, largely in order to ward off his tendency toward homosexuality."[22]

In the ***Romances sans paroles,*** whose original title was *La Mauvaise Chanson*, Verlaine's underlying sense of the inadequacy of the signifier reerupts. He is not just writing about being bad; writing itself is bad. These poems represent not only a rebellion against conventional social expectations but also the cancellation of Verlaine's recent praise of the "chanson" as verbal artifact. He now achieves the summit of his art by freeing himself from the former excesses of metalanguage, specifically from the continual need to depreciate words verbally, a need that had pervaded the ***Fêtes galantes***. He now can evoke the indefinable without needing to dismiss the definable. But as a result, the poems in ***Romances sans paroles*** lack the thread of narrative continuity which had linked the various ***Fêtes galantes*** together into a progressive drama of the disintegration of the word.

The three section titles, "Ariettes oubliées," "Paysages belges," and "Aquarelles," all denote a transposition of the arts which reinforces the word-canceling gesture of the collective title, ***Romances sans paroles***. The nine poems of the first section are untitled; thus the ostensible pretext, which titles so often convey, has been suppressed in favor of impressionistic drift. In the ***Romances sans paroles*** as in the ***Fêtes galantes***, words, removed from human beings and ascribed instead to natural entities, no longer provide a mocking, jarring contrast to human aspirations. We have returned to an elegiac mode wherein nature appears to echo human hopes and desires. The satiric edge of the ***Fêtes galantes*** is lacking.[23]

The pathetic fallacy impregnates the nine "Ariettes oubliées" with anthropomorphism. In the first one, the choir of little voices in the branches expresses the plaintive, humble anthem of two human lovers' souls (p. 191). A murmur of unspecified origin in the second of these poems allows the lyric self to intuit "le contour subtil des voix anciennes" (the subtle contour of ancient voices); "les lueurs musiciennes" (the musical gleams) reveal to him a future dawn. The subtle synesthesias (a singing voice compared to an outline drawn by an artist, light compared to music) imply an overarching network of horizontal correspondences of sense impressions that ultimately derive from the organic unity of nature. The poet's heart and soul become a double eye reflecting "l'ariette . . . de toutes lyres!" (p. 192: the arietta of every lyre!). In the third poem the rain on the town corresponds to the weeping in the speaker's heart. By dispensing with a human verbal message Verlaine restores the harmony of self and externality that had been shattered in the ***Fêtes galantes***, although of course he must use words to do so.

Considered as a group, the "Ariettes oubliées" are what John Porter Houston percipiently identified as "mood poems" when he characterized them as the one clear innovation of French Symbolism.[24] This innovation, however, has its ties to the past; it represents a further deterioration of the vestiges of the religious sentiment that survived, in degenerate form, in the lyric worldview of Romanticism. When at the turn of this century Romanticism was condemned as "split religion," the accusation meant that Romanticism presented free-floating, invertebrate religious sentiment without any doctrinal, institutional, or dogmatic support. But Verlaine's "Symbolism" in these poems further debases the Romantics' material/spiritual correspondences to material/sentimental ones, to a harmony between the order of physical nature and the poet's feelings. Unlike the Christian and the Romantic modes of sensibility, moreover, Verlaine's lacks a social context and therefore entails no revelation, no "message," nothing useful for humanity:

O que nous mêlions, âmes soeurs que nous sommes,
A nos voeux confus la douceur puérile
De cheminer loin des femmes et des hommes,
Dans le frais oubli de ce qui nous exile!

[IV, p. 193][25]

(O let us mingle, kindred spirits that we are, / With our uncertain hopes the boyish sweetness / Of traveling far from women and men, / Newly oblivious of what is exiling us!)

The dreamy swoon so characteristic of the "Ariettes oubliées," where the poet's feelings are in harmony with his surroundings, recalls the infantile bliss of being fed and cradled. These poems are indeed deeply regressive. "Le contour subtil des voix anciennes" in the second poem clearly evokes the voice of the mother recalled from infancy. And in the same poem, the "escarpolette" "balançant jeunes et vieilles heures!" (the child's swing, swaying young and old hours to and fro!) represents not—or at least not only—an alternation between homosexual and heterosexual feelings, as many critics have claimed. Instead, it reflects Verlaine's desire to move back and forth between a remembered infantile relationship with the loved woman and his present involvement with his wife Mathilde. What the poet weeps for in "Il pleure dans mon coeur" is the loss of this blissful past. The predominance of the infantile over the homosexual becomes apparent in the fifth poem when the "air bien vieux" in the "boudoir longtemps parfumé d'Elle" (p. 193: the ancient melody . . . the boudoir filled for a long time with her scent) is metaphorically transformed into "ce berceau soudain / Qui lentement dorlote mon pauvre être" (p. 193: that sudden cradle / Which slowly coddles my poor being). A tune from former days which elicits memories of the poet's past momentarily consoles him. More playfully and subtly, the same motif recurs in the sixth "Ariette" through the mediation of medieval and fairy-tale literature. There the "petit poète jamais las / De la rime non attrapée!" (the little poet who is never weary / Of chasing the rhyme he will never catch!) is a self-image, and rhyme figures the relationship between two separate entities, the first of which engenders the second as a mother engenders a child. The primordial loss of fusion with the mother is the source of the sense of exile and sadness in the seventh poem. This mood also generates the impression of the death of the moon (as a figuration of the mother-imago) and, in the ninth poem, the death of the shadows of trees and of smoke, which figure memories:

Combien, ô voyageur, ce paysage blême
 Te mira blême toi-même,
Et que tristes pleuraient dans les hautes feuillées
 Tes espérances noyées!

[p. 196]

(How much, O traveler, this pale landscape / Caught sight of you, pale yourself, / And how sadly among the high foliage were weeping / Your drowned hopes!)

Language disappoints because it reminds us of the need to earn and to sustain in adult relationships the positive regard the mother unconditionally grants to the infant. Therefore the "Ariettes oubliées" attempt to create the semblance of a regression to a preverbal state, an impression that contrasts sharply with the ostensible modernity of the short, unusual line lengths and the synesthetic network of associations with the other arts. "Regression in the service of the ego" this poetry may be, but it also foreshadows a historical forward movement, away from the antiverbal crisis that marks the first phase of French Symbolism to the second Symbolist generation, characterized by a renewed aspiration to found a unity of the arts and to invent a cosmic, totalizing discourse.

From this point on ***Romances sans paroles*** deteriorates. Superficially the "Paysages belges" section appears to offer an impressionistic series of vignettes in rapid movement, but in fact these vignettes gravitate as a group around the fixed center of a happy home—inn, nest, or château—explicitly mentioned by the first three poems of the group. One could characterize the impossible return to infancy as centripetal, the demands of adult life as centrifugal (in the absence of a coherent sense of identity), and the resulting movement as circular. This motion appears in the next two poems in the form of a merry-go-round and of weathervanes. **"Malines"** combines the poles of movement and immobility in the image of railway cars speeding through the night but each providing at the same time an intimate home:

> Chaque wagon est un salon
> Où l'on cause bas et d'où l'on
> Aime à loisir cette nature . . .
>
> [p. 201]
>
> (Each railway car is a living room / Where you talk in low tones and from which you can / Love this nature at leisure.)

These first two groups of poems are dated from May through August 1872; the last seven poems of the collection, dated from September 1872 through April of the next year, revert to an anecdotal, self-justifying confessional tradition characteristic of Verlaine's later verse and illustrated here most starkly by **"Birds in the Night"** and **"Child Wife."**

Written in prison in 1874 after Verlaine's drunken brutality and his escapades with Rimbaud had irrevocably ended his marriage, **"L'Art poétique"** reintroduces a corrosive subversion of the word through incongruous juxtaposition, self-contradiction, disunity of tone, pleonasm, and hyperpoeticism.[26] Robert Mitchell has pointed out that, except for the nine-syllable lines corresponding to Verlaine's recommendation to use imparisyllabic meters, "the form of the poem is basically unfaithful, and even antithetical, to its substance."[27] Verlaine advocates weaving an airy creation "sans rien en lui qui pèse ou qui pose" (without anything in it that weighs down or comes to rest), but he creates a strongly didactic statement in which twelve exhortations to the reader fill up all but three of the nine stanzas. Repeated and therefore heavy-handed commands to seek "nuance" (the word occurs three times among the twenty-seven words of stanza 4) strikingly subvert the desired effect of delicacy.[28] And from that point on the text is invaded by a decidedly antipoetic diction as in stanzas 5 and 6 the poem evokes that which it wishes to destroy: "tout cet ail de basse cuisine! . . . tords-lui le cou! . . . en train d'énergie . . . elle ira jusqu'où" etc. (all that greasy-spoon garlic! . . . wring its neck! . . . getting energetic . . . how far will it go). Condemning the mechanical repetition of rhyme (i.e., of the same sounds), stanza 7 itself accumulates six *ou*'s in lines 2 and 3, and four *s*'s and *f*'s each in lines 2 through 4. The last two stanzas return to enunciating a "poetical" statement of the ideal described as a free ramble through the fresh morning air "vers d'autres cieux à d'autres amours" (p. 327: toward other skies, to other loves). But even here—if we are to assume that this concluding image of an aimless stroll corresponds to the "music" that Verlaine recommended "above all else" in his first line—Verlaine's putative "musicality" amounts to precisely the opposite of what a musician would understand by that word: the absence of structure and direction.

The jarring incongruity of prescribing a light touch in **"L'Art poétique"** in a language coarsened by pedestrian diction and crude excesses of alliteration and assonance not only conveys an ironic reflection on the claims of poetry but also betrays an inner conflict between faith in poetry and disdain for it as a vehicle for aspirations.[29] Through the ***Romances sans paroles*** Verlaine's poetry—based on a fantasized relationship to an Other whose domain is language—alternates between vulnerable openness and wary mistrust. The losses of his wife Mathilde and of his lover Rimbaud, the shock of these failures of love, robbed love of its justification for Verlaine. No longer having the energy to mistrust, he regressed into a relationship with himself. For a time he tried to aggrandize himself through a religious conversion that seemed to hold the promise of associating his self with a greater self. But transcendence eluded him. Throughout his later collections of verse he remained inextricably entangled in self-justifications of various kinds. He tried to have something to show for his past; he yielded to the rhetoric that must accompany such a stance and sank back into a dilute reworking of the confessional strain of late Romantic elegiac poetry. As Jacques Borel observes, by the time of ***La Bonne Chanson*** Verlaine was already beginning to retreat from the full originality of his personal vision: "He will be impelled forward by Rimbaud, called on in a sense to pursue down to its ultimate consequences an experiment that he had been the first to initiate by having a presentiment of the liberating power of the dream, but away from which, suspecting the dangers that **'Crimen Amoris'** and then **'Mort!'** will denounce, he had already turned into the elegiac comfort of 1870."[30]

Our faith in the referentiality of language—that there exists a real link between the signifier and a signified—depends upon our faith in intersubjectivity, the belief that we share a common code and that each signifier means the same thing to us as to the significant others in our lives. Once Verlaine had experienced "l'incommunicabilité," the impossibility of communication, he attacked the belief in referentiality in three distinct ways in his poetry. At times, as in the theater of the absurd, he depicted a dialogue of the deaf, as in **"Colloque sentimental,"** where each signifier has different referents for different people. At other times he exalted "musicality" over verbality: thus he was attracted to the libretti of Favart, which he studied with Rimbaud, because they provided the model for a form intermediate, so to speak, between language and music, insofar as the importance of the words was minimized by the necessity of tailoring them to the prepotent musical form. Verlaine's marked choice of unusual rhythms augmented the ostensible importance of the "musical"—that is, the rhythmic—dimension of his verse by calling attention to its rhythms so they could not be taken for granted. As Verlaine, like the other Symbolists, was not himself musical and was in fact rather unfamiliar with music, the inspiration that music could provide for his verse had to remain limited.[31] Yet his fascination with musicality represented a positive response to the experience of the emptiness of language, for it implied that one can shift out of an unreliable system into another system that is self-contained. When you name musical notes, for example, your referents are elements of a preexisting structure independent of language; their "meanings" are precisely nonreferential, consisting as they do in internal relationships between the parts of a musical composition.

The pessimistic mode of Verlaine's assault on signification, the one with which he ended, was the specular, narcissistic short circuit in which all signifiers voiced by the poet refer back to the poet himself. In his earlier collections of verse, images of the moon symbolize this condition. The heavenly body corresponds to the poet's body (e.g., the Pierrot's white face explicitly mimics the appearance of the moon), and the moon also recalls the fantasized maternal breast, surviving in the preconscious as the dream screen and existing only to gratify the needs of the imperial self.[32] In the weaker later verse, the confessional tradition back into which Verlaine sinks narrativizes this pessimistic solution of narcissism. If you cannot communicate with others, then you must commune with your own emptiness.

Notes

1. See James Lawler, *The Language of French Symbolism* (Princeton: Princeton University Press, 1969), chap. 2, "Verlaine's 'Naiveté,'" pp. 21–70; and Jean-Pierre Richard, *Poésie et profondeur* (Paris: Seuil, 1955), "Fadeur de Verlaine," pp. 165–85.
2. *La Petite Musique de Verlaine* (Paris: SEDES [for the Société des Etudes Romantiques], 1982).
3. For more sophisticated studies of Verlaine's "musicality," however, see Nicolas Ruwet, "Blancs, rimes, et raisons: Typographie, rimes, et structures linguistiques en poésie," *Revue d'esthéthique*, 1/2 (1979), 397–426; and Eléonore M. Zimmermann, *Magies de Verlaine: Etude de l'évolution poétique de Paul Verlaine* (Paris: Corti, 1967), pp. 11, 20–27, 65, and passim. A detailed data base for such studies has recently been provided by Frédéric S. Eigeldinger, Dominique Godet, and Eric Wehrli, comps., *Table de concordances rythmique et syntaxique des Poésies de Paul Verlaine: "Poèmes saturniens," "Fêtes galantes," "La Bonne Chanson," "Romances sans paroles"* (Geneva: Slatkine, 1985).
4. Henri Peyre, "Poets against Music in the Age of Symbolism," in Marcel Tetel, ed., *Symbolism and Modern Literature: Studies in Honor of Wallace Fowlie* (Durham, N.C.: Duke University Press, 1978), pp. 179–92.
5. See Antoine Adam, *The Art of Paul Verlaine* (New York: New York University Press, 1963), pp. 63, 70, and 84.
6. See Jacques-Henry Bornecque, *Lumières sur les "Fêtes galantes" de Paul Verlaine* (Paris: Nizet, 1959), pp. 50–59, 76–89, 97–103, and 109–10. This quotation appears on p. 50.
7. See Paul Verlaine, *Oeuvres en prose complètes,* ed. Jacques Borel (Paris: Gallimard, 1972), pp. 77–79, 82, 57, 154–61, and 599–612.
8. See the classic theoretical statement by Calvin S. Brown, *Music and Literature: A Comparison of the Arts* (Athens: University of Georgia Press, 1948).
9. Paul Verlaine, "Critique des *Poèmes Saturniens,*" *Revue d'Aujourd'hui,* 3 (March 15, 1890), reproduced in Verlaine, *Oeuvres poétiques complètes*, ed. Yves Le Dantec and Jacques Borel (Paris: Gallimard, 1962). Unless I have indicated otherwise, all subsequent references to Verlaine are from this edition and appear in the text, identified by page number only.
10. In his informative edition of Verlaine's *Poésies* (Paris: Imprimerie Nationale, 1980), Jacques Décaudin refers to "Fadaises" as "an anticipatory 'Fête galante,' which capsizes in anguish and the death wish, a poem of loneliness and sadness" (p. 10).
11. Décaudin, *Poésies*, sees the title of the first poem in the collection, "Votre âme est un paysage choisi," as a clue to the meaning of the entire collection: these are "paysages intérieurs" (p. 19). This observation is congruent with John Porter Houston's identification of the "mood poem" as Verlaine's greatest original creation (see below, n. 24). For a sprightly interpretation of the two poems titled "Nevermore" in the *Poèmes saturniens*, see Jefferson Humphries, *Metamorphoses of the Raven: Literary Overdeterminedness in France and in the South since Poe* (Baton Rouge: Louisiana State University Press, 1985), pp. 60–68. Humphries reads the second poem as "an allegory of its own inadequacy" (p. 67).
12. See Pierre Martino, *Verlaine* (Paris: Boivin, 1951), pp. 71–72 and note.
13. J. S. Chaussivert, "Fête et jeu verlainiens: *Romances sans paroles. Sagesse*," in *Petite Musique de Verlaine*, pp. 49–60.
14. Chaussivert, "Fête et jeu verlainiens," p. 49.
15. For a fuller discussion see Laurence M. Porter, "Text versus Music in the French Art Song: Debussy, Fauré, and Verlaine's 'Mandoline,'" *Nineteenth-Century French Studies*, 12 (Fall 1983-Winter 1984), 138–44; and the companion article (with musical examples) "Meaning in Music: Debussy and Fauré as Interpreters of Verlaine," *Topic: A Journal of the Liberal Arts*, 35 (1981), 26–37.
16. See Georges Zayed, "La Tradition des 'Fêtes galantes' et le lyrisme verlainien," *Aquila: Chestnut Hill Studies in Modern Languages and Literatures*, 1 (1968), 213–46. This rich, sensitive article, which deserves to be much better known, shows how common the term "fêtes galantes" and its associated *commedia dell'arte* figures were before and during Verlaine's time. Zayed celebrates this collection as Verlaine's masterpiece and mentions as sources Victor Hugo's "Fête chez Thérèse" (often mentioned by others), "Passé," and "Lettre"; Théophile Gautier's *Poésies diverses* of 1835; and Théodore de Banville's "Fête galante" in *Les Cariatides*. But none of the twenty-seven examples cited from precursors contains any direct discourse, which so typifies the imagination of Verlaine. Compare, e.g., Gautier's "Le Banc de Pierre" in the first *Parnasse contemporain* of 1866 with the "Colloque sentimental":

   Ce qu'ils disaient la maîtresse l'oublie;
   Mais l'amoureux, coeur blessé, s'en souvient,

Et dans le bois, avec mélancolie,
Au rendez-vous, tout seul, revient.

(What they used to say, the mistress forgets; / But the man who loved her, with a wounded heart, remembers; / And all alone, with melancholy mein, to the grove / Where they used to meet, returns.)

Zayed, like Bornecque, stresses the presence of the memory of Elisa Moncomble: see pp. 237–45.

17. See Philip Wheelwright, *Metaphor and Reality* (Bloomington: Indiana University Press, 1962), pp. 78–86.

18. For sources, see Bornecque, *Lumières sur les "Fêtes galantes,"* pp. 179–83.

19. Claude Cuénot, who also considers the *Fêtes galantes* to be Verlaine's masterpiece, comments on their conclusion: "The frail decor of these painted canvasses is torn apart at the end, no doubt deliberately, by the two pieces called 'En sourdine' [the renunciation of love in the ecstasy of the void] and 'Colloque sentimental' [the excruciating memory of a dead love]": see "Un type de création littéraire: Paul Verlaine," *Studi francesi*, 35 (May-August 1968), 229–45; the quotation appears on p. 235.

In an interesting overview of Verlaine, R. A. York concludes:

"Above all, Verlaine subverts the idea of a coherent and fully intended speech act. Hence his love of inapt register, of excessive pedantry, of implausible personae, of pastiche and irony. Hence his liking for disguised speech acts, most often for utterances which purport to be explanations or justifications of some previous remark, but which prove to be no more than rephrasings of it"

(*The Poem as Utterance* [London and New York: Methuen, 1986], p. 77; see also pp. 61–78).

20. J. S. Chaussivert, however, eloquently defends its artistic merits: see *L'Art verlainien dans "La Bonne Chanson"* (Paris: Nizet, 1973), pp. 7–8, 31–33, 115, and passim. Chaussivert provides a helpful diagram of the collection's structure (p. 31).

21. The roman numerals that appear in citations from *La Bonne Chanson* refer to the numbers of individual poems.

22. In Verlaine, *Oeuvres poétiques complètes,* p. 136 (editor's note).

23. One would expect the contrary, owing to the constant presence of Verlaine's lover Rimbaud—whose own poetry is preeminently satiric—during the composition of *Romances sans paroles*. But cf. Charles Chadwick, *Verlaine* (London: Athlone, 1973), p. 51, who claims that Rimbaud's influence on Verlaine's poetry was negligible. More likely, sexual satisfaction made Verlaine lose his edge.

24. John Porter Houston, *French Symbolism and the Modernist Movement: A Study of Poetic Structures* (Baton Rouge: Louisiana State University Press, 1980), pp. 19–40, esp. 22–23; reviewed by Laurence M. Porter in *Comparative Literature*, 36 (Winter 1984), 94–96.

25. The roman numeral iv refers to the number of this poem in the series of "Ariettes oubliées."

26. See Carol de Dobay Rifelj, *Word and Figure: The Language of Nineteenth-Century French Poetry* (Columbus: Ohio State University Press, 1987), esp. pp. 120–25.

27. Robert Mitchell, "Mint, Thyme, and Tobacco: New Possibilities and Affinities in the *Artes poeticae* of Verlaine and Mallarmé," *French Forum,* 2 (September 1977), 238–54. On "Images d'un sou," also from the "Jadis" section of *Jadis et naguère*, cf. Zimmermann, *Magies de Verlaine*, p. 133.

28. Mitchell, "Mint, Thyme, and Tobacco," pp. 240–43.

29. See Michel Grimaud, "Questions de méthode: Verlaine et la critique structuraliste," *Oeuvres et Critiques,* 9 (1984), 125–26, for detailed comments.

30. Verlaine, *Oeuvres poétiques complètes,* p. 171 (editor's introduction).

31. See once again Peyre, "Poets against Music," cited in n. 4 above.

32. See Jeanne Bem, "Verlaine, poète lunaire: Mythe et langage poétique," *Stanford French Review*, 4 (Winter 1980), 379–94. For a recent discussion of the "Isakower phenomenon" (adult hallucinations of the mother's breast) and the related "dream screen" and "blank dream" experiences, plus a valuable bibliography, see Philip M. Brombert, "On the Occurrence of the Isakower Phenomenon in a Schizoid Disorder," *Contemporary Psychoanalysis*, 20 (1984), 600–601 and 623–24; see also chap. 2, n. 40.

Gretchen Schultz (essay date 1991)

SOURCE: "Lyric Itineraries in Verlaine's 'Almanach pour l'annee passee,'" in *Romance Quarterly*, Vol. 38, No. 2, May, 1991, pp. 139–55.

[*In the following essay, Schultz explores the significance of* "Almanach pour l'année passée"*compared to the rest of Verlaine's poetic output.*]

Paul Verlaine's collection of poems, entitled *Cellulairement*, contains some of his most compelling, indeed some of his most enigmatic, poetry. It marks the culmination of the poetic practice, which he identified as the contradictory cohabitation of dreaminess and precision, set forth in his poem **"Art poétique"**: "Rien de plus cher que la chanson grise / Où l'Indécis au Précis se joint."[1] It marks as well a pivotal event in the poet's life, for as its title suggests, *Cellulairement* was conceived and written in a prison cell in Belgium, between 1873 and 1875, where Verlaine was incarcerated after a dispute with his lover and literary colleague, Arthur Rimbaud. The work was named for the newly instituted "régime cellulaire" which separated prisoners from one another in separate cells, and which was opposed to the traditional "régime commun." An innovation in the nineteenth-century penal institution and imported from the United States, the "régime cellulaire" was thought to be a harsher punishment, and so prisoners confined in this manner generally served shorter terms. Verlaine took this option: "Avec le système d'ici, j'ai, par le fait de mon emprisonnement dans une prison *cellulaire*, six mois de réduction."[2]

Despite its importance both as a literary and as a personal event, *Cellulairement* never appeared as such, for Verlaine, unable to find a publisher, dismantled the collection and eventually distributed its poems among his subsequent volumes of poetry. We hope to retrieve the immediacy of the collection by reassembling some of its poems and studying them together as they existed in the 1875 manuscript. Specifically, in the pages to follow we offer a reading of the series of four sonnets which Verlaine entitled **"Almanach pour l'année passée"** in *Cellulairement*. To consider these poems at the crossroads of lived experience and formal experimentation is to find in them a parallel search for lyric form and identity.

Let us quickly sketch the history of Verlaine's poetic production up to this point, in order to trace the maturation of his writing and in order to present more clearly its constituent factors. His first collection, ***Poèmes saturniens***, was published in 1866, the same year in which the first *Parnasse contemporain* came out. Eight of Verlaine's poems appeared in this anthology, and at this time he numbered himself among the adherents to the Parnasse. His next collection, ***Fêtes galantes*** (1869), continued in the Parnassian line. Inspired by Watteau's paintings, its pastoral pieces exhibited a *préciosité* which the sincerity of Verlaine's later works would belie. His contributions to the second *Parnasse contemporain* (dated 1869, but not released until after the war in 1871) mark the end of his association with the Parnasse. Ultimately, its rigid formality and requirement of objectivity clashed with Verlaine's appreciation of the vague and the imprecise. It was with his next collection, ***La bonne chanson*** (published in 1872, also after a two-year deferral), that he took a definitive step away from the rigidity of the Parnasse movement.

Although ***La bonne chanson*** was dedicated to Mathilde Mauté, his future wife, Verlaine initially intended that ***Romances sans paroles***, his next work published in 1874, be dedicated to Rimbaud. Edmond Lepelletier, Verlaine's lifelong friend, but no admirer of Rimbaud, managed to suppress this dedication, and yet Rimbaud's mark on the work remains. It was Verlaine's unsettling encounter with him which inaugurated the poetic theory described in **"Art poétique."** Together Verlaine and Rimbaud began their study of uneven meters and rhyme gender which would eventually lead them in different directions. Although Rimbaud abandoned verse for the poetic prose of *Une Saison en enfer* and the *Illuminations*, Verlaine continued his experiments with rhythm and rhyme. Uneven meters abound in ***Romances sans paroles***, constrasting with the preponderance of even meters in ***La bonne chanson***. These discoveries were like a poetic homecoming for Verlaine.

Romances sans paroles reflected an era of expansion for Verlaine, an era of real and poetic discovery, for he was continually roving with Rimbaud during the period between 1871–73 when he wrote its poems. They include images of these voyages: the second section of the collection, "Paysages belges," contains poems describing their Belgian adventure. The poems of its third section, "Aquarelles," are of English inspiration, written during their first trip to London, and their English titles (e.g., **"Green," "Child Wife," "A Poor Young Shepherd"**) mark Verlaine's apprenticeship of the English language. "Paysages" and "Aquarelles" are section titles that reflect the importance of the visual in the poems and suggest the classical metaphor of poetry as painting.

At the same time, ***Romances sans paroles*** speaks of pure melody, conveying a newfound sense of poetic freedom in the metaphor of poetry as music. "Sans paroles": Verlaine abandoned the search for meaning in words and gave himself free rein to explore the most musical aspects of poetry, sound and rhythm. The first section of ***Romances sans paroles***, "Ariettes oubliées," also refers to the musicality of this verse. By dividing themselves between the two metaphors of poetry as music and poetry as painting, the section titles attest to the importance of both sound and image in the poems.

Gustave Kahn once said of Verlaine that he wrote "sans décors, ou en tel décor qui n'est qu'un rythme."[3] For Kahn, both poet and art critic (among others, he wrote a book on Fantin-Latour whose "Un Coin de table" captures Verlaine and Rimbaud together in 1872), decor was of the utmost concern not just for the visual arts, but for poetry as well. He called it "la pure mentalité du poète" (p. 86). It is a curious idea that the visual or spatial would somehow be made over into rhythm in the poetry of Verlaine, but one well worth pursuing. If the ***Fêtes galantes*** show Verlaine's sensitivity to the picturesque and ***La bonne chanson*** his predilection for the musical, then ***Romances sans paroles*** begins the marriage of decor and rhythm in his work. Without words, with no indication of scene, its title promises what Kahn would call a decor made of rhythm.

Against the background of the expansiveness, both creative and physical, of ***Romances sans paroles***, *Cellulairement* resounds like a sudden and violent slamming of a door. If a good part of Western Europe comprised the contextual horizon of ***Romances sans paroles,*** *Cellulairement* had only the four small walls of a prison cell in which to germinate. But by opposing the expansiveness of ***Romances sans paroles*** to the confinement of *Cellulairement*, we do not mean to characterize it as representative of closure or poetic regression, for in the latter collection Verlaine continued his study of decor and rhythm. What

Cellulairement reflects instead is the poet's passage from outward-bound discovery to introspection. A place of confinement and punishment, the prison also provides enclosure and security. Victor Brombert draws an analogy between the prison cell and the monastic cell, place of solitary reflection and meditation, both which played so strongly on the poetic imagination of the nineteenth century.[4] Verlaine did in fact make his prison cell a kind of monastic cell, for it was there that he underwent conversion to Catholicism and was moved to compose religious poetry.

As Brombert suggests, the confinement of prison does not shut off movement toward the exterior. On the contrary, it adds to the conceptual opposition between inside and outside a desire for the outside as a real space, previously available and assumed, now denied and thus explicitly coveted. This place which favors contemplation, setting the scene for self-exploration, creates at the same time a scene of aspiration beyond present confines, either through physical escape or spiritual transcendence.

The word "cellulairement," coined as an adverb by Verlaine,[5] tells in what manner the poems were composed: in confinement and in solitude. But it also carries associations which go beyond describing the poetic space of production. Just as ***Romances sans paroles*** evokes lack of verbal impediment, so too does the title *Cellulairement* speak of poetic form as well as evoking the place and manner of composition. On the level of the poem, Kahn spoke of Verlaine's "cellules métriques"—those unexpected rhythms which so often clashed with traditional meters and cesuras in his poetry. In the unity which is a poem there are cells which are smaller still: the rhyming fragments at the end of the poetic line, or the syllable, the smallest constitutive element of French verse. The word "cell" resounds on the many levels of the poem, pointing to the smallest elements of the poem which Verlaine crafted, not in order to confine poetically, but in order to *refine* poetically. Here is some of his densest and most intropective poetry, different from the spirited *élan* characteristic of the ***Romances sans paroles***.

The questions at issue for the poem are multiple and as complex as is the multiple self finding voice in the lyric subject. This subject at times seeks to be situated in space, at other times to escape that very confinement: the spatial contours of Verlaine's poetry run the gamut from frames clearly grounded in referential description to dreamlike musings free of representational images. And the music of his poetry is as unpredictable as the picture it paints: unconventional rhythms strain conventional meters; rarely used meters push for acceptance. Numerous critics have remarked on the formal variety in Verlaine's poetry of this period, where meters, strophic divisions and rhymes are continually found combined in new patterns. The subject acquires its materiality and its voice through the images and sounds of the poem. If lyricism revolves around the representation of the self, then this quest must also take place on formal terrain; as the poem literally takes shape, we discern the seeking self as well.

Let us now turn to the **"Almanach"** to consider these questions. This series poses not only a structural problem by presenting a group of poems sharing the same form, the sonnet, but varying wildly in the practice of that form, it also raises many interesting questions in its kaleidoscopic treatment of representation and subjectivity. Although united formally, these four sonnets offer astounding variety in every other way.

At the end of 1873, Verlaine wrote to Lepelletier from the prison at Mons, and with this letter included the four sonnets which he first entitled "Mon Almanach pour 1874." The sonnets themselves were originally named for the four seasons, suggesting, as well as temporal change, a whole in the unity of the year. This aspect of coherence would not endure, for in the manuscript of *Cellulairement*, when Verlaine retitled the series **"Almanach pour l'année passée,"** he substituted the Roman numerals I-IV for its seasonal titles. And as we know, Verlaine eventually scattered the four seasons of *Cellulairement* to the four winds of his later collections, where all but the first sonnet underwent only minor revisions. It is this dispersal that we seek to reverse in order to return as near as possible to the scene of writing and to the constitution of the Verlainian lyric subject.

From the beginning, then, the **"Almanach"** was not only conceived as a series, but also presented in terms of a unity: the year. The original titles of its poems, **"Printemps," "Été," "Automne," "Hiver,"** tell of the unfolding seasons, a linear, chronological progression. This forward movement in time, the principal aspect of traditional narrative, suggests to the reader that a story will be told. But when read together, the individual poems give little sense of a narrative progression: both in their "content" and their mode of expression they seem diverse and largely disconnected. Their metric makeup ranges from the octosyllables of **"Printemps"** to the highly unusual thirteen-syllable line of **"Hiver."** No meter is repeated, and each sonnet has a different rhyme scheme. Likewise the pastoral scene of **"Printemps"** offers no apparent link to the noisy, smoky picture of London painted in **"Hiver."**

The words we have just used, "scene" and "picture," suggest a comparison with painting. Let us consider for a moment Monet's studies of the cathedral at Rouen, depicted periodically in the changing light of the evolving day. This series offers a skeletal narrative as if with a sequence of still shots: by capturing the same structure at discrete moments of the day, they chart temporal progression. The references to seasons in the titles lead us to expect such pictures or stories corresponding to points in time. But in the poems of the **"Almanach,"** even those descriptive elements that would characterize a season do not consistently appear. For although the country landscape of **"Printemps"** gives us springtime images, **"Hiver"** offers no element that is specifically hibernal. Even **"Automne,"** which can be characterized as an ode to drunken forgetfulness, presents no clear justification for its title. Verlaine changed the title to **"Vendanges"** before publishing it in ***Jadis et***

naguère, offering us a linking clue: the grape harvest supplies the intermediate term between autumn and drunkenness.

We must then conclude that the **"Almanach"** disappoints the promises in its titles of referentiality and narrativity. But let us suggest with Laurent Jenny that poetry, even of the most lyric and nonrepresentational sort, presents a narrative of its own kind. He writes: "Est-ce que les poèmes, si lyriques soient-ils, ne nous racontent pas aussi des 'histoires'? Ce sentiment parfois, à leur lecture, que 'c'est toute une vie' qu'ils narrent en silence, scellée dans le métal de quelques mots. Ce qu'on appelle une 'evocation'. Ou encore cette impression que c'est une histoire 'à sa façon'."[6] He suggests that the broadest, most inclusive definition of narrative would be "un message qui énonce le devenir du sujet," and that poetry as well as prose can be read for such a message. Even if a poem cannot be considered referential to external reality, it is narrative insofar as it carries an itinerary. Jenny is careful to nuance his discussion, to show the difference of lyric narration from prose narration. Although prose generally carries reference to historical time, its story enmeshed in the ticking of the clock and in the march of years, the poem, and above all the modern lyric, does not. The chronology of the poem relies on the order in which it presents its images and events, an order that is not necessarily conditioned by time as we know it. Thus in the sequence of the poem we find the subject in movement, but a movement which is oriented by the unfolding of the poem rather than by time or direction.

Is our conventional notion of the lyric poem not compatible with Jenny's definition of narrative as "le devenir du sujet"? We are conditioned to experience lyric and narrative as distinct modes with radically different principles of composition. Yet the lyric is, fundamentally, an adventure of the self. Its subject is that creature found so fascinating by each of us, the individual in search of self-integration and self-expression. But that fascination assumes different manners of expression, represented by the different genres. The manner of expression of lyricism is to inscribe the drama of the subject, not in the temporal framework of historical narration, but in another way: to experience the "devenir du sujet" through the "devenir du poème." The stuff of the poem, its rhythms and its decor, conspire to situate the subject. Its unfolding images strive to shape the experience of subjectivity. Lyricism traces a certain story of the subject as it weaves itself into the fabric of its discourse. We can then expect to find a *poetic* itinerary in the **"Almanach"** coincident with the narrative of the subject's becoming.

In the title *Cellulairement* we discerned the evocation of a *recueillement*, a privileged word in the nineteenth-century poetic vocabulary which suggests a movement of interiorization. On the level of decor, the **"Almanach"** traces this same movement from without to within, for it begins with the pastoral scene of **"Printemps,"** next moving inside to the hazy interior of **"Été,"** and then shifting to the psychic interiorization of **"Automne"** where the space of the poem goes no farther than "dans la tête" of the speaking subject. If these three poems follow a consistent progression from outside to inside, the final sonnet, **"Hiver,"** takes a step beyond this progression, constituting a crossing-over to "another side" which we hope to clarify during the course of this analysis. This sonnet returns us to an outside scene, but a dream scene which breaks with the referentiality of the previous poems. There exist, on the many levels, representational and metrical, of the **"Almanach,"** parallel itineraries which journey from **"Printemps"** through **"Été"** and **"Automne,"** finally stepping off into uncharted territory with **"Hiver."**

On a metrical level, the sonnets posit another progression which interacts with and sheds light on the narrative movement of the poems. Their different meters and rhyme schemes present a progression which tends from the traditional and regular towards the unconventional and irregular. The meter of these sonnets progresses toward longer and uneven lines. The first two, in octosyllables and alexandrines, are echoed by the last two, in lines of nine and thirteen syllables respectively. If the alexandrine was the conventional meter for the sonnet from Ronsard on and throughout most of the nineteenth century, Elwert tells us that there is also a historical precedent for the octosyllabic sonnet which enjoyed a certain success during the seventeenth century.[7] On the other hand, the nine-syllable line, unusual in itself, had no precedent in the sonnet. And the thirteen-syllable line was practically unheard of before the generation of Banville. Its awkwardness is translated by the title which Verlaine gave to **"Hiver"** when he finally published it in ***Jadis et naguère:*** **"Sonnet boiteux."**

We know from Verlaine's **"Art poétique"** that he considered uneven lines the most malleable and musical of poetic meters: "De la musique avant toute chose / Et pour cela préfère l'impair." At the same time, he was not afraid to take liberties with rhythm in the alexandrine by displacing the cesura, liberties which contributed to the eventual downfall of this *maître vers* and the inauguration of *vers libre*. Thus in tending towards uneven meters in the **"Almanach,"** initially via innovative rhythms in the alexandrine, Verlaine was tending toward what he felt to be at the heart of his poetry, a supple and sinuous music, following no steady or preconditioned beat. With this in mind, we can read the **"Almanach"** as a résumé of the poetic itinerary charted by Verlaine from ***La bonne chanson*** through ***Romances sans paroles*** and *Cellulairement*, his straining of conventional meters with unusual rhythms and ultimately his experimentation with uncommon, uneven meters. As the first example of a thirteen-syllable line in his work, **"Hiver"** once again stands out as a singular poetic statement at the end of the **"Almanach,"** where Verlaine ventures onto an evocative horizon not previously explored.

Rhyme also divides the **"Almanach"** into two halves, the first two poems offering relatively conventional schemes, the last two more unusual ones. While **"Printemps"** and

"Été" comply with the tradition of alternating masculine and feminine rhymes, in **"Automne"** all rhymes are feminine. And although there is alternation of rhyme gender in **"Hiver,"** it operates on the level of the strophe rather than on that of rhyme pair, such that the first quatrain and first tercet consist of solely masculine rhymes, and the second quatrain and second tercet of uniquely feminine rhymes. In the final tercet, rhyme breaks down altogether, making **"Hiver"** the only instance of blank verse in Verlaine's work.

We propose to trace the narrative of the **"Almanach"** as each poem unfolds and as each sonnet gives way to the next, paying particular attention to decor and rhythm. For these are the elements that will delineate the space in which the subject exists and show the modulations of a subjective voice.

I. [**"Printemps"**][8]

La bise se rue à travers
Les buissons tout noirs et tout verts,
Glaçant la neige éparpillée
Dans la campagne ensoleillée.

L'odeur est aigre près des bois,
L'horizon chante avec des voix,
Les coqs des clochers des villages
Luisent crûment sur les nuages.

C'est délicieux de marcher
A travers ce brouillard léger
Qu'un vent taquin parfois retrousse.

Ah! fi de mon vieux feu qui tousse!
J'ai des fourmis dans les talons.
«Voici l'Avril!» Vieux cœur, allons!

"Printemps" has many prosaic elements. Although a sonnet, a fixed-form poem, it is written in rhymed couplets, a rhyme scheme that Verlaine, like many other poets, usually matched with nonfixed, or less lyrical, forms. Indeed, the *rimes plates* of **"Printemps"** seem to contradict the spirit of the sonnet, a highly constrained poetic form. Having no metrical figure of closure, couplets favor forward, linear (proselike) progression, rather than vertical patterns of equivalence expected from the traditional *rimes embrassées* of the sonnet. In fact, when Verlaine retouched **"Printemps"** for eventual inclusion in ***Sagesse*** (III, xi), the tendency of the rhymed couplet toward continuation got the better of him: he added three more distichs, removed strophic divisions, and published it as a twenty-line poem of no fixed form. The version of **"Printemps"** under consideration is significantly different from the published one.

"Printemps," recounted in the third person, begins as pure description and is reminiscent of some of the pastoral travel poems of "Paysages belges," of ***Romances sans paroles***, that were unapologetically representational. Like **"Simples fresques I,"** for example, **"Printemps"** paints a colorful picture of a landscape: there the "verdâtre et rose / Des collines," here the "buissons tout noirs et tout verts." But **"Printemps"** contains more than just these visually descriptive elements; indeed, it runs the gamut of the senses. One feels the icy breeze, smells the bitter wood, hears the song of the horizon. Even taste is implied by the word "délicieux" in line nine. So although the first three strophes of **"Printemps"** form a highly scenic description of an unpeopled landscape, the sensory elements upon which the description depends imply a subject of these perceptions.

"Printemps" begins the subjective itinerary of the **"Almanach"** by charting a gradual progression from the impersonal to the personal, ending with the emergence of the speaking subject in the final tercet. "La bise" is the grammatical subject of the first strophe which contains strictly natural elements and whose objective description is indebted to the Parnasse. The second quatrain moves a step closer to human activity, for here a village enters the decor with its steeples and weather vanes. This strophe offers poetic animation as well, as the horizon is personified, engaged in the human activity of singing. But immediately thereafter, animation is put in question by the rooster, which turns out not to be living, but an inanimate copy. Who is present to smell the acrid underbrush or to see the steeple shining against a backdrop of clouds? Unlike the first strophe where the North wind acts as an agent and interacts with other inanimate natural elements, the second strophe alludes to human presence, a smelling, listening, seeing subject in a human landscape.

Strophe three begins with an echo of the first in the transversal movement signalled by "à travers" which, in both strophes, sets the scene for the enjambement between their first and second lines. But instead of the North wind rushing through the thicket, here there is the decidedly human activity of walking through a fog. The parallelism of the enjambements is bolstered by the repetition of the rhythm of the first two lines (divided into measures of 5/3 and 3/5). This combination forms a lively contrast to the otherwise regular division of the octosyllables of the sonnet into two even measures of four syllables. In retrospect, by virtue of these parallel constructions, an implicit metaphor between the North wind and the not-yet-visible subject is suggested. Although impersonal, perhaps this forceful wind is, after all, anything but inanimate. Indeed, *anima*, meaning breath, more aptly describes the wind which blows through this poem, from the powerful "bise" to the "vent taquin." Figures of life, wind and breath are also figures for rhythm, the modulations of the human voice (represented by the singing horizon), and the gait of the subject wandering through the countryside. The subject, emerging from the blowing wind, follows its rhythm and the path it takes.

But who is the subject of the verb "marcher" and who might be the author of the observation "C'est délicieux"? The enjoyment which this phrase expresses is savored all the more by the dieresis in "délici-eux": although we have yet to glimpse the subject cloaked in mist, this expression of pleasure suggests subjective presence. In line eleven the force of the North wind is mitigated: first a powerful agent, now the wind is seen as a playful companion ("vent taquin"). This personification offers another instance of the animation of impersonal nature against the backdrop of a largely depopulated landscape.

The final strophe erupts with the interjection "Ah!" followed quickly by the inaugurative use of the first person. Unique in this poem, a three-part rhythm divided into uneven measures of one, five and two syllables ("Ah! / fi de mon vieux feu / qui tousse!") marks this turning point, introducing the speaking subject by recreating the unpredictable rhythms of spoken language. The scene moves indoors, if only momentarily, next to a "vieux feu." Although this move inside presages the interior scene of the following sonnet, within the space of the present poem it forms the prelude to a voyage, perhaps preceding the cross-country journey just followed in the first three strophes. Thus the temporal chronology of the events of the poem does not necessarily coincide with its subjective itinerary, which follows the gradual shift in the poem from a landscape of absence to the immediacy of the speaking subject's voice. The spirit of vagabondage (the other side of incarceration) reigns in the penultimate line where the first person subject pronoun is uttered once and for all—"J'ai des fourmis dans les talons"—and is captured by the meandering spirit of the couplets of the poem and the unpredictable itinerary of the wind. Like them, the wandering subject has no other guide than forward progression: one foot placed in front of another, the advance of the poetic line.

II. [**"Été"**[9]]

L'espoir luit comme un brin de paille dans l'étable.
Que crains-tu de la guêpe ivre de son vol fou?
Vois, le soleil toujours poudroie à quelque trou.
Que ne t'endormais-tu, le coude sur la table?

Pauvre âme pâle, au moins cette eau du puits glacé,
Bois-la. Puis dors après. Allons, tu vois, je reste,
Et je dorloterai les rêves de ta sieste,
Et tu chantonneras comme un enfant bercé.

Midi sonne. De grâce, éloignez-vous madame.
Il dort. C'est étonnant[10] comme les pas de femme
Résonnent[11] au cerveau des pauvres malheureux.

Midi sonne. J'ai fait arroser dans la chambre.
Va, dors![12] L'espoir luit comme un caillou dans un creux.
Ah, quand refleuriront les roses de septembre!

"Été" is a sonnet true to the tradition of Ronsard thanks to its alexandrines and rhyme scheme of two quatrains of *rimes embrassées* followed by two tercets composed of a distich and the four final lines in *rimes croisées*. Like **"Printemps," "Été"** respects the rule of alternation of masculine and feminine rhymes. The only way it departs from classic sonnet structure is by not repeating the rhymes of the first quatrain in the second, but for Verlaine there was nothing new in this venial sin of versification, a practice tolerated since Baudelaire. Within this very conventional frame, the only regular sonnet of the series, Verlaine weaves a rather extraordinary web of unusual rhythms. His predilection is for a short measure followed by a long one, as in the first line which is broken after the third syllable: "L'espoir luit / comme un brin de paille dans l'étable."

Much has been written on Verlaine's use of regular and irregular meters, with differing conclusions. Henri Morier, in his article on the "césure verlainienne," counsels the reader to respect the traditional mid-alexandrine break when scanning Verlaine's poetry, in order to appreciate the tension created between the syntax of the poem and its meter.[13] Other critics are moved to ignore the hemistich which Verlaine's alexandrines often seem to disregard themselves, instead scanning the measures of the lines based on syntax of the poem alone. Although these points of view are not necessarily mutually exclusive, Morier is certainly right to suggest that Verlaine was ever conscious of the traditional cesura, even when he chose not to honor it.

The alexandrines of **"Été,"** most of which can be scanned in the conventional manner at the hemistich, offer a relatively steady beat. But the syntax of the poem does battle with this beat, following its own lively rhythms. Michel Serres sees an emergence of order in the images of this poem and in its practice of the alexandrine which echos the insistent ringing of twelve o'clock in its twelve syllables. Order emerges from the erratic movement of the drunken wasp's flight and the disorder of the wisps of straw on the stable floor. At the same time undifferentiated, meaningless noise constitutes the unchanging background against which meter and rhythm come to form a meaningful order. Serres summarizes the movement of **"Été"** in this way: ". . . c'est l'ensemencement du quasi-périodique sur le multiple, de la redondance sur le chaos. . . . Du sommeil à l'éveil. . . . Et de l'inconscient au conscient. . . . Le rhythme apparaît sur le bruit de fond. . . . Midi sonne, advient le temps. . . . Un ordre se forme par le rhythme et la musique."[14] If there is a narrative in this poem, it is one which charts the emergence of regularity, beginning with images of incoherence and urging towards the regular chiming of high noon. Largely governed by the choppy rhythms which seek to imitate patterns of speech, the poem ends in rhythmic coherence with the countdown offered by the three short initial measures of the final tercet: "Midi sonne" (3 syllables), "Va, dors!" (2), "Ah" (1). The emergence of rhythm parallels the emergence of the conscious subject.

The luminous sunshine of **"Printemps"** pierces through a knothole in the decor of **"Été"** and is dispersed in this interior scene: "Vois, le soleil toujours poudroie à quelque trou." It is a scene of interiors in a number of ways: this inside setting is also a highly intimate one, deriving from the subject's direct address, in tender, protective conversation, to an unidentified *tu*. The tone of this poem is quite different from the largely descriptive **"Printemps."** The language of **"Été"** is at once more metaphoric, sprinkled with comparisons, and at the same time less literary thanks to its conversational tone. The concluding tercet of **"Printemps"** marks the transition to this conversational mode. Although **"Été"** is non-descriptive, it carries passing indications of setting: of a table, a room, water to drink and water sprinkled on the dry, dusty dirt floor of the barn. We are still in a country setting, but know not much more: this decor is a mystery that the few references of the speaking subject do as much to confound as they do to clarify. **"Printemps"** and **"Été"** are directly opposed to each other in the sense that the subject is as evasive in the first poem as physical description is in the second, whereas description is foregrounded in **"Printemps,"** as is the first-person speaking subject in **"Été."**

Je is above all defined by verbal interactions, addressing a masculine *tu* in all but the first tercet, where the speaking subject brushes aside an intrusive, feminine *vous*. This subject is a conscious one, as opposed to the troubled sleeper. The continual critical interest in this poem focuses in particular on the mysteries of *who* and *where*, mysteries confounded by the direct address. For if direct address lends immediacy, it also sets the frame of the poem at such an intimate proximity to the conversation that reference to decor is relegated to the margins of the conversation. The speaking subject itself is delineated only in terms of its interlocutors.

Serres suggests that the resounding "pas de femmes" echo the feminine rhymes which are characterized by an additional mute *e*: "Alors la rime féminine ensemence partout son manque ou son supplément, elle produit çà et là l'impair, la musique: c'est étonnant comme les pas de femme résonnent. . . ." The image of these feminine footsteps reverberating in the unfortunate man's head also provides the thread which links **"Été"** to the following sonnet, **"Automne,"** composed entirely of feminine rhymes and confined to the subject's brain. This poetic space is similar to that found in Baudelaire's "Spleen" poems where, for example, "mon triste cerveau" supplies the terrain for intense thought or emotion.

III. [**"Automne"**]

Les choses qui chantent dans la tête
Alors que la mémoire est absente,
Ecoutez, c'est notre sang qui chante . . .
O musique lointaine et discrète!

Ecoutez! c'est notre sang qui pleure
Alors que notre âme s'est enfuie,
D'une voix jusqu'alors inouïe
Et qui va se taire tout à l'heure.

Frère du sang de la vigne rose,
Frère du vin de la veine noire,[15]
O vin, ô sang, c'est l'apothéose!

Chantez, pleurez! Chassez la mémoire
Et chassez l'âme, et jusqu'aux ténèbres
Magnétisez nos pauvres vertèbres.

With **"Automne"** begins the second pair of poems, both written in uneven meters. With the arrival of Verlaine's privileged nine-syllable line (also used in his **"Art poétique"**), we find the song, which was whispered in the first two sonnets, foregrounded. Let us recall the line from **"Printemps,"** "L'horizon chante avec des voix," and this one from **"Été":** "Et tu chantonneras comme un enfant bercé." In the first case a distant accompaniment and in **"Été"** the low murmuring of a child being lulled to sleep, here in **"Automne"** decor has fallen away, giving way to pure music or rhythm: "Les choses qui chantent dans la tête."

The subject that we have been tracing—or the subjects whose accumulation might have something to tell us about subjectivity—undergoes modulation once again in **"Automne."** Here the play of light and visual imagery—the glittering snow of **"Printemps"** or the twig of hay gleaming in the summer sunlight—have disappeared, while voice and sound take over the register of subjectivity. In addition, the shift to plural pronouns tends to undo the effects of intimacy produced by **"Été."** *Je* gives way to *nous*, and *tu* to the implied *vous* of the imperative. But it is unclear whether this *nous* is an authentic one, whether it includes another or others, such as the "frère du sang," or simply serves to blur the identity of this speaking subject whose senses are already blurred by wine, whose blood runs red with *le vin de l'oubli*.

At the same time as plurality marks this subject, absence plays a role in its constitution. The absence of memory and soul is the condition for the song. Unlike the conscious subject of **"Été,"** this one rejects reason and the mental faculties: it is instead "notre sang qui chante." While the referent or referents to *nous* are vague, subjectivity is literally incarnated by the body, and particularly the interior of the body. Beginning "dans la tête" we see this speaking subject from the inside: the blood, the veins, the vertebrae. This *intimacy*, whose etymological sense (from the Latin *INTIMVS*) is "the condition of being inmost or deepest," and is of a wholly different kind from that of **"Été."**

What is the route taken by the three speaking subjects encountered so far? The first, placed in a country setting, translated a sense of pleasure by following the path of the wind and describing the landscape. The second took shape through speech, establishing itself as a distinct, conscious subject in a nonspecific decor. From this conscious subject we shift to the irrationality and incoherence of **"Automne."** Here the voice is highly subjective, for it speaks of its own experience, rather than responding to another's and refers to the sensations of its own body. In **"Automne"** inside is turned out; the most visible decor is all that is usually considered internal: psychological make-up, blood and bones. Its message is a supremely poetic one: the song counts for itself alone. That the subject's specificity gives way to vague plurality, that the song gives way to tears in the second strophe, that the voice in question is both unheard of and unhearable ("inouï")—all this uncertainty and vagueness tell us that the distant music and the intermittent song, its emanation, count for all. The subject has in a sense made itself over into the multiplicity of song. Rhythm, the voice, incarnate in body, in turn make possible subjectivity. The subject's affliction is reminiscent of the anxiety of "tu" in the previous poem: subjective experience has moved to center stage. The song is allowed to represent the subject's distress, and in its conflict the multiple nature of subjectivity is revealed.

The rhythms of **"Automne"** divide the sonnet clearly in two. The changing rhythms of the quatrains are opposed to the consistent division of all the lines of the tercets into two measures of four and five syllables. This steady incantatory beat is reinforced by the repetition in the first tercet: "Frère du sang de la vigne rose, / Frère du vin de la veine noire." Indeed, the content of these lines are as religious as is the litany which their form suggests. The images of the first tercet are clearly Christian: in the passage from wine to blood one reads the transubstantiation of Christ, and the apotheosis suggests another transformation, from human to god.

In fact, the more supernatural and therefore pagan reference to mesmerism in the final tercet continues to deal with transformations, here the transformation of states of consciousness. The starting point of the poem deals with the physiological changes caused by intoxication, changes such as the "seeing double" which leads, perhaps, to the pluralization of the subject pronouns. These final changes are of a more profound sort, operating on the boundaries of absence and presence, of the physical and the psychological.

The imperatives, "Chantez, pleurez! Chassez," chase two enjambements through the final tercet to its enigmatic last command, "Magnétisez nos pauvres vertèbres." "Vertèbre" comes from the Latin verb meaning to turn *(VERTERE)*. From the spinning head of the drunken subject to the multiplication of conscious states, this poem turns, revolves, upon questions of subjectivity. The final plural rhyme, the only one in the poem, hints again at the multiple, if unstable, constitution of this subject.

IV. [**"Hiver"**]

Ah! vraiment c'est triste, ah! vraiment ça finit trop mal.
Il n'est pas permis d'être à ce point infortuné.
Ah! vraiment c'est trop la mort du naïf animal
Qui voit tout son sang couler sous son regard fané.

Londres fume et crie. O quelle ville de la Bible!
Le gaz flambe et nage et les enseignes sont vermeilles.
Et les maisons dans leur ratatinement terrible
Epouvantent comme un sénat[16] de petites vieilles.

Tout l'affreux passé saute, piaule, miaule et glapit
Dans le brouillard rose et jaune et sale des Sohos
Avec des *indeeds* et des *all rights* et des *haôs*.

Non vraiment c'est trop un martyre sans espérance,[17]
Non vraiment cela finit trop mal, vraiment c'est triste:
O le feu du ciel sur cette ville de la Bible!

If **"Automne"** offers the picture of a subject at once split between absence and presence, **"Hiver"** finds the subject completely shattered. The first person has disappeared in favor of the third person, and yet this poem is anything but impersonal, for it is sprinkled with repeated interjections ("Ah! vraiment c'est triste") that point to a speaking subject. Distressed in the previous poem, here the speaking subject expresses something resembling sheer panic. Images of previous poems return in **"Hiver,"** but are made over to coincide with its violent, chaotic tone. The first word, the interjection, "Ah!," introduced the speaking subject in **"Printemps."** But rather than the carefree expression of the first sonnet, or the melancholic hopefulness of **"Été"**—"Ah, quand refleuriront les roses de septembre!"—here this interjection repeated three times in the first quatrain expresses unadulterated despair. Its replacement in the final strophe with the negative "*Non* vraiment c'est trop" [my emphasis] suggests complete resignation.

The repetition of these phrases in the first and final strophes reinforces the frame formed of a scene of violent martyrdom. The blood which sang and flowed freely through veins in **"Automne"** here is spilled under the watchful eye of a dying animal. The "vieux feu qui tousse" of **"Printemps"** is made over in the final image of a fiery sky in **"Hiver."** What is framed in the two central strophes is a landscape, but an entirely different one from that found in **"Printemps."** This cityscape is rendered vivid both visually and phonically in this fierce portrait of London. Colors jump from the page: "vermeille, rose, jaune." The innocuous "brouillard léger" of **"Printemps"** is here transformed into the menacing "brouillard rose et jaune et sale" (reminiscent of Baudelaire's "brouillard sale et jaune" in "Les sept vieillards").

On the level of sound, the song heard throughout the other sonnets has disappeared, giving way here to chaotic, incoherent noise. These noises come from inanimate sources, beginning with the city itself: "Londres fume et crie" and reaching a cacophonous climax with the horrid, shrieking past: "l'affreux passé saute, piaule, miaule et glapit." This last line recalls Baudelaire once more, "Les monstres glapissants, hurlants, grognants, rampants" of "Au lecteur," and along with them all the violence and despair associated with spleen. At the end of this litany of sounds comes perhaps the most incoherent sounds of all: the foreign words, simple interjections, listed in line eleven: "Avec des *indeeds* et des *all rights* et des *haôs*."

It is fitting that **"Hiver"** carry so many references to the preceding poems in the **"Almanach"** (as well as Baudelairian echoes), since it is above all the weight of the past which afflicts its subject. The speaking subject of **"Printemps"** looks forward to the budding season and ends on a note of continuation with "allons." This word is repeated in line six of **"Été"** which also closes with a look to the future: "Ah, quand refleuriront les roses de septembre!" In **"Automne,"** memory is absent and the past is thus effaced. Although these first three sonnets look to the future rather than to the past, **"Hiver"** ends the cycle of seasons and poems and can thus only look back. The past makes a violent return in line nine: "Tout l'affreux passé saute. . . ." This poem is conditioned by a memory which haunts the speaking subject. Irreversible closure blocks off the future: "cela finit trop mal."

If the narrative of the subject throughout these sonnets traces its emergence, coming to consciousness, multiplication in misery and final breakdown, then in its own narrative, **"Hiver"** constitutes a final entropic movement, for the sonnet as well as for the subject. This sonnet, which would be retitled **"Sonnet boiteux,"** has become the unfortunate, limping, pitiful creature seen in the persecuted animal of the third line: ". . . [le] naïf animal / Qui voit tout son sang couler sous un regard fané." The thirteen-syllable line, so close to the supremely symmetrical alexandrine, and yet so far from perfection, suffers from excess: one little syllable is much too much. The self-conscious poem tells us as much with the "trop" which it repeats four times. Likewise, as it is the final syllable that ruins the line, it is the final strophe which spoils the rhyme. The quatrains begin in a regular, if unconventional fashion with *rimes embrassées* alternating rhyme gender between strophes. In the first tercet all we find is the rather odd pairing of two English words ("Sohos" and "haôs"), the first misspelled with a final *-s* and the second barely decipherable to this native speaker. In the final tercet, rhyme has broken down altogether. Again the poem confesses: "cela finit trop mal."

An odd sort of closure this is, for an itinerary ending in a dispersal which the ultimate dismemberment of the manuscript of *Cellulairement* irrevocably confirmed. One could speculate that Verlaine, a lost soul writing from a foreign prison, was moved to chart the emergence of his own despair and the disintegration of his sense of self through his speaking subject. And yet I hesitate to conflate the two, for parallel to this itinerary which seems to follow the unbecoming, rather than the "*devenir* du sujet," exists another movement yearning toward poetic innovation which serves to confirm life rather than subjective death. Verlaine's experimentation with unusual meters, rhythms and rhymes went to the heart of poetry as he understood it: the too much or too little of the feminine rhyme and of the odd meter allowed him to experiment with limits and with margins. That the Verlainian poem might live and breathe, its subject must remain on the margins of representability, for ultimately it is the subject's hesitation between consolidation and dispersal that the poem captures in its own hesitations between precision and uncertainty.

Notes

1. Originally collected in *Cellulairement*, published in *Jadis et naguère*. All references, unless otherwise indicated, are to *Œuvres poétiques complètes* (Paris: Pléiade, 1962).
2. Letter to Lepelletier, dated from Mons, November 24, 1873. *Correspondance de Paul Verlaine*, ed. Ad. van Bever (Paris: Messein, 1922), I, 120–21.
3. Kahn, *Symbolistes et décadents* (Paris: Vanier, 1902), p. 89.
4. *La prison romantique* (Paris: Corti, 1975).
5. Compare the adverbial form of the title of Verlaine's *Parallèlement* (1889).
6. "Le poétique et le narratif," *Poétique* 28 (1976): 440.
7. *Traité de versification française* (Paris: Klincksieck, 1965), p. 178.
8. This version is from the manuscript of *Cellulairement*, described by Ernest Dupuy in "Étude critique sur le texte d'un manuscrit de P. Verlaine," *Revue d'histoire littéraire de la France* 20 (1913): 489–516.
9. I have chosen to reproduce the published versions of the final three sonnets since the variations from *Cellulairement* are minor, intending to polish the poems as well as correct faulty grammar. Substantive changes from the earlier manuscript are indicated in the notes below. "Été" was eventually published as *Sagesse*, III, iii. Cf. Elénore Zimmermann's study of the final three sonnets of the "Almanach" as they illustrate the poetic system elaborated by Verlaine in prison. In *Magies de Verlaine* (Paris: Corti, 1967), pp. 92–109.
10. In *Cellulairement*, read *et c'est affreux* for *c'est étonnant*.
11. In *Cellulairement*, read *Répondent* for *Résonnent.*
12. In *Cellulairement*, read *Il dort*! for *Va, dors*!
13. *Dictionnaire de poétique et de rhétorique* (Paris: P.U.F., 1961), pp. 189–92.
14. "Sciences exactes et littérature," *Dictionnaire historique, thématique et technique des littératures* 2 vols. (Paris: Larousse, 1986), p. 1487.
15. In *Cellulairement*, read Frère du *vin* de la vigne rose, / Frère du *sang* de la veine noire . . .
16. In *Cellulairement*, read *tas noir* for *sénat.*
17. In *Cellulairement*, read *assurance* for *espérance.*

Russell S. King (essay date 1998)

SOURCE: "Verlaine's *Romances sans paroles*: The Inscription of Gender," in *Nineteenth Century French Studies*, Vol. 27, Nos. 1 & 2, Fall 1998 and Winter 1999, pp. 117–31.

[*In the following essay, King discusses Verlaine's sexuality as it appears in the language of his poems.*]

> Je distinguerai donc deux bisexualités, deux façons opposées de penser la possibilité et la pratique de la bisexualité:

> 1. La bisexualité comme fantasme d'un être total qui vient à la place de la peur de la castration, et voile la différence sexuelle . . .
>
> 2. A cette bisexualité fusionnelle, effaçante, qui veut conjurer la castration, j'oppose l'autre bisexualité, celle dont chaque sujet non enfermé dans le faux théâtre de la représentation phallocentrique, institue son univers érotique.
>
> C. Clément, H. Cixous, *La Jeune Née* (155)

> Soyons deux enfants, soyons deux jeunes filles, Eprises de rien et de tout étonnées.
>
> Verlaine, ***Romances sans paroles***[1]

Paul Verlaine's ***Romances sans paroles*** (1874) can be described as a bisexual text in its autobiographical origins, in that the bulk of the twenty one poems are inspired by, or depict, however indirectly, either the heterosexual relationship with the poet's young wife, Mathilde, or the homosexual relationship with the poet Arthur Rimbaud. The immediate biographical context of the Verlaine/Mathilde/ Rimbaud triangle, stretching from Rimbaud's arrival in Paris on 10 September 1871, thirteen months after Verlaine's marriage on 11 August 1870, to the birth of the son Georges on 30 October 1871, and to Verlaine's final meeting with Rimbaud in Stuttgart in January 1875, has been frequently reported, described, dramatized, and is the subject of this paper only as a preliminary.

Few questions, however, have been asked about how gender and Verlaine's sexuality are explicitly or implicitly inscribed into the language of his actual poetry. Can one hypothesize, for example, an "écriture masculine," an "écriture bisexuelle" or an "écriture homosexuelle," which transcends the purely biographical, and sex and sexuality as thematic content? To what extent can writing be defined as masculine, feminine, or, to use Cixous' term, bisexual? Attempts to isolate grammatical, syntactic or lexical features, like those of Robin Lakoff, to which we shall refer later, to define woman's writing have proved controversial and provocative. In an entirely different approach, Hélène Cixous, it would seem, uses the labels masculine and feminine, not as fixed and separate binary categories which relate to sexual difference, man and woman, but as coded metaphors for positions which transcend fixed sexual binaries. Cixous' two definitions of bisexuality are centered around two sorts of binaries: the first seeks to fuse the two sexes into a complete totality—a kind of androgynous bisexuality, whilst the second suggests an unstable, free inter-play between two non-fixed positions, outside of the "false theatre" of phallocentricity, which may be called *masculine* and *feminine* (that is, gender) which may or may not be related to the categories of *male* and *female* (that is, sex). The same question of bisexual identity has been brilliantly scrutinized and theorized more recently by Marjorie Garber's *Vice Versa*, and *Bisexual Politics: Theories, Queries & Visions*, edited by Naomi Tucker. In the former Garber examines how the bisexual has been inscribed into a multiplicity of texts, whilst, in the latter volume of essays, many of the writers specifically challenge traditional binarism which underpins gender studies.

Verlaine's poetry has almost always been read in a largely biographical mode: his successive collections have been seen to relate to, and depict, the prevailing relationships, male or female, of the period of composition: for example ***Les Poèmes saturniens*** and his cousin Elisa, ***La Bonne Chanson*** and his fiancée Mathilde Mauté, ***Romances sans paroles*** and his wife and Rimbaud, ***Amour*** and Lucien Létinois, ***Chansons pour elle*** and Eugénie Krantz, and ***Odes en son honneur*** and Philomène Boudin. These people have always provided a primary context for reading and understanding each of his collections of poems. There is no denying that the increasingly mythicized life of the poet and his relationships contributed enormously to his reputation and fame as a poet in the last ten years of his life, and still today provides a powerfully pleasurable context for reading his poetry. It is however not our context.

Verlaine studies have frequently been forced into a straightjacket of binarism: in the intimate inter-textual reading between the two texts of life and poetry, heterosexuality and homosexuality, security and freedom, idealistic and pornographic writing, and good poetry and bad poetry. In other words few readers and critics have sought to study Verlaine's poetic practice, except with reference to binary structuring within some biographical context.

Before we turn specifically to the opening poems of the ***Romances sans paroles***, it is useful to examine how various writers, namely novelist Francis Carco, academic critic E. A. Carter, and novelist/biographer Henri Troyat, have approached Verlaine.

Francis Carco, in his *Verlaine: Poète maudit* (1948), a "l'homme et l'œuvre" account of the poet, structures his analysis and account of the poet around the squalor of the life and the beauty of the poetry. His psychoanalyzing purpose is founded on the over-protectiveness of the mother and the poet's physical ugliness: "Cette faiblesse n'est que trop excusable. Elle provient de la façon dont l'enfant a été élevé, de sa laideur contre laquelle il n'a jamais rien pu" (233). I have no argument with the novelist's eminently readable and vivid account of the poet, but I contest the manner in which descriptive explanation and glib analysis are provided by a convenient dividing up of the personality into various conflicting selves, responding to different impulses of the traditional binary.

A similar binary approach is proclaimed by A. E. Carter in his choice of subtitle: *Verlaine: a study in Parallels* (1969). Carter begins with an account (a picture, an image) of young Verlaine, aged seven, playing with a young girl on the Esplanade at Metz:

> Its Edenic quality is obvious. With the passage of forty years [when Verlaine wrote about it in his *Confessions*] the Esplanade represented his childhood, a paradise where evil could not enter.
>
> (4)

Carter's analysis is established by contrasting the paradise of childhood with failures and evasions of adulthood. The crisis was already apparent during Verlaine's adolescence: "Already in the tormented adolescent of the Lycée Bonaparte we discover the first symptoms of the bisexual tendency which *afflicted* (my emphasis) Verlaine as a man."(15) The visit to Belgium of Verlaine and Rimbaud is seen in the light of childhood and adulthood:

> To Verlaine, the whole adventure was instinctive and sensuous, an abdication of responsibility: "Je nous voyais comme deux bons enfants," are the words Rimbaud puts into his mouth in *Une Saison en Enfer*, "libres de se promener dans le Paradis de tristesse." Childhood, freedom, Paradise: the three terms give us the essentials. Even the sexual factor played a secondary role by comparison. Emotionally trapped in memories of his first years, Verlaine was forever seeking to combine them with the brutal facts of adulthood. It was an obstinate tropism towards a security he never found.
>
> (98–99)

Henri Troyat, in his *Verlaine* (1993), who too focuses on this interface of biography and poetry, deals extensively but in a fairly straightforward manner with the psychological make-up of the poet and how it fashioned his poetry. For example he writes of the association of Verlaine's liking for pornography, masturbation and writing. Consciousness of his ugliness was the source of his homosexual practices. In his chapter 10, entitled *Déchiré entre Mathilde et "Rimbe,"* Troyat writes:

> Dans cette affaire, il est le faible, le mou, la femelle, Rimbaud, le mâle résolu et rude. Le bonheur de Verlaine est de se soumettre, celui de Rimbaud est de dominer. Comme ils se complètent bien, comme ils ont besoin l'un de l'autre! . . . Parfois cependant, las d'être dominé, pénétré, il inverse les rôles. Mais, la plupart du temps, c'est Rimbaud qui est le mâle dans leur accouplement. Le tempérament de Verlaine le pousse à la soumission. Il lécherait volontiers les pieds du vainqueur. Cela ne l'empêche pas d'être séduit, à ses heures, par l'anatomie féminine. Il apprécie autant un gars bien planté qu'une luronne à la poitrine opulente. Est-ce sa faute si ces deux exigences coexistent en lui, s'il est aussi troublé par les fesses d'un garçon que par celles d'une fille? . . . Il est tour à tour "il" et "elle," un amant avec une sensualité féminine, une maîtresse avec un membre viril. En tout cas, Mathilde ne l'inspire plus. Rimbaud le tient à sa merci. Il lui dispense à la fois les clartés de l'esprit et les ténèbres de la chair.
>
> (158–60)

This bisexual behavior is reported in best dramatic fashion for example in his account of Mathilde's meeting with her husband at the Grand Hotel Liégeois in July 1872:

> En apercevant cette jeune femme à demi nue, il s'embrase de nouveau comme s'il ne l'avait pas dédaignée, rejetée, bafouée pour suivre un homme. Après des étreintes viriles qui l'ont comblé, il a un goût de revenez-y pour la chair lisse et pâle qu'il caresse. Elle lui semble même renouvelée par l'expérience qu'il a eue de l'autre sexe.
>
> (174)

What is significant is that Troyat relies heavily on the poetry to substantiate much of his version of what happened, in this case, on lines from **"Birds in the night"**.

It is as if the warnings of the Anglo-American "new critics" of the 40's and 50's had never existed: against the construction of the life from the literary text, and the interpretation of the literary text from the biography:

> The whole view that art is self-expression pure and simple, the transcript of personal feelings and experiences, is demonstrably false. Even when there is close relationship between the work of art and the life of an author, this must never be construed as meaning that the work of art is a mere copy of life. . . . The biographical approach actually obscures a proper comprehension of the literary process, since it breaks up the order of literary tradition to substitute the life-cycle of an individual.
>
> (Wellek & Warren 78)[2]

As an interested party, even ex-Madame Verlaine, Mathilde, in her *Mémoires d'une vie*, written in 1907–08, argues that Verlaine's poetry is understandable only with reference to the poet's life: "L'œuvre de Verlaine est obscure pour ceux qui ne sont pas très au courant de sa vie, puisque, la plupart du temps, il fait allusion à des événements tout personnels." (Troyat 461)

Yet Troyat paradoxically (given his extensive reliance on actual poems) concludes his biographical study of Verlaine, with the "new critical" stance that recognition of poetic value does not depend on the life, a view which became apparent when François Coppée published his *Choix de poésie* in 1896, which detached poems from the individual collections many of which seemed anchored to parts and persons of his life:

> Et le public, en le lisant, n'a nul besoin, contrairement aux assertions de Mathilde, de connaître les péripéties de l'existence de Verlaine pour comprendre et aimer sa bouleversante confession. Par une mystérieuse magie, cette poésie, la plus individuelle qui soit, est aussi celle de chacun de nous. Comme si Verlaine, en ne parlant que de lui-même, avait exprimé les sentiments de tous.
>
> (Troyat, 461, last paragraph)

Finally I now turn to Jean-Pierre Richard's chapter entitled "Fadeur de Verlaine" in his *Poésie et Profondeur*, in my estimation the most brilliant and insightful study there has been of Verlaine's poetry. As a phenomenologist, Richard's text or object of study is the writing of Verlaine, all poems and non-poetic writings just part of one large macro-text. Verlaine's life is almost entirely bracketed out, and sex/gender issues are never center stage. For our purposes the most relevant passage in his study is relegated to a footnote, probably because it transgresses the principles of phenomenological "new criticism" in speaking of the life of the poet, and also because sex/gender is never relevant to his thesis:

> Cette équivoque [séductions équivoques de la fadeur] n'est peut-être pas sans relation avec cette autre ambi-

> guité qui fit de Verlaine un être sexuellement ambivalent. Peut-être conviendrait-il alors de relier le goût du fané, des brumes et de la continuité sensible à certaines tendances féminines, et de rattacher au contraire le besoin de déchirure et de dissonance au côté viril de sa nature. En face de Verlaine, Rimbaud se situe tout entier du côté masculin du choc et de la dissonance: admirons-le d'avoir reconnu la féminité verlainienne, et d'avoir voulu la nourrir en faisant lire à Verlaine les poésies de Marceline Desbordes-Valmore, dont celui-ci aussitôt s'enthousiasma.
>
> (171–72)

Indeed it now seems that this "supplementary" footnote allows us to "re-write" Richard's study of Verlaine's poetic universe, centered around notions of *fadeur* and *le fané*, as a profoundly gendered one: Verlaine is a "sexually ambivalent being," and his "goût du fané" and taste for mists represent the feminine within him, whilst for Rimbaud, wholly male, the defining masculine traits are breaking (besoin de déchirure), dissonance and shock. Whether Richard is purposely resorting to gender stereotypes to define Verlaine and distinguish him from Rimbaud, there is no obvious hierarchy within the binary, for it is precisely what Richard identifies as the feminine which is valorized, thereby reversing the gender hierarchy and becoming the distinctive feature of what Richard calls "la poésie verlainienne la plus authentique". Richard's study of Verlaine is, arguably, gendered from the outset, in that he focuses on those distinguishing qualities which are traditionally and stereotypically coded as feminine:

> En face des choses l'être verlainien adopte spontanément une attitude de passivité, d'attente. Vers leur lointain inconnu il ne projette pas sa curiosité ni son désir, il ne tente même pas de les dévoiler, de les attirer à lui et de s'en rendre maître; il demeure immobile et tranquille, content de cultiver en lui les vertus de porosité qui lui permettront de mieux se laisser pénétrer par elles quand elles auront daigné se manifester à lui.[. . .] Repos, silence, détente, ouverture. L'œuvre verlainienne illustrerait assez bien un certain quiétisme du sentir.
>
> (165)

Passivity of the subject and openness to the world and sensations are the two essential qualities which characterize this period of his poetry and are radically different from the later poetry which "devient didactique et bavarde," (185) and is little more than rhymed anecdotal verse. They provide a useful point of entry into the gendered approach to Verlaine's writing.[3]

Romances sans paroles (1874) is a heterogeneous collection of poems: the first nine are grouped under the subheading of "Ariettes oubliées," the next five are "Paysages belges," followed by a longer—twenty one quatrains—**"Birds in the Night,"** and the final six poems are "Aquarelles." Let us examine the first poem of the collection:

> Le vent dans la plaine
> Suspend son haleine.
> FAVART

C'est l'extase langoureuse,
C'est la fatigue amoureuse,
C'est tous les frissons des bois
Parmi l'étreinte des brises,
C'est, vers les ramures grises,
Le choeur des petites voix.

O le frêle et frais murmure!
Cela gazouille et susurre,
Cela ressemble au cri doux
Que l'herbe agitée expire . . .
Tu dirais, sous l'eau qui vire,
Le roulis sourd des cailloux.

Cette âme qui se lamente
En cette plainte dormante.
C'est la nôtre, n'est-ce pas?
La mienne, dis, et la tienne,
Dont s'exhale l'humble antienne
Par ce tiède soir, tout bas?

At first reading this is a most unpromising poem as an introduction to the gender issue in Verlaine. In the notes to the Garnier edition of Verlaine's ***Oeuvres poétiques***, Jacques Robichez seems to dismiss (?) it as fairly inconsequential:

> Poème sur rien, poème à personne, la première ariette s'écoute sans qu'il soit besoin de la comprendre. *As you like it* serait peut-être le titre qui lui conviendrait le mieux.
>
> (581)

In *The Athlone Press* edition of the ***Romances sans paroles***, D. Hillery concludes his excellent three page commentary in this way:

> If a meaning has to be found for the poem then it derives from the way in which the poem, admittedly on a miniature scale, copies the patterns of normal existence: the insidious invasion of personal happiness by vague feelings of doubt, culminating in implied disillusion. Verlaine's expression of it is unique (and it is not necessarily a deliberate choice); but it is indeed this common pattern of experience which contributes in a large, and unacknowledged, degree to the special potency of this *ariette*.
>
> (73)

Critics and commentators such as Robichez and Hillery only indirectly or implicitly address the matter of gender, unlike Jean-Pierre Richard. Let us look at two aspects: firstly who speaks and who is the poem's internal addressee? Sex and gender are not abstractions, but are attached to, and define, persons, characters, subjects. Secondly how do they respond to, perceive, accommodate themselves to, the physical world around them?

> Je caresse l'idée de faire . . . un livre de poèmes . . . d'où l'homme sera complètement banni.
>
> (Letter to Lepelletier, 16 May 1873, Lepelletier 323)

The subject/addresser/poetic voice must somehow be sought and identified before gender and sex can be attached to "him". His (?) explicit presence is a matter of pronouns. In this poem the first specific reference to a person is delayed till line 11: but the "tu dirais" is largely a familiar, conversational expression, involving a person admittedly, perhaps a combination of addressee and reader. But the "dis" of line 16 would suggest that the "other person" and addressee are the same, and form the couple, "la nôtre," of line 15.

As far as the subject is concerned, there is no "je," or other first person singular form, except the "la mienne". Thus the subject in terms of a first person singular is blurred, made obscure, relegated to an oblique case. This is produced in many grammatical forms: for example, instead of an active verb, that is, one with subject and object, a nominalisation is preferred which has the double effect of focusing on the nature of the action without involving persons. Thus "étreinte" instead of some form of the verb "étreindre." Similarly the nouns of the preceding lines, "extase," "fatigue" and "frissons" are stripped of pronominal associations.

The subject's relationship with the world is not one of stereotypical idealized masculinity—power, control, action—but the world seems to act on him: this is the notion of passivity which is at the core of Richard's thesis. The four times repeated formulaic opening—"C'est . . . c'est . . . c'est . . . c'est . . .," like the "cela gazouille . . . cela ressemble . . ."—which would in Hugo have suggested rhetorical assertiveness—perhaps now, in Verlaine, connotes groping tentativeness. There is moreover a movement to the distancing, objective third person: "cette âme" instead of "Je me lamente" or even "Mon âme se lamente" at the beginning of the third stanza. In order for the physical sensations—*extase, fatigue, frissons, exhale*—to become emotion-laden—*lamente, plainte, humble*—and the focus of the poem, the actual persons must withdraw, be concealed. Though a human context is implied by all these italicized words, the human presence is merely suggested, through *cette âme, la nôtre, la mienne*, and no firm "persona," character or clear identity emerges or is permitted. However much reading practice of romantic and post-romantic poetry may identify the addresser/speaker, the poetic voice, with that of the actual poet, a biographical reading which substitutes Verlaine for the unspoken "je" overloads the human presence and detracts from the other values (ariette, landscape, sensation, emotion) of the poem and the manner in which the past (ecstasy, love) has faded into the melancholic memory and experience in the present.

The same can be said of the poem's addressee, the partner of *la nôtre, la tienne*. Indeed what is most interesting is that the identity is so blurred that critics have been unable to decide whether this is a "Mathilde" poem or a "Rimbaud" poem:

> Avec ces derniers mots le poème se dissout dans le silence, comme une conversation chuchotée de deux amants, la nuit. Antoine Adam ne doute pas que Verlaine s'adresse à Mathilde dont il implore le retour au foyer. Pourquoi pas à Rimbaud? Il semble qu'une hésitation demeure permise. Et même, faut-il choisir?
>
> (Robichez 581)

Elsewhere, in *Verlaine: Entre Rimbaud et Dieu,* Jacques Robichez spelt out the two readings/contexts of Verlaine's ***Romances sans paroles***, insisting that there is no need to provide the biographical referents:

> Il y a deux façons de lire ces poèmes. La première consiste à les rattacher étroitement aux circonstances de la vie de l'auteur dans le temps de leur composition. On est alors amené à nommer, en marge de chacun d'eux, Rimbaud ou Mathilde, quelquefois Rimbaud et Mathilde. La seconde, sans négliger complètement ces circonstances, distend le rapport qui les relie à chacun des Ariettes. Chaque fois qu'il est possible, elle ne choisit pas entre les deux amours de Verlaine. Elle recherche, non pas l'identification d'un personnage, mais l'évocation volontairement brouillée d'impressions et d'états d'âme. Elle correspond mieux, semble-t-il, aux intentions du poète, et moins mal aux vues de Rimbaud.
>
> (58)

Surely the poem's biographic referentiality—is it Mathilde or Rimbaud?—is not what is important but rather the presence of blurred, obscured personas, relegated to oblique cases, who could be male or female: "la mienne" and "la tienne" which suggest the feminine in French are of course ungendered as far as the persons are concerned. Gender is far more difficult to conceal in French since adjectives must normally reveal a feminine form. For example "Je suis content" and "Je suis contente" gender the subject. There is a quite normal expectation that the gender of the poetic "je" will be the same gender as that of the poet. In other words in Verlaine there is an expectation that the "je" will be male unless some grammatical form indicates otherwise. Part of the play in Baudelaire's "La Beauté" ("Je suis belle, ô mortels, comme un rêve de pierre") derives from this fact. In ***Romances sans paroles***, it is only in the seventh poem that there is any confirmation that the "je" is in fact masculine, and then the grammatical indicator is silent in speech: "Je ne me suis pas consolé."

The same blurring of the personas characterizes te second *ariette*:

> Je devine à travers un murmure,
> Le contour subtil des voix anciennes
> Et dans les lueurs musiciennes,
> Amour pâle, une aurore future!

Perhaps the "voix anciennes" may relate to Mathilde, though the pluralization does remove the specificity, and the "aurore future" could either refer to a future new beginning or reconciliation with Mathilde, or a future free relationship with Rimbaud. Instead of being a solution to be solved by scholar and reader alike, I would argue, like Robichez above, that the absence of specificity, whatever the poem's pre-text, is what is at stake in this poem. It is rather the fused shading of emotion (*amour*) and sensation (sound and sight).

The fourth *ariette* is an even more problematic poem, especially with the future of the feminine plural to refer to the lovers:

> Il faut, voyez-vous, nous pardonner les choses:
> De cette façon nous serons bien heureuses
> Et si notre vie a des instants moroses,
> Du moins nous serons, n'est-ce pas, deux pleureuses.
>
> . . . . .
>
> Soyons deux enfants, soyons deux jeunes filles
> Eprises de rien et de tout étonnées . . .

Who is addressed in line one? The conventional referential supposition is that it is Mathilde, but there is uncertainty about the identity of the "nous"—whether the "nous" of line 1 is the same as the "nous" of line 2—, the "deux pleureuses," the "deux enfants," the "deux jeunes filles": whether it is Verlaine and Mathilde or Verlaine and Rimbaud:

> Jacques Borel se ralliant à l'opinion d'Antoine Adam, estime que c'est un gros "contresens" de voir dans les "deux enfants" de l'Ariette IV, Verlaine et Rimbaud. A son avis il s'agit sans le moindre doute de Verlaine et de Mathilde. On pourrait être beaucoup moins affirmatif. L'hésitation, comme ailleurs, demeure permise, mais il semble que plusieurs présomptions trahissent ici le couple anormal dont une querelle (vers 1) a troublé l'union.
>
> (583)

Again, along with the suggestive and very specific erasure of the masculine in favor of the feminine forms, what is significant is the blurring again of the identities of the personas, with pluralization, and conventional forms such as "âmes soeurs" and "deux enfants." Though there is a glimpse of a narrative scenario, comprising persons and actions, specifics which might begin to constitute an identity are muffled and blurred.

The same can be said of the majority of the poems of ***Romances sans paroles***: even the "Paysages belges" clearly based on, depicting, and written during, the Belgian visit of Verlaine and Rimbaud, with this specificity being signaled by the inclusion of date and place of composition at the end of four of them. **"Walcourt"** is distinguished not only by its absence of verbs, but also by the total absence of first person pronominal forms. The second, **"Charleroi"** hides behind the third personal "on":

> Le vent profond
> Pleure, on veut croire.
>
> . . . . .
>
> On sent donc quoi?

In **"Bruxelles,"** the only explicit presence is the oblique "mes langueurs" in the penultimate line. This pattern extends to almost all the ***Romances sans paroles***, whether the subject addresser's sexual and gender identity, like that of the "other" person. Masculine grammatical markers—"je" with masculine adjective for example—are minimized: in the first *ariette* the "la mienne et la tienne" are feminine in that they refer to the noun "âme" or possibly "plainte." Nonetheless this is a non-masculine tone established throughout the poem, with the strong predominance of feminine nouns.

This poetry with its musical and pictorial expression of sensation and emotion, with the blurring of both subject and object differs enormously from the "other" style of writing of Verlaine, which characterizes most of his later collections, which is found in **"Birds in the Night"** and the **"Child Wife,"** which biographers will categorize as uncontroversially and unmistakably "Mathilde" poems:

> Vous n'avez pas eu toute patience:
> Cela se comprend par malheur, de reste
> Vous êtes si jeune! Et l'insouciance,
> C'est le lot amer de l'âge céleste!
>
> . . . . .
>
> Et vous voyez bien que j'avais raison
> Quand je vous disais, dans mes moments noirs,
> Que vos yeux, foyers de mes vieux espoirs,
> Ne couvaient plus rien que la trahison.

The presence and gendered identity of personas in both these poems are more prominent, and the biographical critic has little problem situating them clearly and specifically within the biographical context. The grammatical pronouns of "je" and "vous" are frequent, focused strongly within the poem's narrative structure. These are poems with strongly identifiable actors, personas. Whether readers consider them to be good poems or not, they much more closely resemble the poetic practice of Verlaine's later and, in the general view, very much inferior poetry. (See Carter 111.)

But in what way is all this blurring of the subject and uncertainty about the identity of the addressee-object gendered and related to "bisexual writing"? I would like to juxtapose the first *ariette* quoted in full above and the section in Cixous' *La Jeune Née*, under the subheading "le masculin futur":

> Il y a des exceptions. Il y en a toujours eu, ce sont ces êtres incertains, poétiques, qui ne se sont pas laissés à l'état de mannequins codés par le refoulement impitoyable de la composante homosexuelle. Hommes ou femmes, êtres complexes, mobiles, ouverts. D'admettre la composante de l'autre sexe les rend à la fois beaucoup plus riches, plusieurs, forts et dans la mesure de cette mobilité, très fragiles. On n'invente qu'à cette condition: penseurs, artistes, créateurs de nouvelles valeurs, "philosophes" à la folle façon nietzchéenne, inventeurs et briseurs de concepts, de formes, les changeurs de vie ne peuvent qu'être agités par des singularités—complémentaires ou contradictoires. ça ne veut pas dire que pour créer il faut être homosexuel. Mais qu'il n'est pas d'-*invention* possible, qu'elle soit

philosophique ou poétique, sans qu'en le sujet inventeur il y ait en abondance de l'autre, du divers, personnes-détachées, personnes-pensées, peuples issus de l'inconscient, et dans chaque désert soudain animé, surgissent de moi qu'on ne se connaissait pas—nos femmes, nos monstres, nos chacals, nos arabes, nos semblables, nos frayeurs. Mais qu'il n'est pas d'invention d'autres JE, pas de poésie, pas de fiction sans qu'une homosexualité (jeu donc de la bisexualité) fasse en moi oeuvre de cristallisation de mes ultra-subjectivités. Je est cette matière personnelle, exubérante, gaie masculine, féminine ou autre en laquelle Je enchante et m'angoisse. Et dans le concert des personnalisations qui s'appellent Je, à la fois on refoule une certaine homosexualité, symboliquement, substitutivement, ça passe par des signes divers, traits comportements, manières gestes, et ça se voit plus nettement encore dans l'écriture.

(153–54)

The relevance of Cixous' thesis of a homosexual or bisexual self which allows this "concert de peronnalisations qui s'appellent Je" would seem to apply more readily to the notion of self and others in Baudelaire, the "sainte prostitution de l'âme" formulated in the prose poem "Les Foules" and illustrated in many others. For Verlaine it rather permits the diminution of the strong male/masculine identity which seeks to know the world through its binary classifications and analyses, control others and the world, and to preserve and assert the self and identity of the strong, assertive, active, masculine "moi" and "je." In the bulk of the ***Romances sans paroles*** therefore the strongly asserted self evaporates, not necessarily becoming others as in Baudelaire, but gives itself up, renounces itself, to allow the experience of sensation and emotion to emerge center-stage.

The other coded gendered feature of Verlaine's writing, consequent on the above renunciation of the assertive, identifiable self, is that the senses, body and the mind, become open and available to the world. This openness to the world, sensational and emotional receptivity, relates of course to the essential "passivity" of Verlaine which has formed the basis of Richard's and others' reading of Verlaine's "better" poetry.

If we turn back to the first ariette of ***Romances sans paroles***, we have found, along with the almost total absence of the lovers, a similar dissolution of the objective world, now relegated to "bois, brises, ramures, voix, l'herbe, eau, cailloux," the first four being a kind of generalized plural and the other singular nouns to a generalized amorphous pseudo-plural. What is now important is precisely bodily sensations: extase langoureuse, fatigue amoureuse, frissons, étreinte then followed by aural pleasures: the "chorus of small voices," and the whole of the second stanza seeks to provide impressions of these invisible sounds:

O le frêle et frais murmure!
Cela gazouille et susurre,
Cela ressemble au cri doux
Que l'herbe agitée expire . . .
Tu dirais, sous l'eau qui vire,
Le roulis sourd des cailloux.

Adjectives (frêle, frais, doux, sourd) and verbs (gazouille, susurre, expire) have been made the principal vehicles of suggested meanings. This is part of a familiar pattern in Verlaine's poetry: a movement from visual sensation, or emotion-sensation within a seen context (woods) to one of sound and thence, in the final stage, to one of reverie: it has now become a spiritual (cette âme) plainte. Objects in themselves are not perceived with precision, specificity, but vaguely, impressionistically.

In a paper on "Synaesthesia in Cixous and Barthes," Claire Oboussier explains how Cixous' thinking might illuminate the poetic practice of Verlaine's privileging of the body and its almost synaesthetic sensations in its openness to the world:

Fox Cixous, therefore, knowledge is never abstracted but always linked directly to the body. Moreover, the partitioning of the senses is both artificial and constraining and should be challenged through different paradigms in writing. In *Illa* ways in which this kind of knowledge should be acquired are developed; a rose should be felt in a rose way; things must be allowed to happen in their own modality instead of being appropriated and abstracted.

(126)

Verlaine's synaesthesia is not a cross-circuiting one, but a form which is founded most particularly on sight and sound, not as interchangeable senses: Verlaine focuses on that interface when sight blurs into an experience of sound/music, thus forming part of the fading, dissolving process formulated in his **"Art poétique"** and exemplified in many of his most celebrated poems.

This bodily and sensual openness to the world is not consistent with the strongly assertive sense of self and subjectivity, as we have seen above. It is also most specifically manifested in a number of syntactic and lexical features which, some years ago, Robin Lakoff[4] analyzed, controversially and provocatively, as characteristic of woman's language in contemporary American speech: "tag" questions such as "C'est la nôtre, n'est-ce pas?" signifying tentativeness, seeking approval, as opposed to a confident masculine assertion or declaration; "empty adjectives" such as "petits," "charmants"; epistemic modal forms such as "peut-être"; and "disfluency" in the form of hesitations, pauses, false starts. These features of feminine unassertiveness and hesitancy have been strongly challenged by some and defended by others as communication facilitators. In the case of Verlaine's poetry they are all strongly present, and are positively valorized. Indeed, in purely linguistic terms, they are at the center of Verlaine's poetic practice which cherishes the suggestive and imprecise, and abhors the declarative, the declamatory, and confidently assertive.

The inscription of gender in Verlaine's poetry differs considerably from the androgynous/hermaphroditic ideals—

Cixous' first kind of bisexuality—which re-emerged in French poetry and writing generally in the late 19th century, from about 1860 onwards. Despite the youth of Rimbaud and others like Lucien Létinois, Verlaine's aesthetic ideal never took the form of the pretty boy who looked like a girl. Nor is Verlaine's bisexuality altogether that of Cixous' second category which recognizes sexual difference but operates a free play between the two sexes. Rather his bisexual writing is more characterized by the elimination of traditional masculine markers, both in terms of grammatical forms, and of the absence of the assertive, active subject who seeks mastery, knowledge and power. His partner, particularly in the so-called "Rimbaud" poems, likewise is similarly somewhat ungendered. In erasing the traditional markers of masculinity and masculine writing, Verlaine privileges and valorizes the feminine, submitting the body to sensation and emotion.

Notes

1. Paul Verlaine, "Il faut, voyez-vous, nous pardonner les choses." This is the fourth "ariette oubliée" (123) in *Romances sans paroles*, in *Oeuvres Poétiques Complètes*, Pléiade, 1951.
2. *Theory of Literature*, first published in 1949.
3. Questions of language in Verlaine's poetry have been addressed, in a totally ungendered way, in Russell S. King, "Le Paysage verbal verlainien," and "Verlaine's Verbal Sensation."
4. *Women's Studies: a Reader*, edited by Stevi Jackson, Section 12: Language and Gender, 401–30.

Works cited

Carco, Francis. *Verlaine—poète maudit*. Paris: Albin Michel, 1948.

Carter, A. E. *Verlaine: a study in Parallels*. Toronto: U of Toronto P, 1969.

Clément, Catherine and Cixous, Hélène. *La Jeune Née*. Paris: 10/18, 1975.

Garber, Marjorie. *Vice Versa: Bisexuality and the Eroticism of Everday Life*. London: Hamish Hamilton, 1995.

Jackson, Stevi, editor. *Women' Studies: a Reader*. Hemel Hempstead, U.K.: Harvester, 1993.

King, Russell S. "Le Paysage verbal verlainien." *Europe* (September-October, 1974): 96–107.

———. "Verlaine's Verbal Sensation." *Studies in Philology* 72 (April 1975): 226–36.

Lepelletier, Edmond. *Paul Verlaine: sa vie, son oeuvre*. Paris: Mercure de France, 1907.

Oboussier, Claire. "Synaethesia in Cixous and Barthes," in *Women and Representation*. Eds Diana Knight and Judith Still. Nottingham: WIF Publications, U of Nottingham, 1995.

Richard, Jean-Pierre. *Poésie et Profondeur.* Paris: Seuil, 1955.

Robichez, Jacques. *Verlaine: entre Rimbaud et Dieu*. Paris: SEDES, 1982.

Troyat, Henri. *Verlaine*. Paris: Flammarion, 1993.

Tucker, Naomi, ed. *Bisexual Politics: Theories, Queries & Visions*. New York: Harrington Park Press, 1995.

Verlaine, Paul. *Oeuvres Poétiques Complètes*. Bibliothèque de la Pléiade. Paris: Gallimard, 1951.

———. *Oeuvres en Prose Complètes*. Ed. Jacques Borel. Bibliothèque de la Pléiade. Paris: Gallimard, 1972.

———. *Oeuvres Poétiques*. Ed. Jacques Robichez. Paris: Garnier, 1969.

———. *Romances sans paroles*, Ed. David Hillery. London: Athone Press, 1976.

Wellek, René and Warren, Austin. *Theory of Literature*. London: Penguin, 1949.

FURTHER READING

Biographies

Lepelletier, Edmond. *Paul Verlaine: His Life-His Work*, translated by E. M. Lang. London: T. Werner Laurie, 1907, 463 pp.

Early biography of Verlaine, written by a close friend.

Richardson, Joanna. *Verlaine*. New York: The Viking Press, 1971, 432 pp.

Critical biography of Verlaine.

Criticism

Harris, Frank. "Talks With Paul Verlaine." *Contemporary Portraits*, pp. 269–82. New York: Brentano's Publishers, 1920.

Recounts discussions the author had with Verlaine.

Minahen, Charles D. "Homosexual Erotic Scripting in Verlaine's *Hombres*." *Articulations of Difference: Gender Studies and Writing in French*, edited by Dominique D. Fisher and Lawrence R. Schehr, pp. 119–35. Stanford, Calif.: Stanford University Press, 1997.

Examines Verlaine's construction of an erotic consciousness in his poetry.

Porter, Laurence M. "Meaning in Music: Debussy and Fauré as Interpreters of Verlaine." *Topic: A Journal of the Liberal Arts* 35 (Fall 1981): 26–37.

Examines Verlaine's poetry and themes as interpreted in the music of Claude Debussy and Gustave Fauré.

Schmidt, Paul. "Visions of Violence: Rimbaud and Verlaine." *Homosexualities and French Literature: Cultural Contexts/Critical Texts*, edited by George Stambolian and Elaine Marks, pp. 228–42. Ithaca and London: Cornell University Press, 1979.

Discusses the poetic dialogue between Verlaine and his lover, the poet Arthur Rimbaud, created by the fetishistic use of certain words and phrases in their poetry.

Stone, Alan. "Introduction." *Royal Tastes: Erotic Writings*, by Paul Verlaine, pp. vii-xiv. New York: Harmony Books, 1984.

Explains the publication history of Verlaine's erotic writings.

Additional coverage of Verlaine's life and career is contained in the following sources published by the Gale Group: *DISCovering Authors Modules: Poets*; and *Nineteenth-Century Literature Criticism*, Vols. 2 and 51.

How to Use This Index

The main references

Calvino, Italo
1923-1985 .... **CLC 5, 8, 11, 22, 33, 39, 73; SSC 3**

list all author entries in the following Gale Literary Criticism series:

BLC = *Black Literature Criticism*
CLC = *Contemporary Literary Criticism*
CLR = *Children's Literature Review*
CMLC = *Classical and Medieval Literature Criticism*
DA = *DISCovering Authors*
DAB = *DISCovering Authors: British*
DAC = *DISCovering Authors: Canadian*
DAM = *DISCovering Authors: Modules*
  DRAM: *Dramatists Module;* ***MST:*** *Most-Studied Authors Module;*
  MULT: *Multicultural Authors Module;* ***NOV:*** *Novelists Module;*
  POET: *Poets Module;* ***POP:*** *Popular Fiction and Genre Authors Module*
DC = *Drama Criticism*
HLC = *Hispanic Literature Criticism*
LC = *Literature Criticism from 1400 to 1800*
NCLC = *Nineteenth-Century Literature Criticism*
NNAL = *Native North American Literature*
PC = *Poetry Criticism*
SSC = *Short Story Criticism*
TCLC = *Twentieth-Century Literary Criticism*
WLC = *World Literature Criticism, 1500 to the Present*

The cross-references

See also CANR 23; CA 85-88;
obituary CA116

list all author entries in the following Gale biographical and literary sources:

AAYA = *Authors & Artists for Young Adults*
AITN = *Authors in the News*
BEST = *Bestsellers*
BW = *Black Writers*
CA = *Contemporary Authors*
CAAS = *Contemporary Authors Autobiography Series*
CABS = *Contemporary Authors Bibliographical Series*
CANR = *Contemporary Authors New Revision Series*
CAP = *Contemporary Authors Permanent Series*
CDALB = *Concise Dictionary of American Literary Biography*
CDBLB = *Concise Dictionary of British Literary Biography*
DLB = *Dictionary of Literary Biography*
DLBD = *Dictionary of Literary Biography Documentary Series*
DLBY = *Dictionary of Literary Biography Yearbook*
HW = *Hispanic Writers*
JRDA = *Junior DISCovering Authors*
MAICYA = *Major Authors and Illustrators for Children and Young Adults*
MTCW = *Major 20th-Century Writers*
SAAS = *Something about the Author Autobiography Series*
SATA = *Something about the Author*
YABC = *Yesterday's Authors of Books for Children*

Literary Criticism Series Cumulative Author Index

Aksenov, Vassily
See Aksyonov, Vassily (Pavlovich)
Akst, Daniel 1956- **CLC 109**
See also CA 161
Aksyonov, Vassily (Pavlovich) 1932- **CLC 22, 37, 101**
See also CA 53-56; CANR 12, 48, 77
Akutagawa, Ryunosuke 1892-1927 **TCLC 16**
See also CA 117; 154
Alain 1868-1951 **TCLC 41**
See also CA 163
Alain-Fournier TCLC 6
See also Fournier, Henri Alban
See also DLB 65
Alarcon, Pedro Antonio de 1833-1891 **NCLC 1**
Alas (y Urena), Leopoldo (Enrique Garcia) 1852-1901 **TCLC 29**
See also CA 113; 131; HW 1
Albee, Edward (Franklin III) 1928- **CLC 1, 2, 3, 5, 9, 11, 13, 25, 53, 86, 113; DA; DAB; DAC; DAM DRAM, MST; DC 11; WLC**
See also AITN 1; CA 5-8R; CABS 3; CANR 8, 54, 74; CDALB 1941-1968; DA3; DLB 7; INT CANR-8; MTCW 1, 2
Alberti, Rafael 1902-1999 **CLC 7**
See also CA 85-88; 185; CANR 81; DLB 108; HW 2
Albert the Great 1200(?)-1280 **CMLC 16**
See also DLB 115
Alcala-Galiano, Juan Valera y
See Valera y Alcala-Galiano, Juan
Alcayaga, Lucila Godoy
See Godoy Alcayaga, Lucila
Alcott, Amos Bronson 1799-1888 **NCLC 1**
See also DLB 1, 223
Alcott, Louisa May 1832-1888 **NCLC 6, 58, 83; DA; DAB; DAC; DAM MST, NOV; SSC 27; WLC**
See also AAYA 20; CDALB 1865-1917; CLR 1, 38; DA3; DLB 1, 42, 79, 223; DLBD 14; JRDA; MAICYA; SATA 100; YABC 1
Aldanov, M. A.
See Aldanov, Mark (Alexandrovich)
Aldanov, Mark (Alexandrovich) 1886(?)-1957 **TCLC 23**
See also CA 118; 181
Aldington, Richard 1892-1962 **CLC 49**
See also CA 85-88; CANR 45; DLB 20, 36, 100, 149
Aldiss, Brian W(ilson) 1925- **CLC 5, 14, 40; DAM NOV; SSC 36**
See also CA 5-8R; CAAS 2; CANR 5, 28, 64; DLB 14; MTCW 1, 2; SATA 34
Alegria, Claribel 1924- **CLC 75; DAM MULT; HLCS 1; PC 26**
See also CA 131; CAAS 15; CANR 66; DLB 145; HW 1; MTCW 1
Alegria, Fernando 1918- **CLC 57**
See also CA 9-12R; CANR 5, 32, 72; HW 1, 2
Aleichem, Sholom TCLC 1, 35; SSC 33
See also Rabinovitch, Sholem
Aleixandre, Vicente 1898-1984
See also CANR 81; HLCS 1; HW 2
Alepoudelis, Odysseus
See Elytis, Odysseus
Aleshkovsky, Joseph 1929-
See Aleshkovsky, Yuz
See also CA 121; 128
Aleshkovsky, Yuz CLC 44
See also Aleshkovsky, Joseph
Alexander, Lloyd (Chudley) 1924- **CLC 35**
See also AAYA 1, 27; CA 1-4R; CANR 1, 24, 38, 55; CLR 1, 5, 48; DLB 52; JRDA; MAICYA; MTCW 1; SAAS 19; SATA 3, 49, 81
Alexander, Meena 1951- **CLC 121**
See also CA 115; CANR 38, 70
Alexander, Samuel 1859-1938 **TCLC 77**
Alexie, Sherman (Joseph, Jr.) 1966- **CLC 96; DAM MULT**
See also AAYA 28; CA 138; CANR 65; DA3; DLB 175, 206; MTCW 1; NNAL
Alfau, Felipe 1902- **CLC 66**
See also CA 137
Alfred, Jean Gaston
See Ponge, Francis
Alger, Horatio Jr., Jr. 1832-1899 **NCLC 8, 83**
See also DLB 42; SATA 16
Algren, Nelson 1909-1981 **CLC 4, 10, 33; SSC 33**
See also CA 13-16R; 103; CANR 20, 61; CDALB 1941-1968; DLB 9; DLBY 81, 82; MTCW 1, 2
Ali, Ahmed 1910- **CLC 69**
See also CA 25-28R; CANR 15, 34
Alighieri, Dante
See Dante
Allan, John B.
See Westlake, Donald E(dwin)
Allan, Sidney
See Hartmann, Sadakichi
Allan, Sydney
See Hartmann, Sadakichi
Allen, Edward 1948- **CLC 59**
Allen, Fred 1894-1956 **TCLC 87**
Allen, Paula Gunn 1939- **CLC 84; DAM MULT**
See also CA 112; 143; CANR 63; DA3; DLB 175; MTCW 1; NNAL
Allen, Roland
See Ayckbourn, Alan
Allen, Sarah A.
See Hopkins, Pauline Elizabeth
Allen, Sidney H.
See Hartmann, Sadakichi
Allen, Woody 1935- **CLC 16, 52; DAM POP**
See also AAYA 10; CA 33-36R; CANR 27, 38, 63; DLB 44; MTCW 1
Allende, Isabel 1942- **CLC 39, 57, 97; DAM MULT, NOV; HLC 1; WLCS**
See also AAYA 18; CA 125; 130; CANR 51, 74; DA3; DLB 145; HW 1, 2; INT 130; MTCW 1, 2
Alleyn, Ellen
See Rossetti, Christina (Georgina)
Allingham, Margery (Louise) 1904-1966 **CLC 19**
See also CA 5-8R; 25-28R; CANR 4, 58; DLB 77; MTCW 1, 2
Allingham, William 1824-1889 **NCLC 25**
See also DLB 35
Allison, Dorothy E. 1949- **CLC 78**
See also CA 140; CANR 66; DA3; MTCW 1
Allston, Washington 1779-1843 **NCLC 2**
See also DLB 1, 235
Almedingen, E. M. CLC 12
See also Almedingen, Martha Edith von
See also SATA 3
Almedingen, Martha Edith von 1898-1971
See Almedingen, E. M.
See also CA 1-4R; CANR 1
Almodovar, Pedro 1949(?)- **CLC 114; HLCS 1**
See also CA 133; CANR 72; HW 2
Almqvist, Carl Jonas Love 1793-1866 **NCLC 42**
Alonso, Damaso 1898-1990 **CLC 14**
See also CA 110; 131; 130; CANR 72; DLB 108; HW 1, 2
Alov
See Gogol, Nikolai (Vasilyevich)
Alta 1942- **CLC 19**
See also CA 57-60
Alter, Robert B(ernard) 1935- **CLC 34**
See also CA 49-52; CANR 1, 47
Alther, Lisa 1944- **CLC 7, 41**
See also CA 65-68; CAAS 30; CANR 12, 30, 51; MTCW 1
Althusser, L.
See Althusser, Louis
Althusser, Louis 1918-1990 **CLC 106**
See also CA 131; 132
Altman, Robert 1925- **CLC 16, 116**
See also CA 73-76; CANR 43
Alurista 1949-
See Urista, Alberto H.
See also DLB 82; HLCS 1
Alvarez, A(lfred) 1929- **CLC 5, 13**
See also CA 1-4R; CANR 3, 33, 63; DLB 14, 40
Alvarez, Alejandro Rodriguez 1903-1965
See Casona, Alejandro
See also CA 131; 93-96; HW 1
Alvarez, Julia 1950- **CLC 93; HLCS 1**
See also AAYA 25; CA 147; CANR 69; DA3; MTCW 1
Alvaro, Corrado 1896-1956 **TCLC 60**
See also CA 163
Amado, Jorge 1912- **CLC 13, 40, 106; DAM MULT, NOV; HLC 1**
See also CA 77-80; CANR 35, 74; DLB 113; HW 2; MTCW 1, 2
Ambler, Eric 1909-1998 **CLC 4, 6, 9**
See also CA 9-12R; 171; CANR 7, 38, 74; DLB 77; MTCW 1, 2
Amichai, Yehuda 1924-2000 **CLC 9, 22, 57, 116**
See also CA 85-88; CANR 46, 60; MTCW 1
Amichai, Yehudah
See Amichai, Yehuda
Amiel, Henri Frederic 1821-1881 **NCLC 4**
Amis, Kingsley (William) 1922-1995 **CLC 1, 2, 3, 5, 8, 13, 40, 44, 129; DA; DAB; DAC; DAM MST, NOV**
See also AITN 2; CA 9-12R; 150; CANR 8, 28, 54; CDBLB 1945-1960; DA3; DLB 15, 27, 100, 139; DLBY 96; INT CANR-8; MTCW 1, 2
Amis, Martin (Louis) 1949- **CLC 4, 9, 38, 62, 101**
See also BEST 90:3; CA 65-68; CANR 8, 27, 54, 73; DA3; DLB 14, 194; INT CANR-27; MTCW 1
Ammons, A(rchie) R(andolph) 1926- **CLC 2, 3, 5, 8, 9, 25, 57, 108; DAM POET; PC 16**
See also AITN 1; CA 9-12R; CANR 6, 36, 51, 73; DLB 5, 165; MTCW 1, 2
Amo, Tauraatua i
See Adams, Henry (Brooks)
Amory, Thomas 1691(?)-1788 **LC 48**
Anand, Mulk Raj 1905- **CLC 23, 93; DAM NOV**
See also CA 65-68; CANR 32, 64; MTCW 1, 2
Anatol
See Schnitzler, Arthur
Anaximander c. 610B.C.-c. 546B.C. **CMLC 22**
Anaya, Rudolfo A(lfonso) 1937- **CLC 23; DAM MULT, NOV; HLC 1**
See also AAYA 20; CA 45-48; CAAS 4; CANR 1, 32, 51; DLB 82, 206; HW 1; MTCW 1, 2
Andersen, Hans Christian 1805-1875 **NCLC 7, 79; DA; DAB; DAC; DAM MST, POP; SSC 6; WLC**
See also CLR 6; DA3; MAICYA; SATA 100; YABC 1

Anderson, C. Farley
See Mencken, H(enry) L(ouis); Nathan, George Jean
Anderson, Jessica (Margaret) Queale 1916- **CLC 37**
See also CA 9-12R; CANR 4, 62
Anderson, Jon (Victor) 1940- **CLC 9; DAM POET**
See also CA 25-28R; CANR 20
Anderson, Lindsay (Gordon) 1923-1994 **CLC 20**
See also CA 125; 128; 146; CANR 77
Anderson, Maxwell 1888-1959 **TCLC 2; DAM DRAM**
See also CA 105; 152; DLB 7, 228; MTCW 2
Anderson, Poul (William) 1926- **CLC 15**
See also AAYA 5, 34; CA 1-4R, 181; CAAE 181; CAAS 2; CANR 2, 15, 34, 64; CLR 58; DLB 8; INT CANR-15; MTCW 1, 2; SATA 90; SATA-Brief 39; SATA-Essay 106
Anderson, Robert (Woodruff) 1917- **CLC 23; DAM DRAM**
See also AITN 1; CA 21-24R; CANR 32; DLB 7
Anderson, Sherwood 1876-1941 **TCLC 1, 10, 24; DA; DAB; DAC; DAM MST, NOV; SSC 1; WLC**
See also AAYA 30; CA 104; 121; CANR 61; CDALB 1917-1929; DA3; DLB 4, 9, 86; DLBD 1; MTCW 1, 2
Andier, Pierre
See Desnos, Robert
Andouard
See Giraudoux, (Hippolyte) Jean
Andrade, Carlos Drummond de CLC 18
See also Drummond de Andrade, Carlos
Andrade, Mario de 1893-1945 **TCLC 43**
Andreae, Johann V(alentin) 1586-1654 **LC 32**
See also DLB 164
Andreas-Salome, Lou 1861-1937 **TCLC 56**
See also CA 178; DLB 66
Andress, Lesley
See Sanders, Lawrence
Andrewes, Lancelot 1555-1626 **LC 5**
See also DLB 151, 172
Andrews, Cicily Fairfield
See West, Rebecca
Andrews, Elton V.
See Pohl, Frederik
Andreyev, Leonid (Nikolaevich) 1871-1919 **TCLC 3**
See also CA 104; 185
Andric, Ivo 1892-1975 **CLC 8; SSC 36**
See also CA 81-84; 57-60; CANR 43, 60; DLB 147; MTCW 1
Androvar
See Prado (Calvo), Pedro
Angelique, Pierre
See Bataille, Georges
Angell, Roger 1920- **CLC 26**
See also CA 57-60; CANR 13, 44, 70; DLB 171, 185
Angelou, Maya 1928- **CLC 12, 35, 64, 77; BLC 1; DA; DAB; DAC; DAM MST, MULT, POET, POP; PC 32; WLCS**
See also AAYA 7, 20; BW 2, 3; CA 65-68; CANR 19, 42, 65; CDALBS; CLR 53; DA3; DLB 38; MTCW 1, 2; SATA 49
Anna Comnena 1083-1153 **CMLC 25**
Annensky, Innokenty (Fyodorovich) 1856-1909 **TCLC 14**
See also CA 110; 155
Annunzio, Gabriele d'
See D'Annunzio, Gabriele
Anodos
See Coleridge, Mary E(lizabeth)
Anon, Charles Robert
See Pessoa, Fernando (Antonio Nogueira)
Anouilh, Jean (Marie Lucien Pierre) 1910-1987 **CLC 1, 3, 8, 13, 40, 50; DAM DRAM; DC 8**
See also CA 17-20R; 123; CANR 32; MTCW 1, 2
Anthony, Florence
See Ai
Anthony, John
See Ciardi, John (Anthony)
Anthony, Peter
See Shaffer, Anthony (Joshua); Shaffer, Peter (Levin)
Anthony, Piers 1934- **CLC 35; DAM POP**
See also AAYA 11; CA 21-24R; CANR 28, 56, 73; DLB 8; MTCW 1, 2; SAAS 22; SATA 84
Anthony, Susan B(rownell) 1916-1991 **TCLC 84**
See also CA 89-92; 134
Antoine, Marc
See Proust, (Valentin-Louis-George-Eugene-) Marcel
Antoninus, Brother
See Everson, William (Oliver)
Antonioni, Michelangelo 1912- **CLC 20**
See also CA 73-76; CANR 45, 77
Antschel, Paul 1920-1970
See Celan, Paul
See also CA 85-88; CANR 33, 61; MTCW 1
Anwar, Chairil 1922-1949 **TCLC 22**
See also CA 121
Anzaldua, Gloria (Evanjelina) 1942-
See also CA 175; DLB 122; HLCS 1
Apess, William 1798-1839(?) **NCLC 73; DAM MULT**
See also DLB 175; NNAL
Apollinaire, Guillaume 1880-1918 **TCLC 3, 8, 51; DAM POET; PC 7**
See also CA 152; MTCW 1
Appelfeld, Aharon 1932- **CLC 23, 47; SSC 42**
See also CA 112; 133; CANR 86
Apple, Max (Isaac) 1941- **CLC 9, 33**
See also CA 81-84; CANR 19, 54; DLB 130
Appleman, Philip (Dean) 1926- **CLC 51**
See also CA 13-16R; CAAS 18; CANR 6, 29, 56
Appleton, Lawrence
See Lovecraft, H(oward) P(hillips)
Apteryx
See Eliot, T(homas) S(tearns)
Apuleius, (Lucius Madaurensis) 125(?)-175(?) **CMLC 1**
See also DLB 211
Aquin, Hubert 1929-1977 **CLC 15**
See also CA 105; DLB 53
Aquinas, Thomas 1224(?)-1274 **CMLC 33**
See also DLB 115
Aragon, Louis 1897-1982 **CLC 3, 22; DAM NOV, POET**
See also CA 69-72; 108; CANR 28, 71; DLB 72; MTCW 1, 2
Arany, Janos 1817-1882 **NCLC 34**
Aranyos, Kakay
See Mikszath, Kalman
Arbuthnot, John 1667-1735 **LC 1**
See also DLB 101
Archer, Herbert Winslow
See Mencken, H(enry) L(ouis)
Archer, Jeffrey (Howard) 1940- **CLC 28; DAM POP**
See also AAYA 16; BEST 89:3; CA 77-80; CANR 22, 52; DA3; INT CANR-22
Archer, Jules 1915- **CLC 12**
See also CA 9-12R; CANR 6, 69; SAAS 5; SATA 4, 85
Archer, Lee
See Ellison, Harlan (Jay)
Arden, John 1930- **CLC 6, 13, 15; DAM DRAM**
See also CA 13-16R; CAAS 4; CANR 31, 65, 67; DLB 13; MTCW 1
Arenas, Reinaldo 1943-1990 **CLC 41; DAM MULT; HLC 1**
See also CA 124; 128; 133; CANR 73; DLB 145; HW 1; MTCW 1
Arendt, Hannah 1906-1975 **CLC 66, 98**
See also CA 17-20R; 61-64; CANR 26, 60; MTCW 1, 2
Aretino, Pietro 1492-1556 **LC 12**
Arghezi, Tudor 1880-1967 **CLC 80**
See also Theodorescu, Ion N.
See also CA 167; DLB 220
Arguedas, Jose Maria 1911-1969 **CLC 10, 18; HLCS 1**
See also CA 89-92; CANR 73; DLB 113; HW 1
Argueta, Manlio 1936- **CLC 31**
See also CA 131; CANR 73; DLB 145; HW 1
Arias, Ron(ald Francis) 1941-
See also CA 131; CANR 81; DAM MULT; DLB 82; HLC 1; HW 1, 2; MTCW 2
Ariosto, Ludovico 1474-1533 **LC 6**
Aristides
See Epstein, Joseph
Aristophanes 450B.C.-385B.C. **CMLC 4; DA; DAB; DAC; DAM DRAM, MST; DC 2; WLCS**
See also DA3; DLB 176
Aristotle 384B.C.-322B.C. **CMLC 31; DA; DAB; DAC; DAM MST; WLCS**
See also DA3; DLB 176
Arlt, Roberto (Godofredo Christophersen) 1900-1942 **TCLC 29; DAM MULT; HLC 1**
See also CA 123; 131; CANR 67; HW 1, 2
Armah, Ayi Kwei 1939- **CLC 5, 33, 136; BLC 1; DAM MULT, POET**
See also BW 1; CA 61-64; CANR 21, 64; DLB 117; MTCW 1
Armatrading, Joan 1950- **CLC 17**
See also CA 114; 186
Arnette, Robert
See Silverberg, Robert
Arnim, Achim von (Ludwig Joachim von Arnim) 1781-1831 **NCLC 5; SSC 29**
See also DLB 90
Arnim, Bettina von 1785-1859 **NCLC 38**
See also DLB 90
Arnold, Matthew 1822-1888 **NCLC 6, 29, 89; DA; DAB; DAC; DAM MST, POET; PC 5; WLC**
See also CDBLB 1832-1890; DLB 32, 57
Arnold, Thomas 1795-1842 **NCLC 18**
See also DLB 55
Arnow, Harriette (Louisa) Simpson 1908-1986 **CLC 2, 7, 18**
See also CA 9-12R; 118; CANR 14; DLB 6; MTCW 1, 2; SATA 42; SATA-Obit 47
Arouet, Francois-Marie
See Voltaire
Arp, Hans
See Arp, Jean
Arp, Jean 1887-1966 **CLC 5**
See also CA 81-84; 25-28R; CANR 42, 77
Arrabal
See Arrabal, Fernando
Arrabal, Fernando 1932- **CLC 2, 9, 18, 58**
See also CA 9-12R; CANR 15
Arreola, Juan Jose 1918- **SSC 38; DAM MULT; HLC 1**

Bakhtin, Mikhail
See Bakhtin, Mikhail Mikhailovich
Bakhtin, Mikhail Mikhailovich 1895-1975 **CLC 83**
See also CA 128; 113
Bakshi, Ralph 1938(?)- **CLC 26**
See also CA 112; 138
Bakunin, Mikhail (Alexandrovich) 1814-1876 **NCLC 25, 58**
Baldwin, James (Arthur) 1924-1987 **CLC 1, 2, 3, 4, 5, 8, 13, 15, 17, 42, 50, 67, 90, 127; BLC 1; DA; DAB; DAC; DAM MST, MULT, NOV, POP; DC 1; SSC 10, 33; WLC**
See also AAYA 4, 34; BW 1; CA 1-4R; 124; CABS 1; CANR 3, 24; CDALB 1941-1968; DA3; DLB 2, 7, 33; DLBY 87; MTCW 1, 2; SATA 9; SATA-Obit 54
Bale, John 1495-1563 **LC 62**
See also DLB 132
Ballard, J(ames) G(raham) 1930- **CLC 3, 6, 14, 36; DAM NOV, POP; SSC 1**
See also AAYA 3; CA 5-8R; CANR 15, 39, 65; DA3; DLB 14, 207; MTCW 1, 2; SATA 93
Balmont, Konstantin (Dmitriyevich) 1867-1943 **TCLC 11**
See also CA 109; 155
Baltausis, Vincas
See Mikszath, Kalman
Balzac, Honore de 1799-1850 **NCLC 5, 35, 53; DA; DAB; DAC; DAM MST, NOV; SSC 5; WLC**
See also DA3; DLB 119
Bambara, Toni Cade 1939-1995 **CLC 19, 88; BLC 1; DA; DAC; DAM MST, MULT; SSC 35; WLCS**
See also AAYA 5; BW 2, 3; CA 29-32R; 150; CANR 24, 49, 81; CDALBS; DA3; DLB 38; MTCW 1, 2; SATA 112
Bamdad, A.
See Shamlu, Ahmad
Banat, D. R.
See Bradbury, Ray (Douglas)
Bancroft, Laura
See Baum, L(yman) Frank
Banim, John 1798-1842 **NCLC 13**
See also DLB 116, 158, 159
Banim, Michael 1796-1874 **NCLC 13**
See also DLB 158, 159
Banjo, The
See Paterson, A(ndrew) B(arton)
Banks, Iain
See Banks, Iain M(enzies)
Banks, Iain M(enzies) 1954- **CLC 34**
See also CA 123; 128; CANR 61; DLB 194; INT 128
Banks, Lynne Reid **CLC 23**
See also Reid Banks, Lynne
See also AAYA 6
Banks, Russell 1940- **CLC 37, 72; SSC 42**
See also CA 65-68; CAAS 15; CANR 19, 52, 73; DLB 130
Banville, John 1945- **CLC 46, 118**
See also CA 117; 128; DLB 14; INT 128
Banville, Theodore (Faullain) de 1832-1891 **NCLC 9**
Baraka, Amiri 1934- **CLC 1, 2, 3, 5, 10, 14, 33, 115; BLC 1; DA; DAC; DAM MST, MULT, POET, POP; DC 6; PC 4; WLCS**
See also Jones, LeRoi
See also BW 2, 3; CA 21-24R; CABS 3; CANR 27, 38, 61; CDALB 1941-1968; DA3; DLB 5, 7, 16, 38; DLBD 8; MTCW 1, 2
Barbauld, Anna Laetitia 1743-1825 **NCLC 50**
See also DLB 107, 109, 142, 158
Barbellion, W. N. P. **TCLC 24**
See also Cummings, Bruce F(rederick)
Barbera, Jack (Vincent) 1945- **CLC 44**
See also CA 110; CANR 45
Barbey d'Aurevilly, Jules Amedee 1808-1889 **NCLC 1; SSC 17**
See also DLB 119
Barbour, John c. 1316-1395 **CMLC 33**
See also DLB 146
Barbusse, Henri 1873-1935 **TCLC 5**
See also CA 105; 154; DLB 65
Barclay, Bill
See Moorcock, Michael (John)
Barclay, William Ewert
See Moorcock, Michael (John)
Barea, Arturo 1897-1957 **TCLC 14**
See also CA 111
Barfoot, Joan 1946- **CLC 18**
See also CA 105
Barham, Richard Harris 1788-1845 **NCLC 77**
See also DLB 159
Baring, Maurice 1874-1945 **TCLC 8**
See also CA 105; 168; DLB 34
Baring-Gould, Sabine 1834-1924 **TCLC 88**
See also DLB 156, 190
Barker, Clive 1952- **CLC 52; DAM POP**
See also AAYA 10; BEST 90:3; CA 121; 129; CANR 71; DA3; INT 129; MTCW 1, 2
Barker, George Granville 1913-1991 **CLC 8, 48; DAM POET**
See also CA 9-12R; 135; CANR 7, 38; DLB 20; MTCW 1
Barker, Harley Granville
See Granville-Barker, Harley
See also DLB 10
Barker, Howard 1946- **CLC 37**
See also CA 102; DLB 13, 233
Barker, Jane 1652-1732 **LC 42**
Barker, Pat(ricia) 1943- **CLC 32, 94**
See also CA 117; 122; CANR 50; INT 122
Barlach, Ernst (Heinrich) 1870-1938 **TCLC 84**
See also CA 178; DLB 56, 118
Barlow, Joel 1754-1812 **NCLC 23**
See also DLB 37
Barnard, Mary (Ethel) 1909- **CLC 48**
See also CA 21-22; CAP 2
Barnes, Djuna 1892-1982 **CLC 3, 4, 8, 11, 29, 127; SSC 3**
See also CA 9-12R; 107; CANR 16, 55; DLB 4, 9, 45; MTCW 1, 2
Barnes, Julian (Patrick) 1946- **CLC 42; DAB**
See also CA 102; CANR 19, 54; DLB 194; DLBY 93; MTCW 1
Barnes, Peter 1931- **CLC 5, 56**
See also CA 65-68; CAAS 12; CANR 33, 34, 64; DLB 13, 233; MTCW 1
Barnes, William 1801-1886 **NCLC 75**
See also DLB 32
Baroja (y Nessi), Pio 1872-1956 **TCLC 8; HLC 1**
See also CA 104
Baron, David
See Pinter, Harold
Baron Corvo
See Rolfe, Frederick (William Serafino Austin Lewis Mary)
Barondess, Sue K(aufman) 1926-1977 **CLC 8**
See also Kaufman, Sue
See also CA 1-4R; 69-72; CANR 1
Baron de Teive
See Pessoa, Fernando (Antonio Nogueira)
Baroness Von S.
See Zangwill, Israel
Barres, (Auguste-) Maurice 1862-1923 **TCLC 47**
See also CA 164; DLB 123
Barreto, Afonso Henrique de Lima
See Lima Barreto, Afonso Henrique de
Barrett, (Roger) Syd 1946- **CLC 35**
Barrett, William (Christopher) 1913-1992 **CLC 27**
See also CA 13-16R; 139; CANR 11, 67; INT CANR-11
Barrie, J(ames) M(atthew) 1860-1937 **TCLC 2; DAB; DAM DRAM**
See also CA 104; 136; CANR 77; CDBLB 1890-1914; CLR 16; DA3; DLB 10, 141, 156; MAICYA; MTCW 1; SATA 100; YABC 1
Barrington, Michael
See Moorcock, Michael (John)
Barrol, Grady
See Bograd, Larry
Barry, Mike
See Malzberg, Barry N(athaniel)
Barry, Philip 1896-1949 **TCLC 11**
See also CA 109; DLB 7, 228
Bart, Andre Schwarz
See Schwarz-Bart, Andre
Barth, John (Simmons) 1930- **CLC 1, 2, 3, 5, 7, 9, 10, 14, 27, 51, 89; DAM NOV; SSC 10**
See also AITN 1, 2; CA 1-4R; CABS 1; CANR 5, 23, 49, 64; DLB 2, 227; MTCW 1
Barthelme, Donald 1931-1989 **CLC 1, 2, 3, 5, 6, 8, 13, 23, 46, 59, 115; DAM NOV; SSC 2**
See also CA 21-24R; 129; CANR 20, 58; DA3; DLB 2; DLBY 80, 89; MTCW 1, 2; SATA 7; SATA-Obit 62
Barthelme, Frederick 1943- **CLC 36, 117**
See also CA 114; 122; CANR 77; DLBY 85; INT 122
Barthes, Roland (Gerard) 1915-1980 **CLC 24, 83**
See also CA 130; 97-100; CANR 66; MTCW 1, 2
Barzun, Jacques (Martin) 1907- **CLC 51**
See also CA 61-64; CANR 22
Bashevis, Isaac
See Singer, Isaac Bashevis
Bashkirtseff, Marie 1859-1884 **NCLC 27**
Basho
See Matsuo Basho
Basil of Caesaria c. 330-379 **CMLC 35**
Bass, Kingsley B., Jr.
See Bullins, Ed
Bass, Rick 1958- **CLC 79**
See also CA 126; CANR 53, 93; DLB 212
Bassani, Giorgio 1916- **CLC 9**
See also CA 65-68; CANR 33; DLB 128, 177; MTCW 1
Bastos, Augusto (Antonio) Roa
See Roa Bastos, Augusto (Antonio)
Bataille, Georges 1897-1962 **CLC 29**
See also CA 101; 89-92
Bates, H(erbert) E(rnest) 1905-1974 **CLC 46; DAB; DAM POP; SSC 10**
See also CA 93-96; 45-48; CANR 34; DA3; DLB 162, 191; MTCW 1, 2
Bauchart
See Camus, Albert
Baudelaire, Charles 1821-1867 **NCLC 6, 29, 55; DA; DAB; DAC; DAM MST, POET; PC 1; SSC 18; WLC**
See also DA3
Baudrillard, Jean 1929- **CLC 60**
Baum, L(yman) Frank 1856-1919 **TCLC 7**
See also CA 108; 133; CLR 15; DLB 22; JRDA; MAICYA; MTCW 1, 2; SATA 18, 100

Baum, Louis F.
See Baum, L(yman) Frank
Baumbach, Jonathan 1933- **CLC 6, 23**
See also CA 13-16R; CAAS 5; CANR 12, 66; DLBY 80; INT CANR-12; MTCW 1
Bausch, Richard (Carl) 1945- **CLC 51**
See also CA 101; CAAS 14; CANR 43, 61, 87; DLB 130
Baxter, Charles (Morley) 1947- **CLC 45, 78; DAM POP**
See also CA 57-60; CANR 40, 64; DLB 130; MTCW 2
Baxter, George Owen
See Faust, Frederick (Schiller)
Baxter, James K(eir) 1926-1972 **CLC 14**
See also CA 77-80
Baxter, John
See Hunt, E(verette) Howard, (Jr.)
Bayer, Sylvia
See Glassco, John
Baynton, Barbara 1857-1929 **TCLC 57**
Beagle, Peter S(oyer) 1939- **CLC 7, 104**
See also CA 9-12R; CANR 4, 51, 73; DA3; DLBY 80; INT CANR-4; MTCW 1; SATA 60
Bean, Normal
See Burroughs, Edgar Rice
Beard, Charles A(ustin) 1874-1948 **TCLC 15**
See also CA 115; DLB 17; SATA 18
Beardsley, Aubrey 1872-1898 **NCLC 6**
Beattie, Ann 1947- **CLC 8, 13, 18, 40, 63; DAM NOV, POP; SSC 11**
See also BEST 90:2; CA 81-84; CANR 53, 73; DA3; DLBY 82; MTCW 1, 2
Beattie, James 1735-1803 **NCLC 25**
See also DLB 109
Beauchamp, Kathleen Mansfield 1888-1923
See Mansfield, Katherine
See also CA 104; 134; DA; DAC; DAM MST; DA3; MTCW 2
Beaumarchais, Pierre-Augustin Caron de 1732-1799 **LC 61; DAM DRAM; DC 4**
Beaumont, Francis 1584(?)-1616 **LC 33; DC 6**
See also CDBLB Before 1660; DLB 58, 121
Beauvoir, Simone (Lucie Ernestine Marie Bertrand) de 1908-1986 **CLC 1, 2, 4, 8, 14, 31, 44, 50, 71, 124; DA; DAB; DAC; DAM MST, NOV; SSC 35; WLC**
See also CA 9-12R; 118; CANR 28, 61; DA3; DLB 72; DLBY 86; MTCW 1, 2
Becker, Carl (Lotus) 1873-1945 **TCLC 63**
See also CA 157; DLB 17
Becker, Jurek 1937-1997 **CLC 7, 19**
See also CA 85-88; 157; CANR 60; DLB 75
Becker, Walter 1950- **CLC 26**
Beckett, Samuel (Barclay) 1906-1989 **CLC 1, 2, 3, 4, 6, 9, 10, 11, 14, 18, 29, 57, 59, 83; DA; DAB; DAC; DAM DRAM, MST, NOV; SSC 16; WLC**
See also CA 5-8R; 130; CANR 33, 61; CDBLB 1945-1960; DA3; DLB 13, 15, 233; DLBY 90; MTCW 1, 2
Beckford, William 1760-1844 **NCLC 16**
See also DLB 39
Beckman, Gunnel 1910- **CLC 26**
See also CA 33-36R; CANR 15; CLR 25; MAICYA; SAAS 9; SATA 6
Becque, Henri 1837-1899 **NCLC 3**
See also DLB 192
Becquer, Gustavo Adolfo 1836-1870
See also DAM MULT; HLCS 1
Beddoes, Thomas Lovell 1803-1849 **NCLC 3**
See also DLB 96
Bede c. 673-735 **CMLC 20**
See also DLB 146
Bedford, Donald F.
See Fearing, Kenneth (Flexner)
Beecher, Catharine Esther 1800-1878 **NCLC 30**
See also DLB 1
Beecher, John 1904-1980 **CLC 6**
See also AITN 1; CA 5-8R; 105; CANR 8
Beer, Johann 1655-1700 **LC 5**
See also DLB 168
Beer, Patricia 1924- **CLC 58**
See also CA 61-64; 183; CANR 13, 46; DLB 40
Beerbohm, Max -1956
See Beerbohm, (Henry) Max(imilian)
Beerbohm, (Henry) Max(imilian) 1872-1956 **TCLC 1, 24**
See also CA 104; 154; CANR 79; DLB 34, 100
Beer-Hofmann, Richard 1866-1945 **TCLC 60**
See also CA 160; DLB 81
Begiebing, Robert J(ohn) 1946- **CLC 70**
See also CA 122; CANR 40, 88
Behan, Brendan 1923-1964 **CLC 1, 8, 11, 15, 79; DAM DRAM**
See also CA 73-76; CANR 33; CDBLB 1945-1960; DLB 13, 233; MTCW 1, 2
Behn, Aphra 1640(?)-1689 **LC 1, 30, 42; DA; DAB; DAC; DAM DRAM, MST, NOV, POET; DC 4; PC 13; WLC**
See also DA3; DLB 39, 80, 131
Behrman, S(amuel) N(athaniel) 1893-1973 **CLC 40**
See also CA 13-16; 45-48; CAP 1; DLB 7, 44
Belasco, David 1853-1931 **TCLC 3**
See also CA 104; 168; DLB 7
Belcheva, Elisaveta 1893- **CLC 10**
See also Bagryana, Elisaveta
Beldone, Phil "Cheech"
See Ellison, Harlan (Jay)
Beleno
See Azuela, Mariano
Belinski, Vissarion Grigoryevich 1811-1848 **NCLC 5**
See also DLB 198
Belitt, Ben 1911- **CLC 22**
See also CA 13-16R; CAAS 4; CANR 7, 77; DLB 5
Bell, Gertrude (Margaret Lowthian) 1868-1926 **TCLC 67**
See also CA 167; DLB 174
Bell, J. Freeman
See Zangwill, Israel
Bell, James Madison 1826-1902 **TCLC 43; BLC 1; DAM MULT**
See also BW 1; CA 122; 124; DLB 50
Bell, Madison Smartt 1957- **CLC 41, 102**
See also CA 111, 183; CAAE 183; CANR 28, 54, 73; MTCW 1
Bell, Marvin (Hartley) 1937- **CLC 8, 31; DAM POET**
See also CA 21-24R; CAAS 14; CANR 59; DLB 5; MTCW 1
Bell, W. L. D.
See Mencken, H(enry) L(ouis)
Bellamy, Atwood C.
See Mencken, H(enry) L(ouis)
Bellamy, Edward 1850-1898 **NCLC 4, 86**
See also DLB 12
Belli, Gioconda 1949-
See also CA 152; HLCS 1
Bellin, Edward J.
See Kuttner, Henry
Belloc, (Joseph) Hilaire (Pierre Sebastien Rene Swanton) 1870-1953 **TCLC 7, 18; DAM POET; PC 24**
See also CA 106; 152; DLB 19, 100, 141, 174; MTCW 1; SATA 112; YABC 1
Belloc, Joseph Peter Rene Hilaire
See Belloc, (Joseph) Hilaire (Pierre Sebastien Rene Swanton)
Belloc, Joseph Pierre Hilaire
See Belloc, (Joseph) Hilaire (Pierre Sebastien Rene Swanton)
Belloc, M. A.
See Lowndes, Marie Adelaide (Belloc)
Bellow, Saul 1915- **CLC 1, 2, 3, 6, 8, 10, 13, 15, 25, 33, 34, 63, 79; DA; DAB; DAC; DAM MST, NOV, POP; SSC 14; WLC**
See also AITN 2; BEST 89:3; CA 5-8R; CABS 1; CANR 29, 53; CDALB 1941-1968; DA3; DLB 2, 28; DLBD 3; DLBY 82; MTCW 1, 2
Belser, Reimond Karel Maria de 1929-
See Ruyslinck, Ward
See also CA 152
Bely, Andrey **TCLC 7; PC 11**
See also Bugayev, Boris Nikolayevich
See also MTCW 1
Belyi, Andrei
See Bugayev, Boris Nikolayevich
Benary, Margot
See Benary-Isbert, Margot
Benary-Isbert, Margot 1889-1979 **CLC 12**
See also CA 5-8R; 89-92; CANR 4, 72; CLR 12; MAICYA; SATA 2; SATA-Obit 21
Benavente (y Martinez), Jacinto 1866-1954 **TCLC 3; DAM DRAM, MULT; HLCS 1**
See also CA 106; 131; CANR 81; HW 1, 2; MTCW 1, 2
Benchley, Peter (Bradford) 1940- **CLC 4, 8; DAM NOV, POP**
See also AAYA 14; AITN 2; CA 17-20R; CANR 12, 35, 66; MTCW 1, 2; SATA 3, 89
Benchley, Robert (Charles) 1889-1945 **TCLC 1, 55**
See also CA 105; 153; DLB 11
Benda, Julien 1867-1956 **TCLC 60**
See also CA 120; 154
Benedict, Ruth (Fulton) 1887-1948 **TCLC 60**
See also CA 158
Benedict, Saint c. 480-c. 547 **CMLC 29**
Benedikt, Michael 1935- **CLC 4, 14**
See also CA 13-16R; CANR 7; DLB 5
Benet, Juan 1927- **CLC 28**
See also CA 143
Benet, Stephen Vincent 1898-1943 **TCLC 7; DAM POET; SSC 10**
See also CA 104; 152; DA3; DLB 4, 48, 102; DLBY 97; MTCW 1; YABC 1
Benet, William Rose 1886-1950 **TCLC 28; DAM POET**
See also CA 118; 152; DLB 45
Benford, Gregory (Albert) 1941- **CLC 52**
See also CA 69-72, 175; CAAE 175; CAAS 27; CANR 12, 24, 49; DLBY 82
Bengtsson, Frans (Gunnar) 1894-1954 **TCLC 48**
See also CA 170
Benjamin, David
See Slavitt, David R(ytman)
Benjamin, Lois
See Gould, Lois
Benjamin, Walter 1892-1940 **TCLC 39**
See also CA 164
Benn, Gottfried 1886-1956 **TCLC 3**
See also CA 106; 153; DLB 56
Bennett, Alan 1934- **CLC 45, 77; DAB; DAM MST**
See also CA 103; CANR 35, 55; MTCW 1, 2
Bennett, (Enoch) Arnold 1867-1931 **TCLC 5, 20**

See also CA 106; 155; CDBLB 1890-1914; DLB 10, 34, 98, 135; MTCW 2

Bennett, Elizabeth
See Mitchell, Margaret (Munnerlyn)

Bennett, George Harold 1930-
See Bennett, Hal
See also BW 1; CA 97-100; CANR 87

Bennett, Hal CLC 5
See also Bennett, George Harold
See also DLB 33

Bennett, Jay 1912- **CLC 35**
See also AAYA 10; CA 69-72; CANR 11, 42, 79; JRDA; SAAS 4; SATA 41, 87; SATA-Brief 27

Bennett, Louise (Simone) 1919- **CLC 28; BLC 1; DAM MULT**
See also BW 2, 3; CA 151; DLB 117

Benson, E(dward) F(rederic) 1867-1940 **TCLC 27**
See also CA 114; 157; DLB 135, 153

Benson, Jackson J. 1930- **CLC 34**
See also CA 25-28R; DLB 111

Benson, Sally 1900-1972 **CLC 17**
See also CA 19-20; 37-40R; CAP 1; SATA 1, 35; SATA-Obit 27

Benson, Stella 1892-1933 **TCLC 17**
See also CA 117; 155; DLB 36, 162

Bentham, Jeremy 1748-1832 **NCLC 38**
See also DLB 107, 158

Bentley, E(dmund) C(lerihew) 1875-1956 **TCLC 12**
See also CA 108; DLB 70

Bentley, Eric (Russell) 1916- **CLC 24**
See also CA 5-8R; CANR 6, 67; INT CANR-6

Beranger, Pierre Jean de 1780-1857 **NCLC 34**

Berdyaev, Nicolas
See Berdyaev, Nikolai (Aleksandrovich)

Berdyaev, Nikolai (Aleksandrovich) 1874-1948 **TCLC 67**
See also CA 120; 157

Berdyayev, Nikolai (Aleksandrovich)
See Berdyaev, Nikolai (Aleksandrovich)

Berendt, John (Lawrence) 1939- **CLC 86**
See also CA 146; CANR 75, 93; DA3; MTCW 1

Beresford, J(ohn) D(avys) 1873-1947 **TCLC 81**
See also CA 112; 155; DLB 162, 178, 197

Bergelson, David 1884-1952 **TCLC 81**

Berger, Colonel
See Malraux, (Georges-)Andre

Berger, John (Peter) 1926- **CLC 2, 19**
See also CA 81-84; CANR 51, 78; DLB 14, 207

Berger, Melvin H. 1927- **CLC 12**
See also CA 5-8R; CANR 4; CLR 32; SAAS 2; SATA 5, 88

Berger, Thomas (Louis) 1924- **CLC 3, 5, 8, 11, 18, 38; DAM NOV**
See also CA 1-4R; CANR 5, 28, 51; DLB 2; DLBY 80; INT CANR-28; MTCW 1, 2

Bergman, (Ernst) Ingmar 1918- **CLC 16, 72**
See also CA 81-84; CANR 33, 70; MTCW 2

Bergson, Henri(-Louis) 1859-1941 **TCLC 32**
See also CA 164

Bergstein, Eleanor 1938- **CLC 4**
See also CA 53-56; CANR 5

Berkoff, Steven 1937- **CLC 56**
See also CA 104; CANR 72

Bermant, Chaim (Icyk) 1929- **CLC 40**
See also CA 57-60; CANR 6, 31, 57

Bern, Victoria
See Fisher, M(ary) F(rances) K(ennedy)

Bernanos, (Paul Louis) Georges 1888-1948 **TCLC 3**
See also CA 104; 130; DLB 72

Bernard, April 1956- **CLC 59**
See also CA 131

Berne, Victoria
See Fisher, M(ary) F(rances) K(ennedy)

Bernhard, Thomas 1931-1989 **CLC 3, 32, 61**
See also CA 85-88; 127; CANR 32, 57; DLB 85, 124; MTCW 1

Bernhardt, Sarah (Henriette Rosine) 1844-1923 **TCLC 75**
See also CA 157

Berriault, Gina 1926-1999 **CLC 54, 109; SSC 30**
See also CA 116; 129; 185; CANR 66; DLB 130

Berrigan, Daniel 1921- **CLC 4**
See also CA 33-36R; CAAE 187; CAAS 1; CANR 11, 43, 78; DLB 5

Berrigan, Edmund Joseph Michael, Jr. 1934-1983
See Berrigan, Ted
See also CA 61-64; 110; CANR 14

Berrigan, Ted CLC 37
See also Berrigan, Edmund Joseph Michael, Jr.
See also DLB 5, 169

Berry, Charles Edward Anderson 1931-
See Berry, Chuck
See also CA 115

Berry, Chuck CLC 17
See also Berry, Charles Edward Anderson

Berry, Jonas
See Ashbery, John (Lawrence)

Berry, Wendell (Erdman) 1934- **CLC 4, 6, 8, 27, 46; DAM POET; PC 28**
See also AITN 1; CA 73-76; CANR 50, 73; DLB 5, 6; MTCW 1

Berryman, John 1914-1972 **CLC 1, 2, 3, 4, 6, 8, 10, 13, 25, 62; DAM POET**
See also CA 13-16; 33-36R; CABS 2; CANR 35; CAP 1; CDALB 1941-1968; DLB 48; MTCW 1, 2

Bertolucci, Bernardo 1940- **CLC 16**
See also CA 106

Berton, Pierre (Francis Demarigny) 1920- **CLC 104**
See also CA 1-4R; CANR 2, 56; DLB 68; SATA 99

Bertrand, Aloysius 1807-1841 **NCLC 31**

Bertran de Born c. 1140-1215 **CMLC 5**

Besant, Annie (Wood) 1847-1933 **TCLC 9**
See also CA 105; 185

Bessie, Alvah 1904-1985 **CLC 23**
See also CA 5-8R; 116; CANR 2, 80; DLB 26

Bethlen, T. D.
See Silverberg, Robert

Beti, Mongo CLC 27; BLC 1; DAM MULT
See also Biyidi, Alexandre
See also CANR 79

Betjeman, John 1906-1984 **CLC 2, 6, 10, 34, 43; DAB; DAM MST, POET**
See also CA 9-12R; 112; CANR 33, 56; CDBLB 1945-1960; DA3; DLB 20; DLBY 84; MTCW 1, 2

Bettelheim, Bruno 1903-1990 **CLC 79**
See also CA 81-84; 131; CANR 23, 61; DA3; MTCW 1, 2

Betti, Ugo 1892-1953 **TCLC 5**
See also CA 104; 155

Betts, Doris (Waugh) 1932- **CLC 3, 6, 28**
See also CA 13-16R; CANR 9, 66, 77; DLBY 82; INT CANR-9

Bevan, Alistair
See Roberts, Keith (John Kingston)

Bey, Pilaff
See Douglas, (George) Norman

Bialik, Chaim Nachman 1873-1934 **TCLC 25**
See also CA 170

Bickerstaff, Isaac
See Swift, Jonathan

Bidart, Frank 1939- **CLC 33**
See also CA 140

Bienek, Horst 1930- **CLC 7, 11**
See also CA 73-76; DLB 75

Bierce, Ambrose (Gwinett) 1842-1914(?) **TCLC 1, 7, 44; DA; DAC; DAM MST; SSC 9; WLC**
See also CA 104; 139; CANR 78; CDALB 1865-1917; DA3; DLB 11, 12, 23, 71, 74, 186

Biggers, Earl Derr 1884-1933 **TCLC 65**
See also CA 108; 153

Billings, Josh
See Shaw, Henry Wheeler

Billington, (Lady) Rachel (Mary) 1942- **CLC 43**
See also AITN 2; CA 33-36R; CANR 44

Binyon, T(imothy) J(ohn) 1936- **CLC 34**
See also CA 111; CANR 28

Bion 335B.C.-245B.C. **CMLC 39**

Bioy Casares, Adolfo 1914-1999 **CLC 4, 8, 13, 88; DAM MULT; HLC 1; SSC 17**
See also CA 29-32R; 177; CANR 19, 43, 66; DLB 113; HW 1, 2; MTCW 1, 2

Bird, Cordwainer
See Ellison, Harlan (Jay)

Bird, Robert Montgomery 1806-1854 **NCLC 1**
See also DLB 202

Birkerts, Sven 1951- **CLC 116**
See also CA 128; 133; 176; CAAE 176; CAAS 29; INT 133

Birney, (Alfred) Earle 1904-1995 **CLC 1, 4, 6, 11; DAC; DAM MST, POET**
See also CA 1-4R; CANR 5, 20; DLB 88; MTCW 1

Biruni, al 973-1048(?) **CMLC 28**

Bishop, Elizabeth 1911-1979 **CLC 1, 4, 9, 13, 15, 32; DA; DAC; DAM MST, POET; PC 3**
See also CA 5-8R; 89-92; CABS 2; CANR 26, 61; CDALB 1968-1988; DA3; DLB 5, 169; MTCW 1, 2; SATA-Obit 24

Bishop, John 1935- **CLC 10**
See also CA 105

Bissett, Bill 1939- **CLC 18; PC 14**
See also CA 69-72; CAAS 19; CANR 15; DLB 53; MTCW 1

Bissoondath, Neil (Devindra) 1955- **CLC 120; DAC**
See also CA 136

Bitov, Andrei (Georgievich) 1937- **CLC 57**
See also CA 142

Biyidi, Alexandre 1932-
See Beti, Mongo
See also BW 1, 3; CA 114; 124; CANR 81; DA3; MTCW 1, 2

Bjarme, Brynjolf
See Ibsen, Henrik (Johan)

Bjoernson, Bjoernstjerne (Martinius) 1832-1910 **TCLC 7, 37**
See also CA 104

Black, Robert
See Holdstock, Robert P.

Blackburn, Paul 1926-1971 **CLC 9, 43**
See also CA 81-84; 33-36R; CANR 34; DLB 16; DLBY 81

Black Elk 1863-1950 **TCLC 33; DAM MULT**
See also CA 144; MTCW 1; NNAL

Black Hobart
See Sanders, (James) Ed(ward)

Blacklin, Malcolm
See Chambers, Aidan

Blackmore, R(ichard) D(oddridge) 1825-1900 **TCLC 27**
See also CA 120; DLB 18

Blackmur, R(ichard) P(almer) 1904-1965 **CLC 2, 24**
See also CA 11-12; 25-28R; CANR 71; CAP 1; DLB 63

Black Tarantula
See Acker, Kathy

Blackwood, Algernon (Henry) 1869-1951 **TCLC 5**
See also CA 105; 150; DLB 153, 156, 178

Blackwood, Caroline 1931-1996 **CLC 6, 9, 100**
See also CA 85-88; 151; CANR 32, 61, 65; DLB 14, 207; MTCW 1

Blade, Alexander
See Hamilton, Edmond; Silverberg, Robert

Blaga, Lucian 1895-1961 **CLC 75**
See also CA 157; DLB 220

Blair, Eric (Arthur) 1903-1950
See Orwell, George
See also CA 104; 132; DA; DAB; DAC; DAM MST, NOV; DA3; MTCW 1, 2; SATA 29

Blair, Hugh 1718-1800 **NCLC 75**

Blais, Marie-Claire 1939- **CLC 2, 4, 6, 13, 22; DAC; DAM MST**
See also CA 21-24R; CAAS 4; CANR 38, 75, 93; DLB 53; MTCW 1, 2

Blaise, Clark 1940- **CLC 29**
See also AITN 2; CA 53-56; CAAS 3; CANR 5, 66; DLB 53

Blake, Fairley
See De Voto, Bernard (Augustine)

Blake, Nicholas
See Day Lewis, C(ecil)
See also DLB 77

Blake, William 1757-1827 **NCLC 13, 37, 57; DA; DAB; DAC; DAM MST, POET; PC 12; WLC**
See also CDBLB 1789-1832; CLR 52; DA3; DLB 93, 163; MAICYA; SATA 30

Blanchot, Maurice 1907- **CLC 135**
See also CA 117; 144; DLB 72

Blasco Ibanez, Vicente 1867-1928 **TCLC 12; DAM NOV**
See also CA 110; 131; CANR 81; DA3; HW 1, 2; MTCW 1

Blatty, William Peter 1928- **CLC 2; DAM POP**
See also CA 5-8R; CANR 9

Bleeck, Oliver
See Thomas, Ross (Elmore)

Blessing, Lee 1949- **CLC 54**

Blight, Rose
See Greer, Germaine

Blish, James (Benjamin) 1921-1975 **CLC 14**
See also CA 1-4R; 57-60; CANR 3; DLB 8; MTCW 1; SATA 66

Bliss, Reginald
See Wells, H(erbert) G(eorge)

Blixen, Karen (Christentze Dinesen) 1885-1962
See Dinesen, Isak
See also CA 25-28; CANR 22, 50; CAP 2; DA3; MTCW 1, 2; SATA 44

Bloch, Robert (Albert) 1917-1994 **CLC 33**
See also AAYA 29; CA 5-8R, 179; 146; CAAE 179; CAAS 20; CANR 5, 78; DA3; DLB 44; INT CANR-5; MTCW 1; SATA 12; SATA-Obit 82

Blok, Alexander (Alexandrovich) 1880-1921 **TCLC 5; PC 21**
See also CA 104; 183

Blom, Jan
See Breytenbach, Breyten

Bloom, Harold 1930- **CLC 24, 103**
See also CA 13-16R; CANR 39, 75, 92; DLB 67; MTCW 1

Bloomfield, Aurelius
See Bourne, Randolph S(illiman)

Blount, Roy (Alton), Jr. 1941- **CLC 38**
See also CA 53-56; CANR 10, 28, 61; INT CANR-28; MTCW 1, 2

Bloy, Leon 1846-1917 **TCLC 22**
See also CA 121; 183; DLB 123

Blume, Judy (Sussman) 1938- **CLC 12, 30; DAM NOV, POP**
See also AAYA 3, 26; CA 29-32R; CANR 13, 37, 66; CLR 2, 15; DA3; DLB 52; JRDA; MAICYA; MTCW 1, 2; SATA 2, 31, 79

Blunden, Edmund (Charles) 1896-1974 **CLC 2, 56**
See also CA 17-18; 45-48; CANR 54; CAP 2; DLB 20, 100, 155; MTCW 1

Bly, Robert (Elwood) 1926- **CLC 1, 2, 5, 10, 15, 38, 128; DAM POET**
See also CA 5-8R; CANR 41, 73; DA3; DLB 5; MTCW 1, 2

Boas, Franz 1858-1942 **TCLC 56**
See also CA 115; 181

Bobette
See Simenon, Georges (Jacques Christian)

Boccaccio, Giovanni 1313-1375 **CMLC 13; SSC 10**

Bochco, Steven 1943- **CLC 35**
See also AAYA 11; CA 124; 138

Bodel, Jean 1167(?)-1210 **CMLC 28**

Bodenheim, Maxwell 1892-1954 **TCLC 44**
See also CA 110; 187; DLB 9, 45

Bodker, Cecil 1927- **CLC 21**
See also CA 73-76; CANR 13, 44; CLR 23; MAICYA; SATA 14

Boell, Heinrich (Theodor) 1917-1985 **CLC 2, 3, 6, 9, 11, 15, 27, 32, 72; DA; DAB; DAC; DAM MST, NOV; SSC 23; WLC**
See also CA 21-24R; 116; CANR 24; DA3; DLB 69; DLBY 85; MTCW 1, 2

Boerne, Alfred
See Doeblin, Alfred

Boethius 480(?)-524(?) **CMLC 15**
See also DLB 115

Boff, Leonardo (Genezio Darci) 1938-
See also CA 150; DAM MULT; HLC 1; HW 2

Bogan, Louise 1897-1970 **CLC 4, 39, 46, 93; DAM POET; PC 12**
See also CA 73-76; 25-28R; CANR 33, 82; DLB 45, 169; MTCW 1, 2

Bogarde, Dirk 1921-1999
See Van Den Bogarde, Derek Jules Gaspard Ulric Niven

Bogosian, Eric 1953- **CLC 45**
See also CA 138

Bograd, Larry 1953- **CLC 35**
See also CA 93-96; CANR 57; SAAS 21; SATA 33, 89

Boiardo, Matteo Maria 1441-1494 **LC 6**

Boileau-Despreaux, Nicolas 1636-1711 **LC 3**

Bojer, Johan 1872-1959 **TCLC 64**

Bok, Edward W. 1863-1930 **TCLC 101**
See also DLB 91; DLBD 16

Boland, Eavan (Aisling) 1944- **CLC 40, 67, 113; DAM POET**
See also CA 143; CANR 61; DLB 40; MTCW 2

Boll, Heinrich
See Boell, Heinrich (Theodor)

Bolt, Lee
See Faust, Frederick (Schiller)

Bolt, Robert (Oxton) 1924-1995 **CLC 14; DAM DRAM**
See also CA 17-20R; 147; CANR 35, 67; DLB 13, 233; MTCW 1

Bombal, Maria Luisa 1910-1980 **SSC 37; HLCS 1**
See also CA 127; CANR 72; HW 1

Bombet, Louis-Alexandre-Cesar
See Stendhal

Bomkauf
See Kaufman, Bob (Garnell)

Bonaventura NCLC 35
See also DLB 90

Bond, Edward 1934- **CLC 4, 6, 13, 23; DAM DRAM**
See also CA 25-28R; CANR 38, 67; DLB 13; MTCW 1

Bonham, Frank 1914-1989 **CLC 12**
See also AAYA 1; CA 9-12R; CANR 4, 36; JRDA; MAICYA; SAAS 3; SATA 1, 49; SATA-Obit 62

Bonnefoy, Yves 1923- **CLC 9, 15, 58; DAM MST, POET**
See also CA 85-88; CANR 33, 75; MTCW 1, 2

Bontemps, Arna(ud Wendell) 1902-1973 **CLC 1, 18; BLC 1; DAM MULT, NOV, POET**
See also BW 1; CA 1-4R; 41-44R; CANR 4, 35; CLR 6; DA3; DLB 48, 51; JRDA; MAICYA; MTCW 1, 2; SATA 2, 44; SATA-Obit 24

Booth, Martin 1944- **CLC 13**
See also CA 93-96; CAAS 2; CANR 92

Booth, Philip 1925- **CLC 23**
See also CA 5-8R; CANR 5, 88; DLBY 82

Booth, Wayne C(layson) 1921- **CLC 24**
See also CA 1-4R; CAAS 5; CANR 3, 43; DLB 67

Borchert, Wolfgang 1921-1947 **TCLC 5**
See also CA 104; DLB 69, 124

Borel, Petrus 1809-1859 **NCLC 41**

Borges, Jorge Luis 1899-1986 **CLC 1, 2, 3, 4, 6, 8, 9, 10, 13, 19, 44, 48, 83; DA; DAB; DAC; DAM MST, MULT; HLC 1; PC 22, 32; SSC 4, 41; WLC**
See also AAYA 26; CA 21-24R; CANR 19, 33, 75; DA3; DLB 113; DLBY 86; HW 1, 2; MTCW 1, 2

Borowski, Tadeusz 1922-1951 **TCLC 9**
See also CA 106; 154

Borrow, George (Henry) 1803-1881 **NCLC 9**
See also DLB 21, 55, 166

Bosch (Gavino), Juan 1909-
See also CA 151; DAM MST, MULT; DLB 145; HLCS 1; HW 1, 2

Bosman, Herman Charles 1905-1951 **TCLC 49**
See also Malan, Herman
See also CA 160; DLB 225

Bosschere, Jean de 1878(?)-1953 **TCLC 19**
See also CA 115; 186

Boswell, James 1740-1795 **LC 4, 50; DA; DAB; DAC; DAM MST; WLC**
See also CDBLB 1660-1789; DLB 104, 142

Bottoms, David 1949- **CLC 53**
See also CA 105; CANR 22; DLB 120; DLBY 83

Boucicault, Dion 1820-1890 **NCLC 41**

Bourget, Paul (Charles Joseph) 1852-1935 **TCLC 12**
See also CA 107; DLB 123

Bourjaily, Vance (Nye) 1922- **CLC 8, 62**
See also CA 1-4R; CAAS 1; CANR 2, 72; DLB 2, 143

Bourne, Randolph S(illiman) 1886-1918 **TCLC 16**
See also CA 117; 155; DLB 63

Bova, Ben(jamin William) 1932- **CLC 45**
See also AAYA 16; CA 5-8R; CAAS 18; CANR 11, 56; CLR 3; DLBY 81; INT CANR-11; MAICYA; MTCW 1; SATA 6, 68

Bowen, Elizabeth (Dorothea Cole) 1899-1973 **CLC 1, 3, 6, 11, 15, 22, 118; DAM NOV; SSC 3, 28**
See also CA 17-18; 41-44R; CANR 35; CAP 2; CDBLB 1945-1960; DA3; DLB 15, 162; MTCW 1, 2
Bowering, George 1935- **CLC 15, 47**
See also CA 21-24R; CAAS 16; CANR 10; DLB 53
Bowering, Marilyn R(uthe) 1949- **CLC 32**
See also CA 101; CANR 49
Bowers, Edgar 1924-2000 **CLC 9**
See also CA 5-8R; CANR 24; DLB 5
Bowie, David CLC 17
See also Jones, David Robert
Bowles, Jane (Sydney) 1917-1973 **CLC 3, 68**
See also CA 19-20; 41-44R; CAP 2
Bowles, Paul (Frederick) 1910-1999 **CLC 1, 2, 19, 53; SSC 3**
See also CA 1-4R; 186; CAAS 1; CANR 1, 19, 50, 75; DA3; DLB 5, 6; MTCW 1, 2
Box, Edgar
See Vidal, Gore
Boyd, Nancy
See Millay, Edna St. Vincent
Boyd, William 1952- **CLC 28, 53, 70**
See also CA 114; 120; CANR 51, 71; DLB 231
Boyle, Kay 1902-1992 **CLC 1, 5, 19, 58, 121; SSC 5**
See also CA 13-16R; 140; CAAS 1; CANR 29, 61; DLB 4, 9, 48, 86; DLBY 93; MTCW 1, 2
Boyle, Mark
See Kienzle, William X(avier)
Boyle, Patrick 1905-1982 **CLC 19**
See also CA 127
Boyle, T. C. 1948-
See Boyle, T(homas) Coraghessan
Boyle, T(homas) Coraghessan 1948- **CLC 36, 55, 90; DAM POP; SSC 16**
See also BEST 90:4; CA 120; CANR 44, 76, 89; DA3; DLBY 86; MTCW 2
Boz
See Dickens, Charles (John Huffam)
Brackenridge, Hugh Henry 1748-1816 **NCLC 7**
See also DLB 11, 37
Bradbury, Edward P.
See Moorcock, Michael (John)
See also MTCW 2
Bradbury, Malcolm (Stanley) 1932- **CLC 32, 61; DAM NOV**
See also CA 1-4R; CANR 1, 33, 91; DA3; DLB 14, 207; MTCW 1, 2
Bradbury, Ray (Douglas) 1920- **CLC 1, 3, 10, 15, 42, 98; DA; DAB; DAC; DAM MST, NOV, POP; SSC 29; WLC**
See also AAYA 15; AITN 1, 2; CA 1-4R; CANR 2, 30, 75; CDALB 1968-1988; DA3; DLB 2, 8; MTCW 1, 2; SATA 11, 64
Bradford, Gamaliel 1863-1932 **TCLC 36**
See also CA 160; DLB 17
Bradley, David (Henry), Jr. 1950- **CLC 23, 118; BLC 1; DAM MULT**
See also BW 1, 3; CA 104; CANR 26, 81; DLB 33
Bradley, John Ed(mund, Jr.) 1958- **CLC 55**
See also CA 139
Bradley, Marion Zimmer 1930-1999 **CLC 30; DAM POP**
See also AAYA 9; CA 57-60; 185; CAAS 10; CANR 7, 31, 51, 75; DA3; DLB 8; MTCW 1, 2; SATA 90; SATA-Obit 116
Bradstreet, Anne 1612(?)-1672 **LC 4, 30; DA; DAC; DAM MST, POET; PC 10**
See also CDALB 1640-1865; DA3; DLB 24
Brady, Joan 1939- **CLC 86**
See also CA 141
Bragg, Melvyn 1939- **CLC 10**
See also BEST 89:3; CA 57-60; CANR 10, 48, 89; DLB 14
Brahe, Tycho 1546-1601 **LC 45**
Braine, John (Gerard) 1922-1986 **CLC 1, 3, 41**
See also CA 1-4R; 120; CANR 1, 33; CDBLB 1945-1960; DLB 15; DLBY 86; MTCW 1
Bramah, Ernest 1868-1942 **TCLC 72**
See also CA 156; DLB 70
Brammer, William 1930(?)-1978 **CLC 31**
See also CA 77-80
Brancati, Vitaliano 1907-1954 **TCLC 12**
See also CA 109
Brancato, Robin F(idler) 1936- **CLC 35**
See also AAYA 9; CA 69-72; CANR 11, 45; CLR 32; JRDA; SAAS 9; SATA 97
Brand, Max
See Faust, Frederick (Schiller)
Brand, Millen 1906-1980 **CLC 7**
See also CA 21-24R; 97-100; CANR 72
Branden, Barbara CLC 44
See also CA 148
Brandes, Georg (Morris Cohen) 1842-1927 **TCLC 10**
See also CA 105
Brandys, Kazimierz 1916- **CLC 62**
Branley, Franklyn M(ansfield) 1915- **CLC 21**
See also CA 33-36R; CANR 14, 39; CLR 13; MAICYA; SAAS 16; SATA 4, 68
Brathwaite, Edward (Kamau) 1930- **CLC 11; BLCS; DAM POET**
See also BW 2, 3; CA 25-28R; CANR 11, 26, 47; DLB 125
Brautigan, Richard (Gary) 1935-1984 **CLC 1, 3, 5, 9, 12, 34, 42; DAM NOV**
See also CA 53-56; 113; CANR 34; DA3; DLB 2, 5, 206; DLBY 80, 84; MTCW 1; SATA 56
Brave Bird, Mary 1953-
See Crow Dog, Mary (Ellen)
See also NNAL
Braverman, Kate 1950- **CLC 67**
See also CA 89-92
Brecht, (Eugen) Bertolt (Friedrich) 1898-1956 **TCLC 1, 6, 13, 35; DA; DAB; DAC; DAM DRAM, MST; DC 3; WLC**
See also CA 104; 133; CANR 62; DA3; DLB 56, 124; MTCW 1, 2
Brecht, Eugen Berthold Friedrich
See Brecht, (Eugen) Bertolt (Friedrich)
Bremer, Fredrika 1801-1865 **NCLC 11**
Brennan, Christopher John 1870-1932 **TCLC 17**
See also CA 117
Brennan, Maeve 1917-1993 **CLC 5**
See also CA 81-84; CANR 72
Brent, Linda
See Jacobs, Harriet A(nn)
Brentano, Clemens (Maria) 1778-1842 **NCLC 1**
See also DLB 90
Brent of Bin Bin
See Franklin, (Stella Maria Sarah) Miles (Lampe)
Brenton, Howard 1942- **CLC 31**
See also CA 69-72; CANR 33, 67; DLB 13; MTCW 1
Breslin, James 1930-
See Breslin, Jimmy
See also CA 73-76; CANR 31, 75; DAM NOV; MTCW 1, 2
Breslin, Jimmy CLC 4, 43
See also Breslin, James
See also AITN 1; DLB 185; MTCW 2
Bresson, Robert 1901(?)-1999 **CLC 16**
See also CA 110; 187; CANR 49
Breton, Andre 1896-1966 **CLC 2, 9, 15, 54; PC 15**
See also CA 19-20; 25-28R; CANR 40, 60; CAP 2; DLB 65; MTCW 1, 2
Breytenbach, Breyten 1939(?)- **CLC 23, 37, 126; DAM POET**
See also CA 113; 129; CANR 61; DLB 225
Bridgers, Sue Ellen 1942- **CLC 26**
See also AAYA 8; CA 65-68; CANR 11, 36; CLR 18; DLB 52; JRDA; MAICYA; SAAS 1; SATA 22, 90; SATA-Essay 109
Bridges, Robert (Seymour) 1844-1930 **TCLC 1; DAM POET; PC 28**
See also CA 104; 152; CDBLB 1890-1914; DLB 19, 98
Bridie, James TCLC 3
See also Mavor, Osborne Henry
See also DLB 10
Brin, David 1950- **CLC 34**
See also AAYA 21; CA 102; CANR 24, 70; INT CANR-24; SATA 65
Brink, Andre (Philippus) 1935- **CLC 18, 36, 106**
See also CA 104; CANR 39, 62; DLB 225; INT 103; MTCW 1, 2
Brinsmead, H(esba) F(ay) 1922- **CLC 21**
See also CA 21-24R; CANR 10; CLR 47; MAICYA; SAAS 5; SATA 18, 78
Brittain, Vera (Mary) 1893(?)-1970 **CLC 23**
See also CA 13-16; 25-28R; CANR 58; CAP 1; DLB 191; MTCW 1, 2
Broch, Hermann 1886-1951 **TCLC 20**
See also CA 117; DLB 85, 124
Brock, Rose
See Hansen, Joseph
Brodkey, Harold (Roy) 1930-1996 **CLC 56**
See also CA 111; 151; CANR 71; DLB 130
Brodsky, Iosif Alexandrovich 1940-1996
See Brodsky, Joseph
See also AITN 1; CA 41-44R; 151; CANR 37; DAM POET; DA3; MTCW 1, 2
Brodsky, Joseph 1940-1996 **CLC 4, 6, 13, 36, 100; PC 9**
See also Brodsky, Iosif Alexandrovich
See also MTCW 1
Brodsky, Michael (Mark) 1948- **CLC 19**
See also CA 102; CANR 18, 41, 58
Brome, Richard 1590(?)-1652 **LC 61**
See also DLB 58
Bromell, Henry 1947- **CLC 5**
See also CA 53-56; CANR 9
Bromfield, Louis (Brucker) 1896-1956 **TCLC 11**
See also CA 107; 155; DLB 4, 9, 86
Broner, E(sther) M(asserman) 1930- **CLC 19**
See also CA 17-20R; CANR 8, 25, 72; DLB 28
Bronk, William (M.) 1918-1999 **CLC 10**
See also CA 89-92; 177; CANR 23; DLB 165
Bronstein, Lev Davidovich
See Trotsky, Leon
Bronte, Anne 1820-1849 **NCLC 4, 71**
See also DA3; DLB 21, 199
Bronte, Charlotte 1816-1855 **NCLC 3, 8, 33, 58; DA; DAB; DAC; DAM MST, NOV; WLC**
See also AAYA 17; CDBLB 1832-1890; DA3; DLB 21, 159, 199
Bronte, Emily (Jane) 1818-1848 **NCLC 16, 35; DA; DAB; DAC; DAM MST, NOV, POET; PC 8; WLC**
See also AAYA 17; CDBLB 1832-1890; DA3; DLB 21, 32, 199
Brooke, Frances 1724-1789 **LC 6, 48**
See also DLB 39, 99
Brooke, Henry 1703(?)-1783 **LC 1**

See also DLB 39
Brooke, Rupert (Chawner) 1887-1915 **TCLC 2, 7; DA; DAB; DAC; DAM MST, POET; PC 24; WLC**
See also CA 104; 132; CANR 61; CDBLB 1914-1945; DLB 19; MTCW 1, 2
Brooke-Haven, P.
See Wodehouse, P(elham) G(renville)
Brooke-Rose, Christine 1926(?)- **CLC 40**
See also CA 13-16R; CANR 58; DLB 14, 231
Brookner, Anita 1928- **CLC 32, 34, 51, 136; DAB; DAM POP**
See also CA 114; 120; CANR 37, 56, 87; DA3; DLB 194; DLBY 87; MTCW 1, 2
Brooks, Cleanth 1906-1994 **CLC 24, 86, 110**
See also CA 17-20R; 145; CANR 33, 35; DLB 63; DLBY 94; INT CANR-35; MTCW 1, 2
Brooks, George
See Baum, L(yman) Frank
Brooks, Gwendolyn 1917-2000 **CLC 1, 2, 4, 5, 15, 49, 125; BLC 1; DA; DAC; DAM MST, MULT, POET; PC 7; WLC**
See also AAYA 20; AITN 1; BW 2, 3; CA 1-4R; CANR 1, 27, 52, 75; CDALB 1941-1968; CLR 27; DA3; DLB 5, 76, 165; MTCW 1, 2; SATA 6
Brooks, Mel CLC 12
See also Kaminsky, Melvin
See also AAYA 13; DLB 26
Brooks, Peter 1938- **CLC 34**
See also CA 45-48; CANR 1
Brooks, Van Wyck 1886-1963 **CLC 29**
See also CA 1-4R; CANR 6; DLB 45, 63, 103
Brophy, Brigid (Antonia) 1929-1995 **CLC 6, 11, 29, 105**
See also CA 5-8R; 149; CAAS 4; CANR 25, 53; DA3; DLB 14; MTCW 1, 2
Brosman, Catharine Savage 1934- **CLC 9**
See also CA 61-64; CANR 21, 46
Brossard, Nicole 1943- **CLC 115**
See also CA 122; CAAS 16; DLB 53
Brother Antoninus
See Everson, William (Oliver)
The Brothers Quay
See Quay, Stephen; Quay, Timothy
Broughton, T(homas) Alan 1936- **CLC 19**
See also CA 45-48; CANR 2, 23, 48
Broumas, Olga 1949- **CLC 10, 73**
See also CA 85-88; CANR 20, 69
Brown, Alan 1950- **CLC 99**
See also CA 156
Brown, Charles Brockden 1771-1810 **NCLC 22, 74**
See also CDALB 1640-1865; DLB 37, 59, 73
Brown, Christy 1932-1981 **CLC 63**
See also CA 105; 104; CANR 72; DLB 14
Brown, Claude 1937- **CLC 30; BLC 1; DAM MULT**
See also AAYA 7; BW 1, 3; CA 73-76; CANR 81
Brown, Dee (Alexander) 1908- **CLC 18, 47; DAM POP**
See also AAYA 30; CA 13-16R; CAAS 6; CANR 11, 45, 60; DA3; DLBY 80; MTCW 1, 2; SATA 5, 110
Brown, George
See Wertmueller, Lina
Brown, George Douglas 1869-1902 **TCLC 28**
See also CA 162
Brown, George Mackay 1921-1996 **CLC 5, 48, 100**
See also CA 21-24R; 151; CAAS 6; CANR 12, 37, 67; DLB 14, 27, 139; MTCW 1; SATA 35
Brown, (William) Larry 1951- **CLC 73**
See also CA 130; 134; INT 133
Brown, Moses
See Barrett, William (Christopher)
Brown, Rita Mae 1944- **CLC 18, 43, 79; DAM NOV, POP**
See also CA 45-48; CANR 2, 11, 35, 62; DA3; INT CANR-11; MTCW 1, 2
Brown, Roderick (Langmere) Haig-
See Haig-Brown, Roderick (Langmere)
Brown, Rosellen 1939- **CLC 32**
See also CA 77-80; CAAS 10; CANR 14, 44
Brown, Sterling Allen 1901-1989 **CLC 1, 23, 59; BLC 1; DAM MULT, POET**
See also BW 1, 3; CA 85-88; 127; CANR 26; DA3; DLB 48, 51, 63; MTCW 1, 2
Brown, Will
See Ainsworth, William Harrison
Brown, William Wells 1813-1884 **NCLC 2, 89; BLC 1; DAM MULT; DC 1**
See also DLB 3, 50
Browne, (Clyde) Jackson 1948(?)- **CLC 21**
See also CA 120
Browning, Elizabeth Barrett 1806-1861 **NCLC 1, 16, 61, 66; DA; DAB; DAC; DAM MST, POET; PC 6; WLC**
See also CDBLB 1832-1890; DA3; DLB 32, 199
Browning, Robert 1812-1889 **NCLC 19, 79; DA; DAB; DAC; DAM MST, POET; PC 2; WLCS**
See also CDBLB 1832-1890; DA3; DLB 32, 163; YABC 1
Browning, Tod 1882-1962 **CLC 16**
See also CA 141; 117
Brownson, Orestes Augustus 1803-1876 **NCLC 50**
See also DLB 1, 59, 73
Bruccoli, Matthew J(oseph) 1931- **CLC 34**
See also CA 9-12R; CANR 7, 87; DLB 103
Bruce, Lenny CLC 21
See also Schneider, Leonard Alfred
Bruin, John
See Brutus, Dennis
Brulard, Henri
See Stendhal
Brulls, Christian
See Simenon, Georges (Jacques Christian)
Brunner, John (Kilian Houston) 1934-1995 **CLC 8, 10; DAM POP**
See also CA 1-4R; 149; CAAS 8; CANR 2, 37; MTCW 1, 2
Bruno, Giordano 1548-1600 **LC 27**
Brutus, Dennis 1924- **CLC 43; BLC 1; DAM MULT, POET; PC 24**
See also BW 2, 3; CA 49-52; CAAS 14; CANR 2, 27, 42, 81; DLB 117, 225
Bryan, C(ourtlandt) D(ixon) B(arnes) 1936- **CLC 29**
See also CA 73-76; CANR 13, 68; DLB 185; INT CANR-13
Bryan, Michael
See Moore, Brian
Bryan, William Jennings 1860-1925 **TCLC 99**
Bryant, William Cullen 1794-1878 **NCLC 6, 46; DA; DAB; DAC; DAM MST, POET; PC 20**
See also CDALB 1640-1865; DLB 3, 43, 59, 189
Bryusov, Valery Yakovlevich 1873-1924 **TCLC 10**
See also CA 107; 155
Buchan, John 1875-1940 **TCLC 41; DAB; DAM POP**
See also CA 108; 145; DLB 34, 70, 156; MTCW 1; YABC 2
Buchanan, George 1506-1582 **LC 4**
See also DLB 152
Buchheim, Lothar-Guenther 1918- **CLC 6**
See also CA 85-88
Buchner, (Karl) Georg 1813-1837 **NCLC 26**
Buchwald, Art(hur) 1925- **CLC 33**
See also AITN 1; CA 5-8R; CANR 21, 67; MTCW 1, 2; SATA 10
Buck, Pearl S(ydenstricker) 1892-1973 **CLC 7, 11, 18, 127; DA; DAB; DAC; DAM MST, NOV**
See also AITN 1; CA 1-4R; 41-44R; CANR 1, 34; CDALBS; DA3; DLB 9, 102; MTCW 1, 2; SATA 1, 25
Buckler, Ernest 1908-1984 **CLC 13; DAC; DAM MST**
See also CA 11-12; 114; CAP 1; DLB 68; SATA 47
Buckley, Vincent (Thomas) 1925-1988 **CLC 57**
See also CA 101
Buckley, William F(rank), Jr. 1925- **CLC 7, 18, 37; DAM POP**
See also AITN 1; CA 1-4R; CANR 1, 24, 53, 93; DA3; DLB 137; DLBY 80; INT CANR-24; MTCW 1, 2
Buechner, (Carl) Frederick 1926- **CLC 2, 4, 6, 9; DAM NOV**
See also CA 13-16R; CANR 11, 39, 64; DLBY 80; INT CANR-11; MTCW 1, 2
Buell, John (Edward) 1927- **CLC 10**
See also CA 1-4R; CANR 71; DLB 53
Buero Vallejo, Antonio 1916-2000 **CLC 15, 46**
See also CA 106; CANR 24, 49, 75; HW 1; MTCW 1, 2
Bufalino, Gesualdo 1920(?)- **CLC 74**
See also DLB 196
Bugayev, Boris Nikolayevich 1880-1934 **TCLC 7; PC 11**
See also Bely, Andrey
See also CA 104; 165; MTCW 1
Bukowski, Charles 1920-1994 **CLC 2, 5, 9, 41, 82, 108; DAM NOV, POET; PC 18**
See also CA 17-20R; 144; CANR 40, 62; DA3; DLB 5, 130, 169; MTCW 1, 2
Bulgakov, Mikhail (Afanas'evich) 1891-1940 **TCLC 2, 16; DAM DRAM, NOV; SSC 18**
See also CA 105; 152
Bulgya, Alexander Alexandrovich 1901-1956 **TCLC 53**
See also Fadeyev, Alexander
See also CA 117; 181
Bullins, Ed 1935- **CLC 1, 5, 7; BLC 1; DAM DRAM, MULT; DC 6**
See also BW 2, 3; CA 49-52; CAAS 16; CANR 24, 46, 73; DLB 7, 38; MTCW 1, 2
Bulwer-Lytton, Edward (George Earle Lytton) 1803-1873 **NCLC 1, 45**
See also DLB 21
Bunin, Ivan Alexeyevich 1870-1953 **TCLC 6; SSC 5**
See also CA 104
Bunting, Basil 1900-1985 **CLC 10, 39, 47; DAM POET**
See also CA 53-56; 115; CANR 7; DLB 20
Bunuel, Luis 1900-1983 **CLC 16, 80; DAM MULT; HLC 1**
See also CA 101; 110; CANR 32, 77; HW 1
Bunyan, John 1628-1688 **LC 4; DA; DAB; DAC; DAM MST; WLC**
See also CDBLB 1660-1789; DLB 39
Burckhardt, Jacob (Christoph) 1818-1897 **NCLC 49**
Burford, Eleanor
See Hibbert, Eleanor Alice Burford
Burgess, Anthony -1993 **CLC 1, 2, 4, 5, 8, 10, 13, 15, 22, 40, 62, 81, 94; DAB**

See also Wilson, John (Anthony) Burgess
See also AAYA 25; AITN 1; CDBLB 1960 to Present; DLB 14, 194; DLBY 98; MTCW 1
Burke, Edmund 1729(?)-1797 **LC 7, 36; DA; DAB; DAC; DAM MST; WLC**
See also DA3; DLB 104
Burke, Kenneth (Duva) 1897-1993 **CLC 2, 24**
See also CA 5-8R; 143; CANR 39, 74; DLB 45, 63; MTCW 1, 2
Burke, Leda
See Garnett, David
Burke, Ralph
See Silverberg, Robert
Burke, Thomas 1886-1945 **TCLC 63**
See also CA 113; 155; DLB 197
Burney, Fanny 1752-1840 **NCLC 12, 54**
See also DLB 39
Burns, Robert 1759-1796 **LC 3, 29, 40; DA; DAB; DAC; DAM MST, POET; PC 6; WLC**
See also CDBLB 1789-1832; DA3; DLB 109
Burns, Tex
See L'Amour, Louis (Dearborn)
Burnshaw, Stanley 1906- **CLC 3, 13, 44**
See also CA 9-12R; DLB 48; DLBY 97
Burr, Anne 1937- **CLC 6**
See also CA 25-28R
Burroughs, Edgar Rice 1875-1950 **TCLC 2, 32; DAM NOV**
See also AAYA 11; CA 104; 132; DA3; DLB 8; MTCW 1, 2; SATA 41
Burroughs, William S(eward) 1914-1997 **CLC 1, 2, 5, 15, 22, 42, 75, 109; DA; DAB; DAC; DAM MST, NOV, POP; WLC**
See also AITN 2; CA 9-12R; 160; CANR 20, 52; DA3; DLB 2, 8, 16, 152; DLBY 81, 97; MTCW 1, 2
Burton, SirRichard F(rancis) 1821-1890 **NCLC 42**
See also DLB 55, 166, 184
Busch, Frederick 1941- **CLC 7, 10, 18, 47**
See also CA 33-36R; CAAS 1; CANR 45, 73, 92; DLB 6
Bush, Ronald 1946- **CLC 34**
See also CA 136
Bustos, F(rancisco)
See Borges, Jorge Luis
Bustos Domecq, H(onorio)
See Bioy Casares, Adolfo; Borges, Jorge Luis
Butler, Octavia E(stelle) 1947- **CLC 38, 121; BLCS; DAM MULT, POP**
See also AAYA 18; BW 2, 3; CA 73-76; CANR 12, 24, 38, 73; CLR 65; DA3; DLB 33; MTCW 1, 2; SATA 84
Butler, Robert Olen (Jr.) 1945- **CLC 81; DAM POP**
See also CA 112; CANR 66; DLB 173; INT 112; MTCW 1
Butler, Samuel 1612-1680 **LC 16, 43**
See also DLB 101, 126
Butler, Samuel 1835-1902 **TCLC 1, 33; DA; DAB; DAC; DAM MST, NOV; WLC**
See also CA 143; CDBLB 1890-1914; DA3; DLB 18, 57, 174
Butler, Walter C.
See Faust, Frederick (Schiller)
Butor, Michel (Marie Francois) 1926- **CLC 1, 3, 8, 11, 15**
See also CA 9-12R; CANR 33, 66; DLB 83; MTCW 1, 2
Butts, Mary 1892(?)-1937 **TCLC 77**
See also CA 148
Buzo, Alexander (John) 1944- **CLC 61**
See also CA 97-100; CANR 17, 39, 69
Buzzati, Dino 1906-1972 **CLC 36**
See also CA 160; 33-36R; DLB 177
Byars, Betsy (Cromer) 1928- **CLC 35**
See also AAYA 19; CA 33-36R, 183; CAAE 183; CANR 18, 36, 57; CLR 1, 16; DLB 52; INT CANR-18; JRDA; MAICYA; MTCW 1; SAAS 1; SATA 4, 46, 80; SATA-Essay 108
Byatt, A(ntonia) S(usan Drabble) 1936- **CLC 19, 65, 136; DAM NOV, POP**
See also CA 13-16R; CANR 13, 33, 50, 75; DA3; DLB 14, 194; MTCW 1, 2
Byrne, David 1952- **CLC 26**
See also CA 127
Byrne, John Keyes 1926-
See Leonard, Hugh
See also CA 102; CANR 78; INT 102
Byron, George Gordon (Noel) 1788-1824 **NCLC 2, 12; DA; DAB; DAC; DAM MST, POET; PC 16; WLC**
See also CDBLB 1789-1832; DA3; DLB 96, 110
Byron, Robert 1905-1941 **TCLC 67**
See also CA 160; DLB 195
C. 3. 3.
See Wilde, Oscar (Fingal O'Flahertie Wills)
Caballero, Fernan 1796-1877 **NCLC 10**
Cabell, Branch
See Cabell, James Branch
Cabell, James Branch 1879-1958 **TCLC 6**
See also CA 105; 152; DLB 9, 78; MTCW 1
Cabeza de Vaca, Alvar Nunez 1490-1557(?) **LC 61**
Cable, George Washington 1844-1925 **TCLC 4; SSC 4**
See also CA 104; 155; DLB 12, 74; DLBD 13
Cabral de Melo Neto, Joao 1920- **CLC 76; DAM MULT**
See also CA 151
Cabrera Infante, G(uillermo) 1929- **CLC 5, 25, 45, 120; DAM MULT; HLC 1; SSC 39**
See also CA 85-88; CANR 29, 65; DA3; DLB 113; HW 1, 2; MTCW 1, 2
Cade, Toni
See Bambara, Toni Cade
Cadmus and Harmonia
See Buchan, John
Caedmon fl. 658-680 **CMLC 7**
See also DLB 146
Caeiro, Alberto
See Pessoa, Fernando (Antonio Nogueira)
Cage, John (Milton, Jr.) 1912-1992 **CLC 41**
See also CA 13-16R; 169; CANR 9, 78; DLB 193; INT CANR-9
Cahan, Abraham 1860-1951 **TCLC 71**
See also CA 108; 154; DLB 9, 25, 28
Cain, G.
See Cabrera Infante, G(uillermo)
Cain, Guillermo
See Cabrera Infante, G(uillermo)
Cain, James M(allahan) 1892-1977 **CLC 3, 11, 28**
See also AITN 1; CA 17-20R; 73-76; CANR 8, 34, 61; DLB 226; MTCW 1
Caine, Hall 1853-1931 **TCLC 97**
Caine, Mark
See Raphael, Frederic (Michael)
Calasso, Roberto 1941- **CLC 81**
See also CA 143; CANR 89
Calderon de la Barca, Pedro 1600-1681 **LC 23; DC 3; HLCS 1**
Caldwell, Erskine (Preston) 1903-1987 **CLC 1, 8, 14, 50, 60; DAM NOV; SSC 19**
See also AITN 1; CA 1-4R; 121; CAAS 1; CANR 2, 33; DA3; DLB 9, 86; MTCW 1, 2
Caldwell, (Janet Miriam) Taylor (Holland) 1900-1985 **CLC 2, 28, 39; DAM NOV, POP**
See also CA 5-8R; 116; CANR 5; DA3; DLBD 17
Calhoun, John Caldwell 1782-1850 **NCLC 15**
See also DLB 3
Calisher, Hortense 1911- **CLC 2, 4, 8, 38, 134; DAM NOV; SSC 15**
See also CA 1-4R; CANR 1, 22, 67; DA3; DLB 2; INT CANR-22; MTCW 1, 2
Callaghan, Morley Edward 1903-1990 **CLC 3, 14, 41, 65; DAC; DAM MST**
See also CA 9-12R; 132; CANR 33, 73; DLB 68; MTCW 1, 2
Callimachus c. 305B.C.-c. 240B.C. **CMLC 18**
See also DLB 176
Calvin, John 1509-1564 **LC 37**
Calvino, Italo 1923-1985 **CLC 5, 8, 11, 22, 33, 39, 73; DAM NOV; SSC 3**
See also CA 85-88; 116; CANR 23, 61; DLB 196; MTCW 1, 2
Cameron, Carey 1952- **CLC 59**
See also CA 135
Cameron, Peter 1959- **CLC 44**
See also CA 125; CANR 50
Camoens, Luis Vaz de 1524(?)-1580
See also HLCS 1
Camoes, Luis de 1524(?)-1580 **LC 62; HLCS 1; PC 31**
Campana, Dino 1885-1932 **TCLC 20**
See also CA 117; DLB 114
Campanella, Tommaso 1568-1639 **LC 32**
Campbell, John W(ood, Jr.) 1910-1971 **CLC 32**
See also CA 21-22; 29-32R; CANR 34; CAP 2; DLB 8; MTCW 1
Campbell, Joseph 1904-1987 **CLC 69**
See also AAYA 3; BEST 89:2; CA 1-4R; 124; CANR 3, 28, 61; DA3; MTCW 1, 2
Campbell, Maria 1940- **CLC 85; DAC**
See also CA 102; CANR 54; NNAL
Campbell, (John) Ramsey 1946- **CLC 42; SSC 19**
See also CA 57-60; CANR 7; INT CANR-7
Campbell, (Ignatius) Roy (Dunnachie) 1901-1957 **TCLC 5**
See also CA 104; 155; DLB 20, 225; MTCW 2
Campbell, Thomas 1777-1844 **NCLC 19**
See also DLB 93; 144
Campbell, Wilfred TCLC 9
See also Campbell, William
Campbell, William 1858(?)-1918
See Campbell, Wilfred
See also CA 106; DLB 92
Campion, Jane CLC 95
See also AAYA 33; CA 138; CANR 87
Camus, Albert 1913-1960 **CLC 1, 2, 4, 9, 11, 14, 32, 63, 69, 124; DA; DAB; DAC; DAM DRAM, MST, NOV; DC 2; SSC 9; WLC**
See also CA 89-92; DA3; DLB 72; MTCW 1, 2
Canby, Vincent 1924- **CLC 13**
See also CA 81-84
Cancale
See Desnos, Robert
Canetti, Elias 1905-1994 **CLC 3, 14, 25, 75, 86**
See also CA 21-24R; 146; CANR 23, 61, 79; DA3; DLB 85, 124; MTCW 1, 2
Canfield, Dorothea F.
See Fisher, Dorothy (Frances) Canfield
Canfield, Dorothea Frances
See Fisher, Dorothy (Frances) Canfield

Author Index

Canfield, Dorothy
See Fisher, Dorothy (Frances) Canfield
Canin, Ethan 1960- **CLC 55**
See also CA 131; 135
Cannon, Curt
See Hunter, Evan
Cao, Lan 1961- **CLC 109**
See also CA 165
Cape, Judith
See Page, P(atricia) K(athleen)
Capek, Karel 1890-1938 **TCLC 6, 37; DA; DAB; DAC; DAM DRAM, MST, NOV; DC 1; SSC 36; WLC**
See also CA 104; 140; DA3; MTCW 1
Capote, Truman 1924-1984 **CLC 1, 3, 8, 13, 19, 34, 38, 58; DA; DAB; DAC; DAM MST, NOV, POP; SSC 2; WLC**
See also CA 5-8R; 113; CANR 18, 62; CDALB 1941-1968; DA3; DLB 2, 185, 227; DLBY 80, 84; MTCW 1, 2; SATA 91
Capra, Frank 1897-1991 **CLC 16**
See also CA 61-64; 135
Caputo, Philip 1941- **CLC 32**
See also CA 73-76; CANR 40
Caragiale, Ion Luca 1852-1912 **TCLC 76**
See also CA 157
Card, Orson Scott 1951- **CLC 44, 47, 50; DAM POP**
See also AAYA 11; CA 102; CANR 27, 47, 73; DA3; INT CANR-27; MTCW 1, 2; SATA 83
Cardenal, Ernesto 1925- **CLC 31; DAM MULT, POET; HLC 1; PC 22**
See also CA 49-52; CANR 2, 32, 66; HW 1, 2; MTCW 1, 2
Cardozo, Benjamin N(athan) 1870-1938 **TCLC 65**
See also CA 117; 164
Carducci, Giosue (Alessandro Giuseppe) 1835-1907 **TCLC 32**
See also CA 163
Carew, Thomas 1595(?)-1640 **LC 13; PC 29**
See also DLB 126
Carey, Ernestine Gilbreth 1908- **CLC 17**
See also CA 5-8R; CANR 71; SATA 2
Carey, Peter 1943- **CLC 40, 55, 96**
See also CA 123; 127; CANR 53, 76; INT 127; MTCW 1, 2; SATA 94
Carleton, William 1794-1869 **NCLC 3**
See also DLB 159
Carlisle, Henry (Coffin) 1926- **CLC 33**
See also CA 13-16R; CANR 15, 85
Carlsen, Chris
See Holdstock, Robert P.
Carlson, Ron(ald F.) 1947- **CLC 54**
See also CA 105; CANR 27
Carlyle, Thomas 1795-1881 **NCLC 70; DA; DAB; DAC; DAM MST**
See also CDBLB 1789-1832; DLB 55; 144
Carman, (William) Bliss 1861-1929 **TCLC 7; DAC**
See also CA 104; 152; DLB 92
Carnegie, Dale 1888-1955 **TCLC 53**
Carossa, Hans 1878-1956 **TCLC 48**
See also CA 170; DLB 66
Carpenter, Don(ald Richard) 1931-1995 **CLC 41**
See also CA 45-48; 149; CANR 1, 71
Carpenter, Edward 1844-1929 **TCLC 88**
See also CA 163
Carpentier (y Valmont), Alejo 1904-1980 **CLC 8, 11, 38, 110; DAM MULT; HLC 1; SSC 35**
See also CA 65-68; 97-100; CANR 11, 70; DLB 113; HW 1, 2
Carr, Caleb 1955(?)- **CLC 86**
See also CA 147; CANR 73; DA3
Carr, Emily 1871-1945 **TCLC 32**
See also CA 159; DLB 68
Carr, John Dickson 1906-1977 **CLC 3**
See also Fairbairn, Roger
See also CA 49-52; 69-72; CANR 3, 33, 60; MTCW 1, 2
Carr, Philippa
See Hibbert, Eleanor Alice Burford
Carr, Virginia Spencer 1929- **CLC 34**
See also CA 61-64; DLB 111
Carrere, Emmanuel 1957- **CLC 89**
Carrier, Roch 1937- **CLC 13, 78; DAC; DAM MST**
See also CA 130; CANR 61; DLB 53; SATA 105
Carroll, James P. 1943(?)- **CLC 38**
See also CA 81-84; CANR 73; MTCW 1
Carroll, Jim 1951- **CLC 35**
See also AAYA 17; CA 45-48; CANR 42
Carroll, Lewis -1898 **NCLC 2, 53; PC 18; WLC**
See also Dodgson, Charles Lutwidge
See also CDBLB 1832-1890; CLR 2, 18; DLB 18, 163, 178; DLBY 98; JRDA
Carroll, Paul Vincent 1900-1968 **CLC 10**
See also CA 9-12R; 25-28R; DLB 10
Carruth, Hayden 1921- **CLC 4, 7, 10, 18, 84; PC 10**
See also CA 9-12R; CANR 4, 38, 59; DLB 5, 165; INT CANR-4; MTCW 1, 2; SATA 47
Carson, Rachel Louise 1907-1964 **CLC 71; DAM POP**
See also CA 77-80; CANR 35; DA3; MTCW 1, 2; SATA 23
Carter, Angela (Olive) 1940-1992 **CLC 5, 41, 76; SSC 13**
See also CA 53-56; 136; CANR 12, 36, 61; DA3; DLB 14, 207; MTCW 1, 2; SATA 66; SATA-Obit 70
Carter, Nick
See Smith, Martin Cruz
Carver, Raymond 1938-1988 **CLC 22, 36, 53, 55, 126; DAM NOV; SSC 8**
See also CA 33-36R; 126; CANR 17, 34, 61; DA3; DLB 130; DLBY 84, 88; MTCW 1, 2
Cary, Elizabeth, Lady Falkland 1585-1639 **LC 30**
Cary, (Arthur) Joyce (Lunel) 1888-1957 **TCLC 1, 29**
See also CA 104; 164; CDBLB 1914-1945; DLB 15, 100; MTCW 2
Casanova de Seingalt, Giovanni Jacopo 1725-1798 **LC 13**
Casares, Adolfo Bioy
See Bioy Casares, Adolfo
Casely-Hayford, J(oseph) E(phraim) 1866-1930 **TCLC 24; BLC 1; DAM MULT**
See also BW 2; CA 123; 152
Casey, John (Dudley) 1939- **CLC 59**
See also BEST 90:2; CA 69-72; CANR 23
Casey, Michael 1947- **CLC 2**
See also CA 65-68; DLB 5
Casey, Patrick
See Thurman, Wallace (Henry)
Casey, Warren (Peter) 1935-1988 **CLC 12**
See also CA 101; 127; INT 101
Casona, Alejandro **CLC 49**
See also Alvarez, Alejandro Rodriguez
Cassavetes, John 1929-1989 **CLC 20**
See also CA 85-88; 127; CANR 82
Cassian, Nina 1924- **PC 17**
Cassill, R(onald) V(erlin) 1919- **CLC 4, 23**
See also CA 9-12R; CAAS 1; CANR 7, 45; DLB 6
Cassirer, Ernst 1874-1945 **TCLC 61**
See also CA 157
Cassity, (Allen) Turner 1929- **CLC 6, 42**
See also CA 17-20R; CAAS 8; CANR 11; DLB 105
Castaneda, Carlos (Cesar Aranha) 1931(?)-1998 **CLC 12, 119**
See also CA 25-28R; CANR 32, 66; HW 1; MTCW 1
Castedo, Elena 1937- **CLC 65**
See also CA 132
Castedo-Ellerman, Elena
See Castedo, Elena
Castellanos, Rosario 1925-1974 **CLC 66; DAM MULT; HLC 1; SSC 39**
See also CA 131; 53-56; CANR 58; DLB 113; HW 1; MTCW 1
Castelvetro, Lodovico 1505-1571 **LC 12**
Castiglione, Baldassare 1478-1529 **LC 12**
Castle, Robert
See Hamilton, Edmond
Castro (Ruz), Fidel 1926(?)-
See also CA 110; 129; CANR 81; DAM MULT; HLC 1; HW 2
Castro, Guillen de 1569-1631 **LC 19**
Castro, Rosalia de 1837-1885 **NCLC 3, 78; DAM MULT**
Cather, Willa -1947
See Cather, Willa Sibert
Cather, Willa Sibert 1873-1947 **TCLC 1, 11, 31, 99; DA; DAB; DAC; DAM MST, NOV; SSC 2; WLC**
See also Cather, Willa
See also AAYA 24; CA 104; 128; CDALB 1865-1917; DA3; DLB 9, 54, 78; DLBD 1; MTCW 1, 2; SATA 30
Catherine, Saint 1347-1380 **CMLC 27**
Cato, Marcus Porcius 234B.C.-149B.C. **CMLC 21**
See also DLB 211
Catton, (Charles) Bruce 1899-1978 **CLC 35**
See also AITN 1; CA 5-8R; 81-84; CANR 7, 74; DLB 17; SATA 2; SATA-Obit 24
Catullus c. 84B.C.-c. 54B.C. **CMLC 18**
See also DLB 211
Cauldwell, Frank
See King, Francis (Henry)
Caunitz, William J. 1933-1996 **CLC 34**
See also BEST 89:3; CA 125; 130; 152; CANR 73; INT 130
Causley, Charles (Stanley) 1917- **CLC 7**
See also CA 9-12R; CANR 5, 35; CLR 30; DLB 27; MTCW 1; SATA 3, 66
Caute, (John) David 1936- **CLC 29; DAM NOV**
See also CA 1-4R; CAAS 4; CANR 1, 33, 64; DLB 14, 231
Cavafy, C(onstantine) P(eter) 1863-1933 **TCLC 2, 7; DAM POET**
See also Kavafis, Konstantinos Petrou
See also CA 148; DA3; MTCW 1
Cavallo, Evelyn
See Spark, Muriel (Sarah)
Cavanna, Betty **CLC 12**
See also Harrison, Elizabeth Cavanna
See also JRDA; MAICYA; SAAS 4; SATA 1, 30
Cavendish, Margaret Lucas 1623-1673 **LC 30**
See also DLB 131
Caxton, William 1421(?)-1491(?) **LC 17**
See also DLB 170
Cayer, D. M.
See Duffy, Maureen
Cayrol, Jean 1911- **CLC 11**
See also CA 89-92; DLB 83
Cela, Camilo Jose 1916- **CLC 4, 13, 59, 122; DAM MULT; HLC 1**
See also BEST 90:2; CA 21-24R; CAAS 10; CANR 21, 32, 76; DLBY 89; HW 1; MTCW 1, 2

Chretien de Troyes c. 12th cent. - **CMLC 10**
See also DLB 208
Christie
See Ichikawa, Kon
Christie, Agatha (Mary Clarissa) 1890-1976 **CLC 1, 6, 8, 12, 39, 48, 110; DAB; DAC; DAM NOV**
See also AAYA 9; AITN 1, 2; CA 17-20R; 61-64; CANR 10, 37; CDBLB 1914-1945; DA3; DLB 13, 77; MTCW 1, 2; SATA 36
Christie, (Ann) Philippa
See Pearce, Philippa
See also CA 5-8R; CANR 4
Christine de Pizan 1365(?)-1431(?) **LC 9**
See also DLB 208
Chubb, Elmer
See Masters, Edgar Lee
Chulkov, Mikhail Dmitrievich 1743-1792 **LC 2**
See also DLB 150
Churchill, Caryl 1938- **CLC 31, 55; DC 5**
See also CA 102; CANR 22, 46; DLB 13; MTCW 1
Churchill, Charles 1731-1764 **LC 3**
See also DLB 109
Chute, Carolyn 1947- **CLC 39**
See also CA 123
Ciardi, John (Anthony) 1916-1986 **CLC 10, 40, 44, 129; DAM POET**
See also CA 5-8R; 118; CAAS 2; CANR 5, 33; CLR 19; DLB 5; DLBY 86; INT CANR-5; MAICYA; MTCW 1, 2; SAAS 26; SATA 1, 65; SATA-Obit 46
Cicero, Marcus Tullius 106B.C.-43B.C. **CMLC 3**
See also DLB 211
Cimino, Michael 1943- **CLC 16**
See also CA 105
Cioran, E(mil) M. 1911-1995 **CLC 64**
See also CA 25-28R; 149; CANR 91; DLB 220
Cisneros, Sandra 1954- **CLC 69, 118; DAM MULT; HLC 1; SSC 32**
See also AAYA 9; CA 131; CANR 64; DA3; DLB 122, 152; HW 1, 2; MTCW 2
Cixous, Helene 1937- **CLC 92**
See also CA 126; CANR 55; DLB 83; MTCW 1, 2
Clair, Rene CLC 20
See also Chomette, Rene Lucien
Clampitt, Amy 1920-1994 **CLC 32; PC 19**
See also CA 110; 146; CANR 29, 79; DLB 105
Clancy, Thomas L., Jr. 1947-
See Clancy, Tom
See also CA 125; 131; CANR 62; DA3; DLB 227; INT 131; MTCW 1, 2
Clancy, Tom CLC 45, 112; DAM NOV, POP
See also Clancy, Thomas L., Jr.
See also AAYA 9; BEST 89:1, 90:1; MTCW 2
Clare, John 1793-1864 **NCLC 9, 86; DAB; DAM POET; PC 23**
See also DLB 55, 96
Clarin
See Alas (y Urena), Leopoldo (Enrique Garcia)
Clark, Al C.
See Goines, Donald
Clark, (Robert) Brian 1932- **CLC 29**
See also CA 41-44R; CANR 67
Clark, Curt
See Westlake, Donald E(dwin)
Clark, Eleanor 1913-1996 **CLC 5, 19**
See also CA 9-12R; 151; CANR 41; DLB 6
Clark, J. P.
See Clark Bekedermo, J(ohnson) P(epper)
See also DLB 117
Clark, John Pepper
See Clark Bekedermo, J(ohnson) P(epper)
Clark, M. R.
See Clark, Mavis Thorpe
Clark, Mavis Thorpe 1909- **CLC 12**
See also CA 57-60; CANR 8, 37; CLR 30; MAICYA; SAAS 5; SATA 8, 74
Clark, Walter Van Tilburg 1909-1971 **CLC 28**
See also CA 9-12R; 33-36R; CANR 63; DLB 9, 206; SATA 8
Clark Bekedermo, J(ohnson) P(epper) 1935- **CLC 38; BLC 1; DAM DRAM, MULT; DC 5**
See also Clark, J. P.; Clark, John Pepper
See also BW 1; CA 65-68; CANR 16, 72; MTCW 1
Clarke, Arthur C(harles) 1917- **CLC 1, 4, 13, 18, 35, 136; DAM POP; SSC 3**
See also AAYA 4, 33; CA 1-4R; CANR 2, 28, 55, 74; DA3; JRDA; MAICYA; MTCW 1, 2; SATA 13, 70, 115
Clarke, Austin 1896-1974 **CLC 6, 9; DAM POET**
See also CA 29-32; 49-52; CAP 2; DLB 10, 20
Clarke, Austin C(hesterfield) 1934- **CLC 8, 53; BLC 1; DAC; DAM MULT**
See also BW 1; CA 25-28R; CAAS 16; CANR 14, 32, 68; DLB 53, 125
Clarke, Gillian 1937- **CLC 61**
See also CA 106; DLB 40
Clarke, Marcus (Andrew Hislop) 1846-1881 **NCLC 19**
Clarke, Shirley 1925- **CLC 16**
Clash, The
See Headon, (Nicky) Topper; Jones, Mick; Simonon, Paul; Strummer, Joe
Claudel, Paul (Louis Charles Marie) 1868-1955 **TCLC 2, 10**
See also CA 104; 165; DLB 192
Claudius, Matthias 1740-1815 **NCLC 75**
See also DLB 97
Clavell, James (duMaresq) 1925-1994 **CLC 6, 25, 87; DAM NOV, POP**
See also CA 25-28R; 146; CANR 26, 48; DA3; MTCW 1, 2
Cleaver, (Leroy) Eldridge 1935-1998 **CLC 30, 119; BLC 1; DAM MULT**
See also BW 1, 3; CA 21-24R; 167; CANR 16, 75; DA3; MTCW 2
Cleese, John (Marwood) 1939- **CLC 21**
See also Monty Python
See also CA 112; 116; CANR 35; MTCW 1
Cleishbotham, Jebediah
See Scott, Walter
Cleland, John 1710-1789 **LC 2, 48**
See also DLB 39
Clemens, Samuel Langhorne 1835-1910
See Twain, Mark
See also CA 104; 135; CDALB 1865-1917; DA; DAB; DAC; DAM MST, NOV; DA3; DLB 11, 12, 23, 64, 74, 186, 189; JRDA; MAICYA; SATA 100; YABC 2
Clement of Alexandria 150(?)-215(?) **CMLC 41**
Cleophil
See Congreve, William
Clerihew, E.
See Bentley, E(dmund) C(lerihew)
Clerk, N. W.
See Lewis, C(live) S(taples)
Cliff, Jimmy CLC 21
See also Chambers, James
Cliff, Michelle 1946- **CLC 120; BLCS**
See also BW 2; CA 116; CANR 39, 72; DLB 157
Clifton, (Thelma) Lucille 1936- **CLC 19, 66; BLC 1; DAM MULT, POET; PC 17**
See also BW 2, 3; CA 49-52; CANR 2, 24, 42, 76; CLR 5; DA3; DLB 5, 41; MAICYA; MTCW 1, 2; SATA 20, 69
Clinton, Dirk
See Silverberg, Robert
Clough, Arthur Hugh 1819-1861 **NCLC 27**
See also DLB 32
Clutha, Janet Paterson Frame 1924-
See Frame, Janet
See also CA 1-4R; CANR 2, 36, 76; MTCW 1, 2; SATA 119
Clyne, Terence
See Blatty, William Peter
Cobalt, Martin
See Mayne, William (James Carter)
Cobb, Irvin S(hrewsbury) 1876-1944 **TCLC 77**
See also CA 175; DLB 11, 25, 86
Cobbett, William 1763-1835 **NCLC 49**
See also DLB 43, 107, 158
Coburn, D(onald) L(ee) 1938- **CLC 10**
See also CA 89-92
Cocteau, Jean (Maurice Eugene Clement) 1889-1963 **CLC 1, 8, 15, 16, 43; DA; DAB; DAC; DAM DRAM, MST, NOV; WLC**
See also CA 25-28; CANR 40; CAP 2; DA3; DLB 65; MTCW 1, 2
Codrescu, Andrei 1946- **CLC 46, 121; DAM POET**
See also CA 33-36R; CAAS 19; CANR 13, 34, 53, 76; DA3; MTCW 2
Coe, Max
See Bourne, Randolph S(illiman)
Coe, Tucker
See Westlake, Donald E(dwin)
Coen, Ethan 1958- **CLC 108**
See also CA 126; CANR 85
Coen, Joel 1955- **CLC 108**
See also CA 126
The Coen Brothers
See Coen, Ethan; Coen, Joel
Coetzee, J(ohn) M(ichael) 1940- **CLC 23, 33, 66, 117; DAM NOV**
See also CA 77-80; CANR 41, 54, 74; DA3; DLB 225; MTCW 1, 2
Coffey, Brian
See Koontz, Dean R(ay)
Coffin, Robert P(eter) Tristram 1892-1955 **TCLC 95**
See also CA 123; 169; DLB 45
Cohan, George M(ichael) 1878-1942 **TCLC 60**
See also CA 157
Cohen, Arthur A(llen) 1928-1986 **CLC 7, 31**
See also CA 1-4R; 120; CANR 1, 17, 42; DLB 28
Cohen, Leonard (Norman) 1934- **CLC 3, 38; DAC; DAM MST**
See also CA 21-24R; CANR 14, 69; DLB 53; MTCW 1
Cohen, Matt(hew) 1942-1999 **CLC 19; DAC**
See also CA 61-64; 187; CAAS 18; CANR 40; DLB 53
Cohen-Solal, Annie 19(?)- **CLC 50**
Colegate, Isabel 1931- **CLC 36**
See also CA 17-20R; CANR 8, 22, 74; DLB 14, 231; INT CANR-22; MTCW 1
Coleman, Emmett
See Reed, Ishmael
Coleridge, Hartley 1796-1849 **NCLC 90**
See also DLB 96
Coleridge, M. E.
See Coleridge, Mary E(lizabeth)
Coleridge, Mary E(lizabeth) 1861-1907 **TCLC 73**
See also CA 116; 166; DLB 19, 98
Coleridge, Samuel Taylor 1772-1834 **NCLC**

Cotes, Cecil V.
See Duncan, Sara Jeannette
Cotter, Joseph Seamon Sr. 1861-1949 **TCLC 28; BLC 1; DAM MULT**
See also BW 1; CA 124; DLB 50
Couch, Arthur Thomas Quiller
See Quiller-Couch, SirArthur (Thomas)
Coulton, James
See Hansen, Joseph
Couperus, Louis (Marie Anne) 1863-1923 **TCLC 15**
See also CA 115
Coupland, Douglas 1961- **CLC 85, 133; DAC; DAM POP**
See also AAYA 34; CA 142; CANR 57, 90
Court, Wesli
See Turco, Lewis (Putnam)
Courtenay, Bryce 1933- **CLC 59**
See also CA 138
Courtney, Robert
See Ellison, Harlan (Jay)
Cousteau, Jacques-Yves 1910-1997 **CLC 30**
See also CA 65-68; 159; CANR 15, 67; MTCW 1; SATA 38, 98
Coventry, Francis 1725-1754 **LC 46**
Cowan, Peter (Walkinshaw) 1914- **SSC 28**
See also CA 21-24R; CANR 9, 25, 50, 83
Coward, Noel (Peirce) 1899-1973 **CLC 1, 9, 29, 51; DAM DRAM**
See also AITN 1; CA 17-18; 41-44R; CANR 35; CAP 2; CDBLB 1914-1945; DA3; DLB 10; MTCW 1, 2
Cowley, Abraham 1618-1667 **LC 43**
See also DLB 131, 151
Cowley, Malcolm 1898-1989 **CLC 39**
See also CA 5-8R; 128; CANR 3, 55; DLB 4, 48; DLBY 81, 89; MTCW 1, 2
Cowper, William 1731-1800 **NCLC 8; DAM POET**
See also DA3; DLB 104, 109
Cox, William Trevor 1928- **CLC 9, 14, 71; DAM NOV**
See also Trevor, William
See also CA 9-12R; CANR 4, 37, 55, 76; DLB 14; INT CANR-37; MTCW 1, 2
Coyne, P. J.
See Masters, Hilary
Cozzens, James Gould 1903-1978 **CLC 1, 4, 11, 92**
See also CA 9-12R; 81-84; CANR 19; CDALB 1941-1968; DLB 9; DLBD 2; DLBY 84, 97; MTCW 1, 2
Crabbe, George 1754-1832 **NCLC 26**
See also DLB 93
Craddock, Charles Egbert
See Murfree, Mary Noailles
Craig, A. A.
See Anderson, Poul (William)
Craik, Dinah Maria (Mulock) 1826-1887 **NCLC 38**
See also DLB 35, 163; MAICYA; SATA 34
Cram, Ralph Adams 1863-1942 **TCLC 45**
See also CA 160
Crane, (Harold) Hart 1899-1932 **TCLC 2, 5, 80; DA; DAB; DAC; DAM MST, POET; PC 3; WLC**
See also CA 104; 127; CDALB 1917-1929; DA3; DLB 4, 48; MTCW 1, 2
Crane, R(onald) S(almon) 1886-1967 **CLC 27**
See also CA 85-88; DLB 63
Crane, Stephen (Townley) 1871-1900 **TCLC 11, 17, 32; DA; DAB; DAC; DAM MST, NOV, POET; SSC 7; WLC**
See also AAYA 21; CA 109; 140; CANR 84; CDALB 1865-1917; DA3; DLB 12, 54, 78; YABC 2
Cranshaw, Stanley
See Fisher, Dorothy (Frances) Canfield
Crase, Douglas 1944- **CLC 58**
See also CA 106
Crashaw, Richard 1612(?)-1649 **LC 24**
See also DLB 126
Craven, Margaret 1901-1980 **CLC 17; DAC**
See also CA 103
Crawford, F(rancis) Marion 1854-1909 **TCLC 10**
See also CA 107; 168; DLB 71
Crawford, Isabella Valancy 1850-1887 **NCLC 12**
See also DLB 92
Crayon, Geoffrey
See Irving, Washington
Creasey, John 1908-1973 **CLC 11**
See also CA 5-8R; 41-44R; CANR 8, 59; DLB 77; MTCW 1
Crebillon, Claude Prosper Jolyot de (fils) 1707-1777 **LC 1, 28**
Credo
See Creasey, John
Credo, Alvaro J. de
See Prado (Calvo), Pedro
Creeley, Robert (White) 1926- **CLC 1, 2, 4, 8, 11, 15, 36, 78; DAM POET**
See also CA 1-4R; CAAS 10; CANR 23, 43, 89; DA3; DLB 5, 16, 169; DLBD 17; MTCW 1, 2
Crews, Harry (Eugene) 1935- **CLC 6, 23, 49**
See also AITN 1; CA 25-28R; CANR 20, 57; DA3; DLB 6, 143, 185; MTCW 1, 2
Crichton, (John) Michael 1942- **CLC 2, 6, 54, 90; DAM NOV, POP**
See also AAYA 10; AITN 2; CA 25-28R; CANR 13, 40, 54, 76; DA3; DLBY 81; INT CANR-13; JRDA; MTCW 1, 2; SATA 9, 88
Crispin, Edmund CLC 22
See also Montgomery, (Robert) Bruce
See also DLB 87
Cristofer, Michael 1945(?)- **CLC 28; DAM DRAM**
See also CA 110; 152; DLB 7
Croce, Benedetto 1866-1952 **TCLC 37**
See also CA 120; 155
Crockett, David 1786-1836 **NCLC 8**
See also DLB 3, 11
Crockett, Davy
See Crockett, David
Crofts, Freeman Wills 1879-1957 **TCLC 55**
See also CA 115; DLB 77
Croker, John Wilson 1780-1857 **NCLC 10**
See also DLB 110
Crommelynck, Fernand 1885-1970 **CLC 75**
See also CA 89-92
Cromwell, Oliver 1599-1658 **LC 43**
Cronin, A(rchibald) J(oseph) 1896-1981 **CLC 32**
See also CA 1-4R; 102; CANR 5; DLB 191; SATA 47; SATA-Obit 25
Cross, Amanda
See Heilbrun, Carolyn G(old)
Crothers, Rachel 1878(?)-1958 **TCLC 19**
See also CA 113; DLB 7
Croves, Hal
See Traven, B.
Crow Dog, Mary (Ellen) (?)- **CLC 93**
See also Brave Bird, Mary
See also CA 154
Crowfield, Christopher
See Stowe, Harriet (Elizabeth) Beecher
Crowley, Aleister TCLC 7
See also Crowley, Edward Alexander
Crowley, Edward Alexander 1875-1947
See Crowley, Aleister
See also CA 104
Crowley, John 1942- **CLC 57**
See also CA 61-64; CANR 43; DLBY 82; SATA 65
Crud
See Crumb, R(obert)
Crumarums
See Crumb, R(obert)
Crumb, R(obert) 1943- **CLC 17**
See also CA 106
Crumbum
See Crumb, R(obert)
Crumski
See Crumb, R(obert)
Crum the Bum
See Crumb, R(obert)
Crunk
See Crumb, R(obert)
Crustt
See Crumb, R(obert)
Cruz, Victor Hernandez 1949-
See also BW 2; CA 65-68; CAAS 17; CANR 14, 32, 74; DAM MULT, POET; DLB 41; HLC 1; HW 1, 2; MTCW 1
Cryer, Gretchen (Kiger) 1935- **CLC 21**
See also CA 114; 123
Csath, Geza 1887-1919 **TCLC 13**
See also CA 111
Cudlip, David R(ockwell) 1933- **CLC 34**
See also CA 177
Cullen, Countee 1903-1946 **TCLC 4, 37; BLC 1; DA; DAC; DAM MST, MULT, POET; PC 20; WLCS**
See also BW 1; CA 108; 124; CDALB 1917-1929; DA3; DLB 4, 48, 51; MTCW 1, 2; SATA 18
Cum, R.
See Crumb, R(obert)
Cummings, Bruce F(rederick) 1889-1919
See Barbellion, W. N. P.
See also CA 123
Cummings, E(dward) E(stlin) 1894-1962 **CLC 1, 3, 8, 12, 15, 68; DA; DAB; DAC; DAM MST, POET; PC 5; WLC**
See also CA 73-76; CANR 31; CDALB 1929-1941; DA3; DLB 4, 48; MTCW 1, 2
Cunha, Euclides (Rodrigues Pimenta) da 1866-1909 **TCLC 24**
See also CA 123
Cunningham, E. V.
See Fast, Howard (Melvin)
Cunningham, J(ames) V(incent) 1911-1985 **CLC 3, 31**
See also CA 1-4R; 115; CANR 1, 72; DLB 5
Cunningham, Julia (Woolfolk) 1916- **CLC 12**
See also CA 9-12R; CANR 4, 19, 36; JRDA; MAICYA; SAAS 2; SATA 1, 26
Cunningham, Michael 1952- **CLC 34**
See also CA 136
Cunninghame Graham, R. B.
See Cunninghame Graham, Robert (Gallnigad) Bontine
Cunninghame Graham, Robert (Gallnigad) Bontine 1852-1936 **TCLC 19**
See also Graham, R(obert) B(ontine) Cunninghame
See also CA 119; 184; DLB 98
Currie, Ellen 19(?)- **CLC 44**
Curtin, Philip
See Lowndes, Marie Adelaide (Belloc)
Curtis, Price
See Ellison, Harlan (Jay)
Cutrate, Joe
See Spiegelman, Art
Cynewulf c. 770-c. 840 **CMLC 23**
Czaczkes, Shmuel Yosef
See Agnon, S(hmuel) Y(osef Halevi)

Dabrowska, Maria (Szumska) 1889-1965 **CLC 15**
See also CA 106
Dabydeen, David 1955- **CLC 34**
See also BW 1; CA 125; CANR 56, 92
Dacey, Philip 1939- **CLC 51**
See also CA 37-40R; CAAS 17; CANR 14, 32, 64; DLB 105
Dagerman, Stig (Halvard) 1923-1954 **TCLC 17**
See also CA 117; 155
Dahl, Roald 1916-1990 **CLC 1, 6, 18, 79; DAB; DAC; DAM MST, NOV, POP**
See also AAYA 15; CA 1-4R; 133; CANR 6, 32, 37, 62; CLR 1, 7, 41; DA3; DLB 139; JRDA; MAICYA; MTCW 1, 2; SATA 1, 26, 73; SATA-Obit 65
Dahlberg, Edward 1900-1977 **CLC 1, 7, 14**
See also CA 9-12R; 69-72; CANR 31, 62; DLB 48; MTCW 1
Daitch, Susan 1954- **CLC 103**
See also CA 161
Dale, Colin TCLC 18
See also Lawrence, T(homas) E(dward)
Dale, George E.
See Asimov, Isaac
Dalton, Roque 1935-1975
See also HLCS 1; HW 2
Daly, Elizabeth 1878-1967 **CLC 52**
See also CA 23-24; 25-28R; CANR 60; CAP 2
Daly, Maureen 1921-1983 **CLC 17**
See also AAYA 5; CANR 37, 83; JRDA; MAICYA; SAAS 1; SATA 2
Damas, Leon-Gontran 1912-1978 **CLC 84**
See also BW 1; CA 125; 73-76
Dana, Richard Henry Sr. 1787-1879 **NCLC 53**
Daniel, Samuel 1562(?)-1619 **LC 24**
See also DLB 62
Daniels, Brett
See Adler, Renata
Dannay, Frederic 1905-1982 **CLC 11; DAM POP**
See also Queen, Ellery
See also CA 1-4R; 107; CANR 1, 39; DLB 137; MTCW 1
D'Annunzio, Gabriele 1863-1938 **TCLC 6, 40**
See also CA 104; 155
Danois, N. le
See Gourmont, Remy (-Marie-Charles) de
Dante 1265-1321 **CMLC 3, 18, 39; DA; DAB; DAC; DAM MST, POET; PC 21; WLCS**
See also Alighieri, Dante
See also DA3
d'Antibes, Germain
See Simenon, Georges (Jacques Christian)
Danticat, Edwidge 1969- **CLC 94**
See also AAYA 29; CA 152; CANR 73; MTCW 1
Danvers, Dennis 1947- **CLC 70**
Danziger, Paula 1944- **CLC 21**
See also AAYA 4; CA 112; 115; CANR 37; CLR 20; JRDA; MAICYA; SATA 36, 63, 102; SATA-Brief 30
Da Ponte, Lorenzo 1749-1838 **NCLC 50**
Dario, Ruben 1867-1916 **TCLC 4; DAM MULT; HLC 1; PC 15**
See also CA 131; CANR 81; HW 1, 2; MTCW 1, 2
Darley, George 1795-1846 **NCLC 2**
See also DLB 96
Darrow, Clarence (Seward) 1857-1938 **TCLC 81**
See also CA 164
Darwin, Charles 1809-1882 **NCLC 57**
See also DLB 57, 166
Daryush, Elizabeth 1887-1977 **CLC 6, 19**
See also CA 49-52; CANR 3, 81; DLB 20
Dasgupta, Surendranath 1887-1952 **TCLC 81**
See also CA 157
Dashwood, Edmee Elizabeth Monica de la Pasture 1890-1943
See Delafield, E. M.
See also CA 119; 154
Daudet, (Louis Marie) Alphonse 1840-1897 **NCLC 1**
See also DLB 123
Daumal, Rene 1908-1944 **TCLC 14**
See also CA 114
Davenant, William 1606-1668 **LC 13**
See also DLB 58, 126
Davenport, Guy (Mattison, Jr.) 1927- **CLC 6, 14, 38; SSC 16**
See also CA 33-36R; CANR 23, 73; DLB 130
Davidson, Avram (James) 1923-1993
See Queen, Ellery
See also CA 101; 171; CANR 26; DLB 8
Davidson, Donald (Grady) 1893-1968 **CLC 2, 13, 19**
See also CA 5-8R; 25-28R; CANR 4, 84; DLB 45
Davidson, Hugh
See Hamilton, Edmond
Davidson, John 1857-1909 **TCLC 24**
See also CA 118; DLB 19
Davidson, Sara 1943- **CLC 9**
See also CA 81-84; CANR 44, 68; DLB 185
Davie, Donald (Alfred) 1922-1995 **CLC 5, 8, 10, 31; PC 29**
See also CA 1-4R; 149; CAAS 3; CANR 1, 44; DLB 27; MTCW 1
Davies, Ray(mond Douglas) 1944- **CLC 21**
See also CA 116; 146; CANR 92
Davies, Rhys 1901-1978 **CLC 23**
See also CA 9-12R; 81-84; CANR 4; DLB 139, 191
Davies, (William) Robertson 1913-1995 **CLC 2, 7, 13, 25, 42, 75, 91; DA; DAB; DAC; DAM MST, NOV, POP; WLC**
See also BEST 89:2; CA 33-36R; 150; CANR 17, 42; DA3; DLB 68; INT CANR-17; MTCW 1, 2
Davies, Walter C.
See Kornbluth, C(yril) M.
Davies, William Henry 1871-1940 **TCLC 5**
See also CA 104; 179; DLB 19, 174
Da Vinci, Leonardo 1452-1519 **LC 12, 57, 60**
Davis, Angela (Yvonne) 1944- **CLC 77; DAM MULT**
See also BW 2, 3; CA 57-60; CANR 10, 81; DA3
Davis, B. Lynch
See Bioy Casares, Adolfo; Borges, Jorge Luis
Davis, B. Lynch
See Bioy Casares, Adolfo
Davis, H(arold) L(enoir) 1894-1960 **CLC 49**
See also CA 178; 89-92; DLB 9, 206; SATA 114
Davis, Rebecca (Blaine) Harding 1831-1910 **TCLC 6; SSC 38**
See also CA 104; 179; DLB 74
Davis, Richard Harding 1864-1916 **TCLC 24**
See also CA 114; 179; DLB 12, 23, 78, 79, 189; DLBD 13
Davison, Frank Dalby 1893-1970 **CLC 15**
See also CA 116
Davison, Lawrence H.
See Lawrence, D(avid) H(erbert Richards)
Davison, Peter (Hubert) 1928- **CLC 28**
See also CA 9-12R; CAAS 4; CANR 3, 43, 84; DLB 5
Davys, Mary 1674-1732 **LC 1, 46**
See also DLB 39
Dawson, Fielding 1930- **CLC 6**
See also CA 85-88; DLB 130
Dawson, Peter
See Faust, Frederick (Schiller)
Day, Clarence (Shepard, Jr.) 1874-1935 **TCLC 25**
See also CA 108; DLB 11
Day, Thomas 1748-1789 **LC 1**
See also DLB 39; YABC 1
Day Lewis, C(ecil) 1904-1972 **CLC 1, 6, 10; DAM POET; PC 11**
See also Blake, Nicholas
See also CA 13-16; 33-36R; CANR 34; CAP 1; DLB 15, 20; MTCW 1, 2
Dazai Osamu 1909-1948 **TCLC 11; SSC 41**
See also Tsushima, Shuji
See also CA 164; DLB 182
de Andrade, Carlos Drummond 1892-1945
See Drummond de Andrade, Carlos
Deane, Norman
See Creasey, John
Deane, Seamus (Francis) 1940- **CLC 122**
See also CA 118; CANR 42
de Beauvoir, Simone (Lucie Ernestine Marie Bertrand)
See Beauvoir, Simone (Lucie Ernestine Marie Bertrand) de
de Beer, P.
See Bosman, Herman Charles
de Brissac, Malcolm
See Dickinson, Peter (Malcolm)
de Campos, Alvaro
See Pessoa, Fernando (Antonio Nogueira)
de Chardin, Pierre Teilhard
See Teilhard de Chardin, (Marie Joseph) Pierre
Dee, John 1527-1608 **LC 20**
Deer, Sandra 1940- **CLC 45**
See also CA 186
De Ferrari, Gabriella 1941- **CLC 65**
See also CA 146
Defoe, Daniel 1660(?)-1731 **LC 1, 42; DA; DAB; DAC; DAM MST, NOV; WLC**
See also AAYA 27; CDBLB 1660-1789; CLR 61; DA3; DLB 39, 95, 101; JRDA; MAICYA; SATA 22
de Gourmont, Remy(-Marie-Charles)
See Gourmont, Remy (-Marie-Charles) de
de Hartog, Jan 1914- **CLC 19**
See also CA 1-4R; CANR 1
de Hostos, E. M.
See Hostos (y Bonilla), Eugenio Maria de
de Hostos, Eugenio M.
See Hostos (y Bonilla), Eugenio Maria de
Deighton, Len CLC 4, 7, 22, 46
See also Deighton, Leonard Cyril
See also AAYA 6; BEST 89:2; CDBLB 1960 to Present; DLB 87
Deighton, Leonard Cyril 1929-
See Deighton, Len
See also CA 9-12R; CANR 19, 33, 68; DAM NOV, POP; DA3; MTCW 1, 2
Dekker, Thomas 1572(?)-1632 **LC 22; DAM DRAM; DC 12**
See also CDBLB Before 1660; DLB 62, 172
Delafield, E. M. 1890-1943 **TCLC 61**
See also Dashwood, Edmee Elizabeth Monica de la Pasture
See also DLB 34
de la Mare, Walter (John) 1873-1956 **TCLC 4, 53; DAB; DAC; DAM MST, POET; SSC 14; WLC**
See also CA 163; CDBLB 1914-1945; CLR 23; DA3; DLB 162; MTCW 1; SATA 16

Author Index

Delaney, Franey
See O'Hara, John (Henry)
Delaney, Shelagh 1939- **CLC 29; DAM DRAM**
See also CA 17-20R; CANR 30, 67; CDBLB 1960 to Present; DLB 13; MTCW 1
Delany, Martin Robinson 1812-1885 **NCLC 93**
See also DLB 50
Delany, Mary (Granville Pendarves) 1700-1788 **LC 12**
Delany, Samuel R(ay, Jr.) 1942- **CLC 8, 14, 38; BLC 1; DAM MULT**
See also AAYA 24; BW 2, 3; CA 81-84; CANR 27, 43; DLB 8, 33; MTCW 1, 2
De La Ramee, (Marie) Louise 1839-1908
See Ouida
See also SATA 20
de la Roche, Mazo 1879-1961 **CLC 14**
See also CA 85-88; CANR 30; DLB 68; SATA 64
De La Salle, Innocent
See Hartmann, Sadakichi
Delbanco, Nicholas (Franklin) 1942- **CLC 6, 13**
See also CA 17-20R; CAAS 2; CANR 29, 55; DLB 6
del Castillo, Michel 1933- **CLC 38**
See also CA 109; CANR 77
Deledda, Grazia (Cosima) 1875(?)-1936 **TCLC 23**
See also CA 123
Delgado, Abelardo (Lalo) B(arrientos) 1930-
See also CA 131; CAAS 15; CANR 90; DAM MST, MULT; DLB 82; HLC 1; HW 1, 2
Delibes, Miguel CLC 8, 18
See also Delibes Setien, Miguel
Delibes Setien, Miguel 1920-
See Delibes, Miguel
See also CA 45-48; CANR 1, 32; HW 1; MTCW 1
DeLillo, Don 1936- **CLC 8, 10, 13, 27, 39, 54, 76; DAM NOV, POP**
See also BEST 89:1; CA 81-84; CANR 21, 76, 92; DA3; DLB 6, 173; MTCW 1, 2
de Lisser, H. G.
See De Lisser, H(erbert) G(eorge)
See also DLB 117
De Lisser, H(erbert) G(eorge) 1878-1944 **TCLC 12**
See also de Lisser, H. G.
See also BW 2; CA 109; 152
Deloney, Thomas 1560(?)-1600 **LC 41**
See also DLB 167
Deloria, Vine (Victor), Jr. 1933- **CLC 21, 122; DAM MULT**
See also CA 53-56; CANR 5, 20, 48; DLB 175; MTCW 1; NNAL; SATA 21
Del Vecchio, John M(ichael) 1947- **CLC 29**
See also CA 110; DLBD 9
de Man, Paul (Adolph Michel) 1919-1983 **CLC 55**
See also CA 128; 111; CANR 61; DLB 67; MTCW 1, 2
DeMarinis, Rick 1934- **CLC 54**
See also CA 57-60, 184; CAAE 184; CAAS 24; CANR 9, 25, 50
Dembry, R. Emmet
See Murfree, Mary Noailles
Demby, William 1922- **CLC 53; BLC 1; DAM MULT**
See also BW 1, 3; CA 81-84; CANR 81; DLB 33
de Menton, Francisco
See Chin, Frank (Chew, Jr.)
Demetrius of Phalerum c. 307B.C.- **CMLC 34**
Demijohn, Thom
See Disch, Thomas M(ichael)
Deming, Richard 1915-1983
See Queen, Ellery
See also CA 9-12R; CANR 3; SATA 24
de Molina, Tirso 1584(?)-1648 **DC 13**
See also HLCS 2
de Montherlant, Henry (Milon)
See Montherlant, Henry (Milon) de
Demosthenes 384B.C.-322B.C. **CMLC 13**
See also DLB 176
de Natale, Francine
See Malzberg, Barry N(athaniel)
de Navarre, Marguerite 1492-1549 **LC 61**
Denby, Edwin (Orr) 1903-1983 **CLC 48**
See also CA 138; 110
Denis, Julio
See Cortazar, Julio
Denmark, Harrison
See Zelazny, Roger (Joseph)
Dennis, John 1658-1734 **LC 11**
See also DLB 101
Dennis, Nigel (Forbes) 1912-1989 **CLC 8**
See also CA 25-28R; 129; DLB 13, 15, 233; MTCW 1
Dent, Lester 1904(?)-1959 **TCLC 72**
See also CA 112; 161
De Palma, Brian (Russell) 1940- **CLC 20**
See also CA 109
De Quincey, Thomas 1785-1859 **NCLC 4, 87**
See also CDBLB 1789-1832; DLB 110; 144
Deren, Eleanora 1908(?)-1961
See Deren, Maya
See also CA 111
Deren, Maya 1917-1961 **CLC 16, 102**
See also Deren, Eleanora
Derleth, August (William) 1909-1971 **CLC 31**
See also CA 1-4R; 29-32R; CANR 4; DLB 9; DLBD 17; SATA 5
Der Nister 1884-1950 **TCLC 56**
de Routisie, Albert
See Aragon, Louis
Derrida, Jacques 1930- **CLC 24, 87**
See also CA 124; 127; CANR 76; MTCW 1
Derry Down Derry
See Lear, Edward
Dersonnes, Jacques
See Simenon, Georges (Jacques Christian)
Desai, Anita 1937- **CLC 19, 37, 97; DAB; DAM NOV**
See also CA 81-84; CANR 33, 53; DA3; MTCW 1, 2; SATA 63
Desai, Kiran 1971- **CLC 119**
See also CA 171
de Saint-Luc, Jean
See Glassco, John
de Saint Roman, Arnaud
See Aragon, Louis
Descartes, Rene 1596-1650 **LC 20, 35**
De Sica, Vittorio 1901(?)-1974 **CLC 20**
See also CA 117
Desnos, Robert 1900-1945 **TCLC 22**
See also CA 121; 151
de Stael, Germaine 1766-1817 **NCLC 91**
See also Stael-Holstein, Anne Louise Germaine Necker Baronn
See also DLB 119
Destouches, Louis-Ferdinand 1894-1961 **CLC 9, 15**
See also Celine, Louis-Ferdinand
See also CA 85-88; CANR 28; MTCW 1
de Tolignac, Gaston
See Griffith, D(avid Lewelyn) W(ark)
Deutsch, Babette 1895-1982 **CLC 18**
See also CA 1-4R; 108; CANR 4, 79; DLB 45; SATA 1; SATA-Obit 33
Devenant, William 1606-1649 **LC 13**
Devkota, Laxmiprasad 1909-1959 **TCLC 23**
See also CA 123
De Voto, Bernard (Augustine) 1897-1955 **TCLC 29**
See also CA 113; 160; DLB 9
De Vries, Peter 1910-1993 **CLC 1, 2, 3, 7, 10, 28, 46; DAM NOV**
See also CA 17-20R; 142; CANR 41; DLB 6; DLBY 82; MTCW 1, 2
Dewey, John 1859-1952 **TCLC 95**
See also CA 114; 170
Dexter, John
See Bradley, Marion Zimmer
Dexter, Martin
See Faust, Frederick (Schiller)
Dexter, Pete 1943- **CLC 34, 55; DAM POP**
See also BEST 89:2; CA 127; 131; INT 131; MTCW 1
Diamano, Silmang
See Senghor, Leopold Sedar
Diamond, Neil 1941- **CLC 30**
See also CA 108
Diaz del Castillo, Bernal 1496-1584 **LC 31; HLCS 1**
di Bassetto, Corno
See Shaw, George Bernard
Dick, Philip K(indred) 1928-1982 **CLC 10, 30, 72; DAM NOV, POP**
See also AAYA 24; CA 49-52; 106; CANR 2, 16; DA3; DLB 8; MTCW 1, 2
Dickens, Charles (John Huffam) 1812-1870 **NCLC 3, 8, 18, 26, 37, 50, 86; DA; DAB; DAC; DAM MST, NOV; SSC 17; WLC**
See also AAYA 23; CDBLB 1832-1890; DA3; DLB 21, 55, 70, 159, 166; JRDA; MAICYA; SATA 15
Dickey, James (Lafayette) 1923-1997 **CLC 1, 2, 4, 7, 10, 15, 47, 109; DAM NOV, POET, POP**
See also AITN 1, 2; CA 9-12R; 156; CABS 2; CANR 10, 48, 61; CDALB 1968-1988; DA3; DLB 5, 193; DLBD 7; DLBY 82, 93, 96, 97, 98; INT CANR-10; MTCW 1, 2
Dickey, William 1928-1994 **CLC 3, 28**
See also CA 9-12R; 145; CANR 24, 79; DLB 5
Dickinson, Charles 1951- **CLC 49**
See also CA 128
Dickinson, Emily (Elizabeth) 1830-1886 **NCLC 21, 77; DA; DAB; DAC; DAM MST, POET; PC 1; WLC**
See also AAYA 22; CDALB 1865-1917; DA3; DLB 1; SATA 29
Dickinson, Peter (Malcolm) 1927- **CLC 12, 35**
See also AAYA 9; CA 41-44R; CANR 31, 58, 88; CLR 29; DLB 87, 161; JRDA; MAICYA; SATA 5, 62, 95
Dickson, Carr
See Carr, John Dickson
Dickson, Carter
See Carr, John Dickson
Diderot, Denis 1713-1784 **LC 26**
Didion, Joan 1934- **CLC 1, 3, 8, 14, 32, 129; DAM NOV**
See also AITN 1; CA 5-8R; CANR 14, 52, 76; CDALB 1968-1988; DA3; DLB 2, 173, 185; DLBY 81, 86; MTCW 1, 2
Dietrich, Robert
See Hunt, E(verette) Howard, (Jr.)
Difusa, Pati
See Almodovar, Pedro
Dillard, Annie 1945- **CLC 9, 60, 115; DAM NOV**
See also AAYA 6; CA 49-52; CANR 3, 43, 62, 90; DA3; DLBY 80; MTCW 1, 2; SATA 10

Dillard, R(ichard) H(enry) W(ilde) 1937- **CLC 5**
See also CA 21-24R; CAAS 7; CANR 10; DLB 5
Dillon, Eilis 1920-1994 **CLC 17**
See also CA 9-12R, 182; 147; CAAE 182; CAAS 3; CANR 4, 38, 78; CLR 26; MAICYA; SATA 2, 74; SATA-Essay 105; SATA-Obit 83
Dimont, Penelope
See Mortimer, Penelope (Ruth)
Dinesen, Isak -1962 **CLC 10, 29, 95; SSC 7**
See also Blixen, Karen (Christentze Dinesen)
See also MTCW 1
Ding Ling CLC 68
See also Chiang, Pin-chin
Diphusa, Patty
See Almodovar, Pedro
Disch, Thomas M(ichael) 1940- **CLC 7, 36**
See also AAYA 17; CA 21-24R; CAAS 4; CANR 17, 36, 54, 89; CLR 18; DA3; DLB 8; MAICYA; MTCW 1, 2; SAAS 15; SATA 92
Disch, Tom
See Disch, Thomas M(ichael)
d'Isly, Georges
See Simenon, Georges (Jacques Christian)
Disraeli, Benjamin 1804-1881 **NCLC 2, 39, 79**
See also DLB 21, 55
Ditcum, Steve
See Crumb, R(obert)
Dixon, Paige
See Corcoran, Barbara
Dixon, Stephen 1936- **CLC 52; SSC 16**
See also CA 89-92; CANR 17, 40, 54, 91; DLB 130
Doak, Annie
See Dillard, Annie
Dobell, Sydney Thompson 1824-1874 **NCLC 43**
See also DLB 32
Doblin, Alfred TCLC 13
See also Doeblin, Alfred
Dobrolyubov, Nikolai Alexandrovich 1836-1861 **NCLC 5**
Dobson, Austin 1840-1921 **TCLC 79**
See also DLB 35; 144
Dobyns, Stephen 1941- **CLC 37**
See also CA 45-48; CANR 2, 18
Doctorow, E(dgar) L(aurence) 1931- **CLC 6, 11, 15, 18, 37, 44, 65, 113; DAM NOV, POP**
See also AAYA 22; AITN 2; BEST 89:3; CA 45-48; CANR 2, 33, 51, 76; CDALB 1968-1988; DA3; DLB 2, 28, 173; DLBY 80; MTCW 1, 2
Dodgson, Charles Lutwidge 1832-1898
See Carroll, Lewis
See also CLR 2; DA; DAB; DAC; DAM MST, NOV, POET; DA3; MAICYA; SATA 100; YABC 2
Dodson, Owen (Vincent) 1914-1983 **CLC 79; BLC 1; DAM MULT**
See also BW 1; CA 65-68; 110; CANR 24; DLB 76
Doeblin, Alfred 1878-1957 **TCLC 13**
See also Doblin, Alfred
See also CA 110; 141; DLB 66
Doerr, Harriet 1910- **CLC 34**
See also CA 117; 122; CANR 47; INT 122
Domecq, H(onorio Bustos)
See Bioy Casares, Adolfo
Domecq, H(onorio) Bustos
See Bioy Casares, Adolfo; Borges, Jorge Luis
Domini, Rey
See Lorde, Audre (Geraldine)
Dominique
See Proust, (Valentin-Louis-George-Eugene-) Marcel
Don, A
See Stephen, SirLeslie
Donaldson, Stephen R. 1947- **CLC 46; DAM POP**
See also CA 89-92; CANR 13, 55; INT CANR-13
Donleavy, J(ames) P(atrick) 1926- **CLC 1, 4, 6, 10, 45**
See also AITN 2; CA 9-12R; CANR 24, 49, 62, 80; DLB 6, 173; INT CANR-24; MTCW 1, 2
Donne, John 1572-1631 **LC 10, 24; DA; DAB; DAC; DAM MST, POET; PC 1; WLC**
See also CDBLB Before 1660; DLB 121, 151
Donnell, David 1939(?)- **CLC 34**
Donoghue, P. S.
See Hunt, E(verette) Howard, (Jr.)
Donoso (Yanez), Jose 1924-1996 **CLC 4, 8, 11, 32, 99; DAM MULT; HLC 1; SSC 34**
See also CA 81-84; 155; CANR 32, 73; DLB 113; HW 1, 2; MTCW 1, 2
Donovan, John 1928-1992 **CLC 35**
See also AAYA 20; CA 97-100; 137; CLR 3; MAICYA; SATA 72; SATA-Brief 29
Don Roberto
See Cunninghame Graham, Robert (Gallnigad) Bontine
Doolittle, Hilda 1886-1961 **CLC 3, 8, 14, 31, 34, 73; DA; DAC; DAM MST, POET; PC 5; WLC**
See also H. D.
See also CA 97-100; CANR 35; DLB 4, 45; MTCW 1, 2
Doppo, Kunikida 1869-1908 **TCLC 99**
See also DLB 180
Dorfman, Ariel 1942- **CLC 48, 77; DAM MULT; HLC 1**
See also CA 124; 130; CANR 67, 70; HW 1, 2; INT 130
Dorn, Edward (Merton) 1929-1999 **CLC 10, 18**
See also CA 93-96; 187; CANR 42, 79; DLB 5; INT 93-96
Dorris, Michael (Anthony) 1945-1997 **CLC 109; DAM MULT, NOV**
See also AAYA 20; BEST 90:1; CA 102; 157; CANR 19, 46, 75; CLR 58; DA3; DLB 175; MTCW 2; NNAL; SATA 75; SATA-Obit 94
Dorris, Michael A.
See Dorris, Michael (Anthony)
Dorsan, Luc
See Simenon, Georges (Jacques Christian)
Dorsange, Jean
See Simenon, Georges (Jacques Christian)
Dos Passos, John (Roderigo) 1896-1970 **CLC 1, 4, 8, 11, 15, 25, 34, 82; DA; DAB; DAC; DAM MST, NOV; WLC**
See also CA 1-4R; 29-32R; CANR 3; CDALB 1929-1941; DA3; DLB 4, 9; DLBD 1, 15; DLBY 96; MTCW 1, 2
Dossage, Jean
See Simenon, Georges (Jacques Christian)
Dostoevsky, Fedor Mikhailovich 1821-1881 **NCLC 2, 7, 21, 33, 43; DA; DAB; DAC; DAM MST, NOV; SSC 2, 33; WLC**
See also DA3
Doughty, Charles M(ontagu) 1843-1926 **TCLC 27**
See also CA 115; 178; DLB 19, 57, 174
Douglas, Ellen CLC 73
See also Haxton, Josephine Ayres; Williamson, Ellen Douglas
Douglas, Gavin 1475(?)-1522 **LC 20**
See also DLB 132
Douglas, George
See Brown, George Douglas
Douglas, Keith (Castellain) 1920-1944 **TCLC 40**
See also CA 160; DLB 27
Douglas, Leonard
See Bradbury, Ray (Douglas)
Douglas, Michael
See Crichton, (John) Michael
Douglas, (George) Norman 1868-1952 **TCLC 68**
See also CA 119; 157; DLB 34, 195
Douglas, William
See Brown, George Douglas
Douglass, Frederick 1817(?)-1895 **NCLC 7, 55; BLC 1; DA; DAC; DAM MST, MULT; WLC**
See also CDALB 1640-1865; DA3; DLB 1, 43, 50, 79; SATA 29
Dourado, (Waldomiro Freitas) Autran 1926- **CLC 23, 60**
See also CA 25-28R, 179; CANR 34, 81; DLB 145; HW 2
Dourado, Waldomiro Autran 1926-
See Dourado, (Waldomiro Freitas) Autran
See also CA 179
Dove, Rita (Frances) 1952- **CLC 50, 81; BLCS; DAM MULT, POET; PC 6**
See also BW 2; CA 109; CAAS 19; CANR 27, 42, 68, 76; CDALBS; DA3; DLB 120; MTCW 1
Doveglion
See Villa, Jose Garcia
Dowell, Coleman 1925-1985 **CLC 60**
See also CA 25-28R; 117; CANR 10; DLB 130
Dowson, Ernest (Christopher) 1867-1900 **TCLC 4**
See also CA 105; 150; DLB 19, 135
Doyle, A. Conan
See Doyle, Arthur Conan
Doyle, Arthur Conan 1859-1930 **TCLC 7; DA; DAB; DAC; DAM MST, NOV; SSC 12; WLC**
See also AAYA 14; CA 104; 122; CDBLB 1890-1914; DA3; DLB 18, 70, 156, 178; MTCW 1, 2; SATA 24
Doyle, Conan
See Doyle, Arthur Conan
Doyle, John
See Graves, Robert (von Ranke)
Doyle, Roddy 1958(?)- **CLC 81**
See also AAYA 14; CA 143; CANR 73; DA3; DLB 194
Doyle, Sir A. Conan
See Doyle, Arthur Conan
Doyle, Sir Arthur Conan
See Doyle, Arthur Conan
Dr. A
See Asimov, Isaac; Silverstein, Alvin
Drabble, Margaret 1939- **CLC 2, 3, 5, 8, 10, 22, 53, 129; DAB; DAC; DAM MST, NOV, POP**
See also CA 13-16R; CANR 18, 35, 63; CDBLB 1960 to Present; DA3; DLB 14, 155, 231; MTCW 1, 2; SATA 48
Drapier, M. B.
See Swift, Jonathan
Drayham, James
See Mencken, H(enry) L(ouis)
Drayton, Michael 1563-1631 **LC 8; DAM POET**
See also DLB 121
Dreadstone, Carl
See Campbell, (John) Ramsey
Dreiser, Theodore (Herman Albert) 1871-1945 **TCLC 10, 18, 35, 83; DA;**

DAC; DAM MST, NOV; SSC 30; WLC
See also CA 106; 132; CDALB 1865-1917; DA3; DLB 9, 12, 102, 137; DLBD 1; MTCW 1, 2
Drexler, Rosalyn 1926- **CLC 2, 6**
See also CA 81-84; CANR 68
Dreyer, Carl Theodor 1889-1968 **CLC 16**
See also CA 116
Drieu la Rochelle, Pierre(-Eugene) 1893-1945 **TCLC 21**
See also CA 117; DLB 72
Drinkwater, John 1882-1937 **TCLC 57**
See also CA 109; 149; DLB 10, 19, 149
Drop Shot
See Cable, George Washington
Droste-Hulshoff, Annette Freiin von 1797-1848 **NCLC 3**
See also DLB 133
Drummond, Walter
See Silverberg, Robert
Drummond, William Henry 1854-1907 **TCLC 25**
See also CA 160; DLB 92
Drummond de Andrade, Carlos 1902-1987 **CLC 18**
See also Andrade, Carlos Drummond de
See also CA 132; 123
Drury, Allen (Stuart) 1918-1998 **CLC 37**
See also CA 57-60; 170; CANR 18, 52; INT CANR-18
Dryden, John 1631-1700 **LC 3, 21; DA; DAB; DAC; DAM DRAM, MST, POET; DC 3; PC 25; WLC**
See also CDBLB 1660-1789; DLB 80, 101, 131
Duberman, Martin (Bauml) 1930- **CLC 8**
See also CA 1-4R; CANR 2, 63
Dubie, Norman (Evans) 1945- **CLC 36**
See also CA 69-72; CANR 12; DLB 120
Du Bois, W(illiam) E(dward) B(urghardt) 1868-1963 **CLC 1, 2, 13, 64, 96; BLC 1; DA; DAC; DAM MST, MULT, NOV; WLC**
See also BW 1, 3; CA 85-88; CANR 34, 82; CDALB 1865-1917; DA3; DLB 47, 50, 91; MTCW 1, 2; SATA 42
Dubus, Andre 1936-1999 **CLC 13, 36, 97; SSC 15**
See also CA 21-24R; 177; CANR 17; DLB 130; INT CANR-17
Duca Minimo
See D'Annunzio, Gabriele
Ducharme, Rejean 1941- **CLC 74**
See also CA 165; DLB 60
Duclos, Charles Pinot 1704-1772 **LC 1**
Dudek, Louis 1918- **CLC 11, 19**
See also CA 45-48; CAAS 14; CANR 1; DLB 88
Duerrenmatt, Friedrich 1921-1990 **CLC 1, 4, 8, 11, 15, 43, 102; DAM DRAM**
See also DuRrenmatt, Friedrich
See also CA 17-20R; CANR 33; DLB 69, 124; MTCW 1, 2
Duffy, Bruce 1953(?)- **CLC 50**
See also CA 172
Duffy, Maureen 1933- **CLC 37**
See also CA 25-28R; CANR 33, 68; DLB 14; MTCW 1
Dugan, Alan 1923- **CLC 2, 6**
See also CA 81-84; DLB 5
du Gard, Roger Martin
See Martin du Gard, Roger
Duhamel, Georges 1884-1966 **CLC 8**
See also CA 81-84; 25-28R; CANR 35; DLB 65; MTCW 1
Dujardin, Edouard (Emile Louis) 1861-1949 **TCLC 13**
See also CA 109; DLB 123
Dulles, John Foster 1888-1959 **TCLC 72**
See also CA 115; 149
Dumas, Alexandre (pere)
See Dumas, Alexandre (Davy de la Pailleterie)
Dumas, Alexandre (Davy de la Pailleterie) 1802-1870 **NCLC 11, 71; DA; DAB; DAC; DAM MST, NOV; WLC**
See also DA3; DLB 119, 192; SATA 18
Dumas, Alexandre (fils) 1824-1895 **NCLC 71; DC 1**
See also AAYA 22; DLB 192
Dumas, Claudine
See Malzberg, Barry N(athaniel)
Dumas, Henry L. 1934-1968 **CLC 6, 62**
See also BW 1; CA 85-88; DLB 41
du Maurier, Daphne 1907-1989 **CLC 6, 11, 59; DAB; DAC; DAM MST, POP; SSC 18**
See also CA 5-8R; 128; CANR 6, 55; DA3; DLB 191; MTCW 1, 2; SATA 27; SATA-Obit 60
Du Maurier, George 1834-1896 **NCLC 86**
See also DLB 153, 178
Dunbar, Paul Laurence 1872-1906 **TCLC 2, 12; BLC 1; DA; DAC; DAM MST, MULT, POET; PC 5; SSC 8; WLC**
See also BW 1, 3; CA 104; 124; CANR 79; CDALB 1865-1917; DA3; DLB 50, 54, 78; SATA 34
Dunbar, William 1460(?)-1530(?) **LC 20**
See also DLB 132, 146
Duncan, Dora Angela
See Duncan, Isadora
Duncan, Isadora 1877(?)-1927 **TCLC 68**
See also CA 118; 149
Duncan, Lois 1934- **CLC 26**
See also AAYA 4, 34; CA 1-4R; CANR 2, 23, 36; CLR 29; JRDA; MAICYA; SAAS 2; SATA 1, 36, 75
Duncan, Robert (Edward) 1919-1988 **CLC 1, 2, 4, 7, 15, 41, 55; DAM POET; PC 2**
See also CA 9-12R; 124; CANR 28, 62; DLB 5, 16, 193; MTCW 1, 2
Duncan, Sara Jeannette 1861-1922 **TCLC 60**
See also CA 157; DLB 92
Dunlap, William 1766-1839 **NCLC 2**
See also DLB 30, 37, 59
Dunn, Douglas (Eaglesham) 1942- **CLC 6, 40**
See also CA 45-48; CANR 2, 33; DLB 40; MTCW 1
Dunn, Katherine (Karen) 1945- **CLC 71**
See also CA 33-36R; CANR 72; MTCW 1
Dunn, Stephen 1939- **CLC 36**
See also CA 33-36R; CANR 12, 48, 53; DLB 105
Dunne, Finley Peter 1867-1936 **TCLC 28**
See also CA 108; 178; DLB 11, 23
Dunne, John Gregory 1932- **CLC 28**
See also CA 25-28R; CANR 14, 50; DLBY 80
Dunsany, Edward John Moreton Drax Plunkett 1878-1957
See Dunsany, Lord
See also CA 104; 148; DLB 10; MTCW 1
Dunsany, Lord -1957 **TCLC 2, 59**
See also Dunsany, Edward John Moreton Drax Plunkett
See also DLB 77, 153, 156
du Perry, Jean
See Simenon, Georges (Jacques Christian)
Durang, Christopher (Ferdinand) 1949- **CLC 27, 38**
See also CA 105; CANR 50, 76; MTCW 1
Duras, Marguerite 1914-1996 **CLC 3, 6, 11, 20, 34, 40, 68, 100; SSC 40**
See also CA 25-28R; 151; CANR 50; DLB 83; MTCW 1, 2
Durban, (Rosa) Pam 1947- **CLC 39**
See also CA 123
Durcan, Paul 1944- **CLC 43, 70; DAM POET**
See also CA 134
Durkheim, Emile 1858-1917 **TCLC 55**
Durrell, Lawrence (George) 1912-1990 **CLC 1, 4, 6, 8, 13, 27, 41; DAM NOV**
See also CA 9-12R; 132; CANR 40, 77; CDBLB 1945-1960; DLB 15, 27, 204; DLBY 90; MTCW 1, 2
Durrenmatt, Friedrich
See Duerrenmatt, Friedrich
DuRrenmatt, Friedrich
See Duerrenmatt, Friedrich
Dutt, Toru 1856-1877 **NCLC 29**
Dwight, Timothy 1752-1817 **NCLC 13**
See also DLB 37
Dworkin, Andrea 1946- **CLC 43, 123**
See also CA 77-80; CAAS 21; CANR 16, 39, 76; INT CANR-16; MTCW 1, 2
Dwyer, Deanna
See Koontz, Dean R(ay)
Dwyer, K. R.
See Koontz, Dean R(ay)
Dwyer, Thomas A. 1923- **CLC 114**
See also CA 115
Dye, Richard
See De Voto, Bernard (Augustine)
Dylan, Bob 1941- **CLC 3, 4, 6, 12, 77**
See also CA 41-44R; DLB 16
E. V. L.
See Lucas, E(dward) V(errall)
Eagleton, Terence (Francis) 1943- **CLC 63, 132**
See also CA 57-60; CANR 7, 23, 68; MTCW 1, 2
Eagleton, Terry
See Eagleton, Terence (Francis)
Early, Jack
See Scoppettone, Sandra
East, Michael
See West, Morris L(anglo)
Eastaway, Edward
See Thomas, (Philip) Edward
Eastlake, William (Derry) 1917-1997 **CLC 8**
See also CA 5-8R; 158; CAAS 1; CANR 5, 63; DLB 6, 206; INT CANR-5
Eastman, Charles A(lexander) 1858-1939 **TCLC 55; DAM MULT**
See also CA 179; CANR 91; DLB 175; NNAL; YABC 1
Eberhart, Richard (Ghormley) 1904- **CLC 3, 11, 19, 56; DAM POET**
See also CA 1-4R; CANR 2; CDALB 1941-1968; DLB 48; MTCW 1
Eberstadt, Fernanda 1960- **CLC 39**
See also CA 136; CANR 69
Echegaray (y Eizaguirre), Jose (Maria Waldo) 1832-1916 **TCLC 4; HLCS 1**
See also CA 104; CANR 32; HW 1; MTCW 1
Echeverria, (Jose) Esteban (Antonino) 1805-1851 **NCLC 18**
Echo
See Proust, (Valentin-Louis-George-Eugene-) Marcel
Eckert, Allan W. 1931- **CLC 17**
See also AAYA 18; CA 13-16R; CANR 14, 45; INT CANR-14; SAAS 21; SATA 29, 91; SATA-Brief 27
Eckhart, Meister 1260(?)-1328(?) **CMLC 9**
See also DLB 115
Eckmar, F. R.
See de Hartog, Jan
Eco, Umberto 1932- **CLC 28, 60; DAM NOV, POP**
See also BEST 90:1; CA 77-80; CANR 12, 33, 55; DA3; DLB 196; MTCW 1, 2
Eddison, E(ric) R(ucker) 1882-1945 **TCLC 15**

See also CA 109; 156
Eddy, Mary (Ann Morse) Baker 1821-1910 **TCLC 71**
See also CA 113; 174
Edel, (Joseph) Leon 1907-1997 **CLC 29, 34**
See also CA 1-4R; 161; CANR 1, 22; DLB 103; INT CANR-22
Eden, Emily 1797-1869 **NCLC 10**
Edgar, David 1948- **CLC 42; DAM DRAM**
See also CA 57-60; CANR 12, 61; DLB 13, 233; MTCW 1
Edgerton, Clyde (Carlyle) 1944- **CLC 39**
See also AAYA 17; CA 118; 134; CANR 64; INT 134
Edgeworth, Maria 1768-1849 **NCLC 1, 51**
See also DLB 116, 159, 163; SATA 21
Edmonds, Paul
See Kuttner, Henry
Edmonds, Walter D(umaux) 1903-1998 **CLC 35**
See also CA 5-8R; CANR 2; DLB 9; MAICYA; SAAS 4; SATA 1, 27; SATA-Obit 99
Edmondson, Wallace
See Ellison, Harlan (Jay)
Edson, Russell CLC 13
See also CA 33-36R
Edwards, Bronwen Elizabeth
See Rose, Wendy
Edwards, G(erald) B(asil) 1899-1976 **CLC 25**
See also CA 110
Edwards, Gus 1939- **CLC 43**
See also CA 108; INT 108
Edwards, Jonathan 1703-1758 **LC 7, 54; DA; DAC; DAM MST**
See also DLB 24
Efron, Marina Ivanovna Tsvetaeva
See Tsvetaeva (Efron), Marina (Ivanovna)
Ehle, John (Marsden, Jr.) 1925- **CLC 27**
See also CA 9-12R
Ehrenbourg, Ilya (Grigoryevich)
See Ehrenburg, Ilya (Grigoryevich)
Ehrenburg, Ilya (Grigoryevich) 1891-1967 **CLC 18, 34, 62**
See also CA 102; 25-28R
Ehrenburg, Ilyo (Grigoryevich)
See Ehrenburg, Ilya (Grigoryevich)
Ehrenreich, Barbara 1941- **CLC 110**
See also BEST 90:4; CA 73-76; CANR 16, 37, 62; MTCW 1, 2
Eich, Guenter 1907-1972 **CLC 15**
See also CA 111; 93-96; DLB 69, 124
Eichendorff, Joseph Freiherr von 1788-1857 **NCLC 8**
See also DLB 90
Eigner, Larry CLC 9
See also Eigner, Laurence (Joel)
See also CAAS 23; DLB 5
Eigner, Laurence (Joel) 1927-1996
See Eigner, Larry
See also CA 9-12R; 151; CANR 6, 84; DLB 193
Einstein, Albert 1879-1955 **TCLC 65**
See also CA 121; 133; MTCW 1, 2
Eiseley, Loren Corey 1907-1977 **CLC 7**
See also AAYA 5; CA 1-4R; 73-76; CANR 6; DLBD 17
Eisenstadt, Jill 1963- **CLC 50**
See also CA 140
Eisenstein, Sergei (Mikhailovich) 1898-1948 **TCLC 57**
See also CA 114; 149
Eisner, Simon
See Kornbluth, C(yril) M.
Ekeloef, (Bengt) Gunnar 1907-1968 **CLC 27; DAM POET; PC 23**
See also CA 123; 25-28R
Ekelof, (Bengt) Gunnar
See Ekeloef, (Bengt) Gunnar
Ekelund, Vilhelm 1880-1949 **TCLC 75**
Ekwensi, C. O. D.
See Ekwensi, Cyprian (Odiatu Duaka)
Ekwensi, Cyprian (Odiatu Duaka) 1921- **CLC 4; BLC 1; DAM MULT**
See also BW 2, 3; CA 29-32R; CANR 18, 42, 74; DLB 117; MTCW 1, 2; SATA 66
Elaine TCLC 18
See also Leverson, Ada
El Crummo
See Crumb, R(obert)
Elder, Lonne III 1931-1996 **DC 8**
See also BLC 1; BW 1, 3; CA 81-84; 152; CANR 25; DAM MULT; DLB 7, 38, 44
Eleanor of Aquitaine 1122-1204 **CMLC 39**
Elia
See Lamb, Charles
Eliade, Mircea 1907-1986 **CLC 19**
See also CA 65-68; 119; CANR 30, 62; DLB 220; MTCW 1
Eliot, A. D.
See Jewett, (Theodora) Sarah Orne
Eliot, Alice
See Jewett, (Theodora) Sarah Orne
Eliot, Dan
See Silverberg, Robert
Eliot, George 1819- **NCLC 4, 13, 23, 41, 49, 89; DA; DAB; DAC; DAM MST, NOV; PC 20; WLC**
See also CDBLB 1832-1890; DA3; DLB 21, 35, 55
Eliot, John 1604-1690 **LC 5**
See also DLB 24
Eliot, T(homas) S(tearns) 1888-1965 **CLC 1, 2, 3, 6, 9, 10, 13, 15, 24, 34, 41, 55, 57, 113; DA; DAB; DAC; DAM DRAM, MST, POET; PC 5, 31; WLC**
See also AAYA 28; CA 5-8R; 25-28R; CANR 41; CDALB 1929-1941; DA3; DLB 7, 10, 45, 63; DLBY 88; MTCW 1, 2
Elizabeth 1866-1941 **TCLC 41**
Elkin, Stanley L(awrence) 1930-1995 **CLC 4, 6, 9, 14, 27, 51, 91; DAM NOV, POP; SSC 12**
See also CA 9-12R; 148; CANR 8, 46; DLB 2, 28; DLBY 80; INT CANR-8; MTCW 1, 2
Elledge, Scott CLC 34
Elliot, Don
See Silverberg, Robert
Elliott, Don
See Silverberg, Robert
Elliott, George P(aul) 1918-1980 **CLC 2**
See also CA 1-4R; 97-100; CANR 2
Elliott, Janice 1931-1995 **CLC 47**
See also CA 13-16R; CANR 8, 29, 84; DLB 14; SATA 119
Elliott, Sumner Locke 1917-1991 **CLC 38**
See also CA 5-8R; 134; CANR 2, 21
Elliott, William
See Bradbury, Ray (Douglas)
Ellis, A. E. CLC 7
Ellis, Alice Thomas CLC 40
See also Haycraft, Anna (Margaret)
See also DLB 194; MTCW 1
Ellis, Bret Easton 1964- **CLC 39, 71, 117; DAM POP**
See also AAYA 2; CA 118; 123; CANR 51, 74; DA3; INT 123; MTCW 1
Ellis, (Henry) Havelock 1859-1939 **TCLC 14**
See also CA 109; 169; DLB 190
Ellis, Landon
See Ellison, Harlan (Jay)
Ellis, Trey 1962- **CLC 55**
See also CA 146; CANR 92
Ellison, Harlan (Jay) 1934- **CLC 1, 13, 42; DAM POP; SSC 14**
See also AAYA 29; CA 5-8R; CANR 5, 46; DLB 8; INT CANR-5; MTCW 1, 2
Ellison, Ralph (Waldo) 1914-1994 **CLC 1, 3, 11, 54, 86, 114; BLC 1; DA; DAB; DAC; DAM MST, MULT, NOV; SSC 26; WLC**
See also AAYA 19; BW 1, 3; CA 9-12R; 145; CANR 24, 53; CDALB 1941-1968; DA3; DLB 2, 76, 227; DLBY 94; MTCW 1, 2
Ellmann, Lucy (Elizabeth) 1956- **CLC 61**
See also CA 128
Ellmann, Richard (David) 1918-1987 **CLC 50**
See also BEST 89:2; CA 1-4R; 122; CANR 2, 28, 61; DLB 103; DLBY 87; MTCW 1, 2
Elman, Richard (Martin) 1934-1997 **CLC 19**
See also CA 17-20R; 163; CAAS 3; CANR 47
Elron
See Hubbard, L(afayette) Ron(ald)
Eluard, Paul TCLC 7, 41
See also Grindel, Eugene
Elyot, Sir Thomas 1490(?)-1546 **LC 11**
Elytis, Odysseus 1911-1996 **CLC 15, 49, 100; DAM POET; PC 21**
See also CA 102; 151; MTCW 1, 2
Emecheta, (Florence Onye) Buchi 1944- **CLC 14, 48, 128; BLC 2; DAM MULT**
See also BW 2, 3; CA 81-84; CANR 27, 81; DA3; DLB 117; MTCW 1, 2; SATA 66
Emerson, Mary Moody 1774-1863 **NCLC 66**
Emerson, Ralph Waldo 1803-1882 **NCLC 1, 38; DA; DAB; DAC; DAM MST, POET; PC 18; WLC**
See also CDALB 1640-1865; DA3; DLB 1, 59, 73, 223
Eminescu, Mihail 1850-1889 **NCLC 33**
Empson, William 1906-1984 **CLC 3, 8, 19, 33, 34**
See also CA 17-20R; 112; CANR 31, 61; DLB 20; MTCW 1, 2
Enchi, Fumiko (Ueda) 1905-1986 **CLC 31**
See also CA 129; 121; DLB 182
Ende, Michael (Andreas Helmuth) 1929-1995 **CLC 31**
See also CA 118; 124; 149; CANR 36; CLR 14; DLB 75; MAICYA; SATA 61; SATA-Brief 42; SATA-Obit 86
Endo, Shusaku 1923-1996 **CLC 7, 14, 19, 54, 99; DAM NOV**
See also CA 29-32R; 153; CANR 21, 54; DA3; DLB 182; MTCW 1, 2
Engel, Marian 1933-1985 **CLC 36**
See also CA 25-28R; CANR 12; DLB 53; INT CANR-12
Engelhardt, Frederick
See Hubbard, L(afayette) Ron(ald)
Engels, Friedrich 1820-1895 **NCLC 85**
See also DLB 129
Enright, D(ennis) J(oseph) 1920- **CLC 4, 8, 31**
See also CA 1-4R; CANR 1, 42, 83; DLB 27; SATA 25
Enzensberger, Hans Magnus 1929- **CLC 43; PC 28**
See also CA 116; 119
Ephron, Nora 1941- **CLC 17, 31**
See also AITN 2; CA 65-68; CANR 12, 39, 83
Epicurus 341B.C.-270B.C. **CMLC 21**
See also DLB 176
Epsilon
See Betjeman, John
Epstein, Daniel Mark 1948- **CLC 7**

See also CA 49-52; CANR 2, 53, 90
Epstein, Jacob 1956- **CLC 19**
See also CA 114
Epstein, Jean 1897-1953 **TCLC 92**
Epstein, Joseph 1937- **CLC 39**
See also CA 112; 119; CANR 50, 65
Epstein, Leslie 1938- **CLC 27**
See also CA 73-76; CAAS 12; CANR 23, 69
Equiano, Olaudah 1745(?)-1797 **LC 16; BLC 2; DAM MULT**
See also DLB 37, 50
ER TCLC 33
See also CA 160; DLB 85
Erasmus, Desiderius 1469(?)-1536 **LC 16**
Erdman, Paul E(mil) 1932- **CLC 25**
See also AITN 1; CA 61-64; CANR 13, 43, 84
Erdrich, Louise 1954- **CLC 39, 54, 120; DAM MULT, NOV, POP**
See also AAYA 10; BEST 89:1; CA 114; CANR 41, 62; CDALBS; DA3; DLB 152, 175, 206; MTCW 1; NNAL; SATA 94
Erenburg, Ilya (Grigoryevich)
See Ehrenburg, Ilya (Grigoryevich)
Erickson, Stephen Michael 1950-
See Erickson, Steve
See also CA 129
Erickson, Steve 1950- **CLC 64**
See also Erickson, Stephen Michael
See also CANR 60, 68
Ericson, Walter
See Fast, Howard (Melvin)
Eriksson, Buntel
See Bergman, (Ernst) Ingmar
Ernaux, Annie 1940- **CLC 88**
See also CA 147; CANR 93
Erskine, John 1879-1951 **TCLC 84**
See also CA 112; 159; DLB 9, 102
Eschenbach, Wolfram von
See Wolfram von Eschenbach
Eseki, Bruno
See Mphahlele, Ezekiel
Esenin, Sergei (Alexandrovich) 1895-1925 **TCLC 4**
See also CA 104
Eshleman, Clayton 1935- **CLC 7**
See also CA 33-36R; CAAS 6; CANR 93; DLB 5
Espriella, Don Manuel Alvarez
See Southey, Robert
Espriu, Salvador 1913-1985 **CLC 9**
See also CA 154; 115; DLB 134
Espronceda, Jose de 1808-1842 **NCLC 39**
Esquivel, Laura 1951(?)-
See also AAYA 29; CA 143; CANR 68; DA3; HLCS 1; MTCW 1
Esse, James
See Stephens, James
Esterbrook, Tom
See Hubbard, L(afayette) Ron(ald)
Estleman, Loren D. 1952- **CLC 48; DAM NOV, POP**
See also AAYA 27; CA 85-88; CANR 27, 74; DA3; DLB 226; INT CANR-27; MTCW 1, 2
Euclid 306B.C.-283B.C. **CMLC 25**
Eugenides, Jeffrey 1960(?)- **CLC 81**
See also CA 144
Euripides c. 485B.C.-406B.C. **CMLC 23; DA; DAB; DAC; DAM DRAM, MST; DC 4; WLCS**
See also DA3; DLB 176
Evan, Evin
See Faust, Frederick (Schiller)
Evans, Caradoc 1878-1945 **TCLC 85**
Evans, Evan
See Faust, Frederick (Schiller)
Evans, Marian
See Eliot, George
Evans, Mary Ann
See Eliot, George
Evarts, Esther
See Benson, Sally
Everett, Percival 1956-
See Everett, Percival L.
Everett, Percival L. 1956- **CLC 57**
See also Everett, Percival
See also BW 2; CA 129
Everson, R(onald) G(ilmour) 1903- **CLC 27**
See also CA 17-20R; DLB 88
Everson, William (Oliver) 1912-1994 **CLC 1, 5, 14**
See also CA 9-12R; 145; CANR 20; DLB 212; MTCW 1
Evtushenko, Evgenii Aleksandrovich
See Yevtushenko, Yevgeny (Alexandrovich)
Ewart, Gavin (Buchanan) 1916-1995 **CLC 13, 46**
See also CA 89-92; 150; CANR 17, 46; DLB 40; MTCW 1
Ewers, Hanns Heinz 1871-1943 **TCLC 12**
See also CA 109; 149
Ewing, Frederick R.
See Sturgeon, Theodore (Hamilton)
Exley, Frederick (Earl) 1929-1992 **CLC 6, 11**
See also AITN 2; CA 81-84; 138; DLB 143; DLBY 81
Eynhardt, Guillermo
See Quiroga, Horacio (Sylvestre)
Ezekiel, Nissim 1924- **CLC 61**
See also CA 61-64
Ezekiel, Tish O'Dowd 1943- **CLC 34**
See also CA 129
Fadeyev, A.
See Bulgya, Alexander Alexandrovich
Fadeyev, Alexander TCLC 53
See also Bulgya, Alexander Alexandrovich
Fagen, Donald 1948- **CLC 26**
Fainzilberg, Ilya Arnoldovich 1897-1937
See Ilf, Ilya
See also CA 120; 165
Fair, Ronald L. 1932- **CLC 18**
See also BW 1; CA 69-72; CANR 25; DLB 33
Fairbairn, Roger
See Carr, John Dickson
Fairbairns, Zoe (Ann) 1948- **CLC 32**
See also CA 103; CANR 21, 85
Fairman, Paul W. 1916-1977
See Queen, Ellery
See also CA 114
Falco, Gian
See Papini, Giovanni
Falconer, James
See Kirkup, James
Falconer, Kenneth
See Kornbluth, C(yril) M.
Falkland, Samuel
See Heijermans, Herman
Fallaci, Oriana 1930- **CLC 11, 110**
See also CA 77-80; CANR 15, 58; MTCW 1
Faludy, George 1913- **CLC 42**
See also CA 21-24R
Faludy, Gyoergy
See Faludy, George
Fanon, Frantz 1925-1961 **CLC 74; BLC 2; DAM MULT**
See also BW 1; CA 116; 89-92
Fanshawe, Ann 1625-1680 **LC 11**
Fante, John (Thomas) 1911-1983 **CLC 60**
See also CA 69-72; 109; CANR 23; DLB 130; DLBY 83
Farah, Nuruddin 1945- **CLC 53; BLC 2; DAM MULT**
See also BW 2, 3; CA 106; CANR 81; DLB 125
Fargue, Leon-Paul 1876(?)-1947 **TCLC 11**
See also CA 109
Farigoule, Louis
See Romains, Jules
Farina, Richard 1936(?)-1966 **CLC 9**
See also CA 81-84; 25-28R
Farley, Walter (Lorimer) 1915-1989 **CLC 17**
See also CA 17-20R; CANR 8, 29, 84; DLB 22; JRDA; MAICYA; SATA 2, 43
Farmer, Philip Jose 1918- **CLC 1, 19**
See also AAYA 28; CA 1-4R; CANR 4, 35; DLB 8; MTCW 1; SATA 93
Farquhar, George 1677-1707 **LC 21; DAM DRAM**
See also DLB 84
Farrell, J(ames) G(ordon) 1935-1979 **CLC 6**
See also CA 73-76; 89-92; CANR 36; DLB 14; MTCW 1
Farrell, James T(homas) 1904-1979 **CLC 1, 4, 8, 11, 66; SSC 28**
See also CA 5-8R; 89-92; CANR 9, 61; DLB 4, 9, 86; DLBD 2; MTCW 1, 2
Farren, Richard J.
See Betjeman, John
Farren, Richard M.
See Betjeman, John
Fassbinder, Rainer Werner 1946-1982 **CLC 20**
See also CA 93-96; 106; CANR 31
Fast, Howard (Melvin) 1914- **CLC 23, 131; DAM NOV**
See also AAYA 16; CA 1-4R, 181; CAAE 181; CAAS 18; CANR 1, 33, 54, 75; DLB 9; INT CANR-33; MTCW 1; SATA 7; SATA-Essay 107
Faulcon, Robert
See Holdstock, Robert P.
Faulkner, William (Cuthbert) 1897-1962 **CLC 1, 3, 6, 8, 9, 11, 14, 18, 28, 52, 68; DA; DAB; DAC; DAM MST, NOV; SSC 1, 35, 42; WLC**
See also AAYA 7; CA 81-84; CANR 33; CDALB 1929-1941; DA3; DLB 9, 11, 44, 102; DLBD 2; DLBY 86, 97; MTCW 1, 2
Fauset, Jessie Redmon 1884(?)-1961 **CLC 19, 54; BLC 2; DAM MULT**
See also BW 1; CA 109; CANR 83; DLB 51
Faust, Frederick (Schiller) 1892-1944(?) **TCLC 49; DAM POP**
See also CA 108; 152
Faust, Irvin 1924- **CLC 8**
See also CA 33-36R; CANR 28, 67; DLB 2, 28; DLBY 80
Fawkes, Guy
See Benchley, Robert (Charles)
Fearing, Kenneth (Flexner) 1902-1961 **CLC 51**
See also CA 93-96; CANR 59; DLB 9
Fecamps, Elise
See Creasey, John
Federman, Raymond 1928- **CLC 6, 47**
See also CA 17-20R; CAAS 8; CANR 10, 43, 83; DLBY 80
Federspiel, J(uerg) F. 1931- **CLC 42**
See also CA 146
Feiffer, Jules (Ralph) 1929- **CLC 2, 8, 64; DAM DRAM**
See also AAYA 3; CA 17-20R; CANR 30, 59; DLB 7, 44; INT CANR-30; MTCW 1; SATA 8, 61, 111
Feige, Hermann Albert Otto Maximilian
See Traven, B.
Feinberg, David B. 1956-1994 **CLC 59**
See also CA 135; 147
Feinstein, Elaine 1930- **CLC 36**

See also CA 69-72; CAAS 1; CANR 31, 68; DLB 14, 40; MTCW 1
Feldman, Irving (Mordecai) 1928- **CLC 7**
See also CA 1-4R; CANR 1; DLB 169
Felix-Tchicaya, Gerald
See Tchicaya, Gerald Felix
Fellini, Federico 1920-1993 **CLC 16, 85**
See also CA 65-68; 143; CANR 33
Felsen, Henry Gregor 1916-1995 **CLC 17**
See also CA 1-4R; 180; CANR 1; SAAS 2; SATA 1
Fenno, Jack
See Calisher, Hortense
Fenollosa, Ernest (Francisco) 1853-1908 **TCLC 91**
Fenton, James Martin 1949- **CLC 32**
See also CA 102; DLB 40
Ferber, Edna 1887-1968 **CLC 18, 93**
See also AITN 1; CA 5-8R; 25-28R; CANR 68; DLB 9, 28, 86; MTCW 1, 2; SATA 7
Ferguson, Helen
See Kavan, Anna
Ferguson, Niall 1967- **CLC 134**
Ferguson, Samuel 1810-1886 **NCLC 33**
See also DLB 32
Fergusson, Robert 1750-1774 **LC 29**
See also DLB 109
Ferling, Lawrence
See Ferlinghetti, Lawrence (Monsanto)
Ferlinghetti, Lawrence (Monsanto) 1919(?)- **CLC 2, 6, 10, 27, 111; DAM POET; PC 1**
See also CA 5-8R; CANR 3, 41, 73; CDALB 1941-1968; DA3; DLB 5, 16; MTCW 1, 2
Fern, Fanny 1811-1872
See Parton, Sara Payson Willis
Fernandez, Vicente Garcia Huidobro
See Huidobro Fernandez, Vicente Garcia
Ferre, Rosario 1942- **SSC 36; HLCS 1**
See also CA 131; CANR 55, 81; DLB 145; HW 1, 2; MTCW 1
Ferrer, Gabriel (Francisco Victor) Miro
See Miro (Ferrer), Gabriel (Francisco Victor)
Ferrier, Susan (Edmonstone) 1782-1854 **NCLC 8**
See also DLB 116
Ferrigno, Robert 1948(?)- **CLC 65**
See also CA 140
Ferron, Jacques 1921-1985 **CLC 94; DAC**
See also CA 117; 129; DLB 60
Feuchtwanger, Lion 1884-1958 **TCLC 3**
See also CA 104; 187; DLB 66
Feuillet, Octave 1821-1890 **NCLC 45**
See also DLB 192
Feydeau, Georges (Leon Jules Marie) 1862-1921 **TCLC 22; DAM DRAM**
See also CA 113; 152; CANR 84; DLB 192
Fichte, Johann Gottlieb 1762-1814 **NCLC 62**
See also DLB 90
Ficino, Marsilio 1433-1499 **LC 12**
Fiedeler, Hans
See Doeblin, Alfred
Fiedler, Leslie A(aron) 1917- **CLC 4, 13, 24**
See also CA 9-12R; CANR 7, 63; DLB 28, 67; MTCW 1, 2
Field, Andrew 1938- **CLC 44**
See also CA 97-100; CANR 25
Field, Eugene 1850-1895 **NCLC 3**
See also DLB 23, 42, 140; DLBD 13; MAICYA; SATA 16
Field, Gans T.
See Wellman, Manly Wade
Field, Michael 1915-1971 **TCLC 43**
See also CA 29-32R
Field, Peter
See Hobson, Laura Z(ametkin)
Fielding, Henry 1707-1754 **LC 1, 46; DA; DAB; DAC; DAM DRAM, MST, NOV; WLC**
See also CDBLB 1660-1789; DA3; DLB 39, 84, 101
Fielding, Sarah 1710-1768 **LC 1, 44**
See also DLB 39
Fields, W. C. 1880-1946 **TCLC 80**
See also DLB 44
Fierstein, Harvey (Forbes) 1954- **CLC 33; DAM DRAM, POP**
See also CA 123; 129; DA3
Figes, Eva 1932- **CLC 31**
See also CA 53-56; CANR 4, 44, 83; DLB 14
Finch, Anne 1661-1720 **LC 3; PC 21**
See also DLB 95
Finch, Robert (Duer Claydon) 1900- **CLC 18**
See also CA 57-60; CANR 9, 24, 49; DLB 88
Findley, Timothy 1930- **CLC 27, 102; DAC; DAM MST**
See also CA 25-28R; CANR 12, 42, 69; DLB 53
Fink, William
See Mencken, H(enry) L(ouis)
Firbank, Louis 1942-
See Reed, Lou
See also CA 117
Firbank, (Arthur Annesley) Ronald 1886-1926 **TCLC 1**
See also CA 104; 177; DLB 36
Fisher, Dorothy (Frances) Canfield 1879-1958 **TCLC 87**
See also CA 114; 136; CANR 80; DLB 9, 102; MAICYA; YABC 1
Fisher, M(ary) F(rances) K(ennedy) 1908-1992 **CLC 76, 87**
See also CA 77-80; 138; CANR 44; MTCW 1
Fisher, Roy 1930- **CLC 25**
See also CA 81-84; CAAS 10; CANR 16; DLB 40
Fisher, Rudolph 1897-1934 **TCLC 11; BLC 2; DAM MULT; SSC 25**
See also BW 1, 3; CA 107; 124; CANR 80; DLB 51, 102
Fisher, Vardis (Alvero) 1895-1968 **CLC 7**
See also CA 5-8R; 25-28R; CANR 68; DLB 9, 206
Fiske, Tarleton
See Bloch, Robert (Albert)
Fitch, Clarke
See Sinclair, Upton (Beall)
Fitch, John IV
See Cormier, Robert (Edmund)
Fitzgerald, Captain Hugh
See Baum, L(yman) Frank
FitzGerald, Edward 1809-1883 **NCLC 9**
See also DLB 32
Fitzgerald, F(rancis) Scott (Key) 1896-1940 **TCLC 1, 6, 14, 28, 55; DA; DAB; DAC; DAM MST, NOV; SSC 6, 31; WLC**
See also AAYA 24; AITN 1; CA 110; 123; CDALB 1917-1929; DA3; DLB 4, 9, 86; DLBD 1, 15, 16; DLBY 81, 96; MTCW 1, 2
Fitzgerald, Penelope 1916- **CLC 19, 51, 61**
See also CA 85-88; CAAS 10; CANR 56, 86; DLB 14, 194; MTCW 2
Fitzgerald, Robert (Stuart) 1910-1985 **CLC 39**
See also CA 1-4R; 114; CANR 1; DLBY 80
FitzGerald, Robert D(avid) 1902-1987 **CLC 19**
See also CA 17-20R
Fitzgerald, Zelda (Sayre) 1900-1948 **TCLC 52**
See also CA 117; 126; DLBY 84
Flanagan, Thomas (James Bonner) 1923- **CLC 25, 52**
See also CA 108; CANR 55; DLBY 80; INT 108; MTCW 1
Flaubert, Gustave 1821-1880 **NCLC 2, 10, 19, 62, 66; DA; DAB; DAC; DAM MST, NOV; SSC 11; WLC**
See also DA3; DLB 119
Flecker, Herman Elroy
See Flecker, (Herman) James Elroy
Flecker, (Herman) James Elroy 1884-1915 **TCLC 43**
See also CA 109; 150; DLB 10, 19
Fleming, Ian (Lancaster) 1908-1964 **CLC 3, 30; DAM POP**
See also AAYA 26; CA 5-8R; CANR 59; CDBLB 1945-1960; DA3; DLB 87, 201; MTCW 1, 2; SATA 9
Fleming, Thomas (James) 1927- **CLC 37**
See also CA 5-8R; CANR 10; INT CANR-10; SATA 8
Fletcher, John 1579-1625 **LC 33; DC 6**
See also CDBLB Before 1660; DLB 58
Fletcher, John Gould 1886-1950 **TCLC 35**
See also CA 107; 167; DLB 4, 45
Fleur, Paul
See Pohl, Frederik
Flooglebuckle, Al
See Spiegelman, Art
Flora, Fletcher 1914-1969
See Queen, Ellery
See also CA 1-4R; CANR 3, 85
Flying Officer X
See Bates, H(erbert) E(rnest)
Fo, Dario 1926- **CLC 32, 109; DAM DRAM; DC 10**
See also CA 116; 128; CANR 68; DA3; DLBY 97; MTCW 1, 2
Fogarty, Jonathan Titulescu Esq.
See Farrell, James T(homas)
Follett, Ken(neth Martin) 1949- **CLC 18; DAM NOV, POP**
See also AAYA 6; BEST 89:4; CA 81-84; CANR 13, 33, 54; DA3; DLB 87; DLBY 81; INT CANR-33; MTCW 1
Fontane, Theodor 1819-1898 **NCLC 26**
See also DLB 129
Foote, Horton 1916- **CLC 51, 91; DAM DRAM**
See also CA 73-76; CANR 34, 51; DA3; DLB 26; INT CANR-34
Foote, Shelby 1916- **CLC 75; DAM NOV, POP**
See also CA 5-8R; CANR 3, 45, 74; DA3; DLB 2, 17; MTCW 2
Forbes, Esther 1891-1967 **CLC 12**
See also AAYA 17; CA 13-14; 25-28R; CAP 1; CLR 27; DLB 22; JRDA; MAICYA; SATA 2, 100
Forche, Carolyn (Louise) 1950- **CLC 25, 83, 86; DAM POET; PC 10**
See also CA 109; 117; CANR 50, 74; DA3; DLB 5, 193; INT 117; MTCW 1
Ford, Elbur
See Hibbert, Eleanor Alice Burford
Ford, Ford Madox 1873-1939 **TCLC 1, 15, 39, 57; DAM NOV**
See also Chaucer, Daniel
See also CA 104; 132; CANR 74; CDBLB 1914-1945; DA3; DLB 162; MTCW 1, 2
Ford, Henry 1863-1947 **TCLC 73**
See also CA 115; 148
Ford, John 1586-(?) **DC 8**
See also CDBLB Before 1660; DAM DRAM; DA3; DLB 58
Ford, John 1895-1973 **CLC 16**

Fuller, Charles (H., Jr.) 1939- **CLC 25; BLC 2; DAM DRAM, MULT; DC 1**
See also BW 2; CA 108; 112; CANR 87; DLB 38; INT 112; MTCW 1
Fuller, John (Leopold) 1937- **CLC 62**
See also CA 21-24R; CANR 9, 44; DLB 40
Fuller, Margaret
See Ossoli, Sarah Margaret (Fuller marchesa d')
Fuller, Roy (Broadbent) 1912-1991 **CLC 4, 28**
See also CA 5-8R; 135; CAAS 10; CANR 53, 83; DLB 15, 20; SATA 87
Fuller, Sarah Margaret 1810-1850
See Ossoli, Sarah Margaret (Fuller marchesa d')
Fulton, Alice 1952- **CLC 52**
See also CA 116; CANR 57, 88; DLB 193
Furphy, Joseph 1843-1912 **TCLC 25**
See also CA 163
Fussell, Paul 1924- **CLC 74**
See also BEST 90:1; CA 17-20R; CANR 8, 21, 35, 69; INT CANR-21; MTCW 1, 2
Futabatei, Shimei 1864-1909 **TCLC 44**
See also CA 162; DLB 180
Futrelle, Jacques 1875-1912 **TCLC 19**
See also CA 113; 155
Gaboriau, Emile 1835-1873 **NCLC 14**
Gadda, Carlo Emilio 1893-1973 **CLC 11**
See also CA 89-92; DLB 177
Gaddis, William 1922-1998 **CLC 1, 3, 6, 8, 10, 19, 43, 86**
See also CA 17-20R; 172; CANR 21, 48; DLB 2; MTCW 1, 2
Gage, Walter
See Inge, William (Motter)
Gaines, Ernest J(ames) 1933- **CLC 3, 11, 18, 86; BLC 2; DAM MULT**
See also AAYA 18; AITN 1; BW 2, 3; CA 9-12R; CANR 6, 24, 42, 75; CDALB 1968-1988; CLR 62; DA3; DLB 2, 33, 152; DLBY 80; MTCW 1, 2; SATA 86
Gaitskill, Mary 1954- **CLC 69**
See also CA 128; CANR 61
Galdos, Benito Perez
See Perez Galdos, Benito
Gale, Zona 1874-1938 **TCLC 7; DAM DRAM**
See also CA 105; 153; CANR 84; DLB 9, 78, 228
Galeano, Eduardo (Hughes) 1940- **CLC 72; HLCS 1**
See also CA 29-32R; CANR 13, 32; HW 1
Galiano, Juan Valera y Alcala
See Valera y Alcala-Galiano, Juan
Galilei, Galileo 1546-1642 **LC 45**
Gallagher, Tess 1943- **CLC 18, 63; DAM POET; PC 9**
See also CA 106; DLB 212
Gallant, Mavis 1922- **CLC 7, 18, 38; DAC; DAM MST; SSC 5**
See also CA 69-72; CANR 29, 69; DLB 53; MTCW 1, 2
Gallant, Roy A(rthur) 1924- **CLC 17**
See also CA 5-8R; CANR 4, 29, 54; CLR 30; MAICYA; SATA 4, 68, 110
Gallico, Paul (William) 1897-1976 **CLC 2**
See also AITN 1; CA 5-8R; 69-72; CANR 23; DLB 9, 171; MAICYA; SATA 13
Gallo, Max Louis 1932- **CLC 95**
See also CA 85-88
Gallois, Lucien
See Desnos, Robert
Gallup, Ralph
See Whitemore, Hugh (John)
Galsworthy, John 1867-1933 **TCLC 1, 45; DA; DAB; DAC; DAM DRAM, MST, NOV; SSC 22; WLC**
See also CA 104; 141; CANR 75; CDBLB 1890-1914; DA3; DLB 10, 34, 98, 162; DLBD 16; MTCW 1
Galt, John 1779-1839 **NCLC 1**
See also DLB 99, 116, 159
Galvin, James 1951- **CLC 38**
See also CA 108; CANR 26
Gamboa, Federico 1864-1939 **TCLC 36**
See also CA 167; HW 2
Gandhi, M. K.
See Gandhi, Mohandas Karamchand
Gandhi, Mahatma
See Gandhi, Mohandas Karamchand
Gandhi, Mohandas Karamchand 1869-1948 **TCLC 59; DAM MULT**
See also CA 121; 132; DA3; MTCW 1, 2
Gann, Ernest Kellogg 1910-1991 **CLC 23**
See also AITN 1; CA 1-4R; 136; CANR 1, 83
Garber, Eric 1943(?)-
See Holleran, Andrew
See also CANR 89
Garcia, Cristina 1958- **CLC 76**
See also CA 141; CANR 73; HW 2
Garcia Lorca, Federico 1898-1936 **TCLC 1, 7, 49; DA; DAB; DAC; DAM DRAM, MST, MULT, POET; DC 2; HLC 2; PC 3; WLC**
See also Lorca, Federico Garcia
See also CA 104; 131; CANR 81; DA3; DLB 108; HW 1, 2; MTCW 1, 2
Garcia Marquez, Gabriel (Jose) 1928- **CLC 2, 3, 8, 10, 15, 27, 47, 55, 68; DA; DAB; DAC; DAM MST, MULT, NOV, POP; HLC 1; SSC 8; WLC**
See also AAYA 3, 33; BEST 89:1, 90:4; CA 33-36R; CANR 10, 28, 50, 75, 82; DA3; DLB 113; HW 1, 2; MTCW 1, 2
Garcilaso de la Vega, El Inca 1503-1536
See also HLCS 1
Gard, Janice
See Latham, Jean Lee
Gard, Roger Martin du
See Martin du Gard, Roger
Gardam, Jane 1928- **CLC 43**
See also CA 49-52; CANR 2, 18, 33, 54; CLR 12; DLB 14, 161, 231; MAICYA; MTCW 1; SAAS 9; SATA 39, 76; SATA-Brief 28
Gardner, Herb(ert) 1934- **CLC 44**
See also CA 149
Gardner, John (Champlin), Jr. 1933-1982 **CLC 2, 3, 5, 7, 8, 10, 18, 28, 34; DAM NOV, POP; SSC 7**
See also AITN 1; CA 65-68; 107; CANR 33, 73; CDALBS; DA3; DLB 2; DLBY 82; MTCW 1; SATA 40; SATA-Obit 31
Gardner, John (Edmund) 1926- **CLC 30; DAM POP**
See also CA 103; CANR 15, 69; MTCW 1
Gardner, Miriam
See Bradley, Marion Zimmer
Gardner, Noel
See Kuttner, Henry
Gardons, S. S.
See Snodgrass, W(illiam) D(e Witt)
Garfield, Leon 1921-1996 **CLC 12**
See also AAYA 8; CA 17-20R; 152; CANR 38, 41, 78; CLR 21; DLB 161; JRDA; MAICYA; SATA 1, 32, 76; SATA-Obit 90
Garland, (Hannibal) Hamlin 1860-1940 **TCLC 3; SSC 18**
See also CA 104; DLB 12, 71, 78, 186
Garneau, (Hector de) Saint-Denys 1912-1943 **TCLC 13**
See also CA 111; DLB 88
Garner, Alan 1934- **CLC 17; DAB; DAM POP**
See also AAYA 18; CA 73-76, 178; CAAE 178; CANR 15, 64; CLR 20; DLB 161; MAICYA; MTCW 1, 2; SATA 18, 69; SATA-Essay 108
Garner, Hugh 1913-1979 **CLC 13**
See also CA 69-72; CANR 31; DLB 68
Garnett, David 1892-1981 **CLC 3**
See also CA 5-8R; 103; CANR 17, 79; DLB 34; MTCW 2
Garos, Stephanie
See Katz, Steve
Garrett, George (Palmer) 1929- **CLC 3, 11, 51; SSC 30**
See also CA 1-4R; CAAS 5; CANR 1, 42, 67; DLB 2, 5, 130, 152; DLBY 83
Garrick, David 1717-1779 **LC 15; DAM DRAM**
See also DLB 84
Garrigue, Jean 1914-1972 **CLC 2, 8**
See also CA 5-8R; 37-40R; CANR 20
Garrison, Frederick
See Sinclair, Upton (Beall)
Garro, Elena 1920(?)-1998
See also CA 131; 169; DLB 145; HLCS 1; HW 1
Garth, Will
See Hamilton, Edmond; Kuttner, Henry
Garvey, Marcus (Moziah, Jr.) 1887-1940 **TCLC 41; BLC 2; DAM MULT**
See also BW 1; CA 120; 124; CANR 79
Gary, Romain **CLC 25**
See also Kacew, Romain
See also DLB 83
Gascar, Pierre **CLC 11**
See also Fournier, Pierre
Gascoyne, David (Emery) 1916- **CLC 45**
See also CA 65-68; CANR 10, 28, 54; DLB 20; MTCW 1
Gaskell, Elizabeth Cleghorn 1810-1865 **NCLC 70; DAB; DAM MST; SSC 25**
See also CDBLB 1832-1890; DLB 21, 144, 159
Gass, William H(oward) 1924- **CLC 1, 2, 8, 11, 15, 39, 132; SSC 12**
See also CA 17-20R; CANR 30, 71; DLB 2, 227; MTCW 1, 2
Gassendi, Pierre 1592-1655 **LC 54**
Gasset, Jose Ortega y
See Ortega y Gasset, Jose
Gates, Henry Louis, Jr. 1950- **CLC 65; BLCS; DAM MULT**
See also BW 2, 3; CA 109; CANR 25, 53, 75; DA3; DLB 67; MTCW 1
Gautier, Theophile 1811-1872 **NCLC 1, 59; DAM POET; PC 18; SSC 20**
See also DLB 119
Gawsworth, John
See Bates, H(erbert) E(rnest)
Gay, John 1685-1732 **LC 49; DAM DRAM**
See also DLB 84, 95
Gay, Oliver
See Gogarty, Oliver St. John
Gaye, Marvin (Penze) 1939-1984 **CLC 26**
See also CA 112
Gebler, Carlo (Ernest) 1954- **CLC 39**
See also CA 119; 133
Gee, Maggie (Mary) 1948- **CLC 57**
See also CA 130; DLB 207
Gee, Maurice (Gough) 1931- **CLC 29**
See also CA 97-100; CANR 67; CLR 56; SATA 46, 101
Gelbart, Larry (Simon) 1928- **CLC 21, 61**
See also Gelbart, Larry
See also CA 73-76; CANR 45
Gelbart, Larry 1928-
See Gelbart, Larry (Simon)
Gelber, Jack 1932- **CLC 1, 6, 14, 79**
See also CA 1-4R; CANR 2; DLB 7, 228

Gellhorn, Martha (Ellis) 1908-1998 **CLC 14, 60**
See also CA 77-80; 164; CANR 44; DLBY 82, 98
Genet, Jean 1910-1986 **CLC 1, 2, 5, 10, 14, 44, 46; DAM DRAM**
See also CA 13-16R; CANR 18; DA3; DLB 72; DLBY 86; MTCW 1, 2
Gent, Peter 1942- **CLC 29**
See also AITN 1; CA 89-92; DLBY 82
Gentile, Giovanni 1875-1944 **TCLC 96**
See also CA 119
Gentlewoman in New England, A
See Bradstreet, Anne
Gentlewoman in Those Parts, A
See Bradstreet, Anne
George, Jean Craighead 1919- **CLC 35**
See also AAYA 8; CA 5-8R; CANR 25; CLR 1; DLB 52; JRDA; MAICYA; SATA 2, 68
George, Stefan (Anton) 1868-1933 **TCLC 2, 14**
See also CA 104
Georges, Georges Martin
See Simenon, Georges (Jacques Christian)
Gerhardi, William Alexander
See Gerhardie, William Alexander
Gerhardie, William Alexander 1895-1977 **CLC 5**
See also CA 25-28R; 73-76; CANR 18; DLB 36
Gerstler, Amy 1956- **CLC 70**
See also CA 146
Gertler, T. CLC 134
See also CA 116; 121
Ghalib NCLC 39, 78
See also Ghalib, Hsadullah Khan
Ghalib, Hsadullah Khan 1797-1869
See Ghalib
See also DAM POET
Ghelderode, Michel de 1898-1962 **CLC 6, 11; DAM DRAM**
See also CA 85-88; CANR 40, 77
Ghiselin, Brewster 1903- **CLC 23**
See also CA 13-16R; CAAS 10; CANR 13
Ghose, Aurabinda 1872-1950 **TCLC 63**
See also CA 163
Ghose, Zulfikar 1935- **CLC 42**
See also CA 65-68; CANR 67
Ghosh, Amitav 1956- **CLC 44**
See also CA 147; CANR 80
Giacosa, Giuseppe 1847-1906 **TCLC 7**
See also CA 104
Gibb, Lee
See Waterhouse, Keith (Spencer)
Gibbon, Lewis Grassic TCLC 4
See also Mitchell, James Leslie
Gibbons, Kaye 1960- **CLC 50, 88; DAM POP**
See also AAYA 34; CA 151; CANR 75; DA3; MTCW 1; SATA 117
Gibran, Kahlil 1883-1931 **TCLC 1, 9; DAM POET, POP; PC 9**
See also CA 104; 150; DA3; MTCW 2
Gibran, Khalil
See Gibran, Kahlil
Gibson, William 1914- **CLC 23; DA; DAB; DAC; DAM DRAM, MST**
See also CA 9-12R; CANR 9, 42, 75; DLB 7; MTCW 1; SATA 66
Gibson, William (Ford) 1948- **CLC 39, 63; DAM POP**
See also AAYA 12; CA 126; 133; CANR 52, 90; DA3; MTCW 1
Gide, Andre (Paul Guillaume) 1869-1951 **TCLC 5, 12, 36; DA; DAB; DAC; DAM MST, NOV; SSC 13; WLC**
See also CA 104; 124; DA3; DLB 65; MTCW 1, 2
Gifford, Barry (Colby) 1946- **CLC 34**
See also CA 65-68; CANR 9, 30, 40, 90
Gilbert, Frank
See De Voto, Bernard (Augustine)
Gilbert, W(illiam) S(chwenck) 1836-1911 **TCLC 3; DAM DRAM, POET**
See also CA 104; 173; SATA 36
Gilbreth, Frank B., Jr. 1911- **CLC 17**
See also CA 9-12R; SATA 2
Gilchrist, Ellen 1935- **CLC 34, 48; DAM POP; SSC 14**
See also CA 113; 116; CANR 41, 61; DLB 130; MTCW 1, 2
Giles, Molly 1942- **CLC 39**
See also CA 126
Gill, Eric 1882-1940 **TCLC 85**
Gill, Patrick
See Creasey, John
Gilliam, Terry (Vance) 1940- **CLC 21**
See also Monty Python
See also AAYA 19; CA 108; 113; CANR 35; INT 113
Gillian, Jerry
See Gilliam, Terry (Vance)
Gilliatt, Penelope (Ann Douglass) 1932-1993 **CLC 2, 10, 13, 53**
See also AITN 2; CA 13-16R; 141; CANR 49; DLB 14
Gilman, Charlotte (Anna) Perkins (Stetson) 1860-1935 **TCLC 9, 37; SSC 13**
See also CA 106; 150; DLB 221; MTCW 1
Gilmour, David 1949- **CLC 35**
See also CA 138, 147
Gilpin, William 1724-1804 **NCLC 30**
Gilray, J. D.
See Mencken, H(enry) L(ouis)
Gilroy, Frank D(aniel) 1925- **CLC 2**
See also CA 81-84; CANR 32, 64, 86; DLB 7
Gilstrap, John 1957(?)- **CLC 99**
See also CA 160
Ginsberg, Allen 1926-1997 **CLC 1, 2, 3, 4, 6, 13, 36, 69, 109; DA; DAB; DAC; DAM MST, POET; PC 4; WLC**
See also AAYA 33; AITN 1; CA 1-4R; 157; CANR 2, 41, 63; CDALB 1941-1968; DA3; DLB 5, 16, 169; MTCW 1, 2
Ginzburg, Natalia 1916-1991 **CLC 5, 11, 54, 70**
See also CA 85-88; 135; CANR 33; DLB 177; MTCW 1, 2
Giono, Jean 1895-1970 **CLC 4, 11**
See also CA 45-48; 29-32R; CANR 2, 35; DLB 72; MTCW 1
Giovanni, Nikki 1943- **CLC 2, 4, 19, 64, 117; BLC 2; DA; DAB; DAC; DAM MST, MULT, POET; PC 19; WLCS**
See also AAYA 22; AITN 1; BW 2, 3; CA 29-32R; CAAS 6; CANR 18, 41, 60, 91; CDALBS; CLR 6; DA3; DLB 5, 41; INT CANR-18; MAICYA; MTCW 1, 2; SATA 24, 107
Giovene, Andrea 1904- **CLC 7**
See also CA 85-88
Gippius, Zinaida (Nikolayevna) 1869-1945
See Hippius, Zinaida
See also CA 106
Giraudoux, (Hippolyte) Jean 1882-1944 **TCLC 2, 7; DAM DRAM**
See also CA 104; DLB 65
Gironella, Jose Maria 1917- **CLC 11**
See also CA 101
Gissing, George (Robert) 1857-1903 **TCLC 3, 24, 47; SSC 37**
See also CA 105; 167; DLB 18, 135, 184
Giurlani, Aldo
See Palazzeschi, Aldo
Gladkov, Fyodor (Vasilyevich) 1883-1958 **TCLC 27**
See also CA 170
Glanville, Brian (Lester) 1931- **CLC 6**
See also CA 5-8R; CAAS 9; CANR 3, 70; DLB 15, 139; SATA 42
Glasgow, Ellen (Anderson Gholson) 1873-1945 **TCLC 2, 7; SSC 34**
See also CA 104; 164; DLB 9, 12; MTCW 2
Glaspell, Susan 1882(?)-1948 **TCLC 55; DC 10; SSC 41**
See also CA 110; 154; DLB 7, 9, 78, 228; YABC 2
Glassco, John 1909-1981 **CLC 9**
See also CA 13-16R; 102; CANR 15; DLB 68
Glasscock, Amnesia
See Steinbeck, John (Ernst)
Glasser, Ronald J. 1940(?)- **CLC 37**
Glassman, Joyce
See Johnson, Joyce
Glendinning, Victoria 1937- **CLC 50**
See also CA 120; 127; CANR 59, 89; DLB 155
Glissant, Edouard 1928- **CLC 10, 68; DAM MULT**
See also CA 153
Gloag, Julian 1930- **CLC 40**
See also AITN 1; CA 65-68; CANR 10, 70
Glowacki, Aleksander
See Prus, Boleslaw
Gluck, Louise (Elisabeth) 1943- **CLC 7, 22, 44, 81; DAM POET; PC 16**
See also CA 33-36R; CANR 40, 69; DA3; DLB 5; MTCW 2
Glyn, Elinor 1864-1943 **TCLC 72**
See also DLB 153
Gobineau, Joseph Arthur (Comte) de 1816-1882 **NCLC 17**
See also DLB 123
Godard, Jean-Luc 1930- **CLC 20**
See also CA 93-96
Godden, (Margaret) Rumer 1907-1998 **CLC 53**
See also AAYA 6; CA 5-8R; 172; CANR 4, 27, 36, 55, 80; CLR 20; DLB 161; MAICYA; SAAS 12; SATA 3, 36; SATA-Obit 109
Godoy Alcayaga, Lucila 1889-1957 **TCLC 2; DAM MULT; HLC 2; PC 32**
See also BW 2; CA 104; 131; CANR 81; HW 1, 2; MTCW 1, 2
Godwin, Gail (Kathleen) 1937- **CLC 5, 8, 22, 31, 69, 125; DAM POP**
See also CA 29-32R; CANR 15, 43, 69; DA3; DLB 6; INT CANR-15; MTCW 1, 2
Godwin, William 1756-1836 **NCLC 14**
See also CDBLB 1789-1832; DLB 39, 104, 142, 158, 163
Goebbels, Josef
See Goebbels, (Paul) Joseph
Goebbels, (Paul) Joseph 1897-1945 **TCLC 68**
See also CA 115; 148
Goebbels, Joseph Paul
See Goebbels, (Paul) Joseph
Goethe, Johann Wolfgang von 1749-1832 **NCLC 4, 22, 34, 90; DA; DAB; DAC; DAM DRAM, MST, POET; PC 5; SSC 38; WLC**
See also DA3; DLB 94
Gogarty, Oliver St. John 1878-1957 **TCLC 15**
See also CA 109; 150; DLB 15, 19
Gogol, Nikolai (Vasilyevich) 1809-1852 **NCLC 5, 15, 31; DA; DAB; DAC; DAM DRAM, MST; DC 1; SSC 4, 29; WLC**
See also DLB 198
Goines, Donald 1937(?)-1974 **CLC 80; BLC 2; DAM MULT, POP**

Green, Hannah
See Greenberg, Joanne (Goldenberg)
Green, Hannah 1927(?)-1996 **CLC 3**
See also CA 73-76; CANR 59, 93
Green, Henry 1905-1973 **CLC 2, 13, 97**
See also Yorke, Henry Vincent
See also CA 175; DLB 15
Green, Julian (Hartridge) 1900-1998
See Green, Julien
See also CA 21-24R; 169; CANR 33, 87; DLB 4, 72; MTCW 1
Green, Julien CLC 3, 11, 77
See also Green, Julian (Hartridge)
See also MTCW 2
Green, Paul (Eliot) 1894-1981 **CLC 25; DAM DRAM**
See also AITN 1; CA 5-8R; 103; CANR 3; DLB 7, 9; DLBY 81
Greenberg, Ivan 1908-1973
See Rahv, Philip
See also CA 85-88
Greenberg, Joanne (Goldenberg) 1932- **CLC 7, 30**
See also AAYA 12; CA 5-8R; CANR 14, 32, 69; SATA 25
Greenberg, Richard 1959(?)- **CLC 57**
See also CA 138
Greene, Bette 1934- **CLC 30**
See also AAYA 7; CA 53-56; CANR 4; CLR 2; JRDA; MAICYA; SAAS 16; SATA 8, 102
Greene, Gael CLC 8
See also CA 13-16R; CANR 10
Greene, Graham (Henry) 1904-1991 **CLC 1, 3, 6, 9, 14, 18, 27, 37, 70, 72, 125; DA; DAB; DAC; DAM MST, NOV; SSC 29; WLC**
See also AITN 2; CA 13-16R; 133; CANR 35, 61; CDBLB 1945-1960; DA3; DLB 13, 15, 77, 100, 162, 201, 204; DLBY 91; MTCW 1, 2; SATA 20
Greene, Robert 1558-1592 **LC 41**
See also DLB 62, 167
Greer, Germaine 1939- **CLC 131**
See also AITN 1; CA 81-84; CANR 33, 70; MTCW 1, 2
Greer, Richard
See Silverberg, Robert
Gregor, Arthur 1923- **CLC 9**
See also CA 25-28R; CAAS 10; CANR 11; SATA 36
Gregor, Lee
See Pohl, Frederik
Gregory, Isabella Augusta (Persse) 1852-1932 **TCLC 1**
See also CA 104; 184; DLB 10
Gregory, J. Dennis
See Williams, John A(lfred)
Grendon, Stephen
See Derleth, August (William)
Grenville, Kate 1950- **CLC 61**
See also CA 118; CANR 53, 93
Grenville, Pelham
See Wodehouse, P(elham) G(renville)
Greve, Felix Paul (Berthold Friedrich) 1879-1948
See Grove, Frederick Philip
See also CA 104; 141, 175; CANR 79; DAC; DAM MST
Grey, Zane 1872-1939 **TCLC 6; DAM POP**
See also CA 104; 132; DA3; DLB 212; MTCW 1, 2
Grieg, (Johan) Nordahl (Brun) 1902-1943 **TCLC 10**
See also CA 107
Grieve, C(hristopher) M(urray) 1892-1978 **CLC 11, 19; DAM POET**
See also MacDiarmid, Hugh; Pteleon
See also CA 5-8R; 85-88; CANR 33; MTCW 1
Griffin, Gerald 1803-1840 **NCLC 7**
See also DLB 159
Griffin, John Howard 1920-1980 **CLC 68**
See also AITN 1; CA 1-4R; 101; CANR 2
Griffin, Peter 1942- **CLC 39**
See also CA 136
Griffith, D(avid Lewelyn) W(ark) 1875(?)-1948 **TCLC 68**
See also CA 119; 150; CANR 80
Griffith, Lawrence
See Griffith, D(avid Lewelyn) W(ark)
Griffiths, Trevor 1935- **CLC 13, 52**
See also CA 97-100; CANR 45; DLB 13
Griggs, Sutton (Elbert) 1872-1930 **TCLC 77**
See also CA 123; 186; DLB 50
Grigson, Geoffrey (Edward Harvey) 1905-1985 **CLC 7, 39**
See also CA 25-28R; 118; CANR 20, 33; DLB 27; MTCW 1, 2
Grillparzer, Franz 1791-1872 **NCLC 1; SSC 37**
See also DLB 133
Grimble, Reverend Charles James
See Eliot, T(homas) S(tearns)
Grimke, Charlotte L(ottie) Forten 1837(?)-1914
See Forten, Charlotte L.
See also BW 1; CA 117; 124; DAM MULT, POET
Grimm, Jacob Ludwig Karl 1785-1863 **NCLC 3, 77; SSC 36**
See also DLB 90; MAICYA; SATA 22
Grimm, Wilhelm Karl 1786-1859 **NCLC 3, 77; SSC 36**
See also DLB 90; MAICYA; SATA 22
Grimmelshausen, Johann Jakob Christoffel von 1621-1676 **LC 6**
See also DLB 168
Grindel, Eugene 1895-1952
See Eluard, Paul
See also CA 104
Grisham, John 1955- **CLC 84; DAM POP**
See also AAYA 14; CA 138; CANR 47, 69; DA3; MTCW 2
Grossman, David 1954- **CLC 67**
See also CA 138
Grossman, Vasily (Semenovich) 1905-1964 **CLC 41**
See also CA 124; 130; MTCW 1
Grove, Frederick Philip TCLC 4
See also Greve, Felix Paul (Berthold Friedrich)
See also DLB 92
Grubb
See Crumb, R(obert)
Grumbach, Doris (Isaac) 1918- **CLC 13, 22, 64**
See also CA 5-8R; CAAS 2; CANR 9, 42, 70; INT CANR-9; MTCW 2
Grundtvig, Nicolai Frederik Severin 1783-1872 **NCLC 1**
Grunge
See Crumb, R(obert)
Grunwald, Lisa 1959- **CLC 44**
See also CA 120
Guare, John 1938- **CLC 8, 14, 29, 67; DAM DRAM**
See also CA 73-76; CANR 21, 69; DLB 7; MTCW 1, 2
Gudjonsson, Halldor Kiljan 1902-1998
See Laxness, Halldor
See also CA 103; 164
Guenter, Erich
See Eich, Guenter
Guest, Barbara 1920- **CLC 34**
See also CA 25-28R; CANR 11, 44, 84; DLB 5, 193
Guest, Edgar A(lbert) 1881-1959 **TCLC 95**
See also CA 112; 168
Guest, Judith (Ann) 1936- **CLC 8, 30; DAM NOV, POP**
See also AAYA 7; CA 77-80; CANR 15, 75; DA3; INT CANR-15; MTCW 1, 2
Guevara, Che CLC 87; HLC 1
See also Guevara (Serna), Ernesto
Guevara (Serna), Ernesto 1928-1967 **CLC 87; DAM MULT; HLC 1**
See also Guevara, Che
See also CA 127; 111; CANR 56; HW 1
Guicciardini, Francesco 1483-1540 **LC 49**
Guild, Nicholas M. 1944- **CLC 33**
See also CA 93-96
Guillemin, Jacques
See Sartre, Jean-Paul
Guillen, Jorge 1893-1984 **CLC 11; DAM MULT, POET; HLCS 1**
See also CA 89-92; 112; DLB 108; HW 1
Guillen, Nicolas (Cristobal) 1902-1989 **CLC 48, 79; BLC 2; DAM MST, MULT, POET; HLC 1; PC 23**
See also BW 2; CA 116; 125; 129; CANR 84; HW 1
Guillevic, (Eugene) 1907- **CLC 33**
See also CA 93-96
Guillois
See Desnos, Robert
Guillois, Valentin
See Desnos, Robert
Guimaraes Rosa, Joao 1908-1967
See also CA 175; HLCS 2
Guiney, Louise Imogen 1861-1920 **TCLC 41**
See also CA 160; DLB 54
Guiraldes, Ricardo (Guillermo) 1886-1927 **TCLC 39**
See also CA 131; HW 1; MTCW 1
Gumilev, Nikolai (Stepanovich) 1886-1921 **TCLC 60**
See also CA 165
Gunesekera, Romesh 1954- **CLC 91**
See also CA 159
Gunn, Bill CLC 5
See also Gunn, William Harrison
See also DLB 38
Gunn, Thom(son William) 1929- **CLC 3, 6, 18, 32, 81; DAM POET; PC 26**
See also CA 17-20R; CANR 9, 33; CDBLB 1960 to Present; DLB 27; INT CANR-33; MTCW 1
Gunn, William Harrison 1934(?)-1989
See Gunn, Bill
See also AITN 1; BW 1, 3; CA 13-16R; 128; CANR 12, 25, 76
Gunnars, Kristjana 1948- **CLC 69**
See also CA 113; DLB 60
Gurdjieff, G(eorgei) I(vanovich) 1877(?)-1949 **TCLC 71**
See also CA 157
Gurganus, Allan 1947- **CLC 70; DAM POP**
See also BEST 90:1; CA 135
Gurney, A(lbert) R(amsdell), Jr. 1930- **CLC 32, 50, 54; DAM DRAM**
See also CA 77-80; CANR 32, 64
Gurney, Ivor (Bertie) 1890-1937 **TCLC 33**
See also CA 167
Gurney, Peter
See Gurney, A(lbert) R(amsdell), Jr.
Guro, Elena 1877-1913 **TCLC 56**
Gustafson, James M(oody) 1925- **CLC 100**
See also CA 25-28R; CANR 37
Gustafson, Ralph (Barker) 1909- **CLC 36**
See also CA 21-24R; CANR 8, 45, 84; DLB 88
Gut, Gom
See Simenon, Georges (Jacques Christian)
Guterson, David 1956- **CLC 91**

See also CA 132; CANR 73; MTCW 2
Guthrie, A(lfred) B(ertram), Jr. 1901-1991 **CLC 23**
See also CA 57-60; 134; CANR 24; DLB 212; SATA 62; SATA-Obit 67
Guthrie, Isobel
See Grieve, C(hristopher) M(urray)
Guthrie, Woodrow Wilson 1912-1967
See Guthrie, Woody
See also CA 113; 93-96
Guthrie, Woody CLC 35
See also Guthrie, Woodrow Wilson
Gutierrez Najera, Manuel 1859-1895
See also HLCS 2
Guy, Rosa (Cuthbert) 1928- **CLC 26**
See also AAYA 4; BW 2; CA 17-20R; CANR 14, 34, 83; CLR 13; DLB 33; JRDA; MAICYA; SATA 14, 62
Gwendolyn
See Bennett, (Enoch) Arnold
H. D. CLC 3, 8, 14, 31, 34, 73; PC 5
See also Doolittle, Hilda
H. de V.
See Buchan, John
Haavikko, Paavo Juhani 1931- **CLC 18, 34**
See also CA 106
Habbema, Koos
See Heijermans, Herman
Habermas, Juergen 1929- **CLC 104**
See also CA 109; CANR 85
Habermas, Jurgen
See Habermas, Juergen
Hacker, Marilyn 1942- **CLC 5, 9, 23, 72, 91; DAM POET**
See also CA 77-80; CANR 68; DLB 120
Haeckel, Ernst Heinrich (Philipp August) 1834-1919 **TCLC 83**
See also CA 157
Hafiz c. 1326-1389(?) **CMLC 34**
Hafiz c. 1326-1389 **CMLC 34**
Haggard, H(enry) Rider 1856-1925 **TCLC 11**
See also CA 108; 148; DLB 70, 156, 174, 178; MTCW 2; SATA 16
Hagiosy, L.
See Larbaud, Valery (Nicolas)
Hagiwara Sakutaro 1886-1942 **TCLC 60; PC 18**
Haig, Fenil
See Ford, Ford Madox
Haig-Brown, Roderick (Langmere) 1908-1976 **CLC 21**
See also CA 5-8R; 69-72; CANR 4, 38, 83; CLR 31; DLB 88; MAICYA; SATA 12
Hailey, Arthur 1920- **CLC 5; DAM NOV, POP**
See also AITN 2; BEST 90:3; CA 1-4R; CANR 2, 36, 75; DLB 88; DLBY 82; MTCW 1, 2
Hailey, Elizabeth Forsythe 1938- **CLC 40**
See also CA 93-96; CAAS 1; CANR 15, 48; INT CANR-15
Haines, John (Meade) 1924- **CLC 58**
See also CA 17-20R; CANR 13, 34; DLB 212
Hakluyt, Richard 1552-1616 **LC 31**
Haldeman, Joe (William) 1943- **CLC 61**
See also Graham, Robert
See also CA 53-56, 179; CAAE 179; CAAS 25; CANR 6, 70, 72; DLB 8; INT CANR-6
Hale, Sarah Josepha (Buell) 1788-1879 **NCLC 75**
See also DLB 1, 42, 73
Haley, Alex(ander Murray Palmer) 1921-1992 **CLC 8, 12, 76; BLC 2; DA; DAB; DAC; DAM MST, MULT, POP**
See also AAYA 26; BW 2, 3; CA 77-80; 136; CANR 61; CDALBS; DA3; DLB 38; MTCW 1, 2
Haliburton, Thomas Chandler 1796-1865 **NCLC 15**
See also DLB 11, 99
Hall, Donald (Andrew, Jr.) 1928- **CLC 1, 13, 37, 59; DAM POET**
See also CA 5-8R; CAAS 7; CANR 2, 44, 64; DLB 5; MTCW 1; SATA 23, 97
Hall, Frederic Sauser
See Sauser-Hall, Frederic
Hall, James
See Kuttner, Henry
Hall, James Norman 1887-1951 **TCLC 23**
See also CA 123; 173; SATA 21
Hall, Radclyffe -1943
See Hall, (Marguerite) Radclyffe
See also MTCW 2
Hall, (Marguerite) Radclyffe 1886-1943 **TCLC 12**
See also CA 110; 150; CANR 83; DLB 191
Hall, Rodney 1935- **CLC 51**
See also CA 109; CANR 69
Halleck, Fitz-Greene 1790-1867 **NCLC 47**
See also DLB 3
Halliday, Michael
See Creasey, John
Halpern, Daniel 1945- **CLC 14**
See also CA 33-36R; CANR 93
Hamburger, Michael (Peter Leopold) 1924- **CLC 5, 14**
See also CA 5-8R; CAAS 4; CANR 2, 47; DLB 27
Hamill, Pete 1935- **CLC 10**
See also CA 25-28R; CANR 18, 71
Hamilton, Alexander 1755(?)-1804 **NCLC 49**
See also DLB 37
Hamilton, Clive
See Lewis, C(live) S(taples)
Hamilton, Edmond 1904-1977 **CLC 1**
See also CA 1-4R; CANR 3, 84; DLB 8; SATA 118
Hamilton, Eugene (Jacob) Lee
See Lee-Hamilton, Eugene (Jacob)
Hamilton, Franklin
See Silverberg, Robert
Hamilton, Gail
See Corcoran, Barbara
Hamilton, Mollie
See Kaye, M(ary) M(argaret)
Hamilton, (Anthony Walter) Patrick 1904-1962 **CLC 51**
See also CA 176; 113; DLB 191
Hamilton, Virginia 1936- **CLC 26; DAM MULT**
See also AAYA 2, 21; BW 2, 3; CA 25-28R; CANR 20, 37, 73; CLR 1, 11, 40; DLB 33, 52; INT CANR-20; JRDA; MAICYA; MTCW 1, 2; SATA 4, 56, 79
Hammett, (Samuel) Dashiell 1894-1961 **CLC 3, 5, 10, 19, 47; SSC 17**
See also AITN 1; CA 81-84; CANR 42; CDALB 1929-1941; DA3; DLB 226; DLBD 6; DLBY 96; MTCW 1, 2
Hammon, Jupiter 1711(?)-1800(?) **NCLC 5; BLC 2; DAM MULT, POET; PC 16**
See also DLB 31, 50
Hammond, Keith
See Kuttner, Henry
Hamner, Earl (Henry), Jr. 1923- **CLC 12**
See also AITN 2; CA 73-76; DLB 6
Hampton, Christopher (James) 1946- **CLC 4**
See also CA 25-28R; DLB 13; MTCW 1
Hamsun, Knut TCLC 2, 14, 49
See also Pedersen, Knut
Handke, Peter 1942- **CLC 5, 8, 10, 15, 38, 134; DAM DRAM, NOV**
See also CA 77-80; CANR 33, 75; DLB 85, 124; MTCW 1, 2
Handy, W(illiam) C(hristopher) 1873-1958 **TCLC 97**
See also BW 3; CA 121; 167
Hanley, James 1901-1985 **CLC 3, 5, 8, 13**
See also CA 73-76; 117; CANR 36; DLB 191; MTCW 1
Hannah, Barry 1942- **CLC 23, 38, 90**
See also CA 108; 110; CANR 43, 68; DLB 6; INT 110; MTCW 1
Hannon, Ezra
See Hunter, Evan
Hansberry, Lorraine (Vivian) 1930-1965 **CLC 17, 62; BLC 2; DA; DAB; DAC; DAM DRAM, MST, MULT; DC 2**
See also AAYA 25; BW 1, 3; CA 109; 25-28R; CABS 3; CANR 58; CDALB 1941-1968; DA3; DLB 7, 38; MTCW 1, 2
Hansen, Joseph 1923- **CLC 38**
See also CA 29-32R; CAAS 17; CANR 16, 44, 66; DLB 226; INT CANR-16
Hansen, Martin A(lfred) 1909-1955 **TCLC 32**
See also CA 167
Hanson, Kenneth O(stlin) 1922- **CLC 13**
See also CA 53-56; CANR 7
Hardwick, Elizabeth (Bruce) 1916- **CLC 13; DAM NOV**
See also CA 5-8R; CANR 3, 32, 70; DA3; DLB 6; MTCW 1, 2
Hardy, Thomas 1840-1928 **TCLC 4, 10, 18, 32, 48, 53, 72; DA; DAB; DAC; DAM MST, NOV, POET; PC 8; SSC 2; WLC**
See also CA 104; 123; CDBLB 1890-1914; DA3; DLB 18, 19, 135; MTCW 1, 2
Hare, David 1947- **CLC 29, 58, 136**
See also CA 97-100; CANR 39, 91; DLB 13; MTCW 1
Harewood, John
See Van Druten, John (William)
Harford, Henry
See Hudson, W(illiam) H(enry)
Hargrave, Leonie
See Disch, Thomas M(ichael)
Harjo, Joy 1951- **CLC 83; DAM MULT; PC 27**
See also CA 114; CANR 35, 67, 91; DLB 120, 175; MTCW 2; NNAL
Harlan, Louis R(udolph) 1922- **CLC 34**
See also CA 21-24R; CANR 25, 55, 80
Harling, Robert 1951(?)- **CLC 53**
See also CA 147
Harmon, William (Ruth) 1938- **CLC 38**
See also CA 33-36R; CANR 14, 32, 35; SATA 65
Harper, F. E. W.
See Harper, Frances Ellen Watkins
Harper, Frances E. W.
See Harper, Frances Ellen Watkins
Harper, Frances E. Watkins
See Harper, Frances Ellen Watkins
Harper, Frances Ellen
See Harper, Frances Ellen Watkins
Harper, Frances Ellen Watkins 1825-1911 **TCLC 14; BLC 2; DAM MULT, POET; PC 21**
See also BW 1, 3; CA 111; 125; CANR 79; DLB 50, 221
Harper, Michael S(teven) 1938- **CLC 7, 22**
See also BW 1; CA 33-36R; CANR 24; DLB 41
Harper, Mrs. F. E. W.
See Harper, Frances Ellen Watkins
Harris, Christie (Lucy) Irwin 1907- **CLC 12**
See also CA 5-8R; CANR 6, 83; CLR 47; DLB 88; JRDA; MAICYA; SAAS 10; SATA 6, 74; SATA-Essay 116
Harris, Frank 1856-1931 **TCLC 24**

Author Index

See also CA 109; 150; CANR 80; DLB 156, 197

Harris, George Washington 1814-1869 **NCLC 23**
See also DLB 3, 11

Harris, Joel Chandler 1848-1908 **TCLC 2; SSC 19**
See also CA 104; 137; CANR 80; CLR 49; DLB 11, 23, 42, 78, 91; MAICYA; SATA 100; YABC 1

Harris, John (Wyndham Parkes Lucas) Beynon 1903-1969
See Wyndham, John
See also CA 102; 89-92; CANR 84; SATA 118

Harris, MacDonald CLC 9
See also Heiney, Donald (William)

Harris, Mark 1922- **CLC 19**
See also CA 5-8R; CAAS 3; CANR 2, 55, 83; DLB 2; DLBY 80

Harris, (Theodore) Wilson 1921- **CLC 25**
See also BW 2, 3; CA 65-68; CAAS 16; CANR 11, 27, 69; DLB 117; MTCW 1

Harrison, Elizabeth Cavanna 1909-
See Cavanna, Betty
See also CA 9-12R; CANR 6, 27, 85

Harrison, Harry (Max) 1925- **CLC 42**
See also CA 1-4R; CANR 5, 21, 84; DLB 8; SATA 4

Harrison, James (Thomas) 1937- **CLC 6, 14, 33, 66; SSC 19**
See also CA 13-16R; CANR 8, 51, 79; DLBY 82; INT CANR-8

Harrison, Jim
See Harrison, James (Thomas)

Harrison, Kathryn 1961- **CLC 70**
See also CA 144; CANR 68

Harrison, Tony 1937- **CLC 43, 129**
See also CA 65-68; CANR 44; DLB 40; MTCW 1

Harriss, Will(ard Irvin) 1922- **CLC 34**
See also CA 111

Harson, Sley
See Ellison, Harlan (Jay)

Hart, Ellis
See Ellison, Harlan (Jay)

Hart, Josephine 1942(?)- **CLC 70; DAM POP**
See also CA 138; CANR 70

Hart, Moss 1904-1961 **CLC 66; DAM DRAM**
See also CA 109; 89-92; CANR 84; DLB 7

Harte, (Francis) Bret(t) 1836(?)-1902 **TCLC 1, 25; DA; DAC; DAM MST; SSC 8; WLC**
See also CA 104; 140; CANR 80; CDALB 1865-1917; DA3; DLB 12, 64, 74, 79, 186; SATA 26

Hartley, L(eslie) P(oles) 1895-1972 **CLC 2, 22**
See also CA 45-48; 37-40R; CANR 33; DLB 15, 139; MTCW 1, 2

Hartman, Geoffrey H. 1929- **CLC 27**
See also CA 117; 125; CANR 79; DLB 67

Hartmann, Sadakichi 1867-1944 **TCLC 73**
See also CA 157; DLB 54

Hartmann von Aue c. 1160-c. 1205 **CMLC 15**
See also DLB 138

Hartmann von Aue 1170-1210 **CMLC 15**

Haruf, Kent 1943- **CLC 34**
See also CA 149; CANR 91

Harwood, Ronald 1934- **CLC 32; DAM DRAM, MST**
See also CA 1-4R; CANR 4, 55; DLB 13

Hasegawa Tatsunosuke
See Futabatei, Shimei

Hasek, Jaroslav (Matej Frantisek) 1883-1923 **TCLC 4**
See also CA 104; 129; MTCW 1, 2

Hass, Robert 1941- **CLC 18, 39, 99; PC 16**
See also CA 111; CANR 30, 50, 71; DLB 105, 206; SATA 94

Hastings, Hudson
See Kuttner, Henry

Hastings, Selina CLC 44

Hathorne, John 1641-1717 **LC 38**

Hatteras, Amelia
See Mencken, H(enry) L(ouis)

Hatteras, Owen TCLC 18
See also Mencken, H(enry) L(ouis); Nathan, George Jean

Hauptmann, Gerhart (Johann Robert) 1862-1946 **TCLC 4; DAM DRAM; SSC 37**
See also CA 104; 153; DLB 66, 118

Haviaras, Stratis CLC 33
See also Chaviaras, Strates

Hawes, Stephen 1475(?)-1523(?) **LC 17**
See also DLB 132

Hawkes, John (Clendennin Burne, Jr.) 1925-1998 **CLC 1, 2, 3, 4, 7, 9, 14, 15, 27, 49**
See also CA 1-4R; 167; CANR 2, 47, 64; DLB 2, 7, 227; DLBY 80, 98; MTCW 1, 2

Hawking, S. W.
See Hawking, Stephen W(illiam)

Hawking, Stephen W(illiam) 1942- **CLC 63, 105**
See also AAYA 13; BEST 89:1; CA 126; 129; CANR 48; DA3; MTCW 2

Hawkins, Anthony Hope
See Hope, Anthony

Hawthorne, Julian 1846-1934 **TCLC 25**
See also CA 165

Hawthorne, Nathaniel 1804-1864 **NCLC 39; DA; DAB; DAC; DAM MST, NOV; SSC 3, 29, 39; WLC**
See also AAYA 18; CDALB 1640-1865; DA3; DLB 1, 74, 223; YABC 2

Haxton, Josephine Ayres 1921-
See Douglas, Ellen
See also CA 115; CANR 41, 83

Hayaseca y Eizaguirre, Jorge
See Echegaray (y Eizaguirre), Jose (Maria Waldo)

Hayashi, Fumiko 1904-1951 **TCLC 27**
See also CA 161; DLB 180

Haycraft, Anna (Margaret) 1932-
See Ellis, Alice Thomas
See also CA 122; CANR 85, 90; MTCW 2

Hayden, Robert E(arl) 1913-1980 **CLC 5, 9, 14, 37; BLC 2; DA; DAC; DAM MST, MULT, POET; PC 6**
See also BW 1, 3; CA 69-72; 97-100; CABS 2; CANR 24, 75, 82; CDALB 1941-1968; DLB 5, 76; MTCW 1, 2; SATA 19; SATA-Obit 26

Hayford, J(oseph) E(phraim) Casely
See Casely-Hayford, J(oseph) E(phraim)

Hayman, Ronald 1932- **CLC 44**
See also CA 25-28R; CANR 18, 50, 88; DLB 155

Haywood, Eliza (Fowler) 1693(?)-1756 **LC 1, 44**
See also DLB 39

Hazlitt, William 1778-1830 **NCLC 29, 82**
See also DLB 110, 158

Hazzard, Shirley 1931- **CLC 18**
See also CA 9-12R; CANR 4, 70; DLBY 82; MTCW 1

Head, Bessie 1937-1986 **CLC 25, 67; BLC 2; DAM MULT**
See also BW 2, 3; CA 29-32R; 119; CANR 25, 82; DA3; DLB 117, 225; MTCW 1, 2

Headon, (Nicky) Topper 1956(?)- **CLC 30**

Heaney, Seamus (Justin) 1939- **CLC 5, 7, 14, 25, 37, 74, 91; DAB; DAM POET; PC 18; WLCS**
See also CA 85-88; CANR 25, 48, 75, 91; CDBLB 1960 to Present; DA3; DLB 40; DLBY 95; MTCW 1, 2

Hearn, (Patricio) Lafcadio (Tessima Carlos) 1850-1904 **TCLC 9**
See also CA 105; 166; DLB 12, 78, 189

Hearne, Vicki 1946- **CLC 56**
See also CA 139

Hearon, Shelby 1931- **CLC 63**
See also AITN 2; CA 25-28R; CANR 18, 48

Heat-Moon, William Least CLC 29
See also Trogdon, William (Lewis)
See also AAYA 9

Hebbel, Friedrich 1813-1863 **NCLC 43; DAM DRAM**
See also DLB 129

Hebert, Anne 1916-2000 **CLC 4, 13, 29; DAC; DAM MST, POET**
See also CA 85-88; 187; CANR 69; DA3; DLB 68; MTCW 1, 2

Hecht, Anthony (Evan) 1923- **CLC 8, 13, 19; DAM POET**
See also CA 9-12R; CANR 6; DLB 5, 169

Hecht, Ben 1894-1964 **CLC 8**
See also CA 85-88; DLB 7, 9, 25, 26, 28, 86; TCLC 101

Hedayat, Sadeq 1903-1951 **TCLC 21**
See also CA 120

Hegel, Georg Wilhelm Friedrich 1770-1831 **NCLC 46**
See also DLB 90

Heidegger, Martin 1889-1976 **CLC 24**
See also CA 81-84; 65-68; CANR 34; MTCW 1, 2

Heidenstam, (Carl Gustaf) Verner von 1859-1940 **TCLC 5**
See also CA 104

Heifner, Jack 1946- **CLC 11**
See also CA 105; CANR 47

Heijermans, Herman 1864-1924 **TCLC 24**
See also CA 123

Heilbrun, Carolyn G(old) 1926- **CLC 25**
See also CA 45-48; CANR 1, 28, 58

Heine, Heinrich 1797-1856 **NCLC 4, 54; PC 25**
See also DLB 90

Heinemann, Larry (Curtiss) 1944- **CLC 50**
See also CA 110; CAAS 21; CANR 31, 81; DLBD 9; INT CANR-31

Heiney, Donald (William) 1921-1993
See Harris, MacDonald
See also CA 1-4R; 142; CANR 3, 58

Heinlein, Robert A(nson) 1907-1988 **CLC 1, 3, 8, 14, 26, 55; DAM POP**
See also AAYA 17; CA 1-4R; 125; CANR 1, 20, 53; DA3; DLB 8; JRDA; MAICYA; MTCW 1, 2; SATA 9, 69; SATA-Obit 56

Helforth, John
See Doolittle, Hilda

Hellenhofferu, Vojtech Kapristian z
See Hasek, Jaroslav (Matej Frantisek)

Heller, Joseph 1923-1999 **CLC 1, 3, 5, 8, 11, 36, 63; DA; DAB; DAC; DAM MST, NOV, POP; WLC**
See also AAYA 24; AITN 1; CA 5-8R; 187; CABS 1; CANR 8, 42, 66; DA3; DLB 2, 28, 227; DLBY 80; INT CANR-8; MTCW 1, 2

Hellman, Lillian (Florence) 1906-1984 **CLC 2, 4, 8, 14, 18, 34, 44, 52; DAM DRAM; DC 1**
See also AITN 1, 2; CA 13-16R; 112; CANR 33; DA3; DLB 7, 228; DLBY 84; MTCW 1, 2

Helprin, Mark 1947- **CLC 7, 10, 22, 32; DAM NOV, POP**
See also CA 81-84; CANR 47, 64; CDALBS; DA3; DLBY 85; MTCW 1, 2

Helvetius, Claude-Adrien 1715-1771 **LC 26**
Helyar, Jane Penelope Josephine 1933-
See Poole, Josephine
See also CA 21-24R; CANR 10, 26; SATA 82
Hemans, Felicia 1793-1835 **NCLC 71**
See also DLB 96
Hemingway, Ernest (Miller) 1899-1961 **CLC 1, 3, 6, 8, 10, 13, 19, 30, 34, 39, 41, 44, 50, 61, 80; DA; DAB; DAC; DAM MST, NOV; SSC 1, 25, 36, 40; WLC**
See also AAYA 19; CA 77-80; CANR 34; CDALB 1917-1929; DA3; DLB 4, 9, 102, 210; DLBD 1, 15, 16; DLBY 81, 87, 96, 98; MTCW 1, 2
Hempel, Amy 1951- **CLC 39**
See also CA 118; 137; CANR 70; DA3; MTCW 2
Henderson, F. C.
See Mencken, H(enry) L(ouis)
Henderson, Sylvia
See Ashton-Warner, Sylvia (Constance)
Henderson, Zenna (Chlarson) 1917-1983 **SSC 29**
See also CA 1-4R; 133; CANR 1, 84; DLB 8; SATA 5
Henkin, Joshua CLC 119
See also CA 161
Henley, Beth CLC 23; DC 6
See also Henley, Elizabeth Becker
See also CABS 3; DLBY 86
Henley, Elizabeth Becker 1952-
See Henley, Beth
See also CA 107; CANR 32, 73; DAM DRAM, MST; DA3; MTCW 1, 2
Henley, William Ernest 1849-1903 **TCLC 8**
See also CA 105; DLB 19
Hennissart, Martha
See Lathen, Emma
See also CA 85-88; CANR 64
Henry, O. TCLC 1, 19; SSC 5; WLC
See also Porter, William Sydney
Henry, Patrick 1736-1799 **LC 25**
Henryson, Robert 1430(?)-1506(?) **LC 20**
See also DLB 146
Henry VIII 1491-1547 **LC 10**
See also DLB 132
Henschke, Alfred
See Klabund
Hentoff, Nat(han Irving) 1925- **CLC 26**
See also AAYA 4; CA 1-4R; CAAS 6; CANR 5, 25, 77; CLR 1, 52; INT CANR-25; JRDA; MAICYA; SATA 42, 69; SATA-Brief 27
Heppenstall, (John) Rayner 1911-1981 **CLC 10**
See also CA 1-4R; 103; CANR 29
Heraclitus c. 540B.C.-c. 450B.C. **CMLC 22**
See also DLB 176
Herbert, Frank (Patrick) 1920-1986 **CLC 12, 23, 35, 44, 85; DAM POP**
See also AAYA 21; CA 53-56; 118; CANR 5, 43; CDALBS; DLB 8; INT CANR-5; MTCW 1, 2; SATA 9, 37; SATA-Obit 47
Herbert, George 1593-1633 **LC 24; DAB; DAM POET; PC 4**
See also CDBLB Before 1660; DLB 126
Herbert, Zbigniew 1924-1998 **CLC 9, 43; DAM POET**
See also CA 89-92; 169; CANR 36, 74; DLB 232; MTCW 1
Herbst, Josephine (Frey) 1897-1969 **CLC 34**
See also CA 5-8R; 25-28R; DLB 9
Heredia, Jose Maria 1803-1839
See also HLCS 2
Hergesheimer, Joseph 1880-1954 **TCLC 11**
See also CA 109; DLB 102, 9
Herlihy, James Leo 1927-1993 **CLC 6**
See also CA 1-4R; 143; CANR 2
Hermogenes fl. c. 175- **CMLC 6**
Hernandez, Jose 1834-1886 **NCLC 17**
Herodotus c. 484B.C.-429B.C. **CMLC 17**
See also DLB 176
Herrick, Robert 1591-1674 **LC 13; DA; DAB; DAC; DAM MST, POP; PC 9**
See also DLB 126
Herring, Guilles
See Somerville, Edith
Herriot, James 1916-1995 **CLC 12; DAM POP**
See also Wight, James Alfred
See also AAYA 1; CA 148; CANR 40; MTCW 2; SATA 86
Herris, Violet
See Hunt, Violet
Herrmann, Dorothy 1941- **CLC 44**
See also CA 107
Herrmann, Taffy
See Herrmann, Dorothy
Hersey, John (Richard) 1914-1993 **CLC 1, 2, 7, 9, 40, 81, 97; DAM POP**
See also AAYA 29; CA 17-20R; 140; CANR 33; CDALBS; DLB 6, 185; MTCW 1, 2; SATA 25; SATA-Obit 76
Herzen, Aleksandr Ivanovich 1812-1870 **NCLC 10, 61**
Herzl, Theodor 1860-1904 **TCLC 36**
See also CA 168
Herzog, Werner 1942- **CLC 16**
See also CA 89-92
Hesiod c. 8th cent. B.C.- **CMLC 5**
See also DLB 176
Hesse, Hermann 1877-1962 **CLC 1, 2, 3, 6, 11, 17, 25, 69; DA; DAB; DAC; DAM MST, NOV; SSC 9; WLC**
See also CA 17-18; CAP 2; DA3; DLB 66; MTCW 1, 2; SATA 50
Hewes, Cady
See De Voto, Bernard (Augustine)
Heyen, William 1940- **CLC 13, 18**
See also CA 33-36R; CAAS 9; DLB 5
Heyerdahl, Thor 1914- **CLC 26**
See also CA 5-8R; CANR 5, 22, 66, 73; MTCW 1, 2; SATA 2, 52
Heym, Georg (Theodor Franz Arthur) 1887-1912 **TCLC 9**
See also CA 106; 181
Heym, Stefan 1913- **CLC 41**
See also CA 9-12R; CANR 4; DLB 69
Heyse, Paul (Johann Ludwig von) 1830-1914 **TCLC 8**
See also CA 104; DLB 129
Heyward, (Edwin) DuBose 1885-1940 **TCLC 59**
See also CA 108; 157; DLB 7, 9, 45; SATA 21
Hibbert, Eleanor Alice Burford 1906-1993 **CLC 7; DAM POP**
See also BEST 90:4; CA 17-20R; 140; CANR 9, 28, 59; MTCW 2; SATA 2; SATA-Obit 74
Hichens, Robert (Smythe) 1864-1950 **TCLC 64**
See also CA 162; DLB 153
Higgins, George V(incent) 1939-1999 **CLC 4, 7, 10, 18**
See also CA 77-80; 186; CAAS 5; CANR 17, 51, 89; DLB 2; DLBY 81, 98; INT CANR-17; MTCW 1
Higginson, Thomas Wentworth 1823-1911 **TCLC 36**
See also CA 162; DLB 1, 64
Highet, Helen
See MacInnes, Helen (Clark)
Highsmith, (Mary) Patricia 1921-1995 **CLC 2, 4, 14, 42, 102; DAM NOV, POP**
See also CA 1-4R; 147; CANR 1, 20, 48, 62; DA3; MTCW 1, 2
Highwater, Jamake (Mamake) 1942(?)- **CLC 12**
See also AAYA 7; CA 65-68; CAAS 7; CANR 10, 34, 84; CLR 17; DLB 52; DLBY 85; JRDA; MAICYA; SATA 32, 69; SATA-Brief 30
Highway, Tomson 1951- **CLC 92; DAC; DAM MULT**
See also CA 151; CANR 75; MTCW 2; NNAL
Higuchi, Ichiyo 1872-1896 **NCLC 49**
Hijuelos, Oscar 1951- **CLC 65; DAM MULT, POP; HLC 1**
See also AAYA 25; BEST 90:1; CA 123; CANR 50, 75; DA3; DLB 145; HW 1, 2; MTCW 2
Hikmet, Nazim 1902(?)-1963 **CLC 40**
See also CA 141; 93-96
Hildegard von Bingen 1098-1179 **CMLC 20**
See also DLB 148
Hildesheimer, Wolfgang 1916-1991 **CLC 49**
See also CA 101; 135; DLB 69, 124
Hill, Geoffrey (William) 1932- **CLC 5, 8, 18, 45; DAM POET**
See also CA 81-84; CANR 21, 89; CDBLB 1960 to Present; DLB 40; MTCW 1
Hill, George Roy 1921- **CLC 26**
See also CA 110; 122
Hill, John
See Koontz, Dean R(ay)
Hill, Susan (Elizabeth) 1942- **CLC 4, 113; DAB; DAM MST, NOV**
See also CA 33-36R; CANR 29, 69; DLB 14, 139; MTCW 1
Hillerman, Tony 1925- **CLC 62; DAM POP**
See also AAYA 6; BEST 89:1; CA 29-32R; CANR 21, 42, 65; DA3; DLB 206; SATA 6
Hillesum, Etty 1914-1943 **TCLC 49**
See also CA 137
Hilliard, Noel (Harvey) 1929- **CLC 15**
See also CA 9-12R; CANR 7, 69
Hillis, Rick 1956- **CLC 66**
See also CA 134
Hilton, James 1900-1954 **TCLC 21**
See also CA 108; 169; DLB 34, 77; SATA 34
Himes, Chester (Bomar) 1909-1984 **CLC 2, 4, 7, 18, 58, 108; BLC 2; DAM MULT**
See also BW 2; CA 25-28R; 114; CANR 22, 89; DLB 2, 76, 143, 226; MTCW 1, 2
Hinde, Thomas CLC 6, 11
See also Chitty, Thomas Willes
Hine, (William) Daryl 1936- **CLC 15**
See also CA 1-4R; CAAS 15; CANR 1, 20; DLB 60
Hinkson, Katharine Tynan
See Tynan, Katharine
Hinojosa(-Smith), Rolando (R.) 1929-
See also CA 131; CAAS 16; CANR 62; DAM MULT; DLB 82; HLC 1; HW 1, 2; MTCW 2
Hinton, S(usan) E(loise) 1950- **CLC 30, 111; DA; DAB; DAC; DAM MST, NOV**
See also AAYA 2, 33; CA 81-84; CANR 32, 62, 92; CDALBS; CLR 3, 23; DA3; JRDA; MAICYA; MTCW 1, 2; SATA 19, 58, 115
Hippius, Zinaida TCLC 9
See also Gippius, Zinaida (Nikolayevna)
Hiraoka, Kimitake 1925-1970
See Mishima, Yukio
See also CA 97-100; 29-32R; DAM DRAM; DA3; MTCW 1, 2
Hirsch, E(ric) D(onald), Jr. 1928- **CLC 79**
See also CA 25-28R; CANR 27, 51; DLB 67; INT CANR-27; MTCW 1
Hirsch, Edward 1950- **CLC 31, 50**
See also CA 104; CANR 20, 42; DLB 120

Hitchcock, Alfred (Joseph) 1899-1980 **CLC 16**
See also AAYA 22; CA 159; 97-100; SATA 27; SATA-Obit 24
Hitler, Adolf 1889-1945 **TCLC 53**
See also CA 117; 147
Hoagland, Edward 1932- **CLC 28**
See also CA 1-4R; CANR 2, 31, 57; DLB 6; SATA 51
Hoban, Russell (Conwell) 1925- **CLC 7, 25; DAM NOV**
See also CA 5-8R; CANR 23, 37, 66; CLR 3; DLB 52; MAICYA; MTCW 1, 2; SATA 1, 40, 78
Hobbes, Thomas 1588-1679 **LC 36**
See also DLB 151
Hobbs, Perry
See Blackmur, R(ichard) P(almer)
Hobson, Laura Z(ametkin) 1900-1986 **CLC 7, 25**
See also CA 17-20R; 118; CANR 55; DLB 28; SATA 52
Hoch, Edward D(entinger) 1930-
See Queen, Ellery
See also CA 29-32R; CANR 11, 27, 51
Hochhuth, Rolf 1931- **CLC 4, 11, 18; DAM DRAM**
See also CA 5-8R; CANR 33, 75; DLB 124; MTCW 1, 2
Hochman, Sandra 1936- **CLC 3, 8**
See also CA 5-8R; DLB 5
Hochwaelder, Fritz 1911-1986 **CLC 36; DAM DRAM**
See also CA 29-32R; 120; CANR 42; MTCW 1
Hochwalder, Fritz
See Hochwaelder, Fritz
Hocking, Mary (Eunice) 1921- **CLC 13**
See also CA 101; CANR 18, 40
Hodgins, Jack 1938- **CLC 23**
See also CA 93-96; DLB 60
Hodgson, William Hope 1877(?)-1918 **TCLC 13**
See also CA 111; 164; DLB 70, 153, 156, 178; MTCW 2
Hoeg, Peter 1957- **CLC 95**
See also CA 151; CANR 75; DA3; MTCW 2
Hoffman, Alice 1952- **CLC 51; DAM NOV**
See also CA 77-80; CANR 34, 66; MTCW 1, 2
Hoffman, Daniel (Gerard) 1923- **CLC 6, 13, 23**
See also CA 1-4R; CANR 4; DLB 5
Hoffman, Stanley 1944- **CLC 5**
See also CA 77-80
Hoffman, William M(oses) 1939- **CLC 40**
See also CA 57-60; CANR 11, 71
Hoffmann, E(rnst) T(heodor) A(madeus) 1776-1822 **NCLC 2; SSC 13**
See also DLB 90; SATA 27
Hofmann, Gert 1931- **CLC 54**
See also CA 128
Hofmannsthal, Hugo von 1874-1929 **TCLC 11; DAM DRAM; DC 4**
See also CA 106; 153; DLB 81, 118
Hogan, Linda 1947- **CLC 73; DAM MULT**
See also CA 120; CANR 45, 73; DLB 175; NNAL
Hogarth, Charles
See Creasey, John
Hogarth, Emmett
See Polonsky, Abraham (Lincoln)
Hogg, James 1770-1835 **NCLC 4**
See also DLB 93, 116, 159
Holbach, Paul Henri Thiry Baron 1723-1789 **LC 14**
Holberg, Ludvig 1684-1754 **LC 6**
Holcroft, Thomas 1745-1809 **NCLC 85**
See also DLB 39, 89, 158
Holden, Ursula 1921- **CLC 18**
See also CA 101; CAAS 8; CANR 22
Holderlin, (Johann Christian) Friedrich 1770-1843 **NCLC 16; PC 4**
Holdstock, Robert
See Holdstock, Robert P.
Holdstock, Robert P. 1948- **CLC 39**
See also CA 131; CANR 81
Holland, Isabelle 1920- **CLC 21**
See also AAYA 11; CA 21-24R, 181; CAAE 181; CANR 10, 25, 47; CLR 57; JRDA; MAICYA; SATA 8, 70; SATA-Essay 103
Holland, Marcus
See Caldwell, (Janet Miriam) Taylor (Holland)
Hollander, John 1929- **CLC 2, 5, 8, 14**
See also CA 1-4R; CANR 1, 52; DLB 5; SATA 13
Hollander, Paul
See Silverberg, Robert
Holleran, Andrew 1943(?)- **CLC 38**
See also Garber, Eric
See also CA 144
Holley, Marietta 1836(?)-1926 **TCLC 99**
See also CA 118; DLB 11
Hollinghurst, Alan 1954- **CLC 55, 91**
See also CA 114; DLB 207
Hollis, Jim
See Summers, Hollis (Spurgeon, Jr.)
Holly, Buddy 1936-1959 **TCLC 65**
Holmes, Gordon
See Shiel, M(atthew) P(hipps)
Holmes, John
See Souster, (Holmes) Raymond
Holmes, John Clellon 1926-1988 **CLC 56**
See also CA 9-12R; 125; CANR 4; DLB 16
Holmes, Oliver Wendell, Jr. 1841-1935 **TCLC 77**
See also CA 114; 186
Holmes, Oliver Wendell 1809-1894 **NCLC 14, 81**
See also CDALB 1640-1865; DLB 1, 189, 235; SATA 34
Holmes, Raymond
See Souster, (Holmes) Raymond
Holt, Victoria
See Hibbert, Eleanor Alice Burford
Holub, Miroslav 1923-1998 **CLC 4**
See also CA 21-24R; 169; CANR 10; DLB 232
Homer c. 8th cent. B.C.- **CMLC 1, 16; DA; DAB; DAC; DAM MST, POET; PC 23; WLCS**
See also DA3; DLB 176
Hongo, Garrett Kaoru 1951- **PC 23**
See also CA 133; CAAS 22; DLB 120
Honig, Edwin 1919- **CLC 33**
See also CA 5-8R; CAAS 8; CANR 4, 45; DLB 5
Hood, Hugh (John Blagdon) 1928- **CLC 15, 28; SSC 42**
See also CA 49-52; CAAS 17; CANR 1, 33, 87; DLB 53
Hood, Thomas 1799-1845 **NCLC 16**
See also DLB 96
Hooker, (Peter) Jeremy 1941- **CLC 43**
See also CA 77-80; CANR 22; DLB 40
hooks, bell CLC 94; BLCS
See also Watkins, Gloria Jean
See also MTCW 2
Hope, A(lec) D(erwent) 1907- **CLC 3, 51**
See also CA 21-24R; CANR 33, 74; MTCW 1, 2
Hope, Anthony 1863-1933 **TCLC 83**
See also CA 157; DLB 153, 156
Hope, Brian
See Creasey, John
Hope, Christopher (David Tully) 1944- **CLC 52**
See also CA 106; CANR 47; DLB 225; SATA 62
Hopkins, Gerard Manley 1844-1889 **NCLC 17; DA; DAB; DAC; DAM MST, POET; PC 15; WLC**
See also CDBLB 1890-1914; DA3; DLB 35, 57
Hopkins, John (Richard) 1931-1998 **CLC 4**
See also CA 85-88; 169
Hopkins, Pauline Elizabeth 1859-1930 **TCLC 28; BLC 2; DAM MULT**
See also BW 2, 3; CA 141; CANR 82; DLB 50
Hopkinson, Francis 1737-1791 **LC 25**
See also DLB 31
Hopley-Woolrich, Cornell George 1903-1968
See Woolrich, Cornell
See also CA 13-14; CANR 58; CAP 1; DLB 226; MTCW 2
Horace 65B.C.-8B.C. **CMLC 39**
See also DLB 211
Horatio
See Proust, (Valentin-Louis-George-Eugene-) Marcel
Horgan, Paul (George Vincent O'Shaughnessy) 1903-1995 **CLC 9, 53; DAM NOV**
See also CA 13-16R; 147; CANR 9, 35; DLB 212; DLBY 85; INT CANR-9; MTCW 1, 2; SATA 13; SATA-Obit 84
Horn, Peter
See Kuttner, Henry
Hornem, Horace Esq.
See Byron, George Gordon (Noel)
Horney, Karen (Clementine Theodore Danielsen) 1885-1952 **TCLC 71**
See also CA 114; 165
Hornung, E(rnest) W(illiam) 1866-1921 **TCLC 59**
See also CA 108; 160; DLB 70
Horovitz, Israel (Arthur) 1939- **CLC 56; DAM DRAM**
See also CA 33-36R; CANR 46, 59; DLB 7
Horton, George Moses 1797(?)-1883(?) **NCLC 87**
See also DLB 50
Horvath, Odon von
See Horvath, Oedoen von
See also DLB 85, 124
Horvath, Oedoen von 1901-1938 **TCLC 45**
See also Horvath, Odon von; von Horvath, Oedoen
See also CA 118
Horwitz, Julius 1920-1986 **CLC 14**
See also CA 9-12R; 119; CANR 12
Hospital, Janette Turner 1942- **CLC 42**
See also CA 108; CANR 48
Hostos, E. M. de
See Hostos (y Bonilla), Eugenio Maria de
Hostos, Eugenio M. de
See Hostos (y Bonilla), Eugenio Maria de
Hostos, Eugenio Maria
See Hostos (y Bonilla), Eugenio Maria de
Hostos (y Bonilla), Eugenio Maria de 1839-1903 **TCLC 24**
See also CA 123; 131; HW 1
Houdini
See Lovecraft, H(oward) P(hillips)
Hougan, Carolyn 1943- **CLC 34**
See also CA 139
Household, Geoffrey (Edward West) 1900-1988 **CLC 11**
See also CA 77-80; 126; CANR 58; DLB 87; SATA 14; SATA-Obit 59

Housman, A(lfred) E(dward) 1859-1936 **TCLC 1, 10; DA; DAB; DAC; DAM MST, POET; PC 2; WLCS**
See also CA 104; 125; DA3; DLB 19; MTCW 1, 2
Housman, Laurence 1865-1959 **TCLC 7**
See also CA 106; 155; DLB 10; SATA 25
Howard, Elizabeth Jane 1923- **CLC 7, 29**
See also CA 5-8R; CANR 8, 62
Howard, Maureen 1930- **CLC 5, 14, 46**
See also CA 53-56; CANR 31, 75; DLBY 83; INT CANR-31; MTCW 1, 2
Howard, Richard 1929- **CLC 7, 10, 47**
See also AITN 1; CA 85-88; CANR 25, 80; DLB 5; INT CANR-25
Howard, Robert E(rvin) 1906-1936 **TCLC 8**
See also CA 105; 157
Howard, Warren F.
See Pohl, Frederik
Howe, Fanny (Quincy) 1940- **CLC 47**
See also CA 117; CAAE 187; CAAS 27; CANR 70; SATA-Brief 52
Howe, Irving 1920-1993 **CLC 85**
See also CA 9-12R; 141; CANR 21, 50; DLB 67; MTCW 1, 2
Howe, Julia Ward 1819-1910 **TCLC 21**
See also CA 117; DLB 1, 189, 235
Howe, Susan 1937- **CLC 72**
See also CA 160; DLB 120
Howe, Tina 1937- **CLC 48**
See also CA 109
Howell, James 1594(?)-1666 **LC 13**
See also DLB 151
Howells, W. D.
See Howells, William Dean
Howells, William D.
See Howells, William Dean
Howells, William Dean 1837-1920 **TCLC 7, 17, 41; SSC 36**
See also CA 104; 134; CDALB 1865-1917; DLB 12, 64, 74, 79, 189; MTCW 2
Howes, Barbara 1914-1996 **CLC 15**
See also CA 9-12R; 151; CAAS 3; CANR 53; SATA 5
Hrabal, Bohumil 1914-1997 **CLC 13, 67**
See also CA 106; 156; CAAS 12; CANR 57; DLB 232
Hroswitha of Gandersheim c. 935-c. 1002 **CMLC 29**
See also DLB 148
Hsi, Chu 1130-1200 **CMLC 42**
Hsun, Lu
See Lu Hsun
Hubbard, L(afayette) Ron(ald) 1911-1986 **CLC 43; DAM POP**
See also CA 77-80; 118; CANR 52; DA3; MTCW 2
Huch, Ricarda (Octavia) 1864-1947 **TCLC 13**
See also CA 111; DLB 66
Huddle, David 1942- **CLC 49**
See also CA 57-60; CAAS 20; CANR 89; DLB 130
Hudson, Jeffrey
See Crichton, (John) Michael
Hudson, W(illiam) H(enry) 1841-1922 **TCLC 29**
See also CA 115; DLB 98, 153, 174; SATA 35
Hueffer, Ford Madox
See Ford, Ford Madox
Hughart, Barry 1934- **CLC 39**
See also CA 137
Hughes, Colin
See Creasey, John
Hughes, David (John) 1930- **CLC 48**
See also CA 116; 129; DLB 14
Hughes, Edward James
See Hughes, Ted
See also DAM MST, POET; DA3
Hughes, (James) Langston 1902-1967 **CLC 1, 5, 10, 15, 35, 44, 108; BLC 2; DA; DAB; DAC; DAM DRAM, MST, MULT, POET; DC 3; PC 1; SSC 6; WLC**
See also AAYA 12; BW 1, 3; CA 1-4R; 25-28R; CANR 1, 34, 82; CDALB 1929-1941; CLR 17; DA3; DLB 4, 7, 48, 51, 86, 228; JRDA; MAICYA; MTCW 1, 2; SATA 4, 33
Hughes, Richard (Arthur Warren) 1900-1976 **CLC 1, 11; DAM NOV**
See also CA 5-8R; 65-68; CANR 4; DLB 15, 161; MTCW 1; SATA 8; SATA-Obit 25
Hughes, Ted 1930-1998 **CLC 2, 4, 9, 14, 37, 119; DAB; DAC; PC 7**
See also Hughes, Edward James
See also CA 1-4R; 171; CANR 1, 33, 66; CLR 3; DLB 40, 161; MAICYA; MTCW 1, 2; SATA 49; SATA-Brief 27; SATA-Obit 107
Hugo, Richard F(ranklin) 1923-1982 **CLC 6, 18, 32; DAM POET**
See also CA 49-52; 108; CANR 3; DLB 5, 206
Hugo, Victor (Marie) 1802-1885 **NCLC 3, 10, 21; DA; DAB; DAC; DAM DRAM, MST, NOV, POET; PC 17; WLC**
See also AAYA 28; DA3; DLB 119, 192; SATA 47
Huidobro, Vicente
See Huidobro Fernandez, Vicente Garcia
Huidobro Fernandez, Vicente Garcia 1893-1948 **TCLC 31**
See also CA 131; HW 1
Hulme, Keri 1947- **CLC 39, 130**
See also CA 125; CANR 69; INT 125
Hulme, T(homas) E(rnest) 1883-1917 **TCLC 21**
See also CA 117; DLB 19
Hume, David 1711-1776 **LC 7, 56**
See also DLB 104
Humphrey, William 1924-1997 **CLC 45**
See also CA 77-80; 160; CANR 68; DLB 212
Humphreys, Emyr Owen 1919- **CLC 47**
See also CA 5-8R; CANR 3, 24; DLB 15
Humphreys, Josephine 1945- **CLC 34, 57**
See also CA 121; 127; INT 127
Huneker, James Gibbons 1857-1921 **TCLC 65**
See also DLB 71
Hungerford, Pixie
See Brinsmead, H(esba) F(ay)
Hunt, E(verette) Howard, (Jr.) 1918- **CLC 3**
See also AITN 1; CA 45-48; CANR 2, 47
Hunt, Francesca
See Holland, Isabelle
Hunt, Kyle
See Creasey, John
Hunt, (James Henry) Leigh 1784-1859 **NCLC 1, 70; DAM POET**
See also DLB 96, 110, 144
Hunt, Marsha 1946- **CLC 70**
See also BW 2, 3; CA 143; CANR 79
Hunt, Violet 1866(?)-1942 **TCLC 53**
See also CA 184; DLB 162, 197
Hunter, E. Waldo
See Sturgeon, Theodore (Hamilton)
Hunter, Evan 1926- **CLC 11, 31; DAM POP**
See also CA 5-8R; CANR 5, 38, 62; DLBY 82; INT CANR-5; MTCW 1; SATA 25
Hunter, Kristin (Eggleston) 1931- **CLC 35**
See also AITN 1; BW 1; CA 13-16R; CANR 13; CLR 3; DLB 33; INT CANR-13; MAICYA; SAAS 10; SATA 12
Hunter, Mary
See Austin, Mary (Hunter)
Hunter, Mollie 1922- **CLC 21**
See also McIlwraith, Maureen Mollie Hunter
See also AAYA 13; CANR 37, 78; CLR 25; DLB 161; JRDA; MAICYA; SAAS 7; SATA 54, 106
Hunter, Robert (?)-1734 **LC 7**
Hurston, Zora Neale 1891-1960 **CLC 7, 30, 61; BLC 2; DA; DAC; DAM MST, MULT, NOV; DC 12; SSC 4; WLCS**
See also AAYA 15; BW 1, 3; CA 85-88; CANR 61; CDALBS; DA3; DLB 51, 86; MTCW 1, 2
Husserl, E. G.
See Husserl, Edmund (Gustav Albrecht)
Husserl, Edmund (Gustav Albrecht) 1859-1938 **TCLC 100**
See also CA 116; 133
Huston, John (Marcellus) 1906-1987 **CLC 20**
See also CA 73-76; 123; CANR 34; DLB 26
Hustvedt, Siri 1955- **CLC 76**
See also CA 137
Hutten, Ulrich von 1488-1523 **LC 16**
See also DLB 179
Huxley, Aldous (Leonard) 1894-1963 **CLC 1, 3, 4, 5, 8, 11, 18, 35, 79; DA; DAB; DAC; DAM MST, NOV; SSC 39; WLC**
See also AAYA 11; CA 85-88; CANR 44; CDBLB 1914-1945; DA3; DLB 36, 100, 162, 195; MTCW 1, 2; SATA 63
Huxley, T(homas) H(enry) 1825-1895 **NCLC 67**
See also DLB 57
Huysmans, Joris-Karl 1848-1907 **TCLC 7, 69**
See also CA 104; 165; DLB 123
Hwang, David Henry 1957- **CLC 55; DAM DRAM; DC 4**
See also CA 127; 132; CANR 76; DA3; DLB 212; INT 132; MTCW 2
Hyde, Anthony 1946- **CLC 42**
See also CA 136
Hyde, Margaret O(ldroyd) 1917- **CLC 21**
See also CA 1-4R; CANR 1, 36; CLR 23; JRDA; MAICYA; SAAS 8; SATA 1, 42, 76
Hynes, James 1956(?)- **CLC 65**
See also CA 164
Hypatia c. 370-415 **CMLC 35**
Ian, Janis 1951- **CLC 21**
See also CA 105; 187
Ibanez, Vicente Blasco
See Blasco Ibanez, Vicente
Ibarbourou, Juana de 1895-1979
See also HLCS 2; HW 1
Ibarguengoitia, Jorge 1928-1983 **CLC 37**
See also CA 124; 113; HW 1
Ibsen, Henrik (Johan) 1828-1906 **TCLC 2, 8, 16, 37, 52; DA; DAB; DAC; DAM DRAM, MST; DC 2; WLC**
See also CA 104; 141; DA3
Ibuse, Masuji 1898-1993 **CLC 22**
See also CA 127; 141; DLB 180
Ichikawa, Kon 1915- **CLC 20**
See also CA 121
Idle, Eric 1943- **CLC 21**
See also Monty Python
See also CA 116; CANR 35, 91
Ignatow, David 1914-1997 **CLC 4, 7, 14, 40**
See also CA 9-12R; 162; CAAS 3; CANR 31, 57; DLB 5
Ignotus
See Strachey, (Giles) Lytton
Ihimaera, Witi 1944- **CLC 46**
See also CA 77-80
Ilf, Ilya TCLC 21

See also Fainzilberg, Ilya Arnoldovich
Illyes, Gyula 1902-1983 **PC 16**
See also CA 114; 109
Immermann, Karl (Lebrecht) 1796-1840 **NCLC 4, 49**
See also DLB 133
Ince, Thomas H. 1882-1924 **TCLC 89**
Inchbald, Elizabeth 1753-1821 **NCLC 62**
See also DLB 39, 89
Inclan, Ramon (Maria) del Valle
See Valle-Inclan, Ramon (Maria) del
Infante, G(uillermo) Cabrera
See Cabrera Infante, G(uillermo)
Ingalls, Rachel (Holmes) 1940- **CLC 42**
See also CA 123; 127
Ingamells, Reginald Charles
See Ingamells, Rex
Ingamells, Rex 1913-1955 **TCLC 35**
See also CA 167
Inge, William (Motter) 1913-1973 **CLC 1, 8, 19; DAM DRAM**
See also CA 9-12R; CDALB 1941-1968; DA3; DLB 7; MTCW 1, 2
Ingelow, Jean 1820-1897 **NCLC 39**
See also DLB 35, 163; SATA 33
Ingram, Willis J.
See Harris, Mark
Innaurato, Albert (F.) 1948(?)- **CLC 21, 60**
See also CA 115; 122; CANR 78; INT 122
Innes, Michael
See Stewart, J(ohn) I(nnes) M(ackintosh)
Innis, Harold Adams 1894-1952 **TCLC 77**
See also CA 181; DLB 88
Ionesco, Eugene 1909-1994 **CLC 1, 4, 6, 9, 11, 15, 41, 86; DA; DAB; DAC; DAM DRAM, MST; DC 12; WLC**
See also CA 9-12R; 144; CANR 55; DA3; MTCW 1, 2; SATA 7; SATA-Obit 79
Iqbal, Muhammad 1873-1938 **TCLC 28**
Ireland, Patrick
See O'Doherty, Brian
Irenaeus St. 130- **CMLC 42**
Iron, Ralph
See Schreiner, Olive (Emilie Albertina)
Irving, John (Winslow) 1942- **CLC 13, 23, 38, 112; DAM NOV, POP**
See also AAYA 8; BEST 89:3; CA 25-28R; CANR 28, 73; DA3; DLB 6; DLBY 82; MTCW 1, 2
Irving, Washington 1783-1859 **NCLC 2, 19; DA; DAB; DAC; DAM MST; SSC 2, 37; WLC**
See also CDALB 1640-1865; DA3; DLB 3, 11, 30, 59, 73, 74, 186; YABC 2
Irwin, P. K.
See Page, P(atricia) K(athleen)
Isaacs, Jorge Ricardo 1837-1895 **NCLC 70**
Isaacs, Susan 1943- **CLC 32; DAM POP**
See also BEST 89:1; CA 89-92; CANR 20, 41, 65; DA3; INT CANR-20; MTCW 1, 2
Isherwood, Christopher (William Bradshaw) 1904-1986 **CLC 1, 9, 11, 14, 44; DAM DRAM, NOV**
See also CA 13-16R; 117; CANR 35; DA3; DLB 15, 195; DLBY 86; MTCW 1, 2
Ishiguro, Kazuo 1954- **CLC 27, 56, 59, 110; DAM NOV**
See also BEST 90:2; CA 120; CANR 49; DA3; DLB 194; MTCW 1, 2
Ishikawa, Hakuhin
See Ishikawa, Takuboku
Ishikawa, Takuboku 1886(?)-1912 **TCLC 15; DAM POET; PC 10**
See also CA 113; 153
Iskander, Fazil 1929- **CLC 47**
See also CA 102
Isler, Alan (David) 1934- **CLC 91**
See also CA 156
Ivan IV 1530-1584 **LC 17**
Ivanov, Vyacheslav Ivanovich 1866-1949 **TCLC 33**
See also CA 122
Ivask, Ivar Vidrik 1927-1992 **CLC 14**
See also CA 37-40R; 139; CANR 24
Ives, Morgan
See Bradley, Marion Zimmer
Izumi Shikibu c. 973-c. 1034 **CMLC 33**
J CLC 25, 58, 65, 123; DAM DRAM; DC 6
See also CA 104; CANR 36, 63; DA3; DLB 232; MTCW 1, 2
J. R. S.
See Gogarty, Oliver St. John
Jabran, Kahlil
See Gibran, Kahlil
Jabran, Khalil
See Gibran, Kahlil
Jackson, Daniel
See Wingrove, David (John)
Jackson, Helen Hunt 1830-1885 **NCLC 90**
See also DLB 42, 47, 186, 189
Jackson, Jesse 1908-1983 **CLC 12**
See also BW 1; CA 25-28R; 109; CANR 27; CLR 28; MAICYA; SATA 2, 29; SATA-Obit 48
Jackson, Laura (Riding) 1901-1991
See Riding, Laura
See also CA 65-68; 135; CANR 28, 89; DLB 48
Jackson, Sam
See Trumbo, Dalton
Jackson, Sara
See Wingrove, David (John)
Jackson, Shirley 1919-1965 **CLC 11, 60, 87; DA; DAC; DAM MST; SSC 9, 39; WLC**
See also AAYA 9; CA 1-4R; 25-28R; CANR 4, 52; CDALB 1941-1968; DA3; DLB 6; MTCW 2; SATA 2
Jacob, (Cyprien-)Max 1876-1944 **TCLC 6**
See also CA 104
Jacobs, Harriet A(nn) 1813(?)-1897 **NCLC 67**
Jacobs, Jim 1942- **CLC 12**
See also CA 97-100; INT 97-100
Jacobs, W(illiam) W(ymark) 1863-1943 **TCLC 22**
See also CA 121; 167; DLB 135
Jacobsen, Jens Peter 1847-1885 **NCLC 34**
Jacobsen, Josephine 1908- **CLC 48, 102**
See also CA 33-36R; CAAS 18; CANR 23, 48
Jacobson, Dan 1929- **CLC 4, 14**
See also CA 1-4R; CANR 2, 25, 66; DLB 14, 207, 225; MTCW 1
Jacqueline
See Carpentier (y Valmont), Alejo
Jagger, Mick 1944- **CLC 17**
Jahiz, al- c. 780-c. 869 **CMLC 25**
Jakes, John (William) 1932- **CLC 29; DAM NOV, POP**
See also AAYA 32; BEST 89:4; CA 57-60; CANR 10, 43, 66; DA3; DLBY 83; INT CANR-10; MTCW 1, 2; SATA 62
James, Andrew
See Kirkup, James
James, C(yril) L(ionel) R(obert) 1901-1989 **CLC 33; BLCS**
See also BW 2; CA 117; 125; 128; CANR 62; DLB 125; MTCW 1
James, Daniel (Lewis) 1911-1988
See Santiago, Danny
See also CA 174; 125
James, Dynely
See Mayne, William (James Carter)
James, Henry Sr. 1811-1882 **NCLC 53**
James, Henry 1843-1916 **TCLC 2, 11, 24, 40, 47, 64; DA; DAB; DAC; DAM MST, NOV; SSC 8, 32; WLC**
See also CA 104; 132; CDALB 1865-1917; DA3; DLB 12, 71, 74, 189; DLBD 13; MTCW 1, 2
James, M. R.
See James, Montague (Rhodes)
See also DLB 156
James, Montague (Rhodes) 1862-1936 **TCLC 6; SSC 16**
See also CA 104; DLB 201
James, P. D. 1920- **CLC 18, 46, 122**
See also White, Phyllis Dorothy James
See also BEST 90:2; CDBLB 1960 to Present; DLB 87; DLBD 17
James, Philip
See Moorcock, Michael (John)
James, William 1842-1910 **TCLC 15, 32**
See also CA 109
James I 1394-1437 **LC 20**
Jameson, Anna 1794-1860 **NCLC 43**
See also DLB 99, 166
Jami, Nur al-Din 'Abd al-Rahman 1414-1492 **LC 9**
Jammes, Francis 1868-1938 **TCLC 75**
Jandl, Ernst 1925- **CLC 34**
Janowitz, Tama 1957- **CLC 43; DAM POP**
See also CA 106; CANR 52, 89
Japrisot, Sebastien 1931- **CLC 90**
Jarrell, Randall 1914-1965 **CLC 1, 2, 6, 9, 13, 49; DAM POET**
See also CA 5-8R; 25-28R; CABS 2; CANR 6, 34; CDALB 1941-1968; CLR 6; DLB 48, 52; MAICYA; MTCW 1, 2; SATA 7
Jarry, Alfred 1873-1907 **TCLC 2, 14; DAM DRAM; SSC 20**
See also CA 104; 153; DA3; DLB 192
Jawien, Andrzej
See John Paul II, Pope
Jaynes, Roderick
See Coen, Ethan
Jeake, Samuel, Jr.
See Aiken, Conrad (Potter)
Jean Paul 1763-1825 **NCLC 7**
Jefferies, (John) Richard 1848-1887 **NCLC 47**
See also DLB 98, 141; SATA 16
Jeffers, (John) Robinson 1887-1962 **CLC 2, 3, 11, 15, 54; DA; DAC; DAM MST, POET; PC 17; WLC**
See also CA 85-88; CANR 35; CDALB 1917-1929; DLB 45, 212; MTCW 1, 2
Jefferson, Janet
See Mencken, H(enry) L(ouis)
Jefferson, Thomas 1743-1826 **NCLC 11**
See also CDALB 1640-1865; DA3; DLB 31
Jeffrey, Francis 1773-1850 **NCLC 33**
See also DLB 107
Jelakowitch, Ivan
See Heijermans, Herman
Jellicoe, (Patricia) Ann 1927- **CLC 27**
See also CA 85-88; DLB 13, 233
Jemyma
See Holley, Marietta
Jen, Gish CLC 70
See also Jen, Lillian
Jen, Lillian 1956(?)-
See Jen, Gish
See also CA 135; CANR 89
Jenkins, (John) Robin 1912- **CLC 52**
See also CA 1-4R; CANR 1; DLB 14
Jennings, Elizabeth (Joan) 1926- **CLC 5, 14, 131**
See also CA 61-64; CAAS 5; CANR 8, 39, 66; DLB 27; MTCW 1; SATA 66
Jennings, Waylon 1937- **CLC 21**
Jensen, Johannes V. 1873-1950 **TCLC 41**
See also CA 170

Jensen, Laura (Linnea) 1948- **CLC 37**
See also CA 103
Jerome, Jerome K(lapka) 1859-1927 **TCLC 23**
See also CA 119; 177; DLB 10, 34, 135
Jerrold, Douglas William 1803-1857 **NCLC 2**
See also DLB 158, 159
Jewett, (Theodora) Sarah Orne 1849-1909 **TCLC 1, 22; SSC 6**
See also CA 108; 127; CANR 71; DLB 12, 74, 221; SATA 15
Jewsbury, Geraldine (Endsor) 1812-1880 **NCLC 22**
See also DLB 21
Jhabvala, Ruth Prawer 1927- **CLC 4, 8, 29, 94; DAB; DAM NOV**
See also CA 1-4R; CANR 2, 29, 51, 74, 91; DLB 139, 194; INT CANR-29; MTCW 1, 2
Jibran, Kahlil
See Gibran, Kahlil
Jibran, Khalil
See Gibran, Kahlil
Jiles, Paulette 1943- **CLC 13, 58**
See also CA 101; CANR 70
Jimenez (Mantecon), Juan Ramon 1881-1958 **TCLC 4; DAM MULT, POET; HLC 1; PC 7**
See also CA 104; 131; CANR 74; DLB 134; HW 1; MTCW 1, 2
Jimenez, Ramon
See Jimenez (Mantecon), Juan Ramon
Jimenez Mantecon, Juan
See Jimenez (Mantecon), Juan Ramon
Jin, Ha
See Jin, Xuefei
Jin, Xuefei 1956- **CLC 109**
See also CA 152; CANR 91
Joel, Billy CLC 26
See also Joel, William Martin
Joel, William Martin 1949-
See Joel, Billy
See also CA 108
John, Saint 7th cent. - **CMLC 27**
John of the Cross, St. 1542-1591 **LC 18**
John Paul II, Pope 1920- **CLC 128**
See also CA 106; 133
Johnson, B(ryan) S(tanley William) 1933-1973 **CLC 6, 9**
See also CA 9-12R; 53-56; CANR 9; DLB 14, 40
Johnson, Benj. F. of Boo
See Riley, James Whitcomb
Johnson, Benjamin F. of Boo
See Riley, James Whitcomb
Johnson, Charles (Richard) 1948- **CLC 7, 51, 65; BLC 2; DAM MULT**
See also BW 2, 3; CA 116; CAAS 18; CANR 42, 66, 82; DLB 33; MTCW 2
Johnson, Denis 1949- **CLC 52**
See also CA 117; 121; CANR 71; DLB 120
Johnson, Diane 1934- **CLC 5, 13, 48**
See also CA 41-44R; CANR 17, 40, 62; DLBY 80; INT CANR-17; MTCW 1
Johnson, Eyvind (Olof Verner) 1900-1976 **CLC 14**
See also CA 73-76; 69-72; CANR 34
Johnson, J. R.
See James, C(yril) L(ionel) R(obert)
Johnson, James Weldon 1871-1938 **TCLC 3, 19; BLC 2; DAM MULT, POET; PC 24**
See also BW 1, 3; CA 104; 125; CANR 82; CDALB 1917-1929; CLR 32; DA3; DLB 51; MTCW 1, 2; SATA 31
Johnson, Joyce 1935- **CLC 58**
See also CA 125; 129
Johnson, Judith (Emlyn) 1936- **CLC 7, 15**
See also Sherwin, Judith Johnson
See also CA 25-28R, 153; CANR 34
Johnson, Lionel (Pigot) 1867-1902 **TCLC 19**
See also CA 117; DLB 19
Johnson, Marguerite (Annie)
See Angelou, Maya
Johnson, Mel
See Malzberg, Barry N(athaniel)
Johnson, Pamela Hansford 1912-1981 **CLC 1, 7, 27**
See also CA 1-4R; 104; CANR 2, 28; DLB 15; MTCW 1, 2
Johnson, Robert 1911(?)-1938 **TCLC 69**
See also BW 3; CA 174
Johnson, Samuel 1709-1784 **LC 15, 52; DA; DAB; DAC; DAM MST; WLC**
See also CDBLB 1660-1789; DLB 39, 95, 104, 142
Johnson, Uwe 1934-1984 **CLC 5, 10, 15, 40**
See also CA 1-4R; 112; CANR 1, 39; DLB 75; MTCW 1
Johnston, George (Benson) 1913- **CLC 51**
See also CA 1-4R; CANR 5, 20; DLB 88
Johnston, Jennifer (Prudence) 1930- **CLC 7**
See also CA 85-88; CANR 92; DLB 14
Joinville, Jean de 1224(?)-1317 **CMLC 38**
Jolley, (Monica) Elizabeth 1923- **CLC 46; SSC 19**
See also CA 127; CAAS 13; CANR 59
Jones, Arthur Llewellyn 1863-1947
See Machen, Arthur
See also CA 104; 179
Jones, D(ouglas) G(ordon) 1929- **CLC 10**
See also CA 29-32R; CANR 13, 90; DLB 53
Jones, David (Michael) 1895-1974 **CLC 2, 4, 7, 13, 42**
See also CA 9-12R; 53-56; CANR 28; CDBLB 1945-1960; DLB 20, 100; MTCW 1
Jones, David Robert 1947-
See Bowie, David
See also CA 103
Jones, Diana Wynne 1934- **CLC 26**
See also AAYA 12; CA 49-52; CANR 4, 26, 56; CLR 23; DLB 161; JRDA; MAICYA; SAAS 7; SATA 9, 70, 108
Jones, Edward P. 1950- **CLC 76**
See also BW 2, 3; CA 142; CANR 79
Jones, Gayl 1949- **CLC 6, 9, 131; BLC 2; DAM MULT**
See also BW 2, 3; CA 77-80; CANR 27, 66; DA3; DLB 33; MTCW 1, 2
Jones, James 1921-1977 **CLC 1, 3, 10, 39**
See also AITN 1, 2; CA 1-4R; 69-72; CANR 6; DLB 2, 143; DLBD 17; DLBY 98; MTCW 1
Jones, John J.
See Lovecraft, H(oward) P(hillips)
Jones, LeRoi CLC 1, 2, 3, 5, 10, 14
See also Baraka, Amiri
See also MTCW 2
Jones, Louis B. 1953- **CLC 65**
See also CA 141; CANR 73
Jones, Madison (Percy, Jr.) 1925- **CLC 4**
See also CA 13-16R; CAAS 11; CANR 7, 54, 83; DLB 152
Jones, Mervyn 1922- **CLC 10, 52**
See also CA 45-48; CAAS 5; CANR 1, 91; MTCW 1
Jones, Mick 1956(?)- **CLC 30**
Jones, Nettie (Pearl) 1941- **CLC 34**
See also BW 2; CA 137; CAAS 20; CANR 88
Jones, Preston 1936-1979 **CLC 10**
See also CA 73-76; 89-92; DLB 7
Jones, Robert F(rancis) 1934- **CLC 7**
See also CA 49-52; CANR 2, 61
Jones, Rod 1953- **CLC 50**
See also CA 128
Jones, Terence Graham Parry 1942- **CLC 21**
See also Jones, Terry; Monty Python
See also CA 112; 116; CANR 35, 93; INT 116
Jones, Terry
See Jones, Terence Graham Parry
See also SATA 67; SATA-Brief 51
Jones, Thom (Douglas) 1945(?)- **CLC 81**
See also CA 157; CANR 88
Jong, Erica 1942- **CLC 4, 6, 8, 18, 83; DAM NOV, POP**
See also AITN 1; BEST 90:2; CA 73-76; CANR 26, 52, 75; DA3; DLB 2, 5, 28, 152; INT CANR-26; MTCW 1, 2
Jonson, Ben(jamin) 1572(?)-1637 **LC 6, 33; DA; DAB; DAC; DAM DRAM, MST, POET; DC 4; PC 17; WLC**
See also CDBLB Before 1660; DLB 62, 121
Jordan, June 1936- **CLC 5, 11, 23, 114; BLCS; DAM MULT, POET**
See also AAYA 2; BW 2, 3; CA 33-36R; CANR 25, 70; CLR 10; DLB 38; MAICYA; MTCW 1; SATA 4
Jordan, Neil (Patrick) 1950- **CLC 110**
See also CA 124; 130; CANR 54; INT 130
Jordan, Pat(rick M.) 1941- **CLC 37**
See also CA 33-36R
Jorgensen, Ivar
See Ellison, Harlan (Jay)
Jorgenson, Ivar
See Silverberg, Robert
Josephus, Flavius c. 37-100 **CMLC 13**
Josiah Allen's Wife
See Holley, Marietta
Josipovici, Gabriel (David) 1940- **CLC 6, 43**
See also CA 37-40R; CAAS 8; CANR 47, 84; DLB 14
Joubert, Joseph 1754-1824 **NCLC 9**
Jouve, Pierre Jean 1887-1976 **CLC 47**
See also CA 65-68
Jovine, Francesco 1902-1950 **TCLC 79**
Joyce, James (Augustine Aloysius) 1882-1941 **TCLC 3, 8, 16, 35, 52; DA; DAB; DAC; DAM MST, NOV, POET; PC 22; SSC 3, 26; WLC**
See also CA 104; 126; CDBLB 1914-1945; DA3; DLB 10, 19, 36, 162; MTCW 1, 2
Jozsef, Attila 1905-1937 **TCLC 22**
See also CA 116
Juana Ines de la Cruz 1651(?)-1695 **LC 5; HLCS 1; PC 24**
Judd, Cyril
See Kornbluth, C(yril) M.; Pohl, Frederik
Juenger, Ernst 1895-1998 **CLC 125**
See also CA 101; 167; CANR 21, 47; DLB 56
Julian of Norwich 1342(?)-1416(?) **LC 6, 52**
See also DLB 146
Junger, Ernst
See Juenger, Ernst
Junger, Sebastian 1962- **CLC 109**
See also AAYA 28; CA 165
Juniper, Alex
See Hospital, Janette Turner
Junius
See Luxemburg, Rosa
Just, Ward (Swift) 1935- **CLC 4, 27**
See also CA 25-28R; CANR 32, 87; INT CANR-32
Justice, Donald (Rodney) 1925- **CLC 6, 19, 102; DAM POET**
See also CA 5-8R; CANR 26, 54, 74; DLBY 83; INT CANR-26; MTCW 2
Juvenal c. 60-c. 13 **CMLC 8**
See also Juvenalis, Decimus Junius
See also DLB 211
Juvenalis, Decimus Junius 55(?)-c. 127(?)
See Juvenal

Juvenis
See Bourne, Randolph S(illiman)

Kacew, Romain 1914-1980
See Gary, Romain
See also CA 108; 102

Kadare, Ismail 1936- **CLC 52**
See also CA 161

Kadohata, Cynthia CLC 59, 122
See also CA 140

Kafka, Franz 1883-1924 **TCLC 2, 6, 13, 29, 47, 53; DA; DAB; DAC; DAM MST, NOV; SSC 5, 29, 35; WLC**
See also AAYA 31; CA 105; 126; DA3; DLB 81; MTCW 1, 2

Kahanovitsch, Pinkhes
See Der Nister

Kahn, Roger 1927- **CLC 30**
See also CA 25-28R; CANR 44, 69; DLB 171; SATA 37

Kain, Saul
See Sassoon, Siegfried (Lorraine)

Kaiser, Georg 1878-1945 **TCLC 9**
See also CA 106; DLB 124

Kaletski, Alexander 1946- **CLC 39**
See also CA 118; 143

Kalidasa fl. c. 400- **CMLC 9; PC 22**

Kallman, Chester (Simon) 1921-1975 **CLC 2**
See also CA 45-48; 53-56; CANR 3

Kaminsky, Melvin 1926-
See Brooks, Mel
See also CA 65-68; CANR 16

Kaminsky, Stuart M(elvin) 1934- **CLC 59**
See also CA 73-76; CANR 29, 53, 89

Kandinsky, Wassily 1866-1944 **TCLC 92**
See also CA 118; 155

Kane, Francis
See Robbins, Harold

Kane, Henry 1918-
See Queen, Ellery
See also CA 156

Kane, Paul
See Simon, Paul (Frederick)

Kanin, Garson 1912-1999 **CLC 22**
See also AITN 1; CA 5-8R; 177; CANR 7, 78; DLB 7

Kaniuk, Yoram 1930- **CLC 19**
See also CA 134

Kant, Immanuel 1724-1804 **NCLC 27, 67**
See also DLB 94

Kantor, MacKinlay 1904-1977 **CLC 7**
See also CA 61-64; 73-76; CANR 60, 63; DLB 9, 102; MTCW 2

Kaplan, David Michael 1946- **CLC 50**
See also CA 187

Kaplan, James 1951- **CLC 59**
See also CA 135

Karageorge, Michael
See Anderson, Poul (William)

Karamzin, Nikolai Mikhailovich 1766-1826 **NCLC 3**
See also DLB 150

Karapanou, Margarita 1946- **CLC 13**
See also CA 101

Karinthy, Frigyes 1887-1938 **TCLC 47**
See also CA 170

Karl, Frederick R(obert) 1927- **CLC 34**
See also CA 5-8R; CANR 3, 44

Kastel, Warren
See Silverberg, Robert

Kataev, Evgeny Petrovich 1903-1942
See Petrov, Evgeny
See also CA 120

Kataphusin
See Ruskin, John

Katz, Steve 1935- **CLC 47**
See also CA 25-28R; CAAS 14, 64; CANR 12; DLBY 83

Kauffman, Janet 1945- **CLC 42**
See also CA 117; CANR 43, 84; DLBY 86

Kaufman, Bob (Garnell) 1925-1986 **CLC 49**
See also BW 1; CA 41-44R; 118; CANR 22; DLB 16, 41

Kaufman, George S. 1889-1961 **CLC 38; DAM DRAM**
See also CA 108; 93-96; DLB 7; INT 108; MTCW 2

Kaufman, Sue CLC 3, 8
See also Barondess, Sue K(aufman)

Kavafis, Konstantinos Petrou 1863-1933
See Cavafy, C(onstantine) P(eter)
See also CA 104

Kavan, Anna 1901-1968 **CLC 5, 13, 82**
See also CA 5-8R; CANR 6, 57; MTCW 1

Kavanagh, Dan
See Barnes, Julian (Patrick)

Kavanagh, Julie 1952- **CLC 119**
See also CA 163

Kavanagh, Patrick (Joseph) 1904-1967 **CLC 22**
See also CA 123; 25-28R; DLB 15, 20; MTCW 1

Kawabata, Yasunari 1899-1972 **CLC 2, 5, 9, 18, 107; DAM MULT; SSC 17**
See also CA 93-96; 33-36R; CANR 88; DLB 180; MTCW 2

Kaye, M(ary) M(argaret) 1909- **CLC 28**
See also CA 89-92; CANR 24, 60; MTCW 1, 2; SATA 62

Kaye, Mollie
See Kaye, M(ary) M(argaret)

Kaye-Smith, Sheila 1887-1956 **TCLC 20**
See also CA 118; DLB 36

Kaymor, Patrice Maguilene
See Senghor, Leopold Sedar

Kazan, Elia 1909- **CLC 6, 16, 63**
See also CA 21-24R; CANR 32, 78

Kazantzakis, Nikos 1883(?)-1957 **TCLC 2, 5, 33**
See also CA 105; 132; DA3; MTCW 1, 2

Kazin, Alfred 1915-1998 **CLC 34, 38, 119**
See also CA 1-4R; CAAS 7; CANR 1, 45, 79; DLB 67

Keane, Mary Nesta (Skrine) 1904-1996
See Keane, Molly
See also CA 108; 114; 151

Keane, Molly CLC 31
See also Keane, Mary Nesta (Skrine)
See also INT 114

Keates, Jonathan 1946(?)- **CLC 34**
See also CA 163

Keaton, Buster 1895-1966 **CLC 20**

Keats, John 1795-1821 **NCLC 8, 73; DA; DAB; DAC; DAM MST, POET; PC 1; WLC**
See also CDBLB 1789-1832; DA3; DLB 96, 110

Keble, John 1792-1866 **NCLC 87**
See also DLB 32, 55

Keene, Donald 1922- **CLC 34**
See also CA 1-4R; CANR 5

Keillor, Garrison CLC 40, 115
See also Keillor, Gary (Edward)
See also AAYA 2; BEST 89:3; DLBY 87; SATA 58

Keillor, Gary (Edward) 1942-
See Keillor, Garrison
See also CA 111; 117; CANR 36, 59; DAM POP; DA3; MTCW 1, 2

Keith, Michael
See Hubbard, L(afayette) Ron(ald)

Keller, Gottfried 1819-1890 **NCLC 2; SSC 26**
See also DLB 129

Keller, Nora Okja 1965- **CLC 109**
See also CA 187

Kellerman, Jonathan 1949- **CLC 44; DAM POP**
See also BEST 90:1; CA 106; CANR 29, 51; DA3; INT CANR-29

Kelley, William Melvin 1937- **CLC 22**
See also BW 1; CA 77-80; CANR 27, 83; DLB 33

Kellogg, Marjorie 1922- **CLC 2**
See also CA 81-84

Kellow, Kathleen
See Hibbert, Eleanor Alice Burford

Kelly, M(ilton) T(errence) 1947- **CLC 55**
See also CA 97-100; CAAS 22; CANR 19, 43, 84

Kelman, James 1946- **CLC 58, 86**
See also CA 148; CANR 85; DLB 194

Kemal, Yashar 1923- **CLC 14, 29**
See also CA 89-92; CANR 44

Kemble, Fanny 1809-1893 **NCLC 18**
See also DLB 32

Kemelman, Harry 1908-1996 **CLC 2**
See also AITN 1; CA 9-12R; 155; CANR 6, 71; DLB 28

Kempe, Margery 1373(?)-1440(?) **LC 6, 56**
See also DLB 146

Kempis, Thomas a 1380-1471 **LC 11**

Kendall, Henry 1839-1882 **NCLC 12**

Keneally, Thomas (Michael) 1935- **CLC 5, 8, 10, 14, 19, 27, 43, 117; DAM NOV**
See also CA 85-88; CANR 10, 50, 74; DA3; MTCW 1, 2

Kennedy, Adrienne (Lita) 1931- **CLC 66; BLC 2; DAM MULT; DC 5**
See also BW 2, 3; CA 103; CAAS 20; CABS 3; CANR 26, 53, 82; DLB 38

Kennedy, John Pendleton 1795-1870 **NCLC 2**
See also DLB 3

Kennedy, Joseph Charles 1929-
See Kennedy, X. J.
See also CA 1-4R; CANR 4, 30, 40; SATA 14, 86

Kennedy, William 1928- **CLC 6, 28, 34, 53; DAM NOV**
See also AAYA 1; CA 85-88; CANR 14, 31, 76; DA3; DLB 143; DLBY 85; INT CANR-31; MTCW 1, 2; SATA 57

Kennedy, X. J. CLC 8, 42
See also Kennedy, Joseph Charles
See also CAAS 9; CLR 27; DLB 5; SAAS 22

Kenny, Maurice (Francis) 1929- **CLC 87; DAM MULT**
See also CA 144; CAAS 22; DLB 175; NNAL

Kent, Kelvin
See Kuttner, Henry

Kenton, Maxwell
See Southern, Terry

Kenyon, Robert O.
See Kuttner, Henry

Kepler, Johannes 1571-1630 **LC 45**

Kerouac, Jack CLC 1, 2, 3, 5, 14, 29, 61
See also Kerouac, Jean-Louis Lebris de
See also AAYA 25; CDALB 1941-1968; DLB 2, 16; DLBD 3; DLBY 95; MTCW 2

Kerouac, Jean-Louis Lebris de 1922-1969
See Kerouac, Jack
See also AITN 1; CA 5-8R; 25-28R; CANR 26, 54; DA; DAB; DAC; DAM MST, NOV, POET, POP; DA3; MTCW 1, 2; WLC

Kerr, Jean 1923- **CLC 22**
See also CA 5-8R; CANR 7; INT CANR-7

Kerr, M. E. CLC 12, 35
See also Meaker, Marijane (Agnes)
See also AAYA 2, 23; CLR 29; SAAS 1

Kerr, Robert CLC 55

Kerrigan, (Thomas) Anthony 1918- **CLC 4, 6**
See also CA 49-52; CAAS 11; CANR 4

Lancaster, Bruce 1896-1963 **CLC 36**
See also CA 9-10; CANR 70; CAP 1; SATA 9
Lanchester, John CLC 99
Landau, Mark Alexandrovich
See Aldanov, Mark (Alexandrovich)
Landau-Aldanov, Mark Alexandrovich
See Aldanov, Mark (Alexandrovich)
Landis, Jerry
See Simon, Paul (Frederick)
Landis, John 1950- **CLC 26**
See also CA 112; 122
Landolfi, Tommaso 1908-1979 **CLC 11, 49**
See also CA 127; 117; DLB 177
Landon, Letitia Elizabeth 1802-1838 **NCLC 15**
See also DLB 96
Landor, Walter Savage 1775-1864 **NCLC 14**
See also DLB 93, 107
Landwirth, Heinz 1927-
See Lind, Jakov
See also CA 9-12R; CANR 7
Lane, Patrick 1939- **CLC 25; DAM POET**
See also CA 97-100; CANR 54; DLB 53; INT 97-100
Lang, Andrew 1844-1912 **TCLC 16**
See also CA 114; 137; CANR 85; DLB 98, 141, 184; MAICYA; SATA 16
Lang, Fritz 1890-1976 **CLC 20, 103**
See also CA 77-80; 69-72; CANR 30
Lange, John
See Crichton, (John) Michael
Langer, Elinor 1939- **CLC 34**
See also CA 121
Langland, William 1330(?)-1400(?) **LC 19; DA; DAB; DAC; DAM MST, POET**
See also DLB 146
Langstaff, Launcelot
See Irving, Washington
Lanier, Sidney 1842-1881 **NCLC 6; DAM POET**
See also DLB 64; DLBD 13; MAICYA; SATA 18
Lanyer, Aemilia 1569-1645 **LC 10, 30**
See also DLB 121
Lao-Tzu
See Lao Tzu
Lao Tzu fl. 6th cent. B.C.- **CMLC 7**
Lapine, James (Elliot) 1949- **CLC 39**
See also CA 123; 130; CANR 54; INT 130
Larbaud, Valery (Nicolas) 1881-1957 **TCLC 9**
See also CA 106; 152
Lardner, Ring
See Lardner, Ring(gold) W(ilmer)
Lardner, Ring W., Jr.
See Lardner, Ring(gold) W(ilmer)
Lardner, Ring(gold) W(ilmer) 1885-1933 **TCLC 2, 14; SSC 32**
See also CA 104; 131; CDALB 1917-1929; DLB 11, 25, 86; DLBD 16; MTCW 1, 2
Laredo, Betty
See Codrescu, Andrei
Larkin, Maia
See Wojciechowska, Maia (Teresa)
Larkin, Philip (Arthur) 1922-1985 **CLC 3, 5, 8, 9, 13, 18, 33, 39, 64; DAB; DAM MST, POET; PC 21**
See also CA 5-8R; 117; CANR 24, 62; CDBLB 1960 to Present; DA3; DLB 27; MTCW 1, 2
Larra (y Sanchez de Castro), Mariano Jose de 1809-1837 **NCLC 17**
Larsen, Eric 1941- **CLC 55**
See also CA 132
Larsen, Nella 1891-1964 **CLC 37; BLC 2; DAM MULT**
See also BW 1; CA 125; CANR 83; DLB 51
Larson, Charles R(aymond) 1938- **CLC 31**
See also CA 53-56; CANR 4
Larson, Jonathan 1961-1996 **CLC 99**
See also AAYA 28; CA 156
Las Casas, Bartolome de 1474-1566 **LC 31**
Lasch, Christopher 1932-1994 **CLC 102**
See also CA 73-76; 144; CANR 25; MTCW 1, 2
Lasker-Schueler, Else 1869-1945 **TCLC 57**
See also CA 183; DLB 66, 124
Laski, Harold J(oseph) 1893-1950 **TCLC 79**
Latham, Jean Lee 1902-1995 **CLC 12**
See also AITN 1; CA 5-8R; CANR 7, 84; CLR 50; MAICYA; SATA 2, 68
Latham, Mavis
See Clark, Mavis Thorpe
Lathen, Emma CLC 2
See also Hennissart, Martha; Latsis, Mary J(ane)
Lathrop, Francis
See Leiber, Fritz (Reuter, Jr.)
Latsis, Mary J(ane) 1927(?)-1997
See Lathen, Emma
See also CA 85-88; 162
Lattimore, Richmond (Alexander) 1906-1984 **CLC 3**
See also CA 1-4R; 112; CANR 1
Laughlin, James 1914-1997 **CLC 49**
See also CA 21-24R; 162; CAAS 22; CANR 9, 47; DLB 48; DLBY 96, 97
Laurence, (Jean) Margaret (Wemyss) 1926-1987 **CLC 3, 6, 13, 50, 62; DAC; DAM MST; SSC 7**
See also CA 5-8R; 121; CANR 33; DLB 53; MTCW 1, 2; SATA-Obit 50
Laurent, Antoine 1952- **CLC 50**
Lauscher, Hermann
See Hesse, Hermann
Lautreamont, Comte de 1846-1870 **NCLC 12; SSC 14**
Laverty, Donald
See Blish, James (Benjamin)
Lavin, Mary 1912-1996 **CLC 4, 18, 99; SSC 4**
See also CA 9-12R; 151; CANR 33; DLB 15; MTCW 1
Lavond, Paul Dennis
See Kornbluth, C(yril) M.; Pohl, Frederik
Lawler, Raymond Evenor 1922- **CLC 58**
See also CA 103
Lawrence, D(avid) H(erbert Richards) 1885-1930 **TCLC 2, 9, 16, 33, 48, 61, 93; DA; DAB; DAC; DAM MST, NOV, POET; SSC 4, 19; WLC**
See also CA 104; 121; CDBLB 1914-1945; DA3; DLB 10, 19, 36, 98, 162, 195; MTCW 1, 2
Lawrence, T(homas) E(dward) 1888-1935 **TCLC 18**
See also Dale, Colin
See also CA 115; 167; DLB 195
Lawrence of Arabia
See Lawrence, T(homas) E(dward)
Lawson, Henry (Archibald Hertzberg) 1867-1922 **TCLC 27; SSC 18**
See also CA 120; 181
Lawton, Dennis
See Faust, Frederick (Schiller)
Laxness, Halldor CLC 25
See also Gudjonsson, Halldor Kiljan
Layamon fl. c. 1200- **CMLC 10**
See also DLB 146
Laye, Camara 1928-1980 **CLC 4, 38; BLC 2; DAM MULT**
See also BW 1; CA 85-88; 97-100; CANR 25; MTCW 1, 2
Layton, Irving (Peter) 1912- **CLC 2, 15; DAC; DAM MST, POET**
See also CA 1-4R; CANR 2, 33, 43, 66; DLB 88; MTCW 1, 2
Lazarus, Emma 1849-1887 **NCLC 8**
Lazarus, Felix
See Cable, George Washington
Lazarus, Henry
See Slavitt, David R(ytman)
Lea, Joan
See Neufeld, John (Arthur)
Leacock, Stephen (Butler) 1869-1944 **TCLC 2; DAC; DAM MST; SSC 39**
See also CA 104; 141; CANR 80; DLB 92; MTCW 2
Lear, Edward 1812-1888 **NCLC 3**
See also CLR 1; DLB 32, 163, 166; MAICYA; SATA 18, 100
Lear, Norman (Milton) 1922- **CLC 12**
See also CA 73-76
Leautaud, Paul 1872-1956 **TCLC 83**
See also DLB 65
Leavis, F(rank) R(aymond) 1895-1978 **CLC 24**
See also CA 21-24R; 77-80; CANR 44; MTCW 1, 2
Leavitt, David 1961- **CLC 34; DAM POP**
See also CA 116; 122; CANR 50, 62; DA3; DLB 130; INT 122; MTCW 2
Leblanc, Maurice (Marie Emile) 1864-1941 **TCLC 49**
See also CA 110
Lebowitz, Fran(ces Ann) 1951(?)- **CLC 11, 36**
See also CA 81-84; CANR 14, 60, 70; INT CANR-14; MTCW 1
Lebrecht, Peter
See Tieck, (Johann) Ludwig
le Carre, John CLC 3, 5, 9, 15, 28
See also Cornwell, David (John Moore)
See also BEST 89:4; CDBLB 1960 to Present; DLB 87; MTCW 2
Le Clezio, J(ean) M(arie) G(ustave) 1940- **CLC 31**
See also CA 116; 128; DLB 83
Leconte de Lisle, Charles-Marie-Rene 1818-1894 **NCLC 29**
Le Coq, Monsieur
See Simenon, Georges (Jacques Christian)
Leduc, Violette 1907-1972 **CLC 22**
See also CA 13-14; 33-36R; CANR 69; CAP 1
Ledwidge, Francis 1887(?)-1917 **TCLC 23**
See also CA 123; DLB 20
Lee, Andrea 1953- **CLC 36; BLC 2; DAM MULT**
See also BW 1, 3; CA 125; CANR 82
Lee, Andrew
See Auchincloss, Louis (Stanton)
Lee, Chang-rae 1965- **CLC 91**
See also CA 148; CANR 89
Lee, Don L. CLC 2
See also Madhubuti, Haki R.
Lee, George W(ashington) 1894-1976 **CLC 52; BLC 2; DAM MULT**
See also BW 1; CA 125; CANR 83; DLB 51
Lee, (Nelle) Harper 1926- **CLC 12, 60; DA; DAB; DAC; DAM MST, NOV; WLC**
See also AAYA 13; CA 13-16R; CANR 51; CDALB 1941-1968; DA3; DLB 6; MTCW 1, 2; SATA 11
Lee, Helen Elaine 1959(?)- **CLC 86**
See also CA 148
Lee, Julian
See Latham, Jean Lee

Author Index

101; DAM MULT; HLCS 2
See also CA 77-80; CANR 71; DLB 113; HW 1, 2
L'Heureux, John (Clarke) 1934- **CLC 52**
See also CA 13-16R; CANR 23, 45, 88
Liddell, C. H.
See Kuttner, Henry
Lie, Jonas (Lauritz Idemil) 1833-1908(?) **TCLC 5**
See also CA 115
Lieber, Joel 1937-1971 **CLC 6**
See also CA 73-76; 29-32R
Lieber, Stanley Martin
See Lee, Stan
Lieberman, Laurence (James) 1935- **CLC 4, 36**
See also CA 17-20R; CANR 8, 36, 89
Lieh Tzu fl. 7th cent. B.C.-5th cent. B.C. **CMLC 27**
Lieksman, Anders
See Haavikko, Paavo Juhani
Li Fei-kan 1904-
See Pa Chin
See also CA 105
Lifton, Robert Jay 1926- **CLC 67**
See also CA 17-20R; CANR 27, 78; INT CANR-27; SATA 66
Lightfoot, Gordon 1938- **CLC 26**
See also CA 109
Lightman, Alan P(aige) 1948- **CLC 81**
See also CA 141; CANR 63
Ligotti, Thomas (Robert) 1953- **CLC 44; SSC 16**
See also CA 123; CANR 49
Li Ho 791-817 **PC 13**
Liliencron, (Friedrich Adolf Axel) Detlev von 1844-1909 **TCLC 18**
See also CA 117
Lilly, William 1602-1681 **LC 27**
Lima, Jose Lezama
See Lezama Lima, Jose
Lima Barreto, Afonso Henrique de 1881-1922 **TCLC 23**
See also CA 117; 181
Limonov, Edward 1944- **CLC 67**
See also CA 137
Lin, Frank
See Atherton, Gertrude (Franklin Horn)
Lincoln, Abraham 1809-1865 **NCLC 18**
Lind, Jakov CLC 1, 2, 4, 27, 82
See also Landwirth, Heinz
See also CAAS 4
Lindbergh, Anne (Spencer) Morrow 1906- **CLC 82; DAM NOV**
See also CA 17-20R; CANR 16, 73; MTCW 1, 2; SATA 33
Lindsay, David 1876(?)-1945 **TCLC 15**
See also CA 113; 187
Lindsay, (Nicholas) Vachel 1879-1931 **TCLC 17; DA; DAC; DAM MST, POET; PC 23; WLC**
See also CA 114; 135; CANR 79; CDALB 1865-1917; DA3; DLB 54; SATA 40
Linke-Poot
See Doeblin, Alfred
Linney, Romulus 1930- **CLC 51**
See also CA 1-4R; CANR 40, 44, 79
Linton, Eliza Lynn 1822-1898 **NCLC 41**
See also DLB 18
Li Po 701-763 **CMLC 2; PC 29**
Lipsius, Justus 1547-1606 **LC 16**
Lipsyte, Robert (Michael) 1938- **CLC 21; DA; DAC; DAM MST, NOV**
See also AAYA 7; CA 17-20R; CANR 8, 57; CLR 23; JRDA; MAICYA; SATA 5, 68, 113
Lish, Gordon (Jay) 1934- **CLC 45; SSC 18**
See also CA 113; 117; CANR 79; DLB 130; INT 117
Lispector, Clarice 1925(?)-1977 **CLC 43; HLCS 2; SSC 34**
See also CA 139; 116; CANR 71; DLB 113; HW 2
Littell, Robert 1935(?)- **CLC 42**
See also CA 109; 112; CANR 64
Little, Malcolm 1925-1965
See Malcolm X
See also BW 1, 3; CA 125; 111; CANR 82; DA; DAB; DAC; DAM MST, MULT; DA3; MTCW 1, 2
Littlewit, Humphrey Gent.
See Lovecraft, H(oward) P(hillips)
Litwos
See Sienkiewicz, Henryk (Adam Alexander Pius)
Liu, E 1857-1909 **TCLC 15**
See also CA 115
Lively, Penelope (Margaret) 1933- **CLC 32, 50; DAM NOV**
See also CA 41-44R; CANR 29, 67, 79; CLR 7; DLB 14, 161, 207; JRDA; MAICYA; MTCW 1, 2; SATA 7, 60, 101
Livesay, Dorothy (Kathleen) 1909- **CLC 4, 15, 79; DAC; DAM MST, POET**
See also AITN 2; CA 25-28R; CAAS 8; CANR 36, 67; DLB 68; MTCW 1
Livy c. 59B.C.-c. 17 **CMLC 11**
See also DLB 211
Lizardi, Jose Joaquin Fernandez de 1776-1827 **NCLC 30**
Llewellyn, Richard
See Llewellyn Lloyd, Richard Dafydd Vivian
See also DLB 15
Llewellyn Lloyd, Richard Dafydd Vivian 1906-1983 **CLC 7, 80**
See also Llewellyn, Richard
See also CA 53-56; 111; CANR 7, 71; SATA 11; SATA-Obit 37
Llosa, (Jorge) Mario (Pedro) Vargas
See Vargas Llosa, (Jorge) Mario (Pedro)
Lloyd, Manda
See Mander, (Mary) Jane
Lloyd Webber, Andrew 1948-
See Webber, Andrew Lloyd
See also AAYA 1; CA 116; 149; DAM DRAM; SATA 56
Llull, Ramon c. 1235-c. 1316 **CMLC 12**
Lobb, Ebenezer
See Upward, Allen
Locke, Alain (Le Roy) 1886-1954 **TCLC 43; BLCS**
See also BW 1, 3; CA 106; 124; CANR 79; DLB 51
Locke, John 1632-1704 **LC 7, 35**
See also DLB 101
Locke-Elliott, Sumner
See Elliott, Sumner Locke
Lockhart, John Gibson 1794-1854 **NCLC 6**
See also DLB 110, 116, 144
Lodge, David (John) 1935- **CLC 36; DAM POP**
See also BEST 90:1; CA 17-20R; CANR 19, 53, 92; DLB 14, 194; INT CANR-19; MTCW 1, 2
Lodge, Thomas 1558-1625 **LC 41**
Lodge, Thomas 1558-1625 **LC 41**
See also DLB 172
Loennbohm, Armas Eino Leopold 1878-1926
See Leino, Eino
See also CA 123
Loewinsohn, Ron(ald William) 1937- **CLC 52**
See also CA 25-28R; CANR 71
Logan, Jake
See Smith, Martin Cruz
Logan, John (Burton) 1923-1987 **CLC 5**
See also CA 77-80; 124; CANR 45; DLB 5
Lo Kuan-chung 1330(?)-1400(?) **LC 12**
Lombard, Nap
See Johnson, Pamela Hansford
London, Jack TCLC 9, 15, 39; SSC 4; WLC
See also London, John Griffith
See also AAYA 13; AITN 2; CDALB 1865-1917; DLB 8, 12, 78, 212; SATA 18
London, John Griffith 1876-1916
See London, Jack
See also CA 110; 119; CANR 73; DA; DAB; DAC; DAM MST, NOV; DA3; JRDA; MAICYA; MTCW 1, 2
Long, Emmett
See Leonard, Elmore (John, Jr.)
Longbaugh, Harry
See Goldman, William (W.)
Longfellow, Henry Wadsworth 1807-1882 **NCLC 2, 45; DA; DAB; DAC; DAM MST, POET; PC 30; WLCS**
See also CDALB 1640-1865; DA3; DLB 1, 59, 235; SATA 19
Longinus c. 1st cent. - **CMLC 27**
See also DLB 176
Longley, Michael 1939- **CLC 29**
See also CA 102; DLB 40
Longus fl. c. 2nd cent. - **CMLC 7**
Longway, A. Hugh
See Lang, Andrew
Lonnrot, Elias 1802-1884 **NCLC 53**
Lopate, Phillip 1943- **CLC 29**
See also CA 97-100; CANR 88; DLBY 80; INT 97-100
Lopez Portillo (y Pacheco), Jose 1920- **CLC 46**
See also CA 129; HW 1
Lopez y Fuentes, Gregorio 1897(?)-1966 **CLC 32**
See also CA 131; HW 1
Lorca, Federico Garcia
See Garcia Lorca, Federico
Lord, Bette Bao 1938- **CLC 23**
See also BEST 90:3; CA 107; CANR 41, 79; INT 107; SATA 58
Lord Auch
See Bataille, Georges
Lord Byron
See Byron, George Gordon (Noel)
Lorde, Audre (Geraldine) 1934-1992 **CLC 18, 71; BLC 2; DAM MULT, POET; PC 12**
See also BW 1, 3; CA 25-28R; 142; CANR 16, 26, 46, 82; DA3; DLB 41; MTCW 1, 2
Lord Houghton
See Milnes, Richard Monckton
Lord Jeffrey
See Jeffrey, Francis
Lorenzini, Carlo 1826-1890
See Collodi, Carlo
See also MAICYA; SATA 29, 100
Lorenzo, Heberto Padilla
See Padilla (Lorenzo), Heberto
Loris
See Hofmannsthal, Hugo von
Loti, Pierre TCLC 11
See also Viaud, (Louis Marie) Julien
See also DLB 123
Lou, Henri
See Andreas-Salome, Lou
Louie, David Wong 1954- **CLC 70**
See also CA 139
Louis, Father M.
See Merton, Thomas

Lovecraft, H(oward) P(hillips) 1890-1937 **TCLC 4, 22; DAM POP; SSC 3**
See also AAYA 14; CA 104; 133; DA3; MTCW 1, 2
Lovelace, Earl 1935- **CLC 51**
See also BW 2; CA 77-80; CANR 41, 72; DLB 125; MTCW 1
Lovelace, Richard 1618-1657 **LC 24**
See also DLB 131
Lowell, Amy 1874-1925 **TCLC 1, 8; DAM POET; PC 13**
See also CA 104; 151; DLB 54, 140; MTCW 2
Lowell, James Russell 1819-1891 **NCLC 2, 90**
See also CDALB 1640-1865; DLB 1, 11, 64, 79, 189, 235
Lowell, Robert (Traill Spence, Jr.) 1917-1977 **CLC 1, 2, 3, 4, 5, 8, 9, 11, 15, 37, 124; DA; DAB; DAC; DAM MST, NOV; PC 3; WLC**
See also CA 9-12R; 73-76; CABS 2; CANR 26, 60; CDALBS; DA3; DLB 5, 169; MTCW 1, 2
Lowenthal, Michael (Francis) 1969- **CLC 119**
See also CA 150
Lowndes, Marie Adelaide (Belloc) 1868-1947 **TCLC 12**
See also CA 107; DLB 70
Lowry, (Clarence) Malcolm 1909-1957 **TCLC 6, 40; SSC 31**
See also CA 105; 131; CANR 62; CDBLB 1945-1960; DLB 15; MTCW 1, 2
Lowry, Mina Gertrude 1882-1966
See Loy, Mina
See also CA 113
Loxsmith, John
See Brunner, John (Kilian Houston)
Loy, Mina CLC 28; DAM POET; PC 16
See also Lowry, Mina Gertrude
See also DLB 4, 54
Loyson-Bridet
See Schwob, Marcel (Mayer Andre)
Lucan 39-65 **CMLC 33**
See also DLB 211
Lucas, Craig 1951- **CLC 64**
See also CA 137; CANR 71
Lucas, E(dward) V(errall) 1868-1938 **TCLC 73**
See also CA 176; DLB 98, 149, 153; SATA 20
Lucas, George 1944- **CLC 16**
See also AAYA 1, 23; CA 77-80; CANR 30; SATA 56
Lucas, Hans
See Godard, Jean-Luc
Lucas, Victoria
See Plath, Sylvia
Lucian c. 120-c. 180 **CMLC 32**
See also DLB 176
Ludlam, Charles 1943-1987 **CLC 46, 50**
See also CA 85-88; 122; CANR 72, 86
Ludlum, Robert 1927- **CLC 22, 43; DAM NOV, POP**
See also AAYA 10; BEST 89:1, 90:3; CA 33-36R; CANR 25, 41, 68; DA3; DLBY 82; MTCW 1, 2
Ludwig, Ken CLC 60
Ludwig, Otto 1813-1865 **NCLC 4**
See also DLB 129
Lugones, Leopoldo 1874-1938 **TCLC 15; HLCS 2**
See also CA 116; 131; HW 1
Lu Hsun 1881-1936 **TCLC 3; SSC 20**
See also Shu-Jen, Chou
Lukacs, George CLC 24
See also Lukacs, Gyorgy (Szegeny von)
Lukacs, Gyorgy (Szegeny von) 1885-1971
See Lukacs, George
See also CA 101; 29-32R; CANR 62; MTCW 2
Luke, Peter (Ambrose Cyprian) 1919-1995 **CLC 38**
See also CA 81-84; 147; CANR 72; DLB 13
Lunar, Dennis
See Mungo, Raymond
Lurie, Alison 1926- **CLC 4, 5, 18, 39**
See also CA 1-4R; CANR 2, 17, 50, 88; DLB 2; MTCW 1; SATA 46, 112
Lustig, Arnost 1926- **CLC 56**
See also AAYA 3; CA 69-72; CANR 47; DLB 232; SATA 56
Luther, Martin 1483-1546 **LC 9, 37**
See also DLB 179
Luxemburg, Rosa 1870(?)-1919 **TCLC 63**
See also CA 118
Luzi, Mario 1914- **CLC 13**
See also CA 61-64; CANR 9, 70; DLB 128
Lyly, John 1554(?)-1606 **LC 41; DAM DRAM; DC 7**
See also DLB 62, 167
L'Ymagier
See Gourmont, Remy (-Marie-Charles) de
Lynch, B. Suarez
See Bioy Casares, Adolfo; Borges, Jorge Luis
Lynch, B. Suarez
See Bioy Casares, Adolfo
Lynch, David (K.) 1946- **CLC 66**
See also CA 124; 129
Lynch, James
See Andreyev, Leonid (Nikolaevich)
Lynch Davis, B.
See Bioy Casares, Adolfo; Borges, Jorge Luis
Lyndsay, Sir David 1490-1555 **LC 20**
Lynn, Kenneth S(chuyler) 1923- **CLC 50**
See also CA 1-4R; CANR 3, 27, 65
Lynx
See West, Rebecca
Lyons, Marcus
See Blish, James (Benjamin)
Lyre, Pinchbeck
See Sassoon, Siegfried (Lorraine)
Lytle, Andrew (Nelson) 1902-1995 **CLC 22**
See also CA 9-12R; 150; CANR 70; DLB 6; DLBY 95
Lyttelton, George 1709-1773 **LC 10**
Maas, Peter 1929- **CLC 29**
See also CA 93-96; INT 93-96; MTCW 2
Macaulay, (Emilie) Rose 1881(?)-1958 **TCLC 7, 44**
See also CA 104; DLB 36
Macaulay, Thomas Babington 1800-1859 **NCLC 42**
See also CDBLB 1832-1890; DLB 32, 55
MacBeth, George (Mann) 1932-1992 **CLC 2, 5, 9**
See also CA 25-28R; 136; CANR 61, 66; DLB 40; MTCW 1; SATA 4; SATA-Obit 70
MacCaig, Norman (Alexander) 1910- **CLC 36; DAB; DAM POET**
See also CA 9-12R; CANR 3, 34; DLB 27
MacCarthy, Sir(Charles Otto) Desmond 1877-1952 **TCLC 36**
See also CA 167
MacDiarmid, Hugh CLC 2, 4, 11, 19, 63; PC 9
See also Grieve, C(hristopher) M(urray)
See also CDBLB 1945-1960; DLB 20
MacDonald, Anson
See Heinlein, Robert A(nson)
Macdonald, Cynthia 1928- **CLC 13, 19**
See also CA 49-52; CANR 4, 44; DLB 105
MacDonald, George 1824-1905 **TCLC 9**
See also CA 106; 137; CANR 80; CLR 67; DLB 18, 163, 178; MAICYA; SATA 33, 100
Macdonald, John
See Millar, Kenneth
MacDonald, John D(ann) 1916-1986 **CLC 3, 27, 44; DAM NOV, POP**
See also CA 1-4R; 121; CANR 1, 19, 60; DLB 8; DLBY 86; MTCW 1, 2
Macdonald, John Ross
See Millar, Kenneth
Macdonald, Ross CLC 1, 2, 3, 14, 34, 41
See also Millar, Kenneth
See also DLBD 6
MacDougal, John
See Blish, James (Benjamin)
MacDougal, John
See Blish, James (Benjamin)
MacEwen, Gwendolyn (Margaret) 1941-1987 **CLC 13, 55**
See also CA 9-12R; 124; CANR 7, 22; DLB 53; SATA 50; SATA-Obit 55
Macha, Karel Hynek 1810-1846 **NCLC 46**
Machado (y Ruiz), Antonio 1875-1939 **TCLC 3**
See also CA 104; 174; DLB 108; HW 2
Machado de Assis, Joaquim Maria 1839-1908 **TCLC 10; BLC 2; HLCS 2; SSC 24**
See also CA 107; 153; CANR 91
Machen, Arthur TCLC 4; SSC 20
See also Jones, Arthur Llewellyn
See also CA 179; DLB 36, 156, 178
Machiavelli, Niccolo 1469-1527 **LC 8, 36; DA; DAB; DAC; DAM MST; WLCS**
MacInnes, Colin 1914-1976 **CLC 4, 23**
See also CA 69-72; 65-68; CANR 21; DLB 14; MTCW 1, 2
MacInnes, Helen (Clark) 1907-1985 **CLC 27, 39; DAM POP**
See also CA 1-4R; 117; CANR 1, 28, 58; DLB 87; MTCW 1, 2; SATA 22; SATA-Obit 44
Mackenzie, Compton (Edward Montague) 1883-1972 **CLC 18**
See also CA 21-22; 37-40R; CAP 2; DLB 34, 100
Mackenzie, Henry 1745-1831 **NCLC 41**
See also DLB 39
Mackintosh, Elizabeth 1896(?)-1952
See Tey, Josephine
See also CA 110
MacLaren, James
See Grieve, C(hristopher) M(urray)
Mac Laverty, Bernard 1942- **CLC 31**
See also CA 116; 118; CANR 43, 88; INT 118
MacLean, Alistair (Stuart) 1922(?)-1987 **CLC 3, 13, 50, 63; DAM POP**
See also CA 57-60; 121; CANR 28, 61; MTCW 1; SATA 23; SATA-Obit 50
Maclean, Norman (Fitzroy) 1902-1990 **CLC 78; DAM POP; SSC 13**
See also CA 102; 132; CANR 49; DLB 206
MacLeish, Archibald 1892-1982 **CLC 3, 8, 14, 68; DAM POET**
See also CA 9-12R; 106; CANR 33, 63; CDALBS; DLB 4, 7, 45; DLBY 82; MTCW 1, 2
MacLennan, (John) Hugh 1907-1990 **CLC 2, 14, 92; DAC; DAM MST**
See also CA 5-8R; 142; CANR 33; DLB 68; MTCW 1, 2
MacLeod, Alistair 1936- **CLC 56; DAC; DAM MST**
See also CA 123; DLB 60; MTCW 2
Macleod, Fiona
See Sharp, William
MacNeice, (Frederick) Louis 1907-1963 **CLC**

1, 4, 10, 53; DAB; DAM POET
See also CA 85-88; CANR 61; DLB 10, 20; MTCW 1, 2
MacNeill, Dand
See Fraser, George MacDonald
Macpherson, James 1736-1796 **LC 29**
See also Ossian
See also DLB 109
Macpherson, (Jean) Jay 1931- **CLC 14**
See also CA 5-8R; CANR 90; DLB 53
MacShane, Frank 1927-1999 **CLC 39**
See also CA 9-12R; 186; CANR 3, 33; DLB 111
Macumber, Mari
See Sandoz, Mari(e Susette)
Madach, Imre 1823-1864 **NCLC 19**
Madden, (Jerry) David 1933- **CLC 5, 15**
See also CA 1-4R; CAAS 3; CANR 4, 45; DLB 6; MTCW 1
Maddern, Al(an)
See Ellison, Harlan (Jay)
Madhubuti, Haki R. 1942- **CLC 6, 73; BLC 2; DAM MULT, POET; PC 5**
See also Lee, Don L.
See also BW 2, 3; CA 73-76; CANR 24, 51, 73; DLB 5, 41; DLBD 8; MTCW 2
Maepenn, Hugh
See Kuttner, Henry
Maepenn, K. H.
See Kuttner, Henry
Maeterlinck, Maurice 1862-1949 **TCLC 3; DAM DRAM**
See also CA 104; 136; CANR 80; DLB 192; SATA 66
Maginn, William 1794-1842 **NCLC 8**
See also DLB 110, 159
Mahapatra, Jayanta 1928- **CLC 33; DAM MULT**
See also CA 73-76; CAAS 9; CANR 15, 33, 66, 87
Mahfouz, Naguib (Abdel Aziz Al-Sabilgi) 1911(?)-
See Mahfuz, Najib
See also BEST 89:2; CA 128; CANR 55; DAM NOV; DA3; MTCW 1, 2
Mahfuz, Najib CLC 52, 55
See also Mahfouz, Naguib (Abdel Aziz Al-Sabilgi)
See also DLBY 88
Mahon, Derek 1941- **CLC 27**
See also CA 113; 128; CANR 88; DLB 40
Mailer, Norman 1923- **CLC 1, 2, 3, 4, 5, 8, 11, 14, 28, 39, 74, 111; DA; DAB; DAC; DAM MST, NOV, POP**
See also AAYA 31; AITN 2; CA 9-12R; CABS 1; CANR 28, 74, 77; CDALB 1968-1988; DA3; DLB 2, 16, 28, 185; DLBD 3; DLBY 80, 83; MTCW 1, 2
Maillet, Antonine 1929- **CLC 54, 118; DAC**
See also CA 115; 120; CANR 46, 74, 77; DLB 60; INT 120; MTCW 2
Mais, Roger 1905-1955 **TCLC 8**
See also BW 1, 3; CA 105; 124; CANR 82; DLB 125; MTCW 1
Maistre, Joseph de 1753-1821 **NCLC 37**
Maitland, Frederic 1850-1906 **TCLC 65**
Maitland, Sara (Louise) 1950- **CLC 49**
See also CA 69-72; CANR 13, 59
Major, Clarence 1936- **CLC 3, 19, 48; BLC 2; DAM MULT**
See also BW 2, 3; CA 21-24R; CAAS 6; CANR 13, 25, 53, 82; DLB 33
Major, Kevin (Gerald) 1949- **CLC 26; DAC**
See also AAYA 16; CA 97-100; CANR 21, 38; CLR 11; DLB 60; INT CANR-21; JRDA; MAICYA; SATA 32, 82
Maki, James
See Ozu, Yasujiro
Malabaila, Damiano
See Levi, Primo
Malamud, Bernard 1914-1986 **CLC 1, 2, 3, 5, 8, 9, 11, 18, 27, 44, 78, 85; DA; DAB; DAC; DAM MST, NOV, POP; SSC 15; WLC**
See also AAYA 16; CA 5-8R; 118; CABS 1; CANR 28, 62; CDALB 1941-1968; DA3; DLB 2, 28, 152; DLBY 80, 86; MTCW 1, 2
Malan, Herman
See Bosman, Herman Charles; Bosman, Herman Charles
Malaparte, Curzio 1898-1957 **TCLC 52**
Malcolm, Dan
See Silverberg, Robert
Malcolm X CLC 82, 117; BLC 2; WLCS
See also Little, Malcolm
Malherbe, Francois de 1555-1628 **LC 5**
Mallarme, Stephane 1842-1898 **NCLC 4, 41; DAM POET; PC 4**
Mallet-Joris, Francoise 1930- **CLC 11**
See also CA 65-68; CANR 17; DLB 83
Malley, Ern
See McAuley, James Phillip
Mallowan, Agatha Christie
See Christie, Agatha (Mary Clarissa)
Maloff, Saul 1922- **CLC 5**
See also CA 33-36R
Malone, Louis
See MacNeice, (Frederick) Louis
Malone, Michael (Christopher) 1942- **CLC 43**
See also CA 77-80; CANR 14, 32, 57
Malory, (Sir) Thomas 1410(?)-1471(?) **LC 11; DA; DAB; DAC; DAM MST; WLCS**
See also CDBLB Before 1660; DLB 146; SATA 59; SATA-Brief 33
Malouf, (George Joseph) David 1934- **CLC 28, 86**
See also CA 124; CANR 50, 76; MTCW 2
Malraux, (Georges-)Andre 1901-1976 **CLC 1, 4, 9, 13, 15, 57; DAM NOV**
See also CA 21-22; 69-72; CANR 34, 58; CAP 2; DA3; DLB 72; MTCW 1, 2
Malzberg, Barry N(athaniel) 1939- **CLC 7**
See also CA 61-64; CAAS 4; CANR 16; DLB 8
Mamet, David (Alan) 1947- **CLC 9, 15, 34, 46, 91; DAM DRAM; DC 4**
See also AAYA 3; CA 81-84; CABS 3; CANR 15, 41, 67, 72; DA3; DLB 7; MTCW 1, 2
Mamoulian, Rouben (Zachary) 1897-1987 **CLC 16**
See also CA 25-28R; 124; CANR 85
Mandelstam, Osip (Emilievich) 1891(?)-1938(?) **TCLC 2, 6; PC 14**
See also CA 104; 150; MTCW 2
Mander, (Mary) Jane 1877-1949 **TCLC 31**
See also CA 162
Mandeville, John fl. 1350- **CMLC 19**
See also DLB 146
Mandiargues, Andre Pieyre de CLC 41
See also Pieyre de Mandiargues, Andre
See also DLB 83
Mandrake, Ethel Belle
See Thurman, Wallace (Henry)
Mangan, James Clarence 1803-1849 **NCLC 27**
Maniere, J.-E.
See Giraudoux, (Hippolyte) Jean
Mankiewicz, Herman (Jacob) 1897-1953 **TCLC 85**
See also CA 120; 169; DLB 26
Manley, (Mary) Delariviere 1672(?)-1724 **LC 1, 42**
See also DLB 39, 80
Mann, Abel
See Creasey, John
Mann, Emily 1952- **DC 7**
See also CA 130; CANR 55
Mann, (Luiz) Heinrich 1871-1950 **TCLC 9**
See also CA 106; 164, 181; DLB 66, 118
Mann, (Paul) Thomas 1875-1955 **TCLC 2, 8, 14, 21, 35, 44, 60; DA; DAB; DAC; DAM MST, NOV; SSC 5; WLC**
See also CA 104; 128; DA3; DLB 66; MTCW 1, 2
Mannheim, Karl 1893-1947 **TCLC 65**
Manning, David
See Faust, Frederick (Schiller)
Manning, Frederic 1887(?)-1935 **TCLC 25**
See also CA 124
Manning, Olivia 1915-1980 **CLC 5, 19**
See also CA 5-8R; 101; CANR 29; MTCW 1
Mano, D. Keith 1942- **CLC 2, 10**
See also CA 25-28R; CAAS 6; CANR 26, 57; DLB 6
Mansfield, Katherine -1923 **TCLC 2, 8, 39; DAB; SSC 9, 23, 38; WLC**
See also Beauchamp, Kathleen Mansfield
See also DLB 162
Manso, Peter 1940- **CLC 39**
See also CA 29-32R; CANR 44
Mantecon, Juan Jimenez
See Jimenez (Mantecon), Juan Ramon
Manton, Peter
See Creasey, John
Man Without a Spleen, A
See Chekhov, Anton (Pavlovich)
Manzoni, Alessandro 1785-1873 **NCLC 29**
Map, Walter 1140-1209 **CMLC 32**
Mapu, Abraham (ben Jekutiel) 1808-1867 **NCLC 18**
Mara, Sally
See Queneau, Raymond
Marat, Jean Paul 1743-1793 **LC 10**
Marcel, Gabriel Honore 1889-1973 **CLC 15**
See also CA 102; 45-48; MTCW 1, 2
March, William 1893-1954 **TCLC 96**
Marchbanks, Samuel
See Davies, (William) Robertson
Marchi, Giacomo
See Bassani, Giorgio
Margulies, Donald CLC 76
See also DLB 228
Marie de France c. 12th cent. - **CMLC 8; PC 22**
See also DLB 208
Marie de l'Incarnation 1599-1672 **LC 10**
Marier, Captain Victor
See Griffith, D(avid Lewelyn) W(ark)
Mariner, Scott
See Pohl, Frederik
Marinetti, Filippo Tommaso 1876-1944 **TCLC 10**
See also CA 107; DLB 114
Marivaux, Pierre Carlet de Chamblain de 1688-1763 **LC 4; DC 7**
Markandaya, Kamala CLC 8, 38
See also Taylor, Kamala (Purnaiya)
Markfield, Wallace 1926- **CLC 8**
See also CA 69-72; CAAS 3; DLB 2, 28
Markham, Edwin 1852-1940 **TCLC 47**
See also CA 160; DLB 54, 186
Markham, Robert
See Amis, Kingsley (William)
Marks, J
See Highwater, Jamake (Mamake)
Marks-Highwater, J
See Highwater, Jamake (Mamake)
Markson, David M(errill) 1927- **CLC 67**
See also CA 49-52; CANR 1, 91

Marley, Bob CLC 17
See also Marley, Robert Nesta
Marley, Robert Nesta 1945-1981
See Marley, Bob
See also CA 107; 103
Marlowe, Christopher 1564-1593 **LC 22, 47; DA; DAB; DAC; DAM DRAM, MST; DC 1; WLC**
See also CDBLB Before 1660; DA3; DLB 62
Marlowe, Stephen 1928-
See Queen, Ellery
See also CA 13-16R; CANR 6, 55
Marmontel, Jean-Francois 1723-1799 **LC 2**
Marquand, John P(hillips) 1893-1960 **CLC 2, 10**
See also CA 85-88; CANR 73; DLB 9, 102; MTCW 2
Marques, Rene 1919-1979 **CLC 96; DAM MULT; HLC 2**
See also CA 97-100; 85-88; CANR 78; DLB 113; HW 1, 2
Marquez, Gabriel (Jose) Garcia
See Garcia Marquez, Gabriel (Jose)
Marquis, Don(ald Robert Perry) 1878-1937 **TCLC 7**
See also CA 104; 166; DLB 11, 25
Marric, J. J.
See Creasey, John
Marryat, Frederick 1792-1848 **NCLC 3**
See also DLB 21, 163
Marsden, James
See Creasey, John
Marsh, Edward 1872-1953 **TCLC 99**
Marsh, (Edith) Ngaio 1899-1982 **CLC 7, 53; DAM POP**
See also CA 9-12R; CANR 6, 58; DLB 77; MTCW 1, 2
Marshall, Garry 1934- **CLC 17**
See also AAYA 3; CA 111; SATA 60
Marshall, Paule 1929- **CLC 27, 72; BLC 3; DAM MULT; SSC 3**
See also BW 2, 3; CA 77-80; CANR 25, 73; DA3; DLB 33, 157, 227; MTCW 1, 2
Marshallik
See Zangwill, Israel
Marsten, Richard
See Hunter, Evan
Marston, John 1576-1634 **LC 33; DAM DRAM**
See also DLB 58, 172
Martha, Henry
See Harris, Mark
Marti (y Perez), Jose (Julian) 1853-1895 **NCLC 63; DAM MULT; HLC 2**
See also HW 2
Martial c. 40-c. 104 **CMLC 35; PC 10**
See also DLB 211
Martin, Ken
See Hubbard, L(afayette) Ron(ald)
Martin, Richard
See Creasey, John
Martin, Steve 1945- **CLC 30**
See also CA 97-100; CANR 30; MTCW 1
Martin, Valerie 1948- **CLC 89**
See also BEST 90:2; CA 85-88; CANR 49, 89
Martin, Violet Florence 1862-1915 **TCLC 51**
Martin, Webber
See Silverberg, Robert
Martindale, Patrick Victor
See White, Patrick (Victor Martindale)
Martin du Gard, Roger 1881-1958 **TCLC 24**
See also CA 118; DLB 65
Martineau, Harriet 1802-1876 **NCLC 26**
See also DLB 21, 55, 159, 163, 166, 190; YABC 2
Martines, Julia
See O'Faolain, Julia
Martinez, Enrique Gonzalez
See Gonzalez Martinez, Enrique
Martinez, Jacinto Benavente y
See Benavente (y Martinez), Jacinto
Martinez Ruiz, Jose 1873-1967
See Azorin; Ruiz, Jose Martinez
See also CA 93-96; HW 1
Martinez Sierra, Gregorio 1881-1947 **TCLC 6**
See also CA 115
Martinez Sierra, Maria (de la O'LeJarraga) 1874-1974 **TCLC 6**
See also CA 115
Martinsen, Martin
See Follett, Ken(neth Martin)
Martinson, Harry (Edmund) 1904-1978 **CLC 14**
See also CA 77-80; CANR 34
Marut, Ret
See Traven, B.
Marut, Robert
See Traven, B.
Marvell, Andrew 1621-1678 **LC 4, 43; DA; DAB; DAC; DAM MST, POET; PC 10; WLC**
See also CDBLB 1660-1789; DLB 131
Marx, Karl (Heinrich) 1818-1883 **NCLC 17**
See also DLB 129
Masaoka Shiki TCLC 18
See also Masaoka Tsunenori
Masaoka Tsunenori 1867-1902
See Masaoka Shiki
See also CA 117
Masefield, John (Edward) 1878-1967 **CLC 11, 47; DAM POET**
See also CA 19-20; 25-28R; CANR 33; CAP 2; CDBLB 1890-1914; DLB 10, 19, 153, 160; MTCW 1, 2; SATA 19
Maso, Carole 19(?)- **CLC 44**
See also CA 170
Mason, Bobbie Ann 1940- **CLC 28, 43, 82; SSC 4**
See also AAYA 5; CA 53-56; CANR 11, 31, 58, 83; CDALBS; DA3; DLB 173; DLBY 87; INT CANR-31; MTCW 1, 2
Mason, Ernst
See Pohl, Frederik
Mason, Lee W.
See Malzberg, Barry N(athaniel)
Mason, Nick 1945- **CLC 35**
Mason, Tally
See Derleth, August (William)
Mass, William
See Gibson, William
Master Lao
See Lao Tzu
Masters, Edgar Lee 1868-1950 **TCLC 2, 25; DA; DAC; DAM MST, POET; PC 1; WLCS**
See also CA 104; 133; CDALB 1865-1917; DLB 54; MTCW 1, 2
Masters, Hilary 1928- **CLC 48**
See also CA 25-28R; CANR 13, 47
Mastrosimone, William 19(?)- **CLC 36**
See also CA 186
Mathe, Albert
See Camus, Albert
Mather, Cotton 1663-1728 **LC 38**
See also CDALB 1640-1865; DLB 24, 30, 140
Mather, Increase 1639-1723 **LC 38**
See also DLB 24
Matheson, Richard Burton 1926- **CLC 37**
See also AAYA 31; CA 97-100; CANR 88; DLB 8, 44; INT 97-100
Mathews, Harry 1930- **CLC 6, 52**
See also CA 21-24R; CAAS 6; CANR 18, 40
Mathews, John Joseph 1894-1979 **CLC 84; DAM MULT**
See also CA 19-20; 142; CANR 45; CAP 2; DLB 175; NNAL
Mathias, Roland (Glyn) 1915- **CLC 45**
See also CA 97-100; CANR 19, 41; DLB 27
Matsuo Basho 1644-1694 **LC 62; DAM POET; PC 3**
Mattheson, Rodney
See Creasey, John
Matthews, (James) Brander 1852-1929 **TCLC 95**
See also DLB 71, 78; DLBD 13
Matthews, Greg 1949- **CLC 45**
See also CA 135
Matthews, William (Procter, III) 1942-1997 **CLC 40**
See also CA 29-32R; 162; CAAS 18; CANR 12, 57; DLB 5
Matthias, John (Edward) 1941- **CLC 9**
See also CA 33-36R; CANR 56
Matthiessen, F(rancis) O(tto) 1902-1950 **TCLC 100**
See also CA 185; DLB 63
Matthiessen, Peter 1927- **CLC 5, 7, 11, 32, 64; DAM NOV**
See also AAYA 6; BEST 90:4; CA 9-12R; CANR 21, 50, 73; DA3; DLB 6, 173; MTCW 1, 2; SATA 27
Maturin, Charles Robert 1780(?)-1824 **NCLC 6**
See also DLB 178
Matute (Ausejo), Ana Maria 1925- **CLC 11**
See also CA 89-92; MTCW 1
Maugham, W. S.
See Maugham, W(illiam) Somerset
Maugham, W(illiam) Somerset 1874-1965 **CLC 1, 11, 15, 67, 93; DA; DAB; DAC; DAM DRAM, MST, NOV; SSC 8; WLC**
See also CA 5-8R; 25-28R; CANR 40; CDBLB 1914-1945; DA3; DLB 10, 36, 77, 100, 162, 195; MTCW 1, 2; SATA 54
Maugham, William Somerset
See Maugham, W(illiam) Somerset
Maupassant, (Henri Rene Albert) Guy de 1850-1893 **NCLC 1, 42, 83; DA; DAB; DAC; DAM MST; SSC 1; WLC**
See also DA3; DLB 123
Maupin, Armistead 1944- **CLC 95; DAM POP**
See also CA 125; 130; CANR 58; DA3; INT 130; MTCW 2
Maurhut, Richard
See Traven, B.
Mauriac, Claude 1914-1996 **CLC 9**
See also CA 89-92; 152; DLB 83
Mauriac, Francois (Charles) 1885-1970 **CLC 4, 9, 56; SSC 24**
See also CA 25-28; CAP 2; DLB 65; MTCW 1, 2
Mavor, Osborne Henry 1888-1951
See Bridie, James
See also CA 104
Maxwell, William (Keepers, Jr.) 1908- **CLC 19**
See also CA 93-96; CANR 54; DLBY 80; INT 93-96
May, Elaine 1932- **CLC 16**
See also CA 124; 142; DLB 44
Mayakovski, Vladimir (Vladimirovich) 1893-1930 **TCLC 4, 18**
See also CA 104; 158; MTCW 2
Mayhew, Henry 1812-1887 **NCLC 31**
See also DLB 18, 55, 190
Mayle, Peter 1939(?)- **CLC 89**
See also CA 139; CANR 64

See also AAYA 25; CDALB 1640-1865; DA3; DLB 3, 74; SATA 59
Menander c. 342B.C.-c. 292B.C. **CMLC 9; DAM DRAM; DC 3**
See also DLB 176
Menchu, Rigoberta 1959-
See also HLCS 2
Menchu, Rigoberta 1959-
See also CA 175; HLCS 2
Mencken, H(enry) L(ouis) 1880-1956 **TCLC 13**
See also CA 105; 125; CDALB 1917-1929; DLB 11, 29, 63, 137, 222; MTCW 1, 2
Mendelsohn, Jane 1965- **CLC 99**
See also CA 154
Mercer, David 1928-1980 **CLC 5; DAM DRAM**
See also CA 9-12R; 102; CANR 23; DLB 13; MTCW 1
Merchant, Paul
See Ellison, Harlan (Jay)
Meredith, George 1828-1909 **TCLC 17, 43; DAM POET**
See also CA 117; 153; CANR 80; CDBLB 1832-1890; DLB 18, 35, 57, 159
Meredith, William (Morris) 1919- **CLC 4, 13, 22, 55; DAM POET; PC 28**
See also CA 9-12R; CAAS 14; CANR 6, 40; DLB 5
Merezhkovsky, Dmitry Sergeyevich 1865-1941 **TCLC 29**
See also CA 169
Merimee, Prosper 1803-1870 **NCLC 6, 65; SSC 7**
See also DLB 119, 192
Merkin, Daphne 1954- **CLC 44**
See also CA 123
Merlin, Arthur
See Blish, James (Benjamin)
Merrill, James (Ingram) 1926-1995 **CLC 2, 3, 6, 8, 13, 18, 34, 91; DAM POET; PC 28**
See also CA 13-16R; 147; CANR 10, 49, 63; DA3; DLB 5, 165; DLBY 85; INT CANR-10; MTCW 1, 2
Merriman, Alex
See Silverberg, Robert
Merriman, Brian 1747-1805 **NCLC 70**
Merritt, E. B.
See Waddington, Miriam
Merton, Thomas 1915-1968 **CLC 1, 3, 11, 34, 83; PC 10**
See also CA 5-8R; 25-28R; CANR 22, 53; DA3; DLB 48; DLBY 81; MTCW 1, 2
Merwin, W(illiam) S(tanley) 1927- **CLC 1, 2, 3, 5, 8, 13, 18, 45, 88; DAM POET**
See also CA 13-16R; CANR 15, 51; DA3; DLB 5, 169; INT CANR-15; MTCW 1, 2
Metcalf, John 1938- **CLC 37**
See also CA 113; DLB 60
Metcalf, Suzanne
See Baum, L(yman) Frank
Mew, Charlotte (Mary) 1870-1928 **TCLC 8**
See also CA 105; DLB 19, 135
Mewshaw, Michael 1943- **CLC 9**
See also CA 53-56; CANR 7, 47; DLBY 80
Meyer, Conrad Ferdinand 1825-1905 **NCLC 81**
See also DLB 129
Meyer, June
See Jordan, June
Meyer, Lynn
See Slavitt, David R(ytman)
Meyer-Meyrink, Gustav 1868-1932
See Meyrink, Gustav
See also CA 117
Meyers, Jeffrey 1939- **CLC 39**
See also CA 73-76; CAAE 186; CANR 54; DLB 111
Meynell, Alice (Christina Gertrude Thompson) 1847-1922 **TCLC 6**
See also CA 104; 177; DLB 19, 98
Meyrink, Gustav TCLC 21
See also Meyer-Meyrink, Gustav
See also DLB 81
Michaels, Leonard 1933- **CLC 6, 25; SSC 16**
See also CA 61-64; CANR 21, 62; DLB 130; MTCW 1
Michaux, Henri 1899-1984 **CLC 8, 19**
See also CA 85-88; 114
Micheaux, Oscar (Devereaux) 1884-1951 **TCLC 76**
See also BW 3; CA 174; DLB 50
Michelangelo 1475-1564 **LC 12**
Michelet, Jules 1798-1874 **NCLC 31**
Michels, Robert 1876-1936 **TCLC 88**
Michener, James A(lbert) 1907(?)-1997 **CLC 1, 5, 11, 29, 60, 109; DAM NOV, POP**
See also AAYA 27; AITN 1; BEST 90:1; CA 5-8R; 161; CANR 21, 45, 68; DA3; DLB 6; MTCW 1, 2
Mickiewicz, Adam 1798-1855 **NCLC 3**
Middleton, Christopher 1926- **CLC 13**
See also CA 13-16R; CANR 29, 54; DLB 40
Middleton, Richard (Barham) 1882-1911 **TCLC 56**
See also CA 187; DLB 156
Middleton, Stanley 1919- **CLC 7, 38**
See also CA 25-28R; CAAS 23; CANR 21, 46, 81; DLB 14
Middleton, Thomas 1580-1627 **LC 33; DAM DRAM, MST; DC 5**
See also DLB 58
Migueis, Jose Rodrigues 1901- **CLC 10**
Mikszath, Kalman 1847-1910 **TCLC 31**
See also CA 170
Miles, Jack CLC 100
Miles, Josephine (Louise) 1911-1985 **CLC 1, 2, 14, 34, 39; DAM POET**
See also CA 1-4R; 116; CANR 2, 55; DLB 48
Militant
See Sandburg, Carl (August)
Mill, John Stuart 1806-1873 **NCLC 11, 58**
See also CDBLB 1832-1890; DLB 55, 190
Millar, Kenneth 1915-1983 **CLC 14; DAM POP**
See also Macdonald, Ross
See also CA 9-12R; 110; CANR 16, 63; DA3; DLB 2, 226; DLBD 6; DLBY 83; MTCW 1, 2
Millay, E. Vincent
See Millay, Edna St. Vincent
Millay, Edna St. Vincent 1892-1950 **TCLC 4, 49; DA; DAB; DAC; DAM MST, POET; PC 6; WLCS**
See also CA 104; 130; CDALB 1917-1929; DA3; DLB 45; MTCW 1, 2
Miller, Arthur 1915- **CLC 1, 2, 6, 10, 15, 26, 47, 78; DA; DAB; DAC; DAM DRAM, MST; DC 1; WLC**
See also AAYA 15; AITN 1; CA 1-4R; CABS 3; CANR 2, 30, 54, 76; CDALB 1941-1968; DA3; DLB 7; MTCW 1, 2
Miller, Henry (Valentine) 1891-1980 **CLC 1, 2, 4, 9, 14, 43, 84; DA; DAB; DAC; DAM MST, NOV; WLC**
See also CA 9-12R; 97-100; CANR 33, 64; CDALB 1929-1941; DA3; DLB 4, 9; DLBY 80; MTCW 1, 2
Miller, Jason 1939(?)- **CLC 2**
See also AITN 1; CA 73-76; DLB 7
Miller, Sue 1943- **CLC 44; DAM POP**
See also BEST 90:3; CA 139; CANR 59, 91; DA3; DLB 143
Miller, Walter M(ichael, Jr.) 1923- **CLC 4, 30**
See also CA 85-88; DLB 8
Millett, Kate 1934- **CLC 67**
See also AITN 1; CA 73-76; CANR 32, 53, 76; DA3; MTCW 1, 2
Millhauser, Steven (Lewis) 1943- **CLC 21, 54, 109**
See also CA 110; 111; CANR 63; DA3; DLB 2; INT 111; MTCW 2
Millin, Sarah Gertrude 1889-1968 **CLC 49**
See also CA 102; 93-96; DLB 225
Milne, A(lan) A(lexander) 1882-1956 **TCLC 6, 88; DAB; DAC; DAM MST**
See also CA 104; 133; CLR 1, 26; DA3; DLB 10, 77, 100, 160; MAICYA; MTCW 1, 2; SATA 100; YABC 1
Milner, Ron(ald) 1938- **CLC 56; BLC 3; DAM MULT**
See also AITN 1; BW 1; CA 73-76; CANR 24, 81; DLB 38; MTCW 1
Milnes, Richard Monckton 1809-1885 **NCLC 61**
See also DLB 32, 184
Milosz, Czeslaw 1911- **CLC 5, 11, 22, 31, 56, 82; DAM MST, POET; PC 8; WLCS**
See also CA 81-84; CANR 23, 51, 91; DA3; MTCW 1, 2
Milton, John 1608-1674 **LC 9, 43; DA; DAB; DAC; DAM MST, POET; PC 19, 29; WLC**
See also CDBLB 1660-1789; DA3; DLB 131, 151
Min, Anchee 1957- **CLC 86**
See also CA 146
Minehaha, Cornelius
See Wedekind, (Benjamin) Frank(lin)
Miner, Valerie 1947- **CLC 40**
See also CA 97-100; CANR 59
Minimo, Duca
See D'Annunzio, Gabriele
Minot, Susan 1956- **CLC 44**
See also CA 134
Minus, Ed 1938- **CLC 39**
See also CA 185
Miranda, Javier
See Bioy Casares, Adolfo
Miranda, Javier
See Bioy Casares, Adolfo
Mirbeau, Octave 1848-1917 **TCLC 55**
See also DLB 123, 192
Miro (Ferrer), Gabriel (Francisco Victor) 1879-1930 **TCLC 5**
See also CA 104; 185
Mishima, Yukio 1925-1970 **CLC 2, 4, 6, 9, 27; DC 1; SSC 4**
See also Hiraoka, Kimitake
See also DLB 182; MTCW 2
Mistral, Frederic 1830-1914 **TCLC 51**
See also CA 122
Mistral, Gabriela
See Godoy Alcayaga, Lucila
Mistry, Rohinton 1952- **CLC 71; DAC**
See also CA 141; CANR 86
Mitchell, Clyde
See Ellison, Harlan (Jay); Silverberg, Robert
Mitchell, James Leslie 1901-1935
See Gibbon, Lewis Grassic
See also CA 104; DLB 15
Mitchell, Joni 1943- **CLC 12**
See also CA 112
Mitchell, Joseph (Quincy) 1908-1996 **CLC 98**
See also CA 77-80; 152; CANR 69; DLB 185; DLBY 96
Mitchell, Margaret (Munnerlyn) 1900-1949 **TCLC 11; DAM NOV, POP**
See also AAYA 23; CA 109; 125; CANR 55; CDALBS; DA3; DLB 9; MTCW 1, 2
Mitchell, Peggy
See Mitchell, Margaret (Munnerlyn)
Mitchell, S(ilas) Weir 1829-1914 **TCLC 36**

See also CA 165; DLB 202
Mitchell, W(illiam) O(rmond) 1914-1998 **CLC 25; DAC; DAM MST**
See also CA 77-80; 165; CANR 15, 43; DLB 88
Mitchell, William 1879-1936 **TCLC 81**
Mitford, Mary Russell 1787-1855 **NCLC 4**
See also DLB 110, 116
Mitford, Nancy 1904-1973 **CLC 44**
See also CA 9-12R; DLB 191
Miyamoto, (Chujo) Yuriko 1899-1951 **TCLC 37**
See also CA 170, 174; DLB 180
Miyazawa, Kenji 1896-1933 **TCLC 76**
See also CA 157
Mizoguchi, Kenji 1898-1956 **TCLC 72**
See also CA 167
Mo, Timothy (Peter) 1950(?)- **CLC 46, 134**
See also CA 117; DLB 194; MTCW 1
Modarressi, Taghi (M.) 1931- **CLC 44**
See also CA 121; 134; INT 134
Modiano, Patrick (Jean) 1945- **CLC 18**
See also CA 85-88; CANR 17, 40; DLB 83
Moerck, Paal
See Roelvaag, O(le) E(dvart)
Mofolo, Thomas (Mokopu) 1875(?)-1948 **TCLC 22; BLC 3; DAM MULT**
See also CA 121; 153; CANR 83; DLB 225; MTCW 2
Mohr, Nicholasa 1938- **CLC 12; DAM MULT; HLC 2**
See also AAYA 8; CA 49-52; CANR 1, 32, 64; CLR 22; DLB 145; HW 1, 2; JRDA; SAAS 8; SATA 8, 97; SATA-Essay 113
Mojtabai, A(nn) G(race) 1938- **CLC 5, 9, 15, 29**
See also CA 85-88; CANR 88
Moliere 1622-1673 **LC 10, 28; DA; DAB; DAC; DAM DRAM, MST; DC 13; WLC**
See also DA3
Molin, Charles
See Mayne, William (James Carter)
Molnar, Ferenc 1878-1952 **TCLC 20; DAM DRAM**
See also CA 109; 153; CANR 83
Momaday, N(avarre) Scott 1934- **CLC 2, 19, 85, 95; DA; DAB; DAC; DAM MST, MULT, NOV, POP; PC 25; WLCS**
See also AAYA 11; CA 25-28R; CANR 14, 34, 68; CDALBS; DA3; DLB 143, 175; INT CANR-14; MTCW 1, 2; NNAL; SATA 48; SATA-Brief 30
Monette, Paul 1945-1995 **CLC 82**
See also CA 139; 147
Monroe, Harriet 1860-1936 **TCLC 12**
See also CA 109; DLB 54, 91
Monroe, Lyle
See Heinlein, Robert A(nson)
Montagu, Elizabeth 1720-1800 **NCLC 7**
Montagu, Elizabeth 1917- **NCLC 7**
See also CA 9-12R
Montagu, Mary (Pierrepont) Wortley 1689-1762 **LC 9, 57; PC 16**
See also DLB 95, 101
Montagu, W. H.
See Coleridge, Samuel Taylor
Montague, John (Patrick) 1929- **CLC 13, 46**
See also CA 9-12R; CANR 9, 69; DLB 40; MTCW 1
Montaigne, Michel (Eyquem) de 1533-1592 **LC 8; DA; DAB; DAC; DAM MST; WLC**
Montale, Eugenio 1896-1981 **CLC 7, 9, 18; PC 13**
See also CA 17-20R; 104; CANR 30; DLB 114; MTCW 1
Montesquieu, Charles-Louis de Secondat 1689-1755 **LC 7**
Montgomery, (Robert) Bruce 1921(?)-1978
See Crispin, Edmund
See also CA 179; 104
Montgomery, L(ucy) M(aud) 1874-1942 **TCLC 51; DAC; DAM MST**
See also AAYA 12; CA 108; 137; CLR 8; DA3; DLB 92; DLBD 14; JRDA; MAICYA; MTCW 2; SATA 100; YABC 1
Montgomery, Marion H., Jr. 1925- **CLC 7**
See also AITN 1; CA 1-4R; CANR 3, 48; DLB 6
Montgomery, Max
See Davenport, Guy (Mattison, Jr.)
Montherlant, Henry (Milon) de 1896-1972 **CLC 8, 19; DAM DRAM**
See also CA 85-88; 37-40R; DLB 72; MTCW 1
Monty Python
See Chapman, Graham; Cleese, John (Marwood); Gilliam, Terry (Vance); Idle, Eric; Jones, Terence Graham Parry; Palin, Michael (Edward)
See also AAYA 7
Moodie, Susanna (Strickland) 1803-1885 **NCLC 14**
See also DLB 99
Mooney, Edward 1951-
See Mooney, Ted
See also CA 130
Mooney, Ted CLC 25
See also Mooney, Edward
Moorcock, Michael (John) 1939- **CLC 5, 27, 58**
See also Bradbury, Edward P.
See also AAYA 26; CA 45-48; CAAS 5; CANR 2, 17, 38, 64; DLB 14, 231; MTCW 1, 2; SATA 93
Moore, Brian 1921-1999 **CLC 1, 3, 5, 7, 8, 19, 32, 90; DAB; DAC; DAM MST**
See also CA 1-4R; 174; CANR 1, 25, 42, 63; MTCW 1, 2
Moore, Edward
See Muir, Edwin
Moore, G. E. 1873-1958 **TCLC 89**
Moore, George Augustus 1852-1933 **TCLC 7; SSC 19**
See also CA 104; 177; DLB 10, 18, 57, 135
Moore, Lorrie CLC 39, 45, 68
See also Moore, Marie Lorena
Moore, Marianne (Craig) 1887-1972 **CLC 1, 2, 4, 8, 10, 13, 19, 47; DA; DAB; DAC; DAM MST, POET; PC 4; WLCS**
See also CA 1-4R; 33-36R; CANR 3, 61; CDALB 1929-1941; DA3; DLB 45; DLBD 7; MTCW 1, 2; SATA 20
Moore, Marie Lorena 1957-
See Moore, Lorrie
See also CA 116; CANR 39, 83
Moore, Thomas 1779-1852 **NCLC 6**
See also DLB 96, 144
Moorhouse, Frank 1938- **SSC 40**
See also CA 118; CANR 92
Mora, Pat(ricia) 1942-
See also CA 129; CANR 57, 81; CLR 58; DAM MULT; DLB 209; HLC 2; HW 1, 2; SATA 92
Moraga, Cherrie 1952- **CLC 126; DAM MULT**
See also CA 131; CANR 66; DLB 82; HW 1, 2
Morand, Paul 1888-1976 **CLC 41; SSC 22**
See also CA 184; 69-72; DLB 65
Morante, Elsa 1918-1985 **CLC 8, 47**
See also CA 85-88; 117; CANR 35; DLB 177; MTCW 1, 2
Moravia, Alberto 1907-1990 **CLC 2, 7, 11, 27, 46; SSC 26**
See also Pincherle, Alberto
See also DLB 177; MTCW 2
More, Hannah 1745-1833 **NCLC 27**
See also DLB 107, 109, 116, 158
More, Henry 1614-1687 **LC 9**
See also DLB 126
More, Sir Thomas 1478-1535 **LC 10, 32**
Moreas, Jean TCLC 18
See also Papadiamantopoulos, Johannes
Morgan, Berry 1919- **CLC 6**
See also CA 49-52; DLB 6
Morgan, Claire
See Highsmith, (Mary) Patricia
Morgan, Edwin (George) 1920- **CLC 31**
See also CA 5-8R; CANR 3, 43, 90; DLB 27
Morgan, (George) Frederick 1922- **CLC 23**
See also CA 17-20R; CANR 21
Morgan, Harriet
See Mencken, H(enry) L(ouis)
Morgan, Jane
See Cooper, James Fenimore
Morgan, Janet 1945- **CLC 39**
See also CA 65-68
Morgan, Lady 1776(?)-1859 **NCLC 29**
See also DLB 116, 158
Morgan, Robin (Evonne) 1941- **CLC 2**
See also CA 69-72; CANR 29, 68; MTCW 1; SATA 80
Morgan, Scott
See Kuttner, Henry
Morgan, Seth 1949(?)-1990 **CLC 65**
See also CA 185; 132
Morgenstern, Christian 1871-1914 **TCLC 8**
See also CA 105
Morgenstern, S.
See Goldman, William (W.)
Moricz, Zsigmond 1879-1942 **TCLC 33**
See also CA 165
Morike, Eduard (Friedrich) 1804-1875 **NCLC 10**
See also DLB 133
Moritz, Karl Philipp 1756-1793 **LC 2**
See also DLB 94
Morland, Peter Henry
See Faust, Frederick (Schiller)
Morley, Christopher (Darlington) 1890-1957 **TCLC 87**
See also CA 112; DLB 9
Morren, Theophil
See Hofmannsthal, Hugo von
Morris, Bill 1952- **CLC 76**
Morris, Julian
See West, Morris L(anglo)
Morris, Steveland Judkins 1950(?)-
See Wonder, Stevie
See also CA 111
Morris, William 1834-1896 **NCLC 4**
See also CDBLB 1832-1890; DLB 18, 35, 57, 156, 178, 184
Morris, Wright 1910-1998 **CLC 1, 3, 7, 18, 37**
See also CA 9-12R; 167; CANR 21, 81; DLB 2, 206; DLBY 81; MTCW 1, 2
Morrison, Arthur 1863-1945 **TCLC 72; SSC 40**
See also CA 120; 157; DLB 70, 135, 197
Morrison, Chloe Anthony Wofford
See Morrison, Toni
Morrison, James Douglas 1943-1971
See Morrison, Jim
See also CA 73-76; CANR 40
Morrison, Jim CLC 17
See also Morrison, James Douglas
Morrison, Toni 1931- **CLC 4, 10, 22, 55, 81, 87; BLC 3; DA; DAB; DAC; DAM MST, MULT, NOV, POP**

See also AAYA 1, 22; BW 2, 3; CA 29-32R; CANR 27, 42, 67; CDALB 1968-1988; DA3; DLB 6, 33, 143; DLBY 81; MTCW 1, 2; SATA 57
Morrison, Van 1945- **CLC 21**
See also CA 116; 168
Morrissy, Mary 1958- **CLC 99**
Mortimer, John (Clifford) 1923- **CLC 28, 43; DAM DRAM, POP**
See also CA 13-16R; CANR 21, 69; CDBLB 1960 to Present; DA3; DLB 13; INT CANR-21; MTCW 1, 2
Mortimer, Penelope (Ruth) 1918-1999 **CLC 5**
See also CA 57-60; 187; CANR 45, 88
Morton, Anthony
See Creasey, John
Mosca, Gaetano 1858-1941 **TCLC 75**
Mosher, Howard Frank 1943- **CLC 62**
See also CA 139; CANR 65
Mosley, Nicholas 1923- **CLC 43, 70**
See also CA 69-72; CANR 41, 60; DLB 14, 207
Mosley, Walter 1952- **CLC 97; BLCS; DAM MULT, POP**
See also AAYA 17; BW 2; CA 142; CANR 57, 92; DA3; MTCW 2
Moss, Howard 1922-1987 **CLC 7, 14, 45, 50; DAM POET**
See also CA 1-4R; 123; CANR 1, 44; DLB 5
Mossgiel, Rab
See Burns, Robert
Motion, Andrew (Peter) 1952- **CLC 47**
See also CA 146; CANR 90; DLB 40
Motley, Willard (Francis) 1909-1965 **CLC 18**
See also BW 1; CA 117; 106; CANR 88; DLB 76, 143
Motoori, Norinaga 1730-1801 **NCLC 45**
Mott, Michael (Charles Alston) 1930- **CLC 15, 34**
See also CA 5-8R; CAAS 7; CANR 7, 29
Mountain Wolf Woman 1884-1960 **CLC 92**
See also CA 144; CANR 90; NNAL
Moure, Erin 1955- **CLC 88**
See also CA 113; DLB 60
Mowat, Farley (McGill) 1921- **CLC 26; DAC; DAM MST**
See also AAYA 1; CA 1-4R; CANR 4, 24, 42, 68; CLR 20; DLB 68; INT CANR-24; JRDA; MAICYA; MTCW 1, 2; SATA 3, 55
Mowatt, Anna Cora 1819-1870 **NCLC 74**
Moyers, Bill 1934- **CLC 74**
See also AITN 2; CA 61-64; CANR 31, 52
Mphahlele, Es'kia
See Mphahlele, Ezekiel
See also DLB 125, 225
Mphahlele, Ezekiel 1919- **CLC 25, 133; BLC 3; DAM MULT**
See also Mphahlele, Es'kia
See also BW 2, 3; CA 81-84; CANR 26, 76; DA3; DLB 225; MTCW 2; SATA 119
Mqhayi, S(amuel) E(dward) K(rune Loliwe) 1875-1945 **TCLC 25; BLC 3; DAM MULT**
See also CA 153; CANR 87
Mrozek, Slawomir 1930- **CLC 3, 13**
See also CA 13-16R; CAAS 10; CANR 29; DLB 232; MTCW 1
Mrs. Belloc-Lowndes
See Lowndes, Marie Adelaide (Belloc)
Mtwa, Percy (?)- **CLC 47**
Mueller, Lisel 1924- **CLC 13, 51**
See also CA 93-96; DLB 105
Muir, Edwin 1887-1959 **TCLC 2, 87**
See also CA 104; DLB 20, 100, 191
Muir, John 1838-1914 **TCLC 28**
See also CA 165; DLB 186
Mujica Lainez, Manuel 1910-1984 **CLC 31**
See also Lainez, Manuel Mujica
See also CA 81-84; 112; CANR 32; HW 1
Mukherjee, Bharati 1940- **CLC 53, 115; DAM NOV; SSC 38**
See also BEST 89:2; CA 107; CANR 45, 72; DLB 60; MTCW 1, 2
Muldoon, Paul 1951- **CLC 32, 72; DAM POET**
See also CA 113; 129; CANR 52, 91; DLB 40; INT 129
Mulisch, Harry 1927- **CLC 42**
See also CA 9-12R; CANR 6, 26, 56
Mull, Martin 1943- **CLC 17**
See also CA 105
Muller, Wilhelm NCLC 73
Mulock, Dinah Maria
See Craik, Dinah Maria (Mulock)
Munford, Robert 1737(?)-1783 **LC 5**
See also DLB 31
Mungo, Raymond 1946- **CLC 72**
See also CA 49-52; CANR 2
Munro, Alice 1931- **CLC 6, 10, 19, 50, 95; DAC; DAM MST, NOV; SSC 3; WLCS**
See also AITN 2; CA 33-36R; CANR 33, 53, 75; DA3; DLB 53; MTCW 1, 2; SATA 29
Munro, H(ector) H(ugh) 1870-1916
See Saki
See also CA 104; 130; CDBLB 1890-1914; DA; DAB; DAC; DAM MST, NOV; DA3; DLB 34, 162; MTCW 1, 2; WLC
Murdoch, (Jean) Iris 1919-1999 **CLC 1, 2, 3, 4, 6, 8, 11, 15, 22, 31, 51; DAB; DAC; DAM MST, NOV**
See also CA 13-16R; 179; CANR 8, 43, 68; CDBLB 1960 to Present; DA3; DLB 14, 194, 233; INT CANR-8; MTCW 1, 2
Murfree, Mary Noailles 1850-1922 **SSC 22**
See also CA 122; 176; DLB 12, 74
Murnau, Friedrich Wilhelm
See Plumpe, Friedrich Wilhelm
Murphy, Richard 1927- **CLC 41**
See also CA 29-32R; DLB 40
Murphy, Sylvia 1937- **CLC 34**
See also CA 121
Murphy, Thomas (Bernard) 1935- **CLC 51**
See also CA 101
Murray, Albert L. 1916- **CLC 73**
See also BW 2; CA 49-52; CANR 26, 52, 78; DLB 38
Murray, Judith Sargent 1751-1820 **NCLC 63**
See also DLB 37, 200
Murray, Les(lie) A(llan) 1938- **CLC 40; DAM POET**
See also CA 21-24R; CANR 11, 27, 56
Murry, J. Middleton
See Murry, John Middleton
Murry, John Middleton 1889-1957 **TCLC 16**
See also CA 118; DLB 149
Musgrave, Susan 1951- **CLC 13, 54**
See also CA 69-72; CANR 45, 84
Musil, Robert (Edler von) 1880-1942 **TCLC 12, 68; SSC 18**
See also CA 109; CANR 55, 84; DLB 81, 124; MTCW 2
Muske, Carol 1945- **CLC 90**
See also Muske-Dukes, Carol (Anne)
Muske-Dukes, Carol (Anne) 1945-
See Muske, Carol
See also CA 65-68; CANR 32, 70
Musset, (Louis Charles) Alfred de 1810-1857 **NCLC 7**
See also DLB 192
Mussolini, Benito (Amilcare Andrea) 1883-1945 **TCLC 96**
See also CA 116
My Brother's Brother
See Chekhov, Anton (Pavlovich)
Myers, L(eopold) H(amilton) 1881-1944 **TCLC 59**
See also CA 157; DLB 15
Myers, Walter Dean 1937- **CLC 35; BLC 3; DAM MULT, NOV**
See also AAYA 4, 23; BW 2; CA 33-36R; CANR 20, 42, 67; CLR 4, 16, 35; DLB 33; INT CANR-20; JRDA; MAICYA; MTCW 2; SAAS 2; SATA 41, 71, 109; SATA-Brief 27
Myers, Walter M.
See Myers, Walter Dean
Myles, Symon
See Follett, Ken(neth Martin)
Nabokov, Vladimir (Vladimirovich) 1899-1977 **CLC 1, 2, 3, 6, 8, 11, 15, 23, 44, 46, 64; DA; DAB; DAC; DAM MST, NOV; SSC 11; WLC**
See also CA 5-8R; 69-72; CANR 20; CDALB 1941-1968; DA3; DLB 2; DLBD 3; DLBY 80, 91; MTCW 1, 2
Naevius c. 265B.C.-201B.C. **CMLC 37**
See also DLB 211
Nagai Kafu 1879-1959 **TCLC 51**
See also Nagai Sokichi
See also DLB 180
Nagai Sokichi 1879-1959
See Nagai Kafu
See also CA 117
Nagy, Laszlo 1925-1978 **CLC 7**
See also CA 129; 112
Naidu, Sarojini 1879-1943 **TCLC 80**
Naipaul, Shiva(dhar Srinivasa) 1945-1985 **CLC 32, 39; DAM NOV**
See also CA 110; 112; 116; CANR 33; DA3; DLB 157; DLBY 85; MTCW 1, 2
Naipaul, V(idiadhar) S(urajprasad) 1932- **CLC 4, 7, 9, 13, 18, 37, 105; DAB; DAC; DAM MST, NOV; SSC 38**
See also CA 1-4R; CANR 1, 33, 51, 91; CDBLB 1960 to Present; DA3; DLB 125, 204, 206; DLBY 85; MTCW 1, 2
Nakos, Lilika 1899(?)- **CLC 29**
Narayan, R(asipuram) K(rishnaswami) 1906- **CLC 7, 28, 47, 121; DAM NOV; SSC 25**
See also CA 81-84; CANR 33, 61; DA3; MTCW 1, 2; SATA 62
Nash, (Frediric) Ogden 1902-1971 **CLC 23; DAM POET; PC 21**
See also CA 13-14; 29-32R; CANR 34, 61; CAP 1; DLB 11; MAICYA; MTCW 1, 2; SATA 2, 46
Nashe, Thomas 1567-1601(?) **LC 41**
See also DLB 167
Nashe, Thomas 1567-1601 **LC 41**
Nathan, Daniel
See Dannay, Frederic
Nathan, George Jean 1882-1958 **TCLC 18**
See also Hatteras, Owen
See also CA 114; 169; DLB 137
Natsume, Kinnosuke 1867-1916
See Natsume, Soseki
See also CA 104
Natsume, Soseki 1867-1916 **TCLC 2, 10**
See also Natsume, Kinnosuke
See also DLB 180
Natti, (Mary) Lee 1919-
See Kingman, Lee
See also CA 5-8R; CANR 2
Naylor, Gloria 1950- **CLC 28, 52; BLC 3; DA; DAC; DAM MST, MULT, NOV, POP; WLCS**
See also AAYA 6; BW 2, 3; CA 107; CANR 27, 51, 74; DA3; DLB 173; MTCW 1, 2
Neihardt, John Gneisenau 1881-1973 **CLC 32**
See also CA 13-14; CANR 65; CAP 1; DLB 9, 54

Nekrasov, Nikolai Alekseevich 1821-1878 **NCLC 11**
Nelligan, Emile 1879-1941 **TCLC 14**
See also CA 114; DLB 92
Nelson, Willie 1933- **CLC 17**
See also CA 107
Nemerov, Howard (Stanley) 1920-1991 **CLC 2, 6, 9, 36; DAM POET; PC 24**
See also CA 1-4R; 134; CABS 2; CANR 1, 27, 53; DLB 5, 6; DLBY 83; INT CANR-27; MTCW 1, 2
Neruda, Pablo 1904-1973 **CLC 1, 2, 5, 7, 9, 28, 62; DA; DAB; DAC; DAM MST, MULT, POET; HLC 2; PC 4; WLC**
See also CA 19-20; 45-48; CAP 2; DA3; HW 1; MTCW 1, 2
Nerval, Gerard de 1808-1855 **NCLC 1, 67; PC 13; SSC 18**
Nervo, (Jose) Amado (Ruiz de) 1870-1919 **TCLC 11; HLCS 2**
See also CA 109; 131; HW 1
Nessi, Pio Baroja y
See Baroja (y Nessi), Pio
Nestroy, Johann 1801-1862 **NCLC 42**
See also DLB 133
Netterville, Luke
See O'Grady, Standish (James)
Neufeld, John (Arthur) 1938- **CLC 17**
See also AAYA 11; CA 25-28R; CANR 11, 37, 56; CLR 52; MAICYA; SAAS 3; SATA 6, 81
Neumann, Alfred 1895-1952 **TCLC 100**
See also CA 183; DLB 56
Neville, Emily Cheney 1919- **CLC 12**
See also CA 5-8R; CANR 3, 37, 85; JRDA; MAICYA; SAAS 2; SATA 1
Newbound, Bernard Slade 1930-
See Slade, Bernard
See also CA 81-84; CANR 49; DAM DRAM
Newby, P(ercy) H(oward) 1918-1997 **CLC 2, 13; DAM NOV**
See also CA 5-8R; 161; CANR 32, 67; DLB 15; MTCW 1
Newlove, Donald 1928- **CLC 6**
See also CA 29-32R; CANR 25
Newlove, John (Herbert) 1938- **CLC 14**
See also CA 21-24R; CANR 9, 25
Newman, Charles 1938- **CLC 2, 8**
See also CA 21-24R; CANR 84
Newman, Edwin (Harold) 1919- **CLC 14**
See also AITN 1; CA 69-72; CANR 5
Newman, John Henry 1801-1890 **NCLC 38**
See also DLB 18, 32, 55
Newton, (Sir)Isaac 1642-1727 **LC 35, 52**
Newton, Suzanne 1936- **CLC 35**
See also CA 41-44R; CANR 14; JRDA; SATA 5, 77
Nexo, Martin Andersen 1869-1954 **TCLC 43**
Nezval, Vitezslav 1900-1958 **TCLC 44**
See also CA 123
Ng, Fae Myenne 1957(?)- **CLC 81**
See also CA 146
Ngema, Mbongeni 1955- **CLC 57**
See also BW 2; CA 143; CANR 84
Ngugi, James T(hiong'o) **CLC 3, 7, 13**
See also Ngugi wa Thiong'o
Ngugi wa Thiong'o 1938- **CLC 36; BLC 3; DAM MULT, NOV**
See also Ngugi, James T(hiong'o)
See also BW 2; CA 81-84; CANR 27, 58; DLB 125; MTCW 1, 2
Nichol, B(arrie) P(hillip) 1944-1988 **CLC 18**
See also CA 53-56; DLB 53; SATA 66
Nichols, John (Treadwell) 1940- **CLC 38**
See also CA 9-12R; CAAS 2; CANR 6, 70; DLBY 82
Nichols, Leigh
See Koontz, Dean R(ay)
Nichols, Peter (Richard) 1927- **CLC 5, 36, 65**
See also CA 104; CANR 33, 86; DLB 13; MTCW 1
Nicolas, F. R. E.
See Freeling, Nicolas
Niedecker, Lorine 1903-1970 **CLC 10, 42; DAM POET**
See also CA 25-28; CAP 2; DLB 48
Nietzsche, Friedrich (Wilhelm) 1844-1900 **TCLC 10, 18, 55**
See also CA 107; 121; DLB 129
Nievo, Ippolito 1831-1861 **NCLC 22**
Nightingale, Anne Redmon 1943-
See Redmon, Anne
See also CA 103
Nightingale, Florence 1820-1910 **TCLC 85**
See also DLB 166
Nik. T. O.
See Annensky, Innokenty (Fyodorovich)
Nin, Anais 1903-1977 **CLC 1, 4, 8, 11, 14, 60, 127; DAM NOV, POP; SSC 10**
See also AITN 2; CA 13-16R; 69-72; CANR 22, 53; DLB 2, 4, 152; MTCW 1, 2
Nishida, Kitaro 1870-1945 **TCLC 83**
Nishiwaki, Junzaburo 1894-1982 **PC 15**
See also CA 107
Nissenson, Hugh 1933- **CLC 4, 9**
See also CA 17-20R; CANR 27; DLB 28
Niven, Larry **CLC 8**
See also Niven, Laurence Van Cott
See also AAYA 27; DLB 8
Niven, Laurence Van Cott 1938-
See Niven, Larry
See also CA 21-24R; CAAS 12; CANR 14, 44, 66; DAM POP; MTCW 1, 2; SATA 95
Nixon, Agnes Eckhardt 1927- **CLC 21**
See also CA 110
Nizan, Paul 1905-1940 **TCLC 40**
See also CA 161; DLB 72
Nkosi, Lewis 1936- **CLC 45; BLC 3; DAM MULT**
See also BW 1, 3; CA 65-68; CANR 27, 81; DLB 157, 225
Nodier, (Jean) Charles (Emmanuel) 1780-1844 **NCLC 19**
See also DLB 119
Noguchi, Yone 1875-1947 **TCLC 80**
Nolan, Christopher 1965- **CLC 58**
See also CA 111; CANR 88
Noon, Jeff 1957- **CLC 91**
See also CA 148; CANR 83
Norden, Charles
See Durrell, Lawrence (George)
Nordhoff, Charles (Bernard) 1887-1947 **TCLC 23**
See also CA 108; DLB 9; SATA 23
Norfolk, Lawrence 1963- **CLC 76**
See also CA 144; CANR 85
Norman, Marsha 1947- **CLC 28; DAM DRAM; DC 8**
See also CA 105; CABS 3; CANR 41; DLBY 84
Normyx
See Douglas, (George) Norman
Norris, Frank 1870-1902 **SSC 28**
See also Norris, (Benjamin) Frank(lin, Jr.)
See also CDALB 1865-1917; DLB 12, 71, 186
Norris, (Benjamin) Frank(lin, Jr.) 1870-1902 **TCLC 24**
See also Norris, Frank
See also CA 110; 160
Norris, Leslie 1921- **CLC 14**
See also CA 11-12; CANR 14; CAP 1; DLB 27
North, Andrew
See Norton, Andre
North, Anthony
See Koontz, Dean R(ay)
North, Captain George
See Stevenson, Robert Louis (Balfour)
North, Milou
See Erdrich, Louise
Northrup, B. A.
See Hubbard, L(afayette) Ron(ald)
North Staffs
See Hulme, T(homas) E(rnest)
Norton, Alice Mary
See Norton, Andre
See also MAICYA; SATA 1, 43
Norton, Andre 1912- **CLC 12**
See also Norton, Alice Mary
See also AAYA 14; CA 1-4R; CANR 68; CLR 50; DLB 8, 52; JRDA; MTCW 1; SATA 91
Norton, Caroline 1808-1877 **NCLC 47**
See also DLB 21, 159, 199
Norway, Nevil Shute 1899-1960
See Shute, Nevil
See also CA 102; 93-96; CANR 85; MTCW 2
Norwid, Cyprian Kamil 1821-1883 **NCLC 17**
Nosille, Nabrah
See Ellison, Harlan (Jay)
Nossack, Hans Erich 1901-1978 **CLC 6**
See also CA 93-96; 85-88; DLB 69
Nostradamus 1503-1566 **LC 27**
Nosu, Chuji
See Ozu, Yasujiro
Notenburg, Eleanora (Genrikhovna) von
See Guro, Elena
Nova, Craig 1945- **CLC 7, 31**
See also CA 45-48; CANR 2, 53
Novak, Joseph
See Kosinski, Jerzy (Nikodem)
Novalis 1772-1801 **NCLC 13**
See also DLB 90
Novis, Emile
See Weil, Simone (Adolphine)
Nowlan, Alden (Albert) 1933-1983 **CLC 15; DAC; DAM MST**
See also CA 9-12R; CANR 5; DLB 53
Noyes, Alfred 1880-1958 **TCLC 7; PC 27**
See also CA 104; DLB 20
Nunn, Kem **CLC 34**
See also CA 159
Nwapa, Flora 1931- **CLC 133; BLCS**
See also BW 2; CA 143; CANR 83; DLB 125
Nye, Robert 1939- **CLC 13, 42; DAM NOV**
See also CA 33-36R; CANR 29, 67; DLB 14; MTCW 1; SATA 6
Nyro, Laura 1947- **CLC 17**
Oates, Joyce Carol 1938- **CLC 1, 2, 3, 6, 9, 11, 15, 19, 33, 52, 108, 134; DA; DAB; DAC; DAM MST, NOV, POP; SSC 6; WLC**
See also AAYA 15; AITN 1; BEST 89:2; CA 5-8R; CANR 25, 45, 74; CDALB 1968-1988; DA3; DLB 2, 5, 130; DLBY 81; INT CANR-25; MTCW 1, 2
O'Brien, Darcy 1939-1998 **CLC 11**
See also CA 21-24R; 167; CANR 8, 59
O'Brien, E. G.
See Clarke, Arthur C(harles)
O'Brien, Edna 1936- **CLC 3, 5, 8, 13, 36, 65, 116; DAM NOV; SSC 10**
See also CA 1-4R; CANR 6, 41, 65; CDBLB 1960 to Present; DA3; DLB 14, 231; MTCW 1, 2
O'Brien, Fitz-James 1828-1862 **NCLC 21**

See also DLB 74
O'Brien, Flann CLC 1, 4, 5, 7, 10, 47
See also O Nuallain, Brian
See also DLB 231
O'Brien, Richard 1942- **CLC 17**
See also CA 124
O'Brien, (William) Tim(othy) 1946- **CLC 7, 19, 40, 103; DAM POP**
See also AAYA 16; CA 85-88; CANR 40, 58; CDALBS; DA3; DLB 152; DLBD 9; DLBY 80; MTCW 2
Obstfelder, Sigbjoern 1866-1900 **TCLC 23**
See also CA 123
O'Casey, Sean 1880-1964 **CLC 1, 5, 9, 11, 15, 88; DAB; DAC; DAM DRAM, MST; DC 12; WLCS**
See also CA 89-92; CANR 62; CDBLB 1914-1945; DA3; DLB 10; MTCW 1, 2
O'Cathasaigh, Sean
See O'Casey, Sean
Occom, Samson 1723-1792 **LC 60**
See also DLB 175; NNAL
Ochs, Phil(ip David) 1940-1976 **CLC 17**
See also CA 185; 65-68
O'Connor, Edwin (Greene) 1918-1968 **CLC 14**
See also CA 93-96; 25-28R
O'Connor, (Mary) Flannery 1925-1964 **CLC 1, 2, 3, 6, 10, 13, 15, 21, 66, 104; DA; DAB; DAC; DAM MST, NOV; SSC 1, 23; WLC**
See also AAYA 7; CA 1-4R; CANR 3, 41; CDALB 1941-1968; DA3; DLB 2, 152; DLBD 12; DLBY 80; MTCW 1, 2
O'Connor, Frank CLC 23; SSC 5
See also O'Donovan, Michael John
See also DLB 162
O'Dell, Scott 1898-1989 **CLC 30**
See also AAYA 3; CA 61-64; 129; CANR 12, 30; CLR 1, 16; DLB 52; JRDA; MAICYA; SATA 12, 60
Odets, Clifford 1906-1963 **CLC 2, 28, 98; DAM DRAM; DC 6**
See also CA 85-88; CANR 62; DLB 7, 26; MTCW 1, 2
O'Doherty, Brian 1934- **CLC 76**
See also CA 105
O'Donnell, K. M.
See Malzberg, Barry N(athaniel)
O'Donnell, Lawrence
See Kuttner, Henry
O'Donovan, Michael John 1903-1966 **CLC 14**
See also O'Connor, Frank
See also CA 93-96; CANR 84
Oe, Kenzaburo 1935- **CLC 10, 36, 86; DAM NOV; SSC 20**
See also CA 97-100; CANR 36, 50, 74; DA3; DLB 182; DLBY 94; MTCW 1, 2
O'Faolain, Julia 1932- **CLC 6, 19, 47, 108**
See also CA 81-84; CAAS 2; CANR 12, 61; DLB 14, 231; MTCW 1
O'Faolain, Sean 1900-1991 **CLC 1, 7, 14, 32, 70; SSC 13**
See also CA 61-64; 134; CANR 12, 66; DLB 15, 162; MTCW 1, 2
O'Flaherty, Liam 1896-1984 **CLC 5, 34; SSC 6**
See also CA 101; 113; CANR 35; DLB 36, 162; DLBY 84; MTCW 1, 2
Ogilvy, Gavin
See Barrie, J(ames) M(atthew)
O'Grady, Standish (James) 1846-1928 **TCLC 5**
See also CA 104; 157
O'Grady, Timothy 1951- **CLC 59**
See also CA 138
O'Hara, Frank 1926-1966 **CLC 2, 5, 13, 78; DAM POET**
See also CA 9-12R; 25-28R; CANR 33; DA3; DLB 5, 16, 193; MTCW 1, 2
O'Hara, John (Henry) 1905-1970 **CLC 1, 2, 3, 6, 11, 42; DAM NOV; SSC 15**
See also CA 5-8R; 25-28R; CANR 31, 60; CDALB 1929-1941; DLB 9, 86; DLBD 2; MTCW 1, 2
O Hehir, Diana 1922- **CLC 41**
See also CA 93-96
Ohiyesa
See Eastman, Charles A(lexander)
Okigbo, Christopher (Ifenayichukwu) 1932-1967 **CLC 25, 84; BLC 3; DAM MULT, POET; PC 7**
See also BW 1, 3; CA 77-80; CANR 74; DLB 125; MTCW 1, 2
Okri, Ben 1959- **CLC 87**
See also BW 2, 3; CA 130; 138; CANR 65; DLB 157, 231; INT 138; MTCW 2
Olds, Sharon 1942- **CLC 32, 39, 85; DAM POET; PC 22**
See also CA 101; CANR 18, 41, 66; DLB 120; MTCW 2
Oldstyle, Jonathan
See Irving, Washington
Olesha, Yuri (Karlovich) 1899-1960 **CLC 8**
See also CA 85-88
Oliphant, Laurence 1829(?)-1888 **NCLC 47**
See also DLB 18, 166
Oliphant, Margaret (Oliphant Wilson) 1828-1897 **NCLC 11, 61; SSC 25**
See also DLB 18, 159, 190
Oliver, Mary 1935- **CLC 19, 34, 98**
See also CA 21-24R; CANR 9, 43, 84, 92; DLB 5, 193
Olivier, Laurence (Kerr) 1907-1989 **CLC 20**
See also CA 111; 150; 129
Olsen, Tillie 1912- **CLC 4, 13, 114; DA; DAB; DAC; DAM MST; SSC 11**
See also CA 1-4R; CANR 1, 43, 74; CDALBS; DA3; DLB 28, 206; DLBY 80; MTCW 1, 2
Olson, Charles (John) 1910-1970 **CLC 1, 2, 5, 6, 9, 11, 29; DAM POET; PC 19**
See also CA 13-16; 25-28R; CABS 2; CANR 35, 61; CAP 1; DLB 5, 16, 193; MTCW 1, 2
Olson, Toby 1937- **CLC 28**
See also CA 65-68; CANR 9, 31, 84
Olyesha, Yuri
See Olesha, Yuri (Karlovich)
Ondaatje, (Philip) Michael 1943- **CLC 14, 29, 51, 76; DAB; DAC; DAM MST; PC 28**
See also CA 77-80; CANR 42, 74; DA3; DLB 60; MTCW 2
Oneal, Elizabeth 1934-
See Oneal, Zibby
See also CA 106; CANR 28, 84; MAICYA; SATA 30, 82
Oneal, Zibby CLC 30
See also Oneal, Elizabeth
See also AAYA 5; CLR 13; JRDA
O'Neill, Eugene (Gladstone) 1888-1953 **TCLC 1, 6, 27, 49; DA; DAB; DAC; DAM DRAM, MST; WLC**
See also AITN 1; CA 110; 132; CDALB 1929-1941; DA3; DLB 7; MTCW 1, 2
Onetti, Juan Carlos 1909-1994 **CLC 7, 10; DAM MULT, NOV; HLCS 2; SSC 23**
See also CA 85-88; 145; CANR 32, 63; DLB 113; HW 1, 2; MTCW 1, 2
O Nuallain, Brian 1911-1966
See O'Brien, Flann
See also CA 21-22; 25-28R; CAP 2; DLB 231
Ophuls, Max 1902-1957 **TCLC 79**
See also CA 113
Opie, Amelia 1769-1853 **NCLC 65**
See also DLB 116, 159
Oppen, George 1908-1984 **CLC 7, 13, 34**
See also CA 13-16R; 113; CANR 8, 82; DLB 5, 165
Oppenheim, E(dward) Phillips 1866-1946 **TCLC 45**
See also CA 111; DLB 70
Opuls, Max
See Ophuls, Max
Origen c. 185-c. 254 **CMLC 19**
Orlovitz, Gil 1918-1973 **CLC 22**
See also CA 77-80; 45-48; DLB 2, 5
Orris
See Ingelow, Jean
Ortega y Gasset, Jose 1883-1955 **TCLC 9; DAM MULT; HLC 2**
See also CA 106; 130; HW 1, 2; MTCW 1, 2
Ortese, Anna Maria 1914- **CLC 89**
See also DLB 177
Ortiz, Simon J(oseph) 1941- **CLC 45; DAM MULT, POET; PC 17**
See also CA 134; CANR 69; DLB 120, 175; NNAL
Orton, Joe CLC 4, 13, 43; DC 3
See also Orton, John Kingsley
See also CDBLB 1960 to Present; DLB 13; MTCW 2
Orton, John Kingsley 1933-1967
See Orton, Joe
See also CA 85-88; CANR 35, 66; DAM DRAM; MTCW 1, 2
Orwell, George -1950 **TCLC 2, 6, 15, 31, 51; DAB; WLC**
See also Blair, Eric (Arthur)
See also CDBLB 1945-1960; DLB 15, 98, 195
Osborne, David
See Silverberg, Robert
Osborne, George
See Silverberg, Robert
Osborne, John (James) 1929-1994 **CLC 1, 2, 5, 11, 45; DA; DAB; DAC; DAM DRAM, MST; WLC**
See also CA 13-16R; 147; CANR 21, 56; CDBLB 1945-1960; DLB 13; MTCW 1, 2
Osborne, Lawrence 1958- **CLC 50**
Osbourne, Lloyd 1868-1947 **TCLC 93**
Oshima, Nagisa 1932- **CLC 20**
See also CA 116; 121; CANR 78
Oskison, John Milton 1874-1947 **TCLC 35; DAM MULT**
See also CA 144; CANR 84; DLB 175; NNAL
Ossian c. 3rd cent. - **CMLC 28**
See also Macpherson, James
Ossoli, Sarah Margaret (Fuller marchesa d') 1810-1850 **NCLC 5, 50**
See also Fuller, Margaret; Fuller, Sarah Margaret
See also CDALB 1640-1865; DLB 1, 59, 73, 83, 223; SATA 25
Ostriker, Alicia (Suskin) 1937- **CLC 132**
See also CA 25-28R; CAAS 24; CANR 10, 30, 62; DLB 120
Ostrovsky, Alexander 1823-1886 **NCLC 30, 57**
Otero, Blas de 1916-1979 **CLC 11**
See also CA 89-92; DLB 134
Otto, Rudolf 1869-1937 **TCLC 85**
Otto, Whitney 1955- **CLC 70**
See also CA 140
Ouida TCLC 43
See also De La Ramee, (Marie) Louise
See also DLB 18, 156
Ousmane, Sembene 1923- **CLC 66; BLC 3**
See also BW 1, 3; CA 117; 125; CANR 81; MTCW 1

Ovid 43B.C.-17 **CMLC 7; DAM POET; PC 2**
See also DA3; DLB 211
Owen, Hugh
See Faust, Frederick (Schiller)
Owen, Wilfred (Edward Salter) 1893-1918 **TCLC 5, 27; DA; DAB; DAC; DAM MST, POET; PC 19; WLC**
See also CA 104; 141; CDBLB 1914-1945; DLB 20; MTCW 2
Owens, Rochelle 1936- **CLC 8**
See also CA 17-20R; CAAS 2; CANR 39
Oz, Amos 1939- **CLC 5, 8, 11, 27, 33, 54; DAM NOV**
See also CA 53-56; CANR 27, 47, 65; MTCW 1, 2
Ozick, Cynthia 1928- **CLC 3, 7, 28, 62; DAM NOV, POP; SSC 15**
See also BEST 90:1; CA 17-20R; CANR 23, 58; DA3; DLB 28, 152; DLBY 82; INT CANR-23; MTCW 1, 2
Ozu, Yasujiro 1903-1963 **CLC 16**
See also CA 112
Pacheco, C.
See Pessoa, Fernando (Antonio Nogueira)
Pacheco, Jose Emilio 1939-
See also CA 111; 131; CANR 65; DAM MULT; HLC 2; HW 1, 2
Pa Chin CLC 18
See also Li Fei-kan
Pack, Robert 1929- **CLC 13**
See also CA 1-4R; CANR 3, 44, 82; DLB 5; SATA 118
Padgett, Lewis
See Kuttner, Henry
Padilla (Lorenzo), Heberto 1932- **CLC 38**
See also AITN 1; CA 123; 131; HW 1
Page, Jimmy 1944- **CLC 12**
Page, Louise 1955- **CLC 40**
See also CA 140; CANR 76; DLB 233
Page, P(atricia) K(athleen) 1916- **CLC 7, 18; DAC; DAM MST; PC 12**
See also CA 53-56; CANR 4, 22, 65; DLB 68; MTCW 1
Page, Thomas Nelson 1853-1922 **SSC 23**
See also CA 118; 177; DLB 12, 78; DLBD 13
Pagels, Elaine Hiesey 1943- **CLC 104**
See also CA 45-48; CANR 2, 24, 51
Paget, Violet 1856-1935
See Lee, Vernon
See also CA 104; 166
Paget-Lowe, Henry
See Lovecraft, H(oward) P(hillips)
Paglia, Camille (Anna) 1947- **CLC 68**
See also CA 140; CANR 72; MTCW 2
Paige, Richard
See Koontz, Dean R(ay)
Paine, Thomas 1737-1809 **NCLC 62**
See also CDALB 1640-1865; DLB 31, 43, 73, 158
Pakenham, Antonia
See Fraser, (Lady) Antonia (Pakenham)
Palamas, Kostes 1859-1943 **TCLC 5**
See also CA 105
Palazzeschi, Aldo 1885-1974 **CLC 11**
See also CA 89-92; 53-56; DLB 114
Pales Matos, Luis 1898-1959
See also HLCS 2; HW 1
Paley, Grace 1922- **CLC 4, 6, 37; DAM POP; SSC 8**
See also CA 25-28R; CANR 13, 46, 74; DA3; DLB 28; INT CANR-13; MTCW 1, 2
Palin, Michael (Edward) 1943- **CLC 21**
See also Monty Python
See also CA 107; CANR 35; SATA 67
Palliser, Charles 1947- **CLC 65**
See also CA 136; CANR 76
Palma, Ricardo 1833-1919 **TCLC 29**
See also CA 168
Pancake, Breece Dexter 1952-1979
See Pancake, Breece D'J
See also CA 123; 109
Pancake, Breece D'J CLC 29
See also Pancake, Breece Dexter
See also DLB 130
Pankhurst, Emmeline (Goulden) 1858-1928 **TCLC 100**
See also CA 116
Panko, Rudy
See Gogol, Nikolai (Vasilyevich)
Papadiamantis, Alexandros 1851-1911 **TCLC 29**
See also CA 168
Papadiamantopoulos, Johannes 1856-1910
See Moreas, Jean
See also CA 117
Papini, Giovanni 1881-1956 **TCLC 22**
See also CA 121; 180
Paracelsus 1493-1541 **LC 14**
See also DLB 179
Parasol, Peter
See Stevens, Wallace
Pardo Bazan, Emilia 1851-1921 **SSC 30**
Pareto, Vilfredo 1848-1923 **TCLC 69**
See also CA 175
Paretsky, Sara 1947- **CLC 135; DAM POP**
See also AAYA 30; BEST 90:3; CA 125; 129; CANR 59; DA3; INT 129
Parfenie, Maria
See Codrescu, Andrei
Parini, Jay (Lee) 1948- **CLC 54, 133**
See also CA 97-100; CAAS 16; CANR 32, 87
Park, Jordan
See Kornbluth, C(yril) M.; Pohl, Frederik
Park, Robert E(zra) 1864-1944 **TCLC 73**
See also CA 122; 165
Parker, Bert
See Ellison, Harlan (Jay)
Parker, Dorothy (Rothschild) 1893-1967 **CLC 15, 68; DAM POET; PC 28; SSC 2**
See also CA 19-20; 25-28R; CAP 2; DA3; DLB 11, 45, 86; MTCW 1, 2
Parker, Robert B(rown) 1932- **CLC 27; DAM NOV, POP**
See also AAYA 28; BEST 89:4; CA 49-52; CANR 1, 26, 52, 89; INT CANR-26; MTCW 1
Parkin, Frank 1940- **CLC 43**
See also CA 147
Parkman, Francis Jr., Jr. 1823-1893 **NCLC 12**
See also DLB 1, 30, 186, 235
Parks, Gordon (Alexander Buchanan) 1912- **CLC 1, 16; BLC 3; DAM MULT**
See also AITN 2; BW 2, 3; CA 41-44R; CANR 26, 66; DA3; DLB 33; MTCW 2; SATA 8, 108
Parmenides c. 515B.C.-c. 450B.C. **CMLC 22**
See also DLB 176
Parnell, Thomas 1679-1718 **LC 3**
See also DLB 94
Parra, Nicanor 1914- **CLC 2, 102; DAM MULT; HLC 2**
See also CA 85-88; CANR 32; HW 1; MTCW 1
Parra Sanojo, Ana Teresa de la 1890-1936
See also HLCS 2
Parrish, Mary Frances
See Fisher, M(ary) F(rances) K(ennedy)
Parson
See Coleridge, Samuel Taylor
Parson Lot
See Kingsley, Charles
Parton, Sara Payson Willis 1811-1872 **NCLC 86**
See also DLB 43, 74
Partridge, Anthony
See Oppenheim, E(dward) Phillips
Pascal, Blaise 1623-1662 **LC 35**
Pascoli, Giovanni 1855-1912 **TCLC 45**
See also CA 170
Pasolini, Pier Paolo 1922-1975 **CLC 20, 37, 106; PC 17**
See also CA 93-96; 61-64; CANR 63; DLB 128, 177; MTCW 1
Pasquini
See Silone, Ignazio
Pastan, Linda (Olenik) 1932- **CLC 27; DAM POET**
See also CA 61-64; CANR 18, 40, 61; DLB 5
Pasternak, Boris (Leonidovich) 1890-1960 **CLC 7, 10, 18, 63; DA; DAB; DAC; DAM MST, NOV, POET; PC 6; SSC 31; WLC**
See also CA 127; 116; DA3; MTCW 1, 2
Patchen, Kenneth 1911-1972 **CLC 1, 2, 18; DAM POET**
See also CA 1-4R; 33-36R; CANR 3, 35; DLB 16, 48; MTCW 1
Pater, Walter (Horatio) 1839-1894 **NCLC 7, 90**
See also CDBLB 1832-1890; DLB 57, 156
Paterson, A(ndrew) B(arton) 1864-1941 **TCLC 32**
See also CA 155; SATA 97
Paterson, Katherine (Womeldorf) 1932- **CLC 12, 30**
See also AAYA 1, 31; CA 21-24R; CANR 28, 59; CLR 7, 50; DLB 52; JRDA; MAICYA; MTCW 1; SATA 13, 53, 92
Patmore, Coventry Kersey Dighton 1823-1896 **NCLC 9**
See also DLB 35, 98
Paton, Alan (Stewart) 1903-1988 **CLC 4, 10, 25, 55, 106; DA; DAB; DAC; DAM MST, NOV; WLC**
See also AAYA 26; CA 13-16; 125; CANR 22; CAP 1; DA3; DLB 225; DLBD 17; MTCW 1, 2; SATA 11; SATA-Obit 56
Paton Walsh, Gillian 1937- **CLC 35**
See also Walsh, Jill Paton
See also AAYA 11; CANR 38, 83; CLR 2, 65; DLB 161; JRDA; MAICYA; SAAS 3; SATA 4, 72, 109
Paton Walsh, Jill
See Paton Walsh, Gillian
Patton, George S. 1885-1945 **TCLC 79**
Paulding, James Kirke 1778-1860 **NCLC 2**
See also DLB 3, 59, 74
Paulin, Thomas Neilson 1949-
See Paulin, Tom
See also CA 123; 128
Paulin, Tom CLC 37
See also Paulin, Thomas Neilson
See also DLB 40
Pausanias c. 1st cent. - **CMLC 36**
Paustovsky, Konstantin (Georgievich) 1892-1968 **CLC 40**
See also CA 93-96; 25-28R
Pavese, Cesare 1908-1950 **TCLC 3; PC 13; SSC 19**
See also CA 104; 169; DLB 128, 177
Pavic, Milorad 1929- **CLC 60**
See also CA 136; DLB 181
Pavlov, Ivan Petrovich 1849-1936 **TCLC 91**
See also CA 118; 180
Payne, Alan
See Jakes, John (William)

Paz, Gil
See Lugones, Leopoldo
Paz, Octavio 1914-1998 **CLC 3, 4, 6, 10, 19, 51, 65, 119; DA; DAB; DAC; DAM MST, MULT, POET; HLC 2; PC 1; WLC**
See also CA 73-76; 165; CANR 32, 65; DA3; DLBY 90, 98; HW 1, 2; MTCW 1, 2
p'Bitek, Okot 1931-1982 **CLC 96; BLC 3; DAM MULT**
See also BW 2, 3; CA 124; 107; CANR 82; DLB 125; MTCW 1, 2
Peacock, Molly 1947- **CLC 60**
See also CA 103; CAAS 21; CANR 52, 84; DLB 120
Peacock, Thomas Love 1785-1866 **NCLC 22**
See also DLB 96, 116
Peake, Mervyn 1911-1968 **CLC 7, 54**
See also CA 5-8R; 25-28R; CANR 3; DLB 15, 160; MTCW 1; SATA 23
Pearce, Philippa CLC 21
See also Christie, (Ann) Philippa
See also CLR 9; DLB 161; MAICYA; SATA 1, 67
Pearl, Eric
See Elman, Richard (Martin)
Pearson, T(homas) R(eid) 1956- **CLC 39**
See also CA 120; 130; INT 130
Peck, Dale 1967- **CLC 81**
See also CA 146; CANR 72
Peck, John 1941- **CLC 3**
See also CA 49-52; CANR 3
Peck, Richard (Wayne) 1934- **CLC 21**
See also AAYA 1, 24; CA 85-88; CANR 19, 38; CLR 15; INT CANR-19; JRDA; MAICYA; SAAS 2; SATA 18, 55, 97; SATA-Essay 110
Peck, Robert Newton 1928- **CLC 17; DA; DAC; DAM MST**
See also AAYA 3; CA 81-84, 182; CAAE 182; CANR 31, 63; CLR 45; JRDA; MAICYA; SAAS 1; SATA 21, 62, 111; SATA-Essay 108
Peckinpah, (David) Sam(uel) 1925-1984 **CLC 20**
See also CA 109; 114; CANR 82
Pedersen, Knut 1859-1952
See Hamsun, Knut
See also CA 104; 119; CANR 63; MTCW 1, 2
Peeslake, Gaffer
See Durrell, Lawrence (George)
Peguy, Charles Pierre 1873-1914 **TCLC 10**
See also CA 107
Peirce, Charles Sanders 1839-1914 **TCLC 81**
Pellicer, Carlos 1900(?)-1977
See also CA 153; 69-72; HLCS 2; HW 1
Pena, Ramon del Valle y
See Valle-Inclan, Ramon (Maria) del
Pendennis, Arthur Esquir
See Thackeray, William Makepeace
Penn, William 1644-1718 **LC 25**
See also DLB 24
PEPECE
See Prado (Calvo), Pedro
Pepys, Samuel 1633-1703 **LC 11, 58; DA; DAB; DAC; DAM MST; WLC**
See also CDBLB 1660-1789; DA3; DLB 101
Percy, Walker 1916-1990 **CLC 2, 3, 6, 8, 14, 18, 47, 65; DAM NOV, POP**
See also CA 1-4R; 131; CANR 1, 23, 64; DA3; DLB 2; DLBY 80, 90; MTCW 1, 2
Percy, William Alexander 1885-1942 **TCLC 84**
See also CA 163; MTCW 2
Perec, Georges 1936-1982 **CLC 56, 116**
See also CA 141; DLB 83
Pereda (y Sanchez de Porrua), Jose Maria de 1833-1906 **TCLC 16**
See also CA 117
Pereda y Porrua, Jose Maria de
See Pereda (y Sanchez de Porrua), Jose Maria de
Peregoy, George Weems
See Mencken, H(enry) L(ouis)
Perelman, S(idney) J(oseph) 1904-1979 **CLC 3, 5, 9, 15, 23, 44, 49; DAM DRAM; SSC 32**
See also AITN 1, 2; CA 73-76; 89-92; CANR 18; DLB 11, 44; MTCW 1, 2
Peret, Benjamin 1899-1959 **TCLC 20**
See also CA 117; 186
Peretz, Isaac Loeb 1851(?)-1915 **TCLC 16; SSC 26**
See also CA 109
Peretz, Yitzkhok Leibush
See Peretz, Isaac Loeb
Perez Galdos, Benito 1843-1920 **TCLC 27; HLCS 2**
See also CA 125; 153; HW 1
Peri Rossi, Cristina 1941-
See also CA 131; CANR 59, 81; DLB 145; HLCS 2; HW 1, 2
Perlata
See Peret, Benjamin
Perrault, Charles 1628-1703 **LC 3, 52; DC 12**
See also MAICYA; SATA 25
Perry, Anne 1938- **CLC 126**
See also CA 101; CANR 22, 50, 84
Perry, Brighton
See Sherwood, Robert E(mmet)
Perse, St.-John
See Leger, (Marie-Rene Auguste) Alexis Saint-Leger
Perutz, Leo(pold) 1882-1957 **TCLC 60**
See also CA 147; DLB 81
Peseenz, Tulio F.
See Lopez y Fuentes, Gregorio
Pesetsky, Bette 1932- **CLC 28**
See also CA 133; DLB 130
Peshkov, Alexei Maximovich 1868-1936
See Gorky, Maxim
See also CA 105; 141; CANR 83; DA; DAC; DAM DRAM, MST, NOV; MTCW 2
Pessoa, Fernando (Antonio Nogueira) 1888-1935 **TCLC 27; DAM MULT; HLC 2; PC 20**
See also CA 125; 183
Peterkin, Julia Mood 1880-1961 **CLC 31**
See also CA 102; DLB 9
Peters, Joan K(aren) 1945- **CLC 39**
See also CA 158
Peters, Robert L(ouis) 1924- **CLC 7**
See also CA 13-16R; CAAS 8; DLB 105
Petofi, Sandor 1823-1849 **NCLC 21**
Petrakis, Harry Mark 1923- **CLC 3**
See also CA 9-12R; CANR 4, 30, 85
Petrarch 1304-1374 **CMLC 20; DAM POET; PC 8**
See also DA3
Petronius c. 20-66 **CMLC 34**
See also DLB 211
Petrov, Evgeny TCLC 21
See also Kataev, Evgeny Petrovich
Petry, Ann (Lane) 1908-1997 **CLC 1, 7, 18**
See also BW 1, 3; CA 5-8R; 157; CAAS 6; CANR 4, 46; CLR 12; DLB 76; JRDA; MAICYA; MTCW 1; SATA 5; SATA-Obit 94
Petursson, Halligrimur 1614-1674 **LC 8**
Peychinovich
See Vazov, Ivan (Minchov)
Phaedrus c. 18B.C.-c. 50 **CMLC 25**
See also DLB 211
Philips, Katherine 1632-1664 **LC 30**
See also DLB 131
Philipson, Morris H. 1926- **CLC 53**
See also CA 1-4R; CANR 4
Phillips, Caryl 1958- **CLC 96; BLCS; DAM MULT**
See also BW 2; CA 141; CANR 63; DA3; DLB 157; MTCW 2
Phillips, David Graham 1867-1911 **TCLC 44**
See also CA 108; 176; DLB 9, 12
Phillips, Jack
See Sandburg, Carl (August)
Phillips, Jayne Anne 1952- **CLC 15, 33; SSC 16**
See also CA 101; CANR 24, 50; DLBY 80; INT CANR-24; MTCW 1, 2
Phillips, Richard
See Dick, Philip K(indred)
Phillips, Robert (Schaeffer) 1938- **CLC 28**
See also CA 17-20R; CAAS 13; CANR 8; DLB 105
Phillips, Ward
See Lovecraft, H(oward) P(hillips)
Piccolo, Lucio 1901-1969 **CLC 13**
See also CA 97-100; DLB 114
Pickthall, Marjorie L(owry) C(hristie) 1883-1922 **TCLC 21**
See also CA 107; DLB 92
Pico della Mirandola, Giovanni 1463-1494 **LC 15**
Piercy, Marge 1936- **CLC 3, 6, 14, 18, 27, 62, 128; PC 29**
See also CA 21-24R; CAAE 187; CAAS 1; CANR 13, 43, 66; DLB 120, 227; MTCW 1, 2
Piers, Robert
See Anthony, Piers
Pieyre de Mandiargues, Andre 1909-1991
See Mandiargues, Andre Pieyre de
See also CA 103; 136; CANR 22, 82
Pilnyak, Boris TCLC 23
See also Vogau, Boris Andreyevich
Pincherle, Alberto 1907-1990 **CLC 11, 18; DAM NOV**
See also Moravia, Alberto
See also CA 25-28R; 132; CANR 33, 63; MTCW 1
Pinckney, Darryl 1953- **CLC 76**
See also BW 2, 3; CA 143; CANR 79
Pindar 518B.C.-446B.C. **CMLC 12; PC 19**
See also DLB 176
Pineda, Cecile 1942- **CLC 39**
See also CA 118
Pinero, Arthur Wing 1855-1934 **TCLC 32; DAM DRAM**
See also CA 110; 153; DLB 10
Pinero, Miguel (Antonio Gomez) 1946-1988 **CLC 4, 55**
See also CA 61-64; 125; CANR 29, 90; HW 1
Pinget, Robert 1919-1997 **CLC 7, 13, 37**
See also CA 85-88; 160; DLB 83
Pink Floyd
See Barrett, (Roger) Syd; Gilmour, David; Mason, Nick; Waters, Roger; Wright, Rick
Pinkney, Edward 1802-1828 **NCLC 31**
Pinkwater, Daniel Manus 1941- **CLC 35**
See also Pinkwater, Manus
See also AAYA 1; CA 29-32R; CANR 12, 38, 89; CLR 4; JRDA; MAICYA; SAAS 3; SATA 46, 76, 114
Pinkwater, Manus
See Pinkwater, Daniel Manus
See also SATA 8
Pinsky, Robert 1940- **CLC 9, 19, 38, 94, 121; DAM POET; PC 27**
See also CA 29-32R; CAAS 4; CANR 58; DA3; DLBY 82, 98; MTCW 2

Raleigh, Richard
See Lovecraft, H(oward) P(hillips)
Raleigh, Sir Walter 1554(?)-1618 **LC 31, 39; PC 31**
See also CDBLB Before 1660; DLB 172
Rallentando, H. P.
See Sayers, Dorothy L(eigh)
Ramal, Walter
See de la Mare, Walter (John)
Ramana Maharshi 1879-1950 **TCLC 84**
Ramoacn y Cajal, Santiago 1852-1934 **TCLC 93**
Ramon, Juan
See Jimenez (Mantecon), Juan Ramon
Ramos, Graciliano 1892-1953 **TCLC 32**
See also CA 167; HW 2
Rampersad, Arnold 1941- **CLC 44**
See also BW 2, 3; CA 127; 133; CANR 81; DLB 111; INT 133
Rampling, Anne
See Rice, Anne
Ramsay, Allan 1684(?)-1758 **LC 29**
See also DLB 95
Ramuz, Charles-Ferdinand 1878-1947 **TCLC 33**
See also CA 165
Rand, Ayn 1905-1982 **CLC 3, 30, 44, 79; DA; DAC; DAM MST, NOV, POP; WLC**
See also AAYA 10; CA 13-16R; 105; CANR 27, 73; CDALBS; DA3; DLB 227; MTCW 1, 2
Randall, Dudley (Felker) 1914-2000 **CLC 1, 135; BLC 3; DAM MULT**
See also BW 1, 3; CA 25-28R; CANR 23, 82; DLB 41
Randall, Robert
See Silverberg, Robert
Ranger, Ken
See Creasey, John
Ransom, John Crowe 1888-1974 **CLC 2, 4, 5, 11, 24; DAM POET**
See also CA 5-8R; 49-52; CANR 6, 34; CDALBS; DA3; DLB 45, 63; MTCW 1, 2
Rao, Raja 1909- **CLC 25, 56; DAM NOV**
See also CA 73-76; CANR 51; MTCW 1, 2
Raphael, Frederic (Michael) 1931- **CLC 2, 14**
See also CA 1-4R; CANR 1, 86; DLB 14
Ratcliffe, James P.
See Mencken, H(enry) L(ouis)
Rathbone, Julian 1935- **CLC 41**
See also CA 101; CANR 34, 73
Rattigan, Terence (Mervyn) 1911-1977 **CLC 7; DAM DRAM**
See also CA 85-88; 73-76; CDBLB 1945-1960; DLB 13; MTCW 1, 2
Ratushinskaya, Irina 1954- **CLC 54**
See also CA 129; CANR 68
Raven, Simon (Arthur Noel) 1927- **CLC 14**
See also CA 81-84; CANR 86
Ravenna, Michael
See Welty, Eudora
Rawley, Callman 1903-
See Rakosi, Carl
See also CA 21-24R; CANR 12, 32, 91
Rawlings, Marjorie Kinnan 1896-1953 **TCLC 4**
See also AAYA 20; CA 104; 137; CANR 74; CLR 63; DLB 9, 22, 102; DLBD 17; JRDA; MAICYA; MTCW 2; SATA 100; YABC 1
Ray, Satyajit 1921-1992 **CLC 16, 76; DAM MULT**
See also CA 114; 137
Read, Herbert Edward 1893-1968 **CLC 4**
See also CA 85-88; 25-28R; DLB 20, 149
Read, Piers Paul 1941- **CLC 4, 10, 25**
See also CA 21-24R; CANR 38, 86; DLB 14; SATA 21
Reade, Charles 1814-1884 **NCLC 2, 74**
See also DLB 21
Reade, Hamish
See Gray, Simon (James Holliday)
Reading, Peter 1946- **CLC 47**
See also CA 103; CANR 46; DLB 40
Reaney, James 1926- **CLC 13; DAC; DAM MST**
See also CA 41-44R; CAAS 15; CANR 42; DLB 68; SATA 43
Rebreanu, Liviu 1885-1944 **TCLC 28**
See also CA 165; DLB 220
Rechy, John (Francisco) 1934- **CLC 1, 7, 14, 18, 107; DAM MULT; HLC 2**
See also CA 5-8R; CAAS 4; CANR 6, 32, 64; DLB 122; DLBY 82; HW 1, 2; INT CANR-6
Redcam, Tom 1870-1933 **TCLC 25**
Reddin, Keith CLC 67
Redgrove, Peter (William) 1932- **CLC 6, 41**
See also CA 1-4R; CANR 3, 39, 77; DLB 40
Redmon, Anne CLC 22
See also Nightingale, Anne Redmon
See also DLBY 86
Reed, Eliot
See Ambler, Eric
Reed, Ishmael 1938- **CLC 2, 3, 5, 6, 13, 32, 60; BLC 3; DAM MULT**
See also BW 2, 3; CA 21-24R; CANR 25, 48, 74; DA3; DLB 2, 5, 33, 169, 227; DLBD 8; MTCW 1, 2
Reed, John (Silas) 1887-1920 **TCLC 9**
See also CA 106
Reed, Lou CLC 21
See also Firbank, Louis
Reese, Lizette Woodworth 1856-1935 **PC 29**
See also CA 180; DLB 54
Reeve, Clara 1729-1807 **NCLC 19**
See also DLB 39
Reich, Wilhelm 1897-1957 **TCLC 57**
Reid, Christopher (John) 1949- **CLC 33**
See also CA 140; CANR 89; DLB 40
Reid, Desmond
See Moorcock, Michael (John)
Reid Banks, Lynne 1929-
See Banks, Lynne Reid
See also CA 1-4R; CANR 6, 22, 38, 87; CLR 24; JRDA; MAICYA; SATA 22, 75, 111
Reilly, William K.
See Creasey, John
Reiner, Max
See Caldwell, (Janet Miriam) Taylor (Holland)
Reis, Ricardo
See Pessoa, Fernando (Antonio Nogueira)
Remarque, Erich Maria 1898-1970 **CLC 21; DA; DAB; DAC; DAM MST, NOV**
See also AAYA 27; CA 77-80; 29-32R; DA3; DLB 56; MTCW 1, 2
Remington, Frederic 1861-1909 **TCLC 89**
See also CA 108; 169; DLB 12, 186, 188; SATA 41
Remizov, A.
See Remizov, Aleksei (Mikhailovich)
Remizov, A. M.
See Remizov, Aleksei (Mikhailovich)
Remizov, Aleksei (Mikhailovich) 1877-1957 **TCLC 27**
See also CA 125; 133
Renan, Joseph Ernest 1823-1892 **NCLC 26**
Renard, Jules 1864-1910 **TCLC 17**
See also CA 117
Renault, Mary -1983 **CLC 3, 11, 17**
See also Challans, Mary
See also DLBY 83; MTCW 2
Rendell, Ruth (Barbara) 1930- **CLC 28, 48; DAM POP**
See also Vine, Barbara
See also CA 109; CANR 32, 52, 74; DLB 87; INT CANR-32; MTCW 1, 2
Renoir, Jean 1894-1979 **CLC 20**
See also CA 129; 85-88
Resnais, Alain 1922- **CLC 16**
Reverdy, Pierre 1889-1960 **CLC 53**
See also CA 97-100; 89-92
Rexroth, Kenneth 1905-1982 **CLC 1, 2, 6, 11, 22, 49, 112; DAM POET; PC 20**
See also CA 5-8R; 107; CANR 14, 34, 63; CDALB 1941-1968; DLB 16, 48, 165, 212; DLBY 82; INT CANR-14; MTCW 1, 2
Reyes, Alfonso 1889-1959 **TCLC 33; HLCS 2**
See also CA 131; HW 1
Reyes y Basoalto, Ricardo Eliecer Neftali
See Neruda, Pablo
Reymont, Wladyslaw (Stanislaw) 1868(?)-1925 **TCLC 5**
See also CA 104
Reynolds, Jonathan 1942- **CLC 6, 38**
See also CA 65-68; CANR 28
Reynolds, Joshua 1723-1792 **LC 15**
See also DLB 104
Reynolds, Michael S(hane) 1937- **CLC 44**
See also CA 65-68; CANR 9, 89
Reznikoff, Charles 1894-1976 **CLC 9**
See also CA 33-36; 61-64; CAP 2; DLB 28, 45
Rezzori (d'Arezzo), Gregor von 1914-1998 **CLC 25**
See also CA 122; 136; 167
Rhine, Richard
See Silverstein, Alvin
Rhodes, Eugene Manlove 1869-1934 **TCLC 53**
Rhodius, Apollonius c. 3rd cent. B.C.- **CMLC 28**
See also DLB 176
R'hoone
See Balzac, Honore de
Rhys, Jean 1890(?)-1979 **CLC 2, 4, 6, 14, 19, 51, 124; DAM NOV; SSC 21**
See also CA 25-28R; 85-88; CANR 35, 62; CDBLB 1945-1960; DA3; DLB 36, 117, 162; MTCW 1, 2
Ribeiro, Darcy 1922-1997 **CLC 34**
See also CA 33-36R; 156
Ribeiro, Joao Ubaldo (Osorio Pimentel) 1941- **CLC 10, 67**
See also CA 81-84
Ribman, Ronald (Burt) 1932- **CLC 7**
See also CA 21-24R; CANR 46, 80
Ricci, Nino 1959- **CLC 70**
See also CA 137
Rice, Anne 1941- **CLC 41, 128; DAM POP**
See also AAYA 9; BEST 89:2; CA 65-68; CANR 12, 36, 53, 74; DA3; MTCW 2
Rice, Elmer (Leopold) 1892-1967 **CLC 7, 49; DAM DRAM**
See also CA 21-22; 25-28R; CAP 2; DLB 4, 7; MTCW 1, 2
Rice, Tim(othy Miles Bindon) 1944- **CLC 21**
See also CA 103; CANR 46
Rich, Adrienne (Cecile) 1929- **CLC 3, 6, 7, 11, 18, 36, 73, 76, 125; DAM POET; PC 5**
See also CA 9-12R; CANR 20, 53, 74; CDALBS; DA3; DLB 5, 67; MTCW 1, 2
Rich, Barbara
See Graves, Robert (von Ranke)
Rich, Robert
See Trumbo, Dalton
Richard, Keith CLC 17

See also Richards, Keith
Richards, David Adams 1950- **CLC 59; DAC**
See also CA 93-96; CANR 60; DLB 53
Richards, I(vor) A(rmstrong) 1893-1979 **CLC 14, 24**
See also CA 41-44R; 89-92; CANR 34, 74; DLB 27; MTCW 2
Richards, Keith 1943-
See Richard, Keith
See also CA 107; CANR 77
Richardson, Anne
See Roiphe, Anne (Richardson)
Richardson, Dorothy Miller 1873-1957 **TCLC 3**
See also CA 104; DLB 36
Richardson, Ethel Florence (Lindesay) 1870-1946
See Richardson, Henry Handel
See also CA 105
Richardson, Henry Handel TCLC 4
See also Richardson, Ethel Florence (Lindesay)
See also DLB 197
Richardson, John 1796-1852 **NCLC 55; DAC**
See also DLB 99
Richardson, Samuel 1689-1761 **LC 1, 44; DA; DAB; DAC; DAM MST, NOV; WLC**
See also CDBLB 1660-1789; DLB 39
Richler, Mordecai 1931- **CLC 3, 5, 9, 13, 18, 46, 70; DAC; DAM MST, NOV**
See also AITN 1; CA 65-68; CANR 31, 62; CLR 17; DLB 53; MAICYA; MTCW 1, 2; SATA 44, 98; SATA-Brief 27
Richter, Conrad (Michael) 1890-1968 **CLC 30**
See also AAYA 21; CA 5-8R; 25-28R; CANR 23; DLB 9, 212; MTCW 1, 2; SATA 3
Ricostranza, Tom
See Ellis, Trey
Riddell, Charlotte 1832-1906 **TCLC 40**
See also CA 165; DLB 156
Ridge, John Rollin 1827-1867 **NCLC 82; DAM MULT**
See also CA 144; DLB 175; NNAL
Ridgway, Keith 1965- **CLC 119**
See also CA 172
Riding, Laura CLC 3, 7
See also Jackson, Laura (Riding)
Riefenstahl, Berta Helene Amalia 1902-
See Riefenstahl, Leni
See also CA 108
Riefenstahl, Leni CLC 16
See also Riefenstahl, Berta Helene Amalia
Riffe, Ernest
See Bergman, (Ernst) Ingmar
Riggs, (Rolla) Lynn 1899-1954 **TCLC 56; DAM MULT**
See also CA 144; DLB 175; NNAL
Riis, Jacob A(ugust) 1849-1914 **TCLC 80**
See also CA 113; 168; DLB 23
Riley, James Whitcomb 1849-1916 **TCLC 51; DAM POET**
See also CA 118; 137; MAICYA; SATA 17
Riley, Tex
See Creasey, John
Rilke, Rainer Maria 1875-1926 **TCLC 1, 6, 19; DAM POET; PC 2**
See also CA 104; 132; CANR 62; DA3; DLB 81; MTCW 1, 2
Rimbaud, (Jean Nicolas) Arthur 1854-1891 **NCLC 4, 35, 82; DA; DAB; DAC; DAM MST, POET; PC 3; WLC**
See also DA3
Rinehart, Mary Roberts 1876-1958 **TCLC 52**
See also CA 108; 166
Ringmaster, The
See Mencken, H(enry) L(ouis)
Ringwood, Gwen(dolyn Margaret) Pharis 1910-1984 **CLC 48**
See also CA 148; 112; DLB 88
Rio, Michel 19(?)- **CLC 43**
Ritsos, Giannes
See Ritsos, Yannis
Ritsos, Yannis 1909-1990 **CLC 6, 13, 31**
See also CA 77-80; 133; CANR 39, 61; MTCW 1
Ritter, Erika 1948(?)- **CLC 52**
Rivera, Jose Eustasio 1889-1928 **TCLC 35**
See also CA 162; HW 1, 2
Rivera, Tomas 1935-1984
See also CA 49-52; CANR 32; DLB 82; HLCS 2; HW 1
Rivers, Conrad Kent 1933-1968 **CLC 1**
See also BW 1; CA 85-88; DLB 41
Rivers, Elfrida
See Bradley, Marion Zimmer
Riverside, John
See Heinlein, Robert A(nson)
Rizal, Jose 1861-1896 **NCLC 27**
Roa Bastos, Augusto (Antonio) 1917- **CLC 45; DAM MULT; HLC 2**
See also CA 131; DLB 113; HW 1
Robbe-Grillet, Alain 1922- **CLC 1, 2, 4, 6, 8, 10, 14, 43, 128**
See also CA 9-12R; CANR 33, 65; DLB 83; MTCW 1, 2
Robbins, Harold 1916-1997 **CLC 5; DAM NOV**
See also CA 73-76; 162; CANR 26, 54; DA3; MTCW 1, 2
Robbins, Thomas Eugene 1936-
See Robbins, Tom
See also CA 81-84; CANR 29, 59; DAM NOV, POP; DA3; MTCW 1, 2
Robbins, Tom CLC 9, 32, 64
See also Robbins, Thomas Eugene
See also AAYA 32; BEST 90:3; DLBY 80; MTCW 2
Robbins, Trina 1938- **CLC 21**
See also CA 128
Roberts, Charles G(eorge) D(ouglas) 1860-1943 **TCLC 8**
See also CA 105; CLR 33; DLB 92; SATA 88; SATA-Brief 29
Roberts, Elizabeth Madox 1886-1941 **TCLC 68**
See also CA 111; 166; DLB 9, 54, 102; SATA 33; SATA-Brief 27
Roberts, Kate 1891-1985 **CLC 15**
See also CA 107; 116
Roberts, Keith (John Kingston) 1935- **CLC 14**
See also CA 25-28R; CANR 46
Roberts, Kenneth (Lewis) 1885-1957 **TCLC 23**
See also CA 109; DLB 9
Roberts, Michele (B.) 1949- **CLC 48**
See also CA 115; CANR 58; DLB 231
Robertson, Ellis
See Ellison, Harlan (Jay); Silverberg, Robert
Robertson, Thomas William 1829-1871 **NCLC 35; DAM DRAM**
Robeson, Kenneth
See Dent, Lester
Robinson, Edwin Arlington 1869-1935 **TCLC 5, 101; DA; DAC; DAM MST, POET; PC 1**
See also CA 104; 133; CDALB 1865-1917; DLB 54; MTCW 1, 2
Robinson, Henry Crabb 1775-1867 **NCLC 15**
See also DLB 107
Robinson, Jill 1936- **CLC 10**
See also CA 102; INT 102
Robinson, Kim Stanley 1952- **CLC 34**
See also AAYA 26; CA 126; SATA 109
Robinson, Lloyd
See Silverberg, Robert
Robinson, Marilynne 1944- **CLC 25**
See also CA 116; CANR 80; DLB 206
Robinson, Smokey CLC 21
See also Robinson, William, Jr.
Robinson, William, Jr. 1940-
See Robinson, Smokey
See also CA 116
Robison, Mary 1949- **CLC 42, 98**
See also CA 113; 116; CANR 87; DLB 130; INT 116
Rod, Edouard 1857-1910 **TCLC 52**
Roddenberry, Eugene Wesley 1921-1991
See Roddenberry, Gene
See also CA 110; 135; CANR 37; SATA 45; SATA-Obit 69
Roddenberry, Gene CLC 17
See also Roddenberry, Eugene Wesley
See also AAYA 5; SATA-Obit 69
Rodgers, Mary 1931- **CLC 12**
See also CA 49-52; CANR 8, 55, 90; CLR 20; INT CANR-8; JRDA; MAICYA; SATA 8
Rodgers, W(illiam) R(obert) 1909-1969 **CLC 7**
See also CA 85-88; DLB 20
Rodman, Eric
See Silverberg, Robert
Rodman, Howard 1920(?)-1985 **CLC 65**
See also CA 118
Rodman, Maia
See Wojciechowska, Maia (Teresa)
Rodo, Jose Enrique 1872(?)-1917
See also CA 178; HLCS 2; HW 2
Rodriguez, Claudio 1934- **CLC 10**
See also DLB 134
Rodriguez, Richard 1944-
See also CA 110; CANR 66; DAM MULT; DLB 82; HLC 2; HW 1, 2
Roelvaag, O(le) E(dvart) 1876-1931 **TCLC 17**
See also Rolvaag, O(le) E(dvart)
See also CA 117; 171; DLB 9
Roethke, Theodore (Huebner) 1908-1963 **CLC 1, 3, 8, 11, 19, 46, 101; DAM POET; PC 15**
See also CA 81-84; CABS 2; CDALB 1941-1968; DA3; DLB 5, 206; MTCW 1, 2
Rogers, Samuel 1763-1855 **NCLC 69**
See also DLB 93
Rogers, Thomas Hunton 1927- **CLC 57**
See also CA 89-92; INT 89-92
Rogers, Will(iam Penn Adair) 1879-1935 **TCLC 8, 71; DAM MULT**
See also CA 105; 144; DA3; DLB 11; MTCW 2; NNAL
Rogin, Gilbert 1929- **CLC 18**
See also CA 65-68; CANR 15
Rohan, Koda
See Koda Shigeyuki
Rohlfs, Anna Katharine Green
See Green, Anna Katharine
Rohmer, Eric CLC 16
See also Scherer, Jean-Marie Maurice
Rohmer, Sax TCLC 28
See also Ward, Arthur Henry Sarsfield
See also DLB 70
Roiphe, Anne (Richardson) 1935- **CLC 3, 9**
See also CA 89-92; CANR 45, 73; DLBY 80; INT 89-92
Rojas, Fernando de 1465-1541 **LC 23; HLCS 1**
Rojas, Gonzalo 1917-
See also HLCS 2; HW 2
Rojas, Gonzalo 1917-
See also CA 178; HLCS 2

Rolfe, Frederick (William Serafino Austin Lewis Mary) 1860-1913 **TCLC 12**
See also CA 107; DLB 34, 156
Rolland, Romain 1866-1944 **TCLC 23**
See also CA 118; DLB 65
Rolle, Richard c. 1300-c. 1349 **CMLC 21**
See also DLB 146
Rolvaag, O(le) E(dvart)
See Roelvaag, O(le) E(dvart)
Romain Arnaud, Saint
See Aragon, Louis
Romains, Jules 1885-1972 **CLC 7**
See also CA 85-88; CANR 34; DLB 65; MTCW 1
Romero, Jose Ruben 1890-1952 **TCLC 14**
See also CA 114; 131; HW 1
Ronsard, Pierre de 1524-1585 **LC 6, 54; PC 11**
Rooke, Leon 1934- **CLC 25, 34; DAM POP**
See also CA 25-28R; CANR 23, 53
Roosevelt, Franklin Delano 1882-1945 **TCLC 93**
See also CA 116; 173
Roosevelt, Theodore 1858-1919 **TCLC 69**
See also CA 115; 170; DLB 47, 186
Roper, William 1498-1578 **LC 10**
Roquelaure, A. N.
See Rice, Anne
Rosa, Joao Guimaraes 1908-1967 **CLC 23; HLCS 1**
See also CA 89-92; DLB 113
Rose, Wendy 1948- **CLC 85; DAM MULT; PC 13**
See also CA 53-56; CANR 5, 51; DLB 175; NNAL; SATA 12
Rosen, R. D.
See Rosen, Richard (Dean)
Rosen, Richard (Dean) 1949- **CLC 39**
See also CA 77-80; CANR 62; INT CANR-30
Rosenberg, Isaac 1890-1918 **TCLC 12**
See also CA 107; DLB 20
Rosenblatt, Joe CLC 15
See also Rosenblatt, Joseph
Rosenblatt, Joseph 1933-
See Rosenblatt, Joe
See also CA 89-92; INT 89-92
Rosenfeld, Samuel
See Tzara, Tristan
Rosenstock, Sami
See Tzara, Tristan
Rosenstock, Samuel
See Tzara, Tristan
Rosenthal, M(acha) L(ouis) 1917-1996 **CLC 28**
See also CA 1-4R; 152; CAAS 6; CANR 4, 51; DLB 5; SATA 59
Ross, Barnaby
See Dannay, Frederic
Ross, Bernard L.
See Follett, Ken(neth Martin)
Ross, J. H.
See Lawrence, T(homas) E(dward)
Ross, John Hume
See Lawrence, T(homas) E(dward)
Ross, Martin
See Martin, Violet Florence
See also DLB 135
Ross, (James) Sinclair 1908-1996 **CLC 13; DAC; DAM MST; SSC 24**
See also CA 73-76; CANR 81; DLB 88
Rossetti, Christina (Georgina) 1830-1894 **NCLC 2, 50, 66; DA; DAB; DAC; DAM MST, POET; PC 7; WLC**
See also DA3; DLB 35, 163; MAICYA; SATA 20
Rossetti, Dante Gabriel 1828-1882 **NCLC 4, 77; DA; DAB; DAC; DAM MST, POET; WLC**
See also CDBLB 1832-1890; DLB 35
Rossner, Judith (Perelman) 1935- **CLC 6, 9, 29**
See also AITN 2; BEST 90:3; CA 17-20R; CANR 18, 51, 73; DLB 6; INT CANR-18; MTCW 1, 2
Rostand, Edmond (Eugene Alexis) 1868-1918 **TCLC 6, 37; DA; DAB; DAC; DAM DRAM, MST; DC 10**
See also CA 104; 126; DA3; DLB 192; MTCW 1
Roth, Henry 1906-1995 **CLC 2, 6, 11, 104**
See also CA 11-12; 149; CANR 38, 63; CAP 1; DA3; DLB 28; MTCW 1, 2
Roth, Philip (Milton) 1933- **CLC 1, 2, 3, 4, 6, 9, 15, 22, 31, 47, 66, 86, 119; DA; DAB; DAC; DAM MST, NOV, POP; SSC 26; WLC**
See also BEST 90:3; CA 1-4R; CANR 1, 22, 36, 55, 89; CDALB 1968-1988; DA3; DLB 2, 28, 173; DLBY 82; MTCW 1, 2
Rothenberg, Jerome 1931- **CLC 6, 57**
See also CA 45-48; CANR 1; DLB 5, 193
Roumain, Jacques (Jean Baptiste) 1907-1944 **TCLC 19; BLC 3; DAM MULT**
See also BW 1; CA 117; 125
Rourke, Constance (Mayfield) 1885-1941 **TCLC 12**
See also CA 107; YABC 1
Rousseau, Jean-Baptiste 1671-1741 **LC 9**
Rousseau, Jean-Jacques 1712-1778 **LC 14, 36; DA; DAB; DAC; DAM MST; WLC**
See also DA3
Roussel, Raymond 1877-1933 **TCLC 20**
See also CA 117
Rovit, Earl (Herbert) 1927- **CLC 7**
See also CA 5-8R; CANR 12
Rowe, Elizabeth Singer 1674-1737 **LC 44**
See also DLB 39, 95
Rowe, Nicholas 1674-1718 **LC 8**
See also DLB 84
Rowley, Ames Dorrance
See Lovecraft, H(oward) P(hillips)
Rowson, Susanna Haswell 1762(?)-1824 **NCLC 5, 69**
See also DLB 37, 200
Roy, Arundhati 1960(?)- **CLC 109**
See also CA 163; CANR 90; DLBY 97
Roy, Gabrielle 1909-1983 **CLC 10, 14; DAB; DAC; DAM MST**
See also CA 53-56; 110; CANR 5, 61; DLB 68; MTCW 1; SATA 104
Royko, Mike 1932-1997 **CLC 109**
See also CA 89-92; 157; CANR 26
Rozewicz, Tadeusz 1921- **CLC 9, 23; DAM POET**
See also CA 108; CANR 36, 66; DA3; DLB 232; MTCW 1, 2
Ruark, Gibbons 1941- **CLC 3**
See also CA 33-36R; CAAS 23; CANR 14, 31, 57; DLB 120
Rubens, Bernice (Ruth) 1923- **CLC 19, 31**
See also CA 25-28R; CANR 33, 65; DLB 14, 207; MTCW 1
Rubin, Harold
See Robbins, Harold
Rudkin, (James) David 1936- **CLC 14**
See also CA 89-92; DLB 13
Rudnik, Raphael 1933- **CLC 7**
See also CA 29-32R
Ruffian, M.
See Hasek, Jaroslav (Matej Frantisek)
Ruiz, Jose Martinez CLC 11
See also Martinez Ruiz, Jose
Rukeyser, Muriel 1913-1980 **CLC 6, 10, 15, 27; DAM POET; PC 12**
See also CA 5-8R; 93-96; CANR 26, 60; DA3; DLB 48; MTCW 1, 2; SATA-Obit 22
Rule, Jane (Vance) 1931- **CLC 27**
See also CA 25-28R; CAAS 18; CANR 12, 87; DLB 60
Rulfo, Juan 1918-1986 **CLC 8, 80; DAM MULT; HLC 2; SSC 25**
See also CA 85-88; 118; CANR 26; DLB 113; HW 1, 2; MTCW 1, 2
Rumi, Jalal al-Din 1297-1373 **CMLC 20**
Runeberg, Johan 1804-1877 **NCLC 41**
Runyon, (Alfred) Damon 1884(?)-1946 **TCLC 10**
See also CA 107; 165; DLB 11, 86, 171; MTCW 2
Rush, Norman 1933- **CLC 44**
See also CA 121; 126; INT 126
Rushdie, (Ahmed) Salman 1947- **CLC 23, 31, 55, 100; DAB; DAC; DAM MST, NOV, POP; WLCS**
See also BEST 89:3; CA 108; 111; CANR 33, 56; DA3; DLB 194; INT 111; MTCW 1, 2
Rushforth, Peter (Scott) 1945- **CLC 19**
See also CA 101
Ruskin, John 1819-1900 **TCLC 63**
See also CA 114; 129; CDBLB 1832-1890; DLB 55, 163, 190; SATA 24
Russ, Joanna 1937- **CLC 15**
See also CA 5-28R; CANR 11, 31, 65; DLB 8; MTCW 1
Russell, George William 1867-1935
See Baker, Jean H.
See also CA 104; 153; CDBLB 1890-1914; DAM POET
Russell, (Henry) Ken(neth Alfred) 1927- **CLC 16**
See also CA 105
Russell, William Martin 1947- **CLC 60**
See also CA 164; DLB 233
Rutherford, Mark TCLC 25
See also White, William Hale
See also DLB 18
Ruyslinck, Ward 1929- **CLC 14**
See also Belser, Reimond Karel Maria de
Ryan, Cornelius (John) 1920-1974 **CLC 7**
See also CA 69-72; 53-56; CANR 38
Ryan, Michael 1946- **CLC 65**
See also CA 49-52; DLBY 82
Ryan, Tim
See Dent, Lester
Rybakov, Anatoli (Naumovich) 1911-1998 **CLC 23, 53**
See also CA 126; 135; 172; SATA 79; SATA-Obit 108
Ryder, Jonathan
See Ludlum, Robert
Ryga, George 1932-1987 **CLC 14; DAC; DAM MST**
See also CA 101; 124; CANR 43, 90; DLB 60
S. H.
See Hartmann, Sadakichi
S. S.
See Sassoon, Siegfried (Lorraine)
Saba, Umberto 1883-1957 **TCLC 33**
See also CA 144; CANR 79; DLB 114
Sabatini, Rafael 1875-1950 **TCLC 47**
See also CA 162
Sabato, Ernesto (R.) 1911- **CLC 10, 23; DAM MULT; HLC 2**
See also CA 97-100; CANR 32, 65; DLB 145; HW 1, 2; MTCW 1, 2
Sa-Carniero, Mario de 1890-1916 **TCLC 83**
Sacastru, Martin
See Bioy Casares, Adolfo

Savan, Glenn 19(?)- **CLC 50**
Sayers, Dorothy L(eigh) 1893-1957 **TCLC 2, 15; DAM POP**
See also CA 104; 119; CANR 60; CDBLB 1914-1945; DLB 10, 36, 77, 100; MTCW 1, 2
Sayers, Valerie 1952- **CLC 50, 122**
See also CA 134; CANR 61
Sayles, John (Thomas) 1950- **CLC 7, 10, 14**
See also CA 57-60; CANR 41, 84; DLB 44
Scammell, Michael 1935- **CLC 34**
See also CA 156
Scannell, Vernon 1922- **CLC 49**
See also CA 5-8R; CANR 8, 24, 57; DLB 27; SATA 59
Scarlett, Susan
See Streatfeild, (Mary) Noel
Scarron
See Mikszath, Kalman
Schaeffer, Susan Fromberg 1941- **CLC 6, 11, 22**
See also CA 49-52; CANR 18, 65; DLB 28; MTCW 1, 2; SATA 22
Schary, Jill
See Robinson, Jill
Schell, Jonathan 1943- **CLC 35**
See also CA 73-76; CANR 12
Schelling, Friedrich Wilhelm Joseph von 1775-1854 **NCLC 30**
See also DLB 90
Schendel, Arthur van 1874-1946 **TCLC 56**
Scherer, Jean-Marie Maurice 1920-
See Rohmer, Eric
See also CA 110
Schevill, James (Erwin) 1920- **CLC 7**
See also CA 5-8R; CAAS 12
Schiller, Friedrich 1759-1805 **NCLC 39, 69; DAM DRAM; DC 12**
See also DLB 94
Schisgal, Murray (Joseph) 1926- **CLC 6**
See also CA 21-24R; CANR 48, 86
Schlee, Ann 1934- **CLC 35**
See also CA 101; CANR 29, 88; SATA 44; SATA-Brief 36
Schlegel, August Wilhelm von 1767-1845 **NCLC 15**
See also DLB 94
Schlegel, Friedrich 1772-1829 **NCLC 45**
See also DLB 90
Schlegel, Johann Elias (von) 1719(?)-1749 **LC 5**
Schlesinger, Arthur M(eier), Jr. 1917- **CLC 84**
See also AITN 1; CA 1-4R; CANR 1, 28, 58; DLB 17; INT CANR-28; MTCW 1, 2; SATA 61
Schmidt, Arno (Otto) 1914-1979 **CLC 56**
See also CA 128; 109; DLB 69
Schmitz, Aron Hector 1861-1928
See Svevo, Italo
See also CA 104; 122; MTCW 1
Schnackenberg, Gjertrud 1953- **CLC 40**
See also CA 116; DLB 120
Schneider, Leonard Alfred 1925-1966
See Bruce, Lenny
See also CA 89-92
Schnitzler, Arthur 1862-1931 **TCLC 4; SSC 15**
See also CA 104; DLB 81, 118
Schoenberg, Arnold 1874-1951 **TCLC 75**
See also CA 109
Schonberg, Arnold
See Schoenberg, Arnold
Schopenhauer, Arthur 1788-1860 **NCLC 51**
See also DLB 90
Schor, Sandra (M.) 1932(?)-1990 **CLC 65**
See also CA 132
Schorer, Mark 1908-1977 **CLC 9**
See also CA 5-8R; 73-76; CANR 7; DLB 103
Schrader, Paul (Joseph) 1946- **CLC 26**
See also CA 37-40R; CANR 41; DLB 44
Schreiner, Olive (Emilie Albertina) 1855-1920 **TCLC 9**
See also CA 105; 154; DLB 18, 156, 190, 225
Schulberg, Budd (Wilson) 1914- **CLC 7, 48**
See also CA 25-28R; CANR 19, 87; DLB 6, 26, 28; DLBY 81
Schulz, Bruno 1892-1942 **TCLC 5, 51; SSC 13**
See also CA 115; 123; CANR 86; MTCW 2
Schulz, Charles M(onroe) 1922-2000 **CLC 12**
See also CA 9-12R; 187; CANR 6; INT CANR-6; SATA 10; SATA-Obit 118
Schumacher, E(rnst) F(riedrich) 1911-1977 **CLC 80**
See also CA 81-84; 73-76; CANR 34, 85
Schuyler, James Marcus 1923-1991 **CLC 5, 23; DAM POET**
See also CA 101; 134; DLB 5, 169; INT 101
Schwartz, Delmore (David) 1913-1966 **CLC 2, 4, 10, 45, 87; PC 8**
See also CA 17-18; 25-28R; CANR 35; CAP 2; DLB 28, 48; MTCW 1, 2
Schwartz, Ernst
See Ozu, Yasujiro
Schwartz, John Burnham 1965- **CLC 59**
See also CA 132
Schwartz, Lynne Sharon 1939- **CLC 31**
See also CA 103; CANR 44, 89; MTCW 2
Schwartz, Muriel A.
See Eliot, T(homas) S(tearns)
Schwarz-Bart, Andre 1928- **CLC 2, 4**
See also CA 89-92
Schwarz-Bart, Simone 1938- **CLC 7; BLCS**
See also BW 2; CA 97-100
Schwitters, Kurt (Hermann Edward Karl Julius) 1887-1948 **TCLC 95**
See also CA 158
Schwob, Marcel (Mayer Andre) 1867-1905 **TCLC 20**
See also CA 117; 168; DLB 123
Sciascia, Leonardo 1921-1989 **CLC 8, 9, 41**
See also CA 85-88; 130; CANR 35; DLB 177; MTCW 1
Scoppettone, Sandra 1936- **CLC 26**
See also AAYA 11; CA 5-8R; CANR 41, 73; SATA 9, 92
Scorsese, Martin 1942- **CLC 20, 89**
See also CA 110; 114; CANR 46, 85
Scotland, Jay
See Jakes, John (William)
Scott, Duncan Campbell 1862-1947 **TCLC 6; DAC**
See also CA 104; 153; DLB 92
Scott, Evelyn 1893-1963 **CLC 43**
See also CA 104; 112; CANR 64; DLB 9, 48
Scott, F(rancis) R(eginald) 1899-1985 **CLC 22**
See also CA 101; 114; CANR 87; DLB 88; INT 101
Scott, Frank
See Scott, F(rancis) R(eginald)
Scott, Joanna 1960- **CLC 50**
See also CA 126; CANR 53, 92
Scott, Paul (Mark) 1920-1978 **CLC 9, 60**
See also CA 81-84; 77-80; CANR 33; DLB 14, 207; MTCW 1
Scott, Sarah 1723-1795 **LC 44**
See also DLB 39
Scott, Walter 1771-1832 **NCLC 15, 69; DA; DAB; DAC; DAM MST, NOV, POET; PC 13; SSC 32; WLC**
See also AAYA 22; CDBLB 1789-1832; DLB 93, 107, 116, 144, 159; YABC 2
Scribe, (Augustin) Eugene 1791-1861 **NCLC 16; DAM DRAM; DC 5**
See also DLB 192
Scrum, R.
See Crumb, R(obert)
Scudery, Madeleine de 1607-1701 **LC 2, 58**
Scum
See Crumb, R(obert)
Scumbag, Little Bobby
See Crumb, R(obert)
Seabrook, John
See Hubbard, L(afayette) Ron(ald)
Sealy, I(rwin) Allan 1951- **CLC 55**
See also CA 136
Search, Alexander
See Pessoa, Fernando (Antonio Nogueira)
Sebastian, Lee
See Silverberg, Robert
Sebastian Owl
See Thompson, Hunter S(tockton)
Sebestyen, Ouida 1924- **CLC 30**
See also AAYA 8; CA 107; CANR 40; CLR 17; JRDA; MAICYA; SAAS 10; SATA 39
Secundus, H. Scriblerus
See Fielding, Henry
Sedges, John
See Buck, Pearl S(ydenstricker)
Sedgwick, Catharine Maria 1789-1867 **NCLC 19**
See also DLB 1, 74
Seelye, John (Douglas) 1931- **CLC 7**
See also CA 97-100; CANR 70; INT 97-100
Seferiades, Giorgos Stylianou 1900-1971
See Seferis, George
See also CA 5-8R; 33-36R; CANR 5, 36; MTCW 1
Seferis, George CLC 5, 11
See also Seferiades, Giorgos Stylianou
Segal, Erich (Wolf) 1937- **CLC 3, 10; DAM POP**
See also BEST 89:1; CA 25-28R; CANR 20, 36, 65; DLBY 86; INT CANR-20; MTCW 1
Seger, Bob 1945- **CLC 35**
Seghers, Anna CLC 7
See also Radvanyi, Netty
See also DLB 69
Seidel, Frederick (Lewis) 1936- **CLC 18**
See also CA 13-16R; CANR 8; DLBY 84
Seifert, Jaroslav 1901-1986 **CLC 34, 44, 93**
See also CA 127; MTCW 1, 2
Sei Shonagon c. 966-1017(?) **CMLC 6**
Sejour, Victor 1817-1874 **DC 10**
See also DLB 50
Sejour Marcou et Ferrand, Juan Victor
See Sejour, Victor
Selby, Hubert, Jr. 1928- **CLC 1, 2, 4, 8; SSC 20**
See also CA 13-16R; CANR 33, 85; DLB 2, 227
Selzer, Richard 1928- **CLC 74**
See also CA 65-68; CANR 14
Sembene, Ousmane
See Ousmane, Sembene
Senancour, Etienne Pivert de 1770-1846 **NCLC 16**
See also DLB 119
Sender, Ramon (Jose) 1902-1982 **CLC 8; DAM MULT; HLC 2**
See also CA 5-8R; 105; CANR 8; HW 1; MTCW 1
Seneca, Lucius Annaeus c. 1-c. 65 **CMLC 6; DAM DRAM; DC 5**
See also DLB 211

Senghor, Leopold Sedar 1906- **CLC 54, 130; BLC 3; DAM MULT, POET; PC 25**
See also BW 2; CA 116; 125; CANR 47, 74; MTCW 1, 2
Senna, Danzy 1970- **CLC 119**
See also CA 169
Serling, (Edward) Rod(man) 1924-1975 **CLC 30**
See also AAYA 14; AITN 1; CA 162; 57-60; DLB 26
Serna, Ramon Gomez de la
See Gomez de la Serna, Ramon
Serpieres
See Guillevic, (Eugene)
Service, Robert
See Service, Robert W(illiam)
See also DAB; DLB 92
Service, Robert W(illiam) 1874(?)-1958 **TCLC 15; DA; DAC; DAM MST, POET; WLC**
See also Service, Robert
See also CA 115; 140; CANR 84; SATA 20
Seth, Vikram 1952- **CLC 43, 90; DAM MULT**
See also CA 121; 127; CANR 50, 74; DA3; DLB 120; INT 127; MTCW 2
Seton, Cynthia Propper 1926-1982 **CLC 27**
See also CA 5-8R; 108; CANR 7
Seton, Ernest (Evan) Thompson 1860-1946 **TCLC 31**
See also CA 109; CLR 59; DLB 92; DLBD 13; JRDA; SATA 18
Seton-Thompson, Ernest
See Seton, Ernest (Evan) Thompson
Settle, Mary Lee 1918- **CLC 19, 61**
See also CA 89-92; CAAS 1; CANR 44, 87; DLB 6; INT 89-92
Seuphor, Michel
See Arp, Jean
Sevigne, Marie (de Rabutin-Chantal) Marquise de 1626-1696 **LC 11**
Sewall, Samuel 1652-1730 **LC 38**
See also DLB 24
Sexton, Anne (Harvey) 1928-1974 **CLC 2, 4, 6, 8, 10, 15, 53, 123; DA; DAB; DAC; DAM MST, POET; PC 2; WLC**
See also CA 1-4R; 53-56; CABS 2; CANR 3, 36; CDALB 1941-1968; DA3; DLB 5, 169; MTCW 1, 2; SATA 10
Shaara, Jeff 1952- **CLC 119**
See also CA 163
Shaara, Michael (Joseph, Jr.) 1929-1988 **CLC 15; DAM POP**
See also AITN 1; CA 102; 125; CANR 52, 85; DLBY 83
Shackleton, C. C.
See Aldiss, Brian W(ilson)
Shacochis, Bob CLC 39
See also Shacochis, Robert G.
Shacochis, Robert G. 1951-
See Shacochis, Bob
See also CA 119; 124; INT 124
Shaffer, Anthony (Joshua) 1926- **CLC 19; DAM DRAM**
See also CA 110; 116; DLB 13
Shaffer, Peter (Levin) 1926- **CLC 5, 14, 18, 37, 60; DAB; DAM DRAM, MST; DC 7**
See also CA 25-28R; CANR 25, 47, 74; CDBLB 1960 to Present; DA3; DLB 13, 233; MTCW 1, 2
Shakey, Bernard
See Young, Neil
Shalamov, Varlam (Tikhonovich) 1907(?)-1982 **CLC 18**
See also CA 129; 105
Shamlu, Ahmad 1925- **CLC 10**
Shammas, Anton 1951- **CLC 55**
Shandling, Arline
See Berriault, Gina
Shange, Ntozake 1948- **CLC 8, 25, 38, 74, 126; BLC 3; DAM DRAM, MULT; DC 3**
See also AAYA 9; BW 2; CA 85-88; CABS 3; CANR 27, 48, 74; DA3; DLB 38; MTCW 1, 2
Shanley, John Patrick 1950- **CLC 75**
See also CA 128; 133; CANR 83
Shapcott, Thomas W(illiam) 1935- **CLC 38**
See also CA 69-72; CANR 49, 83
Shapiro, Jane CLC 76
Shapiro, Karl (Jay) 1913- **CLC 4, 8, 15, 53; PC 25**
See also CA 1-4R; CAAS 6; CANR 1, 36, 66; DLB 48; MTCW 1, 2
Sharp, William 1855-1905 **TCLC 39**
See also CA 160; DLB 156
Sharpe, Thomas Ridley 1928-
See Sharpe, Tom
See also CA 114; 122; CANR 85; DLB 231; INT 122
Sharpe, Tom CLC 36
See also Sharpe, Thomas Ridley
See also DLB 14
Shaw, Bernard
See Shaw, George Bernard
See also BW 1; MTCW 2
Shaw, G. Bernard
See Shaw, George Bernard
Shaw, George Bernard 1856-1950 **TCLC 3, 9, 21, 45; DA; DAB; DAC; DAM DRAM, MST; WLC**
See also Shaw, Bernard
See also CA 104; 128; CDBLB 1914-1945; DA3; DLB 10, 57, 190; MTCW 1, 2
Shaw, Henry Wheeler 1818-1885 **NCLC 15**
See also DLB 11
Shaw, Irwin 1913-1984 **CLC 7, 23, 34; DAM DRAM, POP**
See also AITN 1; CA 13-16R; 112; CANR 21; CDALB 1941-1968; DLB 6, 102; DLBY 84; MTCW 1, 21
Shaw, Robert 1927-1978 **CLC 5**
See also AITN 1; CA 1-4R; 81-84; CANR 4; DLB 13, 14
Shaw, T. E.
See Lawrence, T(homas) E(dward)
Shawn, Wallace 1943- **CLC 41**
See also CA 112
Shea, Lisa 1953- **CLC 86**
See also CA 147
Sheed, Wilfrid (John Joseph) 1930- **CLC 2, 4, 10, 53**
See also CA 65-68; CANR 30, 66; DLB 6; MTCW 1, 2
Sheldon, Alice Hastings Bradley 1915(?)-1987
See Tiptree, James, Jr.
See also CA 108; 122; CANR 34; INT 108; MTCW 1
Sheldon, John
See Bloch, Robert (Albert)
Sheldon, Walter J. 1917-
See Queen, Ellery
See also AITN 1; CA 25-28R; CANR 10
Shelley, Mary Wollstonecraft (Godwin) 1797-1851 **NCLC 14, 59; DA; DAB; DAC; DAM MST, NOV; WLC**
See also AAYA 20; CDBLB 1789-1832; DA3; DLB 110, 116, 159, 178; SATA 29
Shelley, Percy Bysshe 1792-1822 **NCLC 18, 93; DA; DAB; DAC; DAM MST, POET; PC 14; WLC**
See also CDBLB 1789-1832; DA3; DLB 96, 110, 158
Shepard, Jim 1956- **CLC 36**
See also CA 137; CANR 59; SATA 90
Shepard, Lucius 1947- **CLC 34**
See also CA 128; 141; CANR 81
Shepard, Sam 1943- **CLC 4, 6, 17, 34, 41, 44; DAM DRAM; DC 5**
See also AAYA 1; CA 69-72; CABS 3; CANR 22; DA3; DLB 7, 212; MTCW 1, 2
Shepherd, Michael
See Ludlum, Robert
Sherburne, Zoa (Lillian Morin) 1912-1995 **CLC 30**
See also AAYA 13; CA 1-4R; 176; CANR 3, 37; MAICYA; SAAS 18; SATA 3
Sheridan, Frances 1724-1766 **LC 7**
See also DLB 39, 84
Sheridan, Richard Brinsley 1751-1816 **NCLC 5, 91; DA; DAB; DAC; DAM DRAM, MST; DC 1; WLC**
See also CDBLB 1660-1789; DLB 89
Sherman, Jonathan Marc CLC 55
Sherman, Martin 1941(?)- **CLC 19**
See also CA 116; 123; CANR 86
Sherwin, Judith Johnson 1936-
See Johnson, Judith (Emlyn)
See also CANR 85
Sherwood, Frances 1940- **CLC 81**
See also CA 146
Sherwood, Robert E(mmet) 1896-1955 **TCLC 3; DAM DRAM**
See also CA 104; 153; CANR 86; DLB 7, 26
Shestov, Lev 1866-1938 **TCLC 56**
Shevchenko, Taras 1814-1861 **NCLC 54**
Shiel, M(atthew) P(hipps) 1865-1947 **TCLC 8**
See also Holmes, Gordon
See also CA 106; 160; DLB 153; MTCW 2
Shields, Carol 1935- **CLC 91, 113; DAC**
See also CA 81-84; CANR 51, 74; DA3; MTCW 2
Shields, David 1956- **CLC 97**
See also CA 124; CANR 48
Shiga, Naoya 1883-1971 **CLC 33; SSC 23**
See also CA 101; 33-36R; DLB 180
Shikibu, Murasaki c. 978-c. 1014 **CMLC 1**
Shilts, Randy 1951-1994 **CLC 85**
See also AAYA 19; CA 115; 127; 144; CANR 45; DA3; INT 127; MTCW 2
Shimazaki, Haruki 1872-1943
See Shimazaki Toson
See also CA 105; 134; CANR 84
Shimazaki Toson 1872-1943 **TCLC 5**
See also Shimazaki, Haruki
See also DLB 180
Sholokhov, Mikhail (Aleksandrovich) 1905-1984 **CLC 7, 15**
See also CA 101; 112; MTCW 1, 2; SATA-Obit 36
Shone, Patric
See Hanley, James
Shreve, Susan Richards 1939- **CLC 23**
See also CA 49-52; CAAS 5; CANR 5, 38, 69; MAICYA; SATA 46, 95; SATA-Brief 41
Shue, Larry 1946-1985 **CLC 52; DAM DRAM**
See also CA 145; 117
Shu-Jen, Chou 1881-1936
See Lu Hsun
See also CA 104
Shulman, Alix Kates 1932- **CLC 2, 10**
See also CA 29-32R; CANR 43; SATA 7
Shuster, Joe 1914- **CLC 21**
Shute, Nevil CLC 30
See also Norway, Nevil Shute
See also MTCW 2
Shuttle, Penelope (Diane) 1947- **CLC 7**
See also CA 93-96; CANR 39, 84, 92; DLB 14, 40
Sidney, Mary 1561-1621 **LC 19, 39**
Sidney, Sir Philip 1554-1586 **LC 19, 39; DA;**

DAB; DAC; DAM MST, POET; PC 32
See also CDBLB Before 1660; DA3; DLB 167

Siegel, Jerome 1914-1996 **CLC 21**
See also CA 116; 169; 151

Siegel, Jerry
See Siegel, Jerome

Sienkiewicz, Henryk (Adam Alexander Pius) 1846-1916 **TCLC 3**
See also CA 104; 134; CANR 84

Sierra, Gregorio Martinez
See Martinez Sierra, Gregorio

Sierra, Maria (de la O'LeJarraga) Martinez
See Martinez Sierra, Maria (de la O'LeJarraga)

Sigal, Clancy 1926- **CLC 7**
See also CA 1-4R; CANR 85

Sigourney, Lydia Howard (Huntley) 1791-1865 **NCLC 21, 87**
See also DLB 1, 42, 73

Siguenza y Gongora, Carlos de 1645-1700 **LC 8; HLCS 2**

Sigurjonsson, Johann 1880-1919 **TCLC 27**
See also CA 170

Sikelianos, Angelos 1884-1951 **TCLC 39; PC 29**

Silkin, Jon 1930- **CLC 2, 6, 43**
See also CA 5-8R; CAAS 5; CANR 89; DLB 27

Silko, Leslie (Marmon) 1948- **CLC 23, 74, 114; DA; DAC; DAM MST, MULT, POP; SSC 37; WLCS**
See also AAYA 14; CA 115; 122; CANR 45, 65; DA3; DLB 143, 175; MTCW 2; NNAL

Sillanpaa, Frans Eemil 1888-1964 **CLC 19**
See also CA 129; 93-96; MTCW 1

Sillitoe, Alan 1928- **CLC 1, 3, 6, 10, 19, 57**
See also AITN 1; CA 9-12R; CAAS 2; CANR 8, 26, 55; CDBLB 1960 to Present; DLB 14, 139; MTCW 1, 2; SATA 61

Silone, Ignazio 1900-1978 **CLC 4**
See also CA 25-28; 81-84; CANR 34; CAP 2; MTCW 1

Silver, Joan Micklin 1935- **CLC 20**
See also CA 114; 121; INT 121

Silver, Nicholas
See Faust, Frederick (Schiller)

Silverberg, Robert 1935- **CLC 7; DAM POP**
See also AAYA 24; CA 1-4R, 186; CAAE 186; CAAS 3; CANR 1, 20, 36, 85; CLR 59; DLB 8; INT CANR-20; MAICYA; MTCW 1, 2; SATA 13, 91; SATA-Essay 104

Silverstein, Alvin 1933- **CLC 17**
See also CA 49-52; CANR 2; CLR 25; JRDA; MAICYA; SATA 8, 69

Silverstein, Virginia B(arbara Opshelor) 1937- **CLC 17**
See also CA 49-52; CANR 2; CLR 25; JRDA; MAICYA; SATA 8, 69

Sim, Georges
See Simenon, Georges (Jacques Christian)

Simak, Clifford D(onald) 1904-1988 **CLC 1, 55**
See also CA 1-4R; 125; CANR 1, 35; DLB 8; MTCW 1; SATA-Obit 56

Simenon, Georges (Jacques Christian) 1903-1989 **CLC 1, 2, 3, 8, 18, 47; DAM POP**
See also CA 85-88; 129; CANR 35; DA3; DLB 72; DLBY 89; MTCW 1, 2

Simic, Charles 1938- **CLC 6, 9, 22, 49, 68, 130; DAM POET**
See also CA 29-32R; CAAS 4; CANR 12, 33, 52, 61; DA3; DLB 105; MTCW 2

Simmel, Georg 1858-1918 **TCLC 64**
See also CA 157

Simmons, Charles (Paul) 1924- **CLC 57**
See also CA 89-92; INT 89-92

Simmons, Dan 1948- **CLC 44; DAM POP**
See also AAYA 16; CA 138; CANR 53, 81

Simmons, James (Stewart Alexander) 1933- **CLC 43**
See also CA 105; CAAS 21; DLB 40

Simms, William Gilmore 1806-1870 **NCLC 3**
See also DLB 3, 30, 59, 73

Simon, Carly 1945- **CLC 26**
See also CA 105

Simon, Claude 1913- **CLC 4, 9, 15, 39; DAM NOV**
See also CA 89-92; CANR 33; DLB 83; MTCW 1

Simon, (Marvin) Neil 1927- **CLC 6, 11, 31, 39, 70; DAM DRAM**
See also AAYA 32; AITN 1; CA 21-24R; CANR 26, 54, 87; DA3; DLB 7; MTCW 1, 2

Simon, Paul (Frederick) 1941(?)- **CLC 17**
See also CA 116; 153

Simonon, Paul 1956(?)- **CLC 30**

Simpson, Harriette
See Arnow, Harriette (Louisa) Simpson

Simpson, Louis (Aston Marantz) 1923- **CLC 4, 7, 9, 32; DAM POET**
See also CA 1-4R; CAAS 4; CANR 1, 61; DLB 5; MTCW 1, 2

Simpson, Mona (Elizabeth) 1957- **CLC 44**
See also CA 122; 135; CANR 68

Simpson, N(orman) F(rederick) 1919- **CLC 29**
See also CA 13-16R; DLB 13

Sinclair, Andrew (Annandale) 1935- **CLC 2, 14**
See also CA 9-12R; CAAS 5; CANR 14, 38, 91; DLB 14; MTCW 1

Sinclair, Emil
See Hesse, Hermann

Sinclair, Iain 1943- **CLC 76**
See also CA 132; CANR 81

Sinclair, Iain MacGregor
See Sinclair, Iain

Sinclair, Irene
See Griffith, D(avid Lewelyn) W(ark)

Sinclair, Mary Amelia St. Clair 1865(?)-1946
See Sinclair, May
See also CA 104

Sinclair, May 1863-1946 **TCLC 3, 11**
See also Sinclair, Mary Amelia St. Clair
See also CA 166; DLB 36, 135

Sinclair, Roy
See Griffith, D(avid Lewelyn) W(ark)

Sinclair, Upton (Beall) 1878-1968 **CLC 1, 11, 15, 63; DA; DAB; DAC; DAM MST, NOV; WLC**
See also CA 5-8R; 25-28R; CANR 7; CDALB 1929-1941; DA3; DLB 9; INT CANR-7; MTCW 1, 2; SATA 9

Singer, Isaac
See Singer, Isaac Bashevis

Singer, Isaac Bashevis 1904-1991 **CLC 1, 3, 6, 9, 11, 15, 23, 38, 69, 111; DA; DAB; DAC; DAM MST, NOV; SSC 3; WLC**
See also AAYA 32; AITN 1, 2; CA 1-4R; 134; CANR 1, 39; CDALB 1941-1968; CLR 1; DA3; DLB 6, 28, 52; DLBY 91; JRDA; MAICYA; MTCW 1, 2; SATA 3, 27; SATA-Obit 68

Singer, Israel Joshua 1893-1944 **TCLC 33**
See also CA 169

Singh, Khushwant 1915- **CLC 11**
See also CA 9-12R; CAAS 9; CANR 6, 84

Singleton, Ann
See Benedict, Ruth (Fulton)

Sinjohn, John
See Galsworthy, John

Sinyavsky, Andrei (Donatevich) 1925-1997 **CLC 8**
See also CA 85-88; 159

Sirin, V.
See Nabokov, Vladimir (Vladimirovich)

Sissman, L(ouis) E(dward) 1928-1976 **CLC 9, 18**
See also CA 21-24R; 65-68; CANR 13; DLB 5

Sisson, C(harles) H(ubert) 1914- **CLC 8**
See also CA 1-4R; CAAS 3; CANR 3, 48, 84; DLB 27

Sitwell, Dame Edith 1887-1964 **CLC 2, 9, 67; DAM POET; PC 3**
See also CA 9-12R; CANR 35; CDBLB 1945-1960; DLB 20; MTCW 1, 2

Slwaarmlll, H. P.
See Sharp, William

Sjoewall, Maj 1935- **CLC 7**
See also Sjowall, Maj
See also CA 65-68; CANR 73

Sjowall, Maj
See Sjoewall, Maj

Skelton, John 1463-1529 **PC 25**

Skelton, Robin 1925-1997 **CLC 13**
See also AITN 2; CA 5-8R; 160; CAAS 5; CANR 28, 89; DLB 27, 53

Skolimowski, Jerzy 1938- **CLC 20**
See also CA 128

Skram, Amalie (Bertha) 1847-1905 **TCLC 25**
See also CA 165

Skvorecky, Josef (Vaclav) 1924- **CLC 15, 39, 69; DAC; DAM NOV**
See also CA 61-64; CAAS 1; CANR 10, 34, 63; DA3; DLB 232; MTCW 1, 2

Slade, Bernard **CLC 11, 46**
See also Newbound, Bernard Slade
See also CAAS 9; DLB 53

Slaughter, Carolyn 1946- **CLC 56**
See also CA 85-88; CANR 85

Slaughter, Frank G(ill) 1908- **CLC 29**
See also AITN 2; CA 5-8R; CANR 5, 85; INT CANR-5

Slavitt, David R(ytman) 1935- **CLC 5, 14**
See also CA 21-24R; CAAS 3; CANR 41, 83; DLB 5, 6

Slesinger, Tess 1905-1945 **TCLC 10**
See also CA 107; DLB 102

Slessor, Kenneth 1901-1971 **CLC 14**
See also CA 102; 89-92

Slowacki, Juliusz 1809-1849 **NCLC 15**

Smart, Christopher 1722-1771 **LC 3; DAM POET; PC 13**
See also DLB 109

Smart, Elizabeth 1913-1986 **CLC 54**
See also CA 81-84; 118; DLB 88

Smiley, Jane (Graves) 1949- **CLC 53, 76; DAM POP**
See also CA 104; CANR 30, 50, 74; DA3; DLB 227; INT CANR-30

Smith, A(rthur) J(ames) M(arshall) 1902-1980 **CLC 15; DAC**
See also CA 1-4R; 102; CANR 4; DLB 88

Smith, Adam 1723-1790 **LC 36**
See also DLB 104

Smith, Alexander 1829-1867 **NCLC 59**
See also DLB 32, 55

Smith, Anna Deavere 1950- **CLC 86**
See also CA 133

Smith, Betty (Wehner) 1896-1972 **CLC 19**
See also CA 5-8R; 33-36R; DLBY 82; SATA 6

Smith, Charlotte (Turner) 1749-1806 **NCLC 23**
See also DLB 39, 109

Smith, Clark Ashton 1893-1961 **CLC 43**
See also CA 143; CANR 81; MTCW 2

Smith, Dave **CLC 22, 42**
See also Smith, David (Jeddie)
See also CAAS 7; DLB 5

Smith, David (Jeddie) 1942-
See Smith, Dave
See also CA 49-52; CANR 1, 59; DAM POET

Smith, Florence Margaret 1902-1971
See Smith, Stevie
See also CA 17-18; 29-32R; CANR 35; CAP 2; DAM POET; MTCW 1, 2

Smith, Iain Crichton 1928-1998 **CLC 64**
See also CA 21-24R; 171; DLB 40, 139

Smith, John 1580(?)-1631 **LC 9**
See also DLB 24, 30

Smith, Johnston
See Crane, Stephen (Townley)

Smith, Joseph, Jr. 1805-1844 **NCLC 53**

Smith, Lee 1944- **CLC 25, 73**
See also CA 114; 119; CANR 46; DLB 143; DLBY 83; INT 119

Smith, Martin
See Smith, Martin Cruz

Smith, Martin Cruz 1942- **CLC 25; DAM MULT, POP**
See also BEST 89:4; CA 85-88; CANR 6, 23, 43, 65; INT CANR-23; MTCW 2; NNAL

Smith, Mary-Ann Tirone 1944- **CLC 39**
See also CA 118; 136

Smith, Patti 1946- **CLC 12**
See also CA 93-96; CANR 63

Smith, Pauline (Urmson) 1882-1959 **TCLC 25**
See also DLB 225

Smith, Rosamond
See Oates, Joyce Carol

Smith, Sheila Kaye
See Kaye-Smith, Sheila

Smith, Stevie CLC 3, 8, 25, 44; PC 12
See also Smith, Florence Margaret
See also DLB 20; MTCW 2

Smith, Wilbur (Addison) 1933- **CLC 33**
See also CA 13-16R; CANR 7, 46, 66; MTCW 1, 2

Smith, William Jay 1918- **CLC 6**
See also CA 5-8R; CANR 44; DLB 5; MAICYA; SAAS 22; SATA 2, 68

Smith, Woodrow Wilson
See Kuttner, Henry

Smolenskin, Peretz 1842-1885 **NCLC 30**

Smollett, Tobias (George) 1721-1771 **LC 2, 46**
See also CDBLB 1660-1789; DLB 39, 104

Snodgrass, W(illiam) D(e Witt) 1926- **CLC 2, 6, 10, 18, 68; DAM POET**
See also CA 1-4R; CANR 6, 36, 65, 85; DLB 5; MTCW 1, 2

Snow, C(harles) P(ercy) 1905-1980 **CLC 1, 4, 6, 9, 13, 19; DAM NOV**
See also CA 5-8R; 101; CANR 28; CDBLB 1945-1960; DLB 15, 77; DLBD 17; MTCW 1, 2

Snow, Frances Compton
See Adams, Henry (Brooks)

Snyder, Gary (Sherman) 1930- **CLC 1, 2, 5, 9, 32, 120; DAM POET; PC 21**
See also CA 17-20R; CANR 30, 60; DA3; DLB 5, 16, 165, 212; MTCW 2

Snyder, Zilpha Keatley 1927- **CLC 17**
See also AAYA 15; CA 9-12R; CANR 38; CLR 31; JRDA; MAICYA; SAAS 2; SATA 1, 28, 75, 110; SATA-Essay 112

Soares, Bernardo
See Pessoa, Fernando (Antonio Nogueira)

Sobh, A.
See Shamlu, Ahmad

Sobol, Joshua CLC 60

Socrates 469B.C.-399B.C. **CMLC 27**

Soderberg, Hjalmar 1869-1941 **TCLC 39**

Sodergran, Edith (Irene)
See Soedergran, Edith (Irene)

Soedergran, Edith (Irene) 1892-1923 **TCLC 31**

Softly, Edgar
See Lovecraft, H(oward) P(hillips)

Softly, Edward
See Lovecraft, H(oward) P(hillips)

Sokolov, Raymond 1941- **CLC 7**
See also CA 85-88

Solo, Jay
See Ellison, Harlan (Jay)

Sologub, Fyodor TCLC 9
See also Teternikov, Fyodor Kuzmich

Solomons, Ikey Esquir
See Thackeray, William Makepeace

Solomos, Dionysios 1798-1857 **NCLC 15**

Solwoska, Mara
See French, Marilyn

Solzhenitsyn, Aleksandr I(sayevich) 1918- **CLC 1, 2, 4, 7, 9, 10, 18, 26, 34, 78, 134; DA; DAB; DAC; DAM MST, NOV; SSC 32; WLC**
See also AITN 1; CA 69-72; CANR 40, 65; DA3; MTCW 1, 2

Somers, Jane
See Lessing, Doris (May)

Somerville, Edith 1858-1949 **TCLC 51**
See also DLB 135

Somerville & Ross
See Martin, Violet Florence; Somerville, Edith

Sommer, Scott 1951- **CLC 25**
See also CA 106

Sondheim, Stephen (Joshua) 1930- **CLC 30, 39; DAM DRAM**
See also AAYA 11; CA 103; CANR 47, 68

Song, Cathy 1955- **PC 21**
See also CA 154; DLB 169

Sontag, Susan 1933- **CLC 1, 2, 10, 13, 31, 105; DAM POP**
See also CA 17-20R; CANR 25, 51, 74; DA3; DLB 2, 67; MTCW 1, 2

Sophocles 496(?)B.C.-406(?)B.C. **CMLC 2; DA; DAB; DAC; DAM DRAM, MST; DC 1; WLCS**
See also DA3; DLB 176

Sordello 1189-1269 **CMLC 15**

Sorel, Georges 1847-1922 **TCLC 91**
See also CA 118

Sorel, Julia
See Drexler, Rosalyn

Sorrentino, Gilbert 1929- **CLC 3, 7, 14, 22, 40**
See also CA 77-80; CANR 14, 33; DLB 5, 173; DLBY 80; INT CANR-14

Soto, Gary 1952- **CLC 32, 80; DAM MULT; HLC 2; PC 28**
See also AAYA 10; CA 119; 125; CANR 50, 74; CLR 38; DLB 82; HW 1, 2; INT 125; JRDA; MTCW 2; SATA 80

Soupault, Philippe 1897-1990 **CLC 68**
See also CA 116; 147; 131

Souster, (Holmes) Raymond 1921- **CLC 5, 14; DAC; DAM POET**
See also CA 13-16R; CAAS 14; CANR 13, 29, 53; DA3; DLB 88; SATA 63

Southern, Terry 1924(?)-1995 **CLC 7**
See also CA 1-4R; 150; CANR 1, 55; DLB 2

Southey, Robert 1774-1843 **NCLC 8**
See also DLB 93, 107, 142; SATA 54

Southworth, Emma Dorothy Eliza Nevitte 1819-1899 **NCLC 26**

Souza, Ernest
See Scott, Evelyn

Soyinka, Wole 1934- **CLC 3, 5, 14, 36, 44; BLC 3; DA; DAB; DAC; DAM DRAM, MST, MULT; DC 2; WLC**
See also BW 2, 3; CA 13-16R; CANR 27, 39, 82; DA3; DLB 125; MTCW 1, 2

Spackman, W(illiam) M(ode) 1905-1990 **CLC 46**
See also CA 81-84; 132

Spacks, Barry (Bernard) 1931- **CLC 14**
See also CA 154; CANR 33; DLB 105

Spanidou, Irini 1946- **CLC 44**
See also CA 185

Spark, Muriel (Sarah) 1918- **CLC 2, 3, 5, 8, 13, 18, 40, 94; DAB; DAC; DAM MST, NOV; SSC 10**
See also CA 5-8R; CANR 12, 36, 76, 89; CDBLB 1945-1960; DA3; DLB 15, 139; INT CANR-12; MTCW 1, 2

Spaulding, Douglas
See Bradbury, Ray (Douglas)

Spaulding, Leonard
See Bradbury, Ray (Douglas)

Spence, J. A. D.
See Eliot, T(homas) S(tearns)

Spencer, Elizabeth 1921- **CLC 22**
See also CA 13-16R; CANR 32, 65, 87; DLB 6; MTCW 1; SATA 14

Spencer, Leonard G.
See Silverberg, Robert

Spencer, Scott 1945- **CLC 30**
See also CA 113; CANR 51; DLBY 86

Spender, Stephen (Harold) 1909-1995 **CLC 1, 2, 5, 10, 41, 91; DAM POET**
See also CA 9-12R; 149; CANR 31, 54; CDBLB 1945-1960; DA3; DLB 20; MTCW 1, 2

Spengler, Oswald (Arnold Gottfried) 1880-1936 **TCLC 25**
See also CA 118

Spenser, Edmund 1552(?)-1599 **LC 5, 39; DA; DAB; DAC; DAM MST, POET; PC 8; WLC**
See also CDBLB Before 1660; DA3; DLB 167

Spicer, Jack 1925-1965 **CLC 8, 18, 72; DAM POET**
See also CA 85-88; DLB 5, 16, 193

Spiegelman, Art 1948- **CLC 76**
See also AAYA 10; CA 125; CANR 41, 55, 74; MTCW 2; SATA 109

Spielberg, Peter 1929- **CLC 6**
See also CA 5-8R; CANR 4, 48; DLBY 81

Spielberg, Steven 1947- **CLC 20**
See also AAYA 8, 24; CA 77-80; CANR 32; SATA 32

Spillane, Frank Morrison 1918-
See Spillane, Mickey
See also CA 25-28R; CANR 28, 63; DA3; DLB 226; MTCW 1, 2; SATA 66

Spillane, Mickey CLC 3, 13
See also Spillane, Frank Morrison
See also DLB 226; MTCW 2

Spinoza, Benedictus de 1632-1677 **LC 9, 58**

Spinrad, Norman (Richard) 1940- **CLC 46**
See also CA 37-40R; CAAS 19; CANR 20, 91; DLB 8; INT CANR-20

Spitteler, Carl (Friedrich Georg) 1845-1924 **TCLC 12**
See also CA 109; DLB 129

Spivack, Kathleen (Romola Drucker) 1938- **CLC 6**
See also CA 49-52

Spoto, Donald 1941- **CLC 39**
See also CA 65-68; CANR 11, 57, 93

Springsteen, Bruce (F.) 1949- **CLC 17**
See also CA 111

Spurling, Hilary 1940- **CLC 34**
See also CA 104; CANR 25, 52

Tao Lao
See Storni, Alfonsina
Tarantino, Quentin (Jerome) 1963- **CLC 125**
See also CA 171
Tarassoff, Lev
See Troyat, Henri
Tarbell, Ida M(inerva) 1857-1944 **TCLC 40**
See also CA 122; 181; DLB 47
Tarkington, (Newton) Booth 1869-1946 **TCLC 9**
See also CA 110; 143; DLB 9, 102; MTCW 2; SATA 17
Tarkovsky, Andrei (Arsenyevich) 1932-1986 **CLC 75**
See also CA 127
Tartt, Donna 1964(?)- **CLC 76**
See also CA 142
Tasso, Torquato 1544-1595 **LC 5**
Tate, (John Orley) Allen 1899-1979 **CLC 2, 4, 6, 9, 11, 14, 24**
See also CA 5-8R; 85-88; CANR 32; DLB 4, 45, 63; DLBD 17; MTCW 1, 2
Tate, Ellalice
See Hibbert, Eleanor Alice Burford
Tate, James (Vincent) 1943- **CLC 2, 6, 25**
See also CA 21-24R; CANR 29, 57; DLB 5, 169
Tauler, Johannes c. 1300-1361 **CMLC 37**
See also DLB 179
Tavel, Ronald 1940- **CLC 6**
See also CA 21-24R; CANR 33
Taylor, Bayard 1825-1878 **NCLC 89**
See also DLB 3, 189
Taylor, C(ecil) P(hilip) 1929-1981 **CLC 27**
See also CA 25-28R; 105; CANR 47
Taylor, Edward 1642(?)-1729 **LC 11; DA; DAB; DAC; DAM MST, POET**
See also DLB 24
Taylor, Eleanor Ross 1920- **CLC 5**
See also CA 81-84; CANR 70
Taylor, Elizabeth 1912-1975 **CLC 2, 4, 29**
See also CA 13-16R; CANR 9, 70; DLB 139; MTCW 1; SATA 13
Taylor, Frederick Winslow 1856-1915 **TCLC 76**
Taylor, Henry (Splawn) 1942- **CLC 44**
See also CA 33-36R; CAAS 7; CANR 31; DLB 5
Taylor, Kamala (Purnaiya) 1924-
See Markandaya, Kamala
See also CA 77-80
Taylor, Mildred D. CLC 21
See also AAYA 10; BW 1; CA 85-88; CANR 25; CLR 9, 59; DLB 52; JRDA; MAICYA; SAAS 5; SATA 15, 70
Taylor, Peter (Hillsman) 1917-1994 **CLC 1, 4, 18, 37, 44, 50, 71; SSC 10**
See also CA 13-16R; 147; CANR 9, 50; DLBY 81, 94; INT CANR-9; MTCW 1, 2
Taylor, Robert Lewis 1912-1998 **CLC 14**
See also CA 1-4R; 170; CANR 3, 64; SATA 10
Tchekhov, Anton
See Chekhov, Anton (Pavlovich)
Tchicaya, Gerald Felix 1931-1988 **CLC 101**
See also CA 129; 125; CANR 81
Tchicaya U Tam'si
See Tchicaya, Gerald Felix
Teasdale, Sara 1884-1933 **TCLC 4; PC 31**
See also CA 104; 163; DLB 45; SATA 32
Tegner, Esaias 1782-1846 **NCLC 2**
Teilhard de Chardin, (Marie Joseph) Pierre 1881-1955 **TCLC 9**
See also CA 105
Temple, Ann
See Mortimer, Penelope (Ruth)
Tennant, Emma (Christina) 1937- **CLC 13, 52**
See also CA 65-68; CAAS 9; CANR 10, 38, 59, 88; DLB 14
Tenneshaw, S. M.
See Silverberg, Robert
Tennyson, Alfred 1809-1892 **NCLC 30, 65; DA; DAB; DAC; DAM MST, POET; PC 6; WLC**
See also CDBLB 1832-1890; DA3; DLB 32
Teran, Lisa St. Aubin de CLC 36
See also St. Aubin de Teran, Lisa
Terence c. 184B.C.-c. 159B.C. **CMLC 14; DC 7**
See also DLB 211
Teresa de Jesus, St. 1515-1582 **LC 18**
Terkel, Louis 1912-
See Terkel, Studs
See also CA 57-60; CANR 18, 45, 67; DA3; MTCW 1, 2
Terkel, Studs CLC 38
See also Terkel, Louis
See also AAYA 32; AITN 1; MTCW 2
Terry, C. V.
See Slaughter, Frank G(ill)
Terry, Megan 1932- **CLC 19; DC 13**
See also CA 77-80; CABS 3; CANR 43; DLB 7
Tertullian c. 155-c. 245 **CMLC 29**
Tertz, Abram
See Sinyavsky, Andrei (Donatevich)
Tesich, Steve 1943(?)-1996 **CLC 40, 69**
See also CA 105; 152; DLBY 83
Tesla, Nikola 1856-1943 **TCLC 88**
Teternikov, Fyodor Kuzmich 1863-1927
See Sologub, Fyodor
See also CA 104
Tevis, Walter 1928-1984 **CLC 42**
See also CA 113
Tey, Josephine TCLC 14
See also Mackintosh, Elizabeth
See also DLB 77
Thackeray, William Makepeace 1811-1863 **NCLC 5, 14, 22, 43; DA; DAB; DAC; DAM MST, NOV; WLC**
See also CDBLB 1832-1890; DA3; DLB 21, 55, 159, 163; SATA 23
Thakura, Ravindranatha
See Tagore, Rabindranath
Tharoor, Shashi 1956- **CLC 70**
See also CA 141; CANR 91
Thelwell, Michael Miles 1939- **CLC 22**
See also BW 2; CA 101
Theobald, Lewis, Jr.
See Lovecraft, H(oward) P(hillips)
Theodorescu, Ion N. 1880-1967
See Arghezi, Tudor
See also CA 116; DLB 220
Theriault, Yves 1915-1983 **CLC 79; DAC; DAM MST**
See also CA 102; DLB 88
Theroux, Alexander (Louis) 1939- **CLC 2, 25**
See also CA 85-88; CANR 20, 63
Theroux, Paul (Edward) 1941- **CLC 5, 8, 11, 15, 28, 46; DAM POP**
See also AAYA 28; BEST 89:4; CA 33-36R; CANR 20, 45, 74; CDALBS; DA3; DLB 2; MTCW 1, 2; SATA 44, 109
Thesen, Sharon 1946- **CLC 56**
See also CA 163
Thevenin, Denis
See Duhamel, Georges
Thibault, Jacques Anatole Francois 1844-1924
See France, Anatole
See also CA 106; 127; DAM NOV; DA3; MTCW 1, 2
Thiele, Colin (Milton) 1920- **CLC 17**
See also CA 29-32R; CANR 12, 28, 53; CLR 27; MAICYA; SAAS 2; SATA 14, 72
Thomas, Audrey (Callahan) 1935- **CLC 7, 13, 37, 107; SSC 20**
See also AITN 2; CA 21-24R; CAAS 19; CANR 36, 58; DLB 60; MTCW 1
Thomas, Augustus 1857-1934 **TCLC 97**
Thomas, D(onald) M(ichael) 1935- **CLC 13, 22, 31, 132**
See also CA 61-64; CAAS 11; CANR 17, 45, 75; CDBLB 1960 to Present; DA3; DLB 40, 207; INT CANR-17; MTCW 1, 2
Thomas, Dylan (Marlais) 1914-1953 **TCLC 1, 8, 45; DA; DAB; DAC; DAM DRAM, MST, POET; PC 2; SSC 3; WLC**
See also CA 104; 120; CANR 65; CDBLB 1945-1960; DA3; DLB 13, 20, 139; MTCW 1, 2; SATA 60
Thomas, (Philip) Edward 1878-1917 **TCLC 10; DAM POET**
See also CA 106; 153; DLB 98
Thomas, Joyce Carol 1938- **CLC 35**
See also AAYA 12; BW 2, 3; CA 113; 116; CANR 48; CLR 19; DLB 33; INT 116; JRDA; MAICYA; MTCW 1, 2; SAAS 7; SATA 40, 78
Thomas, Lewis 1913-1993 **CLC 35**
See also CA 85-88; 143; CANR 38, 60; MTCW 1, 2
Thomas, M. Carey 1857-1935 **TCLC 89**
Thomas, Paul
See Mann, (Paul) Thomas
Thomas, Piri 1928- **CLC 17; HLCS 2**
See also CA 73-76; HW 1
Thomas, R(onald) S(tuart) 1913- **CLC 6, 13, 48; DAB; DAM POET**
See also CA 89-92; CAAS 4; CANR 30; CDBLB 1960 to Present; DLB 27; MTCW 1
Thomas, Ross (Elmore) 1926-1995 **CLC 39**
See also CA 33-36R; 150; CANR 22, 63
Thompson, Francis Clegg
See Mencken, H(enry) L(ouis)
Thompson, Francis Joseph 1859-1907 **TCLC 4**
See also CA 104; CDBLB 1890-1914; DLB 19
Thompson, Hunter S(tockton) 1939- **CLC 9, 17, 40, 104; DAM POP**
See also BEST 89:1; CA 17-20R; CANR 23, 46, 74, 77; DA3; DLB 185; MTCW 1, 2
Thompson, James Myers
See Thompson, Jim (Myers)
Thompson, Jim (Myers) 1906-1977(?) **CLC 69**
See also CA 140; DLB 226
Thompson, Judith CLC 39
Thomson, James 1700-1748 **LC 16, 29, 40; DAM POET**
See also DLB 95
Thomson, James 1834-1882 **NCLC 18; DAM POET**
See also DLB 35
Thoreau, Henry David 1817-1862 **NCLC 7, 21, 61; DA; DAB; DAC; DAM MST; PC 30; WLC**
See also CDALB 1640-1865; DA3; DLB 1, 223
Thornton, Hall
See Silverberg, Robert
Thucydides c. 455B.C.-399B.C. **CMLC 17**
See also DLB 176
Thumboo, Edwin 1933- **PC 30**
Thurber, James (Grover) 1894-1961 **CLC 5, 11, 25, 125; DA; DAB; DAC; DAM DRAM, MST, NOV; SSC 1**

See also CA 73-76; CANR 17, 39; CDALB 1929-1941; DA3; DLB 4, 11, 22, 102; MAICYA; MTCW 1, 2; SATA 13
Thurman, Wallace (Henry) 1902-1934 **TCLC 6; BLC 3; DAM MULT**
See also BW 1, 3; CA 104; 124; CANR 81; DLB 51
Tibullus, Albius c. 54B.C.-c. 19B.C. **CMLC 36**
See also DLB 211
Ticheburn, Cheviot
See Ainsworth, William Harrison
Tieck, (Johann) Ludwig 1773-1853 **NCLC 5, 46; SSC 31**
See also DLB 90
Tiger, Derry
See Ellison, Harlan (Jay)
Tilghman, Christopher 1948(?)- **CLC 65**
See also CA 159
Tillich, Paul (Johannes) 1886-1965 **CLC 131**
See also CA 5-8R; 25-28R; CANR 33; MTCW 1, 2
Tillinghast, Richard (Williford) 1940- **CLC 29**
See also CA 29-32R; CAAS 23; CANR 26, 51
Timrod, Henry 1828-1867 **NCLC 25**
See also DLB 3
Tindall, Gillian (Elizabeth) 1938- **CLC 7**
See also CA 21-24R; CANR 11, 65
Tiptree, James, Jr. CLC 48, 50
See also Sheldon, Alice Hastings Bradley
See also DLB 8
Titmarsh, Michael Angelo
See Thackeray, William Makepeace
Tocqueville, Alexis (Charles Henri Maurice Clerel, Comte) de 1805-1859 **NCLC 7, 63**
Tolkien, J(ohn) R(onald) R(euel) 1892-1973 **CLC 1, 2, 3, 8, 12, 38; DA; DAB; DAC; DAM MST, NOV, POP; WLC**
See also AAYA 10; AITN 1; CA 17-18; 45-48; CANR 36; CAP 2; CDBLB 1914-1945; CLR 56; DA3; DLB 15, 160; JRDA; MAICYA; MTCW 1, 2; SATA 2, 32, 100; SATA-Obit 24
Toller, Ernst 1893-1939 **TCLC 10**
See also CA 107; 186; DLB 124
Tolson, M. B.
See Tolson, Melvin B(eaunorus)
Tolson, Melvin B(eaunorus) 1898(?)-1966 **CLC 36, 105; BLC 3; DAM MULT, POET**
See also BW 1, 3; CA 124; 89-92; CANR 80; DLB 48, 76
Tolstoi, Aleksei Nikolaevich
See Tolstoy, Alexey Nikolaevich
Tolstoy, Alexey Nikolaevich 1882-1945 **TCLC 18**
See also CA 107; 158
Tolstoy, Count Leo
See Tolstoy, Leo (Nikolaevich)
Tolstoy, Leo (Nikolaevich) 1828-1910 **TCLC 4, 11, 17, 28, 44, 79; DA; DAB; DAC; DAM MST, NOV; SSC 9, 30; WLC**
See also CA 104; 123; DA3; SATA 26
Tomasi di Lampedusa, Giuseppe 1896-1957
See Lampedusa, Giuseppe (Tomasi) di
See also CA 111
Tomlin, Lily CLC 17
See also Tomlin, Mary Jean
Tomlin, Mary Jean 1939(?)-
See Tomlin, Lily
See also CA 117
Tomlinson, (Alfred) Charles 1927- **CLC 2, 4, 6, 13, 45; DAM POET; PC 17**
See also CA 5-8R; CANR 33; DLB 40
Tomlinson, H(enry) M(ajor) 1873-1958 **TCLC 71**
See also CA 118; 161; DLB 36, 100, 195
Tonson, Jacob
See Bennett, (Enoch) Arnold
Toole, John Kennedy 1937-1969 **CLC 19, 64**
See also CA 104; DLBY 81; MTCW 2
Toomer, Jean 1894-1967 **CLC 1, 4, 13, 22; BLC 3; DAM MULT; PC 7; SSC 1; WLCS**
See also Pinchback, Eugene; Toomer, Eugene; Toomer, Eugene Pinchback; Toomer, Nathan Jean; Toomer, Nathan Pinchback
See also BW 1; CA 85-88; CDALB 1917-1929; DA3; DLB 45, 51; MTCW 1, 2
Torley, Luke
See Blish, James (Benjamin)
Tornimparte, Alessandra
See Ginzburg, Natalia
Torre, Raoul della
See Mencken, H(enry) L(ouis)
Torrence, Ridgely 1874-1950 **TCLC 97**
See also DLB 54
Torrey, E(dwin) Fuller 1937- **CLC 34**
See also CA 119; CANR 71
Torsvan, Ben Traven
See Traven, B.
Torsvan, Benno Traven
See Traven, B.
Torsvan, Berick Traven
See Traven, B.
Torsvan, Berwick Traven
See Traven, B.
Torsvan, Bruno Traven
See Traven, B.
Torsvan, Traven
See Traven, B.
Tournier, Michel (Edouard) 1924- **CLC 6, 23, 36, 95**
See also CA 49-52; CANR 3, 36, 74; DLB 83; MTCW 1, 2; SATA 23
Tournimparte, Alessandra
See Ginzburg, Natalia
Towers, Ivar
See Kornbluth, C(yril) M.
Towne, Robert (Burton) 1936(?)- **CLC 87**
See also CA 108; DLB 44
Townsend, Sue CLC 61
See also Townsend, Susan Elaine
See also AAYA 28; SATA 55, 93; SATA-Brief 48
Townsend, Susan Elaine 1946-
See Townsend, Sue
See also CA 119; 127; CANR 65; DAB; DAC; DAM MST
Townshend, Peter (Dennis Blandford) 1945- **CLC 17, 42**
See also CA 107
Tozzi, Federigo 1883-1920 **TCLC 31**
See also CA 160
Tracy, Don(ald Fiske) 1905-1976(?)
See Queen, Ellery
See also CA 1-4R; 176; CANR 2
Traill, Catharine Parr 1802-1899 **NCLC 31**
See also DLB 99
Trakl, Georg 1887-1914 **TCLC 5; PC 20**
See also CA 104; 165; MTCW 2
Transtroemer, Tomas (Goesta) 1931- **CLC 52, 65; DAM POET**
See also CA 117; 129; CAAS 17
Transtromer, Tomas Gosta
See Transtroemer, Tomas (Goesta)
Traven, B. (?)-1969 **CLC 8, 11**
See also CA 19-20; 25-28R; CAP 2; DLB 9, 56; MTCW 1
Treitel, Jonathan 1959- **CLC 70**
Trelawny, Edward John 1792-1881 **NCLC 85**
See also DLB 110, 116, 144
Tremain, Rose 1943- **CLC 42**
See also CA 97-100; CANR 44; DLB 14
Tremblay, Michel 1942- **CLC 29, 102; DAC; DAM MST**
See also CA 116; 128; DLB 60; MTCW 1, 2
Trevanian CLC 29
See also Whitaker, Rod(ney)
Trevor, Glen
See Hilton, James
Trevor, William 1928- **CLC 7, 9, 14, 25, 71, 116; SSC 21**
See also Cox, William Trevor
See also DLB 14, 139; MTCW 2
Trifonov, Yuri (Valentinovich) 1925-1981 **CLC 45**
See also CA 126; 103; MTCW 1
Trilling, Diana (Rubin) 1905-1996 **CLC 129**
See also CA 5-8R; 154; CANR 10, 46; INT CANR-10; MTCW 1, 2
Trilling, Lionel 1905-1975 **CLC 9, 11, 24**
See also CA 9-12R; 61-64; CANR 10; DLB 28, 63; INT CANR-10; MTCW 1, 2
Trimball, W. H.
See Mencken, H(enry) L(ouis)
Tristan
See Gomez de la Serna, Ramon
Tristram
See Housman, A(lfred) E(dward)
Trogdon, William (Lewis) 1939-
See Heat-Moon, William Least
See also CA 115; 119; CANR 47, 89; INT 119
Trollope, Anthony 1815-1882 **NCLC 6, 33; DA; DAB; DAC; DAM MST, NOV; SSC 28; WLC**
See also CDBLB 1832-1890; DA3; DLB 21, 57, 159; SATA 22
Trollope, Frances 1779-1863 **NCLC 30**
See also DLB 21, 166
Trotsky, Leon 1879-1940 **TCLC 22**
See also CA 118; 167
Trotter (Cockburn), Catharine 1679-1749 **LC 8**
See also DLB 84
Trotter, Wilfred 1872-1939 **TCLC 97**
Trout, Kilgore
See Farmer, Philip Jose
Trow, George W. S. 1943- **CLC 52**
See also CA 126; CANR 91
Troyat, Henri 1911- **CLC 23**
See also CA 45-48; CANR 2, 33, 67; MTCW 1
Trudeau, G(arretson) B(eekman) 1948-
See Trudeau, Garry B.
See also CA 81-84; CANR 31; SATA 35
Trudeau, Garry B. CLC 12
See also Trudeau, G(arretson) B(eekman)
See also AAYA 10; AITN 2
Truffaut, Francois 1932-1984 **CLC 20, 101**
See also CA 81-84; 113; CANR 34
Trumbo, Dalton 1905-1976 **CLC 19**
See also CA 21-24R; 69-72; CANR 10; DLB 26
Trumbull, John 1750-1831 **NCLC 30**
See also DLB 31
Trundlett, Helen B.
See Eliot, T(homas) S(tearns)
Tryon, Thomas 1926-1991 **CLC 3, 11; DAM POP**
See also AITN 1; CA 29-32R; 135; CANR 32, 77; DA3; MTCW 1
Tryon, Tom
See Tryon, Thomas
Ts'ao Hsueh-ch'in 1715(?)-1763 **LC 1**
Tsushima, Shuji 1909-1948
See Dazai Osamu
See also CA 107
Tsvetaeva (Efron), Marina (Ivanovna) 1892-1941 **TCLC 7, 35; PC 14**

Vasiliu, Gheorghe 1881-1957
See Bacovia, George
See also CA 123; DLB 220

Vassa, Gustavus
See Equiano, Olaudah

Vassilikos, Vassilis 1933- **CLC 4, 8**
See also CA 81-84; CANR 75

Vaughan, Henry 1621-1695 **LC 27**
See also DLB 131

Vaughn, Stephanie CLC 62

Vazov, Ivan (Minchov) 1850-1921 **TCLC 25**
See also CA 121; 167; DLB 147

Veblen, Thorstein B(unde) 1857-1929 **TCLC 31**
See also CA 115; 165

Vega, Lope de 1562-1635 **LC 23; HLCS 2**

Venison, Alfred
See Pound, Ezra (Weston Loomis)

Verdi, Marie de
See Mencken, H(enry) L(ouis)

Verdu, Matilde
See Cela, Camilo Jose

Verga, Giovanni (Carmelo) 1840-1922 **TCLC 3; SSC 21**
See also CA 104; 123

Vergil 70B.C.-19B.C. **CMLC 9, 40; DA; DAB; DAC; DAM MST, POET; PC 12; WLCS**
See also Virgil
See also DA3; DLB 211

Verhaeren, Emile (Adolphe Gustave) 1855-1916 **TCLC 12**
See also CA 109

Verlaine, Paul (Marie) 1844-1896 **NCLC 2, 51; DAM POET; PC 2, 32**

Verne, Jules (Gabriel) 1828-1905 **TCLC 6, 52**
See also AAYA 16; CA 110; 131; DA3; DLB 123; JRDA; MAICYA; SATA 21

Very, Jones 1813-1880 **NCLC 9**
See also DLB 1

Vesaas, Tarjei 1897-1970 **CLC 48**
See also CA 29-32R

Vialis, Gaston
See Simenon, Georges (Jacques Christian)

Vian, Boris 1920-1959 **TCLC 9**
See also CA 106; 164; DLB 72; MTCW 2

Viaud, (Louis Marie) Julien 1850-1923
See Loti, Pierre
See also CA 107

Vicar, Henry
See Felsen, Henry Gregor

Vicker, Angus
See Felsen, Henry Gregor

Vidal, Gore 1925- **CLC 2, 4, 6, 8, 10, 22, 33, 72; DAM NOV, POP**
See also AITN 1; BEST 90:2; CA 5-8R; CANR 13, 45, 65; CDALBS; DA3; DLB 6, 152; INT CANR-13; MTCW 1, 2

Viereck, Peter (Robert Edwin) 1916- **CLC 4; PC 27**
See also CA 1-4R; CANR 1, 47; DLB 5

Vigny, Alfred (Victor) de 1797-1863 **NCLC 7; DAM POET; PC 26**
See also DLB 119, 192

Vilakazi, Benedict Wallet 1906-1947 **TCLC 37**
See also CA 168

Villa, Jose Garcia 1904-1997 **PC 22**
See also CA 25-28R; CANR 12

Villarreal, Jose Antonio 1924-
See also CA 133; CANR 93; DAM MULT; DLB 82; HLC 2; HW 1

Villaurrutia, Xavier 1903-1950 **TCLC 80**
See also HW 1

Villehardouin 1150(?)-1218(?) **CMLC 38**

Villiers de l'Isle Adam, Jean Marie Mathias Philippe Auguste, Comte de 1838-1889 **NCLC 3; SSC 14**
See also DLB 123

Villon, Francois 1431-1463(?) **LC 62; PC 13**
See also DLB 208

Vine, Barbara CLC 50
See also Rendell, Ruth (Barbara)
See also BEST 90:4

Vinge, Joan (Carol) D(ennison) 1948- **CLC 30; SSC 24**
See also AAYA 32; CA 93-96; CANR 72; SATA 36, 113

Violis, G.
See Simenon, Georges (Jacques Christian)

Viramontes, Helena Maria 1954-
See also CA 159; DLB 122; HLCS 2; HW 2

Virgil 70B.C.-19B.C.
See Vergil

Visconti, Luchino 1906-1976 **CLC 16**
See also CA 81-84; 65-68; CANR 39

Vittorini, Elio 1908-1966 **CLC 6, 9, 14**
See also CA 133; 25-28R

Vivekananda, Swami 1863-1902 **TCLC 88**

Vizenor, Gerald Robert 1934- **CLC 103; DAM MULT**
See also CA 13-16R; CAAS 22; CANR 5, 21, 44, 67; DLB 175, 227; MTCW 2; NNAL

Vizinczey, Stephen 1933- **CLC 40**
See also CA 128; INT 128

Vliet, R(ussell) G(ordon) 1929-1984 **CLC 22**
See also CA 37-40R; 112; CANR 18

Vogau, Boris Andreyevich 1894-1937(?)
See Pilnyak, Boris
See also CA 123

Vogel, Paula A(nne) 1951- **CLC 76**
See also CA 108

Voigt, Cynthia 1942- **CLC 30**
See also AAYA 3, 30; CA 106; CANR 18, 37, 40; CLR 13, 48; INT CANR-18; JRDA; MAICYA; SATA 48, 79, 116; SATA-Brief 33

Voigt, Ellen Bryant 1943- **CLC 54**
See also CA 69-72; CANR 11, 29, 55; DLB 120

Voinovich, Vladimir (Nikolaevich) 1932- **CLC 10, 49**
See also CA 81-84; CAAS 12; CANR 33, 67; MTCW 1

Vollmann, William T. 1959- **CLC 89; DAM NOV, POP**
See also CA 134; CANR 67; DA3; MTCW 2

Voloshinov, V. N.
See Bakhtin, Mikhail Mikhailovich

Voltaire 1694-1778 **LC 14; DA; DAB; DAC; DAM DRAM, MST; SSC 12; WLC**
See also DA3

von Aschendrof, BaronIgnatz
See Ford, Ford Madox

von Daeniken, Erich 1935- **CLC 30**
See also AITN 1; CA 37-40R; CANR 17, 44

von Daniken, Erich
See von Daeniken, Erich

von Hartmann, Eduard 1842-1906 **TCLC 96**

von Heidenstam, (Carl Gustaf) Verner
See Heidenstam, (Carl Gustaf) Verner von

von Heyse, Paul (Johann Ludwig)
See Heyse, Paul (Johann Ludwig von)

von Hofmannsthal, Hugo
See Hofmannsthal, Hugo von

von Horvath, Odon
See Horvath, Oedoen von

von Horvath, Oedoen -1938
See Horvath, Oedoen von
See also CA 184

von Liliencron, (Friedrich Adolf Axel) Detlev
See Liliencron, (Friedrich Adolf Axel) Detlev von

Vonnegut, Kurt, Jr. 1922- **CLC 1, 2, 3, 4, 5, 8, 12, 22, 40, 60, 111; DA; DAB; DAC; DAM MST, NOV, POP; SSC 8; WLC**
See also AAYA 6; AITN 1; BEST 90:4; CA 1-4R; CANR 1, 25, 49, 75, 92; CDALB 1968-1988; DA3; DLB 2, 8, 152; DLBD 3; DLBY 80; MTCW 1, 2

Von Rachen, Kurt
See Hubbard, L(afayette) Ron(ald)

von Rezzori (d'Arezzo), Gregor
See Rezzori (d'Arezzo), Gregor von

von Sternberg, Josef
See Sternberg, Josef von

Vorster, Gordon 1924- **CLC 34**
See also CA 133

Vosce, Trudie
See Ozick, Cynthia

Voznesensky, Andrei (Andreievich) 1933- **CLC 1, 15, 57; DAM POET**
See also CA 89-92; CANR 37; MTCW 1

Waddington, Miriam 1917- **CLC 28**
See also CA 21-24R; CANR 12, 30; DLB 68

Wagman, Fredrica 1937- **CLC 7**
See also CA 97-100; INT 97-100

Wagner, Linda W.
See Wagner-Martin, Linda (C.)

Wagner, Linda Welshimer
See Wagner-Martin, Linda (C.)

Wagner, Richard 1813-1883 **NCLC 9**
See also DLB 129

Wagner-Martin, Linda (C.) 1936- **CLC 50**
See also CA 159

Wagoner, David (Russell) 1926- **CLC 3, 5, 15**
See also CA 1-4R; CAAS 3; CANR 2, 71; DLB 5; SATA 14

Wah, Fred(erick James) 1939- **CLC 44**
See also CA 107; 141; DLB 60

Wahloo, Per 1926- **CLC 7**
See also CA 61-64; CANR 73

Wahloo, Peter
See Wahloo, Per

Wain, John (Barrington) 1925-1994 **CLC 2, 11, 15, 46**
See also CA 5-8R; 145; CAAS 4; CANR 23, 54; CDBLB 1960 to Present; DLB 15, 27, 139, 155; MTCW 1, 2

Wajda, Andrzej 1926- **CLC 16**
See also CA 102

Wakefield, Dan 1932- **CLC 7**
See also CA 21-24R; CAAS 7

Wakoski, Diane 1937- **CLC 2, 4, 7, 9, 11, 40; DAM POET; PC 15**
See also CA 13-16R; CAAS 1; CANR 9, 60; DLB 5; INT CANR-9; MTCW 2

Wakoski-Sherbell, Diane
See Wakoski, Diane

Walcott, Derek (Alton) 1930- **CLC 2, 4, 9, 14, 25, 42, 67, 76; BLC 3; DAB; DAC; DAM MST, MULT, POET; DC 7**
See also BW 2; CA 89-92; CANR 26, 47, 75, 80; DA3; DLB 117; DLBY 81; MTCW 1, 2

Waldman, Anne (Lesley) 1945- **CLC 7**
See also CA 37-40R; CAAS 17; CANR 34, 69; DLB 16

Waldo, E. Hunter
See Sturgeon, Theodore (Hamilton)

Waldo, Edward Hamilton
See Sturgeon, Theodore (Hamilton)

Walker, Alice (Malsenior) 1944- **CLC 5, 6, 9, 19, 27, 46, 58, 103; BLC 3; DA; DAB; DAC; DAM MST, MULT, NOV, POET, POP; PC 30; SSC 5; WLCS**

Welch, (Maurice) Denton 1915-1948 **TCLC 22**
See also CA 121; 148
Welch, James 1940- **CLC 6, 14, 52; DAM MULT, POP**
See also CA 85-88; CANR 42, 66; DLB 175; NNAL
Weldon, Fay 1931- **CLC 6, 9, 11, 19, 36, 59, 122; DAM POP**
See also CA 21-24R; CANR 16, 46, 63; CDBLB 1960 to Present; DLB 14, 194; INT CANR-16; MTCW 1, 2
Wellek, Rene 1903-1995 **CLC 28**
See also CA 5-8R; 150; CAAS 7; CANR 8; DLB 63; INT CANR-8
Weller, Michael 1942- **CLC 10, 53**
See also CA 85-88
Weller, Paul 1958- **CLC 26**
Wellershoff, Dieter 1925- **CLC 46**
See also CA 89-92; CANR 16, 37
Welles, (George) Orson 1915-1985 **CLC 20, 80**
See also CA 93-96; 117
Wellman, John McDowell 1945-
See Wellman, Mac
See also CA 166
Wellman, Mac 1945- **CLC 65**
See also Wellman, John McDowell; Wellman, John McDowell
Wellman, Manly Wade 1903-1986 **CLC 49**
See also CA 1-4R; 118; CANR 6, 16, 44; SATA 6; SATA-Obit 47
Wells, Carolyn 1869(?)-1942 **TCLC 35**
See also CA 113; 185; DLB 11
Wells, H(erbert) G(eorge) 1866-1946 **TCLC 6, 12, 19; DA; DAB; DAC; DAM MST, NOV; SSC 6; WLC**
See also AAYA 18; CA 110; 121; CDBLB 1914-1945; CLR 64; DA3; DLB 34, 70, 156, 178; MTCW 1, 2; SATA 20
Wells, Rosemary 1943- **CLC 12**
See also AAYA 13; CA 85-88; CANR 48; CLR 16; MAICYA; SAAS 1; SATA 18, 69, 114
Welty, Eudora 1909- **CLC 1, 2, 5, 14, 22, 33, 105; DA; DAB; DAC; DAM MST, NOV; SSC 1, 27; WLC**
See also CA 9-12R; CABS 1; CANR 32, 65; CDALB 1941-1968; DA3; DLB 2, 102, 143; DLBD 12; DLBY 87; MTCW 1, 2
Wen I-to 1899-1946 **TCLC 28**
Wentworth, Robert
See Hamilton, Edmond
Werfel, Franz (Viktor) 1890-1945 **TCLC 8**
See also CA 104; 161; DLB 81, 124
Wergeland, Henrik Arnold 1808-1845 **NCLC 5**
Wersba, Barbara 1932- **CLC 30**
See also AAYA 2, 30; CA 29-32R, 182; CAAE 182; CANR 16, 38; CLR 3; DLB 52; JRDA; MAICYA; SAAS 2; SATA 1, 58; SATA-Essay 103
Wertmueller, Lina 1928- **CLC 16**
See also CA 97-100; CANR 39, 78
Wescott, Glenway 1901-1987 **CLC 13; SSC 35**
See also CA 13-16R; 121; CANR 23, 70; DLB 4, 9, 102
Wesker, Arnold 1932- **CLC 3, 5, 42; DAB; DAM DRAM**
See also CA 1-4R; CAAS 7; CANR 1, 33; CDBLB 1960 to Present; DLB 13; MTCW 1
Wesley, Richard (Errol) 1945- **CLC 7**
See also BW 1; CA 57-60; CANR 27; DLB 38
Wessel, Johan Herman 1742-1785 **LC 7**
West, Anthony (Panther) 1914-1987 **CLC 50**
See also CA 45-48; 124; CANR 3, 19; DLB 15
West, C. P.
See Wodehouse, P(elham) G(renville)
West, Cornel (Ronald) 1953- **CLC 134; BLCS**
See also CA 144; CANR 91
West, (Mary) Jessamyn 1902-1984 **CLC 7, 17**
See also CA 9-12R; 112; CANR 27; DLB 6; DLBY 84; MTCW 1, 2; SATA-Obit 37
West, Morris L(anglo) 1916-1999 **CLC 6, 33**
See also CA 5-8R; 187; CANR 24, 49, 64; MTCW 1, 2
West, Nathanael 1903-1940 **TCLC 1, 14, 44; SSC 16**
See also CA 104; 125; CDALB 1929-1941; DA3; DLB 4, 9, 28; MTCW 1, 2
West, Owen
See Koontz, Dean R(ay)
West, Paul 1930- **CLC 7, 14, 96**
See also CA 13-16R; CAAS 7; CANR 22, 53, 76, 89; DLB 14; INT CANR-22; MTCW 2
West, Rebecca 1892-1983 **CLC 7, 9, 31, 50**
See also CA 5-8R; 109; CANR 19; DLB 36; DLBY 83; MTCW 1, 2
Westall, Robert (Atkinson) 1929-1993 **CLC 17**
See also AAYA 12; CA 69-72; 141; CANR 18, 68; CLR 13; JRDA; MAICYA; SAAS 2; SATA 23, 69; SATA-Obit 75
Westermarck, Edward 1862-1939 **TCLC 87**
Westlake, Donald E(dwin) 1933- **CLC 7, 33; DAM POP**
See also CA 17-20R; CAAS 13; CANR 16, 44, 65; INT CANR-16; MTCW 2
Westmacott, Mary
See Christie, Agatha (Mary Clarissa)
Weston, Allen
See Norton, Andre
Wetcheek, J. L.
See Feuchtwanger, Lion
Wetering, Janwillem van de
See van de Wetering, Janwillem
Wetherald, Agnes Ethelwyn 1857-1940 **TCLC 81**
See also DLB 99
Wetherell, Elizabeth
See Warner, Susan (Bogert)
Whale, James 1889-1957 **TCLC 63**
Whalen, Philip 1923- **CLC 6, 29**
See also CA 9-12R; CANR 5, 39; DLB 16
Wharton, Edith (Newbold Jones) 1862-1937 **TCLC 3, 9, 27, 53; DA; DAB; DAC; DAM MST, NOV; SSC 6; WLC**
See also AAYA 25; CA 104; 132; CDALB 1865-1917; DA3; DLB 4, 9, 12, 78, 189; DLBD 13; MTCW 1, 2
Wharton, James
See Mencken, H(enry) L(ouis)
Wharton, William (a pseudonym) CLC 18, 37
See also CA 93-96; DLBY 80; INT 93-96
Wheatley (Peters), Phillis 1754(?)-1784 **LC 3, 50; BLC 3; DA; DAC; DAM MST, MULT, POET; PC 3; WLC**
See also CDALB 1640-1865; DA3; DLB 31, 50
Wheelock, John Hall 1886-1978 **CLC 14**
See also CA 13-16R; 77-80; CANR 14; DLB 45
White, E(lwyn) B(rooks) 1899-1985 **CLC 10, 34, 39; DAM POP**
See also AITN 2; CA 13-16R; 116; CANR 16, 37; CDALBS; CLR 1, 21; DA3; DLB 11, 22; MAICYA; MTCW 1, 2; SATA 2, 29, 100; SATA-Obit 44
White, Edmund (Valentine III) 1940- **CLC 27, 110; DAM POP**
See also AAYA 7; CA 45-48; CANR 3, 19, 36, 62; DA3; DLB 227; MTCW 1, 2
White, Patrick (Victor Martindale) 1912-1990 **CLC 3, 4, 5, 7, 9, 18, 65, 69; SSC 39**
See also CA 81-84; 132; CANR 43; MTCW 1
White, Phyllis Dorothy James 1920-
See James, P. D.
See also CA 21-24R; CANR 17, 43, 65; DAM POP; DA3; MTCW 1, 2
White, T(erence) H(anbury) 1906-1964 **CLC 30**
See also AAYA 22; CA 73-76; CANR 37; DLB 160; JRDA; MAICYA; SATA 12
White, Terence de Vere 1912-1994 **CLC 49**
See also CA 49-52; 145; CANR 3
White, Walter
See White, Walter F(rancis)
See also BLC; DAM MULT
White, Walter F(rancis) 1893-1955 **TCLC 15**
See also White, Walter
See also BW 1; CA 115; 124; DLB 51
White, William Hale 1831-1913
See Rutherford, Mark
See also CA 121
Whitehead, Alfred North 1861-1947 **TCLC 97**
See also CA 117; 165; DLB 100
Whitehead, E(dward) A(nthony) 1933- **CLC 5**
See also CA 65-68; CANR 58
Whitemore, Hugh (John) 1936- **CLC 37**
See also CA 132; CANR 77; INT 132
Whitman, Sarah Helen (Power) 1803-1878 **NCLC 19**
See also DLB 1
Whitman, Walt(er) 1819-1892 **NCLC 4, 31, 81; DA; DAB; DAC; DAM MST, POET; PC 3; WLC**
See also CDALB 1640-1865; DA3; DLB 3, 64, 224; SATA 20
Whitney, Phyllis A(yame) 1903- **CLC 42; DAM POP**
See also AITN 2; BEST 90:3; CA 1-4R; CANR 3, 25, 38, 60; CLR 59; DA3; JRDA; MAICYA; MTCW 2; SATA 1, 30
Whittemore, (Edward) Reed (Jr.) 1919- **CLC 4**
See also CA 9-12R; CAAS 8; CANR 4; DLB 5
Whittier, John Greenleaf 1807-1892 **NCLC 8, 59**
See also DLB 1
Whittlebot, Hernia
See Coward, Noel (Peirce)
Wicker, Thomas Grey 1926-
See Wicker, Tom
See also CA 65-68; CANR 21, 46
Wicker, Tom CLC 7
See also Wicker, Thomas Grey
Wideman, John Edgar 1941- **CLC 5, 34, 36, 67, 122; BLC 3; DAM MULT**
See also BW 2, 3; CA 85-88; CANR 14, 42, 67; DLB 33, 143; MTCW 2
Wiebe, Rudy (Henry) 1934- **CLC 6, 11, 14; DAC; DAM MST**
See also CA 37-40R; CANR 42, 67; DLB 60
Wieland, Christoph Martin 1733-1813 **NCLC 17**
See also DLB 97
Wiene, Robert 1881-1938 **TCLC 56**
Wieners, John 1934- **CLC 7**
See also CA 13-16R; DLB 16
Wiesel, Elie(zer) 1928- **CLC 3, 5, 11, 37; DA; DAB; DAC; DAM MST, NOV; WLCS**

See also AAYA 7; AITN 1; CA 5-8R; CAAS 4; CANR 8, 40, 65; CDALBS; DA3; DLB 83; DLBY 87; INT CANR-8; MTCW 1, 2; SATA 56
Wiggins, Marianne 1947- **CLC 57**
See also BEST 89:3; CA 130; CANR 60
Wight, James Alfred 1916-1995
See Herriot, James
See also CA 77-80; SATA 55; SATA-Brief 44
Wilbur, Richard (Purdy) 1921- **CLC 3, 6, 9, 14, 53, 110; DA; DAB; DAC; DAM MST, POET**
See also CA 1-4R; CABS 2; CANR 2, 29, 76, 93, CDALBS; DLB 5, 169; INT CANR-29; MTCW 1, 2; SATA 9, 108
Wild, Peter 1940- **CLC 14**
See also CA 37-40R; DLB 5
Wilde, Oscar (Fingal O'Flahertie Wills) 1854(?)-1900 **TCLC 1, 8, 23, 41; DA; DAB; DAC; DAM DRAM, MST, NOV; SSC 11; WLC**
See also CA 104; 119; CDBLB 1890-1914; DA3; DLB 10, 19, 34, 57, 141, 156, 190; SATA 24
Wilder, Billy CLC 20
See also Wilder, Samuel
See also DLB 26
Wilder, Samuel 1906-
See Wilder, Billy
See also CA 89-92
Wilder, Thornton (Niven) 1897-1975 **CLC 1, 5, 6, 10, 15, 35, 82; DA; DAB; DAC; DAM DRAM, MST, NOV; DC 1; WLC**
See also AAYA 29; AITN 2; CA 13-16R; 61-64; CANR 40; CDALBS; DA3; DLB 4, 7, 9, 228; DLBY 97; MTCW 1, 2
Wilding, Michael 1942- **CLC 73**
See also CA 104; CANR 24, 49
Wiley, Richard 1944- **CLC 44**
See also CA 121; 129; CANR 71
Wilhelm, Kate CLC 7
See also Wilhelm, Katie Gertrude
See also AAYA 20; CAAS 5; DLB 8; INT CANR-17
Wilhelm, Katie Gertrude 1928-
See Wilhelm, Kate
See also CA 37-40R; CANR 17, 36, 60; MTCW 1
Wilkins, Mary
See Freeman, Mary E(leanor) Wilkins
Willard, Nancy 1936- **CLC 7, 37**
See also CA 89-92; CANR 10, 39, 68; CLR 5; DLB 5, 52; MAICYA; MTCW 1; SATA 37, 71; SATA-Brief 30
William of Ockham 1285-1347 **CMLC 32**
Williams, Ben Ames 1889-1953 **TCLC 89**
See also CA 183; DLB 102
Williams, C(harles) K(enneth) 1936- **CLC 33, 56; DAM POET**
See also CA 37-40R; CAAS 26; CANR 57; DLB 5
Williams, Charles
See Collier, James L(incoln)
Williams, Charles (Walter Stansby) 1886-1945 **TCLC 1, 11**
See also CA 104; 163; DLB 100, 153
Williams, (George) Emlyn 1905-1987 **CLC 15; DAM DRAM**
See also CA 104; 123; CANR 36; DLB 10, 77; MTCW 1
Williams, Hank 1923-1953 **TCLC 81**
Williams, Hugo 1942- **CLC 42**
See also CA 17-20R; CANR 45; DLB 40
Williams, J. Walker
See Wodehouse, P(elham) G(renville)
Williams, John A(lfred) 1925- **CLC 5, 13; BLC 3; DAM MULT**
See also BW 2, 3; CA 53-56; CAAS 3; CANR 6, 26, 51; DLB 2, 33; INT CANR-6
Williams, Jonathan (Chamberlain) 1929- **CLC 13**
See also CA 9-12R; CAAS 12; CANR 8; DLB 5
Williams, Joy 1944- **CLC 31**
See also CA 41-44R; CANR 22, 48
Williams, Norman 1952- **CLC 39**
See also CA 118
Williams, Sherley Anne 1944-1999 **CLC 89; BLC 3; DAM MULT, POET**
See also BW 2, 3; CA 73-76; 185; CANR 25, 82; DLB 41; INT CANR-25; SATA 78; SATA-Obit 116
Williams, Shirley
See Williams, Sherley Anne
Williams, Tennessee 1911-1983 **CLC 1, 2, 5, 7, 8, 11, 15, 19, 30, 39, 45, 71, 111; DA; DAB; DAC; DAM DRAM, MST; DC 4; WLC**
See also AAYA 31; AITN 1, 2; CA 5-8R; 108; CABS 3; CANR 31; CDALB 1941-1968; DA3; DLB 7; DLBD 4; DLBY 83; MTCW 1, 2
Williams, Thomas (Alonzo) 1926-1990 **CLC 14**
See also CA 1-4R; 132; CANR 2
Williams, William C.
See Williams, William Carlos
Williams, William Carlos 1883-1963 **CLC 1, 2, 5, 9, 13, 22, 42, 67; DA; DAB; DAC; DAM MST, POET; PC 7; SSC 31**
See also CA 89-92; CANR 34; CDALB 1917-1929; DA3; DLB 4, 16, 54, 86; MTCW 1, 2
Williamson, David (Keith) 1942- **CLC 56**
See also CA 103; CANR 41
Williamson, Ellen Douglas 1905-1984
See Douglas, Ellen
See also CA 17-20R; 114; CANR 39
Williamson, Jack CLC 29
See also Williamson, John Stewart
See also CAAS 8; DLB 8
Williamson, John Stewart 1908-
See Williamson, Jack
See also CA 17-20R; CANR 23, 70
Willie, Frederick
See Lovecraft, H(oward) P(hillips)
Willingham, Calder (Baynard, Jr.) 1922-1995 **CLC 5, 51**
See also CA 5-8R; 147; CANR 3; DLB 2, 44; MTCW 1
Willis, Charles
See Clarke, Arthur C(harles)
Willy
See Colette, (Sidonie-Gabrielle)
Willy, Colette
See Colette, (Sidonie-Gabrielle)
Wilson, A(ndrew) N(orman) 1950- **CLC 33**
See also CA 112; 122; DLB 14, 155, 194; MTCW 2
Wilson, Angus (Frank Johnstone) 1913-1991 **CLC 2, 3, 5, 25, 34; SSC 21**
See also CA 5-8R; 134; CANR 21; DLB 15, 139, 155; MTCW 1, 2
Wilson, August 1945- **CLC 39, 50, 63, 118; BLC 3; DA; DAB; DAC; DAM DRAM, MST, MULT; DC 2; WLCS**
See also AAYA 16; BW 2, 3; CA 115; 122; CANR 42, 54, 76; DA3; DLB 228; MTCW 1, 2
Wilson, Brian 1942- **CLC 12**
Wilson, Colin 1931- **CLC 3, 14**
See also CA 1-4R; CAAS 5; CANR 1, 22, 33, 77; DLB 14, 194; MTCW 1
Wilson, Dirk
See Pohl, Frederik
Wilson, Edmund 1895-1972 **CLC 1, 2, 3, 8, 24**
See also CA 1-4R; 37-40R; CANR 1, 46; DLB 63; MTCW 1, 2
Wilson, Ethel Davis (Bryant) 1888(?)-1980 **CLC 13; DAC; DAM POET**
See also CA 102; DLB 68; MTCW 1
Wilson, John 1785-1854 **NCLC 5**
Wilson, John (Anthony) Burgess 1917-1993
See Burgess, Anthony
See also CA 1-4R; 143; CANR 2, 46; DAC; DAM NOV; DA3; MTCW 1, 2
Wilson, Lanford 1937- **CLC 7, 14, 36; DAM DRAM**
See also CA 17-20R; CABS 3; CANR 45; DLB 7
Wilson, Robert M. 1944- **CLC 7, 9**
See also CA 49-52; CANR 2, 41; MTCW 1
Wilson, Robert McLiam 1964- **CLC 59**
See also CA 132
Wilson, Sloan 1920- **CLC 32**
See also CA 1-4R; CANR 1, 44
Wilson, Snoo 1948- **CLC 33**
See also CA 69-72
Wilson, William S(mith) 1932- **CLC 49**
See also CA 81-84
Wilson, (Thomas) Woodrow 1856-1924 **TCLC 79**
See also CA 166; DLB 47
Winchilsea, Anne (Kingsmill) Finch Counte 1661-1720
See Finch, Anne
Windham, Basil
See Wodehouse, P(elham) G(renville)
Wingrove, David (John) 1954- **CLC 68**
See also CA 133
Winnemucca, Sarah 1844-1891 **NCLC 79**
Winstanley, Gerrard 1609-1676 **LC 52**
Wintergreen, Jane
See Duncan, Sara Jeannette
Winters, Janet Lewis CLC 41
See also Lewis, Janet
See also DLBY 87
Winters, (Arthur) Yvor 1900-1968 **CLC 4, 8, 32**
See also CA 11-12; 25-28R; CAP 1; DLB 48; MTCW 1
Winterson, Jeanette 1959- **CLC 64; DAM POP**
See also CA 136; CANR 58; DA3; DLB 207; MTCW 2
Winthrop, John 1588-1649 **LC 31**
See also DLB 24, 30
Wirth, Louis 1897-1952 **TCLC 92**
Wiseman, Frederick 1930- **CLC 20**
See also CA 159
Wister, Owen 1860-1938 **TCLC 21**
See also CA 108; 162; DLB 9, 78, 186; SATA 62
Witkacy
See Witkiewicz, Stanislaw Ignacy
Witkiewicz, Stanislaw Ignacy 1885-1939 **TCLC 8**
See also CA 105; 162
Wittgenstein, Ludwig (Josef Johann) 1889-1951 **TCLC 59**
See also CA 113; 164; MTCW 2
Wittig, Monique 1935(?)- **CLC 22**
See also CA 116; 135; DLB 83
Wittlin, Jozef 1896-1976 **CLC 25**
See also CA 49-52; 65-68; CANR 3
Wodehouse, P(elham) G(renville) 1881-1975 **CLC 1, 2, 5, 10, 22; DAB; DAC; DAM NOV; SSC 2**

Author Index

See also AITN 2; CA 45-48; 57-60; CANR 3, 33; CDBLB 1914-1945; DA3; DLB 34, 162; MTCW 1, 2; SATA 22

Woiwode, L.
See Woiwode, Larry (Alfred)

Woiwode, Larry (Alfred) 1941- **CLC 6, 10**
See also CA 73-76; CANR 16; DLB 6; INT CANR-16

Wojciechowska, Maia (Teresa) 1927- **CLC 26**
See also AAYA 8; CA 9-12R, 183; CAAE 183; CANR 4, 41; CLR 1; JRDA; MAICYA; SAAS 1; SATA 1, 28, 83; SATA-Essay 104

Wojtyla, Karol
See John Paul II, Pope

Wolf, Christa 1929- **CLC 14, 29, 58**
See also CA 85-88; CANR 45; DLB 75; MTCW 1

Wolfe, Gene (Rodman) 1931- **CLC 25; DAM POP**
See also CA 57-60; CAAS 9; CANR 6, 32, 60; DLB 8; MTCW 2; SATA 118

Wolfe, George C. 1954- **CLC 49; BLCS**
See also CA 149

Wolfe, Thomas (Clayton) 1900-1938 **TCLC 4, 13, 29, 61; DA; DAB; DAC; DAM MST, NOV; SSC 33; WLC**
See also CA 104; 132; CDALB 1929-1941; DA3; DLB 9, 102; DLBD 2, 16; DLBY 85, 97; MTCW 1, 2

Wolfe, Thomas Kennerly, Jr. 1930-
See Wolfe, Tom
See also CA 13-16R; CANR 9, 33, 70; DAM POP; DA3; DLB 185; INT CANR-9; MTCW 1, 2

Wolfe, Tom CLC 1, 2, 9, 15, 35, 51
See also Wolfe, Thomas Kennerly, Jr.
See also AAYA 8; AITN 2; BEST 89:1; DLB 152

Wolff, Geoffrey (Ansell) 1937- **CLC 41**
See also CA 29-32R; CANR 29, 43, 78

Wolff, Sonia
See Levitin, Sonia (Wolff)

Wolff, Tobias (Jonathan Ansell) 1945- **CLC 39, 64**
See also AAYA 16; BEST 90:2; CA 114; 117; CAAS 22; CANR 54, 76; DA3; DLB 130; INT 117; MTCW 2

Wolfram von Eschenbach c. 1170-c. 1220 **CMLC 5**
See also DLB 138

Wolitzer, Hilma 1930- **CLC 17**
See also CA 65-68; CANR 18, 40; INT CANR-18; SATA 31

Wollstonecraft, Mary 1759-1797 **LC 5, 50**
See also CDBLB 1789-1832; DLB 39, 104, 158

Wonder, Stevie CLC 12
See also Morris, Steveland Judkins

Wong, Jade Snow 1922- **CLC 17**
See also CA 109; CANR 91; SATA 112

Woodberry, George Edward 1855-1930 **TCLC 73**
See also CA 165; DLB 71, 103

Woodcott, Keith
See Brunner, John (Kilian Houston)

Woodruff, Robert W.
See Mencken, H(enry) L(ouis)

Woolf, (Adeline) Virginia 1882-1941 **TCLC 1, 5, 20, 43, 56, 101; DA; DAB; DAC; DAM MST, NOV; SSC 7; WLC**
See also Woolf, Virginia Adeline
See also CA 104; 130; CANR 64; CDBLB 1914-1945; DA3; DLB 36, 100, 162; DLBD 10; MTCW 1

Woolf, Virginia Adeline
See Woolf, (Adeline) Virginia
See also MTCW 2

Woollcott, Alexander (Humphreys) 1887-1943 **TCLC 5**
See also CA 105; 161; DLB 29

Woolrich, Cornell 1903-1968 **CLC 77**
See also Hopley-Woolrich, Cornell George

Woolson, Constance Fenimore 1840-1894 **NCLC 82**
See also DLB 12, 74, 189, 221

Wordsworth, Dorothy 1771-1855 **NCLC 25**
See also DLB 107

Wordsworth, William 1770-1850 **NCLC 12, 38; DA; DAB; DAC; DAM MST, POET; PC 4; WLC**
See also CDBLB 1789-1832; DA3; DLB 93, 107

Wouk, Herman 1915- **CLC 1, 9, 38; DAM NOV, POP**
See also CA 5-8R; CANR 6, 33, 67; CDALBS; DA3; DLBY 82; INT CANR-6; MTCW 1, 2

Wright, Charles (Penzel, Jr.) 1935- **CLC 6, 13, 28, 119**
See also CA 29-32R; CAAS 7; CANR 23, 36, 62, 88; DLB 165; DLBY 82; MTCW 1, 2

Wright, Charles Stevenson 1932- **CLC 49; BLC 3; DAM MULT, POET**
See also BW 1; CA 9-12R; CANR 26; DLB 33

Wright, Frances 1795-1852 **NCLC 74**
See also DLB 73

Wright, Frank Lloyd 1867-1959 **TCLC 95**
See also AAYA 33; CA 174

Wright, Jack R.
See Harris, Mark

Wright, James (Arlington) 1927-1980 **CLC 3, 5, 10, 28; DAM POET**
See also AITN 2; CA 49-52; 97-100; CANR 4, 34, 64; CDALBS; DLB 5, 169; MTCW 1, 2

Wright, Judith (Arundell) 1915-2000 **CLC 11, 53; PC 14**
See also CA 13-16R; CANR 31, 76, 93; MTCW 1, 2; SATA 14

Wright, L(aurali) R. 1939- **CLC 44**
See also CA 138

Wright, Richard (Nathaniel) 1908-1960 **CLC 1, 3, 4, 9, 14, 21, 48, 74; BLC 3; DA; DAB; DAC; DAM MST, MULT, NOV; SSC 2; WLC**
See also AAYA 5; BW 1; CA 108; CANR 64; CDALB 1929-1941; DA3; DLB 76, 102; DLBD 2; MTCW 1, 2

Wright, Richard B(ruce) 1937- **CLC 6**
See also CA 85-88; DLB 53

Wright, Rick 1945- **CLC 35**

Wright, Rowland
See Wells, Carolyn

Wright, Stephen 1946- **CLC 33**

Wright, Willard Huntington 1888-1939
See Van Dine, S. S.
See also CA 115; DLBD 16

Wright, William 1930- **CLC 44**
See also CA 53-56; CANR 7, 23

Wroth, LadyMary 1587-1653(?) **LC 30**
See also DLB 121

Wu Ch'eng-en 1500(?)-1582(?) **LC 7**

Wu Ching-tzu 1701-1754 **LC 2**

Wurlitzer, Rudolph 1938(?)- **CLC 2, 4, 15**
See also CA 85-88; DLB 173

Wyatt, Thomas c. 1503-1542 **PC 27**
See also DLB 132

Wycherley, William 1641-1715 **LC 8, 21; DAM DRAM**
See also CDBLB 1660-1789; DLB 80

Wylie, Elinor (Morton Hoyt) 1885-1928 **TCLC 8; PC 23**
See also CA 105; 162; DLB 9, 45

Wylie, Philip (Gordon) 1902-1971 **CLC 43**
See also CA 21-22; 33-36R; CAP 2; DLB 9

Wyndham, John CLC 19
See also Harris, John (Wyndham Parkes Lucas) Beynon

Wyss, Johann David Von 1743-1818 **NCLC 10**
See also JRDA; MAICYA; SATA 29; SATA-Brief 27

Xenophon c. 430B.C.-c. 354B.C. **CMLC 17**
See also DLB 176

Yakumo Koizumi
See Hearn, (Patricio) Lafcadio (Tessima Carlos)

Yamamoto, Hisaye 1921- **SSC 34; DAM MULT**

Yanez, Jose Donoso
See Donoso (Yanez), Jose

Yanovsky, Basile S.
See Yanovsky, V(assily) S(emenovich)

Yanovsky, V(assily) S(emenovich) 1906-1989 **CLC 2, 18**
See also CA 97-100; 129

Yates, Richard 1926-1992 **CLC 7, 8, 23**
See also CA 5-8R; 139; CANR 10, 43; DLB 2; DLBY 81, 92; INT CANR-10

Yeats, W. B.
See Yeats, William Butler

Yeats, William Butler 1865-1939 **TCLC 1, 11, 18, 31, 93; DA; DAB; DAC; DAM DRAM, MST, POET; PC 20; WLC**
See also CA 104; 127; CANR 45; CDBLB 1890-1914; DA3; DLB 10, 19, 98, 156; MTCW 1, 2

Yehoshua, A(braham) B. 1936- **CLC 13, 31**
See also CA 33-36R; CANR 43, 90

Yellow Bird
See Ridge, John Rollin

Yep, Laurence Michael 1948- **CLC 35**
See also AAYA 5, 31; CA 49-52; CANR 1, 46, 92; CLR 3, 17, 54; DLB 52; JRDA; MAICYA; SATA 7, 69

Yerby, Frank G(arvin) 1916-1991 **CLC 1, 7, 22; BLC 3; DAM MULT**
See also BW 1, 3; CA 9-12R; 136; CANR 16, 52; DLB 76; INT CANR-16; MTCW 1

Yesenin, Sergei Alexandrovich
See Esenin, Sergei (Alexandrovich)

Yevtushenko, Yevgeny (Alexandrovich) 1933- **CLC 1, 3, 13, 26, 51, 126; DAM POET**
See also CA 81-84; CANR 33, 54; MTCW 1

Yezierska, Anzia 1885(?)-1970 **CLC 46**
See also CA 126; 89-92; DLB 28, 221; MTCW 1

Yglesias, Helen 1915- **CLC 7, 22**
See also CA 37-40R; CAAS 20; CANR 15, 65; INT CANR-15; MTCW 1

Yokomitsu, Riichi 1898-1947 **TCLC 47**
See also CA 170

Yonge, Charlotte (Mary) 1823-1901 **TCLC 48**
See also CA 109; 163; DLB 18, 163; SATA 17

York, Jeremy
See Creasey, John

York, Simon
See Heinlein, Robert A(nson)

Yorke, Henry Vincent 1905-1974 **CLC 13**
See also Green, Henry
See also CA 85-88; 49-52

Yosano Akiko 1878-1942 **TCLC 59; PC 11**
See also CA 161

Yoshimoto, Banana CLC 84
See also Yoshimoto, Mahoko

Yoshimoto, Mahoko 1964-
See Yoshimoto, Banana
See also CA 144

PC Cumulative Nationality Index

AMERICAN

Aiken, Conrad (Potter) **26**
Ammons, A(rchie) R(andolph) **16**
Angelou, Maya **32**
Ashbery, John (Lawrence) **26**
Auden, W(ystan) H(ugh) **1**
Baraka, Amiri **4**
Berry, Wendell (Erdman) **28**
Bishop, Elizabeth **3**
Bogan, Louise **12**
Bradstreet, Anne **10**
Brodsky, Joseph **9**
Brooks, Gwendolyn **7**
Bryant, William Cullen **20**
Bukowski, Charles **18**
Carruth, Hayden **10**
Clampitt, Amy **19**
Clifton, (Thelma) Lucille **17**
Crane, (Harold) Hart **3**
Cullen, Countee **20**
Cummings, E(dward) E(stlin) **5**
Dickinson, Emily (Elizabeth) **1**
Doolittle, Hilda **5**
Dove, Rita (Frances) **6**
Dunbar, Paul Laurence **5**
Duncan, Robert (Edward) **2**
Eliot, T(homas) S(tearns) **5, 31**
Emerson, Ralph Waldo **18**
Ferlinghetti, Lawrence (Monsanto) **1**
Forche, Carolyn (Louise) **10**
Frost, Robert (Lee) **1**
Gallagher, Tess **9**
Ginsberg, Allen **4**
Giovanni, Nikki **19**
Gluck, Louise (Elisabeth) **16**
Hammon, Jupiter **16**
Harjo, Joy **27**
Harper, Frances Ellen Watkins **21**
Hass, Robert **16**
Hayden, Robert E(arl) **6**
H. D. **5**
Hongo, Garrett Kaoru **23**
Hughes, (James) Langston **1**
Jeffers, (John) Robinson **17**
Johnson, James Weldon **24**
Kinnell, Galway **26**
Knight, Etheridge **14**
Kumin, Maxine (Winokur) **15**
Kunitz, Stanley (Jasspon) **19**
Levertov, Denise **11**
Levine, Philip **22**
Lindsay, (Nicholas) Vachel **23**
Longfellow, Henry Wadsworth **30**
Lorde, Audre (Geraldine) **12**
Lowell, Amy **13**
Lowell, Robert (Traill Spence Jr.) **3**
Loy, Mina **16**
Madhubuti, Haki R. **5**
Masters, Edgar Lee **1**
McKay, Claude **2**
Meredith, William (Morris) **28**
Merrill, James (Ingram) **28**
Merton, Thomas **10**
Millay, Edna St. Vincent **6**
Momaday, N(avarre) Scott **25**
Moore, Marianne (Craig) **4**
Nash, (Fredric) Ogden **21**
Nemerov, Howard (Stanley) **24**
Olds, Sharon **22**
Olson, Charles (John) **19**
Ortiz, Simon J(oseph) **17**
Parker, Dorothy (Rothschild) **28**
Piercy, Marge **29**
Pinsky, Robert **27**
Plath, Sylvia **1**
Poe, Edgar Allan **1**
Pound, Ezra (Weston Loomis) **4**
Reese, Lizette Woodworth **29**
Rexroth, Kenneth **20**
Rich, Adrienne (Cecile) **5**
Robinson, Edwin Arlington **1**
Roethke, Theodore (Huebner) **15**
Rose, Wendy **13**
Rukeyser, Muriel **12**
Sanchez, Sonia **9**
Sandburg, Carl (August) **2**
Schwartz, Delmore (David) **8**
Sexton, Anne (Harvey) **2**
Shapiro, Karl (Jay) **25**
Snyder, Gary (Sherman) **21**
Song, Cathy **21**
Soto, Gary **28**
Stein, Gertrude **18**
Stevens, Wallace **6**
Stryk, Lucien **27**
Swenson, May **14**
Teasdale, Sara **31**
Thoreau, Henry David **30**
Toomer, Jean **7**
Viereck, Peter (Robert Edwin) **27**
Wakoski, Diane **15**
Walker, Alice (Malsenior) **30**
Walker, Margaret (Abigail) **20**
Wheatley (Peters), Phillis **3**
Whitman, Walt(er) **3**
Williams, William Carlos **7**
Wylie, Elinor (Morton Hoyt) **23**
Zukofsky, Louis **11**

ARGENTINIAN

Borges, Jorge Luis **22, 32**

AUSTRALIAN

Wright, Judith (Arandell) **14**

AUSTRIAN

Trakl, Georg **20**

CANADIAN

Atwood, Margaret (Eleanor) **8**
Bissett, Bill **14**
Ondaatje, (Philip) Michael **28**
Page, P(atricia) K(athleen) **12**

CHILEAN

Neruda, Pablo **4**
Mistral, Gabriela **32**

CHINESE

Li Ho **13**
Li Po **29**
Tu Fu **9**
Wang Wei **18**

CUBAN

Guillen, Nicolas (Cristobal) **23**

ENGLISH

Arnold, Matthew **5**
Auden, W(ystan) H(ugh) **1**
Behn, Aphra **13**
Belloc, (Joseph) Hilaire (Pierre Sebastien Rene Swanton) **24**
Blake, William **12**
Bradstreet, Anne **10**
Bridges, Robert (Seymour) **28**
Bronte, Emily (Jane) **8**
Brooke, Rupert (Chawner) **24**
Browning, Elizabeth Barrett **6**
Browning, Robert **2**
Byron, George Gordon (Noel) **16**
Carew, Thomas **29**
Carroll, Lewis **18**
Chaucer, Geoffrey **19**
Chesterton, G(ilbert) K(eith) **28**
Clare, John **23**
Coleridge, Samuel Taylor **11**
Davie, Donald (Alfred) **29**
Day Lewis, C(ecil) **11**

Donne, John **1**
Dryden, John **25**
Eliot, George **20**
Eliot, T(homas) S(tearns) **5, 31**
Graves, Robert (von Ranke) **6**
Gray, Thomas **2**
Gunn, Thom(son William) **26**
Hardy, Thomas **8**
Herbert, George **4**
Herrick, Robert **9**
Hopkins, Gerard Manley **15**
Housman, A(lfred) E(dward) **2**
Hughes, Ted **7**
Jonson, Ben(jamin) **17**
Keats, John **1**
Kipling, (Joseph) Rudyard **3**
Larkin, Philip (Arthur) **21**
Levertov, Denise **11**
Loy, Mina **16**
Marvell, Andrew **10**
Milton, John **19, 29**
Montagu, Mary (Pierrepont) Wortley **16**
Noyes, Alfred **27**
Owen, Wilfred (Edward Salter) **19**
Page, P(atricia) K(athleen) **12**
Pope, Alexander **26**
Raleigh, Sir Walter **31**
Rossetti, Christina (Georgina) **7**
Sassoon, Siegfried (Lorraine) **12**
Shelley, Percy Bysshe **14**
Sidney, Sir Philip **32**
Sitwell, Dame Edith **3**
Smart, Christopher **13**
Smith, Stevie **12**
Spenser, Edmund **8**
Suckling, John **30**
Swift, Jonathan **9**
Swinburne, Algernon Charles **24**
Tennyson, Alfred **6**
Tomlinson, (Alfred) Charles **17**
Wordsworth, William **4**
Wyatt, Thomas **27**

FILIPINO

Villa, Jose Garcia **22**

FRENCH

Apollinaire, Guillaume **7**
Baudelaire, Charles **1**
Breton, Andre **15**
Gautier, Theophile **18**
Hugo, Victor (Marie) **17**
Laforgue, Jules **14**
Lamartine, Alphonse (Marie Louis Prat) de **16**
Leger, (Marie-Rene Auguste) Alexis Saint-Leger **23**
Mallarme, Stephane **4**
Marie de France **22**
Merton, Thomas **10**
Nerval, Gerard de **13**
Rimbaud, (Jean Nicolas) Arthur **3**
Ronsard, Pierre de **11**
Tzara, Tristan **27**
Valery, (Ambroise) Paul (Toussaint Jules) **9**
Verlaine, Paul (Marie) **2, 32**
Vigny, Alfred (Victor) de **26**
Villon, Francois **13**

GERMAN

Bukowski, Charles **18**
Enzensberger, Hans Magnus **28**
Goethe, Johann Wolfgang von **5**
Heine, Heinrich **25**
Holderlin, (Johann Christian) Friedrich **4**
Rilke, Rainer Maria **2**

GREEK

Elytis, Odysseus **21**
Homer **23**
Pindar **19**
Sappho **5**
Sikelianos, Angelos **29**

HUNGARIAN

Illyes, Gyula **16**

INDIAN

Kalidasa **22**
Tagore, Rabindranath **8**

IRISH

Day Lewis, C(ecil) **11**
Heaney, Seamus (Justin) **18**
Joyce, James (Augustine Aloysius) **22**
McGuckian, Medbh **27**
Swift, Jonathan **9**
Yeats, William Butler **20**

ITALIAN

Dante **21**
Gozzano, Guido **10**
Martial **10**
Montale, Eugenio **13**
Pasolini, Pier Paolo **17**
Pavese, Cesare **13**
Petrarch **8**

JAMAICAN

McKay, Claude **2**

JAPANESE

Hagiwara Sakutaro **18**
Ishikawa, Takuboku **10**
Matsuo Basho **3**
Nishiwaki, Junzaburo **15**
Yosano Akiko **11**

LEBANESE

Gibran, Kahlil **9**

MARTINICAN

Cesaire, Aime (Fernand) **25**

MEXICAN

Juana Ines de la Cruz **24**
Paz, Octavio **1**

NICARAGUAN

Alegria, Claribel **26**
Cardenal, Ernesto **22**
Dario, Ruben **15**

NIGERIAN

Okigbo, Christopher (Ifenayichukwu) **7**

PERSIAN

Khayyam, Omar **8**

POLISH

Milosz, Czeslaw **8**
Zagajewski, Adam **27**

PORTUGUESE

Camões, Luís Vaz de **31**
Pessoa, Fernando (Antonio Nogueira) **20**

ROMAN

Ovid **2**
Vergil **12**

ROMANIAN

Cassian, Nina **17**
Celan, Paul **10**
Tzara, Tristan **27**

RUSSIAN

Akhmatova, Anna **2**
Bely, Andrey **11**
Blok, Alexander (Alexandrovich) **21**
Brodsky, Joseph **9**
Lermontov, Mikhail Yuryevich **18**
Mandelstam, Osip (Emilievich) **14**
Pasternak, Boris (Leonidovich) **6**
Pushkin, Alexander (Sergeyevich) **10**
Tsvetaeva (Efron), Marina (Ivanovna) **14**

SALVADORAN

Alegria, Claribel **26**

SCOTTISH

Burns, Robert **6**
MacDiarmid, Hugh **9**
Scott, Walter **13**

SENEGALESE

Senghor, Leopold Sedar **25**

SINGAPORAN

Thumboo, Edwin **30**

SOUTH AFRICAN

Brutus, Dennis **24**

SPANISH

Fuertes, Gloria **27**
Garcia Lorca, Federico **3**
Jimenez (Mantecon), Juan Ramon **7**

SWEDISH

Ekeloef, (Bengt) Gunnar **23**

SYRIAN

Gibran, Kahlil **9**

WELSH

Thomas, Dylan (Marlais) **2**

PC Cumulative Title Index

Title Index

Title Index

Title Index

Title Index

"A Code of Morals" (Kipling) **3**:190
"Coeur, couronne et miroir" (Apollinaire) **7**:32-6
"La coeur volé" (Rimbaud) **3**:270
"Cogióme sin prevención" (Juana Ines de la Cruz) **24**:234
"Cohorte" (Perse) **23**:254-57
"The Coin" (Teasdale) **31**:350
Coins and Coffins (Wakoski) **15**:338, 344, 356, 369
"Cold" (Cassian) **17**:12, 15
"Cold in the Earth" (Bronte)
See "Remembrance"
"Cold Iron" (Kipling) **3**:171
"Cold-Blooded Creatures" (Wylie) **23**:314
"La colère de Samson" (Vigny) **26**:366, 368, 371, 380-81, 391, 401, 412, 416
"Coleridge" (McGuckian) **27**:101
"Colesberg" (Brutus) **24**:105
"Colin Clout" (Spenser)
See *Colin Clouts Come Home Againe*
Colin Clouts Come Home Againe (Spenser) **8**:336, 367, 387, 396
"The Coliseum" (Poe) **1**:439
"The Collar" (Gunn) **26**:185
"The Collar" (Herbert) **4**:102-03, 112-13, 130-31
"The Collar" (Herrick) **9**:141
Collected Earlier Poems (Williams) **7**:367-69, 374-75, 378, 382, 387-88, 392-94, 406-07, 409
Collected Early Poems (Pound) **4**:355
The Collected Greed, Parts 1-13 (Wakoski) **15**:356
Collected Later Poems (Williams) **7**:370, 375
The Collected Longer Poems of Kenneth Rexroth (Rexroth) **20**:197, 202, 204, 209-10, 214
Collected Lyrics (Millay) **6**:227
Collected Poems (Aiken) **26**:21, 24, 43-5
Collected Poems (Bridges) **28**:74, 77-8
Collected Poems (Camoes) **31**:32
The Collected Poems (Chesterton) **28**:99, 109
Collected Poems (Cummings) **5**:82-4, 87, 107, 111
Collected Poems (Frost) **1**:203
Collected Poems (Graves) **6**:153, 165, 171
Collected Poems (Hardy) **8**:89, 95-6, 98, 101, 118, 124
Collected Poems (Larkin) **21**:256, 258
Collected Poems (Lindsay) **23**:265, 280-82, 285-86, 288, 292, 294
Collected Poems (MacDiarmid)
Collected Poems (Millay) **6**:227
Collected Poems (Milosz)
See *Czeslaw Milosz: The Collected Poems, 1931-1987*
Collected Poems (Moore) **4**:235-36, 238, 247, 254, 271
Collected Poems (Olson) **19**:316
Collected Poems (Pinsky) **27**:168
The Collected Poems (Plath) **1**:406
Collected Poems (Robinson) **1**:467, 469, 480
Collected Poems (Rossetti)
See *The Poetical Works of Christina Georgina Rossetti*
Collected Poems (Sitwell) **3**:299, 301, 303-05, 308, 318-21, 325
Collected Poems (Stevens) **6**:306
Collected Poems (Stryk) **27**:207, 209-10, 212-16
Collected Poems (Tomlinson) **17**:342, 351, 355, 361
Collected Poems (Yeats) **20**:307, 336-37
Collected Poems 1934 (Williams) **7**:360, 372, 402
Collected Poems, 1938 (Graves) **6**:166
Collected Poems, 1955 (Graves) **6**:138, 140-43, 145
Collected Poems, 1909-1935 (Eliot) **5**:173, 176, 179, 211
Collected Poems, 1912-1944 (H. D.) **5**:297, 305
Collected Poems, 1923-1953 (Bogan) **12**:93, 95-6, 120, 125
Collected Poems, 1929-1933 (Day Lewis) **11**:123
Collected Poems, 1940-1978 (Shapiro) **25**:313, 315
Collected Poems, 1947-1980 (Ginsberg) **4**:71-2, 76-9, 83-4, 86, 89
Collected Poems, 1950-1970 (Davie) **29**:101, 111, 122
Collected Poems, 1951-1971 (Ammons) **16**:10, 20, 27, 40, 46, 54, 61
Collected Poems, 1957-1982 (Berry) **28**:25-29, 32, 37-39, 43-4
The Collected Poems of A. E. Housman (Housman) **2**:175-76, 180
The Collected Poems of Christopher Smart (Smart) **13**:347
Collected Poems of Elinor Wylie (Wylie) **23**:304, 306, 312, 314, 330-31
Collected Poems of H. D. (H. D.) **5**:268, 270, 276
The Collected Poems of Hart Crane (Crane) **3**:89-90
The Collected Poems of Henry Thoreau (Thoreau) **30**:182, 185, 187, 189-90, 232, 237, 256, 209-70, 272-76, 281
The Collected Poems of Howard Nemerov (Nemerov) **24**:298-99, 301
The Collected Poems of Jean Toomer (Toomer) **7**:340-41
The Collected Poems of Muriel Rukeyser (Rukeyser) **12**:224, 226, 235
The Collected Poems of Octavio Paz, 1957-1987 (Paz) **1**:374-76
The Collected Poems of Rupert Brooke (Brooke) **24**:52, 54, 61, 71
The Collected Poems of Sara Teasdale (Teasdale) **31**:327, 339, 342, 362
The Collected Poems of Stevie Smith (Smith) **12**:307, 309, 313-17, 320, 327, 346-47, 350, 352
The Collected Poems of Theodore Roethke (Roethke) **15**:281, 283-84, 288
The Collected Poems of Thomas Merton (Merton) **10**:336-337, 345, 348, 351
The Collected Poems of Wallace Stevens (Stevens) **6**:304
The Collected Poems of Wilfred Owen (Owen) **19**:351
Collected Poetry Notebook (Cesaire) **25**:48-9
Collected Shorter Poems, 1927-1957 (Auden) **1**:30
Collected Shorter Poems, 1930-1950 (Auden) **1**:30
Collected Shorter Poems, 1946-1991 (Carruth) **10**:89, 91
The Collected Shorter Poems of Kenneth Rexroth (Rexroth) **20**:197-98, 202, 204-05
Collected Sonnets (Millay) **6**:227
Collected Works (Akhmatova) **2**:19
Collected Works (Rossetti)
See *The Poetical Works of Christina Georgina Rossetti*
The Collected Works of Billy the Kid (Ondaatje) **28**:298, 304, 314-16, 327, 338-39
"Collected Writings" (Borges) **32**:52
A Collection of Celebrated Love Poems (Hagiwara Sakutaro)
See *A Collection of Celebrated Love Poems*
Collection of Short Songs on Innocent Love (Hagiwara Sakutaro)
See *Collection of Short Songs on Innocent Love*
"Collective Dawns" (Ashbery) **26**:144, 153
"College Breakfast Party" (Eliot) **20**:125
"The College Garden" (Bridges) **28**:79-80
"Les collines" (Apollinaire) **7**:12
"Colloque sentimental" (Verlaine) **32**:350, 352, 371, 390, 393, 396
"The Colloquies" (Gozzano) **10**:175, 180
The Colloquies (Gozzano)
See *I Colloqui*
"Colloquy in Black Rock" (Lowell) **3**:201, 216-17, 227
"Colloquy of the Centaurs" (Dario)
See "Coloquio de los centauros"
"Collos. 3.3" (Herbert) **4**:130
Collyn Clout (Skelton) **25**:329-30, 336, 337, 341-42, 348, 356, 374
"La colombe poisnardée et le jet d'eau" (Apollinaire) **7**:18, 20-2
"A Colombia" (Guillen) **23**:127
"Colombine" (Verlaine) **32**:351, 364, 390, 393
"The Colonel" (Forche) **10**:136, 138, 140, 145, 153, 167, 169
"Colonel Fantock" (Sitwell) **3**:293, 301, 325
"Coloquio de los centauros" (Dario) **15**:88, 92, 96, 112, 114
Color (Cullen) **20**:52-54, 56-58, 62, 66-67, 72, 77, 79, 81-83, 85-86
"The Color Sergeant" (Johnson) **24**:142
"The Colored Band" (Dunbar) **5**:134, 147
"The Colored Soldiers" (Dunbar) **5**:129-31, 133-34, 140
"Colors" (Cullen) **20**:65
"The Colors of Night" (Momaday) **25**:199, 202-203, 217-18
The Colossus, and Other Poems (Plath) **1**:380-81, 84, 388-89, 391, 394, 396, 404, 407, 410, 414
"Colour" (Thumboo) **30**:300
"The Colour Shop" (McGuckian) **27**:106
"A Coloured Print by Shokei" (Lowell) **13**:61
"A Coltrane Poem" (Sanchez) **9**:225
"Columbian Ode" (Dunbar) **5**:128
"Combat Cultural" (Moore) **4**:259
"Come" (Smith) **12**:316
"Come Break with Time" (Bogan) **12**:87, 101, 105-06, 122
"Come, Come Now" (Aleixandre) **15**:15
"Come Death" (Smith) **12**:315
"Come Death" (2Smith) **12**:314, 317, 319
"Come In" (Frost) **1**:197, 213, 230
"Come on, Come back" (Smith) **12**:295
"Come Republic" (Masters) **1**:329, 343
"Come se Quando" (Bridges) **28**:76-9
"Come Thunder" (Okigbo) **7**:235
"Come to the Bower" (Heaney) **18**:197
"The Comedian as the Letter C" (Stevens) **6**:293, 295-96, 304, 306, 310, 330, 335
La Comédie de la Mort (Gautier) **18**:143-46, 155, 159, 163
La comédie de la mort (Gautier) **18**:131-32, 134-35, 141, 155
Comedy (Dante)
See *La divina commedia"*
"The Comet" (Aleixandre) **15**:5
"The Comet at Yell'ham" (Hardy) **8**:89
"Comfort" (Browning) **6**:21
"Coming" (Larkin) **21**:238, 244
"Coming Close" (Levine) **22**:220
"Coming Down through Somerset" (Hughes) **7**:166
"The Coming Fall" (Levertov) **11**:185
The Coming Forth by Day of Osiris Jones (Aiken) **26**:8, 11, 57
"Coming Home" (Gallagher) **9**:36
"Coming Home from the Post Office" (Levine) **22**:221, 228
"Coming of Age in Michigan" (Levine) **22**:220, 228
"The Coming of Arthur" (Tennyson) **6**:408
"The Coming of Kali" (Clifton) **17**:24
"The Coming of the End" (Moments of VisionHardy) **8**:92
"The Coming of Wisdom with Time" (Yeats) **20**:338
Coming through Slaughter (Ondaatje) **28**:298
"Commander Lowell 1887-1950" (Lowell) **3**:219, 235

Title Index

Title Index

"A Curious Man's Dream" (Baudelaire)
See "Le rêve d'un curieux"
"Curl Up and Diet" (Nash) **21**:265
"The Current" (Berry) **28**:14-15
"The Curse" (Millay) **6**:211
"A Curse against Elegies" (Sexton) **2**:351
"A Curse for a Nation" (Browning) **6**:27
"The Curse of Cromwell" (Yeats) **20**:326
"Curtain" (Dunbar) **5**:119
"The Curtain" (Wright) **14**:355
"The Curve" (Levertov) **11**:176
"Custodian" (Kumin) **15**:223
"The Customs-Officer's House" (Montale)
See "La casa dei doganieri"
"Cut" (Plath) **1**:385, 392
"A Cutlet" (Stein) **18**:349
"The Cutting Edge" (Levine) **22**:215
"Cutting the Grapes Free" (Piercy) **29**:312
"Cuttings" (Roethke) **15**:291, 296-98, 312
"Cuttings" (LaterRoethke) **15**:260, 297-98, 302, 312, 314
Cuttlefish Bones (Montale)
See *Ossi di seppia*
"Cutty Sark" (Crane) **3**:84, 90, 106
"Cybernetics" (Nemerov) **24**:261, 282-83, 301
"The Cycads" (Wright) **14**:346
"The Cyclads" (Aiken) **26**:36
"The Cycle" (Jeffers) **17**:141
"The Cycle" (Roethke) **15**:265
"The Cyclical Night" (Borges)
See "La noche cíclica"
"Cyclops" (Shelley) **14**:227
"Le cygne" (Baudelaire) **1**:45, 66, 71
Cynthia (Raleigh)
See *The Ocean to Cynthia*
"Cyparissus" (Duncan) **2**:103
"Cypress Avenue" (Davie) **29**:110
"Cyrano en España" (Dario) **15**:80
"Cyrano in Spain" (Dario)
See "Cyrano en España"
"Cythère" (Verlaine) **32**:350
Czeslaw Milosz: The Collected Poems, 1931-1987 (Milosz) **8**:190-91, 197-98, 202, 206-07, 213-15
"D. R." (Zukofsky) **11**:351, 396
"Da, ia lezhu v zemle . . ." (Mandelstam) **14**:151
"Da una torre" (Montale) **13**:113
"Daddy" (Plath) **1**:382-83, 386-87, 392-93, 395-97, 400-02, 406-07, 414
"Daedalus" (Sikelianos) **29**:365-66, 368, 370-71
"The Daemon" (Bogan) **12**:100, 110
"The Daemon of the World" (Shelley) **14**:185
The Daffodil Murderer (Sassoon) **12**:252, 270, 274-77
"Daffodildo" (Swenson) **14**:277, 287
"Daffy Duck in Hollywood" (Ashbery) **26**:153
"The dagger" (Borges)
See "El puñal"
"Daguerreotype Taken in Old Age" (Atwood) **8**:39
"Un dahlia" (Verlaine) **2**:431
"The Dahlia Gardens" (Clampitt) **19**:82, 90-1
"Dahomey" (Lorde) **12**:160
"The Daily Globe" (Nemerov) **24**:278
The Daily Holidays (Cassian) **17**:6
"Les daimons" (Ronsard) **11**:225, 279, 281-82
"The Dainty Monsters" (Ondaatje) **28**:292-93
The Dainty Monsters (Ondaatje) **28**:291-92, 294, 298-99, 318, 327, 331-32, 335
"Daisies Are Broken" (Williams) **7**:406
"The Daisy" (Tennyson) **6**:357, 360
"Daisy Frazer" (Masters) **1**:334
"Daisy-Cutter" (McGuckian) **27**:76, 103
"Daisy's Song" (Keats) **1**:311
"Dakar" (Borges) **32**:38
"Dakar Doldrums" (Ginsberg) **4**:72
"The Dale" (Lamartine)
See "Le vallon"
"Dalhousie Farm" (Meredith) **28**:181
"The Dalliance of the Eagles" (Whitman) **3**:397
"The Dam" (Rukeyser) **12**:210
Dam 'ah wabitisāmah (Gibran) **9**:73, 75, 77-8, 81
"Dämmerung" (Celan) **10**:124-25
"Damned Women" (Baudelaire)
See "Femmes damnées"
"Damon Being Asked a Reason for Loveing" (Behn) **13**:18
"Damon the Mower" (Marvell) **10**:266, 293, 295-97, 315
"The Dampe" (Donne) **1**:130
"The Dance" (Baraka) **4**:16
"Dance" (Cassian) **17**:13
"The Dance" (Crane) **3**:84, 86, 88, 90
"The Dance" (Larkin) **21**:259
"Dance" (Pavese)
See "Balletto"
"The Dance" (Roethke) **15**:266-67, 269, 273, 279
"The Dance at the Phoenix" (Hardy) **8**:99
"The Dance of Death" (Blok)
See "Danse macabre"
"Dance of Death" (Garcia Lorca)
See "Danza de la muerte"
The Dance of Death (Auden) **1**:8
"Dance of the Macabre Mice" (Stevens) **6**:296
"Dance the Orange" (Hayden) **6**:196
"The Dancer" (H. D.) **5**:305
"Dances of Death" (Blok)
See "Danse macabre"
"Dancing on the Grave of a Son of a Bitch" (Wakoski) **15**:346
Dancing on the Grave of a Son of a Bitch (Wakoski) **15**:336, 348, 365
"The Danger of Writing Defiant Verse" (Parker) **28**:350, 363
Dangling in the Tournefortia (Bukowski) **18**:15
"Daniel Bartoli" (Browning) **2**:84
"Daniel Jazz" (Lindsay) **23**:264, 270, 286
"Danny Deever" (Kipling) **3**:170-71, 179, 188-89, 191
"Dans la grotte" (Verlaine) **32**:349, 351, 391, 393
"Dans le restaurant" (Eliot) **5**:185
"Dansa di Narcís" (Pasolini) **17**:281
"Danse macabre" (Blok) **21**:6, 14, 20
"Danse russe" (Williams) **7**:353, 367, 408
"Dante Études, Book Two" (Duncan) **2**:114-16, 127
Dante's Purgatory (Dante)
See *La divina commedia"*
"Danza de la muerte" (Garcia Lorca) **3**:121
"La danza del espiritu" (Cardenal) **22**:131
"Daphnaida" (Spenser) **8**:365, 367
"Daphnis and Chloe" (Marvell) **10**:265, 271, 291-92, 301
"Darest Thou Now O Soul" (Whitman) **3**:378
"Darien" (Graves) **6**:137, 144, 168
"The Dark and the Fair" (Kunitz) **19**:162, 169
"Dark Blood" (Walker) **20**:273, 282
"The Dark Cup" (Teasdale) **31**:358, 360
"Dark Eye in September" (Celan) **10**:112
"Dark Gift" (Wright) **14**:338, 353, 356
"Dark Girl's Rhyme" (Parker) **28**:356
"The Dark Hills" (Robinson) **1**:468
Dark of the Moon (Teasdale) **31**:327, 330, 333, 335, 338, 341, 347, 349, 370-72, 379-80, 389
The Dark One (Tagore)
See *Shyamali*
"The Dark Ones" (Wright) **14**:373
"Dark Prophecy: I Sing of Shine" (Knight) **14**:39
"Dark Song" (Ammons) **16**:4
"Dark Song" (Sitwell) **3**:291
Dark Summer (Bogan) **12**:87, 89, 105-06, 120-23
"Dark Waters of the Beginning" (Okigbo) **7**:231
"Dark Wild Honey" (Swenson) **14**:276
Dark World (Carruth) **10**:71, 91
"Darkling Summer, Ominous Dusk, Rumorous Rain" (Schwartz) **8**:319
"The Darkling Thrush" (Hardy) **8**:98, 105-06, 121, 131
"Darkness" (Aleixandre) **15**:5
"Darkness" (Byron) **16**:86, 89
"Darkness Chex George Whitman" (Ferlinghetti) **1**:183
"Darkness of Death" (Pasternak) **6**:253
"Darling! Because My Blood Can Sing" (Cummings) **5**:108
"Darling Daughters" (Smith) **12**:326
"Darling, It's Frightening! When a Poet Loves ..." (Pasternak) **6**:251
"Darling Room" (Tennyson) **6**:353
"Dary Tereka" (Lermontov) **18**:268, 281, 290, 295
"Dat Dirty Rum" (McKay) **2**:222
"Dat ol' Mare o' Mine" (Dunbar) **5**:134
"Date Lilia" (Hugo) **17**:94
"Dates" (Ondaatje) **28**:327, 331
"Dates: Penkhull New Road" (Tomlinson) **17**:347, 352
"Dative Haruspices" (Rexroth) **20**:215
"A Daughter I" (Levertov) **11**:209
"A Daughter II" (Levertov) **11**:209
"Daughter Moon" (Wakoski) **15**:366
"The Daughter of the Forest" (Gibran)
See "Amām 'arsh al-jamāl"
Daughters of Fire (Nerval)
See *Les filles du feu*
"Daughters with Curls" (Stevens) **6**:292
"David" (Pasolini) **17**:252, 281
"David and Bathsheba in the Public Garden" (Lowell) **3**:205-06, 215
"David's Lamentation for Saul and Jonathan" (Bradstreet) **10**:6
"David's Night at Veliès" (Merrill) **28**:220
"Davy Jones' Door-Bell" (Lindsay) **23**:264
"Dawlish Fair" (Keats) **1**:311
"Dawn" (Borges)
See "Amanecer"
"Dawn" (Brooke) **24**:53, 64, 82
"Dawn" (Dunbar) **5**:125, 128
"Dawn" (Garcia Lorca)
See "La aurora"
"Dawn" (Teasdale) **31**:331
"Dawn" (Thumboo) **30**:301
"Dawn Adventure" (Lowell) **13**:63
"Dawn after Storm" (Zukofsky) **11**:368
"Dawn Bombardment" (Graves) **6**:144
"Dawn Bombardment" (Graves) **6**:144
"The Dawn Wind" (Kipling) **3**:183
"Dawnbreaker" (Hayden) **6**:198
"The Dawning" (Herbert) **4**:102
"Dawn's Rose" (Hughes) **7**:138, 144, 159
"Day" (Ammons) **16**:12
"The Day After" (Soto) **28**:302
"Day and Night" (Montale)
See "Giorno e notte"
"The Day Before the Trial" (Swinburne) **24**:355
Day by Day (Lowell) **3**:231-32
"The Day Dream" (Coleridge) **11**:91, 106
"The Day Is a Poem" (Jeffers) **17**:141
"The Day is Done" (Dunbar) **5**:126
"The Day is Done" (Longfellow) **30**:27, 46, 52, 103, 109
"The Day Is Gone" (Keats) **1**:279
"TH DAY MAY CUM" (Bissett) **14**:34
"The Day of Battle" (Housman) **2**:160
"The Day of Judgement" (Swift) **9**:259, 265, 281, 295
"Day of Kings" (Hugo) **17**:58
"A Day of Sunshine" (Longfellow) **30**:109
"The Day of the Eclipse" (Merrill) **28**:239, 243
"A Day on the Big Branch" (Nemerov) **24**:257, 261
"Day or Night" (Rossetti) **7**:276
"Day Six O'Hare Telephone" (Merton) **10**:336
"Day That I Have Loved" (Brooke) **24**:58, 62, 76
"The Day the Mountains Move" (Yosano Akiko)
See "Yama no ugoku hi"

Title Index

Title Index

Title Index

Title Index

Title Index

Title Index

Title Index

Title Index

Title Index

Title Index

Title Index

Title Index

Title Index

Title Index

Title Index

Title Index

Title Index

Title Index

Title Index

Title Index

ISBN 0-7876-3278-3

90000

9 780787 632785